David Deerhurveloh
Great Medwon
2ⁿᵈ September 2001

The Variety
Almanac
2000

The Editors of *Variety*

Variety Inc.
Peter Bart, Vice President, Editor-in-Chief
Gerry Byrne, Group Vice President, Publisher

The Variety Almanac
Editor: Peter Cowie
Managing Editors: Anthony D'Alessandro (U.S.), Damjana Finci (U.K.)

BXTREE

Acknowledgements

The editors would like to thank the following individuals and organizations for their kind cooperation during the preparation of this book: Bruce Apar, Peter Bart, Nick Burfitt (Taylor Nelson Sofres plc), British Video Association, Gerry Byrne, Marcelo Cajueiro, Gennaro Castaldo (HMV), Maud Clouët (Mediametrie), Tania D'Alessandro, Dan Edelson, Liza Foreman, Phil Gallo, Don Groves, Alex Hamilton, Doug Hopper, Clare Hulton, Charles Isherwood, Dave Kent (Kobal Collection), Anthony Knight (Blockbuster), Karen Kratz (Nielsen), Tania Littlehales (MTV), Geoffrey Macnab, Marcy Magiera, *Video Business*, Phil Matcham (CIN), Thomas O'Neil, Bryan Pearson, Josh Ratcliffe, Nora Rawlinson, *Publishers Weekly*, David Rooney, Keith Sherman & Associates, Inc, Adrian Sington, Michael Speier, Howard Watson (Society of London Theatre), Michael Williams, Mark Wojan (ACNielsen EDI), Matt Wolf, Cecilia Zecchinelli.

First published 2000 by Boxtree
an imprint of Macmillan Publishers Ltd
25 Eccleston Place, London SW1W 9NF
Basingstoke and Oxford

www.macmillan.co.uk

Associated companies throughout the world

ISBN 0 7522 7159 8

Picture credits
1: (top) The Kobal Collection, © Warner Bros., (bottom) Sebastian Lorey/DreamWorks 1999 from The Kobal Collection; 2: (top) Moving Pictures International, (bottom) Stephen F. Morley/HBO; 3: (top) Teresa Isasi/G2 Films, (bottom) DDA Agency; 4: Keith Hamshere © 1999 Danjaq, LLC & United Artists Corporation, Eon Productions Ltd.; 5: (top) © Polygram Filmed Entertainment, (bottom) Laurie Sparham; 6: © Hat Trick Productions Limited; 7: © 1998 Fox Broadcasting Company/Greg Gorman/FOX; 8: (top) Alessandro Pinna Photography, (bottom left) © Catherine Ashmore, (bottom right) © Ivan Kyncl from Peter Thompson Associates; 9: Rob Howard/FAMOUS; 10: (top left) © Julie Ann Smith 1999, Artisan Entertainment, (top right) Suzanne Tenner, Columbia Motion Pictures, (bottom left) Moving Pictures International, (bottom right) Keith Hamshere © 1995 Danjaq, LLC & United Artists Corporation, Eon Productions Ltd; 11: (top) 20th Century Fox, (bottom left) Moving Pictures International, (bottom right) © Miramax International; 12: © 1996 DreamWorks/M.Aronowitz; 13: (top left) Rob Howard/FAMOUS, (top right and bottom left) courtesy of MTV, (bottom right) Rob Howard/FAMOUS; 14: CARLTON/RANK from The Kobal Collection; 15: (top and bottom left) Moving Pictures International, (bottom right) CARLTON/RANK from The Kobal Collection; 16: The Kobal Collection.

9 8 7 6 5 4 3 2 1

A CIP catalogue record for this book is available from the British Library.

Typeset by Blackjacks
Printed by Mackays of Chatham plc, Chatham, Kent

Contents

Introduction

It's an axiom of show business that resilience and adaptability are the keys to survival. Those entertainers with "staying power" have managed to make the shift from vaudeville to radio or from radio to television to film and then, inevitably, into the great playground of cyberspace.

In its nearly century-long history, *Variety* too has demonstrated its talent for shifting gears. Having started as a repository for vaudeville news and reviews, it responded to the winds of change not only in its ever-expanding coverage, but also in its traditionally quirky headlines. *Variety* banners have run the gamut from "Sticks Nix Hick Pix" (1935) and "Wall St Lays an Egg" (1929) to "Lizards Eat Arnold's Lunch" (1993) and "Pic Biz Freaked by Cybergeek's Leaks" (1997).

People often ask me why *Variety* has maintained its "attitude," not only in headlines, but also in its style of reporting, even to the point of building its own arcane vocabulary. People don't quit their jobs in *Variety*, they "ankle" them. A show doesn't open to good business in the pages of *Variety*; unless it's "boffo" it's downright disappointing.

From the outset, *Variety*'s reporters and editors realized they were covering show business, not issues of national security, hence the insistence on bringing a bit of levity to the table. Also, *Variety* was founded as the voice of the working entertainer, not the corporate "suit." Its lexicon thus reflected Shubert Alley, not the Harvard Business School. And the "attitude" worked.

Over the years, *Variety* has not only continually regenerated itself, but has also spun off new ventures. The weekly gave birth in 1933 to *Daily Variety*, published in Los Angeles. That publication last year spawned a sister newspaper, *Daily Variety Gotham*, published each day in New York City. Also born in 1998 was Variety.com, which firmly planted *Variety* onto the web.

All these publications were created in the knowledge that what was once the entertainment industry has been transformed into the global media and entertainment industry. Show business has become inextricably linked with information and technology. And if there's one single trait which defines the practitioners of this industry, it's that they are news junkies – they have an insatiable need for information which they can digest and act upon. Surely there are few sectors of the global economy that are as volatile as this one, or as open to innovation and change.

As the new millennium gets under way, it is *Variety*'s mission not only to meet these information needs, but also to serve where possible as the connective tissue between the world's media communities. Among other things, this means a continued expansion and refining of Variety.com and of other electronic extensions of our newspaper. Though *Variety*'s impact as a print product will continue to grow, our organization must also supply its readers' needs not only for breaking news, but also for abundant back-up data, listings and other information.

In accomplishing this, to be sure, there is a primary need for objectivity and integrity. No newspaper can maintain its viability if it appears to play favorites or to propagate disinformation. This responsibility weighs heavily on *Variety*'s editors and reporters, all of whom want to "get it first," but also, and more importantly, to get it right. The qualifications of *Variety*'s writers have changed markedly in recent years as their jobs have become more demanding. Not only are higher educational credentials necessary, but substantial experience on other respected journals is also required.

It takes sharp minds to penetrate the blizzard of information and misinformation that confronts the typical *Variety* reporter on a daily basis. It is a demanding job because, in writing their pieces, they know full well that any errors they may make will be replicated over and over again by the general press, who look upon *Variety* as a primary information source.

There have been many occasions when *Variety* has been under pressure to "cooperate" with a major industry power player or advertiser – for instance, going back a couple of generations when some major producers would open a play, get it reviewed and then promptly cut back the size of the orchestra, cast, and even the chorus line. *Variety*'s reviewers would revisit the shows a week or so after the opening and re-review it until they were banned from the theaters. They kept sneaking in and filing their stories anyway.

Variety has fought its battles and still maintains its legacy as the "bible of show business," and this scenario will doubtless continue well into the new millennium. After another hundred years or so, the continuing adventures of this "bible" may become downright biblical.

Peter Bart, Editor-in-Chief

The Year in Perspective

The year in showbiz started off like every Hollywood screenplay – with a grabber: Broadway impresario and Livent co-founder Garth Drabinsky was indicted on 16 counts of fraud to conceal his production company's million-dollar losses. The winds of March certainly blew in some change: *Shakespeare in Love* stole the Best Picture Oscar from *Saving Private Ryan*. April showers brought Barry Diller flowers as the USA Networks chief bought the remains of October and Gramercy from Universal Pictures. Summer had a juicy middle as the two movie moguls of steel (Warner Brothers' Terry Semel and Bob Daly) split and another two reconciled (Michael Eisner and Jeffrey Katzenberg settled their court case for the latter's $250 million bonus). Throw in Ricky Martin, Regis Philbin, a fall's bonfire of a merger between CBS and Viacom, along with a surprise summer hit in which a kid sees dead people, and we cap the final year of the millennium – 1999.

The Force will be with the Box Office – Always!

The total box office not only surpassed last year's figure of $6.8 billion, but hit a grand slam, with a historical domestic figure of $7.4 billion. While the usual top fare of Disney kiddie franchises (*Tarzan, Toy Story 2*) and George Lucas pushed the industry's final takings to the maximum, there were various dark horses that rounded out the top $100 million pics of the year, putting the star system to shame for a while.

One of the year's top films proved not Brad Pitt's *Fight Club*, but rather a wiggling handheld pic from a group of fictitious students lost in the forest. *The Blair Witch Project* conned $140 million out of filmgoers' wallets. The big twist in the summer box office was Bruce Willis' unexpected hit *The Sixth Sense*, about a psychologist who counsels a child to come to terms with his visions of dead people. The supernatural movie would go on to gross $453 million globally for the year. Audiences were thrilled with the "paint by numbers" thriller *Double Jeopardy*, an unexpected left-field $114 million hit for Paramount, making a box-office star out of Ashley Judd. Some notable stellar pics hit serious grounders at the box office: Michelle Pfeiffer in *Deep End of the Ocean* and *Story of Us*, Clint Eastwood's *True Crime*, and Nicolas Cage in *8mm*.

1999 would be noted as the year when reclusive directors finally crawled out from under their rocks: Stanley Kubrick, George Lucas, and Terrence Malick. While Malick's *The Thin Red Line* was a Christmas 1998 release Stateside, the long, visually poetic war film would rake in $86 million globally in 1999. Filmgoers waited impatiently for the overdue bows of Lucas' *The Phantom Menace* and Kubrick's *Eyes Wide Shut*. Queues of *Star Wars* fans lined up months in advance at theaters across America. Film-geek websites over the past two years had posted buzz on both films continuously along with "classified" behind-the-scenes photos. When the curtain went up on both films this summer, the grumbles could be heard from as far away as Tupelo, Mississippi. While a technological marvel employing CGI for a majority of the film's scenes, *The Phantom* for many fans lacked the spirit of the original series. (Still that didn't stop everyone from making *Star Wars: Episode I, The Phantom Menace* the world's highest grosser at $920 million.) The film's only other shortcoming was that it failed to return the *Star Wars* franchise to the No. 1 spot at the all-time box office, leaving *Titanic* unsinkable.

Kubrick's Tom Cruise-Nicole Kidman starrer *Eyes Wide Shut* opened respectably in mid-July Stateside with a $20+ million gross, but fizzled rapidly down to a final cume of $56 million. In a three-hour tale of psychosexual confusion, Tom Cruise's star power wasn't enough to galvanize the pic's B.O. performance. Critics – especially Stateside – were lukewarm toward Kubrick's final film.

Studios Tool with the Future

1999 continued Hollywood's developing love affair with the internet. The medium became a vital marketing tool pegged to the success of *The Blair Witch Project*, as moviegoers flooded Artisan's website over the summer. The internet also proved a worthy saviour for aspiring industryites. Sites such as FilmShark.com provided tracking boards, job listings, and expert script coverage for struggling screen writers. Indie filmmakers benefited from such websites as AtomFilms.com and IFILM.com – which enabled them to exhibit their short films while putting them on the track to being discovered. Powersuits such as Jeffrey Katzenberg, Steven Spielberg, and Michael Ovitz showered their dollars upon upstarts such as Pop.com (a comedy shorts website) and Checkout. com (an electronics e-tailer) respectively. The threat of studio cuts didn't scare executives as they were attracted with stock options by nascent industry websites.

The medium continued to stir the stomachs of studio executives with its "rumour mill" websites. The Gocoverage website founded by producers Steve Tisch, Jon Avent, and Howard Baldwin launched and closed in one week, inciting a slew of screams from agents claiming that the website interfered with their script sales. And how about the piracy of blockbuster films? Web surfers in certain sectors of the world delighted in downloading pirated versions of MGM's Bond pic *The World Is Not Enough* and clips of *Sleepy Hollow* before the films even opened!

On top of all of Lucas' hoopla, the helmer was one of the biggest champions of Digital Projection, making *Phantom Menace* the first film to be shown in the futuristic format. Disney and 20th Century Fox and Disney were also leading proponents of the digital projector created by Texas Instruments and JVC, exhibiting such films as Miramax's *An Ideal Husband*. Digital projectors, if a success in the next decade, could make the distribution of films easier, avoiding heavy film cans and preserving director's creations without the usual deterioration of celluloid.

Music: Here It Went,
Oh Lay! Oh Lay! Oh Lay!

Even though the Spice Girls were on hiatus (married or debuting with low-charting solo albums by Geri Halliwell and Melanie Chisholm); the teenybopper kitsch craze wasn't. Witness the year's two topselling albums – the Backstreet Boys with 9.4 million copies of *Millennium* and blonde, cutie newcomer Britney Spears with *Baby One More Time*, at 8.3 million copies. Thank the Disney Channel and Nickelodeon, whose suave programing of such scream teen concerts became the launch pad for the likes of Christine

Aguilera as well as fueling current popular bands such as N'Sync. The webs weren't far behind with attracting the baby boomer crowd to televized concerts of Shania Twain, Garth Brooks, and a Celine Dion Christmas.

Latin pop was the rage for the English-language market, starting with Ricky Martin who had the chicos and chicas "Livin' the Vida Loca." Critically acclaimed film star Jennifer Lopez followed, not to mention the son of Julio Iglesias – Enrique, whose song "Bailamos" was a hit off the *Wild Wild West* soundtrack. Universal's lure of the young Iglesias with a $40 million record contract raised the bar for Latin music artists, putting him in the salary stratosphere with the likes of Janet Jackson ($70 million) and REM ($80 million). By the end of October, retro-Santana had made a comeback to the No. 1 spot with his *Supernatural* album – 28 years after his last No. 1 hit album in 1971. He beat the Beatles' record of 22 years between No. 1 hits. *Supernatural* wound up in the year's 10 topselling albums, having sold 4.7 million copies.

In the end, music-loving CEO Edgar Bronfman would be a happy man as Universal Music was the year's No. 1 recorded music outfit, gobbling up 27% of current album sales – a statistic that paid off in his acquisition of PolyGram music.

Who Wants a Hit TV Show
and Mega-Merger?

After Mafia films had run their course in the early part of the decade with *The Godfather, Part III* and *Casino*, the mobster genre began the television year by raiding the nation's homes – if they were HBO subscribers. Continuing its hit programing, such as *The Larry Sanders Show* and *Gia*, HBO introduced *The Sopranos*. A show that raised the bar on plot and characterization, it focused on New Jersey mafia captain Tony Soprano and the emotional stress that surrounded him – from his wife to his kingpin uncle Junior. Chock full of great acting, the show tapped into the theme that mobsters are people: Tony Soprano suffered from anxiety disorders and sought out therapy with a psychologist played by Lorraine Bracco. (Coincidentally, after a month of the show's play on HBO, Warner Brothers and Village Roadshow would score with the $100 million hit *Analyze This* at the box office where mobster Robert De Niro undergoes psychotherapy with Billy Crystal playing his shrink.) *The Sopranos* picked up this year's highest number of Emmy nominations for a show with a solid 16 and was hailed by television critics, who crowned it with four Television Critics Association Awards including Best Program of the Year.

Meanwhile back on network television, the year's top-rated show was not a sitcom vying to be the next *Seinfeld*; it was, ironically, a gameshow. In mid-February 1999, ABC announced that one of the shows in development was a gameshow adapted from the British production company Celador. No one imagined at the time that *Who Wants To Be A Millionaire?* would become an integral programing tool for the web, not just a summer fill-in as originally planned. With its bow in mid-August, *Who Wants To Be A Millionaire?* drove the alphabet to its first weekly Nielsen household win since the week of the Oscars show in March.

What was the secret to this show's success? Jolly talkshow host Regis Philbin faced contestants one on one with a series of questions, each correct answer leading a player toward the jackpot of $1 million. One of the popular criticisms about the show, and probably its biggest draw, was the simplicity of the multiple-choice questions (One player's million-dollar question was "Name the President who appeared on TV's 'Laugh In.'" Answer: Richard Nixon.). Aside from that, contestants were permitted to rely upon "life lines" to assist them with head-scratching questions; i.e. they could receive a tip from the audience or friends, or could eliminate two of the four answer choices. The clincher was that players ceased playing when they answered a question incorrectly.

When the answers were called for the November sweep wins, the leader was ABC with its first triumph since Disney took over the company in 1995, grabbing a 5.9 rating and 15 share with the coveted 18-49 demo and a 9.9/16 with households. Kudos to Regis and the questions.

In the same vein as Disney-ABC, Viacom and CBS announced their plan to merge, with Viacom buying CBS out mostly in stock. Combined, the two companies were valued at $70 billion. CBS, an older skewing demo web, would now become part of a vertical integration that included Paramount, MTV, Nickelodeon, VH1, and Simon & Schuster publishing. It was almost as if history took a full circle for Viacom was spun out of CBS in the 1970s after federal antitrust laws limited the amount of programing that networks could own. At the time of the merger, the FCC prohibited one company from owning two networks, calling into question the existence of Viacom's UPN network in 2000.

Into 2000 and Beyond

Sure, the Oscar race would be a hard one to predict with the critically acclaimed bows of *American Beauty*, *The Talented Mr. Ripley*, and *The Hurricane*. *Mission: Impossible 2* would finally defy its own production shoot impossibilities and actually open in mid-2000. However, the biggest cliffhanger was in the final month of 1999, when Ted Turner announced that he would love to buy the NBC Network. "I'm like Noah. I want two of everything," the Time Warner mogul announced at the Western Cable Show. Had a merger occurred, the era of the independent television networks would have been at an end. But will the '90s' vertical integration craze for media companies continue (as the massive AOL acquisition of Time Warner in January 2000 certainly suggests)? Will these entertainment multinationals (with their plans of synergy) step on their toes and break up? Will these game shows continue to dominate primetime TV? What will Steven Spielberg choose to direct as his next feature? Set your recordable DVD timer and go to the local "digital theater'" to find out in the twenty-first century. **Anthony D'Alessandro**

> *You have no values, your whole life is nihilism, cynicism, sarcasm and orgasm. In France I could run on that slogan and win.(Caroline Aaron, Woody Allen,* Deconstructing Harry)

Variety 100 Top Stars

1900-1919

Sarah Bernhardt (1844-1923) The "Divine" French thesp emerges as the first superstar-diva of the twentieth century.

Fanny Brice (1891-1951) Popular Ziegfeld Follies actress was universally adored as the radio star of "Baby Snooks."

Eddie Cantor (1892-1964) Vaudeville comic and Ziegfeld's biggest star, who made a smooth transition to the worlds of radio, TV, and film.

Enrico Caruso (1873-1921) First Italian super-tenor laid the groundwork for Luciano Pavarotti and Placido Domingo.

George M. Cohan (1878-1942) All-American actor, playwright, and writer of such songs as "Yankee Doodle Dandy" and "Give My Regards to Broadway."

Harry Houdini (1874-1926) Hungarian-born magician dazzled auds with his numerous escapes featuring straitjackets, coffins, and safes.

Harry Lauder (1892-1964) Scottish entertainer won international renown for his charming stage persona, kilt and a curled walking stick.

1920s

Louis "Satchmo" Armstrong (1901-71) Phenomenal jazz trumpeter who became a household name thanks to spots on TV shows and pics such as *Pennies From Heaven* and *High Society*.

John Barrymore (1882-1942) Roguish stage and film thesp, aka "the profile," best remembered for his legit take on *Hamlet*.

Louise Brooks (1906-85) Enigmatic silent-film siren who played Lulu in *Pandora's Box* with a pageboy hairstyle and timeless sexual appeal.

Charlie Chaplin (1889-1977) Quintessential comic genius of the silent era, the Little Tramp's classics include *City Lights* and *The Great Dictator*.

Marlene Dietrich (1901-92) German-born blonde bombshell, sexual icon, and formidable star of *The Blue Angel* and *Destry Rides Again*.

Greta Garbo (1905-90) Studios' greatest Swedish import transfixed auds in *Flesh and the Devil*, *Queen Christina*, and *Ninotchka*, with her mysterious, unattainable screen persona.

George Gershwin (1898-1937) Composer of "Rhapsody in Blue" and "Porgy and Bess" became as big a star as those who sung and danced to his groundbreaking music.

John Gilbert (1899-1936) Dubbed by MGM as the "Great Lover," the lead actor in *The Big Parade* was left at the altar by none other than Garbo.

Al Jolson (1886-1950) The biggest name on Broadway who gave voice and star power to Warner Bros.' 1927 pic *The Jazz Singer*.

Buster Keaton (1895-1966) Sad-eyed comic star of silent gems such as *The General* (1927) and *Sherlock Jr.*

Mary Pickford (1892-1979) "America's Sweetheart" starred in more than 51 films and turned her popularity into power by co-founding United Artists.

Will Rogers (1879-1935) Rope twirler, humorist, and homespun philosopher whose influence was so immense that politicians followed his lead.

Rudolph Valentino (1895-1926) Italian-born sex symbol and star of *The Sheik* whose sudden death caused a wave of hysteria among female fans.

1930s

Fred Astaire (1899-1987) and **Ginger Rogers** (1911-95) He gave her class, she made him sexy: glorious, once-in-a-century dancing partners of *Top Hat* and *Swing Time*.

James Cagney (1899-1986) Tough-guy star of *The Public Enemy, Angels With Dirty Faces*, and *White Heat* imbued his gangsters with volatility, staccato speech, grace, and a code of honor.

Gary Cooper (1901-61) Laconic, all-American hero who immortalized the title protagonists of *Sergeant York* and *Meet John Doe*.

Joan Crawford (1908-77) Strident, tough-yet-vulnerable female icon who lit up such pics as *The Women* and *Mildred Pierce*.

Bette Davis (1908-89) One of Warner Bros.' biggest contract players whose searing portrayals made strong, emotional women who live by their wits fashionable.

Errol Flynn (1909-59) Swashbuckling star of *Captain Blood* and *The Adventures of Robin Hood* gave roguish charm new meaning.

Clark Gable (1901-60) Ladykiller with a "winking moustache" was crowned "the king" after his star turns in *It Happened One Night*, and *Gone With the Wind*.

Jean Harlow (1911-37) Voluptuous star of *Platinum Blonde* loved for her larger-than-life screen sensuality.

Katharine Hepburn (1907) A combination of breeding, intelligence, and comic timing allowed Oscar's most decorated actress to command respect from critics and moguls alike.

Stan Laurel (1890-1965) and **Oliver Hardy** (1892-1957) Slapstick comedy team took music-hall antics to big screen, creating short film masterpieces that drew new audiences in showings on early TV.

Myrna Loy (1905-93) and **William Powell** (1892-1984) Elegant, sophisticated couple, best remembered for their portrayal of Nick and Nora Charles in *The Thin Man* series.

Marx Brothers: Leonard "Chico" (1887-1961), Adolph "Harpo" (1888-1964), Julius "Groucho" (1890-1977) and Herbert "Zeppo" Marx (1900-79) Zany, anarchy-loving brothers, stars of *Animal Crackers, Duck Soup* and *A Night at the Opera*.

Shirley Temple (1928) Supremely talented child star who winked, mugged, sang, and tap-danced her way into the hearts of filmgoers worldwide.

1940s

Humphrey Bogart (1899-1957) The quintessential film noir gumshoe of *The Big Sleep* and *The Maltese Falcon*, and anti-romantic hero of *Casablanca*.

Bing Crosby (1903-77) Before Sinatra there was Crosby, whose relaxed manner and casual delivery set the standard for crooners.

Henry Fonda (1905-82) Star of *The Grapes of Wrath* and *My Darling Clementine* excelled at projecting honesty and decency on screen.

John Garfield (1913-52) Cocky Bronx streetboy-turned-Group Theater standout (*The Postman Always Rings Twice, Force of Evil*) was a forerunner to the Method actors of the '50s.

Judy Garland (1922-69) Child star-turned tragic diva whose roles in *The Wizard of Oz, Meet Me in St. Louis*, and *A Star Is Born* made her a legend.

Cary Grant (1904-86) The former Archie Leach perfected a screen persona of ultra-sophistication, wry humor, and debonair charm that kept him in demand for decades.

Bob Hope (1903) Affable, English-born comedian is best remembered for his *Road* pics with Bing Crosby, entertaining U.S. troops, and signature song, "Thanks for the Memories."

Laurence Olivier (1907-89) Considered by many the greatest actor of his generation, Olivier also proved a smouldering leading man in *Wuthering Heights* and *Rebecca*.

Gregory Peck (1916) Strong, silent-type star brought dignity and decency to such pics as *Gentleman's Agreement, Roman Holiday*, and *To Kill a Mockingbird*.

Jimmy Stewart (1908-97) One of the most trusted and beloved American actors, who brought an air of unpretentious appeal to *The Philadelphia Story, It's A Wonderful Life*, and several Hitchcock classics.

Hank Williams (1923-53) The father of modern country music and a lyrical influence on artists in all pop and rock fields, singer-songwriter-musician Williams's impact resonated beyond his short life.

1950s

Lucille Ball (1911-89) Brilliant comedienne who changed the TV landscape with her timeless, hugely influential sitcom *I Love Lucy* after 18 years of starring in movies.

Brigitte Bardot (1934) The first of the great French sex kittens, star of Godard's *Contempt* and Roger Vadim's *And God Created Woman*.

Milton Berle (1908) The durable comic performer known as Uncle Milty and Mr. Television, whose long-running eponymous show glued Americans to their TV sets in the '50s.

Chuck Berry (1926) Singer-songwriter-musician helped create rock 'n' roll with rollicking stage shows, seamless guitar, and sly wordplay.

Marlon Brando (1924): The leading exponent of the Method who exploded on the screen with brute force in *A Streetcar Named Desire* and led the way for Dean, Newman, De Niro, and the rest.

Miles Davis (1926-91) The Picasso of jazz managed to revolutionize the medium by mastering several styles – cool, bop, modal, fusion – while attaining the popularity of a rock star.

James Dean (1931-55) Tragic patron saint of lost-boy angst whose troubled screen portrayals (*Rebel Without a Cause, East of Eden, Giant*) and untimely death catapulted him to immortality.

Jackie Gleason (1916-87) His perfectly crafted role as Everyman Ralph Kramden in TV's hugely popular *The Honeymooners* cast a large shadow on the rest of his film and TV career.

Gene Kelly (1912-96) Virtuoso actor-director whose strong, physical approach to dance added immeasurably to such classics as *Singin' in the Rain* and *An American in Paris*.

Grace Kelly (1928-82) Elegant star of *High Noon, Rear Window* and *To Catch a Thief* whose regal beauty translated into the real-life role of princess.

Dean Martin (1917-95) and **Jerry Lewis** (1926) The boozing straight-man singer and his goofy sidekick, respectively, made 16 films together before establishing their individual stardom.

Marilyn Monroe (1926-62) The queen of platinum blonde bombshells whose sex appeal, fragility, public dramas, and mysterious death have made her a goddess for the ages.

Elvis Presley (1935-77) The King's voice, look and moves ignited a national frenzy, made black music accessible to scores of teens, and inspired countless talents, including the Beatles, to pursue rock 'n' roll.

Frank Sinatra (1915-98) Ol' Blue Eyes, the Voice, Chairman of the Board – Sinatra swung like no other and managed to cross over into films with memorable turns in *From Here to Eternity, The Manchurian Candidate,* and *Guys and Dolls.*

Elizabeth Taylor (1932) True Hollywood royalty, Miss Taylor grew up on the screen and matured with each phase of her career: child star, voluptuous leading lady, survivor of numerous doomed romances, and tireless AIDS activist.

John Wayne (1907-79) Larger-than-life thesp of oaters such as *Stagecoach* and *The Searchers,* as well as war pics *Flying Tigers* and *They Were Expendable,* the Duke made over 180 pics during his lifetime.

1960s

Julie Andrews (1935) For ever branded as the magical nanny in *Mary Poppins* and the singing nun in *The Sound of Music,* the gifted British thesp continued to dazzle fans in *S.O.B., Victor/Victoria,* and TV projects.

The Beatles As the first Brit rock group to achieve world prominence, John, Paul, George, and Ringo broke all previous record sales and took popular music to new heights, both artistically and commercially.

Jean-Paul Belmondo (1933) Versatile French thesp moved with aplomb between projects from Jean-Luc Godard's revolutionary *Breathless* to Alain Resnais' elegiac *Stavisky.*

James Brown (1928) Key rhythm and blues innovator who took the electric blues of Chicago giants such as Muddy Waters and Willie Dixon and created his "New Breed" sound which signified Black Pride and urban street sophistication.

Sean Connery (1930) Scottish-born thesp established the template for James Bond in *Dr. No* and *Goldfinger* before stretching his wings in *The Wind and the Lion, The Man Who Would Be King,* and *The Untouchables.*

Bob Dylan (1941) The two greatest innovators of American songwriting of the century were Irving Berlin and Dylan. Unlike Berlin, Dylan was also a performer who cut a swathe as a political-social figure and who influenced the mores and beliefs of his generation.

Audrey Hepburn (1929-93) The epitome of style and elegance, the Dutch-born actress garnered an Oscar nomination with her first lead in *Roman Holiday* before solidifying her stardom in *Breakfast at Tiffany's* and *My Fair Lady.*

Sophia Loren (1934) Italy's most famous screen export, whether starring in high-brow Oscar-winners such as *The Women* or romping with Marcello Mastroianni in *Yesterday, Today and Tomorrow.*

Steve McQueen (1930-80) The ultimate action star of *The Great Escape* and *Bullitt,* whose minimalist approach to acting epitomized machismo, cool, and quiet strength.

Paul Newman (1925) Blue-eyed idol who combined strikingly good looks with strong acting chops in *The Hustler, Hud,* and *Hombre* before becoming one of the decade's most popular stars.

Sidney Poitier (1924) First African-American male to get nominated for an Oscar (*The Defiant Ones*) and then win one (*Lillies in the Field*), he gave strong, dignified performances in *Guess Who's Coming To Dinner?* and *In the Heat of the Night.*

Barbra Streisand (1942) Ever since she wowed audiences on both stage and screen in *Funny Girl,* the Brooklyn-born actress-singer-helmer has remained a consistent force on the stage and screen, while largely calling her own shots.

1970s

Woody Allen (1935) Standup comic and TV writer became America's most consistent and prolific auteur, while creating a screen persona that embodied modern urban neurosis.

Johnny Carson (1925) The king of late-night talk shows ruled NBC's *The Tonight Show* for three decades. Eight years after his last show, TV viewers still miss his deadpan humor and gracious manners.

Clint Eastwood (1930) A man with no name from '60s spaghetti westerns became a steely '70s icon in pics such as *Dirty Harry,* before maturing into an Oscar-winning helmer with *Unforgiven* in the '90s.

Jane Fonda (1937) Henry's smart, sexy, and fiercely independent daughter straddled acting and political activism with unflinching strength before playing Ted Turner's wife in real life.

Elton John (1947) From sensitive singer-composer to flamboyant showman, the Royal Academy of Music alum became a rock giant with top-selling LPs such as *Don't Shoot Me, I'm Only the Piano Player* and *Goodbye Yellow Brick Road.*

Jack Nicholson (1937) Explosive actor with the devilish grin and arching eyebrows established a winning screen persona in *Five Easy Pieces, One Flew Over the Cuckoo's Nest,* and *Chinatown* that is by turns rebellious, sardonic, and fiendishly charming.

Richard Pryor (1940) Brilliant standup comic radically changed rules of American comedy with his brash, raw humor and went on to achieve mainstream film success.

John Travolta (1954) The street-smart Italian kid from New Jersey defined the spirit of the late '70s in the disco hit *Saturday Night Fever* and the nostalgic musical *Grease,* then staged a major comeback in the '90s with *Pulp Fiction* and *Face/Off.*

1980s

Bill Cosby (1937) His part as Dr. Huxtable helped *The Cosby Show* to rule the airwaves for years and established Cos' as one of TV's most positive black role models.

Harrison Ford (1942) After breaking through as Han Solo in *Star Wars* in the '70s, Ford developed into a no-nonsense superstar in actioners spanning three decades.

Mel Gibson (1956) Rugged star of *Mad Max* movies hit his stride with the *Lethal Weapon* series and went on to direct and star in the Oscar-winning *Braveheart* in 1995.

Michael Jackson (1958) Controversial pop star who transitioned from child entertainer to adult phenomenon.

Madonna (1958) An expert in the art of self-reinvention, Madonna Ciccone continues to deliver strong pop albums, as well as occasional film roles such as *Evita* and the forthcoming *The Next Best Thing.*

Eddie Murphy (1961) Street-smart comic went from wildly inventive *Saturday Night Live* sketches to becoming a big box-office draw with the *Beverly Hills Cop* franchise.

Arnold Schwarzenegger (1947) Austrian bodybuilder starred in many blockbuster action pictures and has been a top international B.O. star for nearly 20 years.

Sylvester Stallone (1946) Everyman, Palookaville persona took hold with the crowd-pleasing *Rocky* and ballooned into invincible superhero in the *Rambo* films.

Meryl Streep (1949) Moving from accent to accent, the chameleonesque thesp excelled in such serious dramas as *The French Lieutenant's Woman, Sophie's Choice* and *Out of Africa.*

Oprah Winfrey (1954) With the phenomenally successful daytime talkshow under her belt, one of the most powerful and recognisable faces in TV and publishing continues to target film projects (*Beloved*) and new vehicles (cabler Oxygen).

1990s

Garth Brooks (1962) Country-music star broke through all barriers to become biggest-selling solo recording artist of all time with nearly 100 million in U.S. record sales alone.

Jim Carrey (1962) Rubber-faced comic went from standup sensation in the '80s to the king of screen slapstick in the '90s (*Ace Ventura: Pet Detective*) before gaining critical kudos with helmers Peter Weir and Milos Forman.

Tom Cruise (1962) Cocky, boyish, toothy actor adept at playing callow types who learn their lesson by the end of the movie, Cruise floats atop the $20 million per-pic club.

Leonardo DiCaprio (1974) Young, virtuoso talent who rose to fame with Oscar-nominated role in *What's Eating Gilbert Grape?* and became a global heart-throb as the scrappy romantic in *Titanic.*

Jodie Foster (1962) Intelligent child actress (*Taxi Driver*) grew up to be one of Hollywood's most respected players with Oscar-winning roles in *The Accused* and *The Silence of The Lambs,* and occasional directing jobs.

Whoopi Goldberg (1955) Impishly funny standup comedienne who has starred in more than 60 movies and TV shows, including *The Color Purple* and *Ghost,* for which she won an Oscar.

Tom Hanks (1956) The boyish, affable hero with the trusting face went from bigscreen cut-up to back-to-back Oscar winner (*Philadelphia, Forrest Gump*).

Julia Roberts (1967) Doe-eyed actress with the big smile hit the box-office jackpot with *Pretty Woman, My Best Friend's Wedding,* and *Notting Hill.*

Jerry Seinfeld (1954) The Brooklyn-born standup comic developed and starred in one of the most innovative sitcoms of the '90s (*Seinfeld*), made a lot of money, and quit when the going was good.

Bruce Willis (1955) TV's smart-aleck gumshoe (*Moonlighting*) hit box-office gold playing the guy who can save the world (*Die Hard* series, *Armageddon*) with a smirk on his face, while in 1999 the spooky *The Sixth Sense* elevated his career to a new level.

... January 7 ...
Glenn Close is to star in **A Little Night Music** on Broadway.

Personalities of the Year

Our personalities this year come from both ends of the showbiz spectrum. Julia Roberts' agent must naturally assume that any new film in which she stars will gross north of $100 million, while Eduardo Sanchez and Daniel Myrick, the brains behind *The Blair Witch Project*, made their maiden feature on the skin of, well, a camcorder. Both Judi Dench and Kevin Spacey have revived that dying breed, the character actor, illuminating often only a few minutes on screen with a carefully modulated performance. And, like Madonna before her, Mariah Carey has now reached a stage in superstardom that enables her to cross from recording to screen acting.

Mariah Carey

"I am not Cinderella ... my life has not been a fairy tale," Mariah Carey told the audience at the MGM Grand in Las Vegas when she was named Artist of the Decade at the 1999 *Billboard* Music Awards. To outsiders, a fairytale figure was exactly what she did seem – and not just because of the confetti that rained down on her as she walked on stage to collect her award. In under 10 years the singer-songwriter had sold 120 million albums worldwide and had racked up 14 chart-topping singles on the *Billboard* Hot 100 (only the Beatles and Elvis Presley have done better). No other female artist of the 1990s could match her success: not Madonna, not Celine Dion, not Whitney Houston. Her private life may have been turbulent and some of her business ventures may have wobbled (her record label, Crave, was closed down after only two years in 1999) but none of this affected her recording. Plot her music career on a graph and all you see is a smooth upward curve.

Star stories are supposed to be gilt-edged fables, but Carey's sounds like something dreamed up for a Danielle Steele mini-series. She is the blue-collar heroine who overcame poverty, racial prejudice and a string of broken relationships. Born in Long Island in March 1970, she is the daughter of an Irish-American mother and a black Venezuelan father; her parents divorced when she was three. Her father, an aeronautical engineer, remarried. She lost touch with him and was brought up by her mother, an opera singer. Her childhood was tough. She and her mixed-race family were subjected to continual harassment. There are accounts of their car being bombed and their dog poisoned. Carey's singing ability was evident right from the outset. She often repeats the story of how, as a young child, she heard her mother practising *Rigoletto*, and corrected her when she hit a false note. Although she never learned to read music and didn't progress far with her piano studies, Mariah had such a good ear that she could play pieces instinctively. "From the time Mariah was a tiny girl," her mother has recalled, "she sang on true pitch. She was able to hear a sound and duplicate it exactly."

Legend has it that Lana Turner was discovered as a teenager in Schwab's Drugstore in Hollywood. Carey's lucky break came in equally unlikely circumstances. After leaving school at 17, she moved to Manhattan and took waitressing jobs while she tried to establish herself as a session singer. In 1988, when she was working as a back-up singer for Brenda Starr, one of her demo tapes reached President of Columbia Records, Tommy Mottola. He was so enraptured with her voice that he signed her up immediately and masterminded the release of her first album, *Mariah Carey* (1990). It sold more than six million copies, yielded two chart-topping singles, and won her a Grammy as Best Newcomer. In 1993 Mottola and Carey married. Their wedding (modeled on that of Charles and Diana) cost – or so the gossip columnists claimed – $500,000. She really did seem like the fairytale princess of pop, an impression that subsequent albums such as *Music Box* (1993), *Merry Christmas* (1994) and *Daydream* (1995) did nothing to dispel. They were expertly crafted, but also mawkish and anodyne. Under Mottola's Svengali-like guidance, Carey was presented to the public as a squeaky-clean American songstress. It was a persona she grew to resent. After she split up from Mottola in the summer of 1997 (they were divorced a year later) she set about changing her image and escaping from what she

---

... January 8 ...

Metro-Goldwyn-Mayer emerges victorious in its lawsuit with Sony Pictures Entertainment over the right to make James Bond films.

referred to as "a huge corporate machine." As she put it, "I'm not the little Mariah who sings sweet like syrup songs anymore. I've got a hip-hop edge. So, you can see who I really am and where my previous personality came from ..."

To register the transformation, you only need to glance at her recent album covers. On *Rainbow* (1999) she's shown dressed like a pin-up in skimpy white tank-top and bikini-bottoms. "I've been wearing turtlenecks and snowsuits for too long," she announced. "I know I am scantily clad, but there's nothing rude about this image. Many other artistes are doing it too and nobody questions them." Her choice of collaborators was revealing. Producers Jimmy Jam and Terry Lewis (best known for their work with Janet Jackson), and hip-hop artists Jay-Z, Missy Elliott, Da Brat, and Snoop Dogg all worked on the album. Her new image, as one sardonic journalist observed, was like that of an "R&B Princess Di, a gutsy glamor girl who'd managed to flee an oppressive, high-profile marriage."

Her followers, who continued to buy her records in enormous quantities, weren't fazed in the slightest by the metamorphosis. During late 1999 the relentlessly hardworking Carey toured all over Europe, South America, and the Far East, promoting *Rainbow*. "Fans are the most important thing," she claimed as she conducted numerous interviews, made instore appearances, and answered questions on the web. "Some people tell me that I shouldn't be so close to my fans, that it is dangerous. But I don't care – I have to be."

In her speech at the 1999 *Billboard* Awards, Carey seemed a little nonplussed at being the biggest-selling female artist of the 1990s. "This is all very surreal to me," she admitted. "Honestly, it seems like not too long ago I was a kid in high school with a demo tape and a lot of determination and just the desire to hear my songs on the radio." That ambition has long since been achieved. Now, as movie actress Jennifer Lopez turns to a singing career, Carey looks set to go the other way. Her long-gestating comedy-thriller *Double O Soul*, in which she was supposed to star opposite Chris Tucker (of *Rush Hour* fame), may still be in limbo, but she has already played a cameo in the Chris O'Donnell film *The Bachelor*, and her first starring vehicle, *All That Glitters*, is due to shoot in early 2000. Her role is tailor-made. She is cast as a young singer from a rough background who makes her breakthrough thanks to her demo tape falling into the hands of an influential DJ. Whatever the film's fate at the box office, one prediction can safely be made – the soundtrack album is sure to nestle somewhere near the top of that *Billboard* chart. **Geoffrey Macnab**

Judi Dench

To win an Academy Award and a Tony in the same year is almost unheard of. Ellen Burstyn managed it in 1974-75 for her roles in Martin Scorsese's *Alice Doesn't Live Here Any More*, and the stage production of *Same Time Next Year*. Now, Dame Judi Dench has followed suit. The Oscar was for her startling eight-minute cameo as the Virgin Queen in *Shakespeare in Love* and she followed that up three months later with a Best Actress prize on Broadway for her role in David Hare's *Amy's View*.

Throughout 1999 it was hard to avoid Dench on stage and screen. In the spring we saw her as one of the sharp-tongued English ladies in Franco Zeffirelli's pretty, 1930s-set Tuscan romance, *Tea With Mussolini*. As the year ended she was tussling with the villainous Sophie Marceau and Robbie Carlyle in the new Bond movie, *The World Is Not Enough*, in which she again played M. (When she first took over the role from Bernard Lee in *GoldenEye* (1995) she startled 007 aficionados by describing the world's favorite secret agent as "a sexist, misogynist dinosaur and a relic of the Cold War.")

The British have long cherished Dench as one of their greatest stage stars. She was made a Dame of the British Empire back in 1988. Generally, this is an honor reserved for ageing Grandes Dames of West End theater, but Dench was only 53 when it came her way. The year before, as if to prove that she was still in her salad days, she had appeared opposite Anthony Hopkins in a National Theatre production of *Antony and Cleopatra*. Dench was initially reluctant to take the role, reportedly claiming that her Cleopatra would be a "menopausal dwarf," but director Peter Hall (who describes her as "the greatest speaker of Shakespeare of her generation") talked her into it. Her performance was applauded by one critic for its combination of "carnality, cunning, caprice, and cruelty."

A Yorkshire doctor's daughter, brought up in a strict Quaker household, Dench doesn't seem like a natural diva. Shy, diminutive (she is barely over 5ft tall), and with a nasal-sounding voice, she only switched to acting because she didn't think she would get anywhere as a stage designer. After graduating from the Central School of Drama (where her co-students included Vanessa Redgrave), she quickly established herself as one of the most versatile talents of her generation.

In the course of a career which started way back in 1957 when, as a 23-year-old straight out of drama school, she was cast as Ophelia to John Neville's Hamlet at the Old Vic, Dench has played Shakespeare, Chekhov, and Restoration comedy; Edward Bond and

---

Harold Pinter; musicals and sitcoms. In 1968, she was Sally Bowles in the first West End production of *Cabaret*. Her Lady Macbeth opposite Ian McKellen's Scottish king in a groundbreaking 1975 production is still talked about with awe. ("She made us see Lady Macbeth not as a heartless, ruthless female power politician, but as a woman so in love with her husband that the love was too much for her," observed the director Trevor Nunn. "People remember her sleep-walking scene as the most harrowing ever.")

She has also done a bit of directing for Branagh's Renaissance Theatre Company. Had it not been for a strained Achilles tendon which knocked her out of action for six months, we would even have seen her in Andrew Lloyd Webber's smash hit, *Cats*. In the mid-1980s alone, she was both the doughty matriarch dragging her wagon across the carnage of war-torn Europe in the National Theatre's *Mother Courage* and, at the same time, the demure suburban heroine of TV sitcom, *A Fine Romance* (in which she starred opposite her husband, Michael Williams).

There was only one area in which Dench struggled – cinema. She may have won a British Film Academy award as Most Promising Newcomer for her second feature, *Four in the Morning* (1966), but somehow Dench and movies just didn't go together. At her first film audition, she was told: "Miss Dench, you have everything wrong with your face." For a long period in the 1970s, she was so discouraged she didn't make any films at all. As she explained to *The Times*: "I decided not to do any film work because that would take me away from my daughter all day, whereas in the theater, once you've opened, it's only really evenings." Her film career, she added, had been "so totally disastrous," that she didn't think anybody would notice anyway.

During the 1980s she could occasionally be prised out in front of the movie cameras, but generally only in period films. We saw her opposite Vanessa Redgrave and Ian Holm in David Hare's *Wetherby* in 1985; as the sex-obsessed novelist Miss Lavish in Merchant-Ivory's *A Room With a View* (1986); as the social-climbing Mrs Beaver in Charles Sturridge's Evelyn Waugh adaptation, *A Handful of Dust* (1987); and as Mistress Quickly in Branagh's *Henry V* (1989). The role as Bond's boss came in 1995. It was only really with Mrs Brown, though, that Dench emerged from the pack of consummately gifted British stage actors who play occasional character parts in movies.

When Miramax acquired this modestly budgeted BBC Scotland-produced film about the relationship between the grieving Queen Victoria and her hirsute Scottish gillie, John Brown, the 63-year-old Dench suddenly, and very belatedly, became a full-blown movie star. Her Oscar-nominated performance was rapturously received by American critics. ("Dame Judi, her face clamped in anguish, radiates the stern ecstasy of grief. This queen of English understatement embodies Victoria's belief: that mourning is the only way survivors can consummate their love for the dead," wrote Richard Corliss in *Time*.)

Then came the cameo as Queen Elizabeth, another of Dench's haughty matriarchs with acid tongues, in John Madden's *Shakespeare in Love*. She only appears three times in the film, but it was enough to win her the Oscar and to ensure that by the time she reached Broadway in *Amy's View* less than a month after the Academy Awards, advance ticket sales stood at $3 million. After her Oscar/Tony double, some critics were left asking what she would do for an encore. It was exactly the same question they posed in 1997, when she made history by winning two Olivier Awards, one for acting (*Absolute Hell*) and one for singing (*A Little Night Music*). Past history suggests she'll manage some other equally startling feat soon. **Geoffrey Macnab**

Julia Roberts

Two films. Two blockbusters. That double play belonged to only one actor in 1999, and it wasn't Tom Cruise, Jim Carrey or Mel Gibson. Julia Roberts scored a pair of $100 million grossers with Universal's *Notting Hill* and Paramount's *Runaway Bride*, and, by reaching those money milestones, the closest thing to a sure bet punctuated a decade of dominance.

Having kicked off the 1990s with a starmaking turn in *Pretty Woman*, Roberts approached the millennium as one of the most bankable thesps. A leading lady whose characters blend southern belle sweetness with assertive self-reliance, she has consistently won over every demographic while building a diverse body of work. And her paychecks finally reflect that: Roberts is the highest-paid actress in Hollywood, with an asking price of $20 million.

Roberts' year could be read as strictly a ledger entry, something that bodes well for studios lucky enough to grab her for future roles. But due to today's obsession with gender wars, her status as a power player is much more significant. She's certainly a domestic and international draw, but the Smyrna, Ga. native commands a business that has always been top-heavy with macho prowess. From Errol Flynn and James Dean to John Wayne and Clint Eastwood, viewers have been hooked on testosterone, with femmes faring – at best – nicely. So Roberts' rise is as much a social achievement as it is a financial one, and the industry has never seen anything like it. For as much as Shirley Temple, Marilyn

... January 10 ...
Disney and Paramount's **A Civil Action** is number one at the box office
this weekend with a studio-estimated $14.5 million.

Monroe, and Bette Davis meant to the movies, Roberts' box-office mastery is more impressive: in an era of bottom lines, she's an accessible sex symbol, the fan favorite next door, and a global commodity at the peak of her career.

Hill and *Bride* topped a decade that began on the streets. As a hooker-with-a-heart, she turned *Woman* (1990) into a home run – it has earned $178 million to date – and copped a second Academy Award nomination (she got a nod in 1989 for *Steel Magnolias*).

Roberts then went straight into heavy drama as the loyal caretaker to Campbell Scott in *Dying Young* (1991; $34 million). Though the pic was a B.O. underperformer, her selection proved to be wise: by shifting gears, she refused to become typecast. And although the actress' biggest hits have all been romantic comedies, some of her most critically lauded work has come under niche helmers, including Robert Altman (*Prêt-à-Porter*, 1994), Lasse Hallström (*Something to Talk About*, 1995), Woody Allen (*Everyone Says I Love You*, 1996), and Neil Jordan (*Michael Collins*, 1996).

Although there have been a few misses (*I Love Trouble, Mary Reilly*), there have, it seems, always been more than enough winners to balance things out. She joined Robin Williams and Dustin Hoffman in 1991's *Hook*, Steven Spielberg's fantasy that earned $120 million, and she co-starred in 1993 with Denzel Washington in Alan J. Pakula's *The Pelican Brief* ($101 million). But the stratospheric leap came in 1997. Action ruled with *Men in Black* and *Air Force One*, dinosaurs were at it again in *The Lost World: Jurassic Park*, and it looked like multiplexes were in store for yet another pyrotechnic-heavy, special-effects-stuffed summer. Audiences, however, were hungry for a little lovin', and they got loads of it from director P.J. Hogan and scribe Ron Bass. Sony's *My Best Friend's Wedding* opened on June 20, 1997, to $22 million, and its final take came to $127 million. Roberts was, according to ticketbuyers, back where she belonged, and the receipts proved it. *Wedding* shone the spotlight on Roberts' appeal, and, thanks to breakout performances from Rupert Everett and Cameron Diaz, it went on to become the counter-programing hit of the season. Costly aliens and a giant T-Rex had to make room for a simple tale about a woman in love, and Roberts solidified her spot atop a list that included Michelle Pfeiffer and Demi Moore.

She also linked up that year with Mel Gibson in WB's *Conspiracy Theory*, and although the pic failed to surpass the $100 million mark at home – final domestic B.O. was $76 million – the worldwide box-office tally reached $133 million. Richard Donner's paranoia study reinforced her ability to open a film, and it ended up as one of a few studio pics on several top-10 lists. Not a love-fest, *Stepmom* (1998) came next, and the somber narrative about a woman's battle with cancer – Susan Sarandon co-starred – was Columbia's high-profile Christmas release; it has grossed $91 million to date.

So when the 1999 summer schedule made the rounds and studios began their distribution chess match, the talk, it seemed, was about Roberts. How would U and Par handle, respectively, *Notting Hill* (release date: May 28, 1999) and *Runaway Bride* (July 30)? It wouldn't matter. As *Daily Variety* chief critic Todd McCarthy wrote in his *Bride* review, "What are fans of the biggest female star going to do – not see this picture after having seen, and liked, her last one? Not likely." As Anna Scott, a glamorous starlet who falls for Hugh Grant, Roberts seemed a natural choice. She was playing herself, and people bought it ($116 million). So by July, when *Bride* opened, it wasn't a surprise that everyone wanted more Julia. Also directed by Marshall, the film earned $152 million.

Things had come full circle. A journey that began by Richard Gere's side ended right there, and ten years of (mostly) hits were book-ended by grand slams. She'll try to top 1999 with *Erin Brockovich*, a story that teams her with *The Limey* director Steven Soderbergh, and Terrence Malick's *The Moviegoer* is also on her slate. **Michael Speier**

Eduardo Sanchez and Daniel Myrick

"On October 21, 1994, Heather Donahue, Joshua Leonard, and Michael Williams hiked into Maryland's Black Hills Forest to shoot a documentary on a local legend, The Blair Witch. They were never heard from again. One year later, their footage was found, documenting the students' five-day journey through the Black Hills Forest and capturing the terrifying events that led to their disappearance."

Thus began the big tease which turned *The Blair Witch Project* into the movie phenomenon of 1999. Four or five lines of deadpan prose posted on *The Blair Witch* website – along with journal entries and police reports – tantalized surfers. Was this story for real? Why did those students disappear? "Evidence exists ... log on to www.blairwitch.com to see and hear," was the advice to the curious. By the time of the film's U.S. release in the late summer, the website was receiving two million hits a day. The filmmakers claimed they were using "guerrilla marketing tactics" to push *Blair Witch*. To outsiders, the process seemed closer to alchemy. Somehow, by the end of the year, a low-budget movie made for "about the cost of a decent car" by Haxan Films, a little-known Orlando-

... January 11 ...
Martin Scorsese and Barry Levinson sign with Artist Management Group, the new management-production banner Michael Ovitz, Rick Yorn, and Julie Silverman-Yorn.

based company owned by five University of Central Florida graduates, had racked up U.S. box-office receipts close to $150 million while also breaking records everywhere from the U.K. (where it was unveiled in time for Halloween) to Australia.

This was not a star-driven, high-concept action-adventure. Apart from a little slime on a rucksack, some piles of rocks, rags, teeth, and a few twisted sticks, *Blair Witch* doesn't offer much in the way of special effects. Nor, beyond lots of tiny handprints smeared on the walls of a ruined house and some strange screeches in the night, is there anything to tell us there really *is* a witch in the woods. The film was shot, very shakily, by its three main cast members on a color camcorder and a 16mm black-and-white camera. ("It was supposed to look like a documentary because we didn't have any money," the directors explained.) As the campers give into hunger, cold, and blind terror, their cameras begin to wobble and the stranger the framing becomes. (We're offered, for instance, one of the largest close-ups of the inside of an actor's nostril yet committed to film.) Nobody had heard of Donahue, Leonard or Williams, the three newcomers who lent their names to the characters they played. Nor had they heard of the writer-directors, Eduardo Sanchez and Daniel Myrick.

Who were they? The 35-year-old Myrick was a Florida-based filmmaker whose resumé, pre-*Blair Witch*, seemed little different from that of any other aspiring indie brat. He'd spent ten years in film and video production, working as an editor and a cameraman and directing shorts. He met the 30-year-old Sanchez, a dab hand at web-page design and a former filmset decorator, at the University of Central Florida.

The *Blair Witch* story began in earnest in October 1997 when Myrick and Sanchez sent their three hand-chosen leads (who'd come through an audition process involving 2,000 other actors) into the Maryland woods and left them to fend for themselves for eight days and nights. The actors shot all their own footage and improvized most of the dialog. When they were asleep in their tents, Sanchez and Myrick (who were staying nearby) tried to spook them and left notes about what their characters were supposed to do the next day.

"Scarier than *The Texas Chainsaw Massacre*. Scarier than the shower scene in *Psycho* ... Scarier than the final twist in *Carrie* and the shark attacks in *Jaws*," pronounced *The Washington Post* when the film was released, but there were no sharks or Freddie Kreuger-like killers on the loose. *Blair Witch* used the power of suggestion to terrify its audiences. In interview after interview, Sanchez and Myrick cited *The Omen*, *The*

Exorcist, and various Bigfoot documentaries (full of mysterious tracks in the snow) as their inspiration. This was a back-to-basics horror film, not another teen pic made under what Myrick referred to disparagingly as "the franchise mentality."

If the filmmakers' tactics were subtle, so were those of distributors Artisan, who picked up the film for $1 million at Sundance and committed to release it theatrically. (Myrick and Sanchez later admitted that all they really hoped for originally was "a video or cable deal.")

First off, Artisan targeted the internet. "I think this is the first time that the web has been the most basic and important tool in getting to a movie's audience," Artisan co-president Amir Malin told *Entertainment Weekly*. "Our demographic is 16 to 24, which is exactly the demo that goes online." It helped that there were hours of footage which didn't make it into the final film, but could be used to embellish the Blair Witch myth. This extra material found its way on to the website and into a teaser documentary, *The Curse Of The Blair Witch*, which was broadcast on the Sci-Fi Channel. The film was finally released in the U.S. on July 16, but initially only on 27 screens. That guaranteed that audiences would be fighting for tickets. Once it went wide, its performance was sensational. Its screen average ($26,528) smashed the record ($21,822) established by *Star Wars: Episode 1, The Phantom Menace* only a few weeks before.

Artisan's marketing ingenuity wouldn't have counted for much if the film had been no good. Fortunately, *The Blair Witch Project* really did deliver – all those traumatized-looking movie-goers filing out of the theaters suggested it was just as eerie and unsettling as the hype had proclaimed. Whether Myrick and Sanchez can contrive the same magic a second time remains to be seen. Over the millennium weekend, Artisan and Haxan announced two sequels for the big screen, with the first due out at Halloween this year. In summer 1999, the Haxan team signed a two-year deal with 20th Century Fox TV and Regency TV to make a smallscreen series along *Blair Witch* lines (the working title is *Fearsum*).

Meanwhile Sanchez and Myrick, both still based in Orlando, ended 1999 hard at work on the screenplay for *Heart of Love*, a comedy which they're touting as "one of the most politically incorrect films imaginable." They're not banking on it being another $150 million hit. ("We know we're gonna bomb," Sanchez joked to one interviewer. "We're gonna live with that bomb and nurture it and then watch it explode.") Whatever happens, *The Blair Witch Project* is already a legend – in box-office terms, the biggest little film of all time. **Geoffrey Macnab**

Kevin Spacey

Having invigorated Broadway in 1999 with his role as Theodore Hickman in Eugene O'Neill's *The Iceman Cometh*, Kevin Spacey then wowed audiences as an irked suburbanite in DreamWorks' much-praised *American Beauty*. It was a potent double-take that proved one thing: His 1995 Supporting Actor Oscar win for *The Usual Suspects* was no fluke. And the two achievements not only led to endless critical praise, but also solidified Spacey as one of America's most talented thesps, a respected artisan who can sway between stage and screen – with audiences ever eager to follow.

Spacey's appeal is difficult to pinpoint but easy to understand. There are many things he is not: an idolized sex symbol, a fiery tempered leading man, a manic comedian. He is, however, a detailed craftsman. Well mannered and well spoken, he has built a career out of chameleon-like turns as a sleazy attorney (*A Time to Kill*, 1996) and a southern gent (*Midnight in the Garden of Good and Evil*, 1997).

He can be a patient, rational presence who usually resorts to self-designed reason when other methods fail (*The Negotiator*, 1998) or a nasty, revenge-seeking husband with a confident swagger (*The Ref*, 1994). He can also be an absolute bastard. In *Glengarry Glen Ross* (1992), he played a ruthless boss who preyed upon his underlings. Ditto with *Swimming With Sharks* (1994) and as the voice of the amoral Hopper in *A Bug's Life* (1998). Spacey plays good as well as he plays evil, and it's that range that has made him not only a respected star, but a necessary one; a reliable psychopath is just as valuable as the neighbour down the street.

So *Beauty*, then, afforded the perfect role for Spacey. Both an inspirational loser and a terrible family man, Lester Burnham was someone only he could pull off with such likable enthusiasm. Full of rage and self-esteem, his decisions to drop out of society, pursue underage girls and get high with the local burnout were both comical and somber, and Spacey, who has tackled the role of a lovable jerk so many times before, seemed the ideal choice. Director Sam Mendes constructed a surreal, post-Clinton fairy tale, with anger replacing mini-vans as the American male's most prized possession. Spacey consumed Burnham, taking his midlife crisis to new levels of fear and relief. He was a lost maverick, but one who seemed to have it all together. With funny and meaningful methods, Spacey shone brightest in a movie that contained some of the year's most enduring moments.

The same could be said of his visit to the boards. As Eugene O'Neill's Hickey, Spacey, who always lines his characters with a layered complexity, brought a new depth to an old role. *Iceman* arrived in New York on March 29 after a stint at London's Almeida Theatre, and the response couldn't have been more positive. He wasn't, as many noted, just chasing pipe dreams, he defined them. A preacher of pathetic idealism, he touched everyone in Harry Hope's bar with a sharpened sword that had basked too many times in defeat. Modern-day *angst* was brought to a familiar character, and the result was a classic interpretation filled with a vibrant urgency. And although he didn't take home a Tony Award – Brian Dennehy (*Death of a Salesman*) won the nod – the entertainment world began to look at Spacey as more than just an able vet. They saw an electrifying pro who understood the limitations of different narratives while making other actors better. *Daily Variety* theater critic Charles Isherwood wrote, "Spacey wraps his sardonic, machine-gun monotone around O'Neill's great gusts of language in a manner that invests them with a sly edge. [He is] mesmerizingly suave; he makes sympathy sexy."

Despite Spacey's rising star and his participation in two of the year's most stimulating projects, it's important to note that his road didn't always wind through high-profile valleys. He has had his share of forgettable comedies (*See No Evil, Hear No Evil*, 1989) and pandering TV movies (*When You Remember Me*, 1990). For every one of his recent home runs, there were box-office misses like *Rocket Gibraltar* (1988), *Consenting Adults* (1992), and *Iron Will* (1994). But, like all successful performers, there was definitely one breakout year that transformed Spacey into the popular commodity he has become, and that flash arrived in 1995.

In that *annus mirabilis* Spacey co-starred in three films that couldn't have been more different. As a maniacal killer in David Fincher's *Se7en*, he sucked audiences in with a hypnotic and biblical take on murder. As the slippery Verbal Kint in Bryan Singer's *Suspects* he dazzled with his fast-talking grace under pressure. And in Wolfgang Petersen's *Outbreak* he proved he belonged in a costly action pic. These three projects symbolized not only Hollywood's different directions, but Spacey's ability to go in every one of them. Commercially and critically, Spacey had arrived.

Two years later, in Curtis Hanson's *L.A. Confidential*, he won more kudos as Jack Vincennes, a sleazy lawman, whose motives were as crooked as his desire for celebrity was strong. When the film copped nine Academy Award nominations, Hollywood singled him out as the symbol of complexity and depth of character that elevated the pic above routine crime fare.

He may have hit a peak on stage and screen in '99, but Spacey also has tackled some of television's more memorable roles. Smallscreen versions of *Long Day's*

Journey Into Night and *Darrow* were both indicative of the future, and his role as Mel Prophett on the acclaimed series *Wiseguy* was well received. He has also lent his voice to high-profile docus (*Steve McQueen: The King of Cool*, 1998; *Hitchcock, Shadow of a Genius*, 1999) that have won notoriety as absorbing looks inside Hollywood.

Next up for Spacey is *The Big Kahuna*, directed by John Swanbeck, and Mimi Leder's *Pay It Forward*. **Michael Speier**

> *Fasten your seatbelts, it's*
> *gonna be a bumpy night.*
> *(Bette Davis, All About Eve)*

... January 14 ...

Former Broadway impresario and Livnet co-founder Garth Drabinsky was indicted today by a Manhattan federal court on 16 counts of conspiracy and securities fraud.

Cyberbiz

Entertainment sites make up a significant segment of the worldwide web. Opening one is like peeling an onion; it leads you to another site, another, and another … Most movie and TV sites focus on American topics, and the list below omits the more provincial among them. Each January *Variety* publishes a "Showbiz Online Resource Guide," including a directory of useful sites. The list of selected sites below, however, is aimed at the buff rather than the business surfer. We welcome suggestions for additional sites to include in future editions of the *Almanac*.

(All site URLs are preceded by "www.")

Afionline.com
Covers professional training in film, plus the American Film Institute's Festival and Lifetime Achievement Award events

Allposters.com
More than 35,000 posters are illustrated and often available

AtomFilms.com
Possibly the best place to view short films online that run for two minutes to 20 minutes

Bafta.org
Site of the British Film Academy of Film and Television Arts

Berlinale.de
Excellent site of the Berlin International Film Festival

Bfi.org.uk
Site of the multifaceted British Film Institute

Bvimovies.com
Official site for Buena Vista – ie Disney – movies and ancillary products

Cannes-fest.com
Surprisingly ugly site, but a good resource during the actual Cannes Film Festival each May

Cinemarquee.com
"Virtual" classes in filmmaking, and notes on film financing, plus classifieds, but now straying offtrack into real estate

Cinema-sites.com
Useful portal for accessing databases and film-related sites)

Disney.com
The Magic Kingdom's very own classy site covering everything from theme parks to merchandise

Emmys.org
Official site of the world's leading TV awards, the Emmys

Entertaindom.com
Video-heavy entertainment hub from Time Warner and Warner Bros., featuring animation, live-action shorts, celebrity interviews, and behind-the-scenes programing from film sets

Film.com
Festival reports, interviews, clips, and soundtracks that can be played through your PC

Filmfan.com
Huge emporium of illustrated memorabilia, posters, etc.

Filmfestivals.com
Well-designed survey of the fest landscape, ably cross-indexed, and available in French also. In co-operation with *Moving Pictures* magazine

Filmfinders.com
Aims to be a virtual marketplace for the international film industry

Filmsite.org
Much-praised and awarded site, with reviews, evaluations, posters, and good reference links

Filmworld.co.uk
Eurobuff's dream site, skewed towards U.K. releases in theaters and on DVD, but with useful festival reports from all over the world

Foxmovies.com
Official site for 20th Century Fox Studios

GoodStory.com
New site that offers established and unsigned screenwriters the chance to post loglines or synopses of their scripts for agents and producers to consider

Hollywood.com
Box-office news, trailers, reviews, and video and DVD availability

Hollywoodreporter.com
Industry website out of L.A.

IFILM.com
Broadcasts every short film it receives to enable viewers to pick their favorite shorts

Imdb.com
The "Internet Movie Database," detailing 130,000 movies and 2 million filmographical entries; rather cursory personality profiles

Kencranes.com
Fast-moving, efficient site that offers every DVD under the sun – and, thankfully, all available laserdiscs as well

Mgm.com
Immense site covering every facet of films, TV, and music under the MGM banner

Moviefone.com
Aimed at U.S. users wanting to check showtimes at cinemas, and pre-book tickets. From AOL

Moviegallery.com
Directory of 100,000 films, new and used, available on DVD and video – but no longer laserdisc – and spiced with interviews

Movieweb.com
Roundup of films on current release in theaters and on video in the U.S., plus a good selection of box-office statistics

Mrshowbiz.go.com
Wide-ranging, illustrated survey of current stars and celebrities, movies, music, and TV

Oscars.org
Official AMPAS site, providing all you need to know about not just the Academy Awards but also its archival element and the Margaret Herrick Research Library

Popcorn.com
Brash British site with good industry news. From Carlton TV

Reel.com
Online store for videos, DVD, soundtracks, etc.

Reeluniverse.com
"The Internet is your Theater," with emphasis on indie and foreign-language films, and links to Amazon.com

Screenit.com
Entertainment reviews for parents

ScriptShark.com
A spinoff of FilmShark.com, this site offers budding scribes the opportunity to have their scripts read – for a fee

Showbizdata.com
U.S.-oriented entertainment search engine linked with filmfinders.com

Silentmovies.com
Rather arcane site, with emphasis on U.S. silents only

Spe.sony.com
Official site for Sony Entertainment, films, television, video, and DVD

Thereelsite.com
The emphasis here is on articles, reviews, and essays on predominantly U.S. products

Ultimatemovies.com
Links to official sites for all current theatrical releases

Variety.com
The site for anyone wanting to be up to the minute with industry news – fully revised content every day

Wb.com
Official site for Warner Bros. Studios

... January 16 ...
La Vie Rêvée des Anges wins Best Picture for 1998, along with Best Director and Best Actress at Les Lumières Awards (French equivalent of the Golden Globes).

Film

The Oscars

The Academy Awards in March mark the highpoint of the Hollywood calendar. Watched by billions around the world, the long, sprawling TV show crowns the great and the good for the prior calendar year. *Variety* estimates that an Oscar win can add tens of millions of dollars to a film's eventual gross, and quite a few million dollars to the asking salary of any actor nabbing a statuette.

The awards ceremony is only the climax to a long campaign season, starting for *Variety* in early December (when submissions for the Best Foreign Film Oscars are announced) and the studios begin jockeying for position in the race to win nominations in February. Cassettes – and now DVDs – pile up outside the front doors of Academy members, ads swell the pages of *Variety*, while special screenings are laid on all over Los Angeles, in New York, London, and elsewhere. On the night itself anything can happen, from Marlon Brando sending a Native American princess to pick up his award for *The Godfather*, to a dying John Wayne saying, "Let's get the wagons in a circle," as he presented an Oscar, or to James Cameron declaring himself "King of the World" as he triumphed with *Titanic*.

The Academy Awards have been bestowed since the 1927-28 season. The coveted Best Picture Oscar has been won by many a remarkable film, yet it is ironic that neither *Citizen Kane* nor *Casablanca* (voted the two best films of all time in an American Film Institute poll in 1998) took home that honor.

Academy Awards: 1927-99

1927-28

Picture: *Wings* (Paramount, Lucien Hubbard)
Most artistic quality of production: *Sunrise*
Actor: Emil Jannings, *The Last Command, The Way of the Flesh*
Actress: Janet Gaynor, *Sunrise*
Dramatic direction: Frank Borzage, *Seventh Heaven*
Comedy direction: Lewis Milestone, *Two Arabian Knights*
Writing/adaptation: Benjamin Glazer, *Seventh Heaven*
Writing/original story: Ben Hecht, *Underworld*
Title writing: Joseph Farnham, *Telling the World, The Fair Coed, Laugh, Clown, Laugh*
Cinematography: Charles Rosher, Karl Struss, *Sunrise*
Interior decoration: William Cameron Menzies, *The Dove, The Tempest*
Engineering effects: Roy Pomeroy, *Wings*
Special awards: Charles Chaplin for *The Circus*; Warner Bros. for *The Jazz Singer*

1928-29

Picture: *The Broadway Melody* (MGM)
Actor: Warner Baxter, *In Old Arizona*
Actress: Mary Pickford, *Coquette*
Director: Frank Lloyd, *The Divine Lady, Weary River, Drag*
Writing achievement: Hans Kraly, *The Patriot*
Cinematography: Clyde De Vinna, *White Shadows in the South Seas*
Interior decoration: Cedric Gibbons, *The Bridge of San Luis Rey, The Hollywood Revue*

1930

Film: *All Quiet on the Western Front* (Universal, Carl Laemmle Jr.)
Actor: George Arliss, *Disraeli*
Actress: Norma Shearer, *The Divorcée*
Director: Lewis Milestone, *All Quiet on the Western Front*
Writing achievement: Frances Marion, *The Big House*
Cinematography: Joseph T. Rucker, Willard Van Der Veer, *With Byrd at the South Pole*
Interior decoration: Herman Rosse, *King of Jazz*
Sound recording: *The Big House*

1931

Picture: *Cimarron* (RKO Radio, William LeBaron)
Actor: Lionel Barrymore, *A Free Soul*
Actress: Marie Dressler, *Min and Bill*
Director: Norman Taurog, *Skippy*
Screenplay: Howard Estabrook, *Cimarron*
Original story: John Monk Saunders, *The Dawn Patrol*
Cinematography: Floyd Crosby, *Tabu*
Interior decoration: Max Ree, *Cimarron*
Sound recording: Paramount Sound Dept.

1932

Picture: *Grand Hotel* (MGM, Irving G. Thalberg)
Actor: Wallace Beary (*The Champ*) and Fredric March (*Dr. Jekyll and Mr. Hyde*)
Actress: Helen Hayes, *The Sin of Madelon Claudet*
Director: Frank Borzage, *Bad Girl*
Screenplay: Edwin Burke, *Bad Girl*
Original story: Frances Marion, *The Champ*
Cinematography: Lee Garmes, *Shanghai Express*
Interior decoration: Gordon Wiles, *Transatlantic*
Sound recording: Paramount Sound Dept.
Short/cartoon: *Flowers and Trees* (Walt Disney/Silly Symphonies)
Short/comedy: *The Music Box* (Laurel and Hardy)
Short/novelty: *Wrestling Swordfish* (Mack Sennett/*Cannibals of the Deep*)
Special awards: Walt Disney for creating Mickey Mouse

1933

Film: *Cavalcade* (Fox, Winfield Sheehan)
Actor: Charles Laughton, *The Private Life of Henry VIII*
Actress: Katharine Hepburn, *Morning Glory*
Director: Frank Lloyd, *Cavalcade*
Screenplay: Victor Heerman, Sarah Y. Mason, *Little Women*
Original story: Robert Lord, *One Way Passage*
Cinematography: Charles Lang, *A Farewell to Arms*
Interior decoration: William S. Darling, *Cavalcade*
Assistant director (given to one from each studio): Charles Burton (Paramount), Scott Beal (Universal), Charles Dorian (MGM), Fred Fox (United Artists), Gordon Hollingshead (Warner Bros.), Dewey Starkey (RKO Radio), William Tummel (Fox)
Sound recording: *A Farewell to Arms*
Short/cartoon: *The Three Little Pigs* (Walt Disney/Silly Symphonies)
Short/comedy: *So This Is Harris* (RKO Radio Special/Phil Harris)
Short/novelty: *Krakatoa* (Educational Studio)

1934

Picture: *It Happened One Night* (Columbia, Harry Cohn)
Actor: Clark Gable, *It Happened One Night*
Actress: Claudette Colbert, *It Happened One Night*
Director: Frank Capra, *It Happened One Night*
Screenplay: Robert Riskin, *It Happened One Night*
Original story: Arthur Caesar, *Manhattan Melodrama*
Cinematography: Victor Milner, *Cleopatra*
Score: *One Night of Love*, Victor Schertzinger
Song: "The Continental" from *The Gay Divorcée* (music, Con Conrad, lyrics, Herb Magidson)
Editing: *Eskimo*
Interior decoration: Cedric Gibbons, *The Merry Widow*
Assistant director: John Waters, *Viva Villa!*
Sound recording: *One Night of Love*
Short/cartoon: *The Tortoise and the Hare* (Walt Disney/Silly Symphonies)
Short/comedy: *La Cucaracha* (RKO Radio Special)
Short/novelty: *City of Wax* (Educational/Battle for Life)
Special award: Shirley Temple

1935

Picture: *Mutiny on the Bounty* (MGM, Irving G. Thalberg)
Actor: Victor McLaglen, *The Informer*
Actress: Bette Davis, *Dangerous*
Director: John Ford, *The Informer*
Screenplay: Dudley Nichols, *The Informer*
Original story: Ben Hecht, Charles MacArthur, *The Scoundrel*
Cinematography: Hal Mohr, *A Midsummer Night's Dream*
Score: *The Informer*, Max Steiner
Song: "Lullaby of Broadway" from *Gold Diggers of 1935* (music, Harry Warren, lyrics, Al Dubin)
Editing: *A Midsummer Night's Dream*
Interior decoration: Richard Day, *The Dark Angel*
Dance direction: David Gould, "I've Got a Feeling You Are Fooling" from *Broadway Melody of 1936*, "Straw Hat" from *Folies Bergères*
Assistant director: Clem Beauchamp, Paul Wing, *The Lives of a Bengal Dancer*
Sound recording: *Naughty Marietta*
Short/cartoon: *Three Orphan Kittens* (Walt Disney/Silly Symphonies)
Short/comedy: *How to Sleep* (MGM/Robert Benchley)
Short/novelty: *Wings over Mount Everest* (Educational)
Special award: David Wark Griffith

... January 18 ...
Indian director Shekhar Kapur is to direct **Steinbeck's Point of View**.

1936

Picture: *The Great Ziegfeld* (MGM, Hunt Stromberg)
Actor: Paul Muni, *The Story of Louis Pasteur*
Actress: Luise Rainer, *The Great Ziegfeld*
Supporting actor: Walter Brennan, *Come and Get It*
Supporting actress: Gale Sondergaard, *Anthony Adverse*
Director: Frank Capra, *Mr. Deeds Goes to Town*
Screenplay: Pierre Collings, Sheridan Gibney, *The Story of Louis Pasteur*
Original story: Pierre Collings, Sheridan Gibney, *The Story of Louis Pasteur*
Cinematography: Gaetano (Tony) Gaudio, *Anthony Adverse*
Score: Erich Wolfgang Korngold, *Anthony Adverse*
Song: "The Way You Look Tonight" from *Swing Time* (music, Jerome Kern, lyrics, Dorothy Fields)
Editing: *Anthony Adverse*
Interior decoration: Richard Day, *Dodsworth*
Dance direction: Seymour Felix, "A Pretty Girl Is Like a Melody" from *The Great Ziegfeld*
Assistant director: Jack Sullivan, *The Charge of the Light Brigade*
Sound recording: *San Francisco*
Short/cartoon: *Country Cousin* (Walt Disney/ Silly Symphonies)
Short/one-reel: *Bored of Education* (Hal Roach/Our Gang)
Short/two-reel: *The Public Pays* (MGM/Crime Doesn't Pay)
Short/color: *Give Me Liberty* (Warner/Broadway Brevities)
Special awards: *The March of Time* for having revolutionized the newsreel; W. Howard Green; Harold Rosson for color cinematography, *The Garden of Allah*

1937

Picture: *The Life of Emile Zola* (Warner Bros., Henry Blanke)
Actor: Spencer Tracy, *Captains Courageous*
Actress: Louise Rainer, *The Good Earth*
Supporting actor: Joseph Schildkraut, *The Life of Emile Zola*
Supporting actress: Alice Brady, *In Old Chicago*
Director: Leo McCarey, *The Awful Truth*
Screenplay: Heinz Herald, Geza Herczeg, Norman Reilly Raine, *The Life of Emile Zola*
Original story: William A. Wellman, Robert Carson, *A Star Is Born*
Cinematography: Karl Freund, *The Good Earth*
Score: *100 Men and a Girl*, Universal Studio Music Dept., head, Charles Previn

Song: "Sweet Leilani" from *Waikiki Wedding* (music and lyrics, Harry Owens)
Editing: *Lost Horizon*
Interior decoration: Stephen Goosson, *Lost Horizon*
Dance direction: Hermes Pan, "Fun House" from *A Damsel in Distress*
Assistant director: Robert Webb, *In Old Chicago*
Sound recording: *The Hurricane*
Short/cartoon: *The Old Mill* (Walt Disney/Silly Symphonies)
Short/one-reel: *Private Life of the Gannets* (Educational)
Short/two-reel: *Torture Money* (MGM/Crime Doesn't Pay)
Short/color: *Penny Wisdom* (MGM/Pete Smith Specialities)
Irving G. Thalberg award: Darryl F. Zanuck
Special awards: Mack Sennett; Edgar Bergen; The Museum of Modern Art Film Library; W. Howard Green for color photography, *A Star Is Born*

1938

Picture: *You Can't Take It With You* (Columbia, Frank Capra)
Actor: Spencer Tracy, *Boys Town*
Actress: Bette Davis, *Jezebel*
Supporting actor: Walter Brennan, *Kentucky*
Supporting actress: Fay Bainter, *Jezebel*
Director: Frank Capra, *You Can't Take It With You*
Screenplay: Ian Dalrymple, Cecil Lewis, W.P. Lipscomb for adaptation of George Bernard Shaw's *Pygmalion*
Original story: Eleanore Griffin, Dore Schary, *Boys Town*
Cinematography: Joseph Ruttenberg, *The Great Waltz*
Original score: Erich Wolfgang Korngold, *The Adventures of Robin Hood*
Score: Alfred Newman, *Alexander's Ragtime Band*
Song: "Thanks for the Memory" from *Big Broadcast of 1938* (music, Ralph Rainger, lyrics, Leo Rubin)
Interior decoration: Carl J. Weyl, *The Adventures of Robin Hood*
Editing: *The Adventures of Robin Hood*
Sound recording: *The Cowboy and the Lady*
Short/cartoon: *Ferdinand the Bull* (Walt Disney)
Short/one-reel: *That Mothers Might Live* (MGM miniatures, directed by Fred Zinnemann)
Short/two-reel: *Declaration of Independence* (Warner Bros. Historical Featurette)
Irving G. Thalberg award: Hal B. Wallis
Special awards: Deanna Durbin, Mickey Rooney, youth actors; Harry M. Warner for the production

... January 19 ...
Matthew Perry makes a deal to create, write, and executive-
produce a sitcom called **The Shrink** for ABC.

of historical short subjects; Walt Disney for *Snow White and the Seven Dwarfs*; Oliver Marsh, Allen Davey, color cinematography; *Sweethearts* for special photographic and sound effects; *Spawn of the North*; J. Arthur Ball for the advancement of color photography

1939

Picture: *Gone With the Wind* (MGM, David O. Selznick)

Actor: Robert Donat, *Goodbye Mr. Chips*

Actress: Vivien Leigh, *Gone With the Wind*

Supporting actor: Thomas Mitchell, *Stagecoach*

Supporting actress: Hattie McDaniel, *Gone With the Wind*

Director: Victor Fleming, *Gone With the Wind*

Screenplay: Sidney Howard, *Gone With the Wind*

Original story: Lewis R. Foster, *Mr. Smith Goes to Washington*

Cinematography/b&w: Greg Toland, *Wuthering Heights*

Cinematography/color: Ernest Haller, Ray Rennahan, *Gone With the Wind*

Original score: Herbert Stothart, *The Wizard of Oz*

Score: Richard Hageman, Frank Harling, John Leipold, Leo Shiken, *Stagecoach*

Song: "Over the Rainbow" from *The Wizard of Oz* (music, Harold Arlen, lyrics, E.Y. Harburg)

Interior decoration: Lyle Wheeler, *Gone With the Wind*

Editing: *Gone With the Wind*

Sound recording: *When Tomorrow Comes*

Special effects: *The Rains Came*

Short/cartoon: *The Ugly Duckling* (Walt Disney/Silly Symphonies)

Short/one-reel: *Busy Little Bears* (Paramount Paragraphics)

Short/two-reel: *Sons of Liberty* (Warner Historical Featurette, directed by Michael Curtiz)

Irving G. Thalberg award: David O. Selznick

Special awards: Douglas Fairbanks, first president of the Academy; The Motion Picture Relief Fund presented to Jean Hersholt, president; Judy Garland, screen juvenile; William Cameron Menzies for the use of color for the enhancement of dramatic mood in *Gone With the Wind*; The Technicolor Company for three-color feature production

1940

Picture: *Rebecca* (UA, David O. Selznick)

Actor: James Stewart, *The Philadelphia Story*

Actress: Ginger Rogers, *Kitty Foyle*

Supporting actor: Walter Brennan, *The Westerner*

Supporting actress: Jane Darwell, *The Grapes of Wrath*

Director: John Ford, *The Grapes of Wrath*

Original screenplay: Preston Sturges, *The Great McGinty*

Adapted screenplay: Donald Ogden Stewart, *The Philadelphia Story*

Original story: Benjamin Glazer, John S. Toldy, *Arise My Love*

Cinematography/b&w: George Barnes, *Rebecca*

Cinematography/color: Georges Perinal, *The Thief of Bagdad*

Original score: Leigh Harline, Paul J. Smith, Ned Washington, *Pinocchio*

Score: Alfred Newman, *Tin Pan Alley*

Song: "When You Wish upon a Star" from *Pinocchio* (music, Leigh Harline, lyrics, Ned Washington)

Interior decoration/b&w: Cedric Gibbons, *Pride and Prejudice*

Interior decoration/color: Vincent Korda, *The Thief of Bagdad*

Editing: *Northwest Mounted Police*

Sound recording: *Strike Up the Band*

Special effects: *The Thief of Bagdad*

Short/cartoon: *The Milky Way* (MGM/Rudolph Ising)

Short/one-reel: *Quicker 'N a Wink* (MGM/Pete Smith Specialities)

Short/two-reel: *Teddy the Rough Rider* (Warner Bros. Historical Featurette)

Special awards: Bob Hope; Colonel Nathan Levinson for making possible the mobilization of industry facilities for Army training films

1941

Picture: *How Green Was My Valley* (20th Century Fox, Darryl F. Zanuck)

Actor: Gary Cooper, *Sergeant York*

Actress: Joan Fontaine, *Suspicion*

Supporting actor: Donald Crisp, *How Green Was My Valley*

Supporting actress: Mary Astor, *The Great Lie*

Director: John Ford, *How Green Was My Valley*

Original screenplay: Herman J. Mankiewicz, Orson Welles, *Citizen Kane*

Adapted screenplay: Sidney Buchman, Seton I. Miller, *Here Comes Mr. Jordan*

Original story: Harry Segall, *Here Comes Mr. Jordan*

Cinematography/b&w: Arthur Miller, *How Green Was My Valley*

Cinematography/color: Ernest Palmer, Ray Rennahan, *Blood and Sand*

Dramatic score: Bernard Hermann, "All That Money Can Buy" from *The Devil and Daniel Webster*

Music score: Frank Churchill, Oliver Wallace, *Dumbo*

Song: "The Last Time I Saw Paris" from *Lady Be Good* (music, Jerome Kern, lyrics, Oscar Hammerstein II)

Interior decoration/b&w: Richard Day, Nathan Juran, *How Green Was My Valley*

Interior decoration/color: Cedric Gibbons, Urie McCleary, *Blossoms in the Dust*

Editing: *Sergeant York*

Sound recording: *That Hamilton Woman*

Special effects: *I Wanted Wings*

Short/cartoon: *Lend a Paw* (Walt Disney/Pluto)

Short/one-reel: *Of Pups and Puzzles* (MGM Passing Parade Series)

Short/two-reel: *Main Street on the March* (MGM)

Documentary: *Churchill's Island* (National Film Board of Canada)

Irwing G. Thalberg award: Walt Disney

Special awards: Rey Scott for producing *Kukan*, documentary on war in China; The British Ministry of Information, *Target For Tonight*; Leopold Stokowski and his associates for their unique achievement in the creation of a new form of visualized music in *Fantasia*

1942

Picture: *Mrs. Miniver* (MGM, Sidney Franklin)

Actor: James Cagney, *Yankee Doodle Dandy*

Actress: Greer Garson, *Mrs. Miniver*

Supporting actor: Van Heflin, *Johnny Eager*

Supporting actress: Teresa Wright, *Mrs. Miniver*

Director: William Wyler, *Mrs. Miniver*

Original screenplay: Michael Kanin, Ring Lardner Jr., *Woman of the Year*

Adapted screenplay: George Froeschel, James Hilton, Claudine West, Arthur Wimperis, *Mrs. Miniver*

Original story: Emeric Pressburger, *The Invaders (49th Parallel)*

Cinematography/b&w: Joseph Ruttenberg, *Mrs. Miniver*

Cinematography/color: Leon Shamroy, *The Black Swan*

Dramatic or comedy score: Max Steiner, *Now, Voyager*

Musical score: Ray Heindorf, Heinz Roemheld, *Yankee Doodle Dandy*

Song: "White Christmas" from *Holiday Inn* (music and lyrics, Irving Berlin)

Interior decoration/b&w: Richard Day, *This Above All*

Interior decoration/color: Richard Day, *My Gal Sal*

Editing: *The Pride of the Yankees*

Sound recording: *Yankee Doodle Dandy*

Special effects: *Reap the Wild Wind*

Short/cartoon: *Der Fuehrer's Face* (Walt Disney/Donald Duck)

Short/one-reel: *Speaking of Animals and Their Families* (Paramount/Speaking of Animals)

Short/two-reel: *Beyond the Line of Duty* (Warner Broadway Brevities)

Documentary: *Battle of Midway* (U.S. Navy); *Kokoda Front Line* (Australian News Information Bureau); *Moscow Strikes Back* (Artkino), *Prelude to War* (U.S. Army Special Services/Why We Fight series)

Irving G. Thalberg award: Sidney Franklin

Special awards: Charles Boyer for establishing the French Research Foundation in Los Angeles as a source of reference for the industry; Noel Coward for *In Which We Serve*; MGM for representing the American way of life in the Andy Hardy series

1943

Picture: *Casablanca* (Warner Bros., Hal B. Wallis)

Actor: Paul Lukas, *Watch on the Rhine*

Actress: Jennifer Jones, *Song of Bernadette*

Supporting actor: Charles Coburn, *The More the Merrier*

Supporting actress: Katina Paxinou, *For Whom the Bell Tolls*

Director: Michael Curtiz, *Casablanca*

Original screenplay: Norman Krasna, *Princess O'Rourke*

Adapted screenplay: Julius J. Epstein, Philip G. Epstein, Howard Koch, *Casablanca*

Original story: William Saroyan, *The Human Comedy*

Cinematography/b&w: Arthur Miller, *The Song of Bernadette*

Cinematography/color: Hal Mohr, W. Howard Greene, *The Phantom of the Opera*

Dramatic or comedy score: Alfred Newman, *The Song of Bernadette*

Musical score: Ray Heindorf, *This Is the Army*

Song: "You'll Never Know" from *Hello Frisco, Hello* (music, Hary Warren, lyrics, Mack Gordon)

Interior decoration/b&w: James Basevi, William Darling, *The Song of Bernadette*

Interior decoration/color: Alexander Golitzen, *The Phantom of the Opera*

Editing: *Air Force*

Sound recording: *This Land Is Mine*

Special effects: *Crash Drive*

Short/cartoon: *Yankee Doodle Mouse* (MGM/Hanna-Barbera/Tom & Jerry)

Short/one-reel: *Amphibious Fighters* (Paramount)

Short/two-reel: *Heavenly Music* (MGM)

... January 21 ...

George Clooney is set to become the highest-paid TV actor of all time. He has been offered $1.25 million an episode to stay on in the next series of hospital drama **ER**.

Documentary/feature: *Desert Victory* (British Ministry of Information)

Documentary/short: *December 7th* (U.S. Navy, directed by John Ford, Gregg Toland)

Irwing G. Thalberg award: Hal B. Wallis

Special award: George Pal for *Puppetoons* (stop-motion animation)

1944

Picture: *Going My Way* (Paramount, Leo McCarey)

Actor: Bing Crosby, *Going My Way*

Actress: Ingrid Bergman, *Gaslight*

Supporting actor: Barry Fitzgerald, *Going My Way*

Supporting actress: Ethel Barrymore, *None But the Lonely Heart*

Director: Leo McCarey, *Going My Way*

Original screenplay: Lamar Trotti, *Wilson*

Adapted screenplay: Frank Butler, Frank Cavett, *Going My Way*

Original story: Leo McCarey, *Going My Way*

Cinematography/b&w: Joseph LaShelle, *Laura*

Cinematography/color: Leon Shamroy, *Wilson*

Dramatic or comedy score: Max Steiner, *Since You Went Away*

Musical score: Carmen Dragon, Morris Stoloff, *Cover Girl*

Song: "Swinging on a Star" from *Going My Way* (music, James Van Heusen, lyrics, Johnny Burke)

Interior decoration/b&w: Cedric Gibbons, *Gaslight*

Interior decoration/color: Wiard Ihnen, *Wilson*

Editing: *Wilson*

Sound recording: *Wilson*

Special effects: *Thirty Seconds Over Tokyo*

Short/cartoon: *Mouse Trouble* (MGM/Hanna-Barbera/Tom & Jerry)

Short/one-reel: *Who's Who in Animal Land* (Paramount/Speaking of Animals)

Short/two-reel: *I Won't Play* (Warner Bros. Featurette)

Documentary/feature: *The Fighting Lady* (20th Century Fox, U.S. Navy)

Documentary/short: *With the Marines at Tarawa* (U.S. Marine Corps)

Irwing G. Thalberg award: Darryl F. Zanuck

Special awards: Margaret O'Brien, outstanding child actress of 1944; Bob Hope for his many services to the Academy

1945

Picture: *The Lost Weekend* (Paramount, Charles Brackett)

Actor: Ray Milland, *The Lost Weekend*

Actress: Joan Crawford, *Mildred Pierce*

Supporting actor: James Dunn, *A Tree Grows in Brooklyn*

Supporting actress: Anne Revere, *National Velvet*

Director: Billy Wilder, *The Lost Weekend*

Original screenplay: Richard Schweizer, *Marie-Louise* (Switzerland)

Adapted screenplay: Charles Brackett, Billy Wilder, *The Lost Weekend*

Original story: Charles G. Booth, *The House on 92nd Street*

Cinematography/b&w: Harry Stradling, *The Picture of Dorian Gray*

Cinematography/color: Leon Shamroy, *Leave Her to Heaven*

Dramatic or comedy score: Miklos Rozsa, *Spellbound*

Musical score: Georgie Stoll, *Anchors Aweigh*

Song: "It Might As Well Be Spring" from *State Fair* (music, Richard Rodgers, lyrics, Oscar Hammerstein II)

Interior decoration/b&w: Wiard Ihnen, *Blood on the Sun*

Interior decoration/color: Hans Dreier, Ernst Fegte, *Frenchman's Creek*

Editing: *National Velvet*

Sound recording: *The Bells of St. Mary's*

Special effects: *Wonder Man*

Short/cartoon: *Quiet Please* (MGM/Hanna-Barbera/Tom & Jerry)

Short/one-reel: *Stairway to Light* (MGM/Passing Parade)

Short/two-reel: *A Star in the Night* (Warner Bros. Broadway Brevities, directed by Don Siegel)

Documentary/feature: *The True Glory* (Governments of U.S. and Britain, directed by Carol Reed, Garson Kanin)

Documentary/short: *Hitler Lives?* (Warner Bros., directed by Don Siegel)

Special awards: Walter Wanger; Peggy Ann Garner; *The House I Live In*; Republic Studio

1946

Picture: *The Best Years of Our Lives* (RKO Radio, Samuel Goldwyn)

Actor: Fredric March, *The Best Years of Our Lives*

Actress: Olivia de Havilland, *To Each His Own*

Supporting actor: Harold Russell, *The Best Years of Our Lives*

Supporting actress: Anne Baxter, *The Razor's Edge*

Director: William Wyler, *The Best Years of Our Lives*

Original screenplay: Muriel Box, Sydney Box, *The Seventh Veil*

Adapted screenplay: Robert E. Sherwood, *The Best Years of Our Lives*

Original story: Clemence Dane, *Vacation From Marriage*

Cinematography/b&w: Arthur Miller, *Anna and the King of Siam*

Cinematography/color: Charles Rosher, Leonard Smith, Arthur Arling, *The Yearling*

Dramatic or comedy score: Hugo Friedhofer, *The Best Years of Our Lives*

Musical score: Morris Stoloff, *The Jolson Story*

Song: "On the Atchison Topeka and Santa Fe" from *The Harvey Girls* (music, Harry Warren, lyrics, Johnny Mercer)

Interior decoration/b&w: Lyle Wheeler, William Darling, *Anna and the King of Siam*

Interior decoration/color: Cedric Gibbons, Paul Groesse, *The Yearling*

Editing: *The Best Years of Our Lives*

Sound recording: *The Jolson Story*

Special effects: *Blithe Spirit*

Short/cartoon: *The Cat Concerto* (MGM/Hanna-Barbera/Tom & Jerry)

Short/one-reel: *Facing Your Danger* (Warner Bros. Sports Parade)

Short/two-reel: *A Boy and His Dog* (Warner Bros. Featurettes)

Documentary/short: *Seeds of Destiny* (U.S. War Dept.)

Irving G. Thalberg award: Samuel Goldwyn

Special awards: Laurence Olivier; Harold Russell; Ernst Lubitsch; Claude Jarman Jr.

1947

Picture: *Gentleman's Agreement* (20th Century Fox, Darryl F. Zanuck)

Actor: Ronald Colman, *A Double Life*

Actress: Loretta Young, *The Farmer's Daughter*

Supporting actor: Edmund Gwenn, *Miracle on 34th Street*

Supporting actress: Celeste Holm, *Gentleman's Agreement*

Director: Elia Kazan, *Gentleman's Agreement*

Original screenplay: Sidney Sheldon, *The Bachelor and the Bobby-Soxer*

Adapted screenplay: George Seaton, *Miracle on 34th Street*

Original story: Valentine Davies, *Miracle on 34th Street*

Cinematography/b&w: Guy Greene, *Great Expectations*

Cinematography/color: Jack Cardiff, *Black Narcissus*

Song: "Zip-A-Dee-Doo-Dah" from *Song of the South* (music, Allie Wrubel, lyrics, Ray Gilbert)

Dramatic or comedy score: Miklos Rozsa, *A Double Life*

Musical score: Alfred Newman, *Mother Wore Tights*

Art direction/b&w: John Bryan, *Great Expectations*

Art direction/color: Alfred Junge, *Black Narcissus*

Editing: *Body and Soul*

Sound recording: *The Bishop's Wife*

Special effects: *Green Dolphin Street*

Short/cartoon: *Tweetie Pie* (Warner/Friz Freleng, Tweety & Sylvester)

Short/one-reel: *Goodbye Miss Turlock* (MGM/Passing Parade)

Short/two-reel: *Climbing the Matterhorn* (Monogram Color, Irving Allen)

Documentary/feature: *Design For Death* (RKO Radio)

Documentary/short: First Steps (United Nations Division of Films and Visual Education)

Special awards: James Baskette; *Bill and Coo*, live-action animal film; *Shoeshine* (Italy), outstanding foreign-language film; Colonel William N. Selig and George K. Spoor, early film pioneers

1948

Picture: *Hamlet* (Universal, Rank/Two Cities, Laurence Olivier)

Actor: Laurence Olivier, *Hamlet*

Actress: Jane Wyman, *Johnny Belinda*

Supporting actor: Walter Huston, *The Treasure of the Sierra Madre*

Supporting actress: Claire Trevor, *Key Largo*

Director: John Huston, *The Treasure of the Sierra Madre*

Screenplay: John Huston, *The Treasure of the Sierra Madre*

Original story: Richard Schweizer, David Wechsler, *The Search*

Cinematography/b&w: William Daniels, *The Naked City*

Cinematography/color: Joseph Valentine, William V. Skall, Winton Hoch, *Joan of Arc*

Dramatic or comedy score: Brian Easdale, *The Red Shoes*

Musical score: Johnny Green, Roger Edens, *Easter Parade*

Song: "Buttons and Bows" from *The Paleface* (music and lyrics, Jay Livingstone)

Art direction/b&w: Roger K. Furse, *Hamlet*

Art direction/color: Hein Heckroth, *The Red Shoes*

Costumes/b&w: Roger K. Furse, *Hamlet*

Costumes/color: Dorothy Jeakins, Karinska, *Joan of Arc*

Editing: *The Naked City*

Sound recording: *The Snake Pit*

Special effects: *Portrait of Jennie*

Short/cartoon: *The Little Orphan*

... January 23 ...
Paramount's high-school football romp **Varsity Blues** continues
to lead the B.O. with an estimated $10.6 million.

Short/one-reel: *Symphony of a City* (Movietone Specialty)

Short/two-reel: *Seal Island* (Walt Disney's True Life Adventures)

Documentary/feature: *The Secret Land* (U.S. Navy, MGM)

Documentary/short: *Toward Independence* (U.S. Army)

Irving G. Thalberg award: Jerry Wald

Special awards: *Monsieur Vincent* (France), outstanding foreign-language film; Ivan Jandl, outstanding juvenile performance, *The Search*; Sid Grauman, master showman; Adolph Zukor, for his services to the industry; Walter Wanger, for distinguished services to the industry

1949

Picture: *All the King's Men* (Columbia, Robert Rossen)

Actor: Broderick Crawford, *All the King's Men*

Actress: Olivia de Havilland, *The Heiress*

Supporting actor: Dean Jagger, *Twelve O'Clock High*

Supporting actress: Mercedes McCambridge, *All the King's Men*

Director: Joseph L. Mankiewicz, *A Letter to Three Wives*

Screenplay: Joseph L. Mankiewicz, *A Letter to Three Wives*

Story and screenplay: Robert Pirosh, *Battleground*

Original story: Douglas Morrow, *The Stratton Story*

Cinematography/b&w: Paul C. Vogel, *Battleground*

Cinematography/color: Winton C. Hoch, *She Wore A Yellow Ribbon*

Dramatic or comedy score: Aaron Copland, *The Heiress*

Musical score: Roger Edens, Lennie Hayton, *On the Town*

Song: "Baby, It's Cold Outside" from *Neptune's Daughter* (music and lyrics, Frank Loesser)

Art direction/b&w: John Meehan, Harry Horner, *The Heiress*

Art direction/color: Cedric Gibbons, Paul Groesse, *Little Women*

Costumes/b&w: Edith Head, *The Heiress*

Costumes/color: *Adventures of Don Juan*

Editing: *Champion*

Sound recording: *Twelve O'Clock High*

Special effects: *Mighty Joe Young* (Willis O'Brien, Ray Harryhausen)

Short/cartoon: *For Scentimental Reasons* (Warner/Chuck Jones/Pepe LePew)

Short/one-reel: *Aquatic House-Party* (Grantland Rice Sportlights)

Short/two-reel: *Van Gogh*

Documentary/feature: *Daybreak in Udi* (British Information Service)

Documentary/short: *A Chance to Live* (March of Time); *So Much For So Little* (Public Health Service and Warner Bros. cartoon unit)

Special awards: *The Bicycle Thief* (Italy), outstanding foreign-language film; Bobby Driscoll, outstanding juvenile actor; Fred Astaire; Cecil B. DeMille; Jean Hersholt, for service to the industry

1950

Picture: *All About Eve* (20th Century Fox, Darryl F. Zanuck)

Actor: José Ferrer, *Cyrano de Bergerac*

Actress: Judy Holliday, *Born Yesterday*

Supporting actor: George Sanders, *All About Eve*

Supporting actress: Josephine Hull, *Harvey*

Director: Joseph Mankiewicz, *All About Eve*

Screenplay: Joseph Mankiewicz, *All About Eve*

Story and screenplay: Charles Brackett, Billy Wilder, D.M. Marshman Jr., *Sunset Boulevard*

Original story: Edna Anhalt, Edward Anhalt, *Panic in the Streets*

Cinematography/b&w: Robert Krasker, *The Third Man*

Cinematography/color: Robert Surtees, *King Solomon's Mines*

Dramatic or comedy score: Franz Waxman, *Sunset Boulevard*

Musical score: Adolph Deutsch, Roger Edens, *Annie Get Your Gun*

Song: "Mona Lisa" from *Captain Carey* (music and lyrics, Ray Evans, Jay Livingstone)

Art direction/b&w: Hans Dreier, John Meehan, *Sunset Boulevard*

Art direction/color: Hans Dreier, *Samson and Delilah*

Costumes/b&w: Edith Head, *All About Eve*

Costumes/color: Edith Head, *Samson and Delilah*

Editing: *King Solomon's Mines*

Sound recording: *All About Eve*

Special effects: *Destination Moon*

Short/cartoon: Gerald McBoing-Boing (UPA/Robert Cannon)

Short/one-reel: *Granddad Of Races* (Warner Bros. Sports Parade)

Short/two-reel: *In Beaver Valley* (Disney True-Life Adventures)

Documentary/feature: *The Titan – The Story of Michaelangelo* (Robert Snyder)

Documentary/short: *Why Korea?* (Fox Movietone)

Irving G. Thalberg award: Darryl F. Zanuck

Special awards: George Murphy; Louis B. Mayer; *The Walls of Malapaga* (France/Italy), outstanding foreign-language film

---

... January 24 ...
Shakespeare in Love takes Best Musical/Comedy Award and
Saving Private Ryan Best Drama Award at the 56th Golden Globes.

1951

Picture: *An American in Paris* (MGM, Arthur Freed)
Actor: Humphrey Bogart, *The African Queen*
Actress: Vivien Leigh, *A Streetcar Named Desire*
Supporting actor: Karl Malden, *A Streetcar Named Desire*
Supporting actress: Kim Hunter, *A Streetcar Named Desire*
Director: George Stevens, *A Place in the Sun*
Screenplay: Michael Wilson, Harry Brown, *A Place in the Sun*
Story and screenplay: Alan Jay Lerner, *An American in Paris*
Original story: Paul Dehn, James Bernard, *Seven Days To Noon*
Cinematography/B&W: William C. Mellor, *A Place in the Sun*
Cinematography/color: Alfred Gilks, John Alton, *An American in Paris*
Dramatic or comedy score: Franz Waxman, *A Place in the Sun*
Musical score: Johnny Green, Saul Chaplin, *An American in Paris*
Song: "In the Cool, Cool, Cool, of the Evening" from *Here Comes The Groom* (music, Hoagy Carmichael, lyrics, Johnny Mercer)
Art direction/b&w: Richard Day, *A Streetcar Named Desire*
Art direction/color: Cedric Gibbons, Preston Ames, *An American in Paris*
Costumes/b&w: Edith Head, *A Place in the Sun*
Costumes/color: Walter Plunkett, Irene Sharaff, *An American in Paris*
Editing: *A Place in The Sun*
Sound recording: *The Great Caruso*
Special effects: *When Worlds Collide*
Short/cartoon: *Two Mouseketeers* (MGM/Hanna-Barbera/Tom & Jerry)
Short/one-reel: *World of Kids* (Vitaphone, Novelties, Robert Youngson)
Short/two-reel: *Nature's Half Acre* (Disney True-Life Adventures)
Documentary/feature: *Kon-Tiki* (Norway)
Documentary/short: *Benjy* (Fred Zinnemann, Los Angeles Orthopedic Hospital)
Irving G. Thalberg award: Arthur Freed
Special awards: Gene Kelly; *Rashomon* (Japan), outstanding foreign-language film

1952

Picture: *The Greatest Show on Earth* (Paramount, Cecil B. DeMille)
Actor: Gary Cooper, *High Noon*
Actress: Shirley Booth, *Come Back, Little Sheba*
Supporting actor: Anthony Quinn, *Viva Zapata!*
Supporting actress: Gloria Grahame, *The Bad and the Beautiful*
Director: John Ford, *The Quiet Man*
Screenplay: Charles Schnee, *The Bad and the Beautiful*
Story and screenplay: TEB Clarke, *The Lavender Hill Mob*
Original story: Frederic M. Frank, Theodore St. John, Frank Cavett, *The Greatest Show on Earth*
Cinematography/b&w: Robert Surtees, *The Bad and the Beautiful*
Cinematography/color: Winton C. Hoch, Archie Stout, *The Quiet Man*
Dramatic or comedy score: Dimitri Tiomkin, *High Noon*
Musical score: Alfred Newman, *With a Song in My Heart*
Song: "High Noon (Do Not Forsake Me, Oh My Darlin')" from *High Noon* (music, Dimitri Tiomkin, lyrics, Ned Washington)
Art direction/b&w: Cedric Gibbons, *The Bad and the Beautiful*
Art direction/color: Paul Sheriff, Marcel Vertes, *Moulin Rouge*
Costumes/b&w: Helen Rose, *The Bad and the Beautiful*
Costumes/color: Marcel Vertes, *Moulin Rouge*
Editing: *High Noon*
Sound recording: *Breaking the Sound Barrier*
Special effects: *Plymouth Adventure*, MGM
Short/cartoon: *Johann Mouse* (MGM/Hanna-Barbera/Tom & Jerry)
Short/one-reel: *Light in the Window*
Short/two-reel: Water Birds (Disney True-Life Adventures)
Documentary/feature: *The Sea Around Us* (RKO Radio, Irwin Allen)
Documentary/short: *Neighbors* (National Film Board of Canada, Norman McLaren)
Irving G. Thalberg award: Cecil B. DeMille
Special awards: George Alfred Mitchell; Joseph M. Schenck; Merian C. Cooper; Harold Lloyd; Bob Hope; *Forbidden Games* (France), outstanding foreign-language film

1953

Picture: *From Here to Eternity* (Columbia, Buddy Adler)
Actor: William Holden, *Stalag 17*
Actress: Audrey Hepburn, *Roman Holiday*
Supporting actor: Frank Sinatra, *From Here to Eternity*

Supporting actress: Donna Reed, *From Here to Eternity*

Director: Fred Zinnemann, *From Here to Eternity*

Screenplay: Daniel Taradash, *From Here to Eternity*

Story and screenplay: Charles Brackett, Walter Reisch, Richard Breen, *Titanic*

Original story: Ian McLellan Hunter, *Roman Holiday*

Cinematography/b&w: Burnett Guffey, *From Here to Eternity*

Cinematography/color: Loyal Griggs, *Shane*

Dramatic or comedy score: Bronislau Kaper, *Lili*

Musical score: Alfred Newman, *Call Me Madam*

Song: "Secret Love" from *Calamity Jane* (music, Sammy Fain, lyrics, Paul Francis Webster)

Art direction/b&w: Cedric Gibbons, *Julius Caesar*

Art direction/color: Lyle Wheeler, George W. Davis, *The Robe*

Costumes/b&w: Edith Head, *Roman Holiday*

Costumes/color: Charles LeMaire, Emile Santiago, *The Robe*

Editing: *From Here to Eternity*

Sound recording: *From Here to Eternity*

Special effects: *War of the Worlds*

Short/cartoon: *Toot, Whistle, Plunk, and Boom* (Walt Disney)

Short/one-reel: *The Merry Wives of Windsor Overture* (MGM Overture Series)

Short/two-reel: *Bear Country* (Disney True-Life Adventures)

Documentary/feature: *The Living Desert* (Disney True-Life Adventures)

Documentary/short: *The Alaskan Eskimo* (Disney True-Life Adventures)

Irving G. Thalberg award: George Stevens

Special awards: Pete Smith; 20th Century Fox; Joseph I. Breen

1954

Picture: *On the Waterfront* (Columbia, Sam Spiegel)

Actor: Marlon Brando, *On The Waterfront*

Actress: Grace Kelly, *The Country Girl*

Supporting actor: Edmond O'Brien, *The Barefoot Contessa*

Supporting actress: Eva Marie Saint, *On the Waterfront*

Director: Elia Kazan, *On the Waterfront*

Screenplay: George Seaton, *The Country Girl*

Story and screenplay: Budd Schulberg, *On the Waterfront*

Original story: Philip Yordan, *Broken Lance*

Cinematography/b&w: Boris Kaufman, *On the Waterfront*

Cinematography/color: Milton Krasner, *Three Coins in the Fountain*

Dramatic or comedy score: Dimitri Tiomkin, *The High and the Mighty*

Musical score: Adolph Deutsch, Saul Chaplin, *Seven Brides For Seven Sisters*

Song: "Three Coins in the Fountain" from *Three Coins in the Fountain* (music, Jule Styne, lyrics, Sammy Cahn)

Art direction/b&w: Richard Day, *On the Waterfront*

Art direction/color: John Meehan, *20,000 Leagues Under the Sea*

Costumes/b&w: Edith Head, *Sabrina*

Costumes/color: Sanzo Wada, *Gate of Hell*

Editing: *On the Waterfront*

Sound recording: *The Glenn Miller Story*

Special effects: *20,000 Leagues Under the Sea*

Short/cartoon: *When Magoo Flew* (UPA. Mr. Magoo/Pete Burness)

Short/one-reel: *This Mechanical Age* (Warner Bros., Robert Youngson)

Short/two-reel: *A Time out of War* (Carnival Prods.)

Documentary/feature: *The Vanishing Prairie* (Disney True-Life Adventures)

Documentary/short: *Thursday's Children* (British Information Service)

Special awards: Bausch & Lomb Optical Company; Kemp R. Niver; Greta Garbo; Danny Kaye; Jon Whiteley, Vincent Winter, outstanding juvenile performances, *The Little Kidnappers*; *Gate of Hell* (Japan), best foreign-language film

1955

Picture: *Marty* (UA, Hecht-Hill-Lancaster)

Actor: Ernest Borgnine, *Marty*

Actress: Anna Magnani, *The Rose Tattoo*

Supporting actor: Jack Lemmon, *Mister Roberts*

Supporting actress: Jo Van Fleet, *East of Eden*

Director: Delbert Mann, *Marty*

Screenplay: Paddy Chayefsky, *Marty*

Story and screenplay: William Ludwig, Sonya Levien, *Interrupted Melody*

Original story: Daniel Fuchs, *Love Me or Leave Me*

Cinematography/b&w: James Wong Howe, *The Rose Tattoo*

Cinematography/color: Robert Burks, *To Catch a Thief*

Dramatic or comedy score: Alfred Newman, *Love Is a Many-Splendored Thing*

Musical score: Robert Russell Bennett, Hay Blackton, Adolph Deutsch, *Oklahoma!*

Song: "Love Is a Many-Splendored Thing" from *Love Is a Many-Splendored Thing* (music, Sammy Fain, lyrics, Paul Francis Webster)

... January 26 ...
Ridley and Tony Scott's Scot Free Prods. becomes a part of the crew team behind a new drama series centered on the CART racing-circuit team owned by Paul Newman.

Art direction/b&w: Hal Perira, Tambi Larsen, *The Rose Tattoo*
Art direction/color: William Flannery, *Picnic*
Costumes/b&w: Helen Rose, *I'll Cry Tomorrow*
Costumes/color: Charles LeMaire, *Love Is a Many-Splendored Thing*
Editing: *Picnic*
Sound recording: *Oklahoma!*
Special effects: *The Bridges at Toko-Ri*
Short/cartoon: *Speedy Gonzales* (Warner Bros./Friz Freleng)
Short/one-reel: *Survival City*
Short/two-reel: *The Face of Lincoln* (University of Southern California)
Documentary/feature: *Helen Keller in Her Story*
Documentary/short: *Men Against the Arctic* (Walt Disney)
Special award: *Samurai, The Legend of Musashi* (Japan), outstanding foreign-language film

1956

Picture: *Around the World in 80 Days* (UA, Michael Todd)
Actor: Yul Brynner, *The King and I*
Actress: Ingrid Bergman, *Anastasia*
Supporting actor: Anthony Quinn, *Lust For Life*
Supporting actress: Dorothy Malone, *Written on the Wind*
Director: George Stevens, *Giant*
Original screenplay: Albert Lamorisse, *The Red Balloon*
Adapted screenplay: James Poe, John Farrow, S.J. Perelman, *Around the World in 80 Days*
Original story: Robert Rich, *The Brave One* (note: pseudonym for blacklisted Dalton Trumbo)
Cinematography/b&w: Joseph Ruttenberg, *Somebody Up There Likes Me*
Cinematography/color: Lionel Lindon, *Around the World in 80 Days*
Dramatic or comedy score: Victor Young, *Around the World in 80 Days*
Musical score: Alfred Newman, Ken Darby, *The King and I*
Song: "Whatever Will Be, Will Be" from *The Man Who Knew Too Much* (music and lyrics, Jay Livingstone, Ray Evans)
Art direction/b&w: Cedric Gibbons, *Somebody Up There Likes Me*
Art direction/color: Lyle Wheeler, *The King and I*
Costumes/b&w: Jean Louis, *The Solid Gold Cadillac*
Costumes/color: Irene Sharaff, *The King and I*
Editing: *Around the World in 80 Days*
Sound recording: *The King and I*

Special effects: *The Ten Commandments*
Short/cartoon: *Mister Magoo's Puddle Jumper* (UPA/Pete Burness)
Short/one-reel: *Crashing the Water Barrier* (Warner Bros.)
Short/two-reel: *The Bespoke Overcoat* (Romulus Films, directed by Jack Clayton)
Documentary/feature: *The Silent World* (Jacques-Yves Cousteau)
Documentary/short: *The True Story of the Civil War*
Foreign-language film: *La Strada* (Italy)
Irving G. Thalberg award: Buddy Adler
Jean Hersholt Humanitarian award: Y. Frank Freeman
Special award: Eddie Cantor

1957

Picture: *The Bridge on the River Kwai* (Columbia, Sam Spiegel)
Actor: Alec Guinness, *The Bridge on the River Kwai*
Actress: Joanne Woodward, *The Three Faces of Eve*
Supporting actor: Red Buttons, *Sayonara*
Supporting actress: Miyoshi Umeki, *Sayonara*
Director: David Lean, *The Bridge on the River Kwai*
Original screenplay: George Wells, *Designing Woman*
Adapted screenplay: Pierre Boulle, *The Bridge on the River Kwai*
Cinematography: Jack Hildyard, *The Bridge on the River Kwai*
Score: Malcolm Arnold, *The Bridge on the River Kwai*
Song: "All the Way" from *The Joker is Wild* (music, James Van Heusen, lyrics, Sammy Cahn)
Art direction: Ted Haworth, *Sayonara*
Costume design: Orry-Kelly, *Les Girls*
Editing: *The Bridge on the River Kwai*
Sound: *Sayonara*
Special effects: *The Enemy Below*
Short/cartoon: *Birds Anonymous* (Warner Bros./Friz Freleng/Sylvester & Tweety)
Short/live action: *The Wetback Hound* (Walt Disney)
Documentary/feature: *Albert Schweitzer*
Foreign-language film: *Nights of Cabiria* (Italy)
Jean Hersholt Humanitarian award: Samuel Goldwyn
Special awards: Charles Brackett; B.B. Kahane, Gilbert M. (Bronco Billy) Anderson; The Society of Motion Picture and Television Engineers

1958

Picture: *Gigi* (MGM, Arthur Freed)
Actor: David Niven, *Separate Tables*
Actress: Susan Hayward, *I Want to Live*
Supporting actor: Burl Ives, *The Big Country*
Supporting actress: Wendy Hiller, *Separate Tables*

Director: Vincente Minnelli, *Gigi*
Original screenplay: Nathan E. Douglas, Harold Jacob Smith, *The Defiant Ones*
Adapted screenplay: Alan Jay Lerner, *Gigi*
Cinematography/b&w: Sam Leavitt, *The Defiant Ones*
Cinematography/color: Joseph Ruttenberg, *Gigi*
Dramatic or comedy score: Dimitri Tiomkin, *The Old Man and the Sea*
Musical score: André Previn, *Gigi*
Song: "Gigi" from *Gigi* (music, Frederick Loewe, lyrics, Alan Jay Lerner)
Art direction: William A. Horning, Preston Ames, *Gigi*
Costume design: Cecil Beaton, *Gigi*
Editing: *Gigi*
Sound: *South Pacific*
Special effects: *Tom Thumb*
Short/cartoon: *Knighty Knight Bugs* (Warner Bros./Friz Freleng/Bugs Bunny)
Short/live action: *Grand Canyon* (Walt Disney)
Documentary/feature: *White Wilderness* (Walt Disney)
Documentary/short: *AMA Girls* (Walt Disney)
Foreign-language film: *My Uncle (Mon Oncle)* (France)
Irving G. Thalberg award: Jack L. Warner
Special award: Maurice Chevalier

1959

Picture: *Ben-Hur* (MGM, Sam Zimbalist)
Actor: Charlton Heston, *Ben-Hur*
Actress: Simone Signoret, *Room at the Top*
Supporting actor: Hugh Griffith, *Ben-Hur*
Supporting actress: Shelley Winters, *The Diary of Anne Frank*
Director: William Wyler, *Ben-Hur*
Original screenplay: Russell Rouse, Clarence Green, Stanley Shapiro, Maurice Richlin, *Pillow Talk*
Adapted screenplay: Neil Paterson, *Room at the Top*
Cinematography/b&w: William C. Mellor, *The Diary of Anne Frank*
Cinematography/color: Robert L. Surtees, *Ben-Hur*
Dramatic or comedy score: Miklos Rozsa, *Ben-Hur*
Musical score: André Previn, Ken Darby, *Porgy & Bess*
Song: "High Hopes" from *A Hole in the Head* (music, James Van Heusen, lyrics, Sammy Cahn)
Art direction/b&w: Lyle R. Wheeler, George W. Davis, *The Diary of Anne Frank*
Art direction/color: William A. Horning, *Ben-Hur*
Costumes/b&w: Orry-Kelly, *Some Like It Hot*
Costumes/color: Elizabeth Haffenden, *Ben-Hur*
Editing: *Ben-Hur*

Sound: *Ben-Hur*
Special effects: *Ben-Hur*
Short/cartoon: *Moonbird* (John Hubley)
Short/live action: *The Golden Fish* (Jacques-Yves Cousteau)
Documentary/feature: *Serengeti Shall Not Die* (Germany)
Documentary/short: *Glass* (Bert Haanstra, Holland)
Foreign-language film: *Black Orpheus* (France)
Jean Hersholt Humanitarian award: Bob Hope
Special awards: Lee de Forest; Buster Keaton

1960

Picture: *The Apartment* (UA, Mirisch, Billy Wilder)
Actor: Burt Lancaster, *Elmer Gantry*
Actress: Elizabeth Taylor, *Butterfield 8*
Supporting actor: Peter Ustinov, *Spartacus*
Supporting actress: Shirley Jones, *Elmer Gantry*
Director: Billy Wilder, *The Apartment*
Original screenplay: Billy Wilder, I.A.L. Diamond, *The Apartment*
Adapted screenplay: Richard Brooks, *Elmer Gantry*
Cinematography/b&w: Freddie Francis, *Sons and Lovers*
Cinematography/color: Russell Metty, *Spartacus*
Dramatic or comedy score: Ernest Gold, *Exodus*
Musical score: Morris Stoloff, Harry Sukman, *Song Without End*
Song: "Never on Sunday" from *Never on Sunday* (music and lyrics, Manos Hadjidakis)
Art direction/b&w: Alexander Trauner, *The Apartment*
Art direction/color: Alexander Golitzen, *Spartacus*
Costume design/b&w: Edith Head, *The Facts of Life*
Costume design/color: Valles and Bill Thomas, *Spartacus*
Editing: *The Apartment*
Sound: *The Alamo*
Special effects: *The Time Machine*
Short/cartoon: *Munro* (William L Snyder)
Short/live action: *Day of the Painter* (Little Movies, Ezra R. Baker)
Documentary/feature: *The Horse With the Flying Tail* (Walt Disney)
Documentary/short: *Giuseppina* (James Hill)
Foreign-language film: *The Virgin Spring* (Sweden)
Jean Hersholt Humanitarian award: Sol Lesser
Special awards: Gary Cooper; Stan Laurel; Hayley Mills, outstanding juvenile performance

1961

Picture: *West Side Story* (UA, Mirisch-B&P Enterprises)

... January 28 ...
Cirque du Soleil's **La Nouba** gala premieres at Walt Disney World in Orlando, Florida.

Actor: Maximilian Schell, *Judgment in Nuremberg*
Actress: Sophia Loren, *Two Women*
Supporting actor: George Chakiris, *West Side Story*
Supporting actress: Rita Moreno, *West Side Story*
Director: Robert Wise, Jerome Robbins, *West Side Story*
Original screenplay: William Inge, *Splendor in the Grass*
Adapted screenplay: Abby Mann, *Judgment in Nuremberg*
Cinematography/b&w: Eugene Shuftan, *The Hustler*
Cinematography/color: Daniel L. Fapp, *West Side Story*
Dramatic or comedy score: Henry Mancini, *Breakfast at Tiffany's*
Musical score: Saul Chaplin, Johnny Green, Sid Ramin, Irwin Kostal, *West Side Story*
Song: "Moon River" from *Breakfast At Tiffany's* (music, Henry Mancini, lyrics, Johnny Mercer)
Art direction/b&w: Harry Horner, *The Hustler*
Art direction/color: Boris Leven, *West Side Story*
Costume design/b&w: Piero Gherardi, *La Dolce Vita*
Costume design/color: Irene Sharaff, *West Side Story*
Editing: *West Side Story*
Sound: *West Side Story*
Special effects: *The Guns of Navarone*
Short/cartoon: *Ersatz (The Substitute)* (Zagreb Film, Dusan Vukotic, Yugoslavia)
Short/live action: *Seawards the Great Ships*
Documentary/feature: *Le ciel et la Boue (The Sky Above, the Mud Below)* (Pierre-Dominique Gaisseau, France)
Documentary/short: *Project Hope*
Foreign-language film: *Through a Glass Darkly* (Sweden)
Irving G. Thalberg award: Stanley Kramer
Jean Hersholt Humanitarian award: George Seaton
Special awards: William Hendricks; Fred L. Metzler; Jerome Robbins

1962

Picture: *Lawrence of Arabia* (Columbia, Sam Spiegel)
Actor: Gregory Peck, *To Kill a Mockingbird*
Actress: Anne Bancroft, *The Miracle Worker*
Supporting actor: Ed Begley, *Sweet Bird of Youth*
Supporting actress: Patty Duke, *The Miracle Worker*
Director: David Lean, *Lawrence of Arabia*
Original screenplay: Ennio de Concini, Alfredo Giannetti, Pietro Germi, *Divorce Italian Style*
Adapted screenplay: Horton Foote, *To Kill a Mockingbird*
Cinematography/b&w: Jean Bourgoin, Walter Wottitz, *The Longest Day*

Cinematography/color: Freddie Young, *Lawrence of Arabia*
Original score: Maurice Jarre, *Lawrence of Arabia*
Adapted score: Ray Heindorf, *The Music Man*
Song: "Days of Wine and Roses" from *Days Of Wine And Roses* (music, Henry Mancini, lyrics, Johnny Mercer)
Art direction/b&w: Alexander Golitzen, Henry Bumstead, *To Kill a Mockingbird*
Art direction/color: John Box, *Lawrence of Arabia*
Costume design/b&w: Norma Koch, *What Ever Happened to Baby Jane?*
Costume design/color: Mary Wills, *The Wonderful World of the Brothers Grimm*
Editing: *Lawrence of Arabia*
Sound: *Lawrence of Arabia*
Special effects: *The Longest Day*
Short/cartoon: *The Hole* (John and Faith Hubley)
Short/live action: *Heureux Anniversaire (Happy Anniversary)* (Pierre Etaix)
Documentary/feature: *Black Fox*
Documentary/short: *Dylan Thomas*
Foreign-language film: *Sundays and Cybèle* (France)
Jean Hersholt Humanitarian award: Steve Broidy

1963

Picture: *Tom Jones* (UA-Lopert, Woodfall)
Actor: Sidney Poitier, *Lillies of the Field*
Actress: Patricia Neal, *Hud*
Supporting actor: Melvyn Douglas, *Hud*
Supporting actress: Margaret Rutherford, *The V.I.P.s*
Director: Tony Richardson, *Tom Jones*
Original screenplay: James R. Webb, *How the West Was Won*
Adapted screenplay: John Osborne, *Tom Jones*
Cinematography/b&w: James Wong Howe, *Hud*
Cinematography/color: Leon Shamroy, *Cleopatra*
Original score: John Addison, *Tom Jones*
Adapted score: AndréPrevin, *Irma La Douce*
Song: "Call Me Irresponsible" from *Papa's Delicate Condition* (music, James Van Heusen, lyrics, Sammy Cahn)
Art direction/b&w: Gene Callahan, *America, America*
Art direction/color: John DeCuir (and nine others), *Cleopatra*
Costume design/b&w: Piero Gherardi, *Federico Fellini's 8½*
Costume design/color: Irene Sharaff, Vittorio Nino Novarese, Renie, *Cleopatra*
Editing: *How the West Was Won*
Sound: *How the West Was Won*
Special visual effects: *Cleopatra*
Sound effects: *It's a Mad, Mad, Mad, Mad World*

... January 29 ...
Tony Bui's **Three Seasons** is the big winner at the 1999 Sundance Film Festival.

Short/cartoon: *The Critic* (Ernest Pintoff/Mel Brooks)
Short/live action: *An Occurence at Owl Creek Bridge* (Robert Enrico)
Documentary/feature: Robert Frost: *A Lover's Quarrel with the World* (WGBH Educational Foundation)
Documentary/short: *Chagall*
Foreign-language film: *Federico Fellini's 8½,* (Italy)
Irving G. Thalberg award: Sam Spiegel

1964

Picture: *My Fair Lady* (Warner Bros., Jack L. Warner)
Actor: Rex Harrison, *My Fair Lady*
Actress: Julie Andrews, *Mary Poppins*
Supporting actor: Peter Ustinov, *Topkapi*
Supporting actress: Lila Kedrova, *Zorba the Greek*
Director: George Cukor, *My Fair Lady*
Original screenplay: S.H. Barnett, Peter Stone, Frank Tarlogg, *Father Goose*
Adapted screenplay: Edward Anhalt, *Becket*
Cinematography/b&w: Walter Lassally, *Zorba the Greek*
Cinematography/color: Harry Stradling, *My Fair Lady*
Original score: Richard M. Sherman, Robert B. Sherman, *Mary Poppins*
Adapted score: André Previn, *My Fair Lady*
Song: "Chim Chim Cher-ee" from *Mary Poppins* (music and lyrics, Richard M. Sherman, Robert B. Sherman)
Art direction/b&w: Vassilis Fotopoulos, *Zorba the Greek*
Art direction/color: Gene Allen, Cecil Beaton, *My Fair Lady*
Costume design/b&w: Dorothy Jeakins, *The Night of the Iguana*
Costume design/color: Cecil Beaton, *My Fair Lady*
Editing: *Mary Poppins*
Sound: *My Fair Lady*
Special visual effects: *Mary Poppins*
Sound effects: *Goldfinger*
Short/cartoon: *The Pink Phink* (Friz Freleng/Pink Panther)
Short/live action: *Casals Conducts: 1964*
Documentary/feature: *Jacques-Yves Cousteau's World Without Sun*
Documentary/short: *Nine From Little Rock* (U.S. Information Agency)
Foreign-language film: *Yesterday, Today and Tomorrow* (Italy)
Special awards: William Tutle, makeup; *The 7 Faces of Dr. Lao*

1965

Picture: *The Sound of Music* (20th Century Fox, Argyle, Robert Wise)
Actor: Lee Marvin, *Cat Ballou*
Actress: Julie Christie, *Darling*
Supporting actor: Martin Balsam, *A Thousand Clowns*
Supporting actress: Shelley Winters, *A Patch of Blue*
Director: Robert Wise, *The Sound of Music*
Original screenplay: Frederic Raphael, *Darling*
Adapted screenplay: Robert Bolt, *Doctor Zhivago*
Cinematography/b&w: Ernest Laszlo, *Ship of Fools*
Cinematography/color: Freddie Young, *Doctor Zhivago*
Original score: Maurice Jarre, *Doctor Zhivago*
Adapted score: Irwin Kostal, *The Sound of Music*
Song: "The Shadow of Your Smile" from *The Sandpiper* (music, Johnny Mendel, lyrics, Paul Francis Webster)
Art direction/b&w: Robert Clatworthy, *Ship of Fools*
Art direction/color: John Box, Terry Marsh, *Doctor Zhivago*
Costume design/b&w: Julie Harris, *Darling*
Costume design/color: Phyllis Dalton, *Doctor Zhivago*
Editing: William Reynolds, *The Sound of Music*
Sound: *The Sound of Music*
Special visual effects: *Thunderball*
Sound effects: *The Great Race*
Short/cartoon: *The Dot and the Line* (MGM/Chuck Jones)
Short/live action: *The Chicken (Le Poulet)*, Claude Berri (France)
Documentary/feature:*The Eleanor Roosevelt Story*
Documentary/short: *To Be Alive!* (Johnson Wax Co., for New York World's Fair)
Foreign-language film: *The Shop on Main Street* (Czechoslovakia)
Irving G. Thalberg award: William Wyler
Jean Hersholt Humanitarian award: Edmond L. DePatie
Special award: Bob Hope

1966

Picture: *A Man For All Seasons* (Columbia, Fred Zinnemann)
Actor: Paul Scofield, *A Man For All Seasons*
Actress: Elizabeth Taylor, *Who's Afraid of Virginia Woolf?*
Supporting actor: Walter Matthau, *The Fortune Cookie*
Supporting actress: Sandy Dennis, *Who's Afraid of Virginia Woolf?*

... January 30 ...
Mel Gibson negotiates to star in **Patriot**, the revolutionary war drama for Columbia.

Director: Fred Zinnemann, *A Man For All Seasons*

Original screenplay: Claude Lelouch, Pierre Uytterhoeven, *A Man and a Woman*

Adapted screenplay: Robert Bolt, *A Man For All Seasons*

Cinematography/b&w: Haskell Wexler, *Who's Afraid of Virginia Woolf?*

Cinematography/color: Ted Moore, *A Man For All Seasons*

Original score: John Barry, *Born Free*

Adapted score: Ken Thorne, *A Funny Thing Happened on the Way to the Forum*

Song: "Born Free" from *Born Free* (music, John Barry, lyrics, Don Black)

Art direction/b&w: Richard Sylbert, *Who's Afraid of Virginia Woolf?*

Art direction/color: Jack Martin Smith, Dale Hennesy, *Fantastic Voyage*

Costume design/b&w: Irene Sharaff, *Who's Afraid of Virginia Woolf?*

Costume design/color: Elizabeth Haffenden, Joan Bridge, *A Man For All Seasons*

Editing: *Grand Prix*

Sound: *Grand Prix*

Sound effects: *Grand Prix*

Special visual effects: *Fantastic Voyage*

Short/cartoon: *Herb Alpert and the Tijuana Brass Double Feature* (John and Faith Hubley)

Short/live action: *Wild Wings* (British Transport Films, Edgar Anstey)

Documentary/feature: *The War Game* (BBC Production for the British Film Institute, Peter Watkins)

Documentary/short: *A Year Toward Tomorrow* (Office of Economic Opportunity)

Foreign-language film: *A Man and a Woman* (France)

Irving G. Thalberg award: Robert Wise

Jean Hersholt Humanitarian award: George Bagnall

Special awards: Y. Frank Freeman; Yakima Canutt

1967

Picture: *In the Heat of the Night* (UA, Walter Mirisch)

Actor: Rod Steiger, *In the Heat of the Night*

Actress: Katharine Hepburn, *Guess Who's Coming to Dinner*

Supporting actor: George Kennedy, *Cool Hand Luke*

Supporting actress: Estelle Parsons, *Bonnie and Clyde*

Director: Mike Nichols, *The Graduate*

Original screenplay: William Rose, *Guess Who's Coming to Dinner*

Adapted screenplay: Stirling Silliphant, *In the Heat of the Night*

Cinematography: Burnett Guffey, *Bonnie and Clyde*

Original score: Elmer Bernstein, *Thoroughly Modern Millie*

Adapted score: Alfred Newman, Ken Darby, *Camelot*

Song: "Talk to the Animals" from *Doctor Dolittle* (music and lyrics, Leslie Bricusse)

Art direction: John Truscott, Edward Carrere, *Camelot*

Costume design: John Truscott, *Camelot*

Editing: Hal Ashby, *In the Heat of the Night*

Sound: *In the Heat of the Night*

Sound effects: *The Dirty Dozen*

Special visual effects: *Doctor Dolittle*

Short/cartoon: *The Box* (Brandon Films, Fred Wolf)

Short/live action: *A Place to Stand* (Ontario Dept. of Economics and Development, made for Expo '67)

Documentary/feature: *The Anderson Platoon* (French Broadcasting System, Pierre Schöndörffer)

Documentary/short: *The Redwoods*

Foreign-language film: *Closely Watched Trains* (Czechoslovakia)

Irving G. Thalberg award: Alfred Hitchcock

Jean Hersholt Humanitarian award: Gregory Peck

Special award: Arthur Freed

1968

Picture: *Oliver!* (Columbia, Romulus, John Woolf)

Actor: Cliff Robertson, *Charly*

Actress: Katharine Hepburn, *The Lion in Winter*; Barbra Streisand, *Funny Girl* (tie)

Supporting actor: Jack Albertson, *The Subject Was Roses*

Supporting actress: Ruth Gordon, *Rosemary's Baby*

Director: Carol Reed, *Oliver!*

Original screenplay: Mel Brooks, *The Producers*

Adapted screenplay: James Goldman, *The Lion in Winter*

Cinematography: Pasqualino De Santis, *Romeo and Juliet*

Original score: John Barry, *The Lion in Winter*

Adapted score: John Green, *Oliver!*

Song: "The Windmills Of Your Mind" from *The Thomas Crown Affair* (music, Michel Legrand, lyrics, Alan and Marilyn Bergman)

Art direction: John Box, Terry Marsh, *Oliver!*

Costume design: Danilo Donati, *Romeo and Juliet*

Editing: *Bullitt*

Sound: *Oliver!*

Special visual effects: Stanley Kubrick, *2001: A Space Odyssey*

Short/cartoon: *Winnie the Pooh and the Blustery Day* (Walt Disney)

Short/live action: *Robert Kennedy Remembered*

Documentary/feature: *Journey Into Self* (Western Behavioral Sciences Institute)
Documentary/short: *Why Man Creates* (Saul Bass)
Foreign-language film: *War and Peace* (USSR)
Jean Hersholt Humanitarian award: Martha Raye
Special awards: John Chambers, makeup, *Planet of the Apes;* Onna White, choreography, *Oliver!*

1969

Picture: *Midnight Cowboy* (UA, Jerome Hellman)
Actor: John Wayne, *True Grit*
Actress: Maggie Smith, *The Prime of Miss Jean Brodie*
Supporting actor: Gig Young, *They Shoot Horses Don't They?*
Supporting actress: Goldie Hawn, *Cactus Flower*
Director: John Schlesinger, *Midnight Cowboy*
Original screenplay: William Goldman, *Butch Cassidy and the Sundance Kid*
Adapted screenplay: Waldo Salt, *Midnight Cowboy*
Cinematography: Conrad Hall, *Butch Cassidy and the Sundance Kid*
Dramatic score: Burt Bacharach, *Butch Cassidy and the Sundance Kid*
Musical score: Lennie Hayton, Lionel Newman, *Hello Dolly!*
Song: "Raindrops Keep Fallin' On My Head" from *Butch Cassidy and the Sundance Kid* (music, Burt Bacharach, lyrics, Hal David)
Art direction: John DeCuir, Jack Martin Smith, *Hello, Dolly!*
Costume design: Margaret Furse, *Anne of the Thousand Days*
Editing: *Z*
Sound: *Hello, Dolly!*
Special visual effects: *Marooned*
Short/cartoon: *It's Tough to Be a Bird* (Walt Disney, Ward Kimball)
Short/live action: *The Magic Machines* (Fly-by-Night Prods., Joan Keller Stern)
Documentary/feature: *Arthur Rubinstein – The Love of Life*
Documentary/short: *Czechoslovakia 1968* (U.S. Information Agency)
Foreign-language film: *Z* (France-Algeria)
Jean Hersholt Humanitarian award: George Jessel
Special award: Cary Grant

1970

Picture: *Patton* (20th Century Fox, Frank McCarthy)
Actor: George C. Scott, *Patton*
Actress: Glenda Jackson, *Women in Love*
Supporting actor: John Mills, *Ryan's Daughter*
Supporting actress: Helen Hayes, *Airport*

Director: Franklin J. Schaffner, *Patton*
Original screenplay: Francis Ford Coppola, Edmund H. North, *Patton*
Adapted screenplay: Ring Lardner Jr., *M*A*S*H*
Cinematography: Freddie Young, *Ryan's Daughter*
Score: Francis Lai, *Love Story*
Song score: The Beatles, *Let it Be*
Song: "For All We Know" from *Lovers and Other Strangers* (music, Fred Karlin, lyrics, Robb Royer, James Griffin)
Art direction: Urie McCleary, *Patton*
Costume design: Nino Novares, *Cromwell*
Editing: *Patton*
Sound: *Patton*
Special visual effects: *Tora! Tora! Tora!*
Short/cartoon: *Is It Always Right to Be Right?* (Stephen and Nick Bosustow)
Short/live action: *The Resurrection of Broncho Billy* (University of Southern California, directed by John Carpenter)
Documentary/feature: *Woodstock* (Michael Wadleigh)
Documentary/short: *Interviews With My Lai Veterans* (Joseph Strick)
Foreign-language film: *Investigation of a Citizen Above Suspicion* (Italy)
Irving G. Thalberg award: Ingmar Bergman
Jean Hersholt Humanitarian award: Frank Sinatra
Special awards: Lillian Gish; Orson Welles

1971

Picture: *The French Connection* (20th Century Fox, D'Antoni-Schine-Moore)
Actor: Gene Hackman, *The French Connection*
Actress: Jane Fonda, *Klute*
Supporting actor: Ben Johnson, *The Last Picture Show*
Supporting actress: Cloris Leachman, *The Last Picture Show*
Director: William Friedkin, *The French Connection*
Original screenplay: Paddy Chayefsky, *The Hospital*
Adapted screenplay: Ernest Tidyman, *The French Connection*
Cinematography: Oswald Morris, *Fiddler on the Roof*
Art direction: John Box, *Nicholas and Alexandra*
Costume design: Yvonne Blake, Antonio Castillo, *Nicholas and Alexandra*
Original score: Michel Legrand, *Summer of '42*
Scoring adaptation: John Williams, *Fiddler on the Roof*
Song: "Theme From Shaft", *Shaft* (music and lyrics, Isaac Hayes)
Editing: *The French Connection*

Special visual effects: *Bedknobs and Broomsticks*
Short/animated: *The Crunch Bird*
Short/live action: *Sentinels of Silence*
Documentary/feature: *The Hellstrom Chronicle*
(David L. Wolper, Walon Green)
Documentary/short: *Sentinels of Silence*
Foreign-language film: *The Garden of the Finzi-Continis* (Italy)
Special award: Charles Chaplin

1972

Picture: *The Godfather* (Paramount, Albert S. Ruddy)
Actor: Marlon Brando, *The Godfather*
Actress: Liza Minnelli, *Cabaret*
Supporting actor: Joel Gray, *Cabaret*
Supporting actress: Eileen Heckart, *Butterflies Are Free*
Director: Bob Fosse, *Cabaret*
Original screenplay: Jeremy Larner, *The Candidate*
Adapted screenplay: Mario Puzo, Francis Ford Coppola, *The Godfather*
Cinematography: Geoffrey Unsworth, *Cabaret*
Original score: Charles Chaplin, Raymond Rasch, Larry Russell, *Limelight*
Scoring adaptation: Ralph Burns, *Cabaret*
Song: "The Morning After" from *The Poseidon Adventure* (music and lyrics, Al Kasha, Joel Hirschhorn)
Art direction: Rolf Zehetbauer, *Cabaret*
Costume design: Anthony Powell, *Travels With My Aunt*
Editing: *Cabaret*
Sound: *Cabaret*
Visual effects: *The Poseidon Adventure*
Short/animated: *A Christmas Carol* (ABC, Richard Williams)
Short/live action: *Norman Rockwell's World ... An American Dream*
Documentary/feature: *Marjoe* (Howard Smith, Sarah Kernochan)
Documentary/short: *This Tiny World*
Foreign-language film: *The Discreet Charm of the Bourgeoisie* (France)
Jean Hersholt Humanitarian award: Rosalind Russell
Special awards: Edward Robinson; Charles S. Boren

1973

Picture: *The Sting* (Universal, Tony Bill, Michael and Julia Phillips)
Actor: Jack Lemmon, *Save the Tiger*
Actress: Glenda Jackson, *A Touch of Class*
Supporting actor: John Houseman, *The Paper Chase*
Supporting actress: Tatum O'Neal, *Paper Moon*

Director: George Roy Hill, *The Sting*
Original screenplay: David S. Ward, *The Sting*
Adapted screenplay: William Peter Blatty, *The Exorcist*
Cinematography: Sven Nykvist, *Cries and Whispers*
Original score: Marvin Hamlisch, *The Way We Were*
Scoring adaptation: Marvin Hamlisch, *The Sting*
Song: "The Way We Were" from *The Way We Were* (music, Marvin Hamlisch, lyrics, Alan and Marilyn Bergman)
Art direction: Henry Bumstead, *The Sting*
Costume design: Edith Head, *The Sting*
Editing: *The Sting*
Sound: *The Exorcist*
Short/animated: *Frank Film* (Frank Mouris)
Short/live action: *The Bolero*
Documentary/feature: *The Great American Cowboy* (Keith Merrill)
Documentary/short: *Princeton: A Search For Answers*
Foreign-language film: *Day For Night* (France)
Irving G. Thalberg award: Lawrence Weingarten
Jean Hersholt Humanitarian award: Lew Wasserman
Special awards: Henri Langlois; Groucho Marx

1974

Picture: *The Godfather, Part II* (Paramount, Francis Ford Coppola, Gray Frederickson, Fred Roos)
Actor: Art Carney, *Harry and Tonto*
Actress: Ellen Burstyn, *Alice Doesn't Live Here Anymore*
Supporting actor: Robert De Niro, *The Godfather, Part II*
Supporting actress: Ingrid Bergman, *Murder on the Orient Express*
Director: Francis Ford Coppola, *The Godfather, Part II*
Original screenplay: Robert Towne, *Chinatown*
Adapted screenplay: Francis Ford Coppola, Mario Puzo, *The Godfather, Part II*
Cinematography: Fred Koenenkamp, Joseph Biroc, *The Towering Inferno*
Original score: Nino Rota, Carmine Coppola, *The Godfather, Part II*
Scoring adaptation: Nelson Riddle, *The Great Gatsby*
Song: "We May Never Love Like This Again" from *The Towering Inferno* (music and lyrics, Al Kasha, Joel Hirschhorn)
Art direction: Dean Tavoularis, *The Godfather, Part II*
Costume design: Theoni V. Aldredge, *The Great Gatsby*
Editing: *The Towering Inferno*
Sound: *Earthquake*
Visual effects: *Earthquake*

Short/animated: *Closed Mondays* (Will Vinton)
Short/live action: *One-Eyed Men Are Kings*
Documentary/feature: *Hearts and Minds* (Peter Davis, Bert Schneider)
Documentary/short: *Don't*
Foreign-language film: *Amarcord* (Italy)
Jean Hersholt Humanitarian award: Arthur B. Krim
Special awards: Howard Hawks; Jean Renoir

1975

Picture: *One Flew Over the Cuckoo's Nest* (UA Fantasy Films, Saul Zaentz, Michael Douglas)
Actor: Jack Nicholson, *One Flew Over the Cuckoo's Nest*
Actress: Louise Fletcher, *One Flew Over the Cuckoo's Nest*
Supporting actor: George Burns, *The Sunshine Boys*
Supporting actress: Lee Grant, *Shampoo*
Director: Milos Forman, *One Flew Over the Cuckoo's Nest*
Original screenplay: Frank Pierson, *Dog Day Afternoon*
Adapted screenplay: Lawrence Hauben, Bo Goldman, *One Flew Over the Cuckoo's Nest*
Cinematography: John Alcott, *Barry Lyndon*
Original score: John Williams, *Jaws*
Scoring adaptation: Leonard Rosenman, *Barry Lyndon*
Song: "I'm Easy" from *Nashville* (music and lyrics, Keith Carradine)
Art direction: Ken Adam, *Barry Lyndon*
Costume design: Ulla-Brit Soderlund, Milena Canonero, *Barry Lyndon*
Editing: Verna Fields, *Jaws*
Sound: *Jaws*
Sound effects: *The Hindenburg*
Visual effects: *The Hindenburg*
Short/animated: *Great* (Bob Godfrey)
Short/live action: *Angel and Big Joe*
Documentary/feature: *The Man Who Skied Down Everest*
Documentary/short: *The End of the Game*
Foreign-language film: *Dersu Uzala* (USSR)
Irving G. Thalberg award: Mervyn LeRoy
Jean Hersholt Humanitarian award: Jules C. Stein
Special award: Mary Pickford

1976

Picture: *Rocky* (UA, Irwin Winkler, Robert Chartoff)
Actor: Peter Finch, *Network*
Actress: Faye Dunaway, *Network*
Supporting actor: Jason Robards, *All the President's Men*

Supporting actress: Beatrice Straight, *Network*
Director: John G. Avildson, *Rocky*
Original screenplay: Paddy Chayefsky, *Network*
Adapted screenplay: William Goldman, *All the President's Men*
Cinematography: Haskell Wexler, *Bound For Glory*
Original score: Jerry Goldsmith, *The Omen*
Scoring adaptation: Leonard Rosenman, *Bound For Glory*
Song: "Evergreen" from *A Star Is Born* (music, Barbra Streisand, lyrics, Paul Williams)
Art direction: George Jenkins, *All the President's Men*
Costume design: Danilo Donati, *Fellini's Casanova*
Editing: *Rocky*
Sound: *All the President's Men*
Visual effects: Carlo Rambaldi, *King Kong*, *Logan's Run* (special award – not a tie)
Short/animated: *Leisure* (Film Australia)
Short/live action: *In the Region of Ice* (American Film Institute)
Documentary/feature: *Harlan County, USA* (Barbara Kopple)
Documentary/short: *Number Our Days* (Lynne Littman)
Foreign-language film: *Black and White in Color* (Ivory Coast)
Irving G. Thalberg award: Pandro S. Berman

1977

Picture: *Annie Hall* (UA, Rollins-Joffe)
Actor: Richard Dreyfuss, *The Goodbye Girl*
Actress: Diane Keaton, *Annie Hall*
Supporting actor: Jason Robards, *Julia*
Supporting actress: Vanessa Redgrave, *Julia*
Director: Woody Allen, *Annie Hall*
Original screenplay: Woody Allen, Marshal Brickman, *Annie Hall*
Adapted screenplay: Alvin Sargent, *Julia*
Cinematography: Vilmos Zsigmond, *Close Encounters of the Third Kind*
Original score: John Williams, *Star Wars*
Scoring adaptation: Jonathan Tunick, *A Little Night Music*
Song: "You Light Up My Life" from *You Light Up My Life* (music and lyrics, Joseph Brooks)
Art direction: John Barry, *Star Wars*
Costume design: John Mollo, *Star Wars*
Editing: *Star Wars*
Sound: *Star Wars*
Sound effects: Benjamin Burtt Jr., *Star Wars*
Visual effects: John Dykstra, Richard Edlund, *Star Wars*
Short/animated: *Sand Castle* (National Film Board of Canada, Co Hoedeman)

Short/live action: *I'll Find a Way* (National Film
Board of Canada)
Documentary/feature: *Who Are the DeBolts? And
Where Did They Get 19 Kids?* (John Korty)
Documentary/short: *Gravity Is My Enemy*
Foreign-language film: *Madame Rosa* (France)
Irving G. Thalberg award: Walter Mirisch
Jean Hersholt Humanitarian award: Charlton Heston
Special awards: Margareth Booth, editing; Gordon
E. Sawyer and Sidney P. Solow, service and
dedication to the Academy

1978

Picture: *The Deer Hunter* (Universal, EMI Films,
Michael Cimino)
Actor: John Voight, *Coming Home*
Actress: Jane Fonda, *Coming Home*
Supporting actor: Christopher Walken, *The Deer
Hunter*
Supporting actress: Maggie Smith, *California Suite*
Director: Michael Cimino, *The Deer Hunter*
Original screenplay: Nancy Dowd, Waldo Salt,
Robert C. Jones, *Coming Home*
Adapted screenplay: Oliver Stone, *Midnight Express*
Cinematography: Nestor Almendros, *Days of Heaven*
Original score: Giorgio Moroder, *Midnight Express*
Scoring adaptation: Joe Renzetti, *The Buddy Holly
Story*
Song: "Last Dance" from *Thank God It's Friday*
(music and lyrics, Paul Jabara)
Art direction: Paul Sylbert, *Heaven Can Wait*
Costume design: Anthony Powell, *Death on the Nile*
Editing: *The Deer Hunter*
Sound: *The Deer Hunter*
Visual effects: *Superman*
Short/animated: *Special Delivery* (National Film
Board of Canada)
Short/live action: *Teenage Father* (New Visions Inc.
for the Children's Home Society)
Documentary/feature: *Scared Straight!*
Documentary/short: *The Flight of the Gossamer
Condor*
Foreign-language film: *Préparez vos mouchoirs (Get
Out Your Handkerchiefs)* (France)
Jean Hersholt Humanitarian award: Leo Jaffe
Special awards: Walter Lantz; Laurence Olivier; King
Vidor; The Museum of Modern Art Department
of Film

1979

Picture: *Kramer vs. Kramer* (Columbia, Stanley R.
Jaffe)
Actor: Dustin Hoffman, *Kramer vs. Kramer*

Actress: Sally Field, *Norma Rae*
Supporting actor: Melvyn Douglas, *Being There*
Supporting actress: Meryl Streep, *Kramer vs. Kramer*
Director: Robert Benton, *Kramer vs. Kramer*
Original screenplay: Steve Tesic, *Breaking Away*
Adapted screenplay: Robert Benton, *Kramer vs.
Kramer*
Cinematography: Vittorio Storaro, *Apocalypse Now*
Original score: Georges Delerue, *A Little Romance*
Scoring adaptation: Ralph Burns, *All That Jazz*
Song: "It Goes Like It Goes" from *Norma Rae* (music,
David Shire, lyrics, Norman Gimbel)
Art direction: Philip Rosenberg, Tony Walton, *All
That Jazz*
Costume design: Albert Wolsky, *All That Jazz*
Editing: *All That Jazz*
Sound: Walter Murch, *Apocalypse Now*
Sound editing: Alan Splet, *The Black Stallion*
Visual effects: H.R. Giger, Carlo Rambaldi, *Alien*
Short/animated: *Every Child* (National Film Board of
Canada, Derek Lamb)
Short/live action: *Board and Care*
Documentary/feature: *Best Boy* (Ira Wohl)
Documentary/short: *Paul Robeson: Tribute to an
Artist*
Foreign-language film: *The Tin Drum* (West
Germany)
Irving G. Thalberg award: Ray Stark
Jean Hersholt Humanitarian award: Robert Benjamin
Special awards: Alec Guinness; Hal Elias, for service
to the Academy

1980

Picture: *Ordinary People* (Paramount, Wildwood,
Ronald L. Schwary)
Actor: Robert De Niro, *Raging Bull*
Actress: Sissy Spacek, *Coal Miner's Daughter*
Supporting actor: Timothy Hutton, *Ordinary People*
Supporting actress: Mary Steenburgen, *Melvin and
Howard*
Director: Robert Redford, *Ordinary People*
Original screenplay: Bo Goldman, *Melvin and
Howard*
Adapted screenplay: Alvin Sargent, *Ordinary People*
Cinematography: Geoffrey Unsworth, Ghislain
Cloquet, *Tess*
Score: Michael Gore, *Fame*
Song: "Fame" from *Fame* (music, Michael Gore,
lyrics, Dean Pitchford)
Art direction: Pierre Guffroy, Jack Stevens, *Tess*
Costume design: Anthony Powell, *Tess*
Editing: Thelma Schoonmaker, *Raging Bull*
Sound: *The Empire Strikes Back*

...February 4...
Saudi prince Muhammad Bin Bandur Abdul Aziz's effort to buy the remaining assets of
PolyGram Filmed Entertainment from Seagram Co. breaks down.

Visual effects: Richard Edlund, Denis Muren, *The Empire Strikes Back*
Short/animated: *The Fly* (Ferenc Rofusz, Hungary)
Short/live action: *The Dollar Bottom*
Documentary/feature: *From Mao to Mozart: Isaac Stern in China*
Documentary/short: *Karl Hess: Toward Liberty*
Foreign-language film: *Moscow Does Not Believe in Tears* (USSR)
Special award: Henry Fonda

1981

Picture: *Chariots of Fire* (The Ladd Company, Warner Bros., Enigma, David Puttnam)
Actor: Henry Fonda, *On Golden Pond*
Actress: Katharine Hepburn, *On Golden Pond*
Supporting actor: John Gielgud, *Arthur*
Supporting actress: Maureen Stapleton, *Reds*
Director: Warren Beatty, *Reds*
Original screenplay: Colin Welland, *Chariots of Fire*
Adapted screenplay: Ernest Thompson, *On Golden Pond*
Cinematography: Vittorio Storaro, *Reds*
Score: Vangelis, *Chariots of Fire*
Song: "Arthur's theme" from *Arthur* (music and lyrics, Burt Bacharach, Carole Bayer Sager, Christopher Cross, Peter Allen)
Art direction: Norman Reynolds, *Raiders of the Lost Ark*
Costume design: Milena Canonero, *Chariots of Fire*
Editing: *Raiders of the Lost Ark*
Sound: *Raiders of the Lost Ark*
Sound-effects editing: *Raiders of the Lost Ark*
Makeup: Rick Baker, *An American Werewolf in London*
Visual effects: Richard Edlund, Joe Johnston, *Raiders of the Lost Ark*
Short/animated: *Crac* (Canada)
Short/live action: *Violet*
Documentary/feature: *Genocide*
Documentary/short: *Close Harmony*
Foreign-language film: *Mephisto* (Hungary)
Irving G. Thalberg award: Albert R. "Cubby" Broccoli
Jean Hersholt Humanitarian award: Danny Kaye
Special award: Barbara Stanwyck

1982

Picture: *Gandhi* (Columbia, Indo-British Films, Richard Attenborough)
Actor: Ben Kingsley, *Gandhi*
Actress: Meryl Streep, *Sophie's Choice*
Supporting actor: Louis Gossett Jr., *An Officer and a Gentleman*

Supporting actress: Jessica Lange, *Tootsie*
Director: Richard Attenborough, *Gandhi*
Original screenplay: John Briley, *Gandhi*
Adapted screenplay: Costa-Gavras, Donald Stewart, *Missing*
Cinematography: Billy Williams, Ronnie Taylor, *Gandhi*
Original score: John Williams, *E.T.*
Song score: Leslie Bricusse, Henry Mancini, *Victor/Victoria*
Song: "Up Where We Belong" from *An Officer and a Gentleman* (music, Jack Nitzsche, Buffy Saint-Marie, lyrics, Will Jennings)
Art direction: Stuart Craig, Bob Laing, *Gandhi*
Costume design: John Mollo, Bhanu Athaiya, *Gandhi*
Editing: *Gandhi*
Sound: *Gandhi*
Sound-effects editing: *E.T.*
Visual effects: Carlo Rimbaldi, Dennis Muren, *E.T.*
Short/animated: *Tango* (Film Polski, Zbigniew Rybczynski)
Short/live action: *A Shocking Accident*
Documentary/feature: *Just Another Missing Kid* (Canada)
Documentary/short: *If You Love This Planet* (National Film Board of Canada)
Foreign-language film: *Volver A Empezar (To Begin Again)* (Spain)
Jean Hersholt Humanitarian award: Walter Mirisch
Special award: Mickey Rooney

1983

Picture: *Terms of Endearment* (Paramount, James L. Brooks)
Actor: Robert Duvall, *Tender Mercies*
Actress: Shirley MacLaine, *Terms of Endearment*
Supporting actor: Jack Nicholson, *Terms of Endearment*
Supporting actress: Linda Hunt, *The Year of Living Dangerously*
Director: James L. Brooks, *Terms of Endearment*
Original screenplay: Horton Foote, *Tender Mercies*
Adapted screenplay: James L. Brooks, *Terms of Endearment*
Cinematography: Sven Nykvist, *Fanny and Alexander*
Original score: Bill Conti, *The Right Stuff*
Song score: Michel Legrand, Alan and Marilyn Bergman, *Yentl*
Song: "Flashdance … What a Feeling" from *Flashdance* (music, Giorgio Moroder, lyrics, Keith Forsey, Irene Cara)
Art direction: Anna Asp, *Fanny and Alexander*
Costume design: Marik Vos, *Fanny and Alexander*

…February 5…
Twentieth Century Fox is close to a deal to pick up
The Stanford Prison Experiment, with Leonardo DiCaprio to star.

Editing: *The Right Stuff*
Sound: *The Right Stuff*
Sound-effects editing: *The Right Stuff*
Visual effects: Richard Edlund, Dennis Muren, Ken Ralston, Phil Tippett, *Return of the Jedi*
Short/animated: *Sundae in New York* (Jimmy Picker)
Short/live action: *Boys and Girls*
Documentary/feature: *He Makes Me Feel Like Dancin'* (Emile Ardonlino)
Documentary/short: *Flamenco at 5:15* (National Film Board of Canada)
Foreign-language film: *Fanny and Alexander* (Sweden)
Jean Hersholt Humanitarian award: M.J. "Mike" Frankovich
Special award: Hal Roach

1984

Picture: *Amadeus* (Orion, Saul Zaentz)
Actor: F. Murray Abraham, *Amadeus*
Actress: Sally Field, *Places in the Heart*
Supporting actor: Haing S. Ngor, *The Killing Fields*
Supporting actress: Peggy Ashcroft, *A Passage to India*
Director: Milos Forman, *Amadeus*
Original screenplay: Robert Benton, *Places in the Heart*
Adapted screenplay: Peter Shaffer, *Amadeus*
Cinematography: Chris Menges, *The Killing Fields*
Original score: Maurice Jarre, *A Passage To India*
Song score: Prince, *Purple Rain*
Song: "I Just Called To Say I Love You" from *The Woman In Red* (music and lyrics, Stevie Wonder)
Art direction: Patrizia Von Brandenstein, *Amadeus*
Costume design: Theodor Pistek, *Amadeus*
Editing: *The Killing Fields*
Sound: *Amadeus*
Sound-effects editing: *The River*
Makeup: Paul LeBlanc, Dick Smith, *Amadeus*
Visual effects: Dennis Muren, et al, *Indiana Jones and the Temple Of Doom*
Short/animated: *Charade*
Short/live action: *Up* (Pyramid Films, Mike Hoover)
Documentary/feature: *The Times of Harvey Milk*
Documentary/short: *The Stone Carvers*
Foreign-language film: *Dangerous Moves* (Switzerland)
Jean Hersholt Humanitarian award: David L. Wolper
Special awards: National Endowment for the Arts; James Stewart

1985

Picture: *Out of Africa* (Universal, Sydney Pollack)
Actor: William Hurt, *Kiss of the Spider Woman*

Actress: Geraldine Page, *The Trip to Bountiful*
Supporting actor: Don Ameche, *Cocoon*
Supporting actress: Anjelica Huston, *Prizzi's Honor*
Director: Sydney Pollack, *Out of Africa*
Original screenplay: Earl W. Wallace, William Kelley; story by William Kelley, Pamela Wallace, Earl W. Wallace, *Witness*
Adapted screenplay: Kurt Luedtke, *Out of Africa*
Cinematography: David Watkin, *Out of Africa*
Score: John Barry, *Out of Africa*
Song: "Say You, Say Me" from *White Nights* (music and lyrics, Lionel Richie)
Art direction: Stephen Grimes, *Out of Africa*
Costume design: Emi Wada, *Ran*
Editing: *Witness*
Sound: *Out of Africa*
Sound-effects editing: *Back to the Future*
Makeup: *Mask*
Visual effects: *Cocoon*
Short/animated: *Anna & Bella* (Cilia Van Dijk)
Short/live action: *Molly's Pilgrim*
Documentary/feature: *Broken Rainbow*
Documentary/short: *Witness To War: Dr. Charlie Clements*
Foreign-language film: *The Official Story* (Argentina)
Jean Hersholt Humanitarian award: Charles "Buddy" Rogers
Special awards: Paul Newman; Alex North; John H. Whitney

1986

Picture: *Platoon* (Orion, Hemdale, Arnold Kopelson)
Actor: Paul Newman, *The Color of Money*
Actress: Marlee Matlin, *Children of a Lesser God*
Supporting actor: Michael Caine, *Hannah and Her Sisters*
Supporting actress: Dianne Wiest, *Hannah and Her Sisters*
Director: Oliver Stone, *Platoon*
Original screenplay: Woody Allen, *Hannah and Her Sisters*
Adapted screenplay: Ruth Prawer Jhabvala, *A Room With a View*
Cinematography: Chris Menges, *The Mission*
Score: Herbie Hancock, *Round Midnight*
Song: "Take My Breath Away" from *Top Gun* (music, Giorgio Moroder, lyrics, Tom Whitlock)
Art direction: Gianni Quaranta, Brian Ackland-Snow, *A Room With a View*
Costume design: Jenny Beaven, John Bright, *A Room With a View*
Editing: *Platoon*
Sound: *Platoon*

Sound-effects editing: *Aliens*
Makeup: Chris Walas, Stephan Dupuis, *The Fly*
Visual effects: Stan Winston, *Aliens*
Short/animated: *A Greek Tragedy*
Short/live action: *Precious Images* (Chuck Workman)
Documentary/feature: *Artie Shaw: Time Is All You've Got; Down and Out in America* (tie)
Documentary/short: *Women – For America, For the World*
Foreign-language film: *The Assault* (The Netherlands)
Irving G. Thalberg award: Steven Spielberg
Special award: Ralph Bellamy

1987

Picture: *The Last Emperor* (Columbia, Hemdale, Jeremy Thomas)
Actor: Michael Douglas, *Wall Street*
Actress: Cher, *Moonstruck*
Supporting actor: Sean Connery, *The Untouchables*
Supporting actress: Olympia Dukakis, *Moonstruck*
Director: Bernardo Bertolucci, *The Last Emperor*
Original screenplay: John Patrick Shanley, *Moonstruck*
Adapted screenplay: Mark Peploe, Bernardo Bertolucci, *The Last Emperor*
Cinematography: Vittorio Storaro, *The Last Emperor*
Score: Ryuichi Sakamoti, David Byrne, Cong Su, *The Last Emperor*
Song: "(I've Had) The Time Of My Life" from *Dirty Dancing* (music, Franke Previte, John DeNicola, Donald Markowitz, lyrics, Franke Previte)
Art direction: Ferdinando Scarfiotti, *The Last Emperor*
Costume design: James Acheson, *The Last Emperor*
Editing: *The Last Emperor*
Sound: *The Last Emperor*
Sound-effects editing: *Robocop*
Makeup: Rick Baker, *Harry and the Hendersons*
Visual effects: Dennis Muren, *Innerspace*
Short/animated: *The Man Who Planted Trees* (Société Radio-Canada/Canadian Broadcasting Corporation, Frederic Back)
Short/live action: *Ray's Male Heterosexual Dance Hall*
Documentary/feature: *The Ten-Year Lunch: The Wit and Legend of the Algonquin Round Table*
Documentary/short subject: *Young at Heart*
Foreign-language film: *Babette's Feast* (Denmark)
Irving G. Thalberg award: Billy Wilder

1988

Picture: *Rain Man* (United Artists, Guber-Peters Co., Mark Johnson)

Actor: Dustin Hoffman, *Rain Man*
Actress: Jodie Foster, *The Accused*
Supporting actor: Kevin Kline, *A Fish Called Wanda*
Supporting actress: Geena Davis, *The Accidental Tourist*
Director: Barry Levinson, *Rain Man*
Original screenplay: Ronald Bass, Barry Morrow, story by Barry Morrow, *Rain Man*
Adapted screenplay: Christopher Hampton, *Dangerous Liaisons*
Cinematography: Peter Biziou, *Mississippi Burning*
Score: Dave Grusin, *The Milagro Beanfield War*
Song: "Let the River Run" from *Working Girl* (music and lyrics, Carly Simon)
Art direction: Stuart Craig, *Dangerous Liaisons*
Costume design: James Acheson, *Dangerous Liaisons*
Editing: *Who Framed Roger Rabbit?*
Sound: *Bird*
Sound-effects editing: *Who Framed Roger Rabbit?*
Makeup: *Beetlejuice*
Visual effects: *Who Framed Roger Rabbit?*
Short/animated: *Tin Toy* (Pixar, John Lasseter)
Short/live action: *The Appointment of Dennis Jennings* (Dean Parisot, Seten Wright)
Documentary/feature: *Hotel Terminus: The Life and Time of Klaus Barbie* (Marcel Ophüls)
Documentary/short: *You Don't Have to Die*
Foreign-language film: *Pelle the Conqueror* (Denmark)
Special awards: Eastman Kodak; National Film Board of Canada
Special award/animation direction: Richard Williams, *Who Framed Roger Rabbit?*

1989

Picture: *Driving Miss Daisy* (Warner Bros., Richard Zanuck, Lili Fini Zanuck)
Actor: Daniel Day-Lewis, *My Left Foot*
Actress: Jessica Tandy, *Driving Miss Daisy*
Supporting actor: Denzel Washington, *Glory*
Supporting actress: Brenda Fricker, *My Left Foot*
Director: Oliver Stone, *Born on the Fourth of July*
Original screenplay: Tom Schulman, *Dead Poets Society*
Adapted screenplay: Alfred Uhry, *Driving Miss Daisy*
Cinematography: Freddie Francis, *Glory*
Score: Alan Menken, *The Little Mermaid*
Song: "Under the Sea" from *The Little Mermaid* (music, Alan Menken, lyrics, Howard Ashman)
Art direction: Anton Frust, *Batman*
Costume design: Phyllis Dalton, *Henry V*
Editing: *Born on the Fourth of July*
Sound: *Glory*

Sound-effects editing: *Indiana Jones and the Last Crusade*
Makeup: *Driving Miss Daisy*
Visual effects: Dennis Muren, et al, *The Abyss*
Short/animated: *Balance*
Short/live action: *Work Experience*
Documentary/feature: *Common Threads: Stories From the Quilt* (Robert Epstein, Bill Couturie)
Documentary/short: *The Johnstown Flood*
Foreign-language film: *Cinema Paradiso* (Italy)
Jean Hersholt Humanitarian award: Howard W. Koch
Special award: Akira Kurosawa

1990

Picture: *Dances With Wolves* (Orion, Tig Prods., Jim Wilson, Kevin Costner)
Actor: Jeremy Irons, *Reversal of Fortune*
Actress: Kathy Bates, *Misery*
Supporting actor: Joe Pesci, *GoodFellas*
Supporting actress: Whoopi Goldberg, *Ghost*
Director: Kevin Costner, *Dances With Wolves*
Original screenplay: Bruce Joel Rubin, *Ghost*
Adapted screenplay: Michael Blake, *Dances With Wolves*
Cinematography: Dean Semler, *Dances With Wolves*
Score: John Barry, *Dances With Wolves*
Song: "Sooner or Later" from *Dick Tracy* (music and lyrics, Stephen Sondheim)
Art direction: Richard Sylbert, *Dick Tracy*
Costume design: Franca Squarciapino, *Cyrano De Bergerac*
Editing: *Dances With Wolves*
Sound: *Dances With Wolves*
Sound-effects editing: *The Hunt For Red October*
Makeup: *Dick Tracy*
Short/animated: *Creature Comforts* (Aardman Animations, Nick Park)
Short/live action: *The Lunch Date* (Adam Davidson)
Documentary/feature: *American Dream* (Barbara Kopple)
Documentary/short: *Days of Waiting*
Foreign-language film: *Journey of Hope* (Switzerland)
Irving G. Thalberg award: Richard D. Zanuck, David Brown
Special awards: Sophia Loren; Myrna Loy

1991

Picture: *The Silence of the Lambs* (Orion, Strong Heart, Jonathan Demme)
Actor: Anthony Hopkins, *The Silence of the Lambs*
Actress: Jodie Foster, *The Silence of the Lambs*
Supporting actor: Jack Palance, *City Slickers*
Supporting actress: Mercedes Ruehl, *The Fisher King*

Director: Jonathan Demme, *The Silence of the Lambs*
Original screenplay: Callie Khouri, *Thelma and Louise*
Adapted screenplay: Ted Tally, *The Silence of the Lambs*
Cinematography: Robert Richardson, *JFK*
Score: Alan Menken, *Beauty and the Beast*
Song: "Beauty and the Beast" from *Beauty and the Beast* (music, Alan Menken, lyrics, Howard Ashman)
Art direction: Dennis Gassner, *Bugsy*
Costume design: Albert Wolsky, *Bugsy*
Editing: *JFK*
Sound: Gary Rudstrom, et al, *Terminator 2: Judgment Day*
Sound-effects editing: *Terminator 2: Judgment Day*
Makeup: Stan Winston, Jeff Dawn, *Terminator 2: Judgment Day*
Visual effects: Dennis Muren, Stan Winston, *Terminator 2: Judgment Day*
Short/animated: *Manipulation*
Short/live action: *Session Man*
Documentary/feature: *In the Shadow of the Stars*
Documentary/short: *Deadly Deception: General Electric, Nuclear Weapons, and our Environment*
Foreign-language film: *Mediterraneo* (Italy)
Irving G. Thalberg award: George Lucas
Special award: Satyajit Ray

1992

Picture: *Unforgiven* (Warner Bros., Clint Eastwood)
Actor: Al Pacino, *Scent of a Woman*
Actress: Emma Thompson, *Howards End*
Supporting actor: Gene Hackman, *Unforgiven*
Supporting actress: Marisa Tomei, *My Cousin Vinny*
Director: Clint Eastwood, *Unforgiven*
Original screenplay: Neil Jordan, *The Crying Game*
Adapted screenplay: Ruth Prawer Jhabvala, *Howards End*
Cinematography: Philippe Rousselot, *A River Runs Through It*
Score: Alan Menken, *Aladdin*
Song: "Whole New World" from *Aladdin* (music, Alan Menken, lyrics, Tim Rice)
Art direction: Luciana Arrighi, Ian Whittaker, *Howards End*
Costume design: Eiko Ishioka, *Bram Stoker's Dracula*
Editing: *Unforgiven*
Sound: *The Last of the Mohicans*
Sound-effects editing: *Bram Stoker's Dracula*
Makeup: *Bram Stoker's Dracula*
Visual effects: *Death Becomes Her*
Short/animated: *Mona Lisa Descending a Staircase*

Short/live action: *Omnibus*
Documentary/feature: *The Panama Deception*
(Barbara Trent)
Documentary/short: *Educating Peter*
Foreign-language film: *Indochine* (France)
Jean Hersholt Humanitarian award: Audrey
Hepburn, Elizabeth Taylor
Special award: Federico Fellini

1993
Picture: *Schindler's List* (Universal, Amblin
Entertainment, Steven Spielberg, Gerald R. Molen,
Branko Lustig)
Actor: Tom Hanks, *Philadelphia*
Actress: Holly Hunter, *The Piano*
Supporting actor: Tommy Lee Jones, *The Fugitive*
Supporting actress: Anna Paquin, *The Piano*
Director: Steven Spielberg, *Schindler's List*
Original screenplay: Jane Campion, *The Piano*
Adapted screenplay: Steven Zaillian, *Schindler's List*
Cinematography: Janusz Kaminski, *Schindler's List*
Score: John Williams, *Schindler's List*
Song: "Streets of Philadelphia" from *Philadelphia*
(music and lyrics, Bruce Springsteen)
Art direction: Allan Starski, Ewa Braun, *Schindler's
List*
Costume design: Gabriella Pescucci, *The Age of
Innocence*
Editing: *Schindler's List*
Sound: Gary Rydstrom, *Jurassic Park*
Sound-effects editing: Gary Rydstrom, *Jurassic Park*
Makeup: *Mrs. Doubtfire*
Visual effects: Dennis Muren, Stan Winston, Phil
Tippett, Michael Lantieri, *Jurassic Park*
Short/animated: *The Wrong Trousers* (Aardman
Animations, Nick Park)
Short/live action: *Black Rider* (Germany)
Documentary/feature: *I Am a Promise: The Children
of Stanton Elementary School*
Documentary/short: *Defending our Lives*
Foreign-language film: *Belle Epoque* (Spain)
Jean Hersholt Humanitarian award: Paul Newman
Special award: Deborah Kerr

1994
Picture: *Forrest Gump* (Paramount, Wendy
Finerman, Steve Tisch, Steve Starkey)
Actor: Tom Hanks, *Forrest Gump*
Actress: Jessica Lange, *Blue Sky*
Supporting actor: Martin Landau, *Ed Wood*
Supporting actress: Dianne Wiest, *Bullets Over
Broadway*
Director: Robert Zemeckis, *Forrest Gump*

Original screenplay: Quentin Tarantino, story by
Quentin Tarantino, Roger Avary, *Pulp Fiction*
Adapted screenplay: Eric Roth, *Forrest Gump*
Cinematography: John Toll, *Legends of the Fall*
Score: Hans Zimmer, *The Lion King*
Song: "Can You Feel The Love Tonight?" from *The
Lion King* (music, Elton John, lyrics, Tim Rice)
Art direction: Ken Adams, *The Madness of King
George*
Costume design: Lizzy Gardiner, Tim Chappel, *The
Adventures of Priscilla, Queen of the Desert*
Editing: *Forrest Gump*
Sound: *Speed*
Sound-effects editing: *Speed*
Makeup: Rick Baker, *Ed Wood*
Visual effects: *Forrest Gump*
Short/animated: *Bob's Birthday* (Channel
Four/National Film Board of Canada)
Short/live action: *Franz Kafka's It's a Wonderful Life*
(Peter Capaldi, Ruth Kenley-Letts), *Trevor* (Peggy
Rajski, Randy Stone) (tie)
Documentary/feature: *Maya Lin: A Strong Clear
Vision* (Freida Lee Mock)
Documentary/short: *A Time For Justice* (Southern
Poverty Law Center)
Foreign-language film: *Burnt By the Sun* (Russia)
Irving G. Thalberg award: Clint Eastwood
Jean Hersholt Humanitarian award: Quincy Jones
Special award: Michelangelo Antonioni

1995
Picture: *Braveheart* (Paramount, Icon, Mel Gibson,
Alan Ladd Jr., Bruce Davey)
Actor: Nicolas Cage, *Leaving Las Vegas*
Actress: Susan Sarandon, *Dead Man Walking*
Supporting actor: Kevin Spacey, *The Usual Suspects*
Supporting actress: Mira Sorvino, *Mighty Aphrodite*
Director: Mel Gibson, *Braveheart*
Original screenplay: Christopher McQuarrie, *The
Usual Suspects*
Adapted screenplay: Emma Thompson, *Sense and
Sensibility*
Cinematography: John Toll, *Braveheart*
Musical or comedy score: Alan Menken and Stephen
Schwartz, *Pocahontas*
Dramatic score: Luis Bacalov, *Il Postino*
Song: "Colors Of The Wind" from *Pocahontas*
(music, Alan Menken, lyrics, Stephen Schwartz)
Art direction: Eugenio Zanetti, *Restoration*
Costume design: James Acheson, *Restoration*
Editing: *Apollo 13*
Sound: *Apollo 13*
Sound-effects editing: *Braveheart*

...February 9...
Warner Bros. pays six figures for the spec script **Ton 80** with Madonna attached to star.

Makeup: Peter Frampton, Paul Pattison, Lois
  Burwell, *Braveheart*
Visual effects: *Babe*
Short/animated: *A Close Shave* (Aardman Animation,
  Nick Park)
Short/live action: *Liberman in Love*
Documentary/feature: *Anne Frank Remembered*
  (BBC/Disney)
Documentary/short: *One Survivor Remembers* (HBO)
Foreign-language film: *Antonia's Line* (The
  Netherlands)
Special awards: Kirk Douglas; Chuck Jones

1996
Picture: *The English Patient* (Miramax, Saul Zaentz)
Actor: Geoffrey Rush, *Shine*
Actress: Frances McDormand, *Fargo*
Supporting actor: Cuba Gooding Jr., *Jerry Maguire*
Supporting actress: Juliette Binoche, *The English
  Patient*
Director: Anthony Minghella, *The English Patient*
Original screenplay: Ethan and Joel Coen, *Fargo*
Adapted screenplay: Billy Bob Thornton, *Sling Blade*
Cinematography: John Seale, *The English Patient*
Original musical or comedy score: Rachel Portman,
  Emma
Original dramatic score: Gabriel Yared, *The English
  Patient*
Song: "You Must Love Me" from *Evita* (music,
  Andrew Lloyd Webber, lyrics, Tim Rice)
Art direction: Brian Morris, *The English Patient*
Set direction: Stephanie McMillan, *The English
  Patient*
Costume design: Ann Roth, *The English Patient*
Editing: *The English Patient*
Sound: *The English Patient*
Sound-effects editing: *The Ghost and the Darkness*
Makeup: Rick Baker, David Leroy Anderson, *The
  Nutty Professor*
Visual effects: *Independence Day*
Short/animated: *Quest*
Short/live action: *Dear Diary*
Documentary/feature: *When We Were Kings* (Leon
  Gast and David Sonenberg)
Documentary/short: *Breathing Lessons: The Life and
  Work of Mark O'Brien*
Foreign-language film: *Kolya* (Czech Republic)
Special awards: Volker W. Bahnemann; Michael Kidd;
  Joe Lombardi; Burton "Bud" Stone

1997
Picture: *Titanic* (James Cameron, Jon Landau)
Actor: Jack Nicholson, *As Good As It Gets*

Actress: Helen Hunt, *As Good As It Gets*
Supporting actor: Robin Williams, *Good Will
  Hunting*
Supporting actress: Kim Basinger, *L.A. Confidential*
Director: James Cameron, *Titanic*
Original screenplay: Ben Affleck, Matt Damon, *Good
  Will Hunting*
Adapted screenplay: Brian Helgeland, Curtis Hanson,
  L.A. Confidential
Cinematography: Russell Carpenter, *Titanic*
Original musical or comedy score: Anne Dudley, *The
  Full Monty*
Original dramatic score: James Horner, *Titanic*
Song: "My Heart Will Go On" from *Titanic*
Art direction: Peter Lamont, Michael Ford, *Titanic*
Costume design: Deborah L. Scott, *Titanic*
Editing: *Titanic*
Sound: *Titanic*
Sound-effects editing: *Titanic*
Makeup: Rick Barker, David LeRoy Anderson,
  Men in Black
Visual effects: *Titanic*
Short/animated: *Geri's Game*
Short/live action: *Visas and Virtue*
Documentary/feature: *The Long Way Home* (Rabbi
  Marvin Hier and Richard Tank)
Documentary/short: *A Story of Healing*
Foreign-language film: *Character* (The Netherlands)
Special awards: Pete Clark; Stanley Donen

1998
Picture: *Shakespeare in Love* (David Parfitt, Donna
  Gigliotti, Harvey Weinstein, Edward Zwick,
  Marc Norman)
Actor: Roberto Begnini, *Life Is Beautiful*
Actress: Gwyneth Paltrow, *Shakespeare in Love*
Supporting actor: James Coburn, *Affliction*
Supporting actress: Judy Dench, *Shakespeare in Love*
Director: Steven Spielberg, *Saving Private Ryan*
Original screenplay: Marc Norman, Tom Stoppard,
  Shakespeare in Love
Adapted screenplay: Bill Condon, *Gods and Monsters*
Cinematography: Janusz Kaminski, *Saving Private
  Ryan*
Original musical or comedy score: Stephen Warbeck,
  Shakespeare in Love
Original dramatic score: Nicola Piovani, *Life Is
  Beautiful*
Song: "When You Believe" from *The Prince of Egypt*
  (music and lyrics, Stephen Schwartz)
Art direction: Martin Childs, Jill Quertier,
  Shakespeare in Love
Costume design: Sandy Powell, *Shakespeare in Love*

... February 10 ...
The 49th Berlin International. Film Festival opens with **Aimée & Jaguar**.

Editing: *Saving Private Ryan*
Sound: *Saving Private Ryan*
Sound effects editing: *Saving Private Ryan*
Makeup: Jenny Shircore, *Elizabeth*
Visual effects: *What Dreams May Come*
Short/animated: *Bunny*
Short/live action: *Election Night (Valgaften)*
Documentary/feature: *The Last Days* (James Moll and Ken Lipper)
Documentary/short: *The Personals: Improvisations on Romance in the Golden Years*
Foreign-language film: *Life Is Beautiful* (Italy)
Honorary Oscar: Elia Kazan
Irving G. Thalberg award: Norman Jewison

1999

Picture: *American Beauty* (DreamWorks, A Jinks/Cohen Company Production, Bruce Cohen and Dan Jinks producers)
Actor: Kevin Spacey, *American Beauty*
Actress: Hilary Swank, *Boys Don't Cry*
Supporting actor: Michael Caine, *The Cider House Rules*
Supporting actress: Angelina Jolie, *Girl, Interrupted*

Director: Sam Mendes, *American Beauty*
Original screenplay: Alan Ball, *American Beauty*
Adapted screenplay: John Irving, *The Cider House Rules*
Cinematography: Conrad L. Hall, *American Beauty*
Original score: John Corigliano, *The Red Violin*
Song: "You'll Be in My Heart" from *Tarzan* (music and lyrics, Phil Collins)
Art direction: Rick Heinrichs; Peter Young, *Sleepy Hollow*
Costume design: Lindy Hemming, *Topsy-Turvy*
Editing: *The Matrix*
Sound: *The Matrix*
Sound-effects editing: *The Matrix*
Makeup: Christine Blundell and Trefor Proud, *Topsy-Turvy*
Visual effects: *The Matrix*
Short/animated: *The Old Man and the Sea*
Short/live action: *My Mother Dreams the Satan's Disciples in New York*
Documentary/feature: *One Day in September*
Documentary/short: *King Gimp*
Foreign-language film: *Todo sobre mi madre (All About My Mother)* (Spain)

> *There are three questions you never give an honest answer to: How old do I look?, Do you like my hair? and Was it good for you too?*
> (Jane Leeves, Frasier)

Golden Globe Film Awards: 1999

Motion picture – drama: *American Beauty*, DreamWorks

Motion picture – musical or comedy: *Toy Story 2*, Disney Pixar

Performance by an actress in a motion picture – drama: Hilary Swank, *Boys Don't Cry*

Performance by an actor in a motion picture – drama: Denzel Washington, *The Hurricane*

Performance by an actress in a motion picture – musical or comedy: Janet McTeer, *Tumbleweeds*

Performance by an actor in a motion picture – musical or comedy: Jim Carrey, *Man on the Moon*

Foreign-language film: *All About My Mother* (Spain)

Performance by an actress in a supporting role in a drama, musical, or comedy: Angelina Jolie, *Girl, Interrupted*

Performance by an actor in a supporting role in drama, musical, or comedy: Tom Cruise, *Magnolia*

Director: Sam Mendes, *American Beauty*

Screenplay: Alan Ball, *American Beauty*

Original score: Ennio Morricone, *The Legend of 1900*

Original song: "You'll Be in My Heart" by Phil Collins, *Tarzan*

Critics' Awards

LA Film Critics: 1999

Picture: *The Insider*

Director: Sam Mendes, *American Beauty*

Actor: Russell Crowe, *The Insider*

Actress: Hilary Swank, *Boys Don't Cry*

Supporting actor: Christopher Plummer, *The Insider*

Supporting actress: Chloe Sevigny, *Boys Don't Cry*

Screenplay: Charlie Kaufman, *Being John Malkovich*

Foreign film: *All About My Mother* (Spain)

Documentary: *Buena Vista Social Club*

Animation: *Iron Giant*

Music: Trey Parker, Marc Shaiman, *South Park: Bigger, Longer, and Uncut*

National Board of Review: 1999

Picture: *American Beauty*

Director: Anthony Minghella, *The Talented Mr. Ripley*

Actor: Russell Crowe, *The Insider*

Actress: Janet McTeer, *Tumbleweeds*

Supporting actor: Philip Seymour Hoffman, *Magnolia* and *The Talented Mr. Ripley*

Supporting actress: Julianne Moore, *Magnolia*, *An Ideal Husband*, *Cookie's Fortune*, and *A Map of the World*

Foreign films: *All About My Mother*, *Run Lola Run*, *East-West*, *Cabaret Balkan*, *The Emperor and the Assassin*

Documentary: *Buena Vista Social Club*

Career achievement: Clint Eastwood

Special achievement in filmmaking: Tim Robbins

Freedom of expression award: Michael Mann, *The Insider*

New York Film Critics' Awards: 1999

Picture: *Topsy-Turvy*

Director: Mike Leigh, *Topsy-Turvy*

Actor: Richard Farnsworth, *The Straight Story*

Actress: Hilary Swank, *Boys Don't Cry*

Supporting actor: John Malkovich, *Being John Malkovich*

Supporting actress: Catherine Keener, *Being John Malkovich*

Screenplay: Alexander Payne, *Election*

Cinematography: Freddie Francis, *The Straight Story*

Foreign film: *All About My Mother* (Spain)

Nonfiction film: *Buena Vista Social Club*

First feature: *Being John Malkovich*

Boston Film Critics: 1999

Picture: *Three Kings*

Director: David O. Russell, *Three Kings*

Actor: Jim Carrey, *Man on the Moon*

Actress: Hilary Swank, *Boys Don't Cry*

Supporting actor: Christopher Plummer, *The Insider*

Supporting actress: Chloe Sevigny, *Boys Don't Cry*

Cinematography: Emmanuel Lubezski, *Sleepy Hollow*

Screenplay: Charlie Kaufman, *Being John Malkovich*

Foreign film: *All About My Mother* (Spain)

Documentary: *Hands on a Hardbody*

New filmmaker: Kimberly Peirce, *Boys Don't Cry*

... February 12 ...

Barbra Streisand's and Cis Corman's Barwood Prods. is to join forces with Storyline Entertainment to turn the Jerry Herman musical **Mame** into a three-hour film.

National Awards

European Academy Awards: 1999

European film: *Todo sobre mi madre (All About My Mother)*, Pedro Almodóvar, Spain

European actor: Ralph Fiennes, *Sunshine*, Hungary

European actress: Cecilia Roth, *Todo sobre mi madre (All About My Mother)*, Spain

European screenwriter: István Szabó, Israel Horovitz, *Sunshine*, Hungary

European cinematographer: Lajos Koltai, *Sunshine* and *Legend of 1999*

European achievement in world cinema: Antonio Banderas, Roman Polanski

European lifetime achievement award: Ennio Morricone

European discovery – Fassbinder award: Tim Roth, *War Zone*, U.K.

European documentary award – Prix Arte: *Buena Vista Social Club*, Wim Wenders

European critics' award – Prix FIPRESCI: *Adieu plancher des vaches*, Otar Iosseliani, France

Screen International award for a non-European film: *The Straight Story*, David Lynch (U.S.)

European short film: *Benvenuto in San Salvario*, Enrico Verra

People's Awards

Best director: Pedro Almodóvar, *Todo sobre mi madre (All About My Mother)*

Best actor: Sean Connery, *Entrapment*

Best actress: Catherine Zeta-Jones, *Entrapment*

AFI Australian Film Awards

Film: *Two Hands*, Gregor Jordan

Director: Gregor Jordan, *Two Hands*

Actor: Russell Dykstra, *Soft Fruit*

Actress: Sacha Horler, *Praise*

Supporting actor: Bryan Brown, *Two Hands*

Supporting actress: Sacha Horler, *Soft Fruit*

Original screenplay: Gregor Jordan, *Two Hands*

Adapted screenplay: Andrew McGahan, *Praise*

Foreign film: *Life Is Beautiful* (Italy)

Cinematography: Martin McGrath ACS, *Passion*

Editing: Lee Smith, *Two Hands*

Sound: Toivo Lember, Gethin Creagh, Peter Smith, Wayne Pashely, *In a Savage Land*

Original music score: David Bridie, *In a Savage Land*

Production design: Murray Picknett, *Passion*

Costume design: Terry Ryan, *Passion*

British Academy of Film and Television Awards

Film: *Shakespeare in Love*, David Parfitt, Donna Gigliotti, Harvey Weinstein, Edward Zwick, Marc Norman

The David Lean award for direction: Peter Weir, *The Truman Show*

Original screenplay: Andrew Niccol, *The Truman Show*

Adapted screenplay: Elaine May, *Primary Colors*

Lead actress: Cate Blanchett, *Elizabeth*

Lead actor: Roberto Benigni, *Life Is Beautiful*

Supporting actress: Judi Dench, *Shakespeare in Love*

Supporting actor: Geoffrey Rush, *Shakespeare in Love*

Best foreign film: *Central Station*, Walter Salles (Brazil)

The Anthony Asquith award for film music: David Hirschfelder, *Elizabeth*

The Carl Foreman newcomer's award: Richard Kwietniowski

Cinematography: Remi Adefarosin, *Elizabeth*

Production design: Dennis Gossner

Costume design: Sandy Powell, *Velvet Goldmine*

Editing: David Gamble, *Shakespeare in Love*

Sound: *Saving Private Ryan*

Special visual effects: *Saving Private Ryan*

Makeup and hair: Jenny Shircore, *Elizabeth*

Short film: *Home*

Animated short film: *The Canterbury Tales*

The Orange audience award: *Lock, Stock and Two Smoking Barrels*

French César Awards

Director: Patrice Chereau, *Ceux qui m'aiment prendront le train*

Film: *La vie rêvée des anges*, Erick Zonca

Actor: Jacques Villeret, *Le dîner de cons*

Actress: Elodie Bouchez, *La vie rêvée des anges*

Supporting actor: Daniel Prévost, *Le dîner de cons*

Supporting actress: Dominique Blanc, *Ceux qui m'aiment prendront le train*

Young actor: Bruno Putzulu, *Petits désordres amoureux*

Young actress: Natacha Régnier, *La vie rêvée des anges*

First film: *Dieu seul me voit*

Foreign film: *Life Is Beautiful* (Italy)

Original or adapted screenplay: Francis Veber, *Le dîner de cons*

Music: Tony Gatli, *Gadjo Dio*

Photography: Eric Gauthier, *Ceux qui m'aiment prendront le train*

...February 13...

Shakespeare in Love enjoys a major box-office boost from its 13 Oscar nominations.

Editing: Véronique Lange, *Taxi*
Sets: Jacques Rouxel, *Lautrec*
Costumes: Pierre-Jean Larroque, *Lautrec*
Short film: Xavier Giannoli, *L'Interview*

Chinese Golden Rooster Awards

Film: *Live in Peace*, Hu Bingliu
Director: Hu Bingliu, *Live in Peace*, Saifu Mailisi, Genghis Kahn
Script: Lu Zhuguo, *The Big March: Sweeping Across the Southeast*
Actor: Feng Gong, *Having Fun*
Actress: Tao Hong, *Colors of the Blind*
Supporting actor: Ge Cunzhuang, *Zhou Enlai: A Great Friend*
Supporting actress: Bao Xueyun, *Live in Peace*

Danish Bodil Film Awards

Danish film: *The Celebration*, Thomas Vinterberg
Actor: Holger Ulrich Thomsen, *The Celebration*
Actress: Bodil Jørgensen, *The Idiots*
Supporting actor: Nikolaj Lic Kaas, *The Idiots*
Supporting actress: Anne Louise Hassing, *The Idiots*
American film: *The Ice Storm*, Ang Lee
Non-American film: *My Name Is Joe*, Ken Loach (U.K.)
Special achievement/honorable Bodil: Ove Sprogøe, actor

Finnish Jussi Film Awards

Picture: *Kuningasjätkä*, Markku Pölönen
Director: Markku Pölönen, *Kuningasjätkä*
Actor: Pertti Koivula, *Kuningasjätkä*
Actress: Elena Leeve, *Tulennielijä*
Actor in a supporting role: Peter Franzen, *Kuningasjätkä*
Actress in a supporting role: Tiina Weckström, *Tulennielijä*
Original screenplay: Markku Pölönen, *Kuningasjätkä*
Cinematography: Kjell Lagerroos, *Tulennielijä*

German Film Awards

Film: *Run Lola Run*
Director: Tom Tykwer, *Run Lola Run*
Actor: August Diehl, *23*
Actress (shared): Juliane Koehler, *Aimée & Jaguar*, Maria Schrader, *Aimée & Jaguar* and *Meschugge*
Supporting actor: Herbert Knaup, *Run Lola Run*
Supporting actress: Nina Petri, *Bin ich Schön* and *Run Lola Run*
Cinematography: Frank Griebe, *Run Lola Run*
Editing: Mathilde Bonnefoy, *Run Lola Run*
Foreign film: *Life Is Beautiful* (Italy)

Film music: Niki Reiser, *Meschugge* and *Pünktchen und Anton*
Lifetime achievement award: Egon Günther

Hong Kong Film Awards

Film: *Beastcops*
Director: Gordon Chan, Dante Lam, *Beastcops*
Script: Chan Hing-kai, *Beastcops*
Actor: Anthony Wong, *Beastcops*
Actress: Sandra Ng, *Portland Street Blues*
Supporting actor: Tam Yiu-man, *Beastcops*
Supporting actress: Shu Qi, *Portland Street Blues*

Icelandic Film Awards (Edda Awards)

Film: *Honor of the House*
Director: Guðny Halldórsdóttir, *Honor of the House*
Actor: Ingvar Siugurosson, *Slurpinn & Co*
Actress: Tinna Gunnlaugsdóttir, *Honor of the House*
Score: Hilmar Örn Hilmarsson, *Honor of the House*
Costumes: Thorin María Jónsdóttir, *The Dance*
Makeup: Ragna Fossberg, *Honor of the House*
Lifetime achievement award: Indriði Thorsteinsson

Italian Donatello Awards

Film: *Not of This World*
Director: Giuseppe Tornatore, *The Legend of the Pianist on the Ocean*
Producer: Lionello Cerri, *Not of This World*
Debuting director: Luciano Ligabue, *Radio Freccia*
Actor: Stafano Accorsi, *Radio Freccia*
Actress: Margherita Buy, *Not of This World*
Supporting actor: Fabrizio Bentivoglio, *Of Lost Love*
Supporting actress: Cecilia Dazzi, *Marriages*
Screenplay: Giuseppe Piccioni, Gualtiero Rosell, Lucia Zei, *Not of This World*
Cinematography: Lajos Koltai, *The Legend of the Pianist on the Ocean*
Art direction: Francesco Frigeri, *The Legend of The Pianist on the Ocean*
Costumes: Maurizion Millenotti, *The Legend of the Pianist on the Ocean*
Editing: Esmerelda Calabria, *Not of This World*
Sound: Gaetano Carito, *Radio Freccia*
Foreign film: *Train of Life* (French/Belgian/Romanian/Dutch)

Norwegian Film Awards (Amandas)

Norwegian feature film: *Only Clouds Move the Stars*, Torun Lian
The Amanda Committee's professional award: Randall Meyers, composer
Dramatic television production: *Offshore*, Christian Brym (NRK)

...February 14...
Warner Bros. get a sweet Valentine's Day present as a wave of romance-minded viewers carry **Message in a Bottle** to an estimated $19.1 million.

Actress: Brit Elisabeth Haagensli, *Absolute Hangover*
Actor: Ingar Helge Gimle, *Absolute Hangover*
The Amanda committee's honorary award: Egil
  Monn-Iversen, film composer/producer
Short film: *Eye for an Eye*, Emil Stang Lund
The Amanda committee's honorary award: Toralv
  Maurstad, actor
Nordic Amanda: *Mifune*, Søren Kragh-Jacobsen
  (Denmark)
Foreign film: *Fucking Åmål*, Lukas Moodysson
  (Sweden)

Spanish Goya Awards

Film: *The Girl of Your Dreams*, Fernando Trueba
Director: Fernando Leon, *Neighborhood*
Actor: Fernando Fernan Gomez, *The Grandfather*
Actress: Penelope Cruz, *The Girl of Your Dreams*
Supporting actor: Tony LeBlanc, *Torrente, the Dumb
  Arm of the Law*
Supporting actress: Adriana Ozores, *Time of the
  Brave*
Most promising young actor: Miroslav Taborsky, *The
  Girl of Your Dreams*
Most promising young actress: Marieta Orozco,
  Neighborhood
Original screenplay: Fernando Leon, *Neighborhood*

Adapted screenplay: Luis Marias, *Mensaka*
Cinematography: Juan Antonio Ruiz Anchia,
  Mararria
Original music: Alberto Iglesias, *The Lovers of the
  Arctic Circle*
Live-action short: *A Perfect Day*
European film: *The Boxer* (Ireland)
Spanish-language foreign film: *Southern Lighthouse*
Honorary academy award: Rafael Alonso

Swedish Golden Bug Film Awards

Picture: *Fucking Åmål*, Lukas Moodysson
Director: Lukas Moodysson, *Fucking Åmål*
Actor: Krister Henriksson, *Veranda för en tenor*
Actress: Alexandra Dahlström, Rebecca Liljeberg,
  Fucking Åmål
Script: Lukas Moodysson, *Fucking Åmål*
Photography: Philip Øgaard, *Glasblåsarns barn*
Supporting actor: Thommy Berggren, *Glasblåsarns
  barn*
Supporting actress: Ia Långhammer, *Hela härligheten*
Foreign picture: *Festen*, Thomas Vinterberg
  (Denmark)
Golden bug for creative achievement: Elisabeth
  Sörenson
Short film: *Aligermaas äventyr*, Andra Lasmanis

MTV Movie Awards: 1999

Best movie: *There's Something About Mary*
Best male performance: Jim Carrey, *The Truman
  Show*
Best female performance: Cameron Diaz, *There's
  Something About Mary*
Breakthrough performance (male): James Van Der
  Beek, *Varsity Blues*
Breakthrough performance (female): Katie Holmes,
  Disturbing Behavior
Best villain (tie): Matt Dillon, *There's Something
  About Mary*; Stephen Dorff, *Blade*
Best song from a movie: "I Don't Want to Miss a
  Thing", Aerosmith, *Armageddon*

Best comedic performance: Adam Sandler, *The
  Waterboy*
Best onscreen duo: Jackie Chan and Chris Tucker,
  Rush Hour
Best kiss: Gwyneth Paltrow and Joseph Fiennes,
  Shakespeare in Love
Best action sequence: *Armageddon* (asteroid destroys
  NYC); Michael Bay, director
Best fight: Ben Stiller vs. Puffy the Dog, *There's
  Something About Mary*
Best new filmmaker: Guy Ritchie, *Lock, Stock and
  Two Smoking Barrels*

> *The trouble with real life is
> there's no danger music.*
> (Jim Carrey, The Cable Guy)

... **February 15** ...
Tom Cruise is planning a U.S. remake of **Lock, Stock and Two Smoking Barrels**.

Prizes awarded at major film festivals: 1999

Berlin

Golden Berlin Bear: *The Thin Red Line* (Terrence Malick)

Silver Berlin Bear Jury Grand Prix: *Mifunes sidste sang - Dogme 3* (Søren Kragh-Jacobsen)

Silver Berlin Bear for the best director: Stephen Frears, *The High-Lo Country*

Silver Berlin Bear for the best actress: Juliane Köhler, Maria Schrader, *Aimée and Jaguar*

Silver Berlin Bear for the best actor: Michael Gwisdek, *Nachtgestalten*

Silver Berlin Bear special jury prize for an outstanding single achievement: Marc Norman, Tom Stoppard for their screenplay of *Shakespeare in Love*

Silver Berlin Bear special jury prize for his outstanding artistic achievements: David Cronenberg

The Blue Angel, the prize of the European Academy of Film and TV: Yesim Ustaoglu, *Günese Yolculuk*

The Alfred Bauer Prize for a film debut: *Karnaval*, Thomas Vincent

FIPRESCI Award: *Ça commence aujourd'hui*, Bertrand Tavernier (France)

Special mention: John Toll, director of photography, *The Thin Red Line*

Special mention to the young upcoming actress: Iben Hjejle, *Mifunes sidste sang - Dogme 3*

Special mention for its subject matter: *Ça commence aujourd'hui*, Bernard Tavernier

Silver Berlin Bear for the best short: *Faraon (Pharaoh)*, Sergei Ovtscharov, *Masks*, Piotr Karwas

Cannes

Palme d'Or: *Rosetta*, Luc and Jean-Pierre Dardenne (Belgium/France)

Grand Prix: *L'Humanité*, Bruno Dumont (France)

Actress: Séverine Caneele, *L'Humanité*, Emilie Dequenne, *Rosetta*

Actor: Emmanuel Schotte, *L'Humanité*

Director: Pedro Almodóvar, *All About My Mother* (Spain)

Screenplay: Yuri Arabov, Marina Koreneva, *Moloch* (Russia/Germany)

Jury Prizes: Manoel de Oliveira

Golden camera: *Throne of Death*, Mulai Nair (India)

Critics' Week awards: *Flowers from Another World*, Iciar Bollain (Spain)

FIPRESCI award: *Peau neuve*, Emilie Deleuze (France)

Karlovy Vary

Film: *Jana's Friends*, Arik Kaplun (Israel)

Director: Aleksandr Rogozhkin, *Blockpost* (Russia)

Actor: Hilmar Thate, *Paths in the Night* (Germany)

Actress: Evlyn Kaplun, *Jana's Friends* (Israel)

Audience award: *Fucking Åmål*, director Lukas Moodysson (Sweden)

Special mention: *Cozy Dens*, Jan Hrebejk (Czech Republic)

FIPRESCI prize: *Cozy Dens*, Jan Hrebejk (Czech Republic)

Freedom award: *Outskirts*, director Peter Lucik (Russia)

San Sebastián

Golden Shell: *C'est quoi la vie?*, François Dupeyron (France)

Special jury award: *Jaime*, Antonio-Pedro Vasconcelos (Luxembourg/Portugal/Brasil)

Silver Shell for the best director: Zhang Yang, *Shower* (China), Michel Deville, *La maladie de Sachs* (France)

Silver Shell for the best actress: Aitana Sánchez-Gijón, *Volaverunt* (Spain/France)

Silver Shell for the best actor: Jacques Dufilho, *C'est quoi la vie?* (France)

Award for the best photography: Alfredo Mayo, *Cuando vuelvas a mi lado* (Spain)

Award for best screenplay: Rosalinde and Michel Deville, *La maladie de Sachs* (France)

Special jury mention: Gracia Querejeta, *Cuando vuelvas a mi lado* (Spain), Colin Nutley, *Under the Sun* (Sweden/Finland)

FIPRESCI award: Christina Andreef, *Soft Fruit* (Australia)

Sundance

Grand jury prize (dramatic): *Three Seasons*, Tony Bui

Grand jury prize (documentary): *American Movie*, Chris Smith

Audience award (dramatic): *Three Seasons*, Tony Bui

Audience award (documentary): *Genghis Blues*, Roko Belic

The World Cinema audience award: *Run Lola Run*, Tom Tykwer and *Train of Life*, Radyu Mihaileanu

Filmmakers trophy (dramatic): *Tumbleweeds*, Gavin O'Connor

Filmmakers trophy (documentary): Sing Faster: *The Stagehand's Ring Cycle*, Jon Else

---

Thessaloniki

Best full-length film award (The Golden Alexander): *Shower*, Zhang Yang (China)

Special jury award (Silver Alexander): *Garage Olimpo*, Marco Bechis (Italy/France/Argentina)

Director award: Justin Kerrigan, *Human Traffic* (U.K.)

Screenplay award: Atef Hetata, *Closed Doors* (Egypt/France); Laurent Cantet, Gilles Marchand, *Human Resources*

Actress award: Sawson Badr, *Closed Doors* (Egypt/France)

Actor award: Jean Pierre Darroussin, *Qui plume la lune*, Christine Carrière (France)

Artistic achievement award: *Return of the Idiot*, Sasa Gedeon (Czech Republic)

Special mention: Paddy Connor, actor, Terry Stacey, cinematographer, for *Dream Catcher* (U.S.)

Venice

Golden Lion for best film: *Ye Ge Dou Bu Neng Shao* (*Not One Less*), Zhang Yimou (China)

Jury Grand Prix: *The Wind Will Carry Us*, Abbas Kiarostami (France/Iran)

Special prize for the best director: *Guo Nian Hui Jia* (*Seventeen Years*), Zhang Yuan

Coppa Volpi for best actress: Nathalie Baye, *Une liaison pornographique*

Coppa Volpi for best actor: Jim Broadbent, *Topsy-Turvy*

Marcello Mastroianni award to a young promising actor or actress: Nina Proll, *Nordrand*

Golden medal of the Italian Senate: *Rien à faire*, Marion Vernoux

Luigi de Laurentiis award: *Questo e' il giardino?*, Giovanni Davide Maderna

Special mention: *Bye Bye Africa*, Mahamet Saleh Haroun

FIPRESCI award: *The Wind Will Carry Us*, Abbas Kiarostami (France/Iran)

> *Of course, you won't be able to lie on your back for a while, but then you can lie from any position, can't you?*
> *(Audrey Hepburn speaking to Cary Grant,* Charade*)*

... February 17 ...
Zeitgeist Films picks up U.S. rights to **The Acid House**, a screen adaptation of the book by **Trainspotting** author Irvine Welsh.

Screen Superstars

Variety tends to measure a star by his or her bankability. We've charted the rise and rise in salaries and packages, upfront and backend alike. With several actors and actresses earning north of $20 million an outing, the pressures of finding tomorrow's new talent grow more daunting by the day.

Our Y2K list of current superstars reflects the marketplace as much as editorial opinion. A wonderful actress can often fail to set the B.O. tills ringing. A lousy performer can be swept to fame and fortune by the right vehicle at the right moment. Each of the actors below has the ability to get a movie off the ground; behind the scenes, many are producers in their own right. The filmographies list only the most recent work in each star's career, from the most abstinent (Streisand) to the most prolific (arguably Travolta).

Woody Allen

Real name: Allen Stewart Konigsberg; legal name Heywood Allen. Born on December 1, 1935 in Brooklyn, NY. Married to Soon Yi, Mia Farrow's (his ex-partner's) adopted daughter. Father of three. Angst-ridden actor, writer-director, still one of the most inventive and original filmmakers in the U.S. He won an Oscar for *Annie Hall*. Recent films: *Stuck on You* (2001), *Woody Allen Summer Project 1999* (2000), *Company Man, Picking Up the Pieces, Sweet and Lowdown* (1999) *Celebrity, Wild Man Blues, Antz* (animated, voice only) (1998), *Deconstructing Harry* (1997), *Everyone Says I Love You* (1996), *Mighty Aphrodite* (1995).

Antonio Banderas

Born in Malaga, Spain in 1960. Married to Melanie Griffith, father of Stella. Spanish heart-throb who became an international star after his success in Almodóvar's hit films, and struck gold with *The Mask of Zorro*. Recent films: *Play It to the Bone, The Body, The Sparrow* (2000), *The 13th Warrior, White River Kid, Crazy in Alabama* – director (1999), *The Mask of Zorro* (1998), *Evita* (1996), *Two Much* (1996), *Never Talk to Strangers* (1995), *Assassins* (1995).

Warren Beatty

Birth name: Henry Warren Beatty. Born in Richmond, VA on March 3, 1937. Married to actress Annette Bening, father of three. Actor, producer, writer, director. His virile good looks brought him popularity in the 1960s while later films secured him critical acclaim, Oscar nominations, and finally the Oscar for best direction for *Reds*. Recent films: *Mr. Hughes* (2000), *Town and Country* (1999), *Bulworth* (1998), *Love Affair* (1994), *Bugsy* (1991).

Pierce Brosnan

Born in Drogheda, County Louth, Ireland on May 16, 1953. Engaged to Keely Shaye-Smith. Father of two sons and three stepchildren. Cool, chic, post-modernist James Bond, who reached out to a middle-aged audience with *The Thomas Crown Affair*. Recent films: *Grey Owl, The Match, The Thomas Crown Affair, The World Is Not Enough* (1999), *The Nephew* (1998), *Tomorrow Never Dies, Dante's Peak* (1997), *Mars Attacks!, The Mirror Has Two Faces, The Disappearance of Kevin Johnson, Robinson Crusoe* (1996), *GoldenEye* (1995).

Sandra Bullock

Born in Arlington, VA on July 29, 1965. Appealing, plain-speaking lead with girl-next-door looks who became a megastar after the box-office smash *Speed* in 1994. Also producer. Recent films: *28 Days, Exactly 3:30, Gun Shy, Miss Congeniality* (2000), *Forces of Nature* (1999), *Prince of Egypt* (voice), *Practical Magic, Hope Floats, Making Sandwiches* (1998), *Speed 2: Cruise Control* (1997), *In Love and War, Two if by Sea, A Time to Kill* (1996).

Nicolas Cage

Real name: Nicholas Coppola (nephew of Francis Ford Coppola). Born in Long Beach, CA on July 1, 1964. Married to Patricia Arquette, father of one. Aggressive, engaging actor who after years in the wilderness joined the Hollywood A list with an Oscar-winning performance in Mike Figgis' *Leaving Las Vegas*, and showed a gentler side to his talent in *City of Angels*. Recent films: *Gone in Sixty Seconds, Family Man, Mr. Hughes* (2000) *8 MM, Bringing Out the Dead* (1999), *City of Angels, Snake Eyes* (1998), *Face/Off* (1997), *Con Air* (1997), *The Rock* (1996).

Jim Carrey

Real name: James Eugene Carrey. Born in Jackson Point, Canada on January 17, 1962. Dating Renée Zellweger. Divorced twice, father of one. Became a household name with outrageous, offbeat, physical comedies and proved with *The Truman Show* that he could tackle more serious roles. He has joined the ranks of the highest-paid stars in the history of film. Recent films: *How the Grinch Stole Christmas, Me, Myself, and Irene* (2000), *Man on the Moon* (1999), *The Truman Show, Simon Birch* (1998), *Liar, Liar* (1997), *The Cable Guy* (1996), *Ace Ventura: When Nature Calls, Batman Forever* (1995), *Ace Ventura Pet Detective, The Mask, Dumb and Dumber* (1994).

Jackie Chan

Real name: Chan Kwong-Sang. Born in Hong Kong on April 7, 1954. Agile, intrepid action star who's graduated from Chinese-language chop-socky flicks to Hollywood top billing. Chan does all his own (often terrifying) stunts, which is rare these days. Recent films: *Shanghai Noon* (2000), *Gen-X Cops, The King of Comedy, Gorgeous* (1999), *Mr. Nice Guy, Rush Hour* (1998), *Jackie Chan's First Strike, Operation Condor* (1997), *Rumble in the Bronx* (1996).

George Clooney

Born in Lexington, KY on 6 May, 1961. The sexy star of *ER* finally made a bigscreen impact with the critically acclaimed if modestly performing *Out of Sight*. Recent films: *The Perfect Storm, O Brother, Where Art Thou?* (2000), *Three Kings, South Park: Bigger, Longer and Uncut* (voice) (1999), *The Thin Red Line, Out of Sight, Waiting For Woody* (1998), *The Peacemaker, Batman and Robin* (1997).

Sean Connery

Real name: Thomas Connery. Born in Edinburgh, Scotland on August 25, 1930. Married to Micheline, father of Jason. Enduring star whose post-Bond career has propelled him into production deals and even the possible launch of a Scottish studio. Recent films: *End Game* (2000), *Entrapment* (1999), *Playing by Heart, The Avengers* (1998), *The Rock, Dragonheart* (voice) (1996), *First Knight, Just Cause* (1995).

Kevin Costner

Born in Lynwood, CA on January 18, 1957. Father of three. His star is on the wane after flops and disappointments in the late 1990s, but cast in the right vehicle he's still capable of recapturing the glory years (when his *Dances with Wolves* earned zillions and swept the Oscars). Runs his own production outfit, Tig. Recent films: *13 Days* (2000), *For Love of the Game, Message in a Bottle* (1999), *The Postman* (1997), *Tin Cup* (1996), *Waterworld* (1995), *Wyatt Earp* (1994).

Tom Cruise

Real name: Thomas Cruise Mapother IV. Born in Syracuse, NY on July 3, 1962. Married to Nicole Kidman, father of two adopted children. Matinee idol Tom Cruise showed he was not just a pretty face and by the end of the 1980s had become a genuine star and mature actor. Recent films: *Minority Report, Mission: Impossible 2* (2000), *Magnolia, Eyes Wide Shut* (1999), *Mission: Impossible, Jerry Maguire* (1996), *Interview With the Vampire* (1994), *The Firm* (1993), *A Few Good Men* (1992).

Matt Damon

Born in Cambridge, MA, on October 8, 1970. Strong-willed beneath his all-American-boy exterior, Damon became a household name after *Good Will Hunting* (which he also co-wrote, earning an Oscar in the process). Recent films: *Titan A.E., All the Pretty Horses, The Legend of Bagger Vance, The Third Wheel* (2000), *The Talented Mr. Ripley, Dogma* (1999), *Saving Private Ryan, Rounders* (1998), *Good Will Hunting, John Grisham's The Rainmaker, Chasing Amy* (1997).

Robert De Niro

Born in New York, NY on August 17, 1943. Father of three. De Niro's accelerated slate finds him popping up in two or three movies a year. Nurtured early on by Scorsese and Coppola, he remains a prestige name for any marquee, but is willing to take small, meaty roles with offbeat directors. Recent films: *The Adventures of Rocky and Bullwinkle, Fifteen Minutes, Navy Diver, Meet the Parents, Out of My Feet* (2000), *Analyze This, Flawless* (1999), *Ronin, Great Expectations* (1998), *Jackie Brown, Wag the Dog, Cop Land* (1997), *The Fan, Marvin's Room* (1996), *Heat, Casino* (1995).

Leonardo DiCaprio

Born in Los Angeles on November 11, 1974. Every teenage girl's dream, this handsome young actor is probably the most bankable of contemporary stars after *Titanic*, although he made his mark early on in offbeat work like *What's Eating Gilbert Grape?* and *The Quick and the Dead*. Recent films: *The Beach, Gangs of New York* (2000), *Don's Plum, The Man in the Iron Mask, Celebrity* (1998), *Titanic* (1997), *Marvin's Room, Romeo and Juliet* (1996).

Michael Douglas

Born in New Brunswick, NJ on September 25, 1944.

Divorced, father of one. Engaged to Catherine Zeta-Jones. Son of the great star of the 1940s and 1950s, Kirk Douglas, Michael Douglas became a marquee name with hits as an actor (and producer, e.g. *One Flew Over the Cuckoo's Nest*). Recent films: *Ace in the Hole, One Night at McCools, A Song For David, Still Life* (2000), *Wonder Boys* (1999), *A Perfect Murder* (1998), *The Game* (1997), *The Ghost and the Darkness* (1996), *The American President* (1995), *Disclosure* (1994).

Clint Eastwood

Born in San Francisco, CA on May 31, 1930. Married to Dina Ruiz, father of five. Rugged, durable icon who surged via *Rawhide* and spaghetti westerns to become Hollywood's favorite screen enforcer. Still a hybrid, with his directed-only pics grossing less than his starring vehicles. Recent films: *Space Cowboys, Listening With the Eyes* (2000), *True Crime* (1999), *Absolute Power* (1997), *The Bridges of Madison County* (1995), *A Perfect World, In the Line of Fire* (1993), *Unforgiven* (1992, Oscars for Best Director and Best Film).

Harrison Ford

Born in Chicago, IL on July 13, 1942. Married to Melissa Mathison, father of four. The rugged, po-faced star of Spielberg films has been on all top lists from the biggest stars ever to the sexiest men, since he was first noted in Coppola's *The Conversation*. Recent films: *What Lies Beneath* (2000), *Random Hearts* (1999), *Six Days, Seven Nights* (1998), *Air Force One, The Devil's Own* (1997), *Sabrina* (1995), *Clear and Present Danger* (1994).

Jodie Foster

Real name: Alicia Christian Foster. Born in Los Angeles, CA on November 19, 1962. Mother of one; did not want to reveal the father's name or the manner of conception. Brilliantly gifted double Oscar-winner, intent on finding the right roles and setting up cool projects through her own shingle, Egg, at Paramount. Recent films: *Flora Plum* (2000), *Anna and the King,* (1999), *Contact* (1997), *Nell* (1994), *Home For the Holidays* (director), *Maverick* (1994), *Sommersby* (1993).

Morgan Freeman

Born in Memphis, TN on June 1, 1937. Married to Myrna Colley-Lee, father of four. Late-maturing black star whose engaging gravitas has brought him an Oscar nomination (for *Shawshank*) and increasingly rewarding roles. Recent films: *Third Degree, Long Way to Freedom, Rendezvous With Rama* (2000), *Along Came a Spider, Nurse Betty, Water Damage* (1999),

Deep Impact, Hard Rain (1998), *Amistad, Long Way Home, Kiss the Girls* (1997), *Chain Reaction, Moll Flanders* (1996), *Outbreak, Seven* (1995), *The Shawshank Redemption* (1994), *Unforgiven* (1992).

Richard Gere

Born in Philadelphia, PA on August 31, 1949. Partner: Carey Lowell. Satin-smooth ladykiller who has acquired a fresh lease of life since *Pretty Woman*. Recent films: *Autumn in New York, Listening With the Eyes, Dr. T and the Women* (2000), *Runaway Bride* (1999), *The Jackal, Red Corner* (1997), *Primal Fear* (1996).

Mel Gibson

Born in Peekskill, NY on January 3, 1956. Married to Robyn Moore, father of 7. Handsome, compeling actor and sex symbol, whose breakthrough came with the *Mad Max* movies in Oz. Also a thoughtful director (*The Man Without a Face, Braveheart*) and producer (Icon Productions). Recent films: *The Million Dollar Hotel, The Patriot, Chicken Run, What Women Want* (2000), *Payback* (1999), *Lethal Weapon 4* (1998), *Conspiracy Theory* (1997), *Ransom* (1996), *Braveheart* (1995, Oscars for Best Director and Best Picture), *Maverick* (1994), *The Man Without a Face* (1993).

Hugh Grant

Born in London, England on September 9, 1960. Partner: Liz Hurley. Diffident, laid-back Brit whose upper-crust delivery harks back to the heyday of Ealing Studios, and whose comic timing has brought him international stardom. Recent films: *Woody Allen Summer Project 1999* (2000), *Mickey Blue Eyes, Notting Hill* (1999), *Extreme Measures* (1996), *Sense and Sensibility, Nine Months, The Englishman Who Went Up a Hill But Came Down a Mountain, An Awfully Big Adventure, Restoration* (1995), *Four Weddings and a Funeral, Sirens* (1994).

Gene Hackman

Born in San Bernardino, CA on January 30, 1930. Married to Betsy Arakawa, father of three. Gruff, often abrasive character actor, Hackman has been one of the busiest, most sought-after screen personalities in Hollywood in the three decades since winning an Oscar for *The French Connection*. Recent films: *Third Degree, The Replacements* (2000), *Twilight, Enemy of the State, Antz* (voice) (1998), *Absolute Power* (1997), *Extreme Measures, The Chamber, The Birdcage* (1996).

Tom Hanks

Born in Concord, CA on July 9, 1956. Married to Rita Wilson, father of four. Arguably the most respected

... February 20 ...
Barbara Walters interviews Monica Lewinsky for
ABC's expanded two-hour edition of **20/20**.

Hollywood actor of the 1990s, with back-to-back Oscars for *Philadelphia* and *Forrest Gump*, and nominations for every other award under the sun. At enviable ease in both dramatic and comedy roles. Recent films: *Castaway, Dino* (2000), *The Green Mile, Toy Story 2* (voice) (1999), *You've Got Mail, Saving Private Ryan* (1998), *That Thing You Do!* (1996), *Apollo 13* (1995), *Forrest Gump* (1994), *Philadelphia, Sleepless in Seattle* (1993).

Dustin Hoffman

Born in Los Angeles, CA on August 8, 1937. Married to Lisa Gottsegen, father of six. One of the most versatile and enduring Hollywood stars (and charismatic stage actor), this two-time Oscar winner (*Kramer vs. Kramer* and *Rain Man*) has also been involved in production. Recipient of the 1999 American Film Institute's lifetime achievement award. Recent films: *Cosm, The Messenger: The Story of Joan of Arc* (1999), *Sphere* (1998), *Wag the Dog, Mad City* (1997), *Sleepers, American Buffalo* (1996), *Outbreak* (1995).

Sir Anthony Hopkins

Born in Port Talbot, Wales on December 31, 1937. Married to Jennifer Ann Lynton, father of one. Distinguished stage actor, but a muted presence on screen until *The Silence of the Lambs* (Oscar, 1991) catapulted him to Hollywood stardom. Returns as Hannibal Lecter in 2000. Recent films: *Mission Impossible: 2, Hannibal* (2000), *Instinct, Titus* (1999), *Meet Joe Black, The Mask of Zorro* (1998), *Amistad, The Edge* (1997), *Surviving Picasso, August* (directed only) (1996), *Nixon* (1995).

Jennifer Lopez

Born in the Bronx, New York on July 24, 1970. Twice divorced. After her sizzling performance and on-screen chemistry with co-star George Clooney in *Out of Sight,* Jennifer Lopez became one of the hottest stars in Hollywood. Her singing has also brought her millions. Films: *The Cell, Pluto Nash* (2000), *Thieves* (1999), *Out of Sight, Antz* (voice) (1998), *Anaconda, Blood and Wine, Selena, U Turn* (1997).

Steve Martin

Born in Waco, Texas on August 14, 1945. Suave, Cary Grant-style comedian whose dead-pan, double-taking manner has worked well on a new generation. Recent films: *Bowfinger, Out-of-Towners, Joe Gould's Secret, The Venice Project* (1999), *The Prince of Egypt* (voice) (1998), *The Spanish Prisoner* (1997), *Sgt. Bilko* (1996), *Father of the Bride, Part II* (1995).

Eddie Murphy

Born in Brooklyn, New York on April 3, 1961. Married to Nicole Mitchell, father of three. The most successful of all black stars in Hollywood, Murphy burst on the scene with manic glee in *48 Hrs* (1982) and has never stopped wisecracking since. Recent films: *Nutty II: The Klumps, Pluto Nash, Shrek* (voice) (2000), *Bowfinger, Life* (1999), *Holy Man, Doctor Dolittle* (1998).

Mike Myers

Born in Scarborough, Ontario, Canada on May 25, 1963. His goofy persistence as Austin Powers (a part he both writes and acts) has made Myers one of the biggest draws in the world – on an off day, so to speak. Recent films: *McClintock's Peach, Shrek* (voice), *Sprockets* (2000), *Mystery Alaska, Austin Powers: The Spy Who Shagged Me, Pete's Meteor* (1999), *54* (1998), *Austin Powers: International Man of Mystery* (1997), *Wayne's World 2, So I Married an Axe Murderer* (1993), *Wayne's World* (1992).

Jack Nicholson

Born in Neptune, NJ on April 22, 1937. Partner: Rebecca Broussard; father of four. Actor, director, erstwhile screenwriter, and an enduring star who dominates virtually any movie he appears in. Owns two Best Actor Oscars, for *As Good as It Gets* and *One Flew Over the Cuckoo's Nest* and one Best Supporting Actor statuette (*Terms of Endearment*). Recent films: *As Good as It Gets, Blood and Wine* (1997), *Mars Attacks!, The Evening Star* (1996), *The Crossing Guard* (1995), *Wolf* (1994).

Al Pacino

Real name: Alfredo James Pacino. Born in New York, NY on April 25, 1940. Relationship: Beverly D'Angelo. A star off-Broadway before making debut in *The Panic in Needle Park* and a spectacular breakthrough with *The Godfather* movies. Hit a rough patch in the 1980s, but back on track with a slew of rasping, authoritative, and sardonic performances in recent years. Recent films: *Chinese Coffee, Any Given Sunday, The Insider* (1999), *The Devil's Advocate, Donnie Brasco* (1997), *Looking For Richard* (also directed), *City Hall* (1996), *Heat, Two Bits* (1995).

Gwyneth Paltrow

Born in Los Angeles, CA on September 28, 1973. This fresh, sophisticated, and very talented young actress came of age with her Oscar for *Shakespeare in Love*. Recent films: *Duets, Bounce* (2000), *The Talented Mr. Ripley,* (1999), *Hush, Shakespeare in Love, A Perfect Murder, Great Expectations, Sliding Doors* (1998),

---

Emma, Hard Eight, The Pallbearer (1996), *Jefferson in Paris, Moonlight and Valentino, Seven* (1995).

Brad Pitt

Real name: William Bradley Pitt. Born in Shawnee, OK on December 18, 1963. Relationship with *Friends* star Jennifer Aniston. All-too-handsome blond star who still looks 20, and, like the young Robert Redford, is at his best in the great outdoors. Recent films: *The Guy Ritchie Project, Listening With the Eyes, Urban Townies* (2000), *Fight Club, Being John Malkovich* (1999), *Meet Joe Black* (1998), *Seven Years in Tibet, The Dark Side of the Sun, The Devil's Own* (1997), *Sleepers* (1996), *Twelve Monkeys, Seven* (1995), *Interview With the Vampire, The Favor, Legends of the Fall* (1994).

Robert Redford

Real name: Charles Robert Redford Jr. Born in Santa Monica, CA on August 18, 1937. Partner: Kathy O'Rear; father of three. Actor who has moved from pretty-boy parts in the 1960s to Oscar-winning director (*Ordinary People*) and producer, and now flag-bearer for the indie movement, with his Sundance Institute, Festival, and TV channel well established. Recent films: *The Horse Whisperer* (also directed, 1998), *Up Close and Personal* (1996), *Quiz Show* (directed only, 1994), *Indecent Proposal* (1993).

Keanu Reeves

Real name: Keanu Charles Reeves. Born in Beirut, Lebanon on September 2, 1964. Dating Jennifer Syme. Handsome action hero at home in sci-fi pix whose career bounced back in 1999 with *The Matrix*. Recent films: *Driven, The Replacement* (2000), *The Matrix* (1999), *Me and Will* (1998), *The Devil's Advocate, The Last Time I Committed Suicide* (1997), *Feeling Minnesota, Chain Reaction* (1996).

Julia Roberts

Real name: Julie Fiona Roberts. Born in Smyrna, GA on October 28, 1967. Busy, broad-smiling actress whose forte for screen comedy helped her to stardom with *Pretty Woman* in 1990. Her abiding glamor has remained in tune despite a turbulent private life. Recent films: *Erin Brockovich, The Moviegoer* (2000), *Notting Hill, Runaway Bride* (1999), *Stepmom* (1998), *Conspiracy Theory, My Best Friend's Wedding* (1997), *Everyone Says I Love You, Mary Reilly, Michael Collins* (1996).

Meg Ryan

Real name: Margaret Hyra. Born in Fairfield, CT on November 19, 1961. Married to Dennis Quaid,

mother of Jack Henry. Jockeying Julia Roberts and Jodie Foster for the top spot among female stars. At her best in comedy, but *Courage Under Fire* and *City of Angels* revealed a tough, introspective facet of her talent. Recent films: *Proof of Life, Hanging up* (2000), *You've Got Mail, Hurlyburly, City of Angels* (1998), *Addicted to Love, Two For the Road, Anastasia* (voice) (1997), *Courage Under Fire* (1996), *French Kiss* (1995).

Arnold Schwarzenegger

Born in Graz, Austria on July 30, 1947. Married to Maria Owings Shriver, father of four. The ultimate bodybuilder turned terminator, Schwarzenegger remains among Hollywood's highest-paid stars, although a heart attack interrupted his career during 1998. Recent films: *The Sixth Day* (2000), *End of Days* (1999), *Batman and Robin* (1997), *Eraser, Jingle All the Way* (1996), *Junior, True Lies* (1994).

Will Smith

Born in Philadelphia, PA on September 25, 1968. Married to actress Jada Pinkett, father of one. Actor and singer whose insolent, off-the-cuff delivery recalls the young Eddie Murphy. Thus far, all his screen appearances have been in major hits. Recent films: *The Legend of Bagger Vance* (2000), *Wild Wild West* (1999), *Enemy of the State* (1998), *Men in Black* (1997), *Independence Day* (1996), *Bad Boys* (1995).

Sylvester Stallone

Born in New York, NY on July 6, 1946. Married to model Jennifer Flavin, father of four. The Italian stallion who for more than a decade ruled as the world's leading action star, although he'd prefer to be remembered as the writer-star of Oscar-winning *Rocky*. *Cop Land* suggested he could score in more thoughtful roles. Recent films: *D-tox, Get Carter, The Hunter, Into Thin Air,* (2000), *Antz* (animated, voice) (1998), *An Alan Smithee Film, The Good Life, Cop Land* (1997), *Daylight* (1996), *Assassins, Judge Dredd* (1995).

Sharon Stone

Born in Meadville, PA on March 10, 1958. Married to newspaper executive Phil Bronstein. An overnight sensation in *Basic Instinct* after years in the wilderness, Stone became the siren of the 1990s, the cool, dangerous blonde with lotsa sex appeal and an unusually high IQ to match. But she badly needs a hit. Recent films: *Beautiful Joe* (2000), *The Muse, Gloria, Simpatico, Picking Up the Pieces* (1999), *The Mighty, Sphere, Antz* (animated, voice) (1998), *Diabolique, Last Dance* (1996), *The Quick and the Dead, Casino, Catwalk* (1995).

Meryl Streep

Real name: Mary Louise Streep. Born in Summit, NJ on 22 June, 1949. Married to Don Gummer, mother of four. Coming of age in both *Julia* and *The Deer Hunter*, Streep dominated the 1980s as Hollywood's foremost screen actress, a natural heir to Katharine Hepburn, and with a gift for accents that has thus far encompassed Polish, Danish, Irish, Spanish, and Australian. Took Best Actress Oscar for *Sophie's Choice*, the statuette for best supporting role in *Kramer vs. Kramer*, and has received 11 nominations as actress. Recent films: *Music of the Heart* (1999), *One True Thing, Dancing at Lughnasa* (1998), *Before and After, Marvin's Room* (1996), *The Bridges of Madison County* (1995).

Barbra Streisand

Born in Brooklyn, NY on April 24, 1942. Married to actor James Brolin, mother of one. Singer, actor, director, and superstar entertainer of the American stage, TV, recordings, and films; has her own production company Barwood Films. Now rarely tempted by screen roles, but still boasting the clout to get projects greenlighted. Won the Best Actress Oscar for *Funny Girl*. Recent films: *The Mirror Has Two Faces* (1996), *The Prince of Tides* (1991).

John Travolta

Born in Englewood, NJ on February 18, 1954. Married to Kelly Preston, father of one. After the success of *Saturday Night Fever* and *Grease* in the 1970s, his career sagged, but he made an unexpected comeback in the early 1990s with *Pulp Fiction* and has been among the busiest and highest-paid actors ever since. Recent films: *Battlefield: Earth, Numbers, Standing Room Only* (2000), *The General's Daughter* (1999), *The Thin Red Line, A Civil Action, Primary Colors* (1998), *Mad City, Face/Off, She's So Lovely* (1997), *Michael, Phenomenon* (1996), *Broken Arrow, Get Shorty, White Man's Burden* (1995).

Denzel Washington

Born in Mount Vernon, NY on December 28, 1954. Married to Pauletta Pearson. Actor, producer, and director whose gaze of integrity has brought him the kind of screen and TV roles once inhabited by Sidney Poitier. Won an Oscar for best supporting role in *Glory*. His production company is Mundy Lane Entertainment. Recent films: *Remember the Titans* (2000), *The Bone Collector, The Hurricane* (1999), *The Siege, He Got Game, Fallen* (1998), *The Preacher's Wife, Courage under Fire* (1996).

Robin Williams

Born in Chicago, IL on July 21, 1952. Married to Marsha Garces, father of three. Ebullient, irrepressible comic with extraordinary vocal gifts (e.g. *Aladdin*), Williams is among the most prolific and consistent of stars, finally winning an Oscar for *Good Will Hunting* after nominations for *Good Morning Vietnam* and *Dead Poets Society*. Recent films: *Don't Worry, He Won't Get Far on Foot, The Interpreter* (2000), *Bicentennial Man, Get Bruce, Jakob the Liar* (1999), *Patch Adams, What Dreams May Come* (1998), *Good Will Hunting, Flubber, Deconstructing Harry, Father's Day* (1997), *The Birdcage, Hamlet, Jack, The Secret Agent* (1996).

Bruce Willis

Real name: Walter Bruce Willis. Born in Idar-Oberstein, Germany on March 19, 1955. Married to Demi Moore since 1987, but they separated in 1998. Father of three daughters. After a huge success with the TV series *Moonlighting*, Willis became equally popular as a bigscreen hero with his portrayal of tough, cynical, chain-smoking cops. Teamed up with Stallone and Schwarzenegger to launch the Planet Hollywood chain. Recent films: *Outlaws* (2001), *Unbreakable, The Whole Nine Yards, The Kid* (2000), *Breakfast of Champions, The Sixth Sense, The Story of Us* (1999), *Armageddon, Mercury Rising, The Siege, Apocalypse* (1998), *The Jackal, The Fifth Element* (1997), *Last Man Standing* (1996).

Catherine Zeta-Jones

Real name: Catherine Jones. Born in Swansea, Wales, U.K. on September 25, 1969. Engaged to Michael Douglas. Smouldering young star whose verve and brio brought her instant stardom with *The Mask of Zorro*. Recent films: *Ace in the Hole, High Fidelity* (2000), *Entrapment, The Haunting* (1999), *The Mask of Zorro* (1998).

> *There's no right; there's no wrong.*
> *There's only popular opinion.*
> *(Brad Pitt, 12 Monkeys)*

... **February 23** ...
Madonna is to make her directorial debut with **The Fires**.

International box office: 1999

Title	Gross ($m)
Australia	
1 Star Wars: Episode I – The Phantom Menace	25.6
2 The Sixth Sense	18.7
3 Austin Powers: The Spy Who Shagged Me	14.8
4 The Matrix	14.7
5 Notting Hill	13.8
6 The Mummy	12.0
7 Big Daddy	9.7
8 American Pie	9.4
9 The World Is Not Enough	8.4
10 Toy Story 2	8.0
11 Shakespeare in Love	7.9
12 Runaway Bride	7.8
13 The Rugrats Movie	7.7
14 Tarzan	7.6
15 The Waterboy	7.4
16 Rush Hour	7.3
17 Entrapment	6.5
18 Deep Blue Sea	6.4
19 The Blair Witch Project	6.2
20 Patch Adams	6.0
Brazil	
1 The Sixth Sense	12.7
2 Star Wars: Episode I – The Phantom Menace	10.0
3 Tarzan	7.7
4 The Mummy	7.1
5 Matrix	5.9
6 Notting Hill	5.2
7 Runaway Bride	5.1
8 Life Is Beautiful	4.8
9 End of Days	4.4
10 Shakespeare in Love	4.3
11 What Dreams May Come	3.4
12 A Bug's Life	3.3
13 The Blair Witch Project	3.3
14 Toy Story 2	3.3
15 Entrapment	3.1
16 Scream 2	3.1
17 Payback	2.8
18 Stepmom	2.8
19 Simao, o fantasma trapalhao*	2.6
20 Orfeu*	2.5
* Local production	

Title	Gross ($m)
Canada	
1 Star Wars: Episode I – The Phantom Menace	32.6
2 The Sixth Sense	18.2
3 Austin Powers: The Spy Who Shagged Me	13.7
4 The Matrix	11.2
5 The Blair Witch Project	10.5
6 Toy Story 2	9.7
7 Big Daddy	9.4
8 Runaway Bride	9.3
9 Double Jeopardy	9.1
10 The World Is Not Enough	8.7
11 The Mummy	8.4
12 Tarzan	7.8
13 Patch Adams	7.7
14 Notting Hill	7.4
15 Shakespeare in Love	6.9
16 Stepmom	6.5
17 American Pie	6.5
18 Inspector Gadget	6.2
19 Entrapment	6.0
20 Pokemon: The First Movie	6.0
France	
1 Asterix & Obelix vs. Caesar	52.0
2 Star Wars: Episode 1 – The Phantom Menace	42.0
3 Tarzan	42.0
4 The Matrix	27.0
5 Notting Hill	26.0
6 The World Is Not Enough	20.0
7 The Mummy	18.0
8 A Bug's Life	18.0
9 Wild Wild West	18.0
10 The Messenger: Joan of Arc*	17.0
11 Entrapment	15.0
12 Les Enfants du Marais*	12.0
13 All About My Mother	11.0
14 Runaway Bride	11.0
15 Quasimodo*	10.0
16 Shakespeare in Love	10.0
17 Eyes Wide Shut	9.0
18 The Faculty	9.0
19 Himalaya*	9.0
20 La Buche*	8.0
* Local production	

Title	Gross ($m)
Germany	
1 Star Wars: Episode I – The Phantom Menace	52.2
2 Notting Hill	30.5
3 The Mummy	29.0
4 Runaway Bride	28.8
5 The Matrix	26.5
6 The World Is Not Enough	23.6
7 Tarzan	22.6
8 You've Got Mail	21.0
9 Shakespeare in Love	19.5
10 Rush Hour	18.8
11 Asterix & Obelix vs. Caesar	18.5
12 A Bug's Life	17.6
13 Werner Volles Rooaaa*	15.1
14 Wild Wild West	14.4
15 Message in a Bottle	12.9
16 The Haunting	12.8
17 Cruel Intentions	12.4
18 She's All That	11.9
19 End of Days	11.8
20 Meet Joe Black	11.5
* Local production	

Title	Gross ($m)
Italy	
1 Notting Hill	14.1
2 Shakespeare in Love	12.9
3 The Sixth Sense	12.3
4 That's Life*	11.2
5 Tarzan	11.0
6 The Mummy	10.8
7 Star Wars: Episode I – The Phantom Menace	10.2
8 Eyes Wide Shut	9.3
9 Runaway Bride	7.9
10 Asterix & Obelix vs. Caesar	7.7
11 You've Got Mail	7.3
12 All About My Mother	7.2
13 Life Is Beautiful*	7.0
14 The Matrix	6.9
15 American Pie	6.8
16 Ronin	6.5
17 Message in a Bottle	6.5
18 Entrapment	6.4
19 Meet Joe Black	6.1
20 The Fish in Love*	5.7
* Local production	

Title	Gross ($m)
South Africa	
1 The Matrix	2.55
2 Notting Hill	2.3
3 The World Is Not Enough	2.08
4 Star Wars: Episode I – The Phantom Menace	2.02
5 The Mummy	1.87
6 Entrapment	1.72
7 Deep Blue Sea	1.63
8 Tarzan	1.54
9 Runaway Bride	1.46
10 Enemy of the State	1.42
11 A Bug's Life	1.39
12 Millennium Menace	1.27
13 Austin Powers: The Spy Who Shagged Me	1.24
14 Antz	1.19
15 Payback	1.18
16 Prince of Egypt	1.15
17 Shakespeare in Love	1.15
18 You've Got Mail	1.09
19 Big Daddy	1.06
20 Meet Joe Black	1.03

Title	Gross ($m)
U.K.	
1 Star Wars: Episode I – The Phantom Menace	83.8
2 Notting Hill*	50.6
3 A Bug's Life	48.2
4 Austin Powers: The Spy Who Shagged Me	42.4
5 The World Is Not Enough	38.4
6 The Sixth Sense	33.6
7 Shakespeare in Love	33.5
8 Tarzan	28.7
9 The Mummy	28.6
10 The Matrix	28.4
11 The Blair Witch Project	24.6
12 American Pie	22.9
13 The Rugrats Movie	22.0
14 Little Voice*	13.7
15 Deep Blue Sea	13.4
16 Runaway Bride	12.4
17 East Is East*	11.9
18 Waking Ned Devine	11.6
19 Wild Wild West	11.3
20 Enemy of the State	11.2
* Local production	

All-time B.O. grossing films

When the press reports that a film has grossed $100 million at the U.S. box office in the first 20 days of its release, that does not mean that the producer has received such a sum. The actual return is somewhere between 45% and 55%, although occasionally the distributor can negotiate with the cinema-owners from a position of strength. In 1974, everyone wanted to screen *The Godfather Part II*, so many theater chains were prepared to pay irrevocable advances. The film fared disappointingly, but Paramount did well. In 1993, everyone was clamoring for *Jurassic Park*, so the worldwide distributor, UIP, could exact from the exhibitor up to 90% of the B.O. revenue after deduction of house costs. Where the trade anticipates a flop, or poor business, then that division of the spoils becomes much more even. Each week, *Variety* charts the box-office gross of each new picture in the U.S. and several other territories around the world, because it's a convenient touchstone of achievement.

The list below is up to the end of calendar year 1999.

Title (Studio; Year; Director; Producer)	Gross ($)
Titanic (Par; 1997; James Cameron; J. Cameron/J. Landau)	600,788,188
Star Wars: Episode IV, A New Hope (Fox; 1977; G. Lucas; G. Kurtz)	460,998,007
Star Wars: Episode I, The Phantom Menace (Fox; 1999; G. Lucas; G. Lucas/R.McCallum)	430,443,350
E.T. – The Extra-Terrestrial (U; 1981; S. Spielberg; S. Spielberg/ K. Kennedy)	399,804,539
Jurassic Park (U; 1993; S. Spielberg, K. Kennedy/G. Molen)	357,067,947
Forrest Gump (Par; 1994; R. Zemeckis; W. Finerman/S. Tisch/S. Starkey)	329,693,974
The Lion King (BV; 1994; R. Allens, R. Minkoff; D. Hahn)	312,855,561
Return of the Jedi (Fox; 1983, R. Marquand; H. Kazanjian/G. Lucas)	309,205,079
Independence Day (Fox; 1996; R. Emmerich; D. Devlin)	306,169,268
The Empire Strikes Back (Fox; 1980; I. Kershner; G. Lucas/G. Kurtz)	290,271,960
Home Alone (Fox; 1990; C. Columbus; J. Hughes)	285,761,243
The Sixth Sense (BV/Spyglass; 1999; M.N. Shyamalan; K. Kennedy/ F. Marshall/B. Mendel/S. Mercer)	276,386,495
Jaws (U; 1975; S. Spielberg; R. Zanuck/D. Brown)	260,000,000
Batman (WB; 1989; T. Burton; J. Peters/P. Guber)	251,188,924
Men in Black (Sony; 1997; B. Sonnenfeld; W. Parkes/L. MacDonald)	250,016,330
Raiders of the Lost Ark (Par; 1981; S. Spielberg; F. Marshall/H. Kazanjian/ G.Lucas)	242,374,454
Twister (WB; 1996; J. De Bont; K. Kennedy/I. Bryce/M. Crichton)	241,721,524
Ghostbusters (Col; 1984; I. Reitman)	238,600,000
Beverly Hills Cop (Par; 1984; M. Brest; D. Simpson/J. Bruckheimer)	234,760,478
The Lost World: Jurassic Park (U; 1997; S. Spielberg; G. Molen/C. Wilson)	229,086,123
Mrs. Doubtfire (Fox; 1993; C. Columbus; M. Williams/R. Williams/ M. Radcliffe)	219,195,051
Ghost (Par; 1990; J. Zucker; L. Weinstein)	217,631,306
Aladdin (BV; 1992; John Musker/ Ron Clements)	217,350,219
Saving Private Ryan (DreamWorks; 1998; S. Spielberg; S. Spielberg/ I. Bruce/M. Gordon/G. Levinsohn)	216,335,085
Toy Story 2 (BV; 1999; A. Brannon/ J. Lasseter; S. McArthur/H. Plotkin/ K.R. Jackson)	208,851,257
Back to the Future (U; 1985; R. Zemeckis; B. Gale/N. Canton/S. Spielberg/ F. Marshall/K. Kennedy)	208,242,016
Austin Powers: The Spy Who Shagged Me (New Line; 1999; J. Roach; J. Todd/ S. Todd/D. Moore/M. Myers/J. Lyons/ E. McLeod)	206,040,086
Terminator 2 (TriStar; 1991; J. Cameron; J. Cameron/G.A. Hurd/M. Kassar)	204,843,345

...February 26...
Death of a Salesman is slaying sales records on Broadway.

Armageddon (BV; 1998; M. Bay; J. Bruckheimer)	201,578,182
Gone With the Wind (MGM; 1939; V. Fleming; D. Selznick)	198,648,910
Indiana Jones and the Last Crusade (Par; 1989; S. Spielberg; R. Watts/ G. Lucas/F. Marshall)	197,171,806
Toy Story (BV; 1995; J. Lasseter; R. Guggenheim/B. Arnold)	191,796,233
Dances with Wolves (Orion; 1990; K. Costner; J. Wilson/K. Costner)	184,208,848
Batman Forever (WB; 1995; J. Schumacher; T. Burton/P. MacGregor-Scott)	184,031,112
The Fugitive (WB; 1993; A. Davis; A. Kopelson)	183,875,760
Grease (Par; 1978; R. Kleiser; R. Stigwood/A. Carr)	181,513,510
Liar, Liar (U; 1997; T. Shadyac; B. Grazer)	181,410,615
Mission: Impossible (Par; 1996; B. DePalma; T. Cruise/P. Wagner)	180,981,866
Indiana Jones and the Temple of Doom (Par; 1984; S. Spielberg; R. Watts/ G. Lucas/F. Marshall)	179,870,271
Pretty Woman (BV; 1990; G. Marshall; A. Milchan/S. Reuther)	178,406,268
Tootsie (Col; 1982; S. Pollack; S. Pollack/ D. Richards)	177,200,000
Top Gun (Par; 1986; T. Scott; D. Simpson/ J. Bruckheimer)	176,781,728
There's Something About Mary (Fox; 1998; P. Farrelly/B. Farrelly; F. Beddor/ M. Steinberg/C. Wessler/B. Thomas)	176,483,808
Snow White and the Seven Dwarfs (BV; 1937; D. Hand)	175,263,233
Crocodile Dundee (Par; 1986; P. Faiman; J. Cornell)	174,803,506
Home Alone 2 (Fox; 1992; C. Columbus; J. Hughes)	173,585,516
Air Force One (Sony; 1997; W. Petersen; W. Petersen/G. Katz/A. Bernstein/ J. Shestack)	172,888,056
Rain Man (MGM/UA; 1988; B. Levinson; M. Johnson/P. Guber/J. Peters)	172,825,435
Apollo 13 (U; 1995; R. Howard; B. Grazer)	172,070,496
The Matrix (WB; 1999; The Wachowski Brothers; J. Silver/B. Berman/ B. Osborne/A. Mason II/E. Stoff)	171,479,930
Tarzan (BV; 1999; K. Lima, C. Buck II; B. Arnold)	170,904,824
Three Men and a Baby (BV; 1987; L. Nimoy; T. Fields/R. Cort)	167,780,960
Robin Hood: Prince of Thieves (WB; 1991; K. Reynolds; J. Watson/P. Densham/ R. B. Lewis)	165,493,908
The Exorcist (WB; 1973; W. Friedkin; W.P. Blatty)	165,000,000
Big Daddy (Sony; 1999; D. Dugan; J. Caracciolo Jr./S. Ganis/J. Giarraputo/ A. Sandler/R. Simonds)	163,479,795
Batman Returns (WB; 1992; T. Burton; D. DiNovi/T. Burton)	162,831,698
A Bug's Life (BV; 1998; J. Lasseter/ A. Stanton; K. Reher)	162,798,565
The Waterboy (BV; 1998; F. Coraci; R. Simonds/J. Giarraputo)	161,487,252
The Sound of Music (Fox; 1965; R. Wise)	160,476,331
The Firm (Par; 1993; S. Pollack; S. Rudin/J. Davis)	158,340,292
Fatal Attraction (Par; 1987; A. Lyne; S. Lansing/S. Jaffe)	156,645,693
The Sting (U; 1973; G.R. Hill; T. Bill/ M. and J. Phillips)	156,000,000
Close Encounters of the Third Kind (Col; 1977; S. Spielberg; M. and J. Phillips)	155,691,323
The Mummy (U; 1999; S. Sommers; S. Daniel/J. Jacks/K. Jarre)	155,385,488
Who Framed Roger Rabbit? (BV; 1988; R. Zemeckis; R. Watts/F. Marshall/ S. Spielberg/K. Kennedy)	154,112,492
Jerry Maguire (Sony; 1996; C. Crowe; J. Brooks/L. Mark/R. Sakai/C. Crowe)	153,962,592
Beverly Hills Cop 2 (Par; 1987; T. Scott; D. Simpson/J. Bruckheimer)	153,665,036
Gremlins (WB; 1984; J. Dante; M. Finnell/ S. Spielberg/F. Marshall/K. Kennedy)	153,083,102
Runaway Bride (Par/BV; 1999; G. Marshall; G. Lucchesi/D. Madden/ T. Tannebaum)	152,054,428
Rambo: First Blood II (TriStar; 1985; G. Cosmatos; B. Feitshans/A. Vajna/ M. Kassar)	150,415,432
As Good As It Gets (Sony; 1997; J. L. Brooks; B. Johnson/K. Zea/J. Brooks)	148,266,088
Lethal Weapon 2 (WB; 1989; R. Donner; R. Donner/J. Silver)	147,253,986
True Lies (Fox; 1994; J. Cameron; J. Cameron/S. Austin)	146,282,411
Beauty and the Beast (BV; 1991; G. Trousdale/K. Wise; D. Hahn)	145,863,363
The Santa Clause (BV; 1994; J. Pasquin; B. Reilly/J. Silver/R. Newmyer)	144,833,357
Lethal Weapon 3 (WB; 1992; R. Donner/ J. Silver)	144,731,527

. . . February 27 . . .
Sony's dark thriller **8MM** snuffed out its competition, notching a
$14.3 million studio-estimated three-day gross.

Dr. Dolittle (Fox; 1998; B. Thomas;
J. Davis/J. Singer/D. Friendly)   144,156,609
Rush Hour (New Line; 1998; B. Ratner; R.
Birnbaum/A. Sarkissian/J. Glickman)   144,061,225
101 Dalmatians (BV; 1961;
W. Reitherman; H. Luske/W. Disney)   143,992,148
The Jungle Book (BV; 1967;
W. Reitherman; W. Disney)   141,843,612
National Lampoon's Animal House (U; 1978;
J. Landis; M. Simmons/I. Reitman)   141,600,000
Pocahontas (BV; 1995; M. Gabriel/
E. Goldberg; J. Pentecost)   141,579,773
A Few Good Men (Col; 1992; R. Reiner;
D. Brown/R. Reiner/A. Scheinman)   141,340,178
The Blair Witch Project (Artisan; 1999;
D. Myrick/E. Sanchez II; B. Eick/
R. Cowie/K. Foxe/G. Hale)   140,539,099
Deep Impact (Par; 1998; M. Leder;
R. Zanuck/D. Brown)   140,464,664
Look Who's Talking (TriStar; 1989;
A. Heckerling; J. Krane)   140,088,813
The Rocky Horror Picture Show (Fox;
1975; J. Sharman; M. White/L. Adler)   139,876,417
Sister Act (BV; 1992; E. Ardolino;
T. Schwartz/S. Rudin)   139,605,150
Saturday Night Fever (Par; 1977;
J. Badham; R. Stigwood)   139,486,124
Platoon (Orion; 1986; O. Stone;
A. Kopelson)   138,530,565
Good Will Hunting (Miramax; 1997;
G. Van Sant; L. Bender)   138,433,435
Ransom (BV; 1996; R. Howard; B. Grazer/
S. Rudin/B.K. Hagopian)   136,492,681
Godzilla (Sony; 1998; R. Emmerich;
D. Devlin)   136,314,294
101 Dalmatians (BV; 1996; S. Herek;
J. Hughes/R. Mestres)   136,182,161
Teenage Mutant Ninja Turtles (New Line;
1990; S. Barron; K. Dawson/S. Fields/
D. Chan/R. Chow)   135,265,915
Patch Adams (U; 1998; T. Shadyac;
M. Williams/T. Shadyac)   135,019,563
The Godfather (Par; 1972; F. F. Coppola;
A. Ruddy)   134,966,411
Superman (WB; 1978; R. Donner;
P. Spengler)   134,218,018
The Rock (BV; 1996; M. Bay;
J. Bruckheimer/D. Simpson)   134,069,511
The Silence of the Lambs (Orion; 1991; J.
Demme; E. Saxon/K. Utt/R. Bozman)   130,726,716
Honey I Shrunk the Kids (BV; 1989;
J. Johnston; R. Finkelman Cox/
T.G. Smith)   130,724,172

The Flintstones (U; 1994; B. Levant;
B. Cohen)   130,531,208
Lethal Weapon 4 (WB; 1998;
R. Donner; J. Silver/R. Donner)   130,444,603
An Officer and a Gentleman
(Par; 1982; T. Hackford; M. Elfand)   129,795,549
The Nutty Professor (U; 1996;
T. Shadyac; B. Grazer/R. Simmons)   128,814,019
Coming to America (Par; 1988;
J. Landis; G. Folsey Jr./R. Wachs)   128,152,301
Rocky IV (UA; 1985; Sylvester Stallone)   127,873,414
Dumb and Dumber (New Line; 1994;
P. Farrelly; C. Wessler/B. Krevoy/
S. Stabler)   127,175,374
My Best Friend's Wedding (Sony; 1997;
P. J. Hogan; J. Zucker/R. Bass)   126,813,153
Smokey and the Bandit (U; 1977;
H. Needham; M. Engelberg)   126,737,428
Sleepless in Seattle (TriStar; 1993;
N. Ephron; G. Foster)   126,680,884
The Truman Show (Par; 1998; P. Weir;
S. Rudin/A. Niccol/E.S. Feldman/
A. Schroeder)   125,618,201
Tomorrow Never Dies (MGM; 1997;
R. Spottiswoode; M. Wilson/
B. Broccoli)   125,234,939
Rocky III (UA; 1982; S. Stallone;
I. Winkler/R. Chartoff)   125,049,125
The Birdcage (MGM/UA; 1996;
M. Nichols; M. Nichols)   124,060,553
City Slickers (Col; 1991; R. Underwood;
I. Smith/B. Crystal)   124,033,791
Good Morning Vietnam (BV; 1987;
B. Levinson; M. Johnson/L. Brezner)   123,922,370
Clear and Present Danger (Par; 1994;
P. Noyce; M. Neufeld/R. Rehme)   122,187,717
The Hunt For Red October (Par; 1990;
J. McTiernan; M. Neufeld)   122,012,643
The Bodyguard (WB; 1992; M. Jackson;
L. Kasdan/J. Wilson/K. Costner)   121,945,720
Wayne's World (Par; 1992; P. Spheeris;
L. Michaels)   121,697,323
Speed (Fox; 1994; J. De Bont;
M. Gordon)   121,248,145
Mulan (BV; 1998; B. Cook/T. Bancroft;
P. Coats)   120,620,254
The Mask (New Line; 1994; C. Russell;
B. Engelman)   119,938,730
Hook (TriStar; 1991; S. Spielberg;
K. Kennedy/F. Marshall/G. Molen)   119,654,823
Blazing Saddles (WB; 1974; M. Brooks;
M. Hertzberg)   119,500,000
Total Recall (TriStar; 1990; P. Verhoeven;

B. Feitshans/R. Shusett/M. Kassar/ A.Vajna)	119,394,839
On Golden Pond (U; 1981; M. Rydell; B. Gilbert)	118,710,777
Back to the Future II (U; 1989; R. Zemeckis; B. Gale/N. Canton/ S. Spielberg/F. Marshall/K. Kennedy)	118,450,002
The World Is Not Enough (MGM; 1999; M. Apted; M. Wilson/B. Broccoli)	117,877,025
Basic Instinct (TriStar; 1992; P. Verhoeven; A. Marshall/M. Kassar)	117,727,224
Die Hard 2 (Fox; 1990; R. Harlin; L. Gordon/J. Silver/C. Gordon)	117,540,947
Rocky (UA; 1976; J. Avildsen; R. Chartoff/I. Winkler)	117,235,247
Notting Hill (PFE/U; 1999; R. Michell; R. Curtis/E. Fellner/T. Bevan/ D. Kenworthy)	116,089,678
The Towering Inferno (Fox; 1974; J. Guillerman; I. Allen)	116,000,000
You've Got Mail (WB; 1998; N. Ephron; N. Ephron/L.S. Donner/G. MacBrown/ J. Durk/D. Ephron)	115,757,269
Karate Kid II (Col; 1986; J. Avildsen; J. Weintraub)	115,103,979
American Graffiti (U; 1973; G. Lucas; F.F. Coppola)	115,000,000
Big (Fox; 1988; P. Marshall; J.L. Brooks/ R. Greenhut)	114,968,774
Double Jeopardy (Par; 1999; B. Beresford; L. Goldberg)	114,032,117
Wild Wild West (WB; 1999; B. Sonnenfeld; J. Peters/T. Glaser/ B. Josephson/J. Simon/B. Todman)	113,805,681
The Addams Family (Par; 1991; B. Sonnenfeld; S. Rudin)	113,502,246
Ghostbusters II (Col; 1989; I. Reitman)	112,494,738
Face/Off (Par; 1997; J. Woo; D. Permut/ B. Osborne/T. Chang/C. Godsick)	112,273,211
One Flew Over the Cuckoo's Nest (UA; 1975; M. Forman; M. Douglas/ S. Zaentz)	112,000,000
Twins (U; 1988; I. Reitman)	111,936,388
Doctor Zhivago (MGM; 1965; D. Lean; C. Ponti)	111,721,913
Enemy of the State (BV; 1998; T. Scott; J. Bruckheimer)	111,549,836
The Little Mermaid (BV; 1989; J. Musker/ R. Clements; H. Ashman/J. Musker)	111,543,479
Star Trek IV, The Voyage Home (Par; 1986; L. Nimoy; H. Bennett)	109,713,132
Porky's (Fox; 1982; B. Clark; D. Carmody/B. Clark/M. Simon)	109,492,484
Crocodile Dundee II (Par; 1988; J. Cornell; J. Cornell/J. Scott)	109,306,210
A Time to Kill (WB; 1996; J. Schumacher; A. Milchan/M. Nathanson/ H. Lowry/J.Grisham)	108,766,007
Terms of Endearment (Par; 1983; J. L. Brooks; J. L. Brooks)	108,423,489
Ace Ventura: When Nature Calls (WB; 1995; S. Oedekerk; G. Barber/ J. Robinson/J. Rose)	108,385,533
Superman II (WB; 1981; R. Lester; P. Spengler)	108,185,706
Pulp Fiction (Miramax; 1994; Q. Tarantino; L. Bender)	107,921,755
A League of Their Own (Col; 1992; P. Marshall; R. Greenhut/E. Abbott)	107,533,925
Batman and Robin (WB; 1997; J. Schumacher; P. MacGregor-Scott)	107,325,195
Analyze This (WB; 1999; H. Ramis; B. Berman/C. Brigham/B. Crystal/ J. Rosenthal/P. Weinstein)	106,885,658
Indecent Proposal (Par; 1993; A. Lyne; S. Lansing)	106,614,059
Driving Miss Daisy (WB; 1989; B. Beresford; R. Zanuck/L.F. Zanuck)	106,593,296
GoldenEye (MGM/UA; 1995; M. Campbell; M. Wilson/B. Broccoli)	106,429,941
Love Story (Par; 1970; A. Hiller; H. Minsky)	106,397,186
Kramer vs. Kramer (Col; 1979; R. Benton; S. Jaffe)	106,260,000
The First Wives Club (Par; 1996; H. Wilson; S. Rudin)	105,489,203
Interview With the Vampire (WB; 1994; N. Jordan; D. Geffen/S. Woolley)	105,264,608
George of the Jungle (BV; 1997; S. Weisman; D. Hoberman/J. Kemer/ J. Avnet)	105,263,257
The Graduate (AvcoEmbassy; 1967; M. Nichols; L. Turman)	104,642,560
Phenomenon (BV; 1996; J. Turteltaub; B. Boyle/M. Taylor)	104,632,573
Every Which Way But Loose (WB; 1978; J. Fargo; R. Daley)	104,268,727
Dick Tracy (BV; 1990; W. Beatty)	103,738,726
9 to 5 (Fox; 1980; C. Higgins; B. Gilbert)	103,290,500
Scream (Miramax; 1996; W. Craven; C. Woods/C. Konrad)	103,046,663
Bambi (BV; 1942; D. Hand)	102,797,150
The General's Daughter (Par; 1999; S. West; J. Krane/M. Neufeld)	102,705,852
Mary Poppins (BV; 1964; R. Stevenson; W. Disney)	102,272,727

... March 1 ...
With her "#1's" disc topping the 3 million-unit plateau, Mariah Carey is the first female artist to have eight consecutive albums reach that threshold.

In the Line of Fire (Col; 1993; W. Petersen; J. Apple)	102,243,874
Butch Cassidy and the Sundance Kid (Fox; 1969; G. R. Hill; J. Foreman)	102,118,000
American Pie (U; 1999; P. Weitz; C. Moore II/C. Weitz/W. Zide/C. Perry)	101,800,949
Maverick (WB; 1994; R. Donner; B. Davey/R. Donner)	101,631,272
Sleeping With the Enemy (Fox; 1991; J. Ruben; L. Goldberg)	101,599,005
The Prince of Egypt (DreamWorks; 1998; B. Chapman/S. Hickner/S. Wells I; J. Katzenberg/P. Cox/S. Rabins)	101,413,188
Scream 2 (Miramax; 1997; W. Craven; C. Konrad/M. Maddelena)	101,363,301
Stir Crazy (Col; 1980; S. Poitier; H. Weinstein)	101,300,000
Eraser (WB; 1996; C. Russell; A. Kopelson; A. Kopelson)	101,295,562
Unforgiven (WB; 1992; C. Eastwood; C. Eastwood/D. Valdes)	101,157,447
Con Air (BV; 1997; S. West; J. Bruckheimer)	101,113,571
Contact (WB; 1997; R. Zemeckis; R. Zemeckis/S. Starkey)	100,803,906
The Pelican Brief (WB; 1993; A. J. Pakula; P. J. Brugge)	100,768,056
The Rugrats Movie (Par; 1998; N. Virgien/ I. Kovalyov; A. Klasky/G. Csupo)	100,494,685
Jumanji (TriStar; 1995; J. Johnston; S. Kroopf/W. Teitler)	100,475,249
Casper (U; 1995; B. Silberling; C. Wilson)	100,328,194
Shakespeare in Love (U/Miramax; 1998; J. Madden; D. Parfitt/D. Gigliotti/ H. Weinstein/E. Zwick/M. Norman)	100,317,794
The Hunchback of Notre Dame (BV; 1996; G. Trousdale/K. Wise; D. Hahn)	100,138,851
Seven (New Line; 1995; D. Fincher; A. Kopelson)	100,125,643
Parenthood (U; 1989; R. Howard; B. Grazer)	100,047,830
Die Hard With a Vengeance (Fox; 1995; J. McTiernan; J. McTiernan/M. Tadross)	100,012,499
Hercules (BV; 1997; J. Musker; A. Dewey/ J. Musker/R.Clements)	99,112,101
The Color Purple (WB; 1985; S. Spielberg; S. Spielberg/K. Kennedy/F. Marshall/ Q. Jones/Guber-Peters)	98,467,863
Inspector Gadget (BV; 1999; D. Kellogg; J. Avnet/B. Bernardi/R. Birnbaum/ J. Glickman)	97,403,112
Schindler's List (U; 1993; S. Spielberg; S. Spielberg/B. Lustig/G. Molen)	96,065,768
Dead Poets Society (BV; 1989; P. Weir; S. Haft/P.J. Witt/T. Thomas)	95,860,116
Arthur (WB; 1981; S. Gordon; R. Greenhut)	95,461,682
Michael (NLC; 1996; N. Ephron; S. Daniel/N. Ephron/J. Jacks)	95,365,924
Flashdance (Par; 1983; A. Lyne; D. Simpson/J. Bruckheimer)	94,921,000
The Mask of Zorro (Sony; 1998; M. Campbell; D. Claybourne/D. Foster)	93,805,793
Flubber (BV; 1997; L. Mayfield; J. Hughes/R. Mestres)	92,993,801
Sleepy Hollow (Par; 1999; T. Burton/ P. Guber/F. Coppola)	92,839,722
When Harry Met Sally (Col;1989; R. Reiner; R. Reiner/A. Scheinman)	92,823,546
The Client (WB; 1994; J. Schumacher; A. Milchan/S.Reuther)	92,115,211
Star Trek: First Contact (Par; 1996; J. Frakes; R. Berman)	92,027,888
Kindergarten Cop (U; 1990; I. Reitman; I. Reitman/B. Grazer)	91,457,688
Crimson Tide (BV; 1995; T. Scott; D. Simpson/J. Bruckheimer)	91,387,195
Back to School (Orion; 1986; A. Metter; E. Endler/M. Endler/H. Ramis/C. Russell)	91,258,000
The Haunting (DreamWorks; 1999; J. DeBont)	91,240,529
Stepmom (Sony; 1998; C. Columbus; R. Bass/C. Columbus/M. Barnathan/ W. Finerman)	91,077,127
The Karate Kid (Col; 1984; J. Avildsen; J. Weintraub)	90,815,558
Antz (DreamWorks, 1998; E. Damell/ T. Johnson; B. Lewis/A. Warner/ P. Wooton)	90,646,554
Space Jam (WB; 1996; J. Pytka/T. Cervone; I. Reitman/J. Medjuck/D. Goldberg)	90,418,342
Trading Places (Par; 1983; J. Landis; A. Russo)	90,404,800
Father of the Bride (BV; 1991; C. Shyer; N. Meyers/C. Baum/H. Rosenman)	89,325,780
Lady and the Tramp (BV, 1955; W. Disney)	88,300,000
Waterworld (U; 1995; K. Reynolds; C. Gordon/J. Davis/K. Costner)	88,246,220
The Hand That Rocks the Cradle (BV; 1992; C. Hanson; D. Maden)	88,036,683
Entrapment (Fox; 1999; J. Amiel; R. Bass/ S. Connery/M. Hertzberg/A. Milchan/ I. Smith)	87,704,396
Back to the Future III (U; 1990; R. Zemeckis; B. Gale/S. Spielberg/ K. Kennedy/F. Marshall)	87,666,629

... **March 2** ...
Shakespeare in Love and **Elizabeth** dominate the nominations for this year's BAFTA Film Awards, with 16 and 12 nods apiece.

Out of Africa (U; 1985; S. Pollack;	
S. Pollack)	87,071,205
Naked Gun 2½: The Smell of Fear	
(Par; 1991; D. Zucker; R.K. Weiss)	86,930,411
The War of the Roses (Fox; 1989;	
D. DeVito; J.L. Brooks/A. Milchan)	86,888,546
To Fly (IMAX; 1976; J. Freeman; G.	
MacGillivray; MacGillivray/Freeman)	86,712,384
Presumed Innocent (WB; 1990; A. J. Pakula;	
S. Pollack/M. Rosenberg)	86,303,188
The Ten Commandments (Par; 1956;	
C.B. DeMille; C.B. DeMille)	85,400,000
Stripes (Col; 1981; I. Reitman;	
D. Goldberg/I. Reitman)	85,297,000
Rocky 2 (MGM; 1979; S. Stallone;	
R. Chartoff/I. Winkler)	85,182,160
Aliens (Fox; 1986; J. Cameron; G.A. Hurd)	85,160,248
Dangerous Minds (BV; 1995; J. N. Smith;	
D. Simpson/J. Bruckheimer)	84,919,401
The Poseidon Adventure (Fox; 1972;	
R. Neame; I. Allen)	84,563,118
Pokemon: The First Movie: Mewtwo	
Strikes Back (WB; 1999; M. Haigney/	
K. Yuyama; A. Kahn/T. Mori/M. Kudo)	84,091,099
Cliffhanger (TriStar; 1993; R. Harlin;	
A. Marshall)	84,049,211
The X-Files (Fox; 1998; R. Bowman;	
C. Carter/D. Sackheim)	83,898,313
Steel Magnolias (Col; 1989; H. Ross;	
R. Stark)	83,759,091
Under Siege (WB; 1992; A. Davis;	
A. Milchan/S. Seagal/S. Reuther)	83,563,139
Airplane! (Par; 1980; J. Abrahams/D. Zucker/	
J. Zucker; H.W. Koch/J.Davison)	83,453,539
Patriot Games (Par; 1992; P. Noyce;	
M. Neufeld/R. Rehme)	83,287,363
Disclosure (WB; 1994; B. Levinson;	
B. Levinson/M. Crichton)	83,015,089
Days of Thunder (Par; 1990; T. Scott;	
D. Simpson/J. Bruckheimer)	82,670,733
Mr. Holland's Opus (BV; 1995; S. Herek;	
T. Field/M. Nolin/R. Cort)	82,569,971
Bram Stoker's Dracula (Col; 1992; F. Coppola;	
F. Coppola/F. Fuchs/C. Mulvehill)	82,522,790
Fried Green Tomatoes (U; 1991; J. Avnet;	
J. Avnet/J. Kerner)	82,418,501
Star Trek (Par; 1979; R. Wise;	
G. Roddenberry)	82,300,000
Heaven Can Wait (Par; 1979; W. Beatty/	
B. Henry; W. Beatty)	81,640,278
Peter Pan (BV/RKO; 1953; W. Disney)	81,600,000
Payback (Par; 1999; B. Helgeland;	
S. McEveety/B. Davey)	81,526,121
Die Hard (Fox; 1988; J. McTiernan;	
L. Gordon/J. Silver)	81,350,242
Police Academy (WB; 1984; H. Wilson;	
P. Maslansky)	81,198,894
Cinderella (BV; 1949; W. Jackson;	
W. Disney)	81,100,000
While You Were Sleeping (BV; 1995;	
J. Turtletaub; J. Roth/R. Brinbaum)	81,057,016
Congo (Par; 1995; F. Marshall;	
K. Kennedy/S. Mercer)	81,022,333
Another 48 Hrs (Par; 1990; W. Hill;	
L. Gordon/R. Wachs)	80,818,974
Moonstruck (MGM/UA; 1987;	
N. Jewison; P. Palmer/N. Jewison)	80,640,528
The Wedding Singer (NLC; 1998;	
F. Corachi; R. Simonds/J. Giarraputo)	80,245,725
Footloose (Par; 1984; H. Ross;	
L.J. Rachmil/C. Zasdan/D. Melnick)	80,035,402
A Star Is Born (WB; 1976; F. Pierson;	
J. Peters)	80,000,000

All-time foreign-language films in North America

	Title (U.S./Canadian distributor)	Gross ($m)
1	*Life Is Beautiful* (Miramax)	57.6
2	*Il Postino* (Miramax)	21.8
3	*Like Water For Chocolate* (Miramax)	21.7
4	*I Am Curious (Yellow)* (Grove Press)	20.2
5	*La Dolce Vita* (Astor)	19.5
6	*La Cage aux Folles* (UA)	17.7
7	*Z* (Cinema 5)	15.8
8	*A Man and a Woman* (AA)	14.3
9	*Cinema Paradiso* (Miramax)	12.0
10	*Das Boot* (Triumph)	11.6
11	*Emmanuelle* (Col)	11.5
12	*Federico Fellini's 8½* (Embassy)	10.4
13	*My Life as a Dog* (Skouras/Vivafilm)	10.1
14	*Elvira Madigan* (Cinema 5)	10.1
15	*The Story of O* (AA)	10.0
16	*The Red Violin* (Lions Gate)	10.0
17	*Shall We Dance?* (Miramax)	9.7
18	*Yesterday, Today and Tomorrow* (Embassy)	9.3
19	*Marriage Italian Style* (Embassy)	9.1

...March 3...
Barbara Walters' interview with Monica Lewinsky attracted 74 million viewers, becoming the most-watched news program ever broadcast by a U.S. network.

20	Dear John (Sigma 3)	8.8
21	Cousin, Cousine (Libra)	8.6
22	Cyrano de Bergerac (Orion Classics/CFP)	8.0
23	Belle de Jour (AA/Miramax)	8.0
24	Women on the Verge (Orion Classics)	7.5
25	Fanny and Alexander (Embassy)	7.4
26	Ran (Orion Classics)	7.3
27	Eat Drink Man Woman (Goldwyn)	7.3
28	Run Lola Run (Sony Classics)	7.2
29	Two Women (Embassy)	7.2
30	The Wedding Banquet (Goldwyn)	6.9
31	Diva (UAC)	6.5
32	Swept Away (Cinema 5)	6.0
33	The Garden of the Finzi-Continis (Cinema 5)	6.0
34	Belle Epoque (Sony Classics/CFP)	6.0
35	Mediterraneo (Miramax/Alliance)	5.8
36	La Cage Aux Folles II (UA)	5.8
37	Kolya (Miramax)	5.8
38	King of Hearts (UA/Lopert)	5.7

39	Indochine (Sony Classics)	5.7
40	Central Station (Sony Classics)	5.6
41	Europa Europa (Orion Classics)	5.6
42	Jean de Florette (Orion Classics)	5.5
43	Au Revoir les Enfants (Orion Classics)	5.3
44	Farewell My Concubine (Miramax)	5.2
45	Madame Rosa (Atlantic)	5.2
46	Babette's Feast (Orion Classics)	5.2
47	La Femme Nikita (Goldwyn)	5.0
48	Wings of Desire (Orion Classics/Alliance)	4.9
49	Les Boys (CFP)	4.8
50	The Decline of the American Empire (Cplx/Malo)	4.7
51	Manon des Sources (Orion Classics)	4.7
52	Antonia's Line (First Look/CFP)	4.2
53	Tie Me Up! Tie Me Down! (Miramax)	4.1
54	The Dinner Game (Lions Gate)	4.0

Gross through January 2, 2000

North American top grossers: 1999

Title (U.S./Canadian distributor)	Gross
Star Wars: Episode I – The Phantom Menace (Fox)	430,443,350
The Sixth Sense (BV, Spyglass)	276,386,495
Toy Story 2 (BV)	208,851,257
Austin Powers: The Spy Who Shagged Me (NL)	205,444,716
The Matrix (WB/Village Roadshow)	171,479,930
Tarzan (BV)	170,904,824
Big Daddy (Sony)	163,479,795
The Mummy (U)	155,385,488
Runaway Bride (BV/Par)	152,054,428
The Blair Witch Project (Artisan)	140,539,099
The World Is Not Enough (MGM)	117,877,025
Notting Hill (U)	116,089,678
Double Jeopardy (Par)	114,032,117
Wild Wild West (WB)	113,805,681
Analyze This (WB Village Roadshow)	106,885,658
The General's Daughter (Par)	102,705,852
American Pie (U)	101,800,949
Inspector Gadget (BV)	97,403,112
Shakespeare in Love (Miramax) *	94,078,225
Sleepy Hollow (Par)	92,839,722
The Haunting (DreamWorks)	91,240,529
Patch Adams (U) *	88,575,238
Entrapment (20th)	87,704,396
Pokemon: The First Movie (WB)	84,091,099
Payback (Par)	81,526,121
Stuart Little (Sony)	79,403,127

The Green Mile (WB)	76,682,014
Deep Blue Sea (WB)	73,648,228
American Beauty (DreamWorks)	71,017,815
The Thomas Crown Affair (MGM)	69,282,369
Blue Streak (Sony)	67,760,741
Bowfinger (U)	66,458,770
Life (U)	64,062,587
The Bone Collector (U)	63,739,165
She's All That (Miramax)	63,465,522
End of Days (U)	63,181,290
Three Kings (WB)	59,223,104
A Civil Action (BV) *	56,554,385
Stepmom (BV) *	55,702,051
Eyes Wide Shut (WB)	55,691,208
Never Been Kissed (Fox)	55,474,756
Forces of Nature (DreamWorks)	52,957,800
Varsity Blues (Par)	52,894,169
Message in a Bottle (WB)	52,880,016
You've Got Mail (WB) *	52,059,121
South Park: Bigger, Longer, and Uncut (Par)	52,037,603
Stigmata (MGM)	50,014,865
Life Is Beautiful (Miramax) *	47,457,371
Deuce Bigalow: Male Gigolo (BV)	46,538,329
The Prince of Egypt (DreamWorks) *	46,306,557
Any Given Sunday (WB)	45,752,119
House on Haunted Hill (WB)	40,489,824
The Talented Mr. Ripley (Par/Miramax)	39,771,649
Bicentennial Man (BV) +	39,610,696

... March 4 ...
Buena Vista's Pixar production **A Bug's Life** ascends
to a worldwide gross of $300 million.

Cruel Intentions (Sony)	38,267,302	Bringing Out the Dead (Par)	16,473,449
10 Things I Hate About You (BV)	38,178,166	Star Trek: Insurrection (Par) *	16,292,275
My Favorite Martian (BV)	36,850,101	A Midsummer Night's Dream	
8MM (Sony)	36,610,578	(Fox Searchlight)	16,071,990
Fight Club (Fox)	36,351,732	The Corrupter (NLC)	15,164,492
The Thin Red Line (Fox) *	35,755,689	Election (Par)	14,943,582
A Bug's Life (BV) *	35,209,001	Music of the Heart (Miramax)	14,755,057
For Love of the Game (U)	35,188,641	Elizabeth (Gramercy) *	14,609,738
Instinct (BV)	34,105,207	Tea With Mussolini (MGM)	14,396,340
Mickey Blue Eyes (WB)	33,864,342	A Simple Plan (Par) *	14,312,353
The Best Man (U)	33,581,815	The Messenger:	
The 13th Warrior (BV)	32,698,900	The Story of Joan of Arc (Sony)	14,140,703
October Sky (U)	32,683,932	Virus (U)	14,087,494
Lake Placid (20th)	31,770,413	The Rugrats Movie (Par) *	14,063,693
Random Hearts (Sony)	31,020,443	In Too Deep (Miramax)	14,026,509
Mighty Joe Young (BV) *	30,603,681	The Deep End of the Ocean (Sony)	13,863,848
Superstar (Par)	30,150,814	The Waterboy (BV) *	13,596,215
Mystery Men (U)	29,762,011	The Mod Squad (MGM)	13,263,993
Dogma (Lion's Gate)	28,983,260	Black Mask (Artisan)	12,504,289
The Out of Towners (Par)	28,544,120	The Omega Code (Providence)	12,276,200
The Other Sister (BV)	27,807,627	The King and I (WB)	12,064,440
Galaxy Quest (DreamWorks)	27,311,918	In Dreams (DreamWorks)	12,017,369
Baby Geniuses (Sony)	27,151,490	The Thirteenth Floor (Sony)	11,904,174
The Story of Us (U)	27,100,031	The Adventures of Elmo	
Blast From the Past (NL)	26,613,620	in Grouchland (Sony)	11,651,787
The Insider (BV)	26,135,523	The Muse (USA)	11,614,955
Saving Private Ryan (DreamWorks) *	25,529,826	Wing Commander (Fox)	11,578,059
The Wood (Par)	25,059,642	Chill Factor (WB)	11,263,966
Anna and the King (Fox)	24,732,782	Cookie's Fortune (October)	10,920,544
Arlington Road (Sony)	24,711,498	Office Space (Fox)	10,827,810
T-Rex: Back to the Cretaceous (Imax) *	24,604,821	The Astronaut's Wife (New Line)	10,672,566
Man on the Moon (U)	24,550,700	Drop Dead Gorgeous (New Line)	10,571,408
Mysteries of Egypt (Destination) *	23,670,867	Three to Tango (WB)	10,570,375
The Iron Giant (WB)	23,159,305	Universal Soldier: The Return (Sony)	10,557,566
Edtv (U)	22,508,689	Bats (Destination)	10,155,691
At First Sight (MGM)	22,365,133	Brokedown Palace (Fox Searchlight)	10,115,013
The Faculty (Miramax) *	21,874,186	The Red Violin (Lions Gate/Odeon) *	10,041,136
The Bachelor (New Line)	21,266,456	Dudley Do-Right (U)	9,818,792
Stir of Echoes (Artisan)	21,133,087	Trippin' (October)	9,017,070
Enemy of the State (BV) *	19,521,933	Teaching Mrs. Tingle (Miramax)	8,959,883
Waking Ned Devine (Fox Searchlight) *	19,456,791	Mystery, Alaska (BV)	8,891,623
Doug's 1st Movie (BV)	19,440,449	Pushing Tin (Fox)	8,408,835
Summer of Sam (BV)	19,288,130	Twin Dragons (Miramax)	8,359,717
An Ideal Husband (Miramax)	18,542,974	The Love Letter (DreamWorks)	8,322,608
Everest (McGillivray-Freeman) *	18,468,249	Outside Providence (Miramax)	7,309,628
Being John Malkovich (USA)	18,243,969	Run Lola Run (Sony Classics)	7,217,016
Anywhere But Here (20th)	18,073,180	Africa's Elephant Kingdom (Discovery) *	7,163,315
Drive Me Crazy (20th)	17,786,372	Buena Vista Social Club (Artisan)	6,918,494
The Rage: Carrie 2 (MGM)	17,762,548	Extreme (Imax/BDDJF)	6,861,660
Rushmore (BV) *	17,023,768	200 Cigarettes (Par)	6,852,450
Go (Sony)	16,892,906	Jack Frost (WB) *	6,658,601
True Crime (WB)	16,676,845	Lost and Found (WB)	6,552,255
Muppets from Space (Sony)	16,604,577	Affliction (Lions Gate) *	6,300,172

...March 5...
The Academy chooses Robert De Niro and Martin Scorsese as the
presenters of a Lifetime Achievement Award to Elia Kazan.

Dick (Sony)	6,276,869	There's Something About Mary (Fox) *	2,061,906
Foolish (Artisan)	6,033,999	Besieged (New Line)	2,048,830
Light It Up (20th)	5,744,635	Three Seasons (October)	2,046,492
Central Station (Sony Classics) *	5,630,372	Happy, Texas (Miramax)	2,039,192
Island of the Sharks (Imax) * +	5,206,926	Taal (Eros)	2,020,532
Rush Hour (NL) *	5,121,529	Humsaath Hain (Eros)	2,005,084
Jakob the Liar (Sony)	4,956,401	Crazy in Alabama (Sony)	1,954,202
Hilary and Jackie (October) *	4,870,919	Goodbye Lover (WB)	1,940,299
Gods and Monsters (Lions Gate) *	4,784,211	Tango (Sony Classics)	1,897,948
A Walk on the Moon (Miramax)	4,772,468	The Dreamlife of Angels (Sony Classics)	1,894,570
Mumford (BV)	4,555,460	Pleasantville (New Line) *	1,823,157
Simply Irresistible (Fox)	4,398,989	Romance (Trimark)	1,630,667
Flawless (MGM)	4,394,718	The End of the Affair (Sony)	1,555,329
The Straight Story (BV)	4,377,877	Wildfire (Primesco)	1,512,930
Encounter in the Third Dimension (nWave)	4,269,548	Hurlyburly (New Line) *	1,506,866
The Winslow Boy (Sony Classics)	4,261,721	Dancing at Lughnasa (Sony Classics) *	1,435,428
Detroit Rock City (New Line)	4,217,115	Meet Joe Black (U) *	1,409,298
The Cider House Rules (Miramax)	4,201,516	Hideous Kinky (Stratosphere)	1,368,627
Gloria (Sony)	4,187,867	Asterix & Obelix vs. Caesar (Lions Gate)**	1,304,052
Idle Hands (Sony)	4,146,292	Straight From the Heart (Video Sound)	1,185,000
The Dinner Game (Lion's Gate) *	4,053,712	Psycho (U) *	1,177,768
Playing By Heart (Miramax) *	3,970,078	Get Real (Paramount Classics)	1,152,979
Little Voice (Miramax) *	3,938,250	I Still Know What You Did Last Summer	
Lock, Stock and Two Smoking Barrels		(Sony) *	1,130,738
(Gramercy)	3,897,569	The General (Sony Classics) *	1,121,644
Thrill Ride (Sony Classics) *	3,482,047	This Is My Father (Sony Classics)	1,115,300
Fifty (Warren Miller)	3,392,140	The Siege (Fox) *	1,072,781
Down in the Delta (Miramax) *	3,175,346	Another Day in Paradise (Trimark)	1,036,818
Jawbreaker (Sony)	3,110,751	Tumbleweeds (Fine Line)	1,027,713
The Limey (Artisan)	3,020,829	Twin Falls Idaho (Sony Classics)	1,019,178
Love Stinks (Independent Artists)	2,924,635	King of Masks (Samuel Goldwyn)	1,014,895
Wolves (Primesco) *	2,852,213	Xiu Xiu: The Sent Down Girl	
Boys Don't Cry (Fox Searchlight)	2,697,068	(Stratosphere)	1,010,933
eXistenZ (Alliance/Miramax)	2,692,346	The Castle (Miramax)	1,007,834
Elvis Gratton 2 (Lions Gate) **	2,581,510	Children of Heaven (Miramax)	933,933
Babe: Pig in the City (U) *	2,551,680	Edge of Seventeen (Strand)	868,348
Mansfield Park (Miramax)	2,472,250	Sweet and Lowdown (Sony Classics)	867,523
Princess Mononoke (Miramax)	2,374,107	Nights of Cabiria reissue (Rialto) *	855,038
Fantasia 2000 (BV/Imax)	2,290,525	Illuminata (Artisan)	840,135
Liberty Heights (WB)	2,286,654	Galapagos (Imax)	806,245
Autumn Tale (USA)	2,205,338	Afterlife (Artistic License)	783,103
A Dog of Flanders (WB)	2,165,637	Cradle Will Rock (BV)	769,995
Siegfried and Roy: The Magic Box (Imax)	2,162,167	Magnolia (New Line)	764,945
All About My Mother (Sony Classics) +	2,133,411	Felicia's Journey (Artisan)	761,929
Limbo (Sony)	2,121,569	Wings of Courage (Sony Classics) *	754,888
Trick (Fine Line)	2,121,027	Body Shots (New Line)	752,123
Les Boys II (Lions Gate) * **	2,092,328		
Antz (DreamWorks) *	2,089,514	*1998 gross not included	
Better Than Chocolate (Trimark)	2,076,941	** Canadian film gross converted at C$1=$0.69	
Ravenous (Fox)	2,062,405	+ Still on release at year end	

. . . March 6 . . .
Erick Zonca's debut pic **La Vie Rêvée des Anges (The Dream Life of Angels)**
named Best Film at the 24th edition of the French César Awards.

All-time adjusted domestic B.O. champs
(in $ millions, based on admissions)

1	Gone With the Wind (MGM, 1939)	2,329
2	Snow White and the Seven Dwarfs (BV, 1937)	1,984
3	Bambi (BV, 1942)	1,028
4	Fantasia (BV, 1940)	887.1
5	Star Wars (Fox, 1977)	866.0
6	Pinocchio (BV, 1940)	856.9
7	The Sound of Music (Fox, 1965)	830.5
8	Jaws (U, 1975)	787.8
9	101 Dalmatians (BV, 1961)	784.5
10	The Jungle Book (BV, 1967)	691.9
11	E.T. – The Extra-Terrestrial (U, 1982)	675.2
12	Titanic (Par, 1997)	610.4
13	The Exorcist (WB, 1973)	605.7
14	Doctor Zhivago (MGM, 1965)	578.0
15	The Empire Strikes Back (Fox, 1980)	574.0
16	The Sting (U, 1973)	572.6
17	Cinderella (BV, 1949)	555.4
18	Mary Poppins (BV, 1964)	537.8
19	Lady and the Tramp (BV, 1955)	537.0
20	The Godfather (Par, 1972)	526.5
21	The Ten Commandments (Par, 1956)	511.8
22	The Graduate (Avco, 1967)	510.4
23	Return of the Jedi (Fox, 1983)	506.0
24	Peter Pan (BV, 1953)	498.1
25	Song of the South (BV, 1946)	471.4

Champs by decade

1990s

1	Titanic (Fox, 97)	600.8
2	Star Wars: Episode I – The Phantom Menace (Fox, 99)	430.4
3	Jurassic Park (U, 93)	357.1
4	Forrest Gump (Par, 94)	329.7
5	The Lion King (BV, 94)	312.8
6	Independence Day (Fox, 96)	306.2
7	Home Alone (Fox, 90)	285.8
8	The Sixth Sense (BV, 99)	276.4
9	Men in Black (Sony, 97)	250.1
10	Twister (WB, 96)	241.7

1980s

1	E.T. – The Extra-Terrestrial (U, 82)	399.8
2	Return of the Jedi (Fox, 83)	309.2
3	The Empire Strikes Back (Fox, 80)	290.3
4	Batman (WB, 89)	251.2
5	Raiders of the Lost Ark (Par, 81)	242.4
6	Ghostbusters (Col, 84)	238.6
7	Beverly Hills Cop (Par, 84)	234.8
8	Back to the Future (U, 85)	208.2
9	Indiana Jones and the Last Crusade (Par, 89)	197.2
10	Indiana Jones and the Temple of Doom (Par, 84)	179.9

1970s

1	Star Wars (Fox, 77)	461.0
2	Jaws (U, 75)	260.0
3	Grease (Par, 1978)	181.5
4	The Exorcist (WB, 73)	165.0
5	The Sting (U, 73)	156.0
6	Close Encounters of the Third Kind (Col, 77)	155.7
7	Animal House (U, 78)	141.6
8	Saturday Night Fever (Par, 77)	139.5
9	The Rocky Horror Picture Show (Fox, 75)	139.2
10	The Godfather (Par, 1972)	135.0

1960s

1	The Sound of Music (Fox, 65)	160.5
2	101 Dalmatians (BV, 61)	143.9
3	The Jungle Book (BV, 67)	141.8
4	Doctor Zhivago (MGM, 65)	111.7
5	The Graduate (Avco, 67)	104.6
6	Mary Poppins (BV, 64)	102.3
7	Butch Cassidy and the Sundance Kid (Fox, 69)	96.7
8	Thunderball (UA, 65)	63.6
9	Cleopatra (Fox, 63)	61.8
10	Funny Girl (Col, 68)	55.3

1950s

1	Lady and the Tramp (BV, 55)	88.3
2	The Ten Commandments (Par, 56)	85.4
3	Peter Pan (BV, 53)	81.6
4	Ben-Hur (MGM, 59)	73.2
5	Around the World in 80 Days (UA, 56)	61.1
6	Sleeping Beauty (BV, 59)	50.4
7	The Robe (Fox, 53)	45.2
8	The Bridge on the River Kwai (Col, 57)	41.3
9	South Pacific (Fox, 58)	38.2
10	This is Cinerama (CRC, 52)	36.5

1940s

1	Bambi (BV, 42)	102.8
2	Cinderella (BV, 49)	81.1
3	Fantasia (BV, 40)	76.2
4	Pinocchio (BV, 40)	73.6
5	Song of the South (BV, 46)	56.4

. . . March 7 . . .
Stanley Kubrick dies just five days after having finally delivered **Eyes Wide Shut**.

6	Samson and Delilah (Par, 49)	29.3
7	The Best Years of Our Lives (RKO, 46)	28.5
8	Duel in the Sun (Selznick, 46)	27.8
9	The Bells of St. Mary's (RKO, 45)	23.7
10	The Jolson Story (Col, 47)	22.9

1930s

1	Gone With the Wind (MGM, 39)	198.7
2	Snow White and the Seven Dwarfs (BV, 37)	175.3
3	The Wizard of Oz (MGM, 39)	32.3
4	Modern Times (UA, 36)	27.6
5	King Kong (RKO, 33)	26.3
6	It Happened One Night (Col, 33)	24.2
7	The Adventures of Robin Hood (WB, 38)	22.8
8	Mutiny on the Bounty (MGM, 35)	21.7
9	Jesse James (Fox, 39)	19.4
10	Tarzan, the Ape Man (MGM, 32)	18.8

Pre-Sound

1	The Big Parade (MGM, 25)
2	The Birth of a Nation (Epoch, 15)
3	The Gold Rush (UA, 25)
4	Ben-Hur (MGM, 25)
5	The Four Horsemen of the Apocalypse (MGM, 21)
6	The Singing Fool (WB, 28)
7	What Price Glory? (Fox, 26)
8	Robin Hood (UA, 22)
9	The Jazz Singer (WB, 27)
10	The Covered Wagon (Par, 23)

* Box-office records in the pre-sound era are sketchy at best, so Variety offers its 10 money-winners of that era (including two early sound pics) based on the best information available.

Festivals

Film festivals have proliferated during the past two decades to the point at which no town or city worth its salt can afford to be without some kind of movie event. They have gradually replaced the network of arthouse cinemas that flourished during the 1960s and 1970s – although precious few producers glean any financial compensation for the screening of their films to anything up to 3,000 eager fans.

Film festivals come in all shapes, sizes, and flavors. They range from gargantuan, metropolitan affairs with attendances running into six figures, to tiny specialized gatherings devoted to films on mountaineering or children's issues. There are national festivals, which showcase the entire production of a nation from one year to the next, as well as festivals taking place in political hotspots of the world like Sarajevo, Jerusalem, and Tehran. Specific genres, such as animation, documentaries, thrillers, or even silent movies, all have their watering-holes somewhere in the world. Then there are the television markets, where the mood is strictly suits-and-ties and appointments through the day.

Craziest of all is the mother of all festivals, Cannes, where critics and conmen crowd the Croisette in what Robin Williams once described as "Disneyland designed by Dante." The amount of business achieved at film and TV markets around the globe is hard to quantify, but it certainly runs into the hundreds of millions of dollars. Throughout the year *Variety*'s reporters and reviewers are on the spot to follow developments at such events. We covered the first Cannes Festival in 1946, and we now produce a daily newspaper on site during the Riviera event. Of the approximately 1,100 films reviewed in *Variety* each year, a majority are seen and written about at festivals.

January

International Film Festival of India (New Delhi)
10-20 January 2000
Directorate of Film Festivals, Ministry of Information
   and Broadcasting, 4th Floor, Lok Nayak Bavan,
   Khan Market, New Delhi 110 003, India

Tel: +91-11 461 5953/469 49210/461 7226
Fax: +91-11 462 3430
Festival director: Malti Sahai
Festival programers: Shankar Mohan, S Santhanam
Market and Competition: Golden Peacock for Best
   Film by an Asian director (Rs500,000)

... March 8 ...

While the **Barber of Siberia** sets local box office records in Moscow, its helmer,
Nikita Mikhalkov, grapples with protests from extremist political forces.

Kid Film Festival (Dallas)
10-23 January 2000
6116 N. Central Expwy, Suite 105, Dallas 75206,
Texas, U.S.
Tel: +1-214 821 6300
Fax: +1-214 821 6364
Website: http://www.usafilmfestival.com
Festival director: Ann Alexander
Festival programer: Alonso Duralde

Travelling – Rennes Film Festival
10-17 January 2000
Université Rennes 2, 6 Avenue Gaston Berger,
F-35043 Rennes Cédex, France
Tel: +33-299 141143
Fax: +33-299 141145
E-mail: hussam.hindi@uhb.fr
Festival director/programer: Hussam Hindi
Competition: The Jury Prize (FFr30,000)

13th Stuttgart Filmwinter
(short film, experimental film, documentary, etc)
13-16 January 2000
Wand 5 e.v., Friedrichstraße 23/a, D-70174 Stuttgart,
Germany
Tel: +49-711 226 9160
Fax: +49-711 226 9161
E-mail: wanda@wand 5.de
Festival director: Ulrich Wegenast
Festival programers: Ulrich Wegenast, Martin Wolf
Competition: Norman award (DM 3,000) and
Teamwork award (DM 3,000)

Palm Springs International Film Festival
13-24 January 2000
1700 E. Tahquitz #3, Palm Springs, CA 92262, U.S.
Tel: +1-760 322 2930
Fax: +1-760 322 4087
E-mail: filmfest@ix.netcom.com.
Website: www.psfilmfest.org
Executive director: Craig Prater

Alpe Adria Cinema Film Festival – The Trieste Film Festival (Trieste)
15-22 January 2000
Via S. Rocco 1, 34143 Trieste, Italy
Tel: +39-040 311 153
Fax: +39-040 311 993
E-mail: aac@spin.it
Festival directors and programers: Annamaria
Percavassi, Tiziana Finzi, Sergio Grmek Germani
Competition: Prize for the best feature film
(L10 million)

FIPA (Festival International de Programmes Audiovisuels) (Biarritz)
18-23 January 2000
14 rue Alexandre Parodi, 75010 Paris, France
Tel: +33-1-44 89 99 99
Fax: +33-1-44 89 99 60
Festival president: Marie-France Pisier
Festival programer: Pierre-Henri Deleau
Competition: FIPA d'Or

Solothurn Film Festival
18-23 January 2000
PO Box 140, CH-4502 Solothurn, Switzerland
Tel: +41-32 625 8080
Fax: +41-32 623 6410
E-mail: filmtage@cuenet.ch
Website: www.filmtage-solothurn.ch
Festival director and programer: Ivo Kummer

Tromsø – The Arctic Film Festival
18-23 January 2000
PO Box 285, Tromsø, N-9253 Norway
Tel: +47-77 60 51 50
Fax: +47-77 60 51 51
E-mail: filmfestival@tromsokino.no
Website: www.tromsokino.no/ filmfestival
Festival director: Hans Henrik Berg
Festival programer: Ola Lund Renolen
Competition: Film Most Worthy of Import
(NKr100,000)

Brussels International Film Festival
19-29 January 2000
30 Chaussée de Louvain, B-1210 Brussels, Belgium
Tel: +32-2 227 3980
Fax: +32-2 218 1860
E-mail: infoffb@netcity.be
Website: http://ffb.cinebel.com
Festival director and programer: Christian Thomas
Competition: Crystal Star ($150,000)

Sundance Film Festival (Park City)
20-30 January 2000
PO Box 16450, Salt Lake City, UT 84116, U.S.
Tel: +1-801 328 3456
Fax: +1-801 575 5175
Festival co-directors: Nicola Guillemet and Geoffrey
Gilmore
Festival programer: Geoffrey Gilmore
Competition: Jury Prize (Drama/documentary)
($5,000)

. . . March 9 . . .
Michael Douglas is to produce and topline a feature adaptation
of the 1960s sitcom **My Three Sons** for New Line Cinema.

Future Film Festival
21-25 January 2000
Via Pietralata 55/a, Bologna, Italy 40123
Tel: +39-051 520 629
Fax: +39-051 523 816
E-mail: fff@clarence.com
Festival directors: Giulietta Fara, Andrea Morini,
Andrea Romeo

Premiers Plans (Angers)
21-30 January 2000
54 rue Beaubourg, 75003 Paris, France
Tel: 33-1-42 71 53 70
Fax: 33-1-42 71 47 55
Website: www.anjou.com/premiersplans/
Festival director and programer: Claude-Eric Poiroux
Competition: Grand Prix (FFr100,000)

Slamdance Film Festival (Park City)
22-29 January 2000
6381 Hollywood Blvd, #520, Los Angeles,
CA 90028, U.S.
Tel: +1-213 466 1786
Fax: +1-213 466 1784
Festival director: Peter Baxter
Competition: Grand Jury Award

Golden Globe Awards
23 January 2000
292 South La Cienega Blvd, Suite 316, Beverly Hills,
CA 90211-3055, U.S.
Tel: +1-310 657 1731
Fax: +1-310 657 5576
E-mail: hfpa95@aol.com
Contact: Chantal Dennage

MIDEM (Cannes)
23-27 January 2000
11 rue du Colonel Avia, 75726, Paris, Cédex 15,
France
Tel: +33-1-41 90 44 00
Fax: +33-1-41 90 44 50
Chief executive: Xavier Roy
Market

NATPE (National Association of TV Programming Executives) (New Orleans)
24-27 January 2000
2425 Olympic Blvd, Suite 550E, Santa Monica,
CA 90404, U.S.
Tel: +1-310-453 4440
Fax: +1-310-453 5258
Website: www.natpe.org

Festival director: Nick Orfanopoulos
European Offices: 454 Oakleigh Rd North, London
N20 ORZ, U.K.
Tel: +44-208 361 3793
Fax: +44-208 368 3824
Contact: Pam Mackenzie
Market

Max Ophüls Preis Film Festival
25-30 January 2000
Filmbüro, Max Ophüls Preis, Mainzer Str 8, 66111
Saarbrücken, Germany
Tel: +49-681-39452
Fax: +49-681-905 1943
E-mail: Filmhaus@aol.com
Festival director: Christel Drawer
Competition: Max Ophüls Preis

Gerardmer Fantastic Arts
26-30 January 2000
36 rue Pierret, 92200 Neuilly, France
Tel: +33-1-41 34 2000
Fax: +33-1-47 58 7777
E-mail: publics@imaginet.fr
Festival director: Lionel Chouchan
Festival programer: Daniel Benzakein
Competition: Grand Prix Gerardmer Fantastic Arts

The International Film Festival (Belgrade)
26 January-5 February 2000
Sava Centar, Milentija Popovica 9, 11000 Belgrade,
Yugoslavia
Tel:+381-11 622 555
Fax: +381-11 622 555/555 015
E-mail: ifilm@eunet.yu
Festival director: Dinko Tucakovic
Festival programers: Miroljub Vuckovic, Dragan
Jelicic

International Film Festival Rotterdam
26 January-6 February 2000
Karel Doormanstr. 278 B, PO Box 21696, 3001 AR
Rotterdam, The Netherlands
Tel: +31-10 890 9090
Fax: +31-10 890 9091
E-mail: tiger@iffrotterdam.nl
Website: www.iffrotterdam.nl
Festival director and programer: Simon Field
Market and Competition: Tiger Award ($10,000)

Internationale Filmwochenende (Würzburg)
27-30 January 2000
Gostbertsteige 2, D-97082, Würzburg, Germany

. . . March 10 . . .
A judge imposes sanctions of $4,500 against Garry Shandling's
lawyers in his suit against former manager Brad Grey.

Tel: +49-931 414098/40 85 61
Fax: +49-931 416279
E-mail: ifw24@aol.com
Festival director: Berthold Kremmler
Competition: Audience Award (DM5,000)

Göteborg Film Festival
28 January-6 February 2000
Box 7079, S-402 32 Göteborg, Sweden
Tel: +46-31 410 546
Fax: +46-31 410 063
E-mail: goteborg@filmfestival.org
Website: www.goteborg.filmfestival.org
Festival director and programer: Gunnar Bergdahl
Competition for Scandinavian films only
Göteborgs-Posten's Nordic Film Prize (SEK100,000)

New York Festival (TV Advertising Awards)
28 January 2000
780 King St, Chappaqua, NY 10514, U.S.
Tel: +1-914 238 4481
Fax: +1-914 238 5040
Festival director: Bilha Goldberg

Imagina (Monaco)
31 January- 2 February 2000 (Monaco) and
2-4 February 2000 (Paris)
4 avenue de l'Europe, 94366 Bry-sur-Marne, France
Tel: +33-1 4983 2693
Fax: +33-1 4983 3185
Festival co-ordinator: Jean-Michel Blottière
Competition: Grand Prix Imagina

The Chicago International TV Competition Awards
January 2000
32 West Randolph St, Suite 600, Chicago, IL 60610, U.S.
Tel: +1-312 425 9400
Fax: +1-312 425 0944
E-mail: filmfest@suba.com
web site: www/chicago.ddbn.com/filmfest
Festival director: Michael Kutza
Competition: The Gold Hugo Statue

Networks in the Studio Seminar
January 2000
Ancienne Route, 17A (European Broadcasting
   Union), Grand Saconnex (Geneva) Switzerland
   1218
Tel: +41-22 717 2721/2725
Fax: +41-22 717 2749/10
E-mail: peters@ebu.ch
Website: www.ebu.ch
Festival director: Jean-Jacques Peters

February

Fajr Film Festival
1-11 February 2000
Farhang Cinema, Dr. Shariati Ave, Gholhak, Tehran,
   19139, Iran
Tel: +98-21 200 2088/89/90
Fax: +98-21 267 082
Festival director and programer: S. Daad
Competition: Crystal Simorgh Award ($5,000)

Hungarian Film Week
3-8 February 2000
c/o Filmunio, Varoslygeti Fasor 38, 1068 Budapest,
   Hungary
Tel: +36-1 351 7760
Fax: +36-1 351 7766
E-mail: filmunio@elender.hu
Competition for Hungarian films only

Victoria Independent Film and Video Festival
4-12 February 2000
101-610 Johnson St., Victoria, British Columbia,
   V8W 1M4, Canada
Tel: +1-250 389 0444
Fax: +1-250 380 1547
Website: www.coastnet.com/~cinevic
Festival director: Kathy Kay

Clermont-Ferrand Short Film Festival
4-12 February 2000
26, rue des Jacobins, F-63000 Clermont-Ferrand,
   France
Tel: +33-473 91 65 73
Fax: +33-473 92 11 93
E-mail: festival@gdebussac.fr
Website: www.shortfilm.gdebussac.fr
Festival director: Roger Gonin
Festival programers: Roger Gonin, Christian Guinot
Competition: Grand Prix (FFr20,000)

Berlin International Film Festival
9-20 February 2000
Potsdamer Strasse 5, D-10785 Berlin, Germany
Tel: +49-30 2592 0202
Fax: +49-30 2592 0299
E-mail: info@berlinale.de
Website: www.berlinale.de
Festival director: Moritz de Hadeln
Competition: Golden Bear

. . . March 11 . . .
The Hollywood Foreign Press Assn. approves a rule change that will increase
the number of foreign films eligible for the group's Golden Globe Awards.

European Film Market (Berlin)
9-20 February 2000
Potsdamer Strasse 5, D-10785 Berlin, Germany
Tel: +49-30 2592 0202
Fax: +49-30 25920699
Contact: Beki Probst

International Forum of New Cinema (Berlin)
10-20 February 2000
Budapester Strasse 50, D-10787 Berlin, Germany
Tel: +49-30 254 89246
Fax: +49-30 261 5025
E-mail: forum@forum-ifb.b.shuttle.de;
  10024.327@compuserve.com
Website: www.b.shuttle.de/forum-ifb
Festival director: Ulrich Gregor
Festival programers: Erika and Ulrich Gregor, Klaus
  Dermutz, Erika Richter, Peter B. Schumann,
  Christoph Terhechte, Dorothee Wenner
Non-competitive, but awards are given.
  Wolfgang Staudte Preis (DM20,000)

The Mobius Advertising Awards (Chicago)
10 February 2000
841 North Addison Ave, Elmhurst, 60126-1291 IL,
  U.S.
Tel: +1-630 834 7773
Fax: +1-630 834 5565
E-mail: filmfestivalandmobius awards@compuserve.com
Festival director: J.W. Anderson
Competition: The Mobius Statuette

Portland International Film Festival
11-28 February 2000
1219 SW Park Ave, Portland 97205, OR, U.S.
Tel: +1-503 221 1156
Fax: +1-503 294 0874
E-mail: info@nwfilm.org
Website: www.nwfilm.org
Festival director and programer: Bill Foster
Competition: Audience Award

Mardi Gras Film Festival (Sydney)
12-22 February 2000
94 Oxford St/PO Box 1081, Darlinghurst,
  NSW 2010, Australia
Tel: +61-2 9332 4938
Fax: +61-2 9331 2988
E-mail: info@queerscreen.com.au
Festival director: Tony Grierson
Competition (for Australian and New Zealand
  queer shorts)
My Queer Career Award (A$2,000)

Transmedia '99 - Video Fest
12-20 February 2000
Klosterstr. 68-70, Berlin, Germany, 10179
Tel: +49-30 2472 1907
Fax: +49-30 2472 1909
E-mail: info@transmediale.de
Festival director: Mickey Kwella
Artistic director: Micky Kwella, Susanne Jaschko
Competition: Transmediale Award (DM7,500)

MILIA (Cannes)
14-17 February 2000
BP 572, 11 rue du Colonel Pierre Avia, 75726 Paris
  Cédex 15, France
Tel: +33-1-41 90 44 00
Fax: +33-1-41 90 44 70
Website: www.reedmidem. milia.com
Program manager: Laurine Garaude
Competition and Market: Milia d'Or

Academy Award Nominations
15 February 2000
Academy of Motion Picture Arts and Sciences,
  8949 Wilshire Blvd, Beverly Hills, CA 90211, U.S.
Tel: +1-310 247 3000
Fax: +1-310 859 9351
Contact: Bruce Davis

Monte Carlo Television Festival
17-23 February 2000
4 Blvd de Jardin Exotique, MC-98000, Monaco,
  Monaco
Tel: +377-93 10 40 60
Fax: +377-93 50 70 14
Festival director: David Tomatis
Market and Competition: Golden Nymph Awards
  (Best TV Film, Mini-series, News Reports, News
  Features)

Local Heroes
18-26 February 2000
3rd Floor, 10022 103rd St, Edmonton, Alberta
  T5J 0X2, Canada
Tel: +1-403 421 4084
Fax: +1-403 425 9099
E-mail: filmhero@nsi-canada.ca
Festival director: Cheryl Ashton
Festival programers: Anthony King
Market

Oslo Filmdager
18-25 February 2000
PO Box 1584, Vika, N-0118 Oslo, Norway

... March 12 ...
Rupert Murdoch's entry into Continental Europe is once again stalled.

Tel: +47-22 82 44 00
Fax: +47-22 82 43 68/69
Festival director: Ingeborg Moraus Hanssen

Miami Film Festival
19-28 February 2000
444 Brickell Ave, #229, Miami, FL 33131, U.S.
Tel: +1-305 377 3456
Fax: +1-305 577 9768
E-mail: mff@gate.net
Festival director and programer: Nat Chediak
Competition: Audience Award

Israel Film Festival
22 February-9 March 2000 (New York)
and 28 March-13 April 2000 (Los Angeles)
6404 Wilshire Blvd, #1240, Los Angeles,
　CA 90048, U.S.
Tel: +1-213 966 4166
Fax: +1-213 658 6346
Website: www.israelifilmfestival.com
Festival director: Meir Fenigstein
Competition: Audience Award

American Film Market (AFM)
23 February-1 March 2000
10850 Wilshire Blvd, Los Angeles, CA 90024, U.S.
Tel: +1-310 446 1000
Fax: +1-310 446 1600
Market director: Julie Friedman
Market

International Festival of Tourist Film
23-28 February 2000
ACTL, via Silvio Pellico 6, 20121 Milano, Italy
Tel: +39-02 86 46 40 80
Fax: +39-02 72 02 25 83
E-mail: info@actl.tt
Festival director: Edoardo Croci
Festival programer: Andrea Archidi
Competition

Cinequest Film Festival
24 February-5 March 2000
PO Box 720040, San José, CA 95172-0040, U.S.
Tel: +1-408 995 5033
Fax: +1-408 995 5713
E-mail: sjfilmfest@aol.com
Website: www.cinequest.org
Festival director: Halfdan Hussey
Festival programer: Mike Rabehl
Competition: Maverick Spirit Award

Freedom Film Festival
24 February-2 March 2000
American Cinema Foundation, 9911 W. Pico Blvd.,
　Suite 510, Los Angeles, CA 90035, U.S.
Tel: +1-310 286 9420
Fax: +1-310 286 7914
E-mail: acinema@cinemafoundation.com
Website:www.cinemafoundation.com
Contact: Gary McVey, executive director

Fantasporto
(Oporto International Film Festival)
25 February-4 March 2000
Rua da Constituição 311, P-4200 Oporto, Portugal
Tel: +351-2 507 3880
Fax: +351-2 550 8210
E-mail: fantas@caleida.pt
Website: www.caleida.pt/fantasporto
Festival director: Mário Dorminsky
Festival programer: Beatriz Pacheco-Pereira
Competition: Best Film Award

Brussels Cartoon and Animated Film Festival
28 February-10 March 2000
19 rue de la Rhétorique, 1060 Bruxelles, Belgium
Tel: +32-2 534 4125
Fax: +32-2 534 2279
E-mail: folioscope@skynet.be
Festival directors and programers: Doris Cleven,
　Philippe Moins

Cine Golden Eagle Showcase
February 2000
1001 Connecticut Avenue NW, Suite 638,
　Washington DC 20036, U.S.
Tel: +1-202 785 1136
Fax: +1-202 785 4114
Cine Golden Eagle Award (prof.) & Cine Eagle
　(amateur)
Entry deadline: 1 August and 1 March each year

Mumbai International Film Festival for
Documentary, Short and Animation Films
February 2000
Films Division, Ministry of Information and
　Broadcasting, Government of India, 24-Dr. G.
　Deshmuks Marg, Mumbai-400 026, India
Tel: +91-22 386 4633/387 3655/386 1421/386 1461
Fax: +91-22 386 0308
Festival director: Mr D. Gautaman
Competition and Market
Various categories: Golden Conch (Rs250,000) and
　Silver Conch (Rs100,000)

**PanAfrican Film and TV Festival
of Ouagadougou**
February 2001
Secrétariat Général Permanent du Fespaco, 01BP –
2505 Ouagadougou 01, Burkina Faso
Tel: +226-30 7538
Fax: +226-31 2509
Festival director: Filippe Sawadogo
Competition: Etalon de Yennega (CFA5 million)

March

Viewpoint: Documentary Now
1-8 March 2000
Sint-Annaplein 63, Ghent 9000, Belgium
Tel: +32-9 225 0845
Fax: +32-9 233 7522
E-mail: studio.skoop@net7.be
Festival director: Walther Vander Cruysse
Festival programer: Cis Bierinckx

**Human Rights Watch International
Film Festival (London)**
2-8 March 2000
350 Fifth Ave, 34th Floor, New York, NY 10118, U.S.
Tel: +1-212 216 1264/216 1235
Fax: +1-212 736 1300
E-mail: burres b@hrw.org
Festival director: Bruni Burres
Festival programers: Bruni Burres, Heather Harding

Bradford Film Festival
3-18 March 2000
National Museum of Photography, Film, and
Television, Bradford, BD1 1NQ, U.K.
Tel: +44-1274 773 399
Fax: +44-1274 770 217
Festival director: Bill Lawrence
Festival programer: Chris Fell
Audience Award

Cartagena Film Festival
3-10 March 2000
Baluarte de San Francisco, Calle San Juan de Dios,
A.A. 1834, Cartagena, Colombia.
Tel: +57-5 660 0966
Fax: +57-5 660 0970, 660 1037
Festival director and programer: Victor Nieto
Competition

Guadalajara Film Festival
3-9 March 2000

Estudios Churubusco Azteca, Atletas 2, Edificio Luis
Buñuel, Pasillo A-211, Col. Country Club, 04220
Mexico, D.F., Mexico
Tel: +525-544 6920
Fax: +525-544 6935
Festival director: Susana López Aranda
Festival programer: Leonardo García Tsao

NatFilm Festival
3-19 March 2000
Store Kannikestraede 6, 1169 Copenhagen K,
Denmark
Tel: +45-33 12 0005
Fax: +45-33 12 7505
E-mail: info@natfilm.dk
Website: www.filmfest.dk
Festival director: Peter Wolsgaard
Festival programer: Kim Foss

Showest (Las Vegas)
6-9 March 2000
Suite 708, 116 N Robertson Blvd, Los Angeles, CA
90048, U.S.
Tel: +1-310 657 7724
Fax: +1-310 657 4758
Executive director: Herb Burton
Director: Laura Rooney
Tradeshow

The Production Show
7-9 March 2000
33-39 Bowling Green Lane, London, EC1R 0DA, U.K.
Tel: +44-207 505 8014
Fax: +44-207 505 8020
E-mail: timmac@media.emap.co.uk
Event director: Tim McPhearson

Tampere Film Festival
8-12 March 2000
Box 305, 33101 Tampere, Finland
Tel: +358-3 213 0034
Fax: +358-3 223 0121
E-mail: film.festival@tt.tampere.fi
Website: www.tampere.fi/festival/film
Festival co-directors: Kirsi Kinnunen, Tuula
Kumpunen, Juhani Alanen
Festival programer: Raimo Silius
Market and Competition: Grand Prix (FMk25,000)
and 'Kiss' statuette

Cinéma du Réel
10-19 March 2000
BPI, 19 rue Beaubourg, 75197 Paris, Cédex 04, France

... March 14 ...
Warner Bros.'s mob comedy **Analyze This** drops just 15%
from its opening frame to $15.7 million at the B.O.

Tel: +33-1-44 78 44 21/44 78 45 16
Fax: +33-1-44 78 12 24
E-mail: cinereel@bpi.fr
Festival director and programer: Suzette Glenadel
Competition: Prix du cinéma du réel (FFr50,000)

South by Southwest Film Conference and Festival
10-18 March 2000
PO Box 4999, Austin, TX 78765, U.S.
Tel: +1-512 467 7979
Fax: +1-512 451 0754
E-mail: film@sxsw.com

Start the Millennium
11-12 March 2000
PO BOX 82, Plymouth, U.K. PL4 8XY
Tel: +44-1752 265 562
Fax: +44-1752 265 562
E-mail: start@sundog.zynet.co.uk
Website: http://start.at/start
Festival director: Stuart More
Festival programer: Kayla Parker

Fribourg Film Festival
12-19 March 2000
Rue de Locarno 8, 1700 Fribourg, Switzerland
Tel: +41-26 3222 232
Fax: +41-26 3227 950
E-mail: info@fiff.ch
Festival director and programer: Martial Knaebel
Competition: Grand Prix (SFr25,000)

Poitiers International School Film Festival
13-19 March 2000
1 Place de la Cathédrale, 86000 Poitiers, France
Tel: +33-4 4941 8000
Fax: +33-4 4941 7601
E-mail: festival-poitiers@rihl.org
Website: www.rihl.org
General secretary: François Defaye
Programing supervisor: Bruno Nicora
Competition

San Francisco International Asian-American Film Festival
13-20 March 2000
NAATA, 346 Ninth St, 2nd Floor, San Francisco, CA 94103, U.S.
Tel: +1-415 957 1205/863 0814
Fax: +1-415 957 1520/863 7428
E-mail: festival@naatanet.org
Festival director: Brian Lau
Festival programers: Brian Lau and Linda Blackaby

Ann Arbor Film Festival
14-19 March 2000
PO Box 8232, Ann Arbor, MI 48107, U.S.
Tel: +1-734-995 5356
Fax: +1-734-995 5396
E-mail: vicki@honeyman.org
Festival director and programer: Vicki Honeyman
Competition: Best of Festival ($2,500)

International Festival of Films on Art
14-19 March 2000
640 Saint-Paul St West, Suite 406, Montréal, Québec H3C 1L9, Canada
Tel: +1-514-874 1637
Fax: +1-514-874 9929
Festival director and programer: René Rozon
Competition: Grand Prix (honorary prize)

Action and Adventure Film Festival
15-19 March 2000
6 Place Froisart, Valenciennes, France 59 300
Tel: +33-3 2729 55 40
Fax: +33-3 27 41 67 49
Festival directors and programers: Patricia Lasou, Sylvie Lemaire, Patricia Riquet
Competition: Grand Prize (FF20,000 for the director)

Nordic Film Festival
15-26 March 2000
30 rue de la République, 76000 Rouen, France
Tel: +33-235 98 28 46
Fax: +33-235 70 92 08
Festival director: Jean Michel Mongrédien
Festival programers: Jean Michel Mongrédien, Isabelle Duault
Competition: Grand Jury Award

Cleveland International Film Festival
16-26 March 2000
2510 Market Ave, Cleveland, OH 44113, U.S.
Tel: +1-216 623 3456 ext. 27
Fax: +1-216 623 0103
E-mail: cfs@clevelandfilm.org
Website: www.clevefilmfest.org
Festival director and programer: David W. Wittkowsky
Competition: Roxanne T. Mueller Award

International Animation Film Festival
16-21 March 2000
Int. Trick Film Festival E.V., Teckstraße 56, Stuttgart, Germany 70 190

...March 15...
Latin America's longest-running cinema event, the Cartagena Film Festival, kicks off its 39th edition with seven days of screenings, workshops, and films.

Tel: +49-711 925 460
Fax: +49-711 925 4615
E-mail: info@itfs.de
Website: www.itfs.de
Festival director: Prof. Albert Ade
Festival programer: Ulrich Wegenast, Götz Gruner
Competition: Capital Stuttgart Award/State of
   Baden-Württenberg Award (DM180,000 total)

¡Viva! Spanish Film Festival
16-26 March 2000
70 Oxford St, Manchester, MI 5NH, U.K.
Tel: +44-161 228 7621
Fax: +44-161 200 1506
Festival programer: Linda Pariser

Brussels International Festival of Fantasy Film
17 March-1 April 2000
144 Ave de la Reine, B-1030, Brussels, Belgium
Tel: +32-2 201 1713
Fax: +32-2 201 1469
E-mail: peymey@skypro.be
Festival directors: Delmote Georges, Guy Delmote
Festival programers: Bozzo Annie, Freddy Bozzo-Gigli
Competition: Golden Raven Award (Corbeau d'Or)
   (US $27,000)

Bergamo Film Meeting
18-26 March 2000
Via Giovanni Reich 49, Torreboldone, Bergamo, Italy,
   24020
Tel: +39-35 36 30 87
Fax: +39-35 34 12 55
E-mail: bfm@alasca.it
Festival directors and programers: Emanuela
   Martini, Angelo Signorelli
Competition: Rosa Camuna d'Oro

SporTel (Miami)
20-23 March 2000
6040 Boulevard East Ste. 27 C, West New York,
   NY 07903, U.S.
4 Blvd de Jardin Exotique, MC-98000 Monaco, Monaco
Tel: +377-93 30 20 32
Fax: +377-93 30 20 33
President: Alexandre de Merode
Executive Vice-President: David Tomatis
Market and Competition: Golden Podium Trophy

Royal Television Society Awards
21 March 2000
Holborn Hall, 100 Gray's Inn Rd, London
   WC1X 1AL, U.K.

Tel: +44-207 430 1000
Fax: +44-207 430 0924
Contact: Nicky Harlow

International Short Film Festival (Tübingen)
23-26 March 2000
Osterbergsytr. 9, Tübingen, Germany 72074
Tel: +49-7071 56960
Fax: +49-7071 56 96 96
E-mail: filmtage tuebingen@t-online.de
Festival directors and programers: Jean-Michel
   Sidaine, Dieter Betz

African Film Festival
24-30 March 2000
Via Lazzaroni 8, 20124 Milano, Italy
Tel: +39-02 66 96 258
Fax: +39-02 6671 4338
E-mail: coe@iol.it
Competition: 1st Premio Agip (L15 million)

Creteil International Festival of Women's Films
24 March-2 April 2000
Maison des Arts, Place Salvador Allende, 94000
   Creteil, France
Tel: +33-1-49 80 38 98
Fax: +33-1-43 99 04 10
E-mail: filmsfemmes@wanadoo.fr
Festival director: Jackie Buet
Festival programers: Jackie Buet, Nicole Fernandez
Competition: Jury Prize (FFr25,000)

East Lansing Film Festival
24-27 March 2000
510 Kedzie St, East Lansing, MI 48823, U.S.
Tel: +1-517 336 5802
Fax: +1-517 336 5802
E-mail: swelff@aol.com
Festival director: Susan W. Woods

IVCA Awards 2000
24 March 2000 (London)
IVCA, Bolsover House, 5-6 Clipstone St, London
   W1P 8LD, U.K.
Tel: +44-207 580 0962
Fax: +44-207 436 2606
Chief executive: Wayne Drew
Competition: Grand Prix

Midwest Filmmakers Conference
24-26 March 2000
Cleveland Filmmakers, 1621 Euclid Ave, #428,
   Cleveland, OH 44115-2107, U.S.

... March 16 ...
Actors earned a record $1.63 billion under Screen Actors Guild
contracts in 1998, about $32 million more than in 1997.

Tel: +1-216 623 0400
Fax: +1-216 623 0103
Website: www.clevelandfilm.org
Festival programer: Frank O'Grady

New Directors/New Films
24 March-9 April 2000
The Film Society of Lincoln Center, 70 Lincoln
Center Plaza, New York, NY 10023, U.S.
Tel: +1-212 875 5638
Fax: +1-212 875 5636
Website: www.filmlinc.com
Contact: Sara Bensman

Academy Awards
26 March 2000
Academy of Motion Picture Arts and Sciences, 8949
Wilshire Blvd, Beverly Hills, CA 90211, U.S.
Tel: +1-310 247 3000
Fax: +1-310 271-3395
Academy Awards

Diagonale-Festival of Austrian Films (Graz)
27 March-2 April 2000
Diagonale, Obere Augerterstrasse 1, 1020 Vienna,
Austria
Tel: +43-1 216 1303
Fax: +43-1 216 1303200
E-mail: wien@diagonale.at
Festival directors: Christine Dollhofer, Constantin Wulff
Competition: Grosser Diagonalepreiss (DM30,000)

Festival du Film de Paris
27 March-2 April 2000
7 rue Brunel, 75017 Paris, France
Tel: +33-1 45 72 96 40
Fax: +33-1 45 72 96 41
Website: www.festival-du-film-paris.com
Festival director: Louise Maurin
Festival programer: Olivier Pelisson
Competition: Grand Prix (FFr700 000)

International Film Festival For Young People
27 March-6 April 2000
BP 526, 8 rue Cereurier, Laon, Cédex 02001, France
Tel: +33-3 23 79 39 37
Fax: +33-3 23 79 39 32
Festival director and programer: Florence Dupont
Competition: Grand Prix (FFr30,000)

London Lesbian and Gay Film Festival
30 March-13 April 2000
South Bank, Waterloo, London SE1 8XT, U.K.

Tel: +44-207-815 1323/815 1324
Fax: +44-207-633 0786
E-mail: jane.ivey@bfi.org.uk
Executive director: Adrian Wootton
Festival programers: Briony Hanson, Robin Baker

Newport Beach International Film Festival
30 March-9 April 2000
4000 MacArthur Blvd, 5th Floor, Newport Beach, CA
92660, U.S.
Tel: +1-949 851 6555
Fax: +1-949 851 6556
Website: www.nbiff.org
Festival director: Jeff Conner
Festival programer: Michelle Parsons
Competition and Market: The Jury Award
(US$8,000)

Chicago Latino Film Festival
31 March-12 April 2000
600 South Michigan Ave, Chicago, IL 60605, U.S.
Tel: +1-312 431 1330
Fax: +1-312 360 0629
Festival director: Pepe Vargas
Festival programer: Carolina Posse
Competition: Audience Award

**Schermi d'amore, Sentimental
and Mélo Film Festival**
31 March-9 April 2000
Comune di Verona, Corso Porta Borsari 17, 37121
Verona, Italy
Tel: +39-045 800 5348
Fax: +39-045 803 6205
Festival director: Michele Placido
Festival programer: Paolo Romano
Competition: Best Film

**Thessaloniki Doc Festival
– Images of 21st Century**
31 March-6 April 2000
40 Paparigopoulou Str. Athens, 11473, Greece
Tel: +30-1 645 3669
Fax: +30-1 644 8143
E-mail: newhorizons@filmfestival.gr
Festival director: Dimitri Eipides
Festival programer: Maria Golfinopoulou

Cairo International Film Festival for Children
March 2000
17 Kasr El Nil St, 202 Cairo, Egypt
Tel: +202-392 3562/392 3962
Fax: +202-393 8979

... March 17 ...
Michael Cimino is attached to direct the $35 million **1500**, a Brazilian pic
that may become the costliest film in Latin-American history.

Festival director: Soheir Abdelkader
Competition: Golden Cairo

Cognac International Thriller Film Festival
March 2000
36 rue Pierret, 92200 Neuilly, France
Tel: +33-1-41 34 20 00
Fax: +33-1-47 58 77 77
E-mail: publics@imaginet.fr
Festival director: Lionel Chouchan
Festival programer: Daniel Benzakein
Competition: Grand Prix

Deutsches Kinder-Film and Fernseh-Festival
March 2000 (biannual)
Stiftung Goldener Spatz, Amthorstrasse 11, D-07545
   Gera, Germany
Tel: +49-365 800 4874
Fax: +49-365 800 1344
E-mail: gold-spa@gera-web.de
Festival director and programer: Margret Albers
Market and Competition: Goldener Spatz (Golden
   Sparrow) Award

Femme Totale Film Festival
March 2001
Kleppingstr. 21-23, 44122 Dortmund, Germany
Tel: +49-231 50 25 162
Fax: +49-231 50 25 734
E-mail: femmetotale@compuserve.com
Website: www.inter-net-work.de
Festival director: Silke Johanna Räbiger
Market

Festival of Yugoslav Documentary and Short Film
Jugoslavia Film, Makedonska 22/VI, 11000 Beograd,
   Yugoslavia
Tel: +381-11 324 8554/324 8282
Fax: +381-11 324 8659
Contact: Vojislav Vucinic
Competition: Grand Prix

Hébraïca (Jewish Culture Events)
March 2000
500, Blvde d'Antigone, Montpellier 3400, France
Tel: +33-467 15 08 76/72 32 63
Fax: +33-467 15 08 72/72 32 62
Event director: Janine Gdalia

Music Film Fest
March 2000
37 Ekzarch Yossif Str., Sofia 1000, Bulgaria
Tel: +359-2 980 3911/880 676

Fax: +359-2 529 325
Festival director and programer: Stefan Kitanov

The New York Underground Film Festival
March 2000
225 Lafayette St, Suite 236, New York, NY 10012, U.S.
Tel: +1-212 252 3845
Fax: +1-212 925 3430
E-mail: festival@nyuff.com
Festival director: Ed Halter
Competition: Festival Choice Award ($750)

Minimalen Short Film Festival
March 2000
Box 10830, Innherredsk 73, N-7002 Trondheim, Norway
Tel: +47-73 52 27 57
Fax: +47-73 53 57 40
E-mail: minimalen@mail.link.no
Festival director and programer: Per Fikse
National competition: The Minimalen Festival Award
   (NKr5,000)

PILOTS (Programme for the International Launch of Television Series Workshops) (Sitges)
March 2000
Diputació 279, E-08007 Barcelona, Spain
Tel: +34-93 487 3773
Fax: +34-93 487 3952
Festival director: Pera Fages

San Diego Latino Film Festival
c/o Centro Cultural de la Raza, 2125 Park Blvd, San
   Diego, CA 92101, U.S.
Tel/fax: +1-619 230 1938
E-mail: LatinoFilm@aol.com
Festival director: Ethan van Thilo
Festival programer: Fred Salas

Spotlight
March 2000
Location Office Bodensee-Oberschwaben,
   Ittenbeuren 5, 88212 Ravensburg, Germany
Tel: +49-751 24 758
Fax: +49-751 24 753
Festival director: Dr. Thomas Knubben
Festival programers: Dr. Thomas Knubben,
   Peter Frey
Competition: Spotlight in Gold Award

Seoul Cable and Satellite Festival
March 2000
Korea Exhibition Centre, 159 Samsung-Dong,
   Kangham-gu, Seoul 135-731, Korea

... March 18 ...
A gown Elizabeth Taylor wore to the 1969 Academy Awards sold for $167,500,
the highest-priced item in a closet-clearing auction of Oscar glamour.

Tel: +822-551 1147
Fax: +822-551 1259
E-mail: chonsh@star.koex.co.kr
Festival director: Sang Hwi Chon

April

Aspen Shortfest
5-9 April 2000
110 East Hallam, Suite 102, Aspen, CO 81611, U.S.
Tel: +1-970 925 6882
Fax: +1-970 925 1967
E-mail: lthielen@aspenfilm.org
Festival director: Laura Thielen
Competition: Grand Jury Prize ($2,000)

**Celtic Film and Television Festival
(Portree, Skye)**
5-8 April 2000
249 West George Street, Glasgow, G2 4QE Scotland
March 2000
Tel: +44-141 302 1737
Fax: +44-141 302 1738
E-mail: mail@celticfilm
Festival director: Francis Hendron
Competition: Spirit of the Festival

Canyonlands Film and Video Festival (Moab)
6-9 April 2000
1102 East 5th Avenue, Durango, Co 81301, U.S.
Tel: +1-970 382 9528
E-mail: canyonfilm@hotmali.com
Website: http://moab-utah.com/film
Festival director: Nicholas Brown
Competition: 'Best of Festival' ($1,000)

Dublin Film Festival
6-16 April 2000
1 Suffolk St, Dublin, Ireland
Tel: +353-1 679 2937
Fax: +353-1 679 2939
Festival director and programer: Paul Taylor

**It's All True – International Documentary Film
Festival (São Paulo/Rio de Janeiro)**
7-16 April 2000
Rua Simáo Alvares 784/2, São Paulo, Brasil 05417 020
Tel/fax: +55-11 852 9601
E-mail: itstrue@ibm.net
Festival director: Amir Labaki
Competition: Best documentary

Worldfest Houston
7-16 April 2000
PO Box 56566, Houston, TX 77256, U.S.
Tel: +1-713 965 9955
Fax: +1-713 965 9960
E-mail: Worldfest@aol.com
Website: www.worldfest.org
Festival director: J. Hunter Todd
Market and Competition: Gold Remi Statuette and
    Gold Lone Star

Udine Incontri Cinema
8-15 April 2000
Via Villalta 24, 33100 Udine, Italy
Tel: +39-04 3229 9545
Fax: +39-04 3222 9825
E-mail: cecudine@tin.it
Festival director: Sabrina Baracetti
Festival programers: Derek Elley, Lorenzo Codelli

**Sprockets International
Film Festival for Children**
8-16 April 2000
Suite 1600, 2 Carlton Street, Toronto, M5B 1J3 Canada
Tel: +1-416 967 7371
Fax: +1-416 967 9477
E-mail: sprocket@torfilmfest.ca
Website: www.bell.ca/filmfest
Festival director and programer: Jane Schoettle
Competiton: Silver Sprocket (Canadian$1000)

MIP-TV (Cannes)
10-14 April 2000
Reed Midem Organisation, BP 572, 11 rue du
    Colonel Pierre Abia, Paris 75726, Cedex 15, France
Tel: +33-1-41 90 45 80
Fax: +33-1-41 90 45 70
Program director: André Vaillant
International TV Market

Vue d'Afrique
10-17 April 2000
Les Journées du Cinéma Africain et Creole, 67 rue
    Ste. Catherine Ouest, 5ème étage, Montréal,
    Québec H2X 1Z7, Canada
Tel: +1-514 284 3322
Fax: +1-514 845 0631
Festival director: Gérard Lechene
Competition

Hong Kong International Film Festival
12-27 April 2000
Level 7, Administration Bldg, Hong Kong Cultural

Centre, 10 Salisbury Rd, Tsimshatsui, Kowloon, Hong Kong
Tel: +852-2734 2903
Fax: +852-2366 5206
E-mail: hkiff@hkiff.com.hlc
Festival director: Lo Tak-Sing
Festival programers: Li Cheuk-to, Jacob Wong

The Shadow Line
12-16 April 2000
Via dei Principati 42, 84100 Salerno, Italy
Tel: +39-089 275 3673
Fax: +39-089 255 1125
E-mail: pdantonio@tim.it
Website: www.starnet.it/gff/giffoni.news.html
Festival director: Peppe D'Antonio
Competition: Shadow Line Award (Lira 5,000,000)

Los Angeles Independent Film Festival
13-18 April 2000
5455 Wilshire Blvd, # 1500, Los Angeles, CA, 90036 U.S.
Tel: +1-213 937 9155
Fax: +1-213 937 7770
Website: www.laiff.com
Festival director: Richard Raddon
Festival programer: Thomas Ethan Harris

National Association of Broadcasters – NAB
13-17 April 2000
1771 N Street, NW, Washington DC 20036-2891, U.S.
Tel: +1-202 429 5350
Fax: +1-202 429 5406
President and CEO of NAB: Eddie Fritz

Taos Talking Picture Festival
13-16 April 2000
216M North Pueblo Rd, #216, Taos, NM 87571, U.S.
Tel: +1-505 751 0637
Fax: +1-505 751 7385
E-mail: ttpix@taosnet.com
Website: http://www.taosnet.com/ttpix/
Executive director: Morten Nilssen
Festival programer: Kelly Clement
Competition: The Taos Land Grant Award

Turin International Gay and Lesbian Film Fest
13-19 April 2000
Piaza San Carlo 161, 10123 Turin, Italy
Tel/fax: +39-11 534 888
E-mail: gifilmfest@assioma.com
Festival director: Giovanni Minerba

Festival programers: Angelo Acerbi, Luca Andreotti
Competition: Three jury awards (feature, short, and documentary) and three audience awards

Cartoons on the Bay (Positano)
14-18 April 2000
RAI Trade, Via Umberto Novaro 18, 00195 Roma, Italy
Tel: +39-06 3749 8315
Fax: +39-06 3735 3521
E-mail: cartoonsbay@raitrade.it
Website: www.raitrade.rai.it/cartoonsbay
Festival director: Alfio Basiancich
Competition: Pulcinella Awards

Confrontations
14-21 April 2000
Institut Jean Vigo, 21 rue Mailly, Perpignan, France 66000
Tel: +33-468 66 30 33/34 09 39
Fax: +33-468 35 41 20
Festival director: Michel Cadé
Festival programers: Michel Cadé, José Balaizzone

Italian Film Festival (Glasgow/Edinburgh)
14-30 April 2000
Italian Institute, 82 Nicolson St, Edinburgh, EH8 9EW, U.K.
Tel: +44-131 668 2232
Fax: +44-131 668 2777
Festival director: Richard Mowe
Festival programer: Allan Hunter

Minneapolis International Film Festival
14-29 April 2000
2331 University Ave SE, Suite 130B, Minneapolis, 55414, U.S.
Tel: +1-612 627 4431
Fax: +1-612 627 4111
Website: www.ufilm.org
Festival director and programer: Albert Milgrom
Competition: Best Dramatic Feature

International Film Festival of Uruguay
15-30 April 2000
Lorenzo Carnelli 1311, Montevideo 11 200, Uruguay
Tel: +598-2 408 2460/409 5795
Fax: +598-2 409 4572
E-mail: cinemuy@chasque.apc.org
Festival director: Manuel Martínez Carril
Festival programers: Manuel Martínez Carril, Guillermo Zapiola
Competition: Gran Premio Ciudad de Montevideo

... March 20 ...
Gods and Monsters is named the Best Film at the 14th Independent Spirit Awards.

Istanbul International Film Festival
15-20 April 2000
Istiklal Cad: 146 Luvr Apt., 80070, Istanbul, Turkey
Tel: +90-212-293 3133 (ext. 50)
Fax: +90-212 249 5575
E-mail: filmfest@istfest-tr.org
Website: www.istfest.org
Festival director: Hülya Uçansu
Competition: Golden Tulip Award

**Washington DC International Film Festival
(Filmfest DC)**
19-30 April 2000
Box 21396, Washington DC 20009, U.S.
Tel:+1-202 724 5613
Fax: +1-202 724 6578
E-mail: FilmfestDC@aol.com
Festival director and programer: Anthony Gittens
Competition: Audience Award

San Francisco International Film Festival
20 April-4 May 2000
San Francisco Film Society, 39 Mesa Street, Suite 110,
The Presidio, San Francisco, CA 94129, U.S.
Tel: +1-415 929 5000
Fax: +1-415 921 5032
E-mail: stiff@stiff.org
Festival director: Peter Scarlett
Festival programers: Brian Gordon, Rachel Rosen,
Doug Jones
Competition: Golden Gate Awards for
documentaries, shorts, animation, experimental
works and TV production

Avignon/New York Film Festival
25-30 April 2000
10 Montée de la Tour, 30400 Villeneuve-les-Avignon,
France
Tel: +33-490 25 93 23
Fax: +33-490 25 93 24
Festival director: Jérôme Henry Rudes
Tel: +1-212-343 2675 Fax: +1-212-343 1849
Competition

Media Wave International Festival of Visual Arts
25 April-1 May 2000
Mediawave Foundation, H-9028 Györ, Soprani út 45,
Hungary
Tel: +36-96-449 444/328 888
Fax: +36-96-415 285
Festival director: Jenö Hartyándi
Festival programers: Ildiko Bari, Sandor Kadar

**St Barth Film Festival
(St Jean, St. Barthelemy)**
25-29 April 2000
410 West 24th St, #16K, New York City, NY 10011, U.S.
Tel: +1-212 989 8004
Fax: +1-212 727 1774
E-mail: jpharris@inerative.net
Festival directors and programers: Ellen Lampert-
Greaux, Joshua Harrison
Focus on Caribbean films

Gen Art Film Festival
26 April-2 May 2000
145 W 28th St, Suite 1101, New York, NY, 10001, U.S.
Tel: +1-212 290 0312
Fax: +1-212 290 0254
E-mail: info@genart.org
Festival director: Tobin Heminway
Festival programer: Adam Pincus
Competition: Audience Awards for Best Feature
and Short

Oslo Animation Festival
26-30 April 2000
PO Box 867, Sentrum, N-0104 Oslo, Norway
Tel: +47-23 119 300
Fax: +47-23 119 310
Festival director: Vibeke Christensen
Managing director: Kristine Kjølleberg
Competition: Grand Prize (£1500)

Grenzland Filmtage (Selb)
27-30 April 2000
Postfach 307, D-95622 Wunsiedel, Germany
Tel:+49-923 2 4770
Fax: +49-923 2 4710
E-mail: festival@grenzland-filmtage.de
Festival directors: Adele Tryr, Lena Wilfert

International Short Film Festival Oberhausen
27 April-2 May 2000
Grillostrasse 34, D-46045 Oberhausen, Germany
Tel: +49-208 825 2652
Fax: +49-208 825 5413
E-mail: kurzfilmtage-oberhausen @uni-duisburg.de
Festival director: Lars Henrik Guss
Competition: Grosser Preis der Stadt Oberhausen
(DM10,000)

Philadelphia Festival of World Cinema
27 April-6 May 2000
International House, 3701 Chestnut St, Philadelphia,
19104 PA, U.S.

...March 21...
Oscar night. The fortunes of the Academy of Motion Picture Arts & Sciences rest on the
Oscar statuette. It is pocketing $37 million from ABC for rights to broadcast the event.

Tel: +1-215 895 6593
Fax: +1-215 895 6562
E-mail: pfwc@lihphilly.org
Website: www.libertynet.org/pfwc
Festival director: Phyllis Kaufman
Festival programer: Davbe Kluft

USA Film Festival
27 April-4 May 2000
6116 N. Central Expwy, Suite 105, Dallas, TX 75206, U.S.
Tel: +1-214 821 6300
Fax: +1-214 821 6364
Website: www.usafilmfestival.com
Festival director: Ann Alexander
Festival programer: Alonso Duralde
Competition (only for short films): National Short
Film Video Competition – Grand Prize ($1000)

Hispanic Film Festival of Miami
28 April-7 May 2000
10700 SW 88 Ct. Miami, FL 33176, U.S.
Tel: +1-305 279 1809
E-mail: jangulo@hispanicfilm.com
Website: www.hispanicfilm.com
Festival director: Jaime Angulo
Festival programer: Susan Angulo

International Documentary Film Festival Munich
28 April-7 May 2000
Trogerstrasse 46, D-81675, Munich, Germany
Tel: +49-89 470 3237
Fax: +49-89 470 6611
Festival director and programer: Gudrun Geyer
Competition: Der Dokumentarfilmpreis (DM20,000)

Trento International Festival of Mountain and Exploration Films
28 April-6 May 2000
Via S. Croce 67, 38100 Trento, Italy
Tel: +39-461 98 61 20
Fax: +39-461 23 18 32
Festival director: Antonio Ciembran
Competition: Gran Premio

Ankara International Film Festival
30 April-8 May 2000
Farabi Sokak 29/1, Çankaya, 06690 Ankara, Turkey
Tel: +90-312 468 7745/3892
Fax: +90-312 467 7830
Festival director: Mahmut Tali Öngören
Festival programer: Gökhan Erkihç
Competition: Best Feature and Best European
Documentary

Arizona State University Art Museum Annual Outdoor Film Festival
End of April 2000
ASU Art Museum, Tenth St and Mill Ave, Tempe, AZ
85287-2911, U.S.
Tel: +1-602 965 2787
Fax: +1-602 965 5254
E-mail: spiak@asu.edu
Festival director: John D Spiak
Festival programers: Jurors
Competition: Juror choice award and LeBlanc
audience choice

BAFTA Film Awards
April 2000
195 Piccadilly, London W1V 0LN, U.K.
Tel: +44-207 734 0022
Fax: +44-207 439 0473
Executive director: John Morrell
Competition: Bafta Awards

European Cinema Congress (Wiesbaden)
April 2000
Forum Film Mediengesellschaft GmbH, Wiesbaden,
Germany 65205
Tel: +49-611 723448
Fax: +49-611 723403
E-mail: hdfev@aol.com
Managing director: Wolf Verscheur

Festival of French Cinema
April 2000
Tel Aviv Cinemathèque, 2 Sprintzak Street, Tel Aviv,
Israel
Tel: +972-3 691 7181
Fax: +972-3 696 2841

New England Film and Video Festival
April 2000
1126 Boylston St, #201, Boston, MA 02215, U.S.
Tel: +1-617 536 1540
Fax: +1-617 536 3576
E-mail: devon@bfvf.org
Festival director: Devon Demonte
Competition: Best of Festival ($1,500)

Palm Beach International Film Festival
April 2000
1555 Palm Beach Lakes Blvd., 0403 West Palm Beach,
FL, 33 401, U.S.
Tel: +1-561 233 1044
Fax: +1-561 683 6655
Festival director: Mark Diamond

. . . March 22 . . .
TLC's **FanMail** is the bestselling album for the third consecutive week,
with 203,000 copies of the disc going home with fans.

Singapore International Film Festival

April 2000
29A Keong Saik Rd, Singapore, Singapore 089136
Tel: +65-738 7567
Fax: +65-738 7578
E-mail: filmfest@pacific.net.sg
Festival director: Teo Swee Leng
Festival programer: Philip Cheah
Competition (for Asian features only): Silver Screen
  Award for Best Asian Feature

May

Silver Images Film Festival

1-12 May 2000
Terra Nova Films, 9848 S Winchester Ave, Chicago,
  IL 60643, U.S.
Tel: +1-773 881 6940
Fax: +1-773 881 3368
Festival director and programer: Martha Foster

Visions du Réel Festival International du Cinéma Documentaire

1-7 May 2000
18 rue Juste-Olivier, CP 593, CH-1260 Nyon,
  Switzerland
Tel: +41-22 361 6060
Fax: +41-22 361 7071
Website: www.webdo.ch/ visions_97.html
Festival director: Jean Perret
Competition: Grand Prix Visions du Réel

Santa Barbara Film Festival

2-12 May 2000
1216 State St, Suite 710, Santa Barbara,
  CA 93101, U.S.
Tel: +1-805 963 0023
Fax: +1-805 962 2524
E-mail: sbiff@swest.net
Website: www.sbfilmfestival
Festival director: Rhea A. Lewis
Festival programer: René Missel
Competition: Burning Vision Award (US$10,000)

Days of Independent Film

4-7 May 2000
Schroeckstr. 6, 86152 Augsburg, Germany, 86152
Tel: +49-821 349 1060
Fax: +49-821 349 5218
E-mail: filmbuero@t-online.de
Festival director and programer: Erwin Schleterer

Golden Rose of Montreux

4-9 May 2000
c/o Television Suisse Romande, Quai Ernest-
  Ansermet 20/CP, 234/1211 Geneva 8, Switzerland
Tel: +41-22 708 8599
Fax: +41-22 781 5249
E-mail: gabrielle.bucher@tsr.ch
Festival director: Chris Zoebeli
Secretary General: George Luks
Competition: Golden Rose Award

Toronto Jewish Film Festival

4-11 May
33 Prince Arthur Ave., 2nd Floor, Toronto, M5R 1B2
  Canada
Tel: +1-416 324 8226
Fax: +1-416 324 8668
E-mail: tjff@interlog.com
Festival producer: Helen Zukerman
Festival programer: Shlomo Schwartzberg

Cannes Film Festival

10-21 May 2000
99 Blvd Malesherbes, 75008 Paris, France
Tel: +33-1 45 61 66 00
Fax: +33-1 45 61 97 60
Website: www.cannes-fest.com
Festival president: Pierre Viot
Festival programer: Gilles Jacob
Market and competition: Palme d'Or

Inside Out Lesbian and Gay Film and Video

18-28 May 2000
401 Richmond St W, Suite 456, Toronto, Ontario
  M5V 3A8, Canada
Tel: +1-416 977 6847
Fax: +1-416 977 8025
Festival director: Rachel Giese
Festival programer: Shane Smith
Competition: Bulloch Award ($1,500)

Los Angeles Asian Pacific American Film and Video Festival

18-25 May 2000
Visual Communications, 263 South LA St, Suite 307,
  Los Angeles, CA 90012, U.S.
Tel: +1-213 680 4462
Fax: +1-213 687 4848
e-mail: viscom@vc.apanet.org
Website: http://vc.apanet.org~viscom/
Festival director: Abraham Ferrer

Emden International Film Festival
31 May-7 June 2000
Postfach 2343, 26703 Emden, Germany
Tel: +49-4921 915 533/35
Fax: +49-4921 915 591
Festival directors and programers: Rolf Eckard,
   Thorsten Hecht
Competition for German-language films and north-
   west European feature films: Emden Film Prize
   (DM15,000)

International Film Fest Cinematograph
31 May-4 June 2000
CineVision, c/o Cinematograph, Museumstrasse 31,
   Innsbruck, Austria 6020
Tel: +43-512 580723
Fax: +43-512 581762
E-mail: cinema@nomad.transit.or.at
Program director: Dr. Helmut Groschup

Maui Film Festival
31 May-3 June 2000
P.O. Box 669, Paia, HI 96779, U.S.
Tel: +1-808 579 9996
Fax: +1-808 579 9552
E-mail: mauifilmfestival@mauifilmfestival.com
Website: www.mauifilmfestival.com
Festival director and programer: Barry Rivers

Prix Jeunesse International
31 May-6 June 2000 (biannual)
c/o Bayerischer Rundfunk, D-80300 Munich,
   Germany
Tel: +49-89 59002058
Fax: +49-89 59003053
E-mail: prixjeunesse@papyrus.de
Contact: Ursula von Zallinger, Kirsten Schneid
Competition: Prix Jeunesse International

Cable and Satellite (London)
Mid-May 2000
Oriel House, 26 The Quadrant, Richmond, Surrey,
   TW9 1DL, U.K.
Tel: +44-208 910 7918
Fax: +44-208 910 7866
Contact: Sonya Gent

Cine Latino
May 2000
Osterbergstr. 9, Tübingen, Germany 72074
Tel: +49-7071 56960
Fax: +49-7071 569696
Festival director: Paolo Robert de Carvalho

European Media Art Festival
Early May 2000
Postfach 1861, 49008 Osnabrück, Germany
Tel: +49-541 216 58
Fax: +49-541 283 27
Festival director: Alfred Rotert

**FIFREC (International Film and Student
Directors Festival) – (Cannes)**
May 2000
FIFREC, BP 7144, 30913, Nîmes Cédex, France
Tel: +33-472 02 20 36
Fax: +33-472 02 20 36
Festival director: Jean Sondel
Competition: Crocodil d'Or

International Short Film Festival Kraków
May 2000
Ul Pychowicka 7, 30-364 Kraków, Poland
Tel: +48-12 267 6340
Fax: +48-12 267 1552
Festival director: Janusz Solarz
Festival programer: Tadeusz Lubelsi
Market and Competition: Grand Prix – The Golden
   Dragon Award (PLN12,000)

Málaga Spanish Film Festival
May 2000
Ramos Marin 2-2c, 29012 Málaga, Spain
Tel: +34-95 222 8242
Fax: +34-95 222 7760
Festival director: Salomon Castiel
Competition

Seattle International Film Festival
18 May-11 June 2000
911 Pine St, Seattle, WA 98101, U.S.
Tel: +1-206 464 5830
Fax: +1-206 264 7919
E-mail: mail@seattlefilm.com
Festival director: Darryl Macdonald
Festival programers: Darryl Macdonald,
   Carl Spence
Competition: American Independent Award

June

Las Vegas International Film Festival
1-10 June 2000
2048 Waverly Circle, Las Vegas, NV 89104, U.S.
Tel/fax: +1-702 547 0877
E-mail: iviff@aol.com

... March 24 ...
Miramax is to release a dubbed-in-English version of Roberto Benigni's **Life Is Beautiful**.

Festival director: Diane Phillips
Festival programer: Eileen Harrison

Montreal Sci-fi Film Festival
1-18 June 2000
Centre Cinéma Impérial, 1432 DeBleury St.
Montreal, H3A 2J1, Canada
Tel: +1-514 848 7187
Fax: +1-514 848 3886
E-mail: ccis@colba.net
Website: www.dimensionSF.com
Contact: Sandro Forte

Shots in the Dark, Mystery and Thriller Festival
1-11 June 2000
Broadway Media Centre, 14 Broad St, Nottingham,
NG1 3AL, U.K.
Tel: +44-115 952 6600
Fax: +44-115 952 6622
E-mail: broadway@bwymedia.demon.co.uk
Contact: Gill Henderson

Women's International Film Festival
1-15 June 2000
València 248 prel. 1, Barcelona, 08007 Spain
Tel: +34-93 216 0004
Fax: +34-93 215 3519
E-mail: drac.info@cambrabcn.es
Festival directors and programers: Marya Selva,
Anna Solà

Huesca Film Festival
2-11 June 2000
Avda. Parque, 1 piso, 22002 Huesca, Spain
Tel: +34-974 212582
Fax: +34-974 210065
E-mail: huescafest@fsai.es
Festival director: José María Escriche
Competition: Danzante de Oro (Pta1,000,000)

New York Lesbian and Gay Film Festival
2-12 June 2000
47 Great Jones St., 6th floor New York, NY 10012, U.S.
Tel: +1-212 254 7228
Fax: +1-212 254 8655
E-mail: newfest@idt.net
Website: www.newfestival.org
Festival director: Wellington Love
Festival programer: Basil Tsiokos

**Balticum Film and TV Festival
(Gudhjem, Rønne, Svaneke)**
3-9 June 2000

Skippergade 8, Svaneke, DK- 3940 Denmark
Tel: +45-70 202002
Fax: +45-70 202001
E-mail: balticmediacentre@bmc.dk
Festival director: Bent Nørby Bonde
Festival programer: Karolina Lidin
Competition: Balticum Documentary Award

Annecy International Animated Film Festival
5-10 June 2000
6 avenue des Iles, B.P. 399, 74013 Annecy, Cédex,
France
Tel: +33-4 50 10 09 00
Fax: +33-4 50 10 09 70
Festival director and programer: Jean-Luc Xiberraf
Competition: Grand Prix for Best Animated Feature

Toronto Worldwide Short Film Festival
5-11 June 2000
60 Atlantic Ave, Suite 106, Toronto, Ontario,
M6K 1X9, Canada
Tel: +1-416 535 8506
Fax: +1-416 535 8342
Executive director: Brenda Sherwood
Market and Competition: Cammy Award

**U.S. International Film and Video Festival
(Chicago)**
7-8 June 2000
841 North Addison Ave, Elmhurst, IL 60126-1291,
U.S.
Tel: +1-630 834 7773
Fax: +1-630 834 5565
Festival director: J.W. Anderson
Competition: Gold Camera and Silver Screen Awards

Sydney Film Festival
9-23 June 2000
PO Box 950, Glebe, NSW 2037, Sydney, Australia
Tel: +61-2 9660 3844
Fax: +61-2 9692 8793
E-mail: info@sydfilm-fest.com.au
Festival director and programer: Gayle Lake
Competition: Dendy Awards for Australian Short
Films (A$2,500 for each award)

Florida Film Festival (Maitland)
10-19 June 2000
Enzian Theater, 1300 S. Orlando Ave, Maitland,
FL 32751, U.S.
Tel: +1-407 629 1088 (Ext.222)
Fax: +1-407 629 6870
E-mail address: filmfest@gate.net

... March 25 ...
George Lucas donates $1.5 million to create a new digital studio at
his alma mater, USC's School of Cinema-Television.

President: Sigrid Tiedtke
Executive director: Melanie Gasper
Festival programer: Matthew Curtis
Competition: Grand Jury Prize

International Hamburg Short Film Festival
10-17 June 2000
Kurtzfilmagentur, D-22765 Hamburg, Germany
Tel: +49-40 398 26 122
Fax: +49-40 398 26 123
E-mail: kfa@shortfilm.com
Website: www.shortfilm.com
Festival director: Astrid Kühl
Competition: Hamburg Short Film Prize (DM5,000)

Banff TV Festival
11-16 June 2000
1516 Railway Ave, Canmore, Alberta T1W 1P6, Canada
Tel: +1-403 678 9260
Fax: +1-403 678 9269
E-mail: info@banfftvfest.com
Website: www.banfftvfest.com
Festival director: Pat Ferns
Festival programer: Jerry Ezekiel
Competition: The Banff Rockie

Human Rights Watch International Film Festival
14-29 June 2000
350 Fifth Ave, 34th Floor, New York, NY 10118, U.S.
Tel: +1-212 216 1264/216 1235
Fax: +1-212 736 1300
E-mail: burres b@hrw.org
Festival director: Bruni Burres
Festival programers: Bruni Burres, Heather Harding
Competition: New film dealing with human rights
    themes ($5,000)

Mediterranean Film Festival
14-21 June 2000
Osterbergstr. 9, Tübingen, Germany, 72074
Tel: +49-7071 56960
Fax: +49-7071 56 96 96
E-mail: filmtage.tuebingen@t-online.de
tuebingen@t-online.de
Festival director: Dieter Betz

Midnight Sun Film Festival (Sodankylä)
14-18 June 2000
Malminkatu 36, 00100 Helsinki, Finland
Tel: +358-9 685 2242
Fax: +358-9 694 5560
Festival director: Peter von Bagh

Festival programer: Göran Michelsson

'Message to Man' International Documentary, Short, and Animated Film Festival
15-22 June 2000
Karavannaya 12, St. Petersburg, Russia, 191011
Tel: +7-812 235 2660/230 2200
Fax: +7-812 235 2660/235 3995
Festival director: Mikhail Litviakov
Festival programer: Victor Semenyuk
Competition: Golden Centaur Award ($5,000)

San Francisco Lesbian and Gay Film Festival
15-25 June 2000
346 Ninth St, San Francisco, CA 94103, U.S.
Tel: +1-415 703 8650
Fax: +1-415 861 1404
E-mail: info@frameline.org
Festival director: Michael Lumpkin
Festival programer: Jennifer Morris
Competition: Audience Award

International Advertising Film Festival (Cannes)
19-24 June 2000
27 Mortimer St, London, W1N 7RJ, U.K.
Tel: +44-207 291 8444
Fax: +44-207 291 8400
Website: http:/www.canneslions.com
Festival president: Roger Hatchuel
Market and Competition: Lions Award

Napoli Film Festival
19-27 June 2000
Vico della Quercia 1/A, 80134 Naples, Italy
Tel: +39-081 551 7799
Fax: +39-081 551 4475
E-mail: nafifest@tin.it
Website: www.napolifilmfestival.freeweb.org
Festival director and programer: Mario Violini
Competition: Vesuvio Award

PILOTS (Programme for the International Launch of Television Series Workshops) (Sitges)
20-26 June 2000
Diputació 279, E-08007 Barcelona, Spain
Tel: +34-93 487 3773
Fax: +34-93 487 3952
Festival director: Pera Fages

Festival of Film Schools
21-30 June 2000
Kaiser Str. 39, Munich 80801, Germany

. . . March 26 . . .
Jim Carrey is to star in the split-personality comedy **Me, Myself, and Irene**.

Tel: +49-89 381 9040
Fax: +49-89 381 90426
Festival director: Prof Wolfgang Längsfeld
Competition

Sunny Side of the Doc
21-24 June 2000
3 Square Stalingrad, 13001 Marseille, France
Tel: +33-49 50 4 44 80
Fax: +33-491 84 38 34
E-mail: 100560.1511@compuserve.com
Market director: Olivier Masson
Market

Art Film Festival (Trencianske Teplice)
23-30 June 2000
Konventna 8, Bratislava, Slovak Republic, 81103
Tel: +42-17 5441 9479
Fax: +42-17 5441 1679
E-mail: festival@artfilm.sk
Festival director: Peter Hledik
Festival programer: Vladimir Stric
Market and Competition: Golden Key Award
   ($3,000)

Festival of Festivals (St Petersburg)
23-29 June 2000
10 Kamennoostrovsky Ave, St Petersburg, 197101,
   Russia
Tel: +7-812 237 0304
Fax: +7-812 237 0304/394 5870
Festival director: Alexander Mamontov
Market and Competition: Grand Prix

La Rochelle International Film Festival
23 June-3 July 2000
16 rue Saint Sabin, 75011 Paris, France
Tel: +33-1-48 06 16 66
Fax: +33-1-48 06 15 40
E-mail: festival.de.la.rochelle@ wanadoo.fr
Festival director: Jean-Loup Passek
Festival programers: Sylvie Pras,
   Prune Engler
Market

Showbiz Expo West (Los Angeles)
23-25 June 2000
383 Main Ave, Norwalk, CA 06851, U.S.
Tel: +1-203 840 5945
Fax: +1-203 840 9945
E-mail: ibogardus@reedexpo.com
Festival director: Joe Markam

Filmfest München
24 June-1 July 2000
Internationale München Filmwochen GmbH,
   Kaiserstraße 39, D-80801 Munich, Germany
Tel: +49-89 38 19 040
Fax: +49-89 38 19 04 27/26
Festival director: Eberhard Hauff
No competition, but special awards given. Top TV
   Award, Media Net Award

Marseille 2000 - Documentary Film Festival
24-29 June 2000
3 Square Stalingrad, 13001, Marseille, France
Tel: +33-495 04 44 90
Fax: +33-491 84 38 34
E-mail: 100560.1511@compuserve.com
Festival and market director: Michel Tregan
Competition: Grand Prix (FFr50,000)

Cinema Expo International (Amsterdam)
26-29 June 2000
244 West 49th St, #200, New York, NY 10019, U.S.
Tel: +1-212 246 6460
Fax: +1-212 265 6428
E-mail: sunshine@maestro.com
Website: www.sunshineworldwide.com
Contact: Andrew Sunshine

French-American Film Workshop
(New York/Avignon)
27 June-2 July 2000
10 montée de la Tour, 30400 Villeneuve-les-Avignon,
   France
Tel: +33-490 25 93 23
Fax: +33-490 25 93 24
Festival director: Jérôme Henry Rudes
Tel: +1-212 343 2675
Fax: +1-212 343 1849
Competition

Hong Kong International Film Market
28-30 June 2000
38th Floor, Office Tower Convention Plaza,
   1 Harbour Rd, Wanchai, Hong Kong
Tel: +852-2584 4333
Fax: +852-2824 0249
E-mail: ernest.chan@tdc.org.hk
Market director: Jenny Koo
Market

Cinemanila International Film Festival
30 June-9 July 2000
94-B Scout de Guia, Laging Handa, 1103 Quezon

. . . March 27 . . .
Shakespeare in Love enjoyed a significant box-office boost over the
first post-Oscar weekend with a three-day gross of $4.4 million.

City, Metro Manila, Philippines
Tel: +63-2 411 9436
Fax: +63-2 411 9284
E-mail: miff@cinemanila.com.ph
Festival director: Amable 'Tikoy' Aguiluz VI
Competition: Grand Prize

Adriaticocinema (Bellaria, Rimini, Catolica)
June 2000
Via Gambalunga 27, 47900 Rimini, Italy
Tel: +39-541 226 27/26 399/52 038
Fax: +39-541 24 227
Festival director: Marco Bellocchio
Organising director: Gianfranco Miro Gori
International competition only for film schools

International Bochum Videofestival
Mid-June 2000
Bochumer Videofestival, ASTA Kulturreferat der
  Ruhr-Universität, Universitätstr. 150, 44801
  Bochum, Germany
Tel: +49-234 700 6712
Fax: +49-234 70 16 23
Festival directors: Katarine Keller, Jessica
  Manscheten, Seryosha Vimmer
Competition

Bradford Animation Festival (BAF!)
June 2000
National Museum of Photography, Film and TV,
  Pictureville, Bradford BD1 1NQ, U.K.
Tel: +44-1274 725 347
Fax: +44-1274 723 155
E-mail: c.sawhney@nmsei.ac.uk or c.fell@nmsi.ac.uk
Festival programer: Chris Fell
Competition

Docfest
(New York International Documentary Festival)
June 2000
159 Maiden Lane, New York, NY 10038, U.S.
Tel: +1-212 943 6333
Fax: +1-212 943 6396
E-mail: dockfest@aol.com
Festival director: Gary Pollard

Fantafestival
Viale Gioachino Rossini 9, 00198 Roma, Italy
Tel: +39-6 807 6999
Fax: +39-6 807 7199
Festival directors: Adriano Pintaldi, Alberto Ravagioli
Festival programer: Loris Curci
Competition: Gran Premio FantaFestival

International and Open Russian Film Festivals
Kinotavr (Sochi)
June 2000
35 Arbat, Moscow 121835, Russia
Tel: +7-095 248 0911/248 9187
Fax: +7-095 248 0966
Festival director: Larisa Blank
Festival programer: Michael Ufhaklv
Entry deadline for films: tbc

Norwegian Short Film Festival (Grimstad)
Mid-June 2000
Filmens Hus, Dronningens Gate 16, N-0152 Oslo,
  Norway
Tel: +47-22 47 46 46
Fax: +47-22 47 46 90
Website: http://www.nfi.no/krtf/welcome.html
Festival director: Torunn Nyen
Competition: (Norwegian films only)

Peniscola International Comedy Festival
June 2000
Plaza Constitucion s/n, 12598 Peniscola, Spain
Tel: +34-964 474 901
Fax: +34-964 481 521

Pesaro Film Festival
June 2000
Via Villafranca 20, 00185 Roma, Italy
Tel: +39-6 445 66 43/49 11 56
Fax: +39-6 491 163
E-mail: pesarofilmfest@mclink.it
Website: www.comune.pesaro.ps.it
Festival director and programer: Adriano Aprà

The Prince's Award
Early June 2000
The Prince's Award Foundation, c/o European
  Environment Agency, Kongens Nytorv 6, DK-1050
  Copenhagen K, Denmark
Tel: +45-33 36 7100/7121
Fax: +45-33 36 7199
E-mail: princes.award@eea.dk
Website: www.eea.dk/events/pa97
Director: Tage Mikkelsen
Competition: Prize for producers of the best CD-ROM,
  video, and film on the environment of Europe

Troia International Film Festival (Setúbal)
Early June 2000
Forum Luisa Todi, Av Luisa Todi 65, 2900 Setúbal,
  Portugal
Tel: +351-65 525 908

Fax: +351-65 525 681
Festival director: Mário Ventura
Festival programer: Fernanda Silva
Competition: Golden Dolphin

July

Age d'Or Prize/Prizes for the distribution of quality films in Belgium (Cinédécouverts)
1-15 July 2000
Royal Film Archive, Ravenstein St. 23, B-1000
 Brussels, Belgium
Tel: +32-2 507 8370
Fax: +32-2 513 1272
Festival director and programer: Gabrielle Claes
Competition: The Age d'Or Prize (BFr500,000)

Mostra Internazionale del Cinema Libero/ Il Cinema Ritrovato
(Festival of film restoration from archives from all over the world)
1-8 July 2000
Via Galliera 8, I-40121 Bologna, Italy
Tel: +39-51 237 088
Fax: +39-51 261 680
E-mail: cinaffcr@comune.bologna.it
Festival director: Gianluca Farinelli

International Film Festival for Children and Young People
3-14 July 2000
Lorenzo Carnelli 1311, 11200 Montevideo, Uruguay
Tel: +598-2 408 2460/409 5795
Fax: +598-2 409 4572
E-mail: cinemuy@chasque.apc.org
Festival director and programer: Ricardo Casas
Competition: Guri Award

Cologne Conference
4-7 July 2000
Adolf Grimme Institut, Im Mediapark 5b, 50670
 Köln, Germany
Tel: +49-221 454 3280
Fax: +49-221 454 3289
E-mail: 100776,2621@ compuserve.com
Director: Lutz Hachmeister
Programer: Martina Richter
Market

Karlovy Vary International Film Festival
5-15 July 2000
Panska 1, 110 00 Prague 1, Czech Republic

Tel: +420-2 24 23 54 48
Fax: +420-2 24 23 3408
E-mail: foundation@iffkv.cz
Festival president: Jiri Bartoska
Festival programer: Eva Zaoralova
Competition: Grand Prix Crystal Globe ($20,000)

Jerusalem Film Festival
6-15 July 2000
PO Box 8561, Derech Hebron, Wolfson Gardens,
 Jerusalem 91083, Israel
Tel: +972-2 672 4131
Fax: +972-2 673 3076
E-mail: festival@jer-cin.org.il
Festival director: Lia van Leer
Festival programers: Lia van Leer, Avinoam Harpak
Competition: Jewish Experience Awards

Auckland International Film Festival
7-23 July 2000
PO Box 9544, Wellington, 6035 New Zealand
Tel: +64-4 385 0162
Fax: +64-4 801 7304
E-mail: enzedff@actrix.gen.nz
Festival director: Bill Gosden
Festival programer: Sandra Reid

Taormina International Film Festival
8-15 July 2000
Palazio dei Congressi, 98039 Taormina, Italy
Tel: +39-942 21142
Fax: +39-942 23348
Festival director: Felice Laudadio
Festival programer: Carmelo Marabello
Competition: Cariddi d'Oro and d'Argento – Premio
 Marco Melani (L75 million in total)

Galway Film Fleadh
11-16 July 2000
Cluain Mhuire, Monivea Rd, Galway, Ireland
Tel: +353-91 751655
Fax: +353-91 770746
E-mail: galfleadh@iol.ie
Festival director: Fiona Kilkelly
Program director: Pat Collins
Market

Fant-Asia Festival (Montreal, Toronto)
13-30 July 2000
300 Leo Pariseau Street, Suite 1500 Montréal, Québec
 H2W 2P3, Canada
Tel: +1-514 982 0020
Fax: +1-514 982 0796

E-mail: festival@videotron.ca
Website: www.fantasiafest.com
Festival director: Pierre Corbeil
Festival programers: Mitch Davis, Julien Fonfrede,
   Karin Hussain, Martin Sauvageau
Competition and Market

Puchon Int'l Fantastic Film Festival
13-21 July 2000
Boksagol Cultural Center, Ste 513, 394-2 Sang-I-
   dong, Wonmi-gu, Puchon, Kyonggi-Province,
   Korea 420 031
Tel: +82-32 322 9225
Fax: +82-32 345 6315
E-mail: programming1@yahoo.com
Director general: Myung-Soo Suh
Festival programer: Cassie Yoo, Chosin Zeong
Competition: Grand Prize (The Golden Kebbi
   $3,000)

Wellington Film Festival
14-30 July 2000
PO Box 9544, Wellington 6035, New Zealand
Tel: +64-4 385 0162
Fax: +64-4 801 7304
E-mail: enzedff@actrix.gen.nz
Festival director: Bill Gosden
Festival programer: Sandra Reid

San Francisco Jewish Film Festival
20 July-3 August 2000
346 Ninth St, San Francisco, CA 94103, U.S.
Tel: +1-415 621 0556
Fax: +1-510 548 0536
E-mail: jewishfilm@aol.com
Festival director: Janis Plotkin
Festival programer: Janis Plotkin, Samuel Ball

Melbourne International Film Festival
22 July-8 August 2000
PO Box 2206, Fitzroy 3065, Melbourne, Australia
Tel: +61-3 9417 2011
Fax: +61-3 9417 3804
E-mail: miff@netspace.net.au
Festival director: Sandra Sdraulig
Festival programer: Brett Woodward
Competition (short films only)
Grand Prix for Best Short Film (A$5,000)

Fantasy Film Festival
(Munich-Frankfurt-Cologne-Stuttgart-Hamburg-
Berlin)
27 July-24 August 2000

Rosebud Entertainment, Herzog-Wilhelmstr. 27,
   80331 Munich, Germany
Tel: +49-89 260 22838
Fax: +49-89 260 22839
E-mail: rosebud-entertainment@t-online.de
Festival directors and programers: Rainer Stefan,
   Schorsch Müller

Brisbane International Film Festival
July-August 2000
PO Box 94, Brisbane Albert St., Queensland 4002,
   Australia
Tel: +61-7 3224 4114
Fax: +61-7 3224 6717
E-mail: pftc@pftc.com.au
Website: www.pftc.com.au
Festival director: Gary Ellis
Competition

Giffoni Film Festival
July 2000
Piazza Umberto 1, 84095 Giffoni Valle Piana, Salerno
   Italy
Tel: +39-89 868 544
Fax: +39-89 866 111
E-mail: gilfonif@mcorrino.peoples.it
Festival director and programer: Claudio Gubitosi
Competition: Silver Gryphon Award

Hometown Video Festival
July 2000
The Alliance for Community Media, 666 11th St,
   NW #806, Washington DC 20001, U.S.
Tel: +1-202 393 2650
Fax: +1-202 393 2653
Festival director: Steve Fortriede

International Short Film Festival of
Vila do Conde
July 2000
Auditorio Municipal – Praga da Republica, 4480 Vila
   do Conde, Portugal
Tel: +351-52 641 644
Fax: +351-52 642 871
Festival directors and programers: M. Dias,
   M. Micaelo, R. Maia, D. Oliveira, J. Rodrigues
Market and Competition: Great Prize City of Vila
   do Conde (Pta500,000)

Monitor Awards (New York)
July 2000
2230 Gallows Rd, Suite 310, Dunn Loring,
   VA 22027, U.S.

... March 30 ...
Overall domestic spending for motion pictures in
Hollywood rose 8.9% last year to $2 billion.

Tel: +1-703 319 0800
Fax: +1-703 641 8776
Contact: Julie Chung

Moscow International Film Festival
July 2000
Khokhlovski Pereulok 10/1, Moscow 109028, Russia
Tel: +7-095 917 2486/0944
Fax: +7-095 916 0107
Festival president: Renat Davletiarov
Festival programer: Kiril Razlogov
Competition: Statuette of Saint George

Potsdam Film Fest
July or August 2000
Dianastr. 21, 14482 Potsdam, Germany
Tel: +49-331 706 0369
Fax: +49-331 706 0339
Festival director: Heidrun Podazus
Festival programer: Festival team

Outdoor Short Film Festival
July 2000
4 rue Hector Berlioz, Grenoble 38000, France
Tel: +33-476 544 351
Fax: +33-476 5124 43
Festival director and programer: Michel Warren
Competition: Grand Prix (FFr15,000)

PIA Film Festival
July 2000
5-19 Sanban-cho, Chiyoda-ku, Tokyo 102-0075, Japan
Tel: +81-3 32 65 14 25
Fax:+81-3 32 65 56 59
Festival director and programer: Keiko Araki
Competition: Grand Prize (¥1 million)

Pula Film Festival
July 2000
Matka Laginje 5, Istarsko Narodno Kazaliste, Pula
 52100, Croatia
Tel: +385-52 22380
Fax: +385-52 214 303
Festival director: Ljubo Sikic
Competition: Golden Arena Award

Sopot Film Festival
July 2000
Centar za kulturu Sopot, Kosmajski trg 7, 11450
 Sopot, Yugoslavia
Tel: +381-11 825 1238/825 1315
Fax: +381-11 825 1315
Contact: Zivorad Milosavljevic

Wine Country Film Festival
July 2000
PO Box 303, Glen Ellen, CA 95442, U.S.
Tel: +1-707 996 2536
Fax: +1-707 996 6964
E-mail: wc.filmfest@aol.com
Festival director and programer: Stephen Ashton
Competition: First Feature Award, Blockbusters Film
 Competition

Zanzibar International Film Festival
July 2000
Karume House, PO Box 3032, Zanzibar, Tanzania
Tel: +255-54 33408
Fax: +255-54 33406/33135
E-mail: ziff@zanzibar.org
Festival director: Mark Leveri
Festival programer: Yusuf Mahmoud
Competition: Golden Dhow Award ($5,000)

International Film Festival (Palic)
July 2000
Otvoreni Univerzitet, Trg Cara Jovana Nenada 15,
 24000 Subotica, Yugoslavia
Tel: +381-24 554 726
Fax: +381-24 37116
Festival director: Radoslav Zelenovic
Festival programer: Dinko Tucakovic
Competition: Alexandar Lifka Award

August

Motovun International Film Festival
1-5 August 2000
Trnjanska 11b, Zagreb, 10000, Croatia
Tel/fax: +385-1 611 5841
E-mail: boris.matic@radio101.hr
Festival director: Boris T Matic
Competition: Golden Tower of Motovun

Locarno International Film Festival
2-12 August 2000
Via della Posta 6, 6600 Locarno, Switzerland
Tel: +41-91 756 2121
Fax: +41-91 756 2149
E-mail: info@pardo.ch
Website: www.pardo.ch
Festival director: Marco Müller
Festival programer: Teresa Cavina
Market and Competition: Golden Leopard (SFr30,000)

...March 31...
Jeff Daniels is to star as George Washington in the A&E telepic **The Crossing**,
a high-budget entry from the cable channel.

Dublin Lesbian and Gay Film Festival
3-7 August 2000
6 South William St, Dublin 2, Ireland
Tel: +353-1 492 0597
Fax: +353-1 670 6377
Festival directors and programers: Kevin Sexton,
   Yvonne O'Reilly

Hollywood Film Festival
3-8 August 2000
433 N. Camden Drive, Suite 600, Beverly Hills,
   CA 90210, U.S.
Tel: +1-310 288 1882
Fax: +1-310 475 0193
E-mail: awards@hollywoodawards.com
Festival director and programer: Carlos de Abreu
Competition: Hollywood Discovery Award ($20,000)

Weiterstadt Open Air Filmfest
10-14 August 2000
Bahnhofstrasse 70, D-64331, Weiterstadt, Germany
Tel: +49-615 012 185
Fax: +49-615 014 073
E-mail: sfk@hrzpub.tu-darmstadt.de
Website: www.home.pages.de/~sfk/weiterstadt
Festival director: Jochen Pollitt

Edinburgh International Film Festival
13-27 August 2000
88 Lothian Rd, Edinburgh EH3 9BZ, Scotland, U.K.
Tel: +44-131 228 4051
Fax: +44-131 229 5501
E-mail: info@edfilmfest.org.uk
Website: www.edfilmfest.aug.uk
Festival director and programer: Lizzie Francke

Odense International Film Festival
14-19 August 2000
Vindegade 18, DK-5000 Odense C, Denmark
Tel: +45-6 613 1372 ext.4044
Fax: +45-6 591 4318
Festival director: Christian Braad Thomsen
Competition: Grand Prix (DKr35,000)

São Paulo International Short Film Festival
17-26 August 2000
Rua Simao Alvares 784/2, 05417-020 São Paulo –
   SP, Brazil
Tel/fax: +55-11 852 9601
E-mail: spshort@ibm.net
Festival director: Zita Carvalhosa
Festival programer: Francisco Cesar Filho

Douarnenez Film Festival
19-26 August 2000
20 rue du Firt Rhu - BP 206, Douarnenes, Cédex
   29172 Brittany, France
Tel: +33-2 9892 0921
Fax: +33-2 9892 2810
E-mail: fdz@wanadoo.fr
Website: kerys.com
Festival directors: Erwan Moalic, Carolin Troin
Competition only for Breton films

Espoo Ciné
22-27 August 2000
PO Box 95, Espoo 02101, Finland
Tel:+358-9 466 599
Fax: +358-9 466 458
E-mail: espoocine@cultnet.fi
Festival director: Timo Kuismin

Festival der 'Neue Heimat Film'
23-27 August 2000
Salzgasse 25, 4240 Freistadt, Austria
Tel/fax: +43-79 42 77733
Festival director: Wolfgang Steininger
Festival programers: Wolfgang Steininger, Sylvia
   Platzer
Competition: Preis der Stadt Freistadt (ASch30,000)

Antarctic Film Festival
24-31 August 2000
2543 2nd St, Suite C, Santa Monica, CA 90405, U.S.
Tel/fax: +1-310 396 2759
E-mail: info@antarctic-filmfest.com
Website: www.antarctic-filmfest.com
Festival director: C.T. Pinguino
Festival programmer: Yarrum Ztnim

Chichester Film Festival
24 August-10 September 2000
New Park Film Centre, New Park Rd, Chichester,
   West Sussex, PO19 1XN, U.K.
Tel: +44-1243 786 650/533 081
Fax: +44-1243 533 081
Festival director and programer: Roger Gibson
Competition: Audience Award for Best Preview and
   Best Short

**Austin Gay and Lesbian International
Film Festival**
25 August-7 September 2000
PO Box L, Austin TX, 78713, U.S.
Tel: +1-512 302 9889
Fax: +1-512 302 1088

...April 1 ...
Martin Scorsese and Nick Pileggi to write the script for a feature on
the story of Italian financier Michele Sindona.

E-mail: kino@agliff.org
Website: www.agliff.org
Festival director: Sandra Martinez
Festival programer: Scott Dinger

Edinburgh International Television Festival
25-28 August 2000
2nd Floor, 24 Neal St, London WC2H 9PS, U.K.
Tel: +44-207 379 4519
Fax: +44-207 836 0702
E-mail: eitf@festival.demon.co.uk
Festival director: Fran Barlow

Montreal World Film Festival
25 August-4 September 2000
1432 De Bleury, Montreal H3A 2JI, Canada
Tel: +1-514 848 3883
Fax: +1-514 848 3886
E-mail: ffm@interlink.net
Website: www.ffm-montreal.org
Festival directors and programers: Serge Losique,
    Daniele Cauchard
Market and Competition: Grand Prix of the Americas

Film in Weimar
– Festival of the Eastern European Cinema
26 August-2 September 2000
Etfuster Str. 40, Jena, Germany 07745
Tel: +49-3641 45 06 30
Fax: +49-3641 61 52 34
E-mail: Klaus.Hattenbach@ Jena.Thur.de
Festival director and programer: Klaus Hattenbach

Norwegian International Film Festival
27 August-3 September 2000
PO Box 145, 5501 Haugesund, Norway
Tel: +47-52 73 44 30
Fax: +47-52 73 44 20
E-mail: haugfest@online.no
Festival director: Gunnar Johan Løvvik
Festival programer: Christine Berg
Market

Chicago Underground Film Festival
Mid-August 2000
3109 N. Western Ave, Chicago, IL 60618, U.S.
Tel: +1-773 327 3456
Fax: +1-773 327 3464
E-mail: info@cuff.org
Website: www.cuff.org
Festival director: Bryan Wendorf
Festival programer: Wendy Solomon
Competition

Fantoche International Animation
Film Festival (Baden)
August-September 2001 (biannual)
Ottikerstrasse 53, 8006 Zürich, Switzerland
Tel: +41-1 361 4151
Fax: +41-1 364 0371
E-mail: fantoche@access.ch
Contact: Otto Alder
Competition

Festival of Actors
August 2000
Pavla Orlovica 28 A, 18000 Nis, Yugoslavia
Tel: +381-18 47 757/42 849
Fax: +381-18 23 197
Festival director and programer: Predrag Jelenkovic
Competition: Grand Prix for the Best Actors

Film Screenplay Festival
August 2000
Vrnjacka 20, 36210 Vrnjacka Banja, Yugoslavia
Tel: +381-36 662 398
Fax: +381-36 662 398
Festival director and programer: Milan Nikodijevic
Competition: Best Screenplay Award

Gramado Film Festival
– Latin and Brazilian Cinema
August 2000
Rua dos Andradas 736, 3 Andar, Centro, 90 020 004
    Porto Alegre, Brazil
Tel: +55-51 226 3932
Fax: +55-51 226 3932
E-mail: festival@via-rs.com.br
Festival director: Esdras Rubinn
Market and Competition: Kikito

Hiroshima International Animation Festival
August 2000
4-17 Kako-machi, Naka-ku, Hiroshima 730, Japan
Tel: +81-82 245 0245
Fax: +81-82 245 0246
E-mail: hiroanim@urban.or.jp
Website: www.city.hiroshima.jp
Festival director and programer: Sayoko Kinoshita
Competition: Grand Prix (¥1,000,000)

Hollywood Film Market
August 2000
433 North Camden Drive, #600, Beverly Hills,
    CA 90201, U.S.
Tel: +1-310 288 1882
Fax: +1-310 475 0193

. . . April 2 . . .
Turning Thomas Harris' novel **Hannibal**, his sequel to **The Silence of the Lambs**,
into a motion picture could cost as much as $100 million.

E-mail: awards@ hollywoodfestival.com
Website: www.hollywoodfestival.com
Contact: John Jacobson

International Festival of Tourist, Ecological, and Sport Films – Mefest (Zlatibor)
August 2000
Mefest c/o Film Danas, Bulevar Crvene Armije 38, 11 000 Beograd, Yugoslavia
Tel/fax: +381-11 430 837/444 5677
Festival director: Gavrilo Azinovic
Festival programer: Dinko Tucakovic
Competition: Golden Pine

International Festival "Window into Europe" (Vyborg)
August 2000
Chistoprudni Blvd. 12 A, Room 601, Moscow 123242, Russia
Tel: +7-095 924 8508
Fax: +7-095 924 1331/937 7025
Festival director: Sava Koulish
Competition

Love is Folly (Varna)
August 2000
31 Liuben Karavelov Strasse, Sofia 1000, Bulgaria
Tel: +359-2 665 564
Fax: +359-2 803 791
Festival director and programer: Alexander Grozev
Competition: Golden Aphrodita

Palm Springs International Short Film Festival
August 2000
1700 E. Tahquitz Cyn Way, Palm Springs, CA 92262, U.S.
Tel: +1-760 322 2930
Fax: +1-760 322 4087
E-mail: filmfest@ix.net.com
Executive director: Craig Prater
Artistic director: Paola Freccero
Market and Competition: Best of Festival ($1,000)

Sarajevo Film Festival
18-26 August 2000
Obala Kulina Bana 10, 71000 Sarajevo, Bosnia
Tel: +387-71 524 127/668 186
Fax: +387-71 664 547
Festival director: Mirsad Purivatra
Festival programer: Philippe Bober
Competition: Sarajevo Best Film Award

Urbanworld Film Festival
Early August 2000
375 Greenwich St. New York, NY 10013, U.S.
Tel: +1-212 941 3845
Fax: +1-212 941 3849
E-mail: aphill@aol.com
Festival director: Stacy Spikes
Market and Competition: Best Picture

Yugoslav Film Festival
August 2000
JUK Herceg-Fest, Dvorana Park, Njegoseva bb, 85340 Herceg-Novi, Yugoslavia
Tel: +381-88 22 098
Fax: +381-88 22004
Festival president: Dragan Jankovic
Festival programer: Zoran Zivkovic
Competition: Grand Prix

September

Deauville Festival of American Films
1-10 September 2000
36 rue Pierret, Neuilly 92200, France
Tel: +33-1 46 40 5500
Fax: +33-1 46 40 5539
E-mail: publics@imaginet.fr
Festival directors: Lionel Chouchan, Andre Halimi
Festival programer: Gerome Lesserre
Competition: Grand Prix "Special Deauville"

Latin American Film Festival
1-14 September 2000
79 Wardour St, London W1V 3TH, U.K.
Tel: +44-207 434 3357
Fax: +44-207 287 2112
Festival director and programer: Eva Tarr

Telluride Film Festival
1-4 September 2000
53 South Main St, Suite 212, Hanover, NH 03755, U.S.
Tel: +1-603 643 1255
Fax: +1-603 643 5938
E-mail: Tellufilm@aol.com
Website: www.telluridefilmfestival.com
Festival directors: Bill Pence, Tom Luddy

Internationales Filmfest Oldenburg
6-10 September 2000
Bahnhof Strasse 15, Oldenburg 26122, Germany
Tel: +49-441 925 0855

... April 3 ...
Cameron Diaz is to join Drew Barrymore in **Charlie's Angels**, for the
Columbia feature adaptation of the '70s private-eye series.

Fax: +49-441 925 0856
E-mail: tnt@filmfest-oldenburg.de
Festival director: Torsten Neumann

Toronto International Film Festival
7-16 September 2000
2 Carlton St, Suite 1600, Toronto, Ontario M5B 1J3,
  Canada
Tel: +1-416 967 7371
Fax: +1-416 967 9477
E-mail: tiffg@torfilm fest.ca
Website: www.bell.ca/toronto/filmfest
Contact: Piers Handling
Competition: Audience Award and Air Canada
  People's Choice Award

Focus on Asia Fukuoka International Film Festival
8-17 September 2000
c/o Fukuoka City Hall, 1-8-1 Tenjin, Chuo-ku,
  Fukuoka 810-8620, Japan
Tel: +81-92 733 5170
Fax: +81-92 733 5595
E-mail: info@focus-on-asia.com
Website: www.focus-on-asia.com
Festival director and programer: Tadao Sato

**International Broadcasting Convention,
Amsterdam**
8-12 September 2000
IBC Office, Savoy Place, London WC2R 0BL, U.K.
Tel: +44-207 240 3839
Fax: +44-207 240 3724
E-mail: show@ibc.org.uk
Website: www/ibc.org.uk/ibc/
Contact: Sharon Chapman

**Lucas – International Film Festival for Children
and Young People**
11-17 September 2000
Deutsches Filmmuseum, Schaumainkai 41, D-60596
  Frankfurt am Main, Germany
Tel: +49-69 2123 8833
Fax: +49-69 2123 7881
E-mail: direktion@deutsches-filmmuseum.de
Website: www.deutsches-filmmuseum.de
Festival director: Prof. W. Schobert
Festival programer: Dr. V. Kull
Competition: Lucas Awards (DM5,000 each)

Short Cuts Cologne
13-17 September 2000
c/o Kölner Filmhaus, Maybachstr. 111, 50670 Köln,
  Germany

Tel: +49-221 222 71027
Fax: +49-221 222 71099
E-mail: scc@k-filmhouse.de
Website: www.k-filmhaus.de
Festival director: Stefan Sarasi
Competition: Jury Award and Audience Award

Atlantic Film Festival
15-23 September 2000
c/o CBC 5600 Sackville St, Halifax, Nova Scotia B3J
  3E9, Canada (PO Box 36139)
Tel: +1-902 422 3456
Fax: +1-902 422 4006
E-mail: festival@atlanticfilm.com
Festival director: Gordon Whittaker
Festival programer: Lia Rinaldo
Market and Competition: People's Choice Award

Festival of Fantastic Films (Manchester)
15-17 September 2000
33 Barrington Rd, Altrincham, Cheshire,
  WA14 1H2, U.K.
Tel: +44-161 929 1423
Fax: +44-161 929 1067
Festival director: Gil Lane Young
Festival programer: Harry Nadler
Competition: Award for Best Film

Independent Feature Film Market
15-22 September 2000
104 West 29th St, 12th Floor, New York, NY 10001-
  5310, U.S.
Tel: +1-212 465 8200
Fax: +1-212 465 8525
E-mail: IFPNY@ifp.org
Website: www.ift.org
Festival director: Milton Tabbot
Market: Gordon Parks Independent Film Award
  ($10,000, sponsored by MTV Films)

Umeå International Film Festival
15-20 September 2000
PO Box 43, 90102 Umeå, Sweden
Tel: +46-90 133388
Fax: +46-90 777961
E-mail: info@ff.umea.com
Website: www.ff.umea.com
Festival director: Thom Palmen

Arsenals International Film Forum
16-24 September 2000
PO Box 1626, Märstalu 14, Riga, Latvia LV 1047
Tel: +371-721 0114/722 1620

Fax: +371-782 0445
E-mail: arsenals@ latnet.lv
Website: vip.latnet.lv/arsenals
Festival director: Benita Sarma
Festival programers: Ieva Pitruka, Zaneta Vegnere,
  Anna Rozenvalde

Drama Short Film Festival
17-23 September 2000
Em Bena Ki 71, Athens, Greece
Tel: +30-1 330 2818
Fax: +30-1 330 0309
E-mail: Kinfest@dra.Forthnet.org
Website: www.dramafilmfest.gr
Festival director and programer: Antonis
  Papandopoulos
Competition and Market
Grand Prix (Dr1 million)

Cinefest – The Sudbury International Film Festival
18-24 September 2000
Suite 218, 40 Elm St, Sudbury, Ontario PC3 1S8,
  Canada
Tel: +1-705 688 1234
Fax: +1-705 688 1351
E-mail: cinefest@vianet.on.ca
Website: www.cinefest.com
Executive director and programer: Tammy Frick
Competition: Best Canadian Film ($5,000)

Festival Cinéma Tout Ecran
18-24 September 2000
Maison des Arts du Grütli, 16 rue du Général
  Dufour, Case postale 5305, CH_1211 Genève 11,
  Switzerland
Tel: +41-22 328 8554
Fax: +41-22 329 6809
E-mail: info@cinema-tout-ecran.ch
Festival director: Leo Kaneman
Festival programer: Stéphanie Billeter
Competition: Grand Prix (SFr10,000)

Ottawa International Animation Festival
19-24 September 2000
2 Daly Ave, Suite 140, Ottawa, Ontario K1N 6E2,
  Canada
Tel:+1-613 232 8769
Fax: +1-613 232-6315
E-mail: oiaf@ottawa.com
Website: www.awn.com/ottawa
Festival director: Chris Robinson
Market and Competition: Grand Prize

Fantasy Film Festival
20-24 September 2000
Stora Varvsgatan 11 K1, SE-21119 Malmö, Sweden
Tel: +46-40 122 266
Fax: +46-40 122 264
E-mail: info@fff.se
Website: www.fff.se
Festival director: Magnus Paulsson
Festival programer: Magnus Bjarne
Competition: Jury's Award for Best Feature

Netherlands Film Festival
20-29 September 2000
PO Box 1581, 3500 BN Utrecht, The Netherlands
Tel: +31-30 232 2684
Fax: +31-30 213 3200
E-mail: nedfilmfest@inter.nl.net
Website: www.filmfestival.nl
Festival director: Jacques van Heyningen
Festival programer: Herman de Wit
Market and Competition: Golden Calf ($10,000)

Helsinki Film Festival – Love and Anarchy
21 September-1 October 2000
Unioninkatu 10, FIN-00130 Helsinki, Finland
Tel: +358-9 684 35230
Fax: +358-9 684 35232
E-mail: lanerva@heff.fi
Website: www.heff.fi
Festival director: Pekka Lanerva

San Sebastián International Film Festival
21-30 September 2000
Plaza de Oqendo s/n, 20004 San Sebastián, Spain
Tel: +34-43 48 12 12
Fax: +34-43 48 12 18
Festival director: Diego Galan
Market and Competition: Golden Shell

Bite the Mango Film Festival
22-30 September 2000
National Museum of Photography, Film, and TV,
  Pictureville, Bradford, BD1 1NQ, U.K.
Tel: +44-1274 725 347
Fax: +44-1274 723 155
E-mail: c.sawhney@nmsi.ac.uk or fell@nmsi.ac.uk
Festival director: Bill Lawrence
Festival programer: Irsan Ajeeb
Market: (Trade Festival of South Asian and Black
  Film and TV)

Festival International du Film Francophone
22-30 September 2000

---

175 rue des Brasseurs, B-5000 Namur, Belgium
Tel: +32-81 24 12 36
Fax: +32-81 22 43 84
E-mail: dany.martin-fiff@skynet.be
Website: www.martin.fiff.namur.be
Festival director and programer: Dany Martin
Market and Competition: Golden Bayard for Best
 Film (BFr50,000)

International Festival of New Film and Video
23-30 September 2000
Zagrebacka 35A, PO Box 244, 21000 Split, Croatia
Tel/fax: +385-21 52 59 25
E-mail: split.filmfest@st.tel.hr
Festival director: Branko Karabatic
Competition: Grand Prix

Holland Film Meeting
22-25 September 2000
PO Box 1581, 3500 BN, Utrecht, The Netherlands
Tel: +31-30 232 2684
Fax: +31-30 213 3200
Festival director: Jacques van Heijningen
Competition and Market: Golden Calf Awards

New York Film Festival
22 September-8 October 2000
Film Society of Lincoln Center, 70 Lincoln Center
 Plaza, New York, NY 10023, U.S.
Tel: +1-212 875 5638
Fax: +1-212 875 5610
Website: www.film.linc.com
Festival director: Richard Peña

Vancouver International Film Festival
22 September-8 October 2000
Suite 410, 1008 Homer St, Vancouver V6B 2X1,
 Canada
Tel: +1-604 685 0260
Fax: +1-604 688 8221
E-mail: viff@viff.org
Website: www.viff.org
Festival director: Alan Franey
Festival programer: PoChu AuYeung
Competition: Air Canada Award for Most Popular Film

Panorama of European Cinema
23 September-8 October 2000
Minoos 10-16, 11743 Athens, Greece
Tel: +30-1 929 96001
Fax: +30-1 902 8311
Director: Ninos Mikeldhs
Competition

Film Camera Festival Manaki Brothers (Bitola)
25 September-1 October 2000
Vardar-Film 8 Mart 4, 91000 Skopje, Macedonia
Tel: +389-91 117527/116626
Fax: +389-91 132 150/117 038
E-mail: ffmanaki@unet.com.mk
Festival director: Delco Mihajlov
Festival programer: Blagoja Kunevski
Competition: Golden Camera 300

FilmFest Hamburg
25 September-1 October 2000
Friedensallee 44, D-22765 Hamburg, Germany
Tel: +49-40 399 19000
Fax: +49-40 399 190010
E-mail: filmfest-hamburg @t-online.de
Website: www.filmfesthamburg.de
Festival director: Josef Wutz
Festival programer: Johannes Wachs

Screens on the Bay (Amalfi)
27-29 September 2000
Sacis, Via Teulada 66, 00195 Roma, Italy
Tel: +39-6 3749 8269
Fax: +39-6 370 1343
Contact: Dino Pirretti

MIPCOM JUNIOR (Cannes)
30 September-1 October 2000
Reed Midem Organisation, BP 572, 11 rue du
 Colonel Pierre Avia, 75726 Paris, Cédex 15, France
Tel: +33-1 41 90 45 80
Fax: +33-1 41 90 45 70
Program director: André Vaillant

Aspen Film Fest
September 2000
110 E Hallam, Suite 102, Aspen, CO 81611, U.S.
Tel: +1-970 925 6882
Fax: +1-970 925 1967
E-mail: Ithielen@aspenfilm.org
Festival director: Laura Thielen

Athens International Film Festival
September 2000
Benaki St, 15235 Halandri, Athens, Greece
Tel: +30-1 606 1363/606 1428
Fax: +30-1 601 4137
Festival director: George Tziotzios
Festival programers: George Krassakopoulos, Leda
 Galanou
Competition: Audience Award (Dr2 million)

...April 6...
Abba musical **Mamma Mia** opens in London 25 years to the
day that the group won the Eurovision Song Contest.

BBC British Short Film Festival
September 2000
BBC British Short Film Festival, BBC Television Centre,
  Room A 214, 56 Wood Lane, London W12 7SB, U.K.
Tel: +44-208 743 8000 ext. 62222
Fax: +44-208 740 8540
Festival director and programer: Amanda Casson
Competition: Awards for Best British and Best
  International Productions (£1,000 each)

Breckenridge Festival of Film
September 2000
P.O. Box 718, Riverwalk Center, 150 W. Admas,
  Breckenridge, CO 80424, U.S.
Tel: +1-970 453 6200
Fax: +1-970 453 2692
E-mail: filmfest@brecknet.com
Festival director: Julie Bullock
Festival programer: Terese Keil
Competition

Empire State Exhibitions Film and Video Fest
September 2000
PO Box 177, Mohawk, NY 13407, U.S.
Tel: +1-212 802 4679
Fax: +1-518 581 7614
E-mail: Empirefilm@aol.com
Website: members.aol.com/empirefilm/festival
Festival directors and programers: Michael J
  Zimmerman, Jon Galt
Competition: The "Essey" Award

Festival de Cinéma Internationale Ste-Thérèse/ Ste-Adèle (Ste-Thérèse et Ste-Adèle)
September 2000
34 rue Blainville Ouest, Sainte-Thérèse, Québec
  J7E 1W9, Canada
Tel: +1-514 434 0387
Fax: +1-514 434 7868
E-mail: festival@ odyssee.net
Festival director: André Marion
Festival programer: Frédéric Lapierre
Competition: Best Film Award ($1,000)

Festival Internacional de Cinema (Figueira da Foz)
September 2000
Apartado dos Correios 50407, 1709 Lisboa Codex,
  Portugal
Tel: +351-1 812 6231
Fax: +351-1 812 6228
Festival director: José Viera Marques
Competition: Grande Premio da Figueira da Foz

International Festival of Film and Video for Children and Young Adults (Isfahan)
September 2000
Farhang Cinema, Dr. Shariati Ave, Gholhak, Tehran,
  Iran 19139
Tel: +98-21 200 2088/89/90
Fax: +98-21 267 082
Festival director: S Daad
Festival programer: Jamal Omid
Competition: Golden Butterfly ($1,200)

Mostra Internazionale d'Arte Cinematografica
September 2000
Cà Giustinian, S Marco 1364A, I-Venice 30124, Italy
Tel: +39-41 521 8878/8711
Fax: +39-41 522 7639
E-mail: das@labiennale.it
Website: www.labiennale.org
Festival director: Alberto Barbera
Festival programers: Silvia Menegazzi, Tiziana Finzi,
  Nadia Zande
Competition: Golden Lion Award

Rencontres d'Annecy du Cinéma Italien
September 2000
Bonlieu Scène Nationale, 1 rue Jean Jaurès, BP 294,
  Annecy 74007, France
Tel: +33-450 33 44 00
Fax: +33-450 51 82 09
Festival director: Salvador Garcia
Festival programer: Pierre Todeschini
Competition: Grand Prix des Rencontres

Sub Fiction – 3. Werkleitz Biennale
September 2000
Straße des Friedens 26, 39249, Torintz, Germany
Tel: +49-39298 6750
Fax: + 49-39298 675 55
Website: www.werkleitz.de/sub-fiction
Festival director: Peter Zorn

Showbiz Expo East (New York)
September 2000
383 Main Ave, Norwalk, CT 06951, U.S.
Tel: +1-203 840 5378
Fax: +1-203 840 9378
Contact: Joe Markam

Tacoma Tortured Artists Film Festival
September 2000
728A Pacific Ave, Tacoma, WA 98402, U.S.
Tel: +1-253 627 5932
Fax: +1-253 627 1525

... April 7 ...
Ted Turner's TNT and TBS to jointly shell out $70 million
for 35 pics from DreamWorks' first five years.

E-mail: TacomaFilm@aol.com
Festival director: James Hume
Competition: The Barbie Award ($1,500)

UFVA Student Film and Video Festival
September 2000
Department of Film and Media Arts, Temple
University 011-00, Philadelphia, PA 19122, U.S.
Tel: +1-215 923 3532
Fax: +1-215 204 6740
E-mail: ufva@vm.temple.edu
Website: thunder.ocis.temple.edu/~ddoyon
Festival director: Juan Carlos Rojas
Competition

**Videonale International Video and Media
Festival**
September 2000
Hochstadenring 22, 53 119
Bonn, Germany
Tel/fax: +49-228 69 28 18
Contacts: Ute Hörner, Judith Ruzicka
Competition

Yugoslav Feature Film Festival
September 2000
Zvezda Film, Trg Slobode 2, 21000 Novi Sad, Yugoslavia
Tel: +381-21 615 759
Fax: +381-21 613 759
Festival director: Pavle Milivojev
Competition: Zlatna Arena

October

Dokumentart – European Film Workshop
1-15 October 2000
Holm-Henning-Freier, Rasenstrasse 3, D-17033,
Neubrandenburg, Germany
Tel: +49-395 566 6610/6109
Fax: +49-395 566 6612
E-mail: latuecht@t-online.de
Festival director: Holm-Henning Freeier
Competition: Latücht-Preis (DM7,000)

MIPCOM (Cannes)
2-6 October 2000
BP 572, 11 rue du Colonel Pierre Avia, 75726 Paris,
Cédex 15, France
Tel: +33-1 41 90 45 80
Fax: +33-1 41 90 45 70
Market director: André Vaillant
Market

Mostra Rio – Rio de Janeiro Film Festival
4-18 October 2000
Rua Voluntários da Pátria 97, 22270-000 Botafogo,
Rio de Janeiro, Brazil
Tel: +55-21 539 1505
Fax: +55-21 539 1247
E-mail: ildasan@ibm.net
Website: www.estacao.com.br
Festival director: Nelson Krumholz
Festival programers: Marcelo Mendes, Ilda Santiago

Chicago International Film Festival
5-19 October 2000
32 West Randolph St, Suite 600, Chicago,
IL 60601, U.S.
Tel: +1-312 425 9400
Fax:+1-312 425 0944
E-mail: filmfest@wwa.com
Website: www.chicago.ddbn.com/filmfest/
Festival director: Michael J Kutza
Festival programers: Helen Gramates, Jim Healy,
Michael Kutza
Competition: The Gold Hugo Award

Festival du Film Britannique
2 Blvd Féart, 35800 Dinard, France
Tel: +33-299 88 19 04
Fax: +33-299 46 67 15
Festival director: Thierry de la Fournière
Competition: Hitchcock Award

Leeds International Film Festival
5-20 October 2000
The Town Hall, The Headrow, Leeds, LS1 3AD, U.K.
Tel: +44-113 247 8398
Fax: +44-113 247 8397
E-mail: filmfestival@leeds.gov.uk
Website: www.leedsfilm.com
Festival director: Liz Rymer

Mill Valley Film Festival
5-15 October 2000
38 Miller Ave, Suite 6, Mill Valley, CA 94941, U.S.
Tel: +1-415 383 5256/0990
Fax: +1-415 383 8606
Festival director: Mark Fishkin
Festival programer: Zoë Elton

Warsaw Film Festival
5-16 October 2000
PO Box 816, 00-950 Warsaw 1, Poland
Tel: +48-22 853 3636
Fax: +48-22 853 11 84

...April 8 ...
The Iceman Cometh opens on Broadway, notching some $5.4 million in advance sales.

E-mail: festiv@wff.org.pl
Festival director: Stefan Laudyn

Pusan International Film Festival
6-14 October 2000
Yachting Center, Room 208, # 1393 Woo 1 Dong,
    Haeundoc-Ku, Pusan, Korea 612021
Tel: +82-51 747 3010/1
Fax: +82-51 747 3012
E-mail: piffoo@chollian.net
Website: www.piff.org
Festival director: Kim Dong-Ho
Festival programers: Kim Ji-Seok, Jay Jeon,
    Lee yong-Kwan
Market

Wildscreen
7-13 October 2000
Deanery Rd, College Green, Bristol BS1 5DB, U.K.
Tel: +44-117 909 6300
Fax: +44-117 909 5000
E-mail: wildscreen@gn.apc.org
Website: www.wildscreen.org.uk
Festival director: Jane Krish
Competition: Golden Panda

Cork International Film Festival
8-15 October 2000
Hatfield House, Tobin St, Cork, Ireland
Tel: +353-21 271711
Fax: +353-21 275945
E-mail: ciff@indigo.ie
Website: www.corkfilmfest.org/ciff/
Artistic director: Michael Hannigan
Competition: European Short Film (Ecu7,500)

Bogotá Film Festival
10-18 October 2000
Calle 26 No. 4-92, Santa Fe de Bogotá, Colombia
Tel: +57-1 282 5196
Fax: +57-1 342 2872
E-mail: cidc@coll.telecom.com.co.
Festival director & programer: Henry Laguado
Competition: Golden PreColombian Circle ($1,500)

British Film Festival
10-17 October 2000
8 Passage Digard, F-50100 Cherbourg, France
Tel: +33-233 93 38 94
Fax: +33-233 01 20 78
Festival director and programer:
Competition: Audience Award (FFr20,000)

Flanders International Film Festival
10-21 October 2000
1104 Kortrijksesteenweg, B-9051 Ghent, Belgium
Tel: +32-9 221 8946
Fax: +32-9 221 9074
E-mail: info@filmfestival.be
Website: www.filmfestival.be
Festival director: Jacques Dubrulle
Festival programer: Walter Provo
Competition: Grand Prix of the Flemish Community
    for Best Film (EUR24,790)

Austin Film Festival and Heart of Film Screenwriters
12-19 October 2000
AHFF Inc, 1600 Nueces, Austin, TX 78701, U.S.
Tel: +1-512 478 4795
Fax: +1-512 478 6205
E-mail: austinfilm@aol.com
Website: www.austinfilmfestival.work
Festival directors: Barbara Morgan, Marsha Milam
Competition and Market: Bronze Award ($750 for
    feature film)

Chicago International Children's Film Festival
12-22 October 2000
Facets Multimedia, 1517 West Fullerton Ave,
    Chicago, IL 60614, U.S.
Tel: +1-773 281 9075
Fax: +1-773 929 5437
E-mail: kidsfest@facets.org
Festival director and programer: Rebekah Cowing
Competition: Grand Prize ($2,500)

Denver International Film Festival
12-19 October 2000
1430 Larimer Square, Suite 201, Denver,
    CO 80202, U.S.
Tel: +1-303 595 3456
Fax: +1-303 595 0956
E-mail: DenverFilm@csn.net
Festival director: Ron Henderson

Films from the South
13-22 October 2000
Fimens Hus, Dronningens Gate 16, N-0152, Oslo,
    Norway
Tel: +47-22 47 45 00
Fax: +47-22 47 46 90

International Film Festival Mannheim-Heidelberg
13-21 October 2000

... April 9 ...
Shakespeare in Love was named Best Film, but **Elizabeth** won the
most prizes at the 51st British Academy of Film Awards.

Collini-Center, Galerie, D-68161 Mannheim, Germany
Tel: +49-621 102943
Fax: +49-621 291564
E-mail: ifmh@mannheim-filmfestival.com
Website: www.mannheim-filmfestival.com
Festival director: Dr Michael Koetz
Market and Competition: International Independent
  Award (DM30,000)

Raindance Film Showcase
13-26 October 2000
81 Berwick St, London W1V 3PF, U.K.
Tel: +44-207 287 3833
Fax: +44-207 439 2243
Website: www: ftech.net/n ind film
Festival director: Elliot Grove
Festival programer: Suzanne Ballantyne
Market

Viennale
13-25 October 2000
Stiftgasse 6, A-1070 Vienna, Austria
Tel: +43-1 526 5947
Fax: +43-1 523 4172
E-mail: organisation@viennale.or.at
Festival director and programer: Alex Horwath
Competition: Fipresci Prize

Le Giornate del Cinema Muto (Sacile)
14-21 October 2000
c/o Cineteca del Friuli, Palazzo Gurisatti, Via G. Bini,
  I-33013 Gemona, Italy
Tel: +39-0432 980458
Fax: +39-0432 970542
E-mail: gcm@proxima.conecta.it
Website: www/cinetacadelfriuli.org/gcm/
Festival director: David Robinson
Market

Haifa International Film Festival
14-21 October 2000
142, Hanassi Ave, Haifa, Israel 34633
Tel: +972-4 835 3522
Fax: +972-4 838 4327
Contact: Eliane Aurbach
Competition: The "Golden Anchor" Award for
  Mediterranean Films (NIS75,000)

Prix Europa Berlin
14-21 October 2000
SFB, Berlin 14046, Germany
Tel: +49-30 30 31 1610
Fax: +49-30 30 31 1619

Festival director: PL Braun
Festival programer: Susanne Hoffmann
Competition: Prix Europa TV Programme of the
  Year (Fiction)

Sheffield International Documentary Festival
16-22 October 2000
The Workstation, 15 Paternoster Row, Sheffield,
  S1 2BX, U.K.
Tel: +44-114 276 5141
Fax: +44-114 272 1849
E-mail: info@sidf.co.uk
Festival director: Kathy Loizou
Festival programer: Alex Cooke

Uppsala International Short Film Festival
16-22 October 2000
PO Box 1746, S-751 47 Uppsala, Sweden
Tel: +46-18 12 00 25
Fax: +46-18 12 13 50
E-mail: uppsala@shortfilmfestival.com
Festival director: Åsa Garnert
Festival programer: Christopher Olofsson
Competition: Uppsala Grand Prix (SKr25,000)

Lesbian and Gay Film Festival
17-22 October 2000
Schanzenstr. 45, 20357 Hamburg, Germany
Tel: +49-40 348 0670
Fax: +49-40 34 05 22
Festival programers: Joachim Post, Astrid Lüder,
  Ronald Behm
Competition

Kudzu Film Festival
18-21 October 2000
P.O. Box 1461, Athens, GA 30603, U.S.
Tel: +1-706 227 6090
Fax: +1-706 227 6090

Ökomedia-International Ecology Film Festival
18-22 October 2000
Ökomedia Institut, Habsburger Strasse 9a, 79104
  Freiburg, Germany
Tel: +49-761 52024
Fax: +49-761 555 724
Festival director: Werner Kobe
Competition

Heartland Film Festival
19-29 October 2000
613 N. East St, Indianapolis, IN 46202, U.S.
Tel: +1-317-464 9405

...April 10...
James Cameron's **Titanic** continued to solidify its hold on the mass-American audience,
racking up huge 18.3 ratings in HBO homes during its pay-TV bow.

Fax: +1-317 635 4201
E-mail: hff@pop.iquest.net
Festival director and programer: Jeffrey L. Sparks
Competition: Crystal Heart Award ($100,000)

Bergen International Film Festival
20-27 October 2000
Georgernes verft 3, N-5011 Bergen, Norway
Tel: +47-55 32 25 90
Fax: +47-55 32 37 40
E-mail: tiff@bgnett.no
Festival director: Tor Fosse
Competition

Fort Lauderdale International Film Festival
20 October-14 November 2000
2633 East Sunrise Blvd, Fort Lauderdale, FL 33304-
    3205, U.S.
Tel: +1-954 760 9898
Fax: +1-954 760 9099
E-mail: brofilm@aol.com
Website: www.ftlaudfilmfest.com
Festival director and programer: Greg von Hausch
Competition: Best Film Award

Valladolid International Film Festival
20-28 October 2000
PO Box 646, 47080 Valladolid, Spain
Tel: +34-83 305700/305777
Fax: +34-83 309835
E-mail: festvalladolid@seminci.com
Website: www.seminci.com
Festival director: Fernando Lara
Festival coordinator: Denise O'Keefe
Competition: Golden Spike (Pta3 million)

Cinekid
21-30 October 2000
Weteringschaus 249, NL-1017 XY Amsterdam,
    The Netherlands
Tel: +31-20 624 7110
Fax: +31-20 620 9965
E-mail: englzx@xsyall.nl
Festival director: Sannatte Naeye
Festival programer: Harry Peters
Competition: Cinekid Award (DFl5,000)

International Film Festival "Molodist"
21-29 October 2000
6 Saksagansky Strasse, Kiev, Ukraine, 252033
Tel: +380-44 246 6798
Fax: +380-44 227 4557
E-mail: molodist@gu.kiev.ua

Festival director: Andrei Khalpakhtchi
Festival programer: Alexander Shpilyuk
Competition: Scythian Deer ($10,000)

Kinofilm
23-29 October 2000
48 Princess St, Manchester M1 6HR, U.K.
Tel: +44-161 288 2494
Fax: +44-161 237 3423
Festival director and programer: John Wojowski

London Premiere Screenings
23-27 October 2000
23-24 George St, Richmond, Surrey TW3 1HY, U.K.
Tel: +44-208 948 5522
Fax: +44-208 332 0495
Festival director: Tim Etchells
Market

International Hofer Filmtage
24-29 October 2000
Loth Strasse 28, D-80335 Munich, Germany
Tel: +49-89 129 7422
Fax: +49-89 129 6868
E-mail: info@hofer-filmtage.de
Website: www.hofer-filmtage.de
Festival director and programer: Heinz Badewitz

Cinéma Meditérranéen Montpellier
27 October-5 November 2000
78 Avenue du Pirée, F-34000 Montpellier, France
Tel: +33-4 99 13 73 73
Fax: +33-4 99 13 73 74
E-mail: cinemed@mnet.fr
Website: www.cinemed.tm.fr
Festival director and programer: Pierre Pitiot
Competition: Antigone d'Or ($20,000)

**Festival du Cinéma International en Abitibi-
Témiscamingue (Rouyn-Noranda)**
28 October-2 November 2000
215 Mercier Ave, Rouyn-Noranda, Québec J9X 5W8,
    Canada
Tel: +1-819 762 6212
Fax: +1-819 762 6762
E-mail: fciatt@sympatico.ca
Website: www.telebec.qc.ca/fciat
Festival director and programer: Jacques Matte

Mifed
29 October-2 November 2000
EA Fiera Milano, Largo Domodossola 1, I-20145
    Milano, Italy

...April 11 ...
The Matrix continues to dominate the U.S. B.O. with a
commanding $30.2 million in its second full week.

Tel: +39-2 48 01 29 12/48 01 29 20/48 01 29 42
Fax: +39-2 49 97 70 20
E-mail: mifed @fnd.it
Director: Tullio Galleno
Market

Banff Mountain Film Festival
30 October-5 November 2000
PO Box 1020, Stn 38, Banff, Alberta T0L 0C0,
   Canada
Tel: +1-403 762 6125
Fax: +1-403 762 6277
E-mail: cmc@banffcentre.ab.ca
Website: www.banffcentre.ab.ca/CMC/
Festival director and programer: Bernadette
   McDonald
Market and Competition: Grand Prize (C$12,500)

AFI Los Angeles International Film Festival
October 2000
2021 N. Western Ave, Los Angeles, CA 90027, U.S.
Tel: +1-213 856 7707
Fax: +1-213 462 4049
E-mail: afifest@afionline.org
Festival director: Jon Fitzgerald
Festival programer: Nancy Collet
Competition: Grand Jury Prize/The Studio Prize
   ($20,000)

The Athens Film Festival
October 2000
PO Box 1631, Athens, GA 30603, U.S.
Tel: +1-706 613 7669
Fax: +1-706 613 0959
E-mail: gafilm@negia.net
Festival director: Juanita M Giles
Festival programer: Todd Campbell
Competition: The Kudzu Award

Black Filmworks Festival of Film and Video
October 2000
Black Filmmakers Hall of Fame, 405 14th St, Suite
   515, Oakland, CA 94612, U.S.
Tel: +1-510 465 0804
Fax: +1-510 839 9858
Contact: Felix Curtis
Market and Competition: Best Film ($1,000)

**Canadian International Annual
Film/Video Festival**
(Campbell River, British Columbia)
October 2000
25 Eugenia St, Barrie, Ontario L4M 1P6, Canada

Tel: +1-705 737 2729
Fax: +1-705 733 8232
E-mail: ciaff@canada.com
Festival director: Ben VW Andrews
Festival programer: Kevin Harrison
Competition: Best Amateur, Best Student, Best
   Independent

European Cable Communications
October 2000
The Cable Communications Association, 5th Floor,
   Artillery House, Artillery Row, London SW1P
   1RT, U.K.
Tel: +44-207 222 2900
Fax: +44-207 799 1471
Contact: Sharon Chapman

Feminale Women's Film Festival
October 2000
Hansaring 86, D-50670 Cologne, Germany
Tel: +49-221 130 0225
Fax: +49-221 130 0281
Festival director: Katja Mildenberger
Festival programers: Verena Mundt, Katja
   Mildenberger, Carla D'Espineux

**FCMM (Montreal International Festival of
Cinema and New Media)**
October 2000
3668 Blvd St-Laurent, Montréal, Québec H2X 2V4,
   Canada
Tel: +1-514 843 4725
Fax: +1-514 843 4631
E-mail: montrealfest@fcmm.com
Festival director and programer: Claude Chamberlan

Film and Music Fest
October 2000
Körnerstrasse 3, 33602 Bielefeld, Germany
Tel: +49-521 677 43
Fax: +49-521 677 27
E-mail: eisenstein.filmfestival@t-online-de
Festival director: Prof. Johnen Kurt

Geneva Film Festival "Stars of Tomorrow"
October 2000
35 rue des Bains, CP 5615, CH-1211 Genève 11,
   Switzerland
Tel: +41-22 809 9450
Fax: +41-22 809 9444
Festival director and programer: Gérald Morin
Competition: European Golden Star
   (SFr10,000 each)

The Golden Chest International TV Festival
October 2000
29 San Stefano Str., Sofia, 1000, Bulgaria
Tel: +359-2 946 1034/963 3095
Fax: +359-2 946 1034
Festival director: Valentin Stoyanov
Competition: Grand Prix "Golden Chest"

Golden Knight International Amateur Film and Video Festival
October 2000
Malta Amateur Cine Circle, PO Box 450, Valletta CMR 01, Malta
Tel: +356-222345
Fax: +356-225047
Website: www.global/net.mt/amacc
Festival director: Alfred Stagno Navarra
Festival programer: Vincent Lungaro Mifsud
Competition: Golden Knight

The Golden Rhyton
October 2000
2-A Dondukov Blvd, Sofia 1000, Bulgaria
Tel: +359-2 987 4096/883 831
Fax: +359-2 873 626
E-mail: nfc@mail.bol.bg
Festival director: Dimitar Dereliev
Competition: Grand Prix

The Hamptons International Film Festival
October 2000
3 Newtown Mews, East Hampton, NY 11937, U.S.
Tel: +1-516 324 4600
Fax: +1-516 324 5116
E-mail: hiff@peconic.net
Festival director: Denise Kasell
Festival programers: David Schwartz, Deena Juras, Linda Blackaby, Lynda Hanse
Competition: Golden Starfish Award ($200,000)

IBTS
(International Audio, Video, Broadcasting, Motion Picture and Telecommunications Show)
October 2000 or 2001. It is a biannual event; it may become annual
Via Domenichino 11, 20149, Milan, Italy
Tel: +39-2 481 5541
Fax: +39-2 498 0330
E-mail: mc1703@mclink.it

International Festival of New Film and Video
October 2000
Zagrebacka 35A, PO Box 244, 21000 Split, Croatia
Tel/fax: +385-21 52 59 25
E-mail: split.filmfest@st.tel.hr
Festival director: Branko Karabatic
Competition: Grand Prix

International Leipzig Festival for Documentary and Animated Film
October 2000
PO Box 0940, D-04009 Leipzig, Germany
Tel: +49-341 980 3921
Fax: +49-341 980 6141
Festival director and programer: Fred Gehler
Market and Competition: Golden Dove (DM9,000)

International Short Film Festival
October 2001
Calle de Santa Maria 10, Bajors, 08700 Igualada, Spain
Tel/fax: +34-93 803 4439
Festival director: Miquel Segura
Competition: Grand Award "Miquel Pique" (Pta500,000)

Kidscreen (Milan)
October 2000
Rue des Palais 112, B-1030 Brussels, Belgium
Tel: +32-2 242 5409
Fax: +32-2 242 7427
Market director: Felix van Ginderhuysen
Market

London Programme Market
October 2000
23-24 George St, Richmond, Surrey TW9 1HY, U.K.
Tel: +44-208 948 5522
Fax: +44-208 332 0495
Market director: Jonathan Bainbridge

Mostra de Valencia/Cinema de Mediterrani
October 2000
Plaza del Arzobispo, 2 Bajo, 46003 Valencia, Spain
Tel: +34-96 392 1506
Fax: +34-96 391 5156
Festival director: Luís Fernández
Festival programer: Elena Escriba
Competition: Palmera de Oro (Pta3 million)

New Orleans Film and Video Festival
October 2000
PO Box 50819, New Orleans, 70150 LA, U.S.
Tel: +1-504 523 3818
Fax: +1-504 529 2430
Festival director: Carol Gniady

... April 13 ...
The Peacock pulls the plug on **Another World**, its 35-year-old daytime soap stalwart.

Festival programer: John Despias
Competition: Lumiere Awards

Noosa International Film Festival
October 2000
PO Box 828, Bondi Junction, NSW 1355, Australia
Tel: +61-2 9360 5384
Fax: +61-2 9360 7893
E-mail: noosafilmfest@net.au
Website: www.noosafilmfestival.com
Festival director: Luke Davis

Peachtree International Film Festival (Atlanta)
October 2000
Peachtree International Film Society, 2180 Pleasant
  Hill Rd, #A-5221, Duluth, GA 30096, U.S.
Tel:+1-770 729 8487
Fax: +1-770 263 0652
E-mail: film@peachtreefilm.org
Festival director and programer: Michelle Forren

San Juan Cinemafest
October 2000
PO Box 4543, San Juan, Puerto Rico 00902-4543
Tel: +1-787 721 6125
Fax: +1-787 723 6412
E-mail: JMV333@aol.com
Festival director: Gabriel Suau
Festival programer: Dominique Borrell
Competition: Pitirre

San Luis Obispo International Film Festival
October 2000
PO Box 1449, San Luis Obispo, CA 93401, U.S.
Tel: +1-805 546 3456
Fax: +1-805 781 6799
E-mail: slofilmfest@slonet.org
Festival director: Mary A Harris
Festival programer: Catherine Peacock
Competition: George Sydney Award ($500)

Santa Fe de Bogotà Festival
October 2000
Calle 26, No. 4-92, Santa Fe de Bogotà, Colombia
Tel: +57-1 282 5196
Fax: +57-1 342 2872
Festival director: Henry Laguado
Festival programer: Camilla Lobo-Guerrera

Saint Louis International Film Festival
October 2000
55 Maryland Plaza, Suite A, Saint Louis, 63108-1501
  MS, U.S.

Tel: +1-314 454 0042
Fax: +1-314 454 0540
E-mail: info@sliff.org
Festival director: Delcia Corlew
Festival programer: Audrey Hutti
Competition: "The Mark Twain Banks" Audience
  Choice Award ($1,000)

São Paolo International Film Festival
October 2000
Al. Lorena 937 Cj.303, 01424-001 São Paolo, Brasil
Tel: +55-11 883 5137/30645819
Fax: +55-11 853 7936
E-mail: info@mostra.org
Website: http://www.mostra.org.
Festival director: Leon Cakoff
Festival programers: Leon Cakoff, Renata de Almeida
Market and Competition: Bandeira Paulista Trophy

ShowEast (Orlando)
October 2000
244 West 49th St, #200, New York, NY 10019, U.S.
Tel: +1-212 246 6460
Fax: +1-212 265 6428
Festival directors: Robert and Jimmy Sunshine

Sitges International Fantasy Film Festival
October 2000
Rossello 257 3-E, 08008 Barcelona, Spain
Tel:+34-3 415 3938
Fax: +34-3 237 6521
E-mail: cinsit@arrakis.es
Festival director: Roc Billas
Competition: Best Film Award

Tokyo International Film Festival
Late October/early November 2000
Landic Building No. 2, Ginza, Chuo-ku, Tokyo 104,
  Japan
Tel: +81-3 3563 6305
Fax: +81-3 3563 6310
Festival director: Yasuyoshi Tokuma
Competition: 1.Tokyo Grand Prix – International
  Competition. 2. Tokyo Gold Prize – Young
  Cinema Competition (¥20 million)

Vevey International Comedy Film Festival
October 2000
La Grenette CP 421, 1800 Vevey, Switzerland
Tel: +41-21 925 8032
Fax: +41-21 922 2024
Festival director and programer: Yves Moser
Competition: Golden Cane (SFr6,000)

... April 14 ...
Anthony Newley, the British singer, playwright, composer, and lyricist, dies of cancer.

VIPER – International Film, Video, and Multimedia Festival
October 2000
PO Box 4929, CH-6002 Lucerne, Switzerland
Tel: +41-1 450 6262
Fax: +41-1 450 6261
E-mail: viper@dial.eunet.ch
Festival director and programer: Conny E Voester
Competition: Film Award, Video Award (SF5,000 each)

Virginia Film Festival
Late October
Drama Department, The University of Virginia, Culbreth Rd, Charlottesville, VA 22903, U.S.
Tel: +1-804 982 5277
Fax: +1-804 924 1447
Website: www.virginia.edu/~vafilm
Festival director: Richard Herskowitz

Yamagata International Documentary Film Festival
October 2000
YIDFF, Tokyo Office, Kitagawa Bldg, 4th Fl, 6-42 Kagurazaka, Shinjuku-ku, Tokyo 1620825, Japan
Tel: +81-33266 9704
Fax: +81-33266 9700
E-mail: yidff@bekkoame.ne.jp
Festival director: Yano Kazuyuki
Festival programers: Ono Seiko, Fujioka Asako
Competition: The Grand Prize (The Robert and Frances Flaherty Prize) (¥3,000,000)

November

Cottbus 8th Festival of Young East European Cinema
1-5 November 2000
Bautzner Straße 91, D-03050 Cottbus, Germany
Tel: +49-355 431070
Fax: +49-355 4310 720
Artistic director: Roland Rust
Competition

London Film Festival
2-16 November 2000
National Film Theatre, South Bank, Waterloo, London SE1 8XT, U.K.
Tel: +44-207 815 1322/1323
Fax: +44-207 633 0786
E-mail: sarah.lutton@bfi.org.uk
Website: www.iff.org.uk

Festival director: Adrian Wootton
Deputy director: Sandra Hebron
Competition: Pipresci Jury/Sutherland Prize

Nordic Film Days
2-5 November 2000
Schildstrasse 12, 23552 Lübeck, Germany
Tel: +49-451 122 4102/519
Fax: +49-451 122 4106
E-mail: info@filmtage.luebeck.de
Website: http://filmtage.luebeck.de
Festival director: Andrea Kunsemüller
Competition: NDR Promotion Prize (DM25,000)

Children's Film Festival
3-12 November 2000
Schroeckstr. 6, D-86152 Augsburg, Germany
Tel: +49-821 349 1060
Fax: +49-821 349 5218
Festival director and programer: Ellen Gratza

Hawaii International Film Festival
3-12 November 2000
1001 Bishop St, Pacific Tower, Suite 745, Honolulu, HI 96813, U.S.
Tel: +1-808 528 3456
Fax: +1-808 528 1410
E-mail: hiffinfo@hiff.org
Website: www.hiff.org
Festival director and programer: Christian Gaines
Competition: First Hawaiian Bank Golden Maile Award

Northwest Film and Video Festival
3-10 November 2000
1219 SW Park Ave, Portland, OR 97205, U.S.
Tel: +1-503 221 1156
Fax: +1-503 294 0874
E-mail: info@nwfilm.org
Festival director: Meagan Atiyeh
Competition: Best of Festival ($12,000 in production service awards)

Siena Short Film Festival
Via in Selci 84/A, 00184 Roma, Italy
Tel: +39-06 474 5585
Fax: +39-06 478 85799
E-mail: filmclub@pronet.it
Website: www.comune.siena.it/film/corto.htm
Festival director: Piero Clemente
Festival programer: Barbara Bialkowska
Competition: Best Short Film (L5 million)

. . . April 15 . . .
DreamWorks Pictures pays $1 million for the film rights to **The Fountain Society**, debut novel of **Scream** director Wes Craven, for ImageMovers to produce.

Worldfest – Flagstaff
3-12 November 2000
PO Box 56568, Houston, TX, U.S.
Tel: +1-713 965 9955
Fax: +1-713 965 9960
E-mail: worldfest@aol.com
Website: vannevar.com/worldfest
Festival director: J. Hunter Todd
Festival programer: Maribel Amador
Market and Competition: Golden Palm

SporTel (Monte Carlo)
5-8 November 2000
4 Blvd de Jardin Exotique, MC-98000 Monaco, Monaco
Tel: +377-93 30 20 32
Fax: +377-93 30 20 33
Director: David Tomatis
Market and Competition: Golden Podium Trophy
   (FFr30,000)

Duisburger Filmwoche
6-12 November 2000
Am König-Heinrich-Platz, D-47049 Duisburg,
   Germany
Tel: +49-203 283 4171
Fax: +49-203 283 4130
E-mail: filmwoche.vhs@duisburg.de
Festival director: Werner Ruzicka
Competition: German-speaking documentaries only
German Film Critics Prize (DM10,000)

Ljubljana International Film Festival
6-9 November 2000
Presernova 10, 1000 Ljubljana, Slovenia
Tel: +386-61 176 7150
Fax:+386-61 22 42 79
Festival director: Jelka Stergel
Competition: Kingfisher Prize

Festival de Cine de Alcala de Henares
10-18 November 2000
Plaza del Empecinado 1, Alcala de Henares 28801,
   Spain
Tel: +34-91 881 3934
Fax: +34-91 881 3906
Festival director: Pedro Medina
Competition: Primer Premio Nacional (Pta800,000)

Amiens International Film Festival
10-19 November 2000
MCA, Place Léon Gontier, F-80000 Amiens, France
Tel: +33-322 71 35 70
Fax: +33-322 92 53 04

E-mail: amiensfilmfestival@ burotec.fr
Festival director and programer: Jean-Pierre Garcia
Competition: The Golden Unicorn (FFr50,000)

Festival dei Popoli International Review of Social Documentary Film
10-16 November 2000
Borgo Pinti 82R, I-Firenze 50121, Italy
Tel: +39-55 244 778
Fax: +39-55 241 364
E-mail: fespopol@dada it
Festival director: Mario Simondi
Competition: Award for Best Documentary Film

Foyle Film Weekend
10-19 November 2000
2nd Floor, Northern Counties Building, 8 Custom
   House St, Derry, Northern Ireland, U.K.
Tel: +44-1504 267 432
Fax: +44-1504 371 738
E-mail:shona@iscm.ulst.ac.uk.
Festival director: Shona Kelpie
Competition: (£1,000)

Stockholm International Film Festival
10-19 November 2000
PO Box 3136, Stockholm, 10362 Sweden
Tel: +46-8 677 5000
Fax: +46-8 200590
E-mail: program@cinema.se
Website: www.filmfestivalen.se
Festival director: Git Scheynius
Festival programer: Jacob Abrahamson
Competition: The Bronze Horse

Encontros Internacionais de Cinema Documental
11-17 November 2000
Rua Angola, Olival Basto, 2675 Odivelas, Portugal
Tel: +351-1 938 8407
Fax: +351-1 938 9347
E-mail: amascultura@mail.telepc.pl
Festival director and programer: Manuel Costa e Silva
Competition: Grand Prix for the Best Documentary
   Feature

CineAsia (Hong Kong)
12-14 November 2000
244 West 49th St, #200, New York, NY 10019, U.S.
Tel: +1-212 246 6460
Fax: +1-212 265 6428
E-mail: sunshine@maestro.com
Contact: Jimmy Sunshine

...April 16...
Hot off toplining **The Matrix**, Keanu Reeves is in line for a raise, and sources
say he's asking for a career-best $15 million against a healthy back-end gross.

Birmingham International Film and TV Festival
15-26 November 2000
9 Margaret St, Birmingham B3 3SB, U.K.
Tel: +44-121 212 0777
Fax: +44-121 212 0666
Festival director: Sarah McKenzie
Festival programer: Barbara Chapman
Competition for local filmmakers

Holland Animation Film Festival
15-19 November 2000
Hoogt 4, 3515 GW Utrecht, The Netherlands
Tel: +31-30 233 1733
Fax: +31-30 233 1079
E-mail: haff@knoware.nl
Website: www.awn.com/haff
Festival director and programer: Gerben Schermer
Competition

Turin International Film Festival
17-25 November 2000
Via Monte di Pietá 1, 10121 Torino, Italy
Tel: +39-11 562 3309
Fax: +39-11 562 9796
E-mail: info@torinofilmfest.org
Website: www.torinofilmfest.org
Festival director and programer: Stefano Della Casa
Competition: Best Film ($20,000)

Oulu International Children's Film Festival
20-26 November 2000
Torikatu 8, 90100 Oulu, Finland
Tel: +358-8 881 1293
Fax: +358-8 881 1290
E-mail: raimo.kinisjarvi@ oufilmcenter.inet.fi
Website: www.ouka.fi/oek
Festival director: Pentti Kejonen
Festival programer: Eszter Vuojala
Competition: Star Boy Award (Ecu3,000)

Brief Encounters (Short Film Festival)
22-26 November 2000
PO Box 576, Bristol BS99 2BD, U.K.
Tel: +44-117 922 4628
Fax: +44-117 922 2906
E-mail: brief.encounters@ dial.pipex.com
Contact: Louise Jannings
Competition

Festival des Trois Continents
22-29 November 2000
19a Passage Pommeraye, BP 43302, F-44033, Nantes
    Cédex 1, France

Tel: +33-240 69 74 14
Fax: +33-240 73 55 22
Festival directors and programmers: Alain Jalladeau,
    Philippe Jalladeau
Competition (only for feature films): Montgolfiere
    d'Or (FFr30,000)

**International Documentary Film Festival
Amsterdam (IDFA)**
22-30 November 2000
Kleine Gartmanplantsoen 10, 017 RR Amsterdam
Tel: +31-20 627 3329
Fax: +31-20 638 5388
E-mail: idfa@xs4all.nl
Festival director and programer: Ally Derks
Competition: UPRO Joris Juens Award (Fl25,000)

Gijón International Film Festival for Young People
24 November-1 December 2000
Paseo de Begoña No. 24 entlo, 33205 Gijón, Spain
Tel: +34-98 534 3739
Fax: +34-98 535 4152
E-mail: festcine@las.es
Website: www.las.es/gijonfilmfestival
Festival director: Jose Luis Cienfuegos
Festival programer: Fran Gayo
Competition: Principado de Asturias (Euros11,988)

Junior Dublin Film Festival
26 November-5 December 2000
c/o Irish Film Centre, Eustace St, Dublin 2, Ireland
Tel: +353-1 671 4095
Fax: +353 1 677 8755
E-mail: jdff@indigo.ie
Festival director and programer: Alan Robinson

**Cinemagic International Film Festival
for Young People**
29 November-9 December 2000
4th Floor, 38 Dublin Rd, Belfast BT2 7HN, Northern
    Ireland, U.K.
Tel: +44-1232 311 900
Fax: +44-1232 319 709
Festival director: Shauna McCarthy
Festival programer: Nicki Fulcher
Competition: Cinemagic Young Jury Award (£1,000)

Action and Adventure Film Festival (Antwerp)
November 2000
1104 Kortrijksesteenweg, Ghent, B-9051 Belgium
Tel: +32-9 221 8946
Fax: +32-9 221 9074
E-mail: filmfestival@infoboard.be

. . . April 17 . . .
Life was just a bowl of cherries for Universal and Imagine Entertainment
over the weekend as the comedy reaped an estimated $20.7 million.

Website: www.rug.ac.be/filmfestival/Welcome.html
Contacts: Jacques Dubrulle, Walter Provo, Peter
  Bouckaert, Marian Ponnet

Brynmawr Film Festival
November 2001
Blaenau Gwent Arts Development Office, Beaufort
  Theatre, Beaufort, Ebbw Vale, Gwent NP3 5QQ,
  South Wales, U.K.
Tel: +44-1495 308996
Fax: +44-1495 308996
Festival director and programer: Geoff Cripps

Cairo International Film Festival
November 2000
17th Kasr El Nil St, Cairo, 202 Egypt
Tel: +202-392 3562
Fax: +202-393 8979
Festival director: Saad Eldin Wahba
Competition: Golden Pyramid

Cape Town International Film Festival
November 2000
University of Cape Town, Private Bag, Rondebosch,
  Cape Town 8001, South Africa
Tel: +27-21 4238 257
Fax: +27-21 4242 355
E-mail: filmfest@hiddingh.uct.ac.za
Festival director: James A. Polley
Festival programer: Mignon Coetzee

Cinanima – International Animated Film Festival
November 2000
Apartado 43, 4501 Espinho Codex, Portugal
Tel: +351-2 734 4611
Fax: +351-2 734 6015
Festival director: Antonio Gaio
Festival programer: Organizing Committee Cinanima
Competition: Grand Prize (Esc500)

Cinemania
November 2000
1 Bulgaria Square, National Palace of Culture, 1414
  Sofia, Bulgaria
Tel: +359-2 54 3061/9166 2841
Fax: +359-2 65 7053
Festival director: Christo Droumev

EuropaCinema (Viareggio)
November 2000
Via 20 Settembre 3, 00187 Roma, Italy
Tel: +39-6 420 111 84/42 000 211
Fax: +39-6 4201 0599

Festival director: Monique Veaute
Competition

Festival Internazionale del Cinema di Salerno
November 2000
Casella Postale 137, I-84100 Salerno, Italy
Tel: +39-089 231 953
Fax: +39-089 223 632
Festival director: Ettore Capuano
Festival programer: Mario De Cesare
Competition: Gran Trofeo Golfo di Salerno

Festival of French Cinema (Acapulco)
November 2000
Unifrance, 4 Villa Bosquet, 75007 Paris, France
Tel: +33-1 47 53 95 80/47 53 27 48
Fax: +33-1 47 05 96 55
Contact: Stephan Melchiori

Festival Primer Plano
November 2000
4 Place Darcy, BP 1002, F-21024 Dijon Cédex, France
Tel: +33-3 80 30 59 78
Fax: +33-3 80 50 18 08
Festival director: Laurence Karoibi
Competition

Festival Tous Courts
November 2000
Cité du Livre – 8-10 rue des Allumettes, 13090 Aix en
  Provence, France
Tel: +33-4 42 27 08 64
Fax: +33-4 42 38 47 83
E-mail: aixfilms@club-internet.fr
Festival president: Sir Marc Ripoll
Competition for short films

Film Arts Festival
November 2000
346 Ninth St, 2nd Floor, San Francisco, CA 94103, U.S.
Tel: +1-415 552 8760
Fax: +1-415 552 0882
Festival director: Mark Taylor

The Forum
November/December 2000
Kleine-Gartmanplantsoen 10, 1017 RR Amsterdam,
  The Netherlands
Tel: +31-20 627 3329
Fax: +31-20 638 5388
E-mail: idfa@xs4all.nl
Market director: Jolanda Klarenbeek
Market

Forum of European Cinema (Strasbourg)
November 2000
10 rue Alexandre Parodi, 75010 Paris, France
Tel: +33-1 44 89 99 99
Fax: +33-1 44 89 99 60
Festival director: Peter Fleischmann
Festival programer: Pierre-Henri Deleau

French Film Festival (Edinburgh/Glasgow)
November 2000
French Institute, 13 Randolph Crescent, Edinburgh,
    EH3 8TX, U.K.
Tel: +44-131 225 6191
Fax: +44-131 220 0648
Festival director and programer: Richard Mowe
Competition: Hennessy Audience Award
    (non-monetary)

IberoAmerican Film Festival
November 2000
Casa Colon, Plaza del Punto, 21003 Huelva, Spain
Tel: +34-959 210 170
Fax: +34-959 210 173
E-mail: festihuelva@ayuntamientohuleva.es
Website: www.festihuelva.otd.es
Festival director and programer: Jon Apaolaza
Competition: Colon de Oro (Pta3 million)

**International Festival of
Documentary and Short Films**
November 2000
C/Colón de Larreategui, n° 37-4° drch, 48009 Bilbao,
    Spain
Tel: +34-94 424 8698
Fax: +34-94 424 5624
Festival director: Jaseba Inchaurraga
Festival programer: Maria Angeles Olea
Competition: Grand Premio (Pta400,000)

International Film Festival Bratislava
November 2000
Mosovkeho 16, 81103 Bratislava, Slovakia
Tel: +421-7 5441 0673
Fax: +421-7 5441 0674
Festival programer: Peter Nagel
Competition: first and second films. Entry deadline:
    30 September 1999

International French Film Festival
November 2000
Frierichstrasse 11, D-72074 Tübingen, Germany
Tel: +49-70 71 56960
Fax: +49-70 71 59 96 96

E-mail: filmtage.tuebingen@t-online.de
Festival directors and programers: Dieter Betz,
    Stefanie Schneider
Competition: Flying Camera (DM10,000)

International Biennale Film+Arc Graz
November 2001
Hallerschloszstrasse 21, 8010 Graz, Austria
Tel: +43-316 35 6155
Fax: +43-316 356156
Festival director and programer: Charlotte
    Pöchhacker
Competition: Grand Prix Flm+Arc.Graz
    (ASch100,000)

**International Independent
Film Festival of Ourense**
November 2000
Apartado 664, 32080 Ourense, Spain
Tel: +34-988 224 127
Fax: +34-988 249 561
E-mail: turiour@fegamp.es
Festival director: Luis Rivas
Festival programer: Jorge Maroto
Competition: Calpurnia Prize (Pta1,500,000)

International Sport Film Festival
November 2000
Via Notarbartolo 1/G, 90141 Palermo, Italy
Tel: +39-91 611 4968
Fax: +39-91 611 4968
Festival director: Vito Maggio
Competition: Paladino d'Oro (L5 million)

International Thessaloniki Film Festival
November 2000
Paparigopoulou 40, 11473 Athens, Greece
Tel: +30-1 645 3668/644 8194
Fax: +30-1 644 8143
E-mail: info@filmfestival.gr
Festival director and programer: Michel Demopoulos
Competition: Golden Alexander (Dr12,500,000)

Latino Film Festival of Marin (Larkspur)
November 2000
3100 Kerner Blvd, Suite G, San Rafael,
    CA 94901, U.S.
Tel: +1-415 459 3530
Fax: +1-415 456 0560
E-mail: sperel@linex.com
Festival director and programer: Sylvia Perel
Competition

...April 19...
Saying it was "forced by demand", Blinde Optics announced
it will sell **The Matrix**-inspired sunglasses to the public.

Margaret Mead Film and Video Festival
November 2000
American Museum of Natural History, 79th St at
   Central Park West, New York, 10024 NY, U.S.
Tel: +1-212 769 5305
Fax: +1-212 769 5329
E-mail: meadfest@amnh.org
Festival director: Elaine Charnov

Nature Film Festival Valvert
November 2000
Rue du Laekenveld 27, 1080 Brussels, Belgium
Tel: +32-2 420 3757
Fax: +32-2 420 0255
Festival directors: Sebastian Lob, Marc Van Doornick
Festival programer: Claudine Brasseur
Competition: Aigle de Cristal (BFr100,000)

**News World International Forum
for Broadcast News (Barcelona)**
November 2000
39 St. James's St, London SW1A 1JD, U.K.
Tel: +44-207 491 0880
Fax: +44-207 491 0990
Managing director: Kerry Innes

Northampton Film Festival
November 2000
351 Pleasant St. Suite 137, Northampton, MA 01060, U.S.
Tel: +1-413 586 3471
Fax: +1-413 584 4432
E-mail: filmfest@nohofilm.org
Festival directors and programers: Howard Polonsky,
   Dee DeGeiso
Competition: Northern Arts Entertainment Best of
   Fest Award ($500)

Ohio Independent Film Festival
November 2000
2258 West 10th St, Cleveland, OH 44113, U.S.
Tel: +1-216 781 1755
E-mail: OhioIndieFilmFest@ juno.com
Festival directors and programers: Bernadette
   Gillota, Annetta Marion

Oslo International Film Festival
November 2000
Ebbellsgate 1, N-0183 Oslo, Norway
Tel: +47-22 20 07 66
Fax: +47-22 20 18 03
E-mail: filmfestival@login.eunet.no
Website: http://wit.no/filmfestival
Festival director and programer: Tommy Lørdahl

**Southern African International Film
and Television Market**
(Cape Town)
November 2000
PO Box 1176, Oakland Park, Johannesburg, 2006,
   South Africa
Tel: +27-11 430 8160
Fax: +27-11 430 8249
E-mail: info@sithengi.co.za
Website: www.sithengi.co.za
Contact: Kim Dearham

Taipei Golden Horse Film Festival
November 2000
Floor 7, No. 45, Chilin Rd, Taipei, 104 Taiwan ROC
Tel: +886-22 567 5861
Fax: +886-22 531 8966
E-mail: tghff@ms14.hinet.net
Website: www.goldenhorse.org.tw
Festival director: You-Ning Lee
Festival programer: Johnny Yang

Tranny Fest
November 2000
584 Castro St, Suite 273, San Francisco, CA 94114, U.S.
Tel/fax: +1-415 552 4249
E-mail: trannyfest@aol. com
Festival directors: Christopher Lee and Alison Austin

Verzaubert, Gay, and Lesbian Film Festival
November 2000
Rosebud Entertainment, Herzog Wilhelm Strasse 27,
   80331 Munich, Germany
Tel: +49-89 260 22 838
Fax: +49-89 260 22 839
E-mail: rosebud-entertainment@t-online.de
Festival directors and programers: Schorsch Müller,
   Rainer Stefan

European Short Film Festival
11 Holbein House, Holbein Place, London,
   SW1W 8NH, U.K.
Tel: +44-207 460 3901
Fax: +44-207 259 9278
Contact: Fritz Kohle

December

Camerimage
2-9 December 2000
Rynek Nowomiejski 28, 87-100 Torun, Poland
Tel: +48-56 6522179

Fax: +48-56 27595
Festival director: Marek Zydowicz
Festival programers: Maciej Kruzewski, Marek
  Zydowicz
Competition: The Golden Frog Award

European Film Academy Awards
2 December 2000
Segitzdam 2, D-10969 Berlin, Germany
Tel: +49-30 615 3091
Fax: +49-30 614 3131
Chairman of the European Film Academy: Nik Powell

Black Nights Film Festival
3-10 December 2000
Nafta St 1, Tallinn, Estonia 10152
Tel: +372-2 425 939
Fax: +372-6 431 351
E-mail: filmimax@pb.eepinet.ee
Festival director: Jaak Kilmi
Festival programer: Tlina Rokk

Noir In Festival (Courmayer, Italy)
5-11 December 2000
Via Tirso 90, I-Rome 00198, Italy
Tel: +39-6 884 8030
Fax: +39-6 884 0450
Festival director: Giorgio Gosetti
Festival programer: Maria Teresa Cavina
Competition: Mystery Award

MIP-ASIA (Singapore)
6-8 December 2000 (tbc)
Reed Midem Organisation, 11 rue du Colonel Pierre
  Avia, F-75015, Paris, France
Tel: +33-1-41 90 45 80
Fax: +33-1-41 90 45 70
Program director: André Vaillant
Market

**International Festival of
New Latin American Cinema**
December 2000
Calle 23, No. 1155, Vedado, Havana 10600, Cuba
Tel: +53-7 34169
Fax: +53-7 334 273

Festival president: Alfredo Guevara
Festival director: Iván Giroud
Competition and Market: Coral Prizes

KISH International Film Festival
December 2000
Kish Fress Zone Organization, Kish Street, Africa
  Expressway, Tehran, Iran
Tel: +98-21 879 7480
Fax: +98-21 878 3999
E-mail: kish-free0zone@kfzo.com

New York Exposition of Short Film and Video
December 2000
New York Expo, 532 LaGuardia Place, Suite 330, New
  York, NY 10012, U.S.
Tel: +1-212 505 7742
E-mail: nyexpo@aol.com
Website: www.yrd.com/nyexpo

Forum Festival
Groesslingova 32, 81109 Bratislava, Slovakia
Tel: +421-7 531 0673
Fax: +421-7 532 0647
Festival director: tbc
Competition for first feature film
Main prize (3000m of negative film stock)

Echo Television and Radio Awards (Vienna)
Echo Awards Secretariat, 26-34 Emerald St, London
  WC1N 3QA, U.K.
Tel: +44-207 253 0880
Fax: +44-207 312 0039
E-mail: medianatura@gn.apc.org
Festival director: Mandy Duncan-Smith
Entry information: Lydia Cerbelle

**TV Festival: The Chicago
International TV Competition**
32 West Randolph St, Suite 600, Chicago, Illinois
  60601, U.S.
Tel: +1-312 425 9400
Fax: +1-312 425 0944
E-mail: filmfest@suba.com
Festival director: Michael Kutza
Competition: The Gold Hugo Statue

> *You can't be anally retentive.*
> *You don't have an anus.*
> *(Ben Affleck,* Dogma*)*

... April 21 ...
Eureka, the prototype Euro entertainment conglomerate, is to co-finance its first
Hollywood pic, Robert Redford's $70 million golf movie, **The Legend of Bagger Vance**.

Film Reviews in *Variety*: 1999

Year in, year out, *Variety*'s film reviews are among the most eagerly scanned and saved items in the paper. They have become longer and more searching over the past decade, as the significance attached to a notice in *Variety* has increased within the industry. Often *Variety* is one of the very first publications to review a picture, and this carries with it an unenviable responsibility. A bad review, appearing two days prior to opening, can influence the box office in the U.S. and, for a foreign-language film, materially affect its sales potential. An Italian producer once assailed us in the streets of Cannes, claiming that *Variety*'s savage critique of his new film that week had resulted in a call from the U.S. distributor reducing its offer by $750,000! Conversely, a favorable notice may provoke a rash of phone calls and faxes to the happy producer in Finland or New Zealand – sometimes inquiring about remake rights even before seeing the film.

The following is an alphabetical list of more than half the reviews published in the paper in 1999. Each of these films had either a wide release, or in some way traveled beyond its national borders (to leading festivals, for example). We have abridged them for space purposes, added where relevant some box-office information, and refer readers to our website, Variety.com, for access to the full version. N.B. *All numbers are through to Dec. 31, 1999. All films are 1999 release unless otherwise indicated. Domestic release refers to pictures that debuted in the U.S., Canada, and Puerto Rico.*

All About My Mother

A Warner Sogefilms (in Spain)/Sony Pictures Classics (in U.S.) release of an El Deseo (Spain)/Renn Prods., France 2 Cinema (France) production, in association with Via Digital. (International sales: G2, London.) Produced by Agustin Almodovar. Directed, written by Pedro Almodovar. Camera (color), Affonso Beato; editor, Jose Salcedo; music, Alberto Iglesias; art director, Antxon Gomez; sound (Dolby Digital), Miguel Rejas. Reviewed at Cine Avenida, Madrid, April 13, 1999. (In Cannes Film Festival - competing.)
Cecilia Roth (Manuela), Eloy Azorin (Esteban), Marisa Paredes (Huma Rojo), Penelope Cruz (Sister Rosa), Candela Pena (Nina), Antonia San Juan (La Agrado), Rosa Maria Sarda (Rosa's Mother), Toni Canto (Lola, La Pionera).
Women on the edge of a nervous breakdown are at the heart of Pedro Almodvar's 13th outing, an emotionally satisfying and brilliantly played take on the ups and (mostly) downs of a group of less-than-typical female friends. Subject and style are distinctively the helmer's own, but the energetic kitsch of his early work has now largely given way to thought-provoking melodrama. Manuela, a nurse and single mother in her late 30s raises son Esteban after coming to Madrid from Barcelona 18 years before. Early scenes develop the relationship between the two and emphasize Manuela's emotional dependence on her son. Esteban, a Truman Capote fan and would-be novelist, is writing a story about his mother for a competition. After a theatre visit to see *A Streetcar Named Desire*, he runs into the street to get the autograph of actress Huma Rojo, and is killed by a passing car as Manuela looks on. Wanting to get back in touch with Esteban's father – another Esteban who, in the interim, has become a transvestite – Manuela returns to Barcelona. While there, she becomes friendly with a carnival of women from a goodhearted transsexual to an innocent do-

gooder nun called Sister Rosa. All the women have some emotional burden to bear. Thanks to a genuinely witty script, pic doesn't become depressing as it focuses on the characters' stoic resilience and good.
U.S. release: Nov. 19   U.S. B.O.: $2.1 million

American Beauty

A DreamWorks Pictures release of a Jinks/Cohen production. Produced by Bruce Cohen, Dan Jinks. Co-producers, Stan Wlodkowski, Alan Ball. Directed by Sam Mendes. Screenplay, Alan Ball. Camera (Deluxe color, Technicolor prints; Panavision widescreen), Conrad L. Hall; editors, Tariq Anwar, Christopher Greenbury; music, Thomas Newman; music supervisor, Chris Douridas; production designer, Naomi Shohan; art director, David S. Lazan; set decorator, Jan K. Bergstrom; costume designer, Julie Weiss. Reviewed at the Century Plaza Theater, L.A., Sept. 7, 1999. (In Toronto Film Festival - Gala; Boston Film Festival.) MPAA Rating: R. Running time: 122 mins.
Kevin Spacey (Lester Burnham), Annette Bening (Carolyn Burnham), Thora Birch (Jane Burnham), Wes Bentley (Ricky Fitts), Mena Suvari (Angela Hayes), Peter Gallagher (Buddy Kane), Allison Janney (Barbara Fitts), Scott Bakula (Jim Olmeyer), Sam Robards (Jim Berkley), Chris Cooper (Colonel Fitts).
An acerbic, darkly comic critique of how social conventions can lead people into false, sterile, and emotionally stunted lives, pic is a real American original. This feature represents a stunning introduction for two cinematic freshmen, screenwriter Alan Ball and director Sam Mendes. The landscape of Ball's story is the familiar one of small-town America and how it provides deceptive facades for lives wracked by hostility, tension, non-communication, and perversity.

Lester Burnham is a loser, having lost interest in his job as well as in any meaningful relationship with his beautiful, highly strung, real-estate agent wife, Carolyn, and teenage daughter, Jane. Family life is a sham for all of them, and they deal with it in different ways: Lester admits it, Carolyn refuses to face it, and Jane is just waiting it out until she can fly the coop. Threatened with dismissal from his job, Lester finds things begin changing for him when he becomes smitten by Jane's best friend, Angela, a blonde Lolita with sex on the brain. Exhilarated by the ludicrous prospect of seducing her, Lester begins obsessively pumping iron and smokes dope. Jane releases her emotional frustration with the odd, voyeuristic teenage neighbor, Ricky. Carolyn seeks an outlet in an affair with her real-estate competitor.

The film constantly analyzes the characters' actions and holds them in bold relief just as it moves the story along at a brisk clip. Dialog is tart and the characters are well and deeply drawn, endowed with an inner life that allows the viewer to understand their often rash and unpredictable behavior.
U.S. release: Sept. 15   U.S. B.O.: $71 million

American Pie

A Universal release of a Warren Zide/Craig Perry production. Produced by Zide, Perry, Chris Moore, Chris Weitz. Co-producers, Louis G. Friedman, Chris Bender. Directed by Paul Weitz. Screenplay, Adam Herz. Camera (Deluxe color), Richard Crudo; editor, Priscilla Nedd-Friendly; music, David Lawrence; music supervisor, Gary Jones; production designer/art director, Paul Peters; set designer, Joshua Lusby; set decorator, Amy Wells; costume designer, Leesa Evans. Reviewed at Old Pasadena 8, Pasadena, CA on June 23, 1999. MPAA Rating: R. Running time: 95 mins.
Jason Biggs (Jim), Shannon Elizabeth (Nadia), Alyson Hannigan (Michelle), Chris Klein (Oz), Natasha Lyonne (Jessica), Thomas Ian Nicholas (Kevin), Tara Reid (Vicky), Seann W. Scott (Stifler), Mena Suvari (Heather), Eddie Kaye Thomas (Finch), Eugene Levy (Jim's Dad), Jennifer Coolidge (Stifler's Mom), Chris Owen (Sherman), Clyde Kusatsu (English Teacher), Lawrence Pressman (Coach Marshall).
American Pie has but a single ambition – to be the king of gross-out comedies. Pic is a dream movie for teenage boys as it exploits the comic possibilities of randy adolescence and the desperate urge to "score." Unlike the leering *Animal House-Nerds* sex farces of yore, pic gives ample time to the female p.o.v. One can sense that helmers are trying to figure out how they can one-up films that have come before and set new standards of vulgar hilarity.

The plot follows the exploits of four high-school seniors, sick of their virginity and determined not to carry their burden with them to college. The boys resolve to divest themselves of their innocence by the time they graduate in three weeks. The buddies include Kevin, who looks to be in the best position to get over since he's fondled his blonde girlfriend Vicky; Finch, who has no apparent prospects; Oz, whose advantageous great looks and jock status are mitigated by an underlying propriety and shyness; and Jim an oaf of no particular distinction who has set his sights on exotic Czech student Nadia. Film succeeds in its elementary mission due to its relentless bluntness and fundamental realism about teenage human nature. Largely no-name cast is game and gamy.
U.S. release: June 25   U.S. B.O. $101.8 million

Analyze This

A Warner Bros. release presented in association with Village Roadshow Pictures and NPV Entertainment of a Baltimore/Spring Creek Pictures/Face/Tribeca production. Produced by Paula Weinstein, Jane Rosenthal. Executive producers, Bruce Berman, Chris Brigham, Billy Crystal. Co-producer, Len Amato. Directed by Harold Ramis. Screenplay, Peter Tolan, Ramis, Kenneth Lonergan, story by Lonergan, Tolan.
Robert De Niro (Paul Vitti), Billy Crystal (Ben Sobel), Lisa Kudrow (Laura MacNamara), Joe Viterelli (Jelly), Chazz Palminteri (Primo Sindone), Bill Macy (Isaac Sobel), Leo Rossi (Carlo Mangano), Kyle Sabihy (Michael Sobel), Rebecca Schull (Dorothy Sobel), Molly Shannon (Caroline), Max Casella (Nicky Shivers), Pat Cooper (Salvatore Masiello), Richard Castellano (Jimmy), Jimmie Ray Weeks (FBI Agent Steadman), Elizabeth Bracco (Marie Vitti) Tony Darrow (Moony), Donnamarie Recco (Sheila).
A shrink pushes a mobster to get in touch with the good fella inside him in *Analyze This*, a sometimes funny situation comedy in which the mechanics of the situation eventually overwhelm the comedy. De Niro and Crystal both have moments to shine in this farcical concoction, which never gets much further than playing riffs on the central juxtaposition of the gangster's emotionalism and the psychiatrist's cerebral outlook.

Paul Vitti, an aging patriarch, acknowledges upfront that times have changed with the traditional Mafia. Vitti is one of the city's two top mob kingpins, and suffering from a modern malady entirely alien to the gangland ethos: anxiety attacks. Vitti pretends to his recruited shrink, Ben Sobel, that he's there on behalf of a friend before coercing the doc into being on 24-hour call to attend to his crisis. But when Sobel's unwelcome new patient finds himself not only unable to pull the trigger on his enemies but too preoccupied to perform in the sack, Vitti heads for Florida, precipitating a gangland hit that aborts Sobel's wedding, ups the ante between Vitti and his New York rival and wreaks havoc on Sobel's life. De Niro's precise comic timing and colorful line readings constitute pic's greatest pleasure. But the gradual dilution of fresh humor is further undercut by a queasy sense that the picture is quietly endorsing all the psychoanalytical mumbo jumbo that it has been poking fun at all along.
U.S. release: March 5   U.S. B.O.: $106.9 million

Angela's Ashes

A Paramount release (in U.S.) of a Paramount Pictures and Universal Pictures Intl. presentation of a David Brown/Scott Rudin/Dirty Hands production. Produced by Rudin, Brown, Alan Parker. Executive producers, Adam Schroeder, Eric Steel. Directed by Parker. Screenplay, Laura Jones, Parker, based on the book by Frank McCourt. Camera (Technicolor, Deluxe and Technicolor prints), Michael Seresin; editor, Gerry Hambling; music, John Williams; production designer, Geoffrey Kirkland; supervising art director, Malcolm Middleton; art directors, Jonathan McKinstry, Fiona Daly; set decorator, Jennifer Williams; costume designer, Consolata Boyle; sound (Dolby Digital/DTS), Ken Weston; supervising sound editor, Eddy Joseph; Irish co-producers, Morgan O'Sullivan, James Flynn; line producer, David Wimbury; associate producers, Kit Golden, Doochy Moult; assistant directors, Dennis Maguire, Tommy Gormley; casting, John

---

. . . April 23 . . .
Ingmar Bergman's latest script **The Faithless** is to start shooting with Bergman's long-standing collaborator Liv Ullmann directing.

and Ros Hubbard, Juliet Taylor. Reviewed at Paramount Studios, L.A., Nov. 22, 1999. MPAA Rating: R. Running time: 145 mins.
Emily Watson (Angela), Robert Carlyle (Dad), Joe Breen (Young Frank), Ciaran Owens (Middle Frank), Michael Legge (Older Frank), Ronnie Masterson (Grandma Sheehan), Pauline McLynn (Aunt Aggie), Liam Carney (Uncle Pa Keating), Eanna Macliam (Uncle Pat), Andrew Bennett (Narrator).
Angela's Ashes artfully evokes the realities of Irish poverty, but misses the humor, lyricism and emotional charge of the book. Apparent effort to capture as many of the text's key dramatic moments results in a lengthy succession of short scenes, a structure that sacrifices depth as well as extensive thespian exploration by the talented cast.

The book's opening section, detailing the McCourts' lives in Brooklyn during the Depression, is disposed of in a quick five minutes, just long enough to establish the unemployability of alcoholic Dad, the inability of his perennially pregnant wife, Angela, to cope, and the comparatively upbeat resourcefulness of five-year-old Frank.

When baby Margaret dies, Angela hits the wall, and arrangements are quickly made to get them back where they came from. The family ventures to Limerick, Angela's hometown, where things fare far worse than in New York. Besides local prejudices making it difficult for Dad to work, Frank's twin brothers die. At halfway, a 10-year-old has his literary ability recognized for the first time. Dad leaves for work in England and disappears for good. Angela is forced to compromise herself egregiously, just to support the family, provoking a rift with Frank and his realization, by the time he turns 16, that he's got to return to New York at all costs.

The climactic upswing can't change the fact that the structural streamlining has turned a singular work into a conventional tale of a gifted young man's struggle to lift himself out of oppressive circumstances.
U.S. release: Dec. 25   U.S. B.O.: $186,032

Anna and the King

A 20th Century Fox release of a Fox 2000 Pictures presentation of a Lawrence Bender production. Produced by Lawrence Bender and Ed Albert. Executive producer, Terence Chang. Co-producers, Jon Jashni, G. Mac Brown, Wink Mordaunt, Julie Kirkham. Directed by Andy Tennant. Screenplay, Steve Meerson and Peter Krikes, based upon the diaries of Anna Leonowens. Camera (Technicolor, wide screen), Caleb Deschanel; editor, Roger Bondelli; music, George Fenton; production designer, Luciana Arrighi; art direction, Paul Ghirardani, "Lek" Chaiyan Chunsuttiwat; set decoration, Ian Whittaker; costume designer, Jenny Beavan; sound (Dolby/SDDS), Brian Simmons; associate producer, Eric Angelson; assistant director, Scott Printz; casting, Priscilla John. Reviewed at a sneak preview at the Egyptian, L.A., Nov 27, 1999. MPAA Rating: PG-13. Running time: 147 mins.
Jodie Foster (Anna), Chow Yun-Fat (King Mongkut), Bai Ling (Tuptim), Tom Felton (Louis), Syed Alwi (The Kralahome), Randall Duk Kim (General Alak), Lim Kay Siu (Prince Chowfa), Melissa Campbell (Princess Fa-Ying), Deanna Yusoff (Lady Thiang).
The third version of the popular tale, most notably done as a Rodgers and Hammerstein musical, *The King and I*, in 1956. A schmaltzy, ultra-elaborate, overly long production, all too

consciously conceived as an oldfashioned family entertainment. Watching Andy Tennant's mishmash of a movie is like leafing through a catalog of Hollywood's popular adventures of the last four decades.

Pic begins with the arrival of Anna and her son Louis in 1862 Siam. The young British widow is bound for culture collision. Unbeknownst to Anna, the King's family consists of numerous wives and concubines and no less than 58 children, whom she is meant to educate in a "scientific" way, one that will help place Siam among countries of the modern world. Anna's prejudices against the King, who suffers from a barbarian reputation, are matched by the ruler's own misconceptions about the West in general and women in particular. Predictably, Anna and the King begin to share a growing affection, she discovering his humanity and visionary qualities, he recognizing her enlightenment of his offspring and the monarchy. Foster enjoys a strong chemistry with Yun-Fat who, in his first nonaction role in an American movie, impresses with his handsome presence and dignified stillness. Tennant gives pic a luxuriant treatment, with overwhelming landscapes, massive battles and parades of elephants.
U.S. release: Dec. 17   U.S. B.O.: $24.7 million

Any Given Sunday

A Warner Bros. release of an Ixtlan/The Donners' Co. production. Produced by Lauren Shuler Donner, Clayton Townsend, Dan Halsted. Executive producers, Richard Donner, Oliver Stone. Co-producers, Eric Hamburg, Jonathan Krauss, Richard Rutowski. Directed by Stone. Screenplay, John Logan, Stone, screen story by Daniel Pyne, Logan. Camera (Technicolor, Panavision widescreen), Salvatore Totino; editors, Tom Nordberg, Keith Salmon, Stuart Waks, Stuart Levy; music score, Robbie Robertson, Paul Kelly, Richard Horowitz; music supervisor, Budd Carr; additional music score, Moby, Swizz Beat, Camara Kambon, Tony McAnany; production designer, Victor Kempster; supervising art director, Stella Vaccaro; art director, Derek Hill; set designers, Stephanie Girard, Jeff Adams, Richard Fojo; set decorators, Ron Reiss, Ford Wheeler; costume designer, Mary Zophres; sound (Dolby Digital/DTS/SDDS), Peter Devlin; supervising sound editors, Wylie Stateman, Kelly Cabral; assistant directors, George Parra, Richard Patrick; second unit director/stunt and football coordinator, Allan Graf; second unit camera, Chuck Cohen; additional camera, Keith Smith; casting, Billy Hopkins, Mary Vernieu. Reviewed at the Galaxy Theater, L.A., Dec. 9, 1999. MPAA Rating: R. Running time: 162 mins.
Al Pacino (Tony D'Amato), Cameron Diaz (Christina Pagniacci), Dennis Quaid (Jack "Cap" Rooney), James Woods (Dr. Harvey Mandrake), Jamie Foxx (Willie Beamen), L.L. Cool J. (Julian Washington), Matthew Modine (Dr. Ollie Powers), Jim Brown (Montezuma Monroe), Charlton Heston (AFFA Football Commissioner), Ann-Margret (Margaret Pagniacci), Aaron Eckhart (Nick Crozier), John C. McGinley (Jack Rose), Lauren Holly (Cindy Rooney), Lela Rochon (Vanessa Struthers), Lawrence Taylor (Luther "Shark" Lavay), Bill Bellamy (Jimmy Sanderson), James Karen, Gianni Russo (Christina's Advisers), Elizabeth Berkley (Manie Murphy), Andrew Bryniarski (Patrick Madman Kelly). With: Duane Martin, Clifton Davis, John Daniel, Patrick O'Hara, Jerry A. Sharp, Marty Wright.
Stone evokes the crisis-crammed lives of at least two dozen

. . . **April 24** . . .
Ewan McGregor and Nicole Kidman team up in Baz Luhrmann's **Moulin Rouge**.

characters umbilically connected to the game, from owners, coaches and players to wives, sportscasters and doctors. Among the central preoccupations here are team ethos vs. selfish individualism, the replacement of team and civic loyalty by commercial interests, the decline in respect for tradition and the knowledge that, no matter how good you are, there is always someone younger right behind you anxious to knock you out of the way.

Pic begins by plunging headlong into a bizarre and bitterly fought game in which the Sharks, Miami's "other" team, is hoping to halt a three-game losing streak and keep its hopes alive for the playoffs with three games to go in the season. Their aging star quarterback, Jack "Cap" Rooney is on the disabled list. The third-stringer, Willie Beamen, saves the games with game tactics that rival the coach's own. As the Sharks win, Willie's fame explodes and his cockiness with it. Savvy, veteran coach Tony D'Amato feels that he may not have what it takes to connect with the younger players any more. Christina Pagniacci has inherited the team and possesses a ruthless bottom-line mentality entirely at odds with the old-school approach of her late father. The finale is a 30-minute playoff humdinger in Dallas that's backdropped by loads of off-field drama. Performances are almost all shot through with electricity.

U.S. release: Dec. 25   U.S. B.O.: $45.8 million

Anywhere But Here

A 20th Century Fox release of a Fox 2000 Pictures presentation of a Laurence Mark production. Produced by Mark. Executive producer, Ginny Nugent. Directed by Wayne Wang. Screenplay, Alvin Sargent, based on the novel by Mona Simpson. Camera (Deluxe color, widescreen), Roger Deakins; editor, Nicholas C. Smith; music, Danny Elfman; production designer, Donald Graham Burt; art director, Kevin Constant; set decorator, Barbara Munch; costume designer, Betsy Heiman; sound (Dolby), Joseph Geisinger; associate producer, Petra Alexandria; assistant director, Betsy Magruder; casting, Victoria Thomas. Reviewed at Toronto Film Festival (Gala), Sept. 16, 1999. MPAA Rating: PG-13. Running time: 114 mins.
Susan Sarandon (Adele August), Natalie Portman (Ann August), Eileen Ryan (Lillian), Ray Baker (Ted), John Diehl (Jimmy), Shawn Hatosy (Benny), Bonnie Bedelia (Carol), Caroline Aaron (Gail), Hart Bochner (Josh Spritzer).
Anywhere But Here will draw comparisons to *Alice Doesn't Live Here Anymore* and 1999's *Tumbleweeds*, both of which are more interesting pictures than Wang's; these moralistic sagas revolve around irresponsible or immature middle-aged women who hit the road with their children in search of a better, more meaningful life. Pic is made in the manner of Hollywood weepies of yesteryear. As he has demonstrated in previous work, Wang's sensitive, humanistic approach is best suited to emotional stories about women. A good deal of the film recalls 1937's *Stella Dallas*.

Adele and 14-year-old Ann head toward the promised land of Beverly Hills. Against Ann's will, they're leaving Bay City, Wis., a provincial town Adele finds stifling. Adele is pushing her daughter into acting. They ultimately settle in an apartment in Beverly Hills, and over the course of a year they move from one shabby place to another. There's a basic role reversal: Ann is more realistic and pragmatic than her flighty mom. Ann goes through a painful coming of age, underlined

by her studying in a new school and her eager desire to meet her biological father. Turning point occurs when Adele discovers Ann delivering an audition monolog that mimics her words and gestures. Sarandon's broad rendition makes the material unbearably familiar; this is one of her least subtle performances. Portman is a natural performer who brings rough edges to any role she plays – the movie is inconceivable without her.

U.S. release: Nov. 12   U.S. B.O.: $18.1 million

Arlington Road

A Sony Pictures Entertainment release of a Screen Gems presentation, in association with Lakeshore Entertainment, of a Gorai/Samuelson production. Produced by Peter Samuelson, Tom Gorai, Marc Samuelson. Executive producers, Tom Rosenberg, Sigurjon Sighvatsson, Ted Tannebaum. Co-executive producers, Judd Malkin, Ed Ross. Co-producers, Jean Higgins, Richard S. Wright. Directed by Mark Pellington. Screenplay, Ehren Kruger.
Jeff Bridges (Michael Faraday), Tim Robbins (Oliver Lang), Joan Cusack (Cheryl Lang), Hope Davis (Brooke Wolf), Robert Gossett (FBI Agent Whit Carver), Mason Gamble (Brady Lang), Spencer Treat Clark (Grant Faraday), Stanley Anderson (Dr. Archer Scobee).
An intelligent, insidiously plotted Hitchcockian thriller directed in souped-up, modern expressionistic style. A study of the bland face of evil that culminates in an all-too-plausible attempt at domestic terrorism, this absorbing and surprising political melodrama sometimes tries too hard for its own good, overstressing points when simple understatement would have a more chilling effect. With several intriguing revelations and twists sprung along the way, the script's inevitable action climax is rife with deep irony.

Overall, Bridges and Robbins are in fine form. College prof Michael Faraday begins to become extremely suspicious of his new neighbors, Oliver and Cheryl Lang. Michael's lectures in American history are tainted by his obsession with radical fringe groups (stemming from his wife's murder by an extreme militia group). He begins poking into the background of the overly friendly Langs, soon discovering that Oliver's architectural blueprints are not for the mall job on which he claims to be the structural engineer. At story's midpoint, Michael uncovers Oliver's carefully hidden secret. From here on, the men engage in escalating psychological cat-and-mouse maneuvers, circling warily and threatening each other against a background of superficially innocuous activity that comes across as increasingly ominous. The film doles out Oliver's motivations and intentions in carefully spaced doses, and the full extent of his manipulations is expertly withheld until the very end.

U.S. release: July 9   U.S. B.O.: $24.7 million

Asterix & Obelix vs. Caesar

An AMLF Distribution release (in France) of a Claude Berri presentation of a Katharina-Renn Prods., TF1 Films Prods., AMLF-Pathe, Pathe Video (France)/Bavaria Films, Neue Constantin (Germany)/Melampo Cinematografica, Cecchi Gori Group (Italy) production. (International sales: President Films, Paris.) Produced by Claude Berri. Executive producer, Pierre Grunstein. Executive in charge of production, Patrick Bordier. Co-producers, Dieter Frank, Reinhard Klooss. Directed by Claude Zidi. Screenplay, Zidi,

---

. . . April 25 . . .
Warner Bros.'s **The Matrix** returned in force with a
$16.5 million gross to lead the U.S. marketplace.

Gerard Lauzier, based on characters created by Rene Goscinny and Albert Uderzo. **Christian Clavier (Asterix), Gerard Depardieu (Obelix), Roberto Benign (Detritus), Michel Galabru (Abraracourcix), Claude Pieplu (Panoramix), Daniel Prevost (Prolix), Pierre Palmade (Assurancetourix), Laetitia Casta (Falbala), Arielle Dombasle (Arielle), Sim (Agecanonix), Marianne Sagebrecht (Bonemine), Gottfried John (Caesar), Jean-Pierre Castaldi (Caius Bonus), Jean-Roger Milo (Cetautomatix), Jean-Jacques Devaux (Ordralfabetix). With: Hardy Krueger Jr., Michel Muller, Olivier Achard, Jacques Delaporte.**
This first live-action version of the cartoon books about a bunch of feisty Frenchies battling the might of Rome is a consistently tasty feast, with its detailed re-creation of the period and characters. It's 50 B.C., and Roman troops have cut a swath through Gaul to reach the English Channel. The only burr in Caesar's saddle is a tiny, fortified village in Gaul that continues to resist, thanks to a magic Druid potion that turns its oddball burghers into unbeatable warriors. After dispatching some tax-collecting Romans and hijacking their treasure chest, the 50 villagers send 500 Roman troops packing. Detritus, oily aide of Caesar, resolves to crush the Frenchmen for good by infiltrating a Druid convention in a sacred forest, capturing the head Druid, Panoramix, and torturing him to reveal the magic potion's formula. Asterix and Obelix set out to rescue the old Druid, with Obelix disguised as a Roman who has captured Asterix.

Pic doesn't trade on modern jokes and deliberate anachronisms: it's pure Gallic whimsy. In Claude Zidi's uninflected, straightforward direction, the first quality is completely lost. The script is low on repartee and even lower on real jokes. Apart from Benigni's wildly mugging performance, pic's energy comes from its physical action rather than from the mouths of the characters. The characters simply don't evolve in the way that a movie demands.

Austin Powers: The Spy Who Shagged Me

A New Line Cinema release of an Eric's Boy/Moving Pictures/Team Todd production. Produced by Suzanne Todd, Jennifer Todd, Demi Moore, Eric McLeod, John Lyons, Mike Myers. Executive producers, Erwin Stoff, Michael DeLuca, Donna Langley. Directed by Jay Roach. Screenplay, Myers, Michael McCullers. Camera (color, widescreen), Ueli Steiger; editors, John Poll, Debra Neil-Fisher; music, George S. Clinton; music supervisor, John Houlihan; executive music producer, Danny Bramson; production designer, Rusty Smith; art director, Alexander Hammond; set designers, John Jeffries, Stephen Cooper, Andrew Reeder; set decorator, Sara Andrews-Ingrassia; costume designer, Deena Appel; sound (SDDS/Dolby Digital/DTS), Kenneth McLaughlin; choreography, Marguerite Derricks; associate producer, Emma Chasin; assistant directors, Gary Scott Marcus, Hal Olofsson; second unit camera, Sandi Sissel; casting, Juel Bestrop, Jeanne McCarthy. Reviewed at AMC Kabuki 8, San Francisco, June 8, 1999. MPAA Rating: PG-13. Running time: 95 mins. **Mike Myers (Austin Powers/Dr. Evil/ Fat Bastard), Heather Graham (Felicity Shagwell), Michael York (Basil Exposition), Robert Wagner (Number Two), Rob Lowe (Young Number Two), Seth Green (Scott Evil), Mindy Sterling (Frau Farbissina), Verne J. Troyer (Mini-Me), Elizabeth Hurley (Vanessa), Kristen Johnston (Ivana Humpalot), Gia Carides (Robin Swallows). With: Burt**
Bacharach, Elvis Costello, Will Ferrell, Woody Harrelson, Charles Napier, Willie Nelson, Tim Robbins, Rebecca Romijn-Stamos, Jerry Springer, Fred Willard.
Bigger isn't necessarily better for the follow-up to the 1997 sleeper. Expanded in every aspect save inspiration, pic tickles the funny bone for 95 minutes, yet feels like a quickie where it ultimately counts most – in the writing. Brit intelligence boss Basil Exposition calls in news that the world is again imperilled by arch-nemesis Dr. Evil, whose outer-space exile hasn't lasted long. Rejoining subordinates Frau Farbissina, Number Two and teenage son Scott, the doc now plans to plant a giant laser gun on the moon, picking off urban centers until his ransom demand is met. Yet worse, he's rigged a flunky's time-machine travel to 1969, stealing the "mojo" from the then-cryogenically frozen Austin Powers. Soon Austin himself is tripping back to the Paisley Age, where curvaceous fellow agent Felicity Shagwell is his new ally in preventing Evil domination.

Biggest letdown is that the script just doesn't have it in terms of fresh narrative developments or individual gags. Too many of the latter are simply insistent reprises from part one. Movie in-jokes, jokey product placements and a misguided dependence on soon-to-be-dated pop culture references fill out the rest of a colorful, fast-paced but thin diversion. Sequel's major added characters – Dr. E's mute, diminutive clone Mini-Me and repulsive Scottish hit man Fat Bastard are middling conceits. Myers' two main onscreen personae – Austin and Dr. Evil – delight once again, their tics and incidental reactions often registering as funnier than any actual jokes.
U.S. release: June 11   U.S. B.O.:$205 million

Autumn Tale (Conte d'automne)

A Les Films du Losange release (in France) of a Les Films du Losange/La Sept Cinema production, with participation of Canal Plus, Sofilmka, Rhone-Alpes Cinema. Produced by Margaret Menegoz. Directed, written by Eric Rohmer. Camera (color), Diane Baratier; editor, Mary Stephen; music, Claude Marti, Gerard Pansanel, Pierre Peyras, Antonello Salis; sound (Dolby SR), Pascal Ribier, Frederic de Ravignan, Nathalie Vidal. Reviewed at Club Gaumont screening room, Paris, Aug. 4, 1998. Running time: 112 mins. **Marie Riviere (Isabelle), Beatrice Romand (Magali), Alain Libolt (Gerald), Didier Sandre (Etienne), Alexia Portal (Rosine). With: Stephane Darmon, Aurelia Alcais, Mathieu Davette, Yves Alcais.**
The fourth and final installment in Eric Rohmer's series named after the four seasons, flirts with various semi-devious approaches to matchmaking among the over-40 set. A typically deftly layered meditation on men, women, friendship and the prospect of romance in the Rhone Valley. In the U.S., Rohmer's previous stanza, *A Summer's Tale* (1996), has not yet been distributed.

Pic's initial 45 minutes unspool in a leisurely and deliberate manner before it comes to life – after which its quirky pleasures build to a satisfying denouement. Forty-something Magali and Isabelle have been best friends since childhood. Magali, a widow, feels lonely out in the country but her prospects for meeting a man seem slim.

A complicity unites Magali and Rosine, the firecracker girl-friend of her bland son, Leonce. College student Rosine is still attracted to her previous lover, Etienne, a handsome bachelor more than twice her age who was her high-school teacher. Deciding it never truly will be "over" between her and Etienne until he gets a new girlfriend, Rosine conspires to introduce him to Magali.

Bookshop owner Isabelle lives with her husband of 24 years. Determined to find a suitable guy for Magali, Isabelle secretly places a singles ad. Using her own name but appropriating Magali's background, Isabelle starts to "date" one of the responses, Gerald. Only when she begins to "test drive" Gerald does the crafty humor of Isabelle's machination – and the film itself – kick in.

U.S. release: July 9 U.S. B.O.: $2.1 million

The Bachelor

A New Line Cinema release of a Lloyd Segan Co. production in association with George Street Pictures. Produced by Segan, Bing Howenstein. Executive producers, Michael De Luca, Chris O'Donnell, Donna Langley. Co-producers, Leon Dudevoir, Stephen Hollocker. Directed by Gary Sinyor. Screenplay, Steve Cohen, based on the play *Seven Chances* by Roi Copper Megrue and the screenplay by Clyde Bruckman, Jean Havez, Joseph Mitchell for the film starring and directed by Buster Keaton. Camera (FotoKem color, Deluxe prints), Simon Archer; editor, Robert Reitano; music, David A. Hughes, John Murphy; production designer, Craig Stearns; art director, Randy Moore. Reviewed at New Line Cinema screening room, L.A., Nov. 1, 1999. MPAA Rating: PG-13. Running time: 101 mins.

Chris O'Donnell (Jimmy Shannon), Renee Zellweger (Anne), Hal Holbrook (O'Dell), James Cromwell (Priest), Artie Lange (Marco), Edward Asner (Gluckman), Marley Shelton (Natalie), Sarah Silverman (Carolyn), Stacy Edwards (Zoe), Rebecca Cross (Stacey), Jennifer Esposito (Daphne), Katharine Towne (Monique), Peter Ustinov (Granddad), Mariah Carey (Ilana), Brooke Shields (Buckley).

You don't have to know and love Buster Keaton's 1925 farce *Seven Chances* to dislike the remake *The Bachelor*, although it certainly doesn't hurt. A mirthless and inept romantic comedy about a young man who must marry within a day if he's to inherit $100 million, new pic is woefully misconceived on virtually every level, as it retains awkward vestiges of its source without at least winking at them or coming up with plausible contemporary substitutes. The most memorable sight in Keaton's comedy was that of hundreds of prospective brides in hot pursuit of the would-be heir through the streets. Action climax of this new version reproduces this image and predictably magnifies it.

Jimmy Shannon is a good-looking but otherwise uninteresting confirmed bachelor who, after three years with girl friend Anne, reaches the relationship crossroads where it's time to "shit or get off the pot." When he proposes to Anne by using these words, she storms off in a huff, which leaves Jimmy in the lurch when the videotaped will of his grandfather reveals that he will receive 100 big ones only if he marries by 6:05 p.m. on his 30th birthday. Naturally, his birthday is the very next day. Jimmy spends most of the remaining 27 hours tracking down some of his former girlfriends and discovers how unmercenary they are. The characters could have been given more interest and dimension. O'Donnell's Jimmy is extremely bland, and lacks the comic chops to add humor to his bungled proposals to Anne and to his encounters with former flames.

U.S release: Nov. 5 U.S. B.O.: $21.3 million

The Barber of Siberia

A Michel Seydoux presentation, in association with Intermedia Films, of a Three T Prods. (Russia)/Camera One, France 2 Cinema (France)/Medusa (Italy)/Barrandov Biografia (Czech Republic) production, supported by Eurimages, Goskino (Russia) with the participation of Canal Plus. (International sales: Intermedia Films, London.) Produced by Seydoux. Executive producer, Leonid Vereschagin. Co-producer, Nikita Mikhalkov. Directed by Mikhalkov. Screenplay, Mikhalkov, Rustam Ibragimbekov, in collaboration with Rospo Pallenberg, based on a story by Mikhalkov. Camera (color, Panavision widescreen), Pavel Lebeshev; editor, Enzo Meniconi; music, Edward Nicolai Artemyev; production designer, Vladimir Aronin; art director, V. Murzin; costume designers, Natasha Ivanova, Sergei Struchev; sound (Dolby Digital), Jean Umansky, Andre Rigaut; stunt coordinator, Valery Derkash; assistant director, V. Trakhtenberg; casting, Kate Dowd (international), Tamara Odintsova (Russia). Reviewed at Cannes Film Festival (noncompeting), May 12, 1999. Running time: 176 mins.

Julia Ormond (Jane Callahan), Oleg Menshikov (Andrei Tolstoy), Richard Harris (Douglas McCracken), Alexei Petrenko (Gen. Radlov), Vladimir Ilyin (Capt. Mokin), Alexander Yakovlev (Maximich), Marat Basharov (Polievsky), Daniel Olbrychski (Kopnovsky), Anna Mikhalkova (Dunvasha), Robert Hardy (Forsten), Nikita Mikhalkov (Czar Alexander III), Isabelle Renauld (Czarina), Evgeny Steblov (Grand Duke), Mac MacDonald (Sgt. "Mad Dog" O'Leary). (English and Russian dialog) Overblown, overlong and decidedly underwhelming on every level, helmer's magnum opus is a singular disappointment. Pitching the first half of the film as a broad comedy proves disastrous, as these labored and undisciplined sequences refuse to work.

Pic begins in 1885 Russia as Jane Callahan travels by train to Moscow to help Douglas McCracken, who may be her father. On the way, she meets some boisterous army recruits, among them Andrei Tolstoy who is smitten by her. McCracken has invented a fearsome machine ("The Barber of Siberia") designed for efficient logging of Siberian forests. He needs Jane's help in persuading gullible Gen. Radlov, the officer in charge of the military academy, to seek financial support for the venture from the Grand Duke. At the military academy, Jane meets Tolstoy again while at the same time flirting with Radlov, who soon decides he'd like to marry her. This simple part of the plot takes an inordinate amount of time to unfold, punctuated as it is by strenuously unfunny slapstick scenes and sequences featuring the playfully rowdy cadets. Later on, Jane and Tolstoy finally get to consummate their love, and now the film shifts into high dramatic gear with confessions, misunderstandings and a lengthy separation as Tolstoy is carted off to Siberia for an alleged assault on the Grand Duke. Film's climax stretches on long after one has gotten the point and worked out the supposedly deep, dark secret.

Being John Malkovich

A USA Films (in U.S.)/Universal Pictures Intl. release of a Gramercy Pictures presentation of a Propaganda Films/Single Cell Pictures production. Produced by Michael Stipe, Sandy Stern, Steve Golin, Vincent Landay. Executive producers, Charlie Kaufman, Michael Kuhn. Directed by

Spike Jonze. Screenplay, Kaufman. Camera (color), Lance Acord; editor, Eric Zumbrunnen; music, Carter Burwell; production designer, K.K. Barrett; art director, Peter Andrus. Reviewed at Venice Film Festival (Dreams and Visions), Sept. 2, 1999. Running time: 112 mins.

John Cusack (Craig Schwartz), Cameron Diaz (Lotte Schwartz), Catherine Keener (Maxine), Orson Bean (Dr. Lester), Mary Kay Place (Floris), John Malkovich (John Horatio Malkovich), Charlie Sheen (Charlie).

A metaphysical comic love story about the desire to be someone else and the urge to control another person's thoughts and actions, this maze-like journey touches on questions of love, identity, sex, gender. Yet what makes it so fresh is the decision to treat even the story's most surreal inventions in real, rather than fantastical terms. Talented, esoteric puppeteer Craig Schwartz takes a job as a filing clerk in Manhattan. Though married to frumpy pet-store staffer Lotte, he is mesmerized by his co-worker Maxine, who could not care for him less. Craig stumbles on a weird discovery. Behind a cabinet in his office is a door that leads to a tunnel into John Malkovich's head. From here he views the world through the actor's eyes before being spat out into a ditch off the New Jersey Turnpike. Before long, Craig and Maxine are charging thrill-starved New Yorkers $200 a pop for entry into this portal to Malkovich's brain. But complications arise when characters take the trip and are instantly hooked on "the Malkovich ride." Jonze draws rich, enjoyable performances from the entire cast. Malkovich reveals himself to be a terrific sport, taking shots at his own career, his screen persona, even his looks and body and, more fancifully, his murky past. It's hard to imagine many established actors game enough to allow themselves to be presented in this often questionable way, and equally hard to imagine another name that would fit the conceit so snugly.

U.S. release: Oct. 29   U.S. B.O.: $18.2 million

Beresina or the Last Days of Switzerland

A T&C Film (Zurich)/Pandora Film (Cologne)/Prisma Film (Vienna) co-production. Produced by Marcel Hoehn, Karl Baumgartner, Michael Seeber, Heinz Stussak. Directed by Daniel Schmid. Screenplay, Martin Suter. Camera (color), Renato Berta; editor, Daniela Roderer; music, Carl Hanggi; production designer, Kathrin Brunner; costume designer, Birgit Hutter; sound (Dolby Digital), Luc Yersin. (German dialog) Reviewed at Cannes Film Festival (Un Certain Regard), May 20, 1999. Running time: 108 mins.

Elena Panova (Irina), Geraldine Chaplin (Charlotte De), Martin Benrath (Sturzenegger), Ulrich Noethen (Alfred Waldvogel), Ivan Darvas (Vetterli), Marina Confalone (Benedetta), Stefan Kurt (Burki), Hans Peter Korff (Tschanz), Joachim Tomaschewsky (Von Gunten).

Leading Swiss helmer Daniel Schmid applies his wicked sense of humor to the fatherland in a rollicking socio-political farce that roasts just about everybody in a position of power. You don't have to be Swiss to enjoy Schmid's scathing indictment of corrupt stuffed shirts or to applaud the irresistible rise to power of a Russian callgirl who just wants a Swiss passport. The beautiful young Irina is naively enamored of a fairytale Switzerland full of Heidis and St. Bernards. While she studies Swiss history and culture in the museums, she is pressed into service (by a flighty fashion designer and young shyster lawyer, Waldvogel) as an exotic prostitute who satisfies her

illustrious customers' every perversity. Her clients soon include the cream of Swiss society. Pic uses black humor to expose Swiss high society as a hypocritical facade hiding secrets from money-laundering to pimping, with the banks involved in absolutely everything. One day Irina learns she is being expelled from the country by the powerful friends who no longer find her convenient to have around. The news sends the film into its hilarious final lap, when Irina sets off a chain of events that lead, as title promises, to the last days of Switzerland. In her first screen appearance, Russian-born thesp Panova brightens the role with her enthusiasm.

Best Laid Plans

A 20th Century Fox (in U.K.)/Fox Searchlight Pictures (in U.S.) release of a Fox 2000 Pictures presentation of a Dogstar Films production. Produced by Alan Greenspan, Betsy Beers, Chris Moore, Sean Bailey. Executive producer, Mike Newell. Co-producer, Nancy Paloian-Breznikar. Directed by Mike Barker. Screenplay, Ted Griffin. Camera (FotoKem color, Technicolor London prints), Ben Seresin; editor, Sloane Klevin; music, Craig Armstrong; production designer, Sophie Becher; art director, John R. Zachary; costume designer, Susan Matheson; sound (Dolby), Reinhard Stergar; assistant director, Paul N. Martin; casting, Mali Finn. Reviewed at Warner Village, West End 6, London, June 9, 1999. MPAA Rating: R. Running time: 92 mins.

Alessandro Nivola (Nick), Reese Witherspoon (Lissa), Josh Brolin (Bryce), Rocky Carroll (Bad Ass Dude), Michael G. Hagerty (Charlie), Terrence Howard (Jimmy), Jamie Marsh (Barry), Gene Wolande (Lawyer), Jonathan McMurtry (Vet).

An intriguing, partly successful attempt at semi-stylized modern noir that starts off gangbusters but can't keep the lead over the full stretch. First two reels are undeniably impressive as the camera finds two former college buddies drinking in a bar in Tropico, Nev., a two-bit town that people do their best to escape. Nick is a working-class native; Bryce, a slightly preppy, in-your-face type, is a teacher who's just arrived to take a cushy sinecure. As they chat, a young woman saunters into the joint. Fade out.

Later that night, Nick is summoned to the ritzy home where Bryce is house-sitting. Bryce says he's been threatened with statutory rape by an underage girl he picked up that night. He then confesses he beat her and has the girl handcuffed downstairs. Nick offers to talk to the girl alone, which leads to the pic's first (and best) twist. Pic flashbacks to when Nick and Lissa hooked up, with dreams of leaving Tropico. Nick's chance comes when he participates in a burglary that nets him 10 grand. Things go sour when Nick and his partner are caught by the burglarized hood. Nick must return the loot in five days or else. Desperate, Nick and Lissa plan to steal a banknote from the house Bryce is minding. Final three reels pick up some of the opening's intensity, but the final twist, though clever and unexpected, has a "so-what?" feel to it.

U.S. release: Sept. 10   U.S. B.O.: $27,816

Bicentennial Man

A Buena Vista Pictures release of a Touchstone Pictures and Columbia Pictures presentation of a 1492 Pictures production in association with Laurence Mark Prods. and Radiant Prods. Produced by Wolfgang Petersen, Gail Katz, Neal Miller, Laurence Mark, Columbus, Mark Radcliffe, Michael Barnathan. Executive producer, Dan Kolsrud. Directed by

Chris Columbus. Screenplay, Nicholas Kazan, based on the short story by Isaac Asimov and the novel *The Positronic Man* by Asimov and Robert Silverberg. Camera (Technicolor), Phil Meheux; editor, Neil Travis; music, James Horner; production designer, Norman Reynolds; art directors, Mark Mansbridge, William Hiney, Bruton E. Jones Jr.; set designers, William A. Taliaferro, Geoff Hubbard, Darrell L. Wight, James E. Tocci; set decorator, Anne Kuljian; costume designer, Joseph G. Aulisi; sound (Dolby Digital/SDDS/DTS), Nelson Stoll; supervising sound editor, Robert Shoup; sound designer, Randy Thom; robotic effects, Steve Johnson's XFX; old-age-makeup-effects designer, Greg Cannom; old-age-makeup-effects creator, Keith Vanderlaan's Captive Audiences Prods.; visual-effects, Dream Quest Images; visual-effects supervisor, James E. Price; associate producer, Paula Dupre Pesmen; assistant director, David Sardi; second unit camera, Brian Sullivan; casting, Janet Hirshenson, Jane Jenkins. Reviewed at the Galaxy Theater, L.A., Dec. 8, 1999. MPAA Rating: PG. Running time: 131 mins.

Robin Williams (Andrew), Sam Neill (Sir), Wendy Crewson (Ma'am), Embeth Davidtz (Little Miss/Portia), Oliver Platt (Rupert Burns), Hallie Kate Eisenberg (Little Miss, aged 7), Stephen Root (Dennis Mansky), Lynne Thigpen (Female President), Bradley Whitford (Lloyd), Kiersten Warren (Galatea Robotic/Human), John Michael Higgins (Bill Feingold), George D. Wallace (Male President).

An ambitious tale handled in a dawdling, sentimental way. This long-arc story of a robot's 200-year journey to become a human being benefits from compeling thematic notions and wizardly visual, robotic makeup effects, but bogs down due to slack storytelling and an insipidly conventional approach. Screenplay deals with issues regarding the appropriateness, morality and rights of artificially created entities, the definition of humanity, and the desirability of immortality. From a comic point of view, there is intermittent amusement, but only a handful of outright laughs.

Andrew is a genial, obedient robot that has been acquired by the upscale Bay Area Martin family as a servant. The head of the family, simply called Sir, comes to suspect that there might be more to Andrew than metal, and the robot shows a remarkable aptitude for building elegant clocks. He becomes the closest confidant of one of Sir's daughters, Little Miss, who would marry him rather than her fiancé if he were only human. Sixteen years later, when Sir dies, Andrew embarks upon a long odyssey to locate others of his ilk. Search concludes back in San Francisco, where he finds a femme robot and her owner, Rupert Burns, whose brilliance "upgrades" Andrew to human physical specifications even while remaining a robot. Reunited with an older Little Miss, Andrew also makes the acquaintance of her look-alike granddaughter, Portia. Her love story with Andrew drives the final, time-jumping stretch of the picture.

U.S. release: Dec. 17   U.S. B.O.: $39.6 million

Big Daddy

A Sony Pictures Entertainment release of a Columbia Pictures presentation of an Out of the Blue Entertainment/Jack Giarraputo production. Produced by Sid Ganis, Jack Giarraputo. Executive producers, Adam Sandler, Robert Simonds, Joseph M. Caracciolo. Co-producer, Alex Siskin. Directed by Dennis Dugan. Screenplay, Steve Franks, Tim Herlihy, Sandler; story, Franks. Camera (Technicolor), Theo

Van de Sande; editor, Jeff Gourson; music, Teddy Castellucci; production designer, Perry Andelin Blake; art director, Rick Butler; set decorator, Leslie Bloom; costume designer, Ellen Lutter; sound (Dolby/SDDS), Paul Massey, Chris Boyes; associate producers, Michelle Holdsworth, Allen Covert; assistant director, Glen Trotiner; casting, Roger Mussenden. Reviewed at Westwood Theater, L.A., June 16, 1999. MPAA Rating: PG-13. Running time: 95 mins.

Adam Sandler (Sonny Koufax), Joey Lauren Adams (Layla), Jon Stewart (Kevin), Cole Sprouse, Dylan Sprouse (Julian), Josh Mostel (Mr. Brooks), Leslie Mann (Corinne), Allen Covert (Phil), Rob Schneider (Delivery Guy), Kristy Swanson (Vanessa), Joe Bologna (Mr. Koufax), Peter Dante (Tommy), Jonathan Loughran (Mike), Steve Buscemi (Homeless Guy).

It's typical Sandler territory in the early going as we meet 32-year-old slacker Sonny Koufax, who mostly spends loads of free time and money in the Big Apple, having collected a $200,000 award from a car accident. Girlfriend Vanessa says she wants to go upstate and take some time off to think about their relationship. Sonny's roomie Kevin is about to wing off to a job in China when pint-size, 5-year-old Julian shows up claiming to be his son, which Kevin denies. Kevin leaves Sonny to take care of the kid during the Columbus Day holiday. Before this least-likely dad can sort out things with social services bureaucrat Mr. Brooks, he bonds with Julian in a series of scenes balanced between juvenile comedy and heartwarming affection. Sonny, realizing that his unexpected fatherhood is the ideal lure for Vanessa, poses as Kevin with Mr. Brooks, and gains custody. Even as Sonny and Julian grow closer, Vanessa dumps Sonny for an absurdly older fellow, and Mr. Brooks gets wind of Sonny's ruse. Sonny meets Layla, who besides giving him her heart, provides her pro-bono legal services when Brooks takes Julian away and Sonny fights for custody. The gross-out stuff is balanced with scenes of Sandler's character at moments of repose and thoughtfulness. Result is uneven; the story's more serious intentions often jar with the goofy sideshow.

U.S. release: June 25   U.S. B.O.: $163.5 million

The Big Kahuna

A Lions Gate release of a Trigger Street and Franchise Pictures production. Produced by Kevin Spacey, Elie Samaha, Andrew Stevens. Executive producers, Gerard Guez. Co-producer, Joanne Horowitz. Directed by John Swanbeck. Screenplay, Roger Rueff, based on his play *Hospitality Suite*. Camera (color), Anastas N. Michos; editor, Peggy Davis; music, Christopher Young; production designer, Kalina Ivanov; art director, Frank White III; set decorator, Suzie Goudler; costume designer, Katherine Jane Bryant; sound (Dolby), Jeff Pullman; associate producer, Bernie Morris; assistant director, Amanda Slater. Reviewed at Toronto Film Festival (Special Presentation), Sept. 16, 1999. Running time: 90 mins.

Kevin Spacey (Larry), Danny DeVito (Phil), Peter Facinelli (Bob).

The ethos of American business is scrutinized in *The Big Kahuna*. A terrific ensemble elevates this slightly opened-up stage play to a passable level of bigscreen entertainment. An engaging drama sprinkled with dark humor and sharp observations about the tension between careerism and personal values.

In a Wichita hotel during a manufacturers' convention, three salesmen engage in discussions on the meaning of work

---

... April 29 ...
The American Museum of Moving Pictures acknowledges
Tom Hanks with a Lifetime Achievement Award.

and life – specifically, how religious and ethical beliefs interface with – and impinge on – professional matters. Phil is a burnt-out account manager who is used to life on the road, and is undergoing a painful divorce. There's Bob, a quiet young researcher, who's a happy newly-wed and traveling on business for the first time. Enter Larry, a loud, energetic man who smokes, drinks, and lusts after women. Boasting a unique outlook on life, Larry thrives on confrontation, and it doesn't take long before he gets in Bob's face. Narrative takes place in the course of one evening, while the group waits for potential customer, Dick Fuller (aka the Big Kahuna), to drop by and boost their sales – and dwindling spirits.

Spacey and DeVito are such pros that it's a pleasure to observe their charged but smooth give-and-take dialog. Newcomer Facinelli holds his own in a demanding role full of surprises. What distinguishes pic from works by Arthur Miller and Mamet is its lack of bitterness or cynicism.

The Blair Witch Project

An Artisan release of a Haxan Films presentation. (International sales: Haxan Films, Orlando, Fla.) Produced by Gregg Hale, Robin Cowie. Executive producers, Bob Eick, Kevin J. Foxe. Co-producer, Michael Monello. Directed, written, edited by Daniel Myrick, Eduardo Sanchez. Camera (color/b&w, video and 16mm-to-35mm), Neal Fredericks; music, Tony Cora; production designer, Ben Rock; art director, Ricardo R. Moreno; sound, Dana Meeks. Reviewed at Sundance Film Festival (Midnight), Jan. 25, 1999. Running time: 87 mins.

With: Heather Donahue, Michael Williams, Joshua Leonard, Bob Griffith, Jim King, Sandra Sanchez, Ed Swanson, Patricia Decou.

An intensely imaginative piece of conceptual filmmaking that also delivers the goods as a dread-drenched horror movie, pic puts a clever modern twist on the universal fear of the dark and things that go bump in the night. The way the film was made has everything to do with how it plays out onscreen. An opening title card informs that, in October 1994, three young filmmakers hiked into the Black Hills Forest in Maryland to shoot a documentary about the legend of the Blair Witch. The filmmakers were never heard from again, but a year later their footage was found, an edited version of which constitutes the present feature.

All the visuals are either handheld, often jittery color video images taken by the bossy director, Heather, or black-and-white 16mm shots lensed by the troupe's tyro cameraman, the hippie-ish Joshua; regular guy Michael is along to record sound. The continuous point-of-view shots and, at night, the highly concentrated lighting keep the viewer's range of vision extremely limited, creating a highly claustrophobic feeling and great apprehension over what might suddenly pop into frame. Pic comes across as smart without feeling manipulative except in isolated moments, and serves as a reminder that effective horror stems much more from psychology than from graphic gore.

U.S. release: July 14   U.S. B.O.: $140 million

The Bone Collector

A Universal release of a Universal Pictures and Columbia Pictures presentation of a Bregman production. Produced by Martin Bregman, Louis A. Stroller, Michael Bregman. Executive producers, Michael Klawitter, Dan Jinks. Directed by Phillip Noyce. Screenplay, Jeremy Iacone, based on the novel by Jeffery Deaver. Camera (Deluxe color, Panavision widescreen), Dean Semler; editor, William Hoy; music, Craig Armstrong; production designer, Nigel Phelps; supervising art directors, Claude Pare (Montreal), Jeff Sage (N.Y.); set decorators, Marie-Claude Gosselin (Montreal), Harriet Zucker (N.Y.). Reviewed at World Film Festival, Montreal (World Greats), Aug. 29, 1999. MPAA Rating: R. Running time: 118 mins.

Denzel Washington (Lincoln Rhyme), Angelina Jolie (Amelia Donaghy), Queen Latifah (Thelma), Michael Rooker (Capt. Howard Cheney), Mike McGlone (Det. Kenny Solomon), Luis Guzman (Eddie Ortiz), Leland Orser (Richard Thompson), John Benjamin Hickey (Dr. Barry Lehman), Bobby Cannavale (Steve), Ed O'Neill (Det. Paulie Sellitto).

The obvious difficulties in making an action thriller out of Jeffery Deaver's bestseller *The Bone Collector* aren't entirely surmounted in Phillip Noyce's glossy adaptation. Helmer is on familiar turf with another mainstream suspenser; confident pacing, subterranean atmospherics, and a few false scares maintain middling tension, but pic's smooth handling doesn't really get under the skin in the manner of some other recent serial-killer thrillers.

Brilliant NYPD criminologist Lincoln Rhyme is paralyzed below the shoulders and passes days in unhappy retirement. But Rhyme's former partner, Det. Sellitto, thinks only his uncanny deduction skills can help in finding a serial killer. From collected evidence, Rhyme is able to pinpoint a likely hostage location.

Story throws out its major barrier to credibility as Rhyme insists that beat cop Amelia Donaghy be the one to survey the forensics of the killer's urban dwellings. We're meant to buy that Rhymes perceives a "natural ability" in Donaghy strictly based on her quick thinking that preserved clues during her first encounter with one of the killer's victims. Clues eventually point toward the assailant's recreation of crimes from the turn of the century. Screenplay doesn't provide much in the way of character backstory, or deep relationships, to fully articulate the immobilized protagonist's human dimension. The action is pulse-quickening, but payoff suffers from the weakness of killer's proffered explanation which reveals little satisfying reason for the choice of victims or violent methods.

U.S. release: Nov. 5   U.S. B.O.: $63.7 million

Bowfinger

A Universal release of a Universal and Imagine Entertainment presentation of a Brian Grazer production. Produced by Grazer. Executive producers, Karen Kehela, Bernie Williams. Directed by Frank Oz. Screenplay, Steve Martin. Camera (Deluxe color), Ueli Steiger; editor, Richard Pearson; music, David Newman; music supervisor, Pilar McCurry; production designer, Jackson Degovia; art director, Tom Reta; set designers, Karl Martin, Les Gobruegge, Dawn Snyder; set decorator, K.C. Fox; costume designer, Joseph G. Aulisi; sound (DTS/SDDS/Dolby Digital), Martin Raymond Bolger; stunt coordinator, Bud Davis; associate producer, Kathleen Courtney; assistant director, Michele Panelli-Venetis; casting, Margery Simkin. Reviewed at the Beverly Connection, L.A., Aug. 4, 1999. MPAA Rating: PG-13. Running time: 96 mins.

Steve Martin (Bobby Bowfinger), Eddie Murphy (Kit Ramsey/Jiff Ramsey), Heather Graham (Daisy), Christine Baranski (Carol), Jamie Kennedy (Dave), Adam Alexi-Malle

(Afrim), **Kohl Sudduth** (Slater), **Barry Newman** (Kit's Agent), **Robert Downey Jr.** (Jerry Renfro), **Terence Stamp** (Terry Stricter).

Bobby Bowfinger, a schlock delusional producer-director, has never made it in Hollywood but, at 50, realizes that it's now or never. He sets out to make a sci-fi flick, *Chubby Rain*, and actually gets a commitment from a smarmy studio exec – if he can deliver the world's biggest action star, Kit Ramsey. Egomaniacal actor Ramsey is overwhelmed by a paranoia that is mostly driven by a fear of being attacked by aliens. This serves Bowfinger effectively as he implements a scheme of capturing candid shots of Ramsey in public reacting to the antics of the director's crazed actors. Ramsey becomes terrified that his nemeses have arrived to torment him, and takes refuge in a celebrity retreat center. Bowfinger responds by finding a Ramsey lookalike, Jiff, a bashful, terminally nerdy fellow who's thrilled to help out. Murphy has been brilliantly, brashly funny up 'til now as the arrogant star, but he more than doubles the pleasure once he re-enters the picture as this milquetoast who performs well beyond the call of duty for his director.

Quirky and clever premise provides an ample clothesline on which to hang innumerable gags and jokes, many of which are very funny. But pic is limited by its sketchlike nature and a fundamental lack of grounding in reality. The most notable element linking the characters is a sense of self-delusion so highly developed that it allows them to live in something like a state of expectant bliss.

U.S. release: Aug.13   U.S. B.O.: $66.5 million

Boys Don't Cry

A Fox Searchlight release, in association with the Independent Film Channel, of a Killer Films/Hart Sharp production. Produced by Jeffrey Sharp, John Hart, Eva Kolodner, Christine Vachon. Executive producers, Pamela Koffler, Jonathan Sehring, Caroline Kaplan. Co producer, Morton Swinsky. Directed by Kimberly Peirce. Screenplay, Peirce, Andy Bienen. Camera (Deluxe color), Jim Denault; editors, Lee Percy, Tracy Granger; music, Nathan Larsen; production designer, Michael Shaw; costume designer, Victoria Farrell; sound (Dolby), Mack Melson; associate producer, Bradford Simpson; casting, Billy Hopkins, Suzanne Smith, Kerry Barden, Jennifer McNamara. Reviewed at 20th Century Fox Studios, L.A., Aug. 30, 1999. (In Venice Film Festival - Cinema of the Present; Toronto Film Festival - Contemporary World Cinema; New York Film Festival.) Running time: 116 mins.

Hilary Swank (Brandon Teena), **Chloe Sevigny** (Lana), **Peter Sarsgaard** (John), **Brendan Sexton III** (Tom), **Alison Folland** (Kate), **Alicia Goranson** (Candace), **Matt McGrath** (Lonny), **Rob Campbell** (Brian), **Jeannetta Arnette** (Lana's Mom).

Based on the brutal rape and murder of Teena Brandon (Brandon Teena), this devastatingly powerful tale of a young girl who disguised herself as a boy is anchored by two fully realized performances, by Hilary Swank as the sexual misfit and Chloe Sevigny as her girlfriend. Richly dense narrative touches on many controversial and timely issues – the nature of sexual identity, biology vs. sociology in gender construction, role playing in modern life – as well as offering a perceptive anatomy of homophobia and intolerance in the American heartland.

Set in 1993, 20-year-old Brandon, donning a boyish haircut and attire, arrives in Fall City as a bright newcomer who enchants all those who meet him. Soon he establishes himself as a playful rebel, a sensitive and loyal friend, and an irresistible romantic who seduces lonely, innocent, and underprivileged beauties. Though warned by close friend Lonny that "his" behavior signals big trouble and "folks in Fall City kill fags," Brandon insists that her life – now his life – is on the right track. He soon lays eyes on Lana; it's love at first sight. Last reel is extremely powerful in chronicling the rednecks' reaction when a local newspaper breaks Brandon's story: almost too painful to watch. *Boys* is a breath of fresh air at a time when most American indies have gotten too soft and too close to the mainstream.

U.S. release: Oct. 8   U.S. B.O.: $2.7 million

Breakfast of Champions

A Summit Entertainment/Flying Heart Films presentation of a Sugar Creek Prods. production. (International sales: Summit, Santa Monica.) Produced by David Blocker, David Willis. Directed, written by Alan Rudolph, based on the novel by Kurt Vonnegut Jr. Camera (color), Elliot Davis; editor, Suzy Elmiger; music, Mark Isham; production designer, Nina Ruscio; art director, Randy Eriksen; costume designer, Rudy Dillon; sound (Dolby Digital), Paul P. Soucek, Elizia A. Paley; visual-effects supervisor, Janet Muswell; associate producer, Sandra Tomita; assistant director, Cara Giallanza; casting, Pam Dixon. Reviewed at Berlin Film Festival (competing), Feb. 13, 1999. Running time: 110 mins.

Bruce Willis (Dwayne Hoover), **Albert Finney** (Kilgore Trout), **Nick Nolte** (Harry Le Sabre), **Barbara Hershey** (Celia Hoover), **Glenne Headly** (Francine Pefko), **Lukas Haas** (Bunny Hoover), **Omar Epps** (Wayne Hoobler), **Buck Henry** (Fred T. Barry), **Vicki Lewis** (Grace Le Sabre), **Ken Campbell** (Eliot Rosewater), **Jake Johannsen** (Bill Bailey), **Will Patton** (Moe), **Chip Zien** (Andy Wojeckowzski), **Ken Campbell** (Gilbert), **Owen Wilson** (Monte Rapid), **Alison Eastwood** (Maria Maritmo), **Shawnee Smith** (Bonnie MacMahon), **Kurt Vonnegut Jr.** (Commercials Director).

A hearty meal that starts off tickling the taste buds but ends up smothering them, pic is a game attempt to film Kurt Vonnegut Jr.'s 1976 satire on American greed and commercialism. Pic has some fine individual moments but fails to cohere into a grander, more substantial statement on the themes it aspires to tackle. A manic, social-commentary comedy that was in fashion when the source novel was written but now fits awkwardly into today's blander Hollywood panorama.

First couple of reels are, however, very funny in their parody of a nightmare Middle American burg, here called Midland City. Dwayne Hoover runs the area's most successful car dealership, Exit 11 Motor Village. Underneath his immaculate smile and slick threads, however, Dwayne is a suicidal, troubled man with a pill-popping wife. Dwayne's longtime sales manager, Harry, likes to wear female undies and lives in permanent fear of being unmasked. And Dwayne's secretary, Francine, drags him off for lunchtime quickies but is really more interested in making big bucks than making her boss. If that's not enough, Dwayne is also under investigation by the Environmental Protection Agency for his role in a local pollution scandal. Centered on a span of a few days during Exit 11's "Hawaiian Week" promo, the film follows the disintegration of Dwayne from all-American business legend to a man in desperate need of answers to the whys and wherefores of life.

U.S. release: Sept. 17   U.S. B.O.: $178,287

. . . May 1 . . .

Entrapment dropped an impressive $26.1 million into its cage to easily command the domestic B.O. for the week.

Bringing Out the Dead

A Paramount release of a Paramount and Touchstone Pictures presentation of a Scott Rudin-Cappa/De Fina production. Produced by Rudin, Barbara De Fina. Executive producers, Adam Schroeder, Bruce S. Pustin. Co-producers, Joseph Reidy, Eric Steel. Directed by Martin Scorsese. Screenplay, Paul Schrader, based on the novel by Joe Connelly. Camera (Deluxe color, Panavision widescreen), Robert Richardson; editor, Thelma Schoonmaker; music, Elmer Bernstein; production designer, Dante Ferretti; art director, Robert Guerra; set decorator, William F. Reynolds; costume designer, Rita Ryack; sound (SDDS/DolbyDigital/ DTS), James J. Sabat; supervising sound editor, Philip Stockton; special visual effects, Industrial Light & Magic; associate producers, Jeff Levine, Mark Roybal; assistant director, Joseph Reidy; casting, Ellen Lewis. Reviewed at Paramount Studios, L.A., Oct. 13, 1999. MPAA Rating: R. Running time: 120 mins.

Nicolas Cage (Frank Pierce), Patricia Arquette (Mary Burke), John Goodman (Larry), Ving Rhames (Marcus), Tom Sizemore (Tom Wolls), Marc Anthony (Noel), Mary Beth Hurt (Nurse Constance), Cliff Curtis (Cy Coates), Nestor Serrano (Dr. Hazmat), Aida Turturro (Nurse Crupp), Cynthia Roman (Rose), Afemo Omilami (Griss), Cullen Oliver Johnson (Mr. Burke), Arthur Nascarella (Captain Barney).

Though not as resonant or brilliant as Scorsese's landmark New York films, pic is a decent, well-made movie that displays admirable balance among the dramatic, comic, and absurdist elements that define paramedics' highly demanding jobs. Frank Pierce is a man on the edge, an insomniac loner who works the graveyard shift and undergoes a severe spiritual crisis that may lead to either self-destruction or redemption. Story is set in the early 1990s, when New York City's Emergency Medical Service was in disorder. This background conveys the chaos and wilderness in which paramedics operate: urgent calls, heavy traffic, overcrowded hospitals, hysterical victims, homeless people, pimps, and crackheads to name a few. Haunted by visions of Rose, a girl he failed to save, Frank knows there's nothing like the joy of preventing a death. Each night, Frank teams with a different partner, and his distinctive interactions with each paramedic provide the film's texture – and most entertaining elements, for ultimately the narrative is about survival, or how these pros cope with the miseries inherent in their chores. Cage is in his best role since *Leaving Las Vegas*. Film has been blessed with a large and superlative ensemble of secondary characters, with standout turns from Goodman, Sizemore and Rhames as the three radically different partners. Scorsese and Schrader's pic is the best adaptation imaginable of its source material, and a mature reworking of many of their longtime preoccupations.

U.S. release: Oct. 22   U.S. B.O.: $16.5 million

Children of the Century

A BAC Films release (in France) from Odeon Films of a Les Films Alain Sarde/Alexandre Films/France 2 Cinema production presented with Canal Plus. (International sales: Le Studio Canal Plus, Paris.) Produced by Diane Kurys, Sarde. Executive producer, Robert Benmussa. Directed by Kurys. Screenplay, Francois Olivier Rousseau, Murray Head, Kurys. Camera (color, widescreen), Vilko Filac; editor, Joele Van Effenterre; music, Luis Bacalov; production designer, Bernard Vezat; art director, Maxime Rebiere; costume designer,

Christian Lacroix, in collaboration with Anais Romand; sound (Dolby Digital/SDDS), Jean-Louis Ughetto, Vincent Amardi, Laurent Kossayan; associate producer, Christine Gozlan; assistant director, Marc Baraduc; casting, Gerard Moulevrier. Reviewed at Toronto Film Festival (Special Presentation), Sept. 15, 1999. Running time: 137 mins.

Juliette Binoche (George Sand), Benoit Magimel (Alfred de Musset), Stefano Dionisi (Pagello), Robin Renucci (Buloz), Karin Viard (Marie Dorval), Isabelle Carre (Aimee d'Alton), Arnaud Giovaninetti (Tattet), Denis Podalydes (Sainte-Beuve), Olivier Foubert (Paul), Marie-France Mignal (Mme de Musset).

An old-fashioned costumer that runs out of gas even faster than the tempestuous love affair between writer George Sand and poet Alfred de Musset that it so devotedly recounts. It is the early 1830s, and Baroness Dudevant arrives in Paris with her two children. Having just left her husband and stifling life in the country, she has decided to reinvent herself as a writer with a masculine name, attire, and gestures, outraging Paris with salon readings from her anti-matrimonial texts. This attracts de Musset, a dissolute rich boy given to boozing and carousing in brothels. The two develop a passionate friendship that leads to a torrid affair, with the poet helping the burgeoning literary star revise a troublesome play. De Musset's family disapproves of the match. The couple escape on a winter trip to Venice, which proves taxing as de Musset spirals into a drink-and-opium-fed dissipation. Sand ultimately takes solace in the arms of a doctor, Pagello, who nurses her and, subsequently, de Musset back to health. From there, things go from dire to merely drear for Sand and de Musset.

Script judiciously mines the letters of the two protagonists for telling glimpses into their passions and self-reflections. However, it fails to illuminate the inner life of Sand – in particular, to reveal what it took to undertake her transformation and to suggest how she could tolerate the extraordinary abuse she endured at the hands of de Musset.

The Cider House Rules

A Miramax Films release of a Miramax Intl./FilmColony presentation of a FilmColony production. Produced by Richard N. Gladstein. Executive producers, Bob Weinstein, Harvey Weinstein, Bobby Cohen, Meryl Poster. Co-producers, Alan C. Blomquist, Leslie Holleran. Directed by Lasse Hallstrom. Screenplay, John Irving, based on his novel. Camera (Deluxe color, widescreen), Oliver Stapleton; editor, Lisa Zeno Churgin; music, Rachel Portman; production designer, David Gropman; art director, Karen Schulz-Gropman; set decorator, Beth Rubino; costume designer, Renee Ehrlich Kalfus; sound (SDDS/Dolby Digital), Petur Hliddal; associate producers, Michelle Platt, Lila Yacoub; assistant director, Stephen P. Dunn; casting, Billy Hopkins, Suzanne Smith, Kerry Barden. Reviewed at Venice Film Festival (competing), Sept. 5, 1999. (Also in Deauville Film Festival; Toronto Film Festival - Gala.) Running time: 131 mins.

Tobey Maguire (Homer Wells), Charlize Theron (Candy Kendall), Delroy Lindo (Mr. Rose), Paul Rudd (Wally Worthington), Michael Caine (Dr. Wilbur Larch), Jane Alexander (Nurse Edna), Kathy Baker (Nurse Angela), Erykah Badu (Rose Rose), Kieran Culkin (Buster), Kate Nelligan (Olive Worthington), Heavy D (Peaches), K. Todd Freeman (Muddy), Paz de la Huerta (Mary Agnes).

. . . May 2 . . .
Oliver Reed dies.

One of the most successful attempts yet at filming the work of popular American novelist John Irving. Dealing in habitual Irving themes of family, love and the search to find a place and purpose in the world, pic could have used more dramatic muscle but is nonetheless a touching, old-fashioned charmer that ultimately satisfies.

Opening in the 1930s at St. Cloud's orphanage in the Maine countryside, the story outlines how twice-adopted, twice-returned child Homer Wells was raised with love by Dr. Wilbur Larch, who heads the institution. Trained by Larch as a doctor, Homer helps care for abandoned children and deliver unwanted babies. But his moral qualms prevent him from assisting in the illegal abortions Larch performs. When young World War II pilot Wally Worthington and his pregnant girlfriend, Candy, come to St. Cloud's for an abortion, Homer impulsively decides to leave with them and see the world beyond the orphanage. Not getting as far as the Maine stateline, he takes work at the businesses of Wally's mother and Candy's family. With Wally away at war, love blossoms between Homer and Candy. Wally's return in a wheelchair and Larch's death – leaving the orphanage without a doctor – forces Homer to make complex decisions that will shape his future.

A strong, sensitive actor, Maguire is a fine choice for Irving's quiet hero. Caine also scores in an uncharacteristic role and is easily the film's most memorable supporting turn.

U.S. release: Dec. 10   U.S. B.O.: $4.2 million

A Civil Action

A Buena Vista release of a Touchstone/Paramount Pictures presentation. Produced by Scott Rudin, Robert Redford, Rachel Pfeffer. Executive producers, Steven Zaillian, David Wisnievitz. Directed, written by Steven Zaillian, based on the book by Jonathan Harr. Camera (DeLuxe color), Conrad L. Hall; editor, Wayne Wahrman; music, Danny Elfman; production designer, David Gropman; art director (L.A.), David J. Bomba; set decorator (L.A.), Tracy A. Doyle; costume designer, Shay Cunliffe; sound (Dolby/SDDS), David Macmillan; associate producers, David McGiffert, Henry J. Golas; assistant director, McGiffert; casting, Avy Kaufman. Reviewed at the Beverly Connection, L.A., Dec. 5, 1998. MPAA Rating PG-13. Running time: 112 mins.
John Travolta (Jan Schlichtmann), Robert Duvall (Jerome Facher), Tony Shalhoub (Kevin Conway), William H. Macy (James Gordon), Zeljko Ivanbeck (Bill Crowley), Bruce Norris (William Cheeseman), John Lithgow (Judge Skinner), Kathleen Quinlan (Anne Anderson), Peter Jacobson (Neil Jacobs), Sydney Pollack (Al Eustis).
Based on a true story, pic is a solid and intelligent legal thriller that may be too complex in its issues, and too low-key and unexciting in its style. In 1980s Woburn, Mass., a Boston personal-injury lawyer wages an environmental crusade on behalf of eight innocent families against two large corporations accused of contaminating the town's drinking water. The families' children have died of leukemia as a result of the water. Pic is all but stolen by Robert Duvall, who enriches every scene he is in as Travolta's nemesis, a shrewdly eccentric corporate attorney. An intricately structured film that is downbeat, lacks clear-cut heroes and villains, and is imbued with moral ambiguity in its dissection of the legal profession, corporate ethos, and the disparity of the American class structure.

The film's thematic virtues – its refusal to romanticize the story, to sentimentalize the victims, and to glorify the lawyers – and stylistic devices – quiet, contemplative mood, slow, deliberate pacing – are uncharacteristic in today's Hollywood. Gradually, it becomes clear that the story is not just about the haves and the have-nots, but the sharp hierarchy that prevails within the legal profession: the prestige of the school one attended (Harvard vs. Cornell), the selectivity of private clubs, the contempt for personal-injury lawyers as "ambulance chasers," as Travolta's Jan reveals in his sharp, ironic voiceover narration that runs throughout the film.

U.S. release: Dec. 1998   U.S. B.O.: $57 million

Cookie's Fortune

An October Films release of a Sandcastle 5/Elysian Dreams production. Produced by Robert Altman, Etchie Stroh. Executive producer, Willi Baer. Co-producers, David Levy, James McLindon. Directed by Robert Altman. Screenplay, Anne Rapp.
Glenn Close (Camille Orcutt), Julianne Moore (Cora Duvall), Liv Tyler (Emma Duvall), Chris O'Donnell (Jason Brown), Charles S. Dutton (Willis Richland), Patricia Neal (Jewel Mae "Cookie" Orcutt), Ned Beatty (Lester Boyle), Courtney B. Vance (Otis Tucker), Donald Moffat (Jack Palmer), Lyle Lovett (Manny Hood), Danny Darst (Billy Cox), Matt Malloy (Eddie "The Expert" Pitts), Randle Mell (Patrick Freeman), Niecy Nash (Wanda Carter), Rufus Thomas (Theo Johnson), Ruby Wilson (Josie Martin), Preston Strobel (Ronnie Freeman).
Altman establishes the particulars of the tiny community of Holly Springs, Mississippi. A portly middle-aged black man, Willis, finishes an evening of drinking at a blues dive by lifting a bottle from the establishment, tipsily makes his way to a grand old house and starts cleaning the antique guns in the collection of old Jewel Mae "Cookie" Orcutt. Willis, it develops, is the caretaker for Jewel Mae, who is bit batty and still terribly devoted to her late husband, Buck. Also underway this Good Friday night is a rehearsal for a church-group production of *Salome*, directed by Jewel Mae's obsessive niece, Camille.

On Saturday, a sober Willis discreetly deposits a full bottle of Wild Turkey back on the shelf at the club. Mae takes one of her pistols and joyfully shoots herself, so that she might be reunited with her husband. Camille denies the possibility that a family member could commit suicide, and meddles with the bloody scene to make it look as though her aunt was murdered during a robbery. Camille also does nothing to prevent the local cops from arresting Willis on the basis of transparently misleading circumstantial evidence.

This deceptively modest pic may or not be Robert Altman's best film in years, but it is certainly his most pleasurable. Distinguished by a generosity of spirit most uncommon in the director's work, as well as by Charles S. Dutton's enormously embraceable performance.

U.S. release: Apr. 2   U.S. B.O.: $10.9 million

Cradle Will Rock

A Buena Vista release of a Touchstone Pictures presentation of a Havoc production. (International sales: UGC Intl., Paris.) Produced by Jon Kilik, Lydia Dean Pilcher, Tim Robbins. Executive producers, Louise Krakower, Frank Beacham, Allan Nicholls. Directed, written by Tim Robbins. Camera (Technicolor, Panavision widescreen), Jean Yves

Above: Keanu Reeves in *The Matrix*

Below: Award-winners Annette Bening and Kevin Spacey in *American Beauty*

Above: Emilie Dequenne in *Rosetta*, Palme d'Or winner at the Cannes Festival

Below: Liev Schreiber and John Malkovich in *RKO 281*, the TV film about the making of *Citizen Kane*

Above: Spain's *All About My Mother* swept up numerous awards around the world

Below: European Academy Awards 1999: (from l to r) David Lynch, Ulrich Felsberg, Cecilia Roth, Pedro Almodóvar, Antonio Banderas, and Ennio Morricone

Above: Pierce Brosnan and Robert Carlisle at odds in
the latest James Bond adventure, *The World Is Not Enough*

Above: Hugh Grant and Julia Roberts in the high-grossing *Notting Hill*

Below: Gwyneth Paltrow and Joseph Fiennes dancing in *Shakespeare in Love*, 1999's Best Film winner at both the Academy Awards in Hollywood and the BAFTA Awards in London

Above: The cast of *Father Ted*

Above: Calista Flockhart as Ally McBeal

Above: *Cats* continued to break records for longevity on stages around the world

Below: The British surprise hit musical *Spend, Spend, Spend* delighted audiences in London's West End

Below: Andrew Lloyd Webber's *Whistle Down the Wind*, starring Glenn Carter and Laura-Michelle Kelly

Escoffier; editor, Geraldine Peroni; music, David Robbins, with songs by Marc Blitzstein; production designer, Richard Hoove. Reviewed at Walt Disney Studios, Burbank, May 6, 1999. Running time: 133 mins.

Hank Azaria (Marc Blitzstein), Ruben Blades (Diego Rivera), Joan Cusack (Hazel Huffman), John Cusack (Nelson Rockefeller), Cary Elwes (John Houseman), Philip Baker Hall (Gray Mathers), Cherry Jones (Hallie Flanagan), Angus Macfadyen (Orson Welles), Bill Murray (Tommy Crickshaw), Vanessa Redgrave (Comtesse LaGrange), Susan Sarandon (Margherita Sarfatti), Jamey Sheridan (John Adair), John Turturro (Aldo Silvano), Emily Watson (Olive Stanton), Bob Balaban (Harry Hopkins), Jack Black (Sid), Kyle Gass (Larry), Paul Giamatti (Carlo), Barnard Hughes (Frank Marvel), Barbara Sukowa (Sophie Silvano), John Carpenter (William Randolph Hearst), Gretchen Mol (Marion Davies), Harris Yulin (Chairman Martin Dies), Gil Robbins (Congressman Starnes), Corina Katt (Frida Kahlo).

A vibrant evocation of a rare moment in American history when art and politics were dynamically forged on the same anvil, pic succeeds more often than not in delivering a credible, kaleidoscopic portrait of creative and famous individuals including Orson Welles, John Houseman, Diego Rivera, and Nelson Rockfeller, to name a few. Erring mainly in its occasional tendency toward caricature, this is Tim Robbins' ambitious attempt to make his own *Reds*, a deeply felt homage to a time when artistic activity was driven by passionate commitment much more than by dreams of profit or celebrity.

In the fall of 1936, during the Depression, Marc Blitzstein's musical *Cradle Will Rock* is taken on by a young Welles and Houseman at the height of their celebrated collaboration. The musical enjoys a unique place in legit annals due to the dramatic circumstances of its premiere: with right-wing politicians on the attack and its theater abruptly shut down by authorities on the day of opening, the company led the public on a 21-block march through Manhattan to another venue where the actors, forbidden by their union from setting foot onstage, spontaneously began performing their roles from various spots in the auditorium. Result was a political triumph for the beleaguered Federal Theater. This episode is a larger picture of the cultural landscape during a tumultuous, exciting period. Many of the performances are splendid with standouts all around. This is a rare Hollywood-backed venture, one that goes a long way toward bringing a convulsive period alive more than 60 years later.

U.S. release: Dec. 8   U.S. B.O.: $769,995

Crazy in Alabama

A Sony Pictures Entertainment release of a Columbia Pictures presentation of a Green Moon production in association with Meir Teper. Produced by Teper, Linda Goldstein Knowlton, Debra Hill, Diane Sillan Isaacs. Executive producer, James R. Dyer. Directed by Antonio Banderas. Screenplay, Mark Childress, based on his novel. Camera (Technicolor, Deluxe prints; widescreen), Julio Macat; editors, Maysie Hoy, Robert C. Jones; music, Mark Snow; production designer, Cecilia Montiel; art director, Michael Atwell; set designer, Noelle King; set decorator, Robert Greenfield; costume designer, Graciela Mazon; sound (Dolby/SDDS), Doug Arnold; assistant director, George Parra; casting, Minsdy Marin. Reviewed at Sony Studios, Culver City, Aug. 25, 1999. MPAA Rating: PG-13. Running time: 111 mins.

Melanie Griffith (Lucille), David Morse (Dove), Lucas Black (Peejoe), Cathy Moriarty (Earlene), Meat Loaf Aday (Sheriff John Doggett), Rod Steiger (Judge Mead), Richard Schiff (Norman), John Beasley (Nehemiah), Robert Wagner (Harry Hall), Noah Emmerich (Sheriff Raymond), Sandra Seacat (Meemaw), Paul Ben-Victor (Mackie), Brad Beyer (Jack), Fannie Flagg (Sally), Elizabeth Perkins (Joan Blake), Linda Hart (Madelyn), Paul Mazursky (Walter Schwegmann), Holmes Osborne (Larry Russell), William Converse Roberts (Murphy), David Speck (Wiley).

Yarn combines an often wacky look at Lucille, a Southern bombshell who heads for Hollywood after murdering her husband, with a deadly serious account of racial strife in the South, circa 1965. She totes his severed head along, a fact she readily blurts out to just about everyone she meets along the road.

Curious events are seen from the point of view of Lucille's insightful 13-year-old nephew Peejoe. The low-key, wryly humorous events in the small Alabama town contrast oddly with the coarser nature of Lucille's wild road trip.

Against a background of peaceful voting-rights protests, black teenager Taylor Jackson stages a peaceful defiance by showing up at an all-white public pool with a group of black boys. A head-bashing is triggered by the cops and Taylor's semi-accidental death at the hands of racist Sheriff John Doggett, is witnessed by Peejoe.

The fearless Peejoe informs the sheriff that he'll tell of the man's responsibility for Taylor's death if he doesn't lay off his pursuit of his aunt.

The director has assembled some good thesps and handles them well; there are also signs that he is alert to visual considerations. All the same, the pic could have used a bold stylistic approach, along the lines of such contempo masters of dark comedy as the Coens or Wes Anderson, to fully put it across. Impression instead is that of a potentially talented filmmaker just getting his feet wet.

U.S. release: Oct. 22   U.S. B.O.: $2 million

Cruel Intentions

A Sony release of a Columbia Pictures presentation, in association with Original Film and Newmarket Capital Group, of a Neal H. Moritz production. Produced by Moritz. Executive producer, Michael Fottrell. Co-executive producers, William Tyrer, Bruce Mellon, Chris J. Ball. Co-producer, Heather Zeegen. Directed, written by Roger Kumble. Script suggested by the novel *Les liaisons dangereuses*.

Sarah Michelle Gellar (Kathryn Merteuil), Ryan Phillippe (Sebastian Valmont), Reese Witherspoon (Annette Hargrove), Selma Blair (Cecile Caldwell), Louise Fletcher (Helen Rosemond), Joshua Jackson (Blaine Tuttle), Eric Mabius (Greg McConnell), Sean Patrick Thomas (Ronald Clifford), Swoosie Kurtz (Dr. Greenbaum), Christine Baranski (Bunny Caldwell).

The fourth film to use Choderlos De Laclos' 1782 novel as its basis, this recent update is for the teenage crowd. Nasty, profane and wickedly entertaining, pic is a faithful rendition. Ryan Phillippe is a sexier, seductive Valmont than seen in earlier versions. This black comedy also benefits from a terrific Sarah Michelle Gellar, who's as manipulative and mean-spirited as Glenn Close was.

Set in Manhattan's upper-crust society during summer break, Kathryn Merteuil and the philandering Sebastian

Valmont are wealthy step-siblings who conspire in wagers with seduction and sexual conquest as chief rewards. Dumped by her beau for the innocent Cecile, Kathryn decides to get even, challenging Sebastian to deflower the girl. The point is to turn Cecile into an insatiable tramp. In the meantime, Sebastian sets his sights on Annette, who published an article in *Seventeen* in which she declared herself a virgin until marrying her true love. Holding that Sebastian can't seduce the chaste Annette before school begins, Kathryn agrees to the wager. If Sebastian succeeds, Kathryn will spend a wild night with him, but should he fail, he'll have to forfeit his 1956 Jaguar to her – and face the shame of defeat. What makes the first reel of this version seductively diverting is the sexual tension between Phillipe and Gellar. The first two acts provide the kind of lewd, odious fun seldom encountered in teen films, making pic a guilty pleasure for both young and mature audiences.

U.S. release: Mar. 5   U.S. B.O.: $38.3 million

Deep Blue Sea

A Warner Bros. release in association with Village Roadshow Pictures and Groucho III Film Partnership of an Alan Riche-Tony Ludwig/Akiva Goldsman production. Produced by Goldsman, Ludwig, Riche. Executive producers, Duncan Kennedy, Bruce Berman. Co-producer, Rebecca Spikings. Directed by Renny Harlin. Screenplay, Duncan Kennedy, Donna Powers, Wayne Powers. Camera (Technicolor, Panavision widescreen), Stephen Windon; editors, Frank J. Urioste, Derek G. Brechin, Dallas S. Puett; music, Trevor Rabin; production designer, William Sandell, Joseph Bennett; supervising art directors, Mark W. Mansbridge, Bruce Crone; art directors, Andrew Rothschild, Hector Romero; set designers, Bill Taliaferro, Javier Nava; set decorator, Debra Echard; costume designer, Mark Bridges; sound (Dolby Digital/DTS/SDDS), John Reitz, Dave Campbell, Gregg Rudloff; supervising sound editors, J. Paul Huntsman, Robb Wilson; visual-effects supervisor, Jeffrey A. Okun; shark action supervisor, Walt Conti; special visual-effects and animation, Cinesite, Industrial Light & Magic; additional visual effects and animation, Flash Film Works, Hammerhead Prods.; special-effects supervisor, John Richardson; animatronic sharks effects, Edge Innovations; associate producer/assistant director, Tom Mack; casting, Christine Sheaks. Reviewed at GCC Galaxy Theater, Hollywood, July 23, 1999. MPAA Rating: R.Running time: 105 mins.

Thomas Jane (Carter Blake), Saffron Burrows (Dr. Susan McAlester), Samuel L. Jackson (Russell Franklin), Jacqueline McKenzie (Janice Higgins), Michael Rapaport (Tom Scoggins), Stellan Skarsgard (Jim Whitlock), L.L. Cool J. (Preacher), Aida Turturro (Brenda Kerns).
Powered by exceptional displays of physical filmmaking, *Deep Blue Sea* is pulled back to shore by the usual suspects: weak plotting and weaker dialog. The main draw is a trio of 40-foot killer sharks on the loose.

Except for weak opener, new sharker avoids any comparison to the Spielberg action classic.

Marine biologist Dr. Susan McAlester and her lab technicians experiment with sharks' brain protein in hopes of eliminating Alzheimer's disease in human cells.They are stationed within a former U.S. Navy sub base called Aquatica, off the Baja coast. Her corporate funder, tycoon Russell Franklin,

decides to cut her off, but McAlester angles for a little extra time to show medical results. Wanting to see where his money is going, he flies back to Susan's lair. The subdued sharks suddenly wreak havoc within the base and a series of disastrous events quickly follow, ultimately unleashing a flood and pic's central action sequence.

Though digitized sharks are unevenly realized, to sometimes ferocious and sometimes cartoonish effect, the physical effects here, dominated by the flooding of Aquatica's endless corridors, hatches and tanks, create an astonishing display of characters threatened by the elements. The thrills are such a rush, however, and the balance of digitized and analog effects is generally so satisfying that pic's sheer dumbness finally becomes part of the fun.

U.S. release: July 28   U.S. B.O.: $73.6 million

Deuce Bigalow: Male Gigolo

A Buena Vista Pictures release of a Touchstone Pictures presentation of a Happy Madison production in association with Out of the Blue Entertainment. Produced by Sid Ganis, Barry Bernardi. Executive producers, Adam Sandler, Jack Giarraputo. Co-producers, Alex Siskin, Harris Goldberg. Directed by Mike Mitchell. Screenplay, Goldberg, Rob Schneider. Camera (Technicolor), Peter Lyons Collister; editors, George Bowers, Lawrence Jordan; music, Teddy Castellucci; music supervisor, Michael Dilbeck; production designer, Alan Au; set decorator, F. Beauchamp Hebb; costume designer, Molly Maginnis; sound (Dolby Digital/DTS/SDDS), David Kelson; supervising sound editors, Elmo Weber, Gary S. Gerlich; visual-effects supervisor, John Van Vliet; special-effects coordinator, David Blitstein; animatronic effects, Stan Winston Studio; choreography, Adam M. Shankman; associate producer, Michelle Archer; assistant director, Cara Giallanza; second unit directors, Bruce Hendricks, Collister; second unit camera, Michael Delahoussaye, Charles S. Cohen; casting, Marcia Ross, Donna Morong, Gail Goldberg. Reviewed at Avco Cinema Center, L.A., Dec. 6, 1999. MPAA Rating: R. Running time: 88 mins.

Rob Schneider (Deuce Bigalow), William Forsythe (Detective Chuck Fowler), Eddie Griffin (T.J. Hicks), Arija Bareikis (Kate), Oded Fehr (Antoine Laconte), Gail O'Grady (Claire), Richard Riehle (Bob Bigalow), Jacqueline Obradors (Elaine Fowler). With: Big Boy, Amy Poehler, Dina Platias, Torsten Voges, Deborah Lemen, Bree Tucker, Andrew Shaifer.
A gross-out comedy made by many of the personnel involved with *Big Daddy*. Pic is a sign that the Sandler comedy empire is expanding and reaching new depths of pure stupidity.

Deuce is a barely lovable semiliterate out of step with everyone else, with a passion for tending tropical fish. A gigolo named Antoine, whom poverty-stricken Deuce jealously observes, ends up asking him to care for his ailing Chinese tailbar lionfish in his Malibu pad while he's out of the country.

Deuce winds up destroying his host's fabulous aquarium. Fishtank repairman Neil demands $6,000 to fix it, leaving Deuce with few options. A call to Antoine leads to new career opportunities, and Deuce becomes possibly the world's first temp gigolo. Deuce is hired as a "man-whore" for pimp T.J. Hicks.

The pic's one saving grace is its habit of wasting no time, so in quick succession Deuce encounters a list of T.J.'s mostly ridiculous clients. Deuce's encounters were clearly the inspi-

---

. . . May 5 . . .
Margaret Edson's **Wit** continues to rack up kudos, with the off-Broadway hit being named Best Play of the 1998-99 season by the New York Drama Critics' Circle.

ration for the script, but they play mainly as disconnected skits, linked only by the irritating intrusion of LAPD Detective Fowler.

Pic has an almost pathological fear of sexual content, the last thing to expect from a comedy about an amateur gigolo. Multiple opportunities for laughs between the sheets are traded for dumb physical routines. "SNL" vet Schneider survives fairly well as headliner after several second-banana assignments.

U.S. release: Dec. 10   U.S. B.O.: $46.5 million

Diamonds

A Miramax release (in U.S.) of a Total Film Group (U.S.)/ Cinerenta (Germany) production. (International sales: J&M Entertainment, London.) Produced by Patricia T. Green. Executive producer, Gerald Green. Co-executive producer, Rainer Bienger. Directed by John Asher. Screenplay, Allan Aaron Katz. Camera (color), Paul Elliott; editor, Timothy O'Meara; music, Joel Goldsmith; production designer, Vince Lorenzini; sound (Dolby), Kelly Rush; assistant director, Richard Fox; casting, Dan Parada. Reviewed at Deauville Festival of American Cinema (Panorama), Deauville, France, Sept. 6, 1999. Running time: 91 mins.
Kirk Douglas (Harry), Dan Aykroyd (Lance), Corbin Allred (Michael), Lauren Bacall (Sin-Dee), Kurt Fuller (Moses). With: Jenny McCarthy, Mariah O'Brian, John Landis.

A proudly sentimental story with plenty of unforced humor, *Diamonds* is tailor-made for Kirk Douglas. Old-fashioned but not fuddy-duddyish pic, which reunites Douglas with Lauren Bacall for the first time since 1950's *Young Man With A Horn.* Script is packed with gentle gags and is never maudlin.

Onetime welterweight champion of the world, Harry "The Polish Prince" Agensky, lives on a lake in rural Canada with his son Moses and daughter-in-law. Harry's other son, Lance, is a newspaper columnist in northern California. Lance and son, Michael, drive through snowy vistas to pick up Harry for a family-bonding trip to Banff.

Harry – whose greatest fear is ending up in a retirement home and whose biggest dream is to live on a gorgeous but pricey ranch in the region – had a stroke following the death of his beloved wife of 45 years. Harry contends that decades earlier, a mobster named Duff the Muff paid him with 13 stolen diamonds for throwing a fight. Because Harry's straight-arrow wife refused to let him keep the booty, he and Muff buried the diamonds in the wall of Muff's house in Reno. Determined to recoup the gems, Harry convinces Mikey and Lance to scrap their original plans and drive to Reno instead. Douglas, in his first screen outing since the stroke that initially left him unable to speak, brims with dignity and feisty humor.

U.S. release: Dec. 10 (Oscar Qualification)   U.S. B.O.: $12,865

Dick

A Sony Pictures Entertainment release from Columbia Pictures of a Phoenix Pictures presentation of a Pacific Western production. Produced by Gale Anne Hurd. Executive producer, David Coatsworth. Directed by Andrew Fleming. Screenplay, Fleming, Sheryl Longin.
Kirsten Dunst (Betsy Jobs), Michelle Williams (Arlene Lorenzo), Jim Breuer (John Dean), Will Ferrell (Bob Woodward), Dave Foley (Bob Haldeman), Teri Garr (Helen Lorenzo), Ana Gasteyer (Rose Mary Woods), Devon

Gummersall (Larry Jobs), Dan Hedaya (Dick), Bruce McCulloch (Carl Bernstein), Ted McGinley (Roderick), Ryan Reynolds (Chip), Saul Rubinek (Henry Kissinger), Harry Shearer (G. Gordon Liddy), G.D. Spradlin (Ben Bradlee).

This audaciously imaginative political comedy will have Watergate buffs in particular and babyboomers in general laughing loud and long. Boosted by resourceful comic playing by the young leading women and an appealingly scruffy supporting cast, the film scores seemingly at will.

Pic plunks its innocents down in the middle of a legendary historical event. Ditsy teens Betsy Jobs and Arlene Lorenzo are best friends who receive jobs as the official White House dog walkers, as Nixon's disturbed at the moment over the fact that his dog Checkers doesn't like him. Thus begins the girls' unlikely access to the upper echelons of power and to the most closely guarded secrets at the heart of one of American politics' most sensational scandals. The girls begin to turn on Dick when they realize he's a mean-spirited and prejudiced "potty-mouth," and set out to destroy him by calling Bob Woodward at the *Washington Post.* If the film is devastating toward the White House crew, it is even more scathing toward Woodward and Bernstein, and this gives the picture a real charge. Fleming directs the script with a sharpness that stings but, pleasingly, doesn't eviscerate; the sense of distance from the events helps the laughs go down easily no matter how cutting the humor.

U.S. release: Aug. 4   U.S. B.O.: $6.3 million

Dogma

A View Askew production. (International sales: Miramax Intl., N.Y.) Produced by Scott Mosier. Co-producer, Lara Greenlee. Directed, written by Kevin Smith. Camera (Deluxe color, Panavision widescreen), Robert Yeoman; editors, Smith, Scott Mosier; music, Howard Shore; music supervisor, Randall Poster; production designer, Robert "Ratface" Holtzman. Reviewed at Cannes Film Festival (noncompeting), May 21, 1999. Running time: 135 mins.
Ben Affleck (Bartleby), George Carlin (Cardinal Glick), Matt Damon (Loki), Linda Fiorentino (Bethany), Salma Hayek (Serendipity), Jason Lee (Azrael), Jason Mewes (Jay), Alan Rickman (Metatron), Chris Rock (Rufus), Bud Cort (John Doe Jersey), Alanis Morissette (Woman-God), Kevin Smith (Silent Bob), Jeff Anderson (Gun Salesman), Brian Christopher O'Halloran (Reporter), Janeane Garofalo (Clinic Girl), Betty Aberlin (Nun), Dan Etheridge (Priest at St. Stephens), Guinevere Turner (Bus Station Attendant), Barrett Hackney, Jared Pfenningwerth, Kitao Sakurai (Stygian Triplets).

A vulgar pro-faith comedy rather than a sacrilegious goof, *Dogma* is an extraordinarily uneven film. Pic seriously belabors its assault on the established denominations and institutions, in particular the Roman Catholic Church, that helmer thinks have become too corrupt and calcified to represent the great beliefs they should convey with purity and vigor.

Bethany, a Catholic abortion clinic worker who is feeling a crisis of faith, is recruited by Metatron, a disgruntled angel, to save all of existence by putting a halt to a wicked plan being hatched by two fallen angels, Bartleby and Loki. Latter were kicked out of paradise centuries ago but intend to re-enter heaven by passing under an arch of a New Jersey church, an act which will prove God's fallibility and bring an end to the world. Bethany has no idea why she has been chosen for this task.

She embarks on her journey, acquiring a slew of oddball characters including Rufus, the supposed 13th apostle who was cut out of the Bible, and a celestial muse-stripper named Serendipity. Intensely irreverent jokes and incidents are strewn throughout, making those in the much funnier *Monty Python and the Holy Grail* look timid by comparison.

Smith hardly advances his technical skills: pic has been shot in widescreen and looks ragged and unattractive, where a stylish look and more visual invention would have spiffed up the proceedings. His writing skills and outrageous humor remain visible.

U.S. release: Nov. 2   U.S. B.O.: $29 million

Double Jeopardy

A Paramount Pictures release of a Leonard Goldberg production. Produced by Goldberg. Co-producer, Richard Luke Rothschild. Directed by Bruce Beresford. Screenplay, David Weisberg, Douglas S. Cook. Camera (Deluxe color, Panavision widescreen), Peter James; editor, Mark Warner; music, Normand Corbeil; production designer, Howard Cummings; supervising art director, Andrew Neskoromny; set designers, John Marcynuk, Allan Galajda, Roxanne Methot; costume designers, Rudy Dillon, Linda Bass; sound (Dolby Digital/DTS), Gary Bourgeois, Myron Nettinga; assistant director, Richard Cowan; casting, Deborah Aquila, Sarah Halley Finn. Reviewed at Paramount Studios, L.A., Sept. 16, 1999. MPAA Rating: R. Running time: 105 mins.
Tommy Lee Jones (Travis Lehman), Ashley Judd (Libby Parsons), Bruce Greenwood (Nick Parsons), Annabeth Gish (Angie), Roma Maffia (Margaret Skolowski), Davenia McFadden (Evelyn Lake), Jay Brazeau (Bobby), Gillian Barber (Rebecca Tingely), Benjamin Weir (Matty Parsons, aged 4), Spencer Treat Clark (Matty Parsons, aged 11).

A single-minded and engaging thriller without an afterglow. The old *Death Wish* revenge fantasy formula is turned on its head by making a strong woman the rooting interest to get justice by any means necessary. In the first studio project in which she's front and center throughout, Ashley Judd makes her woman scorned an impressive star turn that is in equal measures sinewy, determinedly focused and graceful, a yin to Tommy Lee Jones' patented gruff yang as the parole officer tracking her down.

Libby and affluent husband Nick appear to be enjoying the high life along with 4-year-old son Matty. Apparently, Nick is in hot financial water and their marriage is shaky. After a romantic evening aboard their new sailboat, Libby wakes up in a bloodstained bed with a knife – but no Nick.

The Coast Guard appears as Libby holds the knife, and soon after she is convicted of murder. Libby realizes that she's been framed by Nick and upon her parole starts planning her revenge. Though title refers to the well-known legal dictum which prevents a previously convicted person from being charged with the same crime a second time, this is apparently news to Libby: it means that Nick can be murdered sans punishment. A Kandinsky painting pops up in the plot for a clever twist in an amusing art-gallery scene that has energy of the best moments from the *Lethal Weapon* series.

U.S. release: Sept. 24   U.S. B.O.: $114 million

Dreaming of Joseph Lees

A 20th Century Fox (in U.K.)/Fox Searchlight (in U.S.) release of a Fox Searchlight Pictures presentation of a Midsummer Films Prods. production, in association with the Isle of Man Film Commission. Produced by Chris Milburn. Executive producer, Mark Thomas. Directed by Eric Styles. Screenplay, Catherine Linstrum. Camera (Deluxe London color prints), Jimmy Dibling; editor, Caroline Limmer; music, Zbigniew Preisner; production designer, Humphrey Jaeger; art director, Lucy Nias; costume designer, Maggie Chappelhow; sound (Dolby), Phil Edward; assistant director, Alison B. Matthews; casting, Liora Reich, Carrie Hilton. Reviewed at Century preview theater, London, July 29, 1999. Running time: 92 mins.
Samantha Morton (Eva), Lee Ross (Harry), Rupert Graves (Joseph Lees), Holly Aird (Maria), Miriam Margolyes (Signora Caldoni), Frank Finlay (Eva's Father), Nick Woodeson (Mr. Dian), Lauren Richardson (Janie), Felix Billson (Robert).

Rising British thesp Samantha Morton provides the heart and soul of this small-scale period meller about a young woman's romantic obsession with a childhood hero. But despite Morton's lustrous, deeply etched performance, the elements don't fully click in this risky venture.

"When I was 14, I fell in love with my cousin, Joseph Lees," says Eva, immediately setting up the story's nut. It's 1958, in the southwestern rural county of Somerset, England, and Eva, in between thinking of the long-absent Lees, a geologist who lost his leg in a quarry accident and disappeared to Italy, works as a clerk in a sawmill, where she's courted by working-class stud Harry. When she hears Lees has come back for a funeral, she's devastated when her dad forbids her to go. Eva moves in with Harry, surrenders her virginity, but demurs from plunging into marriage. The dramatic tumblers fall into place, as Eva meets Lees at a wedding and the pair dance. It's a brief encounter but enough to ignite the fires on both sides.

Pic's result manages to tap a rarefied zone of emotion and feeling that's usually the province of Continental, rather than British, pictures. It's most effective when images and music take over. The final reels lapse into bathos as the frustrated Harry takes desperate measures to compete with Lees.

U.S. release: Oct. 29   U.S. B.O.: $12,044

East-West (Est-Ouest)

A UFD Distribution release (in France) of a UGC YM presentation of a UGC YM, France 3 Cinema (France)/NTV Profit (Russia)/Mate Prods. (Spain)/Gala Films (Bulgaria) production, with participation of Canal Plus, Sofica Sofinergie 5 and CNC. (International sales: UGC, Paris.) Produced by Yves Marmion. Directed by Regis Wargnier. Screenplay, Sergei Bodrov, Rustam Ibragimbekov, Louis Gardel, Wargnier. Camera (color), Laurent Dailland; editor, Herve Schneid; music, Patrick Doyle; art directors, Vladimir Svetozarov, Alexei Levchenko. Reviewed at Locarno Film Festival (noncompeting), Aug. 4, 1999. Running time: 120 mins.
Sandrine Bonnaire (Marie), Oleg Menhikov (Alexei Golovin), Catherine Deneuve (Gabrielle Develay), Sergei Bodrov Jr. (Sasha), Ruben Tapiero (Seryozha, aged 7), Erwan Baynaud (Seryozha, aged 14), Grigori Manukov (Pirogov), Tatyana Dogilova (Olga), Bogdan Stupka (Col. Boyko), Meglena Karalambova (Nina Fyodorovna).
(French and Russian dialog)

Seven years after *Indochine*, Regis Wargnier returns to the field of large-scale romantic melodrama with mixed results. Pic is too often caught between trying to be a sweeping period drama and intimate love story at the same time, with a script that's never fully satisfying on either count. Initially, the performances of Bonnaire and Menshikov do at least create an emotional center for the movie, as wife and husband stick to each other to try to survive.

Action kicks off in June '46: Russians are tempted back by the Soviet government's offer of an amnesty to anyone who skipped the country in the past 30 years. But joys of returning to the motherland are soon cut short when, upon arrival, they are either shot or sent off to gulags. Because of his badly needed skills as a doctor, Alexei Golovin takes a job as chief health officer at a weaving factory in Kiev, and manages to save his French wife, Marie, from a brutal interrogation by the secret police. Their marriage crumbles as Marie realizes she's trapped in the country and that Alexis is cheating on her. Marie befriends fellow tenant Sasha, and left-wing French actress Gabrielle, who's visiting with a touring theater company. Marie's friends attempt to smuggle her out of the country on two different occasions. These climactic moments hint at the powerful, emotional movie this pic could have been.

Election

A Paramount release of an MTV Films production in association with Bona Fide Prods. Produced by Albert Berger, Ron Yerxa, David Gale, Keith Samples. Executive producer, Van Toffler. Co-producers, Jacobus Rose, Jim Burke. Directed by Alexander Payne. Screenplay, Payne, Jim Taylor, based on the novel by Tom Perrotta.

Matthew Broderick (Jim McAllister), Reese Witherspoon (Tracy Flick), Chris Klein (Paul Metzler), Jessica Campbell (Tammy Metzler), Mark Harelik (Dave Novotny), Phil Reeves (Walt Hendricks), Molly Hagan (Diane McAllister), Delaney Driscoll (Linda Novotny), Colleen Camp (Judith R. Flick), Frankie Ingrassia (Lisa Flanagan), Matt Malloy (Vice Principal Ron Bell), Jeanine Jackson (Jo Metzler), Holmes Osborne (Dick Metzler).

Election is a dark, insidiously funny satire on the self-involved ways that otherwise rational people can allow narrow personal agendas to lead them astray to the point of self-destruction. Payne takes on dicey subjects as teacher-student sex, corrupt administrators, lesbianism at parochial girls schools, and the ruthless cruelty of teenagers.

Backstory involves how Mr. Novotny, a math teacher at Carver High, became involved with the school's overachieving goody-goody, Tracy Flick, ultimately losing his position and family. Novotny was the close friend of history teacher Jim McAllister, who loves his job, and is well respected by all at school. Jim can't stand Tracy, who approaches high school as her personal field of conquest. When Tracy runs for student body president; Jim, in an attempt to thwart her, secretly nominates popular, unqualified jock Paul Metzler to run also. Unexpectedly, Paul's lesbian sister, Tammy, decides to run and wins support, promising to abolish student government if elected.

Appalled by her foes' lack of seriousness, the competition just makes Tracy work harder. Meanwhile, Jim, who stresses ethics in his lectures, slips down the ladder in his personal behavior when he has a fling with Novotny's wife, Linda.

Tracy can't help but serve as an object of ridicule – there is a moment of possibly inadvertent poignancy at the end when she can be seen as a Monica Lewinsky in the making. Broderick skillfully offers up a descending Jim. Witherspoon

nails Tracy in a nifty performance that rings true.
U.S. release: Apr. 23   U.S. B.O.: $15 million

Elephant Juice

A Miramax release presented in association with FilmFour of a HAL Films production. Produced by Sheila Fraser Milne. Executive producers, David Aukin, Trea Hoving, Clin Leventhal. Co-producers, Amy Jenkins, Sam Miller. Directed by Miller. Screenplay, Jenkins, based on an idea by Jenkins and Miller. Camera (Technicolor prints, Panavision widescreen), Adrian Wild; editor, Elen Pierce Lewis; music, Tim Atack; music supervisor, Bob Last; production designer, Grant Hicks; art director, Teresa Weston; costumes, Jill Taylor; sound (Dolby), Peter Baldock; assistant director, Richard Whelan; associate producer, Allon Reich; casting, Di Carling. Reviewed at Edinburgh Film Festival (Focus on British Cinema), Aug. 23, 1999. Running time: 86 mins.

Emmanuelle Beart (Jules), Sean Gallagher (Billy), Daniel Lapaine (Will), Daniela Nardini (Daphne), Mark Strong (Frank), Kimberly Williams (Dodie), Lennie James (Graham), Lee Williams (George). With: Kate Gartside, Rebecca Palmer, James Thornton, Sabra Williams.

Pic is as phony as a three-dollar bill – and about as worthless. A London-set relationships ensembler that desperately wants to be hip and penetrating at the same time, pic is a totally uninvolving construct that submerges its few good performances in a sea of banality. It is a look at "modern relationships" among professionals; however, it comes off as posed and shallow.

Seven of the eight principals gather for a dinner party to celebrate the decision of Jules and Will to tie the knot. The movie cuts away into a series of extended flashbacks and flashforwards during which we learn about the characters and, more precisely, who's been canoodling with whom. What several of them do for a living is unclear, but Jules is a smartly dressed business type with a soft heart who's genuinely in love with Will, a born philanderer who has a regular hooker on the side. Will's best friend, Billy, a research scientist, is a shy type who has problems scoring with women, but finally links up with American coffee-shop owner Dodie, who claims to be into tantric sex and is a divorced mother with a young baby.

Heart of the film lies in the emotional travails of Billy and Jules, the first falling head over heels for the cute but tough Dodie, and the second permanently betrayed by the hormonal Will. Miller directs as if he's seen too many relationship movies set in Manhattan.

Elvis Gratton II

A Lions Gate Films release (in Canada) of an ACPAV/Films Cinepix production, with the participation of Telefilm Canada, Quebec government, Reseau TVA, Super Ecran, Canadian government, Harold Greenberg Fund and Animavision. (International sales: Lions Gate Intl., Los Angeles.) Produced by Bernadette Payeur, Christian Larouche. Directed by Pierre Falardeau. Screenplay, Falardeau, Julien Poulin.

Julien Poulin (Bob Gratton), Yves Trudel (Meo), Barry Blake (Donald Bill Clinton), Jacques Theriault (Docteur), Gilles-Philippe Delorme (News Reader), Michele Sirois (Agathe Pichette).

The recent upswing in vulgar bigscreen comedy hits French-Canadian cinema with a vengeance. Pic works best when it makes no bones about its downmarket sense of humor, but the French-language comedy is much less successful when it attempts to hammer home its separatist political message.

Though he died at the end of the original, Bob "Elvis" Gratton rises from the grave. The hospital doctors are perplexed when their high-tech machines show that Gratton's brain is registering absolutely no mental activity. After a few gags at the hospital, Gratton heads to the countryside for a few days of relaxation with Meo. Out of the blue, a stretch limo appears at their rundown country vacation spot and out pops showbiz agent Donald Bill Clinton, a Col. Parker-like Southern swindler who tells Gratton he has to "think big," and signs on to market the singer around the world. Before you can sing "Love Me Tender," Gratton is touring the globe with his cheesy act, a French director arrives to make a biopic, and Gratton and Clinton set up Gratton Intl. Corp. to handle their diversified activities. Lack of a strong story makes for an uneven film, but there's no denying that the first hour contains some of the funnier moments of Canadian cinema from the past few years.

The Emperor and the Assassin

A Sony Pictures Classics (in U.S.)/Pathe Distribution (in France) release of a Le Studio Canal Plus/Pricel/Shin Corp./NDF presentation of a New Wave Co. (Japan)/Beijing Film Studio (China) production, in association with China Film Co-production Corp. (International sales: Le Studio Canal Plus, Paris.) Produced by Chen Kaige, Shirley Kao, Satoru Iseki. Executive producers, Tsuguhiko Kadokawa, Hiromi-tsu Furukawa, Han Sanping. Directed by Kaige. Screenplay, Chen, Wang Peigong. Camera (color), Zhao Fei; editor, Zhou Xinxia; music, Zhao Jiping; production designers, Tu Juhua, Lin Qi; art directors, Yang Shudong, Ji Weihua; set decorators, Yi Zhenzhou, Zhang Xiaoman; costume designers, Mo Xiao-min, Huang Qiuping; sound (DTS Stereo), Tao Jing; chief consultant, Zeng Qinghuai; martial-arts director, Liu Jiacheng; special-effects supervisor, Liu Shaochun; CGI effects, Centro Film (H.K.); associate producers, Philip Lee, Sunmin Park; line producers, Zhang Xia, Bai Yu; executive director, Zhang Jinzhan; assistant directors, Zhang Xijue, Yang Haiquan, Wang Chao. Reviewed at Pathe screening room, Paris, May 6, 1999. (In Cannes Film Festival - competing.) Running time: 160 mins.
Gong Li (Lady Zhao), Zhang Fengyi (Jing Ke), Li Xuejian (Ying Zheng, King of Qin), Sun Zhou (Dan, Prince of Yan), Wang Zhiwen (Marquis Changxin), Chen Kaige (Lu Buwei), Lu Xiaohe (Gen. Fan Yuqi), Gu Yongfei (Queen Mother), Ding Haifeng (Qin Wuyang), Zhao Benshan (Gao Jianli), Pan Changjiang (Prison Official), Zhou Xun (Blind Girl).

Set during the late 3rd century B.C., near the end of the Warring States period when China was a collection of seven rival kingdoms. Pic starts with a bang as Ying Zheng, head of Qin, invades the state of Han. Half-crazed by his dream, Ying outlines a utopian scenario of unification, in which the country will be divided into provinces under good leaders: peace and prosperity will flourish and the barbarians will be held outside a Great Wall.

Next Ying plans to invade the state of Yan – at which point things become complicated, not least because its head was once a childhood friend of Ying. To give Ying a good excuse to invade the place, his longtime lover and confidante, Lady Zhao, hatches the idea of being branded a traitor, fleeing to Yan and hiring a local assassin to kill Ying. When the plot is uncovered, Ying will then be free to destroy Yan. But events back in Qin change the whole scenario.

Helmer seems not to have learnt the lesson of the great historical epics of cinema: simplification at all costs and the rapid establishment of clear conflicts. Dialog is routine, with the thesps giving it occasional resonance through performances that often approach caricature. Spectacular battle scenes and art direction rarely enhance the drama. They're there to dazzle the eyes, period.

U.S. release: Dec. 17   U.S. B.O.: $173,078

End of Days

A Universal release of a Universal and Beacon Pictures presentation. Produced by Armyan Bernstein, Bill Borden. Executive producers, Marc Abraham, Thomas A. Bliss. Co-producers, Paul Deason, Andrew W. Marlowe. Directed by Peter Hyams. Screenplay, Marlowe. Camera (Deluxe color, Panavision widescreen), Hyams; editor, Steve Kemper; music, John Debney; music supervisor, G. Marq Roswell; production designer, Richard Holland; art directors, Charlie Daboub, Teresa Carriker-Thayer (N.Y.); set designers, Al Hobbs, Mike Stassi, Maya Shimoguchi, Julia Levine, Greg Berry; set decorator, Gary Fettis; costume designer, Bobbie Mannix; sound (Dolby Digital/DTS/SDDS), Gene S. Cantamessa; supervising sound editor, Mike Wilhoit; co-supervising sound editor, Kelly L. Oxford; creature-effects supervisor, Stan Winston; special makeup effects, Kurtzman, Nicotero & Berger EFX Group; church miniatures and effects, Hunter-Gratzner Industries; subway train miniature sequence and church pyrotechnic effects, Stirber Visual Network; visual-effects photography, the Chandler Group; visual effects and digital creature, Rhythm and Hues; visual-effects supervisor, John "D.J." Desjardin; stunt coordinator, Steve M. Davison; assistant director, William M. Elvin. Reviewed at the Century Plaza Cinemas, L.A., Nov. 18, 1999. MPAA Rating: R. Running time: 120 mins.
Arnold Schwarzenegger (Jericho Cane), Gabriel Byrne (The Man), Kevin Pollak (Chicago), Robin Tunney (Christine York), CCH Pounder (Det. Margie Francis), Rod Steiger (Father Kovak), Derrick O'Connor (Thomas Aquinas), Miriam Margolyes (Mabel), Udo Kier (Head Priest), Victor Varnado (Albino), Michael O'Hagan (Cardinal), Mark Margolis (Pope).

Star's first outing since Batman and Robin finds him in fine form in a middling vehicle that veers repeatedly from the reasonably exciting to the risibly over-the-top. Alcoholic ex-cop Jericho Cane finds himself thrust into the vortex of a long-prophesized religious battle in which Satan will try to wrest control of the universe from God. With four days to go before Y2K, earthquakes and subterranean fires in Manhattan set the stage for Satan's dazzling entrance. Jericho has been hired to protect Satan aka The Man, and the next day prevents a sniper from killing his employer. The shooter is Thomas Aquinas, a would-be visionary who prattles on about the advent of a thousand years. Meanwhile, 20-year-old Christine York is having frightening visions about her inability to resist a man she's warned is coming for her. Rather too conveniently, Jericho figures out that it's Christine he's meant to protect, and the fleeing twosome track down Aquinas' friend, Father Kovak, who explains it all: Christine, who bears Satan's mark, is meant to give birth to the anti-Christ and, for this to hap-

---

pen, Satan must impregnate her in the hour before the arrival of the new millennium.

Script by Marlowe works in generating occasions for big-scale action and religion-laced horror, while Hyams seems intent on making the pic as relentlessly unnerving as possible. Special effects are groovy, notably the church finale in which all manner of inanimate objects shake, rattle, and roll.
U.S. release: Nov. 24   U.S. B.O.: $63 million

The End of the Affair

A Sony Pictures Entertainment release of a Columbia Pictures presentation of a Stephen Woolley production. Produced by Stephen Woolley, Neil Jordan. Co-producer, Kathy Sykes. Directed, written by Neil Jordan, based on the novel by Graham Greene. Camera (Technicolor), Roger Pratt; editor, Tony Lawson; music, Michael Nyman. Reviewed at TriStar screening room, L.A., Nov. 11, 1999. MPAA Rating: R. Running time: 109 mins.
Ralph Fiennes (Maurice Bendrix), Julianne Moore (Sarah Miles), Stephen Rea (Henry Miles), Ian Hart (Mr. Parkis), Samuel Bould (Lance Parkis), Jason Isaacs (Father Smythe), James Bolam (Mr. Savage), Deborah Findlay (Miss Smythe).
Neil Jordan's brilliant version of Graham Greene's most complex, autobiographical, and finest novel, is a faithful adaptation that captures its haunting spirit and religious nature. Pic's greatest achievement is that it operates successfully on many levels: as a painful deconstruction of a tragic love affair; a mystical thriller with unorthodox twists and turns, and a big secret in the middle; and an undeniably religious drama about sin and redemption.

A passionate woman trapped in a sterile marriage, Sarah Miles falls for Maurice Bendrix, a handsome young novelist, upon meeting him at a party given by her loyal but unexciting civil servant husband, Henry. They begin an illicit, sexually liberating affair that lasts several years. One of their rendezvous occurs during the 1944 Blitz, when a bomb hits Bendrix's house and he is severely injured. Thinking he is dead, Sarah prays to God to save his life, and shortly thereafter inexplicably breaks off their relationship. Pic begins in 1949, with the utterly bereft Bendrix at his typewriter, trying to understand what went wrong. What ensues is a moving chronicle of the end of Bendrix's affair with Sarah, jumping back and forth between the summer of 1939, when they first met, to Sarah's sudden death, seven years later.

In his most accomplished performance to date, Fiennes shines. The film is arguably the finest screen adaptation of a Greene novel since Carol Reed's *The Fallen Idol* and *The Third Man*.
U.S. release: Dec. 3   U.S. B.O.: $1.6 million

Entrapment

A 20th Century Fox release of a Fountainbridge Films and Michael Hertzberg production, presented with New Regency Enterprises. Produced by Sean Connery, Hertzberg, Rhonda Tollefson. Executive producers, Iain Smith, Ron Bass, Arnon Milchan. Directed by Jon Amiel. Screenplay, Bass, William Broyles; story by Bass, Hertzberg.
Sean Connery (Robert "Mac" MacDougal), Catherine Zeta-Jones (Virginia "Gin" Baker), Ving Rhames (Thibadeaux), Will Patton (Hector Cruz), Maury Chaykin (Conrad Greene.
Designed as a romantic caper pic for Y2K, *Entrapment* is preposterous whimsy that sort of gets by thanks to lustrous

settings, slick production values and, especially, its ultra-attractive stars.

After a Rembrandt is stolen from a New York high-rise, insurance investigator Gin Baker convinces her boss, Hector Cruz, that the culprit is legendary art thief Robert "Mac" MacDougal and gets the green light to track him down in London. It's just 14 days before the turn of the millennium. Rather than catch him, she joins forces with him to steal a unique Chinese mask on display at an English museum. All the while, Mac is suspicious of her. After stealing the mask, they hightail it to Malaysia, where Gin is to deliver the artefact to a mad old crime queen. Here she unveils to Mac her strategy for a stupendous bank-computer heist in the Petronas Twin Towers of Kuala Lumpur. Gin believes she can hack in due to the computer changeovers required by the arrival of the year 2000; and if all goes well, she and Mac can funnel $8 billion their way while everyone else is watching midnight fireworks.

Jon Amiel knows the territory well enough to supply glamorous locations and nifty crime-assisting gizmos in a fancy package, but he's neglected to put anything inside the box. That leaves it to the stars, who, to their credit, carry their heavy load with no apparent strain.
U.S. release: Apr. 30   U.S. B.O.: $88 million

Everybody Loves Sunshine

A Lions Gate release of an IAC Holdings Ltd. presentation in association with the Isle of Man Film Commission and BV Films Intl. of a Gothic production. Produced by Joanne Reay. Executive producers, Guy Collins, Heather Playford Denman, Bjorg Veland, Simon Johnson. Directed, written by Andrew Goth. Camera (Deluxe color), Julian Morson; editor, Jeremy Gibbs; music, Nicky Matthew; music supervisor, Extreme Music; production designer, Paul Cross; art director, Helen Xenopolous; costume designer, Ffon Elinor; sound (Dolby Digital), Malcolm Davies; line producer, Paul Frift; assistant director, Ken Shane; casting, Sarah Bird. Reviewed on videotape, L.A., Nov. 17, 1999. Running time: 97 mins.
Goldie (Terry), Andrew Goth (Ray), David Bowie (Bernie), Rachel Shelley (Clare), Clint Dyer (Leon), Sarah Shackleton (Helen), David Baker (Clinton), Paul Hawkyard (Ken), Graham Bryan (Pat), Danny Price (Spider).
Everybody Loves Sunshine, an urban crime drama set in gang-dominated northern England, never manages to be more than third-rate Tarantino. While pic is occasionally visually inventive and has a noteworthy sound and music track, it's a narrative and dramatic calamity. There's lots of flash and violence but little of substance here.

In the opening sequence, protagonists Terry and Ray are released from prison. But Terry and Ray, cousins, lifelong friends and erstwhile gangmates, have different goals. Terry wants to regain control of his gang, which he entrusted during his prison stint to the cool, efficient, ultra-smooth Bernie. Ray wants to go legit.

As Ray starts to explore life beyond the gang, he falls for Clare, a comely and assertive young woman who reawakens his passion and helps him rediscover his tender side. By contrast, Terry re-enters gang life with a vengeance. He makes a fortune selling drugs to kids and strengthens his arsenal with dozens of semi-automatic weapons. He'll terrorize anyone who crosses him, especially a rival gang run by a group of enigmatic Chinese. When Terry sees that Clare is Ray's weakness, he kidnaps and tortures her. And so Ray's fight to get even culminates in an overblown, somewhat predictable bloodbath finale. Neither lead approaches the creepy, buttoned-down intensity of Bowie's Bernie. His character at least has something to work with: a closeted homosexuality that he desperately wants to keep hidden.

Eyes Wide Shut

A Warner Bros. release of a Pole Star production made by Hobby Films Ltd. Produced by Stanley Kubrick. Executive producer, Jan Harlan. Co-producer, Brian W. Cook. Directed by Kubrick. Screenplay, Kubrick, Frederic Raphael, inspired by the novella *Traumnovelle (Dream Story)* by Arthur Schnitzler. Camera (Deluxe London color), Larry Smith; editor, Nigel Galt; music, Jocelyn Pook; production designers, Les Tomkins, Roy Walker; supervising art director, Kevin Phipps; art director, John Fenner. Reviewed at Warner Bros. Studios, Burbank, July 8, 1999. MPAA Rating: R. Running time: 159 mins.
Tom Cruise (Dr. William Harford), Nicole Kidman (Alice Harford), Sydney Pollack (Victor Ziegler), Marie Richardson (Marion), Rade Sherbedgia (Milich), Todd Field (Nick Nightingale), Vanessa Shaw (Domino), Alan Cumming (Desk Clerk), Sky Dumont (Sandor Szavost), Fay Masterson (Sally), Leelee Sobieski (Milich's Daughter), Thomas Gibson (Carl), Madison Eginton (Helena Harford), Louise Taylor (Gayle), Stewart Thorndike (Nuala), Julienne Davis (Mandy), Carmela Marner (Waitress at Gillespie's).
One of the most highly anticipated films of modern times – the last Kubrick picture. Based on Arthur Schnitzler's 1926 novella *Dream Story*, pic remains faithful while also trading in familiar Kubrick concerns such as paranoia, deception, the "masks" people wear, and how difficult it is for intelligent human beings to transcend the base and self-destructive impulses that drive the species.

Modern-day New York is supplanted for the story's early 20th-century Euro setting. Alice Harford confesses to her husband Dr. William Harford a heavy sexual impulse she once had for another man during the earlier part of their marriage. This sends Bill's thoughts into a tizzy. A latenight house call ushers him out of the apartment, and leads to a midnight journey throughout the city whereby he is tempted along the way to cheat on his wife.

He learns of an exclusive costume party, and proceeds out of town to a lavish mansion where an anonymous, rigorously ritualized orgy that eventually puts at risk his own life as well as that of a woman who steps in to save him is taking place. The following day, Bill retraces his steps to make sense of the oddities he experienced the night before – and a murder that might have occurred. Kidman is sensational as she inhabits her character. Cruise gives a limited, emotionally constrained performance.

The career of a great filmmaker comes to a close with a work that, while not his most startling or innovative or subversive, nonetheless sees him striking out in exciting and sometimes new directions with his stylistic confidence and boldness intact.
U.S. release: July 16   U.S. B.O.: $56 million

eXistenZ

Miramax release of an Alliance Atlantis/Serendipity Point Films presentation, in association with Natural Nylon, of a Robert Lantos production. Produced by Lantos, Andras Hamori, David Cronenberg. Co-producers, Damon Bryant, Bradley Adams, Michael McDonald. Directed, written by David Cronenberg. Camera (Deluxe color), Peter Sushitzky; editor, Ronald Sanders; music, Howard Shore; production designer, Carol Spier; art director, Tamara Deverall; costume designer, Denise Cronenberg. Reviewed at Berlin Film Festival (competing), Feb. 16, 1999. Running time: 97 mins.
Jennifer Jason Leigh (Allegra Geller), Jude Law (Ted Pikul), Willem Dafoe (Gas), Ian Holm (Kiri Vinokur), Don McKellar (Yevgeny Nourish), Callum Keith Rennie (Hugo Carlaw), Sarah Polley (Merle), Christopher Eccleston (Levi).
David Cronenberg fans are likely to be disappointed by *eXistenZ*, in which the director parodies some of his past horror outings. This is unquestionably Cronenberg Lite, but there is plenty of fun to be had from the absurdities and convoluted plotting, and a solid cast lends stature to the far-fetched fantasies. Cronenberg's inspiration was the fatwa placed by Iranian hardliners on *Satanic Verses* author Salman Rushdie. Pic takes place in the near future when technology has made video game-playing far more elaborate and exotic.

Pic opens with Allegra Geller, the world's No. 1. gamgramer, taking part in the first demonstration of her game, eXistenZ at her company's – Antenna Research – seminar. An audience member opens fire, wounding Geller and killing her associate Levi. In the ensuing confusion, the assassin himself is killed and Geller escapes in the company of security guard Ted Pikul. Fearful that the assassin was part of a fanatical anti-game group whose members believe in realism above all, and that there is a fatwa against Geller, the fugitives head for the countryside. Hence, a series of strange encounters takes place as Pikul and Geller flee from the realism fanatics and agents of Antenna's rival, Cortical Systematics. Matters are complicated when Geller and Pikul both hook into her copy of eXistenZ: the pair are never quite certain what's real and what isn't – and neither is the viewer.
U.S. release: Apr. 23   U.S. B.O.: $2.7 million

Fantasia/2000

A Buena Vista release from Walt Disney Pictures. Produced by Donald W. Ernst. Executive producer, Roy Edward Disney. *Symphony No. 5* Directed and art directed by Pixote Hunt. Music, Ludwig van Beethoven. *Pines of Rome* Directed by Hendel Butoy. Art directors, Dean Gordon, William Perkins. Music, Ottorino Respighi. *Rhapsody in Blue* Directed, story by Eric Goldberg. Art director, Susan McKinsey Goldberg. Music, George Gershwin; artistic consultant, Al Hirschfeld; co-producer, Patricia Hicks; conductor and supervisor, Bruce Broughton; piano, Ralph Grierson. *Piano Concerto No. 2, Allegro, Opus 102* Directed by Hendel Butoy. Art director, Michael Humphries. Music, Dmitri Shostakovich; ballet choreography, Kendra McCool; piano, Yefim Bronfman; based on the story *The Steadfast Tin Soldier* by Hans Christian Andersen. *Carnival of the Animals (Le Carnival Des Animaux), Finale* Directed, animated, story by Eric Goldberg. Art director, Susan McKinsey Goldberg. Music, Camille Saint-Saens; original concept, Joe Grant. *The Sorcerer's Apprentice* Directed by James Algar. Art directors, Tom Codrick, Charles Philippi, Zack Schwartz. Music, Paul Dukas, conducted by Leopold Stokowski; story development, Perce Pearce, Carl Fallberg; animation supervision, Fred Moore, Vladimir Tytla. *Pomp and Circumstance - Marches 1, 2, 3 and 4* Directed by Francis Glebas. Art director, Daniel Cooper. Music, Edward Elgar;

choral performance, the Chicago Symphony Chorus; feature soprano, Kathleen Battle. *Firebird Suite – 1919 Version* Directed, designed and story by Gaetan Brizzi, Paul Brizzi. Art director, Carl Jones. Music, Igor Stravinsky. Supervising animation director, Hendel Butoy. Host sequences director, Don Hahn. Host sequences written by Hahn, Irene Mecchi, David Reynolds. Live action camera (CFI color, Imax), Tim Suhrstedt; editors, Jessica Ambinder Rojas, Lois Freeman-Fox; music conducted by James Levine, performed by the Chicago Symphony Orchestra; designer, Pixote Hunt; art director, Alison Yerxa; sound (Dolby Digital/SDDS/DTS), Crew Chamberlain; sound designer and supervisor, Gregory King; co-sound designer, Yann Delpuech; visual-effects supervisor, Richard Hollander; digital supervisor, Eric Hanson; associate producer, Lisa C. Cook; co-associate producer, David Lovegren; assistant director, Bill Hoyt; casting, Ruth Lambert, Mary Hidalgo. Reviewed at Edwards Imax Theater, Valencia, Calif., Dec. 16, 1999. MPAA Rating: G. Running time: 75 mins.
Hosts: Steve Martin, Itzhak Perlman, Quincy Jones, Bette Midler, James Earl Jones, Penn & Teller, James Levine, Angela Lansbury.
The beautifully designed and presented package of new animated sequences plus a reprise has shortcomings of its own: this enjoyable follow-up is simply too breezy and lightweight. While it bends over backward not to be "boring" and is significantly more kid-friendly than the original, pic is like a light buffet of tasty morsels rather than a full and satisfying meal; all the episodes are more or less agreeable, but as a whole it lacks a knockout punch, one dynamite sequence that will galvanize viewers. Respighi's *Pines of Rome* unfolds as a New Age celebration of whales, gliding effortlessly through Antarctic waters, up into the air and through the clouds. Several moments are stunning, but this is basically smooth and silky illustration rather than dramatization. Illustrator Al Hirschfeld provides the inspiration for the animated accompaniment to Gershwin's *Rhapsody in Blue*. Result is intriguing and laudable as an ambitious attempt at a *Symphony of a City*.
Pic reaches its arguable peak with Shostakovich's *Piano Concerto No. 2, Allegro, Opus 102*, which provides the backdrop to Hans Christian Andersen's *The Steadfast Tin Soldier*. Brilliantly directed and animated, this seven-minute story of a one-legged toy soldier who rescues a ballerina from a jack-in-the-box is classically conceived but is drawn with a modern edge. The finale of Saint-Saens' *Carnival of the Animals* is half as long as the piece itself, a two-minute frolic involving some pink flamingos and o-yos that reps a briefly diverting throwaway. The most popular reprise, *The Sorcerer's Apprentice*, is still a winner. However, all the technical expertise has not been enough to make the vintage animation look good on the giant Imax screen.
Elgar's *Pomp and Circumstance* unfolds to the surprising and amusing accompaniment of the Noah's Ark story, with Donald Duck as the elderly captain's assistant. The final segment set to Stravinsky's powerful *Firebird Suite*, possesses an overreaching ambition of profundity that simply cannot be supported in a simple seven-minute episode.
U.S. release: Jan. 1, 2000   U.S. B.O.: $2.2 million

Felicia's Journey

An Artisan release (in U.S.) of an Icon Entertainment Intl. presentation of an Icon production, in association with Alliance Atlantis Pictures. (International sales: Icon Entertainment Intl., London.) Produced by Bruce Davey. Executive producers, Paul Tucker, Ralph Kamp. Co-producer, Robert Lantos. Directed, written by Atom Egoyan, based on the novel by William Trevor. Camera (Deluxe color, widescreen), Paul Sarossy; editor, Susan Shipton; music, Mychael Danna; production designer, Jim Clay. Reviewed at Cannes Film Festival (competing), May 17, 1999. Running time: 116 mins.
Bob Hoskins (Hilditch), Elaine Cassidy (Felicia), Arsinee Khanjian (Gala), Peter McDonald (Johnny), Gerard McSorley (Felicia's Father), Brid Brennan (Mrs. Lysaght), Danny Turner (Young Hilditch), Claire Benedict (Miss Calligary).
Lacking the complexity, lyricism, and moral ambiguity of *The Sweet Hereafter*, new pic is perfectly decent, but hardly vintage. Toplined by an understated but effective Bob Hoskins and the terrifically promising Elaine Cassidy, film centers on the fateful encounter between a naive adolescent girl and a serial killer – an encounter that changes both their lives. All of Egoyan's recurrent motifs – the impact of technology on everyday life; alienation and displacement; the meaning of intimacy in interpersonal relationships – are present, but not as well integrated as in his previous movies.
Joseph Ambrose Hilditch, a middle-aged catering manager, lives in a large house in Birmingham, where he watches an old TV cooking programme as he prepares his own elaborate meals. Hilditch's daily routine is subtly intercut with scenes of a young, beautiful girl, Felicia, on a ferry from Ireland, traveling to Birmingham in search of Johnny, with whom she is passionately in love. Johnny has presumably left for England, too, but he left no address. Felicia and Hilditch meet early on, when he recommends a hotel and offers help in locating Johnny. Felicia eventually discovers Hilditch's dubious past. Egoyan shows how two strikingly different individuals are forced to deal with various forms of denial and suppression. Such concerns elevate *Felicia's Journey* from a routine psychosexual thriller to an ambitious drama.
U.S. release: Nov. 12   U.S. B.O.: $761,929

Fight Club

A 20th Century Fox release of a Fox 2000 Pictures, Regency Enterprises presentation of a Linson Films production. Produced by Art Linson, Cean Chaffin, Ross Grayson Bell. Executive producer, Arnon Milchan. Directed by David Fincher. Screenplay, Jim Uhls, based on the novel by Chuck Palahniuk. Camera (Technicolor, Panavision), Jeff Cronenweth; editor, James Haygood; music, the Dust Brothers; production designer, Alex McDowell; art director, Chris Gorak. Reviewed at Venice Film Festival (Dreams and Visions), Sept. 10, 1999. Running time: 139 mins.
Brad Pitt (Tyler Durden), Edward Norton (Narrator), Helena Bonham Carter (Marla Singer), Meat Loaf Aday (Robert Paulsen), Jared Leto (Angel Face).
Rarely has a film been so keyed into its time. On one hand, pic is the perfect reflection of the millennium malaise that pits pervasive nihilism against an urgent need for something to grasp onto; on the other, it caps off a period in which the media and Washington have never been so assiduous in pointing the finger at Hollywood over the impact of screen violence. Screenplay explores existential themes articulately and accessibly, unleashing a steady stream of humor, razor-sharp dialog, droll popular culture references, and wry comments on consumerism, corporate culture, and capitalism.

. . . May 12 . . .
The Senate voted to approve a package of proposals aimed at putting Hollywood under the spotlight of federal investigators and researchers.

Set in an unidentified city, the story's nameless narrator meets enigmatic Tyler Durden, who makes and sells soap for a living. After some male bonding, Tyler amicably picks a fight that seals their union and marks the beginning of a phenomenon that each week attracts new participants. The narrator continues his day job but awaits the charge that comes with fighting each Saturday night within this secret society. Tyler encourages this lost generation of men to access pain as a remedy for contemporary despair and numbness. Pic's climax sets the narrator out to stop a dramatic chain of events, bringing him face to face with discoveries regarding his true nature that provide the story's big twist.

The three leads are uniformly potent, with Norton demanding by far the greatest range. Pitt is cool, charismatic and dynamically physical, while Bonham Carter, spouting acerbic maxims with attitude to burn, demolishes any residue of her buttoned-up Merchant-Ivory image.

U.S. release: Oct. 15   U.S. B.O.: $36.4 million

Flawless

An MGM release of a Tribeca production. Produced by Joel Schumacher, Jane Rosenthal. Executive producer, Neil Machlis. Co-producers, Caroline Baron, Amy Sayres. Directed, written by Schumacher. Camera (Deluxe prints), Declan Quinn; editor, Mark Stevens; music, Bruce Roberts. Reviewed at MGM screening room, Santa Monica, Nov. 11, 1999. MPAA Rating: R. Running time: 112 mins.
Robert De Niro (Walt Koontz), Philip Seymour Hoffman (Rusty), Barry Miller (Leonard Wilcox), Chris Bauer (Jacko), Skipp Sudduth (Tommy), Wilson Jermaine Heredia (Cha-Cha), Nashom Benjamin (Amazing Grace), Scott Allen Cooper (Ivana), Rory Cochrane (Pogo), Daphne Rubin-Vega (Tia), Wanda De Jesus (Karen).

After disappointing big-budget, special-effects movies, Joel Schumacher takes a step in the right direction with a small-scale, intimate seriocomedy centering on the unlikely camaraderie between a macho security guard and a flamboyant transvestite. A more personal and meaningful work than his previous outings, *Flawless* takes Schumacher back to his New York roots of the 1960s and '70s. Unfortunately, this also proves to be one of the film's main problems – in mores and sexual politics, pic is very much grounded in the zeitgeist of the post-Stonewall era.

Set within a racially diverse apartment complex on the Lower East Side, tale introduces retired security guard Walt Koontz, an ultra-conservative man, who is injured and suffers a stroke which paralyzes him. He refuses to leave his apartment for physical therapy, despite medical advice. But under pressure, Walt reluctantly agrees to a rehabilitative program with Rusty, his transvestite neighbor. Thus begins a rather stormy relationship – and a moral odyssey – of two individuals who could not be more different. Schumacher situates the relationship in a routine, uninvolving crime melodrama concerning some missing money.

Plotline deflates the momentum of the central relationship, which lacks nuance and shading and makes the film seem much more shallow than it actually is. In his first co-starring role, Hoffman has many marvelous moments, but ultimately his performance lacks depth.

U.S. release: Nov. 24   U.S. B.O.: $4.4 million

The Florentine

An Initial Entertainment Group presentation of an American Zoetrope and Nazz/March First co-production. Produced by Tom Benson, Nick Stagliano, Chris Penn, Steven Weisman. Executive producers, Francis Ford Coppola, Cindy Cowan, Fred Fuchs. Directed by Stagliano. Screenplay, Damien Gray, Benson, based on the play by Gray and Amy McCarty-Baker. Camera (color), Stephen Kazmierski; editor, Plummy Tucker; music, Marco Beltrami; music supervisors, Lonnie Sill, Tom Eaton; production designer, Stephen McCabe; costume designer, Kasia Maimone; line producer, A. John Rath; casting, Marcia Shulman. Reviewed at L.A. Independent Film Festival, April 19, 1999. Running time: 104 mins.
Michael Madsen (Whitey), Chris Penn (Bobbie), Jeremy Davies (Truby), Tom Sizemore (Teddy Finn), Luke Perry (Frankie), James Belushi (Billy Munucci), Mary Stuart Masterson (Vikki), Hal Holbrook (Smitty), Virginia Madsen (Molly), Maeve Quinlan (Claire), Burt Young (Joe McCollough).

Bar-owner Whitey is a fixture around which a circle of humanity revolves. The old Pennsylvania steel town of Irish Catholic stock is far past its prime, as are the predominantly male characters. Bobbie is unhappily married to Vikki and struggling with mounting bookie debts, inflaming the anger of small-time mobster Joe, who also holds the note on the Florentine bar. Whitey's sister Molly is about to be married, but her ex-beau, a wandering loser, Teddy Finn, has come back, potentially to cause trouble.

Teddy's best buddy, Truby, counsels him to give up any hope of getting Molly back, though Truby has his own woman problems. Meanwhile, Whitey's fairly witless pal, Frankie, blows the cash Whitey has saved for the wedding caterer in a con scheme involving strong, sharp-witted Billy Munucci. In the story's only real movie sequence, Teddy manages to double-cross Billy and save the wedding. Script was made to order for thesps eager to chew into some long dialogs and monologs. While it's raised above the norm by a cast full of heavyweights, pic is ultimately undone by a distracting spread of novelistic story strands and a deadly, repetitive series of two-character dialog scenes. It evidently fazed neither the impressive list of players, nor its backers, that the characters here are the kind of stock, working-class types that were old news in American theater 40 years ago, or that the script is resolutely uncinematic.

Forever Hollywood

A Kodak presentation of an American Cinematheque production in association with Esplanade Prods. Produced by Sasha Alpert. Executive producer, Barbara Zicka Smith. Directed, written by Todd McCarthy. Co-director, Arnold Glassman. Camera (Deluxe color/b&w), Nancy Schreiber; additional camera, Paul Ryan; editor, Glassman; art director, Hernan Camacho; sound (Dolby SRD), Joseph R. Ekins, Beau Baker; sound editor, Warren Kleiman; line producer, Dale Ann Stieber. Reviewed at the Egyptian Theater, L.A., Dec. 3, 1999. Running time: 57 mins.
With: Warren Beatty, Annette Bening, Jeff Bridges, Andre de Toth, Michael Douglas, Clint Eastwood, Mel Gibson, Salma Hayek, Charlton Heston, Samuel L. Jackson, Angela Lansbury, Jack Lemmon, Shirley MacLaine, Edward Norton, Robert Redford, Rob Reiner, Vincent Sherman, Kevin Spacey, Steven Spielberg, Gloria Stuart, Quentin Tarantino, John Travolta, John Waters. Narrator: Sharon Stone.

. . . May 13 . . .
Studio Canal Plus will fully finance a new quartet of pics from American indie filmmakers Kathryn Bigelow, George Romero, John Waters and Abel Ferrara.

A valentine to both the movies and the town with which they've become synonymous, this is a pleasing and at times moving evocation of the glamor, hopefulness, and exuberance that have propeled both the cinema and the city of Hollywood. While glossing over the physical deterioration of the place and making no reference to its current boisterous comeback, helmers have woven together pieces of feature films, home movies, newsreel footage, and contemporary interviews to create a dazzling tapestry that vividly expresses the energy of Hollywood's filmic roots.

McCarthy, *Variety*'s chief film critic, has a solid take on the development of the film industry and the little town that suddenly got big and famous along with the pictures. In the first half of this image- and idea-packed 57-minute opus, helmers focus on a dizzying celebration of the stars and the factories where dreams rolled out like Fords off an assembly line.

Behind-the-scenes footage of impossibly handsome Gary Cooper, otherworldly Marlene Dietrich, boyishly buoyant Mickey Rooney et al., is accompanied by insightful interviews with veteran film figures such as directors Andre de Toth and Vincent Sherman. *Titanic* co-star Gloria Stuart's reminiscing about stumbling upon the shooting of a fairytale picture in Topanga Canyon, while footage of the original silent film rolls, is perhaps the documentary's single most stunning moment. For newcomers eager to be baptized in the waters of the local religion, *Forever* is a blessing.

For Love of the Game

A Universal Pictures release of a Beacon Pictures/Tig Prods./Mirage Enterprises production. Produced by Armyan Bernstein, Amy Robinson. Executive producers, Ron Bozman, Marc Abraham. Directed by Sam Raimi. Screenplay, Dana Stevens, based on the novel by Michael Shaara. Camera (Deluxe color, Panavision widescreen), John Bailey; editors, Eric L. Beason, Arthur Coburn; music, Basil Poledouris; music supervisor, G. Marq Roswell; production designer, Neil Spisak; art directors, Jim Feng, Steve Arnold. Reviewed at Universal Studios screening room, Universal City, September 8, 1999. MPAA Rating: PG-13. Running time: 137 mins.
Kevin Costner (Billy Chapel), Kelly Preston (Jane Aubrey), John C. Reilly (Gus Sinski), Jena Malone (Heather), Brian Cox (Gary Wheeler), J.K. Simmons (Frank Perry), Vin Scully (As Himself), Steve Lyons (As Himself), Carmine D. Giovinazzo (Ken Strout), Bill Rogers (Davis Birch), Hugh Ross (Mike Udall).
As all-American and all-Hollywood as a movie can get, this marks a kind of capper on Costner's baseball trilogy. Film is a highly uneven study of an aging vet in his swansong game in the bigs. A pic has finally nailed the actual playing of the Grand Old Game with remarkable realism, while fans of helmer Sam Raimi will be in shock at the straight style and storytelling.

For Love of the Game ignores the game's grit and eccentricities in favour of a mood of valedictory romance, and this choice will surely turn off sports-fan moviegoers.

Young Michigan little leaguer Billy Chapel grows up and plays for the Detroit Tigers. His designated catcher is against the manager's decision to pitch Chapel against the contending N.Y. Yankees – especially since the last-place Tigers' season is over – but Chapel's life soon gives him motivation. Chapel is stood up by his girlfriend, fashion-mag columnist Jane, and informed by the Tigers' owner that he's selling the ball club and that Chapel will be traded. The knife is twisted further as

he meets morose Jane in Central Park and learns she's moving to London, and that, in any case, he needs the game more than he needs her. Costner is as uneven as the storytelling itself, stone cold at moments, shimmeringly real in others.
U.S. release: Sept. 17   U.S. B.O.: $35.2 million

Galaxy Quest

A DreamWorks Pictures release of a Mark Johnson production. Produced by Johnson, Charles Newirth. Executive producer, Elizabeth Cantillon. Co-producers, Suzann Ellis, Sona Gourgouris. Directed by Dean Parisot. Screenplay, David Howard, Robert Gordon. Camera (Technicolor, Panavision widescreen), Jerzy Zielinski; editor, Don Zimmerman; music, David Newman; production designer, Linda DeScenna; art director, Jim Nedza; set decorator, Ric McElvin; costume designer, Albert Wolsky; sound (Dolby Digital/DTS/SDDS), Lee Orloff; alien makeup and creature effects, Stan Winston; visual-effects supervisor, Bill George; ILM visual-effects producer, Kim Bromley; animation supervisor, Christopher Armstrong; associate producer, Allegra Clegg; assistant director, Vincent Lascoumes; second unit directors, Andy Armstrong, Stefan Fangmeier; second unit camera, David Boyd, Robert La Bonge, David Drzewiecki; casting, Debra Zane. Reviewed at AMC Studio 30 Theater, Houston, Dec. 17, 1999. MPAA Rating: PG. Running time: 104 mins.
Tim Allen (Jason Nesmith), Sigourney Weaver (Gwen DeMarco), Alan Rickman (Alexander Dane), Tony Shalhoub (Fred Kwan), Sam Rockwell (Guy Fleegman), Daryl Mitchell (Tommy Webber), Enrico Colantoni (Mathesar), Robin Sachs (Sarris), Patrick Breen (Quellek), Missi Pyle (Laliari), Jed Rees (Teb), Justin Long (Brandon), Jeremy Howard (Kyle).
A mischievously clever and slickly commercial sci-fi comedy gets impressive mileage from a one-joke premise – stars of a *Star Trek*-type TV series are drafted into battling real extra-terrestrial villains – thanks in large measure to game efforts from a first-rate cast. More ingratiating than uproarious, pic emerges as a pleasant surprise.

A cheesy primetime space opera called *Galaxy Quest* continues to inspire a cult following almost 20 years after its cancellation. Jason Nesmith, the *Quest* equivalent of William Shatner, is an overbearing and unreliable egotist who clearly enjoys the adulation he receives at the conventions because his career has been in total eclipse. On the show, he portrayed Cmdr. Peter Quincy Taggart, an heroic National Space Exploration Agency officer in charge of the starship *Protector*. Nesmith's overshadowed co-stars haven't done much since the series either: Gwen DeMarco did little more than serve as the show's bosomy babe; and Alexander Dane, a cynical Shakespearean actor permanently typecast himself by playing the half-human, half-reptilian Dr. Lazarus.

Nesmith is approached by a group of unusual fans who turn out to be extraterrestrials. Mathesar is leader of the Thermians, naive creatures who assume the earthly TV programmes are documentaries. And, more important, they believe Cmdr. Taggart and his crew are true-blue heroes who can help the Thermians defend themselves against the intergalactic marauders led by the dreaded Sarris. Nesmith and his co-stars are singularly ill-prepared for offscreen heroics.
U.S. release: Dec. 25   U.S. B.O.: $27.3 million

... May 14 ...
Thesp Kevin Sorbo is saying goodbye to **Hercules: The Legendary Journeys** and hello to Gene Roddenberry's brand of sci-fi/action TV.

The General's Daughter

A Paramount release of a Mace Neufeld and Robert Rehme production and a Jonathan D. Krane production. Produced by Neufeld. Executive producer, Krane. Co-producer, Stratton Leopold. Directed by Simon West. Screenplay, Christopher Bertolini, William Goldman, based on the novel by Nelson DeMille. Camera (Deluxe color, Panavision widescreen), Peter Menzies Jr.; editor, Glen Scantlebury; music, Carter Burwell; production designer, Dennis Washington; art directors, Tom Taylor, Ann Harris; set designers, Lorrie Campbell, Lynn Christopher, Beverli Eagen; set decorator, Marvin March; costume designer, Erica Edell Phillips; sound (DTS/Dolby Digital), Tommy Causey; sound designer/supervising sound editor, Stephen Hunter Flick; associate producers, Anson Downes, Linda Favila; assistant director, Steve Danton; casting, Mindy Marin. Reviewed at Paramount Studios, L.A., June 4, 1999. MPAA Rating: R. Running time: 116 mins.

John Travolta (Paul Brenner), Madeleine Stowe (Sarah Sunhill), James Cromwell (General Campbell), Timothy Hutton (Colonel Kent), Leslie Stefanson (Elisabeth Campbell), Daniel von Bargen (Chief Yardley), Clarence Williams III (Colonel Fowler), James Woods (Colonel Moore), Peter Weireter (Belling), Mark Boone Junior (Elkins), John Beasley (Colonel Slesinger), Boyd Kestner (Captain Elby), Brad Beyer (Bransford), John Benjamin Hickey (Captain Goodson), Rick Dial (Cal Seive), Ariyan Johnson (PFC Robbin), John Frankenheimer (General Sonnenberg).

Logically enough considering its source material, pic is the cinematic equivalent of a disposable airplane read, a hokey, kinky military thriller that's twisty and compelling. Paul Brenner is enlisted to solve an unusual and disturbing crime, the murder on the base of Captain Elisabeth Campbell, an expert in psychological operations who also happens to be the beautiful daughter of retiring General Campbell, a distinguished figure now being paged into politics. Prior to the murder, Paul flirts ineffectually with the alluring young woman. Afterward, he's teamed by chance with fellow Criminal Investigation Division vet Sarah Sunhill, with whom he had an affair long ago.

To set the clock ticking in traditional thriller fashion, Paul is told he's got 36 hours to nail the killer before the FBI moves in, and the scandal goes embarrassingly public. Virtually his first order of business is to question, then arrest Elisabeth's commanding officer, the disarmingly insightful and manipulative Colonel Moore. By this time Paul and Sarah have discovered some decidedly freaky facts about Elisabeth's private life.

As in many mysteries, everybody here is a possible suspect: West works the investigative engine forward at a hard-charging, but not annoyingly fast, clip. Travolta delivers another strong performance that effectively carries the picture. Woods delivers a standout supporting turn.

U.S. release: June 18   U.S. B.O.: $102.7 million

Ghost Dog: The Way of the Samurai

A JVC/Bac Films/Le Studio Canal Plus presentation, in association with Pandora Film and ARD/Degeto Film, of a Plywood production. Produced by Richard Guay, Jim Jarmusch. Co-producer, Diana Schmidt. Directed, written by Jarmusch. Camera (Deluxe color), Robby Muller; editor, Jay Rabinowitz; music, RZA; production designer, Ted Berner;

art director, Mario Ventenilla; set decorator, Ronnie von Blomberg; costume designer, John Dunn; sound (Dolby Digital), Drew Kunin; sound designer, Chic Ciccolini III; assistant director, Jude Gorjanc; casting, Ellen Lewis, Laura Rosenthal. Reviewed at Cannes Film Festival (competing), May 18, 1999. Running time: 116 mins.

Forest Whitaker (Ghost Dog), John Tormey (Louie), Cliff Gorman (Sonny Valerio), Henry Silva (Vargo), Isaach de Bankole (Raymond), Tricia Vessey (Louise Vargo), Victor Argo (Vinny), Gene Ruffini (Old Consigliere), Richard Portnow (Handsome Frank), Camille Winbush (Pearline).

A playful but exceedingly wispy piece of doodling that plays minor variations on the declining hit-man genre. As he goes his own way making films about violent loners living outside society, Jarmusch is edging himself further into the margins of the industry with pictures that few people are interested in seeing. Pic has its share of idiosyncratic cleverness and invention, but the overall conception is terribly thin and the scenes lack complexity, extensive character interaction and a sense of meaningful confrontation, despite the large number of killings.

Set in what's identified on license plates as "The Industrial State", Ghost Dog dresses like any other street character and lives in a dismal rooftop shack. He possesses high-tech crime equipment and a fancy assortment of guns. He also lives a meticulously ordered existence by *The Book of the Samurai*. Ghost Dog pledges undying loyalty to Louie, a small-time Italian mobster who saved his life years back during an attack by thugs. Since then, Ghost Dog, whose name refers to his ability to come and go without being noticed or traced, has pulled off a dozen perfect hits for Louie. But when he's seen on his unlucky 13th job, Louie's superiors decide he's got to go and begin sending shooters of their own after him. Ghost Dog commences a methodical campaign to wipe out his many adversaries, resulting in a succession of killing.

Girl, Interrupted

A Sony Pictures Entertainment release of a Columbia Pictures presentation of a Red Wagon production. Produced by Douglas Wick, Cathy Konrad. Executive producers, Carol Brodie, Winona Ryder. Co-producer, Georgia Kacandes. Directed by James Mangold. Screenplay, Mangold, Lisa Loomer, Anna Hamilton Phelan, based on the book by Susanna Kaysen. Camera (Deluxe color), Jack Green; editor, Kevin Tent; music, Mychael Danna; production designer, Richard Hoover; art director, Jeff Knip; set decorator, Maggie Martin; costume designer, Arianne Phillips; sound (Dolby), Jim Stuebe; associate producer, Kaysen; assistant director, Cas Donovan; casting, Lisa Beach. Reviewed at Sony Studios, Culver City, Dec. 1, 1999. MPAA Rating: R. Running time: 127 mins.

Winona Ryder (Susanna), Angelina Jolie (Lisa), Clea Duvall (Georgina), Brittany Murphy (Daisy), Elisabeth Moss (Polly), Jared Leto (Tobias Jacobs), Jeffrey Tambor (Dr. Potts), Vanessa Redgrave (Dr. Wick), Whoopi Goldberg (Valerie), Mary Kay Place (Mrs. Gilcrest).

Based on Susanna Kaysen's memoir of her experience at a mental hospital, this moderately engaging effort imposes a detached, male perspective on the author's firsthand observations. Kaysen's journal presents a difficult challenge for screen adaptation. Not only is it episodic and non-chronological, but it integrates sharp commentary on female adolescence, bourgeois family values and the abuse of authority by the medical profession. What's missing is the author's dark humor and revelatory insights into her ordeal. Pic is unevenly structured and directed, its sensibility only one notch above that of a *Lifetime* telepic.

Confused, insecure and baffled by the changing mores of American society in 1967-68, Susanna appears to be like many other adolescents. When Susanna's upper middle class parents discover that she has taken a whole bottle of aspirin, they urge her to see a psychiatrist. The doctor diagnoses borderline personality disorder. Without a moment of hesitation, he recommends institutionalization at the Claymoore Hospital. But once Susanna lands at the asylum, the story toes a more conventional path. Most of the narrative is set within the confines of the ward, centering on Susanna's interactions and growing friendship with a half-dozen inmates, who are mostly character types rather than full-blooded characters.

Ryder is credibly cast, occasionally rising above the script's limitations. Stealing every scene she's in, Jolie is excellent as the flamboyant, irresponsible girl who turns out to be far more instrumental than the doctors in Susanna's rehabilitation.

U.S. release: Dec. 21   U.S. B.O.: $434,810

Go

A Sony Pictures Entertainment release of a Columbia Pictures presentation of a Banner Entertainment production in association with Saratoga Entertainment. Produced by Paul Rosenberg, Mickey Liddell, Matt Freeman. Co-producers, Paddy Cullen, John August. Directed by Doug Liman. Screenplay, John August.
Desmond Askew (Simon Baines), Taye Diggs (Marcus), William Fichtner (Burke), J.E. Freeman (Victor Sr.), Katie Holmes (Claire Montgomery), Breckin Meyer (Tiny), Jay Mohr (Zack), Timothy Olyphant (Todd Gaines), Sarah Polley (Ronna Martin), Scott Wolf (Adam), James Duval (Singh), Nathan Bexton (Mannie), Jay Paulson (Loop), Jimmy Shubert (Victor Jr.).
Go trades almost exclusively in elements of reckless chic: recreational drug use, low-rent gangsters, the L.A.-Vegas axis, lap dancing, gunplay, plus a hot soundtrack and a scroll-back-the-action plot structure reminiscent of *Pulp Fiction*. Ronna is an overworked L.A. supermarket checkout girl who, over Christmas, agrees to fill in for her Brit co-worker, Simon, so he can holiday in Vegas. Approached by a couple of good-looking young actors, Adam and Zack, who are interested in scoring some drugs, Ronna decides to risk doing business with Simon's dealer, Todd, but ends up betraying him when she senses she's being set up by Adam and Zack in a sting run by Burke.

Ronna escapes by heading for a giant Christmas party and falls upon tragic circumstances. Plot switches to Simon's escapades in Las Vegas where he manages to bed two women, set a hotel room on fire, steal a sports car (equipped with a gun), and wreak havoc at a strip club. Action rewinds one last time to the Adam-Zack duo as they're left with Burke and his ditzy wife Irene for a holiday dinner. A measure of suspense is generated as the three plot resolutions come together. August's script is based on myriad interlinking parts, the sum of which is meant to play up the coincidental connections in life. Pic exerts a magnetic pull due to Sarah Polley, a thesp who effortlessly draws the viewer's attention.

U.S. release: Apr. 9   U.S. B.O.: $16.9 million

The Green Mile

A Warner Bros. release of a Castle Rock Entertainment presentation of a Darkwoods production. Produced by David Valdes, Frank Darabont. Directed, written by Darabont, based on the novel by Stephen King. Camera (Technicolor), David Tattersall; editor, Richard Francis-Bruce; music, Thomas Newman; production designer, Terence Marsh; supervising art director, William Cruse; set designers, Donald Woodruff, Dianne Wager; set decorator, Michael Seirton; costume designer, Karyn Wagner; sound (Dolby Digital/SDDS/DTS), Willie D. Burton; supervising sound editor, Mark Mangini; sound designer, Eric Lindeman; visual-effects supervisor, Charles Gibson; visual effects, Industrial Light & Magic; assistant director, Alan B. Curtiss; second unit director, Charles Gibson; second unit camera, Mark Vargo; present day sequences camera, Gabriel Beristain; casting, Mali Finn. Reviewed at Warner Bros. Studios, Burbank, Nov. 20, 1999. MPAA Rating: R. Running time: 187 mins.
Tom Hanks (Paul Edgecomb), David Morse (Brutus "Brutal" Howell), Bonnie Hunt (Jan Edgecomb), Michael Clarke Duncan (John Coffey), James Cromwell (Warden Hal Moores), Michael Jeter (Eduard Delacroix), Graham Greene (Arlen Bitterbuck), Doug Hutchison (Percy Wetmore), Sam Rockwell ("Wild Bill" Wharton), Barry Pepper (Dean Stanton), Jeffrey DeMunn (Harry Terwilliger), Patricia Clarkson (Melinda Moores), Harry Dean Stanton (Toot-Toot), Dabbs Greer (Old Paul Edgecomb), Eve Brent (Elaine Connelly), William Sadler (Klaus Detterick), Gary Sinise (Burt Hammersmith).
Tale is set within the modest confines of a death row at Cold Mountain Penitentiary in Louisiana in 1935. Presiding over the inmates is head guard Paul Edgecomb, a decent middle-aged man dedicated to maintaining as much calm and dignity as possible on the cell lot. On his staff are his loyal second-in-command guards with the exception of Percy Wetmore, a shrimpy sadist who can get away with his horrible behavior since he's the son of the governor's wife. Except for troublemaker, "Wild Bill Wharton", the prisoners are good hearted. One in particular is John Coffey, a slow, towering, heavily muscled black man who's been convicted of killing two little girls. One day Coffey miraculously cures Edgecomb of his bladder infection by grabbing his crotch. After an odd moment he releases Edgecomb and lets loose from his mouth a flow of flying particles. Edgecomb becomes convinced not only of Coffey's innocence but of his other-worldly healing powers, leading him to hatch an audacious plot to have the inmate secretly cure the cancer-stricken wife of the prison's dignified warden.

Positioning himself as the specialist in adapting Stephen King period prison novels for the screen, Frank Darabont emerges from his five-year hiatus with an intermittently powerful and meticulously crafted drama that falls short of its full potential due to considerable over-length and some shopworn, simplistic notions at its center. Darabont is nothing if not a fastidious storyteller dedicated to fulsome character detailing and sturdy structural carpentry. Helmer proves very adept at lighting numerous long fuses that burn slowly through the yarn's lengthy telling and finally pay off in some big moments, some more satisfying than others. Overall, the ensemble acting is of a high order.

U.S. release: Dec. 10   U.S. B.O.:$76.7 million

... May 16 ...
Universal's **The Mummy** dug up $25.1 million on its second expedition.

Gregory's Two Girls

A FilmFour Distributors release (in U.K.) of a FilmFour presentation, in association with the Scottish Arts Council National Lottery Fund and Kinowelt Filmproduktion, of a Young Lake production. (International sales: FilmFour Intl., London.) Produced by Christopher Young. Directed, written by Bill Forsyth. Camera (Deluxe Color prints), John de Borman; editor, John Gow; music, Michael Gibbs; production designer, Andy Harris; art director, Stephen Wong; costume designer, Kate Carin; sound (Dolby), Louis Kramer; line producer, Alan J. Wands; assistant director, David Gilchrist; casting, Susie Figgis, Nina Gold. Reviewed at Odeon, Clerk Street, Edinburgh, Aug. 22, 1999. (In Edinburgh Film Festival - Focus on British Cinema section; also in Toronto Film Festival - Masters.) Running time: 116 mins.
John Gordon Sinclair (Gregory Underwood), Carly McKinnon (Frances), Dougray Scott (Fraser Rowan), Maria Doyle Kennedy (Bel), Kevin Anderson (Jon), Martin Schwab (Dimitri), Fiona Bell (Maddy Underwood), Hugh McCue (Douglas), John Murtagh (Headmaster), Matt Costello (Detective Gorrie), Jane Stabler (Detective Ritchie).
Bill Forsyth hasn't lost his early gift for observational, character-driven comedy. At the least, though, the back-to-roots *Girls* re-establishes the helmer as a distinctive, still-functioning talent. He hasn't lost his quiet exasperation at the idiocies of contemporary life. Any fears that Forsyth has tried to replicate his much-loved low-budgeter about a gangly teen with the hots for a soccer-mad schoolgirl, are laid to rest early on. *Girls* has a very different feel and texture.

Gregory Underwood is now an English teacher at the same Scottish school. Now in his mid-30s, he is an emotionally underdeveloped but otherwise passionate, committed teacher who lectures his class on the evils of American big business and politics more than English. Gregory has un-teacherly feelings for 16-year-old Frances, who keeps suggesting a clandestine rendezvous. Frances wants Gregory to help her and fellow pupil Douglas get the goods on corrupt businessman Fraser Rowan, a local boy who made his fortune in the States and now runs a tech company in Cumbernauld. The kids ask Gregory, who's an old school chum of Fraser, to get them into his factory. While Gregory is drawn into the kids' scheme, he continues to be tortured by his dangerous crush on Frances and the never-say-die advances of fellow teacher Bel. When the movie needs to push on to its conclusion, it often becomes mired in extraneous sequences and loses both its emotional focus and rhythm.

Grey Owl

A Remstar Distribution release (in Canada) of a Beaver Prods./Allied Filmmakers/Transfilm production. (International sales: Summit Entertainment, Los Angeles.) Produced by Richard Attenborough, Jake Eberts, Claude Leger. Executive producers, Barr Potter, Lenny Young. Co-producer, Diana Hawkins. Directed by Richard Attenborough. Screenplay, William Nicholson. Camera (color, Panavision widescreen), Roger Pratt; editor, Lesley Walker; music, George Fenton; production designer, Anthony Pratt; art director, Claude Pare; costume designer, Renee April; sound, Patrick Rousseau, Jonathan Bates, Gerry Humphreys; casting, Vera Miller, Nadia Rona. Reviewed at the Quartier Latin Cinema, Montreal, Sept. 20, 1999. Running time: 117 mins.

Pierce Brosnan (Archibald Belaney/Grey Owl), Annie Galipeau (Anahareo/Pony), Nathaniel Arcand (Ned White Bear), Vlasta Vrana (Harry Champlin), David Fox (Jim Wood), Charles Powell (Walter Perry). With: Stephanie Cole, Renee Asherson, Stewart Bick, Graham Greene.
Film is based on the true story of Archibald Belaney, an Englishman obsessed with North American Indians who moved to Canada in the early 20th century and began pretending to be an aboriginal. At first a trapper, Archie Grey Owl eventually had a change of heart, transforming himself into an ardent early environmentalist. His book and lectures about life in the wilds of Canada became a huge success. His double life was exposed only after his death in 1938.

In 1936, a reporter from a small-town Ontario newspaper confronts Grey Owl about his dual identity. Story then quickly flashes back to the fateful moment when Grey Owl meets the young Mohawk woman Anahareo, nicknamed Pony.

She is smitten by this handsome character, and the fascination grows stronger when he takes her to the Ojibway village that he comes from. Pony wants to learn more about her heritage and figures Grey Owl is the ticket to her journey of self-discovery. The most satisfying and touching section is the final reel, in which Grey Owl returns home to England and confronts his past in the form of the two stern aunts who raised him.

Attenborough has attempted to craft another *Gandhi*-like biopic with a sociopolitical message, but this ambitious effort falls far short of the seasoned filmmaker's lofty goals. A remarkably lackluster script, oldfashioned direction, and some seriously questionable casting conspire to create a fatally flawed, if sometimes intriguing, pic.

Guinevere

A Miramax release presented in association with Millenium Prods. of a Bandeira Entertainment production. Produced by Jonathan King, Brad Weston. Executive producers, Avi Lerner, Danny Dimbort, Trevor Short, Beau Flynn, Harvey Weinstein, Bob Weinstein, Stefan Simchowitz, John Thompson, Boaz Davidson. Directed, written by Audrey Wells. Camera (CFI color), Charles Minsky; editor, Dody Dorn; music, Christophe Beck; music supervisor, Barklie K. Griggs; production designer, Stephen McCabe; set decorator, Danielle Berman; costume designer, Genevieve Tyrrell; sound (Dolby), Glenn R. Gaines; line producer, Tani Cohen; assistant director, Jim LaClair; casting, Linda Lowy, John Brace. Reviewed at Sundance Film Festival (competing), Jan. 25, 1999. Running time: 104 mins.
Stephen Rea (Connie Fitzpatrick), Sarah Polley (Harper Sloane), Jean Smart (Deborah Sloane), Gina Gershon (Billie), Paul Dooley (Walter), Francis Guinan (Alan Sloane), Jasmine Guy (Linda), Tracy Letts (Zack), Sandra Oh (Cindy), Carrie Preston (Patty), Emily Procter (Susan Sloane), Grace Una (April), Gedde Watanabe (Ed).
Wonderfully acted, *Guinevere* is an emotionally sensitive and insightful look at a romance between a 20-year-old girl and a bohemian photographer more than twice her age. Script has a strongly articulated take on a common type of male-female relationship that is rarely investigated with the nuance and honesty that it is here: sure, the older man is primarily driven by the ego boost of being with a cute young thing, but the woman can get a great deal out of it, too, in terms of knowledge, life experience, and self-confidence. Pic remains win-

... **May 17** ...
Olympus Film International and Enzo Peri announce the preparation of Marguerite Yourcenar's **Memoirs of Hadrian** is to be directed by John Boorman.

ning throughout because it never loses sight of how the relationship is a double-edged sword for both parties.

Stylishly sketching in its heroine's inferiority complex during her sister's elegant wedding party in San Francisco, pic shows Harper Sloane avoiding socializing by hanging out with the wedding photographer, Connie Fitzpatrick, a shaggily attractive Irishman. Connie wins Harper over by sending her a beautiful portrait he took of her. She feels compelled to pay him a visit, and a relationship begins to flame.

Harper learns from one of Connie's former flames that she is probably in for a five-year run with Connie. The photographer has had numerous "Guineveres," as he calls his inamoratas, with near-identical patterns of emotional and artistic growth until the student outgrew the teacher. Fanciful ending, which brings all the Guineveres together, is a striking conceit, but partly feels like it belongs in a different movie.
U.S. release: Sept. 24   U.S. B.O.: $668,099

The Haunting

A DreamWorks Pictures release of a Roth/Arnold production. Produced by Susan Arnold, Donna Arkoff Roth, Colin Wilson. Executive producer, Jan De Bont. Directed by De Bont. Screenplay, David Self, based on *The Haunting of Hill House* by Shirley Jackson. Camera (Technicolor, Panavision widescreen), Karl Walter Lindenlaub; editor, Michael Kahn; music, Jerry Goldsmith; production designer, Eugenio Zanetti; supervising art director, Tomas Voth; art directors, Martin Laing, Troy Sizemore, Jonathan Lee (U.K.). Reviewed at the Village Theater, L.A., July 20, 1999. MPAA Rating: PG-13. Running time: 114 mins.
Liam Neeson (Dr. David Marrow), Catherine Zeta-Jones (Theo), Owen Wilson (Luke Sanderson), Lili Taylor (Nell), Bruce Dern (Mr. Dudley), Marian Seldes (Mrs. Dudley), Alix Koromzay (Mary Lambetta), Todd Field (Todd Hackett), Virginia Madsen (Jane).
No expense has been spared in the attempt to rev up the low-key spookiness of Robert Wise's 1963 MGM film version of Shirley Jackson's *The Haunting of Hill House* to state-of-the-art levels of terror. Jan De Bont's updating merely stands as yet another illustration of the fact that all the money in Hollywood can't buy imagination, resourcefulness, wit, or a decent script. *The Haunting*'s incredibly hokey premise and surpassing inability to elicit shocks and scares prevent it from reaching its full potential.

Main gambit is that the sprawling estate is actually "alive" with menace, a threat that manifests itself in a torrent of heart-stopping sounds, sudden apparitions, shape-changing carvings and statues, mutating walls and ceilings, and so on. Researcher Dr. David Marrow is recruiting several insomniacs for a study of sleep disorders. In reality, he wants to test the theories he has about fear and what better place to do so than in a creepy mansion? He rounds up three volunteers: Nel, Theo, and Luke. They are bores whose few noticeable personality traits are quite irrelevant to anything that goes on. Overall the plot involves each character, with some motivation for sticking around, navigating the considerable inconveniences of the house. The only thing that keeps one going for a time is the sense that the film is going to get better, that something wild and scary is bound to happen eventually.
U.S. release: July 23   U.S. B.O.: $91.2 million

Holy Smoke

A Miramax Films release of a Miramax Intl. presentation of a Jan Chapman production. Produced by Chapman. Executive producers, Bob Weinstein, Harvey Weinstein, Julie Goldstein. Directed by Jane Campion. Screenplay, Anna Campion, Jane Campion. Camera (color), Dion Beebe; editor, Veronika Jenet; music, Angelo Badalamenti; production/costumer designer, Janet Patterson; art director, Tony Campbell; sound designer, Lee Smith; sound (Dolby Digital), Ben Osmo; visual effects, Animal Logic Film; line producer, Catherine Bishop; associate producer, assistant director, Mark Turnbull; casting, Alison Barrett, Billy Hopkins, Suzanne Smith, Kerry Barden. Reviewed at Venice Film Festival (competing), Sept. 3, 1999. (Also in New York Film Festival.) Running time: 114 mins.
Kate Winslet (Ruth), Harvey Keitel (P.J. Waters), Pam Grier (Carol), Julie Hamilton (Mum), Sophie Lee (Yvonne), Daniel Wyllie (Robbie), Paul Goddard (Tim), Tim Robertson (Dad), George Mangos (Yani). With: Kerry Walker, Leslie Dayman, Samantha Murray, Austen Tayshus, Simon Anderson, Genevieve Lemon.
Jane Campion returns to the freewheeling style and idiosyncratic humor of *Sweetie* in perhaps her most challenging work to date. Original in every sense, this often difficult film about family, relationships, sexual politics, spiritual questing, faith and obsession further explores the director's abiding fascinations in excitingly unconventional terms. The story concerns Ruth, a young Australian woman who falls under the spell of a guru and is drawn into an Indian cult, prompting her family to engage a crack American "exit counsellor," P.J. Waters, at great expense to bring her back to Earth. But when the tables are turned, making sex the central issue, the real subject becomes gender relationships, in particular the dynamic of a younger woman with an older man, as the cult buster himself undergoes a radical deprogramming of his beliefs and standards.

There's something persuasive about being in the hands of such an uncompromising filmmaker who refuses to take a predictable course or make things easy by over explaining. As in *Sweetie*, the observation here of the more gauche side of Australian suburbanites is spot-on and bitingly funny. The role takes Winslet far beyond anything she has done before. Showing the kind of courage few young thesps would be capable of and an extraordinary range that sees her swing from crushed vulnerability to abrasiveness and brutality, from animal cunning to unhinged desperation, she holds nothing back.
U.S. release: Dec. 3   U.S. B.O.: $65,328

The Hurricane

A Universal release of a Beacon Pictures presentation of an Azoff Films/Rudy Langlais production. Produced by Armyan Bernstein, John Ketcham, Norman Jewison. Executive producers, Irving Azoff, Tom Rosenberg, Langlais, Thomas A. Bliss, Marc Abraham, William Teitler. Co-producers, Suzann Ellis, Michael Jewison, Jon Jashni. Directed by Norman Jewison. Screenplay, Armyan Bernstein, Dan Gordon, based on the books *The Sixteenth Round* by Rubin "Hurricane" Carter and *Lazarus and the Hurricane* by Sam Chaiton and Terry Swinton. Camera (Deluxe color), Roger Deakins; editor, Stephen Rivkin; music, Christopher Young; music supervisor, G. Marq Roswell; production designer, Philip Rosenberg; art director, Dennis Davenport; set decorator,

Gordon Sim; costume designer, Aggie Guerard Rodgers; sound (Dolby/DTS/SDDS), Bruce Carwardine; supervising sound editors, Michael O'Farrell, Wayne Griffin; assistant director, J.J. Authors; casting, Avy Kaufman. Reviewed at the Beverly Connection, L.A., Nov. 29, 1999. MPAA Rating: R. Running time: 125 mins

Denzel Washington (Rubin "Hurricane" Carter), Vicellous Reon Shannon (Lesra), Deborah Kara Unger (Lisa), Liev Schreiber (Sam), John Hannah (Terry), Dan Hedaya (Della Pesca), Debbi Morgan (Mae Thelma), Clancy Brown (Lt. Jimmy Williams), David Paymer (Myron Bedlock), Harris Yulin (Leon Friedman), Rod Steiger (Judge Sarokin), Garland Whitt (John Artis).

Rubin "Hurricane" Carter was a black boxer who was wrongly convicted of triple murder and sent to prison, where he spent 19 years before being exonerated and released in 1985. In what is easily his most zealous and fully realized performance since *Malcolm X*, Washington elevates the earnest, occasionally simplistic narrative to the level of a genuinely touching moral exposé. *The Hurricane* is so intriguingly plotted and captivatingly acted that it's easy to overlook its dramatic flaws and overall soft gaze. All the thesps do well in the same emotionally truthful vein.

Brief flashbacks recreate the 1966 murder in a Paterson, N.J. bar, leading to the arrest of Carter and a young fan who just happen to be in the wrong place at the wrong time. Under the manipulation of a malevolent cop, Della Pesca, a wounded victim identifies Carter as one of the killers. Cut to Toronto, seven years later, when a black youth named Lesra picks up Carter's autobiography for a quarter. After reading the book, Lesra finds direction and purpose for the first time in his life. A product of poor, illiterate parents, Lesra has been "adopted" by three Canadian students, who take him to their bohemian apartment in Toronto.

Instinctively convinced of Carter's innocence, Lesra begins corresponding with him, soon enlisting his social-activist guardians to mount a full-time campaign for his release.
U.S. release: Dec. 29   U.S. B.O.: $489,552

An Ideal Husband

A Pathe (in U.K.)/Miramax (in U.S.) release of an Icon Entertainment Intl./Pathe Pictures presentation, in association with the Arts Council of England, of a Fragile Films production, in association with Icon Prods., Miramax Films and Le Studio Canal Plus. Produced by Barnaby Thompson, Uri Fruchtmann, Bruce Davey. Executive producers, Susan B. Landau, Ralph Kamp, Andrea Calderwood. Co-producers, Nicky Kentish Barnes, Paul Tucker. Directed, written by Oliver Parker, based on the play by Oscar Wilde.

Rupert Everett (Lord Arthur Goring), Julianne Moore (Mrs. Laura Cheveley), Jeremy Northam (Sir Robert Chiltern), Cate Blanchett (Lady Gertrud Chiltern), Minnie Driver (Mabel Chiltern), John Wood (Earl of Caversham), Lindsay Duncan (Lady Markby), Peter Vaughan (Phipps), Jeroen Krabbe (Baron Arnheim), Ben Pullen (Tommy).

Oscar Wilde's 104-year-old play about emotional and political chicanery shines like a freshly minted coin in Oliver Parker's adaptation. Pic begins at the home of rising young politician Sir Robert Chiltern where a society party is being thrown. We observe Chiltern's adoring wife, Gertrud, herself into femme politics; his younger sister, Mabel; resolute bachelor and "the idlest man in London," Lord Arthur Goring ;

and, fresh in from Vienna, her ultra-poised friend Mrs. Laura Cheveley. Laura whisks Robert off to a drawing room and calmly blackmails the politico into supporting a dodgy scheme (an Argentine canal project) in Parliament so she doesn't lose her sizable stock-market investment. Laura has an incriminating document about a youthful "indiscretion" by Robert. A cynical social butterfly to his fingertips, Arthur is drawn into helping his old friend Robert. As he has already made clear his opposition to the Argentine scheme, Robert knows he would lose his wife along with his career if he suddenly altered his stance.

Boasts smooth-flowing direction, a shrewdly pruned script and a top-flight ensemble cast that visibly relishes both the dialogue and one another's performances. Most modern about this version is that all the characters finally emerge as sympathetic, rather than brittle constructs; and most welcome is the fact that the pic studiously avoids condescending to the characters in a knowing contempo way.
U.S. release: June 18   U.S. B.O.: $18.5 million

The Insider

A Buena Vista release of a Touchstone Pictures presentation of a Mann/Roth production of a Forward Pass picture. Produced by Michael Mann, Pieter Jan Brugge. Co-producer, Michael Waxman. Directed by Mann. Screenplay, Eric Roth, Mann, based on the *Vanity Fair* article "The Man Who Knew Too Much" by Marie Brenner.

Al Pacino (Lowell Bergman), Russell Crowe (Jeffrey Wigand), Christopher Plummer (Mike Wallace), Diane Venora (Liane Wigand), Philip Baker Hall (Don Hewitt), Lindsay Crouse (Sharon Tiller), Debi Mazar (Debbie De Luca), Stephen Tobolowsky (Eric Kluster), Colm Feore (Richard Scruggs), Bruce McGill (Ron Motley), Gina Gershon (Helen Caperelli), Michael Gambon (Thomas Sandefur), Rip Torn (John Scanlon), Lynne Thigpen (Mrs. Williams), Hallie Kate Eisenberg (Barbara Wigand), Michael Paul Chan (Norman the Cameraman), Linda Hart (Mrs. Wigand), Robert Harper (Mark Stern), Nestor Serrano (FBI Agent Robertson), Pete Hamill (N.Y. Times Reporter), Wings Hauser (Tobacco Lawyer), Clifford Curtis (Sheikh Fadlallah), Renee Olstead (Deborah Wigand), Michael Moore (As Himself).

The impact of a challenging story boldly tackled is diminished by serious overlength and an overriding air of self-importance in *The Insider*. This detailed analysis of the ferocious power, implacable arrogance and ultimate vulnerability of corporate America can only be respected for the fearless determination with which it pulls the curtain back on the shameless chicanery of giant profit- and image-minded companies.

Fired from his position as head of research and development at the third-largest U.S. tobacco company; Jeffrey Wigand is pursued by *60 Minutes* producer Lowell Bergman to blow the lid off the deceptions of "The Seven Dwarfs," the heads of the seven major tobacco companies who have denied to a congressional committee that smoking poses any health risks. In doing so, Wigand grapples with breaking a signed confidentiality agreement, which if broken, would discontinue his "hush" money and health benefits, particularly vital as his daughter suffers from a severe form of asthma. Wigand takes the risk with full confidence that Bergman – and, by implication, *60 Minutes* – will be there to back him up and make it all worthwhile in the end. The fact that this confidence is

---

. . . May 19 . . .
U.S. pics have been removed from local theaters in the wake of the anti-American flare-up in China after NATO's bombing of the Chinese Embassy in Belgrade.

misplaced represents the story's biggest shock, one that naturally devastates Wigand but ultimately has a more profound impact on Bergman and the reputation of the most respected show on U.S. television.

Crowe makes Wigand a fascinating and unpredictable enigma, a figure of complicated motives. Pacino invests Bergman with boundless energy and passion for his job, but it's a one-note character. Plummer delivers enormous satisfaction in an authoritative portrait of Mike Wallace, who is gruff, shrewd, arrogant when he needs to be and always extremely smart – except for one crucial moment.

U.S. release: Nov. 5 U.S. B.O.: $26.1 million

Inspector Gadget

A Buena Vista release of a Walt Disney Pictures production in association with Caravan Pictures. Produced by Jordan Kerner, Roger Birnbaum, Andy Heyward. Executive producers, Jon Avnet, Barry Bernardi, Aaron Meyerson, Jonathan Glickman, Ralph Winter. Co-producers, Lou Arkoff, Jean Chalopin. Directed by David Kellogg. Screenplay, Kerry Ehrin, Zak Penn; story, Ehrin, Dana Olsen; based on characters created by Andy Heyward, Jean Chalopin, Bruno Bianchi.

Matthew Broderick (Inspector Gadget/RoboGadget/John Brown), Rupert Everett (Sanford Scolex), Joely Fisher (Brenda/RoboBrenda), Michelle Trachtenberg (Penny), Andy Dick (Kramer), Cheri Oteri (Mayor Wilson), Michael G. Hagerty (Sikes), Dabney Coleman (Chief Quimby), D.L. Hughley (Gadgetmobile Voice), Rene Auberjonois (Artemus Bradford), Frances Bay (Thelma), Don Adams (Voice of Brain).

A joyless and charmless disaster in which state-of-the-art special effects are squandered on pain-in-the-backside folly, pic is loosely based on the 1980s TV cartoon series about a bumbling bionic crime-fighter.

John Brown, an idealistic security guard, longs to join the police. While working at a technological research facility, he springs into action when intruders kill scientist Artemus Bradford and flee with their victim's latest invention. Brown pursues the culprits – evil billionaire Sanford Scolex and his flunky – who counterattack by tossing an explosive into Brown's car. Scolex loses a hand in the resulting conflagration. However, there isn't much left of our hero when he's wheeled into the hospital. So Brenda Bradford, Artemus' daughter, resorts to drastic measures. Applying the experimental technology designed by her father, she implants several thousand handy-dandy devices in the dying security guard, giving him a new lease on life as a gizmo-enhanced cyborg, and renames him Inspector Gadget. Gadget is assigned to the Riverton City police department, whose chief is unimpressed by the prospect of employing him. Even so, Gadget resolves to find the killers of Brenda's father.

Film careens from scene to scene like a Ritalin-deprived problem child. The acrid stench of desperation permeates the enterprise, as actors struggle to convince the audience that louder and broader somehow equal funnier.

U.S. release: July 23 U.S. B.O.: $97.4 million

The Iron Giant

A Warner Bros. release. Produced by Allison Abbate, Des McAnuff. Executive producer, Pete Townshend. Directed by Brad Bird. Screenplay, Tim McCanlies, story, Bird, based on

the book *The Iron Man* by Ted Hughes. Camera (Technicolor), Mark Dinicola; editor, Darren T. Holmes; music, Michael Kamen; production designer, Mark Whiting; art director, Alan Bodner; sound (Dolby DTS; SDDS), Randy Thom; head of animation, Tony Fucile; artistic coordinator, Scott F. Johnston; associate producer, John Walker; casting, Marci Liroff. Reviewed at Warner Bros. Studios, Burbank, July 16, 1999. MPAA Rating: G. Running time: 86 mins.

Voices: Jennifer Aniston (Annie Hughes), Eli Marienthal (Hogarth Hughes), Harry Connick Jr. (Dean McCoppin), Vin Diesel (The Iron Giant), Christopher McDonald (Kent Mansley), James Gammon (Marv Loach/Floyd Turbeaux), Cloris Leachman (Mrs. Tensedge), John Mahoney (General Rogard), M. Emmet Walsh (Earl Stutz).

A visually appealing, well-crafted film, pic is an unalloyed success that works on several levels. Brad Bird's ambitious, intelligent freshman feature, cleverly set in 1950s small-town America, effectively references everything from Cold War ideology to B-movie conventions, but it never loses sight of its central narrative hook, the friendship of a boy and a giant robot. Story's previous incarnations include a 1968 children's book, a 1989 Pete Townshend album, and a stage version at London's Old Vic.

Pic is set in the fictional peaceful town of Rockwell, Maine. When his TV reception suddenly goes awry, 9-year-old outsider Hogarth climbs up on the roof, and spots a massive steel creature with an appetite for metal that leads him through the woods and to a local power plant. When the Iron Giant becomes entangled in the powerlines, the boy saves the creature from certain electrocution. Apparently capable of feelings, the giant thanks the boy by becoming his protector and friend. When word gets out that a mammoth creature of unknown origin may be in their midst, Rockwell officials notify the government. A deeply suspicious fed, Kent Mansley has people believing the creature may be a Russian secret weapon, and he mobilizes government forces to destroy it. With Mansley and the armed forces pursuing the giant and ready to fire, pic sets up a final, suspenseful confrontation that forces the giant into a difficult and heart-tugging decision.

U.S. release: Aug. 4 U.S. B.O.: $23.2 million

Just a Little Harmless Sex

A Phaedra Cinema release of an Isn't It Romantic presentation of a Miss Q production. Produced by Deborah Capogrosso, Rick Rosenthal. Co-producer, Jamie Beardsley. Directed by Rick Rosenthal. Screenplay, Marti Noxon, Roger Miller. Camera (FotoKem color), Bruce Surtees; editor, James Austin Stewart; music, Tito Larriva; music supervisor, Jen Miller; production designer, Amy Danger; art director, Joseph Dunn; set decorator, Dianne Kalem Karis; costume designer, Kelly Zitrick; sound (Dolby), Stewart Pearce; associate producer, Jen Miller; assistant director, Justin Miller; casting, Rene Haynes, Cathy Henderson-Martin, Don Zuckerman. Reviewed on videocassette, L.A., June 9, 1999. Running time: 98 mins.

Alison Eastwood (Laura), Robert Mailhouse (Alan), Rachel Hunter (Marilyn), Kimberly Williams (Alison), Lauren Hutton (Elaine), Tito Larriva (Chuey), Jonathan Silverman (Danny), Jessica Lundy (Terianne), Michael Ontkean (Jeff), William Ragsdale (Brent).

Exactly what constitutes "just a little harmless sex" and how it affects men, women, and relationships are the subjects of this intermittently entertaining, briskly paced romantic comedy.

While love, sex and discord among twentysomethings are hardly novel issues these days, pic crackles with fresh, witty dialog and an engaging cast.

Driving home one rainy night, Alan stops to pick up an attractive stranded motorist who promptly offers him oral sex. As fate would have it, she's a prostitute, and Alan has barely begun to enjoy his first extramarital dalliance when cops arrive and arrest him. Alan's wife, Laura, is awakened to a 3 a.m. call from the police.

Zipping ahead a few days after the incident, Alan and pals Danny and Brent discuss his predicament. How, they ask, could Alan have been so naive? Though Alan craves Laura's forgiveness, she's busy drinking away her woes with free-wheeling girlfriends Ally and Danny's ex, Terianne. Each of the women has her own sex-inflected agenda to fulfill. Determined to apologize, Alan drags Danny and Brent back to his home, but the girls have already left. In their place emerges Laura's estranged mother, Elaine, who wastes no time making sexual overtures to Brent and Danny but advises Alan to go find Laura.

What saves the film from being utterly predictable is its zesty dialog, rife with pop-psychology references to mags like *Cosmo*, and its swift pacing.

U.S. release: Nov. 6 U.S. B.O.: $87,973

La Bûche (Season's Beatings)

A Pathe release (in France) of a Les Films Alain Sarde/TF1 Prods. production, with participation of Canal Plus and Studio Images 6. (International sales: Le Studio Canal Plus, Paris.) Produced by Sarde. Executive producer, Christine Gozlan. Directed by Daniele Thompson. Screenplay, Daniele Thompson, Christopher Thompson. Camera (color, widescreen), Robert Fraisse, Jean Harnois; editor, Isabelle Castro; music, Michel Legrand; art director, Michele Abbe; costume designer, Elisabeth Tavernier; sound, (Dolby Digital), Jean-Pierre Duret, William Flageolet. Reviewed at UGC Cine Cite, Paris, Dec. 13, 1999. Running time: 107 mins.
Claude Rich (Stanislas), Francois Fabian (Yvette), Sabine Azema (Louba), Emmanuelle Beart (Sonia), Charlotte Gainsbourg (Milla), Jean-Pierre Darroussin (Gilbert), Christopher Thompson (Joseph), Isabelle Carre (Annabelle).

Vet scripter Daniele Thompson (*Cousine cousine, Queen Margot*) makes the leap to helming with an enjoyable, if lightweight, ensembler penned with her son. Heavy on personal foibles, sexual peccadilloes, holiday nostalgia, regrets and resentment, comedy follows the various members of a Parisian family over four eventful days before Christmas. Pic's greatest pleasures are in its thesping; the all-star cast puts across an elaborate, if often predictable, mosaic of human behavior.

Following the December funeral of her second husband, Yvette is comforted by her three grown daughters from her first marriage to Russian-Jewish violinist Stanislas. The eldest, Louba, who lives with her father, sings crowd-pleasing bohemian standards at a Russian cabaret; Sonia is a perfectionist bourgeois housewife; and the youngest, Milla, is a hard-charging businesswoman with a tomboy demeanor. After 12 years of trysts with married lover Gilbert, Louba unexpectedly finds herself pregnant for the first time at 42.

Mostly pic bounces from one piece of crisis-fueled shtick to another as characters reassess their lives and relationships, spurred on by the gap between the warmth and harmony the

holidays are supposed to represent and the chaotic reality of their situations. Still, despite the reigning atmosphere of antagonism and emotional subterfuge, script is basically humorous – starting with the ringing of the deceased's cell phone as his coffin is lowered into the grave.

Ladies Room

A Motion Intl. release (in Canada) of a Cine-Roman/Laurem Prods./Transfilm/Smallrain Ltd. production. Produced by Tony Roman, Rene Malo, Claude Leger, Jonathan Vanger. Directed by Gabriella Cristiani. Screenplay, Leila Basen, Andree Pelletier, Genevieve Lefebvre, Natalina Di Leandro, Amanda Roberts, based on an original idea by Roman. Camera (color), Pierre Mignot; editors, Dominique Fortin, Cristiani; music, Simon Carpentier, Jean-Patrick Capdevielle, Richard Tate, Roman; production designer, Perri Gorrara; art director, Pierre Allard; costume designer, Francesca Chamberland. Reviewed at World Film Festival, Montreal (Panorama Canada), Sept. 1, 1999. Running time: 90 mins.
John Malkovich (Roberto), Lorraine Bracco (Gemma), Greta Scacchi (Lucia), Veronica Ferres (Lauren), Molly Parker (Julia), Greg Thomey (Gianco). With: Nanette Workman, Alan Fawcett, Chris MacCabe, Katie Van Camp, Nathalie Lefebvre, Catherine Friesen, John Glasspoole.

Producer Tony Roman's story gambit is intriguing: peeping into the feminine psyche by setting the pic almost entirely in the inner sanctum of a women's washroom. But an impoverished script, wildly uneven acting and erratic direction ensure that *Ladies Room* achieves no insight into the way women think. The pic is about as exciting as standing in line for the ladies room.

There are two main stories in *Ladies Room*. The first involves three theater actresses who are forced to share a bathroom in place of their flooded dressing rooms. Seasoned actress Gemma is shocked by the cynicism of her younger colleague Julia, which leads to a major pre-show argument. Gemma doesn't realize that Julia happens to be having an affair with Gemma's producer-writer boyfriend and is trying to parlay the sex into bigger roles in his productions.

Second tale is set at the opera, where Lauren is meant to meet her Italian lover, Roberto. Roberto has told Lauren he's divorced, but the date turns nasty when Roberto's pregnant wife, Lucia, shows up at the theater. Roberto's two-timing comes to light when Lucia bumps into the weeping Lauren in ... the ladies room.

Pic has little of interest to say about the relations between men and women, and the static washroom setting doesn't help make it more dynamic. Most of the thesps fare quite badly – in large part because they have such weak material to work with.

Liberty Heights

Warner Bros. release of a Baltimore/Spring Creek Pictures production. Produced by Barry Levinson, Paula Weinstein. Executive producer, Patrick McCormick. Directed, written by Levinson. Camera (Technicolor), Chris Doyle; editor, Stu Linder; music, Andrea Morricone; music supervisors, Joel Sill, Allan Mason; production designer, Vincent Peranio; art director, Alan E. Muraoka; set decorator, William A. Cimino; costume designer, Gloria Gresham. Reviewed at Warner Bros. Studios, Burbank, Nov. 3, 1999. MPAA Rating: R. Running time: 127 mins.
Adrien Brody (Van Kurtzman), Ben Foster (Ben Kurtzman), Orlando Jones (Little Melvin), Bebe Neuwirth

---

... May 21 ...

It took 19 nominations, but thesp Susan Lucci finally snags a Daytime Emmy award for Outstanding Lead Actress in the Drama **All My Children**.

(Ada Kurtzman), Joe Mantegna (Nate Kurtzman), Rebekah Johnson (Sylvia), David Krumholtz (Yussel), Richard Kline (Charlie), Vincent Guastaferro (Pete), Justin Chambers (Trey), Carolyn Murphy (Dubbie), James Pickens Jr. (Sylvia's Father), Frania Rubinek (Rose), Anthony Anderson (Scribbles), Kiersten Warren (Annie), Evan Neuman (Sheldon), Kevin Sussman (Alan), Gerry Rosenthal (Murray), Charley Scalies (Louie).

Barry Levinson goes deep with *Liberty Heights*, and the result is a grand slam. Summoning up boyhood memories of the '50s for his fourth "Baltimore picture" and infusing them with mature and pointed observations about race, class and religion in the U.S., this director seems to be rediscovering his voice as a writer, and in the process has made his best film. Pic pinpoints a moment when previously partitioned segments of society began gingerly mixing and influencing one another.

Although it balances and weaves together several storylines and any number of characters, pic is rooted in the eponymous neighborhood, a middle-class enclave so ethnically uniform in 1954 that a teenage boy can observe, "The whole world was Jewish." The film's younger characters must discover that other racial worlds exist beyond the ones in which they grew up. In the Kurtzman family the grownups live by the motto "If they're not Jewish, they're 'the other kind.'" This attitude is not entirely heeded, however, by the two boys, Van and Ben. Ben crosses Wasp and Black territory by falling hard for blonde, blue-eyed goddess Dubbie and befriending the first black student Sylvia. While the boys' mother and grandma hold down the fort at home, their nattily attired, gambling father, Nate, is coping with changing times in dubious ways.

Levinson rotates every one of his main characters, revealing added shadings and complexities. The Wasps, at first seen from the Jews' point of view as privileged and unapproachable royalty, are soon shown to be fighting demons instilled by their status and high expectations. Also put into interesting and unusually bifurcated perspective are the Blacks.

U.S. release: Nov. 17   U.S. B.O.: $2.3 million

Limbo

A Sony Pictures Entertainment release of a Screen Gems presentation of a Green/Renzi production. Produced by Maggie Renzi. Directed, written, edited by John Sayles. **Mary Elizabeth Mastrantonio (Donna De Angelo), David Strathairn (Joe Gastineau), Vanessa Martinez (Noelle De Angelo), Kris Kristofferson (Smilin' Jack), Casey Siemaszko (Bobby Gastineau), Kathryn Grody (Frankie), Rita Taggart (Lou), Leo Burmester (Harmon King), Michael Laskin (Albright).**

After a promising opening in which numerous interesting aspects of life in modern Alaska are laid out, the potentially fascinating social dynamics are dropped in favor of a thinly realized survival tale that falls flat dramatically and cinematically. This rare attempt to say something about the country's largest but possibly least-known state comes as a particular disappointment.

Donna De Angelo is a talented 40ish lounge singer whose bad luck has landed her in Juneau. Donna's sullen teenage daughter Noelle has never known her father. Despite her mother's loving attitude toward her, she has learned not to put any stock in her mom's promises. Donna has at least managed to keep her career going, despite faulty relationships. She meets a local jack-of-all-trades, Joe Gastineau, who has

bounced around a good deal himself. The buildup to their romance is handled in emotionally plausible if leisurely fashion, with time-outs for Donna's singing (Mastrantonio's voicings are exceptionally fine) and assorted sideline vignettes.

Joe's half-brother Bobby, a slick-talking hustler whom Joe hasn't seen in six years, arrives on the scene. Joe, Donna and Noelle join Bobby on a "mysterious business" boat-trip that results in his murder. The threesome wind up stranded on a nearby island with no provisions. Pic's final 45 minutes take place here, and what must have been intended as a stern test of what three people are truly made of quickly turns dull, simplistic and, finally, evasive.

U.S. release: June 4.   U.S. B.O.: $2.1 million

The Limey

An Artisan Entertainment release. Produced by John Hardy, Scott Kramer. Directed by Steven Soderbergh. Screenplay, Lem Dobbs. Camera (CFI color), Ed Lachman; editor, Sarah Flack; music, Cliff Martinez; production designer, Gary Frutkoff; set decorator, Kathryn Peters; costume designer, Louise Frogley; sound (Dolby Digital/DTS/SDDS), Jim Webb; stunt coordinator, John Robotham; assistant director, Gregory Jacobs; casting, Debra Zane. Reviewed at Cannes Film Festival (noncompeting), May 15, 1999. Running time: 90 mins. **Terence Stamp (Wilson), Peter Fonda (Valentine), Lesley Ann Warren (Elaine), Luis Guzman (Ed), Barry Newman (Avery), Joe Dallessandro (Uncle John), Nicky Katt (Stacy), Amelia Heinle (Adhara), Melissa George (Jennifer).**

Soderbergh shows again his ability to take a routine crime meller and make it an accomplished piece of filmmaking that overcomes its routine elements. Pic pays homage to and is full of allusions to 1960s international cinema, a feeling accentuated by the casting of Fonda and Stamp. Helmer must have realized that the script lacks dramatic momentum, for he structures the whole film around these two central characters. Narrative actually resembles a Western, in which two aging criminals must face the rapidly changing conditions around them and must come to terms with their own identity – and mortality.

Leaving London for the first time, after nine years behind bars, Wilson arrives in L.A. to unravel the mystery surrounding the death of his daughter, Jenny. Wilson is an outsider, an ex-con who's totally out of touch with the new world, including the crime milieu, its lingo and subculture. The only clue Wilson has is that Jenny was involved in a love affair with Valentine, an affluent record producer who owns a spectacular house in the Hollywood Hills. A supporting turn by Joe Dallessandro accentuates pic's reflexive nature as a commentary on a bygone era of filmmaking. Whatever deficiencies critics may find in the overextended monologs and terse, often oblique dialog, one has no problem praising the bravura acting of the entire cast.

U.S. release: Oct. 8   U.S. B.O.: $3 million

Looking For an Echo

A Steve Tisch/Paul Kurta production. Produced by Kurta, Martin Davidson. Executive producer, Tisch. Co-producers, Mary Jo Slater, Anthony Esposito. Directed by Martin Davidson. Screenplay, Jeffrey Goldenberg, Robert Held, Davidson. Camera (color), Charles Minsky; editor, Jerrold Lludwig; music producer and supervisor, Kenny Vance; production designer, Andrew Bernard; art director, Stacey

... May 22 ...

Star Wars: Episode 1 – The Phantom Menace vaporized the competition with a seven-day gross of $99.1 million, producing total takings of $140 million in the U.S.

Tanner; set designer, Catherine Moore; costume designer, Sandy Davidson; sound (Dolby Digital), Dan Ferat; associate producers, Tim Christenson, Joel Tuber; assistant director, Joel Tuber; casting, Mary Jo Slater, Lou DiGiamo. Reviewed at Mill Valley Film Festival, Oct. 12, 1999. Running time: 97 mins. **Armand Assante (Vince), Diane Venora (Joanne), Joe Grifasi (Vic), Tom Mason (Augie), Tony Denison (Nappy), Johnny Williams (Pooch), Edoardo Ballerini (Anthony), Christy Romano (Tina), David Vadim (Tommie), Monica Trombetta (Francine), David Margulies (Dr. Ludwig).**

As an Italian-American widower hitting 50 amid numerous unresolved issues, Armand Assante fairly oozes charm – enough to oil the sometimes contrived, if warmhearted, mechanics of *Looking for An Echo*. Protag Vince was once a teen idol – as lead dreamboat in Vinnie and the Dreamers, a Top 10 doo-wop sensation. But he's long since given up the fickle spotlight to raise three children, supporting them as bartender at an upscale watering hole in his native Brooklyn.

His eldest son is now a cop with a family of his own. Still living at home, middle child Anthony is just starting out with his own rising rock band, and the occasionally testy relationship between father and son suggests that Dad misses music-making more than he'll admit. But latter's primary concern is Tina, his youngest child; she's currently hospitalized, battling leukemia. Vinnie's been out of circulation since his wife died from cancer many years back, but his frequent sickroom visits raise the possibility of dating brassy, more-than-willing nurse Joanne, who's raising a teenage daughter alone.

Scenario is most ingratiating and deft when it deals with Vinnie's private sense of disappointment over his long-defunct singing career – a sentiment shared by his former Dreamers, who reunite for a surprise birthday party, and later jaunt off en masse for a giddy, then bittersweet spree in Atlantic City.

The Loss of Sexual Innocence

A Sony Pictures Classics release of a Summit Entertainment presentation, in association with Newmarket capital group, of a Red Mullet production. Produced by Mike Figgis and Annie Stewart. Executive producer, Patrick Wachsberger. Co-producer, Barney Reisaz. Directed, written by Figgis. Camera (color, wide screen), Benoit Delhomme; editor, Matthew Wood; music, Figgis; production design, Giorgio Desideri; costume design, Florence Nicaise; sound (Dolby Digital), Pawel Wdowczak; assistant director, James Bradley; casting, Jina Jay. Reviewed at Sundance Festival (Premiere), Jan. 23, 1998. Running time: 106 mins.
Julian Sands (Nic as adult), Saffron Burrows (Twins), Stefano Dionisi (Lucca), Jonathan Rhys-Meyers (Nic, aged 16), Kelly Macdonald (Susan), Femi Ogumbanjo (Adam), Hanne Klintoe (Eve), Johanna Torrel (Nic's wife),George Moktar (Nic, aged 12), John Cowey (Nic, aged 5).

Truly experimental in concept and form, this is Mike Figgis' most personal and ambitious film, but also his most problematic one. A self-reflective meditation on the fall from grace, the mysterious nature of love and sexuality, and the link between sex and violence, it is an art picture par excellence, one that derives its inspiration from Milton's *Paradise Lost*.

Unfortunately, pic lacks the lyrical quality, emotional pull and superb acting of *Leaving Las Vegas*. Boasting sublime imagery, but no characters to ground his reverie, new pic heavily relies on an opaque narrative and elliptical editing.

Pic centres on the tumultuous life of Nic, a British director about to embark on a new film project in Tunisia, from the early 1950s, growing up in the Crown Colony of Kenya, to the present. Nic's maturation into manhood are presented through four phases of his life. Episodes in Nic's past are shown randomly, though none assumes greater importance than the others. The most emotionally touching chapter is the sexual exploration of teenager Nic with Susan. Almost every sexual act is interrupted by the outside world, be it Susan's father or the police. The narrative is fractured by recreations of the classic parable of Adam and Eve, which is meant as an allegory illuminating turning points in Nic's life. Through imagery and lyrical music, selective glimpses are offered as to what makes Nic the complex, complicated, and unhappy man that he is.
U.S. release: May 28   U.S. B.O.: $311,374

Magnolia

A New Line release of a Joanne Sellar/Ghoulardi Film production. Produced by Sellar. Executive producers, Michael De Luca, Lynn Harris. Co-producer, Daniel Lupi. Directed, written by Paul Thomas Anderson. Camera (Deluxe color, Panavision widescreen), Robert Elswit; editor, Dylan Tichenor; music, John Brion; songs, Aimee Mann; production designers, William Arnold, Mark Bridges; art director, David Nakabayashi; set decorator, Chris Spellman; costume designer, Mark Bridges; sound (Dolby Digital/SDDS), John Pritchett; special-effects supervisor, Lou Carlucci; visual effects supervisor, Joe Letteri; visual-effects producer, Joseph Grossberg; associate producer, Tichenor; assistant director, Adam Druxman; casting, Cassandra Kulukundis. Reviewed at Todd-AO screening room, Santa Monica, Nov. 30, 1999. MPAA Rating: R. Running time: 188 mins.
Jason Robards (Earl Partridge), Julianne Moore (Linda Partridge), Tom Cruise (Frank Mackey), Philip Seymour Hoffman (Phil Parma), John C. Reilly (Officer Jim Kurring), Melora Walters (Claudia Gator), Jeremy Blackman (Stanley Spector), Michael Bowen (Rick Spector),William H. Macy (Donnie Smith), Philip Baker Hall (Jimmy Gator), Melinda Dillon (Rose Gator), Emmanuel Johnson (Dixon).

Paul Thomas Anderson's eagerly awaited followup to *Boogie Nights* confirms his status as one of the most audacious filmmakers in Hollywood today. This imposing tapestry about the mysterious workings of fate and coincidence and the need for interconnection and love interweaves the stories of a dozen characters as they embark on a moral odyssey during one intense day in their tumultuous lives.

A brief prolog, which sets the film's disturbing tone, presents three acts of violence, jumping among a 1911 prison yard, a 1958 tenement and the early 1980s. At the center of the film, set in the San Fernando Valley area of L.A., is dying patriarch Earl Partridge. He's forced to come to terms with his failures – leaving his sick wife and only son, Frank Mackey. Earl's much younger wife Linda can't deal with his impending death. Refusing to see Earl, Frank is a seductive guru who runs popular seminars that teach angry, frustrated men how to get their way with women.

The most emotionally engaging story centers on the travails of a compassionate, religious cop, Jim Kurring and the courtship he has with Claudia, a highly strung woman who's addicted to drugs and loud music. The weakest section is a TV quiz game, hosted by veteran Jimmy Gator, who is Claudia's father. This yarn brings to the surface the conflict between Rick and Stanley Spector, a father living off the brilliance of his genius son. A superlative ensemble including Tom Cruise (in his best dramatic turn to date) gives this meditation on urban alienation the aura of a major work highly in tune with the zeitgeist.

U.S. release: Dec. 17 U.S. B.O.: $764,945

Man on the Moon

A Universal release of a Universal Pictures and Mutual Film Co. presentation of a Jersey Films/Cinehaus production. Produced by Danny DeVito, Michael Shamberg, Stacey Sher. Executive producers, George Shapiro, Howard West, Michael Hausman. Co-executive producer, Bob Zmuda. Directed by Milos Forman. Screenplay, Scott Alexander, Larry Karaszewski. Camera (Deluxe color, Panavision widescreen), Anastas Michos; editors, Christopher Tellefsen, Lynzee Klingman; music, R.E.M.; music supervisor, Anita Camarata; production designer, Patrizia von Brandenstein; art directors, James Truesdale, Ray Kluga (N.Y.); set decorators, Maria Nay, Karin Wiesel (N.Y.); costume designer, Jeffrey Kurland; sound (DTS/SDDS/Dolby Digital), Chris Newman; supervising sound editor, Ron Bochar; associate producers, Scott Ferguson, Pamela Abdy; assistant director, David McGiffert; casting, Francine Maisler, Kathleen Driscoll-Mohler. Reviewed at USA Films screening room, Beverly Hills, Nov. 5, 1999. MPAA Rating: R. Running time: 118 mins.

Jim Carrey (Andy Kaufman), Danny DeVito (George Shapiro), Courtney Love (Lynne Margulies), Paul Giamatti (Bob Zmuda), Vincent Schiavelli (Maynard Smith), Peter Bonerz (Ed Weinberger), Jerry Lawler (As Himself), Gerry Becker (Stanley Kaufman), Leslie Lyles (Janice Kaufman).

Quick biographical droppings suggest that Andy Kaufman was an early blooming weirdo whose initial forays in performing were met with the same quizzical reactions that greeted him throughout his brief career. Hollywood agent George Shapiro takes him on and gets him on TV sitcom *Taxi*. Kaufman is seen as a highly disruptive prima donna, especially in his insistence upon special guest appearances by his gross and vulgar Las Vegas character, Tony Clifton, which he concocted with Bob Zmuda. Although Zmuda was the comic's closest collaborator, the man comes out of nowhere and it's never shown how they got on the same productive wavelength.

Kaufman seems bereft of true personal connections, and certainly of a romantic life, until he meets Lynne Margulies. Script's key exchange has Kaufman complaining to his girlfriend, "You don't know the real me." "There isn't a real you," she says, revealing the film's central insight: There was no "there" there – Kaufman never broke character. Pic ends with the comedian dying of cancer in 1984 at the age of 35.

Once again stretching his acting muscles to inhabit a singular sort of innocent, Carrey gives every indication of having plunged himself deeply into Kaufman's persona. On the one hand, it's a virtuoso turn that unerringly captures his behavioral quirkiness and disquieting vacantness; on the other, there is only so far the performance can go, since true psychological penetration is essentially impossible in Kaufman's case.

U.S. release: Dec. 22 U.S. B.O.: $24.6 million

Mansfield Park

A Miramax release of a Miramax Films/BBC Films presentation, in association with the Arts Council of England, of a Miramax HAL Films production. Produced by Sarah Curtis. Executive producers, Trea Hoving, David Aukin, Colin Leventhal, David M. Thompson, Bob Weinstein, Harvey Weinstein. Directed, written by Patricia Rozema, based on the novel by Jane Austen, her letters and early journals. Camera (Deluxe color), Michael Coulter; editor, Martin Walsh; music, Lesley Barber; production designer, Christopher Hobbs; art director, Andrew Munro; costume designer, Andrea Galer; sound (Dolby Digital), Peter Glossop; makeup designer, Veronica Brebner; associate producer, Allon Reich; assistant director, Mary Soan; second unit camera, Chris Plevin; casting, Gail Stevens. Reviewed at Montreal Film Festival (competing), Aug. 27, 1999. (Also in Toronto Film Festival – Special Presentations.) Running time: 110 mins.

Embeth Davidtz (Mary Crawford), Jonny Lee Miller (Edmund Bertram), Alessandro Nivola (Henry Crawford), Frances O'Connor (Fanny Price), Harold Pinter (Sir Thomas Bertram), Lindsay Duncan (Lady Bertram/Mrs. Price), Sheila Gish (Mrs. Norris), James Purefoy (Tom Bertram), Hugh Bonneville (Mr. Rushworth), Justine Waddell (Julia Bertram), Victoria Hamilton (Maria Bertram), Sophia Myles (Susan), Hilton McRae (Mr. Price), Hannah Taylor Gordon (Young Fanny), Charles Edwards (Yates).

If ever a picture deserved a possessory credit, it's this one, which should have been called *Patricia Rozema's Mansfield Park*. Ten-year-old Fanny is sent by her impoverished parents to live with her mother's sisters, the laudanum-addicted Lady Bertram and snooty Mrs. Norris, at the country mansion Mansfield Park. Lady Bertram's husband, Sir Thomas, is a rich West Indies plantation owner. Fanny is treated as little more than a declasse servant, her only friend being Sir Thomas' son, the kindly, weak Edmund. Pic dissolves to a grownup Fanny, who's now a passionate and prolific amateur writer. Fanny takes a strong liking to Edmund, but is tangled within a love triangle, that of sly brother and sister Henry and Mary Crawford. Mary is after Edmund, as he's the heir to the family fortune, and Sir Thomas agrees to a match between Fanny and Henry.

Janeites are likely to raise more than eyebrows at this often radical reworking of her third novel; pic reinterprets the central character, Fanny Price, as a cross between Austen herself and a tomboyish proto-feminist, throws in some magical realism and gratuitous lesbian frissons to spice up the pot, and too often steps out of its era to adopt a knowing, politically correct, late 20th-century attitude to the society portrayed.

U.S. release: Nov. 18 U.S. B.O.: $2.5 million

A Map of the World

An Overseas Filmgroup presentation of a Kennedy/Marshall Co. production. Produced by Kathleen Kennedy, Frank Marshall. Executive producer, Willi Bar. Co-producer, Lisa Niedenthal. Directed by Scott Elliott. Screenplay, Peter Hedges, Polly Platt, based on the novel by Jane Hamilton. Camera (Deluxe color), Seamus McGarvey; editors, Craig McKay, Naomi Geraghty; music, Pat Metheny; production designer, Richard Toyon; art director, Kei; set decorator, Megan Less; costume designer, Suzette Daigle; sound (Dolby Digital), Claude La Haye; associate producer, Rainer Bienger (Cinerenta); assistant director, Laurie Mirsky; casting, Avy Kaufman. Reviewed at Toronto Film Festival (Special Presentation), Sept. 14, 1999. Running time: 125 mins.

Sigourney Weaver (Alice Goodwin), Julianne Moore (Theresa Collins), David Strathairn (Howard Goodwin), Ron Lea (Dan Collins), Arliss Howard (Paul Reverdy), Chloe Sevigny (Carole Mackessy), Louise Fletcher (Nellie), Dara Perlmutter (Emma), Kayla Perlmutter (Claire), Marc Donato (Robbie).

Sigourney Weaver plays the boldest, most complex role of her career in Scott Elliott's provocative and unsettling but seriously flawed feature debut. Pic displays many virtues: richly nuanced family drama, darkly sarcastic humor, intriguing characters and, above all, bravura acting by Julianne Moore.

In voiceover narration, Alice Goodwin sets the saga's serio-comic tone, establishing her outsider status as well as the trajectory of her future moral and psychological odyssey. Alice juggles her roles as a part-time school nurse, wife to hard-working farmer Howard, and mother of two vivacious daughters. One morning, while watching her friend Theresa's children, Alice gets distracted. A few minutes later, she finds Theresa's two-year-old daughter, Lizzie, floating in the pond next to the house, unconscious. After a few days in a coma, Lizzie dies, a tragedy that tears the two mothers apart and drives them both to severe depression. Amid the turmoil of her guilt and grief, another shocking event occurs: a neighbor's son accuses Alice of sexual abuse. She's put in prison because her husband can't raise the bail.

What begins as a perceptive study of a woman on the verge of a nervous breakdown gradually turns into a disappointingly conventional prison drama, followed by a schematic and obvious court trial. The jail sequences are too long and further hampered by the stereotypical portraits of female prisoners and the uneven acting of the women who portray them.

U.S. release: Dec. 3   U.S. B.O.: $20,872

The Matrix

A Warner Bros. release presented in association with Village Roadshow Pictures-Groucho II Film Partnership of a Silver Pictures production. Produced by Joel Silver. Executive producers, Barrie Osborne, Andrew Mason, Andy Wachowski, Larry Wachowski, Erwin Stoff, Bruce Berman. Co-producer, Dan Cracchiolo. Directed, written by the Wachowski Brothers. Camera, Bill Pope; editor, Zach Staenberg; music, Don Davis; production designer, Owen Paterson; art directors, Hugh Bateup, Michelle McGahey. Reviewed at Warner Bros. Studios, Burbank, CA; March 18, 1999. MPAA Rating: R. Running time: 136 mins.

Keanu Reeves (Neo), Laurence Fishburne (Morpheus), Carrie-Anne Moss (Trinity), Hugo Weaving (Agent Smith), Gloria Foster (Oracle), Joe Pantoliano (Cypher), Marcus Chong (Tank), Paul Goddard (Agent Brown), Robert Taylor (Agent Jones), Julian Arahanga (Apo), Matt Doran (Mouse), Belinda McClory (Switch), Anthony Ray Parker (Dozer).

It's Special Effects 10, Screenplay 0 for *The Matrix*, an eye-popping but incoherent extravaganza of ultra-cool visuals that truly deliver something new to the sci-fi action lexicon. One gives up making any sense of the plot and settles for what the picture undeniably wields in spades, which is a smorgasbord of effects that in some cases goes beyond what the sci-fi audience has ever seen before. Filmmakers have employed a technique they call "bullet-time photography," ultra-fast lensing that, when combined with computer enhancement, allows for altering the speed and trajectories of people and objects, resulting in the live-action equivalent of a Japanese animated film.

The complicated script fleshes out a backstory where there was an all-out war between humans and advanced machines, resulting in the triumph of artificial intelligence in the early 21st century. The underground city of Zion is now the last bastion of humankind, which awaits a "saviour" to disrupt the Matrix, a power field controlled by humanoid computers that have created a "virtual" real world fed by laboratory-controlled human energy. This new world order is enforced by men in black sunglasses led by Agent Smith. A slacker-software expert played by Reeves is tracked down by an underground movement from this future universe in 1999. The troupe is led by the mysterious Morpheus, a wanted techno-terrorist. Morpheus tells the recruit that he is "The One." Reeves joins Morpheus' clan is reconstituted biologically and emerges with the identity of Neo. Upon morphing, Neo is ready to do battle with the forces that have made the world what it has become.

U.S. release: Mar. 31   U.S. B.O.: $171.5 million

The Messenger: The Story of Joan of Arc

A Sony Pictures Entertainment release (in U.S.) of a Columbia Pictures presentation of a Gaumont production. Produced by Patrice Ledoux. Executive producer, Leeloo Prods. Co-producer, Bernard Grenet. Directed by Luc Besson. Screenplay, Andrew Birkin, Besson. Camera, Thierry Arbogast; editor, Sylvie Landra; music, Eric Serra; production designer, Hugues Tissandier; art director (Czech Republic), Alain Paroutaud. Reviewed at the Samuel Goldwyn Theater, Beverly Hills, CA. Oct. 15, 1999. MPAA Rating: R. Running time 148 mins.

Milla Jovovich (Joan of Arc), John Malkovich (Charles VII), Faye Dunaway (Yolande D'Aragon), Dustin Hoffman (The Conscience), Pascal Greggory (The Duke of Alencon), Vincent Cassel (Gilles de Rais), Tcheky Karyo (Dunois), Richard Ridings (La Hire), Desmond Harrington (Aulon).

Besson steers a reasonable middle course in his interpretation of one of history's most singular and mystifying figures. Milla Jovovich adds nothing to the journey other than her tall and skinny physicality, which is not exactly how one has been led to picture France's most famous peasant girl. The lack of a plausible leading lady is enough to sink what is otherwise an eye-catching, although heavily '90s-style, telling of one of history's most frequently filmed stories. Performances overall are serviceable if a bit ragged, with Americans mixing with variously accented Euros on the French side, while the English are portrayed as a crude lot indeed with an overly colloquial penchant for the f-word. The battle scenes, while perhaps a tad skimpy in the numbers of soldiers on view, are nonetheless a feast for the eyes and the main reason to see the film on the big screen.

Pic is the story of an illiterate girl who undertakes a mission from God to help drive the English out of France in the early 15th century, and is later captured and put on trial for heresy and sorcery; the verdict for which is a foregone conclusion unless she recants and abandons her cause. Given the confusing royal history of the time and the certain ignorance of the Hundred Years' War on the part of the contempo public worldwide, scenarists do a perfectly creditable job of streamlining and clarifying the conflict, which proves especially helpful later on when Joan is put on trial. Dustin Hoffman, as the interrogator at Joan's trial, is cast in the weirdest, most disembodied "character" he has ever played,

---

looking like an old rabbi ministering to the tortured Catholic Maid of Lorraine.

U.S. release: Nov. 12   U.S. B.O.: $14.1 million

A Midsummer Night's Dream

A Fox Searchlight release of a Fox Searchlight Pictures and Regency Enterprises production. Produced by Leslie Urdang, Michael Hoffman. Executive producer, Arnon Milchan. Co-producer, Ann Wingate. Directed, written by Michael Hoffman, based on the play by William Shakespeare.
Kevin Kline (Nick Bottom), Michelle Pfeiffer (Titania), Rupert Everett (Oberon), Stanley Tucci (Puck), Calista Flockhart (Helena), Anna Friel (Hermia), Christian Bale (Demetrius), Dominic West (Lysander), David Strathairn (Theseus), Sophie Marceau (Hippolyta), Roger Rees (Peter Quince), Bernard Hill (Egeus), Bill Irwin (Tom Snout), Sam Rockwell (Francis Flute).
Whimsical, intermittently enjoyable, but decidedly unmagical version of Shakespeare's wild romantic comedy. Set in Tuscany at the turn of the century, this modernist comedy brims with ideas and promises but suffers from a lack of coherent vision and diverse acting styles.

Preparations for the wedding of Duke Theseus and Hippolyta are under way, when the Duke is forced to listen to the complaints of opposing sides in a dispute over an arranged marriage. Egeus has promised his daughter Hermia to Demetrius, but she loves Lysander. Hermia plans to elope with her lover to the woods, but her best friend, Helena, who is in love with Demetrius, knows of the plot. Also bound for the same forest are the village's amateur players, searching for a place to rehearse in. Both sets of lovers and the thesps are unaware that the dark forest is home of the fairies, where the trickster Puck administers a powerful love potion that causes the participants to change and mix their partners in an incorrigible, outrageous manner. Indeed, before long, Puck becomes a pawn in the love games of the fairies' king and queen, Oberon and Titania.

Kline overacts physically and emotionally, Flockhart is entertaining in a broad manner and Pfeiffer renders a strenuously theatrical performance. Overall, the Brits give more coherent and resonant performances.

U.S. release: May 14   U.S. B.O.: $16 million

Miss Julie

An MGM/UA release of a Moonstone Entertainment presentation of a Red Mullet production. Produced by Mike Figgis, Harriet Cruickshank. Executive producers, Annie Stewart, Willie Baer, Etchie Stroh. Directed by Mike Figgis. Screenplay, Figgis, Helen Cooper, based on the play by August Strindberg. Camera (color), Benoit Delhomme; editor, Matthew Wood; music, Figgis; production designer, Michael Howells; costume designer, Sandy Powell. Reviewed at Toronto Film Festival (Contemporary World Cinema), Sept. 13, 1999. Running time: 103 mins.
Saffron Burrows (Miss Julie), Peter Mullan (Jean), Maria Doyle Kennedy (Christine).
A solid, intermittently powerful screen adaptation of August Strindberg's play. Figgis' rendition differs radically from the 1951 film version, one of the first international arthouse hits, helmed by the distinguished Swedish stage and film director Alf Sjöberg (aka Ingmar Bergman's mentor - and Garbo's classmate).

On a large Swedish estate in 1894, the nobility lives in feudal splendor, in sharp contrast to the poverty of the peasants and servants. On a hot Midsummer's Eve, the farmhands and domestics gather outdoors for the traditional festivities. The cook, Christine, awaits the arrival of her footman fiancé, Jean. The informal mood is interrupted as soon as Miss Julie orders Jean to wear her father's formal jacket and dance with her. Over the course of a tumultuous and fateful night, Miss Julie and Jean engage in a dynamic, perverse game of role-playing that forces them to drop – and then assume again – the sharp class distinctions between mistress and servant.

Strindberg's bitter play is a psychological dissection of a beautiful but terribly complicated and repressed woman who's still influenced by the ideas of her domineering mother. What's missing from Figgis' version is a more detailed account of Julie's childhood. Figgis concentrates on the here and now of the Julie-Jean relationship – how it changes radically in the course of the night and culminates in sexual seduction. Jean emerges as greedy and hell-bent on improving his lot, consciously using every means he has, including his sex. He exploits Julie's weakness and vulnerability, humiliating her toward self-destruction.

U.S. release: Dec. 10   U.S. B.O.: $13,107

Mumford

A Buena Vista release of a Touchstone Pictures presentation of a Kasdan Pictures production. Produced by Charles Okun, Lawrence Kasdan. Co-producers, Steve Dunn, Linda Goldstein Knowlton, Jon Hutman. Directed, written by Kasdan. Camera (Deluxe color, Technicolor prints; widescreen), Ericson Core; editors, Carol Littleton, William Steinkamp; music, James Newton Howard; production designer, Jon Hutman; art director, Wray Steven Graham; set designer, Dawn Swiderski; set decorator, Beth Rubino; costume designer, Colleen Atwood; sound (Dolby Digital/SDDS/DTS), John Pritchett; supervising sound editor, Robert Grieve; assistant director, Steven Dunn; casting, Jennifer Shull. Reviewed at Toronto Film Festival (Gala), Sept. 11, 1999. MPAA Rating: R. Running time: 112 mins.
Loren Dean (Mumford), Hope Davis (Sofie Crisp), Jason Lee (Skip Skipperton), Alfre Woodard (Lily), Mary McDonnell (Althea Brockett), Pruitt Taylor Vince (Henry Follett), Zooey Deschanel (Nessa Watkins), Martin Short (Lionel Dillard), David Paymer (Dr. Ernest Delbanco), Jane Adams (Dr. Phyllis Sheeler), Dana Ivey (Mrs. Crisp), Kevin Tighe (Mr. Crisp), Ted Danson (Jeremy Brockett), Jason Ritter (Martin Brockett), Elisabeth Moss (Katie Brockett), Robert Stack (As Himself).
Far too polite and genteel, this comedy about a fraudulent psychologist with unorthodox but beneficial couchside manner sees writer-director Lawrence Kasdan operating on only a fraction of his cylinders. Dr. Mumford, who just happens to share his name with the town, has been there for only a short time but has more patients than the longstanding local shrinks. The secret of Mumford's success seems to have something to do with his empathetic listening skills and matter-of-fact frankness, his willingness to calmly point out his patients' foibles and how they're fooling themselves. But in unusual cases, and the only ones in the picture that become remotely interesting, the doc extents himself in special ways. More appealing to Mumford is Sofie Crisp, an attractive young divorcee so overcome with what she believes is Chronic

---

... May 26 ...
Morgan Freeman is to star in a film based on the novel by Ralph Ellison,
Juneteenth, the followup to his classic 1952 novel **Invisible Man.**

Fatigue Syndrome that she can barely leave the house. Mumford's creative solution is to hold sessions while taking her on long walks just to get her moving again. They also begin falling in love.

Given the rather extraordinary absence of conflict and excitement in all of this, Kasdan throws in a little melodrama involving Mumford's lack of proper medical credentials. Leading the effort to expose the fraud is mean-spirited attorney Lionel Dillard, apparently the only patient ever dissatisfied with Mumford's techniques.

There is really very little more than this going on in the film, if anything, Kasdan's direction here is even less energized than his writing.

U.S. release: Sept. 24   U.S. B.O.: $4.6 million

The Mummy

A Universal release of an Alphaville production. Produced by James Jacks, Sean Daniel. Executive producer, Kevin Jarre. Co-producer, Patricia Carr. Directed, written by Stephen Sommers, screen story by Sommers, Lloyd Fonvielle, Jarre. Camera (Deluxe color, Panavision widescreen), Adrian Biddle; editor, Bob Ducsay; music, Jerry Goldsmith; production designer, Allan Cameron; art directors, Tony Reading, Giles Masters, Clifford Robinson, Peter Russell; set decorator, Peter Howitt; costume designer, John Bloomfield; sound (DTS/SDDS/Dolby Digital), Chris Munro; visual-effects supervisor, John Andrew Berton Jr.; special-effects supervisor, Chris Corbould; live action creature-effects supervisor, Nick Dudman; Mummy designed by the ILM Character Design Group; additional visual effects, Cinesite; stunt coordinator, Simon Crane; associate producer, Megan Moran; assistant director, Cliff Lanning; second unit director, Greg Michael; second unit camera, Harvey Harrison; casting, John and Ros Hubbard. Reviewed at Cineplex Odeon Universal City, April 29, 1999. MPAA Rating: PG-13. Running time: 124 mins.
Brendan Fraser (Rick O'Connell), Rachel Weisz (Evelyn), John Hannah (Jonathan), Arnold Vosloo (Imhotep), Kevin J. O'Connor (Beni), Jonathan Hyde (The Egyptologist), Oded Fehr (Ardeth Bay), Erick Avari (The Curator), Stephen Dunham (Henderson), Corey Johnson (Daniels), Tuc Watkins (Burns), Omid Djalili (Warden), Aharon Ipale (Pharaoh), Bernard Fox (Winston), Patricia Velasquez (Anck-Su-Namun), Carl Chase (Hook), Mohammed Afifi (Hangman).

Stephen Sommers' $80 million extravaganza bears almost no relation to Karl Freund's 1932 Boris Karloff starrer or to Terence Fisher's 1959 film. In 1290 B.C. Thebes, Pharaoh's mistress and her lover, trusted priest Imhotep, assassinate the Pharaoh, whereupon she kills herself and he suffers live mummification. Imhotep is buried deep in Hamunaptra near a vast repository of treasures; should he ever be liberated, his malevolent power will unleash 10 plagues upon Egypt.

Story jumps to the mid-1920s. Yank soldier-explorer Rick O'Connell has already been to Hamunaptra in battle, but he's about to be hanged in Cairo when he's rescued by Evelyn, a bumbling museum librarian who pals around with brother Jonathan. They all set out to the burial site, whose location only Rick knows. But they have competition from some American fortune hunters, and fierce, black-garbed natives who have been watching the Mummy's site. Once all the Yanks and Brits turn up, it's a safe bet that the Mummy won't remain

cooped up for much longer. And this being the age of computer-generated imagery, one can be assured that the Mummy will assume numerous forms. Plot developments stem strictly from convenience, not from conviction or logic, and pic fails to deliver any genuine sense of spirit or fun. Scary moments are of the cheating kind, with mummies and such suddenly popping up from out of frame. Pic is loaded with action and incident, but generates zero suspense or surprise.

U.S. release: May 7   U.S. B.O.: $155.4 million

The Muse

A USA Films release of an October Films presentation. Produced by Herb Nanas. Executive producer, Barry Berg. Directed by Albert Brooks. Screenplay, Brooks, Monica Johnson.
Mark Feuerstein (Josh Martin), Steven Wright (Stan Spielberg), Bradley Whitford (Hal), Mario Opinato (European Man), Dakin Matthews (Dr. Jacobson), Concetta Tomei (Nurse Rennert), Albert Brooks (Steven Phillips), Sharon Stone (Sarah), Andie MacDowell (Laura Phillips), Jeff Bridges (Jack Warrick). As themselves: Cybill Shepherd, Lorenzo Lamas, Jennifer Tilly, Rob Reiner, Wolfgang Puck, James Cameron, Martin Scorsese.

The Muse is a beguiling but erratic rumination on the creative process, Hollywood style. Pic is fresh and idiosyncratic in the writing but often flat directorially. Brooks confronts writer's block, and wittily connects it not only to worries associated with the film industry, but also to the Ancient Greek source of inspiration.

Steven Phillips finds he's in desperate need of an artistic boost upon being kicked off the Paramount lot. Soon after Steven spots his close friend, the hugely successful writer Jack Warrick, consorting with a beautiful blonde, Sarah, and learns that she is one of the nine daughters of Zeus and is in cahoots with many of the top names in showbiz. Delighted to be accepted into the fold, he's soon taken aback by her requirements of expensive gifts. Sarah treats Steven like an errand boy and threatens to break him financially, while also dispensing just enough creative tidbits to get him working on a new screenplay. Steven's well-groomed wife, Laura, is suspicious of the muse, until Sarah advises Laura in launching a successful gourmet cookie business. The spotlight eventually falls upon Sarah herself. Who is this woman who receives urgent visits from Hollywood's elite? Where does she come from? Could she actually be a real muse?

Brooks' moping and constant complaining eventually become a drag, but he still has the lion's share of good lines. Stone shows a long-concealed gift for well-timed comedy.

U.S. release: Aug. 27   U.S. B.O.: $11.6 million

Music of the Heart

A Miramax release of a Miramax Films presentation of a Craven/Maddalena Films production. Produced by Marianne Maddalena, Susan Kaplan, Alan Miller, Walter Scheuer. Executive producers, Bob Weinstein, Harvey Weinstein, Sandy Gallin. Co-producer, Stuart Besser. Directed by Wes Craven. Screenplay, Pamela Gray, based on the documentary film *Small Wonders* by Allen and Lana Miller. Camera (Foto-Kem color, Deluxe prints), Peter Deming; editor, Patrick Lussier; music, Mason Daring; production designer, Bruce Miller; art director, Beth Kuhn; costume designer, Susan Lyall; sound (Dolby Digital), Michael Barosky, Todd Toon. Reviewed at Venice Film

---

Festival (Dreams and Visions), Sept. 6, 1999. (Also in Toronto Film Festival - Gala.) Running time: 124 mins.
Meryl Streep (Roberta Guaspari), Aidan Quinn (Brian Sinclair), Angela Bassett (Janet Williams), Cloris Leachman (Assunta Guaspari), Gloria Estefan (Isabel Vasquez), Josh Pais (Dennis), Jay O. Sanders (Dan), Charlie Hofheimer (Nick, aged 17), Kieran Culkin (Lexi, aged 15), Michael Angarano (Nick, aged 7), Henry Dinhofer (Lexi, aged 5). As themselves: Isaac Stern, Itzhak Perlman, Arnold Steinhardt, Mark O'Connor, Michael Tree, Charles Veal Jr., Karen Briggs, Sandra Park, Diane Monroe, Jonathan Feldman.
In 1988 music-loving Roberta Guaspari was abruptly dumped by her husband. She re-enters the workforce soon landing an interview with the principal of an East Harlem school. Roberta proposes she teach violin within the school's music department. Warned by the cynical music teacher that most of the kids don't have the attention span for the art, Roberta nevertheless perseveres and the film culminates with a successful school concert. Ten years pass, and Roberta's violin classes are now a successful feature in three inner-city schools. But budget cuts force the programs' cancellation and all seems lost, until her success story makes the newspapers and a charity concert, known as Fiddlefest, is proposed at Carnegie Hall. It is a great success, with the best of Roberta's '98 class playing alongside some of her original pupils, plus such luminaries as Stern and Perlman, to name a few.

A gloriously sentimental true-life drama, it recalls famous, and successful, films in which a dedicated teacher was able to break through to classrooms of bored or antisocial children. New pic covers no fresh ground; the dramatic arc is wholly predictable and no opportunity for wrenching emotional scenes is avoided. This is a long way from Craven's horror films, but he obviously had his heart in the project and never misses a beat. Streep vividly conveys the colorful approach of the real Roberta Guaspari and even learnt to play the violin for the film.
U.S. release: Oct. 29   U.S. B.O.: $14.8 million

Mystery Men
A Universal release of a Gordon/Richardson/Levin/Dark Horse production. Produced by Lawrence Gordon, Mike Richardson, Lloyd Levin. Executive producer, Robert Engelman. Co-producer, Steven Gilder. Directed by Kinka Usher. Screenplay, Neil Cuthbert, based on the *Dark Horse* comicbook series created by Bob Burden. Camera (Deluxe color), Stephen H. Burum; editor, Conrad Buff; music, Stephen Warbeck; music supervisor, Karyn Rachtman; production designer, Kirk M. Petruccelli; art director, Barry Chusid; set decorator, Victor Zolfo; costume designer, Marilyn Vance; sound (Dolby Digital/DTS), Douglas B. Arnold; visual-effects supervisor, Lori J. Nelson; assistant director, Jeffrey Wetzel; casting, Mindy Marin. Reviewed at the Gotham Cinema, N.Y., July 27, 1999. MPAA Rating: PG-13. Running time: 120 mins.
Hank Azaria (Blue Raja), Janeane Garofalo (Bowler), William H. Macy (Shoveler), Kel Mitchell (Invisible Boy), Paul Reubens (Spleen), Ben Stiller (Mr. Furious), Wes Studi (Sphinx), Greg Kinnear (Captain Amazing), Lena Olin (Dr. Anabel Lee), Geoffrey Rush (Casanova Frankenstein), Tom Waits (Doc Heller), Eddie Izzard (Tony P), Claire Forlani (Monica), Ricky Jay (Vic Weems), Louise Lasser (Violet).
Sharply written, pic that's an amiable spoof of comic book

heroes. It's too bad, then, that its numerous virtues are undercut by a signal failure to follow the leave-'em-wanting-more rule so crucial to comedy. Paean to the world's super-underachievers kicks off in futuristic Champion City with a large-scale robbery that draws three earnest but unlikely saviors. The Blue Raja sports a turban and fights his enemies by flinging forks and spoons, the Shoveler wields a shovel, and Mr. Furious attempts to level opponents with his bad temper. Their bumbling heroics are overshadowed by the arrival of the city's pre-eminent superhero, Captain Amazing, whose success has put all the city's super-villains out of commission. Anxious to retain his renown, he secures the prison release of one his arch-nemesis, Casanova Frankenstein, who promptly plots citywide mayhem and imprisons Amazing.

Blue Raja, the Shoveler and Mr. Furious realize what a challenge faces them and decide to stage a citywide talent search, recruiting the sad-sack talents of Invisible Boy (who is always visible), Spleen (who battles with his flatulence), and the Bowler (who does battle with a bowling ball) to save Champion City from the nefarious Frankenstein.

Pic boasts several action sequences that are expertly handled and laden with dazzling effects. Dialog is hip and consistently funny, and provides the basis for appealing, flavorful performances by pic's expert ensemble. Debuting helmer Kinka Usher gives the production strong pacing and polish.
U.S. release: Aug. 6   U.S. B.O.: $29.8 million

The Nanny
An Istituto Luce release (in Italy) of a Marco and Pier Giorgio Bellocchio presentation of a Filmalbatros production, in association with Istituto Luce in collaboration with RAI Radiotelevisione Italiana. (International sales: RAI Trade, Rome.) Produced by Pier Giorgio Bellocchio. Directed by Marco Bellocchio. Screenplay, Bellocchio, Daniela Ceselli; inspired by the novella by Luigi Pirandello. Camera (Cinecitta color), Giuseppe Lanci; editor, Francesca Calvelli; music, Carlo Crivelli; art director, Marco Dentici; set decorator, Simona Migliotti; costume designer, Sergio Ballo; sound (Dolby Digital), Maurizio Argentieri; assistant director, Ceselli; casting, Fabiola Banzi. Reviewed at Quattro Fontane Cinema, Rome, May 6, 1999. (In Cannes Film Festival - competing.) Running time: 106 mins.
Fabrizio Bentivoglio (Professor Mori), Valeria Bruni Tedeschi (Vittoria), Maya Sansa (Annetta), Jacqueline Lustig (Maddalena), Pier Giorgio Bellocchio (Nardi), Michele Placido (Mori's Patient). With: Gisella Burinato, Elda Alvigini, Eleonora Danco, Fabio Camilli.
The Nanny is a sober, unerringly controlled psychological drama about motherhood and mental frailty set in the early 1900s. Set against a backdrop of subversive uprisings and police repression, the story centers on well-heeled Professor Mori and his young wife, Vittoria, and the instability that grips her and the couple's relationship following their son's birth. When the baby refuses its mother's breast, Mori hires illiterate country girl Annetta to feed and care for the child, requiring her to abandon her own newborn son. Deeply depressed after the birth, Vittoria is further jarred by the wet nurse's presence. While the girl is natural and instinctive with the baby, Vittoria is awkward and removed, incapable not only of providing physical care but also of showing maternal love and affection. She asks Mori to dismiss the girl. When he refuses, Vittoria withdraws without explanation to the country. Despite his

professional experience dealing with emotional disturbances, Mori is unable to intervene and help her. Vittoria's departure brings him into closer contact with the nanny.

The film, for better or worse, bears many of the customary traits of the director's work – the coldly cerebral approach, exasperatingly slow rhythms and penchant for psychoanalytical discourse. But these are largely countered by the warmth and immediacy of the central theme of maternity, the constant motif of breastfeeding, and by three compelling lead performances. Pic is one of the helmer's more satisfying films in recent years.

Never Been Kissed

A 20th Century Fox release of a Fox 2000 presentation of a Flower Films/Bushwood Pictures production. Produced by Sandy Isaac, Nancy Juvonen. Executive producer, Drew Barrymore. Co-producer, Jeffrey Downer. Directed by Raja Gosnell. Screenplay, Abby Kohn, Marc Silverstein.

Drew Barrymore (Josie Geller), David Arquette (Rob Geller), Michael Vartan (Sam Coulson), Molly Shannon (Anita), John C. Reilly (Gus), Garry Marshall (Rigfort), Sean Whalen (Merkin), Leelee Sobieski (Aldys), Jeremy Jordan (Guy Perkins), Jessica Alba (Kirsten), Marley Shelton (Kristin), Jordan Ladd (Gibby).

A likable romantic comedy with an engaging premise and strong cast. Barrymore plays a nerdy journalist on an undercover assignment to revisit high school and report on today's youth. Pic feels like a vintage John Hughes film, with traces of *Sixteen Candles* evident throughout. That's probably a calculated effect, since Gosnell worked closely with Hughes as an editor on the *Home Alone* films.

Josie Geller, a young Chicago newspaper copy-editor, gets the assignment of her dreams when her boss insists she go back to high school to report on today's teens. Though she's spunky enough for the journalism task, she isn't hip enough to fit in high school. Josie's awkwardness makes her anathema to the cool girls. An A student, Josie catches the eye of her English teacher, Sam Coulson. Similarly, Josie's undercover turn prompts her to discover aspects of herself and revisit long-forgotten episodes. Intercut with present-day scenes are flashbacks of Josie's experiences as an awkward teen. Just when it seems that Josie's second go-round in high school is slated to be as much of a failure as her first, her brother Rob enrolls as the one cool person to give her reputation a boost. But Josie's newfound popularity and deepening friendship with Sam are threatened when her editor insists she write an exposé on teacher-student relations, prompting a crucial prom-night decision. Barrymore shines throughout, rendering a thoroughly winning and sympathetic heroine.

U.S. release: April 9   U.S. B.O.: $55.5 million

The Ninth Gate

A Bac Films (in France)/Artisan Entertainment (in U.S.) release of an Artisan Entertainment presentation of an R.P. Prods., Orly Films, TF1 Films Prods. (France)/Kino Vision, Origen Producciones Cinematograficas (Spain) production, with participation of Bac Films, Canal Plus and Via Digital. Produced by Roman Polanski. Executive producers, Wolfgang Glattes, Michael Cheyko. Co-producers, Inaki Nunez, Antonio Cardenal, Alain Vannier, Mark Allan. Directed by Polanski. Screenplay, Enrique Urbizu, John Brownjohn, Polanski, based on the novel *El Club Dumas* by Arturo Perez-Reverte. Camera

(color, widescreen), Darius Khondji; editor, Herve de Luze; music, Wojciech Kilar; production designer, Dean Tavoularis; art director, Gerard Viard; set decorator, Philippe Turlure; costume designer, Anthony Powell; sound (Dolby Digital), Jean-Marie Blondel; special effects, Duboi, Sony Pictures Imageworks, Eclair Numerique, Mikros Images, Effets Films; line producer, Suzanne Wiesenfeld; associate producer, Adam Kempton; assistant director, Michel Cheyko; casting, Howard Feuer. Reviewed at UGC Cine Cite theater, Paris, Aug. 25, 1999. Running time: 127 mins.

Johnny Depp (Dean Corso), Frank Langella (Boris Balkan), Lena Olin (Liana Telfer), Emmanuelle Seigner (The Girl), Barbara Jefford (Baroness Kessler), Jack Taylor (Victor Fargas), Jose Lopez Rodero (Pablo and Pedro Ceniza), James Russo (Bernie). With: Tony Amoni, Willy Holt, Maria Ducceshi, Jacques Collard.

A sardonic detective thriller peppered with carefully crafted pleasures, not the least of which is a snide approach to wealthy people with a decadent streak. Pic's always assured, baroquely funny tone is set in opening sequence, in which an elderly gentleman pens a suicide note before hanging himself. His widow, Liana Telfer, doesn't know that he sold one of his most valuable books – one of only three known copies of *The Nine Gates of the Kingdom of Shadows*. Dean Corso is a crafty, mercenary rare-book broker, who tracks down volumes for wealthy clients. Filthy-rich Manhattanite Boris Balkan now owns the Telfer book, whose author was burnt at the stake in the 1600s for having written and illustrated it in a league with the devil. Balkan engages Corso to examine the other two editions, which are in the possession of a Mr. Fargas in Portugal and a baroness named Kessler in Paris. His mission – on an unlimited expense account – is to compare the three books to ascertain whether any are forgeries. Corso learns that the ancient engravings which illustrate the three copies give a new meaning to underground literature. And somebody will stop at nothing to assemble the clues needed to conjure Satan.

If your story calls for a street-smart American who might be able to beat erudite Europeans at their own centuries-old game, Depp is a good choice. Olin does her determined hellcat routine with gusto. Langella convinces even in the pic's loonier moments.

Notting Hill

A Polygram Filmed Entertainment (in U.K.)/Universal (in U.S.) release of a PFE presentation, in association with Working Title Films, of a Notting Hill Pictures production. Produced by Duncan Kenworthy. Executive producers, Tim Bevan, Richard Curtis, Eric Fellner. Directed by Roger Michell. Screenplay, Curtis. Camera (Deluxe Color prints, widescreen), Michael Coulter; editor, Nick Moore; music, Trevor Jones. Reviewed at Odeon, Leicester Square, London, March 29, 1999. MPAA Rating: PG-13. Running time: 123 mins.

Julia Roberts (Anna Scott), Hugh Grant (William Thacker), Hugh Bonneville (Bernie), Emma Chambers (Honey), James Dreyfus (Martin), Rhys Ifans (Spike), Tim McInnerny (Max), Gina McKee (Bella), Richard McCabe (Tony), Alec Baldwin (Anna's boyfriend). With: Dylan Moran, Roger Frost, Julian Rhind-Tutt, Lorelei King, John Shrapnel, Clarke Peters, Arturo Venegas, Mischa Barton, Henry Goodman, Melissa Wilson, Emma Bernard, Sam West, Ann Beach.

Notting Hill has buckets to spare of that rarest screen commodity – genuine, engaging charm – plus a cast and production values that fully deliver. A romantic comedy, couched as a modern fairytale, about shy bookseller William Thacker who lives and works amidst his circle of friends in London's Notting Hill. William's unspectacular life changes one day when Anna Scott, the planet's most famous film actress, walks in alone and buys a book. She's friendly in a professional way, he's star-struck, and an on-off relationship begins between the two, whereby Thacker deals with the superficiality of Scott's celebrity life, and Scott becomes entranced by the earthiness of Thacker's life. Both Grant and Roberts manage to shed enough of their movie personas to establish the beginnings of a screen chemistry that becomes vital as the film progresses. It's easy to sit back and analyze faults in the pic's construction. As Anna keeps coming and going out of William's tiny universe, you sit there waiting for scripter Curtis to come up with another unlikely reason for the two to cross paths. Though there's still plenty of Curtis' signature humor, especially in his comic observation of the spaces between words, this is very much a kinder, gentler movie – less manic in keeping its audience hooked, more confident in the longer lines of the story's emotional arc, and less reliant on barbed one-liners and eccentric characters per se.

U.S. release: May 28   U.S. B.O.: $116.1 million

The Ogre

A Studio Babelsberg (Berlin)/Renn Prods. (Paris)/Recorded Picture Co. (London) co-production, in association with WDR and France 2 Cinema and with the participation of Canal Plus. Heritage Films (Warsaw), Ufa Babelsberg. (International sales: UGC D.A. Intl., Paris.) Produced by Ingrid Windisch. Executive producers, Claude Berri, Jeremy Thomas, Lew Rywin. Directed by Volker Schlondorff. Screenplay, Jean-Claude Carriere, Schlondorff, based on the novel *The Erl King* by Michel Tournier. Camera (b&w), Bruno de Keyzer; editor, Nicolas Gaster; music, Michael Nyman; production designer, Ezio Frigerio; art direction, Didier Naert; costume designer, Anna Sheppard; sound (Dolby Digital SRD), Karl-Heinz Laabs; creative consultant, Peter Pryzygodda; associate producers, Pierre Couveinhes, Chris Auty; assistant directors, Marek Brodski, Marcel Just; casting, Karin Beewen. Reviewed at Venice Film Festival (competing), Aug. 29, 1996. Running time: 117 mins.
John Malkovich (Abel), Armin Mueller-Stahl (Count of Kaltenhorn), Gottfried John (Chief Forester), Marianne Sagebreeht (Frau Netta), Volker Spengler (Hermann Goering), Heino Ferch (Raufelsen), Dieter Laser (Prof. Blattchen), Agnes Soral (Rachel), Sasha Hanau (Martine). With Caspar Salman, Daniel Smith, Ilja Smoljanski.
(English dialog)
Handsome production, and an attention-grabbing performance from John Malkovich. A gentle giant is forced by evil circumstances to work for the Nazis but eventually redeems himself. Beginning in Paris in 1925 with the traumas of young Abel, a boy forever falling foul of teachers and fellow pupils. When Abel is about to be punished, prays the school will burn down, it in fact does, saving him from punishment, but at the expense of his friend's death. Action shifts forward 14 years, where Abel has become a simple lughead who works in a Parisian garage, lives a quiet life, and has occasional sex with girlfriend Rachel, who dubs him an "ogre" because of his rough lovemaking.

Abel's fondness for children gets him into trouble when he's falsely accused of raping little Martine and imprisoned. The German invasion brings about his release. However, he's sent to the front and promptly taken prisoner. Before long, Abel has become, though still a prisoner, a member of the inner sanctum of German leaders, including Herman Goering and the aristocratic Count Kaltenhorn. He's given the task of recruiting boys to be trained in the army, and he sets out daily on horseback to kidnap youngsters.

The chief problem here is that what works on the page takes on a totally different dimension on screen. Screenplay takes a disappointingly didactic approach, ramming home points that should already be obvious, especially in the final reel.

The Omega Code

A Providence Entertainment release of a TBN Films presentation of a Gener8Xion Entertainment production. Produced by Matthew Crouch, Rob Marcarelli, Lawrence Mortorff. Executive producer, Paul Crouch. Co-producer, Gary M. Bettman. Directed by Rob Marcarelli. Screenplay, Stephan Blinn, Hollis Barton. Camera (FotoKem color), Carlos Gonzalez; editor, Peter Zinner; music, Harry Manfredini; production designer, Mark Harper; set decorator, Jen Tauritz; sound (Dolby Digital THX), David Waelder; special effects coordinator, Ron Trost; biblical prophecy consultant, Hal Lindsey; associate producer, Blinn; assistant director, Nick Goodwin Self. Reviewed at Loews Cineplex Fountains Theater, Houston, Oct. 15, 1999. MPAA Rating: PG-13. Running time: 99 mins.
Casper Van Dien (Gillian Lane), Michael York (Stone Alexander), Michael Ironside (Dominic).
An apocalyptic melodrama produced under the auspices of the Trinity Broadcasting Network. A fictionalized dramatization of the "end times' prophecies" found in the Book of Revelation, script involves the so-called Bible Code, a highly controversial theory that calls for applying mathematical equations to uncover "hidden truths."

Pic is a hamhanded, flatfooted B movie that makes *The Omen* look like *Citizen Kane*. Gillian Lane turned his back on religion at the age of 10. Now he's a wildly successful motivational speaker and author who dismisses God as just another myth. Naturally, he's overdue for a road-to-Damascus experience. Stone Alexander, a famous media mogul and philanthropist, wants to unite all nations in peace, love and currency. To fulfill his ambitions, he has employed henchmen to steal a CD-ROM disc that contains the Bible Code, which he wants to use for nefarious purposes. He is aided by Dominic, an ex-priest who is bitterly jealous when Alexander recruits Lane as his chief consultant. Lane discovers the Bible Code disc in Alexander's underground computer center. Much of the pic focuses on Lane's flight from the authorities after he is framed as Alexander's would-be assassin.

Climax is a straight steal from *Raiders of the Lost Ark*. Apparently, this is meant to signal the rapture, or the end of the world. But the audience doesn't know for certain because, instead of concluding, the pic simply stops. Helmer keeps the pace brisk, often at the expense of offering a coherent narrative. On a tech level, pic manages the near-miraculous feat of appearing cheap and expensive all at once.

U.S. B.O.: $12.3 million

... May 30 ...

The sound of money struck a powerful chord on Broadway this season as both box-office and attendance figures broke records. Total box-office grosses rose to $588,126,585.

One 4 All

A Bac Films release (in France) of a Les Films 13/France 2 Cinema production, with participation of Canal Plus. (International sales: Les Films 26, Paris.) Produced, directed by Claude Lelouch. Screenplay, Lelouch, Pierre Leroux, Pierre Uytterhoeven; story, Lelouch. Camera (color, widescreen), Lelouch; editors, Helene de Luze, Stephane Mazalaigue; music, Francis Lai; art director, Pascal Aubin; costume designer, Dominique Borg; sound (Dolby Digital), Harald Maury, Jean Gargonne, Jean-Charles Martel; assistant director, Laurent Herbiet; casting, Arlette Gordon, Iris Wong. Reviewed at Max Linder Panorama, Paris, Dec. 20, 1999. Running time: 123 mins.

Jean-Pierre Marielle (Bayard), Anne Parillaud (Olga Duclos), Alessandra Martines (Maxime), Marianne Denicourt (Irina Colbert), Alice Evans (Macha Desachy), Olivia Bonamy (Olivia Colbert), Samy Naceri (Sam Morvan), Rudiger Vogler (Oscar), Anouk Aimee (His Wife), Maka Kotto (The President), Constantin Alexandrov (The King of the Night), Andrea Ferreol (His Wife), Francois Perrot (Shady Film Producer). With: Francois Berleand, Emmanuelle Bercot, Sebastien Bihi, Michel Jonasz, Charles Gerard, Firmine Richard.

The elaborate yet easy-to-follow narrative pursues three actresses whose legit careers are going nowhere as they deploy their most seductive thesping skills in a rather less-than-legit ongoing performance: the mercenary pursuit of wealthy men. To repay debts run up in staging a self-financed production of Chekhov's *Three Sisters*, Olga, Irina and Macha accept a suggestion from Irina's younger sister, Olivia, who works at the Concorde check-in desk and has had it with finicky, wealthy passengers. Olivia, who knows which flight will include particularly well-heeled men, puts a new spin on air traffic control by arranging for her friends to be booked in seats right beside their marks. Armed with extensive advance research and a sure-to-lure fake identity, the women can charm guys off their feet and maintain chaste courtships long enough to benefit from their generosity – in the form of gems and cash – before finding an excuse to dump them.

Commissioner Bayard of the Paris vice squad stumbles onto the scam. With the help of enigmatic looker Maxime, he is staking out Russian mobsters who conduct much of their shady business from seats with excellent sightlines of the topless beauties at the Lido.

Scenes in which the three lasses prepare for their roles are a hoot. Pic is shrewdly cast with actors from several generations, and the whole package is involving and entertaining, funny and suspenseful, without a hint of a lull.

Onegin

A Seven Arts Intl. presentation of a Baby Prods. production. (International sales: Seven Arts, Hollywood, Calif.) Produced by Ileen Maisel, Simon Bosanquet. Executive producer, Ralph Fiennes. Directed by Martha Fiennes. Screenplay, Peter Ettedgui, Michael Ignatieff, based on the verse novel by Aleksandr Pushkin.

Ralph Fiennes (Evgeny Onegin), Liv Tyler (Tatyana Larin), Toby Stephens (Vladimir Lensky), Lena Headey (Olga Larin), Martin Donovan (Prince Nikitin), Alun Armstrong (Zaretsky), Irene Worth (Princess Alina), Harriet Walter (Mme. Larina), Jason Watkins (Guillot), Francesca Annis (Katiusha).

Though this is very much an English rather than a Russian *Onegin*, the heart of Pushkin's classic pumps firm and full in debuting director Martha Fiennes' richly textured pic. The film is luxuriantly lensed. However, the movie is not so much concerned with scoring modern points about the moneyed classes as creating a resonant cinematic frame in which to tell a simple, rhapsodic tale of a sophisticate meeting his match in an uncomplicated young woman whose love he initially spurns. Stripping away the dialog into almost Pinteresque exchanges, and giving the well-chosen cast time to develop a physical language for their roles, helmer Fiennes manages to draw the viewer into this particular universe of almost pure emotion.

Headlined by older brother Ralph Fiennes in a commanding performance as the lethargic socialite brought low by a bad case of amorous mistiming, the story is set in 1820s St. Petersburg. Onegin, while at his countryside estate, befriends his neighbor Lensky who drags him along to meet his spirited fiancée, Olga, and her older sister, Tatyana. Onegin is intrigued by Tatyana for her freshness and openness. Tatyana is entranced by Onegin, who speaks his mind. Lensky, sensing the attraction, challenges Onegin to a duel, even though neither his nor Onegin's heart is in it. Onegin ends up reluctantly shooting his friend and, heartbroken, disappears from view. Six years later Onegin returns to St Petersburg society, where he meets a changed Tatyana and asks for a second chance – with devastating results.

U.S. release: Dec. 17   U.S. B.O.: $8,885

Payback

A Paramount Pictures release of an Icon production. Produced by Bruce Davey. Executive producer, Stephen McEveety. Directed by Brian Helgeland. Screenplay, Helgeland, Terry Hayes, based on the novel *The Hunter*, by Richard Stark. Camera (Deluxe color, widescreen), Ericson Core; editor, Kevin Stitt; music, Chris Boardman; production designer, Richard Hoover; art direction, Troy Sizemore; set decorator, Sandy Struth; costume designer, Ha Nguyen. Reviewed at the National Theater, Los Angeles, CA., Feb. 2, 1999. MPAA Rating: R. Running time: 110 mins.

Mel Gibson (Porter), Gregg Henry (Val), Maria Bello (Rosie), Deborah Kara Unger (Lynn), David Paymer (Stegman), Bill Duke (Detective Hicks), Jack Conley (Detective Leary), William Devane (Carter), Kris Kristofferson (Bronson), John Glover (Phil), Lucy Liu (Pearl).

Payback is such a loose reworking of John Boorman's dazzling 1967 noir *Point Blank* that it hardly qualifies as a remake. Even so, *Payback*, which is structured as an action thriller rather than a moody noir, is not an embarrassment, but it's not distinguished, either. Pandering to Gibson's fans, the film vacillates between the dark and sinister and the comic and whimsical – not always to its advantage. Pic is more graphically violent than *Point Blank*: some of the torture scenes approach the level of *Reservoir Dogs*. While the original pic's bold and sparkling elements are nowhere to be found, *Payback* improves on it in its stronger characterizations.

After a smooth heist, Val steals Porter's portion and his druggie wife Lynn. Val shoots Porter, believing that he is dead. Porter is reborn and risks his life to get back his cut of the loot – $70,000, an amount providing a number of comic relief scenes. His efforts take him into an urban underworld, dominated by a secretive syndicate called the Outfit. Script presents Porter as a brutally murderous thief who'll do anything to get his money back, but also a man with an inner code of honor – a gunslinger in the Old West tradition. Indeed, since revenge and justice are the chief motivations for Porter's behavior, *Payback* has all the attributes of an urban Western.

U.S. release: Feb. 5   U.S. B.O.: $81.5 million

Play It to the Bone

A Buena Vista Pictures release of a Touchstone Pictures presentation in association with Shanghai'd Films. Produced by Stephen Chin. Executive producer, David Lester. Directed, written by Ron Shelton. Camera (Technicolor, Panavision widescreen), Mark Vargo; editor, Paul Seydor, Patrick Flannery; music, Alex Wurman; music supervisors, Dawn Soler, Sterling Meredith; production designer, Claire Jenora Bowin; art director, Mary Finn; set decorator, Danielle Berman; costume designer, Kathryn Morrison; sound (Dolby Digital/DTS/SDDS), Art Rochester; supervising sound editor, William Jacobs; makeup designer, Steve LaPorte; boxing trainer and choreography, Darrell Foster; associate producer, Kellie Davis; assistant director, Gordon Boos; second unit camera, David B. Nowell; casting, Victoria Thomas. Reviewed at GCC Beverly Connection, L.A., Dec. 16, 1999. MPAA Rating: R. Running time: 124 mins.

Antonio Banderas (Cesar Dominguez), Woody Harrelson (Vince Boudreau), Lolita Davidovich (Grace Pasic), Tom Sizemore (Joe Domino), Lucy Liu (Lia), Robert Wagner (Hank Goody), Richard Masur (Artie),Willie Garson (Cappie Caplan), Cylk Cozart (Rudy), Jack Carter (Dante Solomon). With: Jim Lampley, George Foreman, Larry Merchant, Darrell Foster, Steve Lawrence, Mitch Halpern, Chuck Hull, Buddy Greco, Kevin Costner, James Woods, Mike Tyson, Rod Stewart.

More disappointing than one of those truncated, overpriced pay-per-view nonevents that have scandalized pro boxing in the '90s, Ron Shelton's foray into the world of pugilists is a woefully under-realized story of smalltime boxers enjoying perhaps their last moment in the spotlight. The hope that Shelton, long Hollywood's premier observer of sports, would bring fresh insight to the sweet science is unfulfilled on nearly every level.

Two contending middleweight fighters are KO'd by life and promoter Joe Domino must find subs in a hurry to fill the opening card of the latest Mike Tyson bout at Vegas' Mandalay Bay Hotel. He contacts lowlife pals and ex-middleweight contenders Cesar and Vince. After protracted and hardly amusing negotiations, Cesar and Vince agree to fight each other for $50,000 each, with the winner earning a bid for the middleweight championship. Pic divides into two dissimilar halves, the first a dawdling road movie in which the protagonists, none of whom is terribly interesting, unload backstory baggage, and the second half the fight itself. Pic's strategy of trying to raise the emotional stakes, so that the culminating fight will be a true main event, serves only to make us impatient for the first-round ring of the bell.

U.S. release: Dec. 25   U.S. B.O.: $10,714

Plunkett & Macleane

A Polygram Filmed Entertainment (in U.K.)/Gramercy (in U.S.) release of a PFE presentation, in association with the Arts Council of England, of a Working Title Films production. Produced by Tim Bevan, Eric Fellner, Rupert Harvey. Executive producers, Gary Oldman, Douglas Urbanski, Selwyn Roberts, Matthew Stillman. Co-producers, Jonathon Finn, Natascha Wharton. Directed by Jake Scott. Screenplay, Robert Wade, Neal Purvis, Charles McKeown, based on an original screenplay by Selwyn Roberts. Camera (Technicolor prints, Panavision widescreen), John Mathieson; editor, Oral Norrie Ottey; music, Craig Armstrong; production designer, Norris Spencer; art directors, Petr Kunc, Jindrich Koci; costume designer, Janty Yates; sound (Dolby Digital), Mark Holding, Ray Merrin, Graham Daniel; stunt coordinator, Pavel Voukoun; second unit director, Spencer; second unit camera, Martin Grosup; assistant directors, Euan Keddie, Mirek Lux; casting, Jina Jay. Reviewed at Odeon, Leicester Square, London, March 29, 1999. Running time: 100 mins.

Robert Carlyle (Will Plunkett),Jonny Lee Miller (Captain James Macleane), Liv Tyler (Lady Rebecca), Ken Stott (Chance), Michael Gambon (Lord Chief Justice Gibson), Alan Cumming (Lord Rochester). With: Terence Rigby, Claire Rushbrook, Jeff Nuttal, Iain Robertson, James Thornton, Nichola McAuliffe, Susan Porrett.

A strikingly designed and lensed but otherwise chaotic costume romp about two highwaymen in 18th-century London. Though amusing in spots, and briefly high-spirited in others, pic is hopelessly dyslexic in basic film grammar, dissipating both its onscreen talent and its premise of an irreverent modern take on costumers into a series of variable set pieces.

The year is 1748, the place London. Plunkett, a bankrupt apothecary turned robber, and Macleane, a down-at-heel aristocrat with a similar career path, meet in Newgate Prison.

The pair form an uneasy partnership, with Plunkett providing the muscle and business brains, and Macleane the tarnished breeding to get them into well-heeled society. Their entree comes in the louche, well-powdered form of Macleane's former acquaintance Lord Rochester, who invites Macleane to a gambling soiree where he crosses eyes with Rebecca, niece of Lord Chief Justice Gibson.

That night, the masked P&M hold up Rebecca and her uncle. As their renown mounts with further robberies, and Parliament gets nervous about law and order, the ruthless Chance, Thieftaker General, is assigned to hunt down the daring duo. Chance's initial attempts are unsuccessful, but then P&M start making mistakes, Macleane courts disaster by trying to romance Rebecca, and Plunkett gets increasingly anxious to make a clean break and head for America.

U.S. release: Oct. 1   U.S. B.O.: $474,901

Pokemon: The First Movie

A Warner Bros. Family Entertainment release of a Kids WB! presentation of a Pikachu Project '98-Shogakukan Inc. production in association with 4Kids Entertainment. Produced by Norman J. Grossfeld, Choji Yoshikawa, Tomoyuki Igarashi, Takemoto Mori. Executive producers, Alfred R. Kahn, Masakazu Kubo, Takashi Kawaguchi. Directed by Kunihiko Yuyama. English adaptation directed by Michael Haigney. Screenplay by Takeshi Shudo, based on characters created by Satoshi Tajiri. English adaptation, Grossfeld, Haigney, John Touhey. Translations, Paul Taylor. Camera (Deluxe color), Hisao Shirai; editors, Toshio Henmi, Yutaka Ito; music, Ralph Schuckett, John Loeffler; art director, Katsuyoshi Kanemura; animation producer, Toshiaki Okuno, Shukachi Kanda; chief animator, Sayuri Ichiishi; animation supervisor, Yoichi Kotabe; digital

animation, Olm Digital; sound (Dolby Digital/DTS/SDDS), Koji Fukushima; associate producers, Kathy Borland, Takashi Miura, Hiroshi Ishikawa, Katsuhito Yamauchi, Tetsu Kayama, Takaaki Kii, Noriyuki Yoshida; assistant directors, Masamitsu Hidaka, Kiyotaka Isako; casting, Jim Malone. Reviewed at Century Plaza Theater, L.A., Nov. 6, 1999. MPAA Rating: G. Running time: 75 mins.
Voices: Veronica Taylor, Philip Bartlett, Rachael Lillis, Eric Stuart, Addie Blaustein, Ikue Otani.
Pic is the phenomenon's foray into features, from the popular TV show. Young Ash Ketchum has a mission to become the world's greatest Pokemon master. Scientists discover that their efforts to bioengineer the rarest Pokemon of all, Mew, have created a monster – which escapes. For the first time in Pokemon history, Mewtwo is a pocket monster with deep inner thoughts, bitter that he is only a warped clone and specimen, and finding that his life's purpose is to purge all those who oppose him. Ash and his pals (with ever-faithful Pikachu, the first Pokemon Ash collected) are interrupted by a rival, who, like Ash, is a Pokemon trainer with several pocket monsters of his own. Mysterious "mistress of the greatest No. 1 trainer" invites eager trainers to remote New Island. These include Ash's perennial rivals known as Team Rocket. Ash and friends find themselves duped as the No. 1 trainer reveals himself to be Mewtwo.

The younger set love the flat animation design, continued here from the series and game, and the only new visual elements include a certain sepulchral darkness in key scenes and digitized backgrounds, which don't match the foreground art. Poor decision by makers of original Japanese version as well as American version to dump the light fun of the series carries over to pic's color scheme, which is downright depressing compared with *Pokemon*'s funky small-screen sunniness.
U.S. release: Nov. 10   U.S. B.O.: $84.1 million

Random Hearts

A Sony Pictures Entertainment release of a Columbia Pictures presentation of a Rastar/Mirage Enterprises production. Produced by Sydney Pollack, Marykay Powell. Executive producers, Ronald L. Schwary, Warren Adler. Directed by Pollack. Screenplay, Kurt Luedtke; adaptation by Darryl Ponicsan, based on the novel by Warren Adler. Camera (Deluxe color), Philippe Rousselot; editor, William Steinkamp; music, Dave Grusin; production designer, Barbara Ling; art director, Chris Shriver; set designer, Scott Murphy; set decorator, Susan Bode; costume designer, Bernie Pollack; Ms. Thomas' clothing designer, Ann Roth; sound (Dolby Digital/SDDS), Danny Michael; supervising sound editor, Scott A. Hecker; assistant director, Denis L. Stewart; casting, David Rubin. Reviewed at Sony Studios, Culver City, Sept. 23, 1999. MPAA Rating: R. Running time: 133 mins.
Harrison Ford (Dutch Van Den Broeck), Kristin Scott Thomas (Kay Chandler), Charles S. Dutton (Alcee), Bonnie Hunt (Wendy Judd), Dennis Haysbert (Detective George Beaufort), Sydney Pollack (Carl Broman), Richard Jenkins (Truman Trainor), Paul Guilfoyle (Dick Montoya), Susanna Thompson (Peyton Van Den Broeck), Peter Coyote (Cullen Chandler), Dylan Baker (Richard Judd), Lynne Thigpen (Phyllis Bonaparte), Kate Mara (Jessica Chandler), Ariana Thomas (Shyla Mumford), Bill Cobbs (Marvin), Susan Floyd (Molly Roll), Edie Falco (Janice).
Random Hearts is about the retroactive discovery of adultery,

but it's a realization that haunts the protagonists throughout the film's protracted running time. The reluctant but eventual lovers are the opposite of starcrossed, two people uncomfortably thrust together solely because their respective spouses are killed in a plane crash on their way to an illicit rendezvous. Sgt. Dutch Van Den Broeck, of the Washington D.C. Internal Affairs police, hits a brick wall in his initial approaches to congresswoman Kay Chandler, who finds that her tragedy appears to be helping her bid for reelection. But when Kay joins Dutch in a quick visit to Miami to observe the seductive setting for what they've learned was a long-term affair between their mutual mates, the media picks up the scent, spelling PR trouble for Kay. The two lunge at each other in a car in an assaultively amorous physical display that is convincingly urgent as an explosion of pent-up feeling.

The dual climaxes involve sex and then gunplay, the former handled in a plausibly understated way, the latter in a manner melodramatically out of keeping with the rest of the drama. Pic is laborious, remote and strangely uninvolving. There is a hushed quality to the enterprise, a sensitivity that feels more intellectual than emotional, an effort to withhold that is meant ultimately to pay off in a surge of feeling that never happens.
U.S. release: Oct. 8   U.S. B.O.: $31 million

Ride With the Devil

A USA Films release of a Universal presentation of a Good Machine production. Produced by Ted Hope, Robert Colesberry, James Schamus. Executive producer, David Linde. Directed by Ang Lee. Screenplay, Schamus, based on the novel *Woe to Live On* by Daniel Woodrell. Camera (Deluxe color, Panavision widescreen), Frederick Elmes; music, Mychael Danna; music supervisor, Alex Steyermark; editor, Tim Squyres; production designer, Mark Friedberg; art director, Steve Arnold; set designers, Jonathan Scott, Steve Lauberth; set decorator, Stephanie Carroll; costume designer, Marit Allen; sound (Dolby Digital SR), Drew Kunin; supervising sound editor, Philip Stockton; associate producer, Anne Carey; assistant director, Bob Huberman; second unit director, David Ellis; second unit camera, Michael Benson; casting, Avy Kaufman. Reviewed at PolyGram screening room, Beverly Hills, Aug. 27, 1999. (In Deauville Film Festival; Toronto Film Festival – Gala; London Film Festival – opening night.) MPAA Rating: R. Running time: 138 mins.
Skeet Ulrich (Jack Bull Chiles), Tobey Maguire (Jake Roedel), Jewel (Sue Lee Shelley), Jeffrey Wright (Daniel Holt), Simon Baker (George Clyde), Jonathan Rhys Meyers (Pitt Mackeson), James Caviezel (Black John), Thomas Guiry (Riley Crawford), Tom Wilkinson (Orton Brown), Jonathan Brandis (Cave Wyatt), Matthew Faber (Turner Rawls), Stephen Mailer (Babe Hudspeth), John Ales (Quantrill), Zach Grenier (Mr. Evans), Margo Martindale (Wilma Brown), Mark Ruffalo (Alf Bowden), Celia Weston (Mrs. Clark).
Impressing once again with the diversity of his choices of subject matter and milieu, Ang Lee has made a brutal but sensitively observed film about the fringes of the Civil War, about the families and neighbors who were divided among themselves along the Missouri-Kansas border. In the anarchic world of Southern-sympathizing Bushwhackers and pro-Union Jayhawkers the conflict is more often personal and haphazard rather than militarily organized.

. . . June 2 . . .
Director Agnieszka Holland has committed to directing the film version of Edgar Hilsenrath's 30-year-old cult novel **The Nazi and the Barber**.

It's 1862 and Jack Bull Chiles, a wholehearted Confederate, and close friend Jake Roedel (whose family is Union, but he's fighting with the Bushwhackers) rove the countryside as guerrilla fighters with a handful of others, donning Union uniforms in order to fool and kill some opponents. The men hole up for a while near the home of a young widow, Sue Lee Shelley, to whom Jack takes a liking. He is soon mortally injured, and the small group moves on to take up residence in the home of a welcoming family, where Sue Lee can wait out her pregnancy and she and the clearly virginal Jake can commence an odd developing courtship. A military raid marks a moral turning point for Jake, whose commitment to personal matters begins to outflank his political motivations at a time when the tide is also decisively turning against the South.

The film takes the time to give voice to numerous interesting perspectives, such as those of the black slave, the embittered rebel farmer and the war widow. Maguire, Ulrich and Wright capably handle the principal parts, and pop star Jewel isn't asked to display much in range.

U.S. release: Nov. 24   U.S. B.O.: $491,069

Rosetta

A USA Films release (in U.S.) release of a Les Films du Fleuve, RTBF, RTBF (Belgium)/ARP Selection (France) production. (International sales: ARP, Paris.) Produced by Luc and Jean-Pierre Dardenne, Michele and Laurent Petin. Directed, written by Luc and Jean-Pierre Dardenne. **Emilie Dequenne (Rosetta), Fabrizio Rongione (Riquet), Anne Yernaux (Rosetta's Mother), Olivier Gourmet (Boss).** Winner of the Palme d'Or and Best Actress Award at Cannes. Pic follows the daily struggles of a tough Belgian teenager with the basic building blocks of life. Pic plays like *Run Lola Run* meets Ken Loach, as the title heroine goes about her chores in a dreary, wintry town. Rosetta is ejected from a job for some unexplained reason. Between trying to care for her alchoholic mom, Rosetta is constantly on the move, as she searches for a job, scavenges for food, and sells off clothes to earn money. She seemingly has no friends or other relatives.

A ray of hope appears in the form of Riquet, who runs a street food stand; he offers her a place to live and makes vaguely romantic approaches to her over a meager meal in his grungy apartment. Thanks to Riquet, Rosetta finally gets a job at the bakery, but then is suddenly replaced under a flimsy excuse by the boss. Determined to get a job at any cost, she ends up betraying the trust and friendliness of Riquet, who's been quietly cheating the bakery's owner.

Pic undoubtedly has some powerful moments, mostly centered on scenes in which Rosetta behaves in shockingly self-protective ways. Helmers pull no dramatic rabbits out of a hat at the end to put any kind of twist or transfiguration on the material. What the movie does have is a striking performance by 18-year-old non-pro Dequenne.

U.S. release: Nov. 5   U.S. B.O.: $196,796

Runaway Bride

A Paramount release of a Paramount and Touchstone Pictures presentation of an Interscope Communications production in association with Lakeshore Entertainment. Produced by Ted Field, Tom Rosenberg, Scott Kroopf, Robert Cort. Executive producers, Ted Tannebaum, David Madden, Gary Lucchesi. Co-producers, Karen Stirgwolt, Richard Wright, Ellen H. Schwartz. Directed by Garry Marshall. Screenplay, Josann

McGibbon, Sara Parriott. Camera (Deluxe color, Panavision widescreen), Stuart Dryburgh; editor, Bruce Green; music, James Newton Howard; music supervisor, Kathy Nelson; production designer, Mark Friedberg; art director, Wray Steven Graham; set designers, Thomas Minton, Charles McCarry; set decorator, Stephanie Carroll; costume designer, Albert Wolsky; sound (DTS/Dolby Digital), Keith A. Wester; supervising sound editor, Robert L. Sephton; assistant director, Ellen H. Schwartz; second unit director, Scott Marshall; second unit camera, Ian Fox; casting, Gretchen Rennell Court. Reviewed at Paramount Studios, L.A., July 22, 1999. MPAA Rating: PG. Running time: 116 mins. **Julia Roberts (Maggie Carpenter), Richard Gere (Ike Graham), Joan Cusack (Peggy Flemming), Hector Elizondo (Fisher), Rita Wilson (Ellie), Paul Dooley (Walter), Christopher Meloni (Coach Bob), Donal Logue (Priest Bob), Reg Rogers (George Bug Guy), Yul Vasquez (Dead Head Gill), Jane Morris (Mrs. Pressman), Lisa Roberts Gillan (Elaine from Manhattan), Kathleen Marshall (Cousin Cindy), Jean Schertler (Grandma).**

Having waited nine years since their 1990 smash *Pretty Woman,* Julia Roberts, Richard Gere and director Garry Marshall score again with an ultra-commercial mainstream romantic comedy that delivers all the laughs and smiles it intends. *USA Today* columnist Ike Graham deals with his imminent deadline by hanging out in a bar. Fortunately, a young man tells him a good story about a Maryland woman with the chronic habit of leaving fiancés at the altar. Unfortunately, the resulting column is so riddled with errors that his boss (and ex-wife), Ellie, fires him. Given a shot at vindication via a freelance magazine piece if he can get the full and real story about this woman, Ike heads for small town, Hale, Md. Approaching her fourth attempted wedding, Maggie Carpenter is none too happy to have Ike cozying up to her family, friends, and ex beaus. Yet she sobers up and agrees to cooperate with the writer. This, of course, leads to the unavoidable recognition of mutual attraction.

Roberts has a perfect role in Maggie. Her face and feelings are accessible without being obvious, she can be goofy, sporty or amorous with ease, and she's radiant almost regardless of circumstances. Gere delivers a loose, disarming, quite appealing portrait of a man who's made a number of mistakes and looks to be an underachiever as he enters middle age. Marshall's timing and sense of fun are in full evidence.

U.S. release: July 30   U.S. B.O.: $152.1 million

Siegfried & Roy: The Magic Box

An Imax Ltd. release of an L-Squared Entertainment production in association with Lexington Road Prods. and Foundry Film Partners. Produced by Michael Lewis. Executive producers, Lou Gonda, Jon Ein, Robert Greenhut, Bernie Yuman. Co-producer, Jini Dayaneni. Directed by Brett Leonard. Screenplay, Lyn Vaus, Leonard. Camera (color, Imax 3-D), Sean MacLeod Phillips; editor, Jonathan P. Shaw; music, Alan Silvestri; production designer, Steve Suchman; sound (Imax DTAC), Miguel Rivera; supervising sound editor, Steve Pederson; visual-effects supervisor, Phillips; visual-effects production designer, Michael Hartog. Reviewed at Sony, Lincoln Square, N.Y., Oct. 13, 1999. Running time: 50 mins. **Narrator: Anthony Hopkins. With: Siegfried Fischbacher, Roy Uwe Ludwig Horn, John Summers, Andrew Dunlap, Dillon McEwin, Cameron Alexander.**

... June 3 ...

Onegin unspools before a local star audience in Moscow's largest cinema three days before Russia marks the 200th anniversary of Pushkin's birth.

Siegfried & Roy: The Magic Box brings to the big Imax screen subjects unbeatably suited to its lavish scale and the slightly surreal effect of 3-D: the stage show and personal legend of phenomenally successful Las Vegas entertainers Siegfried & Roy. Pic's 20 minutes of computer graphics, the most extensive so far in an Imax film, provide an appropriate and alluring storybook visual setting that should help make this one of the most popular Imax 3-D films yet.

Shown separately, the future showmen grow up in a Germany ruined by World War II. Blond, classically Aryan Siegfried climbs mountains and later becomes interested in stage magic, hoping to dispel the gloom of his soldier father. Dark-haired, delicate Roy has a lifelong affinity for animals, beginning with a dog who rescues him from quicksand and continuing with a cheetah, Chico, that he takes with him when he gets a job as a steward on a cruise ship.

On board Roy discovers Siegfried performing magic tricks and asks if he could make a cheetah disappear. Thus is showbiz history made. Pic culminates at S&R's lavish estate outside Vegas, where they live in Arabian Nights splendor and raise their animals, some belonging to endangered species they hope eventually to return to the wild.

U.S. release: Oct. 1   U.S. B.O.: $2.2 million

Simpatico

A Fine Line Features release of an Emotion Pictures production in association with Le Canal Plus. Produced by Dan Lupovitz, Timm Oberwelland, Jean-Francois Fonlupt. Executive producers, Sue Baden-Powell, Joel Lubin, Greg Shapiro. Directed by Matthew Warchus. Screenplay, Warchus, David Nicholls, adapted from the play by Sam Shepard. Camera (color), John Toll; editor, Pasquale Buba; music, Stewart Copeland; production designer, Amy Ancona; art director, Andrew Laws. Reviewed at Variety Club screening room, San Francisco, Sept. 7, 1999. (In Toronto Film Festival – Gala.) MPAA Rating: R. Running time: 106 mins.
Nick Nolte (Vinnie), Jeff Bridges (Carter), Sharon Stone (Rosie), Catherine Keener (Cecilia), Albert Finney (Simms), Shawn Hatosy (Young Vinnie), Liam Waite (Young Carter), Kimberly Williams (Young Rosie).
Bedraggled, booze-swilling Vinnie places a call cross-country to wealthy buddy Carter, alleging that he's been arrested for harassment – and vaguely threatening the disclosure of some long-buried mutual secrets if help isn't proffered pronto. A panicked Carter hurriedly flies to the SoCal backwater where he and Vinnie grew up.

The multimillionaire is soon rattled by his erstwhile pal's evasiveness; he's been footing the bill for Vinnie's squalid lifestyle for many years, paying for his silence about a mysterious cachet of "documents" from a racetrack scam in their youthful history that cost a racing commissioner by the name of Simms his career, family, and dignity. Vinnie says he's willing to turn this incriminating evidence over once and for all if Carter gets him off the hook with Cecilia, a fling who has supposedly pressed charges.

An unbeatable cast lends satisfying emotional texture to *Simpatico*, a melancholy comedy adapted by Brit stage vet turned first-time feature helmer Matthew Warchus (with David Nicholls) from Sam Shepard's 1994 play. Determinedly low-key pic, more impressive in its fine-tuned details than overall resonance. *Simpatico* gets a considerable overhaul in its translation here, one that admirably shakes off the stagy artifi-

ciality that dogged previous Shepard legit-to-screen effort.
U.S. release: Dec. 17   U.S. B.O.: $7,234

The Sixth Sense

Buena Vista release of a Hollywood Pictures presentation of a Spyglass Entertainment production. Produced by Frank Marshall, Kathleen Kennedy, Barry Mendel. Executive producer, Sam Mercer. Directed, written by M. Night Shyamalan. Camera (Technicolor), Tak Fujimoto; editor, Andrew Mondshein; music, James Newton Howard. Reviewed at Walt Disney Studios, Burbank, July 21, 1999. MPAA Rating: PG-13. Running time: 107 mins.
Bruce Willis (Malcolm Crowe), Toni Collette (Lynn Sear), Olivia Williams (Anna Crowe), Haley Joel Osment (Cole Sear), Donnie Wahlberg (Vincent Gray), Glenn Fitzgerald (Sean), Mischa Barton (Kyra Collins), Trevor Morgan (Tommy Tammisino), Bruce Norris (Stanley Cunningham).
A terrific last-minute story twist goes a fair way toward redeeming *The Sixth Sense*. Moody, low-key and semi-pretentious effort is ominous without being scary or suspenseful for most of its running time, but the positioning of a child at the center of otherworldly goings-on has worked many times before. Few pictures have hinged their effectiveness so completely upon information withheld until the last moment.

Distinguished child psychologist Dr. Malcolm Crowe takes an interest in eight-year-old Cole Sear, the unusually bright son of sorely taxed single mother Lynn. Cole is a kid obsessed with toy soldiers and religious figures, prone to violent free-association writing, victimized by divorce trauma, able to envision what happened in certain places years before and, most crucial, capable of seeing and hearing the dead. Malcolm wrestles with Cole to open up.

During Cole's treatment, Malcolm's amorous relationship with his wife Anna significantly sours, and he continuously dwells on how to improve their circumstances. Writer-director M. Night Shyamalan keeps the dramatic temperature low throughout, attempting to make mood and state-of-mind the focus of the film but producing a lot of downtime on a moment-by-moment basis. Osment, who played Forrest Gump Jr., is the standout here, evoking with his straight-faced intelligence some exceptional British moppet thesps over the years.
U.S. release: Aug. 6   U.S. B.O.: $276.4 million

Skin of Man, Heart of a Beast

A Why Not Prods./Arte France Cinema production with participation of Canal Plus, Centre National de la Cinematographie. (International sales: Celluloid Dreams, Paris.) Produced by Pascal Caucheteux. Directed by Helene Angel. Screenplay, Angel, Agnes de Sacy, Jean-Claude Janer. Camera (color), Isabelle Razavet; editors, Laurent Rouan, Eric Renault; music, Philippe Miller, Martin Wheler; art director, Mathieu Menut; costume designer, Catherine Rigault; sound (Dolby Digital), Olivier Mauvezin; assistant director, Philippe Larue; casting, Claude Martin. Reviewed at Locarno Film Festival (competing), Aug. 11, 1999. Running time: 98 mins.
Serge Riaboukine (Francky), Bernard Blancan (Coco), Pascal Cervo (Alex), Maaike Jansen (Marthe), Cathy Hinderchied (Aurelie), Virginie Guinand (Christelle), Jean-Louis Richard (Tac Tac), Guilaine Londez (Annie).
French newcomer Helene Angel examines the crushing effect of violence on a family through the eyes of two children.

... June 4 ...
Director-scribe Tom Shadyac signs an exclusive,
three-year overall deal with Touchstone TV.

Unfolding during summer in the rocky hill country of southern France, the story kicks off with the unexpected return to his family of Coco after disappearing 15 years earlier. While they don't entirely swallow his explanation of having joined the Foreign Legion, he is welcomed back by his mother, his younger brother, Alex, and older sibling, Francky, a burly, womanizing cop recently suspended from the force. While helmer and co-writers plant the seeds early of the violence to come, the script slyly diverts anticipation of it to center on Francky, who is given to wild behavioral swings. But the real threat of danger comes from Coco. The adults appear oblivious to his erratic moods and suspicious ways, but his presence in the house unnerves Francky's angry adolescent daughter, while her five-year-old sister responds to Coco's vulnerability with warmth and trust. Often uncomfortable to watch, the film creates a potent climate of fear as the family reunion inches toward tragedy.

Angel's rigorous, unflinching direction and the story's sharply drawn characters make this for the most part an uncommonly mature first feature. Angel's able direction of the two girls gives the film much of its force and some of its most original touches, particularly in the final scenes, when their resilience crumbles.

Sleepy Hollow

A Paramount release of a Paramount and Mandalay Pictures presentation of a Scott Rudin/American Zoetrope production. Produced by Rudin, Adam Schroeder. Executive producers, Francis Ford Coppola, Larry Franco. Co-producer, Kevin Yagher. Directed by Tim Burton. Screenplay, Andrew Kevin Walker, screen story by Kevin Yagher, Walker, based on the story *The Legend of Sleepy Hollow* by Washington Irving. Camera (Deluxe color), Emanuel Lubezki; editor, Chris Lebenzon; music, Danny Elfman. Production designer, Rick Heinrichs. Reviewed at Paramount Studios, L.A., Nov. 11, 1999. MPAA Rating: R. Running time: 105 mins.
Johnny Depp (Ichabod Crane), Christina Ricci (Katrina Van Tassel), Miranda Richardson (Lady Van Tassel/Crone), Michael Gambon (Baltus Van Tassel), Casper Van Dien (Brom Van Brunt), Jeffrey Jones (Reverend Steenwyck), Christopher Lee (Burgomaster), Richard Griffiths (Magistrate Philipse), Ian McDiarmid (Dr Lancaster), Michael Gough (Notary Hardenbrook), Christopher Walken (Hessian Horseman), Marc Pickering (Young Masbath), Lisa Marie (Lady Crane), Steven Waddington (Killian), Claire Skinner (Beth Killian), Alun Armstrong (High Constable), Mark Spalding (Jonathan Masbath), Jessica Oyelowo (Sarah).
Inspired by Washington Irving's classic story about Ichabod Crane and the Headless Horseman; story departs from the original by introducing Crane not as a teacher but a New York City constable who, by the standards of 1799, is overly concerned with forensic evidence and proof in criminal investigations. He is sent to "detect" the murderer in three grisly beheadings in Sleepy Hollow, a Dutch river community. Crane learns the story of the Hessian Horseman, a German mercenary who slew countless settlers with his unerring swordsmanship on behalf of the English during the Revolutionary War. The town elders insist that the Hessian, back in the form of a ghost, is responsible for the murders, in which the killer leaves behind the bodies but makes off with the heads. Pic is structured along the familiar lines of so many filmed murder sprees before it. As a Burton movie and a distinctive period piece, pic sports many unusual flavors and textures that set it apart, but the film is only momentarily ever about anything other than the plot and atmosphere, giving it limited stature and resonance.

Depp is engaging; more than once he must overcome his shock and natural physical timidity to rise to the occasion of battling the indestructible Hessian, and he conveys these swings with grace and wit. Mostly British players fill out the excellent supporting cast. Technically, *Sleepy Hollow* resides on a mountain top.
U.S. release: Nov. 19   U.S. B.O.: $92.8 million

Snow Falling on Cedars

A Universal release of a Harry J. Ufland, Ron Bass and Kennedy/Marshall production. Produced by Kathleen Kennedy, Frank Marshall, Ufland, Bass, Carol Baum, Lloyd A. Silverman. Co-producers, Richard Vane, David Guterson. Directed by Scott Hicks. Screenplay, Ron Bass, Hicks, based on the novel by Guterson. Camera (Alpha Cine Lab color, Panavision widescreen), Robert Richardson; editor, Hank Corwin; music, James Newton Howard; production designer, Jeannine Oppewall; supervising art director, Bill Arnold; art director, Doug Byggdin; set decorator, Jim Erickson; costume designer, Renee Erlich Kalfus; sound (DTS/SDDS/Dolby Digital), Eric Batut; associate producer, Kerry Heysen; assistant director, Katterli Frauenfelder; second unit director, Frank Marshall; second unit camera, Ray Stella; casting, David Rubin. Reviewed at Polygram screening room, Beverly Hills, Sept. 1, 1999. (In Boston Film Festival; Toronto Film Festival – Gala.) MPAA Rating: PG-13. Running time: 126 mins.
Ethan Hawke (Ishmael Chambers), James Cromwell (Judge Fielding), Richard Jenkins (Sheriff Art Moran), James Rebhorn (Alvin Hooks), Sam Shepard (Arthur Chambers), Eric Thal (Carl Heine Jr.), Max von Sydow (Nels Gudmundsson), Youki Kudoh (Hatsue Miyamoto), Rick Yune (Kazuo Miyamoto), Jan Rudes (Ole Jurgensen), Celia Weston (Etta Heine), Max Wright (Horace Whaley), Arija Barbikis (Susan Marie Heine), Zeljko Ivanek (Dr Whitman), Caroline Kava (Helen Chambers), Zak Orth (Deputy Abel Martinson), Cary-Hiroyuki Tagawa (Zenhichi Miyamoto), Daniel von Bargen (Carl Heine Sr.), Reeve Carney (Young Ishmael Chambers), Anne Suzuki (Young Hatsue Imada).
An impeccably crafted but dramatically dull adaptation of David Guterson's international bestseller. Film mixes the melodrama of a murder trial with flashback slices of poignant romantic memory and angst, as small-town newspaperman Ishmael Chambers is slowly revealed to be far from an impartial observer of the courtroom drama. Intent of the yarn is to reveal the whole sociopolitical fabric of a very American yet ethnically mixed community during the now-idealized post-World War II period, but the script follows a yawningly predictable course in the area of social observations.

A local fisherman is found dead off San Piedro Island in Washington. Kazuo Miyamoto, a young Japanese-American and a childhood friend of the deceased, Carl Heine Jr., is charged with murder. The arrest and ensuing trial, which starts on the ninth anniversary of Pearl Harbor, revive painful memories that have barely begun to heal regarding the treatment of the island's long-established Japanese-American community. Flashbacks recount an illicit love affair between Kazuo's wife, Hatsue, and Ishmael Chambers. A possible motive for the murder is established by tracing Kazuo's lingering anger over a betrayal by Heine's mother, who used the wartime internment of Japanese as an excuse to terminate his family's purchase of some farm land.

All the back-and-forthing becomes wearying, and as the trial chugs toward a climax one wants to stick with it rather than continually being jerked back into the past.

U.S. release: Dec. 22   U.S. B.O.: $133,025

South Park: Bigger, Longer, and Uncut

A Paramount/Warner Bros. release, in association with Comedy Central, of a Scott Rudin/Trey Parker/Matt Stone production. Produced by Parker, Stone. Executive producers, Rudin, Adam Schroeder. Co-producers, Anne Garefino, Deborah Liebling. Directed by Trey Parker. Screenplay, Parker, Matt Stone, Pam Brady.

Voices: Trey Parker (Stan Marsh, Eric Cartman, Mr. Garrison, Mr. Hat, Officer Barbrady), Matt Stone (Kyle Broflovski, Kenny McCormick), Mary Kay Bergman (Mrs. Cartman, Sheila Broflovski, Sharon Manson, Mrs. McCormick, Wendy Testaburger), Isaac Hayes (Chef).

With: Jesse Howell, Anthony Cross-Thomas, Francesca Clifford, Bruce Howell, Deb Adair, Jennifer Howell, George Clooney, Brent Spiner, Minnie Driver, Dave Foley, Eric Idle, Nick Rhodes, Toddy E. Walters, Stewart Copeland, Stanley G. Sawicki, Mike Judge.

Cable TV's most objectionable tykes arrive on the silver screen with considerable aplomb. Third-grade Stan, Kyle, Cartman and Kenny are thrilled to discover their TV faves, Canadian fartistes Terrence and Philip, have a movie at the local 'plex. Uh-oh: It's NC-17. This doesn't go down well at school or at home as Kyle's mom spearheads an anti-Canadian agitprop campaign that lands the celebs in U.S. prison for "corruption of youth." Violent Canuck reprisal follows, with all thesping Baldwin brothers the first to be bombed. Soon, both nations are on the brink of fullscale combat. The boys orchestrate La Resistance, a children's underground aimed at preventing North American war and possible biblical apocalypse. Their efforts culminate at a USO show where Terrence and Philip are to be executed.

Nothing is sacred and no humor too lowbrow in the South Park universe. The screenplay ladles out parodic high doses of xenophobia, knee-jerk patriotism, racism, homophobia and whatever else comes to mind. Biggest development is an expansion of the show's "musical" interludes. These rude ditties are fully orchestrated and lavishly "staged" to hilarious impact. It's hard to dismiss arguments that *South Park* is hardly suitable fare for younger audiences incapable of understanding its subtle, offence-allaying ironies. But *Bigger, Longer, and Uncut* will make it harder still to dismiss, or kill, this cultural mini-phenom – not least because the feature is a more clever diversion than anyone had any right to expect.

U.S. release: June 30   U.S. B.O.: $52 million

Star Wars: Episode 1 – The Phantom Menace

A 20th Century Fox release of a Lucasfilm production. Produced by Rick McCallum. Executive producer, George Lucas. Directed, written by Lucas. Camera (Rank (Deluxe) Film Labs U.K. color, Deluxe prints; Panavision widescreen), David Tattersall; editor, Paul Martin Smith; music, John Williams; production designer, Gavin Bocquet; supervising art director, Peter Russell. Reviewed at the UA Union Square, New York, N.Y., May 7, 1999. MPAA Rating: PG. Running time: 133 mins.

Liam Neeson (Qui-Gon Jinn), Ewan McGregor (Obi-Wan Kenobi), Natalie Portman (Queen Amidala), Jake Lloyd (Anakin Skywalker), Pernilla August (Shmi Skywalker), Frank Oz, (Yoda), Ian McDiarmid (Senator Palpatine), Oliver Ford Davies (Sio Bibble), Hugh Quarshie (Captain Panaka), Ahmed Best (Jar Jar Binks), Samuel L. Jackson (Mace Windu), Ray Park (Darth Maul), Peter Serafinowicz (Voice of Darth Maul), Ralph Brown (Ric Olie), Terence Stamp (Chancellor Valorum), Brian Blessed (Boss Nass), Sofia Coppola (Sache).

As the most widely anticipated and heavily hyped film of modern times, it can scarcely help being a letdown on some levels, but it's too bad that it disappoints on so many. At heart a fanciful and fun movie for young boys, the first installment of the three-part prequel to the original *Star Wars* trilogy is neither captivating nor transporting, for it lacks emotional pull, as well as the sense of wonder and awe that marks the best works of sci-fi/fantasy. Pic has far more visual effects than any film ever made. The fake backdrops remind one that this is just a computer-generated version of the sort of ambiance habitually created some 50 to 60 years ago by most Hollywood pictures. The pod race on Tatooine is the film's action/effects highlight: the sci-fi equivalent of *Ben-Hur's* chariot race.

While rescuing the planet Naboo's teenage queen from the oppressive Trade Federation, Jedi Master Qui-Gon Jinn and apprentice Obi-Wan Kenobi become stranded on the desert planet of Tatooine where they encounter a nine-year-old boy named Anakin Skywalker (the future Darth Vader). Anakin makes a profound impression upon Qui-Gon Jinn, who begins to suspect that the boy is the Chosen One, who will one day bring balance to the Force. The Force keeps being mentioned, but its origins, implications and moral guidelines are never explored, other than in the most simplistic good-vs.-evil terms

U.S. release: May 19   U.S. B.O.: $430.4 million

Stigmata

An MGM release of an FGM Entertainment production. Produced by Frank Mancuso Jr. Directed by Rupert Wainwright. Screenplay, Tom Lazarus, Rick Ramage; story by Lazarus. Camera (color), Jeffrey L. Kimball; editors, Michael R. Miller, Michael J. Duthie; music, Billy Corgan, Elia Cmiral; additional music, Mike Garson; executive music producer, Budd Carr; production designer, Waldemar Kalinowski; art director, Anthony Stabley; set decorator, Florence Fellman; costume designer, Louise Frogley; makeup-effects supervisor, Ve Neill; sound editor, Mark Mangini; line producer, Vikki Williams; assistant director, Benjamin Rosenberg; casting, Wendy Kurtzman. Reviewed at Variety Club screening room, San Francisco, Sept. 8, 1999. MPAA Rating: R. Running time: 103 mins.

Patricia Arquette (Frankie Paige), Gabriel Byrne (Father Andrew Kiernan), Jonathan Pryce (Cardinal Daniel Houseman), Nia Long (Donna Chadway), Thomas Kopache (Father Durning), Rade Sherbedgia (Marion Petrocelli), Enrico Colantoni (Father Dario), Dick Latessa (Father Gianni Delmonico), Portia de Rossi (Jennifer Kelliho), Patrick Muldoon (Steven), Ann Cusack (Dr. Reston).

The horror genre hasn't boasted an *Exorcist* knockoff in some

---

...June 6...

Half a century after its Broadway debut, Arthur Miller's **Death of a Salesman** is the big winner at the 53rd annual Tony Awards.

time, and those who've been suffering the lack will get their fix. Aggressively silly, this possession thriller starts out promising a good-time mix of unintentional laughs and visual hyperbole.

De rigueur Third World prolog is set in a Brazilian village, where Vatican investigator Father Kiernan discovers the "miracle" of a blood-weeping Virgin Mary statue and other strange phenomena that have occurred since a local priest died. A thief steals a rosary from said cleric's corpse; the object is purchased at market by an American tourist, who mails it as a souvenir to her daughter. The recipient is Frankie, a larky 23-year-old Pittsburgh beautician-stylist who spends most of her time out clubbing. Soon Frankie is experiencing spooky visions and seizures that leave her mutilated with Christ-on-the-cross wounds. Father Kiernan is dispatched by his antagonistic superior to examine her once the attacks attract media attention.

There's much somber mumbo-jumbo about a supposed "secret gospel" penned by Jesus Christ, and its apparent cover-up by the Catholic Church. But just what power is possessing Frankie, and why, remains muzzy.

That wouldn't be much of a loss if the script provided some decent twists and thrills. But momentum dissipates as little really happens, beyond Frankie's recurrent bloodletting fits and the rather ridiculous mutual attraction between her and Father K. A fiery, convoluted finale fails to deliver any satisfying payoff.

U.S. release: Sept. 10   U.S. B.O.: $50 million

The Straight Story

A Buena Vista release of an Alain Sarde presentation of a Les Films Alain Sarde/Le Studio Canal Plus/Picture Factory production. (International sales: Le Studio Canal Plus, Paris.) Produced by Sarde, Mary Sweeney, Neal Edelstein. Executive producers, Pierre Edelman, Michael Polaire. Directed by David Lynch. Screenplay, John Roach, Mary Sweeney. Camera (FotoKem color, widescreen), Freddie Francis; editor, Sweeney; music, Angelo Badalamenti; production designer, Jack Fisk; costume designer, Patricia Norris. Reviewed at Cannes Film Festival (competing), May 21, 1999. Running time: 111 mins.
Richard Farnsworth (Alvin Straight), Sissy Spacek (Rose), Jane Galloway Heitz (Dorothy), Everett McGill (Tom the Dealer), Jennifer Edwards-Hughes (Brenda), Barbara Robertson (Derr Woman), John Farley (Thorvald), John Lordan (Priest), Harry Dean Stanton (Lyle).

David Lynch's most mature film to date. The bizarre noir sensibility that has informed all of his movies is nowhere to be found in this quiet, emotionally effective family tale of reconciliation. Richard Farnsworth gives a shining performance in a comeback role that's his most poignant since his Oscar-nominated turn in *Comes a Horseman*. Favoring a gentle, starkly simple narrative, Lynch has directed a visionary film that ranks up there with his finest work, *Eraserhead* and *Blue Velvet*. The film feels like Lynch's nostalgic recollection of his own childhood in rural Montana.

Alvin Straight is a 73-year-old widower who lives with his speech-impaired daughter, Rose, in the town of Laurens, Iowa. Stubbornly proud, he refuses to see a doctor, despite rapidly declining health. He learns that his brother Lyle, who he hasn't seen in 10 years due to vanity and drinking, has had a stroke. Alvin determines to visit him in Wisconsin. Since Alvin has no car or driver's licence, the only mode of trans-

port is his shabby lawn mower. First effort to ride the old machine fails, but, unfazed, Alvin buys a 30-year-old John Deere and hits the road again. Structured as a road movie, pic refreshingly lacks the genre's requisite thrills and comic relief. With only three or four stops along the way, and a minimal number of secondary roles, scripters construct a character who can be described as a gentleman cowboy of the old school, a Westerner who lives by a personal code of ethics.

U.S. release: Oct. 15   U.S. B.O.: $4.0 million

Stuart Little

A Sony Pictures Entertainment release of a Columbia Pictures presentation of a Douglas Wick and Franklin/Waterman production. Produced by Wick. Executive producers, Jeff Franklin, Steve Waterman, Jason Clark. Directed by Rob Minkoff. Screenplay, M. Night Shyamalan, Greg Brooker, based on the book by E.B. White. Camera (Deluxe color), Guillermo Navarro; editor, Tom Finan; music, Alan Silvestri; music supervisor, Elliot Lurie; production designer, Bill Brzeski; art director, Philip Toolin; set decorator, Clay A. Griffith; costume designer, Joseph Porro; sound (Dolby Digital), Lawrence H. Mann; animation supervisor, Henry Anderson; senior visual-effects supervisor, John Dykstra; visual-effects supervisor, Jerome Chen; senior visual-effects producer, Michelle Murdocca; special-effects supervisor, Eric Allard; assistant director, Benita Allen-Honess; casting, Debra Zane. Reviewed at Sony Studios, Culver City, Nov. 21, 1999. MPAA Rating: PG. Running time: 92 mins.
Geena Davis (Mrs. Little), Hugh Laurie (Mr. Little), Jonathan Lipnicki (George Little), Brian Doyle-Murray (Cousin Edgar), Estelle Getty (Grandma Estelle), Julia Sweeney (Mrs. Keeper), Dabney Coleman (Dr. Beechwood). Voices: Michael J. Fox (Stuart Little), Nathan Lane (Snowbell), Chazz Palminteri (Smokey), Steve Zahn (Monty), Jim Doughan (Lucky), David Alan Grier (Red), Bruno Kirby (Mr. Stout), Jennifer Tilly (Mrs. Stout).

Given what a tricky proposition it is to adapt a classic children's book for the screen, this take on E.B. White's *Stuart Little* does a more-than-passable job of resurrecting the story for a new generation. Filmmakers have taken a slick, commercial approach to the material that turns White's magical 1945 tale into a labored feelgood movie. Mr. and Mrs. Little trot off to a Gotham adoption agency, promising to bring home a little brother for their son, George. George is less than thrilled when they return with a mouse named Stuart. Even more irked is family feline Snowbell. Mr. Little reminds the cat that Stuart is family, "and we don't eat family members." Appalled, Snowbell's alley-cat pals insist the mouse must go, so they consult feline crime boss Smokey, who brings in a pair of wayward mice to pose as Stuart's long-lost biological parents. Though saddened at Stuart's departure, the Littles feel he'd be better off with his own kind. What they don't know is that his "parents" are part of an elaborate kidnapping scheme. Stuart's desperate attempts to return home make up much of the final act.

In all tech areas *Stuart Little* is top-notch. The digitally rendered title character is thoroughly convincing, with attention paid to the most minute details. The animals, especially the cats, get all the best lines, making the humans seem dull or dimwitted by comparison.

U.S. release: Dec. 17   U.S. B.O.: $79.4 million

... June 7 ...
Harry Enfield, one of the UK's most popular TV comedians, makes the leap into movies with **Kevin and Perry Go Large**.

The Suburbans

An Ignite Entertainment production in association with Motion Picture Corp. of America. Produced by Michael Burns, Brad Krevoy, J.J. Abrams and Leanna Creel. Executive producers, Marc Butan, Tim Foster, George Linardos. Co-producer, John Saviano. Directed by Donal Lardner Ward. Screenplay, Lardner Ward, Tony Guma. Camera (color), Michael Barrett; editor, Kathryn Himoff; music, Robbie Kondor; music supervisors, Lynn Geller, Sue Jacobs; production designer, Susan Bolles; set decorator, Catherine Pierson; costume designer, Pamela Withers; casting, Sheila Jaffe, Georganne Walken. Reviewed at Sundance Film Festival (Premieres), Jan. 25, 1999. Running time: 81 mins.
Craig Bierko (Mitch), Amy Brenneman (Grace), Antonio Fargas (Magee), Will Ferrell (Gil), Tony Guma (Rory), Jennifer Love Hewitt (Cate), Robert Loggia (Jules), Ben Stiller (Jay Rose), Jerry Stiller (Speedo Silverberg), Donal Lardner Ward (Danny), Bridgette Wilson (Lara).

Promising a *Spinal Tap*-like look at an erstwhile '80s New Wave band reuniting for one last chance at glory, *The Suburbans* instead delivers a mediocre ensemble comedy-drama that's not particularly funny, involving or even nostalgic. Opening flashes back to 1981, when big-haired New Wave popsters the Suburbans – Danny, Rory, Mitch and Gil – hit the top of their fame with a guest spot on *American Bandstand*. But the group turned out to be one-hit wonders, and the members each frittered away fortune as well as fame before settling into less-than-satisfying adult careers. Turning up for Gil's wedding, however, the quartet stages an impromptu reunion at the reception. Also in attendance is slinky young record company talent scout Cate, who confesses the Suburbans had been her childhood faves. Before they know what's hit them, the pushing-40 foursome are gearing up for – hopefully – a second world domination. The film isn't a music-biz satire at all, exploring instead the tedious marital strife between Danny and his loving wife.

Hewitt doesn't evince much talent for comedy; other players who assuredly do are given very little to work with. The one bright spot is a couple of scenes featuring Jerry and Ben Stiller as manic father-and-son music moguls. One suspects the Stillers worked up their own material here, and it's on a level that *The Suburbans* might have reached for more often.
U.S. release: October 29   U.S. B.O.: $10,949

Summer of Sam

A Buena Vista release of a Touchstone presentation of a 40 Acres and a Mule Filmworks production. Produced by Jon Kilik, Spike Lee. Executive producers, Michael Imperioli, Jeri Carroll-Colicchio. Directed by Spike Lee. Screenplay, Victor Colicchio, Michael Imperioli, Lee. Camera (Technicolor), Ellen Kuras; editor, Barry Alexander Brown; music, Terence Blanchard; music supervisor, Alex Steyermark; production designer, Therese DePrez; art director, Nicholas Lundy; set decorator, Denise Lunderman; costume designer, Ruth E. Carter; sound (SDDS/Dolby Digital/DTS), Rolf Pardula; assistant director, Mike Ellis; casting, Aisha Coley. Reviewed at Cannes Film Festival (Directors Fortnight), May 20, 1999. Running time: 142 mins.
John Leguizamo (Vinny), Adrien Brody (Ritchie), Mira Sorvino (Dionna), Jennifer Esposito (Ruby), Anthony LaPaglia (Detective Lou Petrocelli), Bebe Neuwirth (Gloria), Patti LuPone (Helen), Ben Gazarra (Luigi), Joe Lisi (Tony Olives), Michael Badalucco (Son of Sam), Michael Rispoli (Joe T.), John Savage (Simon), Roger Guenveur Smith (Detective Curt Atwater), Saverio Guerra (Woodstock), Brian Tarantino (Bobby Del Fiore), Arthur Nascarella (Mario), Jimmy Breslin (As Himself), Al Palagonia (Anthony), Ken Garito (Brian), Mike Starr (Eddie), Spike Lee (John Jeffries).

Lee's long, ambitious picture is rather too forcefully reminiscent of his best film *Do the Right Thing*, in the way it attempts to stir up both the characters' and the audience's simmering rage and anxiety during a sweltering summer exacerbated by adverse incidents.

Sam's killing spree is taking place in the Bronx, and the Italian characters are brought onstage with relative dispatch. Vinny and Dionna are young working-class marrieds whose nightlife shines on the disco floor. However, their marriage is on the rocks. Ritchie shocks his buddies by materializing as a London-style punk rock musician. As Son of Sam achieves infamy, citizens begin staying indoors; brunettes dye their hair blond and wear wigs because the female victims have all had brown hair. Tempers soar with the temperature as a blackout occurs and riots ensue. Tension in the city reaches its peak on July 29, the first anniversary of the initial killing, when the maniac is expected to strike again.

All of the characters are affected by the atmosphere created by the killings, but aren't directly connected to it. This is not David Berkowitz's story, nor is it a police procedural about how he was caught. Partly because of the Italian milieu, and partly because he's clearly trying to supercharge his scenes, this is the closest Lee has yet come to Scorsese territory.
U.S. release: July 2   U.S. B.O.: $19.3 million

Sunshine

An Alliance Atlantis Motion Picture Distribution release (in U.K., Canada) of an Alliance Atlantis Pictures production in association with Kinowelt (Germany), ISL Film (Canada), Dor Film (Austria). (International sales: Alliance Atlantis Pictures Intl., Santa Monica.) Produced by Robert Lantos, Andras Hamori. Executive producers, Rainer Kolmel, Jonathan Debin. Co-producers, Danny Krausz, Lajos Ovari. Directed by Istvan Szabo. Screenplay, Szabo, Israel Horovitz. Camera (color), Lajos Koltai; editors, Dominique Fortin, Michael Arcand; music, Maurice Jarre; set designer, Atilla Kovacs; costume designer, Pedro Moreno; sound (Dolby Digital), Jane Tattersall, Fred Brennan. Reviewed at Toronto Film Festival (Gala), Sept. 13, 1999. Running time: 180 mins.
Ralph Fiennes (Ignatz Sonnenschein/Sors, Adam Sors, Ivan Sors/Sonnenschein), Rosemary Harris (Older Valerie Sors), Rachel Weisz (Greta Sors), Jennifer Ehle (Young Valerie Sonnenschein/Sors), Molly Parker (Hannah Wippler Sors), Deborah Kara Unger (Carola), James Frain (Young Gustave Sonnenschein/Sors), John Neville (Older Gustave Sors), Miriam Margolyes (Rose Sonnenschein), David de Keyser (Emmanuel Sonnenschein), Mark Strong (Istvan Sors), William Hurt (Andor Knorr). With: Bill Paterson, Rudiger Vogler, Hanns Zischler.

Personal epics tinged with universal themes of power, success and patriotism have been the hallmark of fervently Hungarian director Istvan Szabo throughout his Oscar-winning career. Ralph Fiennes in three distinct and dashing period roles, the tale's geopolitical complexity, and a nagging superficiality born of a wearying amount of narrative infor-

---

mation are included at the expense of memorable character development.

Story is divided into three acts beginning in the late 18th century. After his parents' death from an explosion, Emmanuel Sonnenschein (German for sunshine) settles in Budapest, where he marries Rose and parlays a family herbal tonic into a successful business. They have two boys, one of whom, Ignatz, becomes a sucessful Viennese jurist. He later marries cousin Valerie and produces sons Istvan and Adam. Adam takes up Catholicism to further his athletic career. He marries fellow convert Hannah but is seduced by his brother's wife, Greta, who unsuccessfully pleads with him to flee the coming Nazi Holocaust. Adam and Hannah's only son, Ivan, watches the horrible death of his father in a WWII labor camp. Returning to take revenge on the Fascists. Ivan becomes involved in Communist politics. An ill-advised affair with party wife Carola and subsequent prison term lead to a bittersweet epiphany at the family home in Budapest with an older Valerie and Gustave, who have survived the turbulent postwar period to experience the Hungarian Revolution of 1956.

Superstar

A Paramount release presented in association with SNL Studios. Produced by Lorne Michaels. Executive producers, Robert K. Weiss, Susan Cavan. Co-producers, Erin Fraser, Steven Wayne Koren. Directed by Bruce McCulloch. Screenplay, Steven Wayne Koren, based on a character created by Molly Shannon. Camera (Deluxe color), Walt Lloyd; editor, Malcolm Campbell; music, Michael Gore; music supervisor, Elliot Lurie; production designer, Gregory Keen; art director, Peter Grundy; set decorator, Doug McCullough; costume designer, Eydi Caines-Floyd; sound (Dolby Digital), Dan Munro; supervising sound editors, Randle Akerson, David B. Cohn; associate producer, Albert Botha; assistant director, Lisa Campbell; casting, Phyllis Huffman. Reviewed at AMC Kabuki 8, San Francisco, Oct. 6, 1999. MPAA Rating: PG-13. Running time: 82 mins.
Molly Shannon (Mary Katherine Gallagher), Will Ferrell (Sky), Elaine Hendrix (Evian), Harland Williams (Slater), Mark McKinney (Father Ritley), Glynis Johns (Grandma), Emmy Laybourne (Helen).
With infrequent exceptions, movies derived from recurrent *Saturday Night Live* skits have been a reliable source of mediocrity – and the just mildly funny nature of sketches involving Molly Shannon's Mary Katherine Gallagher character didn't suggest her promotion to feature length would break this pattern. But *Superstar* proves a pleasant surprise.

The figure created by Shannon is a pratfall-prone, exuberantly clumsy, hypergeeky 17-year-old with delusions of showbiz grandeur – though her main "talent" consists of delivering melodramatic monologs from 1970s TV movies. Orphaned (her parents, we learn, died in a tragic step-dancing accident) and raised by a grandmother, she applies a usually misguided pluck to every situation at her cliquish Catholic high school.

Mary Katherine's dream is to become a superstar, and to engineer an equally stellar first kiss. Winning the school's talent contest (a Catholic teenage-magazine-sponsored "Let's Fight Venereal Disease" fundraiser) just might clinch that first goal. But the second is complicated by the fact that her chosen dreamboat, campus football star Sky, is already going out with the perfectly blonde, bitchy and bulimic Evian.

Script drop-kicks entertaining spoofs of *Armageddon* and *Carrie*, as well as funny musical numbers amid the well-tuned, slapsticky high-school satire. Invention flags somewhat after the halfway point, but rallies for Mary Katherine's climactic talent-show extravaganza and some good closing gags.
U.S. release: Oct. 8   U.S. B.O.: $30.2 million

Sweet and Lowdown

A Sony Classics release of a Sweetland Films presentation of a Magnolia Prods. production. Produced by Jean Doumanian. Executive producer, J.E. Beaucaire. Co-executive producers, Jack Rollins, Charles H. Joffe, Letty Aronson. Co-producer, Richard Brick. Directed, written by Woody Allen. Camera (Du Art, Technicolor prints), Zhao Fei; editor, Alisa Lepselter; music, Dick Hyman; production designer, Santo Loquasto; art director, Tom Warren; costume designer, Laura Cunningham Bauer; sound, Les Lazarowitz; assistant director, Richard Patrick; casting, Juliet Taylor, Laura Rosenthal. Reviewed at Venice Film Festival (noncompeting), Sept. 5, 1999. (Also in Toronto Film Festival – Gala.) Running time: 95 mins.
Sean Penn (Emmet Ray), Samantha Morton (Hattie), Uma Thurman (Blanche), Brian Markinson (Bill Shields), Anthony LaPaglia (Al Torrio), Gretchen Mol (Ellie), Vincent Guastaferro (Sid Bishop), John Waters (Mr. Haynes), Constance Schulman (Hazel), Kellie Overbey (Iris), James Urbaniak (Harry), Mark Damon Johnson (Omer), Darryl Alan Reed (Don), Dick Monday (Chester Weems).
A wonderful showcase for presenting some of the great jazz standards the helmer loves so much, pic is a fascinating insight into a vaunting, egotistical, fast lane, amoral character who justifies his actions with the fact that he's an artist – one who loves his guitar more than any human being. Emmet Ray was a little-known jazz guitarist who flourished briefly in the '30s, and is considered by jazz aficionados to be second only to the great Django Reinhardt. This is the second time (after *Zelig*) that Allen has tackled a fictional character's bio. Relayed as a series of reminiscences by a group of real-life jazz experts, pic has the showbiz feel of *Broadway Danny Rose*.

Ray's dealings with women are shabby – he's a self-confessed love-'em-and-leave-'em type who thinks he's a great lover. He finds himself touched by Hattie, a mute, orphaned laundress. We soon learn he's walked out on her and married Blanche, a sultry, elegant writer. It's a mismatch from the start, and Ray trails his wife during her liaisons with a gangster. Ray realizes his mistake with Hattie, giving the film a sweetly melancholic arc.

This is a film in which the usual Allen one-liners are deliberately in short supply. There are occasional jokes and a couple of slapstick sequences, but generally the mood is reflected by the film's apt title. Penn is in formidable form, and Morton and Thurman make beautiful turns as the women in his life.
U.S. release: Dec. 3   U.S. B.O.: $867,523

The Talented Mr. Ripley

A Paramount release of a Paramount Pictures and Miramax Films presentation of a Mirage Enterprises/Timnick Films production. Produced by William Horberg, Tom Sternberg. Executive producer, Sydney Pollack. Co-producer, Paul Zaentz. Directed, written by Anthony Minghella, based on the novel by Patricia Highsmith. Camera (Deluxe color), John Seale; editor, Walter Murch; music, Gabriel Yared; music supervisor, Graham Walker; production designer, Roy Walker; supervising art director, John Fenner; art director, Stefano Ortolani; set decorator, Bruno Cesari; costume designers, Ann Roth, Gary Jones; sound (Dolby Digital/DTS), Ivan Sharrock; supervising sound editor, Pat Jackson; line producer, Alessandro von Normann; associate producer/assistant director, Steve Andrews; casting, David Rubin. Reviewed at Paramount Studios, L.A., Dec. 9, 1999. MPAA Rating: R. Running time: 139 mins.

Matt Damon (Tom Ripley), Gwyneth Paltrow (Marge Sherwood), Jude Law (Dickie Greenleaf), Cate Blanchett (Meredith Logue), Philip Seymour Hoffman (Freddie Miles), Jack Davenport (Peter Smith-Kingsley), James Rebhorn (Herbert Greenleaf), Sergio Rubini (Inspector Roverini), Philip Baker Hall (Alvin MacCarron), Celia Weston (Aunt Joan), Rosario Fiorello (Fausto), Stefania Rocca (Silvana), Ivano Marescotti (Colonnello Verrecchia), Anna Longhi (Signora Buffi), Alessandro Fabrizi (Sergeant Baggio), Lisa Eichhorn (Emily Greenleaf).

Pic centers around attractive, moneyed expat Americans on the loose in the enticing Italy of the late '50s – a world that is appealing to Tom Ripley, a nice, well-spoken, bespectacled kid from New York who's paid by shipbuilding tycoon Herbert Greenleaf to fetch back his son, Dickie, who has been spending his considerable allowance at a rapid pace in Europe. Tom manages to ingratiate himself with Dickie and his writer girlfriend, Marge. He becomes a "double agent," pretending to try to bring the young man home to Mr. Greenleaf but happily sharing in the money he supplies.

On a final boat ride, however, Dickie suddenly erupts, insulting Tom. Tom hits Dickie with an oar, thinking nothing of finishing off the friend he has envied and obsessed over since he arrived in Italy. Tom soon assumes the identity (and bank account) of Dickie.

After Tom is forced to deal with the police investigation, the film starts losing its special quality; it begins being led by the plot and becomes beholden to intricate procedural details, which pushes it into more conventional territory than it has inhabited up to this point.

Unfortunately, the film doesn't end where it should, on a note of ambiguous alarm, instead moving on to a rather unsatisfactory conclusion. Crime dramas like this have generally come to be approached these days in a neo-noirish style, but Minghella takes a gratifyingly nongenre tack, working boldly in a full-bodied dramatic and visual manner that does not pigeonhole the material. Performances are aces top to bottom.
U.S. release: Dec. 25   U.S. B.O.: $39.8 million

Tarzan

A Buena Vista release of a Walt Disney presentation. Produced by Bonnie Arnold. Directed by Kevin Lima, Chris Buck. Screenplay, Tab Murphy, Bob Tzudiker, Noni White, based on the story *Tarzan And The Apes* by Edgar Rice Burroughs. Additional screenplay material, David Reynolds, Jeffrey Stepakoff. Technicolor; editor, Gregory Perler; songs, Phil Collins; score, Mark Mancina; executive music producer, Chris Montan; art director, Daniel St. Pierre; story artistic supervisor, Brian Pimental; layout supervisor, Jean Christophe Poulain; backgrounds supervisor, Doug Ball; clean-up supervisor, Marshall Lee Toomey; visual-effects supervisor, Peter De-Mund; computer-graphics supervisor, Eric Daniels; supervising animator (Tarzan), Glen Keane;

supervising digital background painter, David McCamley; supervising sound editor (Dolby Digital/SDDS/DTS), Per Hallberg; associate producer, Christopher Chase; casting, Ruth Lambert, Mary Hidalgo. Reviewed at Harmony Gold, L.A., June 1, 1999. MPAA Rating: G. Running time: 88 mins.

Voices: Brian Blessed (Clayton), Glenn Close (Kala), Minnie Driver (Jane), Tony Goldwyn (Tarzan), Nigel Hawthorne (Professor Porter), Lance Henriksen (Kerchak), Wayne Knight (Tantor), Alex D. Linz (Young Tarzan), Rosie O'Donnell (Terk).

Tarzan swings, even if it doesn't always soar. Stranded in Africa after a shipwreck and deprived of his parents by a hungry leopard, the infant Tarzan is rescued by female gorilla, Kala, who raises him as her own son. Little Tarzan receives plenty of ribbing from the ape kids for his relative lack of strength and agility. But the "freaky" one soon learns the ropes, and vines. The unspoiled verdant playground is punctured by a party of late-Victorian Brits including the Professor Porter, his spirited daughter Jane, and muscular white hunter Clayton. The first two seem keen to study gorillas, while Clayton's intentions are more threatening and ambiguous. The visitors begin teaching the curious Tarzan about civilization, and the well-behaved wild man begins sensing that Jane may be of interest to him. Some major action leads to a mixed-bag climax involving satisfying revenge, inevitable tragedy and an overly pat happy ending.

Film is intelligently structured and balanced dramatically, and thematic concerns regarding the unavoidable conflict between human society and nature have been shrewdly focused. Use of Collins' songs as a background to the story, rather than as singing numbers works well. Animation work is richly detailed and colorfully conceived, but the computer animation and graphics are often intermingled and combined in ways that are more distracting in their differences than helpful in their vividness. A "thrill ride" approach to action sequences is part of the film's tendency toward overkill.
U.S. release: June 16   U.S. B.O.: $171 million

Tea With Mussolini

(A UIP (in U.K.)/MGM (in U.S.) release of a Medusa Film/Universal Pictures presentation of a Medusa Film, Cattleya, Cineritmo (Rome)/Film & General Prods. (London) production. Produced by Riccardo Tozzi, Giovannella Zannoni, Clive Parsons. Directed by Franco Zeffirelli. Screenplay, John Mortimer, Zeffirelli, based on *The Autobiography of Franco Zeffirelli*. Camera (Cinecitta color), David Watkin; editor, Tariq Anwar; music, Alessio Vlad, Stefano Arnaldi; art directors, Carlo Centolavigna, Gioia Fiorella Mariani; costume designers, Jenny Beavan, Alberto Spiazzi, Anna Anni; sound (Dolby Digital/DTS Stereo), Brian Simmons; associate producer, Pippo Pisciotto; assistant directors, Pisciotto, Roberto Tatti; casting, Emma Style. Reviewed at Plaza 1, London, March 5, 1999. Running time: 116 mins.

Cher (Elsa), Judi Dench (Arabella), Joan Plowright (Mary), Maggie Smith (Hester), Lily Tomlin (Georgie), Baird Wallace (Luca, as a teenager), Charlie Lucas (Luca, as a child), Massimo Ghini (Paolo), Paolo Seganti (Vittorio), Paul Checquer (Wilfred), Tessa Pritchard (Connie), Mino Bellei (Cesare), Claudio Spadaro (Mussolini).

Much tea is consumed but little sympathy evoked in helmer's semi-autobiographical piece. There are some fine individual

---

. . . June 10 . . .

The American Film Institute unveiled its "100 Years...100 Stars" list. Humphrey Bogart and Katharine Hepburn prove America's greatest male and female screen legends.

performances, plus fine period details, but film suffers from a fatal lack of focus and emotional center, reducing potentially involving material to a succession of individual scenes. Where Zeffirelli's alter ego, here called Luca, should provide emotional continuity and a sense of perspective on the bizarre community, he becomes little more than a bystander as the various distaff leads walk in and out of the spotlight.

Spanning 10 years, story starts in Florence in 1935 when cultured Brits were enamored with Italy and Mussolini. Luca is a bastardized, local kid who is taken in by Mary, an Englishwoman. Her circle of elderly Brit friends – dubbed "the scorpions" for their tart wit and snobbish manners – rally round to take care of Luca. With the entrance of Elsa, a rich American collector on a swing through Italy, the film agreeably broadens beyond just a portrait of English eccentrics. Script's episodic structure starts to become apparent, leading to Smith's aristocrat landing a personal "tea" with Mussolini. She wants Benito's personal assurance that they are in no danger from Fascist gangs. Luca is sent to Austria for a "German education," and pic soon leaps to 1940, the war, the women's internment in San Gimignano, and a manufactured climax as the Jewish Elsa is smuggled out of the country.

U.S. release: May 14   U.S. B.O.: $14.4 million

The Thin Red Line
A 20th Century Fox release of a Fox 2000 Pictures presentation from Phoenix Pictures in association with George Stevens Jr. of a Geisler/Roberdeau production. Produced by Robert Michael Geisler, John Roberdeau, Grant Hill. Executive producer, Stevens. Directed, written by Terrence Malick, based on the novel by James Jones. Camera (Atlab color, Technicolor prints; Panavision widescreen), John Toll; editors, Billy Weber, Leslie Jones, Saar Klein; music, Hans Zimmer; production designer, Jack Fisk; art director, Ian Gracie; set decorators, Richard Hobbs, Suza Maybury; costume designer, Margot Wilson; sound (Dolby Digital), Paul "Salty" Brincat; supervising sound editor, J. Paul Huntsman; key military adviser, Mike Stokey; stunt coordinator, Glenn Boswell; associate producers, Michael Stevens, Sheila Davis Lawrence; assistant director, Skip Cosper; second unit director, Gary Capo; casting, Dianne Crittenden. Reviewed at Warner Hollywood Studios, L.A., Dec. 17, 1998. MPAA Rating: R. Running time: 170 mins.
Sean Penn (First Sgt. Edward Welsh), Adrien Brody (Corporal Fife), Jim Caviezel (Private Witt), Ben Chaplin (Private Bell), George Clooney (Captain Charles Bosche), John Cusack (Captain John Gaff), Woody Harrelson (Sergeant Keck), Elias Koteas (Captain James "Bugger" Staros), Jared Leto (Second Lieutenant Whyte), Dash Mihok (Pfc. Doll), Tim Blake Nelson (Private Tills), Nick Nolte (Lieutenant Colonel Gordon Tall), John C. Reilly (Sergeant Storm), Larry Romano (Private Mazzi), John Savage (Sergeant McCron), John Travolta (Brigadier General Quintard), Arie Verveen (Pfc. Dale), David Harrod (Corporal Queen), Tom Jane (Private Ash), Polyn Leona (Melanesian Woman with Child), Miranda Otto (Marty Bell).
Terrence Malick's much-anticipated return after a 20-year hiatus is a complex, highly talented work marked by intellectual and philosophical ambitions. Helmer has made it back with a picture that bears many of his trademark touches, as well as a scope far beyond anything he's done before. Malick's

forte was always for fabulous visuals and haunting moods rather than for coherent storytelling.

The first characters to come to the fore are Pvt. Witt, one of the AWOL soldiers and First Sgt. Welsh, the cynical everyman-for-himself leader of Charlie Company, an Army infantry outfit being sent to replace Marines in the invasion of Japanese-held Guadalcanal. The troop ship is loaded with soldiers, anxious about what awaits them on the island. There are no real character arcs, and as a result, no truly rounded performances. Just as in Malick's previous films, the full meaning of pic is realized only in the numerous, extensive voiceover commentaries. Many of these consist of elemental rhetorical queries into the spiritual bearings of the universe.

Surprised to encounter no initial resistance on the island, the Americans are forced to pursue the Japanese up toward their positions in the hills, resulting in some fierce action, loads of casualties and a resulting refusal by Capt. Staros to obey what he views as Lt. Col. Tall's suicidal order to take one hill by frontal assault. Structurally the film is decidedly lumpy, with confrontations and climaxes coming and going abruptly, and a final 45 minutes in which the dramatic momentum slides noticeably downhill.

U.S. release: Dec. 1998   U.S. B.O.: $36 million

The Third Miracle
A Sony Pictures Classics release of a Franchise Pictures presentation of an American Zoetrope and Haft Entertainment production. Produced by Fred Fuchs, Steven Haft, Elie Samaha. Executive producers, Francis Ford Coppola, Ashok Amritraj, Andrew Stevens. Co-producer, Don Carmody. Directed by Agnieszka Holland. Screenplay, John Romano, Richard Vetere, based on the novel by Vetere. Camera (Deluxe Toronto prints), Jerzy Zielinski; editor, David J. Siegel; music, Jan A.P. Kaczmarek; production designer, Robert De Vico; art director, Andrew M. Stearn; costume designer, Denise Cronenberg; sound (Dolby Digital), Peter Shewchuk; special-effects coordinator, Michael Kavanagh; associate producers, Lisa Wilson, Judi Farkas, Daryl Sancton, Siegel; assistant director, Andrew Shea; casting, Todd Thaler, Clare Walker. Reviewed at Toronto Film Festival (Special Presentation), Sept. 12, 1999. Running time: 119 mins.
Ed Harris (Frank Shore), Anne Heche (Roxane), Armin Mueller-Stahl (Archbishop Werner), Charles Haid (Bishop Cahill), Michael Rispoli (John Leone), James Gallanders (Brother Gregory), Jean-Louis Roux (Cardinal Sarrazin), Ken James (Father Paul Panak), Caterina Scorsone (Maria Witkowski), Barbara Sukowa (Helen). With: Bob Jarvis, Ned Vukovic, Jade Smith, Monique Mojica, Aron Tager, Norma Dell'Agnese, Steve Ferguson, Mark Huisman, Rodger Barton.
Lofty concepts such as loss of faith and 20th-century belief in religious phenomena receive an interesting but far-from-exhaustive workout in *The Third Miracle*, a dramatically uneven pic. Story centers in Chicago 1979, where washed-up priest Frank Shore is taken to meet his old boss, Bishop Cahill, a smooth power-player in the Catholic Church. Shore is a professional postulator – an investigator into reported miracles – who's still burned by an earlier case.

Cahill puts him in charge of a preliminary report on the late Helen O'Regan, an Austrian-born immigrant said to have performed miracles. Her statue is claimed to weep blood on each anniversary of her death. A cult is already building around the woman, and pressing for official sainthood. The movie starts to gain dramatic shape when Shore and Helen's atheistic daughter Roxane ignite a mutual passion and he decides to recommend to Rome that sainthood be conferred upon Helen after witnessing the statue weep blood. Shore's report leads to an official tribunal, at which he's violently opposed by the powerful Archbishop Werner before new evidence is unearthed in Europe by Gregory.

Mueller-Stahl's entrance halfway in puts some badly needed oomph into a picture that thus far has been solidly acted but extremely unfocused. Strongest stuff comes in the final 40 minutes, as the tribunal convenes and the dialog becomes sharper, the arguments crystallize into a series of faceoffs between Shore and Werner.

U.S. release: Dec. 29   U.S. B.O.: $41,549

The Thomas Crown Affair

An MGM release of an Irish DreamTime production. Produced by Pierce Brosnan, Beau St. Clair. Executive producer, Michael Tadross. Co-producer, Roger Paradiso. Directed by John McTiernan. Screenplay, Leslie Dixon, Kurt Wimmer; story, Alan R. Trustman. Camera (Technicolor, Deluxe prints; Panavision widescreen), Tom Priestley; editor, John Wright; music, Bill Conti. Reviewed at MGM screening room, Santa Monica, July 16, 1999. MPAA Rating: R. Running time: 111 mins.

Pierce Brosnan (Thomas Crown), Rene Russo (Catherine Banning), Denis Leary (Detective Michael McCann), Ben Gazzara (Andrew Wallace), Frankie Faison (Detective Paretti), Fritz Weaver (John Reynolds), Charles Keating (Golchan), Mark Margolis (Knutzhorn), Faye Dunaway (The Psychiatrist).

This redo of Norman Jewison's 1968 Steve McQueen hit is an ultrasleek and slick thriller that attempts to justify its existence by shifting the focus from the caper elements to the psychological and emotional factors that compel two hard-shelled professional adversaries to risk a romantic entanglement.

Rich playboy tycoon Thomas Crown is a self-made man who's got it all but can never imagine settling down with one woman because he simply can't trust anyone; what works for him in business is anathema to deep personal involvement. Crown pulls an extraordinary theft of a $100 million Monet from New York's Metropolitan Museum of Art. Insurance company investigator Catherine Banning is positive that Crown is the culprit, and the sultry femme has no qualms about using any means necessary to land her prey. Like her elegant foe, Catherine is quite a hard case; she's undoubtedly snared many men in this same manner over the years, and is perhaps both proud and weary of the fact that she can no longer find one who is her equal. Crown and Catherine suspect they might have met their match in the other. The twists and turns of their relationship are not without interest, especially because of Russo's handling of her part. Lack of detailed characterization is hardly a fatal flaw in this sort of genre piece, but the absence is especially noticeable in light of the story's heightened attention to the nuances of the central romance.

U.S. release: August 6   U.S. B.O.: $69.3 million

Three Kings

A Warner Bros. release presented in association with Village Roadshow Pictures/Village-A.M Film Partnership of a Coast Ridge Films/Atlas Entertainment production. Produced by Charles Roven, Paul Junger Witt, Edward L. McDonnell. Executive producers, Gregory Goodman, Kelley Smith-Wait, Bruce Berman. Co-producers, Douglas Segal, Kim Roth, John Ridley. Directed, written by David O. Russell, story by John Ridley. Camera (Technicolor, Panavision widescreen), Newton Thomas Sigel; editor, Robert K. Lambert; music, Carter Burwell; music supervisor, Ralph Sall; production designer, Catherine Hardwicke; supervising art director, Derek R. Hill; art director, Jann Engel; set decorator, Gene Serdena; costume designer, Kym Barrett; sound (Dolby Digital/DTS/SDDS), Edward Tise; supervising sound editors, Bruce Fortune, John Leveque; associate producer, Alan G. Glazer; assistant director, Julian Wall; second unit director-stunt coordinator, Dan Bradley; second unit camera, Phil Pfeiffer; casting, Mary Vernieu, Anne McCarthy. Reviewed at Warner Bros. Studios, Burbank, Sept. 20, 1999. MPAA Rating: R. Running time: 115 mins.

George Clooney (Archie Gates), Mark Wahlberg (Troy Barlow), Ice Cube (Chief Elgin), Spike Jonze (Conrad Vig), Nora Dunn (Adriana Cruz), Jamie Kennedy (Walter Wogaman), Mykelti Williamson (Colonel Horn), Cliff Curtis (Amir Abdulah), Said Taghmaoui (Captain Said), Judy Greer (Cathy Daitch), Liz Stauber (Debbie Barlow), Holt McCallany (Captain Van Meter).

A Hollywood take on the Gulf War, *Three Kings* does so in an impudently comic, stylistically aggressive and, finally, very thoughtful manner.

It's March 1991, Saddam Hussein is thrown out of Kuwait and a ceasefire has begun. Special Forces Captain Archie Gates, due to retire in two weeks, discovers that three G.I.s have a map that seems to identify the location of an enormous stash of gold bullion snatched from Kuwait by Saddam's army. Gates has no trouble overcoming the younger men's moral scruples about theft merely by mentioning the identity of the man who stole it first, and how it can enhance their postwar lives. Gates leads them to take possession of the bullion. But the four men encounter a confusing situation at their destination. Welcomed with open arms by the Iraqi civilians, who have been encouraged by President Bush to believe that their efforts to overthrow Saddam will receive U.S. support, the soldiers treat them brusquely in their single-minded quest to grab the gold. In the event, the Americans need the locals' help in loading the bullion, and when Iraqi soldiers intervene, they ignore the Yanks and concentrate on the native "rebels" opposed to the dictator.

No Hollywood film in memory has addressed the amorality of American foreign policy, but the sobering final impression here is that, unless the world's most powerful country defines what it stands for, it will stand for nothing other than the threat of brute force and economic coercion.

U.S. release: Oct. 1   U.S. B.O.: $59.2 million

Three Seasons

An October Films release of an Open City Films production. Produced by Jason Kliot, Joana Vicente, Tony Bui. Executive producer, Harvey Keitel. Co-executive producer, Charles Rosen. Co-producer, Timothy Linh Bui. Directed, written by Tony Bui, based on a story by Tony Bui, Timothy Linh Bui. Don Duong (Hai), Nguyen Ngoc Hiep (Kien An), Tran Manh Cuong (Teacher Dao), Harvey Keitel (James Hager), Zoe Bui (Lan), Nguyen Huu Duoc (Woody), Diem Kieu

---

... June 12 ...
Sotheby's is offering the gold-plated statuette (David O. Selznick's 1939 Best Picture Oscar for **Gone With the Wind**) for auction in New York.

(Singing Lotus Woman), Bui Tuong Trac (Man who buys Lotus Flowers).

If looks were everything, the film would rate unqualified raves. Unfortunately, there's precious little to gnaw in the way of text and subtext once you've ogled the visuals. Pic's historic place sits as the first American indie to be shot in Vietnam with native actors. Pic follows interlocking fortunes of five characters: a young flowergirl, Kien An, a street urchin named Woody, a cyclo-driver named Hai, an ex-Marine named Hager, and a self-deluding prostitute named Lan.

Kien takes a job tending and harvesting lotus blossoms at the mysterious Teacher Dao's seemingly abandoned temple. Dao, coping with advanced leprosy, eventually asks the curious Kien to become his hands and take down dictated poems. Cyclo-driver Hai helps Lan escape an unhappy client and then becomes her slavish admirer, neglecting business to shuttle her between tricks. Hai gathers the necessary cash to graduate from lovesick puppy to client by winning a conveniently provided cyclo race. The street gamin wanders the rain-soaked alleys searching for his stolen merchandise case. He thinks the American has taken it, but the American has his own mission: he's searching for the daughter he never knew.

Plot's many contrivances and cliches can almost be forgiven because they're served up with such wide-eyed wonder by Bui. Helmer was obviously on a real-life quest: to rediscover his homeland.

U.S. release: Apr. 30   U.S. B.O.: $2 million

Titus

A Fox Searchlight Pictures release (in U.S.) of a Fox Searchlight and Clear Blue Sky Prods. presentation, in association with Overseas Filmgroup, of a Urania Pictures and NDF Intl. production. (International sales: Overseas Filmgroup, L.A.) Produced by Jody Patton, Conchita Airoldi, Julie Taymor. Executive producer, Paul G. Allen. Co-executive producers, Ellen Little, Robbie Little, Stephen K. Bannon. Co-producers, Adam Leipzig, Michiyo Yoshizaki. Directed, written by Julie Taymor, based on the play *Titus Andronicus* by William Shakespeare. Camera (Deluxe color, widescreen), Luciano Tovoli; editor, Francoise Bonnot; music, Elliot Goldenthal; production designer, Dante Ferretti; supervising art director, Pier Luigi Basile; art directors, Massimo Razzi, Domenico Sica; set decorator, Carlo Gervasi; costume designer, Milena Canonero; sound (Dolby Digital), David Stephenson; supervising sound editor/sound designer, Blake Leyh; visual-effects supervisor, Kent Houston; associate producer, Karen L. Thorson; co-associate producers, Mark D. Bisgeier; Brad Moseley; assistant directors, Antonio Brandt, Guy Travers; casting, Irene Lamb, Ellen Lewis. Reviewed at 20th Century Fox Studios, L.A., Dec. 8, 1999. MPAA Rating: R. Running time: 162 mins.

Anthony Hopkins (Titus Andronicus), Jessica Lange (Tamora), Alan Cumming (Saturninus), Colm Feore (Marcus), James Frain (Bassianus), Laura Fraser (Lavinia), Harry Lennix (Aaron), Angus Macfadyen (Lucius), Matthew Rhys (Demetrius), Jonathan Rhys-Meyers (Chiron), Kenny Doughty (Quintus), Osheen Jones (Young Lucius), Blake Ritson (Mutius),Colin Wells (Martius), Geraldine McEwan (Nurse).

Theatrical wizard Julie Taymor strides boldly into the feature film arena and emerges with a conditional victory. Gutsily

grappling with one of Shakespeare's least performed and most gruesomely melodramatic plays, the lauded director of Broadway's *The Lion King* makes this wild tale of a savage cycle of revenge in imperial Rome accessible and exceedingly vivid. Distinguished by some outstanding thesping and an arresting stylistic approach that successfully mixes ancient, '30s Fascist and modern motifs.

In 400 A.D., a nocturnal ceremony marks the return to Rome of the great general Titus Andronicus, who has spent years in the north fighting the Goths and has triumphantly returned with a prized prisoner, their beautiful queen, Tamora. A proud military man who has lost all but four of his 25 sons in battle, Titus insists upon enacting a religious ritual of executing one of his prisoners, and sets the bloody ball rolling by selecting Tamora's eldest son for the sacrifice. Although her present circumstances prevent it, the enraged Tamora vows revenge, and she is soon afforded the opportunity to pursue it when she unexpectedly becomes the wife of Rome's new emperor, the shifty and impetuous Saturninus.

Taymor pushes through all this twisted scene-setting with a muscular, confident attitude. One observes this heartwarming tale of family togetherness with a certain perverse fascination as the characters continue on their paths of deceit, butchery and, in the case of Titus, feigned madness. The aging general's personal revenge against Tamora is, in a word, delicious, as he serves her and Saturninus a meal that would do Hannibal Lecter proud.

U.S. release: Dec. 25   U.S. B.O.: $86,328

Topsy-Turvy

An October Films (in U.S.)/Pathe Films (in U.K.) release of a Thin Man Films Ltd./The Greenlight Fund/Newmarket Capital Group production. (International sales: United Artists Films.) Produced by Simon Channing-Williams. Directed, written by Mike Leigh. Camera (color), Dick Pope; editor, Robin Sales; music, Carl Davis, based on operas by Arthur Sullivan; musical director, Gary Yershon; production designer, Eve Stewart; costume designer, Lindy Hemming; associate producer, Georgina Lowe; assistant director, Nick Heckstall-Smith. Reviewed at Venice Film Festival (competing), Sept. 2, 1999. (Also in New York, London film festivals.) Running time: 160 mins.

Jim Broadbent (W.S. Gilbert), Allan Corduner (Arthur Sullivan), Lesley Manville (Lucy Gilbert), Eleanor David (Fanny Ronalds), Ron Cook (Richard D'Oyly Carte), Timothy Spall (Richard Temple), Kevin McKidd (Lely), Martin Savage (Grossmith), Shirley Henderson (Leonora Braham), Jessie Bond (Dorothy Atkinson), Wendy Nottingham (Helen Lenoir).

A candidate for the most offbeat of all composer biopics, Mike Leigh's first costumer details exhaustively the artistic partnership of comic-opera team Gilbert and Sullivan and the making of their evergreen *The Mikado*. After 160 minutes full of entertaining acting, barbed Victorian wit and a generous sample of lavishly staged numbers, this loving salute tends to lose dramatic focus in sheer historical detail.

A surprising project for Brit helmer Leigh, a master of intimate British drama, film exudes affection for and identification with its night-and-day artist-heroes, lyricist W.S. Gilbert, irascible but as emotionless as a colonial general, and the expansive, pleasure-loving composer Sir Arthur Sullivan, a European sophisticate pining to write serious opera. Gilbert's

---

inability to express the slightest feeling for his loving wife, Lucy, or his elderly father, given to hallucinations, makes him the less appealing of the two. The conflict between the two men gives the first hour its impetus and interest, lit up with a galaxy of characters gracefully and wittily revolving around them. Several musical numbers introduce the cast of actor-singers, who will be neatly individualized in pic's second half.

Leigh's affectionate sympathy for ordinary people, a hallmark of his movies, comes out in thumbnail portraits of the opera cast. Thesps sing all their own numbers with great showmanship. A consistently persuasive cast keeps pic alive and relevant to their modern-day stage and film descendants.
U.S. release: Dec. 17   U.S. B.O.: $158,696

Toy Story 2

A Buena Vista Pictures release of a Walt Disney Pictures presentation of a Pixar Animation Studios film. Produced Helene Plotkin, Karen Robert Jackson. Executive producer, Sarah McArthur. Directed by John Lasseter. Co-directors, Lee Unkrich, Ash Brannon. Screenplay, Andrew Stanton, Rita Hsiao, Doug Chamberlin, Chris Webb, original story by Lasseter, Pete Docter, Brannon, Stanton. Camera (Monaco Labs color, Technicolor prints), Sharon Calahan; editors, Edie Bleiman, David Ian Salter, Unkrich; music, Randy Newman. Reviewed at the El Capitan Theater, L.A., Nov. 6, 1999. MPAA Rating: G. Running time: 92 mins.
Voices: Tom Hanks (Woody), Tim Allen (Buzz Lightyear), Joan Cusack (Jessie), Kelsey Grammer (Stinky Pete the Prospector), Don Rickles (Mr. Potato Head), Jim Varney (Slinky Dog), Wallace Shawn (Rex), John Ratzenberger (Hamm), Annie Potts (Bo Peep), Wayne Knight (Al McWhiggin), John Morris (Andy), Laurie Metcalf (Andy's Mom), Estelle Harris (Mrs. Potato Head), R. Lee Ermey (Sarge), Jodi Benson (Barbie), Jonathan Harris (The Cleaner), Joe Ranft (Wheezy), Andrew Stanton (Emperor Zurg), Jeff Pidgeon (Aliens).
In the realm of sequels, *Toy Story 2* is to *Toy Story* what *The Empire Strikes Back* was to its predecessor, a richer, more satisfying film in every respect. John Lasseter and his team have conspired to vigorously push the new entry further with fresh characters, broadened scope, boisterous humor and, most of all, a gratifying emotional and thematic depth.

A broken arm causes cowboy doll Woody to be left behind by his owner Andy in the outside world. He winds up in the shop of greedy toy collector Al McWhiggin. There, Woody meets cowgirl Jessie (who later tugs at his heart), Stinky Pete the Prospector and a horse named Bullseye and, in a wonderfully entertaining interlude, learns of his long-ago celebrity on a show called *Woody's Roundup*, a kids' favorite in which Woody and his new acquaintances were puppets. Al's impressive collection of memorabilia was incomplete without Woody, and now he plans to cash in by selling the whole set to a museum in Japan. Locked in a high-rise room, there is nothing Woody can do to save himself, so it's up to spaceman Buzz Lightyear and Andy's other toy figures to rescue him.

A sense of spirited invention permeates the proceedings from top to bottom, and few films so thoroughly deliver the feeling that everyone connected to it was united in pursuit of a single goal and had matchless fun reaching it.
U.S. release: Nov. 19   U.S. B.O.: $208.9 million

Trick

A Fine Line (domestic) and Good Machine (international) release of a Roadside Attraction and Good Machine production. Produced by Eric d'Arbeloff, Jim Fall, Ross Katz. Executive producers, Anthony Bregman, Mary Jane Skalski, Mark Beigelman. Co-producer, Robert Hawk. Directed by Fall. Screenplay, Jason Schafer.
Christian Campbell (Gabriel), John Paul Pitoc (Mark), Tori Spelling (Katherine), Steve Hayes (Perry), Kevin Chamberlin (Perry's Ex), Brad Beyer (Rich), Lorri Bagley (Judy).
Trick is the most appealing and most erotic gay date movie ever made. Delightfully charming film belongs to a new cycle of gay movies that are not about AIDS or social issues, but "simply" deal with situations, such as dating and first love, relevant to everybody. Script's romantic tale recalls classic Hollywood screwball comedies, from the 1930s to more recent ones, such as Scorsese's *After Hours* and *The Daytrippers*.

Gabriel is a young, ambitious musical-theater writer/composer whose romantic life leaves a lot to be desired. After hearing a song from Gab's new musical, colleague Perry feels that something is missing from his work which he believes reflects Gab's barren life. Gab heads out to the local gay bar to loosen up. He is struck by the sight of a gorgeous go-go boy, Mark. Not courageous enough to approach Mark, Gab heads to the subway and bumps in to him. A visual flirtation leads to talk on the subway platform. It feels like the perfect one-night stand, except they have no place to go.

The filmmakers realize that the trick is to present barriers so that Gab and Mark will not consummate their burning desire. Indeed, they pile up so many obstacles that the couple feel there's a conspiracy against them. When Campbell and Pitoc are onscreen, they touch a deep chord, encouraging all viewers to revisit their own first amorous adventure.
U.S. release: July 23   U.S. B.O.: $2.1 million

True Crime

A Warner Bros. release of a Zanuck Co./Malpaso production. Produced by Clint Eastwood, Richard D. Zanuck, Lili Fini Zanuck. Executive producer, Tom Rooker. Directed by Eastwood. Screenplay, Larry Gross, Paul Brickman, Stephen Schiff, based on the novel by Andrew Klavan. Camera (Technicolor), Jack N. Green; editor, Joel Cox; music, Lennie Niehaus; production designer, Henry Bumstead; art director, Jack G. Taylor Jr.; set decorator, Richard Goddard; sound (Dolby Digital/DTS/SDDS), Walt Martin; assistant director, Robert Lorenz; casting, Phyllis Huffman. Reviewed at Warner Bros. Studios, Burbank, March 5, 1999. MPAA Rating: R. Running time: 127 mins.
Clint Eastwood (Steve Everett), Isaiah Washington (Frank Beachum), Denis Leary (Bob Findley), Lisa Gay Hamilton (Bonnie Beachum), James Woods (Alan Mann), Bernard Hill (Luther Plunkitt), Diane Venora (Barbara Everett), Michael McKean (Reverend Shillerman), Michael Jeter (Dale Porterhouse), Mary McCormack (Michelle Ziegler), Hattie Winston (Mrs. Russel), Penny Rae Bridges (Gail Beachum), Francesca Fisher-Eastwood (Kate Everett), John Finn (Reedy), Laila Robins (Patricia Findley), Sydney Poitier (Jane March), Erik King (Pussy Man), Graham Beckel (Arnold McCardle), Frances Fisher (Cecilia Nussbaum), Marissa Ribisi (Amy Wilson), Christine Ebersole (Bridget Rossiter), Anthony Zerbe (Henry Lowenstein).
The struggles of individuals to rise above their profound

...June 14...
Phil Collins mastered enough Spanish, French, German and Italian to croon five songs in those languages for the soundtrack of Disney's **Tarzan**.

weaknesses and those of the society they've created receive absorbingly dramatic treatment in *True Crime*. A capital-punishment yarn that is much more concerned with character issues than with moral or legal matters, Clint Eastwood's latest picture boasts tight storytelling, sharp acting and an eye for unexpected, enlivening detail.

Confined to a 24-hour period and constructed on parallel tracks to follow the fortunes of two men – a black inmate scheduled for execution at midnight and a white newspaper reporter who becomes convinced at the 11th hour that the prisoner is innocent – solid script is plotted in conventional beat-the-clock suspense fashion. But even more than in past outings, Eastwood is concerned with illuminating his character's flaws and idiosyncrasies, as well as his irresponsibility toward those who count on him most. This concentration on attitudes and personality, as well as a heightened awareness of the tenuousness of life and happiness, give the film a richness and weight that go a long way toward compensating for the late-in-the-game contrivances of the plot mechanics.

Eastwood's turn as the amoral scoundrel reporter make this one of the actor's most detailed and insightful performances. Playing the dignified sufferer, Washington mainly must keep himself tightly coiled, but does a fine job with this as well as with his intermittent emotional outbursts. Large cast has been nicely filled down to the smallest roles.

U.S. release: Mar. 19   U.S. B.O.: $16.7 million

Tumbleweeds

Produced by Greg O'Connor. Executive producers, Ted Demme, Joel Stillerman, Greg O'Connor, Gavin O'Connor, Thomas J. Mangan IV. Directed by Gavin O'Connor. Screenplay by Gavin O'Connor, Angela Shelton from a story by Angela Shelton. Camera (color, Fotokem), Dan Stoloff; editor, John Gilroy; sound (Dolby Digital), Chen Harpaz; music, David Mansfield; production designer, Bruce Eric Holtshousen; costume designer, Mimi Maxmen; casting, Todd Thaler. Reviewed at Sundance Film Festival (dramatic competition), Jan. 24, 1999. Running time: 104 mins.
Janet McTeer (Mary Jo Walker), Kimberly J. Brown (Ava Walker), Gavin O'Connor (Jack Ranson), Jay O'Sanders (Dan Miller), Lois Smith (Ginger), Laurel Holloman (Laurie Pendleton), Michael J. Pollard (Mr. Cummings), Noah Emmerich (Vertis Dewey), Ashley Buccille (Zoe Broussard), Cody McMains (Adam Riley).
Tumbleweeds sounds like very familiar terrain: the road pic/coming-of-age number in which an unlucky-in-love mother and precocious child bond through adversity. That shouldn't hurt this exuberant indie's chances. Powered by an uncommon rapport between its femme leads and helmer's rough-hewn sensibility, pic has what it takes to becomes the year's first heartfelt sleeper.

Set mostly in San Diego and taken from an autobiographical story by Angela Shelton, pic also has topnotch production values and a strong supporting cast going for it. Oft-wed Mary Jo Walker and her 12-year-old daughter, Ava start out for another state and another former beau, when things go sour in Mary-Jo's previous relationship. Mother and daughter skip town for, first, Missouri, and then San Diego. In transit, they meet "Marlboro Man" trucker Jack. And so stage is set for yet another start, with new job, new school, new best friends. In a twist on the formula, Ava has a remarkably easy time fitting in, even winning a lead in the school play. Perpetually

horny Mom doesn't fare as well: She runs afoul of her weirdo boss and shacks up with Jack, who turns out to be just as controlling and moody as her ex.

Brit legit star McTeer, in her U.S. screen debut, is a revelation as happily uncouth good-ol'-gal. Brown, already a TV-stage vet, plays Ava as both naturally curious-about-sex adolescent and disapproving parent figure.

U.S. release: Nov. 24   U.S. B.O.: $1 million

Twin Falls Idaho

A Sony Pictures Classics release of a Seattle Pacific Investments and the Fresh Produce Co. presentation in association with Steven J. Wolfe and Sneak Preview Entertainment of a Rena Ronson production. Produced by Marshall Persinger, Ronson, Wolfe. Executive producer, Joyce Schweickert. Co-producer, Paul Torok. Directed by Michael Polish. Screenplay, Mark and Michael Polish. Camera (Deluxe color), M. David Mullen; editor, Leo Trombetta; music, Stuart Matthewman; production designer, Warren Alan Young; art director, Grace Li; set decorator, Alysia D. Allen; costume designer, Bic Owen; sound, Matthew Nicolay; "twin" makeup effects, Gary J. Tunnicliffe; associate producers, David Cohn, Jon Gries, Julie Lynn; assistant director, Andrew Miller. Reviewed at Raleigh Studios, L.A., Jan. 12, 1999. (In Sundance Film Festival – American Spectrum.) Running time: 110 mins.
Michael Polish (Francis Falls), Mark Polish (Blake Falls), Michele Hicks (Penny), Jon Gries (Jay), Patrick Bauchau (Miles), Garrett Morris (Jesus), William Katt (Surgeon), Lesley Ann Warren (Francine), Teresa Hill (Sissy), Ant (Tre), Holly Woodlawn (Flamboyant at Party).
There are a number of fraternal filmmaking teams, but none quite like the Polish brothers, 27-year-old identical twins who play men bound together Siamese-style in this offbeat, atmospheric drama that casts a minor but distinctive spell. The film's best scenes register with an indelible effect reinforced by the brothers themselves, who enjoy a shorthand way of relating to one another.

An intrusion by a trampy-looking young lady, Penny, ushers us into the world of Blake and Francis Falls, conjoined twins who permit the stranded woman to crash in their hotel room. Handsome and well dressed in clothes made to their unusual specifications, the twin Falls are invariably polite and display an ethereal air and an acceptance of the strange hand fate has dealt them. It develops that the pair share some vital organs, but that Blake is as fit as Francis is sickly. Penny stays on to nurse the latter through a bout with flu and nausea.

The twins venture out on Halloween, which Penny observes is the only time when the Falls can be perceived as normal. The evening winds up at Penny's, where a very unusual threesome starts things on a path that leads to discord between the brothers, a money-making public "divorce" scheme proposed by a scummy lawyer and a discreetly affecting denouement in which the spiritual, moral and emotional implications of the twins' potential physical separation all come into play.

U.S. release: July 30   U.S. B.O.:$1 million

The Virgin Suicides

An American Zoetrope production. Produced by Francis Ford Coppola, Julie Costanzo, Chris Hanley, Dan Halsted. Executive producers, Fred Fuchs, Willi Baer. Co-producers,

Fred Roos, Gary Marcus. Directed, written by Sofia Coppola, based on the novel by Jeffrey Eugenides. Camera (CFI, color), Edward Lachman; editors, James Lyon, Melissa Kent; music, Air; music supervisor, Brian Reitzell; production designer, Jasna Stefanovic; costume designer, Nancy Steiner; sound (Dolby Digital), Richard Beggs; casting, John Buchan. Reviewed at Cannes Film Festival (Directors Fortnight), May 19, 1999. Running time: 97 mins.
James Woods (Mr. Lisbon), Kathleen Turner (Mrs. Lisbon), Kirsten Dunst (Lux), John Hartnett (Trip Fontaine), Hannah Hall (Cecilia), Chelse Swain (Bonnie), A.J. Cook (Mary), Leslie Hayman (Therese), Danny DeVito (Dr. Hornicker), Scott Glenn (Father Moody), Jonathan Tucker (Tim), Anthony DeSimone (Chas), Giovanni Ribisi (Narrator).
In her promising directorial debut, Sofia Coppola tackles the issue of teenage suicide with an assured treatment in, effectively employing a seriocomic tone. Set in a Michigan suburb in the early 1970s, this darkly humorous picture benefits from an original narrative structure that views the story from a contemporary male perspective. Though her direction is uneven, she should be credited for avoiding an easier, more satirical approach and steering clear of the trivial, pandering nature of so many current youth pics.

Headed by a quirky high-school math teacher and his religious wife, the Lisbons appear to be a healthy suburban American family. They have five teenage daughters, notably Cecilia, 13, and the fully developed Lux. Cecilia slits her wrists, but Mr. Lisbon naively hopes that her act was just a random accident. Their priest, Father Moody recommends that Cecilia socialize with boys more. Central reel focuses on Lux and her relationship with Trip, the school's hunk, who is smitten with her. After the two consummate their passion at a school dance, and Cecilia commits suicide, the Lisbon family begins to disintegrate, spiraling downward to a creepy state of isolation. Finally, the boys (who are interested in the Lisbon girls) decide to take action and make contact with the secluded girls. Then, late one night, encouraged by Lux, the boys sneak into the Lisbon house. The dark resolution is not only shocking but deeply disturbing.

A Walk on the Moon

A Miramax release of a Punch Productions picture in association with Village Roadshow Pictures, Groucho Film Partnership. Produced by Dustin Hoffman, Tony Goldwyn, Jay Cohen, Neil Koenigsberg, Lee Gottsegen, Murray Schisgal. Executive producers, Graham Burke, Greg Coote. Co-producer, Josette Perotta. Directed by Tony Goldwyn. Screenplay, Pamela Gray. Reviewed at Sundance Festival (Premieres), Jan. 29, 1999. Running time: 107 mins.
Diane Lane (Pearl Kantrowitz), Liev Schreiber (Marty Kantrowitz), Anna Paquin (Alison Kantrowitz), Viggo Mortensen (Walker Jerome), Tovah Feldshuh (Lilian Kantrowitz), Bobby Boriello (Daniel Kantrowitz).
A Walk on the Moon, set at a middle-class Catskills resort in the summer of '69, is just plain loaded – as in heavy-handed and contrived. This effort by Dustin Hoffman's Punch Productions wants to be both women's pic and coming-of-age piece, but isn't successful at either.

Diane Lane, in her most mature role to date, plays Pearl Kantrowitz, a vaguely dissatisfied mother of two who chooses a summer getaway to sow long-dormant oats and take up with a traveling garment salesman named Walker. Though seemingly

happily married to Marty, a TV repairman, Pearl feels "trapped by life" and secretly resents missing the do-your-own-thing '60s. When hubby's job calls him back to the city, Pearl buys a tie-dyed T-shirt, meets up with Walker and partakes of free love and nude swimming at the Woodstock bacchanal.

Teen daughter Alison is ripe for her own sexual awakening. When, among the sea of faces at Woodstock, she spies Mommy acting very, well, un-Mommy-like, Alison becomes understandably miffed. This was supposed to be *her* summer, not Mom's. Poor square Dad, meanwhile, has no idea what's going on, until his tarot-reading mother, also vacationing with the family, tells Sonny what's what.

Problems abound as pic deals with the impact of adultery on a picture-perfect family. Pearl's behavior takes its toll on audience empathy. A David Lean could appeal to all audience members by creating a well-rounded heroine, who, despite her lapses, remains sympathetic.
U.S. release: Mar. 26   U.S. B.O.: $4.8 million

The Way We Laughed (Cosi Ridevano)

A Cecchi Gori Distribuzione release (in Italy) of a Mario and Vittorio Cecchi Gori presentation of a Cecchi Gori Group Tiger Cinematografica production. Produced by Vittorio and Rita Cecchi Gori. Executive producer, Mario Cotone for Pacific Pictures. Directed, written by Gianni Amelio. Camera (Cinecitta color, widescreen), Luca Bigazzi; editor, Simona Paggi; music, Franco Piersanti; production designer, Giancarlo Basili; set decorator, Nello Giorgetti; costume designer, Gianna Gissi; sound (Dolby Digital SR), Alessandro Zanon; assistant directors, Lidia Biondi, Elisabetta Boni, Enzo Di Terlizzi, Gianluca Greco; casting, Nicola Conticello, Lorella Chiapatti. Reviewed at Venice Film Festival (competing), Sept. 9, 1998. (Also in Toronto Film Festival.) Running time: 126 mins.
Giovanni Enrico Lo Verso (Giovanni), Francesco Giuffrida (Pietro), Fabrizio Gifuni (Pelaia), Rosaria Danze (Lucia), Claudio Contartese (Rosario), Domenico Ragusa (Simone), Simonetta Benozzo (Ada), Pietro Paglietti (Battista).
A bittersweet story of fraternal love that also attempts to chart Italy's transformation and resulting loss of innocence. Pic unfolds from the late '50s through 1964, as the country shook off the last vestiges of postwar poverty and became an industrialized economic power. This meticulously crafted new feature deals with immigrants' dreams of a new world of opportunity. Overall, pic is problematically structured, overly protracted and lacking in narrative fluidity.

The film opens with the arrival at Turin station of illiterate Sicilian Giovanni. Giovanni's brother Pietro is already settled in Turin attending school. It quickly becomes apparent after their reunion that the selflessly devoted Giovanni, who treats his younger brother like a son, has an all-consuming emotional investment in steering his brother through school to a teaching career and a life of enlightenment.

The choice to play many of the story's significant encounters offscreen is rather frustrating and the chapter structure makes the characters appear to change overnight, often implausibly. One such jump occurs when Giovanni becomes president of a worker's cooperative. Given that the character is set up as sweet-natured and verging on idiocy, his transition is impossible to swallow.

Pietro is unsatisfyingly drawn. Until the final chapter, he shows only a flicker of recognition of the sacrifices his older

---

...June 16...
The 45th Williamstown Theater Festival announced Gwyneth Paltrow as Rosalind in Shakespeare's **As You Like It** and Ethan Hawke in Tennessee Williams' **Camino Real**.

brother makes on his behalf, and his responses for most of the film remain annoyingly unclear.

Wild Wild West

A Warner Bros. release of a Peters Entertainment/ Sonnenfeld-Josephson production. Produced by Jon Peters, Barry Sonnenfeld. Executive producers, Bill Todman Jr., Joel Simon, Kim LeMasters, Tracy Glaser, Barry Josephson. Co-producers, Graham Place, Doug Lodato. Directed by Sonnenfeld. Screenplay, S.S. Wilson, Brent Maddock, Jeffrey Price, Peter S. Seaman, story by Jim Thomas, John Thomas. Camera (Technicolor), Michael Ballhaus. Editor, Jim Miller; music, Elmer Bernstein; production designer, Bo Welch; art director, Tom Duffield; set designers, Patrick Sullivan, Maya Shimoguchi, Gerald Sullivan, Mariko Braswell; set decorator, Cheryl Carasik; costume designer, Deborah L. Scott; sound (Dolby Digital/DTS/SDDS), Peter Kurland; supervising sound editors, Skip Lievsay, Bobby Mackston; visual-effects supervisor, Eric Brevig; special visual effects, Industrial Light & Magic; additional visual effects, Cinesite; special-effects supervisor, Michael Lantieri; special-effects makeup, Rick Baker; stunt coordinators, Terry J. Leonard, Artie Malesci, Philip Tan; associate producers, Neri Kyle Tannenbaum, Chris Soldo; assistant director, Soldo; second unit directors, Leonard, Brevig; second unit camera, Bill Pope, David Dunlap, Raymond Stella, Chuck Shuman; aerial camera, David Nowell; casting, David Rubin, Ronna Kress. Reviewed at Warner Bros. Studios, Burbank, June 28, 1999. MPAA Rating: PG-13. Running time: 107 mins.

Will Smith (James West), Kevin Kline (Artemus Gordon/ President Grant), Kenneth Branagh (Dr. Arliss Loveless), Salma Hayek (Rita Escobar), Ted Levine (General McGrath), M. Emmet Walsh (Coleman), Bai Ling (Miss East), Rodney A. Grant (Hudson), Garcelle Beauvais (Girl in Water Tower), Musetta Vander (Munitia), Sofia Eng (Miss Lippenreider), Frederique van der Wal (Amazonia).

As refittings of old TV shows go, this was neither the best nor the worst, turning the 1964-68 series into a Jules Verne-like 19th-century quasi-sci-fier equipped with hip references and contemporary attitude. Pic is full of thunderous, cartoonish action and special effects that enable the digital-effects wizards to show off some new moves.

Special government agents James West, a quick draw, and Artemus Gordon, a resourceful inventor, are thrown together by President U.S. Grant to thwart Confederate General "Bloodbath" McGrath, who is allegedly developing a weapons system that threatens the Union. When the duo sneak into a New Orleans masquerade ball, it becomes evident that their real foe is the insidious Dr. Arliss Loveless, a paraplegic military genius intent upon striking back at a world that has ravaged his country and his body. With a plan to design futuristic instruments of destruction, Loveless has kidnaped all the top scientists in the country, one of whom is the father of Rita Escobar, a beauteous saloon "entertainer" who tags along with West and Gordon. Loveless' aim is to kidnap the president and force the repartitioning of the U.S., with much of the West reserved for him. The breezy, quickwitted style that has made most of Sonnenfeld's films entertaining and successful isn't enough to overcome the production's cumbersome mechanics or the unfocused and unpolished nature of the story and script.

U.S. release: June 30   U.S. B.O.: $113.8 million

The Winslow Boy

A Sony Picture Classics release. Produced by Sarah Green. Directed, written by David Mamet, based on the play by Terence Rattigan. Camera (color), Benoit Delhomme; editor, Barbara Tulliver; music, Alaric Jans; production designer, Gemma Jackson; art director, Andrew Munro; set decorator, Trisha Edwards; costume designer, Consolata Boyle; sound, Clive Winter; casting, Ross and John Hubbard. Reviewed at MAC Kabui: 8, San Francisco, April 6, 1999. Running time: 104 mins.

Nigel Hawthorne (Arthur Winslow), Jeremy Northam (Sir Robert Morton), Rebecca Pidgeon (Catherine Winslow), Gemma Jones (Grace Winslow), Guy Edwards (Ronnie Winslow), Matthew Pidgeon (Dickie Winslow), Colin Stinton (Desmond Curry), Aden Gillett (John Watherstone), Sarah Flind (Violet), Neil North (First Lord of the Admiralty), Sara Stewart (Miss Barnes).

Very English, very period and very polite, and a curious project for combustive U.S. playwright-scenarist-turned-film director. The second screen adaptation of Terence Rattigan's 1946 play emerges as an assured drama graced by some superbly cast performers – albeit compromised by a single problematic one. Pic doesn't sport the romantic sweep or plush aesthetics audiences have come to expect from such U.K.-set period pieces.

Story takes place in the years just before the First World War in London. Retired bank manager Arthur Winslow's 13-year-old son, Ronnie, has been expelled from the naval college for allegedly stealing a classmate's pocket money, a charge he denies. Taking the boy's word and infuriated by the dismissal without fair trial, Arthur presses for further inquiry, which naval college authorities flatly refuse. Though Ronnie resettles in a civilian boarding school, his father takes the case as far as the House of Lords, represented by famous, flamboyant attorney Sir Robert Morton. Latter's employ is costly beyond the comfortable but by-no-means rich Winslow clan's means. As the case becomes a national debate, repercussions spiral for each Winslow family member.

Rattigan's carefully orchestrated character dynamics and well-crafted Big Scenes still deliver in this clean adaptation. Smoothly paced, much of this is engrossing. Those looking for trademark "Mamet-speak" here won't find much more than a few instances. Mamet's wife Pidgeon is pic's major problem. Her delivery is so staccato and void of emotional coloring that the character seems cold and supercilious.

U.S. release: Apr. 30   U.S. B.O.: $4.3 million

Wonderland

A Universal release of a Polygram Filmed Entertainment/ BBC Films presentation of a Kismet Films/Revolution Films production. Produced by Michele Camarda, Andrew Eaton. Executive producers, Stewart Till, David M. Thompson. Co-producer, Gina Carter. Directed by Michael Winterbottom. Screen-play, Laurence Coriat. Camera (color, Panavision widescreen), Sean Bobbitt; editor, Trevor Waite; music, Michael Nyman; production designer, Mark Tildesley; costume designer, Natalie Ward; sound, Richard Flynn; line producer, Anita Overlord; assistant director, Nick Laws; casting, Wendy Brazington. Reviewed at Cannes Film Festival (competing), May 13, 1999. Running time: 108 mins.

Shirley Henderson (Debbie), Gina McKee (Nadia), Molly Parker (Molly), Ian Hart (Dan), John Simm (Eddie), Stuart

Townsend (Tim), Kika Markham (Eileen), Jack Shepherd (Bill), Enzo Cilenti (Darren), Sarah-Jane Potts (Melanie), David Fahm (Franklyn), Ellen Thomas (Donna), Peter Marfleet (Jack), Nathan Constance (Alex).

Ironically titled, *Wonderland* is an emotionally rewarding slice of London life reminding one of Mike Leigh's work. Winterbottom's complete control over devices such as available light and a handheld camera shoot, add to the intensely immediate feel of the material.

Pic is the examination of a family in crisis during four days in a London November. Nadia works in a café, lives alone; and meets men via a dating agency with disappointing results. Nadia's older sister Debbie is separated from her drunken husband, Dan, and seeks refuge in a series of fleeting sexual encounters. Her 11-year-old son Jack is victimized by the real-life encounters he witnesses and the escapism of violent television. Molly, the youngest sister, who is pregnant, seems to be the happiest at first. Her life falls apart when her partner, Eddie, quits his cozy job as a kitchen salesman and leaves her. Eileen, the sisters' mother, is being driven to the point of a nervous breakdown by noisy neighbors. Their father, Bill, is sexually frustrated and drifts aimlessly on account of losing his job. The lives of these sad people are not as bleak as might be supposed. The film is suffused with stoic humor and ends on a note of guarded optimism. These people may find life daunting, but they have the will and resilience to survive, and there's no sense of despair. Performances by the ensemble cast are just about flawless.

The World Is Not Enough

An MGM release of an Albert R. Broccoli's Eon Prods. Ltd. presentation. Produced by Michael G. Wilson, Barbara Broccoli. Directed by Michael Apted. Screenplay, Neal Purvis, Robert Wade, Bruce Feirstein, story by Purvis, Wade. Camera (Deluxe color, Panavision widescreen), Adrian Biddle; editor, Jim Clark; music, David Arnold; production designer, Peter Lamont. Reviewed at MGM screening room, Santa Monica, Nov. 10, 1999. MPAA Rating: PG-13. Running time: 125 mins.

Pierce Brosnan (James Bond), Sophie Marceau (Elektra), Robert Carlyle (Renard), Denise Richards (Christmas Jones), Robbie Coltrane (Valentin Zukovsky), Judi Dench (M), Desmond Llewelyn (Q), John Cleese (R), Maria Grazia Cucinotta (Cigar Girl), Samantha Bond (Moneypenny), Michael Kitchen (Tanner), Colin Salmon (Robinson), Goldie (Bull), David Calder (Sir Robert King), Serena Scott Thomas (Dr. Molly Warmflash), Ulrich Thomsen (Davidov), John Seru (Gabor), Claude-Oliver Rudolph (Colonel Akakievich).

Despite an exciting pre-credits high-speed boat chase (the longest Bond prolog ever) and some solid work by the nicely matched Pierce Brosnan and Sophie Marceau, this film sees 007 undone by villainous scripting and misguided casting.

Daft, overcrammed plotting is a shame, because Brosnan grows comfortable in the role, and reveals a strong urge to make the most of his admittedly scant opportunities to invest Bond with interesting shadings and substance. A wealthy industrialist dies and his daughter Elektra inherits his vast holdings, which include an unfinished oil pipeline across Western Asia. Elektra also has a history with Bond's boss M, who botched a rescue attempt of the young woman when she was held by terrorist kidnaper Renard, from whom Elektra escaped. As Elektra seems a likely target of any number of rivals in the former Soviet Union, Bond heads for Azerbaijan to protect her. But just as James and Elektra find one another, Renard turns up in plots to strike Elektra and her oil pipeline. Bimbette Denise Richards, a nuclear weapons expert, turns up to assist 007 with disengaging bombs and – debriefing. She is the token Yank in the cast, cluelessly flailing about among more mature co-stars.

Michael Apted, a name director, adds little flair to the existing franchise. Dramatic sequences are capable but straightforward, although it is possible that Apted might have urged Brosnan in the encouraging direction indicated here.

U.S. release: Nov. 19   U.S. B.O.: $118 million

> *My father was a drunk,*
> *gambler and womanizer.*
> *I worshipped him.*
> *(John Travolta,*
> *The General's Daughter)*

Future Films

As a paper of record, *Variety* tracks the elaborate mating dance involved in every film production, from the acquisition of a novel or a screenplay, through casting and pre-production, the travails of shooting, and the often torturous post-production phase. For many readers our regular listings of "films in the future" in *Daily Variety* contain the first clues to the output and caliber of the forthcoming year in the cinema. Such lists are fraught with peril: stars climb aboard and stars drop out; directors may ankle only a week or two into the shoot; even the film's title can change. By the time you consult this checklist, many of the films will have been released; others may see the light of day only in a video store a year or more into the millennium. By and large, however, this is the lineup for 2000.
The date after each title indicates commencement of principal photography.

13 Days (Beacon Communications) 10/4/99, Los Angeles, Philippines, Washington DC. **Kevin Costner, Bruce Greenwood, Steven Culp.** EXP, Illona Herzberg, Tom Bliss, Michael DeLuca; PROD, Armyan Bernstein, Kevin Costner, Peter Almond; AP, Mary Montiforte; DIR, Roger Donaldson; SCR, David Self; CAM, Roger Deakins; DISTRIB, New Line.
An inside look at how the Kennedy Administration responded to the discovery of offensive Soviet weapons in Cuba, and the pressurized tug-of-war that ensued between the U.S. and the U.S.S.R. during the 13 days of the missile crisis.

15 Minutes (Industry Entertainment) 5/13/99, Los Angeles, New York. **Robert De Niro, Edward Burns.** PROD, John Herzfeld, David Blocker, Keith Addis, Nick Wechsler; DIR-SCR, John Herzfeld; DISTRIB, New Line.
Superstar N.Y. homicide detective Eddie Fleming allows a young, talented N.Y. Fire Dept. Arson Investigator, Jordy Warsaw to team up with him to crack down a pair of Eastern European killers on a rampage through the city.

102 Dalmatians (Cruella Prods.) 11/28/99, London. **Glenn Close, Gerard Depardieu, Alice Evans, Ioan Gruffudd, Tim McInnerney.** PROD, Edward S. Feldman, Patricia Carr; DIR, Kevin Lima; 2 DIR, Micky Moore; SCR, Kristen Buckley; DISTRIB, BV.
In this all-new sequel, Cruella De Vil is released from prison and swears that she will have nothing to do with fur ever again in her life. She, however, cannot keep her promise and soon is plotting another "FUROCIOUS" scheme to get her ultimate Dalmatian coat.

Adventures of Rocky and Bullwinkle (Tribeca/Capella/Universal) 2/16/99, Los Angeles, Placer County, CA; New York, Washington DC. **Jason Alexander, Rene Russo, Robert De Niro, Monica Potter, Randy Quaid, Piper Perabo, June Foray, Keith Scott, Kenan Thompson, Kel Mitchell, Janeane Garofalo, John Goodman, Billy Crystal, Carl Reiner.** EXP, David Nicksay, Tiffany Ward; PROD, Jane Rosenthal, Robert De Niro; SCR, Kenny Lonegran; CAM, Thomas Ackerman; DISTRIB, U.
Boris Badenov and Natasha Fatale have escaped their cartoon experiences and rehatch a plan to take over the world. It's up to Rocket J. Squirrel and Bullwinkle J. Moose to stop them.

All the Pretty Horses (Columbia Pictures/Miramax/Iracus) 3/15/99, San Antonio, TX; Sante Fe, NM. **Matt Damon, Henry Thomas, Lucas Black, Penelope Cruz, Ruben Blades, Bruce Dern, Robert Patrick.** EXP, Robert Salerno; PROD, Mike Nichols; DIR, Billy Bob Thornton; SCR, Ted Tally; CAM, Barry Markowitz; DISTRIB, Sony.
Based on Cormac McCarthy's bestselling novel; pic tells the story of resilient, dispossessed Texas teenager John Grady Cole who sets off on horseback for Mexico and comes of age.

Along Came a Spider (Phase 1/Manhattan Project/Paramount Pictures) 2/22/00. **Morgan Freeman.** PROD, Joe Wizan, David Brown; DIR, Lee Tamahori; SCR, Marc Moss, James Patterson; DISTRIB, Par.
In the prequel to *Kiss the Girls*, Washington DC homicide detective Dr. Alex Cross investigates the kidnaping of two children from an exclusive school by a schizophrenic psychopath.

Antitrust (Cub Two Prods.) 2/14/00, Vancouver, Canada. **Tim Robbins, Ryan Phillippe.** EXP, David Hoberman, Ashok Amritraj, Doc Erickson, Julia Chasman; PROD, Keith Addis, Nick Wechsler, David Nicksay; DIR, Peter Howitt; SCR, Howard Franklin; DISTRIB, MGM.
When Milo graduates from college and lands his dream job writing software at a multibillion-dollar computer company, he couldn't be more thrilled. But as he settles into his new position, Milo uncovers some dark secrets about the firm and soon learns that he can't trust anyone but himself in the high-stakes world of computer technology.

Autumn in New York (Autumn Leaves/Gary Lucchesi Prod/UA) 9/13/99, New York. **Richard Gere, Winona Ryder, Anthony LaPaglia, Elaine Stritch, Sherry Stringfield, Jill Hennessy.** EXP, Ted Tannebaum, Ron Bozman; PROD, Amy Robinson, Gary Lucchesi, Tom Rosenberg; DIR, Joan Chen; SCR, Allison Burnett; DISTRIB, MGM.
Will Keane is the owner of one of New York's hottest restaurants. His confidence and charisma make him a magnet for beautiful women. But try as they may, not one of them can nail him down. That is, until he meets Charlotte Fielding, a unique, passionate, unpredictable and much younger woman who eventually changes his life forever.

Battlefield Earth (Morgan Creek/Franchise Films) 7/5/99, Montreal, Canada. **John Travolta, Barry Pepper, Forest Whitaker, Kim Coates, Sabine Karsenti, Michael Byrne, Richard Tyson.** EXP, Andrew Stevens, Don Carmody, Ashok Amritraj; PROD, Elie Samaha, Jonathan D. Krane, John Travolta; DIR, Roger Christian; SCR, Cory Mandell; DISTRIB, WB.
Science-fiction action-adventure set in A.D. 3000, when humans have become an endangered species living in cages under the ruthless rule of an alien race. A renegade human who has lived free until his twenties is captured by aliens; they make a pet of him because they admire his intelligence. He uses his knowledge of his enemies to help lead a revolt of the human beings against their alien rulers.

Cast Away (Image Movers/Fox 2000/ DreamWorks) 1/18/99, Los Angeles, Russia, Fiji, Hawaii, Nashville, Tennessee. **Tom Hanks, Helen Hunt.** EXP, Joan Bradshaw; PROD, Tom Hanks, Jack Rapke, Steve Starkey; DIR, Robert Zemeckis; SCR, William Broyles Jr.; CAM, Don Burgess; DISTRIB, 20th Century Fox.

A contemporary drama about a man who is isolated and forced to transform himself in order to survive both physically and emotionally.

Charlie's Angels (Mandy Films/Flower Films/Columbia Pictures) 12/6/99. **Drew Barrymore, Cameron Diaz, Lucy Liu, Bill Murray.** PROD, Leonard Goldberg, Drew Barrymore, Nancy Juvonen; SCR, John August, Ryan Rowe, Ed Solomon; DISTRIB, Sony.
They're beautiful, they're brilliant, and they work for Charlie. In a smart, sexy update of the '70s TV show, pic revolves around three female detectives – Natalie the bookworm, Dylan the tough girl, and Alex the class act – as intelligent and multitalented as they are ravishingly gorgeous and utterly disarming.

Chicken Run (Aardman Animations/Pathe/Allied Filmmakers/DreamWorks) Animated, 12/97, Bristol, England. Voices: **Mel Gibson, Julia Sawalha, Miranda Richardson, Jane Horrocks, Imelda Staunton, Benjamin Whitrow, Lynn Ferguson, Tony Haygarth, Timothy Spall, Phil Daniels.** EXP, Jake Eberts, Michael Rose; PROD, David Sproxton, Peter Lord, Nick Park; DIR, Peter Lord, Nick Park; SCR, Karey Kirkpatrick, Jack Rosenthal; DISTRIB, DreamWorks.
At Tweedy's Chicken Farm, any chicken who doesn't make her egg quota can meet a "fowl" fate. But Ginger and her fellow flock are determined to break out before they can be fried, filleted or fricasseed.

D-TOX Sylvester Stallone, Kris Kristofferson, Tom Berenger, Polly Walker, Jeffrey Wright. EXP, Maureen Peyrot; PROD, Brian Grazer, Karen Kehela, Ric Kidney; DIR, Jim Gillespie; SCR, Ron L. Brinkerhoff, Patrick Smith Kelly.
Disgraced FBI agent faces attempts to solve his drinking problem in an isolated detox center in the wilderness. However, when a major snowstorm cuts off the clinic's power and people wind up dead, it becomes clear that there is a cop killer among the group.

Dancing in the Dark (DiNovi Pictures/MGM Pictures) 2/14/00, Mexico, New Orleans. **Angelina Jolie, Antonio Banderas, Thomas Jane.** EXP, Michael S. Glick; PROD, Kate Guinzburg, Denise DiNovi, Carol Lees; DIR-SCR, Michael Cristofer; DISTRIB, MGM.
Set in the exotic world of Cuba in the 1800s, this sexy, suspenseful thriller is about the dangerous and sometimes lethal power of love. Louis Durand is a wealthy coffee merchant who has decided to take an American wife. When he arrives at the docks to meet

---

Julia Russell, he is surprised to find that she is not the plain woman he was expecting. The surprises continue until the story takes a fateful turn.

Get Carter (Franchise Films) 10/15/99, Vancouver, Canada. **Sylvester Stallone, Miranda Richardson, Rachel Leigh Cooke, Michael Caine.** EXP, Don Carmody; PROD, Mark Canton, Elie Samaha, Neil Canton; DIR, Stephen Kaye; SCR, David McKenna; DISTRIB, WB.
Re-make of the '70s British action-thriller of the same name, it is the story of one man's search for redemption, revenge and ultimately his reconnection with his family following his brother's mysterious murder.

Gone in Sixty Seconds (Jerry Bruckheimer Films/Touchstone Pictures) 5/24/99, Los Angeles. **Nicolas Cage, Angelina Jolie, Giovanni Ribisi, Delroy Lindo, Will Patton, Christopher Eccleston, Chi McBride, Scott Caan, Timothy Olyphant, William L. Scott, Vinnie Jones, James Duval, T.J. Cross, Robert Duvall.** EXP, Jonathan Hensleigh, Chad Oman, Barry Waldman, Denice Shakarian Halicki, Robert Stone, Webster Stone; PROD, Jerry Bruckheimer, Mike Stenson; DIR, Dominic Shea; DISTRIB, BV.
Randall "Memphis" Raines is a now-legit former car thief of legendary proportion who is sucked back into a high-stakes caper in order to save his brother's life.

Finding Forrestor (Col) 4/00, New York. **Sean Connery.** EXP, Sean Connery; Rhonda Tollefson; PROD, Laurence Mark; DIR, Gus Van Sant; SCR, Michael Rich; DISTRIB, Sony.
A drama about a unique relationship between an eccentric, reclusive novelist and a young, black, amazingly gifted scholar-athlete.

The Hollow Man (Red Wagon Prod./Columbia Pictures) 4/26/99, Los Angeles, Washington DC. **Elizabeth Shue, Kevin Bacon, Josh Brolin, Kim Dickens, Greg Grunberg, Joey Slotnick, Mary Randle, William Devane.** EXP, Marion Rosenberg; PROD, Douglas Wick, Alan Marshall; DIR, Paul Verhoeven; SCR (tent.), Andrew Marlowe; CAM, Jost Vacano; DISTRIB, Sony.
At a top-secret military lab a group of brilliant young scientists have just unlocked the secret of invisibility. The team's arrogant leader, Sebastien Caine, ignores the risks and decides to test the dangerous procedure on himself – only to discover his fellow scientists are unable to reverse the effect. As his intoxication with his newfound power grows, he comes to believe that his colleagues may be a threat to his very existence.

How the Grinch Stole Christmas (U) 9/7/99, Los Angeles. **Jim Carrey, Taylor Momsen, Jeffrey Tambor, Christine Baranski, Molly Shannon, Bill Irwin.** EXP-2DIR, Todd Hallowell; PROD, Brian Grazer; DIR, Ron Howard; SCR, Peter Seaman, Jeffrey Price; DISTRIB, U.
Jim Carrey is the Grinch in Dr. Seuss' classic children's book brought to life.

I Was Made to Love Her (3 Arts Entertainment/Alphaville Prods./Par) 2/00. **Chris Rock.** PROD, Jim Jacks, Michael Rotenberg, Sean Daniels; DIR, Chris and Paul Weitz; SCR, Chris and Paul Weitz, Chris Rock, Louis C.K., Ali LeRoi, Lance Crouther; DISTRIB, Par.
A struggling standup comic finds himself trapped in the body of an aristocrat, and tries to make it on the standup circuit, much to the consternation of the aristocrat's family.

The Legend of Bagger Vance (Wildwood Enterprises/Allied Production Ltd.) 9/23/99, Savannah, Georgia. **Will Smith, Matt Damon, Charlize Theron, J. Michael Moncrief, Joel Gretsch, Jack Lemmon.** PROD, Robert Redford; Michael Nozik, Jake Eberts; DIR, Robert Redford; SCR, Jeremy Leven, Richard LaGravenese; DISTRIB, DreamWorks.
Based on the novel by Steven Pressfield.

The Lord of the Rings (New Line) 10/11/99, New Zealand. **Elijah Wood, Sean Astin, Dominic Monaghan, Billy Boyd, Sir Ian Holm, Ian McKellen, Viggo Mortensen, John Rhys-Davies, Orlando Bloom, Sean Bean, Liv Tyler, Christopher Lee, Cate Blanchett.** EXP, Mark Ordesky, Harvey Weinstein, Bob Weinstein; PROD, Tim Sanders, Barrie M. Osborne, Peter Jackson; DIR, Peter Jackson; 2DIR, John Mahaffie; SCR, Fran Walsh, Philippa Boyens, Stephen Sinclair, Peter Jackson; DISTRIB, New Line.
Previously an animated film, J.R.R. Tolkien's classic novel is finally brought to life.

Little Nicky (New Line) 11/3/99, New York, Los Angeles. **Adam Sandler, Harvey Keitel, Patricia Arquette, Allen Covert, Tiny Lister.** EXP, Robert Engelman; PROD, Robert Simonds, Jack Giarraputo; DIR, Steven Brill; SCR, Adam Sandler, Tim Herlihy; DISTRIB, New Line.

...June 21...
Barbra Streisand's New York-based production company has optioned the rights to **Romeo & Julie**, novelist Jeanne Ray's story about ill-fated retirement-age lovers.

Little Nicky, a shy, awkward guy, is the son of the Devil and lives in Hell. When Dad decides not to make Nicky's brothers the heirs to Hell, they create it in New York City. Nicky is summoned by his father to save the city and restore the balance of Good and Evil.

The Man Who Cried (Adventure Pictures/ Working Title Films/Le Studio Canal Plus) 9/7/99, Paris, London. **Robert De Niro, Christina Ricci, Johnny Depp, John Turturro, Cate Blanchett.** EXP, Tim Bevan, Eric Fellner; PROD, Sally Potter, Christopher Sheppard; DIR-SCR; Sally Potter. Set in occupied Paris during World War II, a young female transient enters the theater world when she meets a famous opera singer.

Meet the Parents (Tribeca/Universal/ DreamWorks) 11/8/99, New York. **Robert De Niro, Ben Stiller, Teri Polo, Blythe Danner, Nicole Debluff.** PROD, Jane Rosenthal, Nancy Tenenbaum; DIR, Jay Roach; SCR, Jim Herzfeld, John Hamburg; DISTRIB, U. Groom-to-be Greg Focker has a disastrous first meeting with his girlfriend's family – most notably her intimidating father, Jack Byrnes.

Me, Myself and Irene (Fox) 5/11/99, Burlington, Vermont, Rhode Island. **Jim Carrey, Renee Zellweger, Robert Forster, Chris Cooper.** EXP, Charles Wessler, Tom Schulman; PROD, Farrelly Brothers, Bradley Thomas; DIR, Peter Farrelly & Bobby Farrelly; SCR, Farrelly Brothers, Mike Cerrone; CAM, Mark Irwin; DISTRIB, Fox. A split personality cop's alter ego and true persona fall in love with a girl that he's escorting back home.

Mission: Impossible 2 (CW Productions/ Paramount) 4/18/99, Sydney, New South Wales, Australia; New York, Colorado, Spain. **Tom Cruise, Ving Rhames, Anthony Hopkins.** EXP, Terence Chang, Paul Hitchcock; PROD, Tom Cruise, Paula Wagner; DIR, John Woo; SCR, Robert Towne, Michael Tolkin, David Marconi, William Goldman; CAM, Jeffrey Kimball; DISTRIB, Par. The long awaited follow-up to *Mission: Impossible.*

Mission to Mars (Hollywood Pictures) 7/13/99, Vancouver, Canada; Jordan, Canary Islands, Spain. **Gary Sinise, Don Cheadle, Tim Robbins, Jerry O'Connell, Kim Delaney, Connie Nielsen, Elise Neal, Peter Outerbridge.** EXP, Sam Mercer; PROD, Tom Jacobson; DIR, Brian De Palma; SCR, Graham Yost, James E. Thomas, John C. Thomas; CAM,

Stephen Burum; DISTRIB, BV. When the first manned mission to Mars meets with a catastrophic and mysterious disaster, a rescue mission is launched to investigate the tragedy and bring back any survivors.

Numbers (Par) 11/15/99, Harrisburg, Pennsylvania, Los Angeles. **John Travolta, Lisa Kudrow, Ed O'Neill, Tim Roth, Michael Weston, Michael Rapaport, Michael Moore, Chris Cattan, Daryl Mitchell.** EXP, G. Mac Brown; PROD, Jonathan Krane, Andrew Lazar, Sean Daniel, Nora Ephron; 2DIR, Alfonso Gomez-Rejon; SCR, Adam Resnick; DISTRIB, Par. A TV weatherman, down on his luck, schemes with the station's lotto ball girl to rig the state lottery draw.

Nutty Professor 2: The Klumps (Imagine Ent.) 10/5/99, Los Angeles. **Eddie Murphy, Janet Jackson, Larry Miller, John Ales, Jamal Mixon, Melinda McGraw, Gabriel Williams, Anna Maria Horsford.** EXP, Jerry Lewis, Eddie Murphy, Tom Shadyac, James D. Brubaker, Karen Kehela; PROD, Brian Grazer; AP, Arlene Kehela; DIR, Peter Segal; SCR, David Sheffield, Barry Blaustein, Paul Weitz, Chris Weitz; DISTRIB, U. Lovable Sherman Klump is back and so is his alter ego Buddy Love, who is set on threatening Sherman's plans to wed the beautiful Denise Gains.

O Brother, Where Art Thou? (Working Title Films) 6/7/99, Jackson, Mississippi; Los Angeles. **George Clooney, John Turturro, Blake Nelson, Charles Durning, Chris Thomas King, Michael Badalucco, John Goodman, Holly Hunter.** EXP, Eric Fellner, Tim Bevan; PROD, Ethan Coen; DIR-SCR, Joel Coen; SCR, Ethan Coen; CAM, Roger Deakins; DISTRIB, Buena Vista. Set in the 1930s, three men escape from a chain gang and traverse the Deep South trying to shake off a tracker.

The Patriot (Mutual Film Company/Centropolis Ent.) 9/7/99, South Carolina. **Mel Gibson, Heath Ledger, Joely Richardson, Tcheky Karyo, Jason Isaacs, Tom Wilkinson.** EXP, Roland Emmerich, Ute Emmerich, Bill Fay; PROD, Dean Devlin, Mark Gordon, Gary Levinsohn; DIR, Roland Emmerich; 2DIR, Peter Winther; SCR, Robert Rodat; DISTRIB, Sony. Mel Gibson is Benjamin Martin, a reluctant hero who is swept into the American Revolution when the war reaches his home and threatens his family. A hero of the fierce French and Indian conflict, Martin had renounced fighting forever to raise his family in peace. But when the British arrive at his South Carolina home and endanger what he holds most dear, Martin takes up arms alongside his idealistic patriot son, Gabriel and leads a brave rebel militia into battle against a relentless and overwhelming English Army.

Pay It Forward (Bel Air Ent./Tapestry Films) 2/14/00, Los Angeles, Las Vegas. **Kevin Spacey, Helen Hunt, Haley Joel Osment**. EXP, Jonathan Treisman; PROD, Steven Reuther, Peter Abrams, Robert L. Levy; DIR, Mimi Leder; SCR, Leslie Dixon; DISTRIB, WB. For a class project a boy creates a scheme which involves helping three people who must each help three people and so on until everyone is doing something nice for someone. He puts his plan into action and it actually works, though not in the way the boy anticipated, and not until his own world is changed forever.

The Perfect Storm (WB) 7/26/99, Los Angeles, Gloucester, Massachusetts. **George Clooney, Mark Wahlberg, Mary Elizabeth Mastrantonio, John C. Reilly, Diane Lane, William Fichtner, Allen Payne, Karen Allen, Bob Gunton, Cherry Jones**. EXP, Barry Levinson, Duncan Henderson; PROD, Paula Weinstein, Wolfgang Petersen, Gail Katz; DIR, Wolfgang Petersen, 2DIR, David Ellis; SCR, William Wittliff, Bo Goldman; DISTRIB, WB. A riveting drama based on a true story about a disastrous storm at sea and its consequences to the ships and crews in its path.

Red Planet (WB, Village Roadshow) 8/30/99, Jordan, Australia. **Val Kilmer, Carrie-Anne Moss, Tom Sizemore, Simon Baker, Benjamin Bratt, Terence Stamp**. EXP, Charles J.D. Schlissel, Andrew Mason, Chuck Pfarrer; PROD, Mark Canton, Bruce Berman, Jorge Saralegui; DIR, Anthony Hoffman; SCR, Chuck Pfarrer, Jonathan Lemkin; DISTRIB, WB. Set in the near future, a team of American astronauts make the first manned expedition to Mars. Earth has become a dying planet and a new colony on Mars is now humanity's only hope. The astronauts' equipment suffers life-threatening damage and the crew must depend on one another for survival on the hostile surface of Mars.

Remember the Titans (Jerry Bruckheimer Films) 9/27/99, Atlanta. **Denzel Washington, Will Patton, Ethan Suplee**. EXP, Chad Oman, Mike Stenson, Michael Flynn; PROD, Jerry Bruckheimer,

Chad Oman; DIR, Boaz Yakin; SCR, Gregory Allen Howard; DISTRIB, Touchstone Films. In Alexandria, Virginia in 1971 a black football coach and a white football coach learn to work together during the integration of a black school and a white school.

The Replacements (WB./Bel Air Entertainment) 8/10/99, Baltimore, Maryland. **Keanu Reeves, Gene Hackman, Brooke Langton, Orlando Jones, Jon Favreau, Rhys Ifans, Jack Warden, Gailard Sartain, John Madden, Pat Summerall**. EXP, Steve Reuther, Erwin Stoff, Jeffrey Chernov; PROD, Dylan Sellers; DIR, Howard Deutch; SCR, Vince McKewin, Mark Steven Johnson. A comedy about a mismatched crew of outsiders who get a second chance at greatness when they are recruited to play pro football after the regular team goes on strike.

Screwed Norm MacDonald, Dave Chappelle, Elaine Strich, Danny DeVito. PROD, Robert Simonds; DIR-SCR, Scott Alexander and Larry Karaszewski. Abused and underappreciated chauffeur kidnaps his nasty employer's prized pooch with hilarious consequences.

Shaft (Scott Rudin Prods./Par.) 9/21/99, New York City. **Samuel L. Jackson, Vanessa Williams, Richard Roundtree, Christian Bale, Jeffrey Wright, Toni Collette, Dan Hedaya, Busta Rhymes**. EXP, Paul Hall, Steve Nicolaides; PROD, Scott Rudin, John Singleton, Adam Schroeder; DIR, John Singleton; SCR, Richard Price; DISTRIB, Par. An icon for an entire generation of young filmmakers, detective John Shaft now takes on the underbelly of New York in the year 2000.

The Sixth Day (Phoenix Pictures, Columbia Pictures) 12/6/99, Vancouver. **Arnold Schwarzenegger, Tony Goldwyn, Robert Duvall, Michael Rapaport, Michael Rooker, Sarah Wynter, Wendy Crewson**. EXP, David Coatsworth, Dan Petrie Jr.; PROD, Jon Davison, Arnold Schwarzenegger, Mike Medavoy; DIR, Roger Spottiswoode; SCR, Cormac Wibberley, Marianne Wibberly; CAM, Pierre Mignot; DISTRIB, Sony. Pic creates a world of the very near future in which cattle, fish, and even the family pet can be cloned. But cloning humans is illegal – that is until family man Adam Gibson comes home from work one day to find a clone has replaced him.

Space Cowboys (WB) 7/19/99, Mountain View, CA; Houston, TX; Cape Canaveral, FL. **Clint Eastwood, Tommy Lee Jones, James Garner, Donald Sutherland, James Cromwell, William Devane, Marcia Gay Hamilton, Loren Dean, Rade Sherbedgia**. PROD, Clint Eastwood, Andrew Lazar; DIR, Clint Eastwood; SCR, Ken Kaufman, Howard Klausner; DISTRIB, WB.
Four top fighter pilots, now retired, are brought back into service to assist NASA during a major satellite crisis.

State and Main (Green Renzi/El Dorado/UGC International) 9/21/99, Massachusetts. **Alec Baldwin, Charles Durning, Patti Lupone, William H. Macy, Sarah Jessica Parker, David Paymer, Rebecca Pidgeon, Julia Stiles, Philip Seymour Hoffman**. EXP, Alec Baldwin, Jon Cornick; PROD, Sarah Green, Maggi Renzi; DIR-SCR, David Mamet; CAM, Oliver Stapleton; DISTRIB, Fine Line.
Part Hollywood satire, part screwball comedy, pic explores what happens when a cellphone-wielding movie crew invades a quaint New England town. The residents are all too ready to jettison its pastoral grace for showbiz glitz.

U-571 (Dino De Laurentiis, Universal, Canal Plus Image) 1/25/99, Rome, Malta. **Matthew McConaughey, Bill Paxton, Harvey Keitel, Jon Bon Jovi, David Keith, Jake Weber**. EXP, Hal Lieberman; PROD, Dino De Laurentiis, Martha De Laurentiis; DIR, Jonathan Mostow; SCR, Sam Montgomery, David Ayer, Jonathan Mostow; CAM, Oliver Wood; DISTRIB, U.
U.S. forces try to steal a top-secret decoding device from a German U-boat during World War II.

Unbreakable 4/7/99, Philadelphia. **Bruce Willis, Samuel L. Jackson**. EXP, Gary Barber, Roger Birnbaum; PROD, M. Night Shyamalan, Barry Mendel; DIR-SCR, M. Night Shyamalan; DISTRIB, Touchstone Pictures.

From the director of *The Sixth Sense* comes a riveting story about two men: David Dunne, the sole unharmed survivor of a devastating train wreck, and Elijah Price, a stranger who proposes a bizarre explanation for it.

Unconditional Love (Avery Pix) 10/27/99, Chicago, London, Wales. **Kathy Bates, Rupert Everett, Dan Aykroyd, Jonathan Pryce**. EXP, Gil Netter; PROD, Jerry Zucker, Jocelyn Moorhouse, Patty Whitcher; DIR, P.J. Hogan; SCR, P.J. Hogan, Jocelyn Moorhouse; CAM, Remi Adefarasin; DISTRIB, New Line.
An hilarious and heart warming comedy about a middle-aged housewife and a British valet, who unite to avenge the death of a mutual love interest.

What Lies Beneath (Image Movers) 8/23/99, Los Angeles, Vermont. **Harrison Ford, Michelle Pfeiffer, Diana Scarwid, Joe Morton, Amber Valletta, James Remar, Miranda Otto, Katharine Towne**. EXP, Joan Bradshaw, Mark Johnson; PROD, Steve Starkey, Jack Rapke; DIR, Robert Zemeckis; SCR, Clark Gregg; DISTRIB, DreamWorks.
A supernatural thriller about a happily married couple whose idyllic life is threatened by mysterious events.

X-Men (Springwood Prods.) 9/13/99, Toronto, New York, Los Angeles. **Hugh Jackman, Patrick Stewart, Ian McKellen, Halle Berry, Anna Paquin, Tyler Mane, Ray Park, Rebecca Romijn-Stamos, Bruce Davison, Famke Janssen, James Marsden**. EXP, Richard Donnor, Avi Arad, Stan Lee, Tom De Santo; PROD, Lauren Shuler Donner, Ralph Winter; DIR, Bryan Singer; AD, Lee Clearly; SCR, Ed Solomon, Chris McQuarie, Joss Wheadon, David Hayter, Bryan Singer, Tom DeSanto; CAM, Tom Sigel; DISTRIB, 20th Century Fox.
The live-action, bigscreen adaptation of the most popular comicbook series ever.

It's a tiara.
You do wear it on your head.
I just LOVE finding new
places to wear diamonds.
(Norma Varden, Marilyn Monroe,
Gentlemen Prefer Blondes)

... June 24 ...
Michael Mann and Leonardo DiCaprio team up with
Disney on a biopic of Howard Hughes.

Television

TV in its widest sense has always been reported in depth by *Variety*. And as the film and broadcasting industries have interlocked ever more tightly in recent years, so coverage of TV has proved more crucial. We've arrived at a point where the stars of the tube are not just Oprah or "Ally McBeal" but also Rupert Murdoch, Silvio Berlusconi, and Ted Turner. Mighty concerns like France's TF1 and Canal Plus are involved in the financing of American pictures, while Italy's RAI is a co-producer with several countries in Europe.

Cable and satellite have played havoc with the traditional, often complacent lineup of terrestrial broadcasters, in the U.S., and around the world. As a result, the major TV industry gatherings of the year (NATPE, MIP-TV, MIPCOM, etc) have grown by leaps and bounds, with ever more channels seeking ever more product to satisfy audiences across all continents.

TV is a field in which *Variety*'s slanguage has prospered, from "feevee" (pay TV, pay cable, subscription TV), and "fin-syn" (defunct financial interest and syndication rules), to "nets" (TV networks) and "sitcom" (*Variety*'s very own word for situation comedy on TV). The Nielsen ratings appear each week, and continue to be devoured avidly by all industry watchers.

Top all-time U.S. network TV programs

Title, Telecast, Network, Rating

M*A*S*H Special	2/28/83	CBS	60.2		Ed Sullivan	2/9/64	CBS	45.3
Dallas	11/21/80	CBS	53.3		Super Bowl XXVII	1/31/93	NBC	45.1
Roots Pt. VIII	1/30/77	ABC	51.1		Bob Hope Christmas Show	1/14/71	NBC	45.0
Super Bowl XVI Game	1/24/82	CBS	49.1		Roots Pt. III	1/25/77	ABC	44.8
Super Bowl XVII Game	1/30/83	NBC	48.6		Super Bowl XXXII Game	1/25/98	NBC	44.5
XVII Winter Olympics	2/23/94	CBS	48.5		Super Bowl XI Game	1/9/77	NBC	44.4
Super Bowl XX Game	1/26/86	NBC	48.3		Super Bowl XV Game	1/25/81	NBC	44.4
Gone With the Wind-Pt.1					Super Bowl VI Game	1/16/72	CBS	44.2
(Big Event-Pt. 1)	11/7/76	NBC	47.7		XVII Winter Olympics	2/25/94	CBS	44.1
Gone With the Wind-Pt.2					Roots Pt. II	1/24/77	ABC	44.1
(NBC Mon. Mov.)	11/8/76	NBC	47.4		Beverly Hillbillies	1/8/64	CBS	44.0
Super Bowl XII Game	1/15/78	CBS	47.2		Roots Pt. IV	1/26/77	ABC	43.8
Super Bowl XIII Game	1/21/79	NBC	47.1		Ed Sullivan	2/16/64	CBS	43.8
Bob Hope Christmas Show	1/15/70	NBC	46.6		Super Bowl XXIII Game	1/22/89	NBC	43.5
Super Bowl XVIII Game	1/22/84	CBS	46.4		Academy Awards	4/7/70	ABC	43.4
Super Bowl XIX Game	1/20/85	ABC	46.4		Super Bowl XXXI Game	1/26/97	FOX	43.3
Super Bowl XIV Game	1/20/80	CBS	46.3		Thorn Birds Pt. III	3/29/83	ABC	43.2
Super Bowl XXX Game	1/28/96	NBC	46.0		Thorn Birds Pt. IV	3/30/83	ABC	43.1
ABC Sunday Night Movie					CBS NFC Championship Game	1/10/82	CBS	42.9
(The Day After)	11/20/83	ABC	46.0		Beverly Hillbillies	1/15/64	CBS	42.8
Roots Pt. VI	1/28/77	ABC	45.9		Super Bowl VII Game	1/14/73	NBC	42.7
The Fugitive	8/29/67	ABC	45.9		Thorn Birds Pt. II	3/28/83	ABC	42.5
Super Bowl XXI Game	1/25/87	CBS	45.8		Super Bowl IX Game	1/12/75	NBC	42.4
Roots Pt. V	1/27/77	ABC	45.7		Beverly Hillbillies	2/26/64	CBS	42.4
Super Bowl XXVIII Game	1/30/94	NBC	45.5		Super Bowl X Game	1/18/76	CBS	42.3
Cheers	5/20/93	NBC	45.5		Airport (Movie Specials)	11/11/73	ABC	42.3

Love Story (Sun. Night Mov.)	10/1/72	ABC	42.3	*Super Bowl XXVI*	1/26/92	CBS	40.3
Cinderella	2/22/65	CBS	42.3	*Beverly Hillbillies*	1/23/63	CBS	40.3
Roots Pt. VII	1/29/77	ABC	42.3	*Winds of War - Part 2*	2/7/83	ABC	40.2
Beverly Hillbillies	3/25/64	CBS	42.2	*Super Bowl XXXIII*	1/31/99	FOX	40.2
Beverly Hillbillies	2/5/64	CBS	42.0	*Beverly Hillbillies*	4/8/64	CBS	40.1
Super Bowl XXV Game	1/27/91	ABC	41.9	*Beverly Hillbillies*	2/13/63	CBS	40.1
Beverly Hillbillies	1/29/64	CBS	41.9	*Gunsmoke*	2/4/61	CBS	40.1
Super Bowl XXII Game	1/31/88	ABC	41.9	*Gunsmoke*	2/11/61	CBS	40.1
Miss America Pageant	9/9/61	CBS	41.8	*Bonanza*	2/14/65	NBC	40.1
Beverly Hillbillies	1/1/64	CBS	41.8	*Miss America*	9/7/63	CBS	40.0
Super Bowl VIII Game	1/13/74	CBS	41.6	*Dallas (B)*	11/9/80	CBS	40.0
Bonanza	3/8/64	NBC	41.6	*World Series - Game 6*	10/21/80	NBC	40.0
Beverly Hillbillies	1/22/64	CBS	41.5	*All in the Family*	1/15/72	CBS	40.0
Bonanza	2/16/64	NBC	41.4	*Bonanza*	4/4/65	NBC	39.9
Seinfeld	5/14/98	NBC	41.3	*Super Bowl Game V*	1/17/71	NBC	39.9
Super Bowl XXIX Game	1/29/95	ABC	41.3	*Beverly Hillbillies*	12/11/63	CBS	39.9
Bill Cosby Show	1/22/87	NBC	41.3	*Beverly Hillbillies*	3/20/63	CBS	39.7
Academy Awards	4/10/67	ABC	41.2	*Beverly Hillbillies*	3/11/64	CBS	39.7
Winds of War - Part 7	2/13/83	ABC	41.0	*Gunsmoke*	4/15/61	CBS	39.7
Bonanza	2/9/64	NBC	41.0	*World Series - Game 7*	10/22/75	NBC	39.6
Gunsmoke	1/28/61	CBS	40.9	*Beverly Hillbillies*	3/4/64	CBS	39.6
Bonanza	3/28/65	NBC	40.8	*Bonanza*	1/12/64	NBC	39.6
All in the Family	1/8/72	CBS	40.7	*Bonanza*	1/26/64	NBC	39.6
Bonanza	3/7/65	NBC	40.7	*Bonanza*	3/15/64	NBC	39.6
Beverly Hillbillies	2/20/63	CBS	40.6	*Beverly Hillbillies*	2/12/64	CBS	39.6
Beverly Hillbillies	5/1/63	CBS	40.5				
Gunsmoke	2/25/61	CBS	40.5	*Average Audience % rankings based on NTI			
Roots Pt. I	1/23/77	ABC	40.5	Pocketpiece Reports - January 1961 through February 1			
Bonanza	2/2/64	NBC	40.5	1999. Programs under 30 minutes scheduled duration			
Bonanza	2/21/65	NBC	40.4	are excluded.*			
Miss America	9/12/64	CBS	40.3				

1998-99 TV season (through Jan.2/00)

Title, Day, Network, Rating

ER	Thur	NBC	16.3	Family Law	Mon	CBS	9.8
Frasier	Tues	NBC	13.9	Providence	Fri	NBC	9.8
NFL Monday Night Football	Mon	ABC	13.9	Dharma & Greg	Tues	ABC	9.6
Friends	Thur	NBC	13.6	60 Minutes II	Tues	CBS	9.4
60 Minutes	Sun	NBC	13.6	Ally McBeal	Mon	Fox	9.4
Touched by an Angel	Sun	CBS	11.8	Drew Carey Show	Wed	ABC	9.3
NFL Monday Showcase	Mon	ABC	11.6	CBS Wednesday Movie	Wed	CBS	9.1
CBS Sunday Movie	Sun	CBS	11.5	Diagnosis Murder	Thur	CBS	9.1
Everybody Loves Raymond	Mon	CBS	11.5	The West Wing	Wed	NBC	9.1
Jesse	Thur	NBC	11.1	King of Queens	Mon	CBS	8.9
Law and Order	Wed	NBC	11.1	20/20	Fri	ABC	8.8
Stark Raving Mad	Thur	NBC	11.1	Frasier	Tues	NBC	8.8
JAG	Tues	CBS	10.6	Dateline	Mon	NBC	8.7
Judging Amy	Tues	Tues	10.6	Dateline	Fri	NBC	8.6
The Practice	Sun	ABC	10.6	Dateline	Tues	NBC	8.5
Becker	Mon	CBS	10.4	Fox NFL Sunday Post	Sun	Fox	8.5

...June 26 ...
Producer Jerry Bruckheimer, director Michael Bay and screenwriter
Randall Wallace are to work on **Tennessee**, a forthcoming film for Disney.

Dateline	Wed	NBC	8.4	Spin City	Tues	ABC	8.1
Law and Order: SVU	Mon	NBC	8.4	Fox NFL Sunday-Post	Sun	Fox	7.9
Will & Grace	Tues	NBC	8.4	Just Shoot Me	Tues	NBC	7.9
The X-Files	Sun	Fox	8.4	20/20	Mon	ABC	7.7
20/20	Wed	ABC	8.3	Chicago Hope	Thur	CBS	7.7
Ladies Man	Mon	CBS	8.2	Futurama	Sun	Fox	7.5
NBC Sunday Night Movie	Sun	NBC	8.2	Greed 2	Thur	Fox	7.5
Once and Again	Tues	ABC	8.2	Third Watch	Sun	NBC	7.5
Walker, Texas Ranger	Sat	CBS	8.2	Wonderful World of Disney	Sun	ABC	7.5
Nash Bridges	Fri	CBS	8.1				
The Simpsons	Sun	Fox	8.1	*One ratings point = approx. 1.5 million viewers*			

France: top 10 TV programs: 1999

Program	Channel	Date	(% audience)
1. World Cup Rugby France/Australia	TF1	November 6	27.0
2. TF1 20 Heures	TF1	November 19	26.3
3. *Julie Lescaut* (series)	TF1	October 28	22.7
4. *Pretty Woman*	TF1	February 21	21.8
5. *Les Cordier Juge et Flic* (series)	TF1	November 18	21.7
6. Football Match England/France (friendly)	TF1	February 10	21.6
7. *The Fugitive*	TF1	November 21	21.5
8. *Navarro* (series)	TF1	March 18	21.4
9. Football-Championnat Europe des Nations	TF1	March 31	21.3
10. *Une Femme d'Honneur* (series)	TF1	March 11	20.8

Source: Médiamat Médiamétrie

Germany: top 10 TV programs: 1999

Program	Channel	Date	Viewers (millions)
1. Wetten, dass...?	ZDF	February 20	18.16
2. Wetten, dass...?	ZDF	January 23	16.15
3. Wetten, dass...?	ZDF	March 20	15.79
4. Wetten, dass...?	ZDF	November 13	15.28
5. Wetten, dass...?	ZDF	December 11	14.87
6. Formula 1	RTL	April 11	13.69
7. Wetten, dass...?	ZDF	December 11	13.61
8. Champions League	RTL	May 26	13.58
9. European Cup	ZDF	March 31	12.13
10. European Cup	ZDF	October 9	12.06

Period: Jan. 1-Dec. 12 1999
Source: Blickpunkt: Film

Italy: top 10 TV programs: 1999

Program	Channel	Date	Viewers (millions)
1. San Remo Music Festival	RAI1	February 23	16.26
2. San Remo Music Festival	RAI1	February 27	15.62
3. San Remo Music Festival	RAI1	February 25	14.17
4. San Remo Music Festival	RAI1	February 24	13.77

...June 27...
The summer box office continues to sizzle as Sony's **Big Daddy** earns $41.2 million.

5. San Remo Music Festival	RAI1	February 26	13.66
6. Carramba Che Fortuna	RAI1	January 6	12.54
7. Italy-Bellarus (soccer match)	RAI1	March 31	12.33
8. Juventus-Manchester United (soccer match)	Canale 5	April 21	12.12
9. Italy-Denmark (soccer match)	RAI1	September 8	12.05
10. Denmark-Italy (soccer match)	RAI1	March 27	11.97

Period: Jan. 1 - Dec 20 1999

U.K.: top 50 TV programs: 1999

Program	Channel	Date	Viewers (000s)
1. Coronation Street	ITV	March 7	19,815
2. Who Wants To Be A Millionaire?	ITV	March 7	19,207
3. Coronation Street	ITV	January 4	19,029
4. Coronation Street	ITV	January 13	18,218
5. Heartbeat	ITV	February 28	17,008
6. Touch of Frost	ITV	March 21	16,849
7. Coronation Street	ITV	January 1	16,747
8. EastEnders	BBC1	January 7	15,719
9. Big Match/League Final	ITV	May 26	15,616
10. Coronation Street	ITV	December 25	15,505
11. EastEnders	BBC1	October 25	15,402
12. EastEnders	BBC1	January 26	15,382
13. Walking with Dinosaurs	BBC1	October 4	14,996
14. Big Match Champions League	ITV	November 17	14,600
15. EastEnders	BBC1	September 5	14,393
16. Vicar of Dibley	BBC1	December 27	14,367
17. New You've Been Framed	ITV	November 7	13,903
18. EastEnders	BBC1	December 31	13,440
19. Emmerdale	ITV	January 1	13,351
20. *Goldeneye*	ITV	March 10	13,228
21. Emmerdale	ITV	January 19	13,206
22. TV Nightmares	ITV	January 9	13,099
23. Casualty	BBC1	February 13	13,090
24. Emmerdale	ITV	January 14	12,986
25. EastEnders Special	BBC1	February 14	12,966
26. 2000 Today	BBC1	December 31	12,803
27. *Mission: Impossible*	BBC1	December 26	12,798
28. Neighbours from Hell	ITV	January 7	12,769
29. Comic Relief/launch	BBC1	February 4	12,468
30. EastEnders	BBC1	December 25	12,435
31. Who Wants To Be A Xmas Millionaire?	ITV	December 25	12,433
32. Stars in Their Eyes: Result	ITV	June 5	12,393
33. Weather	BBC1	December 25	12,351
34. ITV News Bulletin	ITV	November 17	12,305
35. Before They Were Famous	BBC1	December 25	12,250
36. Lost for Words	ITV	January 3	12,226
37. Stars in Their Eyes Final	ITV	June 5	12,214
38. Total Eclipse	BBC1	August 10	12,186
39. Police, Camera, Action	ITV	January 6	12,003
40. Forgotten	ITV	February 15	12,002
41. Airline	ITV	February 5	11,993

42. Ground Force	BBC1	March 5	11,986
43. Coronation/After Hours	ITV	November 13	11,951
44. Changing Rooms/Xmas	BBC1	December 27	11,877
45. *Tomorrow Never Dies*	ITV	October 13	11,860
46. News and Weather	BBC1	December 25	11,767
47. Where the Heart Is	ITV	April 18	11,699
48. BBC News	BBC1	December 25	11,693
49. Emmerdale	ITV	December 25	11,671
50. Emmerdale	ITV	November 12	11,553

Source: Taylor Nelson Sofres

Golden Globe TV Awards: 1999

Television series – drama: *The Sopranos*, HBO

Television series – musical or comedy: *Sex and the City*, HBO

Performance by an actress in a television series – drama: Edie Falco, *The Sopranos*

Performance by an actor in a television series – drama: James Gandolfini, *The Sopranos*

Performance by an actress in a television series – musical or comedy: Sarah Jessica Parker, *Sex and the City*

Performance by an actor in a television series – musical or comedy: Michael J. Fox, *Spin City*

Mini-series or motion picture made for television: *RKO 281*, HBO

Performance by an actress in a mini-series or a motion picture made for television: Halle Berry, *Introducing Dorothy Dandridge*

Performance by an actor in a mini-series or a motion picture made for television: Jack Lemmon, *Inherit the Wind*

Performance by an actress in a supporting role in a series, mini-series or motion picture made for television: Nancy Marchand, *The Sopranos*

Performance by an actor in a supporting role in a series, mini-series or motion picture made for television: Peter Fonda, *Passion of Ayn Rand*

British Academy of Film and Television Awards: 1999

Best TV Actor: Tom Courtenay, *A Rather English Marriage*

Best TV Actress: Thora Hird for *Talking Heads: Waiting for the Telegram*

Best Light Entertainer: Michael Parkinson, *Parkinson*

Best Drama Series: *The Cops*

Best Drama Serial: *Our Mutual Friend*

Best Single TV Drama: *A Rather English Marriage*

Best Comedy Series: *Father Ted*

Best Comedy Performance: Dermot Morgan, *Father Ted*

Best Factual Series: *The Human Body*

Best Light Entertainment Series: *Who Wants To Be A Millionaire?*

Best TV Documentary: *After Lockerbie*

Best News & Current Affairs Journalism: *Dispatches - Inside the Animal Liberation Front*

Best Foreign TV Program: *The Larry Sanders Show*

Dennis Potter Award: David Renwick

Lew Grade Audience Award: *Goodnight Mr. Tom*

Richard Dimbleby Award: Trevor McDonald

Golden Rose Festival, Montreux: 1999

GOLDEN ROSE: *The League of Gentlemen* (BBC, U.K.)

COMEDY

Silver Rose: *Fiktiv* (Prime Productions, Germany)

Bronze Rose: *Big Train* (Talkback, U.K.)

VARIETY

Silver Rose: *Whatever You Want* (Hat Trick, U.K.)

Bronze Rose: *Diva and the Maestro* (The Multimedia Group of Canada, Canada)

MUSIC

Silver Rose: *Nobody Does It Better* (NVC Arts, U.K.)

Bronze Rose: *Abbey Lincoln Is* (Local Films, France)

. . . June 29 . . .
Some of Hollywood's biggest names gather at Beverly Hills Tennis Club
to fête Billy Wilder, who celebrates his 93rd birthday.

ARTS & SPECIALS
Special Prize of the City of Montreux: *A Hymn for Alvin Ailey* (Thirteen/WNET, U.S.)
SITCOMS
Silver Rose: *Father Ted* (Channel 4, U.K.)
Bronze Rose: *3rd Rock from the Sun* (Carsey-Werner Productions, U.S.)

GAME SHOWS
Silver Rose: *Who Wants To Be A Millionaire?* (Celador Productions, U.K.)
Bronze Rose: *Bring Me the Head of Light Entertainment* (Channel 5, U.K.)

The Emmys

Nicknamed "Oscar's kid sister" by *Variety*, the Emmy statuette was born on January 25, 1949, with awards going to the "Best Film Made for Television" and to the "Most Popular Programs", along with nods to "Most Outstanding Personality", for the best station (KTLA in those days). As television has expanded in range and influence beyond anyone's dreams (or nightmares), so the Emmys have grown in scope to comprise some 250 different awards, covering every conceivable kind of program and technical craftsmanship. Whether it's daytime or primetime, sports or news, films or documentaries, the Emmys acknowledge its achievement. Contenders for nomination are chosen by a broad popular vote of members of NATAS (the National Academy of Television Arts and Sciences). *Variety* Editor-in-Chief Peter Bart likes telling the story of the paper's mounting an industry-wide search for the first Emmy winner – an obscure ventriloquist and puppeteer named Shirley Dinsdale, who was a naive 22-year-old when she won her award. Though her show was promptly picked up by NBC, alas, it flopped. One loyal *Variety* reader found Dinsdale living quietly in Stony Brook, New York, and she told our newspaper, "I didn't know what an Emmy was when I got it and I certainly didn't understand it afterward." Today, an Emmy can help make or break a series, and represents the ultimate accolade for anyone working in American television.

1948
Most popular program: *Pantomime Quiz*, KTLA
Best film made for television: *The Necklace* (*Your Show Time* series)
Outstanding personality: Shirley Dinsdale and puppet Judy Splinters, KTLA
Technical award: Charles Mesak
Station award: KTLA
Special award: Louis McManus

1949
Live show: *The Ed Wynn Show*, KTTV (CBS)
Outstanding live personality: Ed Wynn, KTTV (CBS)
Kinescope show: *Texaco Star Theater*, KNBH (NBC)
Outstanding kinescope personality: Milton Berle, KNBH (NBC)
Film made for and viewed on television: *The Life of Riley*, KNBH (NBC)
Children's show: *Time for Beany*, KTLA
Sports coverage: *USC-UCLA Football*, KECA-TV

(ABC) (winner, according to contemporary press accounts); *Wrestling*, KTLA (Official ATAS winner)
Public service, cultural or educational program: *Crusade in Europe*, KECA-TV (ABC), KTTV (CBS)
Technical award: Harold W. Jury
Commercial: Lucky Strike, N.W. Ayer
Station achievement: KTLA

1950
Dramatic show: *Pulitzer Prize Playhouse*, KECA-TV (ABC)
Variety show: *The Alan Young Show*, KTTV (CBS)
Cultural show: *Campus Chorus and Orchestra*, KTSL
Game and audience-participation show: *Truth or Consequence*, KTTV (CBS)
Children's show: *Time for Beany*, KTLA
Sports program: *Rams Football*, KNBH (NBC)
News program: *KTLA Newsreel*, KTLA
Educational show: *KFI-TV University*, KFI-TV
Special event: *Departure of Marines for Korea*, KFMB-

TV (San Diego), KTLA
Public service: *City at Night*, KTLA
Outstanding personality: Groucho Marx, KNBH
(NBC)
Actor: Alan Young, KTTV (CBS)
Actress: Gertrude Berg, KTTV (CBS)
Technical achievement: KNBH (NBC)
Station achievement: KTLA

1951
Dramatic show: *Studio One*, CBS
Variety show: *Your Show of Shows*, NBC
Comedy show: *The Red Skelton Show*, NBC
Actor: Sid Caesar
Actress: Imogene Coca
Comedian or comedienne: Red Skelton, NBC
Special achievement awards: Senator Estes Kefauver,
AT&T; Jack Burrell, KNBH

1952
Dramatic program: *Robert Montgomery Presents*, NBC
Situation comedy: *I Love Lucy*, CBS
Mystery, action or adventure program: *Dragnet*, NBC
Variety program: *Your Show of Shows*, NBC
Public-affairs program: *See It Now*, CBS
Children's program: *Time for Beany*, KTLA
Audience-participation, quiz or panel program:
What's My Line?, CBS
Actor: Thomas Mitchell
Actress: Helen Hayes
Comedian: Jimmy Durante, NBC
Comedienne: Lucille Ball, CBS
Outstanding personality: Bishop Fulton J. Sheen

1953
New program: (tie) *Make Room for Daddy*, ABC and
U.S. Steel Hour, ABC
Dramatic program: *U.S. Steel Hour*, ABC
Situation comedy: *I Love Lucy*, CBS
Mystery, action or adventure program: *Dragnet*, NBC
Variety program: *Omnibus*, CBS
Program of news or sports: *See It Now*, CBS
Public-affairs program: *Victory at Sea*, NBC
Audience-participation, quiz or panel program: (tie)
This Is Your Life, NBC, and *What's My Line?*, CBS
Children's program: *Kukla, Fran & Ollie*, NBC
Outstanding personality: Edward R. Murrow, CBS
Male star in a regular series: Donald O'Connor,
Colgate Comedy Hour, NBC
Female star in a regular series: Eve Arden, *Our Miss
Brooks*, CBS
Supporting actor in a regular series: Art Carney, *The
Jackie Gleason Show*, CBS

Supporting actress in a regular series: Vivian Vance, *I
Love Lucy*, CBS

1954
Single program of the year: *Operation Undersea,
Disneyland*, ABC
Dramatic series: *U.S. Steel Hour*, ABC
Situation-comedy series: *Make Room for Daddy*, ABC
Mystery or intrigue series: *Dragnet*, NBC
Western or adventure series: *Stories of the Century*,
Syndicated
Cultural, religious or educational program: *Omnibus*,
CBS
Variety series: *Disneyland*, ABC
Daytime program: *Art Linkletter's House Party*, CBS
Audience guest participation or panel
program: *This Is Your Life*, NBC
Children's program: *Lassie*, CBS
Sports program: *Gillette Cavalcade of Sports*, NBC
Actor in a regular series: Danny Thomas, *Make Room
for Daddy*, ABC
Actress in a regular series: Loretta Young, *The Loretta
Young Show*, NBC
Supporting actor in a regular series: Art Carney, *The
Jackie Gleason Show*, CBS
Supporting actress in a regular series: Audrey
Meadows, *The Jackie Gleason Show*, CBS
Single performance by an actor: Robert Cummings,
Twelve Angry Men, CBS
Single performance by an actress: Judith Anderson,
Macbeth, NBC
Male singer: Perry Como, CBS
Female singer: Dinah Shore, NBC
Most outstanding new personality: George Gobel,
NBC
News reporter or commentator: John Daly, ABC
Direction: Franklin Schaffner, *Twelve Angry Men*, CBS
Writing in dramatic material: Reginald Rose, *Twelve
Angry Men*, CBS
Writing in comedy material: James Allardice, Jack
Douglas, Hal Kanter, Harry Winkler, *The George
Gobel Show*, NBC

1955
Single program of the year: *Peter Pan, Producers'
Showcase*, NBC
Dramatic series: *Producers' Showcase*, NBC
Comedy series: *The Phil Silvers Show*, CBS
Action or adventure series: *Disneyland*, ABC
Variety series: *The Ed Sullivan Show*, CBS
Music series: *Your Hit Parade*, NBC
Special event of news program: *A-Bomb Test
Coverage*, CBS

... July 1 ...
Miss Saigon will call it quits on October 30 at the Theatre Royal,
Drury Lane, five weeks after its 10th birthday.

Documentary program: *Omnibus*, CBS
Daytime programming: *Matinee Theatre*, NBC
Audience-participation series: *The $64,000 Question*, CBS
Children's series: *Lassie*, CBS
Single performance by an actor: Lloyd Nolan, *The Caine Mutiny*
Single performance by an actress: Mary Martin, *Peter Pan, Producers' Showcase*, NBC
Continuing performance by an actor: Phil Silvers, *The Phil Silvers Show*, CBS
Continuing performance by an actress: Lucille Ball, *I Love Lucy*, CBS
Actor in a supporting role: Art Carney, *The Honeymooners*, CBS
Actress in a supporting role: Nanette Fabray, *Caesar's Hour*, NBC
Comedian: Phil Silvers, CBS
Comedienne: Nanette Fabray, NBC
Male singer: Perry Como, NBC
Female singer: Dinah Shore, NBC
MC or program host: Perry Como, NBC
News commentator or reporter: Edward R. Murrow, CBS
Specialty act – single or group: Marcel Marceau, NBC
Producer – live series: Fred Coe, *Producers' Showcase*, NBC
Producer – film series: Walt Disney, *Disneyland*, ABC
Director – live series: Franklin Schaffner, *The Caine Mutiny Court-Martial, Ford Star Jubilee*, CBS
Director – film series: Nat Hiken, *The Phil Silvers Show*, CBS
Original teleplay writing: Rod Serling, *Kraft Television Theatre*, NBC
Comedy writing: Nat Hiken, Barry Blitser, Arnold Auerbach, Harvey Orkin, Vincent Bogert, Arnold Rosen, Coleman Jacoby, Tony Webster, Terry Ryan, *The Phil Silvers Show*, CBS
Television adaptation: Paul Gregory, Franklin Schaffner, *The Caine Mutiny Court-Martial, Ford Star Jubilee*, CBS
Commercial campaign: Ford Motor Co.

1956

Single program of the year: *Requiem for a Heavyweight, Playhouse 90*, CBS
New program series: *Playhouse 90*, CBS
Series – one hour or more: *Caesar's Hour*, NBC
Series – half hour or less: *The Phil Silvers Show*, CBS
Public-service series: *See It Now*, CBS
Single performance by an actor: Jack Palance, *Requiem for a Heavyweight, Playhouse 90*, CBS

Single performance by an actress: Claire Trevor, *Dodsworth, Producers' Showcase*, NBC
Actor in a drama series: Robert Young, *Father Knows Best*, NBC
Actress in a drama series: Loretta Young, *The Loretta Young Show*, NBC
Comedian in a series: Sid Caesar, *Caesar's Hour*, NBC
Comedienne in a series: Nanette Fabray, *Caesar's Hour*, NBC
Supporting actor: Carl Reiner, *Caesar's Hour*, NBC
Supporting actress: Pat Carroll, *Caesar's Hour*, NBC
Male personality: Perry Como, NBC
Female personality: Dinah Shore, NBC
Coverage/newsworthy event: *Years of Crisis*, CBS
News commentator: Edward R. Murrow, CBS
Direction – one hour or more: Ralph Nelson, *Requiem for a Heavyweight, Playhouse 90*, CBS
Direction – half hour or less: Sheldon Leonard, *The Danny Thomas Show*, ABC
Teleplay writing – half hour or less: James P. Cavanagh, *Alfred Hitchcock Presents*, CBS
Teleplay writing – one hour or more: Rod Serling, *Requiem for a Heavyweight, Playhouse 90*, CBS
Comedy writing: Nat Hiken, Billy Friedberg, Tony Webster, Leonard Stern, Arnold Rosen, Coleman Jacoby, *The Phil Silvers Show*, CBS

1957

Single program of the year: *The Comedian, Playhouse 90*, CBS
New series: *The Seven Lively Arts*, CBS
Drama series: *Gunsmoke*, CBS
Comedy series: *The Phil Silvers Show*, CBS
Dramatic anthology series: *Playhouse 90*, CBS
Music, variety, audience-participation or quiz show: *The Dinah Shore Chevy Show*, NBC
Public-service program or series: *Omnibus*, ABC, NBC
Single performance by an actor – lead or support: Peter Ustinov, *The Life of Samuel Johnson, Omnibus*, NBC
Single performance by an actress – lead or support: Polly Bergen, *The Helen Morgan Story, Playhouse 90*, CBS
Continuing performance in a series by a man who essentially plays himself: Jack Benny, *The Jack Benny Show*, CBS
Continuing performance in a series by a woman who essentially plays herself: Dinah Shore, *The Dinah Shore Chevy Show*, NBC
Continuing performance by a lead actor in a dramatic or comedy series: Robert Young, *Father Knows Best*, NBC

Continuing performance by a lead actress in a dramatic or comedy series: Jane Wyatt, *Father Knows Best*, NBC

Supporting actor in a drama or comedy series: Carl Reiner, *Caesar's Hour*, NBC

Supporting actress in a drama or comedy series: Ann B. Davis, *The Bob Cummings Show*, CBS, NBC

Coverage of an unscheduled newsworthy event: Rikers Island, New York, plane crash, *World News Round-Up*, CBS

News commentary: Edward R. Murrow, *See It Now*, CBS

Direction – one hour or more: Bob Banner, *The Dinah Shore Chevy Show*, NBC

Direction – half hour or less: Robert Stevens *The Glass Eye*, *Alfred Hitchcock Presents*, CBS

Teleplay writing – one hour or more: Rod Serling, *The Comedian*, *Playhouse 90*, CBS

Teleplay writing – half hour or less: Paul Monash, *The Lonely Wizard*

Comedy writing: Nat Hiken, Billy Friedberg, Phil Sharp, Terry Ryan, Coleman Jacoby, Arnold Rosen, Sidney Zelinka, A.J. Russell, Tony Webster, *The Phil Silvers Show*, CBS

1958-59

Single program of the year: *An Evening with Fred Astaire*, NBC

Dramatic series – one hour or longer: *Playhouse 90*, CBS

Dramatic series – less than one hour: *The Alcoa Hour*, *Goodyear Theatre*, NBC

Special dramatic program: *Little Moon of Alban*, *Hallmark Hall of Fame*, NBC

Comedy series: *The Jack Benny Show*, CBS

Western series: *Maverick*, ABC

Music or variety series: *The Dinah Shore Chevy Show*, NBC

Special music or variety program – one hour or longer: *An Evening with Fred Astaire*, NBC

Public-service program or series: *Omnibus*, NBC

News-reporting series: *The Huntley-Brinkley Report*, NBC

Special news program: *The Face of Red China*, CBS

Panel, quiz or audience-participation series: *What's My Line?*, CBS

Actor in a drama series: Raymond Burr, *Perry Mason*, CBS

Actress in a drama series: Loretta Young, *The Loretta Young Show*, NBC

Actor in a comedy series: Jack Benny, *The Jack Benny Show*, CBS

Actress in a comedy series: Jane Wyatt, *Father Knows Best*, NBC

Single performance by an actor: Fred Astaire, *An Evening with Fred Astaire*, NBC

Single performance by an actress: Julie Harris, *Little Moon of Alban*, *Hallmark Hall of Fame*, NBC

Supporting actor in a drama series: Dennis Weaver, *Gunsmoke*, CBS

Supporting actress in a drama series: Barbara Hale, *Perry Mason*, CBS

Supporting actor in a comedy series: Tom Poston, *The Steve Allen Show*, NBC

Supporting actress in a comedy series: Ann B. Davis, *The Bob Cummings Show*, NBC

Actor in a variety series: Perry Como, *The Perry Como Show*, NBC

Actress in a variety series: Dinah Shore, *The Dinah Shore Chevy Show*, NBC

News commentator: Edward R. Murrow, CBS

Direction of a single dramatic program – one hour or longer: George Schaefer, *Little Moon of Alban*, *Hallmark Hall of Fame*, NBC

Direction of a single program of a drama series – under one hour: Jack Smight, *Eddie*, *Alcoa Hour*, *Goodyear Theatre*, NBC

Direction of a single program of a comedy series: Peter Tewksbury, *Medal for Margaret*, *Father Knows Best*, CBS

Direction of a music or variety program: Bud Yorkin, *An Evening with Fred Astaire*, NBC

Writing of a single dramatic program – one hour or longer: James Costigan, *Little Moon of Alban*, *Hallmark Hall of Fame*, NBC

Writing of a single program of a drama series – less than one hour: Alfred Brenner, Ken Hughes, *Eddie*, *Alcoa Hour*, *Goodyear Theatre*, NBC

Writing of a single program of a comedy series: Sam Perrin, George Balzer, Hal Goldman, Al Gordon, *The Jack Benny Show*, CBS

Writing of a single music or variety program: Bud Yorkin, Herbert Baker, *An Evening with Fred Astaire*, NBC

1959-60

Drama program: *Playhouse 90*, CBS

Humor program: *Art Carney Special*, NBC

Variety program: *The Fabulous Fifties*, CBS

Public-affairs program: *The Twentieth Century*, CBS

News program: *The Huntley-Brinkley Report*, NBC

Music program: *Leonard Bernstein and the New York Philharmonic*, CBS

Children's program: *Huckleberry Hound*, syndicated

Actor in a series – lead or supporting: Robert Stack, *The Untouchables*, ABC

...July 3 ...
Actress Isabelle Huppert is developing a feature adaptation of
Doris Lessing's novel **The Grass Is Singing**.

Actress in a series – lead or supporting: Jane Wyatt, *Father Knows Best*, NBC

Single performance by an actor – lead or supporting: Laurence Olivier, *The Moon and Sixpence*, NBC

Single performance by an actress – lead or supporting: Ingrid Bergman, *The Turn of the Screw*, Ford Startime, NBC

Single performance in a variety or music program or series: Harry Belafonte, *Tonight with Belafonte, The Revlon Revue*, CBS

Directing in drama: Robert Mulligan, *The Moon and Sixpence*, NBC

Directing in comedy: Ralph Levy, Bud Yorkin, *The Jack Benny Hour Special*, CBS

Writing in drama: Rod Serling, *The Twilight Zone*, CBS

Writing in comedy: Sam Perrin, George Balzer, Al Gordon, Hal Goldman, *The Jack Benny Show*, CBS

Writing in documentary field: Howard K. Smith, Av Westin, *The Population Explosion, CBS Report*, CBS

1960-61

Program of the year: *Macbeth, Hallmark Hall of Fame*, NBC

Drama program: *Macbeth, Hallmark Hall of Fame*, NBC

Humor program: *The Jack Benny Show*, CBS

Variety program: *Astaire Time*, NBC

Public-affairs program: *The Twentieth Century*, CBS

News program: *The Huntley-Brinkley Report*, NBC

Children's program: *Aaron Copland's Birthday Party, Young People's Concert*, CBS

Lead actor in a series: Raymond Burr, *Perry Mason*, CBS

Lead actress in a series: Barbara Stanwyck, *The Barbara Stanwyck Show*, NBC

Single performance by a lead actor: Maurice Evans, *Macbeth, Hallmark Hall of Fame*, NBC

Single performance by a lead actress: Judith Anderson, *Macbeth, Hallmark Hall of Fame*, NBC

Supporting actor or actress in a single program: Roddy McDowall, *Not without Honor, Equitable's American Heritage*, NBC

Supporting actor or actress in a series: Don Knotts, *The Andy Griffith Show*, CBS

Performance in a variety or music program or series: Fred Astaire, *Astaire Time*, NBC

Directing in drama: George Schaefer, *Macbeth, Hallmark Hall of Fame*, NBC

Directing in comedy: Sheldon Leonard, *Danny Thomas Show*, CBS

Writing in drama: Rod Serling, *The Twilight Zone*, CBS

Writing in comedy: Sherwood Schwartz, Dave O'Brien, Al Schwartz, Martin Ragaway, Red Skelton, *The Red Skelton Show*, CBS

Documentary writing: Victor Wolfson, *Winston Churchill – The Valiant Years*, ABC

1961-62

Program of the year: *Victoria Regina, Hallmark Hall of Fame*, NBC

Drama program: *The Defenders*, CBS

Humor program: *The Bob Newhart Show*, NBC

Variety or music program: (variety) *The Garry Moore Show*, CBS; (music) *Leonard Bernstein and the New York Philharmonic in Japan*, CBS

News program: *The Huntley-Brinkley Report*, NBC

Educational or public affairs program: *David Brinkley's Journal*, NBC

Daytime program: *Purex Specials for Women*, NBC

Lead actor in a series: E.G. Marshal, *The Defenders*, CBS

Lead actress in a series: Shirley Booth, *Hazel*, NBC

Single performance by a lead actor: Peter Falk, *Dick Powell Theatre*, NBC

Single performance by a lead actress: Julie Harris, *Victoria Regina, Hallmark Hall of Fame*, NBC

Supporting actor: Don Knotts, *The Andy Griffith Show*, CBS

Supporting actress: Pamela Brown, *Victoria Regina, Hallmark Hall of Fame*, NBC

Performance in a variety or music program or series: Carol Burnett, *The Garry Moore Show*, CBS

Directing in drama: Franklin Schaffner, *The Defenders*, CBS

Directing in comedy: Nat Hiken, *Car 54, Where Are You?*, NBC

Writing in drama: Reginald Rose, *The Defenders*, CBS

Writing in comedy: Carl Reiner, *The Dick Van Dyke Show*, CBS

Documentary writing: Lou Hazam, *Vincent Van Gogh: A Self-Portrait*, NBC

1962-63

Program of the year: *The Tunnel*, NBC

Drama program: *The Defenders*, CBS

Humor program: *The Dick Van Dyke Show*, CBS

Variety program: *The Andy Williams Show*, NBC

Music program: *Julie and Carol at Carnegie Hall*, CBS

Panel, quiz or audience-participation program: *College Bowl*, CBS

Documentary program: *The Tunnel*, NBC

Children's program: *Walt Disney's Wonderful World of Color*, NBC

Outstanding achievement in news: *The Huntley-Brinkley Report*, NBC

Outstanding program achievement in news commentary or public affairs: *David Brinkley's Journal,* NBC

Outstanding achievement in international reporting or commentary: Piers Anderton, *The Tunnel,* NBC

Lead actor in a series: E. G. Marshal, *The Defenders,* CBS

Lead actress in a series: Shirley Booth, *Hazel,* NBC

Single performance by a lead actor: Trevor Howard, *The Invincible Mr. Disraeli, Hallmark Hall of Fame,* NBC

Single performance by a lead actress: Kim Stanley, *Ben Casey,* ABC

Supporting actor: Don Knotts, *The Andy Griffith Show,* CBS

Supporting actress: Glenda Farrell, *Ben Casey,* ABC

Performance in a variety or music program or series: Carol Burnett, *Julie and Carol at Carnegie Hall* and *Carol & Company,* CBS

Directing in drama: Stuart Rosenberg, *The Defenders,* CBS

Directing in comedy: John Rich, *The Dick Van Dyke Show,* CBS

Writing in drama: Robert Thom, Reginald Rose, *The Defenders,* CBS

Writing in comedy: Carl Reiner, *The Dick Van Dyke Show,* CBS

1963-64

Program of the year: *The Making of the President 1960,* ABC

Drama program: *The Defenders,* CBS

Comedy program: *The Dick Van Dyke Show,* CBS

Variety program: *The Danny Kaye Show,* CBS

Music program: *The Bell Telephone Hour,* NBC

News program: *The Huntley-Brinkley Report,* NBC

News or public affairs commentary: *Cuba: Parts I and II – the Bay of Pigs and the Missile Crisis, NBC White Paper,* NBC

Documentary program: *The Making of the President 1960,* ABC

Children's program: *Discovery '63-'64,* ABC

Lead actor in a series: Dick Van Dyke, *The Dick Van Dyke Show,* CBS

Lead actress in a series: Mary Tyler Moore, *The Dick Van Dyke Show,* CBS

Single performance by a lead actor: Jack Klugman, *The Defenders,* CBS

Single performance by a lead actress: Shelley Winters, *Two Is the Number, Bob Hope Presents the Chrysler Theater,* NBC

Supporting actor: Albert Paulsen, *One Day in the Life of Ivan Denisovich, Bob Hope Presents the Chrysler Theater,* NBC

Supporting actress: Ruth White, *Little Moon of Alban, Hallmark Hall of Fame,* NBC

Performance in a variety or music program or series: Danny Kaye, *The Danny Kaye Show,* CBS

Directing in drama: Tom Gries, *East Side, West Side*

Directing in comedy: Jerry Paris, *The Dick Van Dyke Show,* CBS

Directing in variety or music: Robert Scheerer, *The Danny Kaye Show,* CBS

Drama writing – original: Ernest Kinoy, *The Defenders,* CBS

Drama writing – adaptation: Rod Serling, *It's Mental Work, Bob Hope Presents the Chrysler Theater,* NBC

Writing in comedy or variety: Carl Reiner, Sam Denoff, Bill Persky, *The Dick Van Dyke Show,* CBS

1964-65

Entertainment programs: *The Dick Van Dyke Show,* CBS; *The Magnificent Yankee, Hallmark Hall of Fame,* NBC; *My Name Is Barbra,* CBS; *What is Sonata Form?, New York Philharmonic Young People's Concerts with Leonard Bernstein,* CBS

News, documentary, information and sports programs: *I, Leonardo da Vinci, Saga of Western Man,* ABC

Outstanding achievement in entertainment (actors and performers): Leonard Bernstein, *New York Philharmonic Young People's Concerts with Leonard Bernstein ,* CBS; Lynn Fontaine, *The Magnificent Yankee, Hallmark Hall of Fame,* NBC; Alfred Lunt, *The Magnificent Yankee, Hallmark Hall of Fame,* NBC; Barbra Streisand, *My Name Is Barbra,* CBS; Dick Van Dyke, *The Dick Van Dyke Show,* CBS

Outstanding achievement in entertainment (writers): David Karp, *The Defenders,* CBS

Outstanding achievement in entertainment (directors): Paul Bogart, *The Defenders,* CBS

Outstanding achievement in news, documentaries, and sports (narrators): Richard Basehart, *Let My People Go,* syndicated

Outstanding achievement in news, documentaries, and sports (directors): John L. Sughrue, *The Louvre,* NBC

Outstanding achievement in news, documentaries, and sports (writers): Sidney Carroll, *The Louvre,* NBC

1965-66

PRIMETIME PROGRAM AWARDS

Drama series: *The Fugitive,* ABC

Single dramatic program: *The Ages of Man,* ABC

Comedy series: *The Dick Van Dyke Show,* CBS

Variety series: *The Andy Williams Show,* NBC

Variety special: *Chrysler Presents the Bob Hope Christmas Special*, NBC

Musical program: Frank Sinatra: *A Man and His Music*, NBC

Children's program: *A Charlie Brown Christmas*, CBS

PERFORMANCE, DIRECTING, AND WRITING

Actor in a drama series: Bill Cosby, *I Spy*, NBC

Actress in a drama series: Barbara Stanwyck, *The Big Valley*, ABC

Actor in a comedy series: Dick Van Dyke, *The Dick Van Dyke Show*, CBS

Actress in a comedy series: Mary Tyler Moore, *The Dick Van Dyke Show*, CBS

Actor in a drama special: Cliff Robertson, *The Game, Bob Hope Presents the Chrysler Theater*, NBC

Actress in a drama: Simone Signoret, *A Small Rebellion, Bob Hope Presents the Chrysler Theater*, NBC

Supporting actor in a drama: James Daly, *Eagle in a Cage, Hallmark Hall of Fame*, NBC

Supporting actress in a drama: Lee Grant, *Payton Place*, ABC

Supporting actor in a comedy: Don Knotts, *The Andy Griffith Show*, CBS

Supporting actress in a comedy: Alice Pearce, *Bewitched*, ABC

Directing in drama: Sydney Pollack, *The Game, Bob Hope Presents the Chrysler Theater*, NBC

Directing in comedy: William Asher, *Bewitched*, ABC

Directing in variety or music: Alan Handley, *The Julie Andrews Show*, NBC

Writing in drama: Millard Lampell, *Eagle in a Cage, Hallmark Hall of Fame*, NBC

Writing in comedy: Bill Persky, Sam Denoff, *The Dick Van Dyke Show*, CBS

Writing in variety: Al Gordon, Hal Goldman, Sheldon Keller, *An Evening with Carol Channing*, CBS

THE AREAS

News and documentary program: *American White Paper: United States Foreign Policy*, NBC

Daytime program: *Camera Three*, CBS; *Wild Kingdom*, NBC

Sports program: *ABC's Wide World of Sports*, ABC

1966-67

PRIMETIME PROGRAM AWARDS

Drama series: *Mission: Impossible*, CBS

Single dramatic program: *Death of a Salesman*, CBS

Comedy series: *The Monkees*, NBC

Variety series: *The Andy Williams Show*, NBC

Variety special: *The Sid Caesar, Imogene Coca, Carl Reiner, Howard Morris Special*, CBS

Music program: *Brigadoon*, ABC

Children's program: *Jack and the Beanstalk*, NBC

PERFORMANCE, DIRECTING, AND WRITING

Actor in a drama series: Bill Cosby, *I Spy*, NBC

Actress in a drama series: Barbara Bain, *Mission:Impossible*, CBS

Single performance by a lead actor in a drama: Peter Ustinov, *Barefoot in Athens, Hallmark Hall of Fame*, NBC

Single performance by a lead actress in a drama: Geraldine Page, *A Christmas Memory, ABC Stage 67*, ABC

Actor in a comedy series: Don Adams, *Get Smart*, NBC

Actress in a comedy series: Lucille Ball, *The Lucy Show*, CBS

Supporting actor in a drama: Eli Wallach, *The Poppy Is Also a Flower, Xerox Special*, ABC

Supporting actress in a drama: Agnes Moorehead, *The Wild, Wild West*, CBS

Supporting actor in a comedy: Don Knotts, *The Andy Griffith Show*, CBS

Supporting actress in a comedy: Frances Bavier, *The Andy Griffith Show*, CBS

Directing in drama: Alex Segal, *Death of a Salesman*, CBS

Directing in comedy: James Frawley, *The Monkees*, NBC

Directing in variety or music: Fiedler Cook, *Brigadoon*, ABC

Writing in drama: Bruce Geller, *Mission: Impossible*, CBS

Writing in comedy: Buck Henry, Leonard Stern, *Get Smart*, NBC

Writing in variety: Mel Brooks, Sam Denoff, Bill Persky, Carl Reiner, Mel Tolkin, *The Sid Caesar, Imogene Coca, Carl Reiner, Howard Morris Special*, CBS

THE AREAS

News and documentary program: *China: The Roots of Madness*, syndicated

Daytime program: *Mutual of Omaha's Wild Kingdom*, NBC

Sports program: *ABC's Wide World of Sports*, ABC

1967-68

PRIMETIME PROGRAM AWARDS

Single dramatic program: *Elizabeth the Queen, Hallmark Hall of Fame*, NBC

Drama series: *Mission: Impossible*, CBS

Comedy series: *Get Smart*, NBC

Music or variety program: *Rowan and Martin's Laugh-In Special*, NBC

Music or variety series: *Rowan and Martin's Laugh-In*, NBC

PERFORMANCE, DIRECTING, AND WRITING

Actor in a drama series: Bill Cosby, *I Spy*, NBC

Actress in a drama series: Barbara Bain, *Mission: Impossible*, CBS

Actor in a drama special: Melvyn Douglas, *Do Not Go Gentle into That Good Night*, CBS Playhouse, CBS

Actress in a drama special: Maureen Stapleton, *Among the Paths to Eden*, Xerox Special, ABC

Actor in a comedy series: Don Adams, *Get Smart*, NBC

Actress in a comedy series: Lucille Ball, *The Lucy Show*, CBS

Supporting actor in a drama special: Milburn Stone, *Gunsmoke*, CBS

Supporting actress in a drama special: Barbara Anderson, *Ironside*, NBC

Supporting actor in a comedy: Werner Klemperer, *Hogan's Heroes*, CBS

Supporting actress in a comedy: Marion Lorne, *Bewitched*, ABC

Directing in drama special: Paul Bogart, *Dear Friends*, CBS Playhouse, CBS

Directing in comedy: Bruce Bilson, *Get Smart*, NBC

Directing in music or variety: Jack Haley, Jr., *Movin' with Nancy*, NBC

Writing in drama: Loring Mandel, *Do Not Go Gentle into That Good Night*, CBS Playhouse, CBS

Writing in comedy: Allan Burns, Chris Hayward, *He & She*, CBS

Writing in music or variety: Chris Beard, Phil Hahn, Jack Hanrahan, Coslough Johnson, Marc London, Paul Keyes, Allan Manings, David Panich, Hugh Wedlock, Digby Wolfe, *Rowan and Martin's Laugh-In*, NBC

THE AREAS

Daytime program: *Today*, NBC

Sports programming (programs): *ABC's Wide World of Sports*, ABC

1968-69

PRIMETIME PROGRAM AWARDS

Single dramatic program: *Teacher, Teacher*, Hallmark Hall of Fame, NBC

Drama series: *N.E.T. Playhouse*, NET

Comedy series: *Get Smart*, NBC

Music or variety series: *Rowan and Martin's Laugh-In*, NBC

Music or variety program: *The Bill Cosby Special*, NBC

PERFORMANCE, DIRECTING, AND WRITING

Actor in a drama special: Paul Scofield, *Male of the Species*, Prudential's On Stage, NBC

Actress in a drama special: Geraldine Page, *The Thanksgiving Visitor*, ABC

Actor in a drama series: Carl Betz, *Judd for the Defence*, ABC

Actress in a drama series: Barbara Bain, *Mission: Impossible*, CBS

Actor in a comedy series: Don Adams, *Get Smart*, NBC

Actress in a comedy series: Hope Lange, *The Ghost and Mrs. Muir*, NBC

Supporting actor: no winner

Supporting actress: Anna Calder-Marshal, *Male of the Species*, Prudential's On Stage, NBC

Supporting actor in a series: Werner Klemperer, *Hogan's Heroes*, CBS

Supporting actress in a series: Susan Saint James, *The Name of the Game*, NBC

Directing in drama: David Green, *The People Next Door*, CBS Playhouse, CBS

Directing in comedy, variety or music: no winner

Writing in drama: J.P. Miller, *The People Next Door*, CBS Playhouse, CBS

Writing in comedy, variety or music: Alan Blye, Bob Einstein, Murray Roman, Carl Gottlieb, Jerry Music, Steve Martin, Cecil Tuck, Paul Wayne, Cy Howard, Mason Williams, *The Smothers Brothers Comedy Hour*, CBS

THE AREAS

Daytime programming: *The Dick Cavett Show*, ABC

Sports programming (programs): *19th Summer Olympic Games*, ABC

1969-70

PRIMETIME PROGRAM AWARDS

New series: *Room 222*, ABC

Single dramatic program: *A Storm in Summer*, Hallmark Hall of Fame, NBC

Drama series: *Marcus Welby, M.D.*, ABC

Comedy series: *My World and Welcome to It*, NBC

Variety or music program (variety and popular music): *Annie, the Woman in the Life of a Man*, CBS

Variety or music program (classical music): *Cinderella*, National Ballet of Canada, NET

Variety or music series: *The David Frost Show*, syndicated

PERFORMANCE, DIRECTING, AND WRITING

Single performance by a lead actor: Peter Ustinov, *A Storm in Summer*, Hallmark Hall of Fame, NBC

Single performance by a lead actress: Patty Duke, *My Sweet Charlie*, NBC

Actor in a drama series: Robert Young, *Marcus Welby, M.D.*, ABC

Actress in a drama series: Susan Hampshire, *The Forsyte Saga*, NET

Actor in a comedy series: William Windom, *My World and Welcome to It*, NBC

Actress in a comedy series: Hope Lange, *The Ghost and Mrs. Muir*, ABC

Supporting actor in drama: James Brolin, *Marcus Welby, M.D.*, ABC

Supporting actress in drama: Gail Fisher, *Mannix*, CBS

Supporting actor in comedy: Michael Constantin, *Room 222*, ABC

Supporting actress in comedy: Karen Valentine, *Room 222*, ABC

Directing in drama: Paul Bogart, *Shadow Game*, CBS

Directing in comedy, variety or music: Dwight A. Hemion, *The Sound of Burt Bacharach, The Kraft Music Hall*, NBC

Writing in drama: Richard Levinson, William Link, *My Sweet Charlie*, NBC

Writing in comedy, variety or music: Gary Belkin, Peter Bellwood, Herb Sargent, Thomas Meehan, Judith Viorst, *Annie, the Woman in the Life of a Man*, CBS

THE AREAS

Daytime programming: *Today*, NBC

Children's programming (programs): *Sesame Street*, NET

Sports programming (programs): *The NLF Games*, CBS; *ABC's Wide World of Sports*, ABC

1970-71

PRIMETIME PROGRAM AWARDS

Outstanding program: *The Andersonville Trial, Hollywood Television Theatre*, PBS

New series: *All in the Family*, CBS

Drama series: *The Senator, The Bold Ones*, NBC

Comedy series: *All in the Family*, CBS

Variety or music program (popular music): *Singer Presents Burt Bacharach*, CBS

Variety or music program (classical music): *Leopold Stokowski, N.E.T. Festival*, PBS

Variety series – music: *The Flip Wilson Show*, NBC

Variety series – talk: *The David Frost Show*, syndicated

PERFORMANCE, DIRECTING, AND WRITING

Single performance by a lead actor: George C. Scott, *The Price, Hallmark Hall of Fame*, NBC

Single performance by a lead actress: Lee Grant, *The Neon Ceiling*, NBC

Actor in a drama series: Hal Holbrook, *The Senator, The Bold Ones*, NBC

Actress in a drama series: Susan Hampshire, *The First Churchills, Masterpiece Theatre*, PBS

Actor in a comedy series: Jack Klugman, *The Odd Couple*, ABC

Actress in a comedy series: Jean Stapleton, *All in the Family*, CBS

Supporting actor in a drama: David Burns, *The Price, Hallmark Hall of Fame*, NBC

Supporting actress in a drama: Margaret Leighton, *Hamlet, Hallmark Hall of Fame*, NBC

Supporting actor in a comedy: Ed Asner, *The Mary Tyler Moore Show*, CBS

Supporting actress in a comedy: Valerie Harper, *The Mary Tyler Moore Show*, CBS

Directing in drama (special program): Fiedler Cook, *The Price, Hallmark Hall of Fame*, NBC

Directing in drama (single program or series): Daryl Duke, *The Senator, The Bold Ones*, NBC

Directing in comedy: Jay Sandrich, *The Mary Tyler Moore Show*, CBS

Directing in variety or music: Mark Warren, *Rowan and Martin's Laugh-In*, NBC

Writing in drama: Joel Oliansky, *The Senator, The Bold Ones*, NBC

Writing in comedy: James L. Brooks, Allan Burns, *The Mary Tyler Moore Show*, CBS

THE AREAS

Daytime programming (programs): *Today*, NBC

Children's programming (programs): *Sesame Street*, PBS

Sports programming (programs): *ABC's Wide World of Sports*, ABC

1971-72

PRIMETIME PROGRAM AWARDS

Outstanding program: *Brian's Song*, ABC

New series: *Elizabeth R, Masterpiece Theatre*, PBS

Drama series: *Elizabeth R, Masterpiece Theatre*, PBS

Comedy series: *All in the Family*, CBS

Variety or music program (variety and popular music): *Jack Lemmon in 'S Wonderful, 'S Marvelous, 'S Gershwin*, NBC

Variety or music program (classical music): *Beethoven's Birthday: a Celebration in Vienna with Leonard Bernstein*, CBS

Variety series (music): *The Carol Burnett Show*, CBS

Variety series (talk): *The Dick Cavett Show*, CBS

PERFORMANCE, DIRECTING, AND WRITING

Single performance by a lead actor: Keith Michell, *Catherine Howard, The Six Wives of Henry VIII*, CBS

Single performance by a lead actress: Glenda Jackson, *Shadow in the Sun, Elizabeth R, Masterpiece Theatre*, PBS

Actor in a drama series: Peter Falk, *Columbo*, NBC

... July 8 ...

The third installment in J.K. Rowling's Harry Potter series, **Harry Potter and the Prisoner of Azkaban** is the fastest-selling novel ever in the U.K.

Actress in a drama series: Glenda Jackson, *Elizabeth R, Masterpiece Theatre*, PBS

Actor in a comedy series: Carroll O'Connor, *All in the Family*, CBS

Actress in a comedy series: Jean Stapleton, *All in the Family*, CBS

Supporting actor in a drama: Jack Warden, *Brian's Song*, ABC

Supporting actress in a drama: Jenny Agutter, *The Snow Goose, Hallmark Hall of Fame*, NBC

Supporting actor in a comedy: Ed Asner, *The Mary Tyler Moore Show*, CBS

Supporting actress in a comedy: (tie) Valerie Harper, *The Mary Tyler Moore Show*, CBS; Sally Struthers, *All in the Family*, CBS

Performer in music or variety: Harvey Korman, *The Carol Burnett Show*, CBS

Directing in drama (series): Alexander Singer, *The Lawyers, The Bold Ones*, NBC

Directing in drama (special): Tom Gries, *The Glass House*, CBS

Directing in comedy: John Rich, *All in the Family*, CBS

Directing in variety or music (series): Art Fisher, *The Sonny and Cher Comedy Hour*, CBS

Directing in comedy, variety or music (special): Walter C. Miller, Martin Charnin, *Jack Lemmon in 'S Wonderful, 'S Marvelous, 'S Gershwin*, NBC

Writing in a drama series: Richard L. Levinson, William Link, *Columbo*, NBC

Writing in a comedy series: Burt Styler, *All in the Family*, CBS

THE AREAS

Daytime drama programming (programs): *The Doctors*, NBC

Children's programming (programs): *Sesame Street*, PBS

Sports programming (programs): *ABC's Wide World of Sports*, ABC

1972-73

PRIMETIME AND DAYTIME PROGRAM AWARDS

New series: *America*, NBC

Drama series: *The Waltons*, CBS

Comedy series: *All in the Family*, CBS

Drama/comedy – limited episodes: *Tom Brown's Schooldays, Masterpiece Theatre*, PBS

Single program: *A War of Children*, CBS

Variety/music series: *The Julie Andrews Hour*, ABC

Variety/music program: *Singer Presents Liza with a "Z,"* NBC

Classical music program: *Sleeping Beauty*, PBS

Daytime drama: *The Edge of Night*, CBS

Daytime program: *Dinah's Place*, NBC

PERFORMANCE, DIRECTING, AND WRITING

Lead actor (drama series – continuing): Richard Thomas, *The Waltons*, CBS

Lead actor (drama/comedy – limited episodes): Anthony Murphy, *Tom Brown's Schooldays, Masterpiece Theatre*, PBS

Lead actress (drama series – continuing): Michael Learned, *The Waltons*, CBS

Lead actress (drama/comedy – limited episodes): Susan Hampshire, *Vanity Fair, Masterpiece Theatre*, PBS

Actor in a comedy series: Jack Klugman, *The Odd Couple*, ABC

Actress in a comedy series: Mary Tyler Moore, *The Mary Tyler Moore Show*, CBS

Single performance by a lead actor: Laurence Olivier, *Long Day's Journey into Night*, ABC

Single performance by a lead actress: Cloris Leachman, *A Brand New Life*, ABC

Supporting actor in drama: Scott Jacoby, *That Certain Summer*, ABC

Supporting actress in drama: Ellen Corby, *The Waltons*, CBS

Supporting actor in comedy: Ted Knight, *The Mary Tyler Moore Show*, CBS

Supporting actress in comedy: Valerie Harper, *The Mary Tyler Moore Show*, CBS

Supporting performer in music or variety: Tim Conway, *The Carol Burnett Show*, CBS

Directing in drama (series): Jerry Thorpe, *Kung Fu*, ABC

Directing in drama (special): Joseph Sargent, *The Marcus-Nelson Murders*, CBS

Directing in comedy: Jay Sandrich, *The Mary Tyler Moore Show*, CBS

Directing in comedy, variety or music (series): Bill Davis, *The Julie Andrews Hour*, ABC

Directing in comedy, variety or music (special): Bob Fosse, *Singer Presents Liza with a "Z,"* NBC

Writing in drama series: John McGreevey, *The Waltons*, CBS

Writing in a comedy series: Michael Ross, Bernie West, Lee Kalcheim, *All in the Family*, CBS

THE AREAS

Outstanding achievement in a daytime drama: Mary Fickett, performer, *All My Children*, ABC

Children's programming (programs): *Sesame Street*, PBS

Sports programming (programs): *ABC's Wide World of Sports*, ABC

INTERNATIONAL AWARD WINNERS

Fiction: *La Cabina*, Televisión Española, Spain

...July 9...

Disney has taken its boldest leap yet toward vertical integration with the consolidation of Disney's TV production arm and ABC's primetime division into a single entity.

Nonfiction: *Horizon: The Making of a Natural History Film*, BBC, U.K.
Directorate award: Charles Curran

1973-74
PRIMETIME PROGRAM AWARDS
Drama series: *Upstairs, Downstairs, Masterpiece Theatre*, PBS
Comedy series: *M*A*S*H*, CBS
Limited series: *Columbo*, NBC
Special: *The Autobiography of Miss Jane Pittman*, CBS
Music/variety series: *The Carol Burnett Show*, CBS
Comedy/variety or music special: *Lily Tomlin*, CBS
Children's special: *Marlo Thomas and Friends in Free to Be... You and Me*, ABC
PERFORMANCE, DIRECTING, AND WRITING
Actor in a drama series: Telly Savalas, *Kojak*, CBS
Actress in a drama series: Michael Learned, *The Waltons*, CBS
Actor in a comedy series: Alan Alda, *M*A*S*H*, CBS
Actress in a comedy series: Mary Tyler Moore, *The Mary Tyler Moore Show*, CBS
Actor in a limited series: William Holden, *The Blue Knight*, NBC
Actress in a limited series: Mildred Natwick, *The Snoop Sisters*, NBC
Actor in a drama: Hal Holbrook, *Pueblo*, ABC
Actress in a drama: Cicely Tyson, *The Autobiography of Miss Jane Pittman*, CBS
Actor of the year – series: Alan Alda, *M*A*S*H*, CBS
Actress of the year – series: Mary Tyler Moore, *The Mary Tyler Moore Show*, CBS
Actor of the year – special: Hal Holbrook, *Pueblo*, ABC
Actress of the year – special: Cicely Tyson, *The Autobiography of Miss Jane Pittman*, CBS
Supporting actor in drama: Michael Moriarty, *The Glass Menagerie*, ABC
Supporting actress in drama: Joanna Miles, *The Glass Menagerie*, ABC
Supporting actor in comedy: Rob Reiner, *All in the Family*, CBS
Supporting actress in comedy: Cloris Leachman, *The Mary Tyler Moore Show*, CBS
Supporting actor of the year: Michael Moriarty, *The Glass Menagerie*, ABC
Supporting actress of the year: Joanna Miles, *The Glass Menagerie*, ABC
Supporting actor in comedy/variety or music: Harvey Korman, *The Carol Burnett Show*, CBS
Supporting actress in comedy/variety or music: Brenda Vaccaro, *The Shape of Things*, NBC
Director of the year – series: Robert Butler, *The Blue Knight*, NBC

Director of the year – special: Dwight Hemion, *Barbra Streisand... and Other Musical Instruments*, CBS
Writer of the year – series: Treva Silverman, *The Mary Tyler Moore Show*, CBS
Writer of the year – special: Fay Kanin, *Tell Me Where It Hurts*, G.E. Theater, CBS
THE AREAS
Outstanding achievement in children's programming: Charles M. Schulz, writer, *A Charlie Brown Thanksgiving*, CBS; William Zaharuk, art director, Peter Ramofski, set decorator, *The Borrowers*, Hallmark Hall of Fame, NBC
Sports programs: *ABC's Wide World of Sports*, ABC
Outstanding achievement: *The Dick Cavett Show*, ABC
DAYTIME AWARDS
Drama series: *The Doctors*, NBC
Drama special: *The Other Woman*, ABC Matinee Today, ABC
Daytime actor of the year: Pat O'Brien, *The Other Woman*, ABC Matinee Today, ABC
Daytime actress of the year: Cathleen Nesbit, *The Mask of Love*, ABC Matinee Today, ABC
Daytime director of the year: H. Wesley Kenney, *Miss Kline, We Love You*, ABC Afternoon Playbreak, ABC
INTERNATIONAL AWARD WINNERS
Fiction: *Mr. Axelford's Angel*, Yorkshire Television, U.K.
Nonfiction: *Aquarius: Hello Dali!* London Weekend Television, U.K.

1974-75
PRIMETIME PROGRAM AWARDS
Drama series: *Upstairs, Downstairs, Masterpiece Theatre*, PBS
Comedy series: *The Mary Tyler Moore Show*, CBS
Limited episodes: *Benjamin Franklin*, CBS
Special – drama or comedy: *The Law*, NBC
Comedy/variety or music series: *The Carol Burnett Show*, CBS
Comedy/variety or music special: *An Evening with John Denver*, ABC
Classical music program: *Profile in Music: Beverly Hills, Festival '75*, PBS
Children's special: *Yes, Virginia There Is a Santa Claus*, ABC
PERFORMANCE, DIRECTING, AND WRITING
Actor in a drama series: Robert Blake, *Baretta*, ABC
Actress in a drama series: Jean Marsh, *Upstairs, Downstairs, Masterpiece Theatre*, PBS
Actor in a comedy series: Tony Randall, *The Odd Couple*, ABC

Actress in a comedy series: Valerie Harper, *Rhoda*, CBS

Actor in a limited series: Peter Falk, *Columbo*, NBC

Actress in a limited series: Jessica Walter, *Amy Prentiss*, NBC

Actor in a special: Laurence Olivier, *Love Among the Ruins*, ABC Theatre, ABC

Actress in a special: Katharine Hepburn, *Love Among the Ruins*, ABC Theatre, ABC

Supporting actor in a drama series: Will Geer, *The Waltons*, CBS

Supporting actress in a drama series: Ellen Corby, *The Waltons*, CBS

Supporting actor in a comedy series: Ed Asner, *The Mary Tyler Moore Show*, CBS

Supporting actress in a comedy series: Betty White, *The Mary Tyler Moore Show*, CBS

Single performance by a supporting actor in a comedy or drama series: Patrick McGoohan, *Columbo*, NBC

Single performance by a supporting actress in a comedy or drama series: Cloris Leachman, *The Mary Tyler Moore Show*, CBS

Supporting actor in a special: Anthony Quayle, *QB VII*, ABC

Supporting actress in a special: Juliet Mills, *QB VII*, ABC

Supporting actor in variety or music: Jack Albertson, *Cher*, CBS

Supporting actress in variety or music: Cloris Leachman, *Cher*, CBS

Directing in drama: Bill Bain, *Upstairs, Downstairs*, *Masterpiece Theatre*, PBS

Directing in comedy: Gene Reynolds, *M*A*S*H*, CBS

Directing in a special: George Cukor, *Love Among the Ruins*, ABC Theatre, ABC

Writing in drama: Howard Fast, *Benjamin Franklin*, CBS

Writing in comedy: Ed Weinberger, Stan Daniels, *The Mary Tyler Moore Show*, CBS

DAYTIME AWARDS

Drama series: *The Young and the Restless*, CBS

Drama special: *The Girl Who Couldn't Lose*, ABC *Afternoon Playbreak*, ABC

Actor in a drama series: Macdonald Carey, *Days of Our Lives*, NBC

Actress in a drama series: Susan Flannery, *Days of Our Lives*, NBC

Directing in a drama series: Richard Dunlap, *The Young and the Restless*, CBS

SPORTS AWARD WINNERS

Sports program: *ABC's Wide World of Sports*, ABC

Sports event: *Jimmy Connors vs. Rod Laver Tennis Challenge*, CBS

INTERNATIONAL AWARD WINNERS

Fiction: *The Evacuees*, BBC, U.K.

Nonfiction: *Inside Story: Marek*, BBC, U.K.

Directorate award: Junzo Imamichi

1975-76

PRIMETIME PROGRAM AWARDS

Drama series: *Police Story*, NBC

Comedy series: *The Mary Tyler Moore Show*, CBS

Limited series: *Upstairs, Downstairs*, *Masterpiece Theatre*, PBS

Drama special: *Eleanor and Franklin*, ABC

Comedy/variety or music series: *NBC's Saturday Night*, NBC

Comedy/variety or music special: *Gypsy in My Soul*, CBS

Classical music program: *Bernstein and the New York Philharmonic*, *Great Performances*, PBS

Children's special: *Huckleberry Finn*, ABC

PERFORMANCE, DIRECTING, AND WRITING

Actor in a drama series: Peter Falk, *Columbo*, NBC

Actress in a drama series: Michael Learned, *The Waltons*, CBS

Actor in a comedy series: Jack Albertson, *Chico and the Man*, NBC

Actress in a comedy series: Mary Tyler Moore, *The Mary Tyler Moore Show*, CBS

Actor in a single performance in a drama or comedy series: Edward Asner, *Rich Man, Poor Man*, ABC

Actress in a single performance in a drama or comedy series: Kathryn Walker, *The Adams Chronicles*, PBS

Actor in a limited series: Hal Holbrook, *Sandburg's Lincoln*, NBC

Actress in a limited series: Rosemary Harris, *Notorious Woman*, *Masterpiece Theatre*, PBS

Actor in a special: Anthony Hopkins, *The Lindbergh Kidnapping Case*, NBC

Actress in a special: Susan Clark, *Babe*, CBS

Supporting actor in a drama series: Anthony Zerbe, *Harry O*, ABC

Supporting actress in a drama series: Ellen Corby, *The Waltons*, CBS

Supporting actor in a comedy series: Ted Knight, *The Mary Tyler Moore Show*, CBS

Supporting actress in a comedy series: Betty White, *The Mary Tyler Moore Show*, CBS

Directing in a drama series: David Greene, *Rich Man, Poor Man*, ABC

Directing in a comedy series: Gene Reynolds, *M*A*S*H*, CBS

Directing in a special: Daniel Petrie, *Eleanor and Franklin*, ABC

... July 11 ...

Universal's comedy **American Pie** grabbed the top spot in the domestic marketplace with a $32 million take.

Writing in a drama series: Sherman Yellen, *The Adams Chronicles*, PBS

Writing in a comedy series: David Lloyd, *The Mary Tyler Moore Show*, CBS

THE AREAS

Outstanding achievement: *Bicentennial Minutes*, CBS

Outstanding achievement in sports programming: Andy Sidaris, Don Ohlmeyer, Roger Goodman, Larry Kamm, Ronnie Hawkins, Ralph Mellanby, directors, *XII Winter Olympic Games*, ABC

DAYTIME AWARDS

Drama series: *Another World*, NBC

Drama special: *First Ladies' Diaries: Edith Wilson*, NBC

Actor in a drama series: *Larry Haines, Search for Tomorrow*, CBS

Actress in a drama series: Helen Gallagher, *Ryan's Hope*, ABC

Directing in a drama series: David Pressman, *One Life to Live*, ABC

INTERNATIONAL AWARD WINNERS

Fiction: *The Naked Civil Servant*, Thames Television, U.K.

Nonfiction: *Reach for Tomorrow*, Nippon Television Network, Japan

Directorate award: Talbot Duckmanton

1976-77

PRIMETIME PROGRAM AWARDS

Drama series: *Upstairs, Downstairs, Masterpiece Theatre*, PBS

Comedy series: *The Mary Tyler Moore Show*, CBS

Limited series: *Roots*, ABC

Special: (tie) *Eleanor and Franklin: The White House Years*, ABC; *Sybil*, NBC

Variety or music series: *Van Dyke and Company*, NBC

Classical program: *American Ballet Theater: Swan Lake, Live from Lincoln Center, Great Performances*, PBS

Children's special: *Ballet Shoes, Piccadilly Circus*, PBS

Outstanding program achievement: *The Tonight Show*, NBC

PERFORMANCE, DIRECTING, AND WRITING

Actor in a drama series: James Garner, *The Rockford Files*, NBC

Actress in a drama series: Lindsay Wagner, *The Bionic Woman*

Actor in a comedy series: Carroll O'Connor, *All in the Family*, CBS

Actress in a comedy series: Beatrice Arthur, *Maude*, CBS

Actor for a single performance in a drama or comedy series: Louis Gossett, Jr., *Roots*, ABC

Actress for a single performance in a drama or comedy series: Beulah Bondi, *The Waltons*, CBS

Actor in a limited series: Christopher Plummer, *The Money-changers*, NBC

Actress in a limited series: Patty Duke Astin, *Captains and the Kings*, NBC

Actor in a special: Ed Flanders, *Harry S. Truman: Plain Speaking*, PBS

Actress in a special: Sally Field, *Sybil*, NBC

Supporting actor in a drama series: Gary Frank, *Family*, ABC

Supporting actress in a drama series: Kristy McNichol, *Family*, ABC

Supporting actor in a comedy series: Gary Burghoff, *M*A*S*H*, CBS

Supporting actress in a comedy series: Mary Kay Place, *Mary Hartman, Mary Hartman*, syndicated

Directing in a drama series: David Greene, *Roots*, ABC

Directing in a comedy series: Alan Alda, *M*A*S*H*, CBS

Directing in a special: Daniel Petrie, *Eleanor and Franklin: The White House Years*, ABC

Writing in a drama series: Ernest Kinoy, William Blinn, *Roots*, ABC

Writing in a comedy series: Allan Burns, James L. Brooks, Ed Weinberger, Stan Daniels, David Lloyd, Bob Ellison, *The Mary Tyler Moore Show*, CBS

DAYTIME AWARDS

Drama series: *Ryan's Hope*, ABC

Actor in a drama series: Val Dufour, *Search for Tomorrow*, CBS

Actress in a drama series: Helen Gallagher, *Ryan's Hope*, ABC

Directing in a drama series: Lela Swift, *Ryan's Hope*, ABC

INTERNATIONAL AWARD WINNERS

Fiction: *The Collection*, Granada Television, U.K.

Nonfiction: *Henry Ford's America*, Canadian Broadcasting

Directorate award: Alphonse Quiment

1977-78

PRIMETIME PROGRAM AWARDS

Drama series: *The Rockford Files*, NBC

Comedy series: *All in the Family*, CBS

Limited series: *Holocaust*, NBC

Special: *The Gathering*, ABC

Variety or music series: *The Muppet Show*, syndicated

Variety or music special: *Bette Midler – Ol' Red Hair is Back*, NBC

Classical program: *American Ballet Theater: Giselle, Live from Lincoln Center*, PBS

... July 12 ...
After objecting to the way Kuala Lumpur was portrayed in **Entrapment**, the Malaysian government intends to issue strict guidelines for foreign films shooting in the country.

Children's special: *Halloween is Grinch Night*, ABC
Informational series: *The Body Human*, CBS
Informational special: *The Great Whales*, *National Geographic Specials*, PBS
Outstanding program achievement: *The Tonight Show*, NBC
PERFORMANCE, DIRECTING, AND WRITING
Actor in a drama series: Ed Asner, *Lou Grant*, CBS
Actress in a drama series: Sada Thompson, *Family*, ABC
Actor in a comedy series: Carroll O'Connor, *All in the Family*, CBS
Actress in a comedy series: Jean Stapleton, *All in the Family*, CBS
Actor in a limited series: Michael Moriarty, *Holocaust*, NBC
Actress in a limited series: Meryl Streep, *Holocaust*, NBC
Actor for a single performance in a series: Barnard Hughes, *Lou Grant*, CBS
Actress for a single performance in a series: Rita Moreno, *The Rockford Files*, NBC
Actor in a special: Fred Astaire, *A Family Upside Down*, NBC
Actress in a special: Joanne Woodward, *See How She Runs*, CBS
Supporting actor in a drama series: Robert Vaughn, *Washington: Behind Closed Doors*, ABC
Supporting actress in a drama series: Nancy Marchand, *Lou Grant*, CBS
Supporting actor in a comedy series: Rob Reiner, *All in the Family*, CBS
Supporting actress in a comedy series: Julie Kavner, *Rhoda*, CBS
Directing in a drama series: Marvin J. Chomsky, *Holocaust*, NBC
Directing in a comedy series: Paul Bogart, *All in the Family*, CBS
Directing in a special: David Lowell Rich, *The Defection of Simas Kudirka*, CBS
Writing in a drama series: Gerald Green, *Holocaust*, NBC
Writing in a comedy series: Bob Weiskopf, Bob Schiller, Barry Harman, Harve Brosten, *All in the Family*, CBS
DAYTIME AWARDS
Drama series: *Days of Our Lives*, NBC
Actor in a drama series: James Pritchett, *The Doctors*, NBC
Actress in a drama series: Laurie Heinemann, *Another World*, NBC
Directing in a drama series: Richard Dunlap, *The Young and the Restless*, CBS

INTERNATIONAL AWARD WINNERS
Fiction: *The Fly*, Televisie Radio Omroep Stichting, Netherlands
Nonfiction: *Four Women*, Canadian Broadcasting
Directorate award: Prix Italia

1978-79
PRIMETIME PROGRAM AWARDS
Drama series: *Lou Grant*, CBS
Comedy series: *Taxi*, ABC
Limited series: *Roots: The Next Generation*, ABC
Special: *Friendly Fire*, ABC
Variety or music series: *Steve & Eydie Celebrate Irving Berlin*, NBC
Informational program: *Scared Straight!*, syndicated
Classical program: *Balanchine IV, Dance in America*, *Great Performances*, PBS
Children's special: *Christmas Eve on Sesame Street*, PBS
Outstanding program achievement – special events: *The 51st Annual Academy Awards*, ABC
Outstanding program achievement – special class: (tie) *The Tonight Show*, NBC; *Lifeline*, NBC
PERFORMANCE, DIRECTING, AND WRITING
Actor in a drama series: Ron Leibman, *Kaz*, CBS
Actress in a drama series: Mariette Hartley, *The Incredible Hulk*, CBS
Actor in a comedy series: Carroll O'Connor, *All in the Family*, CBS
Actress in a comedy series: Ruth Gordon, *Taxi*, ABC
Actor in a limited series or a special: Peter Strauss, *The Jericho Mile*, ABC
Actress in a limited series or a special: Bette Davis, *Strangers: The Story of a Mother and Daughter*, CBS
Supporting actor in a comedy/variety or music series: Robert Guillaume, *Soap*, ABC
Supporting actress in a comedy/variety or music series: Sally Struthers, *All in the Family*, CBS
Supporting actor in a drama series: Stuart Margolin, *The Rockford Files*, NBC
Supporting actress in a drama series: Kristy McNichol, *Family*, ABC
Supporting actor in a limited series or a special: Marlon Brando, *Roots: The Next Generation*, ABC
Supporting actress in a limited series or a special: Esther Rolle, *Summer of My German Soldier*, ABC
Directing in a drama series: Jackie Cooper, *The White Shadow*, CBS
Directing in a comedy/variety or music series: Noam Pitlik, *Barney Miller*, ABC
Directing in a limited series or a special: David Greene, *Friendly Fire*, ABC
Writing in a drama series: Michelle Gallery, *Lou Grant*, CBS

Writing in a comedy/variety or music series: Alan Alda, *M*A*S*H*, CBS

DAYTIME AWARDS

Drama series: *Ryan's Hope*, ABC

Actor in a drama series: Al Freeman, Jr., *One Life to Live*, ABC

Actress in a drama series: Irene Dailey, *Another World*, NBC

Directing in a drama series: Jerry Evans, Lela Swift, *Ryan's Hope*, ABC

INTERNATIONAL AWARD WINNERS

Documentary: *The Secret Hospital*, Yorkshire TV, U.K.

Performing arts: *Elegies for the Deaths of Three Spanish Poets*, U.K.

Popular arts: *Rich Little's Christmas Carol*, Canadian Broadcasting

Drama: *On Giants' Shoulders*, BBC, U.K.

Directorate award: Dr. Frank Stanton

1979-80

PRIMETIME PROGRAM AWARDS

Drama series: *Lou Grant*, CBS

Comedy series: *Taxi*, ABC

Limited series: *Edward & Mrs. Simpson*, syndicated

Variety or music program: *Baryshnikov on Broadway*, ABC

Special: *The Miracle Worker*, NBC

Classical program: *Live from Studio 8H: A Tribute to Toscanini*, NBC

Informational program: *The Body Human: The Magic Sense*, CBS

Outstanding program achievement – special events: *The 34th Annual Tony Awards*, CBS

Outstanding program achievement – special class: *Fred Astaire: Change Partners and Dance*, PBS

Animated program: *Carlton Your Doorman*, CBS

PERFORMANCE, DIRECTING, AND WRITING

Actor in a drama series: Edward Asner, *Lou Grant*, CBS

Actress in a drama series: Barbara Bel Geddes, *Dallas*, CBS

Actor in a comedy series: Richard Mulligan, *Soap*, ABC

Actress in a comedy series: Cathryn Damon, *Soap*, ABC

Actor in a limited series or a special: Powers Boothe, *Guyana Tragedy: The Story of Jim Jones*, CBS

Actress in a limited series or a special: Patty Duke Astin, *The Miracle Worker*, NBC

Supporting actor in a drama series: Stuart Margolin, *The Rockford Files*, NBC

Supporting actress in a drama series: Nancy Marchand, *Lou Grant*, CBS

Supporting actor in a limited series or a special: George Grizzard, *The Oldest Living Graduate*, NBC

Supporting actress in a limited series or a special: Mare Winningham, *Amber Waves*, ABC

Supporting actor in a comedy, variety or music series: Harry Morgan, *M*A*S*H*, CBS

Supporting actress in a comedy, variety or music series: Loretta Swit, *M*A*S*H*, CBS

Directing in a drama series: Roger Young, *Lou Grant*, CBS

Directing in a comedy series: James Burrows, *Taxi*, ABC

Directing in a limited series or a special: Marvin J. Chomsky, *Attica*, ABC

Writing in a drama series: Seth Freeman, *Lou Grant*, CBS

Writing in a comedy series: Bob Colleary, *Barney Miller*, ABC

DAYTIME AWARDS

Drama series: *Guiding Light*, CBS

Actor in a drama series: Douglass Watson, *Another World*, NBC

Actress in a drama series: Judith Light, *One Life to Live*, ABC

Directing in a drama series: Lela Swift, *Ryan's Hope*, ABC

INTERNATIONAL AWARD WINNERS

Documentary: *Fighting Back*, Canadian Broadcasting

Performing arts: *L'Oiseau de Feu*, Société Radio, Canada

Popular arts: *Not the Least of the Nine O'Clock News*, BBC, U.K.

Drama: *A Rod of Iron*, Yorkshire TV, U.K.

Directorate award: Lord Grade of Elstree

Founder's award: Jim Henson

1980-81

PRIMETIME PROGRAM AWARDS

Drama series: *Hill Street Blues*, NBC

Comedy series: *Taxi*, ABC

Limited series: *Shogun*, NBC

Variety, music or comedy program *Lily: Sold Out*, CBS:

Drama special: *Playing for Time*, CBS

Classical program in the performing arts: *Live from Studio 8H: An Evening of Jerome Robbins' Ballets with Members of the New York City Ballet*, NBC

Informational series: *Meeting of Minds*, PBS

Informational special: *The Body Human: The Bionic Breakthrough*, CBS

Children's program: *Donahue and Kids*, NBC

Animated program: *Life is a Circus, Charlie Brown*, CBS

PERFORMANCE, DIRECTING, AND WRITING

Actor in a drama series: Daniel J. Travanti, *Hill Street Blues*, NBC

Actress in a drama series: Barbara Babcock, *Hill Street Blues*, NBC

Actor in a comedy series: Judd Hirsch, *Taxi*, ABC

Actress in a comedy series: Isabel Sanford, *The Jeffersons*, CBS

Actor in a limited series or a special: Anthony Hopkins, *The Bunker*, CBS

Actress in a limited series or a special: Vanessa Redgrave, *Playing for Time*, CBS

Supporting actor in a drama series: Michael Conrad, *Hill Street Blues*, NBC

Supporting actress in a drama series: Nancy Marchand, *Lou Grant*, CBS

Supporting actor in a comedy, variety or music series: Danny DeVito, *Taxi*, ABC

Supporting actress in a comedy, variety or music series: Eileen Brennan, *Private Benjamin*, CBS

Supporting actor in a limited series or a special: David Warner, *Masada*, ABC

Supporting actress in a limited series or a special: Jane Alexander, *Playing for Time*, CBS

Directing in a drama series: Robert Butler, *Hill Street Blues*, NBC

Directing in a comedy series: James Burrows, *Taxi*, ABC

Directing in a limited series or a special: James Goldstone, *Kent State*, NBC

Writing in a drama series: Michael Kozoll, Steven Bochco, *Hill Street Blues*, NBC

Writing in a comedy series: Michael Leeson, *Taxi*, ABC

DAYTIME AWARDS

Drama series: *General Hospital*, ABC

Actor in a drama series: Douglass Watson, *Another World*, NBC

Actress in a drama series: Judith Light, *One Life to Live*, ABC

Directing in a drama series: Marlena Laird, Alan Pultz, Phillip Sogard, *General Hospital*, ABC

INTERNATIONAL AWARD WINNERS

Documentary: *Charters pour l'Enfer (Charters to Hell)*, Société National de Télévision Française, France

Performing arts: *Sweeney Todd: Scenes from the Making of a Musical*, London Weekend TV, U.K.

Popular arts: *Vinicius Para Criancas or Carca de Noe (Noah's Ark)* TV Globo, Brazil

Drama: *A Town Like Alice*, Channel 7, Australia

Directorate award: Sir Huw Wheldon

Founder's award: Roone Arledge, Ms. Shaun Sutton

1981-82

PRIMETIME PROGRAM AWARDS

Drama series: *Hill Street Blues*, NBC

Comedy series: *Barney Miller*, ABC

Limited series: *Marco Polo*, NBC

Drama special: *A Woman Called Golda*, syndicated

Variety, music or comedy program: *Night of 100 Stars*, ABC

Classical program in the performing arts: *La Bohème, Live from the Met*, PBS

Informational series: *Creativity with Bill Moyers*, PBS

Informational special: *Making of Raiders of the Lost Ark*, PBS

Children's program: *The Wave*, ABC

Animated program: *The Grinch Grinches the Cat in the Hat*, ABC

PERFORMANCE, DIRECTING, AND WRITING

Actor in a drama series: Daniel J. Travanti, *Hill Street Blues*, NBC

Actress in a drama series: Michael Learned, *Nurse*, CBS

Actor in a comedy series: Alan Alda, *M*A*S*H*, CBS

Actress in a comedy series: Carol Kane, *Taxi*, ABC

Actor in a limited series or a special: Mickey Rooney, *Bill*, CBS

Actress in a limited series or a special: Ingrid Bergman, *A Woman Called Golda*, syndicated

Supporting actor in a drama series: Michael Conrad, *Hill Street Blues*, NBC

Supporting actress in a drama series: Nancy Marchand, *Lou Grant*, CBS

Supporting actor in a comedy, variety or music series: Christopher Lloyd, *Taxi*, ABC

Supporting actress in a comedy, variety or music series: Loretta Swit, *M*A*S*H*, CBS

Supporting actor in a limited series or a special: Laurence Olivier, *Brideshead Revisited, Great Performances*, PBS

Supporting actress in a limited series or a special: Penny Fuller, *The Elephant Man*, ABC

Directing in a drama series: Harry Harris, *Fame*, NBC

Directing in a comedy series: Alan Rafkin, *One Day at a Time*, CBS

Directing in a limited series or a special: Marvin J. Chomsky, *Inside the Third Reich*, ABC

Writing in a drama series: Steven Bochco, Anthony Yerkovich, Jeffrey Lewis, Michael Wagner, Michael Kozoll, *Hill Street Blues*, NBC

Writing in a comedy series: Ken Estin, *Taxi*, ABC

DAYTIME AWARDS

Drama series: *Guiding Light*, CBS

Actor in a drama series: Anthony Geary, *General Hospital*, ABC

...July 15...

Emmy-winning producer Steven Bochco has teamed up with Paramount Network Television, signing an exclusive five-year, $45-50 million deal to produce television series.

Actress in a drama series: Robin Strasser, *One Life to Live*, ABC

Directing in a drama series: Marlena Laird, Alan Pulitz, Philip Sogard, *General Hospital*, ABC

INTERNATIONAL AWARD WINNERS

Documentary: *Is There One Who Understands Me? The World of James Joyce*, Radio Telefis Eireann, Ireland

Performing arts: *A Lot of Happiness*, Granada TV, U.K.

Popular arts: *Death and Life Severinian*, TV Globo, Brazil

Drama: *A Voyage Round My Father*, Thames TV, U.K.

Directorate award: Akio Morita

Founder's award: Michael Landon

1982-83

PRIMETIME PROGRAM AWARDS

Drama series: *Hill Street Blues*, NBC

Comedy series: *Cheers*, NBC

Limited series: *Nicholas Nickleby*, syndicated

Drama special: *Special Bulletin*, NBC

Variety, music or comedy program: *Motown 25: Yesterday, Today, Forever*, NBC

Classical program in the performing arts: *Pavarotti in Philadelphia: La Bohème*, PBS

Informational series: *The Barbara Walters Specials*, ABC

Informational special: *The Body Human: The Living Code*, CBS

Animated program: *Ziggy's Gift*, ABC

Children's program: *Big Bird in China*, NBC

PERFORMANCE, DIRECTING, AND WRITING

Actor in a drama series: Ed Flanders, *St. Elsewhere*, NBC

Actress in a drama series: Tyne Daly, *Cagney & Lacey*, CBS

Actor in a comedy series: Judd Hirsch, *Taxi*, NBC

Actress in a comedy series: Shelley Long, *Cheers*, NBC

Actor in a limited series or a special: Tommy Lee Jones, *The Executioner's Song*, NBC

Actress in a limited series or a special: Barbara Stanwyck, *The Thorn Birds*, ABC

Supporting actor in a drama series: James Coco, *St. Elsewhere*, NBC

Supporting actress in a drama series: Doris Roberts, *St. Elsewhere*, NBC

Supporting actor in a comedy, variety or music series: Christopher Lloyd, *Taxi*, NBC

Supporting actress in a comedy, variety or music series: Carol Kane, *Taxi*, NBC

Supporting actor in a limited series or a special: Richard Kiley, *The Thorn Birds*, ABC

Supporting actress in a limited series or a special: Jean Simmons, *The Thorn Birds*, ABC

Performance in a variety or music program: Leontyne Price, *Leontyne Price, Zubin Mehta and the New York Philharmonic, Live from Lincoln Center*, PBS

Directing in a drama series: Jeff Bleckner, *Hill Street Blues*, NBC

Directing in a comedy series: James Burrows, *Cheers*, NBC

Directing in a limited series or a special: John Erman, *Who Will Love My Children?*, ABC

Writing in a drama series: David Milch, *Hill Street Blues*, NBC

Writing in a comedy series: Glen Charles, Les Charles, *Cheers*, NBC

DAYTIME AWARDS

Drama series: *The Young and the Restless*, CBS

Actor in a drama series: Robert Woods, *One Life to Live*, ABC

Actress in a drama series: Dorothy Lyman, *All My Children*, ABC

Directing in a drama series: Allen Fristoe, Norman Hall, Peter Miner, David Pressman, *One Life to Live*, ABC

INTERNATIONAL AWARD WINNERS

Documentary: *The Miracle of Life*, Swedish Television, SVT, Sweden

Performing arts: *Dangerous Music*, HTV, Wales, U.K.

Popular arts: *Blackadder: The Archbishop*, BBC, U.K.

Drama: *King Lear*, Granada TV, U.K.

Children's programming: *Fraggle Rock*, Canadian Broadcasting

Directorate award: Robert Marinho

Founder's award: Herbert Brodkin

1983-84

PRIMETIME PROGRAM AWARDS

Drama series: *Hill Street Blues*, NBC

Comedy series: *Cheers*, NBC

Limited series: *Concealed Enemies, American Playhouse*, PBS

Variety, music or comedy program: *The Kennedy Center Honors*, CBS

Drama/comedy special: *Something about Amelia*, ABC

Classical program in the performing arts: *Placido Domingo Celebrates Seville, Great Performances*, PBS

Informational series: *A Walk through the 20th Century with Bill Moyers*, PBS

Informational special: *America Remembers John F. Kennedy*, syndicated

... July 16 ...
John F. Kennedy Jr.'s plane crashes.

Animated program: *Garfield on the Town*, CBS
Children's program: *He Makes Me Feel Like Dancin'*, NBC
PERFORMANCE, DIRECTING, AND WRITING
Actor in a drama series: Tom Selleck, *Magnum, P.I.*, CBS
Actress in a drama series: Tyne Daly, *Cagney & Lacey*, CBS
Actor in a comedy series: John Ritter, *Three's Company*, ABC
Actress in a comedy series: Jane Curtin, *Kate & Allie*, CBS
Actor in a limited series or a special: Laurence Olivier, *King Lear*, syndicated
Actress in a limited series or a special: Jane Fonda, *The Dollmaker*, ABC
Supporting actor in a drama series: Bruce Weitz, *Hill Street Blues*, NBC
Supporting actress in a drama series: Alfre Woodard, *Hill Street Blues*, NBC
Supporting actor in a comedy series: Pat Harrington, *One Day at a Time*, CBS
Supporting actress in a comedy series: Rhea Perlman, *Cheers*, NBC
Supporting actor in a limited series or a special: Art Carney, *Terrible Joe Moran*, CBS
Supporting actress in a limited series or a special: Roxana Zal, *Something about Amelia*, ABC
Performance in a variety or music program: Cloris Leachman, *Screen Actors Guild 50th Anniversary Celebration*, CBS
Directing in a drama series: Corey Allen, *Hill Street Blues*, NBC
Directing in a comedy series: Bill Persky, *Kate & Allie*, CBS
Directing in a limited series or a special: Jeff Bleckner, *Concealed Enemies, American Playhouse*, PBS
Writing in a drama series: John Ford Noonan, John Masius, Ron Fontana, *St. Elsewhere*, NBC
Writing in a comedy series: David Angel, *Cheers*, NBC
DAYTIME AWARDS
Drama series: *General Hospital*, ABC
Actor in a drama series: Larry Bryggman, *As the World Turns*, CBS
Actress in a drama series: Erika Slezak, *One Life to Live*, ABC
Directing in a drama series: Larry Auerbach, George Keathley, Peter Miner, David Pressman, *One Life to Live*, ABC
INTERNATIONAL AWARD WINNERS
Documentary: *The Heart of the Dragon: Remembering*, Channel 4, U.K.

Performing arts: *The Tragedy of Carmen*, Channel 4, U.K.
Popular arts: *Fresh Fields*, Thames TV, U.K.
Drama: *The Jewel in the Crown*, Granada TV, U.K.
Children's programming: *Wind in the Willows*, Thames TV, U.K.
Directorate award: Lord Sidney Bernstein
Founder's award: David L. Wolper

1984-85
PRIMETIME PROGRAM AWARDS
Drama series: *Cagney & Lacey*, CBS
Comedy series: *The Cosby Show*, NBC
Limited series: *The Jewel in the Crown, Masterpiece Theatre*, PBS
Drama/comedy special: *Do You Remember Love?*, CBS
Variety, music or comedy program: *Motown Returns to the Apollo*, NBC
Classical program in the performing arts: *Tosca, Live from the Met*, PBS
Informational series: *The Living Planet: A Portrait of the Earth*, PBS
Informational special: *Cousteau: Mississippi*, syndicated
Animated program: *Garfield in the Rough*, CBS
Children's program: *Displaced Person, American Playhouse*, PBS
PERFORMANCE, DIRECTING, AND WRITING
Actor in a drama series: William Daniels, *St. Elsewhere*, NBC
Actress in a drama series: Tyne Daly, *Cagney & Lacey*, CBS
Actor in a comedy series: Robert Guillaume, *Benson*, ABC
Actress in a comedy series: Jane Curtin, *Kate & Allie*, CBS
Actor in a limited series or a special: Richard Crenna, *The Rape of Richard Beck*, ABC
Actress in a limited series or a special: Joanne Woodward, *Do You Remember Love?*, CBS
Supporting actor in a drama series: Edward James Olmos, *Miami Vice*, NBC
Supporting actress in a drama series: Betty Thomas, *Hill Street Blues*, NBC
Supporting actor in a comedy series: John Larroquette, *Night Court*, NBC
Supporting actress in a comedy series: Rhea Perlman, *Cheers*, NBC
Supporting actor in a limited series or a special: Karl Malden, *Fatal Vision*, NBC
Supporting actress in a limited series or a special: Kim Stanley, *Cat on a Hot Tin Roof, American Playhouse*, PBS

... July 17 ...
The Blair Witch Project opens to $1.5 million on 27 screens with an astonishing $57,700 per screen average.

Performance in a variety or music program: George Hearn, *Sweeney Todd, Great Performances*, PBS

Directing in a drama series: Karen Arthur, *Cagney & Lacey*, CBS

Directing in a comedy series: Jay Sandrich, *The Cosby Show*, NBC

Directing in a limited series or a special: Lamont Johnson, *Wallenberg: A Hero's Story*, NBC

Writing in a drama series: Patricia Green, *Cagney & Lacey*, CBS

Writing in a comedy series: Ed Weinberger, Michael Leeson, *The Cosby Show*, NBC

DAYTIME AWARDS

Drama series: *The Young and the Restless*, CBS

Actor in a drama series: Darnell Williams, *All My Children*, ABC

Actress in a drama series: Kim Zimmer, *Guiding Light*, CBS

Directing in a drama series: John Whitesell II, Bruce Barry, Matthew Diamond, Irene M. Pace, Robert D. Kochman, Joanne Rivituso, Joanne Sedwick, *Guiding Light*, CBS

INTERNATIONAL AWARD WINNERS

Documentary: *28 Up*, Granada TV, U.K.

Performing arts: *Omnibus: The Treble*, BBC, U.K.

Popular arts: *Spitting Image*, Central Independent Television, U.K.

Drama: *Das Boot*, Bavaria Atelier, West Germany

Children's programming: *Supergran*, Tyne Tees TV, U.K.

Directorate award: Leonard H. Goldson

Founder's award: Sir David Attenborough

1985-86

PRIMETIME PROGRAM AWARDS

Drama series: *Cagney & Lacey*, CBS

Comedy series: *The Golden Girls*, NBC

Mini-series: *Peter the Great*, NBC

Drama/comedy special: *Love Is Never Silent, Hallmark Hall of Fame*, NBC

Variety, music or comedy program: *The Kennedy Center Honors*, CBS

Classical program in the performing arts: *Wolf Trap Presents the Kirov: Swan Lake*, PBS

Informational special: *W.C. Fields Straight Up*, PBS

Informational series: (tie) *Laurence Olivier – A Life, Great Performances*, PBS; *Planet Earth*, PBS

Animated program: *Garfield's Halloween Adventure*, CBS

Children's program: *Anne of Green Gables, Wonderworks*, PBS

PERFORMANCE, DIRECTING, AND WRITING

Actor in a drama series: William Daniels, *St. Elsewhere*, NBC

Actress in a drama series: Sharon Gless, *Cagney & Lacey*, CBS

Actor in a comedy series: Michael J. Fox, *Family Ties*, NBC

Actress in a comedy series: Betty White, *The Golden Girls*, NBC

Actor in a mini-series or a special: Dustin Hoffman, *Death of a Salesman*, CBS

Actress in a mini-series or a special: Marlo Thomas, *Nobody's Child*, CBS

Supporting actor in a drama series: John Karlen, *Cagney & Lacey*, CBS

Supporting actress in a drama series: Bonnie Bartlett, *St. Elsewhere*, NBC

Supporting actor in a comedy series: John Larroquette, *Night Court*, NBC

Supporting actress in a comedy series: Rhea Perlman, *Cheers*, NBC

Supporting actor in a mini-series or a special: John Malkovich, *Death of a Salesman*, CBS

Supporting actress in a mini-series or a special: Colleen Dewhurst, *Between Two Women*, ABC

Performance in a variety or music program: Whitney Houston, *The 28th Annual Grammy Awards*, CBS

Guest performer in a drama series: John Lithgow, *Amazing Stories*, NBC

Guest performer in a comedy series: Roscoe Lee Browne, *The Cosby Show*, NBC

Directing in a drama series: Georg Stanford Brown, *Cagney & Lacey*, CBS

Directing in a comedy series: Jay Sandrich, *The Cosby Show*, NBC

Directing in a mini-series or a special: Joseph Sargent, *Love Is Never Silent, Hallmark Hall of Fame*, NBC

Writing in a drama series: Tom Fontana, John Tinker, John Masius, *St. Elsewhere*, NBC

Writing in a comedy series: Barry Fanaro, Mort Nathan, *The Golden Girls*, NBC

DAYTIME AWARDS

Drama series: *The Young and the Restless*, CBS

Actor in a drama series: David Canary, *All My Children*, ABC

Actress in a drama series: Erika Slezak, *One Life to Live*, ABC

Directing in a drama series: Dennis Steinmetz, Rudy Vejar, Frank Pacelli, Randy Robbins, Betty Rothenberg, *The Young and the Restless*, CBS

INTERNATIONAL AWARD WINNERS

Documentary: *Chasing a Rainbow: The Life of Josephine Baker*, Channel Four, U.K.

Performing arts: *Bejart's Kabuki Ballet*, NHK Japan Broadcasting

Popular arts: *Spitting Image*, Central Independent Television, U.K.

Drama: *Shadowlands*, BBC, U.K.

Children's program: *The Kids of Degrassi Street: Griff Gets a Hand*, Canadian Broadcasting

Directorate award: Herbert Schmertz

Founder's award: Donald L. Taffer

1986-87

PRIMETIME PROGRAM AWARDS

Drama series: *L.A. Law*, NBC

Comedy series: *The Golden Girls*, NBC

Mini-series: *A Year in the Life*, NBC

Drama/comedy special: *Promise, Hallmark Hall of Fame*, CBS

Variety, music or comedy program: *The 1987 Tony Awards*, CBS

Classical program in performing arts: *Vladimir Horowitz: The Last Romantic*, PBS

Informational series: (tie) *Smithsonian World*, PBS; *Unknown Chaplin, American Masters*, PBS

Informational special: Dance in America: *Agnes, the Indomitable De Mille, Great Performances*, PBS

Animated program: *Cathy*, CBS

Children's program: *Jim Henson's The Storyteller: Hans My Hedgehog*, NBC

PERFORMANCE, DIRECTING, AND WRITING

Actor in a drama series: Bruce Willis, *Moonlighting*, ABC

Actress in a drama series: Sharon Gless, *Cagney & Lacey*, CBS

Actor in a comedy series: Michael J. Fox, *Family Ties*, NBC

Actress in a comedy series: Rue McClanahan, *The Golden Girls*, NBC

Actor in a mini-series or a special: James Woods, *Promise, Hallmark Hall of Fame*, NBC

Actress in a mini-series or a special: Gena Rowlands, *The Betty Ford Story*, ABC

Supporting actor in a drama series: John Hillerman, *Magnum, P.I.*, CBS

Supporting actress in a drama series: Bonnie Bartlett, *St. Elsewhere*, NBC

Supporting actor in a comedy series: John Larroquette, *Night Court*, NBC

Supporting actress in a comedy series: Jackée Harry, *227*, NBC

Supporting actor in a mini-series or a special: Dabney Coleman, *Sworn to Silence*, ABC

Supporting actress in a mini-series or a special: Piper Laurie, *Promise, Hallmark Hall of Fame*, NBC

Individual performance in a variety or music program: Robin Williams, *A Carol Burnett Special: Carol, Carol, Whoopi & Robin*, ABC

Guest performer in a drama series: Alfre Woodard, *L.A. Law*, NBC

Guest performer in a comedy series: John Cleese, *Cheers*, NBC

Directing in a drama series: Gregory Hoblit, *L.A. Law*, NBC

Directing in a comedy series: Terry Hughes, *The Golden Girls*, NBC

Directing in a mini-series or a special: Glenn Jordan, *Promise, Hallmark Hall of Fame*, NBC

Writing in a drama series: Steven Bochco, Terry Louise Fisher, *L.A. Law*, NBC

Writing in a comedy series: Gary David Goldberg, Alan Uger, *Family Ties*, NBC

DAYTIME AWARDS

Drama series: *As the World Turns*, CBS

Actor in a drama series: Larry Bryggman, *As the World Turns*, CBS

Actress in a drama series: Kim Zimmer, *Guiding Light*, CBS

Drama series directing team: Frank Pacelli, Rudy Vejar, Betty Rothenberg, Randy Robbins, *The Young and the Restless*, CBS

INTERNATIONAL AWARD WINNERS

Documentary: *The Sword of Islam*, Granada TV, U.K.

Performing arts: *The Belle of Amherst*, Thames TV, U.K.

Popular arts: *Alas Smith and Jones*, BBC, U.K.

Drama: *Porterhouse Blue*, Channel Four, U.K.

Children's program: *It's Late: Degrassi Junior High*, CBC, Canada

Directorate award: Jeremy Isaacs

Founder's award: Jacques-Yves Cousteau

1987-88

PRIMETIME PROGRAM AWARDS

Drama series: *thirtysomething*, ABC

Comedy series: *The Wonder Years*, ABC

Mini-series: *The Murder of Mary Phagan*, NBC

Drama/comedy special: *Inherit the Wind*, NBC

Variety, music or comedy program: *Irving Berlin's 100th Birthday Celebration*, CBS

Classical program in the performing arts: *Nixon in China, Great Performances*, PBS

Informational special: *Dear America: Letters Home from Vietnam*, HBO

Informational series: *Buster Keaton: Hard Act to Follow, American Masters*, PBS

Animated program: *A Claymation Christmas Celebration*, CBS

Children's program: *The Secret Garden, Hallmark Hall of Fame*, CBS

Variety/music events programming: *The 60th Annual Academy Awards*, ABC

PERFORMANCE, DIRECTING, AND WRITING

Actor in a drama series: Richard Kiley, *A Year in the Life*, NBC

Actress in a drama series: Tyne Daly, *Cagney & Lacey*, CBS

Actor in a comedy series: Michael J. Fox, *Family Ties*, NBC

Actress in a comedy series: Bea Arthur, *The Golden Girls*, NBC

Actor in a mini-series or a special: Jason Robards, *Inherit the Wind*, NBC

Actress in a mini-series or a special: Jessica Tandy, *Foxfire, Hallmark Hall of Fame*, CBS

Supporting actor in a drama series: Larry Drake, *L.A. Law*, NBC

Supporting actress in a drama series: Patricia Wettig, *thirtysomething*, ABC

Supporting actor in a comedy series: John Larroquette, *Night Court*, NBC

Supporting actress in a comedy series: Estelle Getty, *The Golden Girls*, NBC

Supporting actor in a mini-series or special: John Shea, *Baby M*, ABC

Supporting actress in a mini-series or special: Jane Seymour, *Onassis: The Richest Man in the World*, ABC

Guest performer in a drama series: Shirley Knight, *thirtysomething*, ABC

Guest performer in a comedy series: Beah Richards, *Frank's Place*, CBS

Individual performance in a variety or music program: Robin Williams, *ABC Presents a Royal Gala*, ABC

Director in a drama series: Mark Tinker, *St. Elsewhere*, NBC

Director in a comedy series: Gregory Hoblit, *Hooperman*, ABC

Director in a mini-series or a special: Lamont Johnson, *Lincoln*, NBC

Writing in a drama series: Paul Haggis, Marshall Herskovitz, *thirtysomething*, ABC

Writing in a comedy series: Hugh Wilson, *Frank's Place*, CBS

DAYTIME AWARDS

Drama series: *Santa Barbara*, NBC

Actor in a drama series: David Canary, *All My Children*, ABC

Actress in a drama series: Helen Gallagher, *Ryan's Hope*, ABC

Drama series directing team: Rudy Vejar, Frank Pacelli, Heather Hill, Randy Robbins, Betty Rothenberg, *The Young and the Restless*, CBS

INTERNATIONAL AWARD WINNERS

Documentary: *The Last Seven Months of Anne Frank*, TROS-TV, The Netherlands

Performing arts: *Ken Russell's ABC of British Music*, London Weekend TV, U.K.

Popular arts: *The New Statesman*, Yorkshire TV, U.K.

Drama: *A Very British Coup*, Channel Four, U.K.

Young people's program: *Touch the Sun: Captain Johnno*, Australian Children's Television Foundation

Directorate award: Vittorio Boni

Founder's award: Goar Mestre

1988-89

PRIMETIME PROGRAM AWARDS

Drama series: *L.A. Law*, NBC

Comedy series: *Cheers*, NBC

Mini-series: *War and Remembrance*, ABC

Drama/comedy special: (tie) *Day One*, CBS; *Roe vs. Wade*, NBC

Variety, music or comedy program: *The Tracey Ullman Show*, Fox

Classical program: in the performing arts: *Bernstein at 70!, Great Performances*, PBS

Informational series: *Nature*, PBS

Informational special: *Lillian Gish: The Actor's Life for Me, American Masters*, PBS

Special events: *Cirque du Soleil: The Magic Circus*, HBO; *The 11th Annual Kennedy Center Honors*, CBS; *The 42nd Annual Tony Awards*, CBS, *The American Film Institute Salute to Gregory Peck*, NBC

Animated program – less than one hour: *Garfield: Babes and Bullets*, CBS

Children's program: *Free to Be... a Family*, ABC

PERFORMANCE, DIRECTING, AND WRITING

Actor in a drama series: Carroll O'Connor, *In the Heat of the Night*, NBC

Actress in a drama series: Dana Delany, *China Beach*, ABC

Actor in a comedy series: Richard Mulligan, *Empty Nest*, NBC

Actress in a comedy series: Candice Bergen, *Murphy Brown*, CBS

Actor in a mini-series or a special: James Woods, *My Name Is Bill W., Hallmark Hall of Fame*, ABC

Actress in a mini-series or a special: Holly Hunter, *Roe vs. Wade*, NBC

Supporting actor in a drama series: Larry Drake, *L.A. Law*, NBC

Supporting actress in a drama series: Melanie Mayron, *thirtysomething*, ABC

Supporting actor in a comedy series: Woody Harrelson, *Cheers*, NBC

Supporting actress in a comedy series: Rhea Perlman, *Cheers*, NBC

Supporting actor in a mini-series or a special: Derek Jacobi, *The Tenth Man, Hallmark Hall of Fame*, CBS

Supporting actress in a mini-series or a special: Colleen Dewhurst, *Those She Left Behind*, NBC

Individual performance (variety or music program): Linda Ronstadt, *Canciones de Mi Padre, Great Performances*, PBS

Individual performance (informational programming): Hall Holbrook, host, *Portrait of America*, TBS

Individual performance (special events): Billy Crystal, host, *The 31st Annual Grammy Awards*, CBS

Individual performance (classical music/dance programming): Mikhail Baryshnikov, *Baryshnikov Dances Balanchine, Great Performances*, PBS

Directing in a drama series: Robert Altman, *Tanner '88*, HBO

Directing in a comedy series: Peter Baldwin, *The Wonder Years*, ABC

Directing in a mini-series or a special: Simon Wincer, *Lonesome Dove*, CBS

Writing in a drama series: Joseph Dougherty, *thirtysomething*, ABC

Writing in a comedy series: Diane English, *Murphy Brown*, CBS

DAYTIME AWARDS

Drama series: *Santa Barbara*, NBC

Actor in a drama series: David Canary, *All My Children*, ABC

Actress in a drama series: Marcy Walker, *Santa Barbara*, NBC

Drama series directing team: Frank Pacelli, Heather Hill, Randy Robbins, Rudy Vejar, Betty Rothenberg, Kathryn Foster, *The Young and the Restless*, CBS

INTERNATIONAL AWARD WINNERS

Documentary: *Four Hours in My Lai*, Yorkshire TV, U.K.

Arts documentary: *Gwen – A Juliet Remembered*, BBC, U.K.

Popular arts: *Alexei Sayle's Stuff: Fun with Magnets*, BBC, U.K.

Performing arts: *La Bohème*, Australian Broadcasting

Drama: *Traffic*, Channel Four, U.K.

Young people: *My Secret Identity*, Sunrise Films, Canada

Directorate award: Ted Turner

Citation: Murray Chercover

Founder's award: Paul Fox

1989-90

PRIMETIME PROGRAM AWARDS

Drama series: *L.A. Law*, NBC

Comedy series: *Murphy Brown*, CBS

Mini-series: *Drug Wars: The Camarena Story*, NBC

Drama/comedy special: (tie) *Caroline?, Hallmark Hall of Fame*, CBS; *The Incident*, CBS

Variety, music or comedy series: *In Living Color*, Fox

Variety, music or comedy special: *Sammy Davis, Jr.'s 60th Anniversary Celebration*, ABC

Classical program in the performing arts: *Aida, The Metropolitan Opera Presents*, PBS

Informational series (area award): *Smithsonian World*, PBS

Informational special (area award): *Dance in America: Bob Fosse Steam Heat, Great Performances*, PBS; *Broadway Dreamers: The Legacy of the Group Theatre, American Masters*, PBS

Animated program – one hour or less: *The Simpsons*, Fox

Children's program: *A Mother's Courage: The Mary Thomas Story, The Magical World of Disney*, NBC

PERFORMANCE, DIRECTING, AND WRITING

Actor in a drama series: Peter Falk, *Columbo*, ABC

Actress in a drama series: Patricia Wettig, *thirtysomething*, ABC

Actor in a comedy series: Ted Danson, *Cheers*, NBC

Actress in a comedy series: Candice Bergen, *Murphy Brown*, CBS

Actor in a mini-series or a special: Hume Cronyn, *Age-Old Friends*, HBO

Actress in a mini-series or a special: Barbara Hershey, *A Killing in a Small Town*, CBS

Supporting actor in a drama series: Jimmy Smits, *L.A. Law*, NBC

Supporting actress in a drama series: Marg Helgenberger, *China Beach*, ABC

Supporting actor in a comedy series: Alex Rocco, *The Famous Teddy Z*, CBS

Supporting actress in a comedy series: Bebe Neuwirth, *Cheers*, NBC

Supporting actor in a mini-series or a special: Vincent Gardenia, *Age-Old Friends*, HBO

Supporting actress in a mini-series or a special: Eva Marie Saint, *People Like Us*, NBS

Performance in a variety or music program: Tracey Ullman, *The Best of Tracey Ullman Show*, Fox

Performance in informational programming: *George Burns, A Conversation with...*, Disney

Performance in classical music/dance programming (area award): Brian Boitano, *Carmen on Ice*, HBO; Brian Orser, *Carmen on Ice*, HBO; Katarina Witt, *Carmen on Ice*, HBO

... July 21 ...

NBC is close to a deal to pay Warner Bros. Television an estimated $5 million per episode to keep cornerstone Thursday sitcom **Friends** on the air through mid-2002.

Guest actor in a drama series: Patrick McGoohan, *Columbo*, ABC

Guest actress in a drama series: Viveca Lindfors, *Life Goes On*, ABC

Guest actor in a comedy series: Jay Thomas, *Murphy Brown*, CBS

Guest actress in a comedy series: Swoosie Kurtz, *Carol & Company*, NBC

Directing in a drama series: (tie) Thomas Carter, *Equal Justice*, ABC; Scott Winant, *thirtysomething*, ABC

Directing in a comedy series: Michael Dinner, *The Wonder Years*, ABC

Directing in a mini-series or a special: Joseph Sargent, *Caroline?*, *Hallmark Hall of Fame*, CBS

Writing in a drama series: David E. Kelley, *L.A. Law*, NBC

Writing in a comedy series: Bob Brush, *The Wonder Years*, ABC

DAYTIME AWARDS

Drama series: *Santa Barbara*, NBC

Actor in a drama series: A. Martinez, *Santa Barbara*, NBC

Actress in a drama series: Kim Zimmer, *Guiding Light*, CBS

Drama series directing team: Michael Gliona, Rick Bennewitz, Robert Schiller, Pamela Fryman, Jeanine Guarneri-Frons, *Santa Barbara*, NBC

INTERNATIONAL AWARD WINNERS

Documentary: *J'ai Douze Ans et Je Fais la Guerre*, CAPA Production, France

Arts documentary: *Bookmark: From Moscow to Pietushki*, BBC, U.K.

Performing arts: *The Mahabharata*, Channel Four, U.K.

Popular arts: *Norbert Smith: A Life*, Channel Four, U.K.

Drama: *First and Last*, BBC, U.K.

Children and young people: *Living with Dinosaurs*, Channel Four, U.K.

Directorate award: Henrikas Yushkiavitshus

Founder's award: Joan Ganz Cooney

1990-91

PRIMETIME PROGRAM AWARDS

Drama series: *L.A. Law*, NBC

Comedy series: *Cheers*, NBC

Drama/comedy special or mini-series: *Separate but Equal*, NBC

Variety, music or comedy program: *The 63rd Annual Academy Awards*, ABC

Informational series (area award): *The Civil War*, PBS

Informational special (area award): *Edward R. Murrow: This Reporter*, *American Masters*, PBS

Children's program: *You Can't Grow Home Again: A 3-2-1 Contact Extra*, PBS

Animated program – one hour or less: *The Simpsons*, Fox

Classical program in the performing arts: *Tchaikovsky's 150th Birthday Gala from Leningrad*, PBS

PERFORMANCE, DIRECTING, AND WRITING

Actor in a drama series: James Earl Jones, *Gabriel's Fire*, ABC

Actress in a drama series: Patricia Wettig, *thirtysomething*, ABC

Actor in a comedy series: Burt Reynolds, *Evening Shade*, CBS

Actress in a comedy series: Kirstie Alley, *Cheers*, NBC

Actor in a mini-series or a special: John Gielgud, *Summer's Lease*, *Masterpiece Theatre*, PBS

Actress in a mini-series or a special: Lynn Whitfield, *The Josephine Baker Story*, HBO

Supporting actor in a comedy series: Jonathan Winters, *Davis Rules*, ABC

Supporting actress in a comedy series: Bebe Neuwirth, *Cheers*, NBC

Supporting actor in a drama series: Timothy Busfield, *thirtysomething*, ABC

Supporting actress in a drama series: Magde Sinclair, *Gabriel's Fire*, ABC

Supporting actor in a mini-series or a special: James Earl Jones, *Heat Wave*, TNT

Supporting actress in a mini-series or a special: Ruby Dee, *Decoration Day*, *Hallmark Hall of Fame*, NBC

Guest actor in a drama series: David Opatoshu, *Gabriel's Fire*, ABC

Guest actress in a drama series: Peggy McCay, *The Trials of Rosie O'Neill*, CBS

Guest actor in a comedy series: Jay Thomas, *Murphy Brown*, CBS

Guest actress in a comedy series: Colleen Dewhurst, *Murphy Brown*, CBS

Directing in a drama series: Thomas Carter, *Equal Justice*, ABC

Directing in a comedy series: James Burrows, *Cheers*, NBC

Directing in a mini-series or a special: Brian Gibson, *The Josephine Baker Story*, HBO

Writing in a drama series: David E. Kelley, *L.A. Law*, NBC

Writing in a comedy series: Gary Dontzig, Steven Peterman, *Murphy Brown*, CBS

DAYTIME AWARDS

Drama series: *As the World Turns*, CBS

Actor in a drama series: Peter Bergman, *The Young and the Restless*, CBS

Actress in a drama series: Finola Hughes, *General Hospital*, ABC

Drama series directing team: Rick Bennewitz, Peter Brinckerhoff, Michael Gliona, Robert Schiller, Jeanine Guarneri-Frons, Pamela Fryman, Robin Raphaelian, *Santa Barbara*, NBC

INTERNATIONAL AWARD WINNERS

Documentary: *Cambodia: The Betrayal*, Central Independent Television, U.K.

Arts documentary: *Damned in the U.S.A.*, Channel Four, U.K.

Performing arts: *Le Dortoir*, Canadian Broadcasting

Popular arts: *The Curse of Mr. Bean*, Thames Television, U.K.

Drama: *The Black Velvet Gown*, Tyne Tees TV, U.K.

Children and young people: *The Fool of the World and the Flying Ship*, Cosgrove Hall Productions, U.K.

Directorate award: Henry Becton

Founder's award: Adrian Cowell

1991-92

PRIMETIME PROGRAM AWARDS

Drama series: *Northern Exposure*, CBS

Comedy series: *Murphy Brown*, CBS

Mini-series: *A Woman Named Jackie*, NBC

Made-for-TV movie: *Miss Rose White, Hallmark Hall of Fame*, NBC

Variety, music or comedy series: *The Tonight Show*, NBC

Variety, music or comedy special: *Cirque du Soleil II: A New Experience*, HBO

Informational series (area award): *MGM: When the Lion Roars*, TNT

Informational special (area award): *Abortion: Desperate Choices*, HBO

Animated program – one hour or less: *A Claymation Easter*, CBS

Children's program: *Mark Twain and Me*, Disney

Classical program in the performing arts: *Perlman in Russia*, PBS

PERFORMANCE, DIRECTING, AND WRITING

Actor in a drama series: Chrisopher Lloyd, *Avonlea*, Disney

Actress in a drama series: Dana Delany, *China Beach*, ABC

Actor in a comedy series: Craig T. Nelson, *Coach*, ABC

Actress in a comedy series: Candice Bergen, *Murphy Brown*, CBS

Actor in a mini-series or a special: Beau Bridges, *Without Warning, The James Brady Story*, HBO

Actress in a mini-series or a special: Gena Rowlands, *Face of a Stranger*, CBS

Supporting actor in a comedy series: Michael Jeter, *Evening Shade*, CBS

Supporting actress in a comedy series: Laurie Metcalf, *Roseanne*, ABC

Supporting actor in a drama series: Richard Dysart, *L.A. Law*, NBC

Supporting actress in a drama series: Valerie Mahaffey, *Northern Exposure*, CBS

Supporting actor in a mini-series or a special: Hume Cronyn, *Broadway Bound*, ABC

Supporting actress in a mini-series or a special: Amanda Plummer, *Miss Rose White, Hallmark Hall of Fame*, NBC

Directing in a drama series: Eric Laneuville, *I'll Fly Away*, NBC

Directing in a comedy series: Barnet Kellman, *Murphy Brown*, CBS

Directing in a mini-series or a special: Daniel Petrie, *Mark Twain and Me*, Disney

Writing in a drama series: Andrew Schneider, Diane Frolov, *Northern Exposure*, CBS

Writing in a comedy series: Elaine Pople, Larry Charles, *Seinfeld*, NBC

DAYTIME AWARDS

Drama series: *All My Children*, ABC

Actor in a drama series: Peter Bergman, *The Young and the Restless*, CBS

Actress in a drama series: Erika Slezak, *One Life to Live*, ABC

Drama series directing team: Michael Eilbaum, Bob Schwarz, Casey Childs, Susan Strickler, Carol Sedwick, Mary Madeiras, Janet Andrews, *Another World*, NBC

INTERNATIONAL AWARD WINNERS

Documentary: *To Sell a War*, Canadian Broadcasting

Arts documentary: *José Carreras: A Life Story*, Iambic Productions and Primetime Television, U.K.

Performing arts: *Pictures on the Edge*, Canadian Broadcasting

Popular arts: *Drop the Dead Donkey*, Channel Four, U.K.

Drama: *A Dangerous Man: Lawrence After Arabia*, Enigma Television, U.K.

Children and young people: *Beat That; Hairdressing*, Channel Four, U.K.

Directorate award: Silvio Berlusconi

Founder's award: Bill Cosby

1992-93

PRIMETIME PROGRAM AWARDS

Drama series: *Picket Fences*, CBS

Comedy series: *Seinfeld*, NBC

Mini-series: *Prime Suspect 2, Mystery!*, PBS

... **July 23** ...
Director Nora Ephron and John Travolta are in talks to re-team for Paramount's romantic comedy **Numbers**.

Made-for-TV movie: *Barbarians at the Gate,* HBO

Variety, music or comedy series: *Saturday Night Live,* NBC

Variety, music or comedy special: *Bob Hope: The First 90 Years,* NBC

Informational series (area award): *Healing and the Mind with Bill Moyers,* PBS

Informational special (area award): *Lucy and Desi: A Home Movie,* NBC

Animated program – one hour or less: *Batman: The Animated Series,* Fox

Children's program (area award): *Avonlea,* Disney; *Beethoven Lives Upstairs,* HBO

Classical program in the performing arts: *Tosca in the Settings and at the Times of Tosca,* PBS

PERFORMANCE, DIRECTING, AND WRITING

Actor in a drama series: Tom Skerritt, *Picket Fences,* CBS

Actress in a drama series: Kathy Baker, *Picket Fences,* CBS

Actor in a comedy series: Ted Danson, *Cheers,* NBC

Actress in a comedy series: Roseanne Arnold, *Roseanne,* ABC

Actor in a mini-series or a special: Robert Morse, *Tru, American Playhouse,* PBS

Actress in a mini-series or a special: Holly Hunter, *The Positively True Adventures of the Alleged Texas Cheerleader-Murdering Mom,* HBO

Supporting actor in a comedy series: Michael Richards, *Seinfeld,* NBC

Supporting actress in a comedy series: Laurie Metcalf, *Roseanne,* ABC

Supporting actor in a drama series: Chad Lowe, *Life Goes on,* ABC

Supporting actress in a drama series: Mary Alice, *I'll Fly Away,* NBC

Supporting actor in a mini-series or a special: Beau Bridges, *The Positively True Adventures of the Alleged Texas Cheerleader-Murdering Mom,* HBO

Supporting actress in a mini-series or a special: Mary Tyler Moore, *Stolen Babies,* Lifetime

Guest actor in a drama series: Laurence Fishburne, *Tribeca,* Fox

Guest actress in a drama series: Elaine Stritch, *Law & Order,* NBC

Guest actor in a comedy series: David Clennon, *Dream On,* HBO

Guest actress in a comedy series: Tracey Ullman, *Love & War,* CBS

Directing in a drama series: Barry Levinson, *Homicide,* NBC

Directing in a comedy series: Betty Thomas, *Dream On,* HBO

Directing in a mini-series or a special: James Sadwith, *Sinatra,* CBS

Writing in a drama series: Tom Fontana, *Homicide,* NBC

Writing in a comedy series: Larry David, *Seinfeld,* NBC

DAYTIME AWARDS

Drama series: *The Young and the Restless,* CBS

Actor in a drama series: David Canary, *All My Children,* ABC

Actress in a drama series: Linda Dano, *Another World,* NBC

Drama series directing team: Paul Lammers, Maria Wagner, Dan Hamilton, Charles C. Dyer, Larry Carpenter, Joel Aronowitz, Michael Kerner, *As the World Turns,* CBS

INTERNATIONAL AWARD WINNERS

Documentary: *Disappearing World: We Are All Neighbours,* Granada TV, U.K.; *Monica and Jonas: The Face of the Informer State,* NHK Japan Broadcasting

Arts documentary: *The Wonderful Horrible Life of Leni Riefenstahl,* Omega Films GMBH and Nomad Films, Germany/Belgium

Performing arts: *Concerto,* Channel Four, U.K.

Popular arts: *Absolutely Fabulous,* BBC, U.K.; *Drop the Dead Donkey,* Channel Four, U.K.

Children and young people: *The Penknife,* NOS/AVRO/Bos Bros., The Netherlands

Drama: *Unnatural Pursuits,* BBC, U.K.

Directorate award: André Rousselet

Founder's award: Richard Dunn

1993-94

PRIMETIME PROGRAM AWARDS

Drama series: *Picket Fences,* CBS

Comedy series: *Frasier,* NBC

Mini-series: *Prime Suspect 3, Mystery!,* PBS

Made-for-TV movie: *And the Band Played on,* HBO

Variety, music or comedy series: *Late Show with David Letterman,* CBS

Variety, music or comedy special: *The Kennedy Center Honors,* CBS

Informational series (area award): *Later with Bob Costas,* NBC

Informational special (area award): *I Am a Promise: The Children of Stanton Street Elementary School,* HBO

Animated program – one hour or less: *The Roman City,* PBS

Children's program: *Kids Killing Kids/Kids Saving Kids,* CBS, Fox

Cultural program: *Vladimir Horowitz: A Reminiscence,* PBS

PERFORMANCE, DIRECTING, AND WRITING

Actor in a drama series: Dennis Franz, *NYPD Blue,* ABC

Actress in a drama series: Sela Ward, *Sister,* NBC

Actor in a comedy series: Kelsey Grammer, *Frasier,* NBC

Actress in a comedy series: Candice Bergen, *Murphy Brown,* CBS

Actor in a mini-series or a special: Hume Cronyn, *To Dance with the White Dog, Hallmark Hall of Fame,* NBC

Actress in a mini-series or a special: Kirstie Alley, *David's Mother,* CBS

Supporting actor in a drama series: Fyvish Finkel, *Picket Fences,* CBS

Supporting actress in a drama series: Leigh Taylor-Young, *Picket Fences,* CBS

Supporting actor in a comedy series: Michael Richards, *Seinfeld,* NBC

Supporting actress in a comedy series: Laurie Metcalf, *Roseanne,* ABC

Supporting actor in a mini-series or a special: Michael Goorijan, *David's Mother,* CBS

Supporting actress in a mini-series or a special: Cicely Tyson, *Oldest Living Confederate Widow Tells All,* CBS

Guest actor in a drama series: Richard Kiley, *Picket Fences,* CBS

Guest actress in a drama series: Faye Dunaway, *Columbo,* ABC

Guest actor in a comedy series: Martin Sheen, *Murphy Brown,* CBS

Guest actress in a comedy series: Eileen Heckart, *Love & War,* CBS

Directing in a drama series: Daniel Sackheim, *NYPD Blue,* ABC

Directing in a comedy series: James Burrows, *Frasier,* NBC

Directing in a mini-series or a special: John Frankenheimer, *Against the Wall,* HBO

Writing in a drama series: Ann Biderman, *NYPD Blue,* ABC

Writing in a comedy series: David Angel, Peter Casey, David Lee, *Frasier,* NBC

DAYTIME AWARDS

Drama series: *All My Children,* ABC

Actor in a drama series: Michael Zaslow, *Guiding Light,* CBS

Actress in a drama series: Hillary B. Smith, *One Life to Live,* ABC

Drama series directing team: Bruce Barry, Jo Anne Sedwick, Irene Pace, Brian Mertes, John O'Connell, Matthew Lagle, Scott Riggs, Lisa Connor, *Guiding Light,* CBS

INTERNATIONAL AWARD WINNERS

Documentary: *Life in the Freezer: The Big Freeze,* BBC, U.K.

Arts documentary: *Positive Art,* Australian Broadcasting

Performing arts: *Peter and the Wolf,* BBC, U.K.

Popular arts: *Absolutely Fabulous: Hospital,* BBC, U.K.; *Red Dwarf VI: Gunmen of the Apocalypse,* BBC, U.K.

Drama: *The Bullion Boys,* BBC, U.K.

Children and young people: *Insektors,* France 3, France

Directorate award: Helmut Thoma

Founder's award: Film on Four, Channel Four, U.K.

1994-95

PRIMETIME PROGRAM AWARDS

Drama series: *NYPD Blue,* ABC

Comedy series: *Frasier,* NBC

Mini-series: *Joseph,* TNT

Made-for-TV movie: *Indictment: The McMartin Trial,* HBO

Variety, music or comedy series: *The Tonight Show with Jay Leno,* NBC

Variety, music or comedy special: *Barbra Streisand: The Concert,* HBO

Informational series (area award): *Baseball,* PBS; *TV Nation,* NBC

Informational special (area award): *Taxicab Confessions,* HBO; *U.S. Holocaust Memorial Museum: One Survivor Remembers,* HBO

Animated program – one hour or less: *The Simpsons,* Fox

Children's program (area award): *Going, Going, Almost Gone! Animals in Danger,* HBO

Cultural program: *Verdi's La Traviata with the New York City Opera, Live from Lincoln Center,* PBS

PERFORMANCE, DIRECTING, AND WRITING

Actor in a drama series: Mandy Patinkin, *Chicago Hope,* CBS

Actress in a drama series: Kathy Baker, *Picket Fences,* CBS

Actor in a comedy series: Kelsey Grammer, *Frasier,* NBC

Actress in a comedy series: Candice Bergen, *Murphy Brown,* CBS

Actor in a mini-series or a special: Raul Julia, *The Burning Season,* HBO

Actress in a mini-series or a special: Glenn Close, *Serving in Silence: The Margarethe Cammermeyer Story,* NBC

Supporting actor in a drama series: Ray Walston, *Picket Fences,* CBS

Supporting actress in a drama series: Julianna Margulies, *ER*, NBC

Supporting actor in a comedy series: David Hyde Pierce, *Frasier*, NBC

Supporting actress in a comedy series: Christine Baranski, *Cybill*, CBS

Supporting actor in a mini-series or a special: Donald Sutherland, *Citizen X*, HBO

Supporting actress in a mini-series or a special: (tie) Judy Davis, *Serving in Silence: The Margarethe Cammermeyer Story*, NBC; Shirley Knight, *Indictment: The McMartin Trial*, HBO

Guest actor in a drama series: Paul Winfield, *Picket Fences*, CBS

Guest actress in a drama series: Shirley Knight, *NYPD Blue*, ABC

Guest actor in a comedy series: Carl Reiner, *Mad About You*, NBC

Guest actress in a comedy series: Cyndi Lauper, *Mad About You*, NBC

Directing in a drama series: Mimi Leder, *ER*, NBC

Directing in a comedy series: David Lee, *Frasier*, NBC

Directing in a mini-series or a special: John Frankenheimer, *The Burning Season*, HBO

Writing in a drama series: Lance A. Gentile, *ER*, NBC

Writing in a comedy series: Chuck Ranberg, Anne Flett-Giordano, *Frasier*, NBC

DAYTIME AWARDS

Drama series: *General Hospital*, ABC

Actor in a drama series: Justin Deas, *Guiding Light*, CBS

Actress in a drama series: Erika Slezak, *One Life to Live*, ABC

Drama series directing team: Christopher Goutman, Henry Kaplan, Conal O'Brien, James A. Baffico, Barbara Martin Simmons, Shirley Simmons, Robin Maizes, Sybil Costello, *All My Children*, ABC

INTERNATIONAL AWARD WINNERS

Documentary: *Anne Frank Remembered*, BBC, U.K.; *Contre l'Oubli (Lest We Forget)*, France 2, France

Arts documentary: *Kenzaburo Oe's Long Road to Fatherhood*, NHK Japan Broadcasting

Performing arts: *Carmen*, SVT Channel 1, Sweden

Popular arts: *Don't Forget Your Toothbrush*, Channel Four, U.K.

Drama: *The Politician's Wife*, Channel Four, U.K.

Children and young people: *Little Lord Fauntleroy*, BBC, U.K.; *Wise Up*, Channel Four, U.K.

Directorate award: John Birt

Founder's award: Don Hewitt

1995-96
PRIMETIME PROGRAM AWARDS

Drama series: *ER*, NBC

Comedy series: *Frasier*, NBC

Mini-series: *Gulliver's Travels*, NBC

Made-for-TV movie: *Truman*, HBO

Variety, music or comedy series: *Dennis Miller Live*, HBO

Variety, music or comedy special: *The Kennedy Center Honors*, CBS

Informational series (area award): *Time Life's Lost Civilizations*, NBC

Informational special (area award): *Survivors of the Holocaust*, TBS

Animated program – one hour or less: *A Pinky & the Brain Christmas Special*, WB

Children's program (area award): *Peter and the Wolf*, ABC

Cultural music/dance program: *Itzhak Perlman: In the Fiddler's House, Great Performances*, PBS

PERFORMANCE, DIRECTING, AND WRITING

Actor in a drama series: Dennis Franz, *NYPD Blue*, ABC

Actress in a drama series: Kathy Baker, *Picket Fences*, CBS

Actor in a comedy series: John Lithgow, *3rd Rock from the Sun*, NBC

Actress in a comedy series: Helen Hunt, *Mad About You*, NBC

Actor in a mini-series or a special: Alan Rickman, *Rasputin*, HBO

Actress in a mini-series or a special: Helen Mirren, *Prime Suspect: Scent of Darkness*, PBS

Supporting actor in a drama series: Ray Walston, *Picket Fences*, CBS

Supporting actress in a drama series: Tyne Daly, *Christy*, CBS

Supporting actor in a comedy series: Rip Torn, *The Larry Sanders Show*, HBO

Supporting actress in a comedy series: Julia Louis-Dreyfus, *Seinfeld*, NBC

Supporting actor in a mini-series or a special: Tom Hulce, *The Heidi Chronicles*, TNT

Supporting actress in a mini-series or a special: Greta Scacchi, *Rasputin*, HBO

Guest actor in a drama series: Peter Boyle, *The X-Files*, Fox

Guest actress in a drama series: Amanda Plummer, *The Outer Limits*, Showtime

Guest actor in a comedy series: Tim Conway, *Coach*, ABC

Guest actress in a comedy series: Betty White, *The John Larroquette Show*, NBC

Directing in a drama series: Jeremy Kagan, *Chicago Hope*, CBS

Directing in a comedy series: Michael Lembeck,

Friends, NBC

Directing in a mini-series or a special: John Frankenheimer, *Andersonville*, TNT

Writing in a drama series: David Morgan, *The X-Files*, Fox

Writing in a comedy series: Joe Keenan, Christopher Lloyd, Rob Greenberg, Jack Burditt, Chuck Ranberg, Anne Flett-Giordano, Linda Morris, Vic Rauseo, *Frasier*, NBC

DAYTIME AWARDS

Drama series: *General Hospital*, ABC

Actor in a drama series: Charles Keating, *Another World*, NBC

Actress in a drama series: Erika Slezak, *One Life to Live*, ABC

Directing in a drama series: Heather Hill, Frank Pacelli, Mike Denney, Kathryn Foster, Betty Rothenberg, Sally McDonald, Dan Brumett, Robin Masick Phillips, Randal Hill, Don Jacob, Bob Welsh, *The Young and the Restless*, CBS

INTERNATIONAL AWARD WINNERS

Documentary: *The Pelican of Ramzan the Red*, France; *People's Century-1933: Master Race*, BBC, U.K.; *The Saga of Life: The Unknown World*, Sveriges Television, Sweden

Arts documentary: *The House*, BBC, U.K.

Performing arts: *September Songs: The Music of Kurt Weill*, Canada

Popular arts: *A Close Shave*, BBC, U.K.

Drama: *La Colline aux Mille Enfants*, The Netherlands

Children and young people: *Newsround Extra*, BBC, U.K.; *Wise Up*, Channel Four, U.K.

Directorate award: Herbert Granath

Founder's award: Reg Grundy

1996-97

PRIMETIME PROGRAM AWARDS

Drama series: *Law & Order*, NBC

Comedy series: *Frasier*, NBC

Mini-series: *Prime Suspect 5: Errors of Judgement*, PBS

Made-for-TV movie: *Miss Evers' Boys*, HBO

Variety, music or comedy series: *Tracey Takes on...*, HBO

Variety, music or comedy special: *Chris Rock: Bring the Pain*, HBO

Informational series (area award): *A&E Biography*, A&E; *The Great War and the Shaping of the 20th Century*, PBS

Informational special (area award): *Without Pity: A Film about Abilities*, HBO

Animated program – one hour or less: *The Simpsons*, Fox

Children's program (area award): *How Do You spell God?*, HBO

Cultural music/dance program: *Puccini's La Bohème with the New York City Opera*, PBS

PERFORMANCE, DIRECTING, AND WRITING

Actor in a drama series: Dennis Franz, *NYPD Blue*, ABC

Actress in a drama series: Gillian Anderson, *The X-Files*, Fox

Actor in a comedy series: John Lithgow, *3rd Rock from the Sun*, NBC

Actress in a comedy series: Helen Hunt, *Mad About You*, NBC

Actor in a mini-series or a special: Armand Assante, *Gotti*, NBC

Actress in a mini-series or a special: Alfre Woodard, *Miss Evers' Boys*, HBO

Supporting actor in a drama series: Hector Elizondo, *Chicago Hope*, CBS

Supporting actress in a drama series: Kim Delaney, *NYPD Blue*, ABC

Supporting actor in a comedy series: Michael Richards, *Seinfeld*, NBC

Supporting actress in a comedy series: Kristen Johnston, *3rd Rock from the Sun*, NBC

Supporting actor in a mini-series or a special: Beau Bridges, *The Second Civil War*, HBO

Supporting actress in a mini-series or a special: Diana Rigg, *Rebecca*, PBS

Guest actor in a drama series: Pruitt Taylor Vince, *Murder One*, ABC

Guest actress in a drama series: Dianne Wiest, *Avonlea*, Disney

Guest actor in a comedy series: Mel Brooks, *Mad About You*, NBC

Guest actress in a comedy series: Carol Burnett, *Mad About You*, NBC

Directing in a drama series: Mark Tinker, *NYPD Blue*, ABC

Directing in a comedy series: David Lee, *Frasier*, NBC

Directing in a variety or music program: Don Mischer, *Centennial Olympic Games: Opening Ceremonies*, NBS

Directing in a mini-series or a special: Andrei Konchalovsky, *The Odyssey*, NBC

Writing in a drama series: David Milch, Stephen Gaghan, Michael R. Perry, *NYPD Blue*, ABC

Writing in a comedy series: Ellen DeGeneres, Mark Driscoll, Davba Savel, Tracey Newman, Jonathan Stark, *Ellen*, ABC

Writing in a variety or music program: Chris Rock, *Chris Rock: Bring the Pain*, HBO

Writing in a mini-series or a special: Horton Foote, *William Faulkner's Old Man, Hallmark Hall of Fame*, CBS

DAYTIME AWARDS

Drama series: *General Hospital*, ABC

Actor in a drama series: Justin Deas, *Guiding the Light*, CBS

Actress in a drama series: Jes Walton, *The Young and the Restless*, CBS

Supporting actor in a drama series: Ian Buchanan, *The Bold and the Beautiful*, CBS

Supporting actress in a drama series: Michelle Stafford, *The Young and the Restless*, CBS

Drama series directing team: Heather Hill, Frank Pacelli, Mike Denney, Kathryn Foster, Betty Rothenberg, Sall McDonald, Dan Brumett, Robin Masick Phillips, Randal Hill, Donald Jacob, *The Young and the Restless*, CBS

Drama series writing team: Agnes Nixon, Lorraine Broderick, Millee Taggart, Hal Corley, Frederick Johnson, Jeff Beldner, Christina Covino, Courtney Simon, Karen L. Lewis, Elizabeth Smith, Michelle Patrick, Bettina F. Bradbury, Judith Donato, Kathleen Klein, Jane Owen Murphy, *All My Children*, ABC

SPECIAL AWARDS

NATAS trustees award: Sumner Redstone

NATAS president's award: *Miss Evers' Boys*, HBO

INTERNATIONAL AWARD WINNERS

Drama: *Crossing the Floor*, Channel Four, U.K.

Documentary: *Jerrie & Louise*, CBC, Canada

Arts documentary: Dancing for Dollars: *The Bolshoi in Las Vegas*, Channel Four, U.K.

Children's: *Wise up*, Channel Four, U.K.

Performance arts: *Enter Achilles*, BBC, U.K.

Popular arts: *Lieberg Zaps Himself*, TROS, Netherlands

1997-98

Comedy series: *Frasier*, NBC

Drama series: *The Practice*, ABC

Mini-series: *From the Earth to the Moon*, HBO

Telefilm: *Don King: Only in America*, HBO

Lead actor in a comedy series: Kelsey Grammer, *Frasier*, NBC

Lead actress in a comedy series: Helen Hunt, *Mad About You*, NBC

Lead actor in a drama series: Andre Braugher, *Homicide: Life on the Street*, NBC

Lead actress in a drama series: Christine Lahti, *Chicago Hope*, CBS

Supporting actor in a comedy series: David Hyde Pierce, *Frasier*, NBC

Supporting actress in a comedy series: Lisa Kudrow, *Friends*, NBC

Supporting actor in a drama series: Gordon Clapp, *NYPD Blue*, ABC

Supporting actress in a drama series: Camryn Manheim, *The Practice*, ABC

Lead actor in a mini-series or a movie: Gary Sinise, *George Wallace*, TNT

Lead actress in a mini-series or a movie: Ellen Barkin, *Before Women Had Wings*, ABC

Guest actor in a comedy series: Mel Brooks, *Mad About You*, NBC

Guest actress in a comedy series: Emma Thompson, *Ellen*, ABC

Guest actor in a drama series: John Larroquette, *The Practice*, ABC

Guest actress in a drama series: Cloris Leachman, *Promised Land*, CBS

Supporting actor in a mini-series or a movie: George C. Scott, *12 Angry Men*, Showtime

Supporting actress in a mini-series or a movie: Mare Winningham, *George Wallace*, TNT

Performance in a variety or music program: Billy Crystal, *The 70th Annual Academy Awards*, ABC

Animated program (one hour or less): *The Simpsons* (*Trash of the Titans*), Fox

Variety, music or comedy series: *Late Show with David Letterman*, CBS

Variety, music or comedy special: *The 1997 Tony Awards*, CBS

Directing for a comedy series: Todd Holland, *The Larry Sanders Show*, HBO

Directing for a drama series: Mark Tinker, *Brooklyn South*, CBS; Paris Barclay, *NYPD Blue*, ABC

Directing for a variety or music program: Louis J. Horvitz, *The 70th Annual Academy Awards*, ABC

Directing for a mini-series or a movie: John Frankenheimer, *George Wallace*, TNT

Writing for a comedy series: Peter Tolan, Garry Shandling, *The Larry Sanders Show*, HBO

Writing for a drama series: Nicholas Wootton, David Milch, Bill Clark, *NYPD Blue*, ABC

Writing for a variety or music program: Eddie Feldmann (head writer), Dennis Miller, David Feldman, Leah Krinsky, Jim Hanna, David Weiss, Jose Arroyo, *Dennis Miller Live*, HBO

Writing for a mini-series or a movie: Kario Salem, *Don King: Only in America*, HBO

Classical music-dance program: *Yo-Yo Ma Inspired by Bach*, PBS

Children's program (area award: possibility of one or more than one award): *Muppets Tonight*, Disney Channel; *Nick News Special Edition – What Are You Staring at?*, Nickelodeon

Nonfiction special (area award: possibility of one or more than one award): *Discovery Sunday – Vietnam POWs: Stories of Survival*, Discovery Channel

---

... July 28 ...

Richard Gere and Robert Altman are to work together for the first time in the romantic comedy **Dr. T. And The Women**.

Nonfiction series (area award: possibility of one or more than one award): *The American Experience*, PBS

Cinematography for a series: Constantine Makris, *Law & Order* (*Stalker*), NBC

Cinematography for a mini-series or a movie: Eric Van Haren Noman, *What the Deaf Man Heard*, CBS

Single-camera picture editing for a series: Heather MacDougall, *The X-Files* (*Kill Switch*), Fox

Single-camera picture editing for a mini-series or a movie: Eric Sears, *Gia*, HBO

Multicamera picture editing for a series: Ron Volk, *Frasier* (*Room Service*), NBC

Multicamera picture editing for a mini-series, movie or a special: Richard Daws, Jason Porthouse, *Stomp Out Loud*, HBO

Music composition for a series (dramatic underscore): Christophe Beck, *Buffy the Vampire Slayer* (*Becoming, Part1*), WB

Music composition for a mini-series or a movie (dramatic underscore): Bruce Boughton, *Glory & Honor*, TNT

Music direction: Bill Conti, *The 70th Annual Academy Awards*, ABC

Music and lyrics: Alf Clausen, music; Ken Keeler, lyrics, *The Simpsons* (*You're Checkin' in – a Musical Tribute to the Betty Ford Center*), Fox

Main title theme music: Maribeth Derry, Tom Snow, Robbie Buchana, Richard Barton Lewis, *Fame L.A.*, syndicated

Art direction for a series: Graeme Murray, production designer; Greg Lioewen, art director; Shirley Inget, set decorator, *The X-Files* (*The Post-Modern Prometheus*), Fox

Art direction for a mini-series or a movie: Roger Hall, production designer; John King, supervising art director; Mike Boone, art director; Karen Brookes, set decorator, *Merlin (Part 1)*, NBC

Art direction for a variety or music program: Radny Ser, production designer; Edward L. Rubin, art director; Julie Kaye Fanton, set decorator, *Rodgers & Hammerstein's Cinderella*, ABC

Costume design for a series: Dan Moore, *The Magnificent Seven* (*Working Girls*), CBS

Costume design for a mini-series or a movie: Ann Hollowood, *Merlin (Part 1)*, NBC

Costume design for a variety or music program: Jane Ruhm, *Tracey Takes on… Sports*, HBO and LuEllyn Harper, costume supervisor; Monique Long, key costumer, *NewsRadio* (*Sinking Ship*), NBC

Costuming for a mini-series, movie or a special (area award: possibility of one or no award): Amy Stofsky, costume supervisor, *The Pentagon Wars*, HBO

Sound editing for a series: Walter Newman, supervising sound editor; Darren Wright, Rick Camera, sound editors; Darleen Stoker-Kageyama, Cathy Flynn-Morris, dialog editors; Tom Harris, ADR editor; Michael D. Dittrick, music editor; Casey Crabtree, James Bailey, Foley artists, *ER* (*Exodus*), NBC

Sound editing for a mini-series, movie or a special: Michael Graham, supervising sound editor; Greg Schorer, co-supervising sound editor; Kristi Johns, Suzanne Angel, ADR editors; Bill Bell, Mark Friedgen, Bob Costanza, Rob Webber, Gary Macheel, Rick Steele, Lou Thomas, Adriane Marfiak, Anton Holden, Michael Lyle, David Eichorn, Marke Steele, Tim Terusa, Rusty Tinsley, sound editors; Kim Naves, music editor; Tim Chilton, Jill Schachne, Foley artists, *Rough Riders (Part 2)*, TNT

Sound mixing for a comedy series or a special: Paul Lewis, production mixer; Nello Torri, Kurt Kassulke, Peter R. Kelsey, re-recording mixers, *Ally McBeal* (*Boy of the World*), Fox

Sound mixing for a variety of music series or a special: Edward J. Greene, production mixer; Tom Vicari, music mixer; Robert Douglass, Patrick Baltzell, sound mixers, *The 70th Annual Academy Awards*, ABC

Sound mixing for a drama series: Russell Fager, production mixer; Rusty Russell Smith, William Freesh, re-recording mixers, *Chicago Hope* (*Brain Salad Surgery*), CBS

Sound mixing for a drama, mini-series or a movie: Russell Williams II, production mixer; David E. Fluhr, Adam Jenkins, re-recording mixers, *12 Angry Men*, Showtime

Casting for a series: Lou Digiaimo, Pat Moran, Brett Goldstein, *Homicide: Life on the Street*, NBC

Casting for a mini-series or a movie: Meg Liberman, Marc Hirschfeld, Sharon Klein, Mark Fincannon, Lisa Mae Wells Fincannon, Craig Fincannon, Deborah Brown, *From the Earth to the Moon*, HBO

Choreography: Marguerite Derricks, Peggy Holmes, *Fame L.A.* (*Pilot*), syndicated

Lighting direction (electronic) for a comedy series: Donald A. Morgan, *Home Improvement* (*A Night to Dismember*), ABC

Lighting direction (electronic) for a drama series, variety series, mini-series, movie or a special: Robert Dickinson, lighting designer; Andy O'Reilly, Matt Ford, Bob Barnhart, lighting directors, *The 70th Annual Academy Awards*, ABC

… July 29 …
Stephen Kay will direct Sylvester Stallone in the remake of the classic British gangster thriller **Get Carter**.

Special visual effects for a series: Pedro Pires, *Yo-Yo Ma Inspired by Bach* (*The Sound of the Carceri*), PBS

Special visual effects for a mini-series or a movie: Tim Webber, visual-effects supervising designer; Stefan Lange, visual-effects cameraman; Matthew Cope, visual-effects shoot coordinator; Richard Conway, physical special-effects supervisor; Tim Greenwood, George Roper, Murray Butler, Angus Wilson, Pedro Sabrosa, William Bartlett, Avtar Bains, visual-effects artists, *Merlin* (*Part 1*), NBC

Technical direction/camera/video for a series: Gene Crowe, technical director; Dave Chameides, Hank Geving, Larry Heider, Bob Hieghton, Don Lenzer, Bill Philbin, camera; Chuck Reilly, John O'Brien, video, *ER* (*Ambush*), NBC

Technical direction/camera/video for a special: Emmett Loughran, technical director; Miguel Armstrong, Juan Barrera, Jim Covello, John Feher, Manny Gutierrez, Jake Ostroff, David Smith, Ron Washburn, camera; William Steinberg, video, *The Metropolitan Opera Presents Carmen*, PBS

Makeup for a series: Todd A. McIntosh, John Vulich, John Maldonado, John Wheaton, Gerald Quist, Margi Latinopoulos, Dayne Johnson, Alan Friedman, Carig Reardon, Michael Blake, Robin Beauchesne, Brigette Myre-Ellis, Mark Shostrom, *Buffy the Vampire Slayer* (*Surprise/Innocence*), WB

Makeup for a mini-series, movie or a special: Aileen Seaton, Mark Coulier, *Merlin*, NBC

Hairstyling for a series: Audree Futterman, *Tracey Takes on... Smoking*, HBO

Hairstyling for a mini-series, movie or special: Vicky Phillips, Lynda Gurasich, *From the Earth to the Moon*, HBO

Main title design: Kasumi Mihori, Billy Pittard, Ed Sullivan, *The Wonderful World of Disney*, ABC

Achievement in nonfiction programming – Cinematography: Richard Chisolm, Paul Goldsmith, Buddy Squires, Jerry Cotts, Nick Caloyianis, Jon Else, *National Geographic Special: America's Endangered Species: Don't Say Good-bye*, NBC; Jim Dutcher, *Wolves at Our Door*, Discovery Channel

Achievement in nonfiction programming – Picture editing: Michael Bloecher, William Haugse, *Assassinated: The Last Days of Kennedy and King*, TBS Superstation; Sam Pollard, *4 Little Girls*, HBO; Arnold Glassman, *Frank Capra's American Dream*, American Movie Classics; Lenny Feinstein, *National Geographic Special: America's Endangered Species: Don't Say Good-bye*, NBC; Amanda Zinoman, *Trauma: Life in the ER* (*Wrong Place,*

Wrong Time), TLC; Mike Harvey, Graham Knight, *Vietnam POWs: Stories of Survival*, Discovery Channel

Achievement in nonfiction programming – Sound editing: Patrick M. Griffith, Lisa Hannan, *National Geographic Explorer* (*Rat*), TBS Superstation

Achievement in nonfiction programming – Sound mixing: Jamie Dutcher, *Wolves at Our Door*, Discovery Channel

Commercial: *Apple Computer – Think Different*, TBWA Chiat/Day, ad agency

Individual achievement in animation: Eric Radomski, *Spawn*, HBO

Voiceover performance: Hank Azaria, *The Simpsons*, Fox

INTERNATIONAL AWARD WINNERS

Documentary: *Exile in Sarajevo*, Exile Prods, Australia

Arts documentary: *The War Symphonies: Shostakovich Against Stalin*, Rhombus Media/ZDF/Arte/IDTV, Netherlands

Performing arts: *The Judas Tree*, Landseer/Channel Four, U.K.

Popular arts: *The Vicar of Dibley: Love and Marriage*, Tiger Aspect Prods/BBC, U.K.

Drama: *The Tattooed Widow*, SVT, Sweden

Children's and Young People: *Blabbermouth and Sticky Beak*, Double Exposure/Channel Four, U.K.

1998-99

PRIMETIME PROGRAM AWARDS

Comedy series: *Ally McBeal*, Fox

Drama series: *The Practice*, ABC

Mini-series: *Horatio Hornblower*, A&E

Telefilm: *A Lesson Before Dying*, HBO

Lead actor in a comedy series: John Lithgow, *3rd Rock from the Sun*, NBC

Lead actor in a drama series: Dennis Franz, *NYPD Blue*, ABC

Lead actor in a mini-series or movie: Stanley Tucci, *Winchell*, HBO

Lead actress in a comedy series: Helen Hunt, *Mad About You*, NBC

Lead actress in a drama series: Edie Falco, *The Sopranos*, HBO

Lead actress in a mini-series or movie: Helen Mirren, *The Passion of Ayn Rand*, Showtime

Supporting actor in a comedy series: David Hyde Pierce, *Frasier*, NBC

Supporting actor in a drama series: Michael Badalucco, *The Practice*, ABC

Supporting actor in a mini-series or movie: Peter O'Toole, *Joan of Arc*, CBS

Supporting actress in a comedy series: Kristen Johnston, *3rd Rock from the Sun*, NBC

Supporting actress in a drama series: Holland Taylor, *The Practice*, ABC

Supporting actress in a mini-series or movie: Anne Bancroft, *Deep in My Heart*, CBS

Performance in a variety or music program: John Leguizamo, *John Leguizamo's Freak*, HBO

Directing for a comedy series: Thomas Schlamme, *Sports Night* (pilot), ABC

Directing for a drama series: Paris Barclay, *NYPD Blue* (*Hearts and Souls*), ABC

Directing for a variety or music program: Paul Miller, *1998 Tony Awards*, CBS

Directing for a mini-series or movie: Allan Arkush, *The Temptations*, NBC

Variety, music or comedy series: *Late Show With David Letterman*, CBS

Variety, music or comedy special: *1998 Tony Awards*, CBS

Writing for a comedy series: Jay Kogen, *Frasier* (*Merry Christmas, Mrs. Moskowitz*), NBC

Writing for a drama series: James Manos Jr., David Chase, *The Sopranos* (*College*), HBO

Writing for a variety or music program: Tom Agna, Vernon Chatman, Louis CK, Lance Crouther, Gregory Greenberg, Ali Leroi, Steve O'Donnell, Chris Rock, Frank Sebastiano, Chuck Sklar, Jeff Stilson, Wanda Sykes-Hall, Mike Upchurch, *The Chris Rock Show*, HBO

Writing for a mini-series or movie: Ann Peacock, *A Lesson Before Dying*, HBO

DAYTIME AWARDS

Drama: *General Hospital*, ABC

Game/audience participation show: *Win Ben Stein's Money*, Comedy Central

Children's series: *Disney Presents Bill Nye the Science Guy*, syndicated

Children's special: *The Island on Bird Street*, Showtime

Children's animated program: *Arthur*, PBS

Talkshow: *The Rosie O'Donnell Show*, syndicated

INTERNATIONAL AWARD WINNERS

Drama: *Lost for Words*, Yorkshire TV/Bard Entertainment, UK

Documentary (tie): *Born in the USSR: 14 Up*, Granada/BBC, UK; *Just Like Anyone Else*, Mainichi Broadcasting, Japan

Performing Arts (tie): *Rodgers & Hammerstein's Oklahoma*, RPTA/Iambic Prods./Sky Prods., UK; *Karen Kain: Dancing in the Moment*, CBC, Canada

Arts Documentary (tie): *The Phil: Part 3*, Diverse/Channel Four, UK; *Let It Come Down: The Life of Paul Bowles*, Requisite Prods./Banff Centre for the Arts, Canada

Popular Arts: *Smack the Pony*, Talkback/Channel Four, UK

Children and Young People: *Tell Us About Your Life: Battlefield Doctor*, NHK, Japan

News: *Dispatches: A Witness to Murder*, Hardcash Prods./Channel Four, UK

As the leader of all illegal activities in Casablanca, I am an influential and respected man.
(Sydney Greenstreet, Casablanca)

...July 31...
The Taormina Film Festival wraps a turning-point edition that saw the return of mass audiences for the first time in many years.

Selected Television Reviews from *Variety*: 1999

The '60s
(Mini-series, NBC, Sunday Feb. 7, Monday Feb. 8, 9 p.m.)
Filmed in and around Los Angeles by Lynda Obst Prods. in association with NBC Studios. Executive producer, Lynda Obst; producer, Jim Chory; director, Mark Piznarski; writers, Bill Couturie, Robert Greenfield, Jeffrey Fiskin; camera, Michael O'Shea; production designer, Vincent Jefferds; art director, Dawn Snyder; editor, Robert Frazen; music, Jed Feuer, Brian Adler; sound, Kenn Fuller; casting, Molly Lopata. Running time: 240 mins.
Jerry O'Connell (Brian Herlihy), Josh Hamilton (Michael Herlihy), Julia Stiles (Katie Herlihy), Bill Smitrovich (Bill Herlihy), Annie Corley (Mary Herlihy), Leonard Roberts (Emmet Taylor), Charles S. Dutton (Rev. Willie Taylor), Jordana Brewster (Sarah), David Alan Grier (Fred Hampton), Jeremy Sisto (Kenny), Cliff Gorman (Father Daniel Berrigan), Donovan Leitch (Neal Reynolds), Carnie Wilson (Mama Earth), Rosanna Arquette (Hippie Mother). With: Raynor Scheine, David Denman, Elisabeth Rohm, Mary Leahy, Heath Lourwood, Nushond Lee, Dana Smith, Hannah Whelan, Wavy Gravy.
The '60s is an MTV-styled blast of grainy imagery and classic rock that disconnects from any real sense of profundity or purpose. Filmmakers peer at the '60s through the prism of two fictional historical family composites – one white and middle class, the other Southern and black and ravaged by discrimination. The white family includes the boy who goes off to Vietnam an innocent and returns a disillusioned head case; a rebellious teenage daughter who winds up pregnant and on the streets of Haight-Ashbury; the good son who becomes an antiwar activist; the straitlaced father blindsided by the times; and the strong-willed mother struggling to get her wayward family back together.

The black family (far less defined here) is represented by a black minister in Mississippi and his teenage son whose lives are forever changed in the crossfire of the deadly 1965 Watts Riots. Some edgy, agonizing moments prop up the second installment after an aimless, warp-speed opening two hours that sprints through a montage of Vietnam, the Civil Rights Movement, the JFK assassination, Berkeley, and the British Invasion to name a few. *The '60s* is a collection of disparate images spliced together to look like something impressive. Though it contains a handful of scenes that embody true, raw power, it most often depicts this revolutionary decade as a series of Kodak moments – with nary a wide-angle shot in the bunch.

Action
Filmed in Los Angeles by Columbia TriStar TV. Executive producers, Chris Thompson, Don Reo, Barry Katz, Joel Silver; executive producer (pilot), Ted Demme; producer (pilot), Robert Lloyd Lewis; associate producer, Todd London; director, Demme; writer, Thompson; camera, Herbert Davis; production designer, Steven J. Wolff; editor, Tony Porter; music, Jonathan Wolff, Paul Buckley, Warren Zevon; sound mixer, Robert Janiger; casting, Mary Gail Artz, Barbara Cohen. Running time: 30 mins.
Jay Mohr (Peter Dragon), Illeana Douglas (Wendy Ward), Jarrad Paul (Adam Rafkin), Jack Plotnick (Stuart Glazer), Buddy Hackett (Uncle Lonnie), Lee Arenberg (Bobby G), Cindy Ambuehl (Jane Gianopolis), Michelle Hurd (Gina), Gavin Polone (Dodi), Hector Contreras (Manny Sanchez), Sara Paxton (Sara Dragon), Richard Burgi (Cole Riccardi), Keanu Reeves (As Himself), Johnny Grant (As Himself).
For all of its ugliness of spirit, *Action* breaks from the gate sporting a cinema-quality look and a wicked, stylish loopiness that prove instantly irresistible. Peter Dragon is a contemptuous, abusive producer of action-schlock pics whose ego cannot be contained in Earth's orbit. Dragon is shown already in midseason form, sniping at his ex, insulting every little guy who crosses his path, sparring with agents and sucking up to the stars he needs. In other words, reality is not far afield. Discovering that his studio has just dropped $250,000 on a script from an Adam Rafkin when he thought it was Alan Rifkin, he wails, "You're telling me we spent a quarter of a million dollars for the wrong Jew?" *Action* subsequently shifts gears to caper comedy with the arrival of Wendy Ward. Wendy is a child star turned high-priced call girl whom Dragon inadvertently befriends on the way to the premiere of his new flop, *Slow Torture*.

Action promises to feature a string of star cameos (Keanu Reeves slips in the opener). Buddy Hackett adds a further touch of off-kilter color portraying Dragon's Uncle Lonnie, who also happens to be his chauffeur. Mohr acquits himself splendidly as the ultimate jerk, and his chemistry with the quirky Douglas is right on target.

About the worst thing one can say about *Action* based on its first half-hour is that it's nasty to the core, no doubt too nasty for many tastes.

The 71st Annual Academy Awards
Broadcast live from the Dorothy Chandler Pavilion in Los Angeles by the Academy of Motion Picture Arts & Sciences. Producer, Gilbert Cates; associate producer, Michael B. Seligman; director, Louis J. Horvitz; writers, Rita Cash, Hal Kanter, Buzz Kohan, Whoopi Goldberg, Jon Macks, Billy Martin, Bruce Vilanch; host, Whoopi Goldberg. Production designer, Roy Christopher; music director, Bill Conti; choreographer, Debbie Allen; costume designer, Ray Aghayan; lighting, Robert Dickinson; fashion coordinator, Fred Hayman. Running time: 242 mins.
Presenters, Val Kilmer, Andy Garcia, Liam Neeson, John Travolta, Sophia Loren, Gwyneth Paltrow, Liv Tyler, Nicolas Cage, Ben Affleck, Jim Carrey, Kevin Costner, Uma Thurman, Robert DeNiro, Annette Bening, Anne Heche, Jennifer Lopez, Goldie Hawn, Jack Nicholson, Steve Martin, Chris Rock, Kim Basinger, Denzel Washington, Helen Hunt, Harrison Ford, Robin Williams; performers, Aerosmith, Celine Dion, Andrea Bocelli, Peter Gabriel, Randy Newman, Whitney Houston, Mariah Carey, Allison Moorer.
The film industry wound up doing a fairly convincing impersonation of a class act at the 71st Annual Academy Awards.

The unrepentant Elia Kazan gave a brief, heartfelt acceptance speech. It was, perhaps, foolish to believe that he was going to get booed off the stage by those protesting his naming of names before the House Un-American Activities

Committee in 1952. Roughly half the audience seemed to give Kazan a genteel standing ovation, and only a few were disgusted for all they were worth.

At worst, the presentation was awkward; at best, muted and anticlimactic. Let's not blame Whoopi Goldberg. She trotted out enough glittering rags, turning the broadcast into her own fashion show. That Whoopi's outfits grew increasingly annoying as the hour grew long is almost irrelevant. At least she gave it a good try. Indeed, even as Goldberg's jokes fell flat, she nonetheless proved a spunky hostess, with a smooth sparring style and charming way with an ad-lib.

Roberto Benigni also did his best to keep everybody awake after his *Life Is Beautiful* won Oscars for foreign-language film and best actor. He was so pumped and so ebullient – dancing on chairs and hopping up stairs – that he made Robin Williams look like Gloria Stuart. Yet there's clearly some excess baggage to unload when the show rolls past 240 minutes.

What was with that wacky interpretive dance thing honoring the dramatic score nominees? A *Saving Private Ryan* tap dance? It brings new meaning to the term "War is hell." Next year, Gilbert Cates and company might just bag some of the earnest-but-leaden tributes and leave the focus where it belongs – on the winners.

And the Beat Goes on: The Sonny & Cher Story

Filmed in Los Angeles by the Larry Thompson Organization. Executive producer, Larry A. Thompson; co-executive producer, Mary Bono; producer, Daniel Schneider; co-producer, Ellen Weston; director, David Burton Morris; writer, Weston, based on the book by Sonny Bono; director of photography, Anthony B. Richmond; editor, Michael S. Murphy; production designer, James Agazzi; music, Steve Tyrell; singing voices, Jess Harnell (Sonny), Kelly van Hoose Smith (Cher); casting, Donna Eckholdt. Running time: 120 mins.

Jay Underwood (Sonny Bono), Renee Faia (Cher), Christian Leffler (Phil Spector), Jim Pirri (Buddy Black), Bruce Nozick (Art Rupe), Carl Gilliard (Bumps Blackwell), Walter Franks (Little Richard), Matthew Chaffee (Brian Stone), Thomas Tofel (Charlie Green), Laura Johnson (Georgia LaPierre), Mahrayh Shaine (David Geffen), Tom Frykman (David Letterman). With: Christine Brent, Maurice Chasse, Phill Miller, Vinnie Argiro, Marie Wilson, Susan Ilene Johnson, Duke Moosekian, Larry Milburn.

Smitten and set up for verbal abuse from the moment he laid eyes on Cherilyn Sarkisian LaPierre, Sonny Bono led the life of a Hustler Who Could. In *And the Beat Goes on*, he's depicted as a tenacious, if modestly talented, musical aspirant hellbent on success, whose heart was always in the right place. No matter how accurate that portrait might be, the telepic is stocked with layer upon layer of fluff as it hurries from their meeting to their split-up and eventual reunion on David Letterman's late-night show.

Ellen Weston's script, based on Bono's autobiography, reduces Sonny and Cher to their individual motivations: she wants to see her name in lights; he seeks fame, but doesn't need to be a star. Seeing that his shot at success is intrinsically linked to her stardom, Bono asks "how high" each time Cher even hints that he should jump.

Sonny responded to Cher's every pipedream, *And the Beat Goes on* portends, and found a way to make it all work – as a coffeehouse act, as recording artists, as TV stars, as a Vegas act,

everything except the movies. The biopic plays loose with the facts about how established Bono was in the music biz when he met Cher, where they married, how established Cher was as a solo artist and exactly how big they had become by 1969 when they decided to take a break from the hubbub.

Animal Farm

Filmed in Ireland by Hallmark Entertainment. Executive producer, Robert Halmi; producer, Greg Smith Sr.; co-producer (Ireland), Morgan O'Sullivan; director, John Stephenson; writers, Alan Janes, Martyn Burke, based on the novel by George Orwell; camera, Mike Brewster; editor, Colin Green; music, Richard Harvey; production designer, Brian Ackland-Snow; visual-effects supervisor, Angus Bickerton. Running time: 89 mins.

Pete Postlethwaite (Mr. Jones). Voices: Kelsey Grammer (Snowball), Ian Holm (Squealer), Julia Louis-Dreyfus (Mollie), Julia Ormond (Jessie), Pete Postlethwaite (Benjamin), Paul Scofield (Boxer), Patrick Stewart (Napoleon), Peter Ustinov (Old Major). With: Alan Stanford, Caroline Gray, Gail Fitzpatrick, Joe Taylor, Jimmy Keogh, Noel O'Donovan.

This aesthetically unappealing live-action version appears too dark and political for children; too familiar and simplistic for adults. Perhaps even more important, it lacks the technical accomplishment to pass muster in the age of *Babe*.

The basic plot of this fable about the corruption of power – in which pigs stand in for Stalin and Trotsky and an old plow horse fronts for the strength and basic goodness of common man – is well known. Tired of being underfed and mistreated, the animals on a farm run by drunken Mr. Jones revolt against their repressive master and take control of the land, with the brainy pigs becoming the group's natural leaders.

Idealistic porker Snowball teaches himself to read and write and for a time upholds the principles of freedom and equality passed down by wise Old Major. But ruthless Napoleon insidiously wrestles power from Snowball, scaring him into exile with the help of his vicious constabulary. Under Napoleon's rule, the greedy, manipulative pigs quickly take on the worst traits of humans, exploiting their intellectual superiority over the more gullible animals and driving the farm to ruin. As Napoleon and his henchmen take up residence in the farmhouse and adopt human vices, the tale becomes progressively more unpleasant and distancing.

Heading the flesh-and-blood thesps, Postlethwaite strikes an appropriately caricaturish note. But considering the talent assembled in the voice cast, vocal characterizations of the animals are undistinguished.

Annie

Filmed in Los Angeles by Storyline Entertainment, Columbia TriStar TV, Inc., and Chris Montan Prods. in association with Walt Disney TV. Executive producers, Craig Zadan, Neil Meron, Chris Montan, Marykay Powell; producer, John Whitman; co-producer, Brad Krevoy; director, Rob Marshall; writer, Irene Mecchi; camera, Ralf Bode; production designer, Stephen Hendrickson; music, Charles Strouse, Martin Charnin, Paul Bogaev; choreographer, Marshall; editor, Scott Vickrey; costume designer, Shay Cunliffe; sound, Edward L. Moskowitz; casting, Valorie Massalas. Running time: 120 mins.

Alicia Morton (Annie), Kathy Bates (Miss Hannigan), Alan Cummings (Rooster Hannigan), Audra McDonald (Grace

---

Farrell), Kristin Chenoweth (Lily St. Regis), Victor Garber (Oliver Warbucks), Andrea McArdle (Star-To-Be), Erin Adams (Tessie), Sarah Hyland (Molly), Lalaine (Kate), Nanea Miyata (July), Marissa Rago (Pepper), Danelle Wilson (Duffy).

Latest edition of the classic musical about the plucky Depression-era orphan and her colorful cohorts turns out to be a tuneful surprise that rises entertainingly above any hint of the remake that it is. Straightforward and sufficiently warm without being sappy, this *Annie* is easily the most watchable adaptation in memory. 12-year-old Alicia Morton gives a spiffy performance as Annie. With this level of Broadway talent on board, it's hardly shocking that the cast gives this *Annie* a stagey ambiance in the best sense.

Telepic is about the legendary streetwise ragamuffin whose indomitable spirit brings a little holiday joy to Depression-ravaged Gotham in December 1933. Dumped on the doorstep of the NYC Municipal Orphanage as an infant, Annie is parentless but not hopeless or dreamless. Complicating Annie's sunny view of the world is the dastardly Miss Hannigan. She has been Annie's surrogate mom for 11 years now and runs her orphanage like a military academy. Charles Strouse and Martin Charnin breathe energetic new life into the original songs. And it's a treat to see Andrea McArdle kick up her heels on a lavish rendition of "NYC" a full 20 years after she made her splashy debut as the rambunctious redhead on Broadway.

Becker

(Sitcom, CBS, Monday Nov. 2, 9:30 p.m.) Filmed in Los Angeles by Paramount Network TV. Executive producer, Dave Hackel; producers, Tim Berry, Andy Ackerman; director, Ackerman; writer, Hackel; camera, Tony Askins; editors, Darryl Bates, Skip Collector; music, Bruce Miller; production designer, Roy Christopher; sound, Dana Mark McClure; casting, Sheila Guthrie. Running time: 30 mins. **Ted Danson (Dr. John Becker), Terry Farrell (Regina Costa), Alex Desert (Jake Malinak), Hattie Winston (Margaret Wyborn), Shawnee Smith (Linda), Robert Bailey Jr. (M.J. Johnson), Davenia McFadden (Annette Johnson), Bill Capizzi (Mr. Capelli), Amy Aquino (Beverly Stone). With: Rocky McMurray, Michael Reid Mackay.**

Ted Danson gives the post-*Cheers* sitcom thing a second wind. If the retooled *Becker* feels a bit one-note from the outset, it also percolates with potential. Danson looks far more comfortable in the brash, cynical character of Dr. John Becker than he ever did on his short-lived CBS effort *Ink*. And he has the benefit here of some unusually biting, sacred cow-slapping dialog in the pilot.

Becker is a Bronx doc who holds the world at arm's length and hangs out at a very un-*Cheers*-like diner, where his arrival clears the place of everyone but its comely proprietor, Reggie, and a blind customer named Jake. Becker marches in and launches into a nonstop tirade about talkshows, pollution, used cars, car salesmen, and humanity in general.

But the belligerent doc has a soft spot for an adorable kid named M.J., who is HIV-positive. That diagnosis forces Becker to contact the doctor whose wife he stole. She's now Becker's ex, too. The shot at organized religion almost qualifies *Becker* as courageous. The show wears its pessimism on its sleeve and invites viewers to reject its protagonist. It doesn't feel the need to constantly tap-dance. It dares to stomp a little bit, to have some sting, to risk some political incorrectness.

Beggars and Choosers

Filmed in Vancouver, B.C. by Granada Entertainment USA in association with the H. Beale Co. and Showtime Networks Inc. Executive producers, Lilly Tartikoff, Peter Lefcourt, Kim Fleary, Scott Siegler; producer, Cal Shumiatcher; co-producer, Dan Pasternack; director, Michael Ritchie; writer, Lefcourt.

Brian Kerwin (Rob Malone), Isabella Hofmann (Cecile Malone), Carol Kane (Lydia (L. L.) Luddin), Charlotte Ross (Lori Volpone), Paul Provenza (Parker Meridian), Tuc Watkins (Malcolm Laffley), William McNamara (Brad Advail), Bill Morey (Emory (E. L.) Luddin), Keegan Connor Tracy (Audrey Malone), Alexis Arquette (Larry "Lola" Lencher), Maria Canals (Yolanda), Stuart Margolin (Kendall Gifford), Kaj-Erik Ericksen (Cary Malone), Christopher Kennedy (Marty Hertz), Klodyne Rodney (Latitia Martinez), Sheila Moore (Margaret Hurley), Samantha Ferris (Sandra Cassandra), Bea Arthur (As Herself).

It's clear that if this inside-jokey dramatic comedy series is a *Larry Sanders* wannabe, it's a particularly savvy one that knows of what it satirizes. *Beggars and Choosers* has the earmarks of a savage gem in its own right, slashing as it does sacred cows and spoofing TV's executive culture with wickedly sophisticated abandon. *Beggars* was evidently one of the last things Brandon Tartikoff developed. If anyone knew about the absurdity and chaos of programming a network, it would have been him.

As show opens, things are simply just dreadful for Rob Malone, the embattled programmer of the last-place Luddin Global Television Network (LGT). The overnights he wakes up to every morning are like a horror movie on a continuous loop. Nothing's working. Malone has been given an ultimatum by kinky boss Luddin to boost the numbers or else. Malone's highest-level staffers aren't much help, in part because they would love to see him fail. Meanwhile, on the home front, things are generally good. But 21-year-old daughter Audrey has thrown a wrench in the works, announcing that she is moving in with Parker Meridian, the smug, narcissistic star of LGT's one series hit. Meridian's been bollixing contract negotiations with LGT by asking for the moon.

To be sure, a show that is unlikely to send Showtime subscriptions soaring through the roof.

A Christmas Carol

(Telepic drama, TNT, Sunday Dec. 5, 8 p.m.) Filmed in England by Hallmark Entertainment. Executive producers, Robert Halmi Sr., Patrick Stewart; producer, Dyson Lovell; director, David Jones; writer, Peter Barnes, based on the novel by Charles Dickens; camera, Ian Wilson; production designer, Roger Hall; editor, David Martin; costume designer, Charles Knode; music, Stephen Warbeck; casting, Joyce Gallie. Running time: 120 mins.

Patrick Stewart (Ebenezer Scrooge), Richard E. Grant (Bob Cratchit), Joel Grey (Christmas Past), Ian McNeice (Albert Fezziwig), Saskia Reeves (Mrs. Cratchit), Desmond Barrit (Christmas Present), Bernard Lloyd (Jacob Marley), Tim Potter (Christmas Future), Ben Tibber (Tiny Tim). With: Dominic West, Trevor Peacock, Liz Smith, Elizabeth Spriggs, Kenny Doughty, Laura Fraser, Celia Imrie.

Only Ebenezer Scrooge would knock TNT's *A Christmas Carol*. Handsome, wholesome, and finely tuned, the cable web's take on Charles Dickens' 1843 masterwork is TV at its classiest. Bah humbug? No way.

...August 3...

Producer Scott Rudin has made a mid-six figure deal to turn Michael Cunningham's Pulitzer prize-winning novel **The Hours** into a feature.

Oft-told tales are difficult to pull off, but there are many nifty strokes here that elevate the story above most interpretations. True to the novel, but peppered with sharp special effects that don't encumber the narrative, this one gets it right. And from the wonderful set pieces to the wintry locales, *A Christmas Carol* contains a beauty rarely captured in today's telepic arena. Director David Jones displays a smooth hand that adds mounds of style to the rendition, and his approach to Peter Barnes' script is a tribute to delicate staging.

Miserly Mr. Scrooge intimidates carolers, fends off charity workers and terrorizes his lone employee, Bob Cratchit. But after the spectre of ex-partner Jacob Marley visits him, along with a parade of phantoms, Scrooge's hum gets de-bugged.

Stewart as Scrooge is such a perfect piece of casting that it will be hard to imagine anyone else as the sour ol' tightwad in years to come. His initial inflections are full of genuine antipathy, and his transformation to a goodhearted citizen is entirely believable.

Dennis Miller: The Millennium Special – 1,000 Years, 100 Laughs, 10 Really Good Ones

(Comedy special, HBO, Saturday Dec. 4, 10 p.m.) Recorded at CBS Television City in Hollywood by Home Box Office. Executive producers, Dennis Miller, Kevin Slattery; co-executive producer, Eddie Feldmann; director, Debbie Palacio; writers, Jose Arroyo, David Feldman, Jim Hanna, Leah Krinsky, Dennis Miller, Eddie Feldmann, Jacob Weinstein, David Weiss; production designer, Bruce Ryan; costumes, Jane Ruhm; editor, Michael Karlich; music, Tom Halm, Shelby Berg. Running time: 55 mins.
With: Dennis Miller, Norm Macdonald
The changing of the zeroes seems a topic tailor-made for Dennis Miller's ironic wit, since the hype is so disproportionate to the event's significance. But maybe the Y2K bug and the corresponding apocalyptic panic is too easy a target for Miller; or, then again, maybe he's just saving the best stuff for his weekly show. Instead of skewering the current millennial craze, with its "best of" litanies, Miller provides his own essential guide to the past thousand years. But while his fifth HBO comedy spec provokes some knowing yucks, it seems a little underwhelming for the occasion.

Miller sums up the first 900 years of the millennium in just a few minutes, fast-forwarding through the centuries with some strong quips about the Magna Carta, the Crusades, the burning of Joan of Arc, the launching of Columbus' voyage, etc. He then hones in on the 20th century, placing himself in different eras and taking the audience on a tour with his trademark rants and news of the day. Miller is still the master of the sardonic, but he's taking himself a lot less seriously. If the work isn't as pithy as before, it's certainly always easy to digest.

Excellent Cadavers

Filmed in Rome and Palermo, Sicily, by Tidewater Entertainment. Executive producer, Bill Unger; producer, David Nichols; director, Ricky Tognazzi; writer, Peter Pruce, based on the book by Alexander Stille; camera, Alessio Gelsini Torresi; production designer, Andrea Crisanti; editor, Roberto Silvi; music, Joseph Vitarelli; casting, Beatrice Kruger, Heidi Levitt. Running time: 120 mins.
Chazz Palminteri (Giovanni Falcone), F. Murray Abraham (Tommaso Buscetta), Anna Galiena (Francesca Falcone), Andy Luotto (Paolo Borsellino), Lina Sastri (Agnese Borsellino).
HBO's *Excellent Cadavers* is an admirable, if overly ambitious telepic that avoids Armani-clad movie mobsters and instead investigates the Sicilian muscle behind the Mafia. The true story takes a more sombre approach to organized crime, visiting early- to mid-'80s Italy to unearth the seeds from which a lot of today's gangster activity sprouted.

Cadavers studies Giovanni Falcone, a zealous prosecutor who died after a reasonably successful attempt to bring down the Cosa Nostra. Chazz Palminteri is solid as the determined lawman, and, as the world's most dangerous Don turned snitch, F. Murray Abraham is an intense and likable madman. Their convincing performances more than make up for helmer's uneven treatment that sometimes goes astray while trying to stay focused on the big picture.

In May 1992, Falcone and his wife were killed in Palermo after a bomb destroyed their motorcade. The account then flashes back to 1980, when Falcone was a bankruptcy attorney trying to ascend the Italian court system's ladder. After his mentor is bumped off by local Mafiosi, Falcone and partner Paolo Borsellino continue the cause, becoming outspoken warriors against illegal activity. As time passes, the high-profile bloodbaths become more frequent: delegates and civil servants are routinely whacked, and the public's anger grows.

Falcone catches a break when kingpin Tommaso Buscetta is captured and extradited to Rome. In exchange for his family's guaranteed security, Buscetta agrees to testify about the intricate network of assassins and smugglers.

Family Guy

Filmed in Los Angeles by 20th Century Fox TV and Film Roman. Executive producers, Seth MacFarlane, David Zuckerman; supervising producers, Craig Hoffman, Danny Smith, Gary Janetti; producer, Sherry Gunther; animation producer, John Bush; director, Peter Shin; writer, MacFarlane; editor, Rick Mackenzie; music, Ron Jones, Walter Murphy; sound, Ronnie Cox, Dave Weathers, Larry Stensvold, Pete Elia; casting, Karen Vice Casting. Running time: 30 mins.
Seth MacFarlane (Peter, Stewie, Brian Griffin), Alex Borstein (Lois Griffin), Seth Green (Chris Griffin). Voices: Lori Alan, Butch Hartman, Phil La Marr, Joey Slotnick, Fred Tatasciore, Wally Wingert, Billy West, Carlos Alazraqui.
The boy wonder who created, developed and executive-produced the Fox animated comedy series that's blessed with 1999's coveted post-Super Bowl time slot is Seth MacFarlane. He's 25 and his age is being hyped by Fox as proof of ... well ... something, and his show *Family Guy* is both undeniably clever and utterly bizarre – not always for the better. To see the wildly eccentric, occasionally uproarious premiere, the kid appears to be getting away with everything the *South Park* guys have without the prerequisite of being on cable.

Peter Griffin is the roly-poly patriarch of an oddball crew living in the New England 'burbs. He and his generally disapproving wife, Lois, are parents to three highly toxic kids: teen princess Meg, slacker fatty Chris and a diabolical infant named Stewie. Stewie's raison d'être seems to be to try to kill his mother any way possible. He also speaks with the sophistication, and British tones, of a whiny Rex Harrison. There's also the family dog Brian. He talks. In fact, he's the smart one in this family and basically keeps everyone in line.

...August 4...
Mel Gibson and Jet Li are teaming up to produce a martial-arts syndicated action series being set up at Alliance Atlantis.

Too often, the show bleeds punchlines and gags without bothering to set them up, resulting in a frenzy of outlandishness almost too absurd for its own good.

Futurama

Filmed in Los Angeles by the Curiosity Co. in association with 20th Century Fox Television. Executive producers, Matt Groening, David X. Cohen; co-executive producers, Ken Keeler, Eric Horsted; producers, Lewis Morton, Brian J. Cowan, J. Stewart Burns, Patric M. Verrone, Jason Grode, Claudia Katz; directors, Rich Moore, Gregg Vanzo; writers, Groening, Cohen; art director, Bill Morrison; designer, Serban Cristescu; editor, Paul D. Calder; music, Christopher Tyng; sound, Ronald Cox; casting, Julie Mossberg, Jill Anthony. Running time: 30 mins.
Billy West (Fry), Katey Sagal (Leela), John DiMaggio (Bender), Dick Clark (As Himself), Leonard Nimoy (As Himself). With: Tress MacNeille, Dave Herman, Kath Soucie.
It's obvious from the start that *Futurama* ain't *The Simpsons*. But it pays to remembers that, at the beginning, *The Simpsons* wasn't *The Simpsons*, either. True genius sometimes takes time to develop.

It's 1,000 years in the future, New Year's Eve 2999, where a hapless 25-year-old New York City pizza delivery guy named Fry finds himself after leaping ahead a full millennium, courtesy of a cryogenic time-freeze tank in which he became accidentally trapped. It turns out that the future has not been particularly kind to New York. Everything is now underground, the city's skyline made over by aliens following their successful invasion some centuries before. Fry is soon accosted by Leela, a sassy one-eyed female alien with understandable depth-perception problems. He also links up with Bender, a smoking, boozing kleptomaniac of a robot who wants very badly to kill himself, if only his hard metal shell would allow it.

The future requires people to be implanted with a "career chip" that forces them to adhere to one employment assignment for life. Those who refuse are fired out of a cannon into the sun. Fry nonetheless rejects his assignment of Delivery Boy until he realizes that he can go to work for a company that hustles packages to "all five quadrants of the universe." As the opener ends, he, Leela and Bender have shoved off together on their first mission as an interstellar messenger service.

The 41st Annual Grammy Awards

Broadcast live from the Shrine Auditorium in Los Angeles by Cossette Prods. in cooperation with the National Academy of Recording Arts & Sciences. Executive producer, Pierre Cossette; supervising producer, John Cossette; producers, Ken Ehrlich, Walter C. Miller; coordinating producer, Tisha Fein; director, Miller; writers, Ehrlich, Bruce Vilanch; musical director, Jack Elliott.
The 41st Annual Grammys on CBS conducted itself in an almost courtly way with nary an outburst of anger or profanity – compared to last year's show, when one sore loser took to the stage to rant like a maniac, and one misguided soul displayed the words "SOY BOMB" on his shirtless chest. Heck, Lauryn Hill read from the Old Testament during her best new artist acceptance speech. Not what one would typically associate as generational rage.

The Grammycast was also almost pathologically sloppy, with presenters and categories appearing out of sync with what was being introduced and presenters appearing flustered and awkward. Is it merely coincidental that, of the seven artists who performed just prior to the distribution of an award in their nominated category, six of them won?

The night's most irksome moments clearly were reserved for host Rosie O'Donnell. She was a virtual run-on sentence of painful puns, oafish self-deprecation and misplaced whimsy. At every opportunity, she ludicrously inserted herself and her ill-conceived views into the equation. There were enough high points in the Grammycast to keep hope alive that true magic could ultimately erupt. Surprise country album winners the Dixie Chicks were so refreshingly pumped about winning that it sent the charisma meter soaring. The B.B. King/Eric Clapton duet on "Rock Me Baby" was sweet, while the rousing performance of salsa artist Ricky Martin and his band nearly brought down the house.

Introducing Dorothy Dandridge

Filmed on location in Los Angeles by Esparza/Katz Prods. in association with Berry/Cirrincione. Executive producers, Moctesuma Esparza, Robert Katz, Joshua D. Maurer, Vincent Cirrincione, Halle Berry; producer, Larry Albucher; director, Martha Coolidge; writers, Shonda Rhimes, Scott Abbot; editor, Alan Heim; sound, David MacMillan; music, Elmer Bernstein; camera, Robbie Greenberg; costume design, Shelley Komarov; casting, Aleta Chappelle. Running time: 120 mins.
Halle Berry (Dorothy Dandridge), Brent Spiner (Earl Mills), Obba Babatunde (Harold Nicholas), Loretta Devine (Ruby Dandridge), Cynda Williams (Vivian Dandridge), LaTanya Richardson (Auntie), Tamara Taylor (Geri Nicholas), Alexis Carrington (Lynn), D.B. Sweeney (Jack Dennison), Klaus Maria Brandauer (Otto Preminger), William Atherton (Darryl Zanuck), Sharon Brown (Etta Jones), Andre Carthen (Harry Belafonte), Benjamin Brown (Sidney Poitier).
Introducing Dorothy Dandridge is an enthralling biopic about the first African-American woman to be nominated for a Best Actress Oscar. This film marks a big step in recognizing the contributions of Dandridge, a woman who made Hollywood accessible for other black actors, but, as a biography, it only begins to explore the psyche of such a complex star.

Pic begins with a fading Dandridge recounting her life in one of her notorious latenight phone calls to her best friend, Geri Nicholas. Dandridge made waves by refusing to play stereotypical black roles. Her greatest fame came from landing and nailing the lead role of Carmen in the controversial musical *Carmen Jones* by helmer Otto Preminger. We learn that Dandridge was traumatized by a sexual assault by her mother's lesbian lover. She had two failed marriages and a mentally challenged daughter who had to be institutionalized. While gutsy and determined when it came to her career, Dandridge had a bad head for business and allowed her finances to be colossally mismanaged. The movie ends with her death from a prescription drug overdose at 42, on the eve of her supposed comeback tour.

As Dandridge, Berry is sexy and innocent, breathy and every bit as beautiful as the glamorous star. The role is that of a damaged beauty and Berry hits the mark whether it calls for sultry or sullen. Dance sequences are impeccable, accentuated by a jazzy musical score by Elmer Bernstein.

...August 5...
Robert Downey Jr. is saddled with a three-year prison sentence for violating probation.

It's Like, You Know

Filmed in Los Angeles by 42 Pound Prods. and EWH3 Prods. in association with DreamWorks. Executive producers, Peter Mehlman, Ted Harbert; co-executive producers, Jeff Astroff, Mike Sikowitz; producers, Suzy Mamann Greenberg, Richard Doctorow, Amy Welsh; director, Andy Ackerman; writer, Mehlman; camera, Wayne Kennan; editor, Ron Volk; music, W.G. "Snuffy" Smith; production designer, Brandy Alexander; sound, Norman Webster; casting, Liberman/Hirschfeld Casting, Merri Sugarman. Running time: 30 mins.

Chris Eigeman (Arthur), Jennifer Grey (As Herself), Steven Eckholdt (Robbie), A. J. Langer (Lauren), Evan Handler (Shrug), Elliott Gould (As Himself), Carolyn Hennessey (Cathy), John Kapelos (Mr. Gibson), Nick Bakay (Harvey), Christen Rose (Zoe), Suzanne Lanza (Danna), Ellen Gerstein (Daughter), Victor Brandt (Voice of Airline Pilot).

It's Like, You Know is the ultimate goof on Los Angeles and its stereotypical idiot culture. Reducing L.A. to the equivalent of a vast Club Med for the freshly lobotomized, the comedy's shallow Seinfeld-ians paint Angelenos as so many Evian-sipping, platitude-spouting, minutiae-yammering, horn-honking, money-loving, tan-seeking, angst-riddled, surgically enhanced, self-obsessed bubbleheads. The producers have crafted themselves a truly distinctive piece of cultural satire that goes beyond mere spoof to approach theater-of-the-absurd territory. The show's L.A. jokes are fresh, energetic, and undeniably, consistently clever.

The comedy opens with snobby New York journalist and confirmed L.A.-phobe Arthur flying out to the City of Angels to spend two months researching a book on hating L.A. Arthur is staying in the city with his onetime college roomie Robbie, a Big Apple transplant himself who has made it big in L.A. by backing a pay-per-view scheme that allowed Jewish citizens to watch the High Holy Day services in their living room. So now the blow-dried Robbie spends his days tooling around town with his bald pal Shrug over such show-about-nothing tidbits.

Last, but far from least, there is *Dirty Dancing's* Jennifer Grey. In the show's most inspired gambit, Grey portrays an insecure, irony-poor, next-door neighbour version of herself, seizing on both her famed nose job and her downward career spiral. This took courage for the actress to undertake, and she pulls it off so well as to approach the sublime.

Jack and Jill

Filmed on location in Los Angeles by the Canton Co. in association with Warner Bros. Television. Executive producers, Randi Mayem Singer, Mark Canton; creator, Singer; producer, David Karl Calloway; director, Jim Frawley; writer, Singer; editor, David Ekstrom; music, Roxanne Lippel; sound, Althea Rodgers; casting, Barbara Miller. Running time: 60 mins.

Ivan Sergei (David "Jill" Jillefsky), Amanda Peet (Jacqueline "Jack" Barrett), Jaime Pressly (Audrey Griffin), Sarah Paulson (Elisa Cronkite), Justin Kirk (Barto Zane), Simon Rex (Mikey Russo).

TV love triangles are a lot like the Bermuda triangle – it's dangerous territory and somebody usually gets lost. Singer tries to play both sides of the fence by introducing us to three presumably likable characters caught up in that inbetween stage of post-collegiate real-world initiation and serious adult-oriented commitment. It's a story with a limited shelf life, considering the other web's Sunday movie programming and Fox's *The X-Files.*

The oh-so-clever twist in this one-hour romantic comedy is that Amanda Peet is Jack (for Jacqueline) and Ivan Sergei is Jill as in David Jillefsky. The tired setup begins with Jack, a stilted bride, dumping her wedding gown in the trash as she makes her way for the big city. Coddled by family and friends for most of her life, Jack hopes to claim her independence by moving in with her old high-school friend Audrey. Jack briefly encounters Jill in the hallway of his apartment building, causing Jill to reconsider his decision to move in with his intelligent and beautiful girlfriend Elise. As luck would have it, Jack has just gotten an internship at the newsroom where Elise works and the two women have become fast friends.

What seems like an impossibly awkward situation resolves itself a little too neatly by the end of the first episode. Everybody here is so earnest in their search for themselves, yet no one seems even remotely mature enough for a serious relationship.

Judging Amy

Filmed in Los Angeles by 20th Century Fox TV in association with CBS Prods. Executive producers, Barbara Hall, Joseph Stern, Amy Brenneman, Connie Tavel; co-executive producers, James Hayman, Nicole Yorkin, Dawn Prestwich; producer, Natalie Chaidez; director, Hayman; writer, Hall; camera, Kenneth D. Zunder; production designer, Michael Mayer; editor, Anita Brandt-Burgoyne; music, Peter Himmelman; sound, Robert J. Anderson Jr.; casting, Jeanie Bacharach. Running time: 60 mins.

Amy Brenneman (Amy Gray), Dan Futterman (Vincent Gray), Tyne Daly (Maxine Gray), Richard T. Jones (Bruce Van Exel), Jessica Tuck (Gillian Gray), Marcus Giamatti (Peter Gray), Karle Warren (Lauren Gray), LaTanya Richardson (Lena Railsback), Spencer Garrett (Franklin Dobbs), Tracey Letts (Mr. Kleinman), Jacqueline Schultz (Mrs. Jenkins), David Newsom (Jack Overby).

Tyne Daly has made the psychic leap from buddy cop to domineering mom in this curiously uninvolving hour that seems to exist as a test of just how much crap a young woman can endure from her mother before she will turn to matricide. Indeed, the message that leaps to the fore from the outset of *Judging Amy* is that if you're going to become a judge, it's probably a bad idea to live with someone who reminds you daily that you're clueless. This tension, however, is a poor TV substitute for compelling self-examination. *Judging Amy* tries awfully hard to impart the idea that everyone has mommy problems, even Harvard grads wearing judicial robes.

Amy is legally separated, having just packed up and moved with her darling little daughter, Gillian, from New York to Hartford, Conn. And as she lies in bed, it's day one of her new job as a Superior Court judge.

Problem is, her mother, Maxine, whose home Amy and Lauren now share, is herself a retired judge. The insecure Amy gets the lay of the judging land even as relations with mom heat to a boil. By the end of the premiere, it's possible to feel some hope that this show can overcome its penchant for bogging down in mock dramatics and helmer James Hayman's soft-focus artsy stylings, and merit a second look.

The King of Queens

Filmed in Los Angeles by Hanley Prods. in association with Columbia TriStar TV and CBS Prods. Executive producer,

---

Michael J. Weithorn ; producer, Annette Sahakian Davis; director, Pam Fryman; writers, Weithorn, David Litt; production designer, Scott Heineman; camera, Wayne Kennan; editor, John Doutt; music, Andrew Gross; sound, Kerry Boggio; casting, Lisa Miller Katz. Running time: 30 mins. **Kevin James (Doug Heffernan), Leah Remini (Carrie Heffernan), Jerry Stiller (Arthur Spooner), Lisa Rieffel (Sara Spooner), Victor Williams (Deacon Palmer), Oswalt Richie (Spence Olchin Patton), Larry Romano (Iannucci).** Stand-up Kevin James plays Doug Heffernan, a couch potato who has probably never seen the inside of a Snackwell's box or a can of Diet Coke. If only Doug and his show were funnier.

While plenty of males will no doubt feel a kindred connection with a character for whom watching a football game on his own big screen TV is akin to an afternoon in the sack with Jennifer Lopez, and any show with Jerry Stiller lending support can't be all bad, *The King of Queens* exists as a collection of trappings in search of a pay-off. It has heart but no teeth, charm without chutzpah.

Our hero Doug drives a package delivery truck. Leah Remini, as his wife Carrie, is thin and gorgeous and would probably be way too good for him in real life. James has a certain goofy charisma that's appealing, and Rimini herself brings a lot of spunk.

Intermittently amusing pilot, finds Doug hanging with the guys in his newly revamped basement done up as a sports bar. But their testosterone-spewing nirvana quickly disappears when Leah's recently widowed dad opts to move into the basement rather than a retirement home after burning down his own house. Then Carrie's sexy, self-centered sister Sara, who wants to be an actress, also moves in with them to save a few bucks.

Show inevitably sinks under the weight of stock characters and strained interaction.

Ladies Man

Taped in Los Angeles by Christopher Thompson Prods. in association with Columbia TriStar TV and CBS Prods. Executive producer, Chris Thompson; supervising producer, Bob Heath; producers, Alfred Molina, Joan Hyler; director, James Burrows; writer, Thompson; camera, Tony Askins; production designer, Bernie Vyzga; editor, Peter Chakos; music, Jonathan Wolff; sound, Pete Damski; casting, Renee Rousselot. Running time: 30 mins. **Alfred Molina (Jimmy Stiles), Sharon Lawrence (Donna Stiles), Betty White (Mitzi Stiles), Park Overall (Clair Stiles), Stephen Root (Gene), Mariam Parris (Bonnie Stiles), Katie Volding (Wendy Stiles), Dixie Carter (Peaches), Lisa Darr (Dr. Mandel).** Television producers evidently have some very compelling mother issues. Why else would we have a sitcom trend involving put-upon men and the brassy women who dominate them? It was the concept at the center of NBC's short-lived comedy *Conrad Bloom* last season, and this fall *Ladies Man* is joined by ABC's *Odd Man Out.* Just once, couldn't a woman be driven batty by a bunch of guys? Is that somehow illegal? No, apparently the only thing against the law is that any of these shows be funny.

Ladies Man is no exception. The irony – and in fact, a reason to hope for improvement – is that the show features some good veteran talent in Sharon Lawrence, Betty White and Park

Overall. They portray the wife, mother and ex, respectively, of Stiles. The ladies do their best to make this work, but Molina is way off, despite direction in the pilot from the master himself, James Burrows.

Molina is a 78 RPM disc operating on a 45 RPM series. He's obviously a talent, but the coarseness and awkwardness of the premise doesn't allow for him to blend naturally into the ensemble. The gambit has the well-meaning Jimmy always saying the wrong thing, followed by "What'd I do?" This becomes a virtual mantra while he attempts to coexist in a household alongside his very pregnant wife, his mom, his two belligerent young daughters ... and his ex!

Lansky

Filmed in various locations by HBO Pictures in association with Frederick Zollo Prods. Executive producers, Fred Zollo, Nick Paleologos, David Mamet; producer, Fred Caruso; director, John McNaughton; writer, David Mamet, based in part on the book, "Meyer Lansky: Mogul of the Mob," by Uri Dan, Dennis Eisenberg and Eli Landau; director of photography, John A. Alonzo; production designer, Edward T. McEvoy; editor, Elena Maganini; music, George S. Clinton; casting, Linda Lowy. Running time: 120 mins. **Richard Dreyfuss (Meyer Lansky), Eric Roberts (Ben Siegel aged 40+), Anthony LaPaglia (Charlie Luciano, 30-40), Beverly D'Angelo (Teddy Lansky), Illeana Douglas (Anna Lansky), Francis Guinan (Kefauver), Stanley DeSantis (Rothstein), Jeff Perry (Rosen), Ron Perkins (Polakoff), Maury Gonsberg (Uri Behar), Bill Capizzi (Joe Masseria), Ron Gilbert (Maranzano), Sal Landi (Joe Adonis). With: Max Perlich, Ryan Merriman, Nicky Corello, Joshua Praw, Anthony Medwetz, Matthew Settle, Paul Sincoff, Peggy Jo Jacobs, Peter Siragusa, Dean Norris, Devon Michael, Ron Pacheco, Chris Marquette, Michael Townsend Wright, Jeffrey Sharmat, Mitchell Roche, Jill Holden, Bernard Hiller, Moscu Alcalay, Bert Remsen, Larry Moss, Robert Miano.**

David Mamet, whose signature works like a straitjacket on the subject at hand, signals this to some degree by making empty the core of his Meyer Lansky. Mamet attempts to give Lansky an emotional center, specifically being a Jew without a country on a personal crusade; he creates a victim, and "a gambler." Overall, a confusing, benign account of a man who assimilated his way into power in Italian-American Mob life.

Back story begins with young Lansky witnessing the murder of a Jew and the start of his gambling fixation. Teenage Benny Siegel befriends Lansky and begins tutoring him on how to control the gambling and how to never fight fair. As young men, Lansky, Siegel and Charlie Luciano get their start in the bootlegging business of Arnold Rothstein, the man who fixed the 1919 World Series and was intrigued by Lansky's mental capabilities. Upon Rothstein's murder, Lansky moves up in organized crime with his two pals. Naturally, Lansky is never the one with the gun, the vendetta or the hit ordered – he's keeping the books straight.

Scenes of Lansky's activities in the '40s and '50s are too short to pinpoint his role in the Mafia.

Richard Dreyfuss' lower than low-key portrayal is in constant service to the arid texture of the script. Eric Roberts, as Siegel, and Anthony LaPaglia, as Luciano, bring some enthusiasm to the setting, showing that at least some of these gangsters enjoyed their spoils.

... August 7 ...

Country singer Dolly Parton has paid low six figures for **The Jew Store**, Stella Suberman's family memoir about growing up Jewish in small-town Tennessee.

Larry David: Curb Your Enthusiasm

Filmed in New York and Los Angeles by Hofflund/Polone Prods. in association with Whyaduck Prods. Executive producers, Larry David, Jeff Garlin, Gavin Polone; producer, Mark Farrell; director, Robert B. Weide. Director of photography, Bradley Sellers; editor, Steven Rasch; music, Wendell Yuponce; casting, Marla Garlin. Running time: 120 mins.

Larry David (As Himself), Jeff Garlin (Jeff Greene), Cheryl Hines (Cheryl David), Judy Toll (HBO executive), Allan Wasserman (HBO executive), Becky Thyre (N.Y. girlfriend), Michael Patrick King (HBO publicist), Jeff Yerkes (Scott Gould). With: Linda Bates, Mark Beltzman, Cynthia Caponera, Julie Claire, Donna Cooper, Ed Crasnick, Don Lake, Stefanie Singer, Larry Thigpen, Jason Alexander, Carol Leifer, Richard Lewis, Jerry Seinfeld, Caroline Rhea, Allan Havey, Mike Reynolds, Suzy Soro.

No matter how *Larry David: Curb Your Enthusiasm* is interpreted – an indictment of the people within the entertainment industry or a linear delusion of one of comedy's funniest thinkers – it is the work of genius. Premise is exceedingly simple: a film of David, a former executive producer and main writer of *Seinfeld*, as he prepares for his return to standup comedy after a nearly 10-year absence. Second half would document his show along with anecdotes and tributes from *Seinfeld* alumni.

Manager Jeff Greene makes the initial pitch to two fawning HBO development execs who spew phoniness and delight at every turn. It's the first of David's many encounters with people he finds contemptible; not only is he repulsed over and over again by human interaction, but he wonders what happened to the days when he actually knew men who liked him.

From there he struggles in countless situations – at home with his wife, in a meeting with the HBO execs planning his show, eating breakfast with two comedians to name a few. Onstage he appears at ease despite the testimony of several individuals that he never felt comfortable up there in the first place. Indeed, his road to showbiz success was circuitous. Whereas most comedians work in hopes of getting a sitcom to star in, David's material and persona wound up becoming *Seinfeld*. No matter how much David turns his world upside down, he functions the same.

Law and Order: SVU

Filmed in New York by Wolf Films in association with Studios USA Television. Executive producers, Dick Wolf, Robert Palm; co-executive producers, Peter Jankowski, Ted Kotcheff; producers, David DeClerque, Michael R. Perry; co-producer, Joe Lazarov; director, Jean De Segonzac; director of photography, Anthony Jannelli; production designer, Teresa Carriker-Thayer; editor, Doug Ibold; music, Mike Post; casting, Julie Tucker, Lynn Kressel Casting. Running time: 60 mins.

Dann Florek (Capt. Donald Cragen), Christopher Meloni (Elliot Stabler), Mariska Hargitay (Olivia Benson), Richard Belzer (John Munch), Michelle Hurd (Monique Jeffries), Dean Winters (Brian Cassidy). With: Gordana Rashovich, Isabel Gillies, Elizabeth Ashley, Ned Eisenberg, Tina Benko, Ronald Guttman, Mark Zimmerman, Angie Harmon, Mili Avital.

This *Law & Order* spinoff wastes no time getting to a juicy crime and expertly tucking the necessary character exposition into a handful of scenes that propel the drama. While it

doesn't tarry in introducing characters the way so many ensemble dramas do, it doesn't maximize the presence of two familiar faces – *L&O* vet Dann Florek and *Homicide's* Richard Belzer. But Christopher Meloni and Mariska Hargitay immediately display a solid chemistry that could carry this look at the seedy side of sex drives.

Detectives Elliot Stabler (the calm one) and Olivia Benson (the hothead) are the primaries in the case of a cab driver hacked to death behind the wheel. SVU, which handles sex-based offenses, is dragged in because the perpetrator has also sliced off the genitals, leading the unit on an obvious investigation that becomes the standard-issue wild goose chase.

Detective squad is considered "elite," yet it takes Capt. Cragen to figure out that the cabbie's license has been forged and the detectives are looking for the wrong man. What appears to be a dead end becomes a twist that involves rape, a Serbian national and ethnic cleansing.

First episode lacks the energy and grit of the first season of *Law & Order*, but Anthony Jannelli's camera work reveals the guilty, and director Jean De Segonzac and editor Doug Ibold keep the action taut even when it's apparent exactly where things are headed.

The Magical Legend of the Leprechauns

Filmed at Shepperton Studios, London, by Hallmark Entertainment in association with RTL Television. Executive producer, Robert Halmi Sr.; producer, Paul Lowin; director, John Henderson; writer, Peter Barnes; camera, Clive Tickner; production designer, Simon Holland; editors, Pamela Power, Paul Endacott; music, Richard Harvey; costumes, Anne Hollowood; casting, Lynn Kressel; visual effects, Cinesite (Europe) Ltd. Running time: 240 mins.

Randy Quaid (Jack Woods), Whoopi Goldberg (The Grand Banshee), Roger Daltrey (King Boric), Colm Meaney (Seamus Muldoon), Kieran Culkin (Barney Devine), Zoe Wanamaker (Mary Muldoon), Daniel Betts (Mickey Muldoon), Orla Brady (Kathleen Fitzpatrick), Caroline Carver (Princess Jessica), Frank Finlay (General Bulstrode), Phyllida Law (Lady Margaret), Michael Williams (Father Daley), Harriet Walter (Queen Morag). With: Kevin McKidd, Tony Curran, Gary Lydon, Jonathan Firth, Clive Merrison, Stephen Moore.

Jack Woods, an American businessman, has come to Ireland with the mission of buying up land for some capitalist venture. After settling into a cottage, he goes walking in the woods, where he spies a beautiful woman bathing in a river. Jack discovers the woman is his neighbor, Kathleen, opening the door to one of the pic's parallel love interests.

When he spots a "little person" in his cottage, Jack gives chase, and ends up rescuing the creature when it falls into the river. Jack then figures his way to the leprechaun's cottage, where Seamus Muldoon finally shows himself, explaining that a leprechaun is in permanent debt to any human who helps him. Seamus introduces his wee family, which consists of wife Mary and son Mickey.

Mickey, who, with his pals, invades the ball of the leprechauns' natural enemies, the Trooping Fairies, falls in love with Princess Jessica, a match which will upset both of their families. Their love will ultimately lead to the accidental death of Mickey's best friend and Jessica's cousin.

In leprechaun-land, the ultimate power is the Grand Banshee, who has become so impatient with the constant bickering between the different fairy types that she takes away their immortality as the two sides gear up for war. What the mini doesn't fully capture is the sense of whimsy or rapscallion nature of the leprechauns. With a bland human plotline, the mini as a whole drags along, with only brief moments of offbeat leprechaun humor to give a sense of what could have been.

The Man Show
Taped in Los Angeles by Stone Stanley Prods. in association with Jackhole Industries and the Lapides Entertainment Organization. Executive producers, David G. Stanley, Scott A. Stone, Daniel Kellison, Howard Lapides; supervising producers, Jennifer Heftler, Lisa Page; directors, Dennis Rosenblatt, Hal Gurnee, Shanda Sawyer; head writer, Jimmy Kimmel.

As hosts of Comedy Central's one-joke *The Man Show*, Jimmy Kimmel and Adam Carolla do a remarkable impersonation of men suffering arrested emotional development in fronting a show that purports to be dissing female culture. *The Man Show* pushes the proposition that guys are sick to death of a nation drowning them in a tidal wave of feminization and wimpifying them with all of that equality and soulmate mumbo-jumbo.

Left free from societal niceties, the satiric conceit here is that men will reject all of that namby-pamby affection stuff in blind pursuit of a good beer, a good buzz, a good ballgame, and a good bonk while locking in visually on nature's greatest wonder: cleavage. The only reason men even give women the illusion of involved conversation is to get laid. And there you have it. *The Man Show* stops being funny once you realize that's the whole joke.

The divertingly smug hosts preside over the live studio audience festivities like cheerleaders at a pep rally for the intimacy-challenged. Surrounding them are a group of bouncy, scantily clad young women known as the Juggy Dance Squad, and an oddball named Bill *The Fox* Foster, whose chief talent is to down large volumes of beer. Comedy Central's show illustrates that men haven't grown much more civilized than they were 5 million years ago.

Mary, Mother of Jesus
Filmed in Budapest, Hungary, by the Shriver Family Film Co. Executive producers, Eunice Kennedy Shriver, Bobby Shriver; producer, Howard Ellis; director, Kevin Connor; writer, Albert Ross, based on material by John Goldsmith; camera, Elemer Ragalyi; production designer, Keith Wilson; costume designer, Maria Hruby; art director, Alistair Kay, Zsuzsa Borvendeg; music,Ken Thorne; editor, Barry Peters; sound, Clive Copland; casting, Noel Davis, Zsolt Csutak. Running time: 120 mins.

Pernilla August (Mary of Nazareth), Christian Bale (Jesus of Nazareth), David Threlfall (Joseph), Geraldine Chaplin (Elizabeth), Melinda Kinnaman (Young Mary), Toby Bailiff (Young Jesus), Hywel Bennett (Herod), Christopher Lawford (Rueben), Simone Bendix (Mary Magdalene), Christopher Routh (John the Baptist).With: Crispin Belfrage, Robert Addie, Michael Mears.

NBC's *Mary, Mother of Jesus* is the mother of all Biblepics. A genuinely captivating take on the life of Jesus, the pic comes at things from something of a Lifetime-esque perspective. That is, it presents the tale through the eyes of Mary, focusing on her pride, her passion and her trauma upon her son's crucifixion at the hands of the Romans. Nevertheless, exec producers exhibit great passion and care in crafting such an uncommonly inspiring rendering of the spiritual perennial. *Mary* is genuinely moving, never sailing over the top to drive home its plentiful religious points. Helmer Kevin Connor has consistent superior control over his players and material. Pernilla August hits all of the right notes while establishing a mesmerizing presence as Mary.

Film frames Mary's story from her own childhood, her visit from God and the subsequent Immaculate Conception, as well as Mary's nurturing of her son from birth through resurrection. Jesus is played as a peace-loving youth and a destiny-driven young adult. The climactic moments of *Mary, Mother of Jesus* are played to wrenching effect, particularly the death of Jesus' father Joseph and the crucifixion itself.

What truly distinguishes the production is its very simplicity. It never falls prey to the kind of overheated rapture so common to Biblical epics, illustrating instead the skepticism of the masses and hostility among those in power that would ultimately prove Jesus' undoing.

Noah's Ark
Filmed in Australia by Hallmark Entertainment for Babelsberg Intl. Film Producktion. Executive producer, Robert Halmi Sr.; producer, Stephen Jones; director, John Irvin; writer, Peter Barnes; camera, Mike Molloy; production designer, Leslie Binns; editor, Ian Crafford; music, Paul Grabowsky; costume designer, Marion Boyce; visual effects supervisor, Ernie Farino; sound, Steve Burgess; casting, Lynn Kressel, Maura Fay & Assn., Joyce Nettles. Running time: 240 mins.

Jon Voight (Noah), Mary Steenburgen (Naamah), F. Murray Abraham (Lot), Carol Kane (Sarah), James Coburn (The Peddler), Mark Bazeley (Shem), Jonathan Cake (Japheth), Alexis Denisof (Ham), Emily Mortimer (Esther), Sidney Poitier (Ruth), Sonya Walger (Miriam).

This *Noah's Ark* is the anti-DeMille, more of a "Noah's Lark" that skirts the line of blasphemy to paint a defiantly informal – even self-mocking – portrait of one of the Bible's most hallowed tales. Scribe Peter Barens clearly doesn't see it as his mission to unnecessarily inflate his project's sense of importance. Barnes goes out of his way to make perfectly certain that no one mistakes his verbiage as being in any way related to the Bible. There are indeed times when *Noah's Ark* approaches parody. It's boosted by an unquenchable sense of humor and a buoyant, almost bubbly tone. The oft-told story of world flooding, 40 days and 40 nights of rain and replenishing the earth by saving two of every animal on the massive ark emerges with far greater clarity thanks to Barnes' pointedly eccentric teleplay and helmer John Irvin's spirited, balanced direction.

While Noah is depicted in biblical literature as being a common schmo, Jon Voight's portrayal is a tad too common here to muster much enthusiasm or admiration. The supporting cast does its best to prop up Voight, with Mary Steenburgen and F. Murray Abraham faring best.

Location setting in Australia is lush and evocative. Nevertheless, this is a project that holds substance in as equal esteem as style. The second night ditches some of the irreverence while working to make sense of God's wiping out of humanity – and His ultimate regret over the act.

The Norm Show

Filmed in Burbank by Mohawk Prods. Inc. in association with Warner Bros. TV. Executive producers, Bruce Helford, Deborah Oppenheimer, Bruce Rasmussen, Rob Ulin; producers, Norm Macdonald, Al Lowenstein; director, Andy Cadiff; writers, Helford, Macdonald; camera, Ken Lamkin; art director, John Shaffner; editor, Pam Marshall; music, W. G. "Snuffy" Walden; sound, Larry Stephens; casting, Liberman/Hirschfeld Casting, Brent Benner, Barbara Miller. Running time: 30 mins. **Norm Macdonald (Norm Henderson), Laurie Metcalf (Laurie), Ian Gomez (Danny), Bruce Jarchow (Mr. Curtis), Nikki Cox (Taylor), Kyle Sabihy (Billy), Suanne Spoke (Receptionist), Robert Roy Hofmo (Big Guy), Robert Dolan (Man With Dog).**

The Norm Show is one of those comedies where the grown-ups suffer from arrested development – their maturity having ground to a halt at roughly age 12 – and everyone orbiting the lead character is consumed with that distinctive emperor's-new-clothes brand of denial.

As the show opens, Henderson has been out of pro hockey for six months, having been booted in shame. Seems the league frowns on its athletes gambling and evading their taxes. So he was given a choice: face a jail term or pay his debt to society by pulling five years' worth of community service as a social worker. He shares the office space with Laurie, a by-the-book worker who has slightly more diplomacy than his life-challenged office mate.

Numbingly silly premiere script charts Norm's handling of a curvy client who quits her job at a pizza joint to work at a massage parlor. Like all good social workers, he immediately hits on the idea of becoming one of her customers. Second seg continues to play up the lighter side of social isolation and emotional distress, hitting on such nuggets as client body odor, shyness and how a social worker can boff a client in the building and still hang onto his job. *Saturday Night Live* alum, Norm Macdonald (in his first sitcom) has a certain likability, a little-kid charm that meshes well with his smooth timing, and a decent chemistry with Metcalf.

Now and Again

Filmed in New York City by Picturemaker Prods. in association with Paramount Network TV and CBS Prods. Executive producer/writer/director, Glenn Gordon Caron; producer, Ronald L. Schwary; camera, Ken Kelsch; production designer, Charley Beal; art director, Beth Kuhn; editors, Tim Squyres, Bob Reitano, Marc Laub; sound, Felipe Borrero; music, Doug Como, Narada Michael Walden, Sunny Hilden; casting, Bonnie Finnegan, Steven Jacobs. Running time: 60 mins.

Eric Close (Michael Wiseman), John Goodman (Michael Wiseman, pilot), Margaret Colin (Lisa Wiseman), Dennis Haysbert (Dr. Theodore Morris), Heather Matarazzo (Heather Wiseman), Gerrit Graham (Roger Singer).

It's quirky, it's mesmerizing, it's addictive – *Now and Again* is no ordinary CBS Friday night series. It is so wildly original it defies conventional categorization. From start to finish, the hour keeps viewers entertainingly off-balance. It shifts tones constantly – a sci-fi thriller one minute, a black comedy the next.

In the introduction, an international terrorist known as the Egg Man releases poison gas via eggs that he leaves on a subway car and winds up killing dozens. We then meet Michael Wiseman, a portly middle-aged insurance executive with an

adoring wife and daughter. One night, he gets jostled onto the subway tracks and smashed to bits by the onrushing vehicle. Here's where the high-concept part kicks in. Turns out that Wiseman's intact brain was saved by the government, and, with his permission, it will now get implanted into the head of a hunky, bio-engineered, 26-year-old superhero with lightning speed and the strength of, well, many, many insurance executives. In exchange for this second chance, Wiseman will be kept on the shortest of leashes, closely monitored while doing government dirty-work such as stalking scum like the Egg Man.

The true secret weapon of *Now and Again* is Dennis Haysbert, with his portrayal of Dr. Theodore Morris – the mysterious, Frankenstein responsible for the experiment that is Wiseman. One minute Haysbert is exulting like a medical Don King; the next, he evokes coiled rage and flippant condescension.

The Passion of Ayn Rand

(Drama) A Showtime presentation of a Producers Entertainment Group production. Executive producers, Irwin Meyer, Marilyn Lewis; producer, Peter Cran, Linda Curran Wexelblatt; co-executive producers, Steven Hewitt, Barry Krost, Doug Chapin; director Christopher Menaul; screenplay by Howard Korder, Mary Gallagher, from the book by Barbara Branden; camera (color), Ron Orieux; editor, David Martin; music, Jeff Beal; production designer, Lindsey Hermer-Bell; art director, Edward Bonutto; set decorator, Brendan Smith; costume designer, Resa McConaghy; line producer, Martin Walters; production manager, Carmen Arndt; assistant director, Michael Zenon; casting, Beth Klein, Diane Kerbel. Running time: 104 mins.

Helen Mirren (Ayn Rand), Eric Stoltz (Nathaniel Branden), Julie Delpy (Barbara Branden), Peter Fonda (Frank O'Connor), Sybil Temchen (Caroline), Don McKellar (Richard), David Ferry (Alfred).

The details of a rather thorny personal life are given a warts-and-all baring in this Showtime-produced drama. But a definitive screen treatment of the Russian-born American novelist-philosopher still remains to be made. While earlier effort dwelt too worshipfully on Rand's achievements and ideas, *Passion* shortchanges those aspects while focusing on a domestic quadrangle that's offbeat but a tad soapish.

Screenplay picks up her saga in 1951, when her bestseller *The Fountainhead* has already made her a national celebrity. Living in L.A. with her long-time, wildly overshadowed "Mr. Rand" Frank O'Connor, she is not immune to the kind of gushing admiration offered by attractive collegians Barbara and Nathaniel. Having passed muster, the youngsters are ecstatic at having won such a stellar mentor. Pic portrays Rand as pushing the reluctant Barbara into a doomed marriage with Nathaniel Branden.

Being allowed into Rand's circle of intimates isn't for everyone. The compassion Barbara feels for others is considered "weakness" here. Her insecurities balloon as both husband and mentor treat any dissenting opinion as "wrong" thinking – and dissect it ruthlessly, before colleagues, as the errant soul squirms. Rand's ethos urges followers to build a true "sense of self." But in reality, only those who rebuild themselves in her image and adopt her (arguably fascistic) life views are acknowledged or rewarded. Never as engrossing as it hopes to be, *Passion* is made quite watchable by solid performances down the line.

...August 10...
Francis Ford Coppola will oversee a re-cutting of MGM's $60 million shelved sci-fi thriller **Supernova** due to Walter Hill's departure from the project.

Pirates of Silicon Valley

Filmed in Los Angeles by Haft Entertainment and St. Nick's Prods. in association with TNT. Executive producers, Steven Haft, Nick Lombardo; co-executive producer, Joseph Dougherty; producer-unit production manager, Leanne Moore; director-writer, Martyn Burke.

Noah Wyle (Steve Jobs), Anthony Michael Hall (Bill Gates), Joey Slotnick (Steve Wozniak), John DiMaggio (Steve Ballmer), Josh Hopkins (Paul Allen), Gema Zamprogna (Arlene), Pine Elfman (Gilmore Bodhi), Alan Royal (John Sculley), J. G. Hertzler (Ridley Scott), Wayne Pere (Captain Crunch). With: Sheila Shaw, Gailard Sartain, Allan Kolman, Richard Waltzer, Harris Mann, Clay Wilcox, Marcus Giamatti, Melissa McBride, Jeffrey Nordling, Marc Worden, Lynne Marie Stewart, Nikita Ager, Brian Gattas, Paul Popowich, Doug Cox, Michael Francis Clarke, Michael Bryan French, Gerald McCullouch, Holly Lewis, Robert Phelps, Brooke Radding.

Writer-director Martyn Burke has taken the battle fought in the microchip trenches at the dawn of the computer revolution and turned it into a wildly entertaining geek tragedy with the stylistic feel of true art. Soulful and marinated in a glaze of irony, the result is a complex, mesmerizing character study masquerading as an American success story.

Pirates is about how the greatest technological innovation of the latter half of the 20th century was fueled by a handful of confirmed nerds named Steve Jobs, Steve Wozniak, Bill Gates, Paul Allen and Steve Ballmer – young bucks brassy enough to think they could change the world and naive enough to believe they could deal with the unfathomable wealth and power, and the inevitable fallout, once they did.

The central character in this saga is Jobs (an intense Noah Wyle), who as co-founder of Apple Computer went from acid-dropping, spiritual eccentric with a hippie girlfriend to a megalomaniacal, ruthless, bullying, and paranoid manipulator.

The story casts Bill Gates (played with unassuming restraint by Anthony Michael Hall) as a kind of obsessed peripheral player in the home computer explosion, who slipped in through the front door while no one was looking. One eye-opening facet is the notion that most of what Apple and Microsoft pioneered was either lifted from other sources or stolen outright.

Poodle Springs

Filmed in Los Angeles by Universal TV Entertainment/MCA, Mirage and Avnet/Kerner Prods. Executive producers, Sydney Pollack, William Horberg, Jon Avnet, Jordan Kerner; co-executive producer, Geoff Stier; producer, Tony Mark; director, Bob Rafelson; writer, Tom Stoppard, based on the novel by Raymond Chandler, Robert B. Parker; camera, Stuart Dryburgh; editor, Steven Cohen; music, Michael Small; production designer, Mark Friedberg; costume designer, Melinda Eshelman; sound, Ed Novick; casting, Johanna Ray, Elaine Huzzar. Running time: 95 mins.

James Caan (Philip Marlowe), Dina Meyer (Laura), David Keith (Larry Victor), Tom Bower (Lt. Arnie Burns), Brian Cox (Clayton Blackstone), Julia Campbell (Muffy Blackstone), Joe Don Baker (P.J. Parker), Nia Peeples (Angel), La Joy Farr (Lola), Michael Laskin (Lipschultz), Sam Vlahos (Eddie Garcia), Matt Gallini (J.D.), Robert Wightman (Slim), Thomas F. Duffy (Fatso).

The disappointing *Poodle Springs* illustrates the pitfalls of depicting a character who is well past his prime. In this case, the lens peers in on a tired, cranky Philip Marlowe in the September of his years.

The moody, film noir quality of Chandler adaptations past gives way here to a straight ahead, contemporary approach that's well-crafted and smartly detailed, but essentially bland. And while the story itself holds together well, our hero tosses a monkey wrench into the proceedings by constantly appearing on the verge of full-scale apathy.

Movie opens in 1963, three days after an aging Marlowe has left behind his life of booze and broads for the strangulating security of marriage. His new wife, lovely Laura, is a rich, statuesque socialite, the kind of babe you figure would never go for a $100 a day gumshoe. But go for him she does, and she saves Philip's butt at the outset when he's framed for murder and it's left to Laura to bail him out.

Pretty soon, Marlowe is investigating a sleazy photographer leading a double life, becoming privy to a blackmail scheme involving a stripper named Lola and cavorting with various hookers, thugs, and billionaires. Caan's characterization is more suave than past versions, but so haughtily world-weary that he's difficult to love.

Popular

Filmed on location in Los Angeles by Murphy/Matthews Prods. and Shephard/Robin Prods. in association with Touchstone Television. Executive producers, Ryan Murphy, Gina Matthews, Greer Shephard, Michael M. Robin; producer, Phil Goldfarb; directors, Brian Robbins, Michael Robins; writers, Ryan Murphy, Gina Matthews; camera, Clark Mathis; editor, Ned Bastille; music, Donald Markowitz; casting, Robert J. Ulrich, Eric Dawson, Carol Kritzer. Running time: 60 mins.

Leslie Bibb (Brooke McQueen), Carly Pope (Sam McPherson), Tamara Mello (Lily Esposito), Christopher Gorham (Harrison John), Tammy Lynn (Nicole Julian), Bryce Johnson (Josh Ford), Sara Rue (Carmen Ferrara), Ron Lester (Sugar Daddy), Leslie Grossman (Mary Cherry), Chad Lowe (Luke Grant).

Popular is a hip-sounding and visually entertaining piece that might best be summed up as *The Odd Couple* meets *The Brady Bunch* meets "teensomething." The pains of adolescence are told here from the perspectives of two high-school sophomores; Sam McPherson, a wannabe journalist who tries desperately to not be just another crayon in the box, and Brooke McQueen, a prom queen in the making who dictates the social strata when not obsessing over the number of calories in a grape. Sam is being brought up by her widowed mom, while Brooke is being raised by her divorced father.

Although Pope as Sam is far too pretty to be unpopular, one thing that the creators deftly convey is that high-school popularity is a nebulous force, constantly shifting its tide. Even the esteemed Brooke cannot escape the scrutiny of this "Lord of the Flies"-like environment. The show scores points for being among the few to have a fairly diverse cast, working in characters of not only different ethnicities but of that most dreaded of all high-school creatures, the social outcast.

While the *Dawson's Creek*-like verbose dialog makes for entertaining television, it is far from realistic. But this is high school a la *Ally McBeal*, rife with fantasy segments, colorful visuals and one of the best collaborations of sight and sound this season.

. . . August 11 . . .

The first total eclipse of the sun in Britain since 1927 and the last for the next 90 years.

Providence

Filmed in Los Angeles and Providence, R.I., by John Masius Prods. in association with NBC Studios. Executive producers, John Masius, Bob DeLaurentis; co-executive producer, Michael Fresco; producer, Monica Wyatt; director, Fresco; writer, Masius; camera, Anthony R. Palmieri; production designer, Brandy Alexander; editor, Ron Rosen; music, W.G. Snuffy Walden; sound, Susan Moore-Chong; casting, April Webster, David Bloch. Running time: 60 mins.
Melina Kanakaredes (Dr. Sydney Hansen), Mike Farrell (Jim Hansen), Paula Cale (Joanie Hansen), Seth Peterson (Robbie Hansen), Leslie Silva (Dr. Helen Reynold), Concetta Tomei (Linda Hansen).
Try to imagine the pitch session: "It's a drama about a really saintly Los Angeles where a plastic surgeon grows tired of bobbing celebrity beaks, particularly after her controlling mother drops dead during her very pregnant sister's wedding and she catches her heavy-petting boyfriend in the shower soaping another man's back. So she is compelled to move back home to Providence, R.I., to help care for her sister's kid and keep her scheming brother in line while pulling their veterinarian daddy toward human contact and away from the dogs and hamsters he loves best". "Yes", replied NBC, "that's a winner".

While the sudsy hour fails to click as believable drama or as offbeat entertainment during its opening two stanzas, the creators at least deserve credit for attempting a somewhat daring tightrope walk with a family drama that pushes to be hip. That it succeeds only occasionally is almost less important than the genre-expanding effort itself. But the show very much belongs to the luminous Kanakaredes. She performs sparklingly as Dr. Sydney Hansen.

You get the feeling that there is an intriguing ensemble drama itching to spring from *Providence*, but its early episodes merely reinforce the idea that it's probably a lousy idea to cast a recovering plastic surgeon as a heroine – particularly one who has regular chats with the ghost of her domineering mother.

RKO 281

Filmed in London by Scott Free Prods. in association with WGBH Boston and HBO Pictures. Executive producers, Ridley Scott, Tony Scott; co-executive producers, Diane Minter Lewis, Chris Zarpas; producer, Su Armstrong; director, Benjamin Ross; writer, John Logan; camera, Mike Southon; editor, Alex Mackie; music, John Altman; sound, Clive Derbyshire, Peter Margrave; casting, Lora Kennedy, Joyce Nettles. Running time: 90 mins.
Liev Schreiber (Orson Welles), James Cromwell (William Randolph Hearst), Melanie Griffith (Marion Davies), John Malkovich (Herman Mankiewicz), Brenda Blethyn (Louella Parsons), Roy Scheider (George Schaefer), David Suchet (Louis B. Mayer), Fiona Shaw (Hedda Hopper), Anastasia Hille (Carole Lombard), Simeon Andrews (John Houseman), Liam Cunningham (Gregg Toland), Lucy Cohu (Dolores Del Rio), Angus Wright (Joseph Cotton), Kerry Shale (Bernard Herrmann), Tim Woodward (Jack Warner), Ron Berglas (Selznick), Geoffrey Hutchings (Cohn), Roger Allam (Disney) Jay Benedict (Zanuck).
A telepic that is not unlike *Citizen Kane* itself - a studied yet distorted truth. The triumph of the movie, though, is its depiction of how art can be created when it is unfettered by humility. Helmer streamlines much of the overall story and

steers clear of re-creating the set of *Kane*, except to depict Welles' authoritarian directorial style.

Orson Welles was the self-proclaimed genius who as a mere 24 year old was given complete control over his first Hollywood film. After a few abortive movie ideas, Welles set his sights on media mogul William Randolph Hearst and the backlog of incendiary stories surrounding the newspaper publisher. Both men had massive egos and were handed the keys to their respective kingdoms. Welles was obsessed with what could be; Hearst, 76 at the time, fretted over what might have been.

By bringing Hearst's life, however thinly veiled, to the big screen, Welles started a war that affected just about every major player in Hollywood. In his efforts to stop the film, Hearst had Hollywood gossip columnists Louella Parsons and Hedda Hopper at each other's throats in an attempt to smear Welles, and basically blackmailed several studio heads as he tried to destroy the film.

Schreiber, as Welles, manages to capture the essence of a man of many passions, and creates a nice balance of hubris and self-loathing to give the part real depth. As Hearst, Cromwell is a study in greed and arrogance.

Rogue Trader

A Pathe release (in U.K.) of a Granada and Newmarket Capital Group presentation of a Granada Film/David Paradine production. (International sales: Capitol Films, London.) Executive producers, David Frost, Pippa Cross, Claire Chapman; co-executive producers, William Tyrer, Chris Ball; producers, James Dearden, Paul Raphael, Janette Day; director, James Dearden; writer, Dearden, based on the book *Rogue Trader: How I Brought Down Barings Bank and Shook the Financial World* by Nicholas Leeson and Edward Whitley. Running time: 101 mins.
Ewan McGregor (Nick Leeson), Anna Friel (Lisa Leeson), Yves Beneyton (Pierre Bonnefoy), Betsy Brantley (Brenda Granger), Caroline Langrishe (Ash Lewis), Nigel Lindsay (Ron Baker), Tim McInnerney (Tony Hawes), Irene Ng (Bonnie Lee), Lee Ross (Danny Argyropoulos), Simon Shepherd (Peter Norris), John Standing (Peter Baring), Pip Torrens (Simon Jones), Tom Wu (George Seow), Daniel York (Henry Tan).
Leeson, a bright-eyed young man, lands a job with one of London's stuffiest institutions, at a time when Barings decided it needed some sharp, declassé talent to stay in the game. He is soon posted to Singapore, as the firm's general manager on the Singapore International Money Exchange. It's a time when the Far East is the new economic frontier. Leeson's combination of naivety and arrogance surfaces early when one of his team makes a mistake. As his losses mount, he hides them in a Back Office Error Account which eventually plays a part in the bank's downfall. He also starts trading on the bank's account rather than just clients' – which is fine when he's on a roll but proves fatal when the market goes against him. Impressed with Leeson's paper profits, Barings' management continues to give him carte blanche. But on February 23, 1995, the whole house of cards comes tumbling down, and Leeson and wife make a run for it.

One of the '90s' most iconic true-life stories, telepic could have furnished any one of several gripping scenarios, but this pic isn't among them. Helmer had many routes available to refashion the source material. However, he has gone a retro

...August 12...
Antonio Banderas plans to direct a TV series based on stories by Nobel Laureate Gabriel García Márquez.

route, with a kind of bargain-basement British *Wall Street*. Miscast McGregor is far too boyishly likable in the lead role, and he's surrounded by either wimps or stereotypes.

Rude Awakening

Filmed in Hollywood by Mandalay TV in association with Columbia TriStar TV Distribution. Executive producers, Peter Guber, Scott Sanders, Joe Voci, Pamela Eels, Claudia Lonow; producer, Terri Guarnieri; director, Alan Myerson; writer, Lonow; camera, Alan Walker; editor, John Neal; music, Rick Marotta; art director, Bob Breen; sound, Peter R. Damski; casting, Ulrich Dawson Kritzen. Running time: 30 mins.

Sherilyn Fenn (Billie Frank), Lynn Redgrave (Trudy Frank) Jonathan Penner (Dave), Rain Pryor (Jackie), Richard Lewis (Harve Schwartz), Corinne Bohrer (Tish), Paul Ben Victor (Carl), Julio Oscar Mechoso (Mike), Niecy Nash (Gaynielle), Cheryl Bartel (Kathy), Mitchell Group (Arte), Andrew Shaifer (Bobby), Michael Rapaport (Johnny).

What *That Girl* was to the 1960s, *Rude Awakening* promises to be to the 1990s – for as long as it lasts, anyway. It's why they invented cable: a divertingly raunchy ensemble comedy fronted by a heroine who drinks like a fish, swears like a sailor, has the unfortunate habit of waking up next to men she doesn't know, and who actually admonishes her genitalia.

Painfully dark and creepy, this alcohol-drenched "sipcom" stars the fetching Sherilyn Fenn as Billie Frank. Billie was a teen night-time soap queen in her salad days. But things have sort of disintegrated for her since she began drinking her breakfast. An intervention plotted by Billie's family and friends fails miserably. And she inevitably crashes, both literally and figuratively, smashing her car into a fire hydrant during one of her intoxicated adventures and winding up in a 12-step program. But at her first Addictions Anonymous meeting, Billie discovers that the support community ain't all it's cracked up to be. She's immediately latched onto by a crazed lesbian and another predatory male.

In the cynical gospel according to *Rude Awakening*, every guy is an insensitive, sexist, opportunistic carrier of hormones awaiting his next conquest, and every woman is a single, embittered abuse magnet. The show is so unctuously over the top that it sabotages any intentions it may have of satirizing the concept of self-help and recovery in the 1990s.

Sex and the City

Filmed in New York by HBO. Executive producer, Darren Star; co-executive producers, Barry Jossen, Michael Patrick King; directors Susan Seidelmann (pilot), Alison Maclean ("Models and Mortals"); writer, Star; director of photography, Stuart Dryburgh; editor, Michael Berenbaum; music, Carol Sue Baker; casting, Ellie Kanner (L.A.), Billy Hopkins (N.Y.). Running time: 30 mins.

Sarah Jessica Parker (Carrie), Kim Cattrall (Samantha), Kristin Davis (Charlotte), Cynthia Nixon (Miranda), Chris Noth (Mr. Big), Willie Garson (Stanford Blatch), Ben Weber (Skipper Johnston).

Sex and the City follows four upscale, attractive women through the sexual subway of contemporary Gotham. Single and in their 30s, each is a distinct blend of guile, guts and needfulness, traipsing through the dating world with predictable and even trite results, their chatter constantly hitting on sex, relationships and sex. Some good acting and some

nicely shot romantic interludes provide some redemption for the series, but scripts need to loosen up and inherit some of the playfulness the actresses bring to their roles.

It's a hopeless world out there, but newspaper columnist Carrie Bradshaw is throwing her libido in the laboratory to sort it all out for the masses. The self-described "sexual anthropologist" gets her information from company owner Samantha, willing and able to do anything; art dealer Charlotte, who's on the constant lookout for Mr. Right; lawyer Miranda, a study in the overstudied approach to all things male; and, of course, her own independent activities.

Pilot finds Bradshaw studying women who have sex like men – do the act and feel nothing afterward. "Models" has her observing men and women who only date beauties from the catwalk and magazine pages, asking that age-old question: How much power do beautiful people have? Both episodes play spin the bottle with the issues and land everywhere but the right places. They possess a wanton thirst for either pleasure or interrogation, and predictable actions and consequences abound.

Shake, Rattle & Roll

Filmed in Charlotte, N.C., by CDS Prods. and Phoenix Pictures in association with Morling Manor Media. Executive producers, Mike Medavoy, Spencer Proffer, Mike Robe; producer, Preston Fischer; co-producers, Suzanne DuBarry, Marc B. Lorber; director, story, Robe; writer (part one), Robe; writer (part two) Bill Kerby; director of photography, Alan Caso; production designer, Stephen Marsh; editors, Sabrina Plisco-Morris, John Duffy; music producer, Proffer; music, Patrick Williams; casting, Jason Padura, Natalie Hart. Running time: 240 mins.

Bonnie Somerville (Lyne Danner), Brad Hawkins (Tyler Hart), Samaria Graham (Marsha Stokes), Travis Fine (Mookie Gilliland), Kai Lennox (Dotson), Dana Delany (Elaine Gunn), James Coburn (Morris Gunn), Kathy Baker (Janice Danner), Frank Whaley (Allen Kogan), Gerald McRaney (Howard Danner). With: Troy Donohue, Elinor Donohue, Edd Burns, Erik King, Maggie Gylenhaal, Leo Burmester, Billy Porter, James Brett Rice, Mark Christopher Lawrence, Shawn Wayne Klush, Michael Weaver, Jimmie Ray Weeks, Rodney Williams, Bing Putney, J. Michael Hunter, Corri English, Shane Callahan, Michael Wright, Quint Voncannon.

Shake, Rattle & Roll has the ability to charm the pants off a selected audience – its fictional leads rocking to the top and then finding the summit less than fulfilling. The two key relationships – the friendship of Lyne Danner and Marsha Stokes and the romance between Danner and Tyler Hart – are driven by sharp and well-articulated performances. Overall, telepic is an intoxicating study of youngsters as they blossom alongside rock 'n' roll in the 1950s.

A Little Richard concert fuels Hart's ambition to play rock 'n' roll, and soon his C&W unit is attempting Chuck Berry's "Maybellene" with Danner on piano. Their rock effort is met with disdain by Hart's father and, more glaringly, girlfriend Noreen, who prevents the HartAches from playing a school formal. After graduation, the band heads off for Memphis, where they run into Fats Domino, who gives them some studio time. (By the end , the paths of Hart and Danner will cross with those of Elvis Presley, Bill Haley, Eddie Cochran, Neil Sedaka and an "American Bandstand" producer.) Pic follows

...August 13 ...

X-Files star David Duchovny sued 20th Century Fox, alleging that the studio has cheated him out of $25 million in profits from the TV series.

the band's quick rise, fall and evolutions; particularly their surge into the top-30 with their tune "Baby, Here I Am."

Music throughout is solidly performed by a host of contemporary pop stars: Blink 182, K-Ci & JoJo, and B.B. King to name a few. Original music hits the mark better in the faux '50s songs; the 1960s numbers sound more Broadway than Brill Building.

Snoops

Filmed in Manhattan Beach and Los Angeles by David E. Kelley Prods. in association with 20th Century Fox TV. Executive producer, David E. Kelley; co-executive producer, Alice West; producer/director, Allan Arkush; writer, Kelley; camera, Jamie Anderson; production designer, Jack DeGovia; editor, Neil Mandelberg; sound, Will Yarbrough; casting, Janet Gilmore, Megan McConnell. Running time: 60 mins.
Gina Gershon (Glenn Hall), Paula Marshall (Dana Plant), Danny Nucci (Manny Lott), Paula Jai Parker (Roberta Young), Edward Kerr (Det. Greg McCormack), John Glover (Gary Hyndman), Margo Martindale (Hannah Vaughn), Shareen Mitchell (Lori Hyndman), Sydney Walsh (Lisa Shire), Clayton Landey (Robert Shire), Brett Kolste Miller (Wilson), Carey Scott (Johnson).
Snoops is everything David Kelley shows aren't supposed to be: all flash and dash, smoke and mirrors – and scarcely a thimbleful of substance. Moody music and an antsy, artsy camera mix with esoteric visuals of time-lapse neon, setting the stage for ... well, more music and askew camera angles and neon. With *Snoops*, there truly is no *there*, there.

What the show does have is Gina Gershon, whose high-octane allure remains mostly intact here as she plays Glenn Hall, a savvy seductress of an L.A. private eye who has been known to sleep with targets to get them busted. Opposite Gershon, Paula Marshall is Dana Plant, a cloying, by-the-book homicide detective who sours on conventional police work and on a relationship with her boss. She decides to work for Glenn. She's conservative, disapproving, condescending. She can't possibly get along with Glenn. So naturally, she does. The third link in the detective agency is Manny Lott, a device junkie who digs planting phone bugs and zapping people with tranquilizer guns. He's at least fun to watch, unlike co-worker Roberta, a glorified assistant with a lousy attitude.

Kelley's opening teleplay, directed with panache by fellow Emmy winner Allan Arkush, is bolstered by the presence of the incomparable John Glover in one of his deliciously deranged bad-guy roles. If viewers tune in for an eyeful at first, it's likely they'll find the protagonists pretty much impossible to cheer on.

The Sopranos

Filmed in New Jersey by HBO Prods. in association with Brillstein-Grey Entertainment. Executive producer, creator, David Chase; executive producer, Brad Grey; co-executive producers, Mitchell Burgess, Robin Green; producer, Ilene S. Landress; director, writer, David Chase; director of photography, Alik Sakharov; production designer, Edward Pisoni; editor, Joanna Cappuccilli; casting, Sheila Jaffe, Georgianne Walker. Running time: 60 mins.
James Gandolfini (Tony Soprano), Lorraine Bracco (Dr. Jennifer Melfi), Edie Falco (Carmela), Michael Imperioli (Christopher), Nancy Marchand (Livia Soprano), Stevie Van Zandt (Silvio Dante), Jamie Lynn Sigler (Meadow),
Robert Iler (Anthony Jr.), Dominic Chianese (Uncle Junior), John Ventimiglia (Artie Bucco), Anthony Desando (Brendan Filone), Michael Rispoli ("Jackie" Aprile), Michele DeCesare (Hunter), Katherine Narducci (Charmaine Bucco), John Heard (Vin Makasian).
The mob life, a middle-aged Tony Soprano comes to learn inside his northern New Jersey enclave, isn't the good life anymore. There's a breakdown in the system, within the Soprano family and in Tony's personal definition of manhood; it manifests itself in anxiety attacks that have Soprano making regular trips to psychiatrist Jennifer Melfi. From these visits spin every Soprano tale – some morose, some wickedly funny, all uncommonly personal – and their distinctive tone will capture a patient audience looking for an intelligent episodic that isn't sex and shoot-'em-ups.

This 13-seg series fleshes out the family side of wiseguys in the waste-management and food-service businesses. Tony Soprano's wife Carmela and their kids, Meadow and Anthony Jr., figure dad has cracked and belongs at a nut farm; unbeknownst to anyone, he's already seeing a shrink, a secret that has its own code of silence.

Expository nature of the first two segments allows characters to enter and develop. Once the characters are drawn, director and writer David Chase travels through the mundane and average before making the de rigueur mob stops. Chase acutely composes each individual with nuance. Gandolfini plays Tony Soprano introspectively but without the hushed tones that generally signal a personal crisis in these sorts of roles. Bracco plays Dr. Melfi with a sexy sophistication in his presence; away from her celebrated patient, she has a liveliness that perks up in episode four.

Stark Raving Mad

(Sitcom, NBC, Thurs. Sept. 23, 9:30 p.m.) Filmed in Los Angeles by Steven Levitan Prods. in association with 20th Century Fox TV. Executive producer, Steven Levitan; co-executive producer, Jeffrey Richman; supervising producer, David Goodman; producers, Brian Buckner, Sebastian Jones, Gayle Abrams, Lyn Green, Richard Levine; director, James Burrows; writer, Levitan; camera, Ken Lamkin, Tony Yarlett; production designer, Wendell Johnson; editors, Peter Chakos, Timothy Mozer; music, Steve Hampton, R. Korbin Kraus, John Adair; sound, Russ Gary; casting, Jeff Greenberg. Running time: 30 mins. **Neil Patrick Harris (Henry McNeely), Tony Shalhoub (Ian Stark), Eddie McClintock (Jake Donovan), Heather Paige (Maddie Keller), Marty (Kent Edgar).**
Stark Raving Mad is nothing very special. Its few real laughs look almost like accidents, since the premise itself strains plausibility. And unlike creator/executive producer Steven Levitan's other NBC shows (*Frasier* and *Just Shoot Me*), this one lacks anything resembling magic. In fact, *Stark Raving Mad* is pretty much a one-joke wonder: Neil Patrick Harris (*Doogie Howser, M.D.*) plays Henry McNeely, a fastidious, super-neurotic New York book editor with germ issues who is forced to "unblock" an eccentric bestselling horror novelist named Ian Stark. That's pretty much the whole shebang. It's *The Odd Couple* in Hell. One guy is certifiably bonkers, the other's a classic type A nervous nelly. Pilot director James Burrows takes what he's handed and works to make it irreverent, inspiring a pilot loaded with slapstick and sight gags to help juice Levitan's mediocre teleplay. It's too bad, because

... August 14 ...
The Sixth Sense again leads the marketplace with $39.6 million.
Bowfinger grosses $25.2 million in its first week.

Harris and Shalhoub are both highly capable, charismatic performers. But it seems they will need to shine elsewhere.

The Tempest

Filmed on location in Charleston, S.C., for Bonnie Raskin Prods. in association with NBC Studios. Executive producers, Bonnie Raskin, Jack Bender; co-producers, Todd Sharp, Ronna Slutske; producer, James Bigwood; director, Jack Bender; writer, James Henerson; editor, Steve Lovejoy; camera, Steve Shaw; production design, Stephen Storer; art director, Jack Ballance; costume design, Van Broughton Ramsey; visual effects, the Frame Store; casting, Susan Edelman, Mary Buck. Running time: 120 mins.
Peter Fonda (Gideon Prosper), John Glover (Anthony Prosper), Harold Perrineau Jr. (Ariel), Katherine Heigl (Miranda), John Pyper-Ferguson (Gator Man), Eddie Mills (Frederick Allen), Dennis Redfield (Willy Gonzo), Donzaleigh Abernathy (Ezeli).
Finding a fresh angle while retaining the true message of *The Tempest* always poses a challenge. Telepic has transposed Shakespeare's fairies and sorcery with Creole voodoo in 1851 Mississippi, a tactic that offers unique parallels to the original story of a man who sees his life only through his losses.

Gideon Prosper is a man blinded by sorrow over the death of his wife, who lets the family plantation fall under the reigns of his unscrupulous brother Anthony. His devotion to the study of magic costs him his home and fortune, and he's forced to flee to a remote island in the Bayou with his young daughter Miranda and the runaway slave Ariel.

Flash to 12 years later, on the eve of the battle of Vicksburg. Gideon spends all his energy trying to protect his now-grown daughter and slave from what they want most – to go out and live in the world on their own. Ariel, bound to Gideon by magic and loyalty, wants to fight for the Union, while Miranda, sheltered and lonely, longs to find companionship. When Frederick Allen, a young Union soldier, finds his way to their secluded island, Gideon is forced to reckon with the world that he has abandoned. Viewers looking for a condensed version of this classic are sure to be baffled by this eclectic drama, but ultimately will be rewarded with a captivating and astutely cast film.

Third Watch

Filmed in New York City by John Wells Prods. in association with Warner Bros. TV. Executive producers, John Wells, Christopher Chulack; co-executive producer, John Romano; supervising producer, John Ridley, Brooke Kennedy; producer, Kristin Harms; director, Chulack; writer, Wells; camera, Glenn Kershaw; production designer, Steven Jordan; art director, Charles E. McCarry; editor, Randy Morgan; music, Martin Davich; sound, T.J. O'Mara; casting, John Levey, Jeff Block, Rob Decina. Running time: 60 mins.
Skipp Sudduth (John "Sully" Sullivan), Michael Beach (Monte "Doc" Parker), Coby Bell (Ty Davis Jr.), Molly Price (Faith Yokas), Kim Raver (Kim Zambrano), Bobby Cannavale (Bobby Caffy), Eddie Cibrian (Jimmy Doherty), Anthony Ruivivar (Carlos Nieto), Jason Wiles (Maurice Boscorelli), Dan Moran (Clown Guy).
ER executive producer John Wells attempts to transfer the same pulse-pounding chaos to the world of street trauma that he has managed to harness in the hospital emergency room. The result is something akin to *ER: Life on the Street*, follow-

ing cops, paramedics and firefighters as they save lives and dodge bullets while navigating the urban jungle of Manhattan. As in *ER*, the folks here are unfailingly decent, earnest and heroic, but the interwoven stories feel an awful lot like Wells retreads from the get-go. Making a second primetime hour with virtually an identical style and tone doesn't seem terribly smart. Moreover, the roles of many of the protagonists in the *Third Watch* premiere play like urban cliches: the hardened veteran cop, his raw, bumbling partner, the gunshy rookie paramedic and the hotheaded maverick cop.

These are one exceptionally attractive bunch of public servants save for one, a done-it-all veteran cop named "Sully" Sullivan. He's kind of paunchy and jowly, but it's OK because he's also cynical and jaded. Nothing wrong with that, but it's a little bit silly given the necessities of their jobs. Looking like models wouldn't appear to rank all that high as job prerequisites.

The opening stories mix small talk with large drama, including a woman who goes into screaming labor in a subway car, an infant who gets tossed harrowingly from a burning building, and a devastating mass shooting that concludes the hour.

Time of Your Life

Filmed in Los Angeles and New York City by Keyser/Lippman Prods. in association with Columbia TriStar TV. Executive producers, Amy Lippman, Chris Keyser, Mark B. Perry, Ken Topolsky; co-executive producer, Michael Engler; supervising producer, Ivan Menchell; producers, Paul Marks, Shelley Meals, Ellen Pressman, Jennifer Love Hewitt, Darin Goldberg; director, Engler; writers, Lippman, Keyser.
Jennifer Love Hewitt (Sarah Reeves Merrin), Johnathon Schaech (Maguire), Diego Serrano (J.B.), Jennifer Garner (Romy), Pauley Perrette (Cecilia), Gina Ravera (Joss).
Hewitt's notoriously troubled teen from *Party of Five* gets her own spinoff. Hewitt's performance in the opener of this spectacularly self-indulgent drama is predictably inelegant. She regularly sends the adorableness meter soaring off the scale. But her rendering of the alternately contrived and poignant teleplay resembles one long run-on sentence.

The premiere finds Maguire, a session musician who runs an East Village hangout in N.Y.C, meeting and pretty much instantly falling for the gloriously idealistic Sarah, who has just ditched her orphan family's San Francisco digs for Gotham. Why New York? It's the place that seemingly every young, single TV character heads to find themselves, the theory being that it's easier to clear one's head in an overpopulated, hyper-stimulated environment. Sarah's other key goal: to track down her biological father. This mission makes for the pilot's most maudlin, awkward interludes. Before the first hour is through, Sarah will have cast winsome looks in the directions of virtually every non-transient in Manhattan. Among those she befriends are an aspiring actress named Romy; a wacky bohemian apartment building manager; and the aforementioned Maguire, who looks like a pretty good catch, but not as good as the womanizing hunk she and Romy spy on, voyeur style.

The 53rd Annual Tony Awards

Presented live (delayed three hours PT) from the Gershwin Theater in New York City by Tony Awards Prods. Executive producer, Walter C. Miller; producer-director, Paul Miller;

... August 15 ...

Chanting "Bring Hollywood home", showbiz pros took to protest against the tide of film and TV productions fleeing to foreign locales for cheaper labor and tax incentives.

writers, Bruce Vilanch, Thomas Meehan. Musical director, Elliott Lawrence; set designer, Roy Christopher. Running time: 120 mins.
Performers: Casts of *The Civil War, Parade, Fosse, Annie Get Your Gun, Little Me, Peter Pan, You're a Good Man, Charlie Brown.* **Presenters: Julie Andrews, Carol Burnett, Calista Flockhart, Matthew Broderick, Ben Stiller, Laurence Fishburne, Alec Baldwin, Paul Giamatti, Angela Lansbury, Christian Slater, Sarah Jessica Parker, William Hurt, Christine Baranski, Bea Arthur, Chita Rivera, Stockard Channing, David Hyde Pierce, Swoosie Kurtz, Jason Robards, Kevin Spacey, Elaine Stritch, Scott Wolf, Kevin Kline.**
Sunday night's 53rd annual kudofest managed to push the boredom envelope to fresh new levels of stiffness and tedium, leaving us all to think the unthinkable: maybe they can't do this thing without Rosie O'Donnell, after all. Hostless? Heck, this Tonys was jokeless, clueless, punchless and joyless, too. Maybe going with, like, 22 quasi-hosts isn't such a good idea, you know? Taking a cue from the no-host bar, executive producer Walter Miller and company figured that if Rosie didn't want to host, well, then no one was going to.

There were a few moments of genuine sweetness and magic sprinkled through the two-hour CBS portion of the Tonycast. Heading that list had to be Julie Andrews doing a modest sing-song banter with co-presenter Carol Burnett – to enthusiastic audience response. It was likewise inspiring to hear the beautiful acceptance speech of top featured actress winner Elizabeth Franz, the charming, heartfelt speech of *Death of a Salesman's* Brian Dennehy for his lead actor win and the eloquent speech of featured actor winner Frank Wood.

When your show is designed to honor live performance, one might think that your live ceremony would be more professional, more self-assured than that of the Oscars and the Emmys if for no other reason than the stage is home.

Oprah Winfrey Presents: Tuesday With Morrie
Filmed in Los Angeles and Santa Clarita by Harpo Films. Executive producers, Oprah Winfrey, Kate Forte; supervising producer, Jennifer Ogden; director, Mick Jackson; writer, Tom Rickman, based on the book by Mitch Albom; camera, Theo Van De Sabde; production designer, J. Michael Riva; editor, Carol Littleton; music, Marco Beltrami; sound, Jim Tanenbaum; casting, Mindy Marin. Running time: 120 mins.
Jack Lemmon (Morrie Schwartz), Hank Azaria (Mitch Albom), Wendy Moniz (Janine), Caroline Aaron (Connie), Bonnie Bartlett (Charlotte), Aaron Lustig (Rabbi Al Axelrod), Bruce Nozick (Mr. Schwartz), Ivo Cutzarida (Armand), John Carroll Lynch (Walter Moran), Dan Thiel (Shawn Daley), Kyle Sullivan (Young Morrie), Christian J. Meoli (Aldo).
This film, inspired by sportswriter Mitch Albom's hugely popular book of the same name – which continues, after two years, to hover near the top of the bestseller list – is given a boost by Jack Lemmon, who plays Morrie Schwartz, an irrepressible 78-year-old college professor struck with ALS (Lou Gehrig's disease) and confined to a wheelchair.

It's been 16 years since Albom last spoke with Morrie. His sadness at his mentor's degenerative condition is complicated by his guilt at not having stayed in touch. Albom continues to bury himself in his hyperkinetic worklife, distancing himself from girlfriend Janine, but the image of Morrie haunts him. Dripping with trepidation, he finally pays his dying mentor a visit in Boston.

What Albom discovers is not an embittered old man, but an ebullient, mentally sharp teacher who finds that facing death allows him to "see things with incredible clarity" and inspires him to teach his "final course ... in living." They begin meeting every Tuesday, and their sessions spur Albom to step off the fast track and begin questioning the shallow, ego-banging absurdity of the sports world.

A few sins of the script are more than mitigated, however, by Mick Jackson's focused direction. All in all, *Tuesdays With Morrie* does the book justice – a pretty impressive feat.

The West Wing
Filmed in Los Angeles by John Wells Prods. in association with Warner Bros. TV. Executive producers, John Wells, Aaron Sorkin, Thomas Schlamme; producers, Llewellyn Wells, Kristin Harms; director, Schlamme; writer, Sorkin; camera, Tom Del Ruth; production designer, Ken Hardy; editor, Blake McCormick; music, Roxanne Lippel; sound, Kenneth Ross; casting, Barbara Miller, John Levey, Kevin Scott, Jeff Block. Running time: 60 mins.
Martin Sheen (President Josiah Bartlet), Rob Lowe (Sam Seaborn), John Spencer (Leo McGarry), Moira Kelly (Madeline Hampton), Tim Matheson (Vice President John Hoyle), Richard Schiff (Toby Ziegler), Brad Whitford (Josh Lyman), Allison Janney (C.J. Gregg).
Series pilots simply don't come much slicker – or whiter – than the droll and edgy The West Wing. It would surely be ironic if a darkly comic political drama like The West Wing – which takes us behind the scenes at the White House – carves out its niche as the show that keeps those congressional rascals at bay.

The drama is an original from the outset, blending artful dialog and sharp performances with Schlamme's sure directorial hand to construct an hour of sublime soapiness.

The premiere adroitly introduces its colorful ensemble of characters without ditching entertainment value. There's the Prez (Martin Sheen, whose unrelenting intensity proves an asset here), the frazzled/pretty-boy deputy communications director (a perfect Rob Lowe), the crusty chief of staff (a flawless John Spencer), a loose cannon deputy chief and a smooth-as-silk press secretary. Richard Schiff co-stars as a battle-toughened spin control artist, while the captivating Moira Kelly plays a slick assistant. Tim Matheson joins the fray the following week.

As events unfold in the fast-paced pilot, Lowe's character unwittingly sleeps with a call girl and complicates matters by accidentally swapping pagers with her. Threats are made about someone's head rolling roughly every three minutes or so. What's most noteworthy, however, is that we find ourselves caring about these workaholic administration gophers almost instantly.

Will and Grace
Filmed in Studio City by Everything Entertainment in association with NBC Studios/Three Sisters Entertainment. Executive producers, David Kohan, Max Mutchnick; producers, Tim Kaiser, Johni Marchinko; director, James Burrows; writers, Kohan, Mutchnick; production designer, Bruce Ryan; camera, Tony Askins; editor, Peter Chakos;

... August 16 ...
In its first acquisition as the new specialized division of MGM, United Artists Films negotiates North American rights for **Things You Can Tell Just By Looking At Her**.

sound, Ed Moskowsitz; music, Jonathan Wolff; casting, Tracy Lilienfield. Running time: 30 mins.

Eric McCormack (Will Truman), Debra Messing (Grace Adler), Sean Hayes (Jack McFarland), Megan Mullally (Karen Walker).

While noting that *Will and Grace* is clearly NBC's best new comedy isn't saying terribly much, the show does spring out of the box boasting snappy dialogue, James Burrows' usual masterful directorial work, and a couple of colorful supporting players.

What the show doesn't have is an original premise (ooh, the gay man's best friend is a woman ... and they're neurotic together!), or a compelling dynamic between Messing and co-star Eric McCormack. He's Will, but he looks and acts more like a younger, less cynical Dennis Miller. McCormack also doesn't happen to behave stereotypically gay at least through the first two episodes, which is to say that he possesses no limp wrist or special hankering for Joan Rivers. Mullally, whose work is priceless as a wealthy, pill-popping socialite slumming it as an assistant to interior designer Grace, and Hayes (as Will's flamboyant gay friend Jack) infuse *Will and Grace* with its camp energy.

As the sitcom opens, the charming but bland Will is a Manhattan lawyer still reeling from the recent end of a long-term relationship. Grace is about to marry a guy she's lukewarm about, to Will's chagrin. She nearly weds the guy anyway, seemingly just to spite Will, but she finally wakes up and hears the show tunes. By the inferior second episode, she will be living with her best pal. Chastely, of course.

Y2K

Filmed in Vancouver, B.C., by NBC Studios. Executive producers, David Israel, Pat Caddell; producer, Michael R. Joyce; director, Dick Lowry; writers, Thomas Hines, Jonathan Fernandez; camera, David Geddes; production designer, Sheila Haley; editor, Steve Lovejoy; music, Brad Fiedel; sound, Kevin Sands; casting, Reuben Cannon, Kim Williams, Michelle Allen. Running time: 120 mins.

Ken Olin (Nick Cromwell), Kate Vernon (Alix Cromwell), Joe Morton (Martin Lowell), Jane McGregor (Kelly Cromwell), Michael Suchanek (Donny Cromwell), Ronny Cox (Benjamin Cromwell), Lauren Tom (Ann Lee), Zack Ward (Rick Rothman), Terence Kelly (Roy Jenkins).

Y2K is intended only to stoke the fires of groundless paranoia and further incite cyberpanic – but not to leave anyone really concerned. Ken Olin portrays Nick Cromwell, a "complex systems failure" expert for the government who has a front-row seat to millennial madness on the eve of New Year's 2000. He and his boss, Martin Lowell, conclude that Y2K computer failure will be massive, and decide to ground all commercial aircraft as the century turns. But then things begin to career out of control everywhere as each part of the world reaches the big 2-0-0-0 moment. ATMs stop spitting out bills, right on schedule. Prison doors operated by computer swing open, releasing criminals into the streets. A nuclear meltdown in Sweden kills everyone in the power plant.

Cromwell reacts to all of this by regularly calling his wife and asking with understandable concern about her and the kids. Pretty soon, his courage will be all that stands between us and enough radiation to fry the planet. It leads to *Y2K* devolving into a hackneyed nuke meltdown/race-against-time flick over its final 40 minutes.

With *Y2K*, NBC slaps a big fat exclamation point onto its millennium-closing obsession, airing a film that consistently squeezes little genuine suspense from a phenomenon that is surely the most overhyped of the 1990s.

> *Bags, bags go away,*
> *come again on Doris Day.*
> *(Elizabeth Taylor on seeing*
> *her eye-bags in the mirror*
> *from* The Mirror Crack'd)

...August 17...
Meg Ryan is to star for director Richard Loncraine in
This Man This Woman, a drama scripted by Frederic Raphael.

Index of TV reviews in Variety 1999

20/20: Monica Lewinsky (March 8-14)
The '60s (Feb. 1-7)
Action (Sept. 13-19)
Aftershock: Earthquake in New York (Nov 8-14)
Alice in Wonderland (Feb. 22-28)
Ally (Sept. 27-Oct. 3)
And the Beat Goes on: The Sony and Cher Story
   (Feb. 22-28)
The Apartment Complex (Nov. 1-7)
Atomic Train (May 10-16)
The Awful Truth (April 5-11)
Beggars and Choosers (June 14-20)
The Big Moment (April 5-11)
Bonanno: A Godfather's Story (July 19-25)
Celebrate the Century, Episode 1: 1900-1914
   (May 3-9)
The Century (March 29-April 4)
The Chimp Channel (June 7-13)
A Christmas Carol (Nov. 22-28)
Cleopatra (May 17-23)
Cold Feet (Sept. 27-Oct. 3)
Crusade (June 7-13)
The Devil's Arithmetic (March 29-April 4)
Dilbert (Jan. 25-31)
Double Platinum (May 10-16)
Earthly Possessions (March 15-21)
Everything's Relative (April 12-18)
Execution of Justice (Nov. 29-Dec. 5)
Family Guy (Feb. 1-7)
Family Law (Sept. 20-26)
First Wave (March 22-28)
Freaks and Geeks (Sept. 20-26)
Futurama (March 29-April 4)
Get Real (Sept. 6-12)
GVSE (July 12-18)
Happy Hour (April 5-11)
Harsh Realm (Oct. 4-10)
Having Our Say: The Delany Sisters' First 100 Years
   (Apr. 19-25)
The History of Sex (Aug. 16-22)
The Hoop Life (June 28-July 11)
The Hunt for the Unicorn Killer (May 3-9)
I'll Make Me a World: A Century of African-American
   Arts (Feb. 1-7)
Introducing Dorothy Dandridge (Aug. 16-22)
Investigative Reports: Guns in America
   (June 28-July 11)
It's Like, You Know ... (March 22-28)
Jack & Jill (Sept. 20-26)
The Jack Bull (April 12-18)

Jackie's Back (June 14-20)
The Jesse Ventura Story (May 17-23)
Joan of Arc (May 10-16)
Judging Amy (Sept. 13-19)
Ladies' Man (Sept. 20-26)
The Lady in Question (Dec. 6-12)
The Last Movie: Stanley Kubrick & Eyes Wide Shut
   (Sept. 27-Oct. 3)
Law and Order: Special Victims Unit (Sept. 20-26)
A Lesson Before Dying (May 17-23)
The Lot (Aug. 16-22)
Love & Money (Oct. 4-10)
Love Letters (April 12-18)
The Magical Legend of the Leprechauns (Nov. 8-14)
The Man Show (June 14-20)
Mary, Mother of Jesus (Nov. 8-14)
Mickey Mouse Works (May 3-9)
The Mike O'Malley Show (Sept. 20-26)
Mission Hill (Sept. 20-26)
The Mississippi: River of Song (Feb. 1-7)
Mutiny (March 22-28)
New York: A Documentary Film (Nov. 15-21)
Now and Again (Sept. 20-26)
Odd Man Out (Sept. 20-26)
Once and Again (Sept. 20-26)
Oprah Winfrey Presents: Tuesdays With Morrie
   (Nov. 29-Dec. 5)
Passing Glory (Feb. 15-21)
The Passion of Ayn Rand (May 24-30)
Payne (March 15-21)
Pirates of Silicon Valley (June 14-20)
The PJS (Jan. 11-17)
Popular (Sept. 27-Oct. 3)
Providence (Jan. 11-17)
Red Handed (March 15-21)
Ricky Martin: One Night Only (Nov. 22-28)
RKO 281 (Nov. 15-21)
Roswell (Oct. 4-10)
Safe Harbor (Sept. 20-26)
Sarah, Plain & Tall: Winter's End (Nov. 15-21)
A Season for Miracles (Dec. 6-12)
Shake, Rattle & Roll (Nov. 1-7)
Snoops (Sept. 20-26)
The Sopranos (Jan. 4-10)
Spongebob Squarepants (July 12-18)
Stark Raving Mad (Sept. 20-26)
Stephen King's Storm of the Century (Feb. 15-21)
Strange World (March 8-14)
Swing Vote (Apr. 19-25)
Third Watch (Sept. 20-26)

...August 18...
Denzel Washington is in talks to play the lead in the Jerry Bruckheimer-Disney
project **Remember The Titans**.

Time of Your Life (Oct. 25-31)
Tom Clancy's Netforce (Feb. 1-7)
Too Rich–The Secret Life of Doris Duke (Feb. 15-21)
Total Recall 2070 (March 8-14)
Turks (Jan. 25-31)
Undressed (July 19-25)

The Unexpected Mrs. Pollifax (May 17-23)
The West Wing (Sept. 20-26)
Work with Me (Sept. 27-Oct. 3)
Y2K (Nov. 22-28)
Y2K: The Winter of Our Disconnect (Oct. 25-31)
Zoe, Duncan, Jack & Jane (Jan. 11-17)

> *I am so pathetic,*
> *I even pity myself.*
> *(Yves Montand,*
> *Manon Ses Sources)*

...August 19...
John Turturro and Emily Watson are poised to fall in love in
Marleen Gorris's next film **The Luzhin Defense**.

Theater

Exploring the yellowing pages of *Variety*'s earliest issues, it's evident that theater (and its cheeky cousin, vaudeville) dominated the fledgling world of entertainment during the first two decades of the century. On the one side there was the straight play, opening on Broadway – the "legitimate" theater (quickly dubbed "Legit" in *Variety*'s language). And beyond the fringe, as it were, lay the world of musical theater, descending all the way down to peripheral music halls, old showboats on the Mississippi, and so on – not necessarily "illegitimate" but simply outside the *Variety* bailiwick.

Throughout the century, *Variety* has stayed loyal to the stage, reviewing most of the new productions on Broadway and in London's West End, tracking openings in other major cities, and recording the grosses of shows as they hit "the road" across the United States. As with our film reviews, notices are aimed at a professional readership, but this does not prevent them from aspiring to a serious artistic assessment of the better productions.

This section includes the Tonys and other leading stage awards, some notable Broadway and West End statistics, openings and closings during 1999, and some of *Variety*'s most significant theater reviews during the past year.

Longest-running shows in London

1. *The Mousetrap* (whodunnit): 47 years, 2 months
2. *Cats* (musical): 18 years, 8 months
3. *Starlight Express* (musical): 15 years, 10 months
4. *Les Misérables* (musical): 14 years, 3 months
5. *The Phantom of the Opera* (musical): 13 years, 3 months
6. *Blood Brothers* (musical): 11 years, 6 months
7. *The Woman In Black* (thriller): 10 years, 11 months
8. *Miss Saigon* (musical): 10 years, 4 months
9. *Buddy* (musical): 10 years, 3 months
10. *An Inspector Calls* (play): 4 years, 3 months

As of Dec. 1999

Broadway productions opening and closing: 1999

Openings

Fosse: musical conceived by Richard Maltby Jr., Chet Walker and Ann Reinking with choreography by Bob Fosse, directed by Maltby, opened Jan 14 at the Broadhurst.

You're a Good Man, Charlie Brown: musical revival directed by Michael Mayer, opened Feb 4 at the Ambassador.

Death of a Salesman: play revival directed by Robert Falls, opened Feb 10 at the Eugene O'Neill.

Not About Nightingales: play by Tennessee Williams directed by Trevor Nunn, opened Feb 25 at the Circle in the Square.

Annie Get Your Gun: musical revival directed by Graciela Daniele, opened March 4 at the Marquis.

Band in Berlin: musical written and conceived by Susan Feldman, directed by Patricia Birch and Feldman, opened March 7 at the Helen Hayes.

Night Must Fall: play revival directed by John Tillinger, opened March 8 at the Lyceum.

The Lion in Winter: play revival directed by Michael Mayer, opened March 11 at the Roundabout Stage Right.

Via Dolorosa: play by David Hare directed by Stephen Daldry, opened March 18 at the Booth.

Closer: play written and directed by Patrick Marber, opened March 25 at the Music Box.

The Weir: play by Conor McPherson directed by Ian Rickson, opened April 1 at the Walter Kerr.

The Iceman Cometh: play revival directed by Howard Davies, opened April 8 at Brooks Atkinson.

Marlene: play with music by Pam Gems, directed by Sean Mathias, opened April 11 at the Cort.

Amy's View: play by David Hare directed by Richard Eyre, opened April 15 at the Ethel Barrymore.

... August 20 ...

Disney's Buena Vista Television and Encore Media Group have signed the most expensive pay TV movie output deal in history, a pact that could total $3.4 billion.

The Civil War: musical with music by Frank Wildhorn, book and lyrics by Wildhorn, Gregory Boyd and Jack Murphy, directed by Jerry Zaks, opened April 22 at the St. James.

The Gershwins' Fascinating Rhythm: musical revue conceived by Mark Lamos and Mel Marvin from source material by Deena Rosenberg, directed by Lamos, opened April 25 at the Longacre.

It Ain't Nothin' But The Blues: musical revue by Charles Bevel, Lita Gaithers, Randal Myler, Ron Taylor and Dan Wheetman, based on an original idea by Taylor, directed by Myler, opened April 26 at the Vivian Beaumont.

The Lonesome West: play by Martin McDonagh, directed by Garry Hynes, opened April 27 at the Lyceum.

Ring Round the Moon: play revival directed by Gerald Gutierrez, opened April 28 at the Belasco.

Voices in the Dark: play by John Pielmeier directed by Christopher Ashley, opened Aug 12 at the Longacre.

Kat and the Kings: musical with book and lyrics by David Kramer and music by Taliep Peterson, directed by Kramer, opened Aug 19 at the Cort.

Epic Proportions: play by Larry Coen and David Crane, directed by Jerry Zaks, opened Sept 30 at the Helen Hayes.

Dame Edna: The Royal Tour: special attractions devised and written by Barry Humphries, with additional material by Ian Davidson, opened Oct 17 at the Booth.

Saturday Night Fever: musical featuring songs by the Bee Gees, adapted from the motion picture by Nan Knighton in collaboration with Arlene Phillips, Paul Nicholas and Robert Stigwood, directed by Phillips, opened Oct 21 at the Minskoff.

The Rainmaker: play revival directed by Scott Ellis, opened Nov 11 at the Brooks Atkinson.

The Price: play revival directed by James Naughton, opened Nov 15 at the Royale Theater.

Kiss Me, Kate: musical revival directed by Michael Blakemore, opened Nov 18 at the Martin Beck.

Tango Argentino: musical revue conceived and directed by Claudio Segovia and Hector Orezzoli, opened Nov 17 at the Gershwin.

Putting it Together: musical revue with music and lyrics by Stephen Sondheim, directed by Eric D. Schaeffer, opened Nov at the Ethel Barrymore.

Marie Christine: musical with book, lyrics and music by Michael John LaChiusa, directed by Graciela Daniele, opened Dec 2 at the Vivian Beaumont.

Swing!: musical revue directed by Lynne Taylor-Corbett, opened Dec 9 at the St. James.

Minnelli on Minnelli: revue written and directed by Fred Ebb, opened Dec 8 at the Palace.

Amadeus: play revival directed by Peter Hall, opened Dec 15 at the Music Box.

Waiting in the Wings: play revival directed by Michael Langham, opened Dec 16 at the Walter Kerr.

Jackie Mason: Much Ado About Everything: solo show written and directed by Jackie Mason, opened Dec 30 at the Golden.

Closings

Fool Moon (specialty) closed Jan 3 after 6 previews, 49 performances.

I'm Still Here... Damn it (Solo) closed Jan 3 after 12 previews, 51 performances.

Peter Pan (musical revival) closed Jan 3 after 5 previews, 48 performances.

Bring in 'da Noise, Bring in 'da Funk (musical) closed Jan 10 after 18 previews, 1,130 performances.

On the Town (musical revival) closed Jan 17 after 37 previews, 65 performances.

Swan Lake (musical) closed Jan 24 after 11 previews, 124 performances.

Little Me (musical revival) closed Feb 21 after 50 previews, 101 performances.

Parade (musical) closed Feb 28 after 39 previews, 85 performances.

The Blue Room (play) closed Feb 25 after 15 previews, 81 performances.

The Beauty Queen of Leenane (play) closed March 15 after 11 previews, 374 performances.

Band in Berlin (musical) closed March 21 after 19 previews, 17 performances.

Electra (play revival) closed March 21 after 14 previews, 115 performances.

Titanic (musical) closed March 28 after 28 previews, 804 performances.

Marlene (musical play) closed May 2 after 15 previews, 25 performances.

The Gershwins' Fascinating Rhythm (musical revue) closed May 9 after 27 previews, 25 performances.

The Civil War (musical) closed June 13 after 35 previews, 61 performances.

The Lonesome West (play) closed June 13 after 9 previews, 55 performances.

Not About Nightingales (play) closed June 13 after 13 previews, 125 performances.

Via Dolorosa (play) closed June 13 after 15 previews, 99 performances.

You're a Good Man, Charlie Brown closed June 13 after 13 previews, 150 performances.

The Sound of Music (musical revival) closed June 20 after 38 previews, 533 performances.

...August 21...
Elton John and Tim Rice's Disney musical **Aida** will open on Broadway in March.

Amy's View (play) closed July 18 after 12 previews, 103 performances.

The Iceman Cometh (play revival) closed July 18 after 10 previews, 102 performances.

Art (play) closed Aug 8 after 20 previews, 600 performances.

Closer (play) closed Aug 22 after 17 previews, 172 performances.

Voices in the Dark (play) closed Oct 10 after 12 previews, 68 performances.

Death of a Salesman (play revival) closed Nov 7 after 22 previews, 274 performances.

The Weir (play) closed Nov 28 after 11 previews, 277 performances.

London West End productions opening and closing: 1999

Openings

2 Pianos 4 Hands (Comedy) 7 Oct

4 Steps to Heaven (Piccadilly) 29 July

50 Revolutions (Whitehall) 10 Sept

110 in the Shade (Fortune) 4 July

Act Without Words I (Barbican Pit) 7 Sept

Act Without Words II (Barbican Pit) 2 Sept

Al Murray – The Pub Landlord (New Ambassadors) 3 Oct

Alcina (Coliseum) 29 Nov

Andalusia: The Last Glory – Caraealia Dance Company (Peacock) 7 Oct

Angela Gheorghiu and Roberto Alagna in Concert (Royal Opera House) 27 Dec

Animal Crackers (Lyric) 16 March

Anna Wiess (Whitehall) 22 Nov

Antigone (Old Vic) 11 Oct

Antony and Cleopatra (Shakespeare's Globe) 30 July

Audra McDonald (Donmar Warehouse) 24 Aug

Augustine's Oak (Shakespeare's Globe) 12 Aug

Bad Weather (Barbican Pit) 19 Jan

The Ballad of Solomon Pavey (Shakespeare's Globe) 2 Oct

The Barber of Seville (Peacock) 31 Aug

Bartholomew Fair (Young Vic) 24 Feb

Battle Royal (National Lyttelton) 9 Dec

La Bayadère (Coliseum) 6 July

The Birthday Party (Piccadilly) 26 April

Black on White (Barbican) 1 July

Blast (London Apollo Hammersmith) 14 Dec

La Bohème (Coliseum) 30 Oct

Boris Godunov (Coliseum) 3 Aug

Boyband (Gielgud) 8 June

Breath (Barbican Pit) 17 Sept

The Breathing Show – Bill T. Jones (Sadler's Wells) 10 Nov

Candide (National Olivier) 13 April

The Carmelites (Coliseum) 20 May

Carmen (Coliseum) 1 May

Casper the Musical (Shaftesbury) 8 Dec

Catastrophe (Barbican Pit) 14 Sept

A Celebration of International Choreography (Royal Opera House) 8 Dec

Cinderella (Coliseum) 11 Jan

City – Odessa Stories (Barbican) 1 June

Closer (National Lyttelton) 20 Dec

Collected Stories (Haymarket) 15 Nov

The Colleen Bawn (National Lyttelton) 18 March

The Colour of Justice (Victoria Palace) 3 March

The Colour of Justice (National Lyttelton) 21 Sept

Come and Go (Barbican Pit) 2 Sept

The Comedy of Errors (Shakespeare's Globe) 3 June

Comic Potential (Lyric) 13 Oct

Copenhagen (Duchess) 8 Feb

Cruel Garden: Rambert Dance Company (Sadler's Wells) 26 May

Dancing on Dangerous Ground (Drury Lane) 6 Dec

The Darker Face of the Earth (National Cottesloe) 5 Aug

Defending the Covenant (Apollo) 17 Feb

The Diary of One Who Vanished (National Lyttelton) 3 Nov

Dick Whittington (Sadler's Wells) 21 Dec

Diva on the Verge – Julia Migenes (Peacock) 22 Feb

Don Giovanni (Sadler's Wells) 14 Oct

Don Quixote (Coliseum) 28 July

Dracula – Northern Ballet Theatre (Sadler's Wells) 17 March

Dreaming (Queen's) 15 June

Drummers (New Ambassadors) 6 Sept

East (Vaudeville) 15 Sept

Edward II – Birmingham Royal Ballet (Sadler's Wells) 2 Feb

Endgame (Barbican) 16 Sept

Enio Marcheto (Queen's) 18 Oct

Eurydice (Whitehall) 12 July

Falstaff (Peacock) 28 Aug

Falstaff (Royal Opera House) 6 Dec

Fascinating Aida – Barefaced Chic! (Haymarket) 9 Feb

Figaro's Wedding (Coliseum) 6 Oct

Finian's Rainbow (Fortune) 5 Sept

Footfalls (Barbican Pit) 10 Sept

Forbidden Broadway (Albery) 3 Aug

The Forest (National Lyttelton) 28 Jan

Der Freischutz (Coliseum) 10 Sept

A Funny Thing Happened on the Way to the Forum
(Open Air) 23 July

Furioso: Meryl Tankard Australian Dance Theatre
(Sadler's Wells) 4 May

The Game of Love and Chance (Barbican) 17 June

La Gatta Cenorentala (Sadler's Wells) 2 Nov

Geometry of Miracles (National Lyttelton) 15 April

Giselle (Sadler's Wells) 6 July

Giselle, Paganini (Coliseum) 8 July

The Gin Game (Savoy) 31 March

Good (Donmar Warehouse) 23 March

Goodnight Children Everywhere (Barbican Pit) 23 Feb

Great Balls of Fire (Cambridge) 6 Oct

Gross Indecency – The Three Trials of Oscar Wilde
(Gielgud) 22 March

Gumboots (Lyric) 22 Sept

Hans Liberg (Peacock) 27 Oct

Hansel and Gretel (Sadler's Wells) 31 March

Happy Days (Barbican) 9 Sept

Hay Fever (Savoy) 14 June

Holly Mothers (New Ambassadors) 1 June

Honk! The Ugly Duckling (National Olivier) 16 Dec

Hot Mouth (Peacock) 21 April

I'd Rather Be Right (Fortune) 9 May

I Love You, You're Perfect, Now Change (Comedy)
28 July

The Importance of Being Ernest (Haymarket) 4 Aug

Irek Mukhamedov and Company (Sadler's Wells) 19 Oct

Jane Eyre (New Ambassadors) 25 Nov

Jeffrey Bernard is Unwell (Old Vic) 4 Aug

Jessye Norman (Barbican) 29 July

Jubilee (Her Majesty's) 21 Nov

Julius Caesar (Shakespeare's Globe) 20 May

Juno and the Paycock (Donmar Warehouse) 20 Sept.

Kathakall – King Lear (Shakespeare's Globe) 7 July

Katya Kabanova (Sadler's Wells) 13 Oct

King Lear (Barbican) 28 Oct

King Priam (Coliseum) 20 Oct

Krapp's Last Tape (Barbican Pit) 4 Sept

The Lady in the Van (Queen's) 7 Dec

Last Dance at Dum Dum (New Ambassadors) 14 July

The Last Fattybottypuss in the World (Open Air) 3 Aug

Lenny (Queen's) 9 Aug

Life is a Dream (Barbican) 23 Sept

The Lion King (Lyceum) 19 Oct

The Lion, the Witch and the Wardrobe (Barbican) 29
March

Little Malcolm and His Struggle With the Eunuchs
(Comedy) 20 Jan

Look Back in Anger (National Lyttelton) 15 July

The Love for Three Oranges (Coliseum) 7 Aug

Love Letters (Haymarket) 8 July

Macbeth (Queen's) 3 March

Making Noise Quietly (Whitehall) 19 April

Mamma Mia! (Prince Edward) 6 April

Mark Morris Dance Group (Sadler's Wells) 5 Oct

Measure For Measure (Barbican) 20 Jan

The Memory of Water (Vaudeville) 11 Jan

Mephistopheles (Coliseum) 18 March

The Merchant of Venice (National Cottesloe) 17 June

The Merchant of Venice (National Olivier) 29 Nov

The Merry Wives of Windsor (Open Air) 1 June

Midsummer Night's Dream – Pacific Northwest Ballet
(Sadler's Wells) 25 Feb

Midsummer Night's Dream (Barbican) 10 Dec

Mixed Programme – Pacific Northwest Ballet (Sadler's
Wells) 22 Feb

Mixed Programme – Rambert Dance Company
(Sadler's Wells) 18 May

Money (National Olivier) 3 June

A Month in the Country (Barbican Pit) 4 May

Morphic Resonance (Donmar Warehouse) 18 Feb

Musa Gitana – Paco Peña Flamenco Dance Company
(Peacock) 4 Feb

The Mysteries: The Doomsday (National Cottesloe)
18 Dec

The Mysteries: The Nativity (National Cottesloe)
18 Dec

The Mysteries: The Passion (National Cottesloe) 18 Dec

National Youth Ballet (Sadler's Wells) 8 Nov

Nederlands Dans Theater 1 (Sadler's Wells) 14 June

The New Rocky Horror Show (Victoria Palace) 14
April

Night Life – Scottish Ballet (Sadler's Wells) 3 June

Not I (Barbican Pit) 7 Sept

The Nutcracker (Coliseum) 14 Dec

The Nutcracker (Royal Opera House) 17 Dec

Oh! What a Night (London Apollo Hammersmith)
5 Aug

Ohio Impromptu (Barbican Pit) 14 Sept

Oklahoma! (Lyceum) 21 Jan

On the Road to Baghdad – Green Candle Dance Co
(Sadler's Wells) 9 March

Online (Sadler's Wells) 19 July

Opening Celebration (Royal Opera House) 4 Dec

The Oresteia 1: Home Guard (National Cottesloe)
1 Dec

The Oresteia 2: The Daughter of Darkness (National
Cottesloe) 1 Dec

Orfeo (Coliseum) 17 Sept

Oroonoko (Barbican Pit) 20 Dec

Orpheus and Eurydice (Coliseum) 24 Feb

Our Late Night (New Ambassadors) 21 Oct

The Pajama Game (Victoria Palace) 4 Oct

Parsifal (Coliseum) 13 Feb

Patti Lupone (Donmar Warehouse) 10 Aug

. . . August 23 . . .

Titanic has once again sailed into the Hollywood record books, this time as the
bestselling DVD to date, with more than 1 million units shipped to retailers.

Paul Bunyan (Sadler's Wells) 24 April
Penny For a Song (Whitehall) 30 Sept.
Perfect Days (Vaudeville) 21 June
Peter Grimes (Sadler's Wells) 30 March
Peter Grimes (Coliseum) 12 Nov
A Piece of Monologue (Barbican Pit) 17 Sept
Platonov or The Play With No Name (Barbican) 9 June
Play (Barbican Pit) 2 Sept
Plenty (Albery) 27 April
The Prisoner of Second Avenue (Haymarket) 30 March
Private Lives (National Lyttelton) 13 May
Programme 1 – Rambert Dance Company (Sadler's Wells) 23 Nov
Programme 2 – Rambert Dance Company (Sadler's Wells) 29 Nov
Programme 3 – Rambert Dance Company (Sadler's Wells) 2 Dec
Programme 1 – San Francisco Ballet (Sadler's Wells) 25 Oct
Programme 2 – San Francisco Ballet (Sadler's Wells) 25 Oct
Programme A – Les Ballets Trockadero de Monte Carlo (Peacock) 9 Sept
Programme B – Les Ballets Trockadero de Monte Carlo (Peacock) 14 Sept
Quartet (Albery) 8 Sept
Raymonda (Coliseum) 19 July
The Real Thing (Donmar Warehouse) 2 June
Remember This (National Lyttelton) 15 Oct
The Return of Don Juan, The Arc Dance Company (Sadler's Wells) 1 March
Richard III (Savoy) 18 Jan
Ricky Jay & His 52 Assistants (Old Vic) 22 June
Rigoletto (Coliseum) 4 June
The Riot (National Cottesloe) 11 Feb
Roberto Zucco (Barbican Pit) 7 April
Rockaby (Barbican Pit) 10 Sept
Romeo and Juliet (Royal Festival Hall) 12 Jan
Romeo and Juliet (Sadler's Wells) 16 Nov
Rose (National Cottesloe) 24 June
Der Rosenkavalier (Coliseum) 4 Sept
Rota – Deborak Colker Dance Company (Peacock) 12 May
Rough for Theatre I (Barbican Pit) 10 Sept
Rough for Theatre II (Barbican Pit) 14 Sept
A Saint She Ain't (Apollo) 22 Sept
Salome (Coliseum) 1 April
Sam Brown (Donmar Warehouse) 31 Aug
Scenes From an Execution (Barbican Pit) 22 Sept
Sell Out (New Ambassadors) 1 June
Semele (Coliseum) 19 April
Sensaclones – Compania Sara Baras (Sadler's Wells) 13 Sept

Shazami – DCA (Barbican) 8 July
Shijma – Sankai Juku (Sadler's Wells) 18 Jan
Slava's Snowshow (Piccadilly) 2 March
Sleep With Me (National Cottesloe) 22 April
The Snowman (Peacock) 1 Dec
Some Explicit Polaroids (New Ambassadors) 14 Oct
Song at Twilight (Gielgud) 20 Oct
Songs of the Wanderers – Cloud Gate Dance Theatre (Sadler's Wells) 13 April
Soul Train (Victoria Palace) 22 June
Sparkleshark (National Lyttelton) 7 June
Spartacus (Coliseum) 12 July
Spend Spend Spend (Piccadilly) 12 Oct
Splash Hatch on the E Going Down (Donmar Warehouse) 18 Feb
The Street of Crocodiles (Queen's) 19 Jan
St. Petersburg Legacy (Barbican Pit) 10 June
Strob (Barbican) 19 May
Suddenly Last Summer (Comedy) 14 April
Summerfolk (National Olivier) 3 Sept
Swan Lake (Royal Albert Hall) 16 June
Swan Lake (Coliseum) 26 July
Swan Lake (Sadler's Wells) 28 Oct
Talk of the City (Young Vic) 10 Feb
The Taming of the Shrew (Barbican Pit) 27 Oct
Tango Pasion (Lyric) 26 May
The Tempest (Barbican) 6 Jan
Tess of the D'Urbervilles (Savoy) 10 Nov
That Time (Barbican Pit) 17 Sept
Three Days of Rain (Donmar Warehouse) 2 March
Three Days of Rain (Donmar Warehouse) 9 Nov
Three Sisters (Whitehall) 27 May
Tinka's New Dress (Barbican Pit) 23 June
La Traviata (Sadler's Wells) 12 Oct
Triple Bill – Birmingham Royal Ballet (Sadler's Wells) 10 Feb
Triple Bill – Royal Ballet (Sadler's Wells) 9 July
Troilus and Cressida (National Olivier) 15 March
The Turn of the Screw (Sadler's Wells) 23 July
Twelfth Night (Open Air) 4 June
Two Gentlemen of Verona (National Cottesloe) 5 May
Ute Lemper – Life's a Swindle (Queen's) 25 Oct
Vassa (Albery) 26 Jan
Victory Over the Sun (Barbican Pit) 18 June
Viktor – Tanztheater Wuppertal Pina Bausch (Sadler's Wells) 27 Jan
Viva! City Ballet of London (Peacock) 9 Nov
Volpone (Barbican Pit) 9 Dec
Wadalka Yamato (Peacock) 18 May
Waiting for Godot (Barbican) 1 Sept
West Side Story (Prince of Wales) 25 Jan
What Where (Barbican Pit) 7 Sept
White Oak Dance Project (Sadler's Wells) 9 June

...August 24...
Edward Windsor, better known as Prince Edward, recruits top Hollywood stars to participate in a documentary on the paparazzi being made by his TV company.

Wild Air – Siobhan Davies Dance Company (Sadler's Wells) 29 Sept

The Winter's Tale (Barbican) 12 April

Wizadora – The Magic Adventure (Barbican) 3 Aug

Yernaya – Goddess of the Sea (Barbican Pit) 27 May

Closings

2 Pianos 4 Hands (Comedy) 6 Dec

4 Steps to Heaven (Piccadilly) 2 Oct

50 Revolutions (Whitehall) 25 Sept

110 in the Shade (Fortune) 25 July

Act Without Words I (Barbican Pit) 8 Sept

Act Without Words II (Barbican Pit) 2 Sept

Al Murray – The Pub Landlord (New Ambassadors) 19 Dec

Alarms & Excursions (Gielgud) 6 March

Amadeus (Old Vic) 5 June

Andalusia: The Last Glory – Caraealia Dance Company (Peacock) 9 Oct

Animal Crackers (Lyric) 15 May

Anna Wiess (Whitehall) 18 Dec

Annie (Victoria Palace) 28 Feb

Antigone (Old Vic) 18 Dec

Antony and Cleopatra (Shakespeare's Globe) 26 Sept

Audra McDonald (Donmar Warehouse) 28 Aug

Augustine's Oak (Shakespeare's Globe) 24 Sept

Bad Weather (Barbican Pit) 13 March

The Ballad of Solomon Pavey (Shakespeare's Globe) 3 Oct

The Barber of Seville (Peacock) 4 Sept

The Barber of Seville (Coliseum) 11 Feb

The Bartered Bride (Sadler's Wells) 14 Jan

Bartholomew Fair (Young Vic) 25 March

La Bayadère (Coliseum) 17 July

Beauty and the Beast (Dominion) 11 Dec

Betrayal (National Lyttelton) 7 April

The Birthday Party (Piccadilly) 3 July

Black on White (Barbican) 3 July

Boogie Nights (Savoy) 9 Jan

Boris Godunov (Coliseum) 5 Aug

Boyband (Gielgud) 14 Aug

Breath (Barbican Pit) 18 Sept

The Breathing Show – Bill T. Jones (Sadler's Wells) 10 Nov

The Carmelites (Coliseum) 10 June

Carmen (Coliseum) 1 July

Catastrophe (Barbican Pit) 15 Oct

Cinderella (Coliseum) 16 Jan

City – Odessa Stories (Barbican) 5 June

Cleo, Camping, Emmanuelle and Dick (National Lyttelton) 16 Jan

The Colleen Bawn (National Lyttelton) 27 March

The Colour of Justice (Victoria Palace) 13 March

The Colour of Justice (National Lyttelton) 25 Sept

Come and Go (Barbican Pit) 2 Sept

The Comedy of Errors (Shakespeare's Globe) 25 Sept

Copenhagen (National Cottesloe) 27 Jan

Crease (Cambridge) 4 Sept

Cruel Garden: Rambert Dance Company (Sadler's Wells) 29 May

The Darker Face of the Earth (National Cottesloe) 11 Nov

Defending the Covenant (Apollo) 11 Sept

The Diary of One Who Vanished (National Lyttelton) 6 Nov

Diva on the Verge – Julia Migenes (Peacock) 8 March

Doctor Dolittle (London Apollo Hammersmith) 26 June

Don Giovanni (Sadler's Wells) 16 Oct

Don Quixote (Coliseum) 31 July

Dracula – Northern Ballet Theatre (Sadler's Wells) 27 March

Dreaming (Queen's) 17 July

Drummers (New Ambassadors) 9 Oct

East (Vaudeville) 6 Nov

Edward II Birmingham Royal Ballet (Sadler's Wells) 6 Feb

Endgame (Barbican) 18 Sept

Enio Marcheto (Queen's) 23 Oct

Eurydice (Whitehall) 14 Aug

Falstaff (Peacock) 3 Sept

Falstaff (Royal Opera House) 22 Dec

Fame (Prince of Wales) 16 Jan

Fascinating Aida – Barefaced Chic! (Haymarket) 13 March

Figaro's Wedding (Coliseum) 28 Oct

Filumena (Piccadilly) 27 Feb

Finian's Rainbow (Fortune) 26 Sept

Footfalls (Barbican Pit) 11 Sept

Forbidden Broadway (Albery) 4 Sept

The Forest (National Lyttelton) 1 May

Der Freischutz (Coliseum) 15 Oct

A Funny Thing Happened on the Way to the Forum (Open Air) 31 Aug

Furioso: Meryl Tankard Australian Dance Theatre (Sadler's Wells) 8 May

The Game of Love and Chance (Barbican) 22 June

La Gatta Cenorentala (Sadler's Wells) 6 Nov

Geometry of Miracles (National Lyttelton) 24 April

Giselle (Sadler's Wells) 16 July

Giselle, Paganini (Coliseum) 10 July

The Gin Game (Savoy) 22 May

The Golden Cockerel (Sadler's Wells) 16 Jan

Good (Donmar Warehouse) 22 May

Goodnight Children Everywhere (Barbican Pit) 27 April

Great Balls of Fire (Cambridge) 18 Dec

Gross Indecency – The Three Trials of Oscar Wilde
(Gielgud) 17 April
Guiding Star (National Cottesloe) 5 April
Gumboots (Lyric) 9 Oct
Hans Liberg (Peacock) 6 Nov
Hansel and Gretel (Sadler's Wells) 1 April
Happy Days (Barbican) 11 Sept
Haroun and the Sea of Stories (National Cottesloe)
6 Jan
Hay Fever (Savoy) 11 Sept
Holly Mothers (New Ambassadors) 3 July
Hot Mouth (Peacock) 1 May
I'd Rather Be Right (Fortune) 30 May
An Ideal Husband (Lyric) 6 March
I Love You, You're Perfect, Now Change (Comedy)
25 Sept
The Importance of Being Ernest (Haymarket) 6 Nov
The Innovation of Love (Haymarket) 6 Feb
Into the Woods (Donmar Warehouse) 13 Feb
Irek Mukhamedov and Company (Sadler's Wells) 23 Oct
Jane Eyre (New Ambassadors) 24 Dec
Jeffrey Bernard is Unwell (Old Vic) 25 Sept
Jessye Norman (Barbican) 31 July
Jesus, My Boy (Apollo) 6 Feb
Jubilee (Her Majesty's) 28 Nov
Julius Caesar (Shakespeare's Globe) 21 Sept
Juno and the Paycock (Donmar Warehouse) 6 Nov
Kafka's Dick (Piccadilly) 26 Feb
Kathakall – King Lear (Shakespeare's Globe) 17 July
Katya Kabanova (Sadler's Wells) 15 Oct
King Lear (Barbican) 20 Nov
King Priam (Coliseum) 5 Nov
Krapp's Last Tape (Barbican Pit) 12 Sept
Last Dance at Dum Dum (New Ambassadors) 28 Aug
The Last Fattybottypuss in the World (Open Air) 31 Aug
Lenny (Queen's) 16 Oct
Life is a Dream (Barbican) 2 Oct
The Lion, the Witch and the Wardrobe (Barbican) 8 May
Little Malcolm and His Struggle With the Eunuchs
(Comedy) 13 March
Look Back in Anger (National Lyttelton) 18 Sept
The Love for Three Oranges (Coliseum) 7 Aug
Love Letters (Haymarket) 1 Aug
Love Upon the Throne (Comedy) 9 Jan
Macbeth (Queen's) 5 June
Making Noise Quietly (Whitehall) 22 May
Mark Morris Dance Group (Sadler's Wells) 9 Oct
Measure for Measure (Barbican) 2 March
The Memory of Water (Vaudeville) 22 May
Mephistopheles (Coliseum) 29 April
The Merchant of Venice (Barbican) 6 March
The Merchant of Venice (National Cottesloe) 13 Nov
The Merry Wives of Windsor (Open Air) 4 Sept

Midsummer Night's Dream – Pacific Northwest Ballet
(Sadler's Wells) 27 Feb
Miss Saigon (Drury Lane) 30 Oct
Mixed Programme – Pacific Northwest Ballet (Sadler's
Wells) 24 Feb
Mixed Programme – Rambert Dance Company
(Sadler's Wells) 22 May
Money (National Olivier) 13 Nov
A Month in the Country (Barbican Pit) 8 May
Morphic Resonance (Donmar Warehouse) 27 Feb
Mr. Puntila and His Man Matil (Albery) 9 Jan
Musa Gitana – Paco Peña Flamenco Dance Company
(Peacock) 7 March
National Youth Ballet (Sadler's Wells) 8 Nov
Nederlands Dans Theater 1 (Sadler's Wells) 17 June
The New Rocky Horror Show (Victoria Palace) 6 June
Night Life – Scottish Ballet (Sadler's Wells) 5 June
Not I (Barbican Pit) 8 Sept
The Nutcracker (Coliseum) 9 Jan
The Nutcracker (Lyceum) 9 Jan
Oh! What a Night (London Apollo Hammersmith)
16 Oct
Ohio Impromptu (Barbican Pit) 15 Sept
Oklahoma! (Lyceum) 26 June
On the Road to Baghdad – Green Candle Dance Co
(Sadler's Wells) 14 March
Ondine (Sadler's Wells) 31 July
Opening Celebration (Royal Opera House) 4 Dec
Orfeo (Coliseum) 18 Oct
Orpheus and Eurydice (Coliseum) 31 March
Our Late Night (New Ambassadors) 6 Nov
The Pajama Game (Victoria Palace) 18 Dec
Parsifal (Coliseum) 19 March
Patti Lupone (Donmar Warehouse) 21 Aug
Paul Bunyan (Sadler's Wells) 1 May
Penny For a Song (Whitehall) 6 Nov
Perfect Days (Vaudeville) 4 Sept
Peter Grimes (Sadler's Wells) 3 April
Peter Grimes (Coliseum) 7 Dec
Peter Pan (National Olivier) 20 Jan
A Piece of Monologue (Barbican Pit) 18 Sept
The Pirates of Penzance (Queen's) 9 Jan
Platonov or The Play With No Name (Barbican) 13 June
Play (Barbican Pit) 2 Sept
Plenty (Albery) 24 July
The Prisoner of Second Avenue (Haymarket) 3 July
Private Lives (National Lyttelton) 6 Sept
Programme 1 – Rambert Dance Company (Sadler's
Wells) 27 Nov
Programme 2 – Rambert Dance Company (Sadler's
Wells) 1 Dec
Programme 3 – Rambert Dance Company (Sadler's
Wells) 4 Dec

Programme 1 – San Francisco Ballet (Sadler's Wells) 25 Oct

Programme 2 – San Francisco Ballet (Sadler's Wells) 27 Oct

Programme A – Les Ballets Trockadero de Monte Carlo (Peacock) 18 Sept

Programme B – Les Ballets Trockadero de Monte Carlo (Peacock) 25 Sept

Purgatory (Barbican Pit) 27 March

Raymonda (Coliseum) 21 July

The Real Thing (Donmar Warehouse) 7 Aug

Remember This (National Lyttelton) 23 Nov

Rent (Shaftesbury) 30 Oct

The Return of Don Juan, The Arc Dance Company (Sadler's Wells) 3 March

Richard III (Savoy) 2 March

Ricky Jay & His 52 Assistants (Old Vic) 17 July

Riders to the Sea (Barbican Pit) 27 March

Rigoletto (Coliseum) 3 July

The Riot (National Cottesloe) 28 April

Roberto Zucco (Barbican Pit) 1 May

Rockaby (Barbican Pit) 11 Sept

Romeo and Juliet (Royal Festival Hall) 16 Jan

Romeo and Juliet (Sadler's Wells) 20 Nov

Rose (National Cottesloe) 8 Sept

Der Rosenkavalier (Coliseum) 25 Sept

Rota – Deborak Colker Dance Company (Peacock) 15 May

Rough for Theatre I (Barbican Pit) 11 Sept

Rough for Theatre II (Barbican Pit) 15 Sept

Salome (Coliseum) 20 April

Sam Brown (Donmar Warehouse) 4 Sept

Scenes From an Execution (Barbican Pit) 9 Oct

Sell Out (New Ambassadors) 4 July

Semele (Coliseum) 28 May

Sensaclones – Compania Sara Baras (Sadler's Wells) 25 Sept

The Shadow of the Glen (Barbican Pit) 29 March

Shazami – DCA (Barbican) 17 July

Shijma – Sankai Juku (Sadler's Wells) 22 Jan

Slava's Snowshow (Piccadilly) 10 April

Sleep With Me (National Cottesloe) 17 July

The Snowman (Peacock) 30 Jan

Some Explicit Polaroids (New Ambassadors) 20 Nov

Songs of the Wanderers – Cloud Gate Dance Theatre (Sadler's Wells) 17 April

Sooty's Magical Mystery Show (Savoy) 9 Jan

Soul Train (Victoria Palace) 4 Sept

Sparkleshark (National Lyttelton) 25 June

Spartacus (Coliseum) 24 July

Splash Hatch on the E Going Down (Donmar Warehouse) 27 Feb

St. Petersburg Legacy (Barbican Pit) 12 June

The Street of Crocodiles (Queen's) 20 Feb

Strob (Barbican) 22 May

Suddenly Last Summer (Comedy) 10 July

Summerfolk (National Olivier) 23 Nov

Swan Lake (Royal Albert Hall) 26 June

Swan Lake (Coliseum) 27 July

Swan Lake (Sadler's Wells) 30 Oct

Talk of the City (Young Vic) 27 March

The Taming of the Shrew (Barbican Pit) 20 Nov

Tango Pasion (Lyric) 31 July

The Tempest (Barbican) 4 March

That Time (Barbican Pit) 18 Sept

Things We Do for Love (Duchess) 30 Jan

Three Days of Rain (Donmar Warehouse) 13 March

Three Sisters (Whitehall) 3 July

Tinka's New Dress (Barbican Pit) 10 July

La Traviata (Coliseum) 11 March

La Traviata (Sadler's Wells) 16 Oct

Triple Bill – Birmingham Royal Ballet (Sadler's Wells) 13 Feb

Triple Bill – Royal Ballet (Sadler's Wells) 13 July

Troilus and Cressida (National Olivier) 24 July

The Turn of the Screw Programme (Sadler's Wells) 29 July

Twelfth Night (Open Air) 2 Sept

Two Gentlemen of Verona (Barbican Pit) 28 Jan

Two Gentlemen of Verona (National Cottesloe) 6 May

Ute Lemper – Life's a Swindle (Queen's) 7 Nov

Vassa (Albery) 27 March

Victory over the Sun (Barbican Pit) 20 June

Viktor – Tanztheater Wuppertal Pina Bausch (Sadler's Wells) 27 Jan

Wadalka Yamato (Peacock) 22 May

Waiting for Godot (Barbican) 12 Sept

West Side Story (Prince Edward) 16 Jan

What Where (Barbican Pit) 8 Sept

White Oak Dance Project (Sadler's Wells) 12 June

Wild Air – Siobhan Davies Dance Company (Sadler's Wells) 2 Oct

The Winter's Tale (Barbican) 6 May

Wizadora – The Magic Adventure (Barbican) 7 Aug

Yernaya – Goddess of the Sea (Barbican Pit) 28 May

The Tonys 1947–99

Founded by the American Theater Wing in 1947 in memory of Antoinette Perry, the glamorous Tonys are Broadway's equivalent of the Emmys or the Academy Awards. Off-Broadway shows are not eligible for the awards, however, which is a bone of contention at a time when so much of the best American stage work is performed away from the traditional Broadway houses.

1947

Actors (dramatic): José Ferrer, *Cyrano de Bergerac;* Fredric March, *Years Ago*

Actresses (dramatic): Ingrid Bergman, *Joan of Lorraine;* Helen Hayes, *Happy Birthday*

Actress, supporting or featured (drama): Patricia Neal, *Another Part of the Forest*

Actor, supporting or featured (musical): David Wayne, *Finian's Rainbow*

Author: Arthur Miller, *All My Sons*

Composer: Kurt Weill, *Street Scene*

Director: Elia Kazan, *All My Sons*

Costumes: Lucinda Ballard, *Happy Birthday/ Another Part of the Forest/ Street Scene/ John Loves Mary/ The Chocolate Soldier*

Scenic designer: David Ffolkes, *Henry VIII*

Choreographers: Agnes de Mille, *Brigadoon;* Michael Kidd, *Finian's Rainbow*

Special awards: Dora Chamberlain, Mr. & Mrs. Ira Katzenberg, Jules Leventhal, Burns Mantle, P.A. MacDonald, Vincent Sardi, Sr.

1948

Actors (dramatic): Henry Fonda, *Mister Roberts;* Paul Kelly, *Command Decision;* Basil Rathbone, *The Heiress*

Actresses (dramatic): Judith Anderson, *Medea;* Katharine Cornell, *Antony and Cleopatra;* Jessica Tandy, *A Streetcar Named Desire*

Actor (musical): Paul Hartman, *Angel in the Wings*

Actress (musical): Grace Hartman, *Angel in the Wings*

Play: *Mister Roberts* by Thomas Heggen & Joshua Logan (based on the novel by Thomas Heggen)

Producer: Leland Hayward, *Mister Roberts*

Authors: Thomas Heggen & Joshua Logan, *Mister Roberts*

Costumes: Mary Percy Schenck, *The Heiress*

Scenic designer: Horace Armistead, *The Medium*

Choreographer: Jerome Robbins, *High Button Shoes*

Conductor & musical director: Max Meth, *Finian's Rainbow*

Stage technician: George Gebhardt

Outstanding performance by newcomers: June Lockhart, *For Love or Money;* James Whitmore, *Command Decision*

Outstanding foreign company: The cast of *The Importance of Being Ernest*

Spreading theater to the country while the originals perform in New York: Mary Martin, *Annie Get Your Gun;* Joe E. Brown, *Harvey*

Experiment in theater: Experimental Theater Inc., accepted by John Garfield

Progressive theater operators: Robert W. Dowling, Paul Beisman

Contribution to theater through a publication: Rosalind Gilder, editor, *Theater Arts*

Contribution to development of regional theater: Robert Porterfield, Virginia Barter Theater

Distinguished wing volunteer worker through the war and after: Vera Allen

Special award: George Pierce

1949

Actor (dramatic): Rex Harrison, *Anne of the Thousand Days*

Actress (dramatic): Martita Hunt, *The Madwoman of Chaillot*

Actor, supporting or featured (dramatic): Arthur Kennedy, *Death of a Salesman*

Actress, supporting or featured (dramatic): Shirley Booth, *Goodbye My Fancy*

Actor (musical): Ray Bolger, *Where's Charley?*

Actress (musical): Nanette Fabray, *Love Life*

Play: *Death of a Salesman* by Arthur Miller

Producers (dramatic): Kermit Bloomgarden & Walter Fried, *Death of a Salesman*

Author: Arthur Miller, *Death of a Salesman*

Director: Elia Kazan, *Death of a Salesman*

Musical: *Kiss Me Kate,* book by Bella & Samuel Spewack, music & lyrics by Cole Porter

Producers (musical): Saint-Subber & Lemuel Ayers, *Kiss Me Kate*

Authors (musical): Bella & Samuel Spewack, *Kiss Me Kate*

Composer & lyricist: Cole Porter, *Kiss Me Kate*

Costumes: Lemuel Ayers, *Kiss Me Kate*

...August 28...
The Sixth Sense led the box office for the fourth straight week.

Scenic designer: Jo Mielziner, *Sleepy Hollow/ Summer and Smoke/ Anne of the Thousand Days/ Death of a Salesman/ South Pacific*

Choreographer: Gower Champion, *Lend an Ear*

Conductor & musical director: Max Meth, *As the Girls Go*

1950

Actor (dramatic): Sidney Blackmer, *Come Back, Little Sheba*

Actress (dramatic): Shirley Booth, *Come Back, Little Sheba*

Actor (musical): Ezio Pinza, *South Pacific*

Actress (musical): Mary Martin, *South Pacific*

Actor, supporting or featured (musical): Myron McCormick, *South Pacific*

Actress, supporting or featured (musical): Juanita Hall, *South Pacific*

Play: *The Cocktail Party* by T.S. Eliot, produced by Gilbert Miller

Director: Joshua Logan, *South Pacific*

Musical: *South Pacific*, book by Oscar Hammerstein II & Joshua Logan, music by Richard Rodgers, lyrics by Oscar Hammerstein II, produced by Leland Hayward, Oscar Hammerstein II, Joshua Logan, & Richard Rodgers

Libretto: Oscar Hammerstein II & Joshua Logan, *South Pacific*

Score: Richard Rodgers, *South Pacific*

Costumes: Aline Bernstein, *Regina*

Scenic designer: Jo Mielziner, *The Innocents*

Choreographer: Helen Tamiris, *Touch and Go*

Conductor & musical director: Maurice Abravanel, *Regina*

Stage technician: Joe Lynn, master propertyman, *Miss Liberty*

Special awards: Maurice Evans, Mrs. Eleanor Roosevelt, Brock Pemberton

1951

Actor (dramatic): Claude Rains, *Darkness at Noon*

Actress (dramatic): Uta Hagen, *The Country Girl*

Actor, supporting or featured (dramatic): Eli Wallach, *The Rose Tattoo*

Actress, supporting or featured (dramatic): Maureen Stapleton, *The Rose Tattoo*

Actor (musical): Robert Alda, *Guys and Dolls*

Actress (musical): Ethel Merman, *Call Me Madam*

Actor, supporting or featured (musical): Russell Nype, *Call Me Madam*

Actress, supporting or featured (musical): Isabel Bigley, *Guys and Dolls*

Play: *The Rose Tattoo* by Tennesse Williams, produced by Cheryl Crawford

Director: George S. Kaufman, *Guys and Dolls*

Musical: *Guys and Dolls*, book by Jo Swerling & Abe Burrows, music & lyrics by Frank Loesser, produced by Cy Feuer & Ernest H. Martin

Outstanding musical score: Irving Berlin, *Call Me Madam*

Costumes: Miles White, *Bless You All*

Scenic designer: Boris Aronson, *The Rose Tattoo/ The Country Girl/ Season in the Sun*

Choreographer: Michael Kidd, *Guys and Dolls*

Conductor & musical director: Lehman Engel, *The Consul*

Stage technician: Richard Raven, master electrician, *The Autumn Garden*

Special award: Ruth Green

1952

Actor (dramatic): José Ferrer, *The Shrike*

Actress (dramatic): Julie Harris, *I Am a Camera*

Actor (musical): Phil Silvers, *Top Banana*

Actress (musical): Gertrude Lawrence, *The King & I*

Actor, supporting or featured (dramatic): John Crombwell, *Point of No Return*

Actress, supporting or featured (dramatic): Marian Winters, *I Am a Camera*

Actor, supporting or featured (musical): Yul Brynner, *The King & I*

Actress, supporting or featured (musical): Helen Gallagher, *Pal Joey*

Play: *The Fourposter* by Jan de Hartog

Musical: *The King & I*, book & lyrics by Oscar Hammerstein II, music by Richard Rodgers

Director: José Ferrer, *The Shrike/The Fourposter/ Stalag 17*

Costumes: Irene Sharaff, *The King & I*

Scenic designer: Jo Mielziner, *The King & I*

Choreographer: Robert Alton, *Pal Joey*

Conductor & musical director: Max Meth, *Pal Joey*

Stage technician: Peter Feller, master carpenter, *Call Me Madam*

Special awards: Judy Garland, Edward Kook, Charles Boyer

1953

Actor (dramatic): Tom Ewell, *The Seven Year Itch*

Actress (dramatic): Shirley Booth, *Time of the Cuckoo*

Actor, supporting or featured (dramatic): John Williams, *Dial M For Murder*

Actress, supporting or featured (dramatic): Beatrice Straight, *The Crucible*

Actor (musical): Thomas Mitchell, *Hazel Flagg*

Actress (musical): Rosalind Russell, *Wonderful Town*

Actor, supporting or featured (musical): Hiram Sherman, *Two's Company*

Actress, supporting or featured (musical): Sheila Bond, *Wish You Were Here*

Play: *The Crucible* by Arthur Miller, produced by Kermit Bloomgarden

Director: Joshua Logan, *Picnic*

Musical: *Wonderful Town*, book by Joseph Fields & Jerome Chodorov, music by Leonard Bernstein, lyrics by Betty Comden & Adolph Green, produced by Robert Fryer

Costume designer: Miles White, *Hazel Flagg*

Scenic designer: Raoul Pène Du Bois, *Wonderful Town*

Choreographer: Donald Saddler, *Wonderful Town*

Conductor & musical director: Lehman Engel, *Wonderful Town* and Gilbert & Sullivan Season

Stage technician: Abe Kurnit, *Wish You Were Here*

Special awards: Beatrice Lillie, Danny Kaye, Equity Community Theater

1954

Actor (dramatic): David Wayne, *The Teahouse of the August Moon*

Actress (dramatic): Audrey Hepburn, *Ondine*

Actor, supporting or featured (dramatic): John Kerr, *Tea and Sympathy*

Actress, supporting or featured (dramatic): Jo Van Fleet, *The Trip to Bountiful*

Actor (musical): Alfred Drake, *Kismet*

Actress (musical): Dolores Gray, *Carnival in Flanders*

Actor, supporting or featured (musical): Harry Belafonte, *John Murray Anderson's Almanac*

Actress, supporting or featured (musical): Gwen Verdon, *Can-Can*

Play: *The Teahouse of the August Moon* by John Patrick, produced by Maurice Evans & George Schaefer

Director: Alfred Lunt, *Ondine*

Musical: *Kismet*, book by Charles Lederer & Luther Davis, music by Alexander Borodin, adapted & with lyrics by Robert Wright & George Forrest, produced by Charles Lederer

Costume designer: Richard Whorf, *Ondine*

Scenic designer: Peter Larkin, *Ondine* and *The Teahouse of the August Moon*

Choreographer: Michael Kid, *Can-Can*

Musical conductor: Louis Adrian, *Kismet*

Stage technician: John Davis, *Picnic*

1955

Actor (dramatic): Alfred Lunt, *Quadrille*

Actress (dramatic): Nancy Kelly, *The Bad Seed*

Actor, supporting or featured (dramatic): Francis L. Sullivan, *Witness for the Prosecution*

Actress, supporting or featured (dramatic): Patricia Jessel, *Witness for the Prosecution*

Actor (musical): Walter Slezak, *Fanny*

Actress (musical): Mary Martin, *Peter Pan*

Actor, supporting or featured (musical): Cyril Ritchard, *Peter Pan*

Actress, supporting or featured (musical): Carol Haney, *The Pajama Game*

Play: *The Desperate Hours* by Joseph Hayes, produced by Howard Erskine & Joseph Hayes

Director: Robert Montgomery, *The Desperate Hours*

Musical: *The Pajama Game*, book by George Abbott & Richard Bissell, music & lyrics by Richard Adler & Jerry Ross

Costume designer: Cecil Beaton, *Quadrille*

Scenic designer: Oliver Messel, *House of Flowers*

Choreographer: Bob Fosse, *The Pajama Game*

Conductor & musical director: Thomas Schippers, *The Saint of Bleecker Street*

Stage technician: Richard Rodda, *Peter Pan*

Special award: Proscenium Productions

1956

Actor (dramatic): Paul Muni, *Inherit the Wind*

Actress (dramatic): Julie Harris, *The Lark*

Actor, supporting or featured (dramatic): Ed Begley, *Inherit the Wind*

Actress, supporting or featured (dramatic): Una Merkel, *The Ponder Heart*

Actor (musical): Ray Walston, *Damn Yankees*

Actress (musical): Gwen Verdon, *Phoenix '55*

Actor, supporting or featured (musical): Russ Brown, *Damn Yankees*

Actress, supporting or featured (musical): Lotte Lenya, *The Threepenny Opera*

Play: *The Diary of Anne Frank* by Frances Goodrich & Albert Hackett, produced by Kermit Bloomgarden

Director: Tyrone Guthrie, *The Matchmaker*

Musical: *Damn Yankees* by George Abbott & Douglass Wallop, music by Richard Adler & Jerry Ross, produced by Frederick Brisson, Robert Griffith, & Harold S. Prince in association with Albert B. Taylor

Conductor & musical director: Hal Hastings, *Damn Yankees*

Scenic designer: Peter Larkin, *Inherit the Wind/No Time for Sergeants*

Costume designer: Alvin Colt, *Pipe Dream*

Choreographer: Bob Fosse, *Damn Yankees*

Stage technician: Harry Green, electrician & sound man, *Middle of the Night/Damn Yankees*

...August 30...
Arnold Schwarzenegger is to star in **Seven Men From Now**, a contemporary remake of the 1956 western.

Special awards: City Center, Fourth Street Chekhov Theater, The Shakespearewright, *The Threepenny Opera*, The Theater Collection of the N.Y. Public Library

1957

Actor (dramatic): Fredric March, *Long Day's Journey into Night*
Actress (dramatic): Margaret Leighton, *Separate Tables*
Actor, supporting or featured (dramatic): Frank Conroy, *The Potting Shed*
Actress, supporting or featured (dramatic): Peggy Cass, *Auntie Mame*
Actor (musical): Rex Harrison, *My Fair Lady*
Actress (musical): Judy Holliday, *Bells Are Ringing*
Actor, supporting or featured (musical): Sydney Chaplin, *Bells Are Ringing*
Actress, supporting or featured (musical): Edith Adams, *Li'l Abner*
Play: *Long Day's Journey Into Night* by Eugene O'Neill, produced by Leigh Connell, Theodore Mann, & José Quintero
Director: Moss Hart, *My Fair Lady*
Musical: *My Fair Lady*, book & lyrics by Alan Jay Lerner, music by Frederick Loewe, produced by Herman Levin
Conductor & musical director: Franz Allers, *My Fair Lady*
Scenic designer: Oliver Smith, *My Fair Lady*
Costume designer: Cecil Beaton, *My Fair Lady*
Choreographer: Michael Kidd, *Li'l Abner*
Stage technician: Howard McDonald (posthumous), carpenter, *Major Barbara*
Special awards: American Shakespeare Festival, Stratford, Connecticut; Jean-Louis Barrault-French Repertory; Robert Russell Bennett, William Hammerstein; Paul Shyre

1958

Actor (dramatic): Ralph Bellamy, *Sunrise at Campobello*
Actress (dramatic): Helen Hayes, *Time Remembered*
Actor, supporting or featured (dramatic): Henry Jones, *Sunrise at Campobello*
Actress, supporting or featured (dramatic): Anne Bancroft, *Two For the Seesaw*
Actor (musical): Robert Preston, *The Music Man*
Actress (musical): Thelma Ritter, *New Girl in Town*, Gwen Verdon, *New Girl in Town*
Actor, supporting or featured (musical): David Burns, *The Music Man*
Actress, supporting or featured (musical): Barbara Cook, *The Music Man*

Play: *Sunrise at Campobello* by Dore Schary, produced by Lawrence Langner, Theresa Helburn, Armina Marshall, & Dore Schary
Director: Vincent J. Donehue, *Sunrise at Campobello*
Musical: *The Music Man*, book by Meredith Wilson & Franklin Lacey, music & lyrics by Meredith Wilson, produced by Kermit Bloomgarden & Herbert Greene, in association with Frank Productions
Conductor & musical director: Herbert Greene, *The Music Man*
Scenic designer: Oliver Smith, *West Side Story*
Costume designer: Motley, *The First Gentleman*
Choreographer: Jerome Robbins, *West Side Story*
Stage technician: Harry Romar, *Time Remembered*
Special awards: New York Shakespeare Festival, Mrs. Martin Beck

1959

Actor (dramatic): Jason Robards, Jr., *The Disenchanted*
Actress (dramatic): Gertrude Berg, *A Majority of One*
Actor, supporting or featured (dramatic): Charlie Ruggles, *The Pleasure of His Company*
Actress, supporting or featured (dramatic): Julie Newmar, *The Marriage-Go-Round*
Actor (musical): Richard Kiley, *Redhead*
Actress (musical): Gwen Verdon, *Redhead*
Actor, supporting or featured (musical): Russel Nype, *Goldilocks*
Actress, supporting or featured (musical): Pat Stanley, *Goldilocks*
Play: *J.B.* by Archibald MacLeish, produced by Alfred de Liagre, Jr.
Director: Elia Kazan, *J.B.*
Musical: *Redhead* by Herbert & Dorothy Fields, Sidney Sheldon, & David Shaw, music by Albert Hague, lyrics by Dorothy Fields
Conductor & musical director: Salvatore Dell'Isola, *Flower Drum Song*
Scenic designer: Donald Oenslager, *A Majority of One*
Costume designer: Rouben Ter-Arutunian, *Redhead*
Choreographer: Bob Fosse, *Redhead*
Stage technician: Sam Knapp, *The Music Man*
Special awards: John Gielgud; Howard Lindsay & Russell Crouse; the cast of *La Plume de ma Tante*

1960

Actor (dramatic): Melvyn Douglas, *The Best Man*
Actress (dramatic): Anne Bancroft, *The Miracle Worker*
Actor, supporting or featured (dramatic): Roddy McDowall, *The Fighting Cock*
Actress, supporting or featured (dramatic): Anne Revere, *Toys in the Attic*

...August 31...

Star Wars: Episode I – the Phantom Menace blasts past the $300 million mark abroad, making the prequel the 11th most successful grosser of all time outside North America.

Actor (musical): Jackie Gleason, *Take Me Along*
Actress (musical): Mary Martin, *The Sound of Music*
Actor, supporting or featured (musical): Tom Bosley, *Fiorello!*
Actress, supporting or featured (musical): Patricia Neway, *The Sound of Music*
Play: *The Miracle Worker* by William Gibson, produced by Fred Coe
Director: Arthur Penn, *The Miracle Worker*
Musical: *Fiorello!* by Jerome Weidman & George Abbott, lyrics by Sheldon Harnick, music by Jerry Bock, produced by Robert E. Griffith & Harold S. Prince; *The Sound of Music* by Howard Lindsay & Russell Crouse, lyrics by Oscar Hammerstein II, music by Richard Rodgers, produced by Leland Hayward, Richard Halliday & Rodgers & Hammerstein
Director (musical): George Abbott, *Fiorello!*
Conductor & musical director: Frederick Dvonch, *The Sound of Music*
Scenic designer (dramatic): Howard Bay, *Toys in the Attic*
Scenic designer (musical): Oliver Smith, *The Sound of Music*
Costume designer: Cecil Beaton, *Saratoga*
Choreographer: Michael Kidd, *Destry Rides Again*
Stage technician: John Walters, chief carpenter, *The Miracle Worker*
Special awards: John D. Rockefeller III, James Thurber & Burgess Meredith, *A Thurber Carnival*

1961

Actor (dramatic): Zero Mostel, *Rhinoceros*
Actress (dramatic): Joan Plowright, *A Taste of Honey*
Actor, supporting or featured (dramatic): Martin Gavel, *Big Fish, Little Fish*
Actress, supporting or featured (dramatic): Colleen Dewhurst, *All the Way Home*
Actor (musical): Richard Burton, *Camelot*
Actress (musical): Elizabeth Seal, *Irma la Douce*
Actor, supporting or featured (musical): Dick Van Dyke, *Bye, Bye Birdie*
Actress, supporting or featured (musical): Tammy Grimes, *The Unsinkable Molly Brown*
Play: *Becket* by Jean Anouilh, produced by David Merrick
Director (dramatic): Sir John Gielgud, *Big Fish, Little Fish*
Musical: *Bye, Bye Birdie*, book by Michael Stewart, music by Charles Strouse, lyrics by Lee Adams, produced by Edward Padula in association with L. Slade Brown
Director (musical): Gower Champion, *Bye, Bye Birdie*

Conductor & musical director: Franz Allers, *Camelot*
Scenic designer (dramatic): Oliver Smith, *Becket*
Scenic designer (musical): Oliver Smith, *Camelot*
Costume designer (dramatic): Motley, *Becket*
Costume designer (musical): Adrian & Tony Duquette, *Camelot*
Choreographer: Gower Champion, *Bye, Bye Birdie*
Stage technician: Teddy Van Bemmel, *Becket*
Special awards: David Merrick, The Theater Guild

1962

Actor (dramatic): Paul Scofield, *A Man For All Seasons*
Actress (dramatic): Margaret Leighton, *Night of the Iguana*
Actor, supporting or featured (dramatic): Walter Matthau, *A Shot in the Dark*
Actress, supporting or featured (dramatic): Elizabeth Ashley, *Take Her, She's Mine*
Actor (musical): Robert Morse, *How to Succeed in Business Without Really Trying*
Actress (musical): Anna Maria Alberghetti, *Carnival*; Diahann Carroll, *No Strings*
Actor, supporting or featured (musical): Charles Nelson Reilly, *How to Succeed in Business Without Really Trying*
Actress, supporting or featured (musical): Phyliss Newman, *Subways Are For Sleeping*
Play: *A Man For All Seasons* by Robert Bolt, produced by Robert Whitehead & Roger L. Stevens
Producer (dramatic): Robert Whitehead & Roger L. Stevens, *A Man For All Seasons*
Director (dramatic): Noel Willman, *A Man For All Seasons*
Musical: *How to Succeed in Business Without Really Trying*, book by Abe Burrows, Jack Weinstock, & Willie Gilbert, music & lyrics by Frank Loesser, produced by Cy Feuer & Ernest Martin
Author (musical): Abe Burrows, Jack Weinstock, & Willie Gilbert, *How to Succeed in Business Without Really Trying*
Producer (musical): Cy Feuer & Ernest Martin, *How to Succeed in Business Without Really Trying*
Director (musical): Abe Burrows, *How to Succeed in Business Without Really Trying*
Composer: Richard Rodgers, *No Strings*
Conductor & musical director: Elliot Lawrence, *How to Succeed in Business Without Really Trying*
Scenic designer: Will Steven Armstrong, *Carnival*
Costume designer: Lucinda Ballard, *The Gay Life*
Choreographer: Agnes de Mille, *Kwamina*
Stage technician: Michael Burns, *A Man For All Seasons*
Special awards: Brooks Atkinson, Franco Zeffirelli, Richard Rodgers

1963

Actor (dramatic): Arthur Hill, *Who's Afraid of Virginia Woolf?*

Actress (dramatic): Uta Hagen, *A Man For All Seasons*

Actor, supporting or featured (dramatic): Alan Arkin, *Enter Laughing*

Actress, supporting or featured (dramatic): Sandy Dennis, *A Thousand Clowns*

Actor (musical): Zero Mostel, *A Funny Thing Happened on the Way to the Forum*

Actress (musical): Vivien Leigh, *Tovarich*

Actor, supporting or featured (musical): David Burns, *A Funny Thing Happened on the Way to the Forum*

Actress, supporting or featured (musical): Anna Quayle, *Stop the World – I Want to Get off*

Play: *Who's Afraid of Virginia Woolf?* by Edward Albee, produced by Theater 1963, Richard Barr, & Clinton Wilder

Producer (dramatic): Richard Barr & Clinton Wilder, Theater 1963, *Who's Afraid of Virginia Woolf?*

Director (dramatic): Alan Schneider, *Who's Afraid of Virginia Woolf?*

Musical: *A Funny Thing Happened on the Way to the Forum*, book by Burt Shevelove & Larry Gelbart, music & lyrics by Stephen Sondheim, produced by Harold Prince

Author (musical): Burt Shevelove & Larry Gelbart, *A Funny Thing Happened on the Way to the Forum*

Producer (musical): Harold Prince, *A Funny Thing Happened on the Way to the Forum*

Director (musical): George Abbott, *A Funny Thing Happened on the Way to the Forum*

Composer & lyricist: Lionel Bart, *Oliver!*

Conductor & musical director: Donal Pippin, *Oliver!*

Scenic designer: Sean Kenny, *Oliver!*

Costume designer: Anthony Powell, *The School For Scandal*

Choreographer: Bob Fosse, *Little Me*

Stage technician: Solly Pernick, *Mr. President*

Special awards: W. McNeil Lowry; Irving Berlin; Alan Bennett, Peter Cook, Jonathan Miller & Dudley Moore for *Beyond the Fringe*

1964

Actor (dramatic): Alec Guinness, *Dylan*

Actress (dramatic): Sandy Dennis, *Any Wednesday*

Actor, supporting or featured (dramatic): Hume Cronyn, *Hamlet*

Actress, supporting or featured (dramatic): Barbara Loden, *After the Fall*

Actor (musical): Bert Lahr, *Foxy*

Actress (musical): Carol Channing, *Hello Dolly!*

Actor, supporting or featured (musical): Jack Cassidy, *She Loves Me*

Actress, supporting or featured (musical): Tessie O'Shea, *The Girl Who Came to Supper*

Play: *Luther* by John Osborne, produced by David Merrick

Producer (dramatic): Herman Shumlin, *The Deputy*

Director (dramatic): Mike Nichols, *Barefoot in the Park*

Musical: *Hello, Dolly!* book by Michael Stewart, music & lyrics by Jerry Herman, produced by David Merrick

Author (musical): Michael Stewart, *Hello, Dolly!*

Producer (musical): David Merrick, *Hello, Dolly!*

Director (musical): Gower Champion, *Hello, Dolly!*

Composer & lyricist: Jerry Herman, *Hello, Dolly!*

Conductor & musical director: Shepard Coleman, *Hello, Dolly!*

Scenic designer: Oliver Smith, *Hello, Dolly!*

Costume designer: Freddy Wittop, *Hello, Dolly!*

Choreographer: Gower Champion, *Hello, Dolly!*

Special award: Eva Le Gallienne

1965

Actor (dramatic): Walter Matthau, *The Odd Couple*

Actress (dramatic): Irene Worth, *Tiny Alice*

Actor, supporting or featured (dramatic): Jack Albertson, *The Subject Was Roses*

Actress, supporting or featured (dramatic): Alice Ghostley, *The Sign in Sidney Brustein's Window*

Actor (musical): Zero Mostel, *Fiddler on the Roof*

Actress (musical): Liza Minnelli, *Flora, the Red Menace*

Actor, supporting or featured (musical): Victor Spinetti, *Oh, What a Lovely War*

Actress, supporting or featured (musical): Maria Karnilova, *Fiddler on the Roof*

Play: *The Subject Was Roses* by Frank Gilroy, produced by Edgar Lansbury

Author (dramatic): Neil Simon, *The Odd Couple*

Producer (dramatic): Claire Nichtern, *Luv*

Director (dramatic): Mike Nichols, *Luv* & *The Odd Couple*

Musical: *Fiddler on the Roof*, book by Joseph Stein, music by Jerry Bock, lyrics by Sheldon Harnick, produced by Harold Prince

Author (musical): Joseph Stein, *Fiddler on the Roof*

Producer (musical): Harold Prince, *Fiddler on the Roof*

Director (musical): Jerome Robbins, *Fiddler on the Roof*

Composer & lyricist: Jerry Bock & Sheldon Harnick, *Fiddler on the Roof*

...September 2...

Studios have been kicking the tires of **Gangs Of New York**, the period gangster drama being put together as a vehicle for director Martin Scorsese and Leonardo DiCaprio.

Scenic designer: Oliver Smith, *Baker Street, Luv & The Odd Couple*
Costume designer: Patricia Zipprodt, *Fiddler on the Roof*
Choreographer: Jerome Robbins, *Fiddler on the Roof*
Special awards: Gilbert Miller, Oliver Smith

1966

Actor (dramatic): Hal Holbrook, *Mark Twain Tonight!*
Actress (dramatic): Rosemary Harris, *The Lion in Winter*
Actor, supporting or featured (dramatic): Patrick Magee, *Marat/Sade*
Actress, supporting or featured (dramatic): Zoe Caldwell, *Slapstick Tragedy*
Actor (musical): Richard Kiley, *Man of La Mancha*
Actress (musical): Angela Lansbury, *Mame*
Actor, supporting or featured (musical): Frankie Michaels, *Mame*
Actress, supporting or featured (musical): Beatrice Arthur, *Mame*
Play: *Marat/Sade* by Peter Weiss, produced by David Merrick Arts Foundation
Director (dramatic): Peter Brook, *Marat/Sade*
Musical: *Man of La Mancha*, book by Dale Wasserman, music by Mitch Leigh, lyrics by Joe Darion, produced by Albert W. Selden & Hal James
Director (musical): Albert Marre, *Man of La Mancha*
Composer & lyricist: Mitch Leigh & Joe Darion, *Man of La Mancha*
Scenic designer: Howard Bay, *Man of La Mancha*
Costume designer: Gunilla Palmstierna-Weiss, *Marat/Sade*
Choreographer: Bob Fosse, *Sweet Charity*
Special award: Helen Menken (posthumous)

1967

Actor (dramatic): Paul Rogers, *The Homecoming*
Actress (dramatic): Beryl Reid, *The Killing of Sister George*
Actor, supporting or featured (dramatic): Ian Holm, *The Homecoming*
Actress, supporting or featured (dramatic): Marian Seldes, *A Delicate Balance*
Actor (musical): Robert Preston, *I Do! I Do!*
Actress (musical): Barbara Harris, *The Apple Tree*
Actor, supporting or featured (musical): Joel Grey, *Cabaret*
Actress, supporting or featured (musical): Peg Murray, *Cabaret*
Play: *The Homecoming* by Harold Pinter, produced by Alexander H. Cohen

Director (dramatic): Peter Hall, *The Homecoming*
Musical: *Cabaret*, book by Joe Masteroff, music by John Kander, lyrics by Fred Ebb, produced by Harold Prince in association with Ruth Mitchell
Director (musical): Harold Prince, *Cabaret*
Composer & lyricist: John Kander & Fred Ebb, *Cabaret*
Scene designer: Boris Aronson, *Cabaret*
Choreographer: Ron Field, *Cabaret*
Costume designer: Patricia Zipprodt, *Cabaret*

1968

Actor (dramatic): Martin Balsam, *You Know I Can't Hear You When the Water's Running*
Actress (dramatic): Zoe Caldwell, *The Prime of Miss Jean Brodie*
Actor, supporting or featured (dramatic): James Patterson, *The Birthday Party*
Actress, supporting or featured (dramatic): Zena Walker, *Joe Egg*
Actor (musical): Robert Goulet, *The Happy Time*
Actress (musical): Patricia Routledge, *Darling of the Day*; Leslie Uggams, *Hallelujah, Baby!*
Actor, supporting or featured (musical): Hiram Sherman, *How Now, Dow Jones*
Actress, supporting or featured (musical): Lilliam Hayman, *Hallelujah, Baby!*
Play: *Rosencrantz and Guildenstern Are Dead* by Tom Stoppard, produced by David Merrick Arts Foundation
Director (dramatic): Mike Nichols, *Plaza Suite*
Musical: *Hallelujah, Baby!* book by Arthur Laurentis, music by Jule Styne, lyrics by Betty Comden & Adolph Green, produced by Albert Selden, Hal James, Jane C. Nusbaum, & Harry Rigby
Producer (musical): Albert Selden, Hal James, Jane C. Nusbaum, & Harry Rigby, *Hallelujah, Baby!*
Director (musical): Gower Champion, *The Happy Time*
Composer & lyricist: Jule Styne, Betty Comden & Adolph Green, *Hallelujah, Baby!*
Scenic designer: Desmond Heeley, *Rosencrantz and Guildenstern Are Dead*
Costume designer: Desmond Heeley, *Rosencrantz and Guildenstern Are Dead*
Choreographer: Gower Champion, *The Happy Time*
Special awards: Audrey Hepburn, Carol Channing, Pearl Bailey, David Merrick, Maurice Chevalier, APA-Phoenix Theater, Marlene Dietrich

1969

Actor (dramatic): James Earl Jones, *The Great White Hope*

Actress (dramatic): Julie Harris, *Forty Carats*
Actor, supporting or featured (dramatic): Al Pacino, *Does a Tiger Wear a Necktie?*
Actress, supporting or featured (dramatic): Jane Alexander, *The Great White Hope*
Actor (musical): Jerry Orbach, *Promises, Promises*
Actress (musical): Angela Lansbury, *Dear World*
Actor, supporting or featured (musical): Ronald Holgate, *1776*
Actress, supporting or featured (musical): Marian Mercer, *Promises, Promises*
Play: *The Great White Hope* by Howard Sackler, produced by Herman Levin
Director (dramatic): Peter Dews, *Hadrian VII*
Musical: *1776*, book by Peter Stone, music & lyrics by Sherman Edwards, produced by Stuart Ostrow
Director (musical): Peter Hunt, *1776*
Scenic designer: Boris Aronson, *Zorba*
Costume designer: Louden Sainthill, *Canterbury Tales*
Choreographer: Joe Layton, *George M!*
Special awards: The National Theater Company of Great Britain, The Negro Ensemble Company, Rex Harrison, Leonard Bernstein, Carol Burnett

1970

Actor (dramatic): Fritz Weaver, *Child's Play*
Actress (dramatic): Tammy Grimes, *Private Lives* (Revival)
Actor, supporting or featured (dramatic): Ken Howard, *Child's Play*
Actress, supporting or featured (dramatic): Blythe Danner, *Butterflies Are Free*
Actor (musical): Cleavon Little, *Purlie*
Actress (musical): Lauren Bacall, *Applause*
Actor, supporting or featured (musical): René Auberjonois, *Coco*
Actress, supporting or featured (musical): Melba Moore, *Purlie*
Play: *Borstal Boy* by Frank McMahon, produced by Michael McAloney & Burton C. Kaiser
Director (dramatic): Joseph Hardy, *Child's Play*
Musical: *Applause*, book by Betty Comden & Adolph Green, music by Charles Strouse, lyrics by Lee Adams, produced by Joseph Kipness & Lawrence Kasha.
Director (musical): Ron Field, *Applause*
Scenic designer: Jo Mielziner, *Child's Play*
Costume designer: Cecil Beaton, *Coco*
Choreographer: Ron Field, *Applause*
Lighting designer: Jo Mielziner, *Child's Play*
Special awards: Sir Noel Coward, Alfred Lunt & Lynn Fontaine, New York Shakespeare Festival, Barbra Streisand

1971

Actor (dramatic): Brian Bedford, *The School For Wives*
Actress (dramatic): Maureen Stapleton, *Gingerbread Lady*
Actor, supporting or featured (dramatic): Paul Sand, *Story Theater*
Actress, supporting or featured (dramatic): Rae Allen, *And Miss Reardon Drinks a Little*
Actor (musical): Hal Linden, *The Rothschilds*
Actress (musical): Helen Gallagher, *No, No Nanette*
Actor, supporting or featured (musical): Keene Curtis, *The Rothschilds*
Actress, supporting or featured (musical): Patsy Kelly, *No, No Nanette*
Play: *Sleuth* by Anthony Shaffer, produced by Helen Bonfils, Morton Gottlieb, and Michael White
Producer (dramatic): Helen Bonfils, Morton Gottlieb, and Michael White, *Sleuth*
Director (dramatic): Peter Brook, *A Midsummer Night's Dream*
Musical: *Company*, produced by Harold Prince
Producer (musical): Harold Prince, *Company*
Director (musical): Harold Prince, *Company*
Book (musical): George Furth, *Company*
Lyrics (musical): Stephen Sondheim, *Company*
Score (musical): Stephen Sondheim, *Company*
Scenic designer: Boris Aronson, *Company*
Costume designer: Raoul Pène Du Bois, *No, No Nanette*
Choreographer: Donald Saddler, *No, No Nanette*
Lighting designer: H.R. Poindexter, *Story Theater*
Special awards: Elliot Norton, Ingram Ash, *Playbill*, Roger L. Stevens

1972

Actor (dramatic): Cliff Gorman, *Lenny*
Actress (dramatic): Sada Thompson, *Twigs*
Actor, supporting or featured (dramatic): Vincent Gardenia, *The Prisoner of Second Avenue*
Actress, supporting or featured (dramatic): Elizabeth Wilson, *Sticks and Bones*
Actor (musical): Phil Silvers, *A Funny Thing Happened on the Way to the Forum* (Revival)
Actress (musical): Alexis Smith, *Follies*
Actor, supporting or featured (musical): Larry Blyden, *A Funny Thing Happened on the Way to the Forum* (Revival)
Actress, supporting or featured (musical): Linda Hopkins, *Inner City*
Play: *Sticks and Bones* by David Rabe, produced by New York Shakespeare Festival-Joseph Papp
Director (dramatic): Mike Nichols, *The Prisoner of Second Avenue*

... September 4 ...

The summer of 1999 was the hottest ever. Box office for the 17-week span was a whisker less than $3.1 billion, approximately 19% higher than the record set one year ago.

Musical: *Two Gentlemen of Verona*, produced by New York Shakespeare Festival-Joseph Papp

Director (musical): Harold Prince & Michael Bennett, *Follies*

Book (musical): *Two Gentlemen of Verona* by John Guare & Mel Shapiro

Score (musical): *Follies*, music & lyrics by Stephen Sondheim

Scenic designer: Boris Aronson, *Follies*

Costume designer: Florence Klotz, *Follies*

Choreographer: Michael Bennett, *Follies*

Lighting designer: Tharon Musser, *Follies*

Special awards: The Theater Guild-American Theater Society, *Fiddler on the Roof*, Ethel Merman, Richard Rodgers

1973

Actor (dramatic): Alan Bates, *Butley*

Actress (dramatic): Julie Harris, *The Last of Mrs. Lincoln*

Actor, supporting or featured (dramatic): John Lithgow, *The Changing Room*

Actress, supporting or featured (dramatic): Leora Dana, *The Last of Mrs. Lincoln*

Actor (musical): Ben Vereen, *Pippin*

Actress (musical): Glynis Johns, *A Little Night Music*

Actor, supporting or featured (musical): George S. Irving, *Irene*

Actress, supporting or featured (musical): Patricia Elliot, *A Little Night Music*

Play: *The Championship Season* by Jason Miller, produced by New York Shakespeare Festival-Joseph Papp

Director (dramatic): A.J. Antoon, *The Championship Season*

Musical: *A Little Night Music*, produced by Harold Prince

Director (musical): Bob Fosse, *Pippin*

Book (musical): *A Little Night Music* by Hugh Wheeler

Score (musical): *A Little Night Music*, music & lyrics by Stephen Sondheim

Scenic designer: Tony Walton, *Pippin*

Costume designer: Florence Klotz, *A Little Night Music*

Choreographer: Bob Fosse, *Pippin*

Lighting designer: Jules Fisher, *Pippin*

Special awards: John Lindsay, Mayor of New York City, Actors' Fund of America, Shubert Organization

1974

Actor (dramatic): Michael Moriarty, *Find Your Way Home*

Actress (dramatic): Colleen Dewhurst, *A Moon For the Misbegotten*

Actor, supporting or featured (dramatic): Ed Flanders, *A Moon For the Misbegotten*

Actress, supporting or featured (dramatic): Frances Sternhagen, *The Good Doctor*

Actor (musical): Christopher Plummer, *Cyrano*

Actress (musical): Virginia Capers, *Raisin*

Actor, supporting or featured (musical): Tommy Tune, *Seesaw*

Actress, supporting or featured (musical): Janie Sell, *Over Here!*

Play: *The River Niger* by Joseph A. Walker, produced by Negro Ensemble Co., Inc

Director (dramatic): José Quintero, *A Moon For the Misbegotten*

Musical: *Raisin*, produced by Robert Nemiroff

Director (musical): Harold Prince, *Candide*

Book (musical): *Candide* by Hugh Wheeler

Score: *Gigi*, music by Frederick Loewe, lyrics by Alan Jay Lerner

Scenic designer: Franne & Eugene Lee, *Candide*

Costume designer: Franne Lee, *Candide*

Choreographer: Michael Bennett, *Seesaw*

Lighting designer: Jules Fisher, *Ulysses in Nighttown*

Special awards: Liza Minnelli, Bette Midler, Peter Cook & Dudley Moore, *A Moon For the Misbegotten*, *Candide*, Actors' Equity Association, Theater Development Fund, John F. Wharton, Harold Friedlander

Theater award '74: John F. Wharton, veteran theatrical attorney; Harold Friedlander, the industry's foremost printing expert

1975

Actor (dramatic): John Kani & Winston Ntshona, *Sizwe Banzi Dead and the Island*

Actress (dramatic): Ellen Burstyn, *Same Time, Next Year*

Actor, supporting or featured (dramatic): Frank Langella, *Seascape*

Actress, supporting or featured (dramatic): Rita Moreno, *The Ritz*

Actor (musical): John Cullum, *Shenandoah*

Actress (musical): Angela Lansbury, *Gypsy*

Actor, supporting or featured (musical): Ted Ross, *The Wiz*

Actress, supporting or featured (musical): Dee Dee Bridgewater, *The Wiz*

Play: *Equus* by Peter Shaffer, produced by Kermit Bloomgarden & Doris Cole Abrahams

Director (dramatic): John Dexter, *Equus*

Musical: *The Wiz*, produced by Ken Harper

... **September 5** ...
Steven Spielberg looks set to take over direction of the
unfinished Kubrick film **Artificial Intelligence**.

Director (musical): Geoffrey Holder, *The Wiz*
Book (musical): *Shenandoah* by James Lee Barrett, Peter Udell, & Philip Rose
Score: *The Wiz*, music & lyrics by Charlie Smalls
Scenic designer: Carl Toms, *Sherlock Holmes*
Costume designer: Geoffrey Holder, *The Wiz*
Choreographer: George Faison, *The Wiz*
Lighting designer: Neil Peter Jampolis, *Sherlock Holmes*
Special award: Neil Simon
Theater award '75: Al Hirschfeld

1976

Actor (play): John Wood, *Travesties*
Actress (play): Irene Worth, *Sweet Bird of Youth*
Actor, (featured role – play): Edward Herrmann, *Mrs. Warren's Profession*
Actress (featured role – play): Shirley Knights, *Kennedy's Children*
Actor (musical): George Rose, *My Fair Lady*
Actress (musical): Donna McKechnie, *A Chorus Line*
Actor (featured role – musical): Sammy Williams, *A Chorus Line*
Actress (featured role – musical): Carole Bishop, *A Chorus Line*
Play: *Travesties* by Tom Stoppard, produced by David Merrick, Doris Cole Abrahams, & Burry Fredrik in association with S. Spencer Davids & Eddie Kulukundis
Director (play): Ellis Rabb, *The Royal Family*
Musical: *A Chorus Line*, produced by Joseph Papp, New York Shakespeare Festival
Director (musical): Michael Bennett, *A Chorus Line*
Book (musical): *A Chorus Line* by James Kirkwood & Nicholas Dante
Score: *A Chorus Line*, music by Marvin Hamlisch, lyrics by Edward Kleban
Scenic designer: Boris Aronson, *Pacific Overtures*
Costume designer: Florence Klotz, *Pacific Overtures*
Lighting designer: Tharon Musser, *A Chorus Line*
Choreographer: Michael Bennett & Bob Avian, *A Chorus Line*
Special awards: Mathilde Pincus, Thomas H. Fitzgerald, Circle in the Square, The Arena Stage, Washington, D.C., Richard Burton
Lawrence Langner award: George Abbott

1977

Actor (play): Al Pacino, *The Basic Training of Pavlo Hummel*
Actress (play): Julie Harris, *The Belle of Amherst*
Actor (featured role – play): Jonathan Pryce, *Comedians*
Actress (featured role – play): Trazana Beverley, *For Colored Girls Who Have Considered Suicide/When the Rainbow is Enuf*
Actor (musical): Barry Bostwick, *The Robber Bridegroom*
Actress (musical): Dorothy Loudon, *Annie*
Actor (featured role – musical): Lenny Baker, *I Love My Wife*
Actress (featured role – musical): Delores Hall, *Your Arm's Too Short to Box With God*
Play: *The Shadow Box* by Michael Cristofer, produced by Allan Francis, Ken Marsolais, Lester Osterman, & Leonard Soloway
Director (play): Gordon Davidson, *The Shadow Box*
Musical: *Annie*, produced by Lewis Allen, Mike Nichols, Irwin Meyer, & Stephen R. Friedman
Director (musical): Gene Saks, *I Love My Wife*
Book (musical): *Annie* by Thomas Meehan
Score: *Annie*, music by Charles Strouse, lyrics by Martin Charnin
Scenic designer: David Mitchell, *Annie*
Costume designer: Theoni V. Aldredge, *Annie*; Santo Loquasto, *The Cherry Orchard*
Lighting designer: Jennifer Tipton, *The Cherry Orchard*
Choreographer: Peter Genaro, *Annie*
Special awards: Lily Tomlin, Barry Manilow, Diana Ross, National Theatre for the Deaf, Mark Taper Forum, Equity Library Theatre
Lawrence Langner award: Cheryl Crawford

1978

Actor (play): Barnard Hughes, *Da*
Actress (play): Jessica Tandy, *The Gin Game*
Actor (featured role – play): Lester Rawlins, *Da*
Actress (featured role – play): Ann Wedgeworth, *Chapter Two*
Actor (musical): John Cullum, *On the Twentieth Century*
Actress (musical): Liza Minnelli, *The Act*
Actor(featured role – musical): Kevin Kline, *On the Twentieth Century*
Actress (featured role – musical): Nell Carter, *Ain't Misbehavin'*
Play: *Da* by Hugh Leonard, produced by Lester Osterman, Marilyn Strauss, & Marc Howard
Director (play): Melvin Bernhardt, *Da*
Musical: *Ain't Misbehavin'*, produced by Emanuel Azenberg, Dasha Epstein, The Shubert Organization, Jane Gaynor, & Ron Dante
Director (musical): Richard Maltby, Jr., *Ain't Misbehavin'*
Book (musical): *On the Twentieth Century* by Betty Comden & Adolph Green

Score: *On the Twentieth Century,* music by Cy
Coleman, lyrics by Betty Comden & Adolph Green
Scenic designer: Robin Wagner, *On the Twentieth
Century*
Costume designer: Edward Gorey, *Dracula*
Lighting designer: Jules Fisher, *Dancin'*
Choreographer: Bob Fosse, *Dancin'*
Most innovative production of a revival: *Dracula,*
produced by Jujamcyn Theater, Elizabeth I.
McCann, John Wulp, Victor Lurie, Nelle Nugent, &
Maz Weitzenhoffer
Special award: The Long Wharf Theater, New Haven,
Connecticut
Theater award '78: To the creators, Charles Moss &
Stan Dragoti (of Wells, Rich, Greene, Inc.) of the "I
Love New York Broadway Show tours," and its
sponsor, the New York State Department of
Commerce
Lawrence Langner memorial award for distinguished
lifetime achievement in the American theater:
Irving Berlin

1979

Actor (play): Tom Conti, *Whose Life Is It Anyway?*
Actress (play): Constance Cummings, *Wings*; Carole
Shelley, *The Elephant Man*
Actor (featured role – play): Michael Gough,
Bedroom Farce
Actress (featured role – play): Joan Hickson, *Bedroom
Farce*
Actor (musical): Len Cariou, *Sweeney Todd*
Actress (musical): Angela Lansbury, *Sweeney Todd*
Actor(featured role – musical): Henderson Forsythe,
The Best Little Whorehouse in Texas
Actress (featured role – musical): Carlyn Glynn, *The
Best Little Whorehouse in Texas*
Play: *The Elephant Man* by Bernard Pomerance,
produced by Richmond Crinkely, Elizabeth I.
McCann, & Nelle Nugent
Director (play): Jack Hofsiss, *The Elephant Man*
Musical: *Sweeney Todd,* produced by Richard Barr,
Charles Woodward, Robert Fryer, Mary Lea
Johnson, & Martin Richards
Director (musical): Harold Prince, *Sweeney Todd*
Book (musical): *Sweeney Todd* by Hugh Wheeler
Score: *Sweeney Todd,* music & lyrics by Stephen
Sondheim
Scenic designer: Eugene Lee, *Sweeney Todd*
Costume designer: Franne Lee, *Sweeney Todd*
Lighting designer: Roger Morgan, *The Crucifer of
Blood*
Choreographer: Michael Bennett & Bob Avian,
Ballroom

Special awards: Henry Fonda, Walter F. Diehl, Eugene
O'Neill Memorial Theater Center, Waterford,
Connecticut, American Conservatory Theater, San
Francisco, California
Lawrence Langner memorial award for distinguished
lifetime achievement in the American theater:
Richard Rodgers

1980

Actor (play): John Rubinstein, *Children of a Lesser
God*
Actress (play): Phyllis Frelich, *Children of a Lesser God*
Actor (featured role – play): David Rounds, *Morning's
at Seven*
Actress (featured role – play): Dinah Manoff, *I Ought
to Be in Pictures*
Actor (musical): Jim Dale, *Barnum*
Actress (musical): Patti LuPone, *Evita*
Actor (featured role – musical): Mandy Patinkin,
Evita
Actress (featured role – musical): Priscilla Lopez, *A
Day in Hollywood/A Night in the Ukraine*
Play: *Children of a Lesser God* by Mark Medoff,
produced by Emanuel Azenberg, Shubert
Organization, Dasha Epstein, & Ron Dante
Director (play): Vivian Matalon, *Morning's at Seven*
Musical: *Evita,* produced by Robert Stigwood
Director (musical): Harold Prince, *Evita*
Book (musical): *Evita* by Tim Rice
Score: *Evita,* music by Andrew Lloyd Webber, lyrics
by Tim Rice
Scenic designer: John Lee Beatty, *Talley's Folly,* David
Mitchell, *Barnum*
Costume designer: Theoni V. Aldredge, *Barnum*
Lighting designer: David Hersey, *Evita*
Choreographer: Tommy Tune & Thommie Walsh, *A
Day in Hollywood/A Night in the Ukraine*
Reproduction (play or musical): *Morning's at Seven,*
produced by Elizabeth I. McCann, Nelle Nugent, &
Ray Larson
Special awards: Mary Tyler Moore, *Whose Life Is It
Anyway?,* Actors Theater of Louisville, Kentucky,
Goodspeed Opera House, East Haddam,
Connecticut

1981

Actor (play): Ian McKellen, *Amadeus*
Actress (play): Jane Lapotaire, *Piaf*
Actor (featured role – play): Brian Backer, *The
Floating Light Bulb*
Actress (featured role – play): Swoosie Kurtz, *Fifth of
July*
Actor (musical): Kevin Kline, *The Pirates of Penzance*

Actress (musical): Lauren Bacall, *Woman of the Year*
Actor (featured role – musical): Hinton Battle, *Sophisticated Ladies*
Actress (featured role – musical): Marilyn Cooper, *Woman of the Year*
Play: *Amadeus* by Peter Shaffer, produced by Shubert Organization, Elizabeth I. McCann, Nelle Nugent, & Roger S. Berlind
Director (play): Peter Hall, *Amadeus*
Musical: *42nd Street*, produced by David Merrick
Director (musical): Wilford Leach, *The Pirates of Penzance*
Book (musical): *Woman of the Year* by Peter Stone
Score: *Woman of the Year*, music by John Kander, lyrics by Fred Ebb
Scenic designer: John Bury, *Amadeus*
Costume designer: Willa Kim, *Sophisticated Ladies*
Lighting designer: John Bury, *Amadeus*
Choreographer: Gower Champion, *42nd Street*
Reproduction (play or musical): *The Pirates of Penzance*, produced by Joseph Papp & The New York Shakespeare Festival
Special awards: Lean Horn, Trinity Square Repertory Company, Providence, Rhode Island

1982

Actor (play): Roger Rees, *The Life and Adventures of Nicholas Nickleby*
Actress (play): Zoe Caldwell, *Medea*
Actor (featured role – play): Zakes Mokae, *'Master Harold'… and the Boys*
Actress (featured role – play): Amanda Plummer, *Agnes of God*
Actor (musical): Ben Harney, *Dreamgirls*
Actress (musical): Jennifer Holliday, *Dreamgirls*
Actor (featured role – musical): Cleavant Derricks, *Dreamgirls*
Actress (featured role – musical): Liliane Montevecchi, *Nine*
Play: *The Life and Adventures of Nicholas Nickleby* by David Edgar, produced by James M. Nederlander, The Shubert Organization, Elizabeth I. McCann, & Nelle Nugent
Director (play): Trevor Nunn/John Caird, *The Life and Adventures of Nicholas Nickleby*
Musical: *Nine*, produced by Michel Stuart, Harvey J. Klaris, Roger S. Berlind, James M. Nederlander, Francine LeFrak, & Kenneth D. Greenblatt
Director (musical): Tommy Tune, *Nine*
Book (musical): *Dreamgirls* by Tom Eyen
Score: *Nine*, music & lyrics by Maury Yeston
Scenic designer: John Napier, Dermot Hayes, *The Life and Adventures of Nicholas Nickleby*

Costume designer: William Ivey Long, *Nine*
Lighting designer: Tharon Musser, *Dreamgirls*
Choreographer: Michael Bennett, Michael Peters, *Dreamgirls*
Special awards: The Guthrie Theater, Minneapolis, Minnesota; The Actors' Fund of America
Theater Award '82: Warner Communications, Radio City Music Hall

1983

Actor (play): Harvey Fierstein, *Torch Song Trilogy*
Actress (play): Jessica Tandy, *Foxfire*
Actor (featured role – play): Matthew Broderick, *Brighton Beach Memories*
Actress (featured role – play): Judith Ivey, *Steaming*
Actor (musical): Tommy Tune, *My One and Only*
Actress (musical): Natalia Makarova, *On Your Toes*
Actor (featured role – musical): Charles "Honi" Coles, *My One and Only*
Actress (featured role – musical): Betty Buckley, *Cats*
Play: *Torch Song Trilogy* by Harvey Fierstein, produced by Kenneth Waissman, Martin Markinson, Lawrence Lane, John Glines, BetMar, & Donald Tick
Director (play): Gene Saks, *Brighton Beach Memories*
Musical: *Cats*, produced by Cameron Mackintosh, The Really Useful Company, Inc., David Geffen, and The Shubert Organization
Director (musical): Trevor Nunn, *Cats*
Book: *Cats* by T.S. Eliot
Score: *Cats*, music by Andrew Lloyd Webber, lyrics by T.S. Eliot
Scenic designer: Ming Cho Lee, *K2*
Costume designer: John Napier, *Cats*
Lighting designer: David Hersey, *Cats*
Choreographer: Tommy Tune, Thommie Walsh, *My One and Only*
Reproduction: *On Your Toes*, produced by Alfred de Liagre, Jr., Roger L. Stevens, John Mauceri, Donald R. Seawell, and Andre Pastoria
Special award: Oregon Shakespeare Festival Association, Ashland, Oregon
Theater award '83: The Theater Collection, Museum of the City of New York

1984

Actor (play): Jeremy Irons, *The Real Thing*
Actress (play): Glenn Close, *The Real Thing*
Actor (featured role – play): Joe Mantegna, *Glengarry Glen Ross*
Actress (featured role – play): Christine Baransky, *The Real Thing*
Actor (musical): George Hearn, *La Cage Aux folles*

Actress (musical): Chita Rivera, *The Rink*
Actor (featured role – musical): Hinton Battle, *The Tap Dance Kid*
Actress (featured role – musical): Lila Kedrova, *Zorba*
Play: *The Real Thing* by Tom Stoppard, produced by Emanuel Azenberg, The Shubert Organization, Icarus Productions, Byron Goldman, Ivan Bloch, Roger Berlind, & Michael Codron
Director (play): Mike Nichols, *The Real Thing*
Musical: *La Cage Aux folles*, produced by Allan Carr, Kenneth D. Greenblatt, Marvin A. Krauss, Steward F. Lane, James M. Nederlander, Martin Richards, Barry Brown, & Fritz Holt
Director (musical): Arthur Laurentis, *La Cage Aux folles*
Book (musical): *La Cage Aux folles* by Harvey Fierstein
Score: *La Cage Aux folles*, music & lyrics by Jerry Herman
Scenic designer: Tony Straiges, *Sunday in the Park With George*
Costume designer: Theoni V. Aldredge, *La Cage Aux folles*
Lighting designer: Richard Nelson, *Sunday in the Park With George*
Choreographer: Danny Daniels, *The Tap Dance Kid*
Reproduction: *Death of a Salesman*, produced by Robert Whitehead & Roger L. Stevens
Special awards: Old Globe Theater, San Diego, California, *La Tragédie de Carmen*, Peter Feller, *A Chorus Line*

1985

Actor (play): Derek Jacobi, *Much Ado About Nothing*
Actress (play): Stockard Channing, *Joe Egg*
Actor (featured role – play): Barry Miller, *Biloxi Blues*
Actress (featured role – play): Judith Ivey, *Hurleyburly*
Actor (musical): Category eliminated for 1985
Actress (musical): Category eliminated for 1985
Actor (featured role – musical): Ron Richardson, *Big River*
Actress (featured role – musical): Leilani Jones, *Grind*
Play: *Biloxi Blues* by Neil Simon, produced by Emanuel Azenberg, & the Center Theater Group/Ahmanson Theater, Los Angeles
Director (play): Gene Saks, *Biloxi Blues*
Musical: *Big River*, produced by Rocco Landesman, Heidi Landesman, Rick Steiner, M. Anthony Fisher, & Dodger Productions
Director (musical): Des McAnuff, *Big River*
Book (musical): *Big River* by William Hauptman
Score: *Big River*, music & lyrics by Roger Miller
Scenic designer: Heidi Landesman, *Big River*

Costume designer: Florence Klotz, *Grind*
Lighting designer: Richard Riddel, *Big River*
Choreographer: Category eliminated
Reproduction (play or musical): *Joe Egg*, produced by The Shubert Organization, Emanuel Azenberg, Roger Berlind, Ivan Bloch, & MTM Enterprises, Inc.
Special awards: Yul Brynner, New York State Council on the Arts, Steppenwolf Theater Company, Chicago, Illinois
Lawrence Langner memorial award for lifetime achievement in the theater: Edwin Lester, founder & general manager for 40 years of the Los Angeles Civic Light Opera

1986

Actor (play): Judd Hirsch, *I'm Not Rappaport*
Actress (play): Lily Tomlin, *The Search For Signs of Intelligent Life in the Universe*
Actor (featured role – play): John Mahoney, *The House of Blue Leaves*
Actress (featured role – play): Swoosie Kurtz, *The House of Blue Leaves*
Actor (musical): George Rose, *The Mystery of Edwin Drood*
Actress (musical): Bernadette Peters, *Song & Dance*
Actor (featured role – musical): Michael Rupert, *Sweet Charity*
Actress (featured role – musical): Bebe Neuwirth, *Sweet Charity*
Play: *I'm Not Rappaport* by Herb Gardner, produced by James Walsh, Lewis Allen, & Marin Heinfling
Director (play): Jerry Zaks, *The House of Blue Leaves*
Musical: *The Mystery of Edwin Drood*, produced by Joseph Papp
Director (musical): Wilford Leach, *The Mystery of Edwin Drood*
Book (musical): *The Mystery of Edwin Drood* by Rupert Holmes
Score: *The Mystery of Edwin Drood*, Rupert Holmes
Scenic designer: Tony Walton, *The House of Blue Leaves*
Costume designer: Patricia Zipprodt, *Sweet Charity*
Lighting designer: Pat Collins, *I'm Not Rappaport*
Choreographer: Bob Fosse, *Big Deal*
Special award: American Repertory Theater, Cambridge, Massachusetts

1987

Actor (play): James Earl Jones, *Fences*
Actress (play): Linda Lavin, *Broadway Bound*
Actor (featured role – play): John Randolph, *Broadway Bound*

Actress (featured role – play): Mary Alice, *Fences*
Actor (musical): Robert Lindsay, *Me and My Girl*
Actress (musical): Maryann Plunkett, *Me and My Girl*
Actor (featured role – musical): Michael Maguire, *Les Misérables*
Actress (featured role – musical): Frances Ruffelle, *Les Misérables*
Play: *Fences* by August Wilson, produced by Carole Shorenstein Hays & The Yale Repertory Theater
Director (play): Lloyd Richards, *Fences*
Musical: *Les Misérables* produced by Cameron Mackintosh
Director (musical): Trevor Nunn & John Caird, *Les Misérables*
Book (musical): *Les Misérables* by Alain Boublil & Claude-Michel Schönberg
Score: *Les Misérables*, music by Claude-Michel Schönberg, lyrics by Herbert Kretzmer & Alain Boublil
Scenic designer: John Napier, *Les Misérables*
Costume designer: John Napier, *Starlight Express*
Lighting designer: David Hersey, *Les Misérables*
Choreographer: Gillian Gregory, *Me and My Girl*
Best revival: *All My Sons*, produced by Jay H. Fuchs, Steven Warnick, & Charles Patsos
Special awards: George Abbott, Jackie Mason, San Francisco Mime Troupe
Lawrence Langner memorial award for lifetime achievement in the American theater: Robert Preston (posthumous)

1988

Actor (play): Ron Silver, *Speed-the-Plow*
Actress (play): Joan Allen, *Burn This*
Actor (featured role – play): B.D. Wong, *M. Butterfly*
Actress (featured role – play): L. Scott Caldwell, *Joe Turner's Come and Gone*
Actor (musical): Michael Crawford, *The Phantom of the Opera*
Actress (musical): Joanna Gleason, *Into the Woods*
Actor (featured role – musical): Bill McCutcheon, *Anything Goes*
Actress (featured role – musical): Judy Kaye, *The Phantom of the Opera*
Play: *M. Butterfly* by David Henry Hwang, produced by Stuart Ostrow & David Geffen
Director (play): John Dexter, *M. Butterfly*
Musical: *The Phantom of the Opera* produced by Cameron Mackintosh & The Really Useful Theater Company, Inc.
Director (musical): Harold Prince, *The Phantom of the Opera*
Book (musical): *Into the Woods* by James Lapine

Score (musical): *Into the Woods*, music & lyrics by Stephen Sondheim
Scenic designer: Maria Björnson, *The Phantom of the Opera*
Costume designer: Maria Björnson, *The Phantom of the Opera*
Lighting designer: Andrew Bridge, *The Phantom of the Opera*
Choreographer: Michael Smuin, *Anything Goes*
Revival: *Anything Goes*, produced by Lincoln Center Theater, Gregory Mosher, & Bernard Gersten
Special awards: Brooklyn Academy of Music, South Coast Repertory of Costa Mesa, CA

1989

Actor (play): Philip Bosco, *Lend Me a Tenor*
Actress (play): Pauline Collins, *Shirley Valentine*
Actor (featured role – play): Boyd Gaines, *The Heidi Chronicles*
Actress (featured role – play): Christine Baransky, *Rumors*
Actor (musical): Jason Alexander, *Jerome Robbins' Broadway*
Actress (musical): Ruth Brown, *Black and Blue*
Actor (featured role – musical): Scott Wise, *Jerome Robbins' Broadway*
Actress (featured role – musical): Debbie Shapiro, *Jerome Robbins' Broadway*
Play: *The Heidi Chronicles* by Wendy Wasserstein, produced by The Shubert Organization, Suntory International Corp., James Walsh, & Playwrights Horizons
Director (play): Jerry Zaks, *Lend Me a Tenor*
Musical: *Jerome Robbins' Broadway*, produced by The Shubert Organization, Suntory International Corp., Byron Goldman, & Emanuel Azenberg
Director (musical): Jerome Robbins, *Jerome Robbins' Broadway*
Book (musical): Category eliminated for 1989
Score (musical): Category eliminated for 1989
Scenic designer: Santo Loquasto, *Cafe Crown*
Costume designer: Claudio Segovia & Hector Orezzoli, *Black and Blue*
Lighting designer: Jennifer Tipton, *Jerome Robbins' Broadway*
Choreographer: Cholly Atkins, Henry LeTang, Frankie Manning, & Gayard Nicholas, *Black and Blue*
Revival: *Our Town*, produced by Lincoln Center Theater, Gregory Mosher, & Bernard Gersten
Special awards: Hartford Stage Company, Hartford, Connecticut

---

...September 10...
Miramax Films and Rome-based distributor Medusa Films have teamed up with Giuseppe Tornatore to direct an Italian-language period film, **Malena**.

1990

Actor (play): Robert Morse, *Tru*
Actress (play): Maggie Smith, *Lettice and Lovage*
Actor (featured role – play): Charles Durning, *Cat on a Hot Tin Roof*
Actress (featured role – play): Margaret Tyzack, *Lettice and Lovage*
Actor (musical): James Naughton, *City of Angels*
Actress (musical): Tyne Daly, *Gypsy*
Actor (featured role – musical): Michael Jeter, *Grand Hotel, The Musical*
Actress (featured role – musical): Randy Graff, *City of Angels*
Play: *The Grapes of Wrath* by Frank Galati, produced by The Shubert Organization, Steppenwolf Theater Company, Suntory International Corp., & Jujamcyn Theaters
Director (play): Frank Galati, *The Grapes of Wrath*
Musical: *City of Angels*, produced by Nick Vanoff, Roger Berlind, Jujamcyn Theaters, Suntory International Corp., & The Shubert Organization
Director (musical): Tommy Tune, *Grand Hotel, The Musical*
Book (musical): *City of Angels* by Larry Gelbart
Score (musical): *City of Angels*, music by Cy Coleman, lyrics by David Zippel
Scenic designer: Robin Wagner, *City of Angels*
Costume designer: Santo Loquasto, *Grand Hotel, The Musical*
Lighting designer: Jules Fisher, *Grand Hotel, The Musical*
Choreographer: Tommy Tune, *Grand Hotel, The Musical*
Revival: *Gypsy*, produced by Barry & Fran Weissler, Kathy Levin, & Barry Brown
Special award: Seattle Repertory Theater
Tony honor: Alfred Drake

1991

Actor (play): Nigel Hawthorne, *Shadowlands*
Actress (play): Mercedes Ruehl, *Lost in Yonkers*
Actor (featured role – play): Kevin Spacey, *Lost in Yonkers*
Actress (featured role – play): Irene Worth, *Lost in Yonkers*
Actor (musical): Jonathan Pryce, *Miss Saigon*
Actress (musical): Lea Salonga, *Miss Saigon*
Actor (featured role – musical): Hinton Battle, *Miss Saigon*
Actress (featured role – musical): Daisy Eagan, *The Secret Garden*
Play: *Lost in Yonkers* by Neil Simon, produced by Emanuel Azenberg

Director (play): Jerry Zaks, *Six Degrees of Separation*
Musical: *The Will Rogers Follies*, produced by Pierre Cossette, Martin Richards, Sam Crothers, James M. Nederlander, Stewart F. Lane, Max Weitzenhoffer, & Japan Satellite Broadcasting, Inc.
Director (musical): Tommy Tune, *The Will Rogers Follies*
Book (musical): *The Secret Garden* by Marsha Norman
Score (musical): *The Will Rogers Follies*, music by Cy Coleman, lyrics by Betty Comden & Adolph Green
Scenic designer: Heidi Landesman, *The Secret Garden*
Costume designer: Willa Kim, *The Will Rogers Follies*
Lighting designer: Jules Fisher, *The Will Rogers Follies*
Choreographer: Tommy Tune, *The Will Rogers Follies*
Revival: *Fiddler on the Roof,* produced by Barry & Fran Weissler, Pace Theatrical Group
Special award: Yale Repertory Theater, New Haven, Connecticut
Tony honor: Father George Moore (posthumous)

1992

Actor (play): Judd Hirsch, *Conversations With My Father*
Actress (play): Glenn Close, *Death and the Maiden*
Actor (featured role – play): Larry Fishburne, *Two Trains Running*
Actress (featured role – play): Brid Brennan, *Dancing at Lughnasa*
Actor (musical): Gregory Hines, *Jelly's Last Jam*
Actress (musical): Faith Prince, *Guys and Dolls*
Actor (featured role – musical): Scott Waara, *The Most Happy Fella*
Actress (featured role – musical): Tonya Pinkins, *Jelly's Last Jam*
Play: *Dancing at Lughnasa* by Brian Friel, produced by Noel Pearson, Bill Kenwright, & Joseph Harris
Director (play): Patrick Mason, *Dancing at Lughnasa*
Musical: *Crazy For You*, produced by Roger Horchow & Elizabeth Williams
Director (musical): Jerry Zaks, *Guys and Dolls*
Book (musical): *Falsettos*, by William Finn & James Lapine
Score (musical): *Falsettos*, music & lyrics by William Finn
Scenic designer: Tony Walton, *Guys and Dolls*
Costume designer: William Ivey Long, *Crazy for You*
Lighting designer: Jules Fisher, *Jelly's Last Jam*
Choreographer: Susan Stroman, *Crazy For You*
Revival: *Guys and Dolls* produced by Dodger Productions, Roger Berlind, Jujamcyn Theaters/TV Asahi, Kardana Productions, & The John. F. Kennedy Center for the Performing Arts

---

Special award: The Goodman Theater of Chicago
Tony honor: *The Fantasticks*

1993

Actor (play): Ron Leibman, *Angels in America: Millennium Approaches*
Actress (play): Madeline Kahn, *The Sisters Rosensweig*
Actor (featured role – play): Stephen Spinella, *Angels in America: Millennium Approaches*
Actress (featured role – play): Debra Monk, *Redwood Curtain*
Actor (musical): Brent Carver, *Kiss of the Spider Woman – The Musical*
Actress (musical): Chita Rivera, *Kiss of the Spider Woman – The Musical*
Actor (featured role – musical): Anthony Crivello, *Kiss of the Spider Woman – The Musical*
Actress (featured role – musical): Andrea Martin, *My Favorite Year*
Play: *Angels in America: Millennium Approaches* by Tony Kishner, produced by Jujamcyn Theatres, Mark Taper Forum/Gordon Davidson, Margo Lion, Susan Quint Gallin, Jon B. Platt, The Baruch-Frankel-Viertel Group, Frederick Zollo, & Herb Alpert
Director (play): George C. Wolfe, *Angels in America: Millennium Approaches*
Musical: *Kiss of the Spider Woman – The Musical*, produced by The Live Entertainment Corp. of Canada/Garth Drabinsky
Director (musical): Des McAnuff, *The Who's Tommy*
Book (musical): *Kiss of the Spider Woman – The Musical* by Terrence McNally
Score (musical): *Kiss of the Spider Woman – The Musical*, music by John Kander, lyrics by Fred Ebb & *The Who's Tommy*, music & lyrics by Pete Townshend
Scenic designer: John Arnone, *The Who's Tommy*
Costume designer: Florence Klotz, *Kiss of the Spider Woman – The Musical*
Lighting designer: Chris Parry, *The Who's Tommy*
Choreographer: Wayne Cilento, *The Who's Tommy*
Revival: *Anna Christie*, produced by Roundabout Theater Company & Todd Haimes
Special awards: *Oklahoma! – 50th Anniversary*, La Jolla Playhouse
Tony honors: IATSE, Broadway Cares/Equity Fights AIDS

1994

Actor (play): Stephen Spinella, *Angels in America: Perestroika*
Actress (play): Diana Rigg, *Medea*

Actor (featured role – play): Jeffrey Wright, *Angels in America: Perestroika*
Actress (featured role – play): Jane Adams, *An Inspector Calls*
Actor (musical): Boyd Gaines, *She Loves Me*
Actress (musical): Donna Murphy, *Passion*
Actor (featured role – musical): Jarrod Emick, *Damn Yankees*
Actress (featured role – musical): Audra Ann McDonald, *Carousel*
Play: *Angels in America: Perestroika* by Tony Kushner, produced by Jujamcyn Theater & The Mark Taper Forum/Gordon Davidson, Artistic director with Margo Lion, Susan Quint Gallin, Jon B. Platt, The Baruch-Frankel-Viertel Group, Frederick Zollo, in association with the New York Shakespeare Festival, Mordecai/Cole Productions, & Herb Alpert
Director (play): Stephen Daldry, *An Inspector Calls*
Musical: *Passion*, produced by The Shubert Organization, Capital Cities/ABC, Roger Berlind, & Scott Rudin
Director (musical): Nicholas Hytner, *Carousel*
Book (musical): *Passion* by James Lapine
Original musical score: *Passion*, music & lyrics by Stephen Sondheim
Scenic designer: Bob Crowley, *Carousel*
Costume designer: Ann Hould-Ward, *Beauty and the Beast*
Lighting designer: Rick Fisher, *An Inspector Calls*
Choreographer: Sir Kenneth MacMillan, *Carousel*
Revival: *An Inspector Calls*, produced by Noel Pearson, The Shubert Organization, Capital Cities/ABC, & Joseph Harris
Revival (musical): *Carousel*, produced by Lincoln Center Theater, Andre Bishop, Bernard Gersten, The Royal National Theater, Cameron Mackintosh, & the Rodgers & Hammerstein Organization
Special awards: Jessica Tandy, Hume Cronyn (Lifetime Achievement), McCarter Theater (Regional Theater)

1995

Actor (play): Ralph Fiennes, *Hamlet*
Actress (play): Cherry Jones, *The Heiress*
Actor (featured role – play): John Glover, *Love! Valour! Compassion!*
Actress (featured role – play): Frances Sternhagen, *The Heiress*
Actor (musical): Matthew Broderick, *How to Succeed in Business Without Really Trying*
Actress (musical): Glenn Close, *Sunset Boulevard*
Actor (featured role – musical): George Hearn, *Sunset Boulevard*

Actress (featured role – musical): Gretha Boston, *Show Boat*

Play: *Love! Valour! Compassion!* by Terrence McNally, produced by Manhattan Theater Club, Lynne Meadow, Barry Grove, & Jujamcyn Theaters

Director (play): Joe Mantello, *Love! Valour! Compassion!*

Musical: *Sunset Boulevard*, produced by The Really Useful Company, Inc.

Director (musical): Harold Prince, *Show Boat*

Book (musical): *Sunset Boulevard* by Don Black & Christopher Hampton

Original musical score: Andrew Lloyd Webber, Don Black, & Christopher Hampton, *Sunset Boulevard*

Scenic designer: John Napier, *Sunset Boulevard*

Costume designer: Florence Klotz, *Show Boat*

Lighting designer: Andrew Bridge, *Sunset Boulevard*

Choreographer: Susan Stroman, *Show Boat*

Revival: *The Heiress*, produced by Lincoln Center Theater, Andre Bishop, & Bernard Gersten

Revival (musical): *Show Boat*, produced by LIVENT (U.S.) Inc./Garth Drabinsky

Special awards: Carol Channing, Harvey Sabinson (Lifetime Achievement), Goodspeed Opera House, East Haddam, Connecticut (Regional Theater)

Tony honor: National Endowment for the Arts, Jane Alexander, chairman

1996

Actor (play): George Grizzard, *A Delicate Balance*

Actress (play): Zoe Caldwell, *Master Class*

Actor (featured role – play): Ruben Santiago-Hudson, *Seven Guitars*

Actress (featured role – play): Audra McDonald, *Master Class*

Actor (musical): Nathan Lane, *A Funny Thing Happened on the Way to the Forum*

Actress (musical): Donna Murphy, *The King and I*

Actor (featured role – musical): Wilson Jermaine Heredia, *Rent*

Actress (featured role – musical): Ann Duquesnay, *Bring in 'da Noise/Bring in 'da Funk*

Play: *Master Class* by Terrence McNally

Director (play): Gerald Gutierrez, *A Delicate Balance*

Musical: *Rent*

Director (musical): George C. Wolfe, *Bring in 'da Noise/Bring in 'da Funk*

Book (musical): *Rent* by Jonathan Larson

Original musical score: *Rent*, music & lyrics by Jonathan Larson

Scenic designer: Brian Thomson, *The King and I*

Costume designer: Roger Kirk, *The King and I*

Lighting designer: Jules Fisher & Peggy Eisenhauer, *Bring in 'da Noise/Bring in 'da Funk*

Choreographer: Savion Glover, *Bring in 'da Noise/Bring in 'da Funk*

Revival (play): *A Delicate Balance*

Revival (musical): *A Funny Thing Happened on the Way to the Forum*

Special regional theater award: Alley Theater of Houston

1997

Actor (play): Christopher Plummer, *Barrymore*

Actress (play): Janet McTeer, *A Doll's House*

Actor (featured role – play): Owen Teale, *A Doll's House*

Actress (featured role – play): Lynne Thigpen, *An American Daughter*

Actor (musical): James Naughton, *Chicago*

Actress (musical): Bebe Neuwirth, *Chicago*

Actor (featured role – musical): Chuck Cooper, *The Life*

Actress (featured role – musical): Lillias White, *The Life*

Play: *The Last Night of Ballyhoo* by Alfred Uhry, produced by Jane Harmon, Nina Keneally, Liz Oliver

Director (play): Anthony Page, *A Doll's House*

Musical: *Titanic*, produced by Dodger Endemol Theatricals, Richard S. Pechter, & The John. F. Kennedy Center

Director (musical): Walter Bobbie, *Chicago*

Book (musical): *Titanic* by Peter Stone

Original musical score: *Titanic*, music & lyrics by Maury Yeston

Orchestrations: Jonathan Tunick, *Titanic*

Scenic designer: Stewart Laing, *Titanic*

Costume designer: Judith Dolan, *Candide*

Lighting designer: Ken Billington, *Chicago*

Choreographer: Ann Reinking, *Chicago*

Revival (play): *A Doll's House*, produced by Bill Kenwright, & Thelma Holt

Revival (musical): *Chicago*, produced by Barry Weissler, Fran Weissler, & Kardana Productions, Inc.

Special regional theater award: Berkeley Repertory Theater

1998

Actor (play): Anthony LaPaglia, *A View From the Bridge*

Actress (play): Marie Mullen, *The Beauty Queen of Leenane*

Actor (featured role – play): Tom Murphy, *The Beauty Queen of Leenane*

Actress (featured role – play): Anna Manahan, *The Beauty Queen of Leenane*

Actor (musical): Alan Cummings, *Cabaret*

Actress (musical): Natasha Richardson, *Cabaret*

Actor (featured role – musical): Ron Rifkin, *Cabaret*

Actress (featured role – musical): Audra McDonald, *Ragtime*

Play: *Art* by Yasmina Reza, produced by David Pugh, Sean Connery, & Joan Cullman

Director (play): Garry Hynes, *The Beauty Queen of Leenane*

Musical: *The Lion King*, produced by Disney

Director (musical): Julie Taymor, *The Lion King*

Book (musical): *Ragtime* by Terrence McNally

Original musical score: *Ragtime*, music by Stephen Flaherty, lyrics by Lunn Ahrens

Orchestrations: William David Brohn, *Ragtime*

Scenic designer: Richard Hudson, *The Lion King*

Costume designer: Julie Taymor, *The Lion King*

Lighting designer: Donald Holder, *The Lion King*

Choreographer: Garth Fagan, *The Lion King*

Revival (play): *A View From the Bridge*, produced by Roundabout Theater Company, Todd Haimes, Ellen Richard, Roger Berlind, James M. Nederlander, Nathaniel Kramer, Elizabeth Ireland McCann, Roy Gabay, & Old Ivy Productions

Revival (musical): *Cabaret*, produced by Roundabout Theater Company, Todd Haimes, & Ellen Richard

Special regional theater award: Denver Center Theater Company

1999

Actor (play): Brian Dennehy, *Death of a Salesman*

Actress (play): Judi Dench, *Amy's View*

Actor (featured role – play): Frank Wood, *Side Man*

Actress (featured role – play): Elizabeth Franz, *Death of a Salesman*

Actor (musical): Martin Short, *Little Me*

Actress (musical): Bernadette Peters, *Annie Get Your Gun*

Actor (featured role – musical): Roger Bart, *You're a Good Man Charlie Brown*

Actress (featured role – musical): Kristen Chenoweth, *You're a Good Man Charlie Brown*

Play: *Side Man* by Warren Leight, produced by: Jay Harris, Peter Manning, Roundabout Theater Co., Rodd Haimes, Ellen Richard, Ron Kastner, James Cushing, Joan Stein

Director (play): Robert Falls, *Death of a Salesman*

Musical: *Fosse*, produced by Livent (U.S.) Inc.

Director (musical): Matthew Bourne, *Swan Lake*

Book (musical): Alfred Uhry, *Parade*

Score: Jason Robert Brown, *Parade*

Orchestrations: Ralph Burns & Douglas Besterman, *Fosse*

Scenic designer: Richard hoover, *Not About Nightingales*

Costume designer: Lez Brotherston, *Swan Lake*

Lighting designer: Andrew Bridge, *Fosse*

Choreographer: Matthew Bourne, *Swan Lake*

Revival (play): *Death of a Salesman*, produced by David Richenthal, Jujamcyn Theatres, Allan S. Gordon, Fox Theatricals, Jerry Frankel, The Goodman Theatre

Revival (musical): *Annie Get Your Gun*, produced by Barry and Fran Weissler, Kardana, Michael Watt, Irving Welzer, Hal Luftig

Regional theater award: Crossroads Theatre Company

Olivier Awards: 1999

Best New Play: *The Weir* by Conor McPherson

Best Musical: *Oklahoma!* Music by Richard Rodgers, book and lyrics by Oscar Hammerstein II

Best New Musical: *Kat and the Kings* by David Kramer and Taliep Peterson

Best New Comedy: *Cleo, Camping, Emanuelle and Dick* by Terry Johnson

Best Actor (Play): Kevin Spacey for *The Iceman Cometh*

Best Actress (Play): Eileen Atkins for *The Unexpected Man*

Best Actor (Musical): The cast of *Kat and the Kings*

Best Actress (Musical): Sophie Thompson for *Into the Woods*

Best Supporting Performance (Play): Brendon Coyle for *The Weir*

Best Supporting Performance (Musical): Shuler Hensley for *Oklahoma!*

Best Director: Howard Davies for *The Iceman Cometh*

Best Choreography: Susan Stroman for *Oklahoma!*

Best Sets: Anthony Ward for *Oklahoma!*

Best Costumes: William Dudley for *Amadeus*

Best Lighting: Hugh Vanstone for *The Blue Room*

...September 14...
Aidan Quinn will portray Paul McCartney and Jared Harris will play John Lennon in the telefilm **Two Of Us**.

Stage Reviews: 1999

Below is a selection of reviews from the many theater productions reviewed by *Variety* at home and abroad.

Amadeus

A Kim Poster, PW Prods., Adam Epstein, SFX Theatrical Group and Center Theater Group/Ahamanson Theater presentation, in association with Old Ivy Prods., of a play in two acts by Peter Shaffer. Directed by Peter Hall. Sets and costumes, William Dudley; lighting, Paule Constable; sound, Matt McKenzie; production stage manager, Susie Cordon. Opened Dec 15, 1999. Reviewed Dec. 13. Running time: 165 mins.

David Suchet (Antonio Salieri), Michael Sheen (Wolfgang Amadeus Mozart), Cindy Katz (Constanze Mozart), David McCallum (Emperor Joseph II), J.P. Linton(Count Johann Kilian Von Strack), Terence Rigby (Count Orsini-Rosenberg), Michael Keenan (Baron Van Swieten), Jake Broder, Charles Janasz (The "Venticelli"), John Rainer (Major Domo), William Ryall (Salieri's Valet), Robert Machray (Salieri's Cook), John Towey (Kapellmeister Bonno), Glynis Bell (Teresa Salieri), Kate Miller (Katherina Cavalieri). With: Jeffrey Bean, Geoffrey Blaisdell, Dan Mason, Kevin Orton.

With his wild eyes gaping as he scampers manically about, Michael Sheen's Mozart is like a rabid raccoon. Watching his fevered activities with feigned detachment is David Suchet's Salieri, a velvet wolf coolly stalking his prey. The rivalry between these two beasts is the dramatic pulse of Peter Shaffer's celebrated *Amadeus*, now celebrating its 20th anniversary. It's not the characters but the stage animals – the actors themselves – who must hold the attention in this enduring classic.

Antonio Salieri narrates the play, which follows the two composers' diverging fortunes over a decade at the Viennese court of Emperor Joseph II. In 1781, Salieri is ensconced in the Austrian capital when Mozart arrives from the provinces trailing a glorious history as a performing prodigy and composer. Salieri is soon thoroughly unhinged by the galling contrast between the celestial sounds of Mozart's music and the puerile buffooneries of the man himself. His beef isn't with Mozart but with God: That this womanizing ruffian should be chosen to deliver the music of the heavens, while the devout Salieri is doomed to be the conduit of more mundane sounds, is too cruel to be borne. Salieri vows to take revenge on such an unjust God, and the destruction of Mozart's career will be the instrument of his vengeance.

Amy's View

A Robert Fox, Scott Rudin, Roger Berlind, Joan Cullman, ABC Inc. and the Shubert Organization presentation of a play in two acts by David Hare. Directed by Richard Eyre. Sets and costumes, Bob Crowley; lighting, Mark Henderson; music, Richard Hartley; sound, Scott Myers; projections, Wendall K. Harrington; production stage manager, Susie Cordon. Opened April 15, 1999; reviewed April 13. Running time: 150 mins.

Tate Donovan (Dominic Tyghe), Samantha Bond (Amy Thomas), Anne Pitoniak (Evelyn Thomas), Judi Dench (Esme Allen), Ronald Pickup (Frank Oddie), Maduka Steady (Toby Cole), Willis Sparks (Stage Manager).

Amy and her boyfriend Dominic are expecting Amy's mother, Esme Allen; while the audience anticipate the diminutive and formidable performer for whom the role of Esme was written. If Esme's entrance is by no means without its complications for her daughter, Judi Dench's return to Broadway – after a 40-year absence – is quite simply bliss.

In a performance with as many sharp, funny edges as quietly heart-rending depths, Dench transforms Hare's play – a vigorously smart, if occasionally too discursive, story of an actress's conflicted relationship with her daughter – into a transcendent, moving meditation on the strange and painful journey that is life.

Esme Allen is an actress who has forged a long career on the English stage. But as the play opens in 1979, she is facing an uncertain future, thanks to her advancing age and the culture's declining interest in the art form. Perhaps that's why she takes an instinctive dislike to the handsome, callow Dominic, a film journalist who espouses views that Esme abhors. With Amy's revelation that she's expecting a child, the situation becomes all the more, er, pregnant with potential conflict. For Esme is a woman who takes imperious, offhand pride in her beliefs, and she's dismayed to see her daughter in thrall to a man she can't respect. The play takes place over more than 15 years. The question that reverberates through them all is how to live a moral and happy life. Do principles or people deserve our greatest allegiance, and how do we decide which to choose when our deepest beliefs put us in conflict with those we love?

Annie Get Your Gun

A Barry and Fran Weissler presentation, in association with Kardana, Michael Watt, Irving Welzer and Hal Luftig, of a musical in two acts with music and lyrics by Irving Berlin, book by Herbert and Dorothy Fields, as revised by Peter Stone. Directed by Graciele Daniele. Choreographed by Daniele and Jeff Calhoun. Supervising musical director/vocal and incidental music arranger, John McDaniel. Sets, Tony Walton; costumes, William Ivey Long; lighting, Beverly Emmons; music director/dance music arrangements, Marvin Laird; orchestrations, Bruce Coughlin; sound, G. Thomas Clark; production manager, Arthur Siccardi. Opened March 4, 1999. Reviewed Feb 28. Running time: 155 mins.

Ron Holgate (Buffalo Bill), Tom Wopat (Frank Butler), Valerie Wright (Dolly Tate), Andrew Palermo (Tommy Keeler), Nicole Ruth Snelson (Winnie Tate), Kevin Bailey (Mac/Running Deer), Peter Marx Foster (Charlie Davenport), Ronn Carroll (Wilson/Pawnee Bill), Gregory Zaragoza (Chief Sitting Bull), Bernadette Peters (Annie Oakley), Cassidy Ladden (Jessie Oakley), Mia Walker (Nellie Oakley), Trevor McQueen Eaton (Little Jake), Carlos Lopez (Eagle Feather), Brad Bradley (Dining Car Waiter), Patrick Wetzel (Sleeping Car Porter), Marvin Laird (Band

Leader), Julia Fowler (Mrs. Schuyler Nelson), Jenny-Lynn Suckling (Sylvia Potter-Porter). With: Shaun Amyot, Randy Donaldson, Madeleine Ehlert, Kisha Howard, Adrienne Hurd, Keri Lee, Desiree Parkman, Eric Sciotto, Kelli Bond Severson, Timothy Edward Smith, David Villella.

With one cowboy boot planted firmly in our PC age and the other still covered in dust from 1946, this new revival has a distinct identity crisis. Attempting to bridge a 50-year gap in attitudes toward the man-woman question – to say nothing of the cowboy-Indian one – the purveyors of the revival only complicate matters by adding a layer of textual irony, stepping back from the Irving Berlin musical's admittedly dated charms even as they present them with gusto. The result is a show that wants to wow us with old-style panache even as its stylistic frame seems to argue that that isn't enough. It's no wonder this *Annie Get Your Gun* doesn't quite hit the bull's-eye.

Steering clear of the brassy tomboy style that presumably marked Ethel Merman's performance in the original, Peters' Annie Oakley is a laidback, slightly dim backwoods girl who speaks in a girlish, molasses-thick Southern drawl (which sounds odd with Peters' nasal voice). But when she is singing, hold on to your ten-gallon hat. The accent is wisely abandoned, the constraints of an unconvincingly written character melt away, and she pours more honest emotion and theatrical intelligence into each song than can be found in the flat-footed book.

It's hard to remain engaged by the cornball story when you're constantly aware that the folks up there enacting it aren't really expecting you to be. The dilemma faced by Daniele and company is not a small one, of course. The original Herbert and Dorothy Fields book was probably never more than standard-issue fluff ("not hard to take," faintly praised *Variety* in '46.)

As You Like It

A Williamstown Theater Festival presentation of the play by William Shakespeare in two acts. Directed by Barry Edelstein. Sets, Narelle Sissons; costumes, Anita Yavich; lighting, Rui Rita; music, Mark Bennett; sound, Kurt B. Kellenberger; fight director, J. Steven White; stage manager, Leila Knox; arrangements, Simon Deacon. Opened Aug 5. Reviewed Aug 6. Running time: 180 mins.

Stephen Barker Turner (Oliver), Alessandro Nivola (Orlando), Larry Marshall (Adam), Sterling Brown (Dennis), Byron Jennings (Duke Frederick/Duke Senior), Megan Dodds (Celia), Gwyneth Paltrow (Rosalind), Mark Linn-Baker (Touchstone), Bruce MacVittie (Le Beau), Mark K. Smaltz (Charles), Michael Cumpsty (Jaques), Keith Byron Kirk (Amiens), Tom Bloom (Corin), John Ellison Conlee (Silvius), Angelina Phillips (Phoebe), Lea DeLaria (Audrey), Sam Breslin Wright (William), Denis Holmes (Sir Oliver Martext), David D. Turner (Jaques de Boys). With: Cheryl Lynn Bowers, Kate Moennig, Samuel Baum, Sterling Brown.

Shakespearean drag proved exceptionally rewarding for Gwyneth Paltrow in *Shakespeare in Love*, so it's entirely fitting that the bright young star should return to the stage as Rosalind in the Williamstown Theater Festival's *As You Like It*. Paltrow gives an ardent and appealing performance, full of larking high spirits and smiling charm. Alas, she doesn't succeed in communicating (after only three weeks of rehearsal, granted) the wisdom and emotional maturity that are so central to this extraordinarily rich character. In that respect, her performance is of a piece with Barry Edelstein's production, a

consistently funny if superficial romp through what is perhaps the Bard's most refined and sophisticated comedy.

The play is famously short on plot. By the end of the first act, its onstage action is more or less at an end. The good Duke Senior has been exiled from the court by his usurping brother Frederick; likewise the good Orlando is chased from town by his envious brother Oliver. Duke Senior's daughter Rosalind, too, is unjustly banished by Duke Frederick and is followed by her loyal friend Celia, Frederick's daughter.

They are all victims of strangely arbitrary emotion, and the progress of the play, a series of ruminative or jesting conversations between the court exiles and the rustics of the forest, traces a gentle progress toward righting these and other emotional wrongs, re-establishing the proper emotional and social equilibrium through a many-sided examination of the meanings and manners of another seemingly arbitrary feeling – love.

Bash

An Eric Krebs and Stephen Pevner presentation of three one-act plays by Neil LaBute. Directed by Joe Mantello. Sets, Scott Pask; costumes, Lynette Meyer; lighting, James Vermeulen; sound, Red Ramona; production stage manager, Babette Roberts. Opened June 24, 1999. Reviewed June 22. Running time: 135 mins.

With: Calista Flockhart, Ron Eldard, Paul Rudd.

Neil LaBute (filmmaker of *In the Company of Men*) examines nefarious behaviour among white-collar warriors and urban sophisticates in a collection of three contemporary horror stories.

Medea Redux is a solo work performed by Flockhart as her character reveals the terrible consequences of her own seduction by an older man. She sits at a plain table in a glaring pool of light, facing an unseen interrogator as she unfolds a tale that tours some quietly harrowing terrain before its disappointingly lurid finale.

LaBute's writing is at its finest here. Flockhart's tremulous air, her fluttering hands and gauntly lit features lend an air of disturbing authenticity to a tale that is most affecting when it's least sensational. Eldard is equally fine in a blackly comic turn as a Mormon businessman smoothly recalling the terrible lengths to which he went to ensure his continued employment as a middle manager at the Salt Lake office of a generic conglomerate. This play, *Iphigenia in Orem*, ends with essentially the same tragedy as *Medea Redux*, a supposedly loving parent's murder of his own child.

In *A Gaggle of Saints*, Flockhart and Rudd play two handsome Mormon college students who hit New York for a formal affair one spring weekend and end up embroiled in a gruesomely described gay bashing. Despite performances that flesh out these quiet devils as best they can, we leave *Bash* with no new knowledge of its ostensible subject, the seemingly normal heart's terrible capacity for cruelty. Watching the play is like staring into the souls of statistics, trying to examine the hearts of newspaper headlines.

Blue Heart

A Brooklyn Academy of Music presentation of an Out of Joint production of two one-act plays (one intermission) by Caryl Churchill. Directed by Max Stafford-Clark. Sets and costumes, Julian McGowan; lighting, Johanna Town; sound, Paul Arditti; stage manager, Kim Beringer. Opened Jan 29, 1999. Reviewed Jan 30. Running time: 100 mins.

... September 16 ...

The Fox web greenlights a Muhammad Ali biopic to be produced by Fox TV Studios Pictures and Robert De Niro's Tribeca Productions.

HEART'S DESIRE: June Watson (Alice), Mary Macleod (Maisie), Bernard Gallagher (Brian), Pearce Quigley (Lewis), Sally Rogers (Susy), Alexandra Roberts (Young Australian Woman).
BLUE KETTLE: Pearce Quigley (Derek), June Watson (Mrs. Plant), Mary Macleod (Mrs. Oliver), Sally Rogers (Enid), Doreen Mantle (Mrs. Vane), Anna Wing (Miss Clarence), Bernard Gallagher (Mr. Vane), Gabrielle Blunt (Mother).
Heart's Desire finds a middle-class English family in the kitchen awaiting the return of a daughter from Australia. The suspense Churchill generates as you wonder what could possibly happen next darkens almost into fear. Amid the excitement of anticipation, Maisie suddenly delivers a homely little speech about her fear of death. A trio of terrorists burst in and annihilate the whole family, and the actors take a little longer than usual to start up again.

Although *Blue Kettle* is a more somber play, it's a moving, strangely affirmative piece. In it, a young man named Derek approaches a series of women and pretends to be the son they gave up for adoption decades ago. As the play proceeds, the dialog is insidiously invaded by the words "blue" and "kettle." The final scene, in which one of the women learns that he is not in fact her son, and Derek implores her to love him anyway, is both devastating and uplifting.

The need for emotional connection runs deeper than language, deeper even than blood, Churchill seems to be saying. And just as communication will take place regardless of the syllables used, necessary human connections will be forged and relationships will have meaning even if the pretexts for them are false and meaningless. It's a thought as inspiriting as the theatrical form it comes in is inspired.

Book of Days

A Hartford Stage Co. presentation, produced in collaboration with the Repertory Theater of St. Louis, of a play in two acts by Lanford Wilson. Directed by Marshall W. Mason. Set, John Lee Beatty; costumes, Laura Crow; lighting, Dennis Parichy; sound, Chuck London; stage manager, Denise Yaney. HSC artistic director, Michael Wilson. Opened, reviewed Oct 27, 1999. Running time: 155 mins.
Suzanne Regan (Ruth Hoch), Matthew Rauch (Len Hoch), Jonathan Hogan (Boyd Middleton), Shannon Burkett (Ginger Reed), Dee Hoty (Martha Hoch), Jim Haynie (Walt Bates), Pamela Dunlap (Sharon Bates), Alan Campbell (James Bates), Bellamy Young (Luann Bates), Boris McGiver (Earl), John Lepard (Rev. Bobby Groves), Tuck Milligan (Sheriff Conroy Atkins).
The play begins with the entire cast coming onstage to deliver a series of documentary facts about the town of Dublin, Missouri. We quickly learn that Dublin is dominated by a cheese factory and a fundamentalist church, and that its community theatre is producing *Saint Joan*, directed by Boyd Middleton (Jonathan Hogan). Although Middleton's story is presented as an important element, it really doesn't have much to do with the central storyline, which concerns the mysterious death of the cheese factory's owner Walt Bates (a charismatic Jim Haynie) during a tornado.

Other characters include the son of the murdered cheese millionaire, a womanizer who always wore condoms while having sex with his wife, and thus can have his marriage annulled for lack of consummation, according to local church law. Broadway vet Dee Hoty clearly enjoys her role as Len's

mother, the dean of a junior college who in her youth was stoned at Woodstock. The script has puzzling idiosyncrasies: the repetition of the line "If you listen very carefully," followed by silence and a distant gunshot; the replaying of a scene from act one in act two; and a scene in which one actress briefly impersonates another role. It becomes increasingly odd as it goes along, never more so than in a second-act scene in which churchgoers begin to speak in tongues and have religious fits. The Hartford opening-night audience found the scene a little too hilarious, and the play went out the window.

The Boys From Syracuse

A Reprise! presentation of a musical in two acts, with music by Richard Rodgers, lyrics by Lorenz Hart and book by George Abbott. Concert adaptation by David Ives. Produced by Marcia Seligson. Directed by Arthur Allan Seidelman. Choreographed by Travis Payne. Musical direction by Peter Matz. Sets, Gary Wissmann; costumes, David R. Zyla; lighting, Tom Ruzika; sound, Philip G. Allen; stage manager, Ronn Goswick. Opened and reviewed Sept 22, 1999. Running time: 135 mins.
John Ganun (Police Sergeant), Charlie Dell (Aegeon), Marvin Thornton (Duke of Ephesus), Will Heermance (Guard), Jason Graae (Dromio of Ephesus), Scott Waara (Antipholus of Ephesus), Gus Corrado (Tailor/Goldsmith), Christopher Sieber (Antipholus of Syracuse), David Hyde Pierce (Dromio of Syracuse), Chad Borden (Merchant), Lea DeLaria (Luce), Karen Culliver (Adriana), Tia Riebling (Luciana), Marian Mercer (Sorceress), Ruth Gottschall (Courtesan). With: Christa Jackson, Tera Bonilla, Shannon Pritchard, Sierra A.R. Rein, Bart Doerfler, Tyson Sheedy, Daria Somers, Fred Voss.
Reprise! has scored a triumph with its new production of Rodgers & Hart's *The Boys From Syracuse*. Despite a checkered three-year history, this semi-staged concert series has tastefully revived some wonderful musicals. And this production is best of breed, with an exceptionally talented cast put through the paces by an astute and imaginative director. Rodgers & Hart's 1938 show is one of the glories of the American musicaltheater: witty, irreverent and sweet. The tuner is, after all, home to such classics as "Falling in Love With Love," "This Can't Be Love," "You Have Cast Your Shadow on the Sea" and "Sing For Your Supper," among several other outstanding songs.

Based on Shakespeare's *The Comedy of Errors*, the show tells of two sets of twins accidentally reunited after years of separation. Antipholus and his servant Dromio have lived in Ephesus for years. Their Syracuse-based siblings, who share the same names, are merely passing through. But citizens of Ephesus can't tell the visiting Antipholus and Dromio from their resident siblings. The confusion is grist for this comic mill, made even funnier, of course, because the "twins" don't really look alike. At its center are the twin Dromios, played by the droll Hyde Pierce and the flinty Graae. Graae is the better singer and a more aggressive actor, but the subtler Hyde Pierce possesses fetching puppy-dog charm. In a show of many highlights, there isn't a single song that falls flat.

Boston Marriage

An American Repertory Theater presentation of a play in three acts written and directed by David Mamet. Set, Sharon Kaitz and J. Michael Griggs; costumes, Harriet Voyt; lighting, John Ambrosone; stage managers, Rosetta E.R. Lee and Tara

Hoping to open the doors for U.S. films in China, MPAA chair and CEO Jack Valenti gives a hearty welcome to Chinese Deputy Consul General Deng Ying.

M. Galvin. Artistic director, Robert Brustein. Opened June 9, 1999. Reviewed June 13. Running time: 105 mins.
Rebecca Pidgeon (Claire), Felicity Huffman (Anna), Mary McCann (Catherine, the maid).
Set at the turn of the century in an American city, the play revolves around two women who were once lovers. It does not, however, explore lesbianism. The central characters could just as well be a man and a woman or two men.

This lack of characterization is furthered by Mamet's highly stylized direction, which requires actresses Rebecca Pidgeon (Claire) and Felicity Huffman (Anna) to declaim their dialogue rather than act it. The play begins with Claire visiting Anna to ask her if she may bring the new young woman she's lusting after to Anna's home in order to seduce her. Anna agrees as long as she can watch through a hole in the wall. It turns out that Claire's would-be lover is the daughter of Anna's protector, and when the daughter sees Anna wearing what is actually her mother's necklace, Anna is clearly in a spot of bother. She suggests a seance to explain matters, but by the time the play ends, it appears that much of what has occurred has been a ploy on Anna's part to get Claire back.

It's impossible to decipher a rationale for the amateurish, unfinished-looking set by Sharon Kaitz and J. Michael Griggs, a painterly, pinkish drawing room replete with curlicues and powder-blue furniture that's feminine to the point of being effeminate. All in all, *Boston Marriage* is an artificial Mamet sweetmeat that's as likely to give toothache as pleasure.

Captains Courageous

A Manhattan Theater Club presentation of a musical in two acts with music by Frederick Freyer, book and lyrics by Patrick Cook, based on *Captains Courageous*, courtesy of Turner Entertainment Co. Directed by Lynne Meadow. Musical staging, Jerry Mitchell. Music direction, Robert Gustafson. Set, Derek McLane; costumes, Catherine Zuber; lighting, Brian MacDevitt; sound, Otts Munderloh; orchestrations, Jonathan Tunick; music adviser, Paul Bogaev; music coordinator, Seymour Red Press; dialect coach, Deborah Hecht; production stage manager, Ed Fitzgerald. Artistic director, Meadow. Opened Feb 16, 1999. Reviewed Feb 11. Running time:125 mins.
Erick Buckley (Harris), Dick Decareau (Evans/Eliot), Michael DeVries (Mr. Cheyne/Peters), Brandon Espinoza (Harvey E. Cheyne), J. Lee Flynn (Ollie), Pete Herber (Hemans/Parent), George Kmeck (Walters), Norm Lewis (Doc), Michael X. Martin (Long Jack), Michael Mulhern (Captain Troop), Gary Schwartz (Murphy/Attendant 2), Dan Sharkey (Simon/Teacher), Daniel Siford (Tom Platt/Attendant 1), Jim Stanek (Dan), Erik Stern (Stephens/Principal), Treat Williams (Manuel).
Sweet of spirit, beguilingly old-fashioned and utterly unexciting, the musical *Captains Courageous* has many admirers, but despite Meadow's artful and handsome chamber production, it's hard to see what inspired such enthusiasm for this nicely behaved but rather plain child. Spoiled rich kid Harvey E. Cheyne is kicked out of private school for unruliness, whereupon his neglectful magnate dad agrees to bring him on a transatlantic business voyage.

Espinoza is obnoxious as he torments the crew aboard the ocean liner. When he tries to snag daddy's straying attention by walking along the railing, he falls overboard. He is picked up by Portuguese immigrant fisherman Manuel, one of a larger crew aboard a ship for three months, and not about to head in to port to bring little Harvey back to New York. The persnickety kid is both softened and toughened by learning the value of hard work aboard the ship, and gains the respect of the hard-boiled lads. The fatherly love that Harvey has been denied is slowly born in Manuel.

The storybook predictability is not helped by the score's monotonous tendencies. Freyer writes pretty, subtly insinuating melodies, but most of the songs are either sea-flavored solos or rousing anthems for the full chorus of sailors. Cook's workmanlike lyrics aren't particularly graceful, and the songs begin to seem interchangeable after awhile. Eventually it's not just Derek McLane's turntable set but the show itself that seems to be going in circles.

The Captain's Tiger

A Manhattan Theater Club presentation of a play in one act by Athol Fugard. Directed by Fugard and Susan Hilferty. Sets and costumes, Hilferty; lighting, Dennis Parichy; music, Lulu Van Der Walt; sound, Darron L. West; production stage manager, Susie Cordon. Opened Jan. 19, 1999. Reviewed Jan 17. Running time: 105 mins.
Athol Fugard (The Author), Tony Todd (Donkeyman), Felicity Jones (Betty).
The year is 1952, and Fugard, who also plays the main character (identified only as "The Author" in the programme), has landed on a cargo ship after hitchhiking up the continent from his home in South Africa, and his job as the captain's gofer leaves him with plenty of time to begin the novel he's been itching to write, the story of his mother's disappointed life. When the young writer sits down to his work, his subject rises before him, clad in airy white linens in the full freshness of her youth, as she was captured in a photograph that has always haunted him. This vision – named Betty and played by Felicity Jones – locks horns with the author as he pens the pages of her destiny.

The difficulties the material poses are tied into the remoteness of the two characters who interact with the author, the second being a brooding engine room worker called a Donkeyman (Tony Todd).

"You can't play it safe as a writer," brags the young would-be artist, but the real revelation in those words will ultimately cause him to abandon his novel at the play's end. That ending has a moving resonance – just as *The Glass Menagerie's* Tom will forever be haunted by his sister, so will the author never shake the ghost of his mother – but it's a small wave of emotion that comes only after a long and perhaps too literary journey through a writer's beginnings.

The Civil War

A Pierre Cossette, Pace Theatrical Group/SFX Entertainment, Bomurwil Prods, Kathleen Raitt and Jujamcyn Theaters presentation of a musical in two acts with music by Frank Wildhorn, and book and lyrics by Wildhorn, Gregory Boyd and Jack Murphy. Directed by Jerry Zaks. Musical director, Jeff Lams. Musical staging, Luis Perez. Sets, Douglas W. Schmidt; costumes, William Ivey Long; lighting, Paul Gallo; sound, Karl Richardson; projections, Wendall K. Harrington; orchestrations, Kim Scharnberg; musical supervision, Jason Howland; music coordinator, John Miller; production manager, Peter Fullbright. Opened April 22, 1999. Reviewed April 18. Running time: 125 mins.

... September 18 ...
The Toronto Film Festival closes with **Onegin**, starring Ralph Fiennes.

Michael Lanning (Captain Emmett Lochran), Rod Weber (Sergeant Patrick Anderson), Royal Reed (Sergeant Byron Richardson), Gilles Chiasson (Corporal William McEwen), Ron Sharpe (Private Conrad Bock), Bart Shatto (Private Elmore Hotchkiss), John Sawyer (Private Nathaniel Taylor), Gene Miller (Captain Billy Pierce), Dave Clemmons (Sergeant Virgil Franklin), Mike Eldred (Corporal John Beauregard), David M. Lutken (Corporal Henry Stewart), Anthony Galde (Private Darius Barksdale), Jim Price (Private Cyrus Stevens), Matt Bogart (Private Sam Taylor), Keith Byron (Frederick Douglass), Michel Bell (Kirk Clayton Toler), Cheryl Freeman (Bessie Toler), Lawrence Clayton (Benjamin Reynolds), Wayne W. Pretlow (Exter Thomas), Capathia Jenkins (Harriet Jackson), Cassandra White (Liza Hughes), Leo Burmester (Autolycus Fell), Irene Molloy (Sarah McEwen), Hope Harris (Violet/Nurse), Beth Leavel (Mabel/Mrs. Bixby), David M. Lutkens (Voice of President Lincoln). With: David Michael Felty, Monique Midgette, Raun Ruffin.

In *The Civil War*, all you get is the facile power pop. The creators simply decided to tell no story at all. The show is essentially a song cycle in full battle dress: a series of numbers performed for the audience by a cast of generic soldiers and slaves that never for a moment engage us as dramatic characters. So Wildhorn's songs must carry the full freight of the musical. And blandly pleasant though his melodies are, they aren't up to the essential task of evoking a rich period in history that has inspired innumerable artists and historians over the past century and more. Because they're all written in specifically contemporary styles – pop rock, country rock, contemporary gospel – Wildhorn's songs never convey a palpable sense of this turbulent time. It's hard to be moved by a soldier's lament for the waste of the war when what he's singing reminds you of an Eagles album of the '70s, or a Garth Brooks disc from the '90s. With no real characters to speak of and minimal narrative to shape, it's hard to see what Jerry Zaks was expected to do, other than get the singers on and off the stage gracefully.

Even without an engaging dramatic frame, *Civil War* attracts audiences used to Wildhorn's pumped-up emotionality, but it's a numbing musical that always substitutes self-importance and superficiality for an original or authentically felt examination of a traumatic period in American history.

Closer

A Robert Fox, Scott Rudin, Roger Berlind, Carole Shorenstein Hays, ABC Inc. and the Shubert Organization presentation of a play in two acts written and directed by Patrick Marber. Sets and costumes, Vicki Mortimer; lighting, Hugh Vanstone; music, Paddy Cunneen; sound, Simon Baker; production stage manager, R. Wade Jackson. Opened March 25, 1999. Reviewed March 23. Running time: 130 mins

Anna Friel (Alice), Rupert Graves (Dan), Ciaran Hinds (Larry), Natasha Richardson (Anna).

Closer's dialogue has a raw emotionality rarely heard in art or life. Marber's cast is more than up to the task of bringing the needed nuances to this artful play's complexities. Play is hard to watch; its truths are painful, its honesty makes you wince.

Dan is an obituary writer and aspiring novelist who meets the younger Alice when she steps in front of a taxicab and is sent to the hospital. The play then skips forward more than a year. Alice and Dan are a couple, and Anna, a divorced and world-weary photographer, is snapping Dan for a book jacket.

The sexual attraction between them is instant, but Anna resists. The fourth character in the play is a dermatologist named Larry. It was Larry who treated Alice's injured leg at the hospital, but he enters the play's sexual equation only by cyberchance, when Dan, posing as a woman named Anna in an Internet chat room, suggests a meeting at which the real Anna happens to turn up.

Anna and Larry are united and the lives of all four characters are turned inside out in a masterfully directed scene that brings the subterranean ache of the play into wounding bloom. Dan coolly tells Alice that he and Anna are in love. From here unfolds an elegantly choreographed tale of love, jealousy, pain and revenge that leaves all the characters wounded and one dead.

Company

A Huntington Theater Company presentation of a musical in two acts with music and lyrics by Stephen Sondheim and book by George Furth. Directed by Larry Carpenter. Choreography, Daniel Pelzig; music direction, F. Wade Russo; set, Loren Sherman; costumes, Toni-Leslie James; lighting, Phil Monat; sound, Duncan Edwards; production stage manager, Jennifer Lynn Brown. Huntington producing director, Peter Altman.

Davis Gaines (Robert), Andy Umberger (Harry), Susan Cella (Sarah), John Schiappa (Peter), Teri Bibb (Susan), William Parry (David), Maureen Silliman (Jenny), Dann Fink (Paul), Tia Speros (Amy), Walter Charles (Larry), Karen Mason (Joanne), Kim Lindsay (Kathy), Angela Lockett (Marta), Marie Danvers (April).

Over the years there have been at least four different versions of *Company*. The original was given a sleek, cool, even chilly air by Boris Aronson's high-tech chrome setting. Loren Sherman has gone for an altogether different look, creating a realistic Manhattan Soho loft apartment. This much cozier, homier-looking set, along with a cast that looks less glossy and glamorous than the Broadway original, gives the characters a mite more humanity. Something may be lost in the lack of surface slickness, but something is also gained, even if we don't know any of the characters very well, one of the show's basic flaws.

Other changes from the 1970 original include the elimination of the dance number "Tick Tock," the use of the song "Marry Me a Little," and the cutting of four cast members, the female quartet known as the Vocal Minority. There are now 14 rather than 18 performers in the cast.

Director Larry Carpenter and his cast have done everything in their power to bring the musical to vivid life, starting with Gaines' Bobby. His performance climaxes in the musical's pivotal scene, "The Ladies Who Lunch." Gaines manages to top "Lunch" with his wail of anguish at his inability to commit, to live, which leads into his powerful epiphany "Being Alive." The entire cast works beautifully together in "Side By Side By Side."

Crimes of the Heart

A Falcon Theater presentation of a play in two acts by Beth Henley. Directed by Garry Marshall. Sets, Akeime Mitterlehner; costumes, Karyl Newman; lighting, Dan Weingarten; sound, Steve Goodie; stage manager, Kevin Larkin. Opened and reviewed Oct 20, 1999. Running time: 165 mins.

... September 19 ...
Columbia's action-comedy **Blue Streak** led the weekend box office with an estimated $19.2 million.

Faith Ford (Lenny McGrath), Morgan Fairchild (Chick Boyle), Paul Satterfield (Doc Porter), Stephanie Niznik (Meg McGrath), Crystal Bernard (Babe Botrelle), Jake Wall (Barnette Lloyd).

In launching its "inaugural" season with Beth Henley's Pulitzer Prize-winning *Crimes of the Heart*, Garry Marshall's Falcon Theater has opted for safe and respectable material. Marshall's production of the play is safe and respectable, too, casting a bevy of female TV stars, some shown off to better effect than others.

Like so many other Pulitzer winners, Henley's play seems a bit light these days. Its comedy is well-crafted but utterly predictable, its fey Southern Gothic sensibility a bit too familiar at this point. Indeed, were it not for its length, *Crimes* could be a sitcom.

The story of three discontented sisters reunited by crisis, *Crimes* examines in fairly straightforward fashion how life rarely turns out as we expect. Lenny McGrath is a tightly wound, if sympathetic, spinster. Her sister Meg, also unmarried, fled to California to pursue a singing career, but she has returned to the small Mississippi town of her youth because sister Babe has shot her husband under mysterious circumstances. Though the action takes place over only two days, a host of conflicts get resolved by play's end.

Faith Ford's commanding turn as Lenny most holds our interest. Her tears seem real, her laughter unforced. But it's her earnest, goofy manner, complete with shy smiles, that really beguiles. No one else in the cast is quite that good, though Jake Wall is delightful in his zealous portrayal of Babe's aw-shucks lawyer, Barnette Lloyd.

Dame Edna: The Royal Tour

A Leonard Soloway, Chase Mishkin, Steven M. Levy and Jonathan Reinis presentation of a solo show in two acts devised and written by Barry Humphries, with additional material by Ian Davidson. Set, Kenneth Foy; costumes, Stephen Adnitt; lighting, Jason Kantrowitz; sound, Peter Fitzgerald; production stage manager, James W. Gibbs. Opened Oct 17, 1999. Reviewed Oct 13. Running time: 135 mins.
With: Dame Edna Everage (Barry Humphries), Andrew Ross, Roxane Barlow, Tamlyn Brooke Shusterman.

Dame Edna Everage, the housewife and self-proclaimed megastar from Australia arrives to the Great White Way in her first U.S. stage show. A tastefully garish hybrid of Margaret Thatcher and Liberace, this fantastic comic apparition is ready to conquer after vanquishing much of the rest of the English-speaking world with her deliriously silly vaudeville act marrying (and mocking) bourgeois propriety and show-biz egotism. Dame Edna is not, of course, a dame in any sense of the word. She sprang full-grown from the imagination of the Australian actor and artist Barry Humphries in the late 1950s. Previous U.S. forays via television series on Fox and NBC have been abortive.

In her first U.S. stage show, much of the stage entertainment is a savagely funny give and take across the footlights, as Dame Edna queries various audience members about their lives, lifestyles, eating habits and decorating tastes. She showers the audience with insults and upbraidings, all meant "in a nurturing way."

But Dame Edna has her own troubles to share with her shrink, Dr. Schadenfreude. There's her mysteriously still-unmarried son Kenny, now living in Chelsea after a career as a dress designer; her recalcitrant mother, now happily resting in a "maximum security twilight home;" and her daughter Valmai, of Flatbush, distressingly co-habitating with a "retired Czech tennis player" of the same sex. Humphries' creation makes us laugh because she is a larger-than-life reflection of universal human foibles.

Death of a Salesman

A David Richenthal, Jujamcyn Theaters, Allan S. Gordon and Fox Theatricals presentation, in association with Jerry Frankel and by special arrangement with the Roundabout Theater Co., of the Goodman Theater production of a play in two acts by Arthur Miller. Directed by Robert Falls. Sets, Mark Wendland; costumes, Birgit Rattenborg Wise; lighting, Michael Philippi; music and sound, Richard Woodbury; production stage manager, Joseph Drummond. Opened Feb 10, 1998. Reviewed Feb 8. Running time: 180 mins.
Brian Dennehy (Willy Loman), Elizabeth Franz (Linda), Kevin Anderson (Biff), Ted Koch (Happy), Richard Thompson (Bernard), Kate Buddeke (The Woman), Howard Witt (Charley), Allen Hamilton (Uncle Ben), Steve Pickering (Howard Wagner), Barbara Eda-Young (Jenny), Kent Klineman (Stanley), Stephanie March (Miss Forsythe), Chelsea Altman (Letta).

Fifty years to the day after its opening, Arthur Miller's *Death of a Salesman*, perhaps the defining play of the waning American century, has returned to Broadway on the cusp of the next. This play's trenchant and tender exploration of both the necessity and the tragedy of disillusionment is indeed as resonant as ever, its dissection of an American dreamer as topical as today's stock prices.

Robert Falls' new production is hardworking and admirable. It's solid and respectable without being reverent, as is the Willy Loman of Brian Dennehy, but it only intermittently touches the emotional depths of the play. Its success is fragmentary rather than cumulative, its overall effect somber and ruminative rather than transcendently moving.

Dennehy's physical bulk gives his performance a particular poignancy. For Dennehy's Willy, the American dream is like a drug habit he can't kick, both soothing and corrupting. A sense of growth is missing from his performance: Dennehy's Willy starts out almost where he ends up three hours later, anxious and brooding, with the same hopeful glint in his eyes as he contemplates the meager insurance money he imagines will provide his son with the chance to shortcut his way to specious success. Kevin Anderson is physically perfect for Biff – he looks like a high school Romeo whose good looks have gone slightly to seed – and he's powerful in the play's climax, when Biff and Willy finally, fitfully connect.

The Dinner Party

A Center Theatre Group/Mark Taper Forum presentation of a play in one act by Neil Simon. Directed by John Rando. Set, John Lee Beatty; lighting, Brian MacDevitt; sound, Jon Gottlieb; casting, Stanley Soble, Amy Lieberman, Jay Binder. Opened and reviewed Dec 1, 1999; closes Jan. 16, 2000. Running time: 95 mins.
John Ritter (Claude Pichon), Henry Winkler (Albert Donay), Edward Herrmann Mariette (Andre Bouville), Michelle Sanders (Levieux Annette), Veanne Cox (Yvonne Fouchet), Frances Conroy (Gabrielle Buonocelli).

Divorce, particularly the messy variety in which unfinished

business haunts former spouses for years on end, is the main course at Neil Simon's latest dissection of the middle-aged human condition. Simon brings together a collection of seeming strangers, bound only by the divorce lawyer they shared, and attempts to illuminate the pain and lack of resolution behind three failed marriages. With the weight of a personal memoir, this is a talky and confrontation-driven work that lacks both universal revelations and hearty laughs. It would need more sustenance to break through on Broadway, where comedy has had a tough time of late.

As usual, the characters are making the turn from 40 to 50, superficially well-off and no strangers to the better things in life. Curtain opens on Claude Pichon admiring a fresco at a three-star restaurant in Paris when Albert Donay bursts in, nervous and panicked. The two are in tuxedos and immediately set to talking about the curious nature of this particular party. They don't know each other, they don't know who else is dining and they come from two different walks of life. Once Simon has the guests assembled, the focus is sharpened. Characters are drawn as couples, not quite male-female mirror images, but with a clarity that makes the attraction between each not only plausible but likely. Play comes to a screeching halt as each couple goes through tales of peccadilloes, faux pas and overboard devotion.

Dinner With Friends

A Mitchell Maxwell, Mark Balsam, Ted Tulchin, Victoria Maxwell, Mari Nakachi and Steven Tulchin presentation of a play in two acts by Donald Margulies. Directed by Daniel Sullivan. Sets, Neil Patel; costumes, Jess Goldstein; lighting, Rui Rita; music and sound score, Michael Roth; sound, Peter Fitzgerald; production stage manager, R. Wade Jackson. Opened Nov 4, 1999. Reviewed Nov 3. Running time: 130 mins.
Matthew Arkin (Gabe), Lisa Emery (Karen), Julie White (Beth), Kevin Kilner (Tom).
A couple dissolves a marriage with minimal angst while the breakup of a four-way friendship leaves more lasting despair. In many ways the subtlest and most intelligent examination of the fragile and yet vital bonds of friendship since Yasmina Reza's Art. Even in this less than superbly cast production, Dinner With Friends is a fine play, but one constantly wishes it were a bit finer. But for the same reason, it's hard not to mourn the play's shortcomings as much as one lauds its strengths. In a neat reversal of the Tolstoy dictum, Margulies wittily seems to suggest that all unhappy marriages are alike, while it's the happy ones that show the fine distinctions.

The white canvas of Art that precipitated the near dissolution of a friendship is reflected here as the more everyday matter of a broken marriage. Fortysomething Gabe and Karen are serving a typically elaborate dinner for their friend Beth when she suddenly dissolves in tears, revealing that her husband, Tom, wants out of their marriage. The usual reasons have been given – Beth wails them out between sobs, as White's robustly funny performance establishes itself as the evening's most entertaining: The passion has died, Tom says Beth never understood him anyway, and there's another woman, too. Gabe and Karen spout the usual indignation and murmur the usual coos of sympathy. Gabe and Karen remain shell-shocked as they begin to sort out the significance of the breakup to their own union, questioning the reality of a friendship they thought they'd shared with an equally happy couple.

Enigma Variations

A Center Theater Group presentation, in association with Duncan C. Weldon, Francine Racette and Emanuel Azenberg, of a play in one act by Eric-Emmanuel Schmitt, translated by Roeg Jacob. Directed by Daniel Roussel. Sets, Ming Cho Lee; costumes, Candice Cain; lighting, Robert Wierzel; sound, Jon Gottlieb; music, Edward Elgar, adapted by Karl Fredrik Lundeberg; stage manager, Robin Veith. Opened, reviewed May 5, 1999. Running time: 90 mins.
Donald Sutherland (Abel Znork), Jamey Sheridan (Erik Larsen).
Enigma Variations proves relentlessly compelling. One wouldn't exactly call Schmitt's play a deep work – despite its philosophical pretensions, it's more witty than wise – but it possesses a strange, restless energy that holds one's attention despite deep flaws. Plot centers on the Nobel Prize-winning author Znorko and a provincial newspaper reporter come to interview him, Erik Larsen. Their battle of wits takes place in Znorko's living room on a remote island near the North Pole. Sutherland has the meatier role. Znorko is not only brilliant – tossing off epigrams like no one since Oscar Wilde – but also cold, snobbish and even mean.

Larsen arrives to visit the recalcitrant writer following the publication of Znorko's 21st book, an epistolary novel made up of love letters, and a marked departure from the rest of his oeuvre. At first, Znorko is a predictably terrible host, but a prolonged lack of human contact has made him desirous to connect with almost anyone, and so when Larsen attempts to leave, Znorko implores him to stay.

Schmitt has inserted an overarching mystery into his play, turning out to be its weakest component. As for the thesps, no complaints. But while Enigma may be beautiful to look at, and even to listen to, its lunge south two-thirds through is a bitter disappointment for those hoping that a real play of ideas would grace the stage. Figuring out why that's failed to happen is the real enigma here.

Epic Proportions

A Bob Cuillo, Brent Peek, Robert Barandes, Matthew Farrell and Mark Schwartz presentation, with Philip & Patricia Barry Prods. and Robert Dragotta, of a play in one act by Larry Coen and David Crane. Directed by Jerry Zaks. Sets, David Gallo; costumes, William Ivey Long; lighting, Paul Gallo; sound, Aural Fixation; fight director, Rick Sordelet; technical director, Peter Fulbright; production stage manager, Rick Steiger. Opened Sept 30, 1999. Reviewed Sept 28. Running time: 75 mins.
Michael Carroll (Narrator), Kristin Chenoweth (Louise Goldman), Alan Tudyk (Benny Bennet), Jeremy Davidson (Phil Bennet), Richard Ziman. (Jack, etc.), Ross Lehman (Shel, etc.), Tom Beckett (Octavium, etc.), Ruth Williamson (Queen, Cochette, etc.), Richard B. Shull (D.W. DeWitt).
A broad comedy of slight proportions that needs all the goosing it can get – and it gets plenty – from a crackerjack cast of stage comedians, led by one of Broadway's brightest new lights, Tony-winner Kristin Chenoweth. Set behind the scenes of a grandiose 1930s Egyptian-Biblical picture, play focuses on the huddled masses who carried spears or cried out against the wrath of some Caesar or other in the kind of lavish spectacle in which Cecil B. DeMille once specialized. Supervising this oppressed populace, camped on the set in the desert out-

side Tucson, Ariz., is Louise Goldman, "assistant director in charge of atmosphere personnel," i.e. extras, played by Chenoweth with adorable, preternatural perkiness. The workaday plot is a romantic triangle trifle that develops between Louise and brothers Benny and Phil Bennet, two hard-working extras whose fates diverge in true Hollywood-picture fashion.

Chenoweth's Louise is a no-nonsense kind of girl who likes to keep her dollar-a-day laborers in lines as strict as the waves in her marcelled hair. Some of the play's funniest bits involve Louise's field marshal tactics in eliciting the right groans of mass fear from the extras when they witness the assassination of the emperor Octavium. The play works best in these unabashedly silly moments that recall *The Carol Burnett Show.* One begins to wonder if a real play is ever going to emerge from the scattershot jokes – and yet you almost regret its arrival when it does:

Everybody's Ruby

A Joseph Papp Public Theater/New York Shakespeare Festival presentation of a play in two acts by Thulani Davis. Directed by Kenny Leon. Sets, Marjorie Bradley Kellogg; costumes, Mariann Verheyen; lighting, Tom Sturge; sound, Jeffrey Carlson; music, Dwight Andrews; dramaturg, Shirley Fishman; production stage manager, Lisa Porter. Producer, George C. Wolfe; artistic producer, Rosemarie Tichler. Opened March 9, 1999. Reviewed March 6. Running time: 160 mins.
Phylicia Rashad (Zora Neale Hurston),Beau Gravitte (Dr. C. Leroy Adams), Viola Davis (Ruby McCollum), Crystal Fox (Marie/Waitress/Receptionist), Bernie McInerney (Judge/Pharmacist), Raynor Scheine (Deputy Sheriff Barkley), J.R. Horne (White Citizen/Defense Attorney/Suit), Peggy Scott (White Citizen/Clerk/Mrs. X), Tuck Milligan (White Citizen/William Bradford Huie), James Shanklin (White Citizen/Prosecutor/Suit/Store Owner), Chuck Patterson (Black Citizen/Bartender/ Mechanic), Ron Cephas Jones (Black Citizen/Carpenter), Bryan Webster (Librarian Logan (Beau) Shipp), Bill Nunn (Barber/Sam McCollum).
The play, based on documentary accounts of the Harlem Renaissance author's investigation into the murder of a prominent white Southern doctor by a married black woman, overflows with intrigue, sex, melodramatic suspense and racial and gender politics. Unfortunately, the playwright never establishes a dramatic through-line for her material, which becomes so complicated that even the devoted cast of Kenny Leon's production can't keep it straight.

With her crumpled "old Harlem hat" and portable typewriter in hand, Zora returns to her home state of Florida to report on the case of Ruby McCollum, the woman about to stand trial for shooting Dr. C. Leroy Adams. Not long after the judge denies her request to interview the prisoner, she calls her friend William Bradford Huie, a white reporter with just the right hard-boiled attitude to help her uncover the facts.

Zora and William discover that Ruby and Dr. Adams had a longstanding sexual involvement, which began as a rape but turned into something more consensual. Ruby's husband Sam, who had underhanded business dealings with the doctor, not only condoned but encouraged his wife in the affair. Only when she got pregnant by her lover does his greed give way to rage, but then it's primarily out of frustration with

being saddled with a white man's kid. As both the play's title and subtitle ("Story of a Murder in Florida") suggest, the author has yet to find her narrative focus.

Far East

A Lincoln Center Theater presentation of a play in two acts by A.R. Gurney. Directed by Daniel Sullivan. Sets, Thomas Lynch; costumes, Jess Goldstein; lighting, Rui Rita; music and sound, Dan Moses Schreier; stage manager, Roy Harris. Artistic director, Andre Bishop; executive producer, Bernard Gersten. Opened Jan 11, 1999. Reviewed Jan 8. Running time: 110 mins.
Sonnie Brown (Reader), Michael Hayden ("Sparky" Watts), Bill Smitrovich (James Anderson), Lisa Emery (Julia), Connor Trinneer (Bob Munger), Mia Tagano, Toshiro Akira Yamamoto (Stagehands).
Set on a Japanese naval base in 1954 during a lull in the Korean war, *Far East* draws on Gurney's own history as a naval officer. "Sparky" Watts is an enthusiastic but callow naval officer who is looking for "significant life experiences," as he puts it to his dryly scornful captain. Lisa Emery, as the captain's wife Julia, is perfectly cast, and gives the most delicately rendered performance in the play. Her growing attraction to the handsome young Sparky is of course the unspoken motive in her increasingly strenuous efforts to break up his affair. Instead of a deepening focus on the relationship between Julia and Sparky, and the fissures in her marriage and his affair that it exposes, Gurney has supplied a contrasting subplot, in which it's revealed that Sparky's fellow officer Bob Munger is being blackmailed by a Japanese male lover.

Gurney has an intriguing subject here – the way the American military regimen constricts and warps human experience, even as it superficially seems to broaden it. Perhaps the startling emotional effect of the play's final tableau is connected to the play's determinedly restrained temperature. As Sparky, Julia and Bob take their seats in a transport plane home, each alone and lost in thought, the profound personal implications of their experiences hangs in the air unspoken and unexamined, and somehow the tense and mournful silence communicates much more than the previous two hours of dialogue.

Finian's Rainbow

A Coconut Grove Playhouse presentation, by special arrangement with Rodger Hess Prods., of a musical in two acts with music by Burton Lane; book by E.Y. Harburg and Fred Saidy, revised by Peter Stone; and lyrics by E.Y. Harburg. Directed by Lonny Price. Choreographed by Marguerite Derricks. Musical director, Eric Stern. Sets, Loren Sherman; costumes, Paul Tazewell; lighting, Phil Monat; sound, Kurt Fischer; orchestrations, Ralph Burns; production stage manager, Neil Krasnow. Coconut Grove Playhouse producing artistic director, Arnold Mittelman. Opened in Coconut Grove, Fla. and reviewed Oct 23, 1999. Running time: 170 mins.
Brian Murray (Finian McLonergan), Austin Pendleton (Senator Billy Bob Rawkins), Kate Jennings (Sharon McLonergan), Denis O'Hare (Grant Ogh), Tina Ou (Susan Mahoney), J. Robert Spencer (Woody Mahoney), Don Stephenson (Buzz Collins), Joseph Webster (Howard Franklin), Terri White (Upstairs Maid). With: Kate Baldwin, Andrew Boyer, Cyrus Akeem Brooks, Angela

Brydon, Dioni Michelle Collins, Kim Craven, Christopher F. Davis, Stephanie Fittro, Asmeret Ghebremichael, Derric Harris, Scott Hislop, Denis Jones, Trent Armand Kendall, Vicky Lambert, Rosa Janae Lee, James Ludwig, Brandi Chavonne Massey, Wes Pope, Eric Riley.

Story opens in a travelogue over the overture by a sharp 18-piece orchestra. The journey depicts Finian McLonergan (Brian Murray) and his daughter Sharon (Kate Jennings Grant) en route from Ireland throughout America (including some odd backtracking) before arriving in Rainbow Valley near Fort Knox. There, Finian gives farmer Woody Mahoney (J. Robert Spencer) the cash needed to prevent the auction of land to Sen. Rawkins for back taxes.

Finian gets a small plot of land from Woody for his favour. There, he buries a pot of magical gold he's stolen from the leprechaun Ogh back in Ireland. Soon, Finian is playing cupid for his daughter and Woody, while awaiting the gold's magic to spread prosperity to the poor sharecroppers throughout the valley.

Murray delivers a warm, congenial performance as Finian, speckled with a subtle brand of wit. Grant and Spencer bring rustic qualities to the romantic leads, exhibiting real polish in their musical turns. Denis O'Hare gives the production its comic spark as the leprechaun Ogh. The humour lies more in O'Hare's brisk, boyish delivery than the jokes themselves.

Costumes, lighting and sound are first-rate. Loren Sherman's scenery evokes the sharecroppers' Rainbow Valley in multicolored pastel rags representing the sky, plus a large tree and giant-sized foliage. But clunky wagons representing fallen leaves, which transport singers during their vocal reveries, deserve to stay in Miami.

Fiorello!

Reprise! Broadway's Best in Concert presents a musical play in two acts, music by Jerry Bock, book by George Abbott and Jerome Weidman, lyrics by Sheldon Harnick, directed by Glenn Casale. Musical direction, Peter Matz; choreography, Kay Cole; scenic design, Gary Wissman; costume design, David R. Zyla; lighting design, Tom Ruzika, Steven Young; sound design, Philip G. Allen. Conductor/keyboard, Matz; associate musical director/pianist, Gerald Sternback; producing artistic director, Marcia Seligson. Opened and reviewed Nov 10, 1999; closes Nov 21. Running time: 130 mins.

Tony Danza (Fiorello LaGuardia), Amy Pietz (Marie), Jennifer Westfeldt (Thea), Lenny Wolpe (Ben), Suzanne Blakeslee (Dora), Mike Hagerty (Floyd), Ron Orbach (Morris), Brian Stepanek (Neil), Pamela Blair (Mitzi). Ensemble: Eddie Driscoll, Joshua Finkel, Daniel Guzman, Julie Janney, Carol Kline, George McDaniel, Stefanie Morse, Diane Vincent.

There are eons of evolutionary strata separating the lovable but dimly lit boxer-cabbie Tony Banta (*Taxi*) from the brilliant and aggressive little gadfly Fiorello LaGuardia, who rose to become mayor of New York. Tony Danza makes the transition from his best-known role with aplomb in this bare-bones but dynamic reprise: Broadway's Best in Concert revival of the 1959 Pulitzer Prize-winning musical that also took top Tony and N.Y. Drama Critics' Circle honors.

Danza captures the pugnacious, driving ambition of the little lawyer of Italian and Jewish heritage, who combined a fiercely intense integrity with an unwavering belief in himself and his ability to lead. Danza does not possess the most secure

vocal instrument but instills an infectious sincerity into his renderings of the workers' strike anthem, *Unfair*, and his political call to arms, *The Name's LaGuardia*. Danza's take-charge LaGuardia is complemented perfectly by Amy Pietz and Jennifer Westfeldt as the two women in his life. Music director Peter Matz and his accomplished onstage miniorchestra create seamless, period-evoking accompaniment to the whole proceedings.

Floyd Collins

A Bridewell Theater Co. presentation of a musical in two acts with music and lyrics by Adam Guettel, book and additional lyrics by Tina Landau. Directed by Clive Paget. Musical director, Nicholas Mojsiejenko. Choreography, Caroline Salem. Set and costumes, Louise Belson; lighting, Robert Bryan; musical supervisor, Mark Warman; sound, Steve Barnes; dialect coach, Rick Lipton. Musical numbers: "The Ballad of Floyd Collins," "The Call," "Where a Man Belongs," "Lucky," "Daybreak," "I Landed on Him," "Heart an' Hand," "The Riddle Song," "Is That Remarkable?," "The Carnival," "Through the Mountain," "Git Comfortable," "The Dream," "How Glory Goes." Opened July 13, 1999 in London. Reviewed July 12. Running time: 160 mins.

Nigel Richards (Floyd Collins), Ian Burford (Lee Collins), Anna Francolini (Nellie Collins), Jill Martin (Miss Jane), Craig Purnell (Homer Collins), Jeremy David (Skeets Miller), Philip Wrigley (Ed Bishop). With: Derek Bell, Colin Hill, Scott Fleming, Sam Mancuso, Keith Merrill, Christopher Key.

Floyd Collins ups the monomaniacal stakes, pitting its title character's sweaty determination against the ever-spiraling chaos above ground that finds his family, a local reporter and even society at large in varying degrees of anticipation, frenzy and collapse.

It's possible, too, that Guettel and Landau have given Floyd a passage or two of self-revelation too many: this is one character so busy explaining himself that there's disconcertingly little left for the audience to intuit. Nor do the lyrics avoid bathos, whether in Floyd's wish for feminine company – here borne out via a fantasy sequence that prompts the production's most embarrassing moment – or in his address to a long-absent mama whom he envisions, her arms outstretched.

A first glimpse of Louise Belson's cheesy set – a winding staircase adjoining intersecting pipework that marks out Floyd's "cave" – doesn't instill confidence; nor does the singing of the cast, most of whom sound as if they learned their American rustic vowel sounds by hanging out at *Whistle Down the Wind*. One doesn't, of course, expect this company to have creative artistry bred in their bones to the extent that Guettel so clearly does in his. (It's characteristic of the evening that in the name role, Richards sings loudly but not especially tunefully.) But it's essential to *Floyd Collins* that the music soars even as Floyd descends ever lower beneath ground. Otherwise, as is sadly the case here, he's not the only one left with a sinking feeling.

Fosse

A Livent (U.S.) Inc. presentation of a musical in three acts conceived by Richard Maltby Jr., Chet Walker and Ann Reinking, with choreography by Bob Fosse. Directed by Maltby. Co-directed and choreographed by Reinking.

Choreography recreated by Walker. Artistic adviser, Gwen Verdon. Sets and costumes, Santo Loquasto; lighting, Andrew Bridge; sound, Jonathan Deans; musical arrangements and supervision, Gordon Lowry Harrell; musical director, Patrick S. Brady; orchestrations, Ralph Burns and Douglas Besterman. Musical numbers: "Life Is Just a Bowl of Cherries," "Fosse's World," "Bye Bye Blackbird," "From the Edge," "Percussion 4," "Big Spender," "Crunchy Granola Suite," "I Wanna Be a Dancin' Man," "Shoeless Joe From Hannibal, Mo.," "Steam Heat," "I Gotcha," "Rich Man's Frug," "Cool Hand Luke," "Nowadays/The Hot Honey Rag," "Glory," "Manson Trio," "Mein Herr," "Take Off With Us - Three Pas de Deux," "Razzle Dazzle," "Who's Sorry Now?," "There'll Be Some Changes Made," "Mr. Bojangles," "Finale." Opened Jan. 14, 1999. Reviewed Jan. 12. Running time: 145 mins.

With: Valarie Pettiford, Jane Lanier, Eugene Fleming, Desmond Richardson, Sergio Trujillo, Kim Morgan Greene, Mary Ann Lamb, Dana Moore, Elizabeth Parkinson, Scott Wise, Julio Agustin, Brad Anderson, Andy Blankenbuehler, Bill Burns, Marc Calamia, Holly Cruikshank, Lisa Gajda, Scott Jovovich, Christopher R. Kirby, Dede LaBarre, Susan Lamontagne, Deborah Leamy, Shannon Lewis, Mary MacLeod, Brad Musgrove, Sean Palmer, Michael Paternostro, Rachelle Rak, Josh Rhodes, Lainie Sakakura, Alex Sanchez, J. Kathleen Watkins.

Fosse celebrates at length and in high style the long moment of a director-choreographer of unique and indelible gifts, as distinctive a dance artist as Broadway has produced. The show is an abundant collection of dances created by Fosse over the course of four decades and in almost as many mediums, including career landmarks from musicals *The Pajama Game*, *Damn Yankees*, *Sweet Charity*, *Chicago* and *Dancin'*, and selections from the shows that famously won him showbiz's triple crown in 1973: the movie *Cabaret*, the TV special *Liza With a Z* and Broadway's *Pippin*. But it's also, at times, a subtle and artfully crafted comment on the forces that drove him and the endless striving that led to his untimely death in 1987. One of the sad ironies of Fosse's career – and paradoxically one of the driving engines of his genius – was an unshakable feeling that nothing was ever enough.

If *Fosse* has a fault, it is a slavish need to include a virtual encyclopedia of Fosse's creations; the result is a feeling of superabundance that begins to set in when we're treated to the sixth piece from *Dancin'*. Fosse's dance vocabulary, while distinctly his own, was undeniably limited. So while it's enjoyable to see the ways he combined and recombined certain gestures across the course of the decades, the sheer volume of numbers on display here sometimes points up the confining nature of his repertoire of moves.

The Gershwins' Fascinating Rhythm

A Music Makers, Columbia Artists and Manny Kladitis presentation of a musical revue in one act with music and lyrics by George and Ira Gershwin, conceived for the stage by Mark Lamos and Mel Marvin from source material by Deena Rosenberg. Directed by Lamos. Musical direction and supervision, Cynthia Kortman. Choreography, David Marques. Sets, Michael Yeargan; costumes, Paul Tazewell; lighting, Peggy Eisenhauer; sound, Abe Jacob; orchestrations, Larry Hochman; musical and vocal arrangements, Mel Marvin; additional arrangement, Paul J. Ascenzo, Joseph Church; music coordinator, Michael Keller; production stage manager, Alan Hall. Opened April 25, 1999. Reviewed April 21. Running time: 95 mins.

With: Michael Berresse, Darius de Haas, Chris Ghelfi, Tim Hunter, Adriane Lenox, Karen Lifshey, Jill Nicklaus, Orfeh, Sara Ramirez, Patrick Wilson.

Fascinating it most assuredly is not, unless you're the kind who ogles car accidents. A strained and wholly unnecessary attempt to prove that the songs of dear old George and Ira are still young, fun and sexy, sexy, sexy. This revue might well have been called *Smokey George and Ira's Cafe*. But boomers aren't likely to thrill to its desperately funkified arrangements of classic tunes, and Gershwin lovers will be aghast. Consequently, the show doesn't have a prayer, even in this weak Broadway musical season.

In both its design and overall conception, the revue recalls various variety shows from the '70s and early '80s, from *Sonny and Cher* to, heaven help us, *Solid Gold*, from its lighting to its costumes. But the show's visual deficiencies would easily be forgiven if its musical achievements were accomplished. But here, too, unfortunately, a lack of taste prevails. Certainly the Gershwins' wealth of music is amply represented: In an intermissionless hour and a half (which feels a lot longer), the show's dozen performers race through 27 songs. But the subtle charms of all too many of them are squandered by self-conscious attempts to dress them up in contemporary musical styles. The greatest damage is done to Ira's lyrics, which are lost in the music mix and drained of wit by the often overblown performances.

Hedda Gabler

A Geffen Playhouse presentation of the play in two acts by Henrik Ibsen, adapted by Jon Robin Baitz, from a literal translation by Anne-Charlotte Hanes Harvey. Directed by Daniel Sullivan. Set, Riccardo Hernandez; costumes, Dunya Ramicova; lighting, Pat Collins; sound, Jon Gottlieb; production stage manager, Peter Van Dyke. Producing director, Gilbert Cates; managing director, Lou Moore. Opened, reviewed March 24, 1999 (runs through April 18). Running time: 140 mins.

Rosemary Murphy (Aunt Julia Tesman), Marjorie Lovett (Berta), Byron Jennings (George Tesman), Annette Bening (Hedda Gabler), Paul Guilfoyle (Judge Brack), Carolyn McCormick (Thea Elvsted), Patrick O'Connell (Eilert Lovborg).

Over a century after Ibsen penned his dark portrait of domestic despair, the play's central role remains a challenge to actresses – a character at once independently modern and a victim of her day. The new adaptation attempts to bridge the gap between 19th century mores and contemporary psychology, with mixed results.

Hedda Gabler is an imperious, demanding woman bent upon deflecting that awareness of her own doom. Yet she entered the situation with eyes wide open, marrying Tesman with no hopes – or illusions – of love. Tesman is a good-hearted, naive scholar consumed with "utterly vital minutiae." While his rival, Lovborg, brilliantly imagines the future, Tesman excels at collating the archival data he relentlessly collects. In a crucial paradox, she is a materialist, intent on building a high profile for herself and Tesman in society, yet she also harbors romantic, if ill-defined, ideals of courage and glory. At first, Hedda wounds others simply because she can. But as Lovborg and Mrs. Elvsted appear on the scene, unwit-

---

... September 24 ...

Former Seinfeld sidekick Michael Richards will reunite with a trio of former Seinfeld staffers to create a new sitcom.

tingly presenting themselves as pawns, Hedda engineers their destruction because she believes she must. Longing to "control someone's destiny" – in part because she sees no option that would allow her to shape her own – she plots a strategy that is, in her tormented understanding of the way things are, a matter of survival.

In her first stage work since 1988's New York production of *Coastal Disturbances*, Bening is a strong presence. She is the harrowing center of an effective, if too muted, *Hedda Gabler*.

Hedwig and the Angry Inch

A Canon Theatricals/Susan Dietz and Joan Stein presentation in association with David Bowie of a one-act musical with text by John Cameron Mitchell, song and lyrics by Stephen Trask. Director, Peter Askin. Set, James Youmans; costumes, Fabio Toblini; lighting, Kevin Adams; sound, Phil Harris; musical staging, Jerry Mitchell;. Opened, reviewed Oct 31, 1999. Running time: 105 mins.
Michael Cerveris (Hedwig), Miriam Shor (Yitzak). With: Stephen Trask, Theodore Liscinski, III, Paul Livingston, Sid Sosa.
The title character of the off-Broadway hit musical is a partially emasculated transvestite from East Germany with a sordid story of love found and lost. Michael Cerveris delivers a superb performance in this polished, energetic mix of monologue, rock concert, German-style cabaret and downtown performance art.

Hedwig's unparalleled identity crisis and effortless charisma capture the essence of glam-rock in a way that the film *Velvet Goldmine* never touched, and take it into a political and global context. Hedwig tells us how, in a botched sex-change operation, he sacrificed most of his appendage to escape communist East Berlin, only to watch on TV from a mobile home in Kansas as the Berlin Wall crumbled just a year later.

The theme of emancipation runs throughout, and provides the key to a moving if abstract ending. But Mitchell and Trask also layer in some philosophical depth with the song "Origin of Love," which recounts Plato's fanciful notion of humans having been split in two and forced to seek out their severed other halves. Hedwig desperately seeks this metaphorical long-lost love, but, given that he has been doubly split, is especially uncertain of where to find it or what his "other half" will look like. Trask's music here alternates among various styles, from punk to hard rock to folk to less categorizable hybrid sounds. The songs are also extremely effective in advancing Hedwig's narrative and communicating the character's emotional states.

Howie the Rookie

A Bush Theater presentation of a play in two acts by Mark O'Rowe. Directed by Mike Bradwell. Sets and costumes, Es Devlin; lighting, Simon Bennison; stage manager, Adrian Pagan. Artistic director, Brid Dukes. Opened in Dublin March 23, 1999. Reviewed March 25. Running time: 100 mins.
Aidan Kelly (The Howie Lee), Karl Shiels (The Rookie Lee).
Superficially, *Howie the Rookie* resembles McPherson's early plays in its format and its setting. But while McPherson's plays were character, *Howie the Rookie* is a language- and plot-driven affair, an outrageous, event-packed thrill ride through a blue-collar urban dystopia.

The play is set on two subsequent days in the lives of the Howie Lee and the Rookie Lee, two working-class acquaintances caught up in a series of gangland feuds over, among other things, a scabies-infected mattress and a pair of Siamese fighting fish. First enemies and then, briefly, allies, the two lads narrate their antics in a breathless staccato poetry: "Bottom of the loop, hang a U, Ginger Boy grabbin' the roof rack for dear life an' back up we go, this time sittin' inside the van, 'stead of hangin' out the side door, two thick monkeys."

The exhilaration of the language ironically underlines the dead-end desperation of the characters' lives; with nothing to do but scrabble over petty possessions and overblown grudge matches, the denizens of this world inevitably turn on and destroy each other. While these acts of violence make sense in the world O'Rowe describes, the layering on of a truly senseless tragedy involving the Howie's younger brother takes matters too far into melodrama, a lone false step in an otherwise well-plotted tale. Despite the few flaws in play and production, this is very assured work from an early-career writer.

Hughie

A Center Theatre Group/Music Center of Los Angeles County, Mark Taper Forum and Gordon Davidson presentation of a one-act play by Eugene O'Neill. Directed by Al Pacino. Set, David Gallo; costumes, Candice Donnelly; lighting, Donald Holder; sound, Jon Gottlieb; stage manager, Jon Gottlieb. Opened, reviewed July 27, 1999. Running time: 60 mins.
Paul Benedict (Charlie Hughes), Al Pacino (Eric Smith).
Eugene O'Neill might be surprised to learn he wrote so funny a work as *Hughie*. Rarely has the sacred umbilical cord between actor and audience been in such need of severing.

Dissolute gambler Eric Smith enters stage right to face night clerk Charlie Hughes. He tells the night clerk, who is new on the job, that for the past four or five days "I've been off on a drunk." Eric's only friend, the previous night clerk Hughie, has just died. The fun times continue when the night clerk gives voice to his many interior monologues, these asides coming to us through the echo chamber of electronic amplification. Obviously, he isn't listening to a word Eric says – until the play's very end, when it is too late and he replaces Hughie as the gambler's new dupe. Eric Smith is some piece of work, one of O'Neill's smaller, nastier creations. He can brag of nothing but booze, gambling and escaping the love of women who tried "to make a sucker" out of him. Pacino's direction pushes *Hughie* from the realistic to the expressionistic, two styles O'Neill experimented with throughout his career. With his signature eye-popping and arms flailing in a voluminous costume, Pacino is, for the most part, the classic sad sack as Eric Smith, and when he cons the new night clerk into replacing Hughie in a game of dice, he is, finally, the sly fox.

The Hunchback of Notre Dame

A Stella presentation, in association with Walt Disney Theatrical Prods., of a musical in two acts with music by Alan Menken, lyrics by Stephen Schwartz, book by James Lapine, German-language version by Michael Kunze. Based on Victor Hugo's *Notre Dame de Paris*. Directed by Lapine. Musical director, Klaus Wilhelm. Choreography by Lar Lubovitch. Sets, Heidi Ettinger; costumes, Sue Blane; lighting, Rick Fisher; sound, Tony Meola; projections, Jerome Sirlin; makeup and masks, Michael Ward; fight director, B.H. Barry; technical director, Ulf Maschek;

... September 25 ...
Paramount's **Double Jeopardy** leads the weekend
box office with an estimated $23.7 million.

musical supervisor and arranger, Michael Kosarin; orchestrations, Michael Starobin; dance arranger, Glen Kelly; stage manager, William Metz. Based on the film by Tab Murphy, Irene Mecchi, Bob Tzudiker and Noni White and Jonathan Roberts. Opened in Berlin June 5, 1999. Reviewed June 12. Running time: 150 mins.

Drew Sarich Frollo (Quasimodo), Jens Janke Esmeralda (Norbert Lamla Clopin), Fredrik Lycke Antoine (Judy Weiss Phoebus), Valentine Zahn (Tamas Ferkay Charles), Yvonne Ritz-Andersen (Loni), Carlo Lauber (Domdekan). With: David Oliver, Eladio Pamaran, Zoltan Tombor, Christopher Murray, Frank Logemann, Andreas Gergen, Andre Bauer, Ulrich Talle, Wolfgang Holtzel, Fabian Aloise, Ben Kazlauskaz, Andrew Gardner, Seth Lerner, Franc Tima, Gerald Michel, Christian Stuppeck, Philip Hogan, Scott Owen, Dominic Fortin, Petra Weidenbach, Luz Tolentino, Stephanie Reese, Ruby Rosales, Barbara Raunegger, Vera Bolten, Alyssa Preston, Inez Timmer, Sandy Nagel, Elena Frid, Coleen Besett, Patricia Gressley, Birge Funke, Danielle Gormann, Karin Sang.

Musical theater stagecraft scales dizzying heights in the Berlin world premiere of *The Hunchback of Notre Dame.* Further tinkering and some inevitable recasting will tell whether a show whose design often reaches to the skies is ready to take off. What's missing is the imprint of a director, like Julie Taymor, who brings to her work a purely joyous love of theater capable of moving millions. Or maybe it's just that Lapine's passions are in fact too private to deliver the affective goods on a scale to match a physical production that leaves no doubt how the show's $25 million budget was spent.

Set designer Heidi Ettinger's ever-shifting array of cubes join Jerome Sirlin's projections to conjure the medieval world of the Parisian bell tower inhabited by Quasimodo, his unyielding master Frollo and a trio of very chatty gargoyles who lead this show's answer to "Be Our Guest," the sprightly "A Guy Like You." A triangular love story finds Quasimodo and Frollo vying for the gypsy girl Esmeralda, whose fate lies with neither man. The prevailing tone is the most sombre of the three Disney film-to-stage shows yet. So why isn't the show as a whole more affecting? The answer lies in part with Stephen Schwartz and Alan Menken's Oscar-nommed score, which is actually at its best in the Weillian strains of Clopin's opener, "The Bells of Notre Dame." Elsewhere, away from its liturgical impulses, the music tilts toward the generic.

The Iceman Cometh

An Allan S. Gordon, Bill Haber, Ira Pittelman, Elan McAllister, Trigger Street Prods. and Emanuel Azenberg presentation of a play in three acts by Eugene O'Neill. Directed by Howard Davies. Sets and costumes, Bob Crowley; lighting, Mark Henderson; sound, John A. Leonard; music, Paddy Cunneen; production stage manager, Steven Zweigbaum. Opened April 8, 1999. Reviewed April 5. Running time: 260 mins.

Tony Danza (Rocky Pioggi), Tim Pigott-Smith (Larry Slade), Stephen Singer (Hugo Kalmar), Michael Emerson (Willie Oban), James Hazeldine (Harry Hope), Clarke Peters (Joe Mott), Robert Sean Leonard (Don Parritt), Patrick L. Godfrey (Cecil Lewis, The Captain), Ed Dixon (Piet Wetjoen, The General), Paul Giamatti (James Cameron (Jimmy Tomorrow)), Richard Riehle (Pat McGloin), Jeff Weiss (Ed Mosher), Catherine Kellner (Margie), Dina

Spybey (Pearl), Katie Finneran (Cora), Skip Sudduth (Chuck Morello), Kevin Spacey (Theodore Hickman (Hickey)), Steve Ryan (Moran), Ned Van Zandt (Lieb).

Often considered an oversized, typically O'Neillian slab of lugubriousness, *Iceman* is here revealed as a black comedy that celebrates the vivifying light of life shining even in the bleakest depths. With a knockout cast that infuses virtually all of the play's many characters with the warmth of real human beings, pulsating with irrepressible life even as they deaden their bruised souls with liquor, Davies and his company flood the stage with a kind of human illumination that only casts into stronger relief the deadly darkness at the play's core.

The slumped, dishevelled and half-dressed men pour into the chairs of Harry Hope's bar-room, forming a picturesque, painterly array. And as they swim back to consciousness, their sodden banter about booze and dreams of past and future glories takes on an unmistakably comic rhythm – these bottom-feeders perform a kind of vaudeville of despair and delusion, each taking a turn to strut his dismal stuff before his appreciative audience of fellow losers.

Enter Hickey, the traveling salesman whose arrival to celebrate Harry's birthday the gang has been awaiting since dawn. Spacey's performance is a commanding, casually charismatic turn. Of course Hickey's tragedy is that his love brings with it a chill from beyond the grave. For in forcing his friends to face life without illusions, Hickey is giving them over to death. The denizens of Harry Hope's don't dream because they're miserable weaklings and frauds, but because they're fully human. Where is the tragedy in hope, after all? It's only the dead who don't dream.

The Importance of Being Earnest

The Pasadena Playhouse presents a play in three acts by Oscar Wilde. Directed by Sheldon Epps. Sets, John Iacovelli; costumes, Dana Rebecca Woods; lighting, Victor En Yu Tan; sound, Frederick W. Boot; stage manager, Lea Chazin. Opened May 16, 1999. Reviewed May 15. Running time: 150 mins.

Robert Curtis Brown (John Worthing), Patrick Dempsey (Algernon Moncrief), David Purdham (Rev. Canon Chasuble), Morgan Rusler (Lane/Merrima), Shirley Knight (Lady Bracknell), Kaitlin Hopkins (Gwendolen Fairfa), Lina Patel (Cecily Cardew), Carolyn Seymour (Miss Prism).

Oscar Wilde's *The Importance of Being Earnest* is among those charmed plays that endlessly repays our consideration. It doesn't matter how often one has heard its jokes, quips and banter: Smiles and laughter will inevitably follow, as they do in Sheldon Epps' new production of the work at the Pasadena Playhouse. Yet there's nothing funny about Epps' rigid, unimaginative staging, complete with such "classy" touches as musical interludes by Debussy and an endless supply of tacky bric-a-brac.

The plot of *Earnest* is one of those delectable confections melding mistaken identity with thwarted love, but the real reward is Wilde's rotund language, polished to a high gloss. Indeed, many of the lines are so famous, thesps must avoid tipping their hand in delivering them. That's only one of many acting problems in the production.

At the centre of the comedy are wealthy idlers Jack Worthing and Algernon Moncrieff. They should be irresistibly charming. Brown comes close, and delivers most of his lines with relish.

Dempsey's Algernon is painful to watch and worse to listen to. His English accent is variable, and when it does stay put, Dempsey sounds more like a member of the working class than a swell. Casting Shirley Knight as the imperious Lady Bracknell was also a miscalculation. A fine actress, Knight possesses an enviable vulnerability – it's one of her claims to greatness – but that quality is entirely at odds with what Lady Bracknell represents.

It Ain't Nothin' But the Blues

An Eric Krebs, Jonathan Reinis, Lawrence Horowitz, Anita Waxman, Elizabeth Williams, CTM Prods. and Anne Squadron presentation, in association with Lincoln Center Theater, of the Crossroads Theater Co./San Diego Repertory Theater/Alabama Shakespeare Festival production of a musical revue in two acts by Charles Bevel, Lita Gaithers, Randal Myler, Ron Taylor and Dan Wheetman, based on an original idea by Taylor. Directed by Myler. Musical director, Wheetman. Set, Robin Sanford Roberts; lighting, Don Darnutzer; sound, Edward Cosla; production stage manager, Doug Hosney; movement, Donald McKayle. Opened April 26, 1999. Running time: 120 mins. **With: "Mississippi" Charles Bevel, Gretha Boston, Carter Calvert, Eloise Laws, Gregory Porter, Ron Taylor, Dan Wheetman.**

At the tail end of a Broadway musical season to leave you singing the blues, along comes a surprise contender, that gives rise to far happier feelings. It's not a traditional book musical, but this pleasingly unpretentious revue has soul and spirit to spare. In the hands of a fiercely gifted set of singers with deep affection for the songs they're performing, it adds up to two hours of pure musical pleasure.

The show is a sort of Blues 101, a sung history of the musical genre that traces it from its roots in African chants through its refinement in the American South and on to the various ancillary genres it influenced. As the show itself relates in some fairly light-handed historical narration, the blues has had a pronounced influence in shaping the country's musical culture: from Branson, Mo., to Motown to the Apollo Theater to Broadway, there are few popular musical genres that haven't been touched by the stirring soul of a sound that was born of pain but finds expression in joyful release.

Three of the show's seven principal performers – "Mississippi" Charles Bevel, Ron Taylor and Dan Wheetman – are also its authors (along with Lita Gaithers and Randal Myler, who also directs). This lends a personal touch that helps to humanize an occasionally slick, prefab feeling that is of course at odds with the down-home nature of the music.

James Joyce's The Dead

A Playwrights Horizons presentation, by special arrangement with Gregory Mosher and Arielle Tepper, of a musical in one act with book by Richard Nelson, music by Shaun Davey and lyrics conceived and adapted by Richard Nelson and Davey. Directed by Nelson and Jack Hofsiss. Choreography by Sean Curran. Sets, David Jenkins; costumes, Jane Greenwood; lighting, Jennifer Tipton; sound, Scott Lehrer; orchestrations, Davey; musical direction, Charles Prince; production stage manager, Kelley Kirkpatrick. Artistic director, Tim Sanford. Opened Oct 28, 1999. Reviewed Oct 25. Running time: 100 mins.

Sally Ann Howes (Aunt Julia Morkan), Marni Nixon (Aunt Kate Morkan), Emily Skinner (Mary Jane Morkan), Christopher Walken (Gabriel Conroy), Blair Brown (Gretta Conroy), Brian Davies (Mr. Browne), Stephen Spinella (Freddy Malins), Paddy Croft (Mrs. Malins), Alice Ripley (Miss Molly Ivors), John Kelly (Bartell D'Arcy), Brooke Sunny Moriber (Lily), Dashiell Eaves (Michael), Daisy Eagan (Rita/Young Julia), Daniel Barrett (Cellist), Louise Owen (Violinist).

A stage version of *The Dead* arrives, in a production that features one of the more extraordinary casts to be seen in New York this season. Joyce's story begins as a tribute to the generous embrace of Irish hospitality, and was inspired by his recollections of musical evenings at the home of his own great aunts. In the story, they become Julia and Kate Morkan, aunts of Gabriel Conroy who live with their niece Mary Jane. The ladies are hosting an annual dinner dance to celebrate the Feast of the Epiphany, and have collected about them friends and family and pupils – all three ladies are teachers of voice or music.

Joyce's story is a tribute to the joys and solaces of music, and its power to unlock the secrets of the heart. Turning Joyce's tale into a stage musical thus might seem a natural and relatively smooth process, but in fact it's a delicate operation – Joyce is a deeply lyrical writer, so adding music to his story is a bit like interpolating new notes into a composer's symphony. When Shaun Davey's music is embroidering Richard Nelson's mostly faithful, intelligent adaptation of the story, it is charming and effective. Most of the numbers are folk songs performed by the characters to entertain the party.

The resulting show is always thoughtful and admirable and honorable, occasionally wonderful. But it is also flawed; too much of the simple, subtle poetry of Joyce's story is diluted by some key missteps and a fairly disastrous piece of miscasting (particularly deadpan Walken who sabotages the emotional arc of the play).

Jane Eyre

A La Jolla Playhouse presentation of a musical in two acts based on the novel by Charlotte Bronte, with music and lyrics by Paul Gordon, book and additional lyrics by John Caird. Directed by Caird and Scott Schwartz. Musical direction, Steven Tyler. Sets, John Napier; costumes, Andreane Neofitou; lighting, Chris Parry; sound, Tom Clark and Mark Menard; orchestrations, Larry Hochman; stage manager, Lori M. Doyle. Opened July 25, 1999. Reviewed July 31. Closes Aug. 29. Running time: 180 mins.

Marla Schaffel (Jane Eyre), Tiffany Scarritt (Young Jane Eyre), Anne Allgood (Mrs. Reed/Lady Ingram), Nell Balaban (Grace Poole/Amy Eshton), James Barbour (Edward Rochester), Lauren Campbell (Schoolgirl), Elizabeth DeGrazia (Blanche Ingram), Bruce Dow (Robert), Megan Drew (Helen Burns), Kelly Felthous (Schoolgirl), Marguerite MacIntyre (Miss Scatcherd/Mrs. Dent/Bertha), Bill Nolte (Richard Mason), Jayne Paterson (Jane's Mother/Mary Ingram), Don Richard (Brocklehurst/Colonel Dent/Vicar), Joelle Shapiro (Adele), Mary Stout (Mrs. Fairfax), Rachel Ulanet (Louisa Eshton), Christopher Yates (Jane's Father/Mr. Eshton/St. John Rivers), Lee Zarrett (John Reed/Young Lord Ingram).

Musicals that sound silly on paper not infrequently emerge better onstage. That's certainly the case with *Jane Eyre*. At three hours (there are 18 songs in the first act alone), it is simply too long. It is also resolutely grim and largely without substantial musical virtues; none of Paul Gordon's tunes play in your head on the way out. Still, something about this show makes for an entertaining evening despite the longueurs.

Jane Eyre's faults will have to be fixed before this show gains any sort of Broadway credibility. First, the chronological imbalances need rectifying. After opening at a fast clip recounting the horrors of the protagonist's early years, show slows down once Jane enters the service of Edward Rochester within his eerie manor house. Comic relief shows up in the persons of housekeeper Miss Fairfax and Blanche Ingram, Rochester's putative fiancee. But humor doesn't jibe with this show's grave tenor. With seemingly every detail of the Bronte novel's later chapters recounted, the show bogs down in a morass of gothic romanticism.

John Caird's book is riddled with cliches. Some of Gordon's pleasant if unremarkable pop-inflected numbers will have to go, too. Co-directors will find the model for their show in its earliest numbers, which are not only snappy and even stirring, but also well-choreographed and cleverly presented.

Show has a real asset in the low-key Schaffel, who sings Jane with conviction and ample, if not overwhelming, vocal power.

Juno and the Peacock

A Noel Pearson presentation of a play in three acts by Sean O'Casey. Directed by Garry Hynes. Sets and costumes, Francis O'Connor; lighting, Mick Hughes; sound, John A. Leonard for Aura Sound; music, Paddy Cunneen; production manager, Paul Tucker. Opened in London, reviewed Sept. 9, 1999. Running time: 150 mins.
Cillian Murphy (Johnny Boyle), Dawn Bradfield (Mary Boyle), Marie Mullen (Juno Boyle), David Wilmot (Jerry Devine), Michael Gambon ("Captain" Boyle), John Kavanagh (Joxer Daly), Declan Conlan (Charles Bentham), Brid Brennan (Maisie Madigan), Pat Leavy (Mrs. Tancred), Derry Power ("Needle" Nugent), Mark Dunne (First Irregular/Sewing Machine Man), Paddy Mooney (Coal Block Vendor/Second Removal Man), Jer O'Leary (Male Neighbor/First Removal Man), Eileen Fennell (Female Neighbor), Daniel Rowan (Irregular Mobilizer), Gavin Kelly (Second Irregular).
First act establishes "life as usual" chez Boyle, as daughter Mary prepares to meet her beau, mother Juno readies herself for work, and son Johnny frets and sulks by the fire, ever-fearing (presciently) that he'll be victimized by the Republican cause that his injury has forced him to leave behind.

Into their tatty sitting room falls the drink-soaked Captain, as ever in the company of his feckless sidekick, Joxer Daly. Gambon's performance and his appearance embrace and highlight the character's contradictions. Dawn Bradfield is a surprisingly pale Mary at first, and Brid Brennan simply seems miscast as the lusty upstairs neighbor Maisie Madigan, while Cillian Murphy fails to make something more interesting out of what is a one-note character in Johnny.

In the transitional second act, the Boyles' overspending starts to catch up with them and the style of performance seems to tighten around their reducing circumstances, bringing home O'Casey's virulent indictment of the nouveau bourgeoisie.

All is nearly forgiven with the stunning image that opens the final act: Mick Hughes' faint lighting streams through open slats in O'Connor's walls onto the Boyles' now-empty flat, revealing Mullen slumped on a packing crate and Bradfield leaning despairing on the fireplace. Hynes' rationale is now clear – she's playing up the extreme comedy in the first act to offset the extreme tragedy of the last – but the current problem is that some of her performers simply can't pull it off.

Kat and the Kings

A Harriet Newman Leve and Judith & David Rosenbauer presentation, in association with Richard Frankel, Marc Routh, Willette Klausner, Kardana-Swinsky Prods., David Kramer, Taliep Peterson and Renaye Kramer, by special arrangement with Paul Elliott, Nick Salmon and Lee Menzies, of a musical in two acts with book and lyrics by David Kramer and music by Taliep Peterson. Direction, musical staging, Kramer. Choreography, Jody J. Abrahams, Loukmaan Adams. Sets, costumes, Saul Radomsky; lighting, Howard Harrison; sound, Orbital Sound/Sebastian Frost; music supervision, Gary Hind; music director, Jeff Lams; music coordinator, John Miller; arrangements, Peterson; production stage manager, Pat Sosnow. Opened Aug 19, 1999. Reviewed Aug 17. Running time: 130 mins.
Terry Hector (Kat Diamond), Kim Louis (Lucy Dixon), Jody J. Abrahams (Young Kat Diamond), Loukmaan Adams (Bingo), Junaid Booysen (Ballie), Alistair Izobell (Magoo).
If sheer exuberance could carry the day, *Kat and the Kings* might sail right into the Broadway history books powered by delightfully buoyant performances from its young South African cast. The loose-limbed, limber-voiced kids who animate the stage in this story of the rise and fall of a doo-wop group in 1950s Cape Town are giving the most infectiously joyous performances in town. The cast's ingratiating talents cannot disguise the faults of this eager-to-please but rather deflatingly inconsequential show.

The musical tells the fictional story of the Cavalla Kings, a vocal quartet who style themselves after the great early R&B-rock groups. Show's creators loosely based the material on the life of Salie Daniels, the leader of a similar singing group who performed the role of the elder Kat Diamond, the show's narrator, in previous runs. Sadly, Daniels died recently, and while his replacement, Terry Hector, is entirely winning, one suspects Daniels' personal connection to the material gave the show some grounding gravitas that is sorely missing from its cheerily simplistic book and lyrics.

The tale begins with Kat, now a shoeshine man in 1999 Cape Town, recalling with nostalgia the beginnings of the Cavalla Kings. His younger self rises beside him on Saul Radomsky's bare-bones set, and together they narrate a saga that hits many of the usual rags-to-riches touchstones, albeit with a distinctive historical backdrop (apartheid) that occasionally impinges on the youthful showbiz high jinks.

Kiss Me, Kate

A Roger Berlind and Roger Horchow presentation of a musical in two acts with music and lyrics by Cole Porter, book by Sam and Bella Spewack. Directed by Michael Blakemore. Choreography, Kathleen Marshall. Musical director, Paul Gemignani. Sets, Robin Wagner; costumes, Martin Pakledinaz; lighting, Peter Kaczorowski; sound, Tony Meola; orchestrations, Don Sebesky; dance arrangements, David

---

Chase; fight direction, B.H. Barry; production supervision, Steven Zweigbaum; production manager, Arthur Siccardi. Musical numbers: "Another Op'nin' Another Show," "Why Can't You Behave," "Wunderbar," "So in Love," "We Open in Venice," "Tom, Dick or Harry," "I've Come to Wive It Wealthily in Padua," "I Hate Men," "Were Thine That Special Face," "Cantiamo D'Amore," "Kiss Me, Kate," "Too Darn Hot," "Where Is the Life That Late I Led," "Always True to You (in My Fashion)," "From This Moment On," "Bianca," "Brush Up Your Shakespeare," "I Am Ashamed That Women Are So Simple." **Adriane Lenox (Hattie), Stanley Wayne Mathis (Paul), Eric Michael Gillett (Ralph, Stage Manager), Amy Spanger (Lois Lane), Michael Berresse (Bill Calhoun), Marin Mazzie (Lilli Vanessi), Brian Stokes Mitchell (Fred Graham), John Horton (Harry Trevor), Robert Ousley (Pops, Stage Doorman), Jerome Vivona (Cab Driver), Lee Wilkof (First Man), Michael Mulhern (Second Man), Ron Holgate (Harrison Howell), "Taming of the Shrew" Players: Amy Spanger (Bianca, Lois Lane), John Horton (Baptista, Harry Trevor), Kevin Neil McCready (Gremio, First Suitor), Darren Lee (Hortensio, Second Suitor), Michael Berresse (Lucentio, Bill Calhoun), Marin Mazzie (Katharine, Lilli Vanessi), Brian Stokes (Petruchio, Fred Graham), Jerome Vivona (Mitchell Nathaniel), Vince Pesce (Gregory), Blake Hammond (Philip), Michael X. Martin (Haberdasher). With: Eric Michael Gillett, Patty Goble, JoAnn M. Hunter, Nancy Lemenager, Carol Lee Meadows, Elizabeth Mills, Linda Mugleston, Cynthia Sophiea.**

Boasting the great Cole Porter's greatest score, the musical has been absent from Broadway in the half-century since its 1951 closing. Contemporary reality melts away, thoughts of the plaguing new millennium recede, and the audience is transported back to the days when the musical was a land of easygoing enchantment, where trifling romantic shenanigans and comic shtick were spun into gold-plated entertainment, borne aloft on melodies as hummable as they were durable, and lyrics that tickled all the way home.

The original book has been spruced up with a few sly jokes that bear a recent date-stamp, but the musical's plot is still a bantamweight sparring with a heavyweight score. With two bright new Broadway stars (Marin Mazzie and Brian Stokes Mitchell) blessed with heaven-sent voices center stage, this musical is a trip to the moon. They play actors Fred Graham and Lilli Vanessi, formerly married, currently at daggers drawn, and thrown together by circumstances in a touring musical adaptation of *The Taming of the Shrew* that's bogged down in Baltimore. This rekindling love is thrown off course when a bouquet intended for Fred's new plaything, the ingenue Lois Lane, falls into Lilli's hands. Much mayhem ensues, nudged along by a pair of poker-faced gangsters played with impeccable deadpan by Lee Wilkof and Michael Mulheren. The duo are wry comic gems, with "Brush Up Your Shakespeare" neatly functioning as their own personal curtain call.

Last Dance at Dum Dum

An Ambassador Theater Group, Royal Court Theater, Mark Goucher and Guy Chapman Prods. Ltd. presentation of a play in two acts by Ayub Khan-Din. Directed by Stuart Burge. Sets and costumes, Tim Hatley; lighting, Mark Henderson; sound, John Leonard and Frank Bradley. Opened July 14, 1999 in London. Reviewed July 17. Running time: 120 mins.

Madhur Jaffrey (Muriel Marsh), Avril Elgar (Daphne Willows), Paul Bazely (Elliot Mukherjee), Sheila Burrell (Violet Wallis), Rashid Karapiet (Mr. Jones), Madhav Sharma (Mr. Chakravatty), Nicholas Le Prevost (Bertie Marsh), Diana Fairfax (Lydia Buller-Hughes).

The peeling colonial bungalow where the play is set houses a community on the verge of extinction, both individually and metaphorically, with the compound's motley inhabitants fiddling – well, dancing – while Calcutta really does burn. As conceived, the characters are either self-conscious eccentrics or merely ciphers, and several of them look as if their best scenes have been edited out.

Comic relief is supplied mostly by Violet (Sheila Burrell, inflecting her lines with a zest Maggie Smith might recognize, with a newly arrived Englishwoman, Lydia Buller-Hughes (Diana Fairfax at her most gracious), on hand to act as resident nurse and (often muffled) voice of pragmatism. It's typical of the play's shorthand approach to character that Lydia's relationship to her native England is encapsulated in an unconvincing swipe at Mrs. Thatcher, even as the houseboy Elliot (Paul Bazely), by contrast, has to bear more than his fair share of the ultimately AWOL plot. Khan-Din's eye for detail remains acute – in an overdue return to the London theater, Jaffrey is at her least stagy recalling how Muriel's mother used to brush her elbows with bleach – but the larger brushstrokes are a blur. Is the play requiem (as the title suggests) or tribute to a tribe under siege? The play never lets on, beyond announcing the obvious ("that was then, and this is now," and so on) and leaving its faux-Chekhovian impulses flailing in the summer heat.

Lenny

A Kim Poster, PW Prods. and Joan Worth presentation, in association with the Peter Hall Co., of a play in two acts by Julian Barry. Directed by Peter Hall. Sets and costumes, William Dudley; lighting, Rick Fisher; music, Roger Kellaway; sound, Rick Clarke; choreography, Vincent Paterson. Opened in London, reviewed Aug 9, 1999. Running time: 155 mins.

Eddie Izzard (Lenny Bruce), David Ryall (The Judge), Elizabeth Berkley (Rusty Blaine). With: Stephen Noonan, James Hayes, Sandra Caron, Matt Devereaux, Annette McLaughlin.

If it's possible to be simultaneously miscast and mesmerizing, Eddie Izzard manages exactly that in *Lenny*, Peter Hall's overinflated revival of Julian Barry's irritatingly thin and protracted 1971 Broadway play. Best known as the genial transvestite British comedian who is slowly adding to his reputation overseas, the fleshy Izzard couldn't seem further removed from the wiry edginess of the late, great and deeply American Lenny Bruce. The problem is that Lenny was fuelled by anger, whereas Izzard works by febrile animation. Nor is one ever unaware of the tension between the subject and the star, with the result that Lenny gets accommodated to Izzard's persona at least as much as Izzard is subsumed by Bruce.

The routines are the raison d'etre of *Lenny*, which is the story of "a stubborn shmuck" (his mother's phrase) who became America's answer to Jonathan Swift. Indeed, Barry's script wastes no hagiographic time invoking any and all comparisons, Aristophanes included, rather as if we couldn't be trusted to see beyond words like "cocksucker," "nigger" and "yid" to the very real moralist beneath. A truthteller cut short in his prime, Lenny knew, negate words and you negate the

---

Michael Douglas and Rene Russo are to star in the romantic comedy **As Told To**.

truth; his was a world in which silence was the real scare. As a drama, what information does *Lenny* impart? Nothing that hasn't fed dozens of comparable tales of fierce and fleeting lives, with the difference that Barry's structure is so hokey and diffuse that it starts to test our natural interest in the topic.

The Lion in Winter

A Roundabout Theater Co. presentation of a play in two acts by James Goldman. Directed by Michael Mayer. Sets, David Gallo; costumes, Michael Krass; lighting, Kenneth Posner; sound, Mark Bennett; production stage manager, Gary Mickelson. Artistic director, Todd Haimes. Opened March 11, 1999. Reviewed March 10. Running time: 130 mins.
Laurence Fishburne (Henry II), Emily Bergl (Alais), Keith Nobbs (John), Neal Huff (Geoffrey), Chuma Hunter-Gault (Richard Lionheart), Stockard Channing (Eleanor), Roger Howarth (Philip). Servants: Jeff Croteau, Dan Maceyak, Benjamin Nurick.

The 1968 film version is a sword that cuts all sorts of ways for the new Broadway revival of James Goldman's play. The play is a literary conceit of sorts: The musty historical drama dusted off, dressed up in latter-day neuroses and half-played for laughs. There's a certain rude pleasure in seeing historical figures, normally treated with reverence onstage, taken down a peg or two and exposed in all their squalid naturalness. The play's wit is mostly garden-variety sarcasm in chain mail and fancy language, its pretensions to high drama and poetry slightly embarrassing.

Only the redoubtable Stockard Channing manages to hold her own against memories of her film rival, the Oscar-winning Hepburn. She plays Eleanor of Aquitaine, estranged wife of Henry II, who has been released from genteel captivity in her own castle to attend a family gathering, where Henry plans to announce which of his three sons will be heir to the kingdom. Henry's favorite is the youngest, John, a sniveling bundle of teenage angst. Eleanor is allied with Richard, the eldest and strongest. Middle child Geoffrey is the bitterest of the trio, and tries to improve his position by playing everyone against each other.

Fishburne's Henry is never authoritative enough to counterbalance Channing's charismatic queen; it's hard not to think Eleanor could wipe the floor with him at any moment. The rest of the lackluster cast struggles with varying levels of success.

The Lion King

A Disney presentation of a musical in two acts with music and lyrics by Elton John and Tim Rice, with additional music and lyrics by Lebo M., Mark Mancina, Jay Rifkin, Julie Taymor and Hans Zimmer, book by Roger Allers and Irene Mecchi, adapted from the screenplay by Mecchi, Jonathan Roberts, and Linda Woolverton. Directed by Julie Taymor. Sets, Richard Hudson; costumes, Taymor; lighting, Donald Holder; mask and puppet design, Taymor and Michael Curry; choreography, Garth Fagan; sound, Tony Meola; hair and makeup design, Michael Ward; music supervisor, Joseph Church; orchestrations, Robert Elhai and David Metzger; music director/conductor, Colin Welford. Based on the Disney film *The Lion King*, directed by Roger Allers and Rob Minkoff, produced by Don Hahn. Opened in London, reviewed Oct 19, 1999. Running time: 165 mins.
Josette Bushell-Mingo (Rafiki), Cornell John (Mufasa), Dawn Michael (Sarabi), Gregory Gudgeon (Zazu), Rob
Edwards (Scar), Luke Youngblood (Young Simba), Dominique Moore (Young Nala), Stephanie Charles (Shenzi), Paul J. Medford (Banzai), Christopher Holt (Ed), Simon Gregor (Timon), Martyn Ellis (Pumbaa), Roger Wright (Simba), Paulette Ivory (Nala).

This is a musical whose scenic *coup de théâtres* are as frequently found in shadows and silhouettes as they are in big statements, of which *The Lion King*, the jutting promontory of Pride Rock notwithstanding, has gratefully little.

If the look of the show is ever more astounding, its text most certainly is not, with the result that one is aware of the production not so much enhancing the core material as deflecting attention away from the frequent inanity of it. For all the putative affinities to *Hamlet* and a rather droll T.S. Eliot quip, *The Lion King* is no more interested in language than the more directly Eliot-inspired *Cats*. It's Taymor and Co.'s genius, however, that such a shortfall hardly matters set against an abiding interest in a realm beyond language – the wordless wonder of theatricality at its most primal.

The performers for the most part are distinctive parts of an enchanting whole whose lapses – the Chippendale-ish contortions of "Be Prepared," accompanied by jets of steam; the inevitable treacle of "Can You Feel the Love Tonight" – are so brief that barely a moment has passed before another exotic image or sound is holding us transfixed. That's the prevailing method of a musical that points the way forward by harking all the way back via an appeal to the imagination, which is where the theater's enduring power to transform truly lies.

The Lonesome West

A Randall L. Wreghitt and Steven M. Levy presentation, in association with Norma Langworthy, Gayle Francis, Dani Davis & Jason Howland, Joan Stein & Susie Dietz, Everett King and Pace Theatrical Group/SFX Entertainment/Jon B. Platt, of the Druid Theater Co./Royal Court Theater production of a play in two acts by Martin McDonagh. Directed by Garry Hynes. Sets and costumes, Francis O'Connor; lighting, Tharon Musser; music, Paddy Cunneen; sound, Paul Arditti; special effects, Gregory Meeh; production stage manager, Matthew Silver. Opened April 27, 1999. Reviewed April 23. Running time: 140 mins.
Maeliosa Stafford (Coleman Connor), Brian F. O'Byrne (Valene Connor), David Ganly (Father Welsh), Dawn Bradfield (Girleen Kelleher).

Martin McDonagh's *The Lonesome West* is the third play in his Leenane trilogy (*Beauty Queen* was the first). And while the production is marked by the same fastidious affection for McDonagh's rhythmic, colorful language and bizarre comic characterizations, the play itself is rather small beer.

The two characters locked in a protracted battle of wills in this case are brothers Coleman and Valene Connor. Valene's behaviour indicates some kind of arrested development. The cynical, cooler Coleman is more recognizably human, although having shot and killed their father would have to be seen as a larger demerit than Valene's quirky pettiness. The play opens on the day of the late patriarch's funeral, as the local priest Father Welsh joins them in their glum sitting parlour for a wee drink. It's Father Welsh who's in need of comfort. He's riddled with self-doubts after the violent death of yet another of his parishioners.

The play never works up the harrowing dramatic force that *Beauty Queen* managed to achieve, despite that play's equal

---

doses of savage comedy. McDonagh spends so much time serving up his characters' subhuman behaviour that their humanity gets utterly lost. Eventually, as the brothers' increasingly violent acts of retribution drive the plot forward, the play begins to resemble a *Road Runner* cartoon crossed with Sam Shepard's *True West*, also a wild west comedy about fraternal angst. Funny, yes, but eventually monotonous.

Look Back in Anger

A Classic Stage Co. presentation of a play by John Osborne in two acts. Directed by Jo Bonney. Set, Narelle Sissons; costumes, Kaye Voyce; lighting, James Vermeulen; sound, Ken Travis; fight director, J. Steven White; production stage manager, Janet Takami. Opened Oct 17, 1999 in New York. Reviewed Oct 14. Running time: 150 mins.
Reg Rogers (Jimmy Porter), James Joseph O'Neill (Cliff Lewis), Enid Graham (Alison Porter), Angelina Phillips (Helena Charles), Michael Lombard (Colonel Redfern).
Reg Rogers' Jimmy is imbued with the more detached attitudinizing of the slacker generation. Slouching morosely about the room, barely able to keep his lolling head erect, and only finding the energy for enunciation when he's speaking in faux-posh tones. Rogers does have a nimble physical grace and the bad-boy charm of a goofy standup comic, but it's impossible to fathom what the upper-class Alison responds to in Jimmy, which may be why Enid Graham's Alison is so dry and distanced.

As Alison's friend Helena, whose contempt for Jimmy is suddenly overtaken by desire, Angelina Phillips has moments of nicely crisp wit and effectiveness. James Joseph O'Neill is a muted presence as the kindly Cliff, witness and mediator in the Porter marriage. Unfortunately, the whole cast is plagued by accent problems.

Both Graham and Rogers are finest in the play's last moments. Their hearts are finally in a broken accord, and the actors give a full-throttle honesty to the scene that finally brings the evening to a tense and tender climax.

But Bonney ends the play on a tentative note, as Alison draws back the hand she reaches out to Jimmy. It's an understandable adjustment for our era, when Alison's submission to Jimmy's abusiveness seems almost pathological. And yet it also mitigates the scene's (and the play's) impact, and is emblematic of the tempered tone that here presides over a play that should hold nothing back.

The Madras House

A Shaw Festival presentation of a play in two acts by Harley Granville Barker. Directed by Neil Munro. Sets, Peter Hartwell; costumes, Christina Poddubiuk; lighting, Erica Hassell, music, Paul Sportelli. Opened in Niagara-on-the-Lake, Ontario, reviewed July 7, 1999. Running time: 145 mins.
Blair Williams (Philip Madras), Ben Carlson (Major Hippisley Thomas), Jenny L. Wright (Maid/Clara/Mannequin), Lynne Cormack (Julia/Mrs. Brigstock), Laurie Paton (Laura/Miss Chancellor/Mannequin), Jane Perry (Emma/Mannequin/Maid), Shauna Black (Jane/Miss Yates/Mannequin), Donna Belleville (Mrs. Katherine Huxtable), Michael Ball (Mr. Henry Huxtable), Jillian Cook (Mrs. Amelia Madras), Phillippa Domville (Minnie/Jessica Madras), William Vickers (Mr. Brigstock), Mark McGrinder (Belhaven), George Dawson (Mr. Windlesham), Douglas E. Hughes (Eustace Perrin State), Peter Millard (Constantine Madras).

There is a clear central theme that rests with the story of Philip Madras, a fashion house owner who opts to sell his absentee father's business and turn to the less exploitative (so he thinks) arena of politics. Philip may view himself as a reformer, but he is also a product of a marriage that taught him to "dislike men and despise women" and he is driven to unravel the mysteries of the opposite sex by talking to them "man to man." His successes and failures form some of the play's most interesting exchanges and highlight this surprisingly sensitive text about the actual price of early women's liberation.

Among Munro's inventive touches: a stenographer's chair center-stage in act one on which matriarch Katherine Huxtable perches and swivels as she controls her family and interrogates visitors; long silences that punctuate frenetic and often over-lapping dialogue; a spectacular set of mirrored, swinging doors by Peter Hartwell that form the backdrop of the set; a recorded reading by Munro himself of the lengthy character introductions and room descriptions; and disciplined ensemble work that parts like the Red Sea to let speeches and moments take effect.

In fact, Munro's ease with this dramaturgically complex work lends him the confidence to experiment, and overall he navigates smoothly through the many changes in tone and lack of traditional narrative, giving full rein to the play's ideas and issues.

Mamma Mia!

A Judy Craymer, Richard East and Bjorn Ulvaeus for Littlestar presentation, in association with Universal, of a musical in two acts with music and lyrics by Benny Andersson and Bjorn Ulvaeus with Stig Anderson, and book by Catherine Johnson. Directed by Phyllida Lloyd. Musical director, Martin Lowe. Choreography, Anthony van Laast. Sets and costumes, Mark Thompson; lighting, Howard Harrison; sound, Andrew Bruce and Bobby Aitken; musical supervisor, additional orchestrations and arrangements, Martin Koch. Musical numbers: "Money, Money, Money," "Mamma Mia," "Chiquitita," "Dancing Queen," "Lay All Your Love on Me," "Super Trouper," "Gimmie, Gimmie, Gimmie," "Name of the Game," "Voulez-Vous," "Thank You For the Music," "Summer Night City," "Under Attack," "One of Us," "S.O.S.," "Does Your Mother Know," "Knowing Me, Knowing You," "Our Last Summer," "Slipping Through My Fingers," "Winner Takes It All," "Take a Chance on Me," "I Do, I Do, I Do," "I Have a Dream." Opened April 6, 1999 in London. Reviewed April 12. Running time: 150 mins.
Lisa Stokke (Sophie Sheridan), Siobhan McCarthy (Donna Sheridan), Louise Plowright (Tanya), Jenny Galloway (Rosie), Andrew Langtree (Sky), Nicholas Colicos (Bill Austin), Paul Clarkson (Harry Bright), Nigel Harman (Eddie), Hilton McRae (Sam Carmichael). With: Tom Magdich, Neal Wright, Eliza Lumley, Melissa Gibson, James Barron, Simon Bishop, Andy Couchman, Wendy Mae Brown, Karen Shenaz David, Lori Haley Fox, Nick Haswell, Melissa Jacques, Drew Jaymson, Anne-Marie McCormack, Stephen McGlynn, Leah-Sue Morland, Joseph Noble, Richard Pettyfer, Caroline Sheen, Scarlett Strallen, Emma Jay Thomas, Timothy Walton, Annette Yeo.
A soggy mother-daughter drama gets folded into some buoyant and kitschy Europop in *Mamma Mia!*, the new ABBA show. Essentially an excuse to get the audience on its feet for

the sort of clap-happy finale that these days is de rigueur on either side of the Atlantic, *Mamma Mia!* achieves its decidedly modest aim with gusto. Still, the fact that it isn't better written, acted or staged will dismay those hoping for something more than a West End equivalent of *Footloose*. In the old days, a musical's book and score attempted some kind of unity, so that one flowed naturally and liltingly from the other. No more: if the audience at *Mamma Mia!* greets most of the numbers with affectionate chuckles (and occasional applause), that's due to the essential incongruity of a show that works (or not) by its very absurdity.

Young Sophie wants to discover which of three possible candidates was her father, and so invites them all to her island wedding, much to the chagrin of Donna, who has lived a hard life as a single mom. *Mamma Mia!* puts its central character through enough of a wringer to suggest that this show could take over where *Blood Brothers* left off in the Aggrieved Mother sweepstakes. No one expects ABBA to be Stephen Sondheim, but even by their standards, the lyrics to, say, *Our Last Summer* are pretty stupefying.

Marlene

A Ric Wanetik and Frederic B. Vogel presentation of a play in two acts by Pam Gems. Directed by Sean Mathias. Set, John Arnone; costumes, David C. Woolard; lighting, Mark Jonathan; sound, Peter J. Fitzgerald; musical direction, Kevin Amos; production stage manager, Arthur Gaffin. Opened April 11, 1999. Reviewed April 8. Running time: 125 mins. **Mary Diveny (Mutti), Margaret Whitton (Vivian), Sian Phillips (Marlene Dietrich).**

Sian Phillips' gives a fairly convincing impersonation of Marlene Dietrich. The show surrounding her eerie impression is staggeringly inept, often incoherent and always dull. With her taut, milk-white skin clinging to glass-cutting cheekbones, and a figure that looks suitably statuesque in the famous flesh-colored, beaded gown of Dietrich's concert years, Phillips does indeed look strikingly like the late-period Marlene represented in the play. And she's got Dietrich's husky bleat of a singing voice down pat. Without a workable vehicle to support Phillips' faux-Marlene, the actress is lost. It's a sad Broadway stumble for a performer with a long and distinguished career in the U.K.

Gems' scattered script finds Dietrich backstage at a Paris concert in 1969, accompanied by her friend Vivian, apparently a playwright who's moonlighting as Marlene's lapdog. Vivian scurries around attending to madame's whims and setting up her wan wisecracks while the play's third character, a mute called Mutti, skulks in the shadows. Mutti is a survivor of Dachau. The monologs about the trauma of the war and Dietrich's decision to abandon allegiance to her homeland have some shape and interest.

The rest of the play is a bizarre, meandering concoction of bitchy or reverent showbiz anecdotes and pathetically tired musings on love and the cinematic art. It's often hard to tell what the woman is going on about, and harder still to care.

Martin Guerre

The West Yorkshire Playhouse in association with Cameron Mackintosh presents a musical in two acts, book by Alain Boublil and Claude-Michel Schonberg, music by Schonberg, lyrics by Boublil and Stephen Clark. Directed by Conall Morrison. Sets, John Napier; costumes, Andreane Neofitou;

lighting, Howard Harrison; sound, Andrew Bruce; musical staging and choreography, David Bolger; musical supervisor, Martin Koch; musical director, David Shrubsole; orchestrator, William David Brohn; fight director, John Waller. Musical numbers: "Live With Somebody You Love," "Your Wedding Day," "The Deluge," "I'm Martin Guerre," "Without You As A Friend," "The Conversion," "God's Anger," "How Many Tears," "Dear Louison," "Welocome To the Land," "The Confession," "The Seasons Turn," "Don't," "All the Years," "The Holy Fight," "The Dinner," "The Revelation," "The Day Has Come," "If You Still Love Me," "The Courtroom," "Who?", "All That I Love," "The Imposter Is Here," "The Final Witness," "The Verdict," "Justice Will Be Done," "Benoit's Lament," "Why?", "You Will Be Mine," "How Many Tears" (reprise), "Live With Somebody You Love" (reprise). Opened Dec 8, 1998 in Leeds, Yorkshire (through Feb 13, 1999); reviewed Jan 7, 1999. Running time: 2 hrs, 45 min.
Stephen Weller (Martin Guerre), Matthew Cammelle (Arnaud du Thil), Joanna Riding (Bertrande de Rols), Maurice Clark (Guillaume), Michael Bauer (Pierre Guerre), Kerry Washington (Madame de Rols), Gareth Snook (Father Dominic), Terry Kelly (Benoit). With: Valery Terrone, Kate McCahill, Andrew Morton, John Tobias, Lorraine Chappell, Sophie Caton, Kathryn Akin, ChristianJon Billett, Julian Duncan, Adam Jones, Daniel Hinchliffe, Natasha Kellett, Lisa Peace, Geoffrey Abbott, Jonathan Penton.

Martin Guerre undeniably works on one level – that of tearjerker, as it chronicles a love triangle involving three individuals struggling to find their hearts in a 16th-century French village marked out mostly by hate. Thrown into an arranged marriage while barely into his teens, Martin leaves behind virgin-bride Bertrande to fight in the Religious Wars, where he befriends fellow combatant, Arnaud du Thil. Seven years have passed as the show opens amid gunfire to find the comrades singing of the importance of love when Martin is struck down, but not before passing on to Arnaud news of his own fraught past as whipping-boy (literally) of a ceaselessly vengeful, hysteria-driven town.

Arriving in rural Artigat after Martin's presumed death, Arnaud brings with him a welcome outburst of rain, thereby ending a lengthy drought. More elementally crucial is his ability to satisfy Bertrande in a way that the barely pubescent Martin never could. And yet it's not just the earth colours of John Napier's bare-timbered set that may ground an audience awaiting the rapturous flight of such authentically tragic musicals as *West Side Story* or *Sweeney Todd*, both of which *Martin Guerre* recalls in passing though at least director Morrison no longer implicates the audience, *Sweeney Todd*-style, as Culprits of sorts during "The Imposter Is Here."

If one can now greatly admire *Martin Guerre* without really loving it, that's because it seems destined forever to lack the sex and wit that accompany even the bleakest narratives, without which no deftly shaded study in grey can ever emerge in all its colours.

The Merchant of Venice

A Royal National Theater presentation of a play by William Shakespeare in two acts. Directed by Trevor Nunn. Sets and costumes, Hildegard Bechtler; lighting, Peter Mumford; music, Steven Edis; sound, Paul Groothuis; choreography, Lynne Page. Opened June 17, 1999; reviewed July 19. Running time: 210 mins.

... October 2 ...

Spurred by Gérard Depardieu's triumphant TV appearance in **The Count Of Monte Cristo**, other French stars sign up for smallscreen projects.

Henry Goodman (Shylock), David Bamber (Antonio), Alexander Hanson (Bassanio), Gabrielle Jourdan (Jessica), Richard Henders (Gratiano), Daniel Evans (Lorenzo), Peter de Jersey (Salerio), Mark Umbers (Solanio), Andrew French (Launcelot Gobbo), Oscar James (Old Gobbo), Derbhle Crotty (Portia), Alex Kelly (Nerissa). With: Michael Wildman, David Burt, John Nolan, Ceri Ann Gregory, Leigh McDonald, Raymond Coulthard, Jack James, Liam McKenna, Charles Millham, Chu Omambala, David Arneil. Nunn works not by altering what, post-Holocaust, remains a problematic source but via absolute fidelity to the shifting moods of a play whose moments of good cheer, as everyone knows, exact an awful price. Antonio is in dire straits: indebted to the usurer Shylock. Should he fail to repay him, Shylock may take a pound of his flesh.

Gratiano may possess a "skipping spirit," but that's only as long as he's hanging out with his mates Bassanio, Salerio and Solanio. Present these suited anti-Semites with the Jew Shylock, however, and they can't go in for the kill enough amid a community that finds even Shylock's servant, Launcelot Gobbo, ready to crack a joke at his master's expense.

Gratiano is a sartorially well turned-out thug who thinks with his fists: Significantly, he throws a playful punch to Alex Kelly's Nerissa, newly got up in legal garb as male clerk to Portia in her own masculine disguise. Sharing a Yiddish exchange with Jessica, Shylock is stripped of everything that matters, starting with family and faith. Though the Jew-baiting in *Merchant* is what resounds through the centuries, it's possible to read the play in its entirety as a so-called "comedy" of reconciliation that leaves at least some of its inhabitants a wreck. Shylock is exiled, but his presence lives on in those unexpected final notes floated by a daughter lost to him in a play that on this occasion sings no less troublingly to us today.

Minnelli on Minnelli

A Radio City Entertainment, LM Concerts, Scott Nederlander and Stewart F. Lane presentation of a concert in two acts written and directed by Fred Ebb. Musical director, Bill LaVorgna. Choreography, John DeLuca. Sets, John Arnone; costumes, Bob Mackie; lighting, Howell Binkley; sound, Peter J. Fitzgerald; projections, Batwin + Robin; film sequence, Jack Haley Jr.; musical arrangements and supervision, Billy Stritch and Marvin Hamlisch; vocal arranger, Stritch; dance music arrangements, David Krane and Peter Howard; production stage manager, Karl Lengel. Opened Dec 8, 1999. Reviewed Dec 7. Running time: 140 mins.
There's something ineffably strange and sad and moving about the manner in which Liza Minnelli's life and career have echoed her mother's. The Palace itself hosted one of Judy Garland's most legendary rallies, when Garland returned triumphantly to the New York stage in 1951 after being fired from MGM.

So let us judge *Minnelli on Minnelli* first as a comeback, a chance for Minnelli to reassert her viability as an entertainer; to vanquish demons and erase tabloid headlines. She gives a warm, energetic performance, touring breezily through an eclectic songbook culled from pictures ranging from 1946's *Ziegfeld Follies* to 1970's *On a Clear Day You Can See Forever.* Minnelli's decision to frame the concert as a tribute to her father's movies has an advantage: it allows her to perform material new to her, and thus not risk comparisons with past performances of her vocally punishing standard repertoire.

For the truth is Minnelli's voice has deteriorated. All voices do, of course. She still has a unique instrument that could not be mistaken for anyone else's, as well as decisive, dramatic phrasing and distinctive elocution.

Minnelli on Minnelli is ultimately as much support group as it is a concert. It may seem odd to ask audiences to pay for the privilege of providing an entertainer with emotional succor, but Liza's fans seem eager to give back a small measure of the pleasure they've been given by the performer over the years.

Much Ado About Everything

A Jyll Rosenfeld and Fred Krohn presentation of a performance by Jackie Mason. Written and directed by Jackie Mason. Produced by Raoul Lionel Felder and Jon Stoll. Lighting, Stan Crocker; sound; Christopher Cronin; stage manager, Don Myers; company manager, Kathy Lowe. Opened Dec 29, 1999; reviewed Dec 28. Running time: 135 mins.
Despite the title of his fifth Broadway show, Jackie Mason takes on anything, not everything. As he travels willy-nilly over the cultural landscape, what the standup comedian chooses to skewer is nearly as significant as what he omits. Bill Clinton's affair with Monica Lewinsky inspires the longest riff, Al Gore and George W. Bush receive a passing glance, and Bill Bradley and John McCain are not mentioned at all. The singing styles of Bing Crosby and Frank Sinatra are parodied, while those of Puff Daddy and Ricky Martin are still hovering under the comic's radar. High points of the show include dead-on impersonations of William F. Buckley, the Inkspots, Jesse Jackson, Henry Kissinger and Ed Sullivan, who single-handedly postponed Mason's career for two or three decades.

Ten percent of *Much Ado About Everything* could have been written and performed a year ago. And maybe it was: the show comes to Broadway via a London run. The other 90 percent seems freeze-dried in another era. Mason, who makes much of his scabrous political incorrectness, rarely delivers on that promise. One topic is absolutely sacred: Mr. Mason himself. He tells us that the critics and editors of the New York Times resurrected his career in the late 1980s, when he appeared in his first Broadway show, *The World According to Me*. Overall, what David Letterman and Jay Leno offer for free, Jackie Mason calls a Broadway show and charges $65.

The Price

A David Richenthal presentation of a play in two acts by Arthur Miller. Directed by James Naughton. Set, Michael Brown; costumes, Laurie A. Churba; lighting, Rui Rita; sound, Jerry M. Yager; production stage manager, Grayson Meritt. Opened Nov 15, 1999. Reviewed Nov 11. Running time: 150 mins.
Jeffrey DeMunn (Victor Franz), Lizbeth Mackay (Esther Franz), Bob Dishy (Gregory Solomon), Harris Yulin (Walter Franz).
Though Arthur Miller's *The Price* is not among his greatest plays – it lacks the unity of purpose and dramatic thrust that mark his most forceful masterpieces – it is nevertheless a seriously engaging symposium on the moral price paid for success and the emotional cost of failure. Play explores in salutary fashion the definitions of the terms of American achievement, and their effects on the family. Naughton's staging is forthright and sensitive, and boasts a solid cast.

Its setting is a Manhattan brownstone's attic, filled to the rafters with furniture. An aged Jewish antique dealer Gregory

Solomon arrives to make a bid on the furniture of the long-deceased father of Victor Franz. A career cop who's contemplating retirement, Victor is trying to decide what he can afford to do with the rest of his life, spurred on by a wife who has had enough of sacrifice.

Solomon is a sly charmer who relies on the pathos of his advanced age to convince Victor to take the price he offers. The dynamics of this scene prove to be a reflection of the relationship that shaped Victor's disappointed life. Victor's estranged brother Walter arrives and the siblings begin to spar about what Victor has sacrificed for their father, and what Walter has gained in life.

The brothers' bargaining with the past ultimately ends in a disordered jumble of recrimination and regret. The play's conclusion suggests that they're both doomed to continue searching for answers that cannot be purchased. When the curtain falls, only the most meaningless of the play's many transactions – the sale of the furniture – has been completed.

The Prisoner of Second Avenue

A Duncan C. Weldon, Allan S. Gordon, Bill Haber, Ira Pittelman, Elan V. McAllister and Emanual Azenberg presentation of a play in two acts by Neil Simon. Directed by David Taylor. Sets and costumes, Simon Higlett; lighting, Mick Hughes; sound, Paul Arditti. Opened March 30, 1999. Reviewed March 27. Running time: 125 mins.
Richard Dreyfuss (Mel Edison), Marsha Mason (Edna Edison), Harry Ditson (Harry Edison), Frances Jeater (Pearl), Janet Legge (Jessie), Frances Cuka (Pauline).
Richard Dreyfuss looks as if he is having the time of his life in the London staging of *The Prisoner of Second Avenue*, and for as long as he's onstage – coupled with a gracious sparring partner in Marsha Mason – the audience has a ball, too. It's not merely that Neil Simon's overextended moan of a play seems oddly dated in the currently gung-ho New York of Rudy Giuliani. But Simon's dramatic carpentry seems surprisingly shoddy coming from someone whose craftsmanship over time has been so expert. The revival provides for a bravura comic performance from Dreyfuss, an actor who has aged rather better than Simon's play.

Mel Edison inveighs against the high-rise hell that is life in Apt. 14-A in an anonymous Second Avenue tower. But you also ache for a man inelegantly fired after 22 years on a job who might take greater joy from being stuck at home if only the toilet didn't forever need jiggling. Mel stalks the living room in an attempt to ascertain how much the burglars grabbed while his Edna was out for a clearly protracted "five minutes." *Prisoner* has a situation but not much of a plot, and David Taylor's direction can't finesse those portions of the play. Luckily, the play recovers just as Mel's energy does, in time for a satisfying finish that presses into service a key prop to suggest that revenge is merely a snowfall away.

Private Lives

A Royal National Theater production of the Noël Coward comedy in three acts. Directed by Philip Franks. Sets and costumes, Stephen Brimson Lewis; lighting, Howard Harrison; music, Matthew Scott; choreography, Marguerite Porter; fight director, Malcolm Ranson; sound, Adam Rudd; staff director, Frank Nealon. Opened in London and reviewed May 13, 1999. Running time: 165 mins.
Juliet Stevenson (Amanda Prynne), Anton Lesser (Elyot Chase), Dominic Rowan (Victor Prynne), Rebecca Saire (Sibyl Chase), Darlene Johnson (Louise).
So accomplished and cunning is Coward's structure that audiences this time around could well think they are seeing the actual 1903 comedy. But even as Brimson Lewis dazzles us with a Dufy-inspired frontcloth and then a Paris flat for the second and third acts that pays sly homage to virtually every artistic movement of the early 20th century, one is still left with two leading performers who have quite simply landed in the wrong play. And without a commanding, stylish and – most crucially – a sexually charged pair of warring lovers, *Private Lives* comes awfully close to resembling a public spectacle.

There's a presentational quality, of course, to the sparring between Amanda Prynne and Elyot Chase, the once-married couple who take a bruise or two to discover that they will forever be one another's best audience, no matter how scarred they may get in the process. What are Amanda and Elyot but an incipient (and younger) version of George and Martha from *Who's Afraid of Virginia Woolf?*, with the divorced pair's new spouses, Sibyl and Victor, as a fledgling Nick and Honey? The obvious difference has to do with that defining Coward gloss which laces the comedy with pain and rue.

Director Franks has moments that reward his attention to the shifting moods of Coward's text. But where is the elegance, the finesse, the grace required for what, after all, must first and foremost be an exercise in style? It's as if both actors are so busy playing subtext that they don't allow the charm covering over the play's very real cruelties to come forth.

Putting It Together

A Cameron Mackintosh presentation, in association with the Mark Taper Forum, of a musical revue in two acts, with music and lyrics by Stephen Sondheim. Directed by Eric D. Schaeffer. Musical staging, Bob Avian. Musical director, Paul Raiman. Set and costumes, Bob Crowley (Carol Burnett's costume, Bob Mackie); lighting, Howard Harrison; sound Andrew Bruce, Mark Menard; projections, Wendall K. Harrington; orchestrations, Jonathan Tunick. Opened Nov 21, 1999. Reviewed Nov 18. Running time: 120 mins.
Carol Burnett (The Wife), George Hearn (The Husband), John Barrowman (The Younger Man), Ruthie Henshall (The Younger Woman), Bronson Pinchot (The Observer).
Burnett's specialty in loopy caricature and vaudevillian shtick are at several removes from the cool ironies that characterize Sondheim's dryer brand of wit. But a comic genius is a comic genius, and in fact Burnett's liberating touch provides much of the sparkle – and, more intriguingly, the heart – in *Putting It Together*, a sleek, more stylish Broadway reworking of the Sondheim revue from 1992.

Her romantic opposite in the show's musical game of quadrille is Broadway veteran George Hearn (they are called the Husband and the Wife in the cast list, Amy and Charlie elsewhere). They are joined at a party that sets the vague whisper of a narrative in motion by the Younger Woman and the Younger Man.

Sondheim songs from some 13 works are woven together to suggest the brittle marriage of the older couple coming almost, but not quite, to grief when the husband's eye strays toward the charms of the Younger Woman. A highlight of the first act is "Lovely," from *A Funny Thing Happened on the Way to the Forum*, in which the lively rapport between Burnett and Henshaw is first established.

... October 4 ...
Tom Hanks is to executive-produce **West Point**, an hour-long drama for Fox Broadcasting.

Henshall is as a performer of major gifts. She's all sultry languor crooning "Sooner or Later," the rather bland torch song from *Dick Tracy*, and later savvily tackles the tongue-in-cheek lyrics of "More," also from the film.

The underlying problem is that Sondheim does not generally write songs – he writes shows. There is inevitably much lost when portions of his musicals are mixed and matched as they are here, though Eric D. Schaeffer's slick direction avoids any seriously jarring changes of tone or style.

Quartet

A Michael Codron presentation of an Yvonne Arnaud Theater, Guildford, production of a play in two acts by Ronald Harwood. Directed by Christopher Morahan. Sets and costumes, Tim Goodchild; lighting, Robin Carter; sound, John A. Leonard; repetiteur, Frances Hills. Opened in London and reviewed Sept 8, 1999. Running time: 130 mins. **Stephanie Cole (Cecily Robson), Alec McCowen (Reginald Paget), Donald Sinden (Wilfred Bond), Angela Thorne (Jean Horton).**

Quartet is best enjoyed as an acting exercise that allows three of its four established performers to prove to an adoring audience that – rather like the people they are playing – there's life in the old girls (and boys) yet. Unlike its celebrated forbear, *Quartet* doesn't establish the slightest resonance between these singers' offstage lives and their task at hand. The new play has little on its mind beyond a build-up to a climactic stunt: the recreation by the cast of the third act quartet from Giuseppe Verdi's *Rigoletto*.

As a result, *Quartet* trades on situation rather than plot and treads murkiest water when it tries to fuel a scenario that is essentially anecdotal; hence, the inevitably recollection-heavy script. The chief victim of Harwood's structure is Angela Thorne, playing Jean Horton, a one-time diva with a bad hip who was married briefly to the fastidious Reginald Paget, whose own sexual history emerges piecemeal in act two. Just watch McCowen forsake, however briefly, Reg's reticent facade to lash out at the (unseen) rest home employee who denies him marmalade at breakfast. Sinden, in turn, saves his most savory flourish for the end of the first act, playing a man of boundless appetite who stops the show with the single word, "lunch." It's at such moments that *Quartet*, however reheated its dramaturgy, could not be more delicious.

The Rainmaker

A Roundabout Theater Co. presentation of a play in two acts by N. Richard Nash. Directed by Scott Ellis. Sets, James Noone; costumes, Jess Goldstein; lighting, Peter Kaczorowski; music, Louis Rosen; sound, Brian Ronan; special effects, Gregory Meeh; fight choreographer, David Leong; production stage manager, Lori M. Doyle. Artistic director, Todd Haimes. Opened Nov 11, 1999. Reviewed Nov 9. Running time: 135 mins.
Jayne Atkinson (Lizzie Curry), Jerry Hardin (H.C. Curry), John Bedford Lloyd (Noah Curry), David Aaron Baker (Jim Curry), Randle Mell (File), Bernie McInerney (Sheriff Thomas), Woody Harrelson (Bill Starbuck). With: Eric Axen, Scott McTyer Cowart, David Harbour, Brian Ibsen, Rey Lucas, Donovan McGrath, Dustin Tucker, Jason Winther.

With disappointingly pallid performances from film and TV star Woody Harrelson and Jayne Atkinson in the principal roles, director Scott Ellis' parched and poky staging treats *The Rainmaker* with a tasteful reserve that is presumably aiming at a soft naturalism but succeeds only in draining the play of much of its satisfying sentimental charge.

Set in the rural Midwest in 1936, Lizzie Curry is a sweet, spunky and socially awkward woman whose lack of matrimonial prospects is a continual worry to her widowed father H.C. and her two brothers. With its emphasis on Lizzie's "plainness" and her pathetic inability to get a man, the plot may strike contemporary audiences as hopelessly dated or even quaintly. The drying up of Lizzie's prospects is symbolized by the drought that is plaguing the region, and hope for both appears on the horizon with the arrival of a slick character calling himself Bill Starbuck, a tall drink of moonshine who claims he can make the rain fall for the bargain price of a hundred bucks. The family gradually falls under the spell of this sweet-talking charlatan, with Lizzie, of course, falling hardest of all. *The Rainmaker* ends with the timely arrival of a much-desired downpour, a watery deluge that should be accompanied by an equal rush of feeling on the part of the audience. Alas, in this new Broadway revival, only the water arrives on cue – the heart stands still.

A Raisin in the Sun

A Williamstown Theater Festival presentation of a play by Lorraine Hansberry in two acts. Directed by Jack Hofsiss. Set, Michael McGarty; costumes, Karen Perry; lighting, Rui Rita; sound, Matthew Spiro; choreographer, Sandra Burton; stage manager, C.A. Clark; musical director, Charles Alterman; production manager, Stephen Judd. Williamstown Theater Festival producer, Michael Ritchie. Opened July 22, 1999 in Williamstown, Mass. Reviewed July 25. Running time: 175 mins.
Viola Davis (Ruth Younger), James Sneed (Travis Younger), Ruben Santiago-Hudson (Walter Lee Younger, Brother), Kimberly Elise (Beneatha Younger, Sister), Gloria Foster (Lena Younger, Mama), Dion Graham (Joseph Asagai), Donn Swaby (George Murchison), Peter Maloney (Karl Lindner). With: Joseph Edward, Shannon Walker Williams, Gina Coleman, Mya Fisher, Andrew Coutermarsh, Rey Lucas, Andrew Leeds, Ivan McClellan.

The production is singularly blessed with its actresses, beginning with Viola Davis as Ruth Younger, the long-suffering wife of 35-year-old chauffeur Walter Lee Younger (Ruben Santiago-Hudson), and Kimberly Elise as Walter Lee's 20-year-old sister Beneatha, an idealist and God-denier who wants to be a doctor. Both are absolutely right, vital and alive.

Strictly speaking, Gloria Foster is quite wrong for the role of the household matriarch. She's nobody's idea of a "colored" cleaning woman in 1940s–50s Chicago – she's too grand, studied and monumental, and sometimes deliberate to the point of slowing down the production. And yet her performance is fascinating. As the deeply frustrated Walter Lee, perhaps the play's most difficult role, Santiago-Hudson is also richly believable, as are Dion Graham and Donn Swaby as the two men in Beneatha's life.

Jack Hofsiss' direction is sensitive and astute, drawing the audience into sympathy with the dilemmas faced by the Youngers as they get ready to become the first black family in a white neighborhood, despite attempts by its "improvement" association to buy them off. By the end of the play, the audience has grown to know the Youngers and wish them well.

Saturday Night Fever

A Robert Stigwood presentation of a musical in two acts based on the Paramount/RSO Picture based on a story by Nik Cohn, screenplay by Norman Wexler. Stage adaptation by Nan Knighton, in collaboration with Arlene Phillips, Paul Nicholas and Stigwood, featuring songs by the Bee Gees. Directed and choreographed by Phillips. Music director, Martyn Axe. Sets, Robin Wagner; costumes, Andy Edwards (Broadway costumes by Suzy Benzinger); lighting, Andrew Bridge; sound, Mick Potter; dance and vocal arrangements, musical supervision, Phil Edwards; orchestrations, Nigel Wright; music coordinator, William Meade; fight director, J. Allen Suddeth; production stage manager, Perry Cline. Opened Oct 21, 1999. Reviewed Oct 19. Running time: 155 mins

James Carpinello (Tony Manero), Paige Price (Stephanie Mangano), Orfeh (Annette), Paul Castree (Bobby C.), Sean Palmer (Joey), Andy Blankenbuehler (Double J), Richard H. Blake (Gus), Bryan Batt (Monty), Casey Nicholaw (Frank Manero), Suzanne Costallos (Flo Manero/Lucille), Jerry Tellier (Frank Junior), Frank Mastrone (Fusco/Al), David Coburn (Jay Langhart/Becker). With: Miles Alden, Michael Balderrama, Andre Ward, Chris Ghelfi, Daniel Jerod Brown, Brian J. Marcum, Rick Spaans, Ottavio, Drisco Fernandez, David Robertson, Karine Plantadit-Bageot, Natalie Willes, Jeanine Meyers, Angela Pupello, Aliane Baquerot, Rebecca Sherman, Paula Wise, Shannon Beach, Deanna Dys, Jennifer Newman, Danielle Jolie, Stacey Martin, Kristoffer Cusick, Karl du Hoffmann, Roger Lee Israel, Anne Nicole Biancofiore, Marcia Urani, Gina Philistine.

This mindless, heartless and tasteless show is like a TV set playing bad reruns that you can't turn off. The stage adaptation is virtually a line-by-line transcription of the screenplay original. This literal-mindedness bespeaks a lack of imagination on the part of this musical's creators that extends to every aspect of the production. The show's authors have managed to squander its still affecting spirit. The movie had sensitivity and grit.

The local disco was the place where Tony Manero could escape the disappointments of his life, and imagine himself into a new nirvana – the joy and self-respect the dancing gave him he distilled into the courage that might allow him to envision a different future for himself. All that emotional subtext has evaporated from the material. To be fair, much of the loss might have been inevitable – the movie's soul was mostly written in the depths of Travolta's wounded eyes, in the nervously arch nasal whine of Karen Lynn Gorney, playing Tony's ambitious dancing partner Stephanie Mangano.

The show's creators concentrate on the far easier task of replicating its record-breaking soundtrack. But these pop songs weren't created to tell a story or define characters; they were written to pack the dance floor. The performers make little impression in the overwhelmingly synthetic environment of the show.

Saturday Night!

A Pegasus Players production of a musical in two acts. Book by Jules J. Epstein. Music and lyrics by Stephen Sondheim. Directed by Gary Griffin. Sets, Jeff Bauer; lights, Shannon McKinney; costumes, Shifra Werch; sound, Steve Mezger; production stage manager, Katie Klemme. Musical numbers: "Saturday Night," "Class," "Delighted I'm Sure," "Love's a Bond," "Isn't It," "In the Movies," "Exhibit A," "A Moment With You," "Montana Chem," "So Many People," "One Wonderful Day," "I Remember That," "All for You," "That Kind of Neighborhood," "What More Do I Need." Opened May 19, 1999 in Chicago; reviewed May 22, 1999. Running time: 160 mins.

Ian Brennan (Gene Gorman), Elizabeth Sayre Yeats (Helen Fogel), Nico Tricoci (Dino), Christopher LoDuca (Artie), Charles Karvelas (Ray), Patrick Sarb (Ted), Philip Dawkins (Bobby/Major Domo/Elevator Boy), Elic Ryan Bramlett (Hank/Male Vocalist), Samantha Fitschen (Celeste), Harriet Nzinga Plumpp (Mildred), Bill Tisdale (Eugene Gorman), Susan Kokot (Florence/Dakota Doran), Derek Hasentrab (Attendant/Clune/Headwaiter), Paul Hofmann (Mr. Fletcher/Mr. Fisher).

The show centers on "the Gang," a bunch of youthful, lower-middle-class neighborhood wannabes who would all like to make a big killing on Wall Street and trade their lonely Saturday nights in Flatbush for hot dates on Park Avenue.

Chief dreamer is Gene, a Billy Liar-type who almost talks his way into a Plaza ballroom and falls for a beautiful woman in the lobby. Plot complications arise when Gene's various shady moneymaking schemes blow up in his face, and he ends up persona non grata with the neighborhood boys and Celeste, a kind of collective surrogate mother. Everything, 'natch, works out fine.

There's an engaging social realism about this thoughtful show, which dramatizes the pervasive underbelly of economic expansion. Although the awkward cop-shop climax could use more work, the book is otherwise well-paced and humorous, replete with assorted wise guys and gals all hustling their way forward in the time-honored Yankee tradition. Fans of *Marry Me a Little* know the quality of the title number, "Saturday Night," and most of the rest of the score lives up to that mark. Griffin's youthful players give this show everything in their arsenal.

All *Saturday Night* really needs now is a little further TLC and an injection of cash. It's no hidden masterpiece but it is a very workable, charming and tuneful little musical.

Spend Spend Spend

A Pola Jones, Michael Watt and Joop van den Ende presentation, in association with Hat Trick Prods. and Theater Royal, Plymouth, of a musical in two acts based on the book by Viv Nicholson and Stephen Smith, with music by Steve Brown, book and lyrics by Brown and Justin Greene. Directed by Jeremy Sams. Musical direction, Dane Preece. Choreography, Craig Revel Horwood. Sets and costumes, Lez Brotherston; lighting, Mark Henderson; sound, Rick Clarke; orchestrations, John Cameron. Musical numbers: "Salon Mystique," "Ice Cream Girl," "I'll Take Care of Thee," "Upstairs in My Room," "Sexual Happening," "Special Day," "Boy Next Door," "Scars of Love," "John Collier," "The Win," "Two Rooms," "Spend Spend Spend," "Miner's Arms," "Garforth," "Drinking in America," "Canary in a Cage," "Who's Gonna Love Me?", "Dance of the Suits," "Pieces of Me," "Brand New Husband," "Spent Spent Spent," "Finale." Opened in London, reviewed Oct 12, 1999. Running time: 145 mins.

Barbara Dickson (Viv), Steven Houghton (Keith), Rachel Leskovac (Young Viv), Jeff Shankley (George). With: Rebecca Barnes, Lorraine Chappell, Susan Fay, Jane Fowler, Marjorie Keys, Gary Milner, Craig Nicholls, Stuart Nurse, Stuart Pendred, Robin Samson, Nicola Sloane, Duncan

Smith, Jamie Somers, Mary Stockley, Paul Thornley, Alexander Pepe, Alana Asher, Liam O'Byrne, Sophie Wallis, Bethanie Snell, Andrew Stylianou.

Spend Spend Spend is rarely more refined or inquiring than the brash and restless Yorkshire woman at its core, which may go down well with the *Blood Brothers* audience that would seem this show's logical (and sizable) local market but renders its international appeal virtually nil.

The link to the long-running Liverpudlian tuner extends a shared (if comparably naively expressed) obsession with class and extends to the star casting here of Barbara Dickson, who was the defining West End Mrs. Johnstone in the Willy Russell mainstay. The Job-like northern English stoicism of that show might seem to be worlds removed from the booze-soaked, sex-obsessed mining environs where *Spend Spend Spend* takes place. At heart, though, both shows are moralistic dirges packaged for popular consumption.

One learns as much from the sight of the suddenly wealthy Viv's possessions sliding on (and, following her downfall, off) the stage as one does from the faintly unpleasant egoism of Young Viv, whom newcomer Rachel Leskovac plays as a stumpily determined, grasping youth with the belt and physique of a northern English Elaine Paige.

In the end, however, even Sams can't allay the emotional phoniness of material that wants to have it both ways, chastising Viv as excess incarnate at the same time that it is exalting her true British grit.

For all its determinedly high spirits on behalf of a hapless woman's sad life, it's hard not to leave *Spend Spend Spend* without feeling somewhat appalled.

Spinning into Butter

Goodman Theater production of a drama in two acts. Written by Rebecca Gilman. Directed by Les Waters. Sets, Linda Buchanan; lights, Robert Christen; costumes, Brigit Rattenborg Wise; sound, Rob Milburn and Larry Schanker; production stage manager, Kimberly Osgood. Artistic director, Robert Falls. Opened May 16, 1999 in Chicago; reviewed May 19. Running time: 140 mins.

Mary Beth Fisher (Dean Sarah Daniels), Andrew Nararro (Patrick Chibas), Jim Leaming (Ross Collins), Robert Brueler (Dean Burton Strauss), Mary Ann Thebus (Dean Catherine Kenney), Matt DeCaro (Mr. Myers), Bruch Reed (Greg Sullivan).

Set on a bucolic but hardly diverse Vermont, action here revolves around a liberal, single, thirtysomething dean of students named Sarah Daniels (played by Mary Beth Fisher). After a romantic affair with a dissembling faculty member goes sour, Dean Daniels' world further falls apart when she hears that someone has been pinning racist notes on the dorm-room door of one of the college's few African-American students.

The news that there is an overt racist in their midst provokes much soul-searching among the various old-world, backbiting teachers and administrators who make up Gilman's cast of characters. In typical academic fashion, the school sets up focus groups and forums, but the minority students balk. By the surprise end of the play, the whole community has been swallowed by a self-made crisis that threatens its very foundation.

The most arresting section of the play comes in the second act when the increasingly self-aware Daniels has a lengthy monolog in which she reveals her own racist thoughts in such excruciating detail that the suddenly silent Goodman audience seemed to be in the midst of a collective squirm.

The overly long script could easily lose about 15 minutes from its second act. And Gilman's ending – composed of a telephone call – is unsatisfying. But those problems could easily be fixed by a remarkable and nervy young playwright who likes to churn up complacency.

Swing!

A Marc Routh, Richard Frankel, Steven Baruch, Tom Viertel, Lorie Cowen Levy/Stanley Shopkorn, Jujamcyn Theaters in association with BB Promotions, Dede Harris/Jeslo Prods., Libby Adler Mages/Mari Glick, Douglas L. Meyer/James D. Stern and Pace Theatrical Group/SFX presentation of a musical revue in two acts directed and choreographed by Lynne Taylor-Corbett. Production supervised by Jerry Zaks. Music director, Jonathan Smith. Sets, Thomas Lynch; costumes, William Ivey Long; lighting, Kenneth Posner; sound, Peter Fitzgerald; original concept, Paul Kelly; flying, Antigravity Inc.; orchestrations, Harold Wheeler; music supervisor, Michael Rafter; music coordinator, John Miller; production stage manager, Karen Armstrong. Opened in New York Dec 9, 1999. Reviewed Dec 6. Running time: 110 mins.

Featuring: Ann Hampton Callaway, Everett Bradley, Laura Benanti, Casey MacGill and the Gotham City Gates, Michael Gruber. With: Laureen Baldovi, Kristine Bendul, Carol Bentley, Caitlin Carter, Geralyn Del Corso, Desiree Duarte, Beverly Durand, Erin East, Scott Fowler, Ryan Francois, Kevin Michael Gaudin, Edgar Godineaux, Aldrin Gonzalez, Janine LaManna, Rod McCune, J.C. Montgomery, Arte Phillips, Robert Royston, Carlos Sierra-Lopez, Jenny Thomas, Keith Lamelle Thomas, Maria Torres.

Are these girls getting frequent flier miles? The women of *Swing!*, a bouncy new revue that celebrates the American dance craze that's in vogue again, spend an awful lot of time airborne. In two hours of song and dance, some of them never seem to hit the ground. High altitudes, high spirits and high energy are the watchwords of this exuberant show, which features some top-flight talent not normally found under a proscenium: jazz vocalist and songwriter Ann Hampton Callaway, British pop singer-songwriter Everett Bradley, retro big band leader Casey MacGill and his Gotham City Gates. The fleet, astonishingly agile team of dancers includes both Broadway hoofers and dancers who've made their names as swing-dancing champs, some of whom provide their own choreography.

Swing! doesn't feel processed and packaged in the manner of some revues. The people onstage display a real connection to this music. The show's format is straightforward, alternating ensemble dances and pas de deux with song solos or duets, the occasional comic novelty number thrown in for good measure. *Swing!* succeeds admirably in its attempt to put a contemporary shine on the sights and sounds of another era. *Swing!* is a pleasing and polished tribute to a particular time and tempo, a lively party that boasts an infectious spirit that mingles nostalgia with a joy in music that's entirely ageless.

Tallulah

A Coconut Grove Playhouse presentation, by arrangement with Duncan C. Weldon and Tony Fantozzi, of a play in two acts by Sandra Ryan Heyward. Directed by Michael Lessac. Sets, Loren Sherman; costumes, Ilona Somogyi; lighting, Phil

Monat; music and sound, Michael Jay; stage managers, Naomi Littman, Karen Moore. Coconut Grove Playhouse producing artistic director, Arnold Mittelman. Opened in Miami and reviewed Jan 8, 1999. Running time: 120 mins. **Kathleen Turner (Tallulah Bankhead).**

The script is a trove of shock-effect bon mots and salty vignettes that complement the play's progression. Author Heyward gives full exposure to Bankhead's ego, eccentricities, sexual proclivities and substance abuse as she regales a few close friends (the audience) in her boudoir before, and after, a lavish reception. Yet though the star tipples throughout, Heyward wisely avoids the use of alcoholic reverie to induce dramatic conflict.

The story finds Bankhead at her home in Bedford Village, N.Y., in 1947, where she will host a fundraising reception for President Harry S. Truman later that evening. In between party prep and girl talk with her "visitors," Bankhead is on the phone having a young brute, Marlon Brando, fired from her current project, Jean Cocteau's The Eagle Has Two Heads, and comforting a despondent friend, Tennessee Williams. The unspoken irony is that, shortly, Eagle will flop and Brando will become a star in Williams' A Streetcar Named Desire.

The presidential reception also flops. After intermission, the emotionally stricken Bankhead intermittently conducts a midlife assessment that leads her to reconsider a script she'd tossed aside. It's for the celebrity radio programme The Big Show, evoked at the finale as her comeback, which gave Bankhead an extension of her celebrity status. Turner, who seemed at times oddly out of place in the collective environment of Indiscretions on Broadway in '95, easily commands the stage with a three-dimensional – Turner-as-Bankhead-as-Turner – performance.

The Taming of the Shrew

A Joseph Papp Public Theater/New York Shakespeare Festival presentation of the play in two acts by William Shakespeare. Directed by Mel Shapiro. Sets, Karl Eigsti; costumes, Marina Draghici; lighting, Brian MacDevitt; sound, Tom Morse; music, Mark Bennett; choreographer, Naomi Goldberg; fight director, J. Steven White; dramaturg, John Dias; production stage manager, James Latus. Producer, George C. Wolfe; artistic producer, Rosemarie Tichler.Opened as part of New York fest, July 1, 1999. Reviewed June 27. Running time: 165 mins.
Olga Merediz (Lady/Haberdasher), Max Wright (Christopher Sly), Magaly Colimon (Hostess), Ramon Deocampo (Bartholomew), Scott Denny (Lucentio), Peter Jacobson (Tranio), Tom Mardirosian (Baptista Minola), MacIntyre Dixon (Gremio), Allison Janney (Katherina), Reg E. Cathey (Hortensio), Erika Alexander (Bianca), Danyon Davis (Biondello), Jay O. Sanders (Petruchio), Mario Cantone (Grumio), Stephen Mo Hannan (Tailor), Don Mayo (Vincentio), Ramon Deocampo (Officer), Erica Schwartz (Stage Manager). With: Evan Robertson, Dion Flynn, Jesse Pennington, Chad Smith, Rio Puertollano.
The Public Theater has come up with the theatrical alternative: the Bard as reinterpreted by the Three Stooges. And just as moviegoers flocked to Big Daddy, the Central Park audience at the performance reviewed guffawed right along with Mel Shapiro's shamelessly broad take on the Bard's prototypical battle of the sexes. Even Shakespeare's broadest of comedies are laced with complex emotional textures and richly

conceived characterizations, all of which Shapiro's Shrew eschews in favor of an attempt at the biggest, baddest jokes possible – with many of them the director's invention. The result, despite some undeniably ripe moments, is eventually an exhausting air of desperation.

Taming of the Shrew rises or falls on the strengths of its principal combatants, the virago Katherina and the putative bully who tames her, Petruchio, and it is here that Shapiro's knockabout directorial style does the most damage. Both actors' portrayals do not seem to have been given much encouragement to find a sense of the coherent characters in the text. Protag performers lack a sense of deep connection with the lover who first appears as a combatant but is ultimately revealed as a soul mate. If we do not feel that Petruchio's brutishness and humiliating trickery serve to inspire Katherina to reveal the real feeling in her heart, a feeling answered in Petruchio's own – well, then, it's just brutishness and humiliation.

Three Days of Rain

A Donmar Warehouse presentation of a play in two acts by Richard Greenberg. Directed by Robin Lefevre. Sets and costumes, Tom Piper; lighting, David Plater; sound, Rob Tory. Opened in London and reviewed March 2, 1999. Running time: 140 mins.
Colin Firth (Walker/Ned), Elizabeth McGovern (Nan/Lina), David Morrissey (Pip/Theo).
A semi-estranged brother and sister reunite in act one following a family death only to draw conclusions about their parents (dad, in particular) that are movingly disproved once the action reverses 35 years to 1960 New York in the second act.

Greenberg has always located the blight beneath his characters' well-spoken badinage, and so he does again here, cannily folding a play about emotional bequest into an intricate tale that depends for one of its key plot points on a literal bequest.

While the second act fizzes with reverberant emotions that make one want to replay the first half alongside it, there's a patness about Greenberg's resolution, however suspenseful the author's juxtaposition of then-vs.-now. The real discovery is Elizabeth McGovern as Walker's aggrieved sister, Nan, and her incipiently alcoholic mother, Lina, who has the dubious distinction (or so her children see it) of being a Zelda Fitzgerald wannabe. It's mildly amusing to hear McGovern, now an American expatriate in London, put an English spin on words like "recovery," just as it's astonishing to witness the continued growth of a onetime Oscar nominee who has gained enormously in confidence and charm since her days as a Hollywood soubrette. It's Lina's blight to be saved and damned at once, but it's part of McGovern's ongoing resurrection that her work as "a very intriguing alcoholic" has made her a very intriguing actress.

Tongue of a Bird

A Center Theater Group/Mark Taper Forum and Joseph Papp Public Theater presentation of the drama in two acts by Ellen McLaughlin. Directed by Lisa Peterson. Sets, Rachel Hauck; costumes, Candice Cain; lighting, Mary Louise Geiger; music & sound, Gina Leishman; production stage manager, Mary K Klinger. Reviewed Jan 13. Opened Jan 14, 1999, closed Feb 7. Running time: 135 mins.
Ashley Johnson (Charlotte), Cherry Jones (Maxine), Diane Venora (Dessa), Marian Seldes (Zofia), Sharon Lawrence (Evie).

Although best known to many theatergoers as the original Angel in Tony Kushner's *Angels in America*, Ellen McLaughlin is also a playwright. Her latest work takes place largely in the clouds, which is apt, for that's where McLaughlin's head is. To be sure, her play has its strengths – a mostly superb cast, some fine writing and a few compelling ideas – yet success eludes this work. The reasons are myriad, but they begin and end with McLaughlin's pretentious script.

Set in the present-day Adirondacks, the action centres on Maxine (a luminous Cherry Jones), a search-and-rescue pilot with a flawless record: in her Cessna, she's found everyone she's ever looked for. Dessa (the overripe Diane Venora) knows this and hires the flyer to find her kidnapped daughter Charlotte (the winsome Ashley Johnson). But looking for this lost little girl takes its toll on Maxine, who has unresolved mother-daughter issues and a cantankerous, Old World grandmother (the always excellent Marian Seldes) to worry about.

Still, the story is sound and the themes are worthy, though hardly fresh. But taking a page from Kushner's playwriting book, McLaughlin lards her effort with grandiose speechifying, which would not be so bad were it not so relentless. Barely a scene goes by without one character or another aiming at profundity. As a result, the best scenes get lost among the dross, because McLaughlin's good and bad writing sound much the same after a while.

Via Dolorosa

A Lincoln Center Theater presentation of the Royal Court Theater production of a play in one act by David Hare. Directed by Stephen Daldry. Set, Ian MacNeil; lighting, Rick Fisher; sound, Paul Arditti; stage manager, Karen Armstrong. Opened March 18, 1999. Reviewed March 16. Running time: 100 mins.
With: David Hare.

David Hare's *Via Dolorosa* is a daring piece of theatre. Hare cheerfully admits his limited experience as a performer, and one of the charms of the show is his slightly awkward stage presence. And his subject is not a solipsistic jaunt through his own life in the theater, but territory far removed from the milieu of an esteemed and prolific British playwright: the fractious land of Israel and the West Bank. The play is ultimately a testament to art's capacity to enlarge our vision of the world to embrace even the most alien of cultures, to forge an intimate connection with people whose struggles are not our own but are in some measure profoundly universal.

The show was inspired by a series of trips Hare took to Israel. Hare's tour is guided by a series of vividly drawn personalities for whom politics and religion are the bread and butter of daily intercourse. The landmarks of Israel's past are all touched upon: the invention of the Zionist movement; the Six-Day war; the Oslo accord; the assassination of Yitzhak Rabin. But there's nothing dense or lecturely about the show: Hare's dramatic gifts combine happily with the passionate personalities he enthusiastically impersonates to turn the complexities of the narrative into engaging theater. Instead of the traditional personal history, Hare offers history personalized.

Waiting in the Wings

An Alexander H. Cohen, Chase Mishkin, Max Cooper, Leonard Soloway, Steven M. Levy presentation of a play in two acts by Noël Coward, as revisited by Jeremy Sams.

Directed by Michael Langham. Sets, Ray Klausen; costumes, Alvin Colt; lighting, Ken Billington; sound, Peter Fitzgerald; dialect coach, Elizabeth Smith; production manager, Beverley Randolph. Opened Dec 16, 1999. Reviewed Dec 15. Running time: 145 mins.
Rosemary Harris (May Davenport), Rosemary Murphy (Cora Clarke), Elizabeth Wilson (Bonita Belgrave), Patricia Connolly (Maudie Melrose), Helena Carroll (Deirdre O'Malley), Bette Henritze (Claire Almina), Helen Stenborg (Sarita Myrtle), Lauren Bacall (Lotta Bainbridge), Victoria Boothby (Topsy Baskerville), Barnard Hughes (Osgood Meeker), Sybil Lines (Dora), Crista Moore (Zelda Fenwick), Anthony Cummings (Alan Banfield), Dana Ivey (Sylvia Archibald), Simon Jones (Perry Lascoe), Amelia Campbell (Doreen), Geddeth Smith (Ted), Collin Johnson (Ambulance Man).

In celebration of the 100th anniversary of the famed British playwright and performer's birth, Noël Coward is posthumously receiving the kind of birthday present that would have pleased him most: a hit show. This gift comes in the guise of one of his later, most roundly dismissed plays of the 1960's.

Director Michael Langham and playwright Jeremy Sams, who is credited rather obscurely with revisiting Coward's play, have molded the production into a charming showcase for a tremendously gifted cast, including a dozen or so actresses of a certain age who contribute funny, affecting and meticulously defined performances that turn a slick but trifling piece of writing into a rewarding evening of theatre.

Waiting is the 1960 equivalent of a situation comedy. Coward assembles a cast of diversely typed characters, in this case retired English actresses and their caretakers, and sets them down in a closed environment, a charity home called the Wings. As the ladies reminisce, chatter and wisecrack, you can feel the playwright floundering for a plot, and settling for a trio of subplots: the feud between longtime resident May Davenport and new arrival Lotta Bainbridge; the ladies' cherished desire to build a solarium, and the undercover journalist who ruffles their feathers but ultimately comes to their aid; and the rapprochement between Lotta and her estranged son Alan. Headliners Bacall and Harris certainly have their work cut out for them on a stage enlivened by such fine work. Bacall uses her inimitable, chilly drawl to powerhouse effect on some of Coward's crisper witticisms.

The Weir

A Thomas Viertel, Richard Frankel, Steven Baruch, Marc Routh, Jujamcyn Theaters, Manhattan Theater Club and Turnstyle/Ambassador Theater Group presentation of the Royal Court Theater production of a play in one act by Conor McPherson. Directed by Ian Rickson. Sets and costumes, Rae Smith; lighting, Paule Constable; sound, Paul Arditti; production stage manager, Brian Meister. Opened April 1, 1999. Reviewed March 30. Running time: 115 mins.
Jim Norton (Jack), Brendan Coyle (Brendan), Kieran Ahern (Jim), Dermot Crowley (Finbar), Michelle Fairley (Valerie).
The Olivier award-winning London hit is a haunting, insinuatingly spellbinding play. The play's setting is a dingy local pub in an Irish backwater town. Constant patron Jack is disgusted to learn that the Guinness tap is out of order. Also inspiring Jack's eloquent Irish scorn is the arrival of a less frequent customer of the bar, Finbar, a local who abandoned the area to make his fortune in the nearest town.

... October 9 ...

Miramax Films agrees to co-finance and handle domestic distribution for Martin Scorsese's **Gangs Of New York**, the dark period picture set to star Leonardo DiCaprio.

He's squiring around a young woman who's purchased a house in the neighbourhood. Just as curious about this woman are Jim, the bar's only other regular, and Brendan, its proprietor.

McPherson has a flawless ear for naturally poetic language that brings out the quiet truth of characters without recourse to revelatory speechifying. The centrepiece of the play is a series of monologues in which the men recount tales of supernatural experience. More haunting than the tales themselves is an unspoken irony: the contrast between the ghosts, who ceaselessly cleave to life, and the denizens of the bar, who have not found the courage – or simply the occasion – to fully embrace it.

The woman's tale awakens in the men a dormant empathy that brings from each a hesitantly expressed desire to comfort her as the tragedy dwarfs their own muted unhappiness. It also brings out the best in this astonishing group of actors, who turn the play's emotional climax into a tremendously moving picture of the intimacy that shared grief can bring about.

You're a Good Man, Charlie Brown

A Michael Leavitt, Fox Theatricals, Jerry Frankel, Arthur Whitelaw and Gene Persson presentation of a musical in two acts with music, book and lyrics by Clark Gesner, based on the comic strip Peanuts by Charles M. Schulz. Directed by Michael Mayer. Musical supervision, arrangements and additional material by Andrew Lippa. Choreographed by Jerry Mitchell. Music director, Kimberly Grigsby. Sets, David Gallo; costumes, Michael Krass; lighting, Kenneth Posner; sound, Brian Ronan; orchestrations, Michael Gibson;

production stage manager, James Harker. Opened Feb 4, 1999. Reviewed Jan 31. Running time: 110 mins. **Kristin Chenoweth (Sally), Stanley Wayne Mathis (Schroeder), B.D. Wong (Linus), Roger Bart (Snoopy), Ilana Levine (Lucy), Anthony Rapp (Charlie Brown).**

You're a Good Man, Charlie Brown arrives on Broadway following a 30-year history as a beloved off-Broadway sleeper hit and a favorite of high schools and summer camps.

Musical centers on the constant enumeration of Charlie's faults: his lonely lunch hours, lack of valentines and rejection by his own dog. Anthony Rapp and his fellow performers are a generally jubilant bunch, giving their all to putting across a score that is sturdy enough to withstand years of revivals without being brilliant. New songs blend in smoothly, with Sally's *My New Philosophy* probably the best. In the surefire role of Schulz's beagle with attitude, Roger Bart delivers the show's other standout performance, using a wicked but endearing leer to suggest Snoopy's devious charm.

In the part of Sally, C.B.'s little sister and a role not in the original version of the musical, Kristin Chenoweth is a daffy, delirious delight. She shines brightest here because she effortlessly gives off the illusion of being a kid acting like an adult, while most of the other performers are clearly adults acting like kids, a more heavy-handed effect.

But despite the high-quality polish and hard work from the creative team behind this revival, musical is still a mere trifle whose pleasant impression barely outlasts its brief running time. Folks returning for nostalgic purposes may be surprised to find that a show that has long lingered in their memory turns out to be so forgettable.

*Lunch is for wimps.
(Michael Douglas,
Wall Street)*

Above: Mariah Carey at the MTV European Awards

Above: Eduardo Sanchez and Daniel Myrick
Below: Kevin Spacey

Above: Julia Roberts in *My Best Friend's Wedding*
Below: Dame Judi Dench

Above: Catherine Zeta-Jones in *Entrapment*
Below: Michael Douglas

Below: Matt Damon in *The Talented Mr. Ripley*

Above: George Clooney in *The Peacemaker*

Above: Fatboy Slim (aka Norman Cook) at the MTV European Awards

Above: Whitney Houston at the MTV European Awards
Below: Christina Aguilera at the MTV European Awards

Below: Sir Elton John

Opposite: Anthony Newley
Below: Stanley Kubrick

Above: Oliver Reed
Below: Ernie Wise

Above: Sir Dirk Bogarde

Index of theater shows reviewed in *Variety* 1999

Drums on the Dyke (Sept 27–Oct 3)
East Is East (May 31–June 6)
Easy Virtue (July 26–Aug 1)
EFX (March 22–28)
Elsa Edgar (Dec 20–Jan 2)
Enigma Variations (May 10–16)
Epic Proportions (Oct 4–10)
The Eros Trilogy (Feb 15–21)
Everybody's Ruby (March 15–21)
The Exact Center of the Universe (April 12–18)
Exactly Like You (April 19–25)
An Experiment With an Air Pump (Nov 1–7)
Faith Prince: Leap of Faith (concert) (Sept 27–Oct 3)
Fame: The Musical (Feb 1–7)
Far East (Jan 18–24)
Finian's Rainbow (Nov 1–7)
The First Picture Show (San Francisco) (June 14–20)
The First Picture Show (Los Angeles) (Aug 16–22)
    (same production)
Fit to Print: Remotely Controlled (Sept 6–12)
Die Fledermaus (opera) (Jan 11–17)
Floyd Collins (July 19–25)
Forbidden Broadway (March 29–April 4)
Force of Nature (April 26–May 2)
The Forest (Feb 8–14)
Fosse (Broadway) (Jan 18–24)
Fosse (Chicago) (Sept 27–Oct 3)
Four Nights in Knaresborough (Nov 15–21)
Freedomland (Jan 4–10)
The Freedom of the City (Dublin) (May 3–9)
The Freedom of the City (New York, Lincoln Center
    Festival) (July 19–25)
Fully Committed (Oct 4–10)
A Funny Thing Happened on the Way to the Forum
    (Aug 9–15)
Furthest From the Sun (Sept 27–Oct 3)
The Gathering (Aug 9–15)
Gemini (June 21–27)
The Gershwins' Fascinating Rhythm (April 26–May 2)
Gertrude and Alice: A Likeness to Loving (June 14–20)
Gimmick (May 10–16)
Give Me Your Answer, Do! (April 26–May 2)
The Glace Bay Miners' Museum (Dec 6–12)
The Glass Menagerie (Jan 11–17)
Glenn (Sept 13–19)
The Glory of Living (Jan 25–31)
The Golden Ass (opera) (May 17–23)
Good (March 29–April 4)
Good Bones (Feb 1–7)
Goodnight Children Everywhere (May 31–June 6)
Goosebumps – Live on Stage (Jan 4–10)
Guiding Star (Jan 18–24)
Gum (April 5–11)

Halfway Home (March 8–14)
Having (March 1–7)
Hay Fever (June 21–27)
Hedda Gabler (March 29–April 4)
Hedwig and the Angry Inch (Oct 18–24)
Henry V (Sept 13–19)
Henry V: A Musical Scenario After Shakespeare (concert)
    (June 7–13)
High Life (Feb 1–7)
Hinton Battle: Largely Live! (Aug 30–Sept 5)
Hotel of Two Worlds (Nov 1–7)
A Hotel on Marvin Gardens (Oct 18–24)
A Hotel Room in the Town of NN (June 21–27)
The Hothouse (March 1–7)
House Arrest: An Introgression (April 26–May 2)
House/Lights (March 8–14)
Howie the Rookie (April 5–11)
The Hunchback of Notre Dame (June 21–27)
Hurrah at Last (June 7–13)
Hushabye Mountin (May 3–9)
I Am the One That I Want (July 19–25)
The Iceman Cometh (April 12–18)
If Love Were All (June 14–20)
If Memory Serves (Dec 20–Jan 2)
The Importance of Being Earnest (New Haven, Conn.)
    (May 17–23)
The Importance of Being Earnest (London) (Aug 23–29)
In the Blood (Nov 29–Dec 5)
Indian Ink (March 8–14)
The Inmates (June 28–July 11)
The Invisible Man (Jan 4–10)
The Iphigenia Cycle (Feb 1–7)
It Ain't Nothin' But the Blues (May 3–9)
It's All True (Jan 18–24)
Jacques Brel Is Alive and Well and Living in Paris (April
    5–11)
James Joyce's The Dead (Nov 1–7)
James Naughton: Street of Dreams (Feb 15–21)
Jane Eyre (Aug 9–15)
Jar the Floor (Aug 23–29)
The Jazz Singer (Nov 8–14)
Jekyll and Hyde (May 3–9)
The Jew of Malta (Nov 8–14)
Jolson Sings Again (March 15–21)
Joseph and the Amazing Technicolor Dreamcoat
    (Millburn, N.J.) (June 21–27)
Joseph and the Amazing Technicolor Dreamcoat (San
    Francisco) (Dec 20–Jan 2)
Juno and the Paycock (Dublin) (Sept 20–26)
Juno and the Paycock (London) (Oct 4–10)
Kafka's Dick (Jan 11–17)
Kat and the Kings (Aug 23–29)
Key West (July 26–Aug 1)

... October 12 ...
Richard Donner is to direct **Timeline**, based on Michael Crichton's new thriller.

Kilt (May 3–9)
King Hedley II (Dec 20–Jan 2)
King Lear (Dec 20–Jan 2)
Kiss Me, Kate (Nov 22–28)
The Lady and the Van (Dec 13–19)
Lake Hollywood (May 3–9)
Last Dance at Dum Dum (Aug 9–15)
The Last Station (Aug 9–15)
Last Train to Nibroc (Dec 6–12)
Legacy (March 22–28)
Lenny (Aug 16–22)
The Life of Galileo (Oct 25–31)
Lift Off (March 1–7)
The Lion in Winter (March 15–21)
The Lion King (Oct 25–31)
Lips (May 3–9)
Lives of the Saints (Philadelphia) (Feb 8–14)
Lives of the Saints (Stockbridge, Mass.) (Sept 6–12)
  same performers
Lobster Alice (Oct 18–24)
The Lonesome West (May 3–9)
Look Back in Anger (London) (Aug 2–8)
Look Back in Anger (New York Off Broadway)
  (Oct 25–31)
Lost Creek Township (April 26–May 2)
Love in the Title (March 22–28)
Love, Janis (Aug 23–29)
Love's Labor's Lost (Aug 16–22)
Lyrebird: Tales of Helpmann (March 8–14)
Macbeth (London) (March 8–14)
Macbeth (New York) (March 22–28)
The Madras House (July 19–25)
The Magic Fire (April 5–11)
A Majority of One (Feb 8–14)
Mamma Mia! (April 26–May 2)
Marathan (Dec 6–12)
Marlene (April 19–25)
Martin Guerre (Leeds, England)(Jan 11–17)
Martin Guerre (Minneapolis, Minn.) (Oct 4–10)
Mary Christine (Dec 6–12)
Maybe Baby, It's You (Nov 15–21)
Measure for Measure (June 28–July 11)
The Merchant of Venice (Aug 2–8)
Merton of the Movies (July 12–18)
A Midsummer Night's Dream (June 28–July 11)
The Mineola Twins (Feb 22–28)
Minnelli on Minnelli (Dec 13–19)
The Misanthrope (Feb 22–28)
Missing Footage (May 17–23)
Misterman (May 31–June 6)
Mnemonic (Oct 4–10)
Moby Dick/Rehearsed (Aug 2–8)
Money (July 12–18)

Morning, Noon and Night (Chicago) (Sept 27–Oct 3)
Morning, Noon and Night (New York) (Nov 15–21)
Morning Star (May 10–16)
Morphic Resonance (March 1–7)
Moses und Aron (opera) (Feb 22–28)
Mother Russia (May 17–23)
Mozart! (Oct 25–31)
Night Must Fall (March 15–21)
No, No, Nanette (Aug 16–22)
Not About Nightingales (March 1–7)
La Nouba (Feb 8–14)
O. Henry's Lovers (Oct 25–31)
The Odyssey (Oct 25–31)
On the Jump (June 7–13)
On the Twentieth Century (June 21–27)
Oo–bla–dee (April 5–11)
Our Father (Dec 13–19)
Over & Over (Feb 15–21)
The Pajama Game (May 17–23)
Paradise Hotel (Jan 25–31)
Peggy Sue Got Married (Aug 2–8)
Perfect Days (June 28–July 11)
Phedre (Jan 11–17)
The Play's the Thing (Sept 6–12)
Plenty (May 10–16)
Portia Coughlan (Feb 1–7)
Preaching to the Perverted (Oct 18–24)
A Preface to the Alien Garden (March 29–April 4)
The Presentment (April 5–11)
The Price (Williamstone, Mass.) (Aug 30–Sept 5)
The Price (New York) (Nov 22–28) (same production)
The Prisoner of Second Avenue (April 5–11)
Private Lives (May 24–30)
Putting It Together (Nov 29–Dec 5)
Quartet (Sept 13–19)
The Rainmaker (Nov 15–21)
A Raisin in the Sun (Aug 2–8)
The Real Thing (June 14–20)
Rebecca (Sept 6–12)
Red (April 5–11)
Red Corners (Jan 25–31)
Red White and Tuna (March 29–April 4)
Remember This (Nov 22–28)
Resident Alien (Nov 22–28)
The Resistible Rise of Arturo Ui (July 12–18)
Resurrection (opera) (May 10–16)
Richard II (Sept 6–12)
Richard III (London) (Feb 8–14)
Richard III (Lennox, Mass.) (July 26–Aug 1)
The Right Size in Do You Come Here Often?
  (Sept 20–26)
Ring Round the Moon (May 3–9)
The Rivals (Jan 4–10)

The Road to Hell (Nov 15–21)
Rocky Horror Show (Feb 8–14)
Romeo and Juliet: The Musical (Aug 23–29)
Rose (July 19–25)
Rosencrantz and Guildenstern Are Dead (July 12–18)
Running Man (Nov 1–7)
Sail Away (Nov 15–21)
A Saint She Ain't (May 17–23)
Saturday Night (May 31–June 6)
Saturday Night Fever (Oct 25–31)
Scent of the Roses (Nov 22–28)
Shoot the Piano Player (Aug 16–22)
Shyster (Dec 13–19)
A Simple Heart (April 12–18)
Sisters Matsumoto (Feb 1–7)
Sleep With Me (May 3–9)
The Smell of the Kill (Feb 15–21)
Some Explicit Polaroids (Oct 25–31)
Some Voices (Jan 11–17)
Song at Twilight (Nov 29–Dec 5)
Space (Dec 13–19)
Speer (March 15–21)
Spend Spend Spend (Oct 18–24)
Spinning into Butter (May 31–June 6)
Spirit: A Journey in Dance, Drums and Song
  (Oct 25–31)
Spread Eagle (Jan 4–10)
Spring Storm (Nov 29–Dec 5)
Starr's Last Tape (Sept 6–12)
Stars in Your Eyes (Nov 1–7)
The Stone Angel (March 1–7)
A Streetcar Named Desire (Sept 20–26)
Suddenly Last Summer (April 19–25)
Summer (opera) (Sept 6–12)
Summer '69 (Aug 30–Sept 5)
The Summer Moon (Nov 15–21)
Surfers (April 19–25)
Susannah (April 12–18)
Sweeney Todd (Nov 1–7)
Swing! (Dec 13–19)
Swingstep (June 14–20)
Syncopation (Dec 20–Jan 2)
Tallulah (Jan 18–24)
The Taming of the Shrew (New York, Off Broadway)
  (July 12–18)
The Taming of the Shrew (Williamston, Mass.)
  (July 19–25)
Tango Argentino (Nov 29–Dec 5)
Tartuffe (San Francisco) (June 28–July 11)
Tartuffe (New York, Off Broadway) (Aug 30–Sept 5)
Temporary Help (Sept 27–Oct 3)
Tennessee Williams Remembered (June 7–13)
La Terrasse (June 14–20)

Tess of the D'Urbervilles (Nov 15–21)
That Championships Season (April 26–May 2)
That Summer (Aug 9–15)
They've Got Death Bound Up (Sept 6–12)
The Threepenny Opera (Sept 20–26)
Things Fall Apart (March 8–14)
Things You Shouldn't Say Past Midnight (May 17–23)
This Lime Tree Bower (May 24–30)
Three Days of Rain (March 8–14)
Thunder Knocking on the Door (Jan 4–10)
Thwak (June 28–July 11)
Time After Time (Jan 4–10)
Tis Pity She's a Whore (Nov 1–7)
Tongue of a Bird (April 12–18)
The Trestle at Pope Lick Creek (July 12–18)
The Trial of Her Inner Thigh (June 28–July 11)
Tristan und Isolde (opera) (Dec 6–12)
The Triumph of Love (Sept 6–12)
Troilus and Cressida (March 22–28)
Trudy Blue (Dec 6–12)
Trust (April 5–11)
The Turn of the Screw (March 29–April 4)
Two for the Show (Jan 11–17)
Two Sisters and a Piano (March 1–7)
Uncle Vanya (July 12–18)
Up, Up and Away: The Songs of Jimmy Web (Jan 25–31)
The Valladolid Debate (March 15–21)
Valparaiso (March 1–7)
Vassa (Feb 15–21)
Very Heaven (May 17–23)
Via Dolorosa (March 22–28)
Vicki Sue Robinson – Behind the Beat (May 17–23)
A View From the Bridge (opera) (Nov 1–7)
Voices in the Dark (Stamford, Conn) (Aug 2–8)
Voices in the Dark (Broadway) (Aug 16–22) same pro-
  duction
Waiting in the Wings (Boston)(Nov 22–28)
Waiting in the Wings (New York – same production)
  (Dec 20–Jan 2)
The Water Engine/Mr. Happiness (Nov 1–7)
The Weir (April 5–11)
The Whisperers (May 10–16)
The Who's Tommy: Broadway in Concert (April 12–18)
Winter (June 21–27)
The Winter's Tale (May 17–23) (St Petersburg, Fla)
The Winter's Tale (June 7–13) (London) (a Maly Drama
  Theater of St. Petersburg production in Russian)
Wonderland (June 21–27)
Working (March 29–April 4)
Wrong Mountain (Nov 8–14)
Y2K (Dec 13–19)
You Be Ted and I'll Be Sylvia (Sept 20–26)
You're a Good Man, Charlie Brown (Feb 8–14)

...October 14...
Kate Winslet is to play the tragic heroine of Emile Zola's novel **Thérèse Raquin**.

Music

Although never figuring as large in *Variety*'s universe as film and broadcasting, the music scene has been covered for most of this century in fair depth by the paper. Until the 1960s there were several pages each week devoted to music. The section waned because legendary Editor Abel Green paid comparatively little heed to it. During the past few years, current Editor-in-Chief Peter Bart has resurrected *Variety*'s music coverage, in the form of news analysis and longer investigative pieces. Indeed, never before has there been so much synergy between the various sectors of entertainment. Elton John is involved in film production; Madonna and Sting have appeared in starring roles on screen; Andrew Lloyd Webber's *Phantom of the Opera* has grossed $3 billion worldwide.

The rise of MTV and the abiding importance of the Grammys are reflected in this section.

All-time U.S. bestselling singles

1. "Candle in the Wind 1997," Elton John, MCA (1997)
2. "I Will Always Love You," Whitney Houston, Arista (1992)
3. "Macarena," Los Del Rio, RCA (1995)
4. "We Are the World," Various, Columbia (1985)
5. "Whomp (There It Is)," Tag Team, Life (1993)
6. "I Do It For You," Bryan Adams, A&M (1991)
7. "Gangsta's Paradise," Coolio, (1995)
8. "Hound Dog," Elvis Presley, (1956)
9. "How Do I Live," LeAnn Rines, Curb (1998)
10. "I'll Be Missing You," Puff Daddy, Bad Boy/Arista (1998)

All-time U.S. bestselling albums

1. *Greatest Hits 1971–1975*, Eagles, Elektra
2. *Thriller*, Michael Jackson, Epic
3. *The Wall*, Pink Floyd, Columbia
4. *Rumours*, Fleetwood Mac, Warner Bros.
5. *Greatest Hits Vols. I&II*, Billy Joel, Columbia
6. *The Beatles*, The Beatles, Capitol
7. *Led Zeppelin IV*, Led Zeppelin, Swan Song
8. *Back in Black*, AC/DC, Atco
9. *Boston*, Boston, Epic
10. *No Fences*, Garth Brooks, Capitol Nashville

Top 10 U.S. singles: 1999

1. "Believe," Cher, Warner Bros.
2. "Nobody's Supposed to Be Here," Deborah Cox, Arista
3. "I'm Your Angel," R. Kelly & Celine Dion, Jive
4. "... Baby One More Time," Britney Spears, Jive
5. "Genie in a Bottle," Christina Aguilera, RCA
6. "Heartbreak Hotel," Whitney Houston (w/Faith Evans, Kelly Price), Arista
7. "Summer Girls," LFO, Logic/Arista
8. "If You Had My Love," Jennifer Lopez, WORK/ERG
9. "Livin' La Vida Loca," Ricky Martin, C2
10. "Angel of Mine," Monica, Arista

Top 10 U.S. albums: 1999

1. *Millennium*, Backstreet Boys, Jive
2. *Baby One More Time*, Britney Spears, Jive
3. *Ricky Martin*, Ricky Martin, Sony/C2
4. *Come on Over*, Shania Twain, Mercury Nashville
5. *Significant Other*, Limp Bizkit, Interscope
6. *Supernatural*, Santana, Arista
7. *Devil Without a Cause*, Kid Rock, Atlantic/Lava
8. *Fanmail*, TLC, Arista/La Face
9. *Christine Aguilera*, Christine Aguilera, RCA
10. *Wide Open Spaces*, Dixie Chicks, Sony/Monument

...October 15...
Former **Seinfeld** scribe-showrunners, Alec Berg and Jeff Schaffer, have landed a six-episode commitment from Fox Broadcasting for a new half-hour comedy.

All-time U.K. bestselling singles

1. "Something About .../Candle in the Wind," Elton John, Rocket (1997)
2. "Do They Know It's Christmas," Band Aid, Mercury (1984)
3. "Bohemian Rhapsody," Queen, EMI (1975)
4. "Mull of Kintyre," Wings, Capitol (1977)
5. "River of Babylon/Brown Girl in the Ring," Boney M, Atlantic/Hansa (1978)
6. "Relax," Frankie Goes to Hollywood, ZTT (1983)
7. "She Loves You," The Beatles, Parlaphone (1963)
8. "You're the One That I Want," John Travolta/Olivia Newton John, RSO (1978)
9. "Unchained Melody," Robson Green & Jerome Flynn, RCA (1995)
10. "Mary's Boy Child," Boney M, Atlantic/Hansa (1978)

All-time U.K. bestselling albums

1. *Sgt Pepper's Lonely Hearts Club Band*, The Beatles, Parlaphone (1967)
2. *Bad*, Michael Jackson, Epic (1987)
3. *Stars*, Simply Red, East West (1991)
4. *Brothers in Arms*, Dire Straits, Vertigo (1985)
5. *Greatest Hits Volume One*, Queen, Parlaphone (1981)
6. *Thriller*, Michael Jackson, Epic (1982)
7. *(What's the Story) Morning Glory?*, Oasis, Creation (1995)
8. *The Immaculate Collection*, Madonna, Sire (1990)
9. *The Very Best of Elton John*, Elton John, Rocket (1990)
10. *... But Seriously*, Phil Collins, Virgin (1989)

Top 10 U.K. singles: 1999

1. "Baby One More Time," Britney Spears, Jive
2. "Blue (Da Ba Dee)," Eiffel 65, Eternal
3. "The Millennium Prayer," Cliff Richard, Papillion
4. "Mambo No. 5 (A Little Bit of ...)," Lou Bega, RCA
5. "9 PM (Till I Come)," ATB, Sound of Ministry
6. "Livin' La Vida Loca," Ricky Martin, Columbia
7. "That Don't Impress Me Much," Shania Twain, Mercury
8. "Sweet Like Chocolate," Shanks & Bigfoot, Pepper
9. "Flat Beat," Mr. Oizo, F Communications
10. "When the Going Gets Tough," Boyzone, Polydor

Top 10 U.K. albums: 1999

1. *Come On Over*, Shania Twain, Mercury
2. *By Request*, Boyzone, Polydor
3. *The Man Who*, Travis, Independiente
4. *Gold – Greatest Hits*, ABBA, Polydor
5. *Performance and Cocktails*, Stereophonics, V2
6. *I've Been Expecting You*, Robbie Williams, Chrysalis
7. *Steptacular*, Steps, Jive
8. *Talk on Corners*, Corrs, Atlantic
9. *Westlife*, Westlife, RCA
10. *On How Life Is*, Macy Gray, Epic

Source: CIN (based on guesstimates, BPI certs and record-company data)

The 34th Annual Academy of Country Music Awards

Artist of the decade: Garth Brooks
Album of the year: *Wide Open Spaces*, Dixie Chicks
Single record of the year: "This Kiss," Faith Hill
Song of the year: "Holes in the Floor of Heaven," Steve Wariner
Video of the year: "This Kiss," Faith Hill
Entertainer of the year: Garth Brooks
Top female vocalist: Faith Hill
Top male vocalist: Tim McGraw
Top vocal duo/group: Dixie Chicks
Top new female vocalist: Jo Dee Messina
Top new male vocalist: Mark Wills

Top new vocal duo/group: Dixie Chicks
Vocal event of the year: "Just to Hear You Say That You Love Me," Faith Hill & Tim McGraw
Pioneer award: Glen Campbell
Double diamond album award: Shania Twain

Billboard Music Awards: 1999

1999 Billboard century award: Emmylou Harris
Artist achievement award: Aerosmith
Artist of the decade: Mariah Carey
Artist of the year: Backstreet Boys
Album of the year: *Millennium*, Backstreet Boys
Male artist of the year: Ricky Martin
Female artist of the year: Britney Spears
New artist of the year: Britney Spears
Album artist of the year: Backstreet Boys
Albums artist duo/group of the year: Backstreet Boys
Female albums artist of the year: Britney Spears
Hot 100 singles male artist of the year: Ricky Martin
Hot 100 singles female artist of the year: Britney Spears
R&B artist of the year: R. Kelly
R&B albums artist of the year: DMX
R&B album of the year: *400 Degreez*, Juvenile
R&B single of the year: "Fortunate," Maxwell
Rap artist of the year: Jay-Z

Rap single of the year: "Who Dat," JY Money/Solé
Country artist of the year: Dixie Chicks
Country albums artist of the year: Dixie Chicks
Country albums artist duo/group of the year: Dixie Chicks
Modern rock artist of the year: The Offspring
Modern rock track of the year: "My Own Worst Enemy," Lit
Rock artist of the year: Creed
Rock track of the year: "One," Creed
Adult contemporary track of the year: "Angel," Sarah McLachlan
Catalog artist of the year: Metallica
Catalog album of the year: *Metallica*, Metallica

In addition, Red Hot Chili Peppers were presented with a special award for setting an all-time Billboard record for the most weeks at No.1 on Modern Rock Tracks chart, with their song "Scar Tissue."

MTV Awards since inception

1984
GENERAL CATEGORY WINNERS
Video of the year: The Cars, "You Might Think"
Male video: David Bowie, "China Girl"
Female video: Cyndi Lauper, "Girls Just Want to Have Fun"
Concept video: Herbie Hancock, "Rockit"
Group video: ZZ Top, "Legs"
Stage performance in a video: Van Halen, "Jump"
Overall performance in a video: Michael Jackson, "Thriller"

PROFESSIONAL CATEGORY WINNERS
Special effects in a video: Herbie Hancock, "Rockit"
Art direction in a video: Herbie Hancock, "Rockit"
Editing in a video: Herbie Hancock, "Rockit"
Cinematography in a video: The Police, "Every Breath You Take"
Choreography in a video: Michael Jackson, "Thriller"
Direction in a video: ZZ Top, "Sharp Dressed Man," Tim Newman, director
Most experimental video: Herbie Hancock, "Rockit"

SPECIAL AWARD WINNERS
Special recognition award: Quincy Jones, in honor of his overall contribution to the entire music universe

Video vanguard awards: The Beatles, David Bowie, Richard Lester
Viewers choice award: Michael Jackson, "Thriller"

1985
GENERAL CATEGORY WINNERS
Video of the year: Don Henley, "The Boys of Summer"
Male video: Bruce Springsteen, "I'm on Fire"
Female video: Tina Turner, "What's Love Got to Do With It?"
Group video: USA for Africa, "We Are the World"
Concept video: Glenn Frey, "Smuggler's Blues"
Overall performance in a video: Philip Bailey and Phil Collins, "Easy Lover"
Stage performance in a video: Bruce Springsteen, "Dancing in the Dark"
New artist in a video: 'Til Tuesday, "Voices Carry"

PROFESSIONAL CATEGORY WINNERS
Special effects in a video: Tom Petty and The Heartbreakers, "Don't Come Around Here No More," Tony Mitchell, Kathy Dougherty, Peter Cohen
Art direction in a video: Don Henley, "The Boys of Summer," Bryan Jones

Editing in a video: Art of Noise, "Close (to the Edit)," Zbigniew Rybczynski

Cinematography in a video: Don Henley, "The Boys of Summer," Pascal Lebeque

Choreography in a video: Elton John, "Sad Songs," David Atkins

Direction in a video: Don Henley, "The Boys of Summer," John Baptiste Mondino, director

Most experimental video: Art of Noise, "Close (to the Edit)," Zbigniew Rybczynski

SPECIAL AWARD WINNERS

Special recognition award: Bob Geldof

Video vanguard awards: David Byrne, Kevin Godley and Lol Creme, Russell Mulcahy

Viewers choice award: USA for Africa, "We Are the World"

1986
GENERAL CATEGORY WINNERS

Video of the year: Dire Straits, "Money For Nothing"

Male video: Robert Palmer, "Addicted to Love"

Female video: Whitney Houston, "How Will I Know?"

Group video: Dire Straits, "Money For Nothing"

Concept video: A-Ha, "Take on Me"

Overall performance in a video: David Bowie and Mick Jagger, "Dancing in the Streets"

Stage performance in a video: Bryan Adams and Tina Turner, "It's Only Love"

New artist in a video: A-Ha, "Take on Me"

PROFESSIONAL CATEGORY WINNERS

Special effects in a video: A-Ha, "Take on Me," Michael Patterson

Art direction in a video: ZZ Top, "Rough Boy," Ron Cobb

Editing in a video: A-Ha, "The Sun Always Shines on TV," David Yardley

Cinematography in a video: A-Ha, "The Sun Always Shines on TV," Oliver Stapleton

Choreography in a video: Prince and the Revolution, "Raspberry Beret," Prince

Direction in a video: A-Ha, "Take on Me," Steven Barron

Most experimental video: A-Ha, "Take on Me," Steven Barron

SPECIAL AWARD WINNERS

Special recognition award: Bill Graham and Jack Healey, executive directors Amnesty International

Video vanguard awards: Madonna and Zbigniew Rybcznski

Viewers choice award: A-Ha, "Take on Me"

1987
GENERAL CATEGORY WINNERS

Video of the year: Peter Gabriel, "Sledgehammer," producer – Adam Whittaker

Male video: Peter Gabriel, "Sledgehammer"

Female video: Madonna, "Papa Don't Preach"

Group video: Talking Heads, "Wild Wild Life"

Concept video: Peter Gabriel/Stephen Johnson, "Sledgehammer"

Stage performance in a video: Bon Jovi, "Livin' on a Prayer"

Overall performance in a video: Peter Gabriel, "Sledgehammer"

New artist in a video: Crowded House, "Don't Dream It's Over"

New video from a film: Talking Heads, "Wild Wild Life"

PROFESSIONAL CATEGORY WINNERS

Special effects in a video: Peter Gabriel, "Sledgehammer," Stephen Johnson, Peter Lord

Art direction in a video: Peter Gabriel, "Sledgehammer," Stephen Johnson, Stephen Quay, Tim Quay

Editing in a video: Peter Gabriel, "Sledgehammer," Stephen Johnson, Colin Green

Cinematography in a video: Robbie Nevil, "C'est la vie," Mark Plummer

Choreography in a video: Janet Jackson, "Nasty," Paula Abdul

Direction in a video: Peter Gabriel, "Sledgehammer," Stephen Johnson

Most experimental video: "Sledgehammer"

SPECIAL AWARD WINNERS

Special recognition award: Elton John and Bernie Taupin

Video vanguard awards: Julien Temple, Peter Gabriel

Viewers choice award: U2, "With or Without You"

1988
GENERAL CATEGORY WINNERS

Video of the year: INXS, "Need You Tonight/Mediate," producers, Julie Stone, Anna Grieves, Michael Hamlyn

Male video: Prince, "U Got the Look"

Female video: Suzanne Vega, "Luka"

Group video: INXS, "Need You Tonight/Mediate"

Concept video: Pink Floyd, "Learning to Fly"

Stage performance in a video: Prince, "U Got the Look"

New artist in a video: Guns 'N Roses, "Welcome to the Jungle"

... October 18 ...
David Mamet is signed up to direct **The Heist** with Danny DeVito, Tommy Lee Jones and Gene Hackman set to star.

New video from a film: Los Lobos, "La Bamba"

PROFESSIONAL CATEGORY WINNERS

Special effects in a video: Squeeze, "Hourglass," Jim Francis, Dave Barton

Art direction in a video: Squeeze, "Hourglass," Clive Crotty, Mick Edwards

Editing in a video: INXS, "Need You Tonight/Mediate," Richard Lowenstein

Cinematography in a video: Sting, "We'll Be Together," Bill Pope

Choreography in a video: Janet Jackson, "The Pleasure Principle," Barry Lather

Direction in a video: George Michael, "Father Figure," Andy Morahan, George Michael

Breakthrough video: INXS, "Need You Tonight/Mediate"

SPECIAL AWARD WINNERS

Video vanguard awards: Michael Jackson

Viewers choice award: INXS, "Need You Tonight/Mediate"

1989
GENERAL CATEGORY WINNERS

Video of the year: Neil Young, "This Note's For You"

Male video: Elvis Costello, "Veronica"

Female video: Paula Abdul, "Straight Up"

Group video: Living Colour, "Cult of Personality"

Rap video: D.J. Jazzy Jeff & The Fresh Prince, "Parents Just Don't Understand"

Dance video: Paula Abdul, "Straight up"

Heavy-metal video: Guns 'N Roses, "Sweet Child 'O Mine"

Postmodern video: R.E.M., "Orange Crush"

Stage video: Living Colour, "Cult of Personality"

New artist video: Living Colour, "Cult of Personality"

Video from a film: U2 with BB King, "When Love Comes to Town"

PROFESSIONAL CATEGORY WINNERS

Direction in a video: Madonna, "Express Yourself," David Fincher

Choreography in a video: Paula Abdul, "Straight Up"

Special effects in a video: Michael Jackson, "Leave Me Alone," Jim Blashfield

Art direction in a video: Madonna, "Express Yourself," Vance Lorenzini

Breakthrough video: Art of Noise featuring Tom Jones, "Kiss"

SPECIAL AWARD WINNERS

Video vanguard: George Michael

International video award: Chayanne, "Este ritmo se baila asi"

Viewers choice award: Madonna, "Like a Prayer"

1990
GENERAL CATEGORY WINNERS

Video of the year: Sinead O'Connor, "Nothing Compares 2 U"

Male video: Don Henley, "The End of the Innocence"

Female video: Sinead O'Connor, "Nothing Compares 2 U"

Group video: B 52's, "Love Shack"

Rap video: M.C. Hammer, "U Can't Touch This"

Heavy-metal video: Aerosmith, "Janie's Got a Gun"

Postmodern video: Sinead O'Connor, "Nothing Compares 2 U"

Dance video: M.C. Hammer, "U Can't Touch This"

New artist video: Michael Penn, "No Myth"

Video from a film: Billy Idol, "Cradle of Love", *Ford Fairlane*

PROFESSIONAL CATEGORY WINNERS

Direction in a video: Madonna, "Vogue," David Fincher

Choreography in a video: Janet Jackson, "Rhythm Nation," Janet Jackson/Anthony Thomas

Special effects in a video: Tears for Fears, "Sowing the Seeds of Love," Jim Blashfield

Cinematography in a video: Madonna, "Vogue," Pascal Lebeque

Art direction in a video: B 52's, "Love Shack," Martin Lasowitz

Breakthrough video: Tears for Fears, "Sowing the Seeds of Love," Jim Blashfield

Editing in a video: Madonna, "Vogue," Jim Haygood

SPECIAL AWARD WINNERS

Video vanguard: Janet Jackson

Viewers choice award: Aerosmith, "Janie's Got a Gun"

INTERNATIONAL VIDEO AWARD WINNERS

Midnight Oil "Blue Sky Mine" (Australia), Titas "Flores" (Brazil), Gloria Estefan "Oye mi canto" (Internacional), The Creeps "Ooh I Like It" (Europe), Kome Kome Club "Funk Fujiyama" (Japan)

1991
GENERAL CATEGORY WINNERS

Video of the year: R.E.M., "Losing My Religion"

Male video: Chris Isaak, "Wicked Game"

Female video: Janet Jackson, "Love Will Never Do Without You"

Group video: R.E.M., "Losing My Religion"

Rap video: LL Cool J, "Mama Said Knock You Out"

Long-form music video: Madonna, "Immaculate Collection"

Metal/hard-rock video: Aerosmith, "The Other Side"

Alternative-music video: Jane's Addiction, "Been Caught Stealing"

Dance video: C+C Music Factory, "Gonna Make You Sweat (Everybody Dance Now)"

New artist video: Jesus Jones, "Right Here, Right Now"

Video from a film: Chris Isaak, "Wicked Game" (*Wild at Heart*)

PROFESSIONAL CATEGORY WINNERS

Direction in a video: R.E.M., "Losing My Religion," Tarsem

Choreography in a video: C+C Music Factory, "Gonna Make You Sweat," Jamale Graves

Special effects in a video: Faith No More, "Falling to Pieces," David Faithfull, Ralph Ziman

Cinematography in a video: Chris Isaak, "Wicked Game" (Concept), Rolf Kesterman

Art direction in a video: R.E.M., "Losing My Religion," José Montana

Breakthrough video: R.E.M., "Losing My Religion," Tarsem

Editing in a video: R.E.M., "Losing My Religion," Robert Duffy

SPECIAL AWARD WINNERS

Video vanguard: Bon Jovi, Wayne Isham

Viewers choice award: Queensryche, "Silent Lucidity"

INTERNATIONAL VIDEO AWARD WINNERS

Cui Jian "Wild in the Snow" (Asia), Yothu Yindi "Treaty (Filthy Lucre Mix)" (Australia), Sepultera "Orgasmatron" (Brazil), Roxette "Joyride" (Europe), Franco De Vita "No Basta" (Internacional), Flipper's Guitar "Groove Tube" (Japan)

1992

GENERAL CATEGORY WINNERS

Video of the year: Van Halen, "Right Now"

Male video: Eric Clapton, "Tears in Heaven"

Female video: Annie Lennox, "Why"

Group video: U2, "Even Better than the Real Thing"

Rap video: Arrested Development, "Tennessee"

Metal/hard-rock video: Metallica, "Enter Sandman"

Alternative-music video: Nirvana, "Smells Like Teen Spirit"

Dance video: Prince & The New Power Generation, "Cream"

New artist video: Nirvana, "Smells Like Teen Spirit"

Video from a film: Queen, "Bohemian Rhapsody" (Wayne's World)

PROFESSIONAL CATEGORY WINNERS

Direction in a video: Van Halen, "Right Now," Mark Fenske

Choreography in a video: En Vogue, "My Lovin' (You're Never Gonna Get It)," Travis Payne, Frank Gatson, Lavelle Smith

Special effects in a video: U2, "Even Better Than the Real Thing," Simon Taylor

Cinematography in a video: Guns 'N Roses, "November Rain," Mike Southon/Daniel Pearl

Art direction in a video: Red Hot Chili Peppers, "Give It Away," Nick Goodman

Breakthrough video: Red Hot Chili Peppers, "Give It Away," Stephane Sednaoui

Editing in a video: Van Halen, "Right Now," Mitchell Sinoway

SPECIAL AWARD WINNERS

Video vanguard award: Guns 'N Roses

Viewers choice award: Red Hot Chili Peppers, "Under the Bridge"

INTERNATIONAL VIDEO AWARD WINNERS

Christina "Jring Mai Glua" (Asia), Diesel "Man Alive" (Australia), Nenhum de Nos "Ao meu Redor" (Brazil), The Cure "Friday I'm in Love" (Europe), El General "Muevelo" (Internacional)

1993

GENERAL CATEGORY WINNERS

Video of the year: Pearl Jam, "Jeremy"

Male video: Lenny Kravitz, "Are You Gonna Go My Way?"

Female video: k.d. lang, "Constant Craving"

Group video: Pearl Jam, "Jeremy"

Rap video: Arrested Development, "People Everyday"

R&B video: En Vogue, "Free Your Mind"

Metal/hard-rock video: Pearl Jam, "Jeremy"

Alternative-music video: Nirvana, "In Bloom" (Version 1-Dresses)

Dance video: En Vogue, "Free Your Mind"

New artist in a video: Stone Temple Pilots, "Plush"

Video from a film: Alice in Chains, "Would?"

PROFESSIONAL CATEGORY WINNERS

Direction in a video: Pearl Jam, "Jeremy," Mark Pellington

Choreography in a video: En Vogue, "Free Your Mind," Frank Gatson/Lavelle Smith/Travis Payne

Special effects in a video: Peter Gabriel, "Steam," Real

. . . October 20 . . .
Liza Minnelli announces that her new show will celebrate all
10 film musicals directed by her father, Vincente Minnelli.

World Productions/Colossal Pictures

Cinematography in a video: Madonna, "Rain," Harris Savides

Art direction in a video: Madonna, "Rain," Jan Peter Flack

Breakthrough video: Los Lobos, "Kiko & the Lavender Moon," Ondrej Rudavsky

Editing in a video: Peter Gabriel, "Steam," Douglas Jines

SPECIAL AWARD WINNERS

Viewers choice award: Aerosmith, "Livin on the Edge"

INTERNATIONAL VIDEO AWARD WINNERS

Indus Creed "Pretty Child (MTV Asia), Titas "Sera que e isso que eu necessito" (MTV Brazil), Luis Miguel "America" (MTV Internacional), George Michael "Killer/Papa Was a Rolling Stone" (MTV Europe)

1994

GENERAL CATEGORY WINNERS

Video of the year: Aerosmith, "Cryin'"

Male video: Tom Petty & The Heartbreakers, "Mary Jane's Last Dance"

Female video: Janet Jackson, "If"

Group video: Aerosmith, "Cryin"

Rap video: Snoop Doggy Dogg, "Doggy Dogg World"

Metal/hard-rock video: Soundgarden, "Black Hole Sun"

Alternative-music video: Nirvana, "Heart-shaped Box"

Dance video: Salt-N-Pepa with En Vogue, "Whatta Man"

New artist in a video: Counting Crows, "Mr. Jones"

R&B video: Salt-N-Pepa with En Vogue, "Whatta Man"

Video from a film: Bruce Springsteen, "Streets of Philadelphia"

PROFESSIONAL CATEGORY WINNERS

Direction in a video: R.E.M., "Everybody Hurts," Jake Scott

Special effects in a video: Peter Gabriel, "Kiss That Frog," Brett Leonard/Angel Studios

Editing in a video: R.E.M., "Everybody Hurts," Pat Sheffield

Choreography in a video: Salt-N-Pepa with En Vogue, "Whatta Man," Frank Garson/Randy Connors

Art direction in a video: Nirvana, "Heart-shaped Box," Bernadette Disanto

Cinematography in a video: R.E.M., "Everybody Hurts," Harris Savides

Breakthrough video: R.E.M., "Everybody Hurts," June Gutterman

SPECIAL AWARD WINNERS

Special recognition award: Rolling Stones

Video vanguard award: Tom Petty

Viewers choice award: Aerosmith, "Cryin'"

INTERNATIONAL WINNERS

Sepultura "Territory" (MTV Brazil), Take That "Babe" (MTV Europe), Hide "Eyes Love You" (MTV Japan), Los Fabulos Cadillacs "Matador" (MTV Latino)

1995

GENERAL CATEGORY WINNERS

Video of the year: TLC, "Waterfalls"

Male video: Tom Petty & The Heartbreakers, "You Don't Know How It Feels"

Female video: Madonna, "Take a Bow"

Group video: TLC, "Waterfalls"

Rap video: Dr. Dre, "Keep Their Heads Ringin'"

R&B video: TLC, "Waterfalls"

Hard-rock video: White Zombie, "More Human Than Human"

Alternative-music video: Weezer, "Buddy Holly"

Dance video: Michael Jackson & Janet Jackson, "Scream"

New artist in a video: Hootie & The Blowfish, "Hold My Hand"

Video from a film: Seal, "Kiss From a Rose"

PROFESSIONAL CATEGORY WINNERS

Direction in a video: Weezer, "Buddy Holly," Spike Jonze

Choreography in a video: Michael Jackson & Janet Jackson, "Scream," Lavelle Smith/Travis Payne/Tina Landon/Sean Cheeseman

Special effects in a video: Rolling Stones, "Love Is Strong," Fred Raimondi

Cinematography in a video: Rolling Stones, "Love Is Strong," Gary Walker/Mike Trim

Art direction in a video: Michael Jackson & Janet Jackson, "Scream," Tom Foden

Breakthrough video: Weezer, "Buddy Holly," Spike Jonze

Editing in a video: Weezer, "Buddy Holly," Spike Jonze

SPECIAL AWARD WINNERS

Video vanguard awards: R.E.M.

Viewers choice award: TLC, "Waterfalls"

...October 21...
Twenty-one years after his last No.1 album,
Carlos Santana is back on top with **Supernatural**.

INTERNATIONAL AWARD WINNERS

Denada "Sambutlah" (MTV Asia), Os paralamas do sucesso "Uma Brasileira" (MTV Brazil), U2 "Hold Me, Thrill Me, Kiss Me, Kill Me" (MTV Europe), Chage & Aska "Something There" (MTV Japan), Café Tacuba "La Ingrata" (MTV Latino), Faye Wong "Chess" (MTV Mandarin)

1996

GENERAL CATEGORY WINNERS

Video of the year: The Smashing Pumpkins, "Tonight, Tonight"

Male video: Beck, "Where It's At"

Female video: Alanis Morissette, "Ironic"

Group video: Foo Fighters, "Big Me"

Rap video: Coolio Featuring LV, "Gangsta's Paradise (Dangerous Minds)"

R&B video: Fugees, "Killing Me Softly"

Hard-rock video: Metallica, "Until It Sleeps"

Alternative-music video: The Smashing Pumpkins, "1979"

Dance video: Coolio, "1, 2, 3, 3 (Sumpin' New)"

New artist in a video: Alanis Morissette, "Ironic"

Video from a film: Coolio Featuring LV, "Gangsta's Paradise (Dangerous Minds)"

PROFESSIONAL CATEGORY WINNERS

Direction in a video: The Smashing Pumpkins, "Tonight, Tonight," Jonathan Dayton & Valerie Faris

Choreography in a video: Bjork, "It's Oh So Quiet," Michael Rooney

Special effects in a video: The Smashing Pumpkins, "Tonight, Tonight," Chris Staves

Cinematography in a video: The Smashing Pumpkins, "Tonight, Tonight," Declan Quinn

Art direction in a video: The Smashing Pumpkins, "Tonight, Tonight," K.K. Barrett & Wa

Breakthrough video: The Smashing Pumpkins, "Tonight, Tonight," Jonathan Dayton & Valerie Faris

Editing in a video: Alanis Morissette, "Ironic," Scott Grey

SPECIAL AWARD WINNERS

Viewers choice award: Bush, "Glycerine"

INTERNATIONAL AWARD WINNERS

Tai Ji Boys "Come Back Home" (MTV Asia), Skank "Garota Nacional" (MTV Brazil), George Michael "Fastlove" (MTV Europe), Colonial Cousins "Sa ni dha pa" (MTV India), Kuroyume "Pistol" (MTV Japan), Soda Stereo "Ella uso mi cabeza como un revolver" (MTV Latino), Nana Tang "Freedom" (MTV Mandarin)

1997

GENERAL CATEGORY WINNERS

Video of the year: Jamiroquai, "Virtual Insanity"

Male video: Beck, "Devil's Haircut"

Female video: Jewel, "You Were Meant For Me"

Group video: No Doubt, "Don't Speak"

Rap video: The Notorious B.I.G, "Hypnotize"

R&B video: Puff Daddy & the Family, "I'll Be Missing You (Featuring Faith Evans & 112)"

Rock video: Aerosmith, "Falling in Love (Is Hard on the Knees)"

Alternative-music video: Sublime, "What I Got"

Dance video: Spice Girls, "Wannabe"

New artist in a video: Fiona Apple, "Sleep to Dream"

Video from a film: Will Smith, "Men in Black"

PROFESSIONAL CATEGORY WINNERS

Direction in a video: Beck, "The New Pollution"

Choreography in a video: Beck, "The New Pollution"

Special effects in a video: Jamiroquai, "Virtual Insanity"

Cinematography in a video: Jamiroquai, "Virtual Insanity"

Art direction in a video: Jamiroquai, "Virtual Insanity"

Breakthrough video: Jamiroquai, "Virtual Insanity"

Editing in a video: Beck, "Devil's Haircut"

SPECIAL AWARD WINNERS

Viewer's choice winner: Prodigy, "Breathe"

Video vanguard: Mark Romanek; L. L. Cool J.

INTERNATIONAL AWARD WINNERS

Eraserheads "Ang Huling el bimbo" (MTV Asia), Skank "E uma partida de futebol" (MTV Brazil), Prodigy "Breathe" (MTV Europe), Asha Bhonsle "O mere sona re" (MTV India), Chara "Yasashii Kimochi" (MTV Japan), Cafe Tecuba "Chilanga Banda" (MTV Latino), Mavis Fan "Bartender Angel" (MTV Mandarin)

1998

GENERAL CATEGORY WINNERS

Video of the year: Madonna, "Ray of Light"

Male video: Will Smith, "Just the Two of Us"

Female video: Madonna, "Ray of Light"

Group video: Backstreet Boys, "Everybody (Backstreet's Back)"

Rap video: Will Smith, "Gettin' Jiggy With It"

Dance video: Prodigy, "Smack My Bitch Up"

Rock video: Aerosmith, "Pink"

Alternative-music video: Green Day, "Time of Your Life (Good Riddance)"

New artist in a video: Natalie Imbruglia, "Torn"

... October 22 ...
Robert DeNiro is close to getting $15 million
for **The Score**, a Mandalay Pictures' suspenser.

Video from a film: Aerosmith, "I Don't Want to Miss a Thing"
R&B video: Wyclef Jean Featuring Refugee Allstars, "Gone till November"

PROFESSIONAL CATEGORY WINNERS
Direction in a video: Madonna, "Ray of Light"
Choreography in a video: Madonna, "Ray of Light"
Special effects in a video: Madonna, "Frozen"
Art direction in a video: Bjork, "Bachelorette"
Editing in a video: Madonna, "Ray of Light"
Cinematography in a video: Fiona Apple, "Criminal"
Breakthrough video: Prodigy, "Smack My Bitch Up"

VIEWER'S CHOICE
Puff Daddy & the Family Featuring the Lox, Lil'Kim, the Notorious B.I.G. & Fuzzbubble, "It's All About the Benjamins (Rock Remix)"

1999
GENERAL CATEGORY WINNERS
Video of the year: Lauryn Hill, "Doo Wop (That Thing)"
Male video: Will Smith, "Miami"
Female video: Lauryn Hill, "Doo Wop (That Thing)"
Group video: TLC, "No Scrubs"
Rap video: Jay-Z featuring Ja & Amil-Lion, "Can I Get a..."
R&B video: Lauryn Hill, "Doo Wop (That Thing)"
Hip Hop video: Beastie Boys, "Intergalactic"
Dance video: Ricky Martin, "Livin' La Vida Loca"
Rock video: KoRn, "Freak on a Leash"
Pop video: Ricky Martin, "Livin' La Vida Loca"
New artist in a video: Eminem, "My Name Is"
Video from a film: Madonna, "Beautiful Stranger"

PROFESSIONAL CATEGORY WINNERS
Direction in a video: Fatboy Slim, "Praise You"
Choreography in a video: Fatboy Slim, "Praise You"
Special effects in a video: Garbage, "Special"
Art direction in a video: Lauryn Hill, "Doo Wop (That Thing)"
Editing in a video: KoRn, "Freak on a Leash"
Cinematography in a video: Marilyn Manson, "The Dope Show"
Breakthrough video: Fatboy Slim, "Praise You"

VIEWERS CHOICE
Backstreet Boys, "I Want It That Way"

INTERNATIONAL AWARD WINNERS
Parokya Ni Edgar "Harana" (MTV South East Asia), Silverchair "Anthem for the Year 2000 (MTV Australia), Raimundos "Mulher de Fases" (MTV Brasil), A.R. Rahman "Dil Se" (MTV India), H.O.T. "Make a Line (MTV Korea), Ricky Martin "Livin' La Vida Loca" (MTV Latin America, north service), Ricky Martin "Livin' La Vida Loca" (MTV Latin America, south service), Shino Lin "Irritated" (MTV Mandarin), Ricky Martin "Livin' La Vida Loca" (MTV Russia)

MTV Europe Awards

1998
London/Milan 13 November
Male: Robbie Williams
Group: Spice Girls
Dance: Prodigy
Song: Natalie Imbruglia, "Torn"
Rock: Aerosmith
Female: Madonna
Pop "new": Spice Girls
Breakthrough artist: All Saints
Rap: Beastie Boys
Album "new": Madonna, *Ray of Light*
Video: Massive Attack, "Tear Drop"
Select U.K.: Five
Select north: Eagle Eye Cherry
Select central: Thomas D – Franka Potente
Select southern: Bluevertigo
Free your mind: B-92 (Independent Serbian radio station)

1999
London/Dublin 11 November
Female: Britney Spears
Dance: Fatboy Slim
Hip Hop: Eminem
Rock: The Offspring
R&B: Whitney Houston
Nordic act: Lene Marlin
Group: Backstreet Boys
Pop: Britney Spears
German act: Xavier Naidoo
Male: Will Smith
Album: Boyzone, *By Request*
Italian act: Elio e le Storie Tese
Brakthrough artist: Britney Spears
UK & Ireland act: Boyzone
Song: Britney Spears, "...Baby One More Time"
Video: Blur, "Coffee & TV"
Free your mind: Bono

The Grammys

The most glamorous and established of all the music awards, the Grammys are even more difficult to call than the Academy Awards. In the words of Thomas O'Neil (author of *Variety's The Grammys: The Ultimate Unofficial Guide to Music's Highest Honor*): "Predicting nominees has been a shattering experience ever since 1995, when it was decreed that the contenders for best record, song, album, and new artist would no longer be chosen by a vote of the 9,000 members of the National Academy of Recording Arts & Sciences. The membership can still cast its ballots and narrow each category down to 20 choices, but the selection of the final five is trusted to a veiled gang of 25 music experts." Just about every category imaginable carries a statuette – rock, rap, country, movie music, jazz, classical, you name it.

1958

Album: *The Music From Peter Gunn* (TV series soundtrack) Henry Mancini, RCA
Record: "Nel Blu dipinto di blu (Volare)," Domenico Modugno, Decca
Song (songwriter's award): "Nel Blu dipinto di blu (Volare)," Domenico Modugno, (lyrics collaborator Franco Miggliacci)
Vocal performance, male: Perry Como, "Catch a Falling Star," RCA
Vocal performance, female: Ella Fitzgerald, *Ella Fitzgerald Sings the Irving Berlin Song Book*, Verve
Performance by a vocal group or chorus: Louis Prima, Keely Smith, "That Old Black Magic," Capitol
Performance by a dance band: Count Basie, *Basie*, Roulette
Performance by an orchestra: Billy May, *Billy May's Big Fat Brass*, Capitol
Country and western performance: Kingston Trio, "Tom Dooley," Capitol
Composition, more than 5 minutes : "Cross Country Suite," Nelson Riddle
Rhythm and blues performance: Champs, "Tequila," Challenge
Jazz performance, individual: Ella Fitzgerald, *Ella Fitzgerald Sings the Irving Berlin Song Book*, Verve
Jazz performance, group: Count Basie, *Basie*, Roulette
Classical performance, orchestra (conductor's award): Felix Slatkin conducting the Hollywood Bowl Symphony, *Gaîté Parisienne*, Capitol
Classical performance, operatic or choral: Roger Wagner Chorale, *Virtuoso*, Capitol
Classical performance, vocal soloist (with or without orchestra): Renata Tebaldi, *Recital of Songs and Arias*, London

1959

Album: *Come Dance With Me*, Frank Sinatra, Capitol
Record: "Mack the Knife," Bobby Darin, Atco
Song (songwriter's award): "The Battle of New Orleans," Jimmy Driftwood
New artist: Bobby Darin
Vocal performance, male: Frank Sinatra, *Come Dance With Me*, Capitol
Vocal performance, female: Ella Fitzgerald, "But Not For Me," Verve
Performance by a vocal group or chorus: Mormon Tabernacle Choir, Richard Condi conducting: "Battle Hymn of the Republic," Columbia
Performance by a top 40 artist: Nat King Cole, "Midnight Flyer," Capitol
Rhythm and blues performance: Dinah Washington, "What a Difference a Day Makes," Mercury
Jazz performance, soloist: Ella Fitzgerald, *Ella Swings Lightly*, Verve
Jazz performance, group: Jonah Jones, *I Dig Chicks*, Capitol
Country and western performance: Johnny Horton, "The Battle of New Orleans," Columbia
Folk performance: Kingston Trio, *The Kingston Trio at Large*, Capitol
Performance by a dance band: Duke Ellington, *Anatomy of a Murder*, Columbia
Performance by an orchestra: David Rose and His Orchestra with André Previn, *Like Young*, MGM
Musical composition, more than 5 minutes: *Anatomy of a Murder*, Duke Ellington, Columbia
Classical performance, orchestra (conductor's award): Charles Munch conducting the Boston Symphony, *Debussy: Images For Orchestra*, RCA
Classical performance, opera cast or choral: Erich Leinsdorf conducting the Vienna Philharmonic

(solos: Peters, London, Della, Casa), *Mozart: The Marriage of Figaro*, RCA

Classical performance, vocal soloist (with or without orchestra): Jussi Björling, *Björling in Opera*, London

Special trustees awards for artists and repertoire contribution: Record of the year: "Mack the Knife," Bobby Darin – Ahmet Ertegun, A&R producer, Atco

Album of the year: *Come Dance With Me*, Frank Sinatra – Dave Cavanaugh, A&R producer, Capitol

1960

Album: *Button Down Mind*, Bob Newhart, Warner Bros.

Record: "Theme from *A Summer Place*," Percy Faith, Columbia

Song (songwriter's award): "Theme from *Exodus*," Ernest Gold

New artist: Bob Newhart

Vocal performance, album, male: Ray Charles, *Genius of Ray Charles*, Atlantic

Vocal performance, single or track, male: Ray Charles, "Georgia on My Mind," ABC

Vocal performance, album, female: Ella Fitzgerald, *Mack the Knife, Ella in Berlin*, Verve

Vocal performance, single or track, female: Ella Fitzgerald, *Mack the Knife*, Verve

Performance by a pop single artist: Ray Charles, "Georgia on My Mind," ABC

Performance by a vocal group: Eydie Gormé, Steve Lawrence, "We Got Us," ABC

Performance by a chorus: Norman Luboff Choir, *Songs of the Cowboy*, Columbia

Performance by a band for dancing: Count Basie, *Dance With Basie*, Roulette

Performance by an orchestra: Henry Mancini, *Mr. Lucky*, RCA

Country and western performance: Marty Robbins, "El Paso," Columbia

Folk performance: Harry Belafonte, "Swing Dat Hammer," RCA

Rhythm and blues performance: Ray Charles, "Let the Good Times Roll," Atlantic

Jazz composition, more than 5 minutes (composer's award): *Sketches of Spain*, Miles Davis, Gil Evans, Columbia

Jazz performance, solo or small group: André Previn, *West Side Story*, Contempo

Jazz performance, large group: Henry Mancini, *The Blues and the Beat*, RCA

Classical performance, orchestra (conductor's award): Fritz Reiner conducting the Chicago

Symphony, *Bartók: Music for Strings, Percussion and Celesta*, RCA

Classical opera production: *Puccini: Turandot*, Erich Leinsdorf conducting the Rome Opera House Chorus and Orchestra (solos: Tebaldi, Nilsson, Björling, Tozzi) RCA

Classical performance, vocal soloist: Leontyne Price, *A Program of Song*, RCA

Contemporary classical composition: *Orchestral Suite from Tender Land*, Aaron Copland, RCA

1961

Album: *Judy at Carnegie Hall*, Judy Garland, Capitol

Record: "Moon River," Henry Mancini, RCA

Song (songwriter's award): "Moon River," Henry Mancini, Johnny Mercer

New artist: Peter Nero

Solo vocal performance, male: Jack Jones, "Lollipops and Roses," Kapp

Solo vocal performance, female: Judy Garland, *Judy at Carnegie Hall*, Capitol

Performance by a vocal group: Lambert, Hendricks and Ross, *High Flying*, Columbia

Performance by a chorus: Johnny Mann Singers (Si Zentner Orchestra) *Great Band With Great Voices*, Liberty

Rock and roll recording: "Let's Twist Again," Chubby Checker, Parkway

Rhythm and blues recording: "Hit the Road Jack," Ray Charles, ABC-Paramount

Original jazz composition (composer's award): "African Waltz," Galt MacDermot, Riverside

Jazz performance by a soloist or small group, instrumental: André Previn, *André Previn Plays Harold Arlen*, Contemporary

Jazz performance by a large group, instrumental: Stan Kenton, *West Side Story*, Capitol

Country and western recording: "Big Bad John," Jimmy Dean, Columbia

Folk recording: *Belafonte Folk Singers at Home and Abroad*, Belafonte Folk Singers, RCA

Instrumental theme or instrumental version of song (composer's award): "African Waltz," Galt MacDermot, Roulette

Album, classical: *Stravinsky Conducts, 1960: Le Sacre du printemps, Pétrouchka*, Igor Stravinsky conducting the Columbia Symphony, Columbia

Contemporary classical composition (composer's award) (tie): *Discantos*, Laurindo Almeida, Capitol and *Movements for Piano and Orchestra*, Igor Stravinsky; and Columbia

Classical performance, orchestra (conductor's award): Charles Munch conducting the Boston

Symphony, *Ravel: Daphnis and Chloé*, RCA

Opera recording (conductor's award): *Puccini: Madame Butterfly*, Gabriele Santini conducting Rome Opera Chorus and Orchestra (solos: de los Angeles, Björling, Pirazzini, Sereni) Capitol

Classical performance, vocal soloist: Joan Sutherland (Molinari-Pradelli conducting the Royal Opera House Orchestra) *The Art of Prima Donna*, London

1962

Album: *The First Family*, Vaughn Meader, Cadence

Record: "I Left My Heart in San Francisco," Tony Bennett, Columbia

Song (songwriter's award): "What Kind of Fool Am I?," Leslie Bricusse, Anthony Newley

New artist: Robert Goulet

Solo vocal performance, male: Tony Bennett, "I Left My Heart in San Francisco," Columbia

Solo vocal performance, female: Ella Fitzgerald, *Ella Swings Brightly With Nelson Riddle*, Verve

Performance by a vocal group: Peter, Paul and Mary, "If I Had a Hammer," Warner Bros.

Performance by a chorus: New Christy Minstrels, *Presenting the New Christy Minstrels*, Columbia

Rock and roll recording: "Alley Cat," Bent Fabric, Atco

Rhythm and blues recording: "I Can't Stop Loving You," Ray Charles, ABC-Paramount

Original jazz composition (composer's award): Vince Guaraldi, "Cast Your Fate to the Winds," Fantasy

Jazz performance by a soloist or small group, instrumental: Stan Getz, "Desafinado," Verve

Jazz performance by a large group, instrumental: Stan Kenton, *Adventures in Jazz*, Capitol

Country and western recording: "Funny Way of Laughin'," Burl Ives, Decca

Folk recording: "If I Had a Hammer," Peter, Paul and Mary, Warner Bros.

Instrumental theme (composer's award): "A Taste of Honey," Bobby Scott, Ric Marlow, Reprise

Album, classical: *Columbia Records Presents Vladimir Horowitz*, Vladimir Horowitz, Columbia

Classical composition by a contemporary composer: Igor Stravinsky, *The Flood*

Classical performance, orchestra (conductor's award): Igor Stravinsky conducting the Columbia Symphony, *Stravinsky: The Firebird Ballet*, Columbia

Opera recording (conductor's award): *Verdi: Aida*, Georg Solti conducting the Rome Opera House Orchestra and Chorus (solos: Price, Vickers, Gorr, Merrill, Tozzi) RCA

Classical performance, vocal soloist (with or without orchestra): Eileen Farrell (Bernstein conducting the New York Philharmonic) *Wagner: Götterdämmerung, Brünnhilde's Immolation Scene; Wesendonck: Songs*, Columbia

1963

Album: *The Barbra Streisand Album*, Barbra Streisand, Columbia

Record: "The Days of Wine and Roses," Henry Mancini, RCA

Song (songwriter's award): "The Days of Wine and Roses," Johnny Mercer, Henry Mancini, RCA

New artist: Swingle Singers

Vocal performance, male: Jack Jones, "Wives and Lovers," Kapp

Vocal performance, female: Barbra Streisand, *The Barbra Streisand Album*, Columbia

Performance by a vocal group: Peter, Paul and Mary, "Blowin' in the Wind," Warner Bros.

Performance by a chorus: Swingle Singers, *Bach Greatest Hits*, Philips

Rock and roll recording: "Deep Purple," Nino Tempo, April Stevens, Atco

Rhythm and blues recording: "Busted," Ray Charles, ABC-Paramount

Original jazz composition (composer's award): Ray Brown, Steve Allen, "Gravy Waltz," Dot

Instrumental jazz performance by a soloist or a small group: Bill Evans, *Conversations With Myself*, Verve

Instrumental jazz performance by a large group: Woody Herman Band, *Encore: Woody Herman, 1963*, Philips

Country and western recording: "Detroit City," Bobby Bare, RCA

Folk recording: Peter, Paul and Mary, "Blowin' in the Wind," Warner Bros.

Instrumental theme (composer's award): "More (Theme from *Mondo Cane*)," Riz Ortolani, Nino Oliviero, Norman Newell, United Artists

Album, classical: *Britten: War Requiem*, Benjamin Britten conducting the London Symphony Orchestra and Chorus (solos: Vishnevskaya, Pears, Fischer-Dieskay; David Willocks directing the Bach Choir; Edward Chapman directing the Highgate School Choir, London

Classical composition by a contemporary composer: Benjamin Britten, *War Requiem*, London

Classical performance, orchestra (conductor's award): Erich Leinsdorf conducting the Boston Symphonic Orcestra, *Bartók: Concerto for Orchestra*, RCA

Most promising new classical artist: André Watts, pianist, Columbia

---

...**October 26**...

Director Jonathan Demme is targeting to remake **Charade** with Will Smith.

Classical performance, vocal soloist: Leontyne Price, *Great Scenes from Gershwin's Porgy and Bess,* RCA

1964

Album: *Getz/Gilberto,* Stan Getz, João Gilberto, Verve

Record: "The Girl From Ipanema," Stan Getz, Astrud Gilberto, Verve

Song (songwriter's award): "Hello Dolly!" Jerry Herman

New artist: Beatles

Vocal performance, male: Louis Armstrong, "Hello Dolly!" Kapp

Vocal performance, female: Barbra Streisand, "People," Columbia

Performance by a vocal group: The Beatles, *A Hard Day's Night,* Capitol

Performance by a chorus: Swingle Singers, *The Swingle Singers Going Baroque,* Philips

Rock and roll recording: "Downtown," Petula Clark, Warner Bros.

Rhythm and blues recording: "How Glad I Am," Nancy Wilson, Capitol

Original jazz composition (composer's award): Lalo Schifrin, "The Cat," Verve

Instrumental jazz performance by a small group or soloist with small group: Stan Getz, *Getz/Gilberto,* Verve

Instrumental jazz performance by a large group or soloist with large group: Laurindo Almeida, *Guitar from Ipanema,* Capitol

Country and western album: *Dang Me/Chu-a-Lug,* Roger Miller, Smash

Country and western single: "Dang Me," Roger Miller, Smash

Country and western song (songwriter's award): "Dang Me," Roger Miller, Smash

New country and western artist: Roger Miller, Smash

Country and western vocal performance, male: Roger Miller, "Dang Me," Smash

Country and western vocal performance, female: Dottie West, "Here Comes My Baby," RCA

Folk recording: *We'll Sing in the Sunshine,* Gale Garnett, RCA

Instrumental composition (other than jazz) (composer's award): Henry Mancini, "*The Pink Panther* Theme," RCA

Album, classical: *Bernstein: Symphony No. 3 ("Kaddish"),* Leonard Bernstein conducting the New York Philharmonic, Columbia

Classical composition by a contemporary composer: Samuel Barber, *Piano Concerto,* Columbia

Classical performance, orchestra (conductor's award): Erich Leinsdorf conducting the Boston Symphony, *Mahler: Symphony No. 5 in C Sharp Minor; Berg: Wozzeck Excerpts* (solo: Phylis Curtin) RCA

Most promising new artist: Marilyn Horne, mezzo-soprano, London

Opera recording (conductor's award): *Bizet: Carmen,* Herbert von Karajan conducting the Vienna Philharmonic Orchestra and Chorus (solos: Price, Corelli, Merrill, Freni) RCA

Classical performance, vocal soloist (with or without orchestra): Leontyne Price (Reiner conducting the Chicago Symphony) *Berlioz: Nuits d'été; Falla: El amor brujo,* RCA

1965

Album: *September of My Years,* Frank Sinatra, Reprise

Record: "A Taste of Honey," Herb Alpert and the Tijuana Brass, A&M

Song (songwriter's award): "The Shadow of Your Smile (Theme from *The Sandpiper*)," Paul Francis Webster, Johnny Mandel

New artist: Tom Jones

Vocal performance, male: Frank Sinatra, "It Was a Very Good Year," Reprise

Vocal performance, female: Barbra Streisand, *My Name is Barbra,* Columbia

Performance by a vocal group: Anita Kerr Quartet, *We Dig Mancini,* RCA

Performance by a chorus: Swingle Singers, *Anyone For Mozart?* Philips

Contemporary (R&R) single: "King of the Road," Roger Miller, Smash

Contemporary (R&R) vocal performance, male: Roger Miller, "King of the Road," Smash

Contemporary (R&R) vocal performance, female: Petula Clark, "I Know the Place," Warner Bros.

Contemporary (R&R) performance by a group (vocal or instrumental): Statler Brothers, "Flowers on the Wall," Columbia

Rhythm and blues recording: "Papa's Got a Brand New Bag," James Brown, King

Original jazz composition (composer's award): Lalo Schifrin, "Jazz Suite on the Mass Texts," RCA

Jazz performance by a small group or soloist with small group: Ramsey Lewis Trio, *The "In" Crowd,* Cadet

Jazz performance by a large group or soloist with large group: Duke Ellington Orchestra, *Ellington '66,* Reprise

Country and western album: *The Return of Roger Miller,* Roger Miller, Smash

Country and western single: "King of the Road," Roger Miller, Smash

---

October 27

Marilyn Monroe's personal items go on the block at Christie's Rockefeller Center location. The gown in which she sang "Happy Birthday, Mr. President" was sold for $1.3 million.

Country and western song (songwriter's award): "King of the Road," Roger Miller, Smash

New country and western artist: Statler Brothers, Columbia

Country and western vocal performance, male: Roger Miller, "King of the Road," Smash

Country and western vocal performance, female: Jody Miller, "Queen of the House," Capitol

Folk recording: *An Evening with Belafonte/Makeba*, Harry Belafonte, Miriam Makeba, RCA

Instrumental performance (non-jazz): Herb Alpert and the Tijuana Brass, "A Taste of Honey," A&M

Album, classical: *Horowitz at Carnegie Hall, an Historic Return*, Vladimir Horowitz, Columbia

Composition by a contemporary classical composer: Charles Ives, *Symphony No. 4*, Columbia

Classical performance, orchestra (conductor's award): Leopold Stokowski conducting the American Symphony, *Ives: Symphony No. 4*, Columbia

Most promising new recording artist: Peter Serkin, pianist, RCA

Opera recording (conductor's award): *Berg: Wozzeck*, Karl Böhm conducting the Orchestra of German Opera Berlin, (solos: Fischer-Dieskay, Lear, Wunderlich) Deutsche Grammophon

Classical vocal performance (with/without orchestra): Leontyne Price, (Leinsdorf conducting the Boston Symphony) Strauss: *Salome; The Egyptian Helen*, RCA

1966

Album: *Sinatra: A Man and His Music*, Frank Sinatra, Reprise

Record: "Strangers in the Night," Frank Sinatra, Reprise

Song (songwriter's award): "Michelle," John Lennon, Paul McCartney, Capitol

Vocal performance, male: Frank Sinatra, "Strangers in the Night," Reprise

Vocal performance, female: Eydie Gormé, "If He Walked Into My Life," Columbia

Performance by a vocal group: Anita Kerr Quartet, "A Man and a Woman," Warner Bros.

Performance by a chorus: Ray Conniff and Singers, "Somewhere My Love (Lara's Theme from *Dr. Zhivago*)," Columbia

Contemporary (R&R) recording: "Winchester Cathedral," New Vaudeville Band, Fontana

Contemporary (R&R) solo vocal performance (male or female): Paul McCartney, "Eleanor Rigby," Capitol

Contemporary (R&R) group performance (vocal or instrumental): The Mamas and the Papas, "Monday, Monday," Dunhill

Rhythm and blues recording: "Crying Time," Ray Charles, ABC-Paramount

Rhythm and blues solo vocal performance (male or female): Ray Charles, "Crying Time," ABC-Paramount

Rhythm and blues group performance (vocal or instrumental): Ramsey Lewis, "Hold It Right There," Cadet

Original jazz composition (composer's award): Duke Ellington, "In the Beginning God," RCA

Instrumental jazz performance by a group or soloist with group: Wes Montgomery, "Goin' out of My Head," Verve

Country and western recording: "Almost Persuaded," David Houston, Epic

Country and western vocal performance (male): David Houston, "Almost Persuaded," Epic

Country and western vocal performance (female): Jeannie Seely, "Don't Touch Me," Monument

Country and western song (songwriter's award): "Almost Persuaded," Billy Sherrill, Glenn Sutton, Epic

Folk recording: *Blues in the Street*, Cortelia Clark, RCA

Instrumental theme (composer's award): "*Batman* Theme," Neal Hefti, RCA

Instrumental performance (other than jazz): Herb Alpert and the Tijuana Brass, "What Now My Love?," A&M

Album, classical: *Ives: Symphony No.1 in D Minor*, Morton Gould conducting the Chicago Symphony, RCA

Classical performance, orchestra (conductor's award): Erich Leinsdorf conducting the Boston Symphony, *Mahler: Symphony No. 6 in A Minor*, RCA

Opera recording (conductor's award): *Wagner: Die Walküre*, Georg Solti conducting the Vienna Philharmonic, London

Classical performance, vocal soloist: Leontyne Price, *Prima Donna*, RCA

1967

Album: *Sgt. Pepper's Lonely Hearts Club Band*, Beatles, Capitol

Record: "Up, Up and Away," 5th Dimension, Soul City

Song (songwriter's award): "Up, Up and Away," Jimmy Webb, Soul City

New artist: Bobby Gentry

Vocal performance, male: Glen Campbell, "By the Time I Get to Phoenix," Capitol

---

... October 28 ...
Nearly 40 years after the studio mounted its first adaptation of the work, 20th Century Fox is set to return to F. Scott Fitzgerald's **Tender Is The Night**.

Vocal performance, female: Bobbie Gentry, "Ode to Billie Joe," Capitol

Performance by a vocal group: 5th Dimension, "Up, Up and Away," Soul City

Performance by a chorus: Johnny Mann Singers, "Up, Up and Away," Soul City

Contemporary single: "Up, Up and Away," 5th Dimension, Soul City

Contemporary album: *Sgt. Pepper's Lonely Hearts Club Band*, Beatles, Capitol

Contemporary solo vocal performance, male: Glen Campbell, "By the Time I Get to Phoenix," Capitol

Contemporary solo vocal performance, female: Bobbie Gentry, "Ode to Billie Joe," Capitol

Contemporary group performance (vocal or instrumental): 5th Dimension, "Up, Up and Away," Soul City

Rhythm and blues recording: "Respect," Aretha Franklin, Atlantic

Rhythm and blues solo vocal performance, male: Lou Rawls, "Dead End Street," Capitol

Rhythm and blues solo vocal performance, female: Aretha Franklin, "Respect," Atlantic

Rhythm and blues group performance (vocal or instrumental): Sam and Dave, "Soul Man," Stax

Instrumental jazz performance by a small group or soloist with small group (7 or fewer): Cannonball Adderley Quintet, *Mercy, Mercy, Mercy*, Capitol

Instrumental jazz performance by a large group or soloist with large group (8 or more): Duke Ellington, "Far East Suite," RCA

Country and western recording: "Gentle on My Mind," Glen Campbell, Capitol

Country and western solo vocal performance, male: Glen Campbell, "Gentle on My Mind," Capitol

Country and western solo vocal performance, female: Tammy Wynette, "I Don't Wanna Play House," Epic

Country and western performance by a duo, trio or group (vocal or instrumental): Johnny Cash, June Carter, "Jackson," Columbia

Country and western song (songwriter's award): "Gentle on My Mind," John Hartford, RCA

Folk performance: John Hartford, "Gentle on My Mind," RCA

Instrumental theme (composer's award): "Mission: Impossible," Lalo Schifrin, Dot

Instrumental performance: Chet Atkins, *Chet Atkins Picks the Best*, RCA

Album, classical (tie): *Berg: Wozzeck*, Pierre Boulez conducting the orchestra and chorus of the Paris National Opera (solos: Berry Strauss, Uhl, Doench) Columbia; and *Mahler: Symphony No.8*

in E Flat Major ("*Symphony of a Thousand*"), Leonard Bernstein conducting the London Symphony with soloists and choruses, Columbia

Classical performance, orchestra (conductor's award): Igor Stravinsky conducting the Columbia Symphony, *Stravinsky: Firebird and Pétrouchka Suites*, Columbia

Opera recording: *Berg: Wozzeck*, Pierre Boulez conducting the orchestra and chorus of the Paris National Opera (solos: Berry Strauss, Uhl, Doench) Columbia

Classical performance, vocal soloist: Leontyne Price, *Prima Donna, Vol 2*, RCA

1968

Album: *By the Time I Get to Phoenix*, Glen Campbell, Capital

Record: "Mrs. Robinson," Simon and Garfunkel, Columbia

Song (songwriter's award): "Little Green Apples," Bobby Russell

New artist: José Feliciano

Contemporary pop vocal performance, male: José Feliciano, "Light My Fire," RCA

Contemporary pop vocal performance, female: Dionne Warwick, "Do You Know the Way to San José," Scepter

Contemporary pop vocal performance by a duo or group: Simon and Garfunkel, "Mrs. Robinson," Columbia

Contemporary pop performance by a chorus: Alan Copeland Singers, "Mission: Impossible/Norwegian Wood," ABC

Contemporary pop performance, instrumental: Mason Williams, "Classical Gas," Warner Bros.

Rhythm and blues vocal performance, male: Otis Redding, "(Sittin' on) The Dock of the Bay," Volt

Rhythm and blues vocal performance, female: Aretha Franklin, "Chain of Fools," Atlantic

Rhythm and blues performance by a duo or group (vocal or instrumental): The Temptations, "Cloud Nine," Gordy

Rhythm and blues song (songwriter's award): "(Sittin' on) The Dock of the Bay," Otis Redding, Steve Cropper, Volt

Instrumental jazz performance by a small group or soloist with small group: Bill Evans Trio, *Bill Evans at the Montreux Jazz Festival*, Verve

Instrumental jazz performance by a large group or soloist with large group: Duke Ellington, *And His Mother Called Him Bill*, RCA

Country solo vocal performance, male: Johnny Cash, "Folsom Prison Blues," Columbia

Country solo vocal performance, female: Jeannie C. Riley, "Harper Valley P.T.A.," Plantation

Country performance by a duo or group (vocal or instrumental): Flatt and Scruggs, "Foggy Mountain Breakdown," Columbia

Country song (songwriter's award): "Little Green Apples," Bobby Russell

Folk performance: Judy Collins, "Both Sides Now," Elektra

Instrumental theme (composer's award): "Classical Gas," Mason Williams, Warner Bros.

Classical performance, orchestra (conductor's award): Pierre Boulez conducting the New Philharmonia Orchestra, *Boulez Conducts Debussy*, Columbia

Opera recording: *Mozart: Così fan tutte*, Erich Leinsdorf conducting the New Philharmonia Orchestra and Ambrosian Opera Chorus (solos: Price, Troyanos, Raskin, Milnes, Shirley, Flagello) RCA

Classical performance, vocal soloist: Montserrat Caballé, (Cillario conducting the RCA Italian Opera Orchestra and Chorus) *Rossini Rarities*, RCA

1969

Album: *Blood Sweat and Tears*, Blood Sweat and Tears, Columbia

Record: "Aquarius/Let the Sunshine in," 5th Dimension, Soul City

Song (songwriter's award): "Games People Play," Joe South

New artist: Crosby, Stills and Nash

Contemporary vocal performance, male: Harry Nilsson, "Everybody's Talkin'," United Artists

Contemporary vocal performance, female: Peggy Lee, "Is That All There Is?" Capitol

Contemporary vocal performance by a group: 5th Dimension, "Aquarius/Let the Sunshine in," Soul City

Contemporary performance by a chorus: Percy Faith Orchestra and Chorus, "Love Theme from *Romeo and Juliet*," Columbia

Contemporary song (songwriter's award): "Games People Play," Joe South

Contemporary instrumental performance: "Variations on a Theme by Erik Satie," Blood Sweat and Tears, Columbia

Rhythm and blues song (songwriter's award): "Color Him Father," Richard Spencer

Rhythm and blues vocal performance, male: Joe Simon, "The Chokin' Kind," Sound Stage

Rhythm and blues vocal performance, female: Aretha Franklin, "Share Your Love With Me," Atlantic

Rhythm and blues vocal performance by a duo or group: Isley Brothers, "It's Your Thing," T-Neck

Rhythm and blues instrumental performance: King Curtis, "Games People Play," Atco

Instrumental jazz performance by a small group or soloist with small group (7 or fewer): Wes Montgomery, *Willow Weep For Me*, Verve

Instrumental jazz performance by a large group or soloist with large group (8 or more): Quincy Jones, "Walking in Space," A&M

Country song (songwriter's award): "A Boy Named Sue," Shel Silverstein

Country vocal performance, male: Johnny Cash, "A Boy Named Sue," Columbia

Country vocal performance, female: Tammy Wynette, "Stand By Your Man," Epic

Country performance by a duo or group : Waylon Jennings, Kimberlys, "MacArthur Park," RCA

Country instrumental performance: Danny Davis and the Nashville Brass, *The Nashville Brass Featuring Danny Davis Play More Nashville Sounds*, RCA

Folk performance: Joni Mitchell, *Clouds*, Warner Bros.

Instrumental theme (composer's award): *Midnight Cowboy*, John Barry

Album, classical: *Switched-on Bach* (*Virtuoso Electronic Performance of Branden Concerto No. 3, Air on a G String, Jesu, Joy of Man's Destiny, etc.*, performed on Moog synthesizer) Walter Carlos, Columbia

Classical performance, orchestra (conductor's award): Pierre Boulez conducting the Cleveland Orchestra, *Boulez Conducts Debussy, Vol. 2, Images pour orchestre*, Columbia

Opera recording: *Wagner: Siegfried*, Herbert von Karajan conducting the Berlin Philharmonic (solos: Thomas, Stewart, Stolze, Dernesch, Keleman, Dominguez, Gayer, Ridderbush) Deutsche Grammophon

Classical performance, vocal soloist: Leontyne Price (Schippers conducting the New Philharmonia) *Barber: Two Scenes from "Anthony and Cleopatra"*; *Knoxville: Summer of 1915*, RCA

1970

Album: *Bridge Over Troubled Water*, Simon and Garfunkel, Columbia

Record: "Bridge Over Troubled Water," Simon and Garfunkel, Columbia

Song (songwriter's award): "Bridge Over Troubled Water," Paul Simon

---

. . . October 30 . . .
Calista Flockhart is to reprise her roles in Neil LaBute's
Bash at the Canon Theater in Beverly Hills.

New artist: Carpenters

Contemporary vocal performance, male: Ray Stevens, "Everything Is Beautiful," Barnaby

Contemporary vocal performance, female: Dionne Warwick, "I'll Never Fall in Love Again," Scepter

Contemporary vocal performance by a duo, group or chorus: The Carpenters, "Close to You," A&M

Contemporary song (songwriter's award): "Bridge Over Troubled Water," Paul Simon

Contemporary instrumental performance: Henry Mancini, *Theme From "Z" and Other Film Music*, RCA

Rhythm and blues song (songwriter's award): "Patches," Ronald Dunbar, General Johnson

Rhythm and blues vocal performance, male: B.B. King, "The Thrill Is Gone," ABC

Rhythm and blues vocal performance, female: Aretha Franklin, "Don't Play That Song," Atlantic

Rhythm and blues performance by a duo or group (vocal or instrumental): Delfonics, "Didn't I (Blow Your Mind This Time)?," Philly Groove

Jazz performance by a small group or soloist with small group (7 or fewer): Bill Evans, *Alone*, MGM

Jazz performance by a large group or soloist with large group (8 or more): Miles Davis, *Bitches Brew*, Columbia

Country song (songwriter's award): "My Woman, My Woman, My Wife," Marty Robbins

Country instrumental performance: Chet Atkins, Jerry Reed, *Me and Jerry*, RCA

Country vocal performance, male: Ray Price, "For the Good Times," Columbia

Country vocal performance, female: Lynn Anderson, "Rose Garden," Columbia

Country vocal performance by a duo or group: Johnny Cash, June Carter, "If I Were a Carpenter," Columbia

Instrumental composition (composer's award): Alfred Newman, "*Airport* Love Theme"

Album, classical: *Berlioz: Les Troyens*, Colin Davis conducting the Royal Opera House Orchestra and Chorus (solos: Vickers, Veasy, Lindholm) Philips

Classical performance, orchestra (conductor's award): Pierre Boulez conducting the Cleveland Orchestra, *Stravinsky: Le Sacre du printemps*, Columbia

Opera recording: *Berlioz: Les Troyens*, Colin Davis conducting the Royal Opera House Orchestra and Chorus (solos: Vickers, Veasey, Lindholm) Philips

Classical performance, vocal soloist: Dietrich Fischer-Dieskay (Gerlad Moore, accompanist) *Schubert: Lieder*, Deutsche Grammophon

1971

Album: *Tapestry*, Carole King, Ode

Record: "It's Too Late," Carole King, Ode

Song (songwriter's award): "You've Got a Friend," Carole King

New artist: Carly Simon

Pop vocal performance, male: James Taylor, "You've Got a Friend," Warner Bros.

Pop vocal performance, female: Carole King, "Tapestry," Ode

Pop vocal performance by a duo, group or chorus: Carpenters, *Carpenters*, A&M

Pop instrumental performance: Quincy Jones, *Smackwater Jack*, A&M

Rhythm and blues song (songwriter's award): "Ain't No Sunshine," Bill Withers

Rhythm and blues vocal performance, male: Lou Rawls, "A Natural Man," MGM

Rhythm and blues vocal performance, female: Aretha Franklin, "Bridge Over Troubled Water," Atlantic

Rhythm and blues performance by a duo or group (vocal or instrumental): Ike and Tina Turner, "Proud Mary," United Artists

Jazz performance by a soloist: Bill Evans, *The Bill Evans Album*, Columbia

Jazz performance by a group: Bill Evans, *The Bill Evans Album*, Columbia

Jazz performance by a big band: Duke Ellington, "New Orleans Suite," Atlantic

Country song (songwriter's award): "Help Me Make It Through the Night," Kris Kristofferson

Country vocal performance, male: Jerry Reed, "When You're Hot, You're Hot," RCA

Country vocal performance, female: Sammi Smith, "Help Me Make It Through the Night," Mega

Country vocal performance, duo or group: Conway Twitty, Loretta Lynn, "After the Fire Is Gone," Decca

Country instrumental: Chet Atkins, *Snowbird*, RCA

Ethnic or traditional recording (including traditional blues): *They Call Me Muddy Waters*, Muddy Waters, Chess

Instrumental composition (composer's award): Michel Legrand, "Theme from *Summer of '42*," Warner Bros.

Album, classical: *Horowitz Plays Rachmaninov* (études tableaux, piano music, sonatas) (solo: Vladimir Horowitz) Columbia

Classical performance, orchestra (conductor's award): Carlo Maria Giulini conducting the Chicago Symphony, *Mahler: Symphony No. 1 in D Major*, Angel

Opera recording: *Verdi: Aida*, Erich Leinsdorf conducting the London Symphony; John Alldis

...October 31...
House On Haunted Hill makes the biggest debut ever
within two days of Halloween with $15.1 million.

Choir (solos: Price, Domingo, Milnes, Bumbry, Raimondi) RCA

Classical performance, vocal soloist: Leontyne Price (Garvey accompanist) *Leontyne Price Sings Robert Schumann*, RCA

1972

Album: *The Concert for Bangla Desh*, George Harrison, Ravi Shankar, Bob Dylan, Leon Russell, Ringo Starr, Billy Preston, Eric Clapton, Klaus Voormann, and others, Apple

Record: "The First Time Ever I Saw Your Face," Roberta Flack, Atlantic

Song (songwriter's award): "The First Time Ever I Saw Your Face," Ewan MacColl

New artist: America

Pop vocal performance, male: Nilsson, "Without You," RCA

Pop vocal performance, female: Helen Reddy, "I Am a Woman," Capitol

Pop vocal performance by a duo, group or chorus: Roberta Flack, Donny Hathaway, "Where Is the Love?," Atlantic

Pop instrumental performance by an instrumental performer: Billy Preston, "Outa-Space," A&M

Pop instrumental performance with vocal coloring: Isaac Hayes, *Black Moses*, Enterprise

Rhythm and blues song (songwriter's award): "Papa Was a Rolling Stone," Barrett Strong, Norman Whitfield

Rhythm and blues vocal performance, male: Billy Paul, "Me and Mrs. Jones," Philadelphia International

Rhythm and blues vocal performance, female: Aretha Franklin, *Young, Gifted and Black*, Atlantic

Rhythm and blues vocal performance by a duo, group or chorus: Temptations, "Papa Was a Rolling Stone," Gordy/Motown

Rhythm and blues instrumental performance: Temptations, Paul Riser, "Papa Was a Rolling Stone," Gordy/Motown

Jazz performance by a soloist: Gary Burton, *Alone at Last*, Atlantic

Jazz performance by a group: Freddie Hubbard, *First Light*, CTI

Jazz performance by a big band: Duke Ellington, "Togo Brava Suite," United Artists

Country song (songwriter's award): "Kiss an Angel Good Mornin'," Ben Peters

Country vocal performance, male: Charley Pride, *Charley Pride Sings Heart Songs*, RCA

Country vocal performance, female: Donna Fargo, "Happiest Girl in the Whole U.S.A.," Dot

Country vocal performance by a duo or group: Statler Brothers, "Class of '57," Mercury

Country instrumental performance: Charlie McCoy, *The Real McCoy*, Monument

Instrumental composition (composer's award): Michel Legrand, "Brian's Song," Bell

Album, classical: *Mahler: Symphony No. 8 in E Flat Major ("Symphony of a Thousand")* Georg Solti conducting the Chicago Symphony, Vienna Boys' Choir, Vienna State Opera Chorus, Vienna Singverein Chorus and soloists, London

Classical performance, orchestra (conductor's award): Georg Solti conducting the Chicago Symphony, *Mahler: Symphony No. 7 in E Minor*, London

Opera recording: *Berlioz: Benvenuto Cellini*, Colin Davis conducting the BBC Symphony; Chorus of Covent Garden (solos: Gedda, Eda-Pierre, Soyer, Berbie) Philips

Classical performance, vocal soloist: Dietrich Fischer-Dieskau (Richter, accompanist) *Brahms: Die Schone Magelone*, Angel

1973

Album: *Innervisions*, Stevie Wonder, Tamla/Motown

Record: "Killing Me Softly With His Song," Roberta Flack, Atlantic

Song (songwriter's award): "Killing Me Softly With His Song," Norman Gimbel, Charles Fox

New artist: Bette Midler

Pop vocal performance, male: Stevie Wonder, "You Are the Sunshine of My Life," Tamla/Motown

Pop vocal performance, female: Roberta Flack, "Killing Me Softly With His Song," Atlantic

Pop vocal performance by a duo, group or chorus: Gladys Knight and the Pips, "Neither One of Us (Wants to Be the First to Say Goodbye)," Soul/Motown

Pop instrumental performance: Eumir Deodato, "Also Sprach Zarathustra (*2001*)," CTI

Rhythm and blues vocal performance, male: Stevie Wonder, "Superstition," Tamla/Motown

Rhythm and blues vocal performance, female: Aretha Franklin, "Master of Eyes," Atlantic

Rhythm and blues vocal performance by a duo, group or chorus: Gladys Knight and the Pips, "Midnight Train to Georgia," Buddah

Rhythm and blues instrumental performance: Ramsey Lewis, "Hang on Sloopy," Columbia

Rhythm and blues song (songwriter's award): "Superstition," Stevie Wonder

Jazz performance by a soloist: Art Tatum, *God Is in the House*, Onyx

---

Jazz performance by a group: Supersax, *Supersax Plays Bird*, Capitol

Jazz performance by a big band: Woody Herman, *Giant Steps*, Fantasy

Country vocal performance, male: Charlie Rich, "Behind Closed Doors," Epic/Columbia

Country vocal performance, female: Olivia Newton-John, "Let Me Be There," MCA

Country vocal performance by a duo or group: Kris Kristofferson, Rita Coolidge, "From the Bottle to the Bottom," A&M

Country instrumental performance: Eric Weissberg, Steve Mandell, "Dueling Banjos," Warner Bros.

Country song (songwriter's award): "Behind Closed Doors," Kenny O'Dell

Instrumental compostion (composer's award): Gato Barbieri, "Last Tango in Paris"

Album, classical: *Bartók: Concerto for Orchestra*, Pierre Boulez conducting the New York Philharmonic, Columbia

Classical performance, orchestra (conductor's award): Pierre Boulez conducting the New York Philharmonic, *Bartók: Concerto for Orchestra*, Columbia

Opera recording: *Bizet: Carmen*, Leonard Bernstein conducting the Metropolitan Opera Orchestra and Manhattan Opera Chorus (solos: Horne, McCracken, Maliponte, Krause) Deutsche Grammophon

Classical performance, vocal soloist: Leontyne Price (Downes conducting the New Philharmonia), *Puccini: Heroines (La Bohème, La Rondine, Tosca, Manon Lescaut)*, RCA

1974

Album: *Fulfillingness' First Finale*, Stevie Wonder, Tamla/Motown

Record: "I Honestly Love You," Olivia Newton-John, MCA

Song (songwriter's award): "The Way We Were," Marilyn and Alan Bergman, Marvin Hamlisch

New artist: Marvin Hamlisch

Pop vocal performance, male: Stevie Wonder, *Fulfillingness' First Finale*, Tamla/Motown

Pop vocal performance, female: Olivia Newton-John, "I Honestly Love You," MCA

Pop vocal performance by a duo, group or chorus: Paul McCartney and Wings, "Band on the Run," Apple/Capitol

Pop instrumental performance: Marvin Hamlisch, "The Entertainer," MCA

Rhythm and blues song (songwriter's award): "Living for the City," Stevie Wonder

Rhythm and blues vocal performance, male: Stevie Wonder, "Boogie on Reggae Woman," Tamla/Motown

Rhythm and blues vocal performance, female: Aretha Franklin, "Ain't Nothing Like the Real Thing," Atlantic

Rhythm and blues vocal performance by a duo, group or chorus: Rufus, "Tell Me Something Good," ABC

Rhythm and blues instrumental performance: MFSB, "TSOP (The Sound of Philadelphia)," Philadelphia International/Epic

Jazz performance by a soloist: Charlie Parker, *First Recordings!* Onyx

Jazz performance by a group: Oscar Peterson, Joe Pass, Niels Pedersen, *The Trio*, Pablo

Jazz performance by a big band: Woody Herman, *Thundering Herd*, Fantasy

Country song (songwriter's award): "A Very Special Love Song," Norris Wilson, Billy Sherrill

Country vocal performance, male: Ronnie Milsap, "Please Don't Tell Me How the Story Ends," RCA

Country vocal performance, female: Anne Murray, "Love Song," Capitol

Country vocal performance by a duo or group: Pointer Sisters, "Fairytale," Blue Thumb

Country instrumental performance: Chet Atkins, Merle Travis, *The Atkins-Travis Travelling Show*, RCA

Instrumental composition (composer's award): Mike Oldfield, "Tubular Bells" (Theme from *The Exorcist*)

Album, classical: *Berlioz: Symphonie Fantastique*, Georg Solti conducting the Chicago Symphony, London

Classical performance, orchestra (conductor's award): Georg Solti conducting the Chicago Symphony, *Berlioz: Symphonie Fantastique*, London

Opera recording: *Puccini: La Bohème*, Georg Solti conducting the London Philharmonic (solos: Caballé, Domingo, Nilnes, Blegen, Raimondi) RCA

Classical performance, vocal soloist: Leontyne Price, *Leontyne Price Sings Richard Strauss*, RCA

Producer: Thom Bell

1975

Album: *Still Crazy After All These Years*, Paul Simon, Columbia

Record: "Love Will Keep Us Together," Captain and Tennille, A&M

Song (songwriter's award): "Send in the Clowns," Stephen Sondheim

---

... **November 2** ...
ITV has picked up four episodes of a new night-time
variety series to be hosted by Jerry Springer.

New artist: Natalie Cole

Pop vocal performance, male: Paul Simon, *Still Crazy After All These Years*, Columbia

Pop vocal performance, female: Janis Ian, "At Seventeen," Columbia

Pop vocal performance by a duo, group or chorus: The Eagles, "Lyin' Eyes," Asylum

Pop instrumental performance: Van McCoy and The Soul City Symphony, "The Hustle," Avco

Rhythm and blues song (songwriter's award): "Where Is the Love?," H.W. Casey

Rhythm and blues vocal performance, male: Ray Charles, "Living For the City," Crossover

Rhythm and blues vocal performance, female: Natalie Cole, "This Will Be," Capitol

Rhythm and blues vocal performance by a duo, group or chorus: Earth, Wind and Fire, "Shining Star," Columbia

Rhythm and blues instrumental performance: Silver Convention, "Fly, Robin, Fly," Midland/RCA

Jazz performance by a soloist: Dizzy Gillespie, *Oscar Peterson and Dizzy Gillespie*, Pablo

Jazz performance by a group: Return to Forever featuring Chick Corea, *No Mystery*, Polydor

Jazz performance by a big band: Phil Woods with Michel Legrand and His Orchestra, *Images*

Country song (songwriter's award): "(Hey Won't You Play) Another Somebody Done Somebody Wrong Song," Chips Moman, Larry Butler

Country vocal performance, male: Willie Nelson, "Blue Eyes Crying in the Rain," Columbia

Country vocal performance, female: Linda Ronstadt, "I Can't Help It (If I'm Still in Love With You)," Capitol

Country vocal performance by a duo or group: Kris Kristofferson, Rita Coolidge, "Lover Please," Monument

Country instrumental performance: Chet Atkins, "The Entertainer," RCA

Instrumental composition (composer's award): Michel Legrand, *Images*

Album, classical: *Beethoven: Symphonies (9) Complete*, Sir Georg Solti conducting the Chicago Symphony, London

Classical performance, orchestra (conductor's award): Pierre Boulez conducting the New York Philharmonic, *Ravel: Daphnis et Chloé*, Columbia

Opera recording: *Mozart: Così fan tutte*, Colin Davis conducting the Chorus and Orchestra of the Royal Opera House, Covent Garden (solos: Caballé, Baker, Gedda, Ganzarolli, Van Allen, Cotrubas) Philips

Classical performance, vocal soloist: Janet Baker

(Bernstein conducting the Israel Philharmonic), *Mahler: Kindertötenlieder*, Columbia

Producer: Arif Mardin

1976

Album: *Songs in the Key of Life*, Stevie Wonder, Tamla/Motown

Record: "This Masquerade," George Benson, Warner Bros.

Song (songwriter's award): "I Write the Songs," Bruce Johnston

New artist: Starland Vocal Band

Pop vocal performance, male: Stevie Wonder, *Songs in the Key of Life*, Tamla/Motown

Pop vocal performance, female: Linda Ronstadt, *Hasten Down the Wind*, Asylum

Pop vocal performance by a duo, group or chorus: Chicago, "If You Leave Me Now," Columbia

Pop instrumental performance: George Benson, *Breezin'*, Warner Bros.

Rhythm and blues song (songwriter's award): "Lowdown," Boz Scaggs, David Paich

Rhythm and blues vocal performance, male: Stevie Wonder, "I Wish," Tamla/Motown

Rhythm and blues vocal performance, female: Natalie Cole, "Sophisticated Lady (She's a Different Lady)," Capitol

Rhythm and blues vocal performance by a duo, group or chorus: Marilyn McCoo, Billy Davis, Jr., "You Don't Have to Be a Star (to Be in My Show)," ABC

Rhythm and blues instrumental performance: George Benson, "Theme from *Good King Bad*," CTI

Jazz vocal performance: Ella Fitzgerald, *Fitzgerald and Pass ... Again*, Pablo

Jazz performance by a soloist: Count Basie, *Basie and Zoot*, Pablo

Jazz performance by a group: Chick Corea, *The Leprechaun*, Polydor

Jazz performance by a big band: Duke Ellington, *The Ellington Suites*, Pablo

Country song (songwriter's award): "Broken Lady," Larry Garlin

Country vocal performance, male: Ronnie Milsap, "(I'm a) Stand By My Woman Man," RCA

Country vocal performance, female: Emmylou Harris, *Elite Hotel*, Reprise

Country vocal performance by a duo or group: Amazing Rhythm Aces, "The End Is Not in Sight (The Cowboy Tune)," ABC

Country instrumental performance: Chet Atkins, Les Paul, *Chester and Lester*, RCA

Instrumental composition: *Bellavia*, Chuck Mangione

... November 3 ...
Warner Bros. and Village Roadshow gear up an
updated remake of the 1972 chamber drama **Sleuth**.

Album, classical: *Beethoven: The Five Piano Concertos*, Daniel Barenboim conducting the London Philharmonic (solo: Rubinstein), RCA

Classical performance, orchestral (conductor's award): Sir Georg Solti conducting the Chicago Symphony, *Strauss: Also Sprach Zarathustra*, London

Opera recording: *Gershwin: Porgy and Bess*, Lorin Maazel conducting the Cleveland Orchestra and Chorus (solos: Mitchell, White) London

Classical performance, vocal soloist: Beverly Sills (Kostelanetz conducting the London Symphony), *Music of Victor Herbert*, Angel

Producer: Stevie Wonder

1977

Album: *Rumours*, Fleetwood Mac, Warner Bros.

Record: "Hotel California," Eagles, Asylum

Song (songwriter's award): "Love Theme From *A Star Is Born* (Evergreen)," Barbra Streisand, Paul Williams

New artist: Debby Boone

Pop vocal performance, male: James Taylor, "Handy Man," Columbia

Pop vocal performance, female: Barbra Streisand, "Love Theme From *A Star Is Born* (Evergreen)," Columbia

Pop vocal performance by a duo, group or chorus: Bee Gees, "How Deep Is Your Love?," RSO

Pop instrumental performance: London Symphony, John Williams, conductor *Star Wars*, 20th Century

Rhythm and blues song (songwriter's award): "You Make Me Feel Like Dancing," Leo Sayer, Vini Poncia

Rhythm and blues vocal performance, male: Lou Rawls, *Unmistakably Lou*, Philadelphia International/Epic

Rhythm and blues vocal performance, female: Thelma Houston, "Don't Leave Me This Way," Motown

Rhythm and blues vocal performance by a duo, group or chorus: Emotions, "Best of My Love," Track, Columbia

Rhythm and blues instrumental performance: Brothers Johnson, "Q," A&M

Jazz vocal performance: Al Jarreau, *Look to the Rainbow*, Warner Bros.

Jazz instrumental performance by a soloist: Oscar Peterson, *The Giants*, Pablo

Jazz instrumental performance by a group: *Phil Woods, The Phil Woods Six – Live from the Showboat*, RCA

Jazz performance by a big band: Count Basie and His Orchestra, *Prime Time*, Pablo

Country song (songwriter's award): "Don't It Make My Brown Eyes Blue," Richard Leigh

Country vocal performance, male: Kenny Rogers, "Lucille," United Artists

Country vocal performance, female: Crystal Gayle, "Don't It Make My Brown Eyes Blue," United Artists

Country vocal performance by a duo or group with vocal: Kendalls, "Heaven's Just a Sin Away," Ovation

Country instrumental performance: Hargus "Pig" Robbins, *Country Instrumentalist*, Elektra

Instrumental composition (composer's award): "Main Title from *Star Wars*," John Williams

Album, classical: *Concert of the Century* (recorded live at Carnegie Hall May 18, 1976) (solos: Leonard Bernstein, Vladimir Horowitz, Isaac Stern, Mstislav Rostropovich, Dietrich Fischer-Dieskau, Yehudi Menuhin, Lyndon Woodside) Columbia

Classical performance, orchestra (conductor's award): Carlo Maria Guilini conducting the Chicago Symphony, *Mahler: Symphony No. 9 in D Major*, Deutsche Grammophon

Opera recording: *Gershwin: Porgy and Bess*, John De Main conducting the Houston Grand Opera Production (solos: Albert, Dale, Smith, Shakesnider, Lane, Brice, Smalls) RCA

Classical performance, vocal soloist: Janet Baker (Marriner conducting the Academy of St. Martin-in-the-Fields) *Bach: Arias*, Angel

Producer: Peter Asher

1978

Album: *Saturday Night Fever* (soundtrack), Bee Gees, David Shire, Yvonne Elliman, Tavares, Kool and the Gang, K.C. and the Sunshine Band, MFSB, Trammps, Walter Murphy, Ralph MacDonald, RSO

Record: "Just the Way You Are," Billy Joel, Columbia

Song (songwriter's award): "Just the Way You Are," Billy Joel

New artist: A Taste of Honey

Pop vocal performance, male: Barry Manilow, "Copacabana (At the Copa)," Artista

Pop vocal performance, female: Anne Murray, "You Needed Me," Capitol

Pop vocal performance by a duo, group or chorus: Bee Gees, *Saturday Night Fever*, RSO

Pop instrumental performance: Chuck Mangione, *Children of Sanchez*, A&M

Rhythm and blues song (songwriter's award): "Last Dance," Paul Jabara

Rhythm and blues vocal performance, male: George Benson, "On Broadway," Warner Bros.

... November 4 ...
Barbra Streisand is to receive the Hollywood Foreign Press Association's
Cecil B. DeMille Career Achievement Award.

Rhythm and blues vocal performance, female: Donna Summer, "Last Dance," Casablanca

Rhythm and blues vocal performance by a duo, group or chorus: Earth, Wind and Fire, *All 'n' All,* Columbia

Rhythm and blues instrumental performance: Earth, Wind and Fire, "Runnin'," Columbia

Jazz vocal performance: Al Jarreau, *All Fly Home,* Warner Bros.

Jazz instrumental performance by a soloist: Oscar Peterson, *Montreux '77, Oscar Peterson Jam,* Pablo

Jazz instrumental performance by a group: Chick Corea, *Friends,* Polydor

Jazz instrumental performance by a big band: Thad Jones, Mel Lewis, *Live in Munich,* Horizon/A&M

Country song (songwriter's award): "The Gambler," Don Schlitz

Country vocal performance, male: Willie Nelson, "Georgia on My Mind," Columbia

Country vocal performance, female: *Here You Come Again,* Dolly Parton, RCA

Country vocal performance by a duo or group: Waylon Jennings, Willie Nelson, "Mammas, Don't Let Your Babies Grow Up to Be Cowboys," RCA

Country instrumental performance: Asleep at the Wheel, "One O'Clock Jump," Capitol

Instrumental composition: "Theme from *Close Encounters of the Third Kind,*" John Williams

Album, classical: *Brahms: Concerto for Violin in D Major,* Carlo Maria Giulini conducting the Chicago Symphony (solo: Itzhak Perlman) Angel

Classical performance, orchestra (conductor's award): Herbert von Karajan, conducting the Berlin Philharmonic, *Beethoven: Symphonies (9) (Complete)* Deutsche Grammophon

Opera recording: *Lehár: The Merry Widow,* Julius Rudel conducting the New York City Opera Orchestra and Chorus (solos: Sills, Titus) Angel

Classical performance, vocal soloist: Luciano Pavarotti, *Luciano Pavarotti, Hits from Lincoln Center,* London

Producer: Bee Gees, Albhy Galuten, Karl Richardson

1979

Album: *52nd Street,* Billy Joel, Columbia

Record: "What a Fool Believes," Doobie Brothers, Warner Bros.

Song (songwriter's award): "What a Fool Believes," Kenny Loggins, Michael McDonald

New artist: Rickie Lee Jones

Pop vocal performance, male: Billy Joel, *52nd Street,* Columbia

Pop vocal performance, female: Dionne Warwick, "I'll Never Love This Way Again," Artista

Pop vocal performance by a duo, group or chorus: Doobie Brothers, *Minute by Minute,* Warner Bros.

Pop instrumental performance: Herb Alpert, "Rise," A&M

Rock vocal performance, male: Bob Dylan, "Gotta Serve Somebody," Columbia

Rock vocal performance, female: Donna Summer, "Hot Stuff," Casablanca

Rock vocal performance by a duo or group with vocal: The Eagles, "Heartache Tonight," Asylum

Rock instrumental performance: Wings, "Rockestra Theme," Columbia

Rhythm and blues song (songwriter's award): "After the Love Has Gone," David Foster, Jay Graydon, Bill Champlin

Rhythm and blues vocal performance, male: Michael Jackson, "Don't Stop till You Get Enough," Epic

Rhythm and blues vocal performance, female: Dionne Warwick, "Déjà vu," Artista

Rhythm and blues vocal performance by a duo, group or chorus: Earth, Wind and Fire, "After the Love Has Gone," ARC/CBS

Rhythm and blues instrumental performance: Earth, Wind and Fire, "Boogie Wonderland," ARC/CBS

Disco recording: "I Will Survive," Gloria Gaynor, Polydor

Jazz fusion performance (vocal or instrumental): Weather Report, *8:30,* ARC/CBS

Jazz vocal performance: Ella Fitzgerald, *Fine & Mellow,* Pablo

Jazz instrumental performance by a soloist: Oscar Peterson, *Jousts,* Pablo

Jazz instrumental performance by a group: Gary Burton, Chick Corea, *Duet,* ECM/Warner Bros.

Jazz instrumental performance by a big band: Duke Ellington, *At Fargo, 1940 Live,* Book-of-the-Month

Country song (songwriter's award): "You Decorated My Life," Bob Morrison, Debbie Hupp

Country vocal performance, male: Kenny Rogers, "The Gambler," United Artists

Country vocal performance, female: Emmylou Harris, *Blue Kentucky Girl,* Warner Bros.

Country vocal performance by a duo or group: Charlie Daniels Band, "The Devil Went Down to Georgia," Epic

Country instrumental performance: Doc and Merle Watson, "Big Sandy/Leather Britches," track, United Artists

Instrumental composition (composer's award): "Theme from *Superman (Main Title),*" John Williams

Classical album: *Brahms: Symphonies (4) (Complete),*

... November 5 ...
Wim Wenders' **The Million Dollar Hotel** is to open the 50th Berlin Intl. Film Festival.

Sir Georg Solti conducting the Chicago Symphony Orchestra, London

Classical orchestral recording (conductor's award): *Brahms: Symphonies (4) (Complete)*, Sir Georg Solti conducting the Chicago Symphony, London

Opera recording: *Britten: Peter Grimes*, Colin Davis conducting the Orchestra and Chorus of the Royal Opera House, Covent Garden (solos: Vickers, Harper, Summers) Philips

Classical performance, vocal soloist: Luciano Pavarotti (Bologna Orchestra) *O Sole Mio (Favorite Neapolitan Songs)* London

Classical producer: James Mallinson

Producer: Larry Butler

1980

Album: *Christopher Cross*, Christopher Cross, Warner Bros.

Record: "Sailing," Christopher Cross, Warner Bros.

Song (songwriter's award): "Sailing," Christopher Cross

New artist: Christopher Cross

Pop vocal performance, male: Kenny Loggins, "This Is It," Columbia

Pop vocal performance, female: Bette Midler, "The Rose," Atlantic

Pop vocal performance by a duo, group or chorus: Barbra Streisand, Barry Gibb, "Guilty," Columbia

Pop instrumental performance: Bob James, Earl Klugh, *One on One*, Columbia

Rock vocal performance, male: Billy Joel, *Glass Houses*, Columbia

Rock vocal performance, female: Pat Benatar, *Crimes of Passion*, Chrysalis

Rock performance by a duo, group with a vocal: Bob Seger and the Silver Bullet Band, *Against the Wind*, Capitol

Rock instrumental performance: The Police, "Regatta de Blanc," A&M

Rhythm and blues song (songwriter's award): "Never Knew Love Like This Before," Reggie Lucas, James Mtume

Rhythm and blues vocal performance, male: George Benson, *Give Me the Night*, Warner Bros./Qwest

Rhythm and blues vocal performance, female: Stephanie Mills, "Never Knew Love Like This Before," 20th Century

Rhythm and blues vocal performance by a duo or group: Manhattans, "Shining Star," Columbia

Rhythm and blues instrumental performance: George Benson, "On Broadway," Warner Bros./Qwest

Jazz fusion performance (vocal or instrumental): Manhattan Transfer, "Birdland," Atlantic

Jazz vocal performance, male: George Benson, "Moody's Mood," Warner Bros./Qwest

Jazz vocal performance, female: Ella Fitzgerald, *A Perfect Match/Ella and Basie*, Pablo

Jazz instrumental performance by a soloist: Bill Evans, *I Will Say Goodbye*, Fantasy

Jazz instrumental performance by a group: Bill Evans, *We Will Meet Again*, Warner Bros.

Instrumental jazz performance by a big band: Count Basie and His Orchestra, *On the Road*, Pablo

Country song (songwriter's award): "On the Road Again," Willie Nelson

Country vocal performance, male: George Jones, "He Stopped Loving Her Today," Epic

Country vocal performance, female: Anne Murray, "Could I Have This Dance," Capitol

Country performance by a duo or group with vocal: Roy Orbison, Emmylou Harris, "That Lovin' You Feelin' Again," Warner Bros.

Country instrumental performance: Gilley's Urban Cowboy Band, "Orange Blossom Special/Hoedown," Full Moon/Asylum

Instrumental composition: "The Empire Strikes Back," John Williams

Classical album: *Berg: Lulu (Complete)*, Pierre Boulez conducting the Orchestre de l'Opéra de Paris (solos: Teresa Stratus, Yvonne Minton, Franz Mazura, Toni Blankenheim) Deutsche Grammophon

Classical performance, orchestra (conductor's award): Bruckner: *Symphony No. 6 in A Major*, Sir Georg Solti conducting the Chicago Symphony, London

Opera recording: *Berg: Lulu (Complete)*, Pierre Boulez conducting the Orchestre de l'Opéra de Paris (solos: Teresa Stratus, Yvonne Minton, Franz Mazura, Toni Blankenheim) Deutsche Grammophon

Classical performance, vocal soloist: Leontyne Price (Henry Lewis conducting the Philharmonic Orchestra), *Prima Donna, Vol. 5, Great Soprano Arias from Handel to Britten*, RCA

Classical producer: Robert Woods

Producer: Phil Ramone

1981

Album: *Double Fantasy*, John Lennon, Yoko Ono, Geffen/Warner Bros.

Record: "Bette Davis Eyes," Kim Carnes, EMI-America

Song (songwriter's award): "Bette Davis Eyes," Donna Weiss, Jackie DeShannon

New artist: Sheena Easton

Pop vocal performance, male: Al Jarreau, *Breaking Away*, Warner Bros.

Pop vocal performance, female: Lena Horne, *Lena Horne: The Lady and Her Music Live on Broadway*, Qwest/Warner Bros.

Pop performance by a duo or group with vocal: Manhattan Transfer, "Boy From New York City," Atlantic

Pop instrumental performance: Mike Post featuring Larry Carlton, "Theme from *Hill Street Blues*," Elektra/Asylum

Rock vocal performance, male: Rick Springfield, "Jessie's Girl," RCA

Rock vocal performance, female: Pat Benatar, "Fire and Ice," Chrysalis

Rock performance by a duo or group with vocal: The Police, "Don't Stand So Close to Me," A&M

Rock instrumental performance: The Police, "Behind My Camel," A&M

Rhythm and blues song (songwriter's award): "Just the Two of Us," Bill Withers, William Salter, Ralph MacDonald

Rhythm and blues vocal performance, male: James Ingram, "One Hundred Ways," A&M

Rhythm and blues vocal performance, female: Aretha Franklin, "Hold on, I'm Comin'," track, Arista

Rhythm and blues vocal performance by a duo or group: Quincy Jones, *The Dude*, A&M

Rhythm and blues instrumental performance: David Sanborn, "All I Need Is You," Warner Bros.

Jazz fusion performance (vocal or instrumental): Grover Washington, Jr., *Winelight*, Elektra/Asylum

Jazz vocal performance, male: Al Jarreau, "Blue Rondo à la Turk," track, Warner Bros.

Jazz vocal performance, female: Ella Fitzgerald, *Digital III at Montreux*, Pablo Live

Jazz performance by a duo or group: Manhattan Transfer, "Until I Met You (Corner Pocket)," track, Atlantic

Jazz instrumental performance by a soloist: John Coltrane, *Bye Bye Blackbird*, Pablo

Jazz instrumental performance by a group: Chick Corea, Gary Burton, *Chick Corea and Gary Burton in Concert, Zurich, October 28, 1979*, ECM

Jazz instrumental performance by a big band: Gerry Mulligan and his Orchestra, *Walk on the Water*, DRG

Country song (songwriter's award): "9 to 5," Dolly Parton

Country vocal performance, male: Ronnie Milsap, "(There's) No Gettin' Over Me," RCA

Country vocal performance, female: Dolly Parton, "9 to 5," RCA

Country performance by a duo or group with vocal: Oak Ridge Boys, "Elvira," MCA

Country instrumental performance: Chet Atkins, *Country After All These Years*, RCA

Instrumental composition (composer's award): "Theme from *Hill Street Blues*," Mike Post

Classical album: *Mahler: Symphony No. 2 in C Minor*, Sir Georg Solti conducting the Chicago Symphony Orchestra and Chorus (solos: Isobel Buchanan, Mira Zakai) London

Classical orchestral recording: *Mahler: Symphony No. 2 in C Minor*, Sir Georg Solti conducting the Chicago Symphony, London

Opera recording: *Janácek: From the House of the Dead*, Sir Charles Mackerras conducting the Vienna Philharmonic (solos: Jiri Zahradnicek, Vaclav Zidek, Ivo Zidek) London

Classical performance, vocal soloist: Joan Sutherland, Marilyn Horne, Luciano Pavarotti (Richard Bonynge conducting the New York City Opera Orchestra), *Live from Lincoln Center Sutherland, Horne, Pavarotti*, London

Classical producer: James Mallinson

Producer (other than classical): Quincy Jones

Music video: *Michael Nesmith in Elephant Parts*, Michael Nesmith, Pacific Arts Video

1982

Album: *Toto IV*, Toto, Columbia/CBS

Record: "Rosanna," Toto, Columbia

Song (songwriter's award): "Always on My Mind," Johnny Christopher, Mark James, Wayne Thompson

New artist: Men at Work

Pop vocal performance, male: Lionel Richie, "Truly," Motown

Pop vocal performance, female: Melissa Manchester, "You Should Hear How She Talks About You," Arista

Pop performance by a duo or group with vocal: Joe Cocker, Jennifer Warnes, "Up Where We Belong," Island

Pop instrumental performance: Ernie Watts, "Chariots of Fire" (theme, dance version), Qwest/Warner Bros.

Rock vocal performance, male: John Cougar, "Hurts So Good," Riva/Polygram

Rock vocal performance, female: Pat Benatar, "Shadows of the Night," Chrysalis

Rock performance by a duo or group with vocal: Survivor, "Eye of the Tiger," Scotti Brothers/CBS

Rock instrumental performance: A Flock of Seagulls, "D.N.A.," Jive/Arista

Rhythm and blues song (songwriter's award): "Turn Your Love Around," Jay Graydon, Steve Lukather, Bill Champli

Rhythm and blues vocal performance, male: Marvin Gaye, "Sexual Healing," Columbia/CBS

Rhythm and blues vocal performance, female: Jennifer Holliday, "And I Am Telling You I'm Not Going," Geffen/Warner Bros.

Rhythm and blues vocal performance by a duo or group (tie): Dazz Band, "Let It Whip," Motown; and Earth, Wind and Fire, "Wanna Be With You," ARC/CBS

Rhythm and blues instrumental performance: Marvin Gaye, "Sexual Healing," Columbia/CBS

Jazz fusion performance (vocal or instrumental): Pat Metheny Group, *Offramp*, ECM/Warner Bros.

Jazz vocal performance, male: Mel Tormé, *An Evening with George Shearing and Mel Tormé*, Concord Jazz

Jazz vocal performance, female: Sarah Vaughan, *Gershwin Live!* CBS

Jazz vocal performance by a duo or group: Manhattan Transfer, "Route 66," Atlantic

Jazz instrumental performance by a soloist: Miles Davis, *We Want Miles*, Columbia

Jazz instrumental performance by a group: Phil Woods Quartet, *"More" Live*, Adelphi

Jazz instrumental performance by a big band: Count Basie and His Orchestra, *Warm Breeze*, Pablo Today

Country song (songwriter's award): "Always on My Mind," Johnny Christopher, Mark James, Wayne Thompson

Country vocal performance, male: Willie Nelson, "Always on My Mind," Columbia/CBS

Country vocal performance, female: Juice Newton, "Break It to Me Gently," Capitol

Country performance by a duo or group with vocal: Alabama, *Mountain Music*, RCA

Country instrumental performance: Roy Clark, "Alabama Jubilee," Churchill

Instrumental composition: "Flying (Theme from *E.T. The Extra-Terrestrial*)," John Williams

Classical album: *Bach: The Goldberg Variations*, Glenn Gould, CBS

Classical orchestral recording (conductor's award): *Mahler: Symphony No. 7 in E Minor ("Song of the Night")* James Levine conducting the Chicago Symphony, RCA

Opera recording: *Wagner: Der Ring des Nibelungen*, Pierre Boulez conducting the Bayreuth Festival Orchestra (solos: Gwyneth Jones, Jeannine Altmeyer, Orton Wenkel, etc) Philips

Classical performance, vocal soloist: Leontyne Price (Zubin Mehta conducting the Israel Philharmonic), Verdi: Arias (*Leontyne Price Sings Verdi*) London

Classical producer: Robert Woods

Producer (other than classical): Toto

Music video: *Olivia Physical*, Olivia Newton-John, MCA Video

1983

Album: *Thriller*, Michael Jackson, Epic/CBS

Record: "Beat It," Michael Jackson, Epic/CBS

New song (songwriter's award): "Every Breath You Take," Sting

New artist: Culture Club

Pop vocal performance, male: Michael Jackson, *Thriller*, Epic/CBS

Pop vocal performance, female: Irene Cara, "Flashdance ... What a Feeling," Casablanca/Polygram

Pop performance by a duo or group with vocal: Police, "Every Breath You Take," A&M

Pop instrumental performance: George Benson, "Being With You," Warner Bros.

Rock vocal performance, male: Michael Jackson, "Beat It," Epic/CBS

Rock vocal performance, female: Pat Benatar, "Love Is a Battlefield," Chrysalis

Rock performance by a duo or group with vocal: Police, *Synchronicity*, A&M

Rock instrumental performance: Sting, *Brimstone & Treacle*, A&M

New Rhythm and blues song (songwriter's award): "Billie Jean," Michael Jackson

Rhythm and blues vocal performance, male: Michael Jackson, "Billie Jean," Epic/CBS

Rhythm and blues vocal performance, female: Chaka Khan, *Chaka Khan*, Warner Bros.

Rhythm and blues vocal performance by a duo or group: Rufus and Chaka Khan, "Ain't Nobody," Warner Bros.

Rhythm and blues instrumental performance: Herbie Hancock, "Rockit," Columbia

Jazz fusion performance (vocal or instrumental): Pat Metheny Group, *Travels*, ECM/Warner Bros.

Jazz vocal performance, male: Mel Tormé, *Top Drawer*, Concord Jazz

Jazz vocal performance, female: Ella Fitzgerald, *The Best Is Yet to Come*, Pablo Today

Jazz vocal performance by a duo or group: Manhattan Transfer, "Why Not!" Atlantic

Jazz instrumental performance by a soloist: Wynton Marsalis, *Think of One*, Columbia

Jazz instrumental performance by a group: Phil Woods Quartet, *At the Vanguard*, Antilles/Island

... **November 8** ...

Following a hotly contested campaign, William Daniels is elected president of the Screen Actors Guild.

Jazz instrumental performance by a big band: Rob McConnell and the Boss Brass, *All in Good Time*, Dark Orchid

New country song (songwriter's award): "Stranger in My House," Mike Reid

Country vocal performance, male: Lee Greenwood, "I.O.U." MCA

Country vocal performance, female: Anne Murray, "A Little Good News," Capitol

Country performance by a duo or group with vocal: Alabama, *The Closer You Get*, RCA

Country instrumental performance: New South, "Fireball," Sugar Hill

Instrumental composition: "Love Theme from *Flashdance*," Giorgio Moroder

Classical album: *Mahler: Symphony No. 9 in D Major*, Sir Georg Solti conducting the Chicago Symphony, London

Classical orchestral recording: *Mahler: Symphony No. 9 in D Major*, Sir Georg Solti conducting the Chicago Symphony, London

Opera recording (tie): *Verdi: La Traviata (Original Soundtrack)*, James Levine conducting the Metropolitan Opera Orchestra and Chorus (solos: Teresa Strates, Placido Domingo, Cornell MacNeil), Elektra; and *Mozart: Le Nozze di Figaro*, Sir Georg Solti conducting the London Philharmonic Orchestra (solos: Kiri Te Kanawa, Lucia Popp, etc) London

Classical performance, vocal soloist: Leontyne Price, Marilyn Horne (Levine conducting the Metropolitan Opera Orchestra), *Leontyne Price and Marilyn Horne in Concert at the Met*. RCA

Classical producer: Marc J. Aubort, Joanna Nickrenz

Producer (other than classical): Quincy Jones, Michael Jackson

Music video, short film: *Girls on Film/Hungry Like the Wolf*, Duran Duran, EMI Music Video/Sony

Video album: *Duran Duran*, Duran Duran, Thorn EMI Video, Disc-Pioneer Artists

1984

Album: *Can't Slow Down*, Lionel Richie, Motown

Record: "What's Love Got to Do With It?," Tina Turner, Capitol

Song (songwriter's award): "What's Love Got to Do With It?," Graham Lyle, Terry Britten

New artist: Cyndi Lauper

Pop vocal performance, male: Phil Collins, "Against All Odds (Take a Look at Me Now)," Atlantic

Pop vocal performance, female: Tina Turner, "What's Love Got to Do With It?," Capitol

Pop performance by a duo or group with vocal: Pointer Sisters, "Jump (For My Love)," Planet

Pop instrumental performance: Ray Parker, Jr., "Ghostbusters," Arista

Rock vocal performance, male: Bruce Springsteen, "Dancing in the Dark," Columbia/CBS

Rock vocal performance, female: Tina Turner, "Better Be Good to Me," Capitol

Rock performance by a duo or group with vocal: Prince and the Revolution, *Purple Rain*, Warner Bros.

Rock instrumental performance: Yes, "Cinema," Atco

New Rhythm and blues song (songwriter's award): "I Feel For You," Prince

Rhythm and blues vocal performance, male: Billy Ocean, "Caribbean Queen (No More Love on the Run)," Jive/Arista

Rhythm and blues vocal performance, female: Chaka Khan, "I Feel For You," Warner Bros.

Rhythm and blues vocal performance by a duo or group: James Ingram, Michael McDonald, "Yah Mo B There," Qwest

Rhythm and blues instrumental performance: Herbie Hancock, *Sound-System*, Columbia/CBS

Jazz fusion performance (vocal or instrumental): Pat Metheny Group, *First Circle*, ECM

Jazz vocal performance: Joe Williams, *Nothin' but the Blues*, Delos

Jazz instrumental performance by a soloist: Wynton Marsalis, *Hot House Flowers*, Columbia/CBS

Jazz instrumental performance by a group: Art Blakey and the Jazz Messengers, "New York Scene," Concord Jazz

Jazz instrumental performance by a big band: Count Basie and His Orchestra, *88 Basie Street*, Pablo

Country song (songwriter's award): "City of New Orleans," Steve Goodman

Country vocal performance, male: Merle Haggard, "That's the Way Love Goes," Epic

Country vocal performance, female: Emmylou Harris, "In My Dreams," Warner Bros.

Country performance by a duo or group with vocal: Judds (Wynnona and Naomi) "Mama He's Crazy," RCA

Country instrumental performance: Ricky Skaggs, "Wheel Hoss," Epic/CBS

Instrumental composition (composer's award) (tie): "The Natural," Randy Newman; and "Olympic Fanfare and Theme," track from *The Official Music of the XXIIIrd Olympiad at Los Angeles*, John Williams

Classical album: *Amadeus* (soundtrack), Neville Mariner conducting the Academy of St. Martin-in-the-Fields, Fantasy

Classical orchestral recording: *Prokofiev: Symphony No. 5 in B Flat, Op. 100,* Leonard Slatkin conducting the St. Louis Symphony, RCA

Opera recording: *Bizet: Carmen* (film soundtrack), Lorin Maazal conducting the Orchestre National de France, (solos: Julia Migenes-Johnson, Placido Domingo, etc), Erato

Classical performance, vocal soloist: Jessye Norman, José van Dam, Heather Harper (Pierre Boulez conducting the members of the Ensemble Intercontemporain and BBC Symphony), *Ravel: Songs of Maurice Ravel,* CBS

Classical producer: Steven Epstein

Producer (other than classical) (tie): David Foster; Lionel Richie, James Anthony Carmichael

Music video, short film: *David Bowie,* David Bowie, Sony/Picture Music

Video album: *Making Michael Jackson's "Thriller,"* Michael Jackson, Vestron Music Video

1985

Album: *No Jacket Required,* Phil Collins, Atlantic

Record: "We Are the World," USA for Africa, Columbia/CBS

Song (songwriter's award): "We Are the World," Michael Jackson, Lionel Richie

New artist: Sade

Pop vocal performance, male: Phil Collins, *No Jacket Required,* Atlantic

Pop vocal performance, female: Whitney Houston, "Saving All My Love For You," Arista

Pop performance by a duo or group with vocal: USA for Africa, "We Are the World," Columbia/CBS

Pop instrumental performance: Jan Hammer, "*Miami Vice* Theme," MCA

Rock vocal performance, male: Don Henley, "The Boys of Summer," Geffen

Rock vocal performance, female: Tina Turner, "One of the Living," Capitol

Rock performance by a duo or group with vocal: Dire Straits, "Money For Nothing," Warner Bros.

Rock instrumental performance: Jeff Beck, "Escape," Epic/CBS

Rhythm and blues song (songwriter's award): "Freeway of Love," Narada Michael Walden, Jeffrey Cohen

Rhythm and blues vocal performance, male: Stevie Wonder, *In Square Circle,* Tamla/Motown

Rhythm and blues vocal performance, female: Aretha Franklin, "Freeway of Love," Arista

Rhythm and blues vocal performance by a duo or group: Commodores, "Nightshift," Gordy/Motown

Rhythm and blues instrumental performance: Ernie Watts, *Musican,* Qwest

Jazz vocal performance, male: Jon Hendricks, Bobby McFerrin, "Another Night in Tunisia," from *Vocalese* (Manhattan Transfer), Atlantic

Jazz vocal performance, female: Cleo Laine, *Cleo at Carnegie the 10th Anniversary Concert,* DRG

Jazz vocal performance by a duo or group: Manhattan Transfer, *Vocalese,* Atlantic

Jazz instrumental performance by a soloist: Wynton Marsalis, "Black Codes From the Underground," Columbia/CBS

Jazz instrumental performance by a group: Wynton Marsalis Group, *Black Codes From the Underground,* Columbia/CBS

Jazz instrumental performance by a big band: John Barry, Bob Wilber, *The Cotton Club* (film soundtrack), Geffen

Jazz fusion performance (vocal or instrumental): David Sanborn, *Straight to the Heart,* Warner Bros.

Country song (songwriter's award): "Highwayman," Jimmy L. Webb

Country vocal performance, male: Ronnie Milsap, "Lost in the Fifties Tonight (In the Still of the Night)," RCA

Country vocal performance, female: Rosanne Cash, "I Don't Know Why You Don't Want Me," CBS

Country performance by a duo or group with vocal: Judds, *Why Not Me,* RCA

Country instrumental performance: Chet Atkins, Mark Knopfler, "Cosmic Square Dance," Columbia/CBS

Instrumental composition: "*Miami Vice* Theme," Jan Hammer

Classical album: *Berlioz: Requiem,* Robert Shaw conducting the Atlanta Symphony Orchestra and Chorus (solo: John Aler), Telarc

Classical orchestral recording (conductor's award): *Fauré: Pelléas et Mélisande,* Robert Shaw conducting the Atlanta Symphony Orchestra and Chorus, Telarc

New classical artist: Chicago Pro Musica

Opera recording: *Schoenberg: Moses und Aron,* Sir Georg Solti conducting the Chicago Symphony Orchestra and Chorus (solos: Franz Mazura, Philip Langridge), London

Classical performance, vocal soloist: John Aler (Shaw conducting the Atlanta Symphony Orchestra and Chorus), *Berlioz: Requiem,* Telarc

Classical producer: Robert E. Woods

Producer (other than classical): Phil Collins, Hugh Padgham

Music video, short form: *We Are the World, the Video Event,* USA for Africa, Tom Trbovich, director, RCA/Columbia Pictures Home Video

---

... November 10 ...
The Beverly Hills outlet of Christie's auction house is planning to put on the block the Oscar that Herman J. Mankiewicz won in 1941 for his screenplay of **Citizen Kane**.

1986

Album: *Graceland*, Paul Simon, Warner Bros.

Record: "Higher Love," Steve Winwood, Island

Song (songwriter's award): "That's What Friends Are For," Burt Bacharach, Carole Bayer Sager

New artist: Bruce Hornsby and the Range

Pop vocal performance, male: Steve Winwood, "Higher Love," Island

Pop vocal performance, female: Barbra Streisand, *The Broadway Album*, Columbia/CBS

Pop vocal performance by a duo or group with vocal: Dionne Warwick, Elton John, Gladys Knight and Stevie Wonder, "That's What Friends Are For," Arista

Pop instrumental performance (orchestra, group or soloist): Harold Faltermeyer, Steve Stevens, "*Top Gun* Anthem," Columbia/CBS

Rock vocal performance, male: Robert Palmer, "Addicted to Love," Island

Rock vocal performance, female: Tina Turner, "Back Where You Started," Capitol

Rock performance by a duo or group with vocal: Eurythmics, "Missionary Man," RCA

Rock instrumental performance: Art of Noise Featuring Duane Eddy, "Peter Gunn," China/Chrysalis

Rhythm and blues song (songwriter's award): "Sweet Love," Anita Baker, Louis A. Johnson, Gary Bias

Rhythm and blues vocal performance, male: James Brown, "Living in America," Scotti Brothers/CBS

Rhythm and blues vocal performance, female: Anita Baker, *Rapture*, Elektra

Rhythm and blues vocal performance by a duo or group: Prince and the Revolution, "Kiss," Paisley Park

Rhythm and blues instrumental performance: Yellowjackets, "And You Know That," MCA

Jazz vocal performance, male: Bobby McFerrin, "Round Midnight," Columbia/CBS

Jazz vocal performance, female: Diane Schuur, *Timeless*, GRP

Jazz vocal performance by a duo or group: 2+2 Plus (Clare Fischer and His Latin Jazz Sextet), *Free Fall*, Discovery

Jazz instrumental performance by a soloist: Miles Davis, *Tutu*, Warner Bros.

Jazz instrumental performance by a group: Wynton Marsalis, *J Mood*, Columbia/CBS

Jazz instrumental performance by a big band: Tonight Show Band With Doc Severinsen, *The Tonight Show Band With Doc Severinsen*, Amherst

Jazz fusion performance (vocal or instrumental): Bob James, David Sanborn, *Double Vision*, Warner Bros.

Country song (songwriter's award): "Grandpa (Tell Me 'bout the Good Old Days)," Jamie O'Hara

Country vocal performance, male: Ronnie Milsap, *Lost in the Fifties Tonight*, RCA

Country vocal performance, female: Reba McEntire, "Whoever's in New England," MCA

Country performance by a duo or group with vocal: Judds, "Grandpa (Tell Me 'bout the Good Old Days)," RCA

Country instrumental performance: Ricky Skaggs, "Raisin' the Dickens," Epic/CBS

Instrumental composition (composer's award): *Out of Africa* (film soundtrack), John Barry

Classical album: *Horowitz: The Studio Recordings, New York 1985*, Vladimir Horowitz, Deutsche Grammophon

Classical orchestral recording (conductor's award): *Liszt: A Faust Symphony*, Sir Georg Solti conducting the Chicago Symphony Orchestra, London

Opera recording: *Bernstein: Candide*, John Mauceri conducting the New York City Opera Orchestra and Chorus (solos: Erie Mills, Maris Clement, etc), New World

Classical performance, vocal soloist: Kathleen Battle (Previn conducting the Royal Philharmonic Orchestra), *Kathleen Battle Sings Mozart*, Angel

Classical producer: Thomas Frost

Producer (other than classical): Jimmy Jam, Terry Lewis

Music video, short form: *Dire Straits Brothers in Arms*, Dire Straits, various directors, Warner Reprise Video

1987

Album: *The Joshua Tree*, U2, Island

Record: "Graceland," Paul Simon, Warner Bros.

Song (songwriter's award): "Somewhere Out There," James Horner, Barry Mann, Cynthia Weil

New artist: Jody Watley

Pop vocal performance, male: Sting, *Bring on the Night*, A&M

Pop vocal performance, female: Whitney Houston, "I Wanna Dance With Somebody (Who Loves Me)," Arista

Pop vocal performance by a duo or group with vocal: Bill Medley, Jennifer Warnes, "(I've Had) The Time of My Life," BMG Music/RCA

Pop instrumental performance: Larry Carlton, "Minute by Minute," MCA

Rock vocal performance, solo: Bruce Springsteen, *Tunnel of Love*, Columbia/CBS

Rock performance by a duo or group with vocal: U2, *The Joshua Tree*, Island

Rock instrumental performance: Frank Zappa, *Jazz From Hell*, Barking Pumpkin

Rhythm and blues song (songwriter's award): "Lean on Me," Bill Withers

Rhythm and blues vocal performance, male: Smokey Robinson, "Just to See Her," Motown

Rhythm and blues vocal performance, female: Aretha Franklin, *Aretha*, Arista

Rhythm and blues vocal performance by a duo or group: Aretha Franklin, George Michael, "I Knew You Were Waiting (for Me)," Arista

Rhythm and blues instrumental performance: David Sanborn, "Chicago Song," Warner Bros.

Jazz vocal performance, male: Bobby McFerrin, "What Is This Thing Called Love?," Blue Note

Jazz vocal performance, female: Diane Schuur, *Diane Schuur and the Count Basie Orchestra*, GRP

Jazz instrumental performance by a soloist: Dexter Gordon, *The Other Side of 'Round Midnight*, GRP

Jazz instrumental performance by a group: Wynton Marsalis, *Marsalis Standard Time, Vol 1*, Columbia/CBS

Jazz instrumental performance by a big band: Duke Ellington Orchestra conducted by Mercer Ellington, *Digital Duke*, GRP

Jazz fusion performance (vocal or instrumental): Pat Metheny Group, *Still Life (Talking)*, Geffen

Country song (songwriter's award): "Forever and Ever, Amen," Paul Overstreet, Don Schlitz

Country vocal performance, male: Randy Travis, *Always and Forever*, Warner Bros.

Country vocal performance, female: K.T. Oslin, "'80s Ladies," BMG Music/RCA

Country performance by a duo or group with vocal: Dolly Parton, Linda Ronstatdt, Emmylou Harris, *Trio*, Warner Bros.

Country vocal performance, duet: Ronnie Milsap, Kenny Rogers, "Make No Mistake, She's Mine," BMG Music/RCA

Country instrumental performance: Asleep at the Wheel, "String of Pars," Epic

New age performance: Yusef Lateef, *Yusef Lateef's Little Symphony*, Atlantic

Instrumental composition: "Call Sheet Blues," Dexter Gordon, Wayne Shorter, Herbie Hancock, Ron Carter, Billy Higgins

Classical album: *Horowitz in Moscow*, Vladimir Horowitz, Deutsche Grammophon

Orchestral recording (conductor's award): *Beethoven: Symphony No. 9 in D Minor ("Choral")*, Sir Georg Solti conducting the Chicago Symphony Orchestra, London

Opera recording: *R. Strauss: Ariadne auf Naxos*, James Levine conducting the Vienna Philharmonic (solos: Anna Tomowa-Sintow, Kathleen Battle, etc), Deutsche Grammophon

Classical performance, vocal soloist: Kathleen Battle (James Levine, accompanist), *Kathleen Battle Salzburg Recital*, Deutsche Grammophon

Classical producer: Robert Woods

Producer (other than classical): Narada Michael Walden

Performance music video: *The Prince's Trust All-Star Rock Concert*, David C. Croft, director, MGM Home Video

Concept music video: *Land of Confusion*, Genesis, John Lloyd, Jim Yukich, directors, Atlantic Video

1988

Album: *Faith*, George Michael

Record: "Don't Worry, Be Happy," Bobby McFerrin, EMI/Manhattan

Song (songwriter's award): "Don't Worry, Be Happy," Bobby McFerrin

New artist: Tracy Chapman

Pop vocal performance, male: Bobby McFerrin, "Don't Worry, Be Happy," EMI/Manhattan

Pop vocal performance, female: Tracy Chapman, "Fast Car," Elektra

Pop vocal performance by a duo or group with vocal: Manhattan Transfer, *Brasil*, Atlantic

Pop instrumental performance: David Sanborn, *Close-Ups*, Reprise

Rock vocal performance, male: Robert Palmer, "Simply Irresistible," EMI/Manhattan

Rock vocal performance, female: Tina Turner, *Tina Live in Europe*, Capitol

Rock performance by a duo or group with vocal: U2, "Desire," Island

Rock instrumental performance: Carlos Santana, *Blues For Salvador*, Columbia/CBS

Rhythm and blues song (songwriter's award): "Giving You the Best That I Got," Anita Baker, Skip Scarborough, Randy Holland

Rhythm and blues vocal performance, male: Terence Trent D'Arby, *Introducing the Hardline According to Terence Trent D'Arby*, Columbia/CBS

Rhythm and blues vocal performance, female: Anita Baker, "Giving You the Best That I Got," Elektra

Rhythm and blues vocal performance by a duo or group: Gladys Knight and the Pips, "Love Overboard," MCA

Rhythm and blues instrumental performance: Chick Corea, "Light Years," GRP

Jazz vocal performance, male: Bobby McFerrin, "Brothers," MCA

... November 12 ...

Ashley Judd and Matthew McConaughey will star in the romantic drama **Dexterity**.

Jazz vocal performance, female: Betty Carter, *Look What I Got!* Verve

Jazz vocal performance by a duo or group: Take 6, "Spread Love," Reprise

Jazz instrumental performance by a soloist: Michael Brecker, *Don't Try This at Home*, MCA-Impulse

Jazz instrumental performance by a group: McCoy Tyner, Pharoah Sanders, David Murray, Cecil McBee, Roy Haynes, *Blues For Coltrane: A Tribute to John Coltrane*, MCA-Impulse

Jazz instrumental performance by a big band: Gil Evans and the Monday Night Orchestra, *Bud and Bird*, Intersound

Jazz fusion performance: Yellowjackets, *Politics*, MCA

Country song (songwriter's award): *Hold Me*, K.T. Oslin, RCA

Country vocal performance, male: Randy Travis, *Old 8 x 10*, Warner Bros.

Country vocal performance, female: K.T. Oslin, "Hold Me," RCA

Country performance by a duo or group with vocal: Judds, "Give a Little Love," RCA

Country instrumental performance: Asleep at the Wheel, "Sugarfoot Rag," Epic

Instrumental composition: "The Theme from *L.A. Law*," Mike Post, Polydor

Classical album: *Verdi, Requiem and Operatic Choruses*, Robert Shaw conducting the Atlanta Symphony Orchestra and Chorus, Telarc

Orchestral recording (conductor's award): *Rorem: String Symphony*, Robert Shaw conducting the Atlanta Symphony Orchestra and Chorus; and *Sunday Morning, Eagles*, Louis Lane conducting the Atlanta Symphony, New World

Opera recording: *Wagner: Lohengrin*, Sir Georg Solti conducting the Vienna State Opera Choir and Vienna Philharmonic (solos: Placido Domingo, Dietrich Fischer-Dieskau, etc), London

Classical performance, vocal soloist: Luciano Pavarotti, tenor (Emerson Buckley conducting the Symphonic Orchestra of Amelia Romagna "Arturo Toscanini"), *Luciano Pavarotti in Concert*, CBS Masterworks

Classical producer: Robert Woods

Producer (other than classical): Neil Dorfsman

Performance music video: *Where the Streets Have No Name*, U2, Meiert Avis, director, Island

Concept music video: *Fat*, Weird Al Yankovic, Jay Levey, director, Rock 'n' Roll/Epic

1989

Album: *Nick of Time*, Bonnie Raitt, Capitol

Record: "Wind Beneath My Wings," Bette Midler, Atlantic

Song (songwriter's award): "Wind Beneath My Wings," Larry Henley, Jeff Silbar

New artist: Milli Vanilli (award revoked)

Pop vocal performance, male: Michael Bolton, "How Am I Supposed to Live Without You?," Columbia/CBS

Pop vocal performance, female: Bonnie Raitt, "Nick of Time," Capitol

Pop vocal performance by a duo or group with vocal: Linda Ronstadt, Aaron Neville, "Don't Know Much," Elektra

Pop instrumental performance: Neville Brothers, "Healing Chant," A&M

Rock vocal performance, male: Don Henley, *The End of the Innocence*, Geffen

Rock vocal performance, female: Bonnie Raitt, *Nick of Time*, Capitol

Rock performance by a duo or group with vocal: Travelling Wilburys, *Travelling Wilburys, Vol. 1*, Wilbury

Rock instrumental performance: Jeff Beck, Terry Bozzio, Tony Hymas, *Jeff Beck's Guitar Shop with Terry Bozzio and Tony Hymas*, Epic

Rhythm and blues song (songwriter's award): "If You Don't Know Me by Now," Kenny Gamble, Leon Huff

Rhythm and blues vocal performance, male: Bobby Brown, "Every Little Step," MCA

Rhythm and blues vocal performance, female: Anita Baker, *Giving You the Best That I Got*, Elektra

Rhythm and blues vocal performance by a duo or group: Soul II Soul, "Back to Life," Virgin

Rhythm and blues instrumental performance: Soul II Soul, "African Dance," Virgin

Jazz fusion performance: Pat Metheny Group, *Letter From Home*, Geffen

Jazz vocal performance, male: Harry Connick, Jr., *When Harry Met Sally*, Columbia/CBS

Jazz vocal performance, female: Ruth Brown, *Blues on Broadway*, Fantasy

Jazz vocal performance by a duo or group: Dr. John, Rickie Lee Jones, "Makin' Whoopee," Warner Bros.

Jazz instrumental performance by a soloist (on a jazz recording): Miles Davis, *Aura*, Columbia/CBS

Jazz instrumental performance by a group: Chick Corea Akoustic Band, *Chick Corea Akoustic Band*, GRP

Jazz instrumental performance by a big band: Miles Davis, *Aura*, Columbia/CBS

Country song (songwriter's award): "After All This Time," Rodney Crowell, Columbia

Country vocal performance, male: Lyle Lovett, *Lyle Lovett and His Large Band*, MCA

... November 13 ...

An exhibition featuring vintage photographs by helmer Monte Hellman and modernist montages by Maryse Alberti opens in the New Alchemy Art Gallery in Hollywood.

Country vocal performance, female: k.d. lang, *Absolute Torch and Twang*, Sire

Country performance by a duo or group with vocal: Nitty Gritty Dirt Band, *Will the Circle Be Unbroken?, Vol. 2*, Universal

Country instrumental performance: Randy Scruggs, Nitty Gritty Dirt Band, "Amazing Grace," Universal

Instrumental composition: "*The Batman* Theme," Danny Elfman (Sinfonia of London Orchestra), Warner Bros.

Classical album: *Bartók: 6 String Quartets*, Emerson String Quartet, Deutsche Grammophon

Orchestral performance (conductor's award): Leonard Bernstein conducting the New York Philharmonic, *Mahler: Symphony No. 3 in D Minor*, Deutsche Grammophon

Opera recording: *Wagner: Die Walküre*, James Levine conducting the Metropolitan Opera Orchestra (solos: Lakes, Moll, etc), Deutsche Grammophon

Classical performance, vocal soloist: Dawn Upshaw, soprano (David Zinman conducting the Orchestra of St. Luke's) *Knoxville: Summer of 1915*, Elektra/Nonesuch

Classical producer: Robert Woods

Producer (other than classical): Peter Asher

Music video, short form: *Leave Me Alone*, Michael Jackson, Jim Blashfield, director, Epic

Music video, long form: *Rhythm Nation*, Janet Jackson, Dominic Sena, Jonathan Dayton, Valerie Faris, directors, A&M

1990

Album: *Back on the Block*, Quincy Jones, Qwest

Record: "Another Day in Paradise," Phil Collins, Atlantic

Song (songwriter's award): "From a Distance," Julie Gold

New artist: Mariah Carey

Pop vocal performance, male: Roy Orbison, "Oh Pretty Woman," Virgin

Pop vocal performance, female: Mariah Carey, "Vision of Love," Columbia/CBS

Pop vocal performance by a duo or group with vocal: Linda Ronstadt, Aaron Neville, "All My Life," Electra

Pop instrumental performance: Angelo Badalementi, "*Twin Peaks* Theme," Warner Bros.

Rock vocal performance, male: Eric Clapton, "Bad Love," Reprise/Duck

Rock vocal performance, female: Alannah Myles, "Black Velvet," Atlantic

Rock performance by a duo or group with vocal: Aerosmith, "Janie's Got a Gun," Geffen

Rock instrumental performance: Vaughn Brothers, "D/FW," Epic Associated

Rhythm and blues song (songwriter's award): "U Can't Touch This," James Miller, M.C. Hammer

Rhythm and blues vocal performance, male: Luther Vandross, "Here and Now," Epic

Rhythm and blues vocal performance, female: Anita Baker, *Compositions*, Elektra

Rhythm and blues vocal performance by a duo or group: Ray Charles, Chaka Khan, "I'll Be Good to You," Qwest

Jazz vocal performance, male: Harry Connick, Jr., *We Are in Love*, Columbia/CBS

Jazz vocal performance, female: Ella Fitzgerald, *All That Jazz*, Pablo

Jazz instrumental performance by a soloist: Oscar Peterson, *The Legendary Oscar Peterson Trio Live at the Blue Note*, Telarc

Jazz instrumental performance by a group: Oscar Peterson, *The Legendary Oscar Peterson Trio Live at the Blue Note*, Telarc

Jazz instrumental performance by a big band: Count Basie Orchestra, "Basie's Bag," Warner Bros.

Jazz fusion performance: Quincy Jones, various artists, "Birdland," Qwest/Warner Bros.

Country song (songwriter's award): "Where've You Been?," Jon Vezner, Don Henry

Country vocal performance, male: Vince Gill, "When I Call Your Name," MCA

Country vocal performance, female: Kathy Mattea, "Where've You Been?," Mercury

Country performance by a duo or group with vocal: Kentucky Headhunters, *Pickin' on Nashville*, Mercury

Country instrumental performance: Chet Atkins, Mark Knopfler, "So Soft Your Goodbye," Columbia/CBS

Instrumental composition: "Change of Heart," Pat Metheny

Classical album: *Ives; Symphony No.2; The Gong on the Hook and Ladder (Fireman's Parade on Main Street); Central Park in the Dark; The Unanswered Question*, Leonard Bernstein conducting the New York Philharmonic, Deutsche Grammophon

Orchestral performance (conductor's award): Leonard Bernstein conducting the Chicago Symphony Orchestra, *Shostakovich: Symphonies No.1, Op. 10, and No. 7 ("Leningrad"), Op. 60*, Deutsche Grammophon

Opera recording: *Wagner: Das Rheingold*, James Levine conducting the Metropolitan Opera Orchestra (solos: Morris, Ludwig, etc), Deutsche Grammophon

---

... November 14 ...
The low-budget **Pokemon: The First Movie** earned $52.1 million
in its first five days, $32.4 million of it over the weekend.

Classical vocal performance: José Carreras, Placido Domingo, Luciano Pavarotti, tenors (Zubin Mehta conducting the Orchestra del Maggio Musicale Fiorentino and Orchestra del Teatro dell'Opera di Roma), *Carreras, Domingo, Pavarotti in Concert*, London

Classical producer: Adam Stern

Producer (other than classical): Quincy Jones

Music video, short form: *Opposites Attract*, Paula Abdul; Michael Patterson, Candice Reckinger, directors, Virgin

Music video, long form: *Please Hammer Don't Hurt 'Em, the Movie*, M.C. Hammer, Rupert Wainwright, director, Fragile Films

1991

Album: *Unforgettable*, Natalie Cole, Elektra Entertainment

Record: "Unforgettable," Natalie Cole (with Nat King Cole), Elektra

Song (songwriter's award): "Unforgettable," Irving Gordon

New artist: Marc Cohn

Pop vocal performance, male: Michael Bolton, "When a Man Loves a Woman," Columbia

Pop vocal performance, female: Bonnie Raitt, "Something to Talk About," Capitol

Pop performance by a duo or group with vocal: R.E.M., "Losing My Religion," Warner Bros.

Pop instrumental performance: Michael Kamen conducting the Greater Los Angeles Orchestra, *Robin Hood: Prince of Thieves*, Morgan Creek

Rock song (songwriter's award): "Soul Cages," Sting

Rock vocal performance, solo: Bonnie Raitt, *Luck of the Draw*, Capitol

Rock performance by a duo or group with vocal: Bonnie Raitt, Delbert McClinton, "Good Man, Good Woman," Capitol

Rock instrumental performance: Eric Johnson, "Cliffs of Dover," Capitol

Rhythm and blues song (songwriter's award): "Power of Love/Love Power," Luther Vandross, Marcus Miller, Teddy Vann

Rhythm and blues vocal performance, male: Luther Vandross, *Power of Love*, Epic

Rhythm and blues vocal performance, female (tie): Lisa Fischer, "How Can I Ease the Pain?," Electra; and Patti LaBelle, *Burnin'*, MCA

Rhythm and blues vocal performance by a duo or group: Boyz II Men, *Cooleyhighharmony*, Motown

Contemporary jazz performance (vocal or instrumental): Manhattan Transfer, "Sassy," Columbia

Jazz vocal performance: Take 6, *He Is Christmas*, Reprise

Jazz instrumental performance, solo: Stan Getz, "I Remember You," Emarcy

Jazz instrumental performance, group: Oscar Peterson Trio, *Saturday Night at the Blue Note*, Telarc

Large jazz ensemble performance: Dizzy Gillespie and the United Nation Orchestra, *Live at the Royal Festival Hall*, Enja

Country song (songwriter's award): "Love Can Build a Bridge," Naomi Judd, John Jarvis, Paul Overstreet

Country vocal performance, male: Garth Brooks, *Ropin' the Wind*, Capitol

Country vocal performance, female: Mary Chapin Carpenter, "Down at the Twist and Shout," Columbia

Country performance by a duo or group with vocal: Judds, "Love Can Build a Bridge," RCA

Country instrumental performance: Mark O'Connor, *The New Nashville Cats*, Warner Bros.

Instrumental composition: "Basque," (James Galway), Elton John

Classical album: *Bernstein: Candide*, Leonard Bernstein conducting the London Symphony Orchestra (solos: Hadley, Anderson, etc), Deutsche Grammophon

Orchestral performance (conductor's award): Daniel Barenboim conducting the Chicago Symphony Orchestra, *Corigliano: Symphony No. 1*, Erato/Elektra International Classics

Opera recording: *Wagner: Götterdämmerung*, James Levine conducting the Metropolitan Opera Orchestra and Chorus (solos: Behrens, Studer, etc), Deutsche Grammophon

Classical vocal performance: Dawn Upshaw, soprano, *The Girl With Orange Lips*, Elektra/Nonesuch

Classical producer: James Mallinson

Producer (other than classical): David Foster

Music video, short form: *Losing My Religion*, R.E.M.; Tarsem, director, Warner Bros.

Music video, long form: *Madonna: Blonde Ambition World Tour Live*, Madonna; David Mallet, Mark "Aldo" Miceli, directors, Pioneer LDCA Inc.

1992

Album: *Unplugged*, Eric Clapton, Reprise

Record: "Tears in Heaven," Eric Clapton, Reprise

Song (songwriter's award): "Tears in Heaven," Eric Clapton, Will Jennings

New artist: Arrested Development

Pop vocal performance, male: Eric Clapton, "Tears in Heaven," Reprise

---

Pop vocal performance, female: k.d. lang, "Constant Craving," WB/Sire

Pop performance by a duo or group with vocal: Celine Dion, Peabo Bryson, "Beauty and the Beast," Epic

Pop instrumental performance: Richard Kaufman conducting the Nuremberg Symphony Orchestra, "Beauty and the Beast," Varèse Sarabande

Rock song (songwriter's award): "Layla," Eric Clapton, Jim Gordon

Rock vocal performance, male: Eric Clapton, *Unplugged*, Reprise

Rock vocal performance, female: Melissa Etheridge, "Ain't It Heavy," Island

Rock performance by a duo or group with vocal: U2, *Achtung Baby*, Island

Rock instrumental performance: Stevie Ray Vaughan, Double Trouble, "Little Wing," Epic

Rhythm and blues song (songwriter's award): "The End of the Road," L.A. Reid, Babyface, Daryl Simmons

Rhythm and blues vocal performance, male: Al Jarreau, *Heaven and Earth*, Reprise

Rhythm and blues vocal performance, female: Chaka Khan, *The Woman I Am*, Warner Bros.

Rhythm and blues vocal performance by a duo or group: Boyz II Men, "The End of the Road," Motown

Rhythm and blues instrumental performance: Miles Davis, *Doo-Bop*, Warner Bros.

Contemporary jazz performance, instrumental: Pat Metheny, *Secret Story*, Geffen

Jazz vocal performance: Bobby McFerrin, "Round Midnight," Blue Note

Jazz instrumental solo: Joe Henderson, "Lush Life," Verve

Jazz instrumental performance (individual or group): Branford Marsalis, *I Heard You Twice the First Time*, Columbia

Large jazz ensemble performance: McCoy Tyner Big Band, *The Turning Point*, Verve

Country song (songwriter's award): "I Still Believe in You," Vince Gill, John Barlow Jarvis

Country vocal performance, male: Vince Gill, "I Still Believe in You," MCA

Country vocal performance, female: Mary Chapin Carpenter, "I Feel Lucky," Columbia

Country performance by a duo or group with vocal: Emmylou Harris, Nash Ramblers, *Emmylou Harris and the Nash Ramblers at the Ryman*, RCA

Country instrumental performance: Chet Atkins, Jerry Reed, *Sneakin' Around*, Columbia

Instrumental composition: "Harlem Renaissance Suite," Benny Carter

Classical album: *Mahler: Symphony No. 9*, Leonard Bernstein conducting the Berlin Philharmonic Orchestra, Deutsche Grammophon

Orchestral performance (conductor's award): Leonard Bernstein conducting the Berlin Philharmonic Orchestra, *Mahler: Symphony No. 9*, Deutsche Grammophon

Opera recording: *R. Strauss: Die Frau ohne Schatten*, Sir Georg Solti conducting the Vienna Philharmonic (solos: Domino, Varady, etc.), London

Vocal classical performance: Kathleen Battle, soprano (Margo Garett, accompanist), *Kathleen Battle at Carnegie Hall*, Deutsche Grammophon

Classical producer: Michael Fine

Producer (other than classical) (tie): Daniel Lanois, Brian Eno; and L.A. Reid, Babyface

Music video, short form: *Digging in the Dirt*, Peter Gabriel, John Downer, director, Geffen

Music video, long form: *Diva*, Annie Lennox; Sophie Muller, director, 6 West Home Video

1993

Album: *The Bodyguard* (soundtrack), Whitney Houston, Arista

Record: "I Will Always Love You," Whitney Houston, Arista

Song (songwriter's award): "A Whole New World (*Aladdin*'s Theme)," Alan Menken, Tim Rice

New artist: Toni Braxton

Pop vocal performance, male: Sting, "If I Ever Lose My Faith in You," A&M

Pop vocal performance, female: Whitney Houston, "I Will Always Love You," Arista

Pop performance by a duo or group with vocal: Peabo Bryson, Regina Belle, "A Whole New World (*Aladdin*'s Theme)," Columbia and Walt Disney

Pop instrumental performance: Bruce Hornsby, Branford Marsalis, "Barcelona Mona," RCA

Rock song (songwriter's award): "Runaway Train," David Pirner

Rock vocal performance, solo: Meat Loaf, "I'd Do Anything For Love (But I Won't Do That)," MCA

Rock performance by a duo or group with vocal: Aerosmith, "Livin' on the Edge," Geffen

Rock instrumental performance: Zappa's Universe Rock Group Featuring Steve Vai, "Sofa," Verve

Rhythm and blues song (songwriter's award): "That's the Way Love Goes," Janet Jackson, James Harris III, Terry Lewis

Rhythm and blues vocal performance, male: Ray Charles, "A Song For You," Warner Bros.

Rhythm and blues vocal performance, female: Toni Braxton, "Another Sad Love Song," La Face

...November 16...
Robert De Niro is to produce, and possibly direct and star in,
There's Something About Miranda for MGM.

Rhythm and blues vocal performance by a duo or group: Sade, "No Ordinary Love," Epic

Contemporary jazz performance, instrumental: Pat Metheny Group, *The Road to You*, Geffen

Jazz vocal performance: Natalie Cole, *Take a Look*, Elektra

Jazz instrumental solo: Joe Henderson, "Miles Ahead," Verve

Jazz instrumental performance (individual or group): Joe Henderson, *So Near, So Far (Musing For Miles)*, Verve

Large jazz ensemble performance: Miles Davis, Quincy Jones, *Miles and Quincy Live at Montreux*, Warner Bros.

Country song (songwriter's award): "Passionate Kisses," Lucinda Williams

Country vocal performance, male: Dwight Yoakam, "Ain't That Lonely Yet," Reprise

Country vocal performance, female: Mary Chapin Carpenter, "Passionate Kisses," Columbia

Country performance by a duo or group with vocal: Brooks and Dunn, "Hard Workin' Man," Arista

Country instrumental performance: Asleep at the Wheel, "Red Wing," Liberty

Instrumental composition: "Forever in Love," Kenny G.

Classical album: *Bartók: The Wooden Prince and Cantata Profana*, Pierre Boulez conducting the Chicago Symphony Orchestra and Chorus (John Aler, tenor; John Tomlison, baritone), Deutsche Grammophon

Orchestral performance (conductor's award): Pierre Boulez conducting the Chicago Symphony, *Bartók: The Wooden Prince*, Deutsche Grammophon

Opera recording: *Handel: Semele*, John Nelson conducting the English Chamber Orchestra and Ambrosian Opera Chorus (solos: Battle, Horne, etc), Philips Classics

Vocal classical performance: Arleen Auger, soprano (Joel Revzen accompanist), *The Art of Arleen Auger*, Koch International

Classical producer: Judith Sherman

Producer (other than classical): David Foster

Music video, short form: *Steam*, Peter Gabriel, Steven R. Johnson, director, Geffen

Music video, long form: *Ten Summoner's Tales*, Sting, Doug Nichol, director, A&M

1994

Album: *MTV Unplugged*, Tony Bennett, Columbia

Record: "All I Wanna Do," Sheryl Crow, A&M

Song (songwriter's award): "Streets of Philadelphia," Bruce Springsteen

New artist: Sheryl Crow

Pop vocal performance, male: Elton John, "Can You Feel the Love Tonight?," Hollywood

Pop vocal performance, female: Sheryl Crow "All I Wanna Do," A&M

Pop performance by a duo or group with vocal: All-4-One, "I Swear," Blitzz/Atlantic

Pop instrumental performance: Booker T and the MGs, *Cruisin'*, Columbia

Pop album: *Longing in Their Hearts*, Bonnie Raitt, Capitol

Rock song (songwriter's award): "Streets of Philadelphia," Bruce Springsteen

Rock vocal performance, male: Bruce Springsteen, "Streets of Philadelphia," Columbia/Epic

Rock vocal performance, female: Melissa Etheridge, "Come to My Window," Island

Rock performance by a duo or group with vocal: Aerosmith, *Crazy*, Geffen

Rock instrumental performance: Pink Floyd, "Marooned," Columbia

Rhythm and blues song (songwriter's award): "I'll Make Love to You," Babyface

Rhythm and blues vocal performance, male: Babyface, "When Can I See You?," Epic

Rhythm and blues vocal performance, female: Toni Braxton, "Breathe Again," LaFace Records

Rhythm and blues vocal performance by a duo or group: Boyz II Men, "I'll Make Love to You," Motown

Rhythm and blues album: *II*, Boyz II Men, Motown

Contemporary jazz performance: Brecker Brothers, "Out of the Loop," GRP

Jazz vocal performance: Etta James, *Mystery Lady (Songs of Billie Holiday)*, Private Music

Jazz instrumental solo: Benny Carter, "Prelude to a Kiss," MusicMasters Jazz

Jazz instrumental performance (individual or group): Ron Carter, Herbie Hancock, Wallace Roney, Wayne Shorter, Tony Williams, *A Tribute to Miles*, Reprise/Qwest

Large jazz ensemble performance: McCoy Tyner Big Band, *Journey*, Birdology/Verve

Country song (songwriter's award): "I Swear," Gary Baker, Frank J. Myers

Country album: *Stones in the Road*, Mary Chapin Carpenter, Columbia

Country vocal performance, male: Vince Gill, "When Love Finds You," MCA

Country vocal performance, female: Mary Chapin Carpenter, "Shut Up and Kiss Me," Columbia

Country performance by a duo or group with vocal: Asleep at the Wheel, Lyle Lovett, "Blues for Dixie," Liberty

---

Country instrumental performance: Chet Atkins, "Young Thing," Columbia

Instrumental composition: "African Skies," Michael Brecker

Classical album: *Bartók: Concerto for Orchestra: 4 Orchestral Pieces, Op. 12*, Pierre Boulez conducting the Chicago Symphony Orchestra, Deutsche Grammophon

Orchestral performance (conductor's award): Pierre Boulez conducting the Chicago Symphony Orchestra, *Bartók: Concerto for Orchestra: 4 Orchestral Pieces, Op. 12*, Deutsche Grammophon

Opera recording: *Floyd: Susannah*, Kent Nagano conducting the Orchestra of the Opéra de Lyon (solos: Jerry Hadley, Samuel Ramey, etc), Virgin Classics

Classical vocal performance: Cecilia Bartoli, *The Impatient Lover*, London

Classical producer: Andrew Cornall

Producer (other than classical): Don Was

Music video, short form: *Love Is Strong*, Rolling Stones, David Fincher, director, Virgin

Music video, long form: *Zoo TV – Live from Sydney*, U2, David Mallet, director, Polygram Video

1995

Album: *Jagged Little Pill*, Alanis Morissette, Maverick/Reprise

Record: "Kiss From a Rose," Seal, ZTT/Sire/Warner Bros.

Song (songwriter's award): "Kiss From a Rose," Seal

New artist: Hootie and the Blowfish

Pop album: *Turbulent Indigo*, Joni Mitchell, Reprise

Pop vocal performance, male: Seal, "Kiss From a Rose," ZTT/Sire/Warner Bros.

Pop vocal performance, female: Annie Lennox, "No More 'I Love You's,'" Arista

Pop performance by a duo or group with vocal: Hootie and the Blowfish, "Let Her Cry," Atlantic

Pop instrumental performance: Los Lobos, "Mariachi Suite," Epic Soundtrax

Rock album: *Jagged Little Pill*, Alanis Morissette, Maverick/Reprise

Rock song (songwriter's award): "You Oughta Know," Glen Ballard, Alanis Morissette

Rock vocal performance, male: Tom Petty, "You Don't Know How It Feels," Warner Bros.

Rock vocal performance, female: Alanis Morissette, "You Oughta Know," Maverick/Reprise

Rock performance by a duo or group with vocal: Blues Traveller, "Run-Around," A&M

Rock instrumental performance: Allman Brothers Band, "Jessica," Epic

Rhythm and blues album: *Crazysexycool*, TLC, LaFace

Rhythm and blues song (songwriter's award): "For Your Love," Stevie Wonder

Rhythm and blues vocal performance, male: Stevie Wonder, "For Your Love," Motown

Rhythm and blues vocal performance, female: Anita Baker, "I Apologize," Elektra

Rhythm and blues vocal performance by a duo or group: TLC, "Creep," LaFace

Rhythm and blues instrumental performance: Miles Davis, *Doo-Bop*, Warner Bros.

Contemporary jazz performance: Pat Metheny Group, *We Live Here*, Geffen

Jazz vocal performance: Lena Horne, *An Evening With Lena Horne*, Blue Note

Jazz instrumental solo: Michael Brecker, "Impressions," Impulse!

Jazz instrumental performance (individual or group): McCoy Tyner Trio Featuring Michael Brecker, *Infinity*, Impulse!

Large jazz ensemble performance: GRP All-Stars Big Band, Tom Scott, *All Blues*, GRP

Country album: *The Woman in Me*, Shania Twain, Mercury Nashville

Country song (songwriter's award): "Go Rest High on That Mountain," Vince Gill

Country vocal performance, male: Vince Gill, "Go Rest High on That Mountain," MCA

Country vocal performance, female: Alison Krauss, "Baby, Now That I've Found You," Rounder

Country performance by a duo or group with vocal: Mavericks, "Here Comes the Rain," MCA

Country instrumental performance: Asleep at the Wheel, "Hightower," Capitol Nashville

Instrumental composition: "A View From the Side," Bill Holman

Classical album: *Debussy: La Mer; Nocturnes; Jeux; etc.*, Pierre Boulez conducting the Cleveland Orchestra, Cleveland Orchestra Choir, Franklin Cohen, clarinet, Deutsche Grammophon

Orchestral performance (conductor's award): Pierre Boulez conducting the Cleveland Orchestra, *Debussy: La Mer*, Deutsche Grammophon

Opera recording: *Berlioz: Les Troyens*, Charles Dutoit conducting the Montreal Symphony Orchestra, (solos: Lakes, Pollet, etc), London

Classical vocal performance: Sylvia McNair, soprano (Christopher Hogwood conducting the Academy of Ancient Music), Philips Classics

Classical producer: Steven Epstein

Producer (other than classical): Babyface

Music video, short form: *Scream*, Michael Jackson, Janet Jackson, Mark Romanek, director, Epic

---

... November 18 ...
Screenwriter actress Carrie Fisher has signed on with Digital Entertainment Network to pen two columns.

Music video, long form: *Secret World Live*, Peter Gabriel, François Girard, director, Geffen Home Video

1996

Album: *Falling Into You*, Celine Dion, 550 Music/Epic
Record: "Change the World," Eric Clapton, Reprise
Song (songwriter's award): "Change the World," Gordon Kennedy, Wayne Kirkpatrick, Tommy Sims
New artist: LeAnn Rimes
Pop vocal performance, male: Eric Clapton, "Change the World," Reprise
Pop vocal performance, female: Toni Braxton, "Unbreak My Heart," LaFace
Pop performance by a duo or group with vocal: Beatles, "Free As a Bird," Capitol
Pop instrumental performance: Bela Fleck and the Flecktones, "The Sinister Minister," Warner Bros.
Rock vocal performance, male: Beck, "Where It's At," DGC
Rock vocal performance, female: Sheryl Crow, "If It Makes You Happy," A&M
Rock performance by a duo or group with vocal: Dave Matthews Band, "So Much to Say," RCA
Rock instrumental performance: Jimmie Vaughan, Eric Clapton, Bonnie Raitt, Robert Cray, B.B. King, Buddy Guy, Dr. John and Art Neville, "SRV Shuffle," Epic
Rhythm and blues album: *Words*, Tony Rich Project, LaFace
Rhythm and blues song (songwriter's award): "Exhale (Shoop Shoop)," Babyface
Rhythm and blues vocal performance, male: Luther Vandross, "Your Secret Love," Epic/LV
Rhythm and blues vocal performance, female: Toni Braxton, "You're Makin' Me High," LaFace
Rhythm and blues performance by a duo or group with vocal: Fugees, "Killing Me Softly With His Song," Ruffhouse/Columbia
Contemporary jazz performance: Wayne Shorter, *High Life*, Verve
Jazz vocal performance: Cassandra Wilson, *New Moon Daughter*, Blue Note
Jazz instrumental solo: Michael Brecker, "Cabin Fever," Impulse
Jazz instrumental performance (individual or group): Michael Brecker, *Tales From the Hudson*, Impulse
Large jazz ensemble performance: Count Basie Orchestra, *Live at Manchester Craftsmen's Guild*, Jazz MCG
Country album: *The Road to Ensenada*, Lyle Lovett, Curb/MCA

Country song (songwriter's award): "Blue," Bill Mack
Country vocal performance, male: Vince Gill, "Worlds Apart," MCA
Country vocal performance, female: LeAnn Rimes, "Blue," MCG/Curb
Country performance by a duo or group with vocal: Brooks and Dunn, "My Maria," Arista/Nashville
Country instrumental performance: Chet Atkins C.G.P., "Jam Man," Columbia Records
Instrumental composition: "Manhattan (Island of Lights and Love)," Herbie Hancock, Jean Hancock
Classical album: *Corigliano: Of Rage and Remembrance (Symphony No. 1, etc.)*, Leonard Slatkin conducting the National Symphony Orchestra, Male Choir of the Oratorio Society of Washington, D.C., Male Chorus of the Choral Arts Society of Washington, RCA Victor Red Seal
Orchestral performance (conductor's award): Michael Tilson Thomas conducting the San Francisco Symphony, *Prokofiev: Romeo and Juliet (Scenes from the Ballet)*, RCA Victor Red Seal
Opera recording: *Britten: Peter Grimes*, Richard Hickox conducting the London Opera, London Symphony Chorus and City of London Sinfonia (solos: Langridge, Opie, Watson), Chandos
Classical vocal performance: Bryn Terfel, bass-baritone (James Levine conducting the Metropolitan Opera Orchestra), *Opera Arias*, Deutsche Grammophon
Classical producer: Joanna Nickrenz
Producer (other than classical): Babyface
Music video, short form: "Free As a Bird," Beatles, Kevin Godley, director, Capitol
Music video, long form: *The Beatles Anthology*, Beatles, Geoff Wonfor, director, Capitol Video/Turner Home Entertainment

1997

Album: *Time Out of Mind*, Bob Dylan, Columbia
Record: "Sunny Came Home," Shawn Colvin, Columbia
Song (songwriter's award): "Sunny Came Home," Shawn Colvin, John Leventhal
New artist: Paula Cole
Pop album: *Hourglass*, James Taylor, Columbia
Pop vocal performance, male: Elton John, "Candle in the Wind 1997," Rocket
Pop vocal performance, female: Sarah McLachlan, "Building a Mystery," Epic
Pop performance by a duo, or group with vocal: Jamiroquai "Virtual Insanity," Work Group
Pop collaboration with vocal: John Lee Hooker, Van Morrison, "Don't Look Back," Pointblank/Virgin

---

... **November 19** ...
Broadway's **Death Of A Salesman** revival marks its 300th and final performance with a taping for Showtime.

Traditional pop vocal performance: Tony Bennett, *Tony Bennett on Holiday*, Columbia

Pop instrumental performance: Sarah McLachlan, "Last Dance," Arista

Dance recording: "Carry on," Donna Summer, Giorgio Moroder, Interhit

Rock album: *Blue Moon Swamp*, John Fogerty, Warner Bros.

Rock song (songwriter's award): "One Headlight," Jacob Dylan

Rock vocal performance, male: Bob Dylan, "Cold Irons Bound," Columbia

Rock vocal performance, female: Fiona Apple, "Criminal," Work Group

Pop performance by a duo, or group with vocal: Wallflowers, "One Headlight," Interscope

Rock instrumental performance: Chemical Brothers, "Block Rockin' Beats," Astralwerks

Hard rock performance: Rage Against the Machine, "People of the Sun," Epic

Metal performance: Tool, "Aenema," Zoo/Volcano

Alternative music performance: Radiohead, *OK Computer*, Capitol

Rhythm and blues album: *Baduizm*, Erykah Badu, Kedar/Universal

Rhythm and blues song (songwriter's award): "I Believe I Can Fly," R. Kelly

Rhythm and blues vocal performance, male: R. Kelly, "I Believe I Can Fly," Jive/Atlantic/Warner Sunset

Rhythm and blues vocal performance, female: Erykah Badu, "On and on," Kedar/Universal

Rhythm and blues performance by a duo or group with vocal: Blackstreet, "No Diggity," Interscope

Rap album: *No Way Out*, Puff Daddy and the Family, Bad Boy

Rap solo performance: Will Smith, "Men in Black," Columbia/Sony

Rap performance by a duo or group: Puff Daddy and Faith Evans Featuring 112, "I'll Be Missing You," Bad Boy

Contemporary jazz performance: Randy Brecker *Into the Sun*, Concord Vista

Jazz vocal performance: Dee Dee Bridgewater, *Dear Ella*, Verve

Jazz instrumental solo: Doc Cheatham, Nicholas Payton, "Stardust," Verve

Jazz instrumental performance (individual or group): Charlie Haden, Pat Metheny, *Beyond the Missouri Sky*, Verve

Large jazz ensemble performance: Joe Henderson Big Band, *Joe Henderson Big Band*, Verve

Latin jazz performance: Roy Hargrove's Crisol, *Habana*, Verve

Country album: *Unchained*, Johnny Cash, American

Country song (songwriter's award): "Butterfly Kisses," Bob Carlisle, Randy Thomas

Country vocal performance, male: Vince Gill, "Pretty Little Adriana," MCA Nashville

Country vocal performance, female: Trisha Yearwood, "How Do I Live?," MCA Nashville

Country performance by a duo or group with vocal: Alison Krauss and Union Station, "Looking in the Eyes of Love," Rounder

Country collaboration with vocal: Trisha Yearwood, Garth Brooks, "In Another's Eyes," MCA Nashville

Country instrumental performance: Alison Krauss and Union Station, "Little Liza Jane," Rounder

Rock gospel album: *Welcome to the Freak Show*, DC Talk, ForeFront

Pop/contemporary gospel album: *Much Afraid*, Jars of Clay, Silvertone/Essential

Southern, country or bluegrass gospel album: *Amazing Grace 2: A Country Salute to Gospel*, various artists, Sparrow

Traditional soul gospel album: *I Couldn't Hear Nobody Pray*, Fairfield Four, Warner Bros, Nashville

Contemporary soul gospel album: *Brothers*, Take 6, Warner-Alliance

Gospel album by a choir of chorus: *God's Property From Kirk Franklin's Nu Nation*, God's Property; Kirk Franklin, choir director, B-Rite

Traditional folk album: *L'Amour ou la folie*, BeauSoleil, Rhino

Contemporary folk album: *Time Out of Mind*, Bob Dylan, Columbia

Traditional blues album: *Don't Look Back*, John Lee Hooker, Pointblank/Virgin

Contemporary blues album: *Señor Blues*, Taj Mahal, Private Music

Bluegrass album: *So Long So Wrong*, Alison Krauss and Union Station, Rounder

Latin pop performance: Luis Miguel, *Romance*, WEA Latina

Latin rock/alternative performance: Los Fabulosos Cadillacs, *Fabulosos Calavera*, BMG U.S. Latin

Tropical Latin performance: Ry Cooder, *Buena Vista Social Club*, World Circuit/Nonesuch

Mexican-American/Tejano music performance: La Mafia, *En tus Manos*, Sony Discos

Reggae album: *Fallen Is Babylon*, Ziggy Marley and the Melody Makers, Elektra/EEG

Polka album: *Living on Polka Time*, Jimmy Sturr, Rounder

New age album: *Oracle*, Michael Hedges, Windham Hill

... November 20 ...
Sophia Loren (65) was voted the most beautiful woman
in the world in a poll carried out by a cosmetics firm.

World music album: *Nascimento*, Milton Nascimento, Warner Bros.

Instrumental arrangement: Bill Holman, "Straight, No Chaser," (Bill Holman Band), JVC Music

Instrumental composition (composer's award): "Aung San Suu Kyi," Wayne Shorter

Musical show album: *Chicago, New Broadway Cast*, Fred Ebb, lyricist, John Kander, composer, RCA Victor

Instrumental composition written for a motion picture or TV (composer's award): "The English Patient," Gabriel Yared

Song written specifically for a motion picture or TV: "I Believe I Can Fly," R. Kelly (*Space Jam*)

Instrumental arrangement accompanying vocal(s): Slide Hampton, "Cotton Tail," (Dee Dee Bridgewater), Verve

Classical album: *Premieres – Cello Concertos (Works of Danielpour, Kirchner, Rouse)*, Yo-Yo Ma, violoncello, David Zinman conducting the Philadelphia Orchestra, Sony Classical

Orchestral performance (conductor's award): Pierre Boulez conducting the Cleveland Orchestra and Chorus, *Berlioz: Symphonie Fantastique, Tristia*, Deutsche Grammophon

Chamber music performance: Emerson String Quartet, *Beethoven: The String Quartets*, Deutsche Grammophon

Small ensemble performance (with or without conductor): Claudio Abbado conducting members of the Berliner Philharmonic, "Hindemith: Kammermusik No. 1 with Finale 1921, Op. 24, No., 1," track from *Hindemith: Kammermusik Nos. 1,4 and 5*, EMI Classics

Classical performance, instrumental soloist(s) (with orchestra): Yo-Yo Ma, violoncello (David Zinman conducting the Philadelphia Orchestra) *Premieres – Cello Concertos, (Works of Danielpour, Kirchner, Rouse)*, Sony Classical

Classical performance, instrumental soloist(s) (without orchestra): Janos Starker, cello, *Bach: Suites for Solo Cello Nos. 1–6*, RCA Victor Red Seal

Opera recording: *Wagner: Die Meistersinger von Nürnberg*, Sir Georg Solti conducting the Chicago Symphony Orchestra and Chorus, (solos: Lippert, Mattila, etc), London

Choral performance: Robert Shaw conducting the Atlanta Symphony Orchestra and Chorus, *Adams: Harmonium; Rachmaninov: The Bells*, Telarc

Classical vocal performance: Cecilia Bartoli, mezzo-soprano (James Levine, piano), *An Italian Songbook (Works of Bellini, Donizetti, Rossini)*, London

Contemporary composition: "El Dorado," John Adams

Engineered recording, classical: Michael Bishop, Jack Renner, *Copland: The Music of America*, Telarc

Classical producer: Stephen Epstein

Spoken comedy album: *Roll With the New*, Chris Rock, DreamWorks

Spoken word or nonmusical album: *Charles Kuralt's Spring*, Charles Kuralt, Simon and Schuster Audioworks

Musical album for children: *All Aboard!* John Denver, Sony Wonder

Spoken word album for children: *Winnie the Pooh*, Charles Kuralt (A.A. Milne), Penguin Audiobooks

Engineered album (other than classical): Frank Filipetti, *Hourglass* (James Taylor), Columbia

Remixer: Frankie Knuckles

Recording package (art director's award): Hugh Brown, Al Q, Jeff Smith, *Titanic: Music as Heard on the Fateful Voyage* (various artists), Rhino

Recording package, boxed (art director's award): Hugh Brown, David Gorman, Rachel Gutek, *Beg, Scream and Shout! The Big Ol' Box of '60s Soul* (various artists), Rhino

Album notes (annotator's award): John Fahey, Luis Kemnitzer, Jon Pankake, Chuck Pirtle, Jeff Place, Neil V. Rosenberg, Luc Sante, Peter Stampfel, Eric Von Schmidt, *Anthology of American Folk Music (1997 Edition Expanded)*, Smithsonian Folkways

Historical album: *Anthology of American Folk Music (1997 Edition Expanded)* (various artists), Smithsonian Folkways

Producer (other than classical): Babyface

Music video, short form: *Got Till It's Gone*, Janet Jackson, Mark Romanek, director, Virgin

Music video, long form: *Jagged Little Pill*, Alanis Morissette, Alanis Morissette, Steve Purcell, directors, Warner/Reprise Video/Maverick

1998

Record: "My Heart Will Go on," Celine Dion, 550 Music/Sony Classical

Album: *The Miseducation of Lauryn Hill*, Lauryn Hill, Ruffhouse/Columbia Records

Song (songwriters' award): "My Heart Will Go on," James Horner and Will Jennings

New artist: Lauryn Hill

Pop vocal performance, male: Eric Clapton, "My Father's Eyes," Reprise Records

Pop vocal performance, female: Celine Dion, "My Heart Will Go on," 550 Music/Sony Classical

Pop performance by a duo or group with vocal: The Brian Setzer Orchestra, "Jump Jive an' Wail," Interscope Records

Pop collaboration with vocals: Elvis Costello and Burt Bacharach, "I Still Have That Other Girl," Mercury Records

Pop instrumental performance: The Brian Setzer Orchestra, "Sleepwalk," Interscope Records

Dance recording: "Ray of Light," Madonna, Maverick/Warner Bros. Records

Pop album: *Ray of Light*, Madonna, Maverick/Warner Bros. Records

Traditional pop vocal performance: Patti Page, "Live at Carnegie Hall - The 50th Anniversary Concert," DRG Records

Female rock vocal performance: Alanis Morissette, "Uninvited," Warner Sun-set/Reprise Records

Male rock vocal performance: Lenny Kravitz, "Fly Away," Virgin Records America

Rock performance by a duo or group with vocal: Aerosmith, "Pink," Columbia

Hard rock performance: Jimmy Page and Robert Plant, "Most High, "Atlantic

Metal performance: Metallica, "Better Than You," Elektra/EEG

Rock instrumental performance: Pat Metheny Group, "The Roots of Confidence," Warner Bros

Rock song (songwriter's award): "Uninvited," Alanis Morissette

Rock album: *The Globe Sessions*, Sheryl Crow, A&M

Alternative music performance: Beastie Boys, *Hello Nasty*, Grand Royal/Capitol

Rhythm and blues vocal performance, male: Stevie Wonder, "St. Louis Blues," Verve

Rhythm and blues vocal performance, female: Lauryn Hill, "Doo Wop (That Thing)," Ruffhouse/Columbia

Rhythm and blues performance by a duo or group with vocal: Brandy and Monica, "The Boy Is Mine," Atlantic and Arista

Rhythm and blues song (songwriter's award): "Doo Wop (That Thing)," Lauryn Hill

Rhythm and blues album: *The Miseducation of Lauryn Hill*, Lauryn Hill, Ruffhouse/Columbia

Traditional rhythm and blues vocal performance (albums only): Patti LaBelle, Live! One Night Only, (MCA)

Rap solo performance: Will Smith, "Gettin' Jiggy Wit It," Columbia

Rap performance by a duo or group: Beastie Boys, "Intergalactic," Grand Royal

Rap album: *Vol. 2 Hard Knock Life*, Jay-Z; Joe Quinde, engineer/mixer, Roc-A-Fella/Def Jam

Country vocal performance, male: Vince Gill, "If You Ever Have Forever in Mind," MCA Nashville

Country vocal performance, female: Shania Twain, "You're Still the One," Mercury Records Nashville

Country performance by a duo or group with vocal: Dixie Chicks, "There's Your Trouble," Monument Records

Country collaboration with vocals: Clint Black, Joe Diffie, Merle Haggard, Emmylou Harris, Alison Krauss, Patty Loveless, Earl Scruggs, Ricky Skaggs, Marty Stuart, Pam Tillis, Randy Travis, Travis Tritt and Dwight Yoakam, "Same Old Train," Columbia Nashville

Country instrumental performance: Randy Scruggs and Vince Gill, "A Soldier's Joy," Reprise

Country song (songwriter's award): "You're Still the One," Shania Twain

Country album: *Wide Open Spaces*, Dixie Chicks, Monument Records

Bluegrass album of the year: *Bluegrass Rules!*, Ricky Skaggs and Kentucky Thunder, Rounder/Skaggs Family Records

New age album: *Landmarks*, Clannad, Atlantic Records

Contemporary jazz performance: Pat Metheny Group, "Imaginary Day," Warner Bros. Records

Jazz vocal performance: Shirley Horn, "I Remember Miles," Verve

Jazz instrumental solo: Chick Corea and Gary Burton, "Rhumbata," Stretch Records

Jazz instrumental instrumental performance (individual or group): Herbie Hancock, "Gershwin's World," Verve

Large jazz ensemble performance: Count Basie Orchestra, "Count Plays Duke," MAMA Records

Latin jazz performance: Arturo Sandoval, "Hot House," N2K Encoded Music

Rock gospel album: *You Are There*, Ashley Cleveland, Cadence/204 Records

Pop contemporary gospel album: *This Is My Song*, Deniece Williams, Harmony Records

Southern, country of bluegrass gospel album: *The Apostle – Music From and Inspired by the Motion Picture*, Various Artists: Peter Afterman, John Huie and Ken Levitan, MCA

Traditional soul gospel album: *He Leadeth Me*, Cissy Houston, House of Blues Music

Contemporary soul gospel album: *The Nu Nation Project*, Kirk Franklin, Gospo Centric Records

Gospel album by a choir or chorus: *Reflections*, The Associates, Warner Alliance Records

Latin pop performance: Ricky Martin, "Vuelve," Sony Latin

Latin rock/alternative performance: Mana, "Suenos Liquidos," WEA Latina

Tropical Latin performance: Marc Anthony, "Contra La Corriente," RMM Records

Mexican-American music performance: Los Super Seven, "Los Super Seven," RCA Records Nashville

Tejano music performance: Flaco Jimenez, "Said and Done," Barb Wire Productions/Virgin Records America

Traditional blues album: *Any Place I'm Going*, Otis Rush, House Of Blues Records

Contemporary blues album: *Slow Down*, Keb' Mo', Okeh/550 Music

Traditional folk album: *Long Journey Home*, The Chieftains With Various Artists, Wicklow Records

Contemporary folk album: *Car Wheels on a Gravel Road*, Lucinda Williams, Mercury Records

Reggae album: Friends, Sly and Robbie, EastWest Records America/EEG

World music album: *Quanta Live*, Gilberto Gil, Atlantic/Mesa Records

Polka album: *Dance With Me*, Jimmy Sturr and His Orchestra, Rounder Records

Musical album for children: *Elmopalooza!* The Sesame Street Muppets With Various Artists, Sony Wonder Records)

Spoken word album for children: *The Children's Shakespeare*, Various artists including Jim Belushi, Linda Hamilton, etc., Dove Audio

Spoken word album: *Still Me*, Christopher Reeve, Random House Audio Books

Spoken comedy album: *The 2000 Year Old Man in the Year 2000*, Mel Brooks and Carl Reiner, Rhino Records

Musical show album: *The Lion King*, Lebo M, Mark Mancina, Tim Rice, Jay Rifkin, Julie Taymor and Hans Zimmer, lyricists; Elton John, Lebo M, Mark Mancina, Jay Rifkin and Hans Zimmer, composers, Walt Disney Records

Instrumental composition (composer's award): "Almost 12," Bela Fleck, Future Man and Victor Lemonte Wooten, Warner Bros. Records

Instrumental composition written for a motion picture or for television (composer's award): "Saving Private Ryan," John Williams, DreamWorks Records

Song written for a motion picture or for television (songwriter's award): "My Heart Will Go on," (From Titanic) – James Horner and Will Jennings, 550 Music and Sony Classical

Instrumental arrangement: Don Sebesky, "Waltz For Debby," RCA Victor

Instrumental arrangement with accompanying vocal(s): Herbie Hancock, Robert Sadin and Stevie Wonder, "St. Louis Blues," Verve

Recording package: Kevin Reagan, art director, "Ray of Light" (Madonna) Maverick/Warner Bros. Records

Boxed recording package: Jim Kemp and Virginia Team, art directors, "The Complete Hank Williams" (Hank Williams) Mercury Records Nashville

Album notes: Bob Belden, Todd Coolman and Michael Cuscuna, album notes writers, *Miles Davis Quintet 1965–1968* (Miles Davis Quintet), Columbia/Legacy Records

Historical album: *The Complete Hank Williams*, Colin Escott and Kira Florita, compilation, Mercury Records Nashville

Engineered album, non-classical: Tchad Blake, Trina Shoemaker and Andy Wallace, engineers, *The Globe Sessions*, (Sheryl Crow) A&M

Producer of the year: Rob Cavallo

Remixer of the year, non-classical: David Morales

Engineered album, classical: "Barber: Prayers of Kierkegaard/Vaughan Williams: Dona Nobis Pacem/Bartok: Cantata Profana" – Jack Renner, engineer (Robert Shaw, conductor) Telarc

Producer of the year, classical: Steven Epstein

Classical album: *Barber: Prayers of Kierkegaard/Vaughan Williams: Dona Nobis Pacem/Bartok: Cantata Profana*, Robert Shaw, conductor; James Mallinson, producer; Richard Clement, tenor; Nathan Gunn, baritone; Carmen Pelton, soprano; Atlanta Symphony Orchestra Choir; Atlanta Symphony Orchestra, Telarc

Orchestral performance (award to conductor and orchestra): Pierre Boulez, conducting Chicago Symphony Orchestra, *Mahler: Sym. No. 9*, Deutsche Grammophon

Opera recording: *Bartok: Bluebeard's Castle*, Pierre Boulez conducting Chicago Symphony Orchestra, Deutsche Grammophon

Choral performance: Robert Shaw conducting Atlanta Symphony Orchestra Choir, *Barber: Prayers of Kierkegaard/Vaughan Williams: Dona Nobis Pacem/Bartok: Cantata Profana*, Telarc

Instrumental soloist performance (with orchestra): Anne-Sophie Mutter, violin, Kryzysztof Penderecki conducting London Symphony Orchestra, *Prenderecki: Violin Con. No. 2 Metamorphosen*, Deutsche Grammophon

Instrumental soloist performance (without orchestra): Murray Perahia, piano, *Bach: English Suites Nos. 1, 3 & 6*, Sony Classical

Chamber music performance: Andre Previn, piano; Gil Shaham, violin, *American Scenes* (Works of Copland, Previn, Barber, Gershwin), Deutsche Grammophon

Small ensemble performance (with or without conductor): Steve Reich and Musicians, "Reich: Music for 18 Musicians," Nonesuch

---

... November 23 ...
Besting a record 1994 tally, 47 nations have submitted pics for
Oscar consideration as 1999's Best Foreign-language Film.

Classical vocal performance: Renee Fleming, soprano (Jeffrey Tate, conductor; English Chamber Orchestra), *The Beautiful Voice* (Works of Charpentier, Gounod, Massenet, Flotow, etc.) London

Classical contemporary composition: "Penderecki: Violin Con. No. 2 Metamorphosen," Krzysztof Penderecki

Classical crossover album: *Soul of the Tango - The Music of Astor Piazzolla*, Libertango; Mumuki; Milonga Del Angel, etc., Yo-Yo Ma, cello; Jorge Calandrelli, conductor, Sony Classical

Music video, short form: *Ray of Light*, Madonna; Jonas Akerlund, video director, Maverick/Warner Bros. Records

Music video, long form: *Rock and Roll Heart*, Lou Reed; Timothy Greenfield-Sanders, video director, Fox Lorber Associates, Inc./WinStar Home Entertainment

1999

Record: "Smooth," Santana, Arista Records

Album: *Supernatural*, Santana, Arista Records

Song (songwriters' award): "Smooth," Santana

New artist: Christina Aguilera

Pop vocal performance, female: Sarah McLachlan, "I Will Remember You," Arista Records

Pop vocal performance, male: Sting, "Brand New Day," A&M Records

Pop performance by a duo or group with vocal: Santana, "Maria Maria," Arista Records

Pop collaboration with vocals: Santana, "Smooth," Arista Records

Pop instrumental performance: Santana, "El Farol," Arista Records

Pop Dance recording: "Believe," Brian Rawling & Mark Taylor, producers/mixers

Pop album: *Brand New Day*, Sting, A&M Records

Traditional pop vocal performance: Tony Bennett, "Bennet Sings Ellington – Hot & Cool," RPM Records/Columbia

Female rock vocal performance: Sheryl Crow, "Sweet Child of Mine," C2 Records/Sony Music Soundtrax

Male rock vocal performance: Lenny Kravitz, "American Woman," Maverick Records

Rock performance by a duo or group with vocal: Santana, "Put Your Lights on," Arista Records

Hard rock performance: Metallica, "Whiskey in the Jar," Elektra Entertainment Group

Metal performance: Black Sabbath, "Iron Man," Epic Records

Rock instrumental performance: Santana, "The Calling," Arista Records

Rock song: "Scar Tissue," Red Hot Chili Peppers

Rock album: *Supernatural*, Santana, Arista Records

Alternative music performance: Beck, *Mutations*, DGC Records

Rhythm and blues vocal performance, female: Whitney Houston, "It's Not Right But It's OK," Arista Records

Rhythm and blues vocal performance, male: Barry White, "Staying Power," Private Music

Rhythm and blues performance by a duo or group with vocal: TLC, "No Scrubs," LaFace Records

Rhythm and blues song: "No Scrubs," TLC

Rhythm and blues album: *Fanmail*, TLC, LaFace Records

Traditional rhythm and blues vocal performance: Barry White, "Staying Power," Private Music

Rap solo performance: Eminem, "My Name Is," Aftermath/Interscope Records

Rap performance by a duo or group: The Roots, "You Got Me," MCA Records

Rap album: *The Slim Shady LP*, Eminem, Aftermath/Interscope Records

Country vocal performance, female: Shania Twain, "Man! I Feel Like a Woman!", Mercury Records Nashville

Country vocal performance, male: George Jones, "Choices," Asylum Records

Country performance by a duo or group with vocal: Dixie Chicks, "Ready to Run," Monument Records and Columbia/Sony Music Soundtrax

Country collaboration with vocals: Emmylou Harris, Linda Ronstadt & Dolly Parton, "After the Gold Rush," Asylum Records

Country instrumental performance: Asleep at the Wheel, "Bob's Breakdowns," DreamWorks Records Nashville

Country song: "Come on Over," Shania Twain

Country album: *Fly*, Dixie Chicks, Monument Records

Bluegrass album of the year: *Ancient Tones*, Ricky Skaggs and Kentucky Thunder, Skaggs Family Records

New age album: *Celtic Solistice*, Paul Winter & Friends, Living Music

Contemporary jazz performance: David Sanborn, "Inside," Elektra Entertainment Group

Jazz vocal performance: Diana Krall, "When I Look in Your Eyes," Verve

Jazz instrumental solo: Wayne Shorter, "In Walked Wayne," Verve

Jazz instrumental performance (individual or group): Gary Burton, Chick Corea, Pat Metheny, Roy Haynes & Dave Holland, "Like Minds," Concord Jazz

---

...November 24...
Le Studio Canal Plus has officially committed to fully financing the Good Machine picture **Human Nature**.

Large jazz ensemble performance: The Bob Florence Limited Edition, "Serendipity 18," MAMA Records

Latin jazz performance: Poncho Sanchez, "Latin Soul," Concord Picante Records

Rock gospel album: *Pray*, Rebecca St. James, ForeFront Records

Pop contemporary gospel album: *Speechless*, Steven Curtis Chapman, Sparrow Records

Southern, country or bluegrass gospel album: *Kennedy Center Homecoming*, Bill & Gloria Gaither and Their Homecoming Friends, Spring House Music Group

Traditional soul gospel album: *Christmas With Shirley Caesar*, Shirley Caesar, Myrrh Records

Contemporary soul gospel album: *Mountain High ... Valley Low*, Yolanda Adams, Elektra Entertainment Group

Gospel album by a choir or chorus: *High & Lifted Up*, The Brooklyn Tabernacle Choir, Atlantic Records

Latin pop performance: Rubeen Blades, "Tiempos," Sony Discos

Latin rock/alternative performance: Chris Perez Band, "Resurrection," Hollywood Records

Traditional tropical Latin performance: Tito Puente, "Mambo Birdland," RMM Records

Salsa performance: Los Van Van, "Llego ... Van Van: Van Van Is Here," Havana Caliente/Atlantic Records

Merengue performance: Elvis Crespo, "Pintame," Sony Tropical Records

Mexican-American performance: Plácido Domingo, "100 Años de Mariachi," EMI Latin/Saragoza

Tejano music performance: Los Palominos, "Por eso te amo," Sony Discos

Traditional blues album: *Blues on the Bayou*, B.B. King, MCA Records

Contemporary blues album: *Take Your Shoes Off*, The Robert Cray Band, Rykodisc

Traditional folk album: *Press on*, June Carter Cash, Risk/Small Hairy Dog Records

Contemporary folk album: *Mule Variations*, Tom Waits, Anti/Epitaph Records

Reggae album: *Calling Rastafari*, Burning Spear, Heartbeat Records

World music album: *Livro*, Caetano Veloso, Nonesuch Records

Polka album: *Polkasonic*, Brave Combo, Cleveland International Records

Musical album for children: *The Adventures of Elmo in Goruchland*, various artists, Sony Wonder

Spoken word album for children: *Listen to the Storyteller*, Wynton Marsalis, Graham Greene & Kate Winslet, Steven Epstein & David Frost, producers, Sony Classical

Spoken word album: *The Autobiography of Martin Luther King, Jr.*, LeVar Burton (with Martin Luther King, Jr.), time Warner Audiobooks

Spoken comedy album: *Bigger & Blacker*, Chris Rock, DreamWorks Records

Musical show album: *Annie Get Your Gun*, Stephen Ferrera & John McDaniel, producers; Irving Berlin, lyricist & composer (The New Broadway cast including Bernadette Peters & Tom Wopat), Angel Records

Soundtrack album: *Tarzan*, Phil Collins, Walt Disney Records

Instrumental composition written for a motion picture or for television: "A Bug's Life", Randy Newman, composer, Walt Disney Records

Song written for a motion picture or for television: "Beautiful Stranger," Madonna, Maverick Records

Instrumental composition: "Joyful Noise Suite," Don Sebesky, composer, RCA Victor/BMG Classics

Instrumental arrangement: Don Sebesky, "Chelsea Bridge," RCA Victor/BMG Classics

Instrumental arrangement with accompanying vocal(s): Charlie Haden, Quartet Weat featuring Shirley Horn, "Lonely Town," Verve

Recording package: Ray Benson, Sally Carns & Buddy Jackson (art directors), "Asleep at the Wheel" (Ride with Bob), DreamWorks Records Nashville

Boxed recording package: Ron Jaramillo & Arnold Levine (art directors), "Miles Davis – The Complete Bitches Brew Sessions" (Miles Davis), Columbia/Legacy Records

Album notes: Bob Blumenthal, album notes writer, *John Coltrane – The Classic Quartet – Complete Impulse!*, John Coltrane, Impulse! Records

Historical album: *The Duke Ellington Centennial Edition – the Complete RCA Victor Recordings (1927–1973)*, Orrin Keepnews & Steven Lasker, compilation producers, RCA Victor/BMG Classics

Engineered album, non-classical: Al Schmitt, engineer, *When I Look in Your Eyes*, Diana Krall, Verve

Producer of the year: Walter Afanasieff

Remixer of the year, non-classical: Club 69 (Peter Rauhofer)

Engineered album, classical: *Stravinsky: Firebird; The Rite of Spring; Perséphone*, Markus Heiland, engineer (Michael Tilson Thomas, conductor), RCA Victor Red Seal

Producer of the year, classical: Adam Abeshouse

Classical album: *Stravinsky: Firebird; The Rite of Spring; Perséphone*, Michael Tilson Thomas, conductor; Andreas Neubronner, producer (Vance George, choir director; Joyce Keil, choir director;

... November 25 ...

The Catholic League, the nation's largest Catholic lay organization, has taken aim at the new Arnold Schwarzenegger movie, **End of Days**.

Stuart Neill, tenor; Sharon J. Paul, choir director; Ragazzi, The Peninsula Boys Choir; San Francisco Symphony Choir; San Francisco Girls Choir; Stephanie Cosserat, narrator; San Francisco Symphony), RCA Victor Red Seal

Orchestral performance: Michael Tilson Thomas, conductor, *Stravinsky: Firebird; The Rite of Spring; Perséphone,* San Francisco Symphony, RCA Victor Red Seal

Opera recording: *Stravinsky: The Rake's Progress,* John Eliot Gardiner, conductor, London Symphony Orchestra, Deutsche Grammophon

Choral performance: Robert Shafer, conductor, The Washington Orchestra, *Britten: War Requiem,* The Washington Chorus

Instrumental soloist performance (with orchestra): Martha Argerich, piano; Charles Dutoit, conductor (Orch. Sym. de Montreal), *Prokofiev: Piano Cons. Nos. 1 & 3/Bartók: Piano Con. No. 3,* EMI Classics

Instrumental soloist performance (without orchestra): Vladimir Ashkenazy, piano, *Shostakovich: 24 Preludes & Fugues, Op. 87,* Decca

Chamber music performance: Anne-Sophie Mutter, violin; Lambert Orkis, piano, *Beethoven: The Violin Sonates (nos. 1-3, Op. 12; Nos. 1-3, Op. 30; Spring*

Sonata, Etc), Deutsche Grammophon

Small ensemble performance: "Color of Love" (Works of Thomas, Stucky, Tavener, Rands, etc.) Chanticleer; Joseph Jennings, conductor, Teldec Classics International

Classical vocal performance: Thomas Quasthoff, baritone; Anne Sofie von Otter, mezzo soprano (Claudio Abbado, conductor; Berliner Phil.), *Mahler: Des Knaben Wunderhorn,* Deutsche Grammophon

Classical contemporary composition: "Boulez: Répons," Pierre Boulez, composer, Deutsche Grammophon

Classical crossover album: *Schickele: Hornsmoke (Piano Con. No. 2 in F Maj. Ole; Brass Calendar; Hornsome – A Horse Opera),* The Chestnut Brass Co.; Peter Schickele, piano & narrator (Cynthia Carr, horn), Newport Classic

Music video, short form: *Freak on a Leash,* Korn; Jonathan Dayton, Valerie Faris, Todd McFarlane & Graham Morris, video directors, Immortal/Epic Records

Music video, long form: *Bands of Gypsys – Live at Fillmore East,* Jimi Hendrix, Bob Smeaton, video director, MCA Records/Experience Hendrix

> *For me the cinema is not a slice of life, but a piece of cake.*
> *(Alfred Hitchcock)*

Selected Music Reviews from *Variety*: 1999

Roy Haynes

Jazz; Catalina Bar & Grill, 105 seats. Reviewed: Jan. 5, 1999
Band: Roy Haynes, Ron Blake, David Kikoski, Dwayne Burno.

Drummer Roy Haynes, a couple months shy of his 73rd birthday, continues to create an impressive and muscular brand of jazz with a simpatico unit adept at fervent music-making. For more than 90 minutes, Haynes demonstrated his polyrhythmic dexterity within the context of song rather than through bombastic solos and overblown delivery. Quite delightfully, it was never apparent the drummer was the leader.

Historians have already begun reassessing Haynes' place in the jazz drumming canon. His elevated stature owes more to recent performances and the many facets of last year's charming Dreyfus disc *Praise* than to longevity: in 50-years-plus, he has sat behind a diverse roster – Sarah Vaughan, Oliver Nelson and Eric Dolphy at the top – and showcased his own talents in 1960s recordings such as "We Three," which included Phineas Newborn Jr. at his pianistic peak.

His program at Catalina's was rife with short, punchy pieces with soloing kept to compact blocks. Each band member plays with a dramatic sense of urgency, particularly pianist David Kikoski whose driving clusters worked as solo excursions and counterpoint to Ron Blake's big tenor sound. Blake, who co-leads the Caribbean-influenced ensemble 21st Century, doubles on soprano sax and leans toward the broadness of John Coltrane in this setting.

In a handful of their soul-funk numbers, he rocked with Texas-sized authority; on a pair of Thelonious Monk tunes, Blake and Haynes turned playful and gave each a jarring edge. More than anything, this is a fun band to watch and hear.

The surprising cornerstone of *Praise* is a tender take on the Cat Stevens ballad "Morning Has Broken." Haynes and his unit don't work in those sorts of hushed tones once they take the bandstand, yet at every step there are nuanced elements giving this band its distinctiveness.

Renee Fleming

Recital; Dorothy Chandler Pavilion, L.A. Music Center, 3,201 seats. Presented by the Los Angeles Philharmonic. Reviewed: Jan. 6, 1999.
Pianist, Helen Yorke. Program: songs by Schubert, Glinka, Liszt, Mendelssohn, Wolf, Richard Strauss, Debussy, Barber; encores by Gershwin, Ellington, Dvorak, Strauss.

As Renee Fleming sang the "Song to the Moon" from Antonin Dvorak's fairytale opera *Russalka*, one of four encores following her vocal recital, the walls of the Dorothy Chandler Pavilion seemed to vanish as a near-capacity audience bathed in pure and audible moonlight. From any standpoint – vocal beauty, charm of stage presence, intelligence and generosity in program-building – Fleming's first-ever Los Angeles appearance proclaimed the presence of an artist as close to perfection as perfection ever gets.

In a generation of young singers – Jane Eaglen, Deborah Voigt, Sharon Sweet, Cecilia Bartoli, et al – bent on drying the tears of those mired in lamentation for opera's golden past, Fleming has somehow managed her current recital tour in the midst of a staggering operatic season: the tragic Blanche in Andre Previn's middling-successful *A Streetcar Named Desire* in San Francisco and top roles in two new Metropolitan Opera productions, Mozart's *Marriage of Figaro* and Carlisle Floyd's *Susannah*.

Adept no less at managing her career than at performance, Fleming removed herself from yet a third Met assignment, as Violetta in Franco Zeffirelli's overstuffed staging of *La Traviata*; rare indeed in these days of the super-hype is the singer who can recognize enough as enough. Last year's London disc, Grammy-nominated this week, is properly titled *The Beautiful Voice*. But even "beautiful" doesn't say it all. What was astounding about Fleming's solo recital here was her ability to mirror a variety of musical styles with uncanny accuracy: the vulnerability of Schubert's Gretchen at her spinning-wheel, the clutching, tragic outcries in Hugo Wolf's portrayals of Goethe's Mignon, the suave elegance in Debussy's Verlaine settings, the whipped cream and bratwurst of Richard Strauss at his banal worst.

In all of this, the strong, insinuating work of pianist Helen Yorke was another defining element. By insisting that Yorke share in all the stage bows out front, Fleming demonstrated an awareness seldom encountered of the partnership that the magical repertory of the art song truly entails.

Culture Club

Pop; Universal Amphitheater, 6,251 seats. Presented by Universal Concerts. Reviewed: Jan. 6, 1999
Band: Boy George, Roy Hay, Mikey Craig, Jon Moss, Zee Cowling, Kezan Frost, Richie Stevens, John Themis, Chaz Kkoshi.

The London-based dance-pop group Culture Club had an impact on U.S. singles charts for a few years in the early 1980s, but the band's sordid legend, gender-bending style and modest musical influence lives on, with forever-running VH1 specials and – now that the four core members have finally put personal differences aside in time to cash in – a reunion tour.

The group's always entertaining singer-songwriter, Boy George, was regal on Wednesday in black, fairytale queen's garb, complete with glittering crown, and his voice on songs like "It's a Miracle" and "Victims" was as rich and as smoothly anguished as ever. But surprisingly, neither he nor his stand-offish bandmates made much effort to create any excitement for the mostly thirty-something fans beyond just playing the songs, which were augmented by backing vocalists and musicians, not to mention a few technical tricks to fatten their sound.

"Tonight is all about nostalgia," said George, stating the obvious, "to a time when Joan Collins ruled the Earth."

Universal was about 90 per cent full for this first of two shows rescheduled from the summer (the second night was sold out, having been offered for sale first). The 75-minute program leaned heavily on updated versions of all the band's hits, like opener "Church of the Poison Mind," a reggae-frosted "Do You Really Want to Hurt Me" and, during the encore, the No. 1 hit "Karma Chameleon." A couple less interesting new songs were thrown in as well, including the dull "I Just Wanna Be Loved," which hit the top 5 in the U.K. last year but was justifiably ignored by U.S. radio.

. . . November 27 . . .
Kevin Spacey is in final talks to star for Steve Reuther's Bel Air
in **Pay It Forward** to be directed next year by Mimi Leder.

Two of the show's highlights were non-band songs: an intense version of "The Crying Game," the Dave Berry hit that Boy George covered for the movie of the same name, and a show-ending, nearly note-for-note version of David Bowie's "Starman."

Vic Chesnutt & Lambchop

Bowery Ballroom, 500 capacity.
Musicians: Vic Chesnutt, Kurt Wagner, Paul Niehaus, Mark Nevers, Alex McManus, Dennis Cronin, Deanna Varagona, John Delworth, Jonathan Marx, Marc Trovillion, C. Scott Chase, Paul Burch, Allen Lowery.
Is the world ready for a kinder, gentler Vic Chesnutt? Judging by the rapt attention afforded the "new and improved" model Saturday night, the answer would seem to be a rousing "yes."

Chesnutt, reliant on a wheelchair as the result of an early-'80s auto accident, has often come across as a sort of charmingly evil twin to Christopher Reeve. He's waxed bitter, spiteful and snotty, but seldom about his own condition – his misanthropy has always been more cosmic than that. But while the singer-guitarist's earlier material – like the self-eviscerating "Stupid Preoccupations," his opening number while seated alone on the Bowery Ballroom's spacious stage – was almost obsessively personal, he's changed his approach, as evidenced by his allegorical new release, *The Salesman and Bernadette.*

That break with the past was crystal clear at this gig, and not just because most of the material was drawn from *Salesman.* Most telling was his decision to forgo his usual stripped-down perf in favour of the big-band backing (13 pieces) of Nashville indie orchestra Lambchop. For the most part, the marriage was a happy one. Augmented by horns, vibraphone and multiple layers of guitar, such slow, shuffling songs as "Mysterious Tunnel" and "Parade" were elevated from sullen to stately. The mere presence of a stageful of musicians buoyed Chesnutt.

At times, however, the wall of sound was a bit too dense. Chesnutt's voice, a high, lonesome whine that wouldn't sound out of place on a '20s-vintage country-blues field recording, couldn't cut through brassier, brighter songs such as "Duty Free." On these, he sounded like an unwelcome guest at his own party.

Still, it was refreshing to see Chesnutt escape the black cloud that seemed destined to hover over his head, without dimming the intensity of his craft. In a too-brief opening set, Lambchop displayed a combination of virtuosity and off-kilter charm, thanks, in large part, to the low-key loopiness of leader Kurt Wagner. Like a parallel-universe Jimmy Webb, with a mile-wide streak of cynicism, Wagner builds grand sonic structures that are every bit as smart as they are sentimental.

George Thorogood & the Destroyers

Blues-rock; House of Blues, 999 capacity. Reviewed: Jan. 10, 1999
Band: George Thorogood, Bill Blough, Jeff Simon, Hank Carter; guest: Waddy Wachtel.
Perhaps finding inspiration in this hallowed venue for the new studio album he will record later this year, guitarist George Thorogood blew the roof off the joint with a hits-filled 90-minute set that found Lonesome George to be as bad as he ever was.

After a blistering six-song opening that included faves "I Drink Alone" and "Who Do You Love" as well as a rousing reading of one of the band's signature concert tunes, John Lee Hooker's "One Bourbon, One Scotch, One Beer," the ever-spirited Thorogood was just getting warmed up. "Let's start the show," said the already sweat-soaked singer-guitarist as he shed his snakeskin jacket, grabbed a slide and launched into another series of classic rock tunes extolling fast living that he and the boys could no doubt play in their sleep, among them "Gearjammer," the much-licensed "Bad to the Bone" and "Move It on Over."

Little has changed with most of these road-tested blues numbers over the years, and the few recent Thorogood originals, such as "Get a Haircut," that were played didn't match up that well with the older ones.

But no matter. This was a party of convention and reverence, and the boisterous and happy audience members got in these familiar mirthful anthems exactly what they came to hear, all of it capped by the contented "Rocking My Life Away," a fitting ending for Thorogood, who once again proved he's found in the blues his true calling.

The Flying Dutchman

Opera Pacific presented Richard Wagner's one-act opera, text by the composer. Segerstrom Hall, Orange County Performing Arts Center, Costa Mesa, 2,977 seats. Running time: 155 mins. Reviewed: Jan. 19, 1999.
Conductor, John DeMain; director and set designer, Keith Warner; costumes, Candice Donnelly; lighting, Marcus Dilliard. Mark Delavan (The Dutchman), Jeanne-Michele Charbonnet (Senta), Charles Austin (Daland), Ian DeNolfo (Erik), Steven Tharp (Steersman), Erin Wood (Mary).
Once again, opera-going in and around Los Angeles has become pleasurable, even thrilling. The turnaround came this week, not with the gloom-beset L.A. Opera at the Music Center, but a worthwhile hour's drive further south, where a mostly superb singing ensemble, brilliant and incisive conducting and a gimmick-laden staging that now and then almost made sense brought Richard Wagner's *Dutchman* into port under full sail.

Shortest and most ear-friendly of Wagner's momentous music dramas, *Dutchman* nevertheless tends to lure stage directors into rough waters, from Jean-Pierre Ponnelle's much-booed surrealist San Francisco staging in the 1970s to Julie Taymor's 1995 fling in Los Angeles that included a ballet for dress dummies. In his Opera Pacific debut, British director Keith Warner has seen the work as a kind of dream-with-in-a-dream.

His stage set, a vast open space instantly transformable by lights and scrims from a spook-infested shipboard to dowdy dwelling, heightens the unreality. At one memorable moment, the floor splits apart and the Dutchman's ghostly, ghastly sailors rise up in a mighty swirl from diabolical depths.

His Senta, the sea captain's daughter haunted by visions of the Dutchman whose curse she hopes to lift, is already onstage at the start, done up in a flaming-red cocktail gown of modern design, writhing and levitating, reaching out toward an image of her phantom lover. They finally meet, an act and a half later, but perhaps not. Now she sees him, now she doesn't; he has a way of going invisible. Like most ghost stories, Warner's contrived narrative overlay does burden the credulity at times.

There are no problems dealing with musical matters, however, from John DeMain's surging, spirited leadership to the overpowering, immensely dramatic, ebony-voiced Dutchman of Mark Delavan, to the smaller-voiced but intelligent Captain Daland of Charles Austin and the Senta of Jeanne-Michele Charbonnet – all three in their Opera Pacific debuts. Everything worked: the interaction of the cast, the lusty, brawling choral ensemble, the harrowing D-minor billowings in Wagner's stupendous orchestration.

Founded in 1987 by impresario David DiChiera as the Western outpost of his Detroit and Dayton companies, Opera Pacific has ridden its own rough billows in recent years, with its last artistic director, Patrick Veitch, hardly long enough in office to unpack. DeMain's recently announced accession to that post – after 18 years as music director at the Houston Grand Opera and several guest stints at Opera Pacific – implies an attainment of stability rare in local operatic circles in recent months. It couldn't happen to a better conductor, or a more promising opera company.

Irma Thomas

R&B; Levon Helm's American Cafe, New Orleans, 690 capacity. Reviewed: Jan. 27, 1999.
Irma Thomas Band: The Soldiers.
Since the late 1980s, when Irma Thomas purchased the Lion's Den as a venue for her in-town weekend performances, the singer dubbed the Soul Queen of New Orleans has earned a reputation for staying behind. Her admirable dedication to the less-touristy spots of the city and to maintaining Crescent City flavor notwithstanding, Thomas appears to be rounding a corner in her career. She's seemingly adopted Levon Helm's month-old club – half a block from the House of Blues – as her French Quarter home, where she dresses up her act and performs in a venue where she doesn't know most of the guests' names.

To some degree, Thomas' move is spurred by the Grammy nomination for her Rounder Records album *Sing It!*, a trio affair featuring Marcia Ball and Tracy Nelson. Then again, there's the insularity of the New Orleans music scene, in which an artist can play gigs seven nights a week and never shake her image in the outside world; in Thomas's case, it's that she's a two-song woman – "You Can Have My Husband (But Please Don't Mess With My Man)" and "Time Is on My Side," one of her B-sides that the Rolling Stones turned into a hit. Certainly it forces some degree of formality on Thomas, and as much as she accepts that, it's drowned in the feel-good attitude of a quality bar band.

Thomas' voice is a pure treasure. As proven on a half-dozen albums this decade, her delivery is a unique blend of conviction and spiritual purity; her voice, regardless of the material or backing, beams from a teenage soul unburdened by a multitude of heartaches and disappointments. Her first of two sets touched on her history – rousing versions of "Don't Mess With My Man" and "Hip Shakin' Mama" – but her more joyous numbers demonstrated how well Thomas can put a song over on a mostly non-native audience waiting for the familiar. "Sing It!," a gospel number given a funky, second line interpretation, was a steaming showstopper; her borrowed yet blessed New Orleans medley, which included "Iko Iko" and "Hey Pocky Way," was sharp and full-bodied, a reminder of how far the Neville Brothers have drifted from telling it like it is.

On ballads, Thomas flashed some of her country charm and rolled through some wonderful tales of romantic unsteadiness. The seven-piece band, featuring three horns, hit the ballads with an uncharacteristic thud, yet proved their mettle in the funkier arrangements.

Blues festivals have been Thomas's main venues outside Louisiana, and there's still some fest hokum in her set – particularly in the stage patter – but she brings on the treats found only in the friendliest confines: singing "Happy Birthday," fulfilling requests and signing autographs between sets.

And starting in the grand tradition of a pair of instrumentals before intro'ing the singer, the band sparkled on a bizarre medley of blues, gospel and the disco ditty "To Be Real" before playing the blues with a leaden and fuzzy '60s rock approach. None of that off-kilter melding, funny enough, was even hinted at when Thomas was onstage.

David S. Ware Quartet

Jazz. Reviewed: Jan. 28, 1999.
Musicians: David S. Ware, Matthew Shipp, William Parker, Susie Ibarra.
It's exceedingly rare to see a regularly gigging jazz combo made up entirely of musicians that could – indeed, on occasion, do – act as leaders themselves. Miles Davis fronted one, as did John Coltrane. And while it might seem presumptuous to mention tenor saxophonist David S. Ware in the same breath as those giants, his quartet may very well be similarly revered decades down the road.

Ware, who's finally drawing some mainstream notice after nearly three decades of underground repute, carries on the tradition of Sonny Rollins: capable of unskeining blinding bursts of freeform noise, he's equally comfortable slipping in a soothing ballad when the mood strikes.

That mellow mood didn't strike particularly often on this evening, though Ware's quartet did play with considerable restraint. Bassist William Parker and pianist Matthew Shipp edged from mathematical parrying into an elegant West Coast groove, setting the stage for the first of Ware's meditative solos on "Estheticmetric," culled from his recent Columbia release *Go See the World*.

Ware seldom dove headlong into the atonal, preferring to skim its surface, while still kicking up quite a wake on pieces like "Rapturelodic." His style, which permeates the quartet, combines precision with a decidedly Eastern sense of circular time. As such, his solos can careen into what seem like blind alleys, yet still return to the theme he'd been working.

Each of his bandmates manifested a similar ability, particularly drummer Susie Ibarra. One of the most consistently underrated percussionists around, Ibarra is that rarest of creatures – a truly free drummer. She almost never lapses into timekeeping, instead traversing cymbals, hi-hats – even the wood of her kit – with terpsichorian grace, snaking subtle filigrees between the melodic cracks.

Over the course of the set's 90 minutes, Ware pulled out a half-dozen jaw-dropping solos – drawing a rousing ovation for each. But in contrast to many similar jazz shows, the leader's periods of silence never felt like down time, which speaks volumes about the quality of the quartet.

Geoff Muldaur

Folk-blues; McCabe's, 150 seats. Reviewed: Feb. 6, 1999.
The wondrous sense of rediscovery that sat at the core of the

'60s folk revival weaves its way, in breathtaking fashion, through the current work of folkie Geoff Muldaur, a guitarist returning to the recording and touring fold 17 years since his last disc. Those who started following Muldaur 30-plus years ago during his days with Jim Kweskin's Jug Band helped pack the house; he responded with resplendent readings of material written and inspired by great, under-appreciated blues performers.

Muldaur, more than most well-travelled troubadours, is an uncommonly dexterous guitarist who draws reams of finger-picked blues and jazz textures out of the instrument. He employs the styles of blues musicians who recorded in Louisiana and Texas after World War I, favoring the ones with gospel backgrounds and a quiver in their voices. Not quite comfortable in front of an audience, he performs with an engaging ease – an everyman, if you will – and had this concert extended beyond the two 50-minute sets, he wouldn't have lost a soul.

Much of Muldaur's new Hightone disc, a graceful ode to the American South titled *The Secret Handshake*, made its way into the show, none more sentimentally touching than "Just a Little While to Stay Here," a ballad heard in New Orleans after a funeral that is arguably the most tender recording of 1998. Muldaur introduced each song by its composer or interpreter, the names of Bobby Charles, Blind Willie Johnson, Sleepy John Estes, Dock Boggs and Vera Hall falling on knowing ears. While his stories could use a little expanding, he is clearly tapping into significant musical *terroir* that, quite unfortunately for anyone with an appreciation for pre-electric blues, seems to get explored only now and again. Muldaur, quite magically, has made it his calling card.

The Rolling Stones

Rock 'n' roll; The Pond of Anaheim, 19,400 seats. Presented by Tommy Hilfiger and VH1. Reviewed: Feb. 9, 1999.
Band: Mick Jagger, Keith Richards, Ron Wood, Charlie Watts, Darryl Jones, Chuck Leavell; Bernard Fowler, Bobby Keys, Andy Snitzer, Lisa Fischer, Blondie Chaplin, Michael Davis, Kent Smith.
Mick Jagger, Keith Richards and the Rolling Stones – on their first all-arena U.S. tour since 1978 – learned long ago that the key to these scaled-down shows is pacing and timing. Without the giant inflatable women and the fireworks of their outdoor stadium concerts, these comparably intimate shows live and die for two hours almost solely by the music.

And so, at the first of two sold-out Pond appearances ("Welcome to wherever we are," Jagger said), the Rolling Stones, still going strong after more than 35 years, eased the spirited audience gradually into the mood of bigger things to come with a low-key opening run of "Jumping Jack Flash" and "Respectable."

The opening segment culminated with a nice read of 1971's rarely played "Moonlight Mile," a ballad that put the crowd back in their seats, and with the country-rock of "Sweet Virginia," with Jagger on harmonica, which drew applause for its California lyrical reference. A venomous "Some Girls" kicked the show into higher gear a half-hour in. The sneering Jagger – currently ensnared in bitter divorce proceedings with Jerry Hall – found new provocation in lines like, "Some women give me children that I never asked them for," spitting them out with all the attitude he could muster. "Let's go back to Zuma Beach," he improvised at song's end.

Guitarists Richards and Ron Wood locked into a number of classic instrumental duels, often facing each other down just in front of the smiling, steady-playing Watts. Jagger, lamentably, shared little onstage time or space with Richards or anyone else, and instead spent most of his time separated from his mates on the large, unadorned open stage, engaged in his usual, age-mocking aerobic routine.

During a strong version of "Out of Control," from 1997's *Bridges to Babylon* (Virgin), Richards got in Jagger's face and aggressively slashed his guitar parts while the latter blew harmonica. But the stand-offish frontman appeared to not even look at his longtime songwriting partner.

The clean look of the stage (broken only by eight windmill-like light rigs decorated in the tour's yellow-and-black look) afforded everyone, including those seated behind the band, an unobstructed view. A host of horn players, back-up singers and other musicians – most of them veterans of many Rolling Stones tours – used hidden ramps on the stage to easily come and go as the set list (which is roughly identical one night to the next) would call for.

As has become ritual at these types of big-name shows, the core band (including bassist Darryl Jones and keyboardist Chuck Leavell) performed a short, toned-down mid-show set on a small stage in the middle of the venue floor. Jagger dedicated a bratty "Route 66" to the song's author, Bobby Troup, who died earlier this week, but the B-stage portion was highlighted by a showstopping version of the classic "Midnight Rambler."

The brisk 21-song show (which neither exceeded nor fell short of expectation) also featured a pair of tunes sung by Richards – oldie "Before They Make Me Run" and the newer "Thief in the Night" – and included an encore just before midnight of "Sympathy For the Devil," updated into a sort of marching version that could be called "Sympathy '99."

Bayou to Bourbon Street

Indigenous Louisiana; Royce Hall, 1,838 seats. Presented by UCLA Performing Arts.
Performers: Beausoleil featuring Michael Doucet (David F. Doucet, Jimmy Breaux, Billy Ware, Tommy Alesi, Al Tharp); the Dirty Dozen Brass Band (Gregory Davis, Efram Towns, Kevin Harris, Roger Lewis, Terence Higgins, Richard Knox, Julius McKee); Geno Delafose and French Rockin' Boogie (John Dela-fose Jr., Germaine Jack, John Esprite, Joseph Chavis).
No, Royce Hall did not come close to resembling Mardi Gras, the boozy, bacchanalian affair held in the out of doors that's impossible to create outside the boundaries of the Gulf Coast states. But the music dragged in from rural and urban Fat Tuesday celebrations stood up well in a concert presentation void of any party surroundings. Some of that testimony goes to the strength of the artists, the rest to the durability of the music.

Each of the acts – the Cajun conquistadors Beausoleil, New Orleans brass-band modernists the Dirty Dozen and keeper of the Cajun/Creole zydeco flame, Geno Delafose – drew heavily on their Louisiana legacy in 45-minute sets, as music from Professor Longhair, zydeco progenitor Amede Ardoin and Cajun composer Dewey Balfa founds its way into the contemporary repertoire of each.

Beausoleil, the middle performer, stretched furthest the boundaries of his domain – Cajun fiddle music – and produced several fascinating hybrids, including a dense surf-

Cajun instrumental and a rollicking fiddle tune with a Bo Diddley beat that came and went with an air of delight. Beausoleil's leader Michael Doucet has long used tradition as a springboard and the songs he premiered from the group's new album, *Cajunization* (released in March by Rhino), are loaded with rock 'n' roll shadings; a mid-tempo instrumental ballad, dedicated to their late bassist Tommy Comeaux, retains the charm of lyrical Cajun fiddle music while enveloping a host of American roots music influences.

Openers Dirty Dozen had the tough task of rousing the relatively full hall. Smartly, they did so without relying on tourist faves and instead exposed the audience to '40s and '50s soul man Dave Bartholomew, Longhair and the unique arranging that a brass band can bring to a familiar piece – in this case, Henry Mancini's "Baby Elephant Walk."

Geno Delafose, backed by an electric band and an animated washboard player, closed the evening on a buoyant note. An adept accordionist, he syncopates his melody lines to keep the edges smooth in this relatively herky-jerky dance genre. Delafose is a fine bridge between the black and white cultures of the Bayou; his artistic strides are subtle in nature (until the band hit a grindingly mundane 12-bar blues) yet strong enough to suggest he has a future beyond weekend dances in his home parish.

Naive and Sentimental Music

The Los Angeles Philharmonic presented the world premiere performance of John Adams' orchestral work *Naive and Sentimental Music*. Performed Feb. 19–21; reviewed Feb. 19, 1999. Running time: 48 mins.
Conductor, Esa-Pekka Salonen. Also on program: Symphony No. 7, *Le Midi* (Haydn); Cello Concerto in A minor (Schumann) with Heinrich Schiff, soloist.
A recent survey tagged 52-year-old John Adams as the most-often-performed living American composer, a statistic slightly skewed by Adams' large output of short, curtain-raiser pieces, most notably the fox trot "The Chairman Dances" from the opera *Nixon in China*. But Adams' output of large-scale, complex pieces also surges onward, and his latest (and, so far, longest) orchestral work, introduced last weekend by the Los Angeles Philharmonic under Esa-Pekka Salonen and co-commissioned by the Vancouver and Sydney Symphonies and the Frankfurt-based Ensemble Modern, carries his considerable art to a dazzling new level.

Naive and Sentimental Music takes its title from an essay by German poet Friedrich Schiller, a rumination on the distinction between the instinctive (naive) artist and the innovative (sentimental). In three movements running 48 minutes, scored for a huge orchestra – including percussion gadgets by the dozen, an electronic sampler, guitar, piano and the more "normal" symphonic instruments in vast array – the music starts from near-silence, builds to a mighty climax, assumes a ruminative mood in a soft-toned slow movement, and roars once again to a grandiose peroration in a heaven-storming finale. Some in the near-capacity audience during Friday night's premiere performance made for the exit doors with the dazed, what-hit-me expression often seen at new-music events. Many more, however, remained to cheer.

Massachusetts-born, New Hampshire-raised and Bay Area-based, Adams came on the scene some 20 years ago as a skilled exponent of the so-called minimalist persuasion, producing extended works built out of endlessly repeating small rhythmic and melodic cells splendidly epitomized in the long piano work "Phrygian Gates," recently released on a stunning Telarc disc by Los Angeles pianist Gloria Cheng-Cochran. Since the early 1980s, however, he has moved across other stylistic landscapes. Nothing could be farther from his early minimalist stance than the wondrously extended, breath-stopping arch of melody at the start of *Naive and Sentimental*, intoned by a solo flute over a quiet, throbbing accompaniment of harps and guitar.

At a time when the undertaking of a new and challenging large-scale orchestral work – one which, Adams admits, "behaves like a symphony" even if he hasn't labeled it as such – smacks of the foolhardy, Adams has created an impressive, fearless masterpiece that will stand out in an already distinguished career. Here and there the work partakes of some well-chosen assistance; ghostly echoes from another of this century's milestones, Igor Stravinsky's spellbinding *Rite of Spring*, resound not far beneath the music's gleaming surface. Intricately bound into Adams' new work, these emanations vibrate in distinguished company.

Kirk Franklin

R&B/Hip-hop; Universal Amphitheater. Presented by Kmart & Universal Concerts. Reviewed: Feb. 19, 1999.
Kirk Franklin with: CeCe Winans, Trin-I-Tee 5:7, The Family, 1NC, Steps of Praise Band: Bobby Sparks, Jerome Allen, Steve Lewis, Keith Anderson, Erick Morgan.
Hip-hop evangelist Kirk Franklin spoke loudly and carried a big (musical) stick at the near-full Universal Ampthitheater, the first of his two weekend shows, where he proved that large groups of young people can be motivated to expressions of love and tolerance, especially when they're spoken to in a language they can understand.

Fronting an ambitious production that in some ways felt more like a rock concert than a gospel show, the Grammy-nominated Franklin led as many as 20 vocalists, eight dancers and seven musicians through a three-hour spectacle (with short intermission) that featured, among other things, complete strangers in the audience hugging one another en masse.

Franklin said you can "praise the Lord any way you want," then gave witness with a fast-paced show that successfully linked contemporary R&B and rap styles with traditional Christian dogma. Many of the numbers featured were taken from Franklin's recent GospoCentric/Interscope album, *The Nu Nation Project* – his fourth consecutive platinum-certified release – but the concert versions of these inspirationals outperformed their recorded cousins by virtue of the passion and joy apparent in the performers' voices and smiling faces.

Franklin sang and rapped and danced and even played some respectable piano, but most of the evening's best performances were courtesy of the constantly changing and interacting group of singers who surrounded him on the big, busy stage, highlighted by CeCe Winans' powerful song of heavenly faith triumphing over a broken heart.

The show came to a rousing close with a high-energy rendering of the crossover hit "Stomp," complete with sample of George Clinton's "One Nation Under a Groove," that brought the kids in the audience to their feet and into the aisles for a group revival dance.

Bob Dylan

Las Vegas House of Blues, Mandalay Bay Hotel. Reviewed: March 2, 1999.

... December 1 ...
Jodie Foster is to topline **The Leni Riefenstahl Project** (working title).

Band: Bob Dylan, Bucky Baxter, Dave Kemper, Tony Garnier, Larry Campbell; guest: Bono.

The magnitude of the stage at the latest House of Blues outpost – within the Mandalay Bay hotel in Las – seemed to hold Bob Dylan's attention for a good three songs as he inaugurated the venue with a solid 80-minute show that found him smiling at the audience, twisting out dance steps and checking the ornamentation of the room. With a capacity nearly double the Sunset Strip venue, the Las Vegas House of Blues sacrifices no intimacy due to the extraordinarily wide stage that sits five and a half feet up from the floor, and a second-floor balcony – with seats(!) – that's a combination of opera-house, choir loft and observatory. To boot, there's an enormous crystal chandelier that would put to shame any production of *Phantom of the Opera*.

Reasons for suspecting the venue could well become Las Vegas's premier music hall are threefold: sightlines exceed those of the L.A. club; the sound system not only made Dylan decipherable but the instruments nicely separated in the mix; and, as any veteran of the Hard Rock's the Joint and the other House of Blues will tell you, the presence of permanent seating is a plus.

Dylan and his quartet brought out the best in the room's acoustics, splitting the 14-song set 70/30 between electric and acoustic numbers. A separate show earlier in the evening with the Blues Brothers band sounded harsh and muffled in comparison, the soloing instruments often out of whack volume-wise with the rhythm section.

Known for wildly altering his set lists from night to night – and having just concluded a two-month tour of colleges – Dylan stuck to crowd-pleasers as he addressed a packed, and talkative, house of diehard fans, locals and the comped cronies of the hotel. An encore of "Knockin' on Heaven's Door," with U2's Bono on guitar and improvising a lyrical tribute to the rock bard, certainly caught everyone's attention.

Dylan started the evening with robust and grinding versions of "Gotta Serve Somebody" and "Million Miles," rounded the edges of "Stuck Inside of Mobile With the Memphis Blues Again" and "It Ain't Me, Babe" to draw out pop textures, played the ubiquitous "Silvio" and closed the evening with a churning version of Buddy Holly's "Not Fade Away." Curiously, Dylan turned in a credible version of the Grateful Dead's "Friend of the Devil."

Fatboy Slim; Dub Pistols

Presented by Goldenvoice. Reviewed: March 11, 1999.
Performers: (Fatboy Slim) Norman Cook; (Dub Pistols) Barry Ashworth, Jon Carter.

Right about now, as the song goes, DJ Norman Cook of Brighton, England, is the toast of the club and dance music world.

His big-beat smash from last summer, "The Rockafeller Skank" – recorded as Fatboy Slim, the best-known of his many musical aliases – has already established itself as an instant dance-floor classic. Cook wins awards about as often as they're handed out lately (including Best Dance Act at the Brit Awards), and he's arguably the most sought-after remixer in the business.

With all that riding on his shoulders, Cook, 35, booked this one-off DJ gig – coming two nights before an appearance at a Miami dance music industry confab, his only other current U.S. date – and set out to transform the Palladium into a big

Hollywood rave, no easy task under any circumstances. But Cook worked the packed-in and initially hesitant crowd for nearly two hours, mixing techno and hip-hop slices into a charged set that gained energy as it went, building to an exciting hands-in-the-air, post-midnight climax that managed to finally get everyone dancing.

After early evening opening turns from the DJ Gearwhore and local radio jock Jason Bentley, the two-man London dub team Dub Pistols tried to get the place going with their funky mix of Latin, hip-hop, punk and reggae records, as also heard on their 1998 debut album *Point Blank* (1500/A&M). But there was no vibe in the place as kids jockied for position around the diamond-shaped stage, centered on the venue's floor beneath video screens that showed the same Dub Pistols logo over and over.

The tall and crew-cut Cook took the stage – which featured four turntables and many travel cases filled with cherished vinyl – as the Pistols were mixing a final reggae jam. Dressed in a loud party shirt and baggy trousers, his cheerleader-like antics brought some much-needed life to the crowd, which spent most of the evening standing and staring at the stage, as if at a rock concert.

His opening strike included a sample of the guitar riff from "(I Can't Get No) Satisfaction" by the Rolling Stones, driven by a forceful hip-hop beat, that segued back and forth into a tease of a key groove from "The Rockafeller Skank," a tune that would reappear throughout the set. The defining characteristics of Cook's unique approach are big, obvious vocal and instrumental hooks, many lifted from unexpected sources, which are set to accelerating, high energy electronic beats.

The long show closed in fine fashion as Cook went on a vibrant bender, mixing more snippets of "Rockafeller Skank" around a James Brown hook and around his anxious remix of the Beastie Boys' "Body Movin'," followed by finale "Praise You," from Fatboy Slim's latest album *You've Come a Long Way, Baby* (Astralwerks), which featured the voice of children's author Camille Yarborough.

Marilyn Manson; Hole

Presented by Universal Concerts/Bill Silva/KROQ. Reviewed: March 14, 1999.
Bands: (MM) Manson, Twiggy Ramirez, Ginger Fish, John 5, Pogo; (H) Courtney Love, Eric Erlandson, Melissa Auf de Mar, Patty Schemel.

Anticipated as an evening of high drama, this pairing of the most antagonistic and self-absorbed characters in all of pop music ultimately crashed and burned. First, Hole chose to end its involvement in the two-week-old U.S. tour, which was supposed to run through the spring, with Sunday's Forum show, and second, an injury to Marilyn Manson 35 minutes into the gig has led to the postponement of at least three concerts.

Hole presented its music with more vigour and authority than in many of the band's past L.A. gigs, as the members worked hard to win over a partisan crowd of mostly male Manson supporters. "You'll get your burning crosses," singer Courtney Love told the crowd, referring to one of Manson's stage stunts. Indeed, a cross made of video screens bearing the band's name was set on fire following a sinister cover of the Eurythmics' "Sweet Dreams (Are Made of This)." It elicited howls of pleasure from the young audience.

Manson, barely dressed in a see-through black nylon bodysuit, wandered about the stage on stilts during "Mechanical

Animals," the title track from his latest Interscope album. Perhaps he should have stayed on the stilts: on the next song, "Rock Is Dead," Manson jumped from a side platform, appeared to trip over a piece of equipment and landed hard on the floor, where he remained in a fetal position while his bandmates finished the song.

An announcement of "technical difficulties" was made after about five minutes of darkness and silence; it was followed with, "We will be unable to continue with the show due to a major injury to our artist," revealed later to be a sprained ankle. Shows this week in San Diego, Las Vegas and Phoenix, which supposedly were going to take place with only Manson and opener Monster Magnet on the bill, have now been postponed.

Sadly, none of those shows would feature Hole, who impressed with an aggressive, punk-tinged set of songs, mostly from the band's two DGC albums, highlighted by opener "Violet" and an encore perf of acoustic "Northern Star," a tribute to Love's late husband, Nirvana singer-guitarist Kurt Cobain. A surprise acoustic version of the Beatles' "You've Got to Hide Your Love Away" suffered from Love's limited vocal skill.

The show was punctuated by the usual Love comments as she took aim at the media (repeatedly and cryptically urging the crowd to "stop reading magazines") and Manson, whose music she dismissed. "I just don't want to deal," she said as a way to explain her band's exit from the tour.

Jeff Beck

Presented by Delsener/Slater. Reviewed: March 19, 1999.
Musicians: Jeff Beck, Jennifer Batten, Randy Hope-Taylor, Steve Alexander.
Frank Zappa may have titled an album *Shut Up and Play Your Guitar*, but of all of rock's original six-string heroes, only Jeff Beck still walks that walk unwaveringly – a fact that's kept him from attaining the mass success of peers like Eric Clapton and Jimmy Page, while making him even more revered by his cadre of fans.

These devotees would have hung on Beck's every word Friday, had he uttered any. The lack of verbal communication didn't seem to dampen any spirits in the sold-out venue, though: In fact, the all-instrumental two-hour set was greeted with the sort of rapt attention (not to mention a fair amount of old-school air-guitar accompaniment) rarely seen at large-hall gigs these days. Beck certainly didn't disappoint anyone who came expecting an evening of unreconstructed guitar heroics. Drawing primarily from *Who Else*, his first solo studio album in nearly a decade, he alternated between panoramic forays and more typically jagged tone-clusters – even bringing the two together on pieces like the incendiary "Blast From the East."

Yes, Beck has a tendency to favour technique over emotion, as borne out by the number of crisp, pristine solos he was able to toss off without breaking a sweat, cracking a smile or involving his band mates in the least. That coolness derailed a few numbers, most notably "Brush With the Blues," the non-committal title of which pretty much reflects the detached sound. Even so, the 55-year-old guitarist manages to take more chances than just about any of his surviving peers. Like Bob Dylan, he's constantly tinkering with his best-known material, often – as with a raving rendition of "Beck's Bolero" – rebuilding it from the ground up.

His capriciousness isn't limited to his own material, either:

midway through the set, Beck began plucking out a version of the Beatles' "A Day in the Life" that wouldn't have been out of place on a supermarket Muzak channel until he unleashed a torrent of feedback-laced skronk that replicated the dramatic swell that bisected the original.

If that sounds old-fashioned, in many ways, it is. But thanks to Beck's refusal to ride the nostalgia wave, it wasn't even remotely out of date.

Pink Martini

Presented by KCRW/Laura Connelly. Reviewed: March 19, 1999.
Band: Thomas Lauderdale, China Forbes, Robert Taylor, Gavin Bondy, John Wagner, Richard Rothfus, Brian Davis, Doug Smith, Derrick Rieth, Pansy Chang.
Three nights of packed houses point to the power of the indefinable – no matter how Pink Martini gets described, there's always an element being overlooked, a reliance on phrases such as lounge, cosmopolitan rumba or neo-classical that only tells part of this rich story. Impressive at every musician's station, the ensemble produces music that's charming and elegant, a tribute to leader Thomas Lauderdale's adept handling of Cuban rumba and Parisian cafe tunes and his ability to balance them with a bit of Carnival disco, a quickie from composer Heitor Villa-Lobos and "Que Sera Sera."

Popular on the party circuit at last year's Cannes Film Festival, the Portland, Ore. band has been championed by the indie public radio crowd, leading to sales of 50,000 for their self-released album, *Sympathique*. Friday's perf, taped and broadcast Saturday evening on KCRW, conveyed the sophistication of the disc and a newfound crispness made all the more profound by the exact and nuanced bass playing of John Wagner as well as a rock-solid four-member percussion team.

Show began with "Bolero," Lauderdale's careful orchestration reminiscent of the work of Mexican bandleader Juan Garcia Esquivel. Lauderdale, his back to the audience with the piano front and center, drove the band with a steady hand, moving from the rumba of "Amado Mio" to the Spanish overtones of "Andalucia" and the dreamy "Aspetta Mi." The wealth of instrumentation was truly maximized, with bongos, trombone, guitar and cello called upon to give each piece a distinct mien.

Cellist Pansy Chang supplied the heavy drama – the best example was a tense duet with bowed bass against a rising drum background – but singer China Forbes held sway with an intoxicating sultriness. She imbued each of the 14 vocal tunes with a sensual finesse and turned "Que Sera Sera" into an otherworldly affair as the band kept march time with chiming percussion and colored the Doris Day hit with an abrupt brass presentation.

Lincoln Center Jazz Orchestra

Presented by UCLA Performing Arts. Reviewed: March 20, 1999.
Band: Wynton Marsalis, Seneca Black, Ryan Kisor, Marcus Printup, Wayne Goodman, Wycliffe Gordon, Ron Westray, Wess Anderson, Ted Nash, Walter Blanding Jr., Victor Goines, Joe Temperley, Farid Bar-ron, Rodney Whitaker, Herlin Riley.
Thick and fast come the anniversaries. The upcoming (April 29) centenary of the incomparable Edward "Duke" Ellington means that great wads of his music are now being played. It

also means the continuation of the argument: Was he merely the century's greatest jazz composer, or should he be more exalted as the inventor of the only purely "American" music of our time? Lincoln Center's 10-year-old Jazz Orchestra, headed by master-trumpeter-educator-tub-thumper Wynton Marsalis, argued the matter on both sides before a sold-out Royce Hall audience, leaving it unresolved, as it should be.

Suave, swanky and eloquent, the LCJO. whose music-stand logo is startlingly readable as "LSD," builds its Ellington repertory from original sources, which include copious recordings and well-documented charts. The orchestrations, handed over to a superlative new band, glisten and gleam: the needle-sharp brass performance in "Braggin' in Brass," the slithering clarinets in "The Mooche," the winds and brass in parallel harmonies worthy of Ravel everywhere in Ellington, but most lustrous at this concert in the slow, haunting oozings of "Mood Indigo."

An evening of the Ellington sound, so nobly revived, soothed the spirit and awakened the pride. If this is the way "American" music is supposed to sound, even in three-minute sound-bites occasioned by the restrictions of the 10-inch, 78-rpm shellac disc of old – so be it.

Still, there were problems, the inevitable ones that arise when new musicians take on old charts. The purely institutional virtuosity, awesome as some of it was at Royce, makes the whole venture sound slick and easy when it should thrill. To note that Wess Anderson's alto sax didn't quite attain the height of Johnny Hodges, or that trumpeter Ryan Kisor's "Concerto for Cootie" fell a millimeter or two short of its dedicatee, is to belabor the obvious.

The program offered welcome quantities of everybody's favorite Ellington: "Take the A-Train," "Sophisticated Lady" and a spectacular, steaming rendition of "Cottontail"; it stretches no point to envision the staying power of these imperishables. Of the excerpts among the evening's offerings from the "orchestral suites" (including, most implausibly, an orchestration of some of Grieg's *Peer Gynt* music that merely added to the work's turgidity), matters of longevity are in greater doubt; Ellington was never quite the symphonist he aimed at being. What Ellington was good at, he was the best there was, and his heritage is in good hands.

Neil Young
Presented by Avalon. Reviewed: March 22, 1999.
Old CSNY fans (and there were plenty helping to pack the Wiltern Theater) probably still delight in Neil Young's humorous song introduction on the *4-Way Street* live album, "This one starts out slow and fizzles out altogether." An apt description of Monday's show, a dark and brooding evening that showcased more than a half-dozen new songs, a lot of curveballs and a couple of numbers that just plain droned. On one level, Young's to be admired for continually expanding the concept of what his concerts are about, his performance exact in its execution; on another, he tests an audience's patience by not giving a fuller picture of his 34-year career.

As in 1992, when Young's solo acoustic tour preceded the release of *Harvest Moon*, one of his most commercially successful albums, and *Unplugged*, this 16-city tour eventually will give way to a Crosby, Stills, Nash & Young album and tour in the summer. That tour, naturally, precludes a Young solo disc, but perhaps could raise his profile enough to warrant the first of the much-delayed eight-CD boxed sets. Let's hope.

Young, who long has been fearless about premiering unfamiliar material, debuted seven songs Monday, many of them in line with the chipper milieu of C,S&N. Most were forward-looking love songs about making plans and holding out hope for love's winning ways. All are written with an uncommon directness that resonates with a non-fictional truth: "Slowpoke," for example, is light-hearted and heavy on easy rhyme schemes; others reflected on the fate of the traveller and that curious balance of making a living on the road and still stoking the home fires. Who but Young can take a line as benign as "nice to see you" and turn it into something so charmingly romantic?

At least a pair of the new numbers, however, had a striking ring of familiarity that even Young acknowledged. "This next one," he said in an introduction, "sounds a lot like the last one." It's been noted before that great composers steal and, indeed, Young has gone back to "Old Man" to use that song's hook in a new tune and to "Heart of Gold," from which he has taken the metered strumming and relationship of the chords and applied it to "Slowpoke." These songs need additional fleshing out.

Following the '92 touring model, too, Young used this acoustic opportunity to radically alter songs on the pump organ (mesmerizingly slow renditions of "Long May You Run" and "After the Gold Rush"), revive a rarely played favorite ("Don't Let it Bring You Down"), a couple of obscurities ("Ambulance Blues" from 1974 and '75's "Albuquerque") and a classic from his days with Buffalo Springfield 30 years ago ("On the Way Home").

Young broke the evening into two 50-minute sets and four encores, the first batch rich in selection and affecting moods. His voice is still potent and nasally, the songs seemingly never changed from their original keys – impressive, considering a good half of them were recorded more than two decades ago. The guitar and piano playing, as always, were sharp.

The second set found him playing under dim red and blue lights and, in at least one occasion, in darkness. The music, appropriately enough, matched the texture – "Ambulance Blues," a knee-jerk reaction of a song Young wrote during a personal down time, wobbled along for 10 minutes, only to be followed by "Old King" and an extended telling of a hound dog's story that lacked a solid pay-off. That he was accompanying himself on his guitar-banjo hybrid kept the mood less than buoyant.

Yet when Young sat at the piano to perform his melancholic and heartbreaking "Philadelphia," the song that gave Jonathan Demme's film its true musical character, the audience was reminded of how film and music can make a marriage work, a distant cry from the songs performed the night before on the Academy Awards.

Silverchair
Presented by House of Blues/Universal Concerts/ Hewitt/Silva. Reviewed: April 1, 1999.
Band: Daniel Johns, Chris Juannou, Ben Gillies.
The three teenaged members of platinum-selling Australian rock band Silverchair went to conspicuous lengths to overcome their juvenile reputation with an updated sound and more thoughtful songwriting approach on their just-released third album, but in concert the trio remains a mundane act alluring to youngsters only.

Silverchair opened their show at the House of Blues – which enjoyed an early sell-out for this booking – with the

... December 4 ...
Pedro Almodóvar's **All About My Mother** wins the
Best Film statuette at the European Film Awards in Berlin.

dramatic "Emotion Sickness," from their new album *Neon Ballroom* (Epic), another earnest stab by singer-guitarist Daniel Johns at explaining why it's so hard being a nice guy like him in an unjust world. But deeper meaning in this or any other of the band's simplistic songs was of little consequence to the boisterous and insatiable crowd, who jumped and screamed throughout the 75-minute show, occasionally shaking the club's walls and fixtures.

"Thank you, San Francisco," dead-panned Johns, before leading the band (which also occasionally included new touring keyboard player Sam Holloway, formerly of impressive Aussie group Cordrazine) into "Suicidal Dream," from Silverchair's 1995 multimillion-selling "Frogstomp" album. The song – with its gloomy theme – earned smiles and cheers as if the band were singing about summer vacation. Johns further tried to create a tense mood toward the set's end, warning of youthful revolution in "Anthem for the Year 2000" – in which he was all but growling his apocalyptic words – and recalling Kurt Cobain in the punk-fueled "Satin Sheets."

Despite Silverchair's commendable intentions – which also included rearranging early hit "Tomorrow" into a solo acoustic turn for Johns – the show never shed the weight of the band's mostly underachieving songs and unremarkable grunge sound.

Sheryl Crow

Presented by Nederlander. Reviewed: April 2, 1999.
Band: Sheryl Crow, Peter Stroud, Mike Rowe, Jim Bogios, Tim Smith, Matt Brubeck, Lorenza Ponce.
An ambitious stage set and a well-designed, impeccably executed light show carried the weight for much of Sheryl Crow's polished yet emotionally uninvolving opening night concert. Crow subjected her admirably crafted material to heavy, nuance-free renditions throughout her nearly two-hour show; when the over-worked "All I Wanna Do," a song that saturated the U.S. five years ago, comes across as a breath of fresh air, comparatively speaking, the artist is in trouble.

Crow's recording career has moved along an impressive trajectory, each disc an unqualified, ambitiously artistic success capable of fulfilling commercial expectations. Released six months ago, *The Globe Sessions* – the million-selling A&M disc from which much of the concert material was drawn – finds Crow balancing her established sensitivity with a developing toughness. In concert, however, that toughness became dense and unappealing by the end of the first hour – guitarist Peter Stroud employed clichéd riffs, the sweetness brought in by cellist Matt Brubeck and violinist Lorenza Ponce turned harsh and sour, and Crow lifted her voice to a screech, all of which put the brakes on the momentum generated in the show's earliest moments.

Fortunately, it started well. Sultry and a bit cocky, Crow wasted no time getting to her invigorating and catchy "My Favorite Mistake": it was her second number, with the three walls behind her a delightful triptych of silent films, still images and floating, cloud-like bursts of color. Ambient lighting and bouncing spotlights added energy and provided a distinct visual for each number.

Crow, staying front and center, alternated between guitar and bass; on the latter instrument, she has given herself a real job and truly blossomed, playing punchy and effective lines with uncommon meatiness. As a guitarist, though, she sticks to basic strumming and striking poses. (She has a real fondness for holding the instrument on her lap as she squats during the hard-rock tunes, proving, once again, that you can take the guitarist out of the heartland but ...)

It's curious that Crow, accomplished on so many levels and seemingly without compromise, sells only her best-known material to the audience. "If It Makes You Happy" was delivered with an impressive swagger that would've made Keith Richards proud; "Strong Enough," the first encore, was played hushed and with delicate care; "Leaving Las Vegas," placed between two grinding numbers, showed how well she can work off a standard, beat-driven track.

Early in her career, her concerts seemed split between the songs she appeared to really care about and those she regarded with indifference. She hasn't changed. Despite her signaling early on that a rowdy evening was in store, the audience was willing to go the distance with her. (The occasional blind-the-audience lighting was to blame for some of it.) A little loosening up and taking cues from the audience – staples of the singer-songwriter tradition – could go a long way toward raising Crow's concerts to a level on par with her albums.

Eagle Eye Cherry opened the evening with a spry set that closed with his former top 10 hit "Save Tonight."

Mercury Rev

Presented by Goldenvoice. Reviewed: April 6, 1999.
Band: Jonathan Donahue, Sean (Grasshopper) Mackiowiak, Adam Snyder, Suzanne Thorpe, Dave Fridmann, Jimmy Chambers.
It's little surprise that Mercury Rev's spacy electronic effort *Deserter's Song* winds up on Richard Branson's V2 label – it's a valuable update of the progressive-thinking rock bands of the early '70s that were the bread and butter of Branson's then-fledgling Virgin imprint. Matching Mole, Robert Wyatt's earliest solo recordings and, up on the pedestal, Hatfield and the North gave Virgin its edge over the other so-called visionaries; with little historical obedience in their dreamy keyboard-woodwind-guitar sound, Mercury Rev finally has found a home away from rough pseudo-psychedelia.

After three albums, buffeted by EPs and singles, Mercury Rev came up with one of 1998's overlooked gems in *Deserter's Songs*. The Buffalo, N.Y., band, long attached to the hard-edge psychedelic school that includes the Flaming Lips, now prefers a far softer sound rooted in Velvet Underground chord progressions and tempos with the otherworldly textures of the theremin and chamberlin layered on top.

Tuesday's well-attended concert found its best moments when the depth of the new material was exposed fully. Nothing felt quite as fragile as the recorded versions, but up against older and grittier songs, numbers such as "Tonite It Shows" and "Opus 40" floated above the rest during the 90-minute show.

Sean (Grasshopper) Mackiowiak brought an intriguing assortment of guitar styles to the fore. He seemingly has been influenced by everyone and anyone, playing rough with some Neil Young-inspired licks on one solo and turning to compact soul riffs on the next. The airiness of the music, an effect enhanced by two keyboards, gives him sufficient room to string together uncommon thoughts on the guitar, much like Phil Miller did more than 25 years ago in Hatfield and the North.

The band performs April 19 at Gotham's Bowery Ballroom with Garth Hudson and Levon Helm, two members of the Band who helped keep "Deserter's Songs" grounded.

... December 5 ...
Pixar/Disney's **Toy Story 2** again dominates the weekly box office, grossing $27.8 million, nearly three times as much as its closest competitors.

Alanis Morissette

Presented by Universal Concerts. Reviewed: April 6, 1999.
Band: Nick Lashley, Chris Chaney, Gary Novak, Joel Shearer, Deron Johnson.
Closing the U.S. portion of her 1999 world tour at a sold-out Universal Amphitheater, recent Grammy Award winner Alanis Morissette made the most of her finite musical talents with a spirited 90-minute performance that progressively gained in poise as it unfolded.

Tentative at first, the 24-year-old Canadian star took the stage – following an instrumental intro jam from her hard-rocking all-male band – and performed the intense "Baba," a captivating opening song taken from her second American album, last year's *Supposed Former Infatuation Junkie* (Maverick/Reprise), that challenges the religions of the world. Dressed in a glittering sleeveless plum top with a skirt over black pants, and with her long hair held in an ever-unraveling ponytail, Morissette bounded and awkwardly danced about while she lustily sang her wordy songs of deceit, heartache, lost love and obsession. She often sang her confessional and confrontational lyrics as if she was about to break out in a scream, like during the hypnotic "Sympathetic Character," which floated lithely over bass player Chris Chaney's dub foundation even as Morissette seemed consumed by her rage for a former lover.

The SRO and VIP-heavy (Farrah Fawcett, Nicolas Cage, Jenna Elfman, Woody Harrelson, No Doubt) crowd – which endured an hour-long delay at show's opening due to a weather-related power outage in the Universal City area – was restrained by Morissette's fans' standards, probably also due to the large percentage of industry-related ticket holders. Hits such as "Hand In My Pocket," a reworked "All I Really Want" and, during the first of two encores, "Ironic" did bring louder cheers, though. Show ended just after midnight with an unplugged-style set (featuring stand-up bass and small drum kit) that closed with the semi-autobiographical "U R."

Morissette has yet to develop an onstage personality that matches the burning intensity of much of her recorded work, but her many onstage faults (such as the unfortunate harmonica and flute playing during a number of songs) in some ways actually add to her inescapable appeal. World tour continues to Canada, Europe and Japan.

The Residents

Experimental rock; Irving Plaza, New York; April 5–7, 1999.
Reviewed: April 5.
Whenever this high-concept aggregation stages a live show, which isn't often – this was their first Gotham appearance in nine years – the result is equal parts performance art, post-Python put-on and innovative synthesis of eclectic musical idioms.

This evening's performance, built around songs from the early winter release *Wormwood*, embraced all of the above, along with a dash of genuine edginess inherent in the project's concept – essentially an almost blasphemous retelling of well-known Bible stories. As ever, the Residents (who, after more than 25 years together, have yet to reveal their faces or names publicly) played in costume – in this case, faux priest robes topped, of course, with their traditional eyeball masks. The core quartet, who employed standard rock instrumentation, rather than the electronic devices more common in their work, was augmented by a pair of neon-clad singers and a narrator who introduced each song, Greek-chorus style.

Although the tales chosen for deconstruction were, by and large, well known, the Residential spin put on the circumcision-obsessed "Dinah and the Unclean Skin" and Gamelan-embellished "Bathsheba Bathes" gave pause. Likewise, the genre-jumping musical borrowings – a snippet of Harry Partch here, a swath of Bill Monroe there – kept the synapses firing throughout the two-hour performance.

The Residents have always been better appreciated as theorists than accomplished musicians, and this evening's events didn't challenge that rep much. That said, the guitar playing was snappy enough, providing a nice counterpoint for the keyboard yammering that underpinned many songs, especially a brief encore set of oldies-but-goodies (highlighted by "Walter Westinghouse"). Some of the vignettes (notably "Judas Saves" and "In the Beginning," into which was incorporated the overture from *Jesus Christ Superstar*) bordered on the sophomoric – a problem that often plagues post-mod Bible berating.

But when the brimstone level was just right (as on the frankly creepy "Hanging by His Hair"), the extravaganza was fully riveting – even if you don't subscribe to the theory that "penis manipulation and babe-bashing" are all the Bible has to offer.

Billy Joel

Reviewed: April 8, 1999.
Band: Dave Rosenthal, David Santos, Michael Mellett, Mark Rivera, Liberty DeVitto, Crystal Taliefero, Tommy Byrnes.
Fresh from his induction into the Rock and Roll Hall of Fame, Billy Joel made his first foray in six years to Southern California with a satisfying show that had nothing new to offer, but the graybeard made up for his lack of fresh material with amusing self-deprecating stories on his failed marriages and how his height-challenged physique makes it tough to date supermodels.

Although the Long Island, N.Y., native son put together a song list that almost everyone in the nearly sold-out cavernous Arrowhead Pond had heard before, the 19-tune set contained several that seem to have held up extremely well over the years. "You May Be Right," from the *Glass Houses* album, and "My Life," from the 1978 hit disc *52nd Street*, were songs that could easily have been discarded by Joel when putting together his show and replaced with newer material from his last album, 1993's *River of Dreams*. These tunes, however, have survived the passage of time and were actually more vibrant than in years past.

The older material was well received by the crowd that's not as spry as it used to be. It was tough to find a concert-goer less than 30 years old, which, considering the length of Joel's career and his upcoming 50th birthday, shouldn't be all that surprising. His days as a reckless youth jumping on pianos are long gone, but his showmanship and storytelling make up for that.

Joel began things with his standard opener, the piano-driven "Angry Young Man," before heading into the somewhat stale "Movin' Out." Joel's voice sounded fine, and the band (which included longtime drummer Liberty DeVitto, who ventured around the stage during the encores after being sequestered behind his drum kit for the majority of the night) was as tight as ever, but by now they easily could play these numbers in their sleep.

It was evident that the highlight for the musicians was the medley that incorporated songs from the 1940s through the

'80s, logical bookends for the 1989 hit "We Didn't Start the Fire." In offering a couple of verses of each, Joel and the band broke into imitations of Sinatra, Elvis, the Beach Boys, the Beatles, Jimi Hendrix, Led Zeppelin, the Eagles and the Police. Obviously not as polished playing these tunes as their own material, Joel and the band seemed to relish the moments of spontaneity.

The show closed with "Scenes From an Italian Restaurant." Joel then played two encores, "Only the Good Die Young" and the sing-along "Piano Man," which made all the Orange County baby-boomers feel young again.

Built to Spill

Presented by Goldenvoice. Reviewed: April 9, 1999.
Band: Doug Martsch, Brett Nelson, Scott Plouf, Jim Roth.
Over and over again, semi-reclusive Built to Spill leader Doug Martsch has declared that he has little interest in achieving fame for his fabulous band, and evidently he means it. But now that Built to Spill's live shows attain the same riveting, eccentric energy as his fractured recordings – as the band so deftly demonstrated to a packed and appreciative Roxy crowd on Friday – the matter of popularity may no longer be in his control.

Since its 1993 debut album, the Idaho-based group has been a college and indie-rock favorite because of Martsch's uncanny ability to combine some of Neil Young's best qualities (biting lyrics, corrosive guitar work, oddly pitched singing voice) and a little Billy Corgan (wicked walls of guitar sound) into strange and beautiful melodic noise. At the first of two sold-out weekend shows, Built to Spill played 14 convoluted tunes (most from its two Warner Bros. albums, the new *Keep It Like a Secret* and 1997's *Perfect From Now On*) that confirmed the band's place near the top of the cutting-edge pop heap.

After shaking off problems with his stage monitors during the otherwise riveting opening pair of "The Plan" and "Center of the Universe" (the first two songs on the new album), Martsch directed, in his own low-key way, an intriguing and complex set of heartfelt, anxiety-filled songs constructed around his twisted songwriting sensibilities. Cascading sweeps of emotion-driven guitar and vocal parts recalled Kurt Cobain's cunning, while bassist Brett Nelson and drummer Scott Plouf helped create powerful aural abstractions, full of unexpected structure twists and tempo turns.

Guitarist Jim Roth of opening band the Delusions remained onstage for the entire 80-minute, encoreless performance, complimenting the majestic songs with haunting slide parts. Brett Netson of Caustic Resin joined on third guitar for a mighty three-song finale climaxing with an extended read of the new song "Broken Chairs" that again brought to mind Young, as well as the guitar work in classic rocker "Layla."

Cesar Rosas

Reviewed: April 10, 1999.
Band: Cesar Rosas, Aaron Ballesteros, Jimmy Baca, Steve Falomir, Eddie Baytos.
Side projects by members of Los Lobos have been in steady supply this year, with Cesar Rosas exploring the simple pleasures of regional roots rock, blues and soul on his solo album *Soul Disguise* (Rykodisc). While Rosas' first musical love may sound overly familiar on disc, it's a natural for a live setting, particularly when performed with the spark and affection that the lone wolf and his backing ensemble lavish upon it.

Rosas, emanating cool as always behind his trademark goatee and sunglasses, entertained diehard Lobos fans with a 90-minute set featuring selections from his new album, a few beloved traditional Mexican songs and a handful of his better-known contributions to his full-time band. His backing ensemble was extraordinarily tight, particularly impressive in that this represents a side project more than an ongoing concern.

The evening offered a largely no-muss, no-fuss approach to Rosas' tasty musical stew, which is clearly how he believes such pure music should be attacked. One wonders what he makes of his fellow Lobos' more dissonant noodling. He does not say much from the stage and there's little swagger behind his fiery, if economic, guitar solos; Rosas may saunter or, more often, stand immobile and drink in his own playing, like B.B. King. Rosas' Los Lobos composition "That Train Don't Stop Here," from *Kiko*, was occasion for an extended jam. But beyond that, only accordionist Jimmy Baca was allowed other solos; other than "Train" and "Volver," performances of Rosas' songs were short, sweet and to the point.

One thing's for certain – Rosas isn't much for ballads. There are only a couple on his new album, and none were performed Saturday night. Were it not for the welcome interludes of norteno music, the programming choice could've made for a pretty one-note show.

Ensemble Intercontemporain

UCLA Performing Arts, the Association Française d'Action Artistique and the Cultural Services of the French Embassy in the U.S. presented the Ensemble Contemporain. Reviewed: April 11, 1999.
Music director, David Robertson; soloist, Alain Damiens, clarinetist.
A dedication to hard-core contemporary music may earn just rewards in heaven; here on Earth, however, the take tends toward the meagre. Yet the new-music ensembles survive; some even manage to draw full houses. Starting a six-campus U.S. tour at UCLA's Schoenberg Hall on Sunday, the Parisian Ensemble Intercontemporain offered a take-no-prisoners program to a cheering capacity crowd that had braved both a howling rainstorm and the knotty musical patterns of Elliott Carter and Pierre Boulez.

Founded in 1976 by France's Ministry of Culture as an adjunct to IRCAM, Boulez's electronic-music research centre, to fulfill his vision of an ensemble expert in the music of its own time – and with Boulez still listed as president – the Ensemble has been led since 1992 by Santa Monica-born David Robertson, 41, who leaves in 2000 to head the Symphony Orchestra of Lyon.

The "classics" on this inaugural tour program were by Boulez – the pair of prickly pieces collectively titled "Derive" – and Carter's Clarinet Concerto, composed in 1997 for, and played by, the Ensemble's first clarinetist Alain Damiens. Music by Philippe Hurel and Unsuk Chin, both involving the interaction of computer technology and live performers, filled out the challenging playbill. The 30-minute "Xi" by Korea-born Chin drew the major ovation: imaginative, capricious music that at key moments surrounds the audience with the clickety-clack and mighty roarings of computer-generated sound.

Challenging? If not altogether decked out in measurable amounts of insinuating charm, the four works still impressed by the skill and variety of their manipulations – especially by the fluency with which the wheels went round in Carter's recent

---

major score. Here both the 90-year-old composer and the mid-dle-aged soloist seemed to be having the time of their lives.

Divas Live '99

Presented by VH1. Reviewed: April 13, 1999.
Performers: Tina Turner, Cher, Elton John, Whitney Houston, LeAnn Rimes, Brandy, Faith Hill, Chaka Khan, Mary J. Blige.
Sequels: you can rarely sit through 'em, and you could easily live without 'em. While "Divas Live '99," the follow-up to the ratings-boosting extravaganza that VH1 presented last year, didn't sink to the level of say, *Friday the 13th Part VI*, the high-glitz, low-content presentation won't make anyone forget the original.

Where the first "Divas" allowed a quintet of A-list songstresses alternately to strut their solo stuff and team up in various permutations, this edition cut back considerably on the interaction, leaving less room for vocal fireworks or bouts of diva-like one-upmanship. When these moments were allowed to flourish – as when Brandy and Faith Hill mugged through Bryan Adams' melodramatic "Everything I Do (I Do It For You)" – the performances seemed more suited to the live stage than the television presentation, which is admitted-ly a tough balance to strike.

Tina Turner did the best job of walking that tightrope, working the crowd feverishly during "Proud Mary" and sum-moning up an appropriately claws-out tone when joining Elton John (with whom she reportedly tussled during rehearsals) for "The Bitch is Back." It was a bit disappointing to hear honorary diva John concentrate on songs from *Aida* rather than his earlier catalog, but he did manage to throw in a few surprises during his rendition of "I'm Still Standing."

Spontaneity, however, wasn't the order of the day, as evi-denced by the sprinkling of vocal embellishments that might well have come from the "Diva in a Can" product posited by one of the ersatz commercials delivered up by *Saturday Night Live* cast members Molly Shannon and Cheri Oteri. Cher's "Believe" was the most egregious example of taped trickery, but several of the other performers were clearly beneficiaries of the stuff as well.

If you were (to paraphrase Naughty by Nature) "down with O.T.T." – as in Over the Top – it might have been possi-ble to appreciate the soulless vocal acrobatics that Whitney Houston unleashed during her overlong set. Otherwise, her scenery-chewing grew old quickly, reaching its nadir on "Ain't No Way," a poorly conceived tribute to last year's superdiva Aretha Franklin.

It's Delightful, It's Delicious, It's DeLaria

Opened in New York and reviewed April 12, 1999.
Band: Lea DeLaria, Whitney Ashe, Mary Ann McSweeney, Barbara Merjan.
With her miniature Mack truck figure, pierced nostril, spiky black hair and boxy men's suit, Lea DeLaria's certainly not your average chanteuse. But then DeLaria is not your average anything. The firebrand lesbian comic proved her bravura vocal chops in the ill-fated Public Theater revival of *On the Town*, and now she's headlining a month of Mondays at Joe's Pub even as she continues to star in Paul Rudnick's *The Most Fabulous Story Ever Told*.

If you thought her energy might be depleted by eight *Fabulous* performances a week, you'd be mistaken: DeLaria

rolled through an intriguing repertoire of a dozen jazz and pop standards with pizzazz to spare. In between numbers she served up generous helpings of her take-no-prisoners come-dy, lambasting the whiny women of folk music and the monotonous house blare of gay discos, or suggesting we save all the money we're spending to bomb Serbia and just buy Kosovo. The combination was revealing. You could see that her finely honed sense of comic rhythms informs her perco-lating, free-form scatting, for instance.

The show is mostly songs – "I love music; it's my life," DeLaria said early on, and she is indeed a sensitive interpreter. Her nicely chosen repertoire pays homage to her varied influ-ences. A self-confessed Judy Garland fanatic (a comic high-light of the show is the tale of how said obsession landed her a coveted Gotham apartment with two gay male roomies), she delivered a stylized rendition of "Get Happy" that segued from cool, African rhythms to snazzy jazz riffs. Also from the Garland songbook was "Alone Together," a somber lament that tested the limits of the brassy contralto's vocal gifts, but was sung with intense feeling. Billie Holiday is another clear influence, and Holiday standard "Everything Happens to Me" benefited from DeLaria's slow-burning, sly humor: "Your answer was goodbye ... (cool pause) ... and there was even postage due."

Other highlights included a venture into blues territory with a smouldering "Empty Bed Blues" and a ribald "Lady, Be Good," crooned to an understandably nonplused young woman in the audience to whom she'd taken a shine. DeLaria's back-up trio – Whitney Ashe on piano, MaryAnn McSweeney on bass and drummer Barbara Merjan – gave smooth, attentive support. For an encore, DeLaria brought her *On the Town* co-star Jesse Tyler Ferguson onstage to join her (or rather react to her) in a full-throttle swing through what's now become her signature tune: Bernstein, Comden and Green's "I Can Cook, Too." As the audience's emphatic reception proved, the show may have closed, but the song is hers for good.

Korn; Rob Zombie

Presented by Live 105. Reviewed: April 13, 1999.
Bands: (K) Jonathan Davis, Fieldy, Munky, Head, David; (RZ) Rob Zombie, Blasko, Riggs, Tempesta.
Just as grunge seemed to render '80s heavy metal ludicrous, the former's eventual fadeout led taste-mongers to pronounce guitar noise in general outmoded. But there always will be a kind of rock fan (mostly male, white and under 21) whose need to channel aggression requires a head-banging sound-track. Korn already had built up a huge following before last year's third CD, *Follow the Leader*, and attendant "Family Values" tour finally forced the trendmeisters to pay attention. The band's current tour with Rob Zombie is labeled "Rock Is Dead" – a sarcastic single-digit salute to those who've under-estimated the form's stubborn resilience.

Both acts have participated in the revivification of metal by incorporating elements of rap. The mix can be glib in some hands, but Korn, especially, manages to avoid wannabe status thanks to Jonathan Davis's impassioned, non-imitative vocals, and to fairly complex song structures driven by a very tight rhythm section. More concerned with raw everyday emotions than the usual puerile metal fantasies, the quintet at its best as in their notorious, harrowing child-abuse-themed "Daddy" – makes music whose sheer intensity transcends a limited palette.

... December 8 ...
David Bowie entertains a 1,500-strong crowd with
sounds old and new in Copenhagen, Denmark.

By now they're easily capable of commanding an arena aud with few gimmicks. The Oakland, Calif., show opened with select fans being led to stand behind two-tiered prison bars, where they remained throughout; the only other extra was a video screen overhead, where stage action close-ups, vid clips and miscellany was edited so expertly that it sometimes overwhelmed the stage antics.

A black-kilt-clad Davis (playing his trademark bagpipes just briefly to poor effect in an otherwise crisp sound mix) proved a compelling frontman, and the band was in potent and precise form. The hour-long set held interest by varying pace, interspersing thrashy faves like "Blind," "Ball Tongue," "A.D.I.D.A.S." and "Got the Life" with pieces like their moody cover of War's "Low Rider." Appealing to an inherently adolescent constituency (one still thrilled to flash halter-topped cleavage and pick a fight, any fight, in public) Korn has the chops and smarts to suggest they might one day take metal all the way to the grown-ups' table.

There's no risk of that with erstwhile White Zombie leader Rob Zombie, an improbable commercial survivor whose brand of horror rock traces lineage back through '80s punk gothics the Misfits, peak '70s Alice Cooper and '60s curio Screaming Lord Sutch. For kids raised on teen slasher pics, the mix of menace and camp irony in musical form is a natural fit. No matter that the music (a simple, sometimes catchy amalgam of chant-along hard rock with industrial/techno/punk flourishes) is seldom distinguished, particularly in its slurry live form. What does matter is that it's good theater.

The long-tressed Zombie roamed around a very busy stage filled by two dominatrix-type femme dancers, a robotic "giant mechanical friend" called the Creeper, shooting flames, and so forth. The video screen pumped out images from animated and German silent pics as Rob screamed hoarsely through the likes of "Superbeast" and "Living Dead Girl." It was all good fun, if no more threatening than an Ed Wood film festival.

Salt-n-Pepa

Reviewed: April 16, 1999.
Band: Cheryl "Salt" James, Sandy "Pepa" Denton, Dee Dee "Spinderella" Roper.
New York-based trio Salt-n-Pepa ruled the hip-hop roost in the late '80s and early '90s with a high-stepping and empowered approach that produced a string of hit anthems. But SNP has been in artistic and commercial decline over the past few years, and that slide was punctuated at the near-full (but rather subdued) House of Blues with a tepid and altogether unspectacular performance that showed the veteran group's best days are clearly behind it.

Backed by a male rapper and a spirited co-ed dance crew, Salt-n-Pepa hit the stage running in matching yellow and black jumpsuits, working a succession of dance moves during songs such as "RU Ready," from the group's underwhelming 1997 effort *Brand New* (London/Red Ant). But the show's early energy quickly dissipated, and subsequent big hits like "Let's Talk About Sex," which featured DJ Spinderella in a lead vocal role, and "Shoop" were delivered in a rote manner that failed to ignite the blase audience.

Despite being tagged a "Greatest Hits" tour, many of the group's best or most popular songs were either omitted here, or, as in opener "Push It," performed in abbreviated or cursory versions.

'N Sync

Presented by Nederlander. Reviewed: April 18, 1999.
Band: Joshua (JC) Chasez, Justin Timberlake, Chris Kirkpatrick, Lance Bass, Joey Fatone.
Screaming is nothing new – Elvis heard it, the Beatles heard it, George Michael heard it and, seemingly, 'N Sync lives for it. When the 6-to-16-year-old girls that make up the vast majority of their audience let the shrieking fly, the Orlando, Fla., quintet appeared to be at their most content, kicking it up a notch as they headed into another flurry of impressively choreographed moves and perfect-pitch harmonies.

There's a good possibility no one will remember their names in 2010, save for Justin Timberlake, but as clean-cut entertainment goes, 'N Sync had the shtick down pat: it's Disneyland in concert format. They paid tribute to pop acts (Jackson 5, Kool & the Gang and the fictional Wonders) that came before them, smoothly balanced dance numbers and ballads with the hits, and when they closed with a cover of Christopher Cross's banal "Sailing," the singers were hoisted above the stage and then floated out over the audience. Everything went according to plan: from the fireworks and numerous costume changes to historical photo montages and the expert execution of a Jackson 5 medley and Adam Schlesinger's magical make-believe hit "That Thing You Do." And the audience screamed. Material, however, is the band's weak point and the muddy sound mix of 'N Sync's six backing musicians emphasized a booming electronic drum and the standard trap kit.

With so little melody in evidence, far too many of 'N Sync's more upbeat numbers came off half-baked except for "Crazy For You," a gem in this genre that the boys played to the dramatic hilt. 'N Sync spread the spotlight across its five members but clearly JC Chasez and Timberlake are the true leaders. Chasez, though, addresses the crowd as if it were a bit older and familiar with adult romance and pained expressions, suggesting that five years down the line he hopes to pick up the drop-off from Michael Bolton.The star here is Timberlake, who exuded charisma and brought an actorly quality to his every step and sentence; he sang with the same precision as he danced, each move more exact and telling than those of his bandmates. Each visit to the microphone was greeted with screams (surprise, surprise) and he instinctively knew how long to bask in it and when to kick the show back into high gear. It felt like he was in control here, much more so than the others, even though it was no secret to anyone in the audience that every little step and speech was planned down to the last comma.

Impressively, even when Timberlake was dancing in the back of the pack, he attracted attention. Their openers, Tatyana Ali and the Sugar Hill Gang, sang to prerecorded backing tracks. Ali and her dancers showed promise; Sugar Hill Gang showed how tired, even if it's rap, bubble-gum music appears 20 years removed from its heyday. Still, there seems to be no stemming the tide of teen pop acts, and the industry has to embrace them if for no other reason than to woo preteens and teenagers to record stores, developing that important retail ritual at an early age.

'N Sync's debut album is at No. 16 after 55 weeks on the album chart with more than 6 million shipped. Charting higher, thanks to girl consumers, are Britney Spears and B*Witched; boys are in this, too, driving sales of Eminem's debut and *The Matrix* soundtrack. In addition, six of the top

20 singles are by popular teen acts. Somehow, it all proves there is life after New Kids on the Block.

The Living End

Presented by Goldenvoice. Reviewed: Apr. 18, 1999.
Band: **Chris Cheney, Scott Owen, Trav Demsey.**
Australian trio the Living End, which smartly combines the aggressive edge of pop-punk with the cool swagger of rockabilly, opened many eyes and ears recently by supporting – with considerable aplomb – a series of amphitheater-size shows for the Offspring, including at Universal two weeks ago where some thought they bested the headliner. But it was at the sold-out and sweaty Roxy on Monday, the Melbourne-based group's only headlining Stateside gig before the start of a Euro tour later this month, where the Living End showed its true potential with a ferocious performance in front of a happy if slightly befuddled young audience.

The band's singer-guitarist Chris Cheney is somewhat comparable to Green Day's Billie Joe Armstrong in both sound and sneering appearance, but Cheney and mates never slowed down for any ballads, and Cheney's blitzing, precision guitar playing at the Roxy bore more pleasing eclectic references than Armstrong ever does. Buoyant bassist Scott Owen played his stand-up double bass with rowdy authority and handled it as if it were his dancefloor partner, even playing (during Aussie hit "Second Solution") while standing on it. His ability to bring swing, blues, ska and boogie flow to the various two-minute songs gave them added breadth. The group has been playing together for seven-plus years (though impressive drummer Trav Demsey is a recent addition), and it showed at the Roxy, where songs from the band's new self-titled Reprise album, like the Stray Cats-flavoured "Bloody Mary" and the reggae-tinged alt-rock radio hit "Prisoner of Society" ("We don't need no one / To tell us what to do") were delivered with an exemplary sense of instrumental cohesion.

The 14-song set also included a supercharged, bass-slapping version of '80s hit "Tainted Love" by Soft Cell; "Save the Day," which recalled the energy of the Sex Pistols; and the exuberant "From Here on In," taken from a 1995 EP, which Cheney intro'd by proclaiming Hollywood the "world's party capital." The crowd here didn't live up to the praise, though, as many of the kids left as soon as the hit single was heard midset. The perf closed on a high note, during a one-song encore, as the former cover band pulled a ferocious rendition of Eddie Cochran's classic – though to the KROQ crowd at the Roxy, obscure – "Twenty Flight Rock" out of its bag of tricks.

The Smashing Pumpkins

Presented by Goldenvoice/Avalon. Reviewed: April 24, 1999.
Band: **Billy Corgan, James Iha, D'Arcy Wretzky, Jimmy Chamberlin.**
About this time last year, the Smashing Pumpkins looked like a band without much of a future, having lost a key original member and seeing sales of their mellow, new-direction *Adore* album fall short of previous efforts. Rumours even began to circulate that Billy Corgan, the band's strikingly bald singer, guitarist, songwriter and acknowledged leader, was about to embark on a solo career.

But the Chicago quartet's explosive display at the sweltering Roxy on Saturday (the finale of a two-week club tour) signalled a return to the guitar-heavy, big-rock formula that first made the group popular in the early part of the decade, most-

ly eschewing – at least for this evening – the more dulcet songwriting that marked last year's artistically and commercially disappointing *Adore* (Virgin). Powerhouse drummer Jimmy Chamberlin – who was fired from the Pumpkins in July 1996 following his misdemeanor arrest in the overdose death of the band's then-touring keyboardist – proved his irreplaceable musical worth to the group and its fans with a propulsive performance that fueled this show's impressive momentum.

The nearly two-hour, low-frills production – after a well-received set from new local space rockers Queens of the Stone Age – began appropriately enough with Chamberlin's gunshot intro of "I Am One," a driving heavy-rock song from the Pumpkins' 1991 debut *Gish* (Caroline) that drew ecstatic cheers from the packed-in throng, which was bathed for the opening in blinding white light. What followed was a triumphant and confidently performed sampling of well-known album cuts ("Zero," "Soma") and B-sides ("La Dolly Vita") from throughout their sizable song catalog, as well as at least eight new tunes that indicated a welcome return to form, leaving last July's disappointing Universal Amphitheater show a distant memory.

Chamberlin's significant presence was probably felt most at the Roxy during the anthemic "Ava Adore," which rose above the programd vibe found on the album version with a palpable new sense of bandwide purpose. An absorbing rework of the hit "Today," from the Pumpkins' breakthrough 1993 *Siamese Dream* album, featured an understated vocal refinement from Corgan (who wore a long-sleeve black pullover and a black kilt) that reinforced the song's melancholic theme.

The second of three encores included a brief solo acoustic turn from Corgan with the reflective new song "God Knows." The evening finished with a roar as the band gave a transcendental read of the mighty guitar workout "Geek USA" that climaxed with a furious six-string battle between Corgan and James Iha.

Lenny Kravitz; Black Crowes

Presented by Avalon/Coors Light. Reviewed: April 23, 1999.
Bands (LK): **Kravitz, Craig Ross, Cindy Blackman, Jack Daley, Harold Todd, Michael Hunter, George Laks, Nehemiah Heild; (BC): Chris Robinson, Rich Robinson, Steve Gorman, Eddie Harsch, Sven Pipien, Audley Freed.**
Retro rockers Lenny Kravitz and the Black Crowes proved a logical and successful pairing that had the somewhat dubious honour of being the first out of the gate among this year's summer shed tours. The chilly light rain, however, that began to fall during the Crowes' "Wiser Time" should serve to remind organizers that April is indeed not summer, even in Southern California.

Crowes frontman Chris Robinson continues to render his hip-swaggering impression of Faces-era Rod Stewart better than the latter can, prancing and twirling among his rough 'n' ready bandmates through several numbers from their latest release, *By Your Side* (Columbia). An attempt to return to the multi-platinum success of the bluesy rock 'n' roll of their debut, 1990's *Shake Your Moneymaker*, the overdrive of "Stop Kicking My Heart Around" and the heavy dual-slide guitar groove of "HorseHead" garnered ample crowd response but have thus far failed to spur the sales that "Jealous Again" and "Hard to Handle" did for the band out of the box.

Robinson, as is his wont, also took a moment or two to preach to the assembled masses (with keyboardist Eddie Harsch providing gospel organ accentuations) about peace and love and the power and glory of music – and having a resultant good time, as did Kravitz.

Equally brazen in his willingness to wear his influences on his sleeves, Kravitz's riff-heavy amalgam of Led Zep bombast and sweet '70s Sly Stone soul fit nicely alongside the Robinson brothers' rave-ups and lone ballad ("She Talks to Angels"). But Kravitz upped the funk ante as headliner, backed by the powerful display of drummer Cindy Blackman, with a short solo that the entire band actually stayed to watch reverentially.

What Kravitz had over the Crowes on this night was a hit single on radio and musicvid stations, "Fly Away," sandwiched in an oddly paced encore between "Let Love Rule," during which Kravitz left the stage to exhort the crowd to sing along, and "Are You Gonna Go My Way," which featured an anticlimactic jam.

Gomez

Presented by Paul McGuigan at the Troubadour. Reviewed: April 26, 1999.

Band: Ian Ball, Ben Ottewell, Tom Gray, Olly Peacock, Paul Blackburn, Dejan Everett.

The lithe and cacophonous guitar lines that make up much of the concluding numbers on Gomez's *Bring It On*, one of the most significant debut albums of the '90s, made for an intriguing starting point at a sold-out Whisky on Monday.

Beyond the calming melodies that are its forte, the tactic exposed a core, less prevalent on its recordings, based on riffs established more than 25 years ago. The band plays off Jimi Hendrix and Robbie Krieger, the chords of Count Five's garage classic "Psychotic Reaction" and the mantra-chorus of Manu Dibango's African funk gem "Soul Makossa" – and, on one occasion, an electric sitar – to create a wild and swirling take on modern psychedelia. This is the first British band that could feel at home on a HORDE tour.

Virgin Records act Gomez takes its three-guitar front-line and toys with the blend of acoustic and electric, repeated lead lines and soothing strumming. The music is far more commanding than the musicians, who appear comfy and laissez-faire, right in line with their casual pub-going dressing style. The band, which has just finished its second album, rose above the Brit pack last year after taking home the prestigious Mercury Music Prize for album of the year in 1998. (In the U.S., the band's most-heard work is its version of the Beatles' "Getting Better" for Philips Electronics ads.)

The debut disc lacks the hallmarks of contemporary Britpop or the genre's harder-edged offshoots and when members launch into the droll, and lyrically accurate, "Tijuana Lady," the band seems undoubtedly American. That they can then spin around and leap between the Talking Heads' "Road to Nowhere" and their own neo-funk "Love Is Better Than a Warm Trombone," it's a pleasant exercise in diversity rather than a scramble for an eclectic identity.

While the material from *Bring It On* – and the grand baritone of Ben Ottewell – shaped the evening, new material finds Gomez venturing into three-part harmonies and expanding on the drinking-and-singing nature of a good-time folk tune such as "Get Myself Arrested." They continue on a hippie vibe singing about water and moons, the energy level culled from a sense of weariness as much as their impeccable "Get Miles" and "Whippin' Piccadilly" spring from youthful jitters. Clearly, they're casting their own future out of an immediate and visceral past.

Underworld

Presented by Goldenvoice. Reviewed: May 1, 1999.

Band: Darren Emerson, Karl Hyde, Rick Smith.

The debate, and it was continuing in the lengthy lines leading into the Santa Monica Civic, concerned the pop nature of Underworld's new V2 disc, *Beaucoup of Fish*, and how it would make its way into the band's always vibrant, industrial-strength rhythmic mix. The answer emerged two-fold, as a swirling and driving 30-minute opener delivered all the goods, from orchestrated sweeps to varying dance beats – the purest update yet of Phil Spector's "symphonies for the kids" concept. Isolated numbers with fewer movements, fine on their own, felt incomplete, however, against such majestic musical constructions.

The Brits manipulate melodies with a sure hand: as they float in and out, some linger and some melt into the rhythm, yet it all feels complete and enriching. Paired with a stunning array of visuals hurtling by on five screens, Underworld's kick-off was so compelling on every level that you thought other bands just don't matter.

Buoyed by a thorough command of dynamics, Underworld's music has an incomparable pull. Sometimes hidden within the massive beats and sometimes layered over a relentless sputtering, Underworld's non-rhythmic sounds have a sense of familiarity. The uniqueness is in the placement. Programmer Rick Smith and DJ Darren Emerson, fiddling with banks of electronics all evening, constantly left room for human elements such as Karl Hyde's voice, which can eerily approximate the blues singer Howlin' Wolf, and traditional orchestra instruments to envelope the audience. They responded in a most un-dancelike fashion: they clapped to the beat.

"Cups," the driving mid-tempo tune from *Beaucoup of Fish* that has been earning Underworld airplay on alternative-rock and college radio, was slipped in about an hour into the show. The screens, which were dominated by words such as "salty" and "suck" and images shot from a moving vehicle, gave way to peaceful shots – a bird alone in the sky, a rippling wave and the word "happiness." As is their wont, Underworld managed to calm down the whole affair with this peaceful package of images and sound before sliding slightly awkwardly into a skewed reggae rhythm and, eventually, the standard steel-hard pogo meter.

Still, at almost every step the band challenged the precepts of electronic music by daringly embracing a pop mentality. As good as the sound was Saturday, Hyde's vocals weren't always clear, but at one point his manipulated voice could be heard twisting a chant of "I triumph" into "I try." On both comments, Underworld stands correct.

Mike Ness

Presented by Goldenvoice. Reviewed: May 3, 1999.

Band: Chris Lawrence, Sean Greaves, Jonny Ray Bartel, Charlie Quintana.

After fronting the Orange County-roots punk band Social Distortion for nearly 20 years, the most surprising thing about singer-songwriter Mike Ness's recently launched solo career is that it took him this long to do it.

Social D. (on hiatus) is known for a confrontational punk-rock style that, unlike most of its peers, regularly uses country and other acoustic-based styles as a launching point for its often-angry examinations of youth, family, relationships and society. However, the punk coat, with its repetitions and

... December 11 ...

The Insider is named Best Picture of the Year by the Los Angeles Film Critics Association.

inherent lack of dynamic, was all but stripped away by Ness, 37, in this solo arrangement at the El Rey, the first of three sold-out shows. The stand-up bass and slide guitar players – Jonny Ray Bartel and Chris Lawrence – effectively buttressed the singer's impassioned vocals with brisk upbeat country and blues flavours. The tattooed Ness delivered, with his trademark nasal vocals, much of the same intensity here as he does at Social D. shows, but without all the in-your-face fury.

The 90-minute show featured many of the songs from Ness's fine debut solo release, *Cheating at Solitaire* (Time Bomb), like the Johnny Cash-inspired "Ballad of a Lonely Man," as well as altered versions of some Social D. favorites and a few choice cover tunes, like a mournful read of Hank Williams' "You Win Again" and Cash's "Ring of Fire"; most of them expressed similar sentiments of uphill struggle, temptation and inner conflict. The tour's backing band, ably anchored by drummer Charlie Quintana (Bob Dylan, Joan Osborne), played with a much more laid-back, countrified approach than the on-hand fans of Social Distortion – who turned out in large numbers wearing Social D. jackets and T-shirts – were accustomed to hearing, and the crowd was thusly tempered throughout much of the performance; patrons in front of the band were seated instead of pressed up against the stage, adding to the mellow mood in the room.

But a four-song encore that included Ness performing Social Distortion's "Bad Luck" by himself, as well as a version of "Ball and Chain" that echoed *Exile on Main Street*-era Rolling Stones, brought the house to its feet for a rousing close.

Shania Twain; Leahy

Promoted by Universal Concerts with Andrew Hewitt and Bill Silva Presents. Reviewed: May 6, 1999.
Bands: (Twain) Roddy Chiong, Cory Churko, Allison Cornell, Brent Barcus, Marc Muller, Randall Waller, Hardy Hemphill, Andy Chichon, J.D. Blair, with El Camino Real High School Camarata (8), Wilson High School Band (4); (Leahy) Siobheann, Donnell, Marie, Frank, Agnes, Doug, Erin and Angus Leahy.
Marketing and the fiddles and steel guitar in her backing band notwithstanding, Shania Twain has so little to do with "country," she makes Garth Brooks look and sound like Porter Wagoner. Still, who's to argue over labels, with the most recent two of the Canadian's three albums certified 10 million sellers? Certainly not the near-capacity Thursday night Hollywood Bowl audience.

Recording for Mercury Nashville Records (now part of the Universal Music Group behemoth), Twain's music echoes a broad background in pop styles and her presentation reflects, at least in part, the influences of her husband, seasoned rock – and now Twain – producer Robert John "Mutt" Lange and manager Jon Landau: Twain's stage set and overall presentation wouldn't surprise anybody who's seen a high-level arena-rock act since the early '80s: smoke, flash pots and Vari-Lites all in place on a nice, clean stage, video screens to either side, and the band outfitted in costumes more likely to be found on Bryan Adams or Def Leppard than, even, Reba McEntire.

The songs, too, are more "rock" than "country," whatever either means these days. Such titles as "Whose Bed Have Your Boots Been Under," "Honey, I'm Home" and "Black Eyes, Blue Tears" (dealing with spousal abuse) clearly resonate with her substantially female audience, and Twain and her powerfully electric band are nothing if not rousing. Much of the music is

at a slightly above medium tempo, with the ballads "You're Still the One" and, especially, the witty acoustic shuffle "No One Needs to Know" welcome respites. Eight singers from Woodland Hills' El Camino Real High School and four percussionists identified as "The Wilson High School Band" appeared to add flavour to "God Bless the Child" (not the Billie Holiday song) and "If You're Not in It For Love, Get Outta Here," respectively. The musical presentation of the show is so slick as to appear almost mechanical, so every once in a while Twain broke the momentum by chatting with members of the audience.

Leahy is a nine-member family band from Ontario, Canada, of Irish descent and specializing in Celtic-influenced music; its records are released Stateside on the Virgin sub Narada, and it has been featured on a PBS special. Reduced to eight for this stop with sister Julie evidently at home, writing, the siblings (aged 19 to early 30s) play keyboards, bass, guitar and a whole lot of fiddles; stepdance; and occasionally sing.

The group's music is certainly more traditional than the present-day Corrs, though there are occasional surprises such as a jazzy piano solo from Marie (who later on played fiddle upside-down, dancing, and with the bow between her legs at various spots during her featured number, and she's not even the principal fiddler). It's a pretty spectacular sight and sound, and Twain (who invited them to join her for one song) is to be commended for bringing them along.

Beck

Presented by Goldenvoice. Reviewed: May 8, 1999.
Band: Justin Meldal-Johnsen, Joey Waronker, Smokey Hormel, Roger Manning, David Brown, David Ralicke, DJ Swamp, Gyvind Kang, Martin Tillman, Jay Dee Maness.
The fashionable music of would-be renaissance man Beck Hansen is an unabashedly derivative consummation of all the many styles and sounds that he's been immersed in since an early age by his artistic family, and each time he takes the stage, this unpredictable son of Echo Park tends to focus on one or another of those disparate styles.

At the first of two sold-out shows at the Wiltern on Saturday, Beck visited his tender, folky side – as also recently expressed on his 1998 *Mutations* (DGC/Bong Load) album – with a low-key, mostly hip-hop-free performance that, despite all its obvious musical references, was utterly without irony.

Backed by a group that included his usual concert band, as well as small string and horn sections, Beck and his oft-present acoustic guitar sang sad, yet hopeful, songs that were far more revealing lyrically than his more popular alternative-rock material. But when strung together in a seriously-toned, nearly two-hour production, these personal and indulgent tunes – like the ho-hum faux-swing of "Tropicalia," or the twangy country of "Rowboat," from his 1994 release *Stereopathetic Soul Manure* (Flipside) – made for a less engaging time than the memorable and far more fun shows of his 1996 "Odelay" tour.

It was generally only during the few modern-rock-oriented numbers, like the flea market sounds of encore "Devil's Haircut" or the *Austin Powers*-like silliness of "Deadweight" – from the *Life Less Ordinary* soundtrack (London) – that either the crowd or Beck seemed fully energized. The pretty "Girl Dreams," from his 1994 *One Foot In the Grave* (K) album, was performed by Beck without the rest of the band and stood out as one of the show's highlights.

Smart use by the band of pedal steel guitar, a pair of sitars (during the dour "Nobody's Fault But My Own"), and a variety of wind instruments (sax, flute, trombone) added spice and tension to the otherwise leisurely proceedings, which, along with earlier shows in Hawaii and Las Vegas, mark the only U.S. shows dedicated to *Mutations.*

Cranberries

Presented by KROQ/ Avalon/ Universal/Hewitt/Silva.
Reviewed: May 19, 1999.
Band: Dolores O'Riordan, Noel Hogan, Mike Hogan, Fergal Lawlor, Steve de Marchi, Russell Burton.
Mellow Irish rockers the Cranberries are – like the bitter Cape Cod fruit that shares their name – an acquired taste and clearly not for everybody, and at the sold-out Wiltern on Wednesday the band gave a whimsical albeit trying performance of bland pop, which was just what the vociferous crowd came to hear.

Following a nearly three-year lay-off, the quartet (often supplemented by a keyboardist and second guitar player) wrapped an eight-city U.S. theater sked here to promote *Bury the Hatchet* (Island), their fourth album that, just like the other three, is full of songs of personal obsession and self-righteous exhortation. Awkward singer Dolores O'Riordan (who also played acoustic and electric guitar as well as some keyboards) has an angelic voice that she ill-treated by lurching into jolting yodels and other vocal faux pas. Her dryly peppy delivery remains devoid of soul, even though some of the new songs she sang celebrate the recent birth of her first child.

O'Riordan, 28, whose unique waddle-walk while she played scored points for originality, often left the stage before the songs ended, appearing disinterested, and she frequently began singing the next song from off-stage. The other band members – including brothers Noel and Mike Hogan on guitar and bass – gave an equally uninspired effort, mostly standing in place and bashing out the simple songs no doubt exactly as they rehearsed them. Touring guitarist Steve de Marchi had the unfortunate luck of playing most of the time in near-darkness, even as he sang harmony vocals.

The worshipful fans, though, were caught up in what they perceived as the spirituality of it all, and they gave the most popular songs – like the boring "Ode to My Family," from 1994's breakthrough album *No Need to Argue*, big hit "Zombie" and show opener and current single "Promises" – rousing receptions that shook the balcony and at times nearly drowned out the band.

The band used dramatic and colorful lights and futuristic stage props to full effect, giving the otherwise dull songs, which draw inspiration from traditional Irish music as well as such contemporary sources as Sinead O'Connor, some needed sense of passion.

Charles Lloyd

Presented inhouse. Reviewed: May 21, 1999.
Band: Charles Lloyd, John Abercrombie, Marc Johnson, Billy Higgins.
Thirty years after turning on both jazz and rock auds, Charles Lloyd's reputation in jazz circles has never been better. He has an absorbing new album, *Voice in the Night* (ECM), and is surrounding himself with musicians of real stature, all of them leaders in their own right.

Yet even with the all-star firepower on hand – essentially a

duplication of the new CD's line-up, with Marc Johnson replacing Dave Holland on bass – much of Lloyd's first set at the Jazz Bakery Friday night didn't quite ignite. The 61-year-old Lloyd is sticking exclusively with the tenor sax these days, and it is paying off at times with some of the most human, emotionally involving playing of his life. Wearing a black hat and looking a bit irritated ("Hay fever," he mumbled), Lloyd was most effective when emitting a variety of moans, shrieks and multiphonic effects within the bop context in mid-solo.

Yet much of the potential energy of the first set was scattered among spiritual indulgences that didn't quite come off, unfocused soloing from guitarist John Abercrombie, and some surprisingly self-indulgent Billy Higgins drum solos. Faulty balances, an ongoing problem in the tricky acoustic space of the Bakery, laid waste to a good deal of the opening number. Things did improve midway through the set, though Abercrombie and Johnson could be heard properly only when Higgins opted for crisper, sparer textures.

Eventually, Abercrombie got into the right gear, crawling thoughtfully through Higgins' joyous polyrhythms, while Johnson displayed some swinging chromatic ideas in a fine bass solo. The music-making came together wholeheartedly in the final number, Lloyd's Mexican folk-song-flavoured "Dorotea's Studio," in which Johnson displayed a lot of wily, lyric fun in his bowed bass solo. With pros like these interacting with one another, it was just a matter of waiting them out.

Wilco

Band: Jeff Tweedy, Jay Bennett, John Stirratt, Ken Coomer, Leroy Bach.
Wilco's scheduled two-night stand at the House of Blues was cut short an evening by the death of frontman Jeff Tweedy's mother-in-law. The tragedy was not mentioned during the show, though Tweedy expressed regret about the cancellation. Still, the loss appeared not to have any effect – positive or negative – on Tweedy's performance, which blended charisma and a regular-guy demeanor in equal measures.

In the group's first L.A. date in two years, Tweedy and company delivered a highly spirited 80-minute set followed by about 25 minutes of encores. They proved a tight-enough unit, but not so rigidly in sync that some scruffy charm wasn't evident. Though much of Tweedy's songwriting focuses on the dark side of human experience, the mood sustained Monday evening was nonetheless one of exhilaration.

The band presented most of the material from its latest album, *Summerteeth* (a curious omission was "Via Chicago," perhaps the best song on the CD), with the usual smattering from past discs *A.M.* and *Being There* and the much-lauded collaboration with Billy Bragg on Woody Guthrie songs, *Mermaid Avenue.* For good measure, the band also performed one song from Tweedy's days in the seminal alt-country ensemble Uncle Tupelo, "New Madrid" from the band's final album, *Anodyne*, though in large part, the countrified twang of Wilco's early days was eschewed in favor of a more straight-ahead rock approach.

The virtues of *Summerteeth* have divided fans somewhat violently: One group declares that with this album, Wilco has sold out; others cheer the band's ability to weld complex textures onto sunny pop pastiches. While it's true that *Summerteeth* features some of Wilco's most pop-accented tunes, the Beatlesesque and Beach Boys influences have cropped up often in its previous work, so the new album

---

shouldn't be any real surprise. On the other hand, in the past Wilco has been at its best when luxuriating in an exquisite melancholy, so the cheeriness of the recent work can feel slightly manufactured.

Ultimately, were the band truly interested in mega-platinum status, it'd do something about Tweedy's raspy vocals, and that's obviously unlikely. Like Paul Westerberg, his voice is not a finely tuned instrument, and therefore probably not a palatable one for fans of slick, mainstream pop. It is, however, a highly expressive one, providing added emotional impact when it's cracking slightly.

At its best, Wilco indulges its pop-country sensibility in an agreeably disparate sonic landscape, bringing an ordered cacophony into Tweedy's songs to lend them an added resonance. "Hotel Arizona," "Shot in the Arm," the Dylan-esque "Passenger Side" and "Hoodoo Voodoo" were among the numbers given an added sonic jolt of jangling discord in Monday's show. For the most part, though, songs were given economical, straightforward renderings – only one, "Forget the Flowers," received a workout utterly unlike its recorded iteration.

Tweedy proved he's a charismatic frontman – when the mood strikes, he'll do a Pete Townshend jump or a judo kick, the classic, basic stuff of live rock. Yet he respects the music too much to affect mere postures in concert. The band, which wasn't even introduced during the set, remained mainly in the background, with only a handful of virtuoso flourishes. Jay Bennett's most ambitious guitar solos came during the unlikely pair of songs "Christ for President" and "Casino Queen."

Seal; Joan Jones

Presented by Nederlander Concerts. Reviewed: May 25, 1999. **Seal's band: Seal, Mike Landau, Tony Levin, Brian Blade, David Sancious, Mike Harvey, Paul Mabin. Joan Jones' band: Jones, Michael Gross, Jimmy Couri.**
Seal's simple but heartfelt message of love and peace among the races isn't always best served on his albums, which tend to be a bit too calculatedly polished and, like late-period Peter Gabriel, misrepresent the singer himself as a bit desultory and detached. But like Gabriel, of whom Seal's sexy, soulful voice is reminiscent, when you put him in a live setting, the songs come alive and the singer seems afire. British-born Sealhenry Samuel's 105-minute set at the Greek Theater Tuesday night was both elegantly mounted, thanks to a tastefully evocative light show, and passionately delivered to a congregation of the faithful.

On disc, Seal seems to operate on two predictable speeds: dance-hall manic and ballad luxuriant; the two often meet for a hybrid pace somewhere in between. When he introduces a song as being "about hope and togetherness," he hasn't given you a clue as to what the song might actually be – all his numbers address those concerns. With a crack live band backing him, featuring legendary session man Tony Levin (who has also played bass for Gabriel), drummer Brian Blade and keyboardist David Sancious, the music had more rhythmic kick than Seal's recorded output has usually managed. Guitarist Mike Landau gave a number of songs, including "Bring It On," "When a Man Is Wrong" and the recent single "Human Beings," a fierce urgency not found on disc. Of course, Seal himself was also responsible for the newfound vibrancy.

Emerging onstage in a dapper charcoal suit and black shirt, he quickly shed his jacket and shoes in order to prowl the stage with an irresistibly pantherlike sensuality as he poured his heart and vocal chords into espousing his vision of a love-

sated, utopian world and the ready obstacles (such as in "Lost My Faith") that stand in understanding's way.

Together, however, Seal and his band gave electrifying new edges to the songs "Latest Craze" and "Newborn Friend" – tunes which are merely pleasant in recorded form, but brought the crowd to its feet in their live renditions. And, predictably, Seal's animated versions of his singles "Kiss From a Rose," "Prayer For the Dying" and "Crazy," which closed the show, elicited justly ecstatic responses from his audience.

Joan Jones, the former front woman for L.A. cult band SUN60 who is currently enjoying popularity thanks to her song "Everyday Down" on the *Felicity* soundtrack as well as her solo debut disk *Starlite Criminal*, opened with a modest set boasting a bigger sound than the three onstage musicians would have suggested. Jones is a quintuple threat: in addition to singing and songwriting, she plays acoustic guitar, keyboards and a somewhat gratuitous mini-trumpet. She performs her songs, usually about locating and finding satisfaction with one's identity, with more passion than the material sometimes suggests.

Still, her onstage turn as a local hero (she recalled hiding in the trees surrounding the Greek to watch acts in her youth) offers hope that she can find a niche audience of teenage girls who find Jewel too callow, but aren't quite ready for Ani DiFranco.

Lucia di Lammermoor

L.A. Opera presented Gaetano Donizetti's three-act opera; libretto by Salvatore Cammarano, based on Walter Scott's novel *The Bride of Lammermoor*.
Conductor, Richard Bonynge with the L.A. Opera Orchestra and Chorus; director, Jonathan Alver; production from Opera New Zealand, John Verryt and Claire Hewitt. Sumi Jo (Lucia di Lammermoor), Frank Lopardo (Edgardo), Gino Quilico (Enrico), Jamie Offenbach (Raimondo). With Charles Castronovo, Megan Dey-Toth, Gabriel Gonzales.
Lucy, the heroine of Walter Scott's *Bride of Lammermoor*, suffers an unhappy fate. So, for some unexplained reason these days, does the opera Gaetano Donizetti fashioned out of Scott's panorama of Scottish melancholy. The L.A. Opera's previous *Lucia*, in 1993, had the heroine literally climbing walls. The L.A. Opera's new version, brought up from Opera New Zealand and staged by original director Jonathan Alver, stretches the credulity somewhat less strenuously. It looks the way it sounds.

That, alas, is only sometimes for the best. Much has been trumpeted about Sumi Jo, the slender Korea-born coloratura soprano whose Queen of the Night (in Mozart's *Magic Flute*) had earned cheers; the sad fact, if Wednesday's opening night performance can be judged, is that she's not ready. She produced a fine, gleaming thread of tone which, however, wandered painfully off pitch that night; worse for this role, her singing never seemed to own the stage, a crucial matter in this opera, made even more difficult by the tendency of her tenor, Frank Lopardo in his local debut, to yell.

Designer John Verryt has furnished the production with a believable suggestion of stern Scottish walls and doorways. But lighting designer Duane Schuler has cloaked them almost consistently in near-darkness until the end, when the sad graveyard choristers suddenly face a blinding-red projected cloudscape. Director Alver's staging also bears a fair resemblance to goings-on in Scott's novel, at least until the crucial

... December 14 ...
Paul McCartney performs in Liverpool in the dingy Cavern Club for the first time for 36 years. Three hundred fans crammed into the subterranean club.

Mad Scene, where party guests around the forlorn Lucia mass into a chorus line that looks like nothing so much as a Hi-De-Ho number from an old MGM musical.

Saddest of all was the spineless, the real word is clunky, conducting of Richard Bonynge, whose real impact was in the fact that his *Lucia di Lammermoor* was performed complete, without the defacements of generations of excisions that included the omission of entire scenes.

Uneven cast, quirky production and all, the full-length *Lucia* didn't seem a minute too long.

Randy Newman

Reviewed: May 26, 1999.

"My career is stagnating," a casually dressed Randy Newman joked late in his first of three nights at House of Blues, lamenting the lack of geographical distance between this stage and the club he started in, the Troubadour.

Well, it's his own fault. Newman's impressive turn to film, which has resulted in 12 Oscar noms, has kept him from recording new pop tunes for 11 years, and as much as the pop game has changed in that time, there still remains a spot for this master of the ironic and sublime. The singular mirror Newman holds up to society not only improves with age, his new material sheds an equally vivid light on the perils of man, divorced and remarried, raised in the rock 'n' roll subculture and fascinated with European history. As he moves from rednecks to missing an ex-wife to aging rock stars to Baltimore, the audience is reminded over and over how Newman's sophistication and clarity in music and lyrics stand alone in rock's canon.

His best recordings were always the sparest ones and in this solo piano setting, everything benefited from that focused treatment. Newman started with the old – "It's Money That I Love," "Birmingham," the gentle "Marie," and "Short People" – before turning to music from his new DreamWorks disc, *Bad Love*. Maturity, in Newman's case, is no buzzword for aging. He sees the goofiness of older men with young wives in "The World Isn't Fair," rock stars not knowing when to hang it up in "I'm Dead (But I Don't Know It)" and tackles 500 years of history in "The Great Nations of Europe," which was intriguingly followed by his Cold War bomb-scare ditty, "Political Science."

As much as the first person has dominated his writing, Newman was always assimilating a character, none better than the people of his brilliant 1974 disc *Gold Old Boys*. In *Bad Love's* songs the "I" is that of a well-meaning realist with dark shadings and a sarcastic response to all of life's riddles. For once, Newman's writing about himself.

Thirty-three songs – "Lonely at the Top," Louisiana" and the new "My Country" were stellar – filled close to two hours and Newman's running commentary was as pinpoint as the lyrics. At 55, he seemingly understands romance better than ever – but he always keeps you wondering. After a rushed performance of his kinky "You Can Leave Your Hat On," the song best known for its steamy appearance in *9½ Weeks*, Newman noted, "As I get older, I take (that song) more seriously." Somehow, that's reassuring.

Tom Ze

Reviewed: May 27, 1999.

Band: Tom Ze, John McEntire, John Herndon, Douglas McCombs, Jeff Parker, Dan Fliegel.

Tropicalismo, Brazil's late '60s revolution in film, theater and music that tackled cultural and political paragons, has affect-ed – and infected – a host of arty rock bands looking for that left-field edge. Tom Ze, the obscure yet adventurous member of the class, has moved from David Byrne reclamation project to cause celebre among the likes of Sean Lennon and world music radio programmers, who have paved the way for his first full U.S. tour at the age of 62.

Ze (pronounced Zay) is the left-wing absurdist of the group that produced Caetano Veloso, Gilberto Gil and Gal Costa. His music, which has been issued in original and remixed forms on Byrne's LuakaBop label, holds little of the captivating Bahian sway associated with tropicalismo, instead emphasizing heavy, and at times industrial, percussion. Ze's songs jab and jump, the band blurting or grooving before giving him a capella room to sing in baby-speak, gargle or recreate the night air of mountain country.

Using the Chicago band Tortoise to, quite impressively, back him onstage, Ze gave a disjointed performance that had a pace almost as discomforting as his music. His voice is usually free of sensual undertones; he uses it to enrich the pinging sounds of mandolin and vibes that dominate the melodies of the music or else elongates his phrases as a counterpoint to the rigid rhythms.

Animated, he introduces songs in charming broken English and lets his actions explain the songs – some are sexual, some are full of anguish, some are just strange, some are little more than a minute long. Near the end of the show, he appeared dressed in hardhat, goggles, rubber gloves and plastic coat and, with a hammer, beat a rhythm on one musician's head as the musician did the same to Ze. The band joined in by getting cymbal-like sounds out of trowels as lights were shut and sparks flew from both sides of the stage. Whether the theatrics have any meaning is anyone's guess.

Beyond the antics, though, this Brazilian Beefheart provides contempo acts such as Beck, High Llamas and Tortoise with the sort of feedback American bands got from the Rolling Stones in 1960s. His collages built of rock 'n' roll elements – and this includes Deep Purple's "Smoke on the Water" riff and the Beatles' "Hey Jude" sing-along – and Brazilian traditions come off worthy of emulation and dissection by rock's arty sect. The route to Ze, clearly exemplified by the youthfulness of the audience, is not through traditional Brazilian outposts but through nightclub turntables.

Blondie

Presented by Universal Concerts. Reviewed: May 28, 1999.

Band: Debbie Harry, Chris Stein, Clem Burke, James Destri, Leigh Foxx, Paul Carbonara.

The reunited Blondie overcame early sound problems at the near-full Universal Amphitheater – part of the influential group's first U.S. tour in 16 years – and offered a program that did articulate justice to their impressive catalog of new-wave pop-punk songs. Unfortunately, the show revealed little about what made the Gotham group itself so appealing in the first place.

The 100-minute program mixed big hits (encore "Heart of Glass," one of the group's four No. 1s), obscure tracks (the excellent "Union City Blue") and a couple from Blondie's mediocre new *No Exit* (Beyond Records) album, including the infectious standout song "Maria." The evening opened slowly (following a turn from local 550 Music rock act Dangerman) with a pair of fan favorites, the 1979 top 40 hit "Dreaming" and "Hanging on the Telephone" that found Blondie in a tentative stage mood while the thin sound mix (most unusual at Universal) was rectified.

Harry, 53, remains the focal point of the group, though the matronly vocalist wisely has retooled her previously sexually charged demeanor to a more refined and mature character. Dressed in a matching tight skirt and sweater outfit, the singer smartly worked the range of material at her disposal, from the excellent mid-set cover of "The Tide is High" to the jazzy new "Boom Boom in the Zoom Zoom Room" (a song much better than its title), with a steady aplomb. But she and the rest of the band were far less animated here than they were at a private performance at the El Rey in February (at the "200 Cigarettes" premiere), moving through this evening with a workman-like effort that caught fire only toward the finale. Impressive drummer Burke, however, was a constant source of distraction, laying down a succession of fiery beats that propelled the group's performance.

Two of Blondie's most popular numbers, the groundbreaking hip-hop-meets-rock of 1981's "Rapture" (which found the high-heel-clad Harry doing some middle-age headbanging) and the irresistible "One Way or Another," brought the regular set to a close in roaring fashion, though the overall effort this night failed to recapture the raw excitement of the group's heyday.

Elvis Costello

Presented by Universal Concerts/Silva-Hewitt. Reviewed: June 1, 1999.
Band: Elvis Costello, Steve Nieve.
Carrying neither the weight nor hoopla of Elvis Costello's pairing with Burt Bacharach nor his first go-round with pianist Steve Nieve, the singer's current tour is a relaxed affair aimed at re-introducing his rock-solid catalog. The Bacharach co-productions from *Painted From Memory*, his first disc for Mercury Records, are given prominence through wellrehearsed dramatic introductions and their melancholic nature, but the acoustic reworkings of vintage Costello are the real attention-grabbers.

Costello and Nieve, the longtime pianist of the Attractions, perform with an ease that wasn't so apparent three years ago at the Troubadour (*Daily Variety*, May 17, 1996). There they dropped out the extra instrumentation and played their parts; here they've found new wrinkles in songs, dropped in a few lines from another song ("Gloria" was a delight) and made savvy decisions when it comes to reworking ("Waiting For the End of the World") or playing it straight (the Bacharach material and the show-opening "Temptation").

The two unveiled their first songwriting collaboration, a short, dark number chronicling the morning after a night of passion that sounds as if it were removed from a song cycle. Costello's voice was agile and strong: the new number required a tempered delivery far different from the vocally huge Bacharach songs and the tender ballads "God's Comic," "Pads, Paws and Claws" and the warhorse "Alison."

With no album to sell, this was certainly a fans' show, one that pulled long-ignored tunes out of the closet and dusted them off for a new showing. None was better than "Radio Sweetheart," introduced as the first song he ever wrote, which segued into Van Morrison's "Jackie Wilson Said (I'm in Heaven When You Smile)."

A grand and energetic performance, Costello convincingly sold it to the last row of the house.

Van Morrison

Presented by Universal Concerts at Universal Amphitheater. Reviewed: June 4, 1999.
Band: Van Morrison, Matt Holland, Richie Buckley, David Hayes, Johnny Scott, Geraint Watkins, Jon Allair, Bobby Irwin, Mark Isham.
In a sprawling introduction to much of his new Pointblank album *Back on Top*, Van Morrison made an ambitious run at cementing himself as the Belfast Bluesman in front of an overly enthusiastic crowd. Morrison began by hinting at an evening of best-loved works – show started with a softly swinging "Moondance" and a straightforward "Days Like This" – but quickly turned to rarely heard music of the last five years, eventually thanking the audience for accepting his "eclectic set." As he did with "Listen to the Lion" in the 1970s when Morrison was one of rock's most significant artists, the singer added a healthy dose of vocal improvisation to his gently paced two-hour show.

The first stretch came on song three, "In the Afternoon," in which Morrison turned his gentle and sweet beseeching of "wanna make love to you in the afternoon" into a fugue for the vintage blues number "Don't You Make Me High (Don't You Feel My Leg)" and a lukewarm reading of James Brown's "Sex Machine." Along the way – this was the first of several songs that stretched beyond the eight-minute mark – he invoked the name of Big Joe Turner and rattled off some of his best-known numbers, harping on the brilliant "TV Mama."

Morrison, dressed in the black hat, suit and shades he seemingly hasn't taken off in five years, posits himself as a cross between Little Milton and James Brown. The songwriting, however, is a unique mix of the spiritual and the secular, delivered with an uncommon sense of bliss, a concept superficially difficult to reconcile with the blues. But Morrison, whose *Back on Top* album holds the attention start to finish, does so with aplomb these days after a dozen years of mixed success in the PolyGram family.

As usual, Morrison's stage movements were compact and pretty much limited to him turning his back to the audience to chain smoke while his adept musicians took solos. Overall, the band excelled at the atmospheric works such as "Philosophers Stone" and "Burning Ground," a track from 1997's *The Healing Game* that he turned into an exercise in word play to close out the main portion of the concert. They lacked the grit, however, to milk the desperation out of Sonny Boy Williamson's "Help Me."

Guest trumpeter Mark Isham, a member of Morrison's band in the early 1980s who was in town for a gig with his Silent Way Project, provided several delicious solos that tilted those pieces to the jazz side. Geraint Watkins' work on the organ was continually refreshing.

Taj Mahal opened the concert with a grab-bag of 20th century music that he turned into goodtime blues, Louis Armstrong's Betty Boop hit from 1932, "I'll Be Glad When You're Dead You Rascal You," and Horace Silver's "Senor Blues" being the highlights.

Mary Chapin Carpenter; Shawn Colvin

Presented by Nederlander. Reviewed: June 6, 1999.
Bands: (Carpenter) John Jennings, Jon Carroll, Duke Levine, Dave Mattacks; (Colvin) Stewart Smith.
Hitting Los Angeles a week after the release of her compilation album *Party Doll and Other Favorites* (Columbia), Mary

---

...December 16...

Julie Andrews sues New York's Mount Sinai Hospital, claiming her singing voice was ruined by the botched surgery two years ago.

Chapin Carpenter retained the album's flair by rearranging a few of her best-known numbers, showing a nice rock 'n' roll edge with Mick Jagger's "Party Doll" and taking a witty swipe at the divas with a hilarious ditty.

Carpenter, who put her most popular hit, "Passionate Kisses," in the No. 2 slot, continues to deliver sharp and friendly performances, backed by a band that has a fine sense of place. Nothing over the top, nothing cloying and no twang: Though country radio is the source of her greatest hits, Carpenter clearly has no artistic relationship with contemporary Nashville. In fact, Carpenter's show in many ways leaned much more toward the confessional style of singer-songwriters such as opener Shawn Colvin.

Carpenter, whose stories contain a bit of self-deprecation, paints characters with a history of leaving the scene of emotional mishap. At her most tender musically, there's a lot of bleakness in the message. "Almost Home," her new single, concerns the shedding of emotional baggage – a sign that her songwriting is taking on new dimensions. Lyrics were changed here and there to reflect, perhaps, a more mature attitude toward the subject matter. In "He Thinks He'll Keep Her," she gave the story a happy ending, taking the woman deserted in her mid-30s out of the "typing pool" and putting her next to the "swimming pool."

Carpenter bookended her show with stark and slow versions of "The Hard Way" and "Come on Come on" and then emphasized the songs from *Party Doll* – "Down at the Twist and Shout," "I Feel Lucky," "Shut Up and Kiss Me." Throughout the evening, Colvin and her guitarist, Stewart Smith, would join the ensemble, giving the vocals and backing added nuance and depth. Backed only by Jon Carroll's piano, the two women – Carpenter singing, Colvin pantomiming – paired on a number that poked fun at Madonna, Mariah Carey, Shania Twain and Celine Dion. Each phrase was more hilarious than the last.

Colvin opened with a seven-song set that was free-and-easy, considerably less controlled than her performances with her band. In a solo setting, she still projects the complete package – the songwriting, the vocals, the stage presence – that has made her such a vital artist in the 1990s.

Ojai Festival

Ojai Festivals Ltd. presented the 52nd annual Ojai Festival. Six concerts, June 4–6, plus three Sundowner events June 2–3.
Artistic director, Ernest Fleischmann; music director, Esa-Pekka Salonen with the Helsinki new-music ensemble Toimii, the Los Angeles Philharmonic, the Los Angeles Philharmonic New Music Ensemble; pianist Olli Mustonen, singers Laura Claycomb and Denyce Graves.
Tucked into a valley north-east of Ventura (which served filmmaker Frank Capra as a site for the original version of *Lost Horizon*), the town of Ojai (population 7,500) is no more than a 90-minute drive from downtown Los Angeles. One weekend a year, however, as this rural enclave of horse farms and orange groves hosts one of the world's most sophisticated and adventurous music festivals, it might as well be the far side of the moon.

This past weekend was one such time. Founded in 1947, the Ojai Festival has from its inception concentrated on the cutting-edge musical repertory more grandiose European festivals would fear to touch. Ojai thrives on true grit. This year's offerings consisted of an extraordinary (and spectacularly successful) feat of bridge building: America meets Finland, and finds much in common.

For his first-ever Ojai stint, Esa-Pekka Salonen brought over the intrepid new-music ensemble Toimii, which he and Magnus Lindberg founded in Helsinki in 1981; Toimii, in turn, brought over a week's worth of new music that was mostly stupendous: music by Salonen himself and his two near-contemporaries Lindberg and Kaija Saariaho. They also brought an hour's worth of delicious operatic spoof for a morning family concert, whose catalog of delectables included the rare spectacle of Salonen himself, in a bunny costume, screeching out a few notes in the soprano stratosphere while leaping after invisible butterflies.

Of the new works, Lindberg's 30-minute "Kraft" made the crowd immediately woozy with its huge sound panorama that enlisted both the Toimii membership and the Los Angeles Philharmonic in full panoply. Much of the piece was techno-derived and enlisted percussion instruments galore (including a gathering of banged-upon auto parts worthy of early John Cage) as musicians dashed to improvised performance spaces all around the audience area while twittering piccolos serenaded (and were serenaded by) Ojai's regular avian contingent. The work dates from 1985 (and was recorded on the Finlandia label two years later); this was its U.S. premiere and the ground at Ojai still may be shaking.

Lindberg's music made a lot of noise at Ojai; it also included a cello concerto that showcased the phenomenal talent of Toimii's cellist Anssi Karttunen, who was kept busy the next night by another killer solo work, *Amers* by Saariaho. A new work by Salonen himself, *Five Images After Sappho*, won hearts with subtler means: music of elegant, long melodic flow, set for soprano and small ensemble. Salonen had composed the cycle for Dawn Upshaw, but that most lovable of singers underwent emergency spine surgery and was replaced by another American soprano less well known but eminently capable, Laura Claycomb. Remember her name.

A program by the Philharmonic's own New Music Ensemble (also founded in 1981) had the aspect of an East–West confrontation: John Adams' *Chamber Symphony*, much of it vibrating with a quasi-European contrapuntal intricacy, as close to bridge-building work as anything of Adams. A program by Finnish pianist Olli Mustonen, Bach and Shostakovich preludes and fugues interwoven, was Ojai's most expendable item; the young pianist works with an absurd range of stage mannerisms, which have now begun to permeate the sounds he makes: false shadings, mannered accentuations, the old-time style more salon than Salonen that one had thought (hoped, even) was a thing of the distant past.

Old 97's

Reviewed: June 3, 1999.
Band: Rhett Miller, Murry Hammond, Ken Bethea, Philip Peeples.
Texas-based alternative country-rockers Old 97's boldly lived up to their ample reputation as live performers in a stimulating, pop-grounded concert at the House of Blues on Thursday and proved that they're blessed with far too many skills to be casually lumped into any one genre.

The energetic music known as "alt-country" is supposedly too honky-tonk for rockers and (heaven forbid) too rocking for country fans, but the quartet happily bridged those two not-so-distant musical worlds with a rare grasp of what makes both styles tick.

"It takes a worried man ... to sing a worried song," sang frontman Rhett Miller during the shuffling "Big Brown Eyes," and to hear his rich, empathetic vocals (most of the songs were taken from the band's four albums, in particular their two recent Elektra titles) was to know that this guy has done plenty of worrying.

Opening the 105-minute program with the ribald boogie stomp "Barrier Reef," a tale of one more drunken romantic affair, the Old 97's sashayed through a pleasing program reflecting the band members' myriad influences. From a cover of Bill Monroe's bluegrass gem "My Sweet Blue-Eyed Darling" to eclectic songs from their just-released album *Fight Songs* – like the punked-up rocker "Oppenheimer," the heartbreaking but beautiful, traditional country ballad "Lonely Holiday," and "What We Talk About," with its pleasing harmony vocals – the 97's passionately crafted passionately a show for all contemporary music lovers.

Exene Cervenka of X reprised her biting vocal role on the regular set-closing "Four Leaf Clover" (which she originally performed on 1997's *Too Far to Care* album), and the show closed with a five-song encore capped triumphantly with what's fast becoming the band's signature live song, the propulsive "Time Bomb."

The Moffatts

Reviewed: June 4, 1999.
Band: Scott, Clint, Dave and Bob Moffatt.
They may not like the comparison, but the Moffatts, who made a big impression on their curious young fans at the Roxy, are Canada's answer to Hanson, a cute and cuddly group of smiling high school-aged brothers who sing well together, write many of their own songs and play their own instruments. And to judge by the pre-teen female screams at this early Friday night show at the near-full Sunset Strip club, that combination could be all it takes to make these guys big stars.

The group, which has already released a couple of hit albums north of the border, is made up of 15-year-old triplets Clint (bass), Dave (keys) and Bob (drums), and their year-older brother Scott on guitar. The four sibs sang, with a fair amount of harmonious success, nothing but love songs – that is, other than covers of recent hits by Blur and Collective Soul – and, besides Bob, each had his turn to take lead vocals and be the object of the girls' attention.

The Moffatts (here in their first formal American concert appearance) played nearly all of the lovesick songs from their slickly produced debut U.S. album – *Chapter I: A New Beginning* (Capitol), which hits stores today – including first single "Until You Loved Me," one of four tracks produced by Glen Ballard (*Clubland*, Alanis Morissette).

The boys demonstrated only a rudimentary command of their instruments (poor drummer Bob often couldn't keep up with his brothers' enthusiasm) during the 16-song perf, but they held a firm grip on their new fans, many of whom heard about this show only the night before, when the group guested on a local top 40 radio station.

Karen Fineman

Reviewed: June 9, 1999.
Band: Karen Fineman, Michael Orland, Jay Condiotti, Trey Henry, Mark Z. Stevens.

Karen Fineman, the former Beverly Hills High schoolgirl who made an auspicious debut as Cosette in the 1988 West Coast premiere of *Les Miz*, has evolved into an elegant solo artist who instills every song with a sumptuous blend of passion, humor, power and finesse. Aided by the economical, understated guidance of director Clifford Bell, Fineman's 15-number act is woven together with light-hearted autobiographical patter that only occasionally crosses over into self-indulgence. Fineman's musical journey is enhanced greatly by the instrumental support of the four-piece ensemble led by musical director-pianist Michael Orland.

Fineman immediately establishes her vocal fluidity and range, opening with a soaring medley of "Something's Coming" (Bernstein/Sondheim) and "I Can See It" (Jones/Schmidt). The singer-actress shifts into a pop persona, offering vibrant, full-throated renditions of Lindy Robbins' country-tinged "Having the Time of Your Life" and a flat-out sultry outing on "Fever," featuring the adroit Shelly Mann-esque hand percussion work of drummer Mark Z. Stevens.

As she guides the audience through her early years as a child of Rodeo Drive and beyond, Fineman displays a keen wit and adroit comic timing, crooning over her teenage infatuation with Starbuck's "Taylor," the full-maned "latte boy who brings me java, he brings me joy." Later, she reveals how her taste in men has matured in "He's Bald," a bolero-rhythmed ode to follicly deprived older men. Her wordy reminiscence about being asked to be a Preparation-H spokeswoman creates unnecessary overkill as a set up for the seldom heard Cy Coleman/Dorothy Fields ballad, "Something Better Than This."

The highlights are Fineman's musical excerpts from *Les Miz*, *City of Angels* (in which she performed on Broadway) and *Promises, Promises*, her recent Reprise Series co-starring effort opposite Jason Alexander. Explaining that she now has the chance to sing the songs she didn't get to do in these shows, Fineman performs an emotion-rich "I Dreamed a Dream" and assumes her best torch song persona, belting out "With Every Breath I Take," while perched seductively on Orland's piano.

Tom Waits

Presented by Avalon. Reviewed: June 13, 1999.
Band: Tom Waits, Smokey Hormel, Larry Taylor, Andrew Borger, Dan Magough.
With a well-chosen assortment of roughed-up, blues-based numbers to compliment the gritty tone of material from the new *Mule Variations*, Tom Waits has created an archetype for the 21st century bluesman. The Waits that performed the second of three sold-out nights at the Wiltern is the welcome remnant of the jazzbo hipster who took an artsy side-road in the late '80s and then disappeared for much of this decade, only to return scuffed and emotionally richer.

Waits' plunge into the blues began in 1978 with the under-rated *Blue Valentine*, and he has kept himself knee-deep in the genre's primordial, gut-bucket elements throughout his career, even while masking them in artifice. The two stellar L.A. blues musicians on his team, guitarist Smokey Hormel and bassist Larry Taylor, provide Waits with a perfect bed to riff over and keep a boot-stomping beat. Best of all, his trademark rasp has become malleable, even refined and tuneable, and his off-the-wall humor, based on loads of factoids, makes him one of rock's most endearing musical comics.

....December 18 ...
Milla Jovovich is to star in **Kingdom Come**, an MGM film set in the Old West.

Sunday's 23-song show found its strength in the emotional tugs Waits has mastered; there might not be anyone as capable as he at making a precise alignment between song lyrics and musical settings. The *Mule Variations* material is an example of mood-swinging perfection: the only thing creepier than the banging and creaking that accompanies "What's He Building?" is the neighbour he describes; *Get Behind the Mule* clanks at a reaper's pace; and "Hold On," a tale of broken dreams, draws unfeigned on the raise-the-power-within style of folk music he has mined for 15 years.

Beyond a few lines of "Step Right Up" that made their way into the version of "Black Rider" he sang as he entered the theater from the rear, Waits confined his selections to cuts from *Mule* and his last four proper albums. He spent much of the night front-and-center doing contortionist dance steps before rolling out an upright piano for a glorious, low-key set of five songs that included a gracious reading of "Innocent When You Dream."

Waits gave the greatest care to the *Mule* works, particularly the simple "Picture in a Frame" and the robust shouter "Filipino Box Spring Hog." He hasn't slowed by being away from the stage for most of the last 10 years, and older songs such as "Shore Leave" and "16 Shells From 30-6" were pumped with a stark freshness. His landmark "Time," which closed the two-hour, 15-minute concert, felt as lived-in as ever.

While his "tour" has yet to expand beyond its first five dates, Waits, 49, has seen his stature grow by leaps and bounds recently through heavy media saturation that includes a "Storytellers" seg on VH1. *Mule Variations* debuted in the top 30 and appears on its way to being his bestselling album yet. His audience, though, is still that ultimate definition of devoted cult and it's unclear if he's penetrating Gen X and younger.

A former Angeleno who now lives up north, he allowed a bit of his own history to sneak in between the bits of offbeat patter ("Around the house we have a saying: the beatings will stop once morale is raised"). As he reminisced about Union and Western avenues, it didn't feel like a man getting homesick – this is an artist who never stops observing life.

Al Green; Deniece Williams

Reviewed: Jun. 11, 1999.
Performers: (Al Green) Anthony Smith, Wayne Tucker, Darryl Wells, Bobby Summers, Darryl Wells Jr., Jock Westbrook, Harvey Jones, Linda Jones, John Sancster, Anthony Royal, Dennis Bates, Warren Gaston; Deniece Williams.
It wasn't so much a concert as a lovefest. Al Green – or rather, the Rev. Al Green – the hugely gifted soul hitmaker of the early 1970s who chucked the scene to become a preacher and gospel singer 20 years ago, is back in the spotlight after recent TV guest turns as the singer in Ally McBeal's hallucinations. And his fans, some of whom looked like they weren't even born the last time he topped the charts, were out in droves to cheer and grab at him at the sold-out Greek Theater.

Being only human, Green didn't discourage them. In fact, he practically gave himself up to them and, as a result, seemed to lose control of his show. Resplendent in a white suit, he threw all of his crowd-pleasing tactics out there as soon as he could. He performed a few nifty dance steps. He waded into the crowd, shaking hands, receiving impassioned hugs from some overstimulated female admirers. He let the audience sing many of his old hits, exclaiming, "You know the songs

better than I do – and I wrote 'em!" He sang in front of old videos of his younger self in action. And he repeated these stunts again and again to the point of redundancy instead of using them sparingly to build the show's momentum.

Another problem could be summed up in two words – the band. Why do Green's hits for Hi Records sound so good today? A good deal of the credit should go to producer Willie Mitchell who put together a fabulously grooving studio band for Green to react to. The group Green fielded was a pedestrian outfit with a cluttered sound that rarely managed anything resembling a groove. Again, the key word is "sparing" – knowing what to leave out and when.

Make no mistake, at 53, Green remains an irresistibly charismatic, energetic performer, still in proud possession of a uniquely keening vocal style. When he focuses his attention and doesn't merely stand aside and lead discordant crowd singalongs, Green is still a mother of an interpreter, especially in his gospel set – like his impassioned, freely unpredictable turn on "Amazing Grace." But outdoors, one could not feel the one-on-one intimacy that still seduces record listeners. And why did he waste scarce time on a useless lounge-style medley of other soul singers' hits when he had more great, sexy originals to draw upon?

Earlier, Deniece Williams, another R&B veteran, laid down a sleek, early 1980s, gospel-flavoured set with appealing hits like "It's Gonna Take a Miracle" and "Let's Hear It For the Boy."

Wild Wild Wango Tango

Presented by Pepsi/Rio Casino/KIIS FM. Reviewed: June 12, 1999.
Performers: Ricky Martin, 98 Degrees, Britney Spears, Will Smith, Enrique Iglesias, Blondie, MC Hammer, UB40, Shaggy, Nancy Sinatra, Fabrice Morvan.
In only five party-driven numbers, Ricky Martin proved what all the media fuss is about. Martin was faced with jump-starting an audience that had baked for up to nine hours at radio station KIIS' annual hit parade in Dodger Stadium. And he rewarded their patience with a fiery perf that put several exclamation points on the end of this mixed show. He's a rare breed in the teen-plus market as he sings pure original songs that draw in influences as disparate as Latin beat and David Bowie vocals. After a day that found its highlights in two veteran acts, Blondie and UB40, Martin was the sign that contemporary pop can be more than excessive samples and one-note singers.

That rare item, a sex symbol with singing talent, Martin was the one performer that solved the riddle of involving video imagery without allowing it to overwhelm the act. He performed with a lively 10-piece band and a handful of salsa dancers, beginning with the smash "Livin' La Vida Loca," copying the tone and choreography of the video without becoming a slave to its script. The "Vida Loca" character was retained for powerful renditions of "Shake Your Bon-Bon" and "The Cup of Life," which he performed on the Grammy telecast in February, beginning a love affair with the English-speaking public that has even landed him on the cover of *Time*.

Martin far outshone the mainstays of the KIIS playlist and the two acts – Will Smith and Enrique Iglesias – pulled in to support the Warner Bros. pic *Wild Wild West*. Smith, reunited with old partner DJ Jazzy Jeff, refuses to remove himself from his video image, choosing to duplicate live his videos for *Men in Black*, *Goin' to Miami* and *Wild Wild West*. Latter perf even

... December 19 ...
Richard Attenborough receives the first BBC/BAFTA
Lifetime Achievement Tribute at a ceremony in London.

included rapper Kool Moe Doe, whose "Wild Wild West" sample is paired with Stevie Wonder's "I Wish" throughout the song, and singer Dru Hill, also in the video.

Iglesias, whose week-old "Bailamos" is already a top 5 Latin track, gave a mannered performance that held little of the sex appeal that Universal Music Group is banking on. The choreography gave Iglesias no out and his wandering offstage after one tune was one of the odder moments of the day.

98 Degrees, the second-billed teen act, played their sweet ballads after opening with their one uptempo hit, "Heat It Up." Dressed in camouflage pants and Rambo-esque ammo vests, the quartet stuck to their best-known numbers – "Invisible Man," "All Because of You" and new single "I Do" – and then attempted to exhibit an edginess by performing a medley of Offspring's "Fly For a White Guy," Eminem's "My Name Is" and Prince's "1999." They should stick to the ballads.

Britney Spears, who sang over a prerecorded track, was the day's biggest disappointment. Her voice lacked character and Spears exhibited none of the skills necessary to maintain the momentum the fans supplied when she was introduced. Her five dancers were rudimentary and Spears' dancing skills were far below that. Her hits, "Sometimes" and "... Baby One More Time," came across as bland and uninvolving.

The crowd was apathetic and unresponsive early on in Blondie's 45-minute set. But they pulled them back in with "Call Me" and "One Way or Another." Singer Debbie Harry sounded sharp and the extraordinary drummer Clem Burke supplied the day's finest organic beats.

A year shy of a score in recording, UB40 is still a premier interpreter of pop music in classic reggae style. Their manner is endearing and perfect for a summer day; their command of the pace over 50 minutes should be a shining example to the younger performers on the bill. Touring in support of the third volume of *Labour of Love* (Virgin), UB40 hit all the high points with "I Can't Help Falling in Love With You," "Red, Red Wine" and "Here I Am (Come and Take Me)" before closing with Peter Tosh's "Legalize It," a point that was lost on this crowd of youngsters and families.

Perhaps most surprising was the energetic set from M.C. Hammer, one of three "Behind the Music" subjects on the bill. Hammer rapped vigorously throughout, all the while keeping pace with his team of dancers, and ventured through the audience while performing. He still loves to base his music on turn of the '80s funk – Parliament, Grace Jones – and he wholeheartedly dived into his biggest hits, "Can't Touch This" and "Too Legit to Quit," before turning to his new church-based self and "That's Right We Pray."

Fabrice Morvan, late of Milli Vanilli and now a KIIS DJ, played a couple of songs from his upcoming CD and even tossed in a tender version of MV's "Blame It on the Rain." Nancy Sinatra was completely out of place. Jamaican Shaggy opened the day with a lot of rhymes that involve the word "boombastic" and, like Hammer and Smith, leaned on vintage R&B by toasting (Jamaica's precursor to rap) over Booker T. & the MG's "Green Onions" and Marvin Gaye's "Let's Get It On."

Sonic Youth/New York Art Quartet
Presented by KnitMedia. Reviewed: June 13, 1999.
Sonic Youth: Thurston Moore, Kim Gordon, Lee Ranaldo, Steve Shelley, Ikue Mori. NYAQ: Milford Graves, John Tchicai, Roswell Rudd, Reggie Workman, Amiri Baraka.
It's been more than 30 years since the New York Art Quartet

released a pair of albums that serve as holy grails of sorts to aficionados of free jazz – and almost that long since its members shared a stage under that moniker. As such, this show, which closed out the 1999 Bell Atlantic Jazz Festival, was one of the more anticipated performances of the season.

To say the least, the principals delivered the goods, offering up nearly 90 minutes of rollercoaster improvisation infused with old-school Afrocentrism and a playful sense of jazz as spectacle – replete with tantric chants and Eastern dance. They also coaxed a rare concert appearance from a long-ago collaborator, poet Amiri Baraka.

Baraka proved a riveting presence, alternating between free-associative declamations – among them a scorching litany of racial epithets that would send shivers down the spine of the most hardcore rapper – and prepared texts. In between, he and drummer Milford Graves traded off measures of an avant-garde sort of scat singing that conjured images of Albert Ayler as a vocalist. At the opposite end of the stage, alto player John Tchicai and trombonist Roswell Rudd duelled giddily through both propulsive stretches of skronk and more lyrical passages held in place by Rudd's meditative musings.

Graves proved to be the real star of the show, however, switching from weightless brushstrokes to pounding mallet work – even taking an oversized stick to the stage itself at one point for some of the most remarkable rhythm-making extant.

In the wake of this performance, a mere rock show would have been a disastrous anticlimax – but Sonic Youth's meandering sprawl of a set could hardly be dubbed "rock." Nineteen years into its existence, the quartet (joined onstage by Ikue Mori) seems to have come full circle, shelving the punky stance and kitsch culture worship of its commercial peak and returning to the avowedly experimental, atonal bent of its earliest work.

Admittedly, the band operates on a less assaultive level than it did when fresh out of the boot camp of Glen Branca's guitar army. Feedback shrieks have given way to slow, detuned progressions in which notes are slowly extracted, as if from amber. The effect was positively hypnotic on a pair of as-yet untitled pieces that opened the set, significantly less so on the distended, sample-laden 15-minute intro appended to "Xpressway to Yr. Skull," the one older number proffered during the hour-long set.

Skunk Anansie
Reviewed: June 14, 1999.
Band: Skin, Martin "Ace" Kent, Cass Lewis, Mark Richardson.
London-based quartet Skunk Anansie, led by striking frontwoman Skin, thoroughly rocked the sold-out Troubadour with a ferocious and unrelenting display, wrapping on a promising note a short U.S. campaign to promote the group's third album.

The bald and athletic Skin (born Deborah Dyer 31 years ago) is an intimidating beauty in the tradition of Grace Jones, and, stalking the stage like some barely caged cat, she worked her elastic voice to wide-ranging effect, never better than during the mid-set perf of the new song "Secretly," a sweeping ballad that showed the delicate vocal power at her command.

The rest of Skunk Anansie – which formed in London in 1994 and released its first album later that year – showed what three years of almost constant international touring can do for a band as they powered, with plenty of Led Zep-informed riffage, through 15 songs taken from all three of the group's politicized albums with a steady and overwhelming precision.

More than just standard, '70s-affected hard rock, however, the music of Skunk Anansie bears updated elements of punk, reggae and hip-hop as well as a smattering of African and Eastern influences, giving added heft to songs such as the vindictive "I Can Dream," the bluesy "Lately," the dramatic flip-off "We Don't Need Who You Think You Are" and the pained "Twisted." Another highlight, first single "The Skank Heads," was an in-your-face rocker tailor-made for inciting crowds of kids to mosh about, as they often struggled to do at the packed club.

A three-song encore of older songs featured some of the group's more political material, including "We Love Your Apathy" and, from their 1994 debut album *Paranoid & Sunburnt*, the chilling tale "Little Baby Swastikkka."

Jonny Lang; Patty Griffin

Presented by Avalon. Reviewed: June 15, 1999.
Bands: (JL) Paul Diethelm, Doug Nelson, Bruce McCabe, Billy Thommes; (PG) Doug Lancio, Frank Swart, John Deaderick, Billy Beard.
No matter how often one hears young blues singer-guitarist Jonny Lang perform, it remains difficult to believe that he's still just a teenager.

Tuesday's rousing display at the Wiltern was further proof of his uncanny capacity to draw from the musical past and make it so appealing to folks his own age. Further, while Lang's technical skill and pleasantly gruff voice may, by now, be old news, at the still-tender age of 19 the North Dakota-bred musician has begun to explore an instinctive vision of those places in his playing where guitar notes can go, a stunning ability that was on full display at the packed and appreciative theater.

Songs from both of Lang's pleasing A&M albums – 1996's *Lie to Me* and last year's *Wander This World* – filled the 105-minute program. The subject matter covered little in the way of new or interesting lyrical ground, but the affable blond guitarist's delivery was enough to earn and keep the attention of all in the house, including a very vocal young female contingent often missing from blues shows.

Lang set the bold tone for the evening early in his generous set with a vigorous workout of the classic "Good Morning Little School Girl," featuring a fiery song-ending solo, which segued into the crowd pleasing "A Quitter Never Wins." Most stirring, though, were his remarkable guitar solos, elements of which recalled B.B. King, Jeff Beck, Stevie Ray Vaughn and the late Roy Buchanan. Second guitarist Paul Diethelm was no slouch either (nor the rest of the backing band), engaging Lang in a number of spectacular instrumental duels.

Opener Patty Griffin and her fine band, at their final show touring with Lang, also gave an impressive and enthusiastic performance, playing songs from her fine 1998 A&M album *Flaming Red*, culminating with a stunning rendition of "Mary" (dedicated to her grandmother) that featured a duet between Griffin and Lang that was oozing with chemistry.

Brad Mehldau

Reviewed: June 15, 1999.
For all the comparisons to Bill Evans that pianist Brad Mehldau has endured in his explorations of the trio format, Mehldau fears not and stays in the Evans path as he tackles solo material. Granted, he doesn't follow the m.o. of Evans by recording solo and then overdubbing himself on a second piano, but he maintains the tone of Evans' highly cerebral originals and creates work that holds a charm distinct from his group work.

Mehldau, a 28-year-old who did his studying at Berklee, performed his new Warners disc *Elegiac Cycle* in his first set Tuesday, playing the compositions of others in the second. He says the new music is about death and "how music confronts us with our mortality." That said, Mehldau certainly kept the mood dark and much of the music very slow. Much of this is closed-in and abstract. And he serves up many of his conceits in couplets of notes played by the right hand against a left that alternates between a roar and a bath.

Strongest works were those influenced by real figures. His "Elegy for William Burroughs and Allen Ginsburg" was free of metre and often disturbing, using neo-classical flourishes to move out of the rougher edges only to return to an intriguing dialogue between the two hands. On "Good-bye Storyteller," dedicated to his late mentor Fred Myrow, he created a deliberate and pensive mood through broad yet gentle brush-strokes.

This work requires a definite focus and Largo works harder than any other club in town to allow that focus to happen. Mehldau is given a reverence by the audience that's a bit premature in his career, but his willingness to extend ideas beyond the well-defined walls of jazz at corporate labels is greatly deserving of praise.

Cibo Matto

Presented by Goldenvoice. Reviewed: June 16, 1996.
Band: Yuka Honda, Miho Hatori, Sean Lennon, Timmo Ellis, Duma Love.
Stereo Type A, Cibo Matto's worthy third album, shows how far leaders Miho Hatori and Yuka Honda have developed as global musical alchemists. Hoping for that melange of bossa-nova, lounge, hip-hop and good old-fashioned American pop to be laid out in a fashion similar to the record proved a bit much. Still, Wednesday's sold out show was vast improvement over the New York/Tokyo band's tours that followed 1996's now classic *Viva! La Woman*, even if the audience responded lethargically.

Now a quintet with Sean Lennon on bass and Duma Love on percussion, the band's sound not only gets fleshed out, but the rhythmic elements also have a greater place in the foreground. When Hatori emphasizes the child-high pitch of her voice, the wisps of innocence over the percolating beats create a sumptuous and unique brand of pop music. A poor, and at times hideous, sound mix clouded some of Hatori's charms and turned Honda's keyboards to mush, preventing the show from replicating the textured nuances of the new disc. As the evening rolled on, Cibo Matto went for increasingly rougher material until Hatori was screaming – a twist far removed from the attractive figure she cuts on softer tunes and during her raps.

Stereo Type A (Warner Bros.) debuted this week at No. 171 on sales of 7,250, a number that doesn't reflect the rabid attention paid this band by its young and ethnically diverse audience. Better acoustics rather than any tweaks of the act will help Cibo Matto develop into the first Japanese pop band with a career beyond novelty hits.

Paul Simon; Bob Dylan

Presented by Nederlander/SFX Entertainment. Reviewed: June 20, 1999.
Bands: (PS) Mark Stewart, Vincent Nguini, Jay Ashby, Chris Botti, Tony Cedras, Steve Gadd, Allain Mallet, Andy Snitzer, Bakithi Kumalo, Steve Shehan, Jamey Haddad; (BD) Larry Campbell, Dave Kemper, Tony Garnier, Charlie Sexton.

Artists working their way through greatest-hits concerts usually struggle with lifting a performance beyond rote renditions. The critical community, naturally, cringes at the thought of yet another superstar mindlessly working his or her way through a decades-old song at the expense of new material. Yet, Bob Dylan and Paul Simon, with no new discs to peddle, did justice to their great bodies of work in this brilliant yet unlikely pairing – even teaming up masterfully on "Sounds of Silence" and "Knockin' on Heaven's Door."

In opening the show – they alternate the headlining spot in this 22-city tour – Dylan devoted eight of his 12 songs to classics from the 1960s. He bookended his set with a pair of tunes that characterize the energy level of his last two years of constant touring: the rousing gospel-bluegrass number "Hallelujah, I'm Ready to Go" and Buddy Holly's Bo Diddley-inspired "Not Fade Away."

Simon, on the other hand, began with a dramatic reworking of one of his best-known pieces, "Bridge Over Troubled Water," orchestrating the intro with a gong and cello. Backed by his usual large band, which featured a number of players from his 1991 unit, Simon made use of their percussive heft in a set dominated by material from *Rhythm of the Saints* and *Graceland*. Whereas Dylan used his harmonica as a melodic, soloing instrument and adjusted his phrasing to the point where lyrics don't rhyme, Simon pushed along "Mrs. Robinson" to country trucking-song rhythm and magnified the Latin undercurrent in "Late in the Evening" before turning it into a jubilant blues.

Both performers were animated and smiling, the Pond's stunningly clear acoustics driving home their significance as songwriters. For many, this wasn't just familiar music, these were songs that have affected the way we approach life. Dylan has been consistently impressive in the 1990s in removing the simple, nostalgic impulse that a familiar song triggers, forcing the audience to listen, on this night, intently to "Mr. Tambourine Man," "It's All Over Now, Baby Blue" and, in duet with Simon, "Knockin' on Heaven's Door." (They also partnered on a medley of "I Walk the Line" and "Blue Moon of Kentucky").

For his part, Simon turned on the power on "Boy in the Bubble," "Me and Julio Down by the Schoolyard" and "Graceland," a masterpiece that should eventually be recognized as one of the finest songs composed in the 20th century. His horn section, led by trumpeter Chris Botti, whose third contempo jazz album has just been released on Verve, provided tremendous shading throughout the evening that included only one song from his Broadway endeavour, *The Capeman*, which he said "was really good." The song, "Trailways Bus," hints at the quality of the music and lyrics of *Capeman*; its failure was strictly the lack of a gripping story.

KROQ Weenie Roast

Presented by KROQ. Reviewed: June 19, 1999.
Bands: Red Hot Chili Peppers, Metallica, Limp Bizkit, Blink 182, Sugar Ray, Live, Kid Rock, Smash Mouth, Orgy, Pennywise, Moby, Lo-Fidelity Allstars, Living End, Freestylers, Lit.

KROQ's annual Weenie Roast benefit concert has less and less the feel of a single-minded event (the plentiful Hawaiian decor aside) and increasingly the vibe of a musical free-for-all. At this year's sold-out event, all-out anarchy – both onstage and in the sun-baked audience – often seemed just a moment away.

The always-impressive line-up this time was heavy on the testosterone, which made for a long, rowdy, messy and fun day for the 15,000-plus attendees, who started arriving around noon for second-stage turns from local young rock band Lit, DJ crew the Freestylers and Australian pop-punks the Living End. Mainstage got going around 3 p.m. with veteran punk outfit Pennywise, modern goth group Orgy and Orange County rock band Smash Mouth delivering well-received short sets, followed by the rap-metal noise of smart-mouthed Detroit singer Kid Rock, who, despite his band's weak music, was the first act to get ticketholders up and jumping.

Pennsylvania cerebral rockers Live and O.C. party band Sugar Ray followed with decent mid-afternoon turns, mostly dominated by familiar radio hits, but both played low-energy sets compared to the rest of the line-up. A new Live song, "The Dolphin's Cry," and Sugar Ray's series of heavy metal song snippets – think Iron Maiden and Twisted Sister – were the respective highlights.

Porn star Janine (of *Blondage* fame) introduced the popular teen punk band Blink-182, whose bassist Mark Hoppus performed the first couple of songs with only his bass between the crowd and his naked frame. The band's exuberant display, promoting their new top-10 MCA album *Enema of the State*, sparked a venue-wide food fight. Many on hand were clearly Limp Bizkit partisans. Singer Fred Durst repeatedly barked at the crowd to rush the stage, but few took his advice, though some did light a large bonfire on the grass. The group's upcoming sophomore album is one of the most anticipated rock releases of the season.

Metallica, otherwise on break between legs of a European tour, were the clear stars of the day. The veteran Bay Area group played a powerhouse though straightforward set of Metalli-hits, including "Battery" and "Master of Puppets," as well as the usual dose of cover songs, including opener "So What" by Anti-Nowhere League and the latest addition to the band's repertoire: "Die, Die My Darling," by the Misfits.

Red Hot Chili Peppers, not surprisingly, had a tough time playing right after Metallica (a tough assignment for any band), and recurrent sound problems as well as visible tension between the band members, didn't help matters. During the group's fourth song – "Around the World," from the Chili Peppers' excellent new *Californication* (WB) album – bassist Flea was so fed up with tech problems he tossed his instrument into the mosh pit, inciting a frenzy that resulted in a number of permanent seats becoming unbolted from the concrete and being passed overhead. The Peppers closed on a high note with a ferocious take on oldie "Me and My Friends," followed by an onstage tantrum by Flea, who took all his frustrations out on the band's rented equipment.

Dave Brubeck

Presented by JVC Jazz Festival. Reviewed: June 20, 1999.
Performers: Dave Brubeck, James Moody, Bobby Militello, Alec Dankworth, Randy Jones, Chris Brubeck.

... December 22 ...
The government of Thailand reaffirms its decision to ban **Anna And The King**, saying the film is disrespectful and contains several inappropriate scenes.

The ever-familiar and always comforting big block chords of Dave Brubeck, marked by his ever-present and resourceful gentle wit and imagination, dominated a richly layered JVC Carnegie Hall program of original compositions and familiar standards. At 79, the legendary pianist-composer displayed the wonderfully complex harmonic structure that has become a trademark, slipping into varying tempos and jaunty patterns of stride and waltzing invention with confidence and ease.

Those always memorable fat chords and rolling arpeggios dominated the Disney opener, "Someday My Prince Will Come," followed by the premiere of Brubeck's new dancing rumba, "A Time of Our Madness." A new minor blues, "You Can Run, But You Can't Hide," was heightened by an imaginative bass solo by Alec Dankworth. "Marian McPartland," a sprightly original tribute to pal and host of the syndicated public radio broadcast "Piano Jazz," was marked with a playful, swinging edge. Recalling his historic tour behind the Iron Curtain in the 1950s, Brubeck offered a graceful unaccompanied Chopin variation, followed by the ensemble in a bracing second take.

Second half was on more familiar terrain, with guest James Moody's tenor sax caressing the Jimmy Van Heusen standard "Polka Dots and Moonbeams" with his fat, warm sound and giving off a fervent romantic allure. Moody also added his trademark humorous spin on "Pennies From Heaven." Centerpiece was a Duke Ellington centennial tribute. Kicking off with "Things Ain't What They Used to Be," and a melancholy trombone interlude by son Chris Brubeck on "I Got It Bad (and That Ain't Good)," the ensemble soared with "Take the A-Train." It was the long evening's most spirited turn, finding Brubeck in a wonderfully hard, swinging mood and pushed fervently by the crisp support of his colleagues.

Anticipated closing rousers included David Brubeck's own timeless classic "Blue Rondo a la Turk," a racing ensemble blues turn motivated by its fiercely driving and infectious intro, and marked by the richly layered solos of Bobby Militello's singing alto sax and Chris Brubeck's bracing trombone. Paul Desmond's classic waltz "Take Five" has lost none of its infectious appeal over the years. The musicians sailed comfortably on familiar turf, framing Randy Jones' long inventive drum solo with a jubilant and driving spirit.

Three Fish
Presented by Goldenvoice. Reviewed: June 21, 1999.
Band: Robbi Robb, Jeff Ament, Richard Steverud, Cary Ecklund.
The music of Three Fish – an occasional jam band featuring Pearl Jam bassist Jeff Ament – is a mostly mellow melange of Middle Eastern-flavoured rock that's imbibed with spiritual lyrics influenced by the 13th-century mystical poet Rumi, all graciously rendered by three friends who formed the group while on a camping trip.

At the two-thirds full Troubadour on Monday the worldly band (supplanted by "Fourth Fish" Cary Ecklund on keys and percussion) offered a joyful program that was much-needed relief from the noxious music which otherwise currently dominates the commercial rock world. Dreadlocked South African-born singer Robbi Robb, also of rock band Tribe After Tribe, sang of "lovers in the dark" and "sailing ships" and "secret places" in his particular spooky style, while trading with Ament on a series of guitars, basses and other strange and wonderful stringed instruments, no doubt collected during their pilgrimage to Egypt.

The dozen or so mostly mid-tempo songs were taken from Three Fish's two exhilarating Epic releases, 1996's self-titled effort and the recently issued *The Quiet Table*, where the band further progressed into a cosmic realm of otherworldly musical exploration.

Sir George Martin; Hollywood Bowl Orchestra
Presented by Los Angeles Philharmonic Association.
Reviewed: June 25, 1999.
Performers: The Bangles (Susanna Hoffs, Vicki Peterson, Debbi Peterson, Michael Steele), Stewart Copeland, Andy Summers, Manuel Barrueco, Pip Clarke, Brad Delp, Peter Case, Adam Duritz, Trevor Rabin, Armand Sabal-Lecco, George Dearing, Tim Heintz, Rob Laufer, Zephyr: Voices Unbound, Hollywood Bowl Orchestra conducted by Sir George Martin. Emcee: Michael York.
Opening night galas at the Hollywood Bowl used to mean Beethoven or Mahler under the stars, and the realization that these weren't real openings at all – not after weeks of "pre-season" concerts. Well, things have changed in Cahuenga Pass – suddenly, startlingly. The "gala" opening is now the real McCoy, the first concert of the Bowl season. And rather than lead with a fistful of European symphonic music, the Bowl celebrated the music of a different European tradition – the Beatles – as conducted by their producer/catalyst, Sir George Martin.

One blanched at the tedious way in which the concert began, with cliché after overheated cliché tumbling forth at great length from actor Michael York. Yet Sir George, in his first appearance here since a 1973 date with the rock group America, lent an air of dignity and graciousness to the affair after the tasteless hullabaloo of the build-up. Martin talked personably, with obviously unique insight and eloquence, about his experiences with the Beatles; he clearly remains in genuine awe of their talent. He turned out to be a very competent conductor, displaying a clear, restrained beat and quiet authority. And despite problems with balance, he did preside over some memorable musical passages – along with others that did not come off well outdoors.

The publicity suggested that we were going to hear rare public performances of the orchestrations that Martin made for the Beatles' now-historic recordings. Well, it's not that simple, for Martin's contributions were not always performable, self-contained orchestrations. They could be decorations, inserts, brilliant extrapolations of suggestions made by the Beatles, or outright collaborations – and many were not written for a symphony orchestra.

So a lot of what was heard at the Bowl lacked the spirit and feel of Martin's charts on the records – the "Eleanor Rigby" music for string octet blown up to symphonic proportions, the thrilling pair of crescendos from "A Day in the Life" surrounded by unnaturally bombastic backing for the rest of the song. Other songs that did not have orchestral writing on the records received the treatment anyway. They could be restrained and tasteful ("Yesterday"), resourceful (Martin transcribing his famous speeded-up piano solo from "In My Life" for strings), or merely gaudy symphonic pops ("I Want to Hold Your Hand").

There was a brave attempt at the deliciously loony chart for "I Am the Walrus," but it was cut off by an abrupt concert ending just before it got really wild, as was "All You Need is Love." The biggest irony was hearing Martin conduct what amounted to the Phil Spector-ized chart for "The Long and

---

Winding Road," which Martin once pointedly derided as "laden with treacle." The results, alas, confirmed his astute assessment. But some original artifacts, such as the closing medley to the *Abbey Road* album and "For No One" – with its horn call superbly played by John Reynolds – came off pretty well. Easily the most authentic moment in the show – and to my ears, the most moving – was Sir George ardently conducting a suite from his own wonderfully melodic symphonic score for the film *Yellow Submarine*, where the Hollywood Bowl Orchestra could finally be heard clearly.

As the evening unfolded, Martin introduced a hodgepodge of guest rock, pop and classical performers – including two-thirds of the Police (Andy Summers on guitar, Stewart Copeland on overly aggressive drums) – who served up the John Lennon, Paul McCartney and George Harrison melodies with varying degrees of success.

The much-touted reunion of the Bangles – singing together for the first time in 10 years – was a bit of a bust; they were often out of tune and out of their depth, though "Across the Universe" was all right. Brad Delp (of Boston) contented himself with decent McCartney impressions; Peter Case conjured a faint facsimile of Lennon. Classical guitarist Manuel Barrueco had no trouble with the intricate filigree of "Here Comes the Sun" – though he, too, differed in pitch with the orchestra – and British violinist Pip Clarke performed a "Because" mini-concerto.

While quibbling over details is a favorite sport among millions of Beatleologists, ultimately those timeless tunes were sturdy enough to sweep the 13,489 customers away. And thanks to a few self-appointed female screamers in the boxes, Beatlemania circa 1964–65 (the years of the Fab Four's Bowl appearances) was sometimes at our throats again.

Gordon Lightfoot

Reviewed: June 24, 1999.
Band: Gordon Lightfoot, Terry Clements, Mike Heffernan, Rick Haynes, Barry Keane.
"Work through the repertoire here," said Gordon Lightfoot as he began his performance at the Greek Theater. As always, nothing else would be necessary. No opening act. No effusive showbiz patter. No special effects. Just a Canadian troubadour who has stayed with the same band over the years while compiling one of the deepest song catalogs in the business.

Lightfoot's place in the scheme of 20th century pop and folk music received a big boost with the release this month of the handsome *Gordon Lightfoot Songbook*, a four-CD box set from Rhino/Warner Archives. Those who have overlooked Lightfoot, now 60, should sample any portion of this box, for they will be jolted by the emotional range and quality of his songs over more than 35 years. His output has decreased since the mid-1980s, yet the quality remains amazingly consistent.

What proved most astonishing was that some of the best, most moving songs of the night were ones from last year's *A Painter Passing Through* album (Reprise). The disarmingly autobiographical title song is a gorgeous thing, the equal of virtually anything he's done in the past, and Lightfoot's insistent, folk-based, signature grooves and drones were as potent as ever in "Boathouse" and "Uncle Toad Said."

There's no getting around the fact that Lightfoot's voice has changed continuously over the decades; the delivery is more clipped, the tone more constricted (no doubt affected by some recent gigs in Nevada desert resorts). But it doesn't matter much, for he still puts the songs over with low-key savvy and obvious affection, with no hint of going into autopilot even when performing tunes he plays every time out ("The Wreck of the Edmund Fitzgerald," "Don Quixote," "If You Could Read My Mind," etc.). The band remains a fine-tuned engine, with Rick Haynes' inventive bass lines on "Edmund Fitzgerald" registering unusually well in this space.

With his new anthology very much in mind, Lightfoot was in a reminiscing mood in the second half, telling droll stories, including one about how Elvis changed the words in "Early Morning Rain."

Mary's Danish

Reviewed: June 28, 1999.
Band: Julie Ritter, Gretchen Seager, David King, Chris Wagner, Louis Gutierrez, James Bradley Jr., Michael Barbera.
There likely were several reasons why the members of early-'90s L.A. heroes, Mary's Danish, decided to get back together for this one-off gig at the House of Blues, but the usual motivations – such as a new album or even a record contract – were definitely not part of the equation.

The near-sell-out perf – part of the L.A. Music Week spotlighting the city's musical diversity – was a welcome return for the talented co-ed band, which was just one of many deserving local groups chewed up and spit out by the music industry in the last few years. In fact, the wheels for this show were put into motion by a weekly newspaper article in March which retold the band's bewildering history as part of a bigger examination of the sad overall state of the industry.

Playing here to a rousing reception and with all six original members together for the first time in more than six years (plus stand-by utility man Michael Babera), this reheated Danish was full of energetic flavour and nearly as good as back in the day, but the perf also was a reminder of why the band's music wasn't more successful in the first place. The group's eclectic funk-rock approach, which includes two duelling and polar opposite female vocalists, was brought to life by the House of Blues' kind sound system and was no doubt further propelled by the apparently unexpected hero's welcome accorded the reunited musicians by the happy fans. Show, comprising mostly songs from MD's three albums, was highlighted by snappy local radio favorites "Don't Crash the Car Tonight" and "Julie's Blanket" (a trib to singer Julie Ritter). It also included a couple songs from Battery Acid – the little-known Mary's Danish spin-off that featured singer Gretchen Seager and her husband, guitarist Louis Gutierrez – as well as a medley of "Foxy Lady" and "Dazed and Confused," and even one ("Bed") from Ritter's just-issued and self-released solo album.

As the 90-minute show (partly composed of a set-list voted on by fans at Ritter's web site) progressed, however, the band's shortcomings became more and more apparent. These shortcomings include the feeling that many of the songs simply go nowhere and completely indecipherable vocals. Also, a new song or two would have been nice.

Mary's Danish may have gotten a raw deal from the corporate world, but they did accomplish more than most bands do, and, as was made clear by the members' on-stage camaraderie, the music can be its own reward.

Richard Thompson

Reviewed: June 30, 1999.
Band: Richard Thompson, Danny Thompson, Teddy Thompson, Pete Zorn, Michael Jerome.
After folk-rock guitarist Richard Thompson, onstage at his sold-out show at the Roxy, announced that he was going to concentrate on new material, he joked that his audience's reaction couldn't have been any blanker had he announced he was performing "Springtime for Hitler" from Mel Brooks' *The Producers.* Self-deprecating cheek aside, Thompson thoroughly assuaged any scepticism that might have existed in the crowd and quite likely ensured a number of first-day sales of his upcoming CD by the time he concluded his two-hour set (including a 20-minute encore).

Thompson, a venerable, crafty songwriter who for 30 years has maintained a fan base that falls in the "diminutive but loyal" category, has maintained an admirable level of excellence in his recorded output. His most recent efforts have been somewhat melodically anemic, but *Mock Tudor* (Capitol), signifies a heartening return to form. Touted as a look back at Thompson's life in London from the '60s to the '80s, the new work features only a couple of tunes that suggest any real reminiscing. "Uninhabited Man" elliptically concerns fallen fellow musicians (two singers whom Thompson had dated died in accidents in the '70s). "Sights of Sounds of London Town," destined to be a future fan favorite, offers a portrait of a gallery of luckless rogues; introducing the song, Thompson drolly announced that it was "sponsored by the London Tourist Authority."

Instead, *Mock Tudor* has Thompson doing what he does best – harsh, alternately cynical and heartbreaking reflections on love and life. Producers Tom Rothrock and Rob Schnapf, who have worked with Beck, the Foo Fighters and Elliott Smith, have punched up Thompson's sound without forcing a strained, more "contemporary" sensibility upon him, and the result is perhaps his most consistently satisfying effort since 1991's *Rumor and Sigh.*

Thompson's concert got off to a rocky start, however, when his band took the stage but drummer Michael Jerome was nowhere to be found. Initially nonplused, Thompson quickly settled into a brief acoustic set. He dueted with his son Teddy (a vocalist as expressive as his pop, with a contract of his own with Virgin) on "Persuasion," a song Thompson collaborated on with Tim and Neil Finn (whom Thompson, taking a shot at his employers, referred to as "former Capitol recording artists").

Once Jerome surfaced, the group exploded into *Mock Tudor*'s opening number, "Cooksferry Queen." The ensemble immediately worked up a head of steam – the rhythm section of Jerome and Thompson's brother Danny, on stand-up bass, propelled the music with muscle and authority all evening – and the show's false start was quickly forgotten. In all, nine songs from the upcoming album were featured, with Thompson offering particularly impassioned performances and incendiary guitar solos in new numbers "Two-Faced Love" and "Hard on Me."

Older material was eventually incorporated into the set. The ballad "Jennie" was re-imagined into something more brawny yet still wistfully evocative; "Al Bowlly's in Heaven" evinced even more of a jazz flavour, benefiting from superb soloing from Danny Thompson and versatile instrumentalist Pete Zorn on clarinet. "She Twists the Knife Again" was given a typically blistering reading, but the biggest crowd-pleaser was

"1952 Vincent Black Lightning," in which Thompson proved he didn't need to solo on electric guitar to be electrifying.

Thompson largely eschewed material from his inspired years with ex-wife Linda (it must be interesting psycho-drama for Teddy to perform those numbers with his mom absent). Only "I Want to See the Bright Lights Tonight" made it into the set before the encore, but the evening did conclude with the one-two punch of "Wall of Death" and "A Man in Need."

Widespread Panic

Reviewed: June 30, 1999.
Band: John Bell, Dave Schools, Todd Nance, Michael Houser, Domingo Ortiz, John Hermann.
The increasingly popular Athens, Ga., based Widespread Panic, which played the last of three sold-out shows at massive Red Rocks Amphitheater near Denver earlier in the week, brought its big, warm Southern rock sound – and an even bigger entourage of loyal followers – to the intimate House of Blues Wednesday for the first of two hot-ticket shows, previewing the group's upcoming sixth studio album.

The three-hour, 15-minute extravaganza, offered as two sets with a short intermission, barely acknowledged the fine material on *Til the Medicine Takes* (Capricorn). Instead, the group packed the show with such fan-approved concert faves as 1991's "C. Brown" and the always wonderful "Traveling Light" (from the 1988 *Space Wrangler* debut), which opened the concert and set the evening's jubilant tone.

The new album introduces fresh elements to WP's soaring sound and backs away from the old-school guitar-jam approach. That sense of exploration was scratched at here with the country swagger of "Blue Indian" and the compact stomp of "Climb to Safety." Most of the evening, though, was dedicated to freeform excursions built around cuts such as live standard "Greta" (during which everyone in the house seemed to be dancing or smoking something usually not allowed in the venue) and the festive "Tall Boy," both from 1997's *Bombs & Butterflies.*

This U.S. preview tour wraps July 27 and 28 at Gotham's Roseland Ballroom. Band then heads for Europe and returns for a full U.S. campaign later in the year.

Joe Strummer and the Mescaleros

Presented by Delsener-Slater. Reviewed: June 30, 1999.
Musicians: Joe Strummer, Antony Genn, Martin Slattery, Gerard Lynch, Pablo Cook, Scott Shields.
It's been more than two decades since Joe Strummer drew punk rock's generational line in the sand, railing that there'd be "No Elvis, Beatles or Rolling Stones in 1977." And while the former Clash frontman has turned down plenty of offers to cash in by reuniting the band, the first New York show by his newly formed group bore telltale signs of nostalgia.

Ostensibly a sneak preview of the first release from the Mescaleros (Strummer's first recording since 1989's *Earthquake Weather*), the sweaty set approached oldies-revue status, thanks to a heaping helping of back-catalog crowd favorites. Strummer, still wiry and intense at 46, looked delighted at the prospect of dusting off long-dormant songs like "London Calling," but the Mescaleros' execution was decidedly hit or miss. False starts and fluctuating energy levels dogged the band midset, particularly during "Rock the Casbah," which was undercut by equipment problems that rendered Strummer's guitar-slashing all but inaudible – a problem offset by the volume of the audience sing-along.

Interestingly, the band fared much better on the more intricate material from bygone days: a brooding "Straight to Hell" transfixed even the most dedicated whoopers in the crowd, while "White Man in Hammersmith Palais" – propelled by Strummer's raspy whispers – was both sinister and uplifting.

Most of the new material previewed could pass for out-takes from the Clash's sprawling, experimental "Sandinista," steeped as it is in dub reggae and murmuringly psychedelic soul arrangements. Strummer managed to disguise the songs' relative similarity by doling them out judiciously, separated by more diverse Clash classics. Still, a brace of the more recent compositions stood out. "Yalla Yalla" boomed with dubwise rhythms, while "Andy Jones" – which Strummer introduced as "a song about soccer" – avoided the pitfalls of the sports chant, and delivered both sharp hooks and incisive diatribes. In short, it doesn't seem that Strummer will have to look backward for much longer.

The Go-Go's

Reviewed: July 8, 1999.
Band: Belinda Carlisle, Charlotte Caffrey, Jane Wiedlin, Gina Schock, Kathy Valentine. Special guests: Berlin, the Lunachicks.
When the weather turns especially warm, the time is right for reunion tours and golden oldies nights, and on this muggy evening in July, the Go-Go's fit the bill. The first self-contained all-female rock ensemble ever to top the charts has reunited to play a brief summer tour. This concert was their first local appearance since 1989 and their first in a large L.A. venue in 15 years.

Opening with the semi-instrumental "Surfin' and Spying" and segueing into "Head Over Heels," the band established its patented perky groove, albeit slowed down a notch, and despite an abbreviated rehearsal schedule (Carlisle missed the first two weeks of the band's reunion practices), they were suitably disciplined. Sticking mostly to the songs from their debut disc *Beauty and the Beat* and their radio hits, the Go-Go's turned in a standard set with a few interesting exceptions. Dipping back into the songbook of their club days, they performed the punked out, X-like "Fun With Ropes," as well as the Capitols oldie "Cool Jerk," complete with Carlisle's hilarious patter and parody lyrics about the true intention of their reunion ("We need big bucks for tummy tucks," explained the singer). Instrumentally, the group was carried by powerful drummer Gina Schock and the surprisingly raunchy lead guitar work of Charlotte Caffrey, whose fills sounded like a surfed-out Johnny Thunders or a crazed Duane Eddy – good show!

Back-up dancers, a slightly extended "We Got the Beat" (with Carlisle blowing the lyrics and losing it on the high notes), "Turn to You" with cocktail lounge jazz introduction – it's the stuff a one-off get together is made of. The rain stayed away, the audience sang and danced in their seats, and the Go-Go's are halfway to the facelifts and boob jobs Carlisle claimed they're working for. What else could you want?

Robert Cray/John Lee Hooker/Keb' Mo'

Presented by the Greek Theater and the New Dodge.
Reviewed: July 9, 1999.
Bands: The Robert Cray Band (Robert Cray, Andrew Love, Wayne Jackson, Carl Severin, Kevin Hayes, Jim Pugh), John Lee Hooker and Coast to Coast Blues Band, Keb' Mo'.
They called this four-hour triple-header a World Class Rock and Blues Festival – no doubt inspired by the "world class rock" slogan of 103.1 FM – and the tag wasn't too far off the mark. The audience heard a revitalized Robert Cray Band, a still-spry, 81-year-old John Lee Hooker and Kevin Moore (who prefers to be called Keb' Mo'), who offered up a master class of genre mixing – the most interesting set of the night.

Keb' Mo' came out alone with his slippery slide dobro a la Robert Johnson, but before long, the L.A. native and his band were throwing all kinds of things into the pot. At one point or another, he successfully mixed a country influence with R&B, a Cajun accordion with a stomping rocker, a 6/8 shuffle with an early-'80s Paul Simon feel. Yet the stylistic blends that came off best were those allied to strong song material, often drawing soundscapes of the Delta or offering wise words of self-help.

Though 1998's well-chosen anthology *The Best of Friends* (Pointblank) was a powerful chronicle of Hooker's renewed vitality in the 1990s, it also led listeners to wonder whether he is only as good as the company he keeps these days. Yet in the early going, while the Coast to Coast Blues Band tried to find its bearings, it was the Hook who kept the show alive on sheer mannerisms alone – those weird atonal electric guitar janglings, the mumbled vocals that could still convey a touch of menace on "Crawlin' King Snake." When the band finally kicked into gear with a killer full-throttle boogie after warming up with a rocking "Boom Boom," Hooker merely puttered around the stage in his role as presiding cheerleader for the single most infectious moment of the mini-festival.

For Cray, his primary inspiration these days comes straight from '60s–'70s vintage Memphis, and that resulted in a powerhouse set of Stax and Hi Records riffs, grooves and mannerisms – even some Steve Cropper-like guitar from the leader. Enlivened by the pair of Memphis Horns (Andrew Love, tenor sax; Wayne Jackson, trumpet) and Jim Pugh's galvanic organ, Cray's band provided a tight, precise backdrop for his strong, soulful vocals which, following the sinewy groove of "Right Next Door," included some first-class blues howling.

Pavement

Presented by Goldenvoice. Reviewed: July 8.
Band: Steve Malkmus, Scott Kannberg, Mark Ibold, Bob Nastanovich, Steve West.
Nothing turns a good college-rock band into a great one more quickly than a plenteous dose of conflict. And with lots of open hostility on the El Rey stage Thursday, slacker heroes Pavement took ill vibes, mixed in their distinctive brand of alt-country-blues-rock and crafted the kind of engaging show that the 10-year-old band's fans crave but rarely get anymore.

Instead of setting and keeping a slow and methodical pace, as has been Pavement's tendency over the last couple of years, singer-guitarist and embattled leader Steve Malkmus kept everybody guessing at this second of two sold-out shows with a seemingly random approach to the evening's song list, which ultimately included more of the band's straight-up rockers than usual.

That sort of onstage captaining may have irritated his bandmates (all five members of Pavement reside in different parts of the country, by the way), but for the audience the net effect was positive. In fact, after the show, many of the band's mostly male fans declared the concert to be one of their best local shows in quite some time. At the least, it was their weirdest.

Following the unusual beats and Dead-inspired jamming of "Speak, See, Remember" from Pavement's recently issued fifth studio album, *Terror Twilight* (Matador), Malkmus took an unscheduled bathroom break, leaving his surprised bandmates to wait for him with their instruments at the ready. After Malkmus sprinted back onstage, the eccentric (and now-relieved) singer launched into the rowdy "Conduit For Sale," from the group's 1992 debut, though his mates were clearly expecting to play something else.

When guitarist Scott Kannberg (known to fans as Spiral Stairs) took lead vocals during the encore on 1995's "Kennel District," Malkmus could be seen making goofy faces, as if unable to give up the spotlight to someone else, even his childhood friend Kannberg. Of course, that's just the sort of anti-rock-star posturing and smug attitude that fans have come to love.

The amusing 80-minute show, which opened with the obscure 1992 track "Frontwards," ended with a rare display of unity during a lengthened version of the combustible "Fight This Generation," a quiet-to-loud love song that seemed an apt finale for this unexpectedly dynamic production.

Cher
Presented by Delsener-Slater Enterprises. Reviewed: July 13, 1999.
Band: Paul Mirkovich, David Barry, Don Boyette, Stacy Campbell, Pattie Darcy Jones, Mark Schulman, Darrell Smith.
Taking the stage under an atomic mantilla of red curls, swathed in a medieval mishmash of chain mail and synthetic fabrics of more recent invention, and sporting suede boots fit for a stroll on the tundra, Cher soon defuses one's slack-jawed amusement (or is it horror?) at her ensemble by registering her own. "How do you like my Braveheart-meets-Bozo outfit?" she slyly asks, freezing withering sarcasms on spectators' lips. That's Cher for you: showmanship unafraid of tastelessness, combined with a healthy sense of the ridiculous. This irresistible mixture was amply displayed Tuesday night, as the performer's latest tour stopped at Madison Square Garden for a single night in front of an enthusiastic sell-out crowd.

If anything can explain this icon's genius for thriving through three decades and more of dubious decisions, mediocre musical output and the occasional, career-saving collision with the Zeitgeist, it's probably her humor. Humor, and the perspective it brings, gives her an ability to look at her latest obsession with a jaundiced eye. Cher doesn't stick with a bad idea – or any idea – for too long; she drops it when it's not working and moves on. "What was I thinking?" could be the paradoxical motto of a career that has outlasted most of her contemporaries'. (By the way, some advice: the Gothic moment is over.)

Her current concert is thus a fascinating trip through varied stylistic terrain, with each segue accompanied by an appropriate switch of the sartorial gears. Musically, she's always been a little out of step – it's fitting that her current hit single "Believe" has made her a disco queen 20-some years after she first jumped on the bandwagon – but she makes up in Vegas flash and determination what she may lack in musical savvy and vocal subtlety. It's been said that you leave some current Broadway shows humming the scenery; at a Cher concert, you leave humming the sequins.

Of which there are, thank heaven and Bob Mackie, plenty on display during the diva's 90 minutes or so onstage. The *Mad Max* vision she opens the show with (singing U2's "I Still Haven't Found What I'm Looking For") gives way to an Adam Antish pirate glam ensemble over a classic Mackie body stocking for a smoothly techno-fied version of Bon Jovi's "We All Sleep Alone." Most dazzling is the explosion of silver beading she dons to perform her '70s disco fizzle "Take Me Home" as colored lights play across a giant plastic lava lamp and inflated pillows in the background.

At 53, Cher still possesses the rare physique that is flattered by flesh-colored Lycra, and she swaggers and wags her wigs with the tireless energy of a performer half her age – or indeed half her daughter's age, which is probably closer to the average of today's arena-fillers. Her sexy contralto bellow has gained a husky sandpaper edge over the decades and remains a forceful if less than nuanced instrument. (The perfection of the vocals on many songs did suggest lip-synching, but if Cher, spawner of a thousand drag queens, can't lip-synch with impunity, who on Earth can?)

The crowd warmly received the hits as well as the star's cherished misses. In performance, she is as committed to her techno-disco nuggets from what she dryly calls her "new, cool" album ("Believe" and the catchy "Strong Enough") as she is to the rock ones of her last musical comeback ("I Found Someone" and "If I Could Turn Back Time"). Clearly, the woman has never met an anthem she didn't like.

As a whole, the show certainly doesn't compare in stylishness to the artfully designed arena performances of Madonna, an equally tireless if more tasteful taker of the cultural temperature. Cher's dancers are able, but the choreography is mostly generic Vegas gyrating, and the set comprises a mostly slapdash array of typical pieces without any unifying style. In any case, fans probably come to Cher for an audience with an icon, not a memorable aesthetic experience. And she delivers a show that is both glaringly flashy and spiced with flashes of real intimacy (of a bomb album, she wryly admitted, "I think four of my gay friends bought this one, and that's it."). Ageless in her fame, and famously ageless, she remains a compelling presence, a performer who is somehow most appealing when she's on the way back, as she always seems to be: the underdog as superstar.

The show opened with a brief, appealing set by R&B trio Wild Orchid, and a longer performance from Cyndi Lauper, herself a career survivor of considerable pluck, and a gifted vocalist and musician whose songs supplied some of the heart that Cher mostly displayed when she wasn't singing.

Bruce Springsteen and the E Street Band
Reviewed: July 15, 1999.
Band: Bruce Springsteen, Clarence Clemons, Nils Lofgren, Danny Federici, Steven Van Zandt, Max Weinberg, Patti Scialfa, Gary Tallent, Roy Bittan.
Bruce Springsteen has been no stranger to hype over the years, having been dubbed the savior of rock 'n' roll more than two decades ago. Well, rock 'n' roll is no closer to being saved now than it was when those words were first uttered – and the second coming of Broo-ooce and the E Street Band isn't likely to change that.

... December 27 ...
Pedro Almodóvar's **All About My Mother** earns
14 nominations for Spain's 14th Goya Awards.

As an exercise in nostalgia, however, the first leg (in Rutherford, N.J.) of this month-long homecoming party was hard to fault. While he tried to steer his audience to nuggets of lesser renown through much of the evening, Springsteen proved most effective when stomping through the hits with the same marathoner's tirelessness he demonstrated back in the '70s.

A European warm-up tour notwithstanding, the band showed signs of rust on its first few numbers, particularly "My Love Will Not Let You Down" and "Darkness on the Edge of Town." Thanks in part to an attractively overhauled arrangement, "The River" saw the E Streeters hit their stride – one that was maintained through a passel of uptempo tracks highlighted by "Badlands." Unfortunately, Springsteen didn't leave enough room for those faster-paced numbers, breaking momentum with maudlin pieces like "Streets of Philadelphia" and the as-yet-unrecorded "Freehold" (a sullen Jersey set piece that harkens back to his earliest days).

When he did pick up the pace, Springsteen often seemed forced – a complaint that could never have been lodged against him at his peak. Where stream-of-consciousness ad libs once livened songs like "Tenth Avenue Freezeout," the ones proffered for this occasion were dated, shot through with bar-band colorlessness.

There were moments when the band truly let loose, when Springsteen and guitarist Steve Van Zandt achieved perfect synchronicity, as on the brassy "Murder Incorporated" and an encore rendition of "Thunder Road." But too often, the Boss seemed bent on asserting his status as one of rock's true serious artists – or, worse yet, one of its elder statesmen.

Lilith Fair

Presented by Universal Concerts. Reviewed: July 17, 1999.
Bands: Sarah McLachlan, Sheryl Crow, Pretenders, Dixie Chicks, Mya, Luscious Jackson, Sixpence None the Richer, Beth Orton, Cibo Matto, others.
Whatever scenarios singer-songwriter Sarah McLachlan dreamed of when, in 1997, she launched the first of what would prove to be three Lilith Fair tours, chances are pretty good this gloriously sunny Saturday afternoon at the Rose Bowl more than lived up to them.

The event's well-rounded collection of musicians was an improvement over last year's more sleepy line-up and included the rousing country-rock of Dixie Chicks; the steady, always-inspired classic rock of the Pretenders; enthused singing and dancing from 18-year-old R&B sensation Mya; and star turns from headliners Sheryl Crow and McLachlan.

Following earlier B-Stage and Village Stage performances – highlighted by Cibo Matto's candy pop and low-lighted by Sixpence None the Richer's bland melodies – the mainstage perfs kicked off under a blazing sun with the edgy dance-rock of Gotham's Luscious Jackson. Now a trio, the ladies sampled their new Grand Royal/Capitol album, *Electric Honey*. They were followed in the late afternoon by Interscope's Mya, who drew cheers from the supportive crowd thanks to an impressive display of tap-dancing accompanying the funky R&B jams taken from her excellent 1998 eponymous debut album.

Just edging out Crow for best set of the day was the Pretenders, led by the gritty Chrissie Hynde, who smartly mixed a hearty 8-song batch of old favorites such as "Talk of the Town," "Middle of the Road" and "Back on the Chain Gang" with tracks from their just-issued new Warner Bros. album *Viva el Amor* like "Popstar" and "Human." A song or two from

their 20-year-old landmark first album, say, "Precious" or "Brass in Pocket," would have made the perf complete.

Crow and her tight band started strong, opening with "A Change," from her self-titled 1996 A&M album, and peaking midset, when Beth Orton (who was impressive on the second stage as well) joined for a duet of "Train in Vain" by the Clash, a song notable here for its key "stand by your man" lyric. Stevie Nicks joined in on the fun two songs later, for a crowd-pleasing duet with Crow of the urgent "Strong Enough," from Crow's 1993 debut.

As was the case for the previous two years of Lilith, Sarah McLachlan's hour-long closing set of poignant love songs – mostly taken from her four distinguished Arista albums – were a bit anti-climactic at the end of the long, hot, rocking day. Yet songs like the angelic "Sweet Surrender" and "Building a Mystery" proved soothing and dreamy accompaniment as the big, eclectic crowd caught its collective breath, awaiting the traditional big show close.

Practically every musician who played on all three stages this day joined in for a celebratory encore reading of the 1969 Jackie DeShannon hit "Put a Little Love in Your Heart," an appropriately warm ending to a festival that will surely be missed next summer.

Sugar Ray

Presented by Nederlander. Reviewed: July 20, 1999.
Band: Mark McGrath, Rodney Shepherd, Stan Frazier, Murphy, DJ Homicide.
Orange County party-rockers Sugar Ray – whose concerts can either be really good or really bad, depending on where and when you see them – were in their festive element at the sold-out Greek on Tuesday, and in this pressure-free, three-band setting, the five overachieving musical hooligans made the most of their talents with an energetic and self-deprecating effort.

As part of an overall dull bill that also featured opening act Fastball and headliner the Goo Goo Dolls, Sugar Ray – the only one of the three groups that doesn't take themselves seriously – acquitted themselves well this balmy evening with a crowd-pleasing mix of the hard-rock, hip-hop and ballads found on their three platinum-plus Lava/Atlantic albums.

Vocalist and center-of-attention Mark McGrath, sporting a slick new hairstyle, told the raucous and often screaming crowd that his voice was hurting him again (like it always is when the band plays L.A., he said), but that doesn't really matter anymore because McGrath's singing voice is hardly the reason most people go to a Sugar Ray show. During rock songs like "RPM" and opener "Glory," the muscular and popular frontman made up for his lack of vocal dexterity with an exhaustive, non-stop flurry of onstage aerobic activity that brought the youngish crowd – which was lured here by no less than three competing local radio stations – out of their plastic seats.

Slower tunes like the melancholic "Fly " – which this time was dedicated to John F. Kennedy Jr. and included a kindergarten-aged girl who jumped into McGrath's arms during the song – and "Every Morning" became big sing-a-longs that brought beaming smiles (and even some tears) to the musicians' faces.

The skilled samples and scratches executed by DJ Homicide – who rode on and off the stage on his bicycle – added much-needed seasoning to the muddy, guitar-heavy sound mix.

... December 28 ...

Gong Li is to be the president of the international jury for the 50th anniversary edition of the Berlin Film Festival.

Kula Shaker

Presented by Nederlander. Reviewed: July 21, 1999.
Band: Crispian Mills, Alonza Bevan, Jay Darlington, Paul Winter-Hart, Brett Findlay.
Much-hyped U.K. rockers Kula Shaker gave an unexpectedly ferocious display of straight-ahead rock 'n' roll at the near-capacity Mayan Theater.

Band mixed Brit rock and pop references from the 1960s and '70s (the Beatles, Pink Floyd, King Crimson, the Who) with a worldly dose of exotic instruments and Indian vocal chants for an impressive and liberating 75-minute production that skipped the indulgent extremes of their L.A. debut three years ago.

Quintet was led by intense singer-guitarist Crispian Mills, the son of actress Hayley Mills and director Roy Boulting. He attacked this performance with the attitude of a just-uncaged animal, slashing wildly at his guitar as his band followed along with a series of mystical jams and powerful grooves. The 15-song show actually peaked at the start as the band launched the gig with a ferocious three-song punch featuring "Hey Dude," from their 1996 debut *K*, a cover of Hawkwind's 30-year-old tune "Hurry on Sundown" and the driving organ-fueled "303."

The set slowly mellowed as it unfolded; moody tracks such as "Shower Your Love," from the band's new album, *Peasants, Pigs and Astronauts* (Columbia), their 1997 alt-radio hit "Tattva" and an interesting cover of Deep Purple's "Hush" surged with psychedelic flow, while encore "Great Hosannah" closed the evening with a long and satisfying jam.

Jake Andrews

Reviewed: July 27, 1999.
Band: Jake Andrews, Mike Sconce, Alvino Bennett.
The first signing to vet producer John Porter's Sire-distributed Jericho label, Jake Andrews is a sharp and sturdy blues guitarist cast in the Texas mold created by Stevie Ray Vaughan. Vaughan's spectre will certainly hang over Andrews but not curse him as this young, sharp-dressed Texan gets more gigs under his belt. As he boldly proved toward the middle of his 75-minute set, he does bring some new and interesting ideas to the table.

Andrews, 18, playing overly loud to an enthusiastic throng, started on a high note with two basic shuffles. Playing the title track of the disc *Time to Burn*, Andrews stretched out with a fluid mix of chords and simple lead lines, the individual notes signalling a bitter sting within a dense pattern – a move he would repeat often as he gave each shuffle its own personality. From start to finish, bassist Mike Sconce and new drummer Alvino Bennett were always on the same page as Andrews, holding steady in a musical style that only works when the timing is dead on.

At his best, Andrews exhibited a flair for breaking up the rock-steady meter. On one number, Bennett started in a New Orleans second-line rhythm before segueing to the Bo Diddley beat as Andrews wandered unconstrained by the rhythmic limitations. He delved into a jazzy improvisation that demonstrated his ability to move rapidly around the fret board without sounding cliched and then showcased a dynamic sound that's far more open prairie than urban grit.

Andrews has honed his skills on Austin's stages for nine years and attracted fans such as the late Albert Collins and Jimmie Vaughan. His rock 'n' roll numbers lack the compositional depth of his blues numbers, but it is encouraging that

his starting point includes a few risks – a sign that he's on his way to more adventurous work.

Whitney Houston

Presented by Universal Concerts. Reviewed: July 29, 1999.
Band: Michael Baker, Myron McKinley, Jetro DaSilva, Jubu Smith, Alex Evans, Taku Hirano, Gary Houston, Sharlotte Gibson, Valerie Pinkston, Cindy Mizelle. Guests:Monica, Bobby Brown.
Wasting no time to establish her new hip-hop-flavored style, Whitney Houston knocked out three tunes from her new *My Love Is Your Love* album at a sold-out Universal Amphitheater, providing a point of view far removed from that of the over-the-top balladry for which she has come to be known. In her first tour in five years, Houston appeared incredibly at ease performing a wide range of material, proffering herself believably as mother, friend and religious believer. Casual in her rapport with the audience, yet exquisitely dressed, Houston offered spectacular vocals without being forced into a histrionic showcase on every other phrase.

She and musical director Michael Baker put together a show that impressed at almost every turn. Her hip-hop numbers – "Get It Back," "Heartbreak Hotel" and "If I Told You That" opened the concert – hold water thanks to the maturity of the lyrics and the twisting nature of beats that never lose track of the melodies.

Houston isn't attempting, a month shy of turning 36, to play a young woman's game – she expresses adult concerns in her songs, embracing acceptance, compromise and forgiveness instead of distance and a doe-eyed concept of love. Not surprisingly, the privacy-invasion tune "In My Business" was given a defiant, and very diva-like, staging in which her four dancers swarmed around her with cameras as she attempted to fight them off. Husband Bobby Brown lent some comic relief at the end of the bit, grabbing a camera and taking a picture of Houston's behind.

That sort of good-natured fun went a long way toward presenting Houston in a new light. Separately, she turned her back to the audience and touched up her make-up as the band played the opening introduction to a song, and when she asked the audience to sing the endless "shoop shoop" chorus from her "Waiting to Exhale" hit, she didn't worry about insulting the fans whose enthusiasm and singing were lacking. The woman's got a sense of humor. And after several comments about the strength of their marriage, Houston, Brown and daughter Bobbi Kristina engaged in a bit of improvised singing that bore all the signs of a happy family. Best of all, not one moment of her show felt overly stagy.

Musically, Houston divided the evening into relatively neat segments: new hip-hop, hit ballads, hit dance numbers (this section was preceded by the one costume change), a pair of gospel numbers and the finale, "I Will Always Love You," which, surprisingly, was the only song on which she saw fit to flash her impressive vocal range. Encore for was current fiery single "It's Not Right But It's OK."

Houston stuck to the arrangements of her records, save for an updated version of "I Wanna Dance With Somebody (Who Loves Me)," which was given a suitable house groove. When she dove into a pair of gospel numbers, Myron McKinley switched from electronic keyboards to the acoustic piano and altered the evening's timbre, giving the musical accompaniment a human edge in line with Houston's message of togetherness, prayer and family. Her ballads could use more pure instruments in the backing; the electronics get the job done in reproducing the record, but when an artist like Houston is giving that extra effort, as she appeared to be on this night, there shouldn't be anything hindering the complete delivery.

Kenny Garrett

Reviewed: July 28, 1999.
Band: Kenny Garrett, Nick Smith, Nat Reeves, Marcus Baylor. Guest: Roy Hargrove.
The approach is not unlike that of a major league hitter who likes fastballs on the first pitch: the action is immediate and the results often scintillating, the rare breathtaking moment in a baseball game. The alto saxophonist Kenny Garrett stood sideways to audience, whispered a count and bam! Like a hitter smacking the ball toward the bleachers, he and the band were off and running with abandon for 15 minutes on Herbie Hancock's "One Finger Snap."

Having come to prominence in one of Miles Davis's later bands, Garrett, a consistent poll winner for his alto saxophone playing, is a fireball in a live setting. On his recent Warner Bros. outing, *Simply Said*, and the handful that preceded it, by contrast, he stresses melody and coherence, venturing into the light side of rap, funk and the music of John Coltrane.

On this, the second set of the second night, Garrett displayed a wondrous sense of invention as he tackled Coltrane's "Giant Steps" with far more intensity than he did on record, venturing unaccompanied with focus intact and showcasing his band, particularly the light touch of pianist Nick Smith.

Venturing into his own compositions, Garrett began to simmer on numbers such as "Charlie Brown Goes to South Africa," which is exactly that – Vince Guaraldi with funky polyrhythms – and his spin on beat poetry, "Back Where You Started." Garrett's key foil is drummer Marcus Baylor, who kept time within a flurry of patterns that were sometimes too sprawling for the music while his solos were welcome flights of hard-nosed drumming. But the evening got an added spark when ace trumpeter Roy Hargrove approached the stage from the side and began a duel with Garrett that continued through the final three numbers. Hargrove clearly pushed Garrett without upstaging him, a demonstration of the rewards only jazz can deliver when the musical environment is perfect.

Allman Brothers Band

Presented by Nederlander and NASCAR. Reviewed: July 31, 1999.
Band: Gregg Allman, Dickey Betts, Jaimoe, Butch Trucks, Marc Quinones, Derek Trucks, Oteil Burbridge.
Summer after summer in the 1990s, the Allman Brothers have been a sure thing, but on the occasion of their 30th anniversary, they pushed the performance a little bit harder, and the results were stupendous.

Reason No. 1: in Derek Trucks, nephew of drummer Butch and leader of his own band prior to joining the Allmans in March, gives co-leader Dicky Betts an extra push during instrumental breaks, presenting original challenges to which Betts responds time and again. Different from former guitarist Warren Haynes, who brought an overbearing muscular quality to new material but stuck to recreations of Duane Allman's work, Trucks gives even the warhorses such as "Statesboro Blues" a personal twist – for such a young player, he has considerable command of the slide guitar and this

genre. Show toppers were extended versions of the chestnut "Blue Sky" and 1975 instrumental "High Falls."

Reason No. 2: Gregg Allman has given up smoking and is singing considerably more than he did on his last two visits. Arguably the best white blues singer alive, he made a strong case on emotional, driving versions of "Please Call Home" (from his 1973 solo debut), "Black Hearted Woman" and the closer of the 135-minute show, "Whipping Post."

As always, the band gave a thorough overview, including material from virtually every album, this time slightly favoring their 1969 debut and 1970's "Idlewild South." The Allmans have also added an intermission to the proceedings (more time to check out NASCAR gear?), which provided some breathing room before the show's acoustic portion, which on this occasion started with "Seven Turns." (In the past, an uncomfortable shifting of players and instruments was required.)

Band premiered one new number, "J.J.'s Alley," overloaded with winding guitar riffs in search of a chord progression. While it sounded distinct from the rest of the material, its essence was uniquely Allman, further proof that no other band possesses the magic of this still vital unit.

Iron Maiden

Presented by Nederlander. Reviewed: July 30, 1999.
Band: Bruce Dickinson, Steve Harris, Dave Murray, Adrian Smith, Janick Jers, Steve Harris, Nicko McBrain.
Veteran British hard rockers Iron Maiden gathered what's left of L.A.'s old-school metal faithful at the Greek on Friday and treated the scruffy sold-out crowd to an ear-piercing, eye-popping barrage of headbanging selections mostly lifted from the band's classic '80s albums.

Group's now-wrapped SRO U.S. itinerary boasted the return of vocalist Bruce Dickinson, and both parties were far better for the reunion; Dickinson's post-Maiden solo career went nowhere, and the band floundered creatively and commercially in the mid-'90s with replacement vocalist Blaze Bayley. Prodigal guitarist Adrian Smith also made his return to Maiden on this tour (which promotes an upcoming best-of album and videogame), giving the group a new, unrelenting triple-guitar attack. (Smith's replacement, Janick Jers, remains with the band despite Smith's return.)

Following warm-up sets from heavy bands Monster Magnet, Soulfly and Puya, the headliners hit the Greek stage to the strident strains of "Aces High" and lustily proceeded with satisfying versions of old faves like "2 Minutes to Midnight," the dramatic, immortality-seeking "Powerslave" and oldie "Phantom of the Opera," which Dickinson intro'd by recalling Maiden's glory days appearances at the Long Beach Arena. The group also sprinkled newer material, like the nightmarish "Fear of the Dark," throughout the set, though with far less effect on the crowd.

The genre's usual stage effects, including lots of foglike smoke and blinding flash-pot explosions, were supplemented by Iron Maiden's trademark set decor, which resembled a haunted castle, and the production's ever-changing backdrops, which featured numerous stimulating visuals. Evening also saw the mid-show return of bloodthirsty group mascot Eddie, a 14-foot-tall rotting zombie who staggered about the stage swatting at band members. Show closed strongly with a trio of songs from Maiden's excellent 1982 album *The Number of the Beast*, capped by a quick version of "Run to the Hills."

... December 30 ...

The year ends with the showbiz industry handing out 3,182 trophies at 332 ceremonies.

Rodelinda

A Music Academy of the West presentation of George Frideric Handel's three-act opera; text by Antonio Salvi and Nicola Francesco Haym after Pierre Corneille. Opened at Lobero Theater, Santa Barbara, and reviewed Aug. 6. Running time: 3 hours, 30 mins.
Conducted by Randall Behr; directed by Christopher Mattaliano; designed by Troy Hourie, James Scott, Trevor Norton; Karen Wierzba (Rodelinda), Bejun Mehta (Bertarido), Lance Clinker (Grimoaldo), Daesan No (Garibaldo), Edyta Kulczak (Eduige), Anne-Marie Seager (Umulfo).
Founded in 1947 by legendary soprano Lotte Lehmann, Santa Barbara's Music Academy of the West produces a summer workshop and festival that's ever-growing and ever-more cherishable. And while Lehmann is said to have had little use for operas composed before the time of her beloved Mozart, this summer's homage to Baroque master George Frideric Handel ranks high in the Academy's half-century's-plus achievement annals.

Composed in 1725 when Handel could do no wrong in the eyes of opera-mad London, *Rodelinda* stands apart from its composer's other works: The opera's plot unfolds on a human scale rather than in the world of gods, goddesses, magicians and monsters. Queen Rodelinda believes her husband, Bertarido, has been killed by usurpers; actually, he is living incognito, gathering forces for his return to bed and throne. Some three hours later, this happens (with a share of hairbreadth near-fatal misunderstandings along the way). As befits the scenario, Handel has created music unusual in its warmth and sensuous beauty; a love-duet at the act two curtain, all mellifluous thirds and sixths, could pass as the most beautiful of all his music.

For Santa Barbara's first Handelian excursion, director Christopher Mattaliano developed a setting that is elegant but simple, marked by a smooth managing of exits and entrances to offset the episodic nature of Baroque opera. His villains smoke cigarettes; heroes and villains brandish up-to-date handguns. James Scott's military get-up and simple gowns did not represent a particular time or place. In the pit, Randall Behr's expert small ensemble, backed by a properly placed harpsichord, gave out the proper sounds for a Handelian orchestra.

Casts for Santa Barbara's one-per-summer operas are drawn from young professionals, who work under the academy's faculty led by voice program director Marilyn Horne, an ardent supporter of restoring Handel to the repertory. A distant cousin of conductor Zubin Mehta, Bejun Mehta sang with an ease that belied the brevity of his career. Part of a highly skilled cast – Karen Wierzba's Rodelinda overcame a couple of inevitable one-note disasters in what is a killer role – Mehta stole the show. He may next hone his art of grand thievery on Sept. 26 in the New York City Opera's first-ever production of Handel's *Ariodante*. Although the world may want for adequate romantic tenors and Wagnerian sopranos, in the countertenor department with Mehta alongside Americans Brian Asawa and David Daniels, the ranks are brimming and golden.

Regina Carter; Dee Dee Bridgewater; Ray Brown; Clayton-Hamilton Jazz Orchestra

Presented by the Los Angeles Philharmonic Assn. Reviewed: Aug. 6, 1999.
Bands: (Ray Brown) Brown, Geoff Keezer, Karriem Riggins; (Clayton-Hamilton Jazz Orchestra) John Clayton, Jeff Clayton, Jeff Hamilton, Charles Owens, Rickey Woodard, Keith Fiddmont, Lee Callet, Isaac Smith, Ira Nepus, George Bohanon, Maurice Spears, Oscar Brashear, Eugene (Snooky) Young, Clay Jenkins, Bobby Rodriguez, Bijon Watson, Bill Cunliffe, Christopher Luty, Jim Hershman; Regina Carter; Dee Dee Bridgewater.
If the will to swing is a crucial component of jazz – as Wynton Marsalis endlessly reminds us – then this edition of Lexus Jazz at the Bowl was an undoubted success. It was precisely this quality that carried the first half of the evening, fuelled by the rhythmic engines of two superb piano trios, whose momentum spilled over into the big band second half.

One of the trios – John Clayton (bass), Bill Cunliffe (piano), Jeff Hamilton (drums) – provided a solid launching pad for the Bowl solo debut of fast-rising violinist Regina Carter. Carter, whose new Verve album is *Rhythms of the Heart*, has plenty of room to run, for few jazz violinists emerge due to the sheer difficulty of mastering the instrument and the rigorous classical training violinists undergo that usually has little or nothing to do with improvisation and swing.

Carter retains some of the formalities of the classical world – standing stock still with a studious look, throwing in classical arpeggios as a cadenza. But when she unleashed her silky-smooth tone, gently teasing glides, ample box of quotes and subtle swing on "Lady Be Good," there was little doubt that jazz is firmly in her bloodstream. Later on, she handled herself with aplomb before the roaring Clayton-Hamilton Jazz Orchestra.

Earlier, Ray Brown's laconically witty trio broke convincingly out of the piano trio rut with some creative arrangements – a slow, irresistibly breezy "Honeysuckle Rose," and a get-down, soul-jazz treatment of "Reunion Blues." The lift provided by the Brown trio also brought out the best in Dee Dee Bridgewater, whose Ella-like scatting was especially energizing when thrown into a dialogue with Brown on "Bye Bye Blackbird." She took some chances, stretching "Cherokee" way out of shape at an extremely slow tempo before snapping back into place, and seemed even more comfortable reacting to the big band in some Ellington tunes.

Indeed, the CHJO is settling nicely into its role as the Bowl's resident jazz anchor, and co-leader John Clayton is encouraging his team to have some fun. Their best moment was an informal blues, "Shout Me Out," on which the two soloists, tenor saxophonist Charles Owens and trombonist Isaac Smith, were cracking up their colleagues (and many in the audience) with some zany, out-there, yet firmly musical flights.

Rage Against the Machine

Presented by Goldenvoice. Reviewed: August 3, 1999.
Band: Zack de la Rocha, Tom Morello, Tim Bob, Brad Wilk.
L.A.'s politically minded metal-punk-rap band Rage Against the Machine followed recent festival appearances at Woodstock '99 and the Mt. Fuji Festival in Japan with their first headlining concert of 1999 at Honolulu's Blaisdell Arena, where the quartet effectively packaged songs from their seven-year, multi-platinum-selling career along with two strong tunes tabbed for their forthcoming third album.

Twelve-song show opened with "Bombtrack," the incendiary lead track from the group's memorable 1992 self-named debut, with the band sounding a little rusty and looking just a bit tentative. But the enthusiastic welcome accorded the band and the unrelenting mosh-pit, quickly changed the band's collective mood. The two new songs were among the highlights of the one-hour, 45-minute production. "Testify" (a working title, according to band members) found dread-locked singer-shouter Zack de la Rocha warning that "He who controls the past, controls the future," while skilled guitarist Tom Morello produced strange and wonderful feedback-laced sounds from his instrument.

Of the older Rage tracks, 1992's "Know Your Enemy" and "Bullet in the Head" created the usual mosh-pit bedlam, as did 1996's "Bulls on Parade" and "People of the Sun," from No. 1 album *Evil Empire* (Epic). None of the bombastic tunes boasted even one chord change, and powerhouse drummer Wilk fell behind the beat more than once, but in the grand and overwhelming atmosphere of a solid Rage Against the Machine live performance, those are trivial complaints.

Gotham's blues bastards the Jon Spencer Blues Explosion opened the show with a blistering hour-long effort, though it took a few songs to win over the sceptical crowd.

Jerry Goldsmith; L.A. Philharmonic

Presented by the Los Angeles Philharmonic Assn. Reviewed: Aug. 6, 1999.

Friday marked a homecoming of sorts for Jerry Goldsmith. The veteran composer for 180 films has won an Oscar, received another 17 nominations and won five Emmys, conducted major symphony orchestras around the world including London and Carnegie Hall, and built a reputation as one of the movies' most versatile and respected music writers. But he had never conducted an orchestra in public in his home-town, which happens to be Los Angeles.

Goldsmith, who turned 70 in February, finally got his wish, conducting the L.A. Phil. in a two-night stand at the Hollywood Bowl. The two-hour, 30-minute program show-cased two dozen of his themes for movies and TV from the past 40 years, mixing scores for celebrated films (*Chinatown*, *Patton*) with memorable music from nearly forgotten ones (*The Wind and the Lion*) and recent commercial hits (*The Mummy*).

Missing among his more famous works were the Oscar-winning music for *The Omen* and his avant-garde score for *Planet of the Apes*. The former demands a choir, and the absence of the latter can be excused by the fact that picnick-ing weekend Bowl audiences aren't usually in the mood for complex exercises in atonality. Emphasis was on the upbeat and familiar.

Goldsmith, closely identified with the *Star Trek* franchise via scores for four of the movies and themes for two of the TV series, even had a Klingon deliver his baton at the top of the show. (Later on, more costumed characters appeared: Disney's Mickey Mouse and Mulan led the audience in a sur-prise "Happy Birthday" singalong to the maestro.)

The Philharmonic shone on Goldsmith's more lyrical compositions such as the love themes from *Chinatown* and *The Russia House*, but demonstrated a decided lack of energy in the more aggressive material, notably the opening *Star Trek* music. Highlights were two long medleys of classic themes that, for families present, bridged the generations (the 1960s' *Sand Pebbles* with the 1980s' *Basic Instinct* in the film medley; *Dr. Kildare* with *Star Trek: Voyager* in the TV medley).

The inevitable airplane obbligato came just minutes late: Instead of passing overhead during the theme from *Air Force*

One, it ruined an exquisite piano-violin duet in Goldsmith's next number, the tender theme for *A Patch of Blue*. Music from last summer's Disney smash *Mulan* (mostly the songs, which Goldsmith didn't write), the new Oscar fanfare and a powerful suite from *L.A. Confidential* rounded out the film excerpts.

The Phil. commissioned a new piece to accompany the fireworks in Cahuenga Pass. Goldsmith's "Fireworks: A Celebration of Los Angeles" was designed to portray, in the composer's words, "the energy, the fun, the casualness" of L.A. His nine-minute ode to the city was alternately lighthearted and dramatic, dignified and exciting (and unfortunately, often obscured by the noise of the fireworks).

The composer's between-tune tales ranged from amusing (a story about pal Sean Connery emulating his ponytail in *Medicine Man*) to bizarre (a report that Panamanian dictator Manuel Noriega surrendered to authorities only after hearing Goldsmith's *Patton* theme played repeatedly over loudspeak-ers). As a conductor, his style wasn't flamboyant; instead of playing to the crowd, focus was on eliciting a solid perfor-mance from the orchestra, a result of years of studio-con-ducting experience.

Bad Company

Presented by Nederlander. Reviewed: Aug. 8, 1999.
Band: Paul Rodgers, Mick Ralphs, Boz Burrell, Simon Kirke.
The four original members of Bad Company wrapped their first U.S. tour in nearly 20 years at the sold-out Greek, where the blues-rockers gave a decent if incomplete accounting of why they're considered among the elite of the classic rock era. Kicking off the program, appropriately enough, with "Can't Get Enough," from their excellent 1974 self-named debut album, the graying musicians hit the stage all smiles, perhaps a step slower than in their 1970s heyday, but still able to cre-ate a mighty musical force. Bad Co. blazed through such hits as "Feel Like Making Love," which was given new life by the aggressive playing of animated bassist Boz Burrell, the dra-matic "Shooting Star" (a bit disappointing because of Mick Ralphs' weak guitar solo), and their old beach song "Seagull," performed solo acoustic by frontman Paul Rodgers, whose soulful singing voice is still among the best in rock.

Satisfying show's one failing was the inclusion of five non-hits in the 14-song set, including two new songs from the band's recently released *Anthology* (Elektra) album that are hardly worth mentioning. Unplayed gems like "Good Lovin' Gone Bad," "Burning Sky" or "Run With the Pack" would have made the show complete. Band instead chose to perform the acoustic "Soul of Love" from one of Rodgers' solo albums and Freddie King's blues instrumental "Hideaway."

Rodgers' piano was rolled out for the encore, which includ-ed the beautiful love song "Silver, Blue & Gold" and the smouldering '74 classic "Bad Company."

Al Kooper

Joe's Pub. Reviewed: Aug. 9, 1999.
It would be a stretch to call Al Kooper one of rock's over-looked masters, but the 40-year veteran has certainly built up a body of work expansive enough to be considered one of the music's master craftsmen, able to take just about any material and build something memorable.

The Brooklyn native mined material culled from his '60s stint with the Blues Project, his work with Blood, Sweat and Tears and his solo career for a two-hour homecoming gig in the Public Theater's jewel box of a new lounge. Although the evening was billed as part of the "Piano Night" series, the typically contrary Kooper began his set by strapping on an electric guitar and launching into the Blues Project favorite "I Can't Keep From Cryin' Sometimes." Demonstrating impressive vocal chops, he segued from the growling tone of that number to the lush melodrama of "Just One Smile" without missing a beat.

Remarkably, Kooper's falsetto seems to have grown sharper with the passing years, as borne out by an encore rendition of the gospel classic "A Brighter Day." The intimate setting afforded the singer the opportunity to spin some lengthy yarns that showed off his raconteur side. But like many artists, Kooper faltered in judging his own work, which led to the airing of decidedly dated oldies such as the bubblegum "Violets at Dawn" (the Blues Project's first ever offering) and the grandiose Blood, Sweat and Tears groaner "The Modern Adventures of Plato, Diogenes and Freud."

Kooper fared much better when he stuck to more emotionally direct tunes from those earlier days. "I Can't Quit Her" proved to be positively wrenching. Similarly, his more contemporary material, especially "Going, Going Gone," came off as sharp and sardonic.

REM
Presented by Nederlander Concerts. Reviewed: Aug. 9, 1999.
Band: Peter Buck, Michael Stipe, Mike Mills, Joey Waronker, Ken Stringfellow, Scott McCoy.
Velvet Goldmine, the bomb of a film that Michael Stipe executive produced more than a year ago, must have taught him a lesson about rock 'n' roll: it ain't all that serious. Eighteen years after REM reintroduced regionalism and abstraction to rock 'n' roll and one year after drummer Bill Berry departed what is arguably the finest record-making unit of the last two decades, REM delivered a show with humor and bite.

The questionable facet of Stipe and company has long been its ability to execute in concert what they so expertly put down on tape. As has been true in past tours, it's not so much the new album that dictates the flavour of the evening but the most recent predecessors, in this case 1996's *New Adventures in Hi-Fi* and 1994's *Monster*. On each of those records, REM made a concerted diversion into grittier material that relied on density of sound rather than the airiness they had seemingly trademarked in the 1980s.

The softer material from *Up*, their first with hired hand Joey Waronker subbing for Berry, meshed well with the more energetic songs; the Brian Wilson-inspired "At My Most Beautiful" is a graceful and melodic step forward from two of their grandest hits, "Man on the Moon" and "Losing My Religion," all of which were among Monday's highlights. *Up*'s "Walk Unafraid," on the other hand, is the most dissonant and churning song REM has ever penned, which worked exquisitely as an adventurous bridge between the more popular "Finest Worksong" and "Man on the Moon," which was dedicated to Andy Kaufman biopic director Milos Forman.

Show was the band's first on the U.S. leg after an extensive overseas tour that ended two weeks ago in Slovenia. They began with a ferocious burst of energy, delivering impassioned versions of "Lotus" and "What's the Frequency, Kenneth?" with Stipe careening about the stage as an over-enthusiastic madman. Lights stayed on Stipe throughout the evening – there were moments when the band couldn't even be seen from midway back in the crowd – and his comfort level onstage alternates with the change of songs. And he still loves to play the mysterious figure: when he introduced a song as guitarist Peter Buck's favorite, the crowd was blessed with the gliding "Sweetness Follows"; the song he introduced as his fave had the audience scratching its collective head trying to decipher lyrics of the obscure "E-Bow the Letter" from *New Adventures*. As Berry's replacement, Waronker brings considerable punch to the band's sound that fortunately avoids anything bombastic. Waronker lifted the final third of the droll "Everybody Hurts" and, throughout the evening, supplied a locked-in beat that has eluded REM for years.

As has been their wont, show was 90 minutes long with a half-hour of encores that included Stipe demonstrating his pedestrian acoustic guitar skills on the new "Falls to Climb," a breakneck version of "End of the World" and Stipe goofing on Elvis with a verse of the King's "Suspicious Minds." The band debuted one as-yet unrecorded number, "The Great Beyond," that would not have been out of place on 1994's *Monster*.

Moby
Presented by Universal/Hewitt/Silva. Reviewed: Aug. 12, 1999.
Band: Greta Brinkman, Scott Farssetto.
Gotham-based techno star Moby did everything but sell soda and popcorn during his concert at the very sold-out Mayan Theater on Thursday, where the multi-instrumentalist composer gave a high-energy clinic in genre splitting and splicing. The bald, 33-year-old musician started the first song of the 100-minute show on acoustic guitar as he and his small backing band laid down a relatively straight-ahead rock groove. But it wasn't long before he began to alternate instruments (keyboards, bongo drums, electric guitar) and musical styles as fast as the crowd could keep up. He's called a techno artist, but Moby's concert blend of punk, dance, R&B, funk and house music, not to mention the mix of dance beats and folk and blues samples found on his acclaimed new *Play* album (V2), indicate an artist much more complex than that simple tag would indicate.

Fun concert, which featured opening act Boom Boom Satellites, gained momentum, volume and intrigue as it went along; the second half of the show concentrated more on the exhilarating grooves found on Moby's early-'90s recordings, like the infectious "Bring Back My Happiness," which had the crowd dancing en masse. Regular set closed with a string of tunes from *Play*, including the colliding musical worlds of "Natural Blues" and the propulsive "Bodyrock." Encores included club hit "Feeling So Real."

Stand-Up Opera
A Ninad Prods. presentation, in association with Duane Poole, of a comedy revue with music in two acts performed by B.J. Ward. Opened and reviewed Aug. 13, 1999. Running time: 1 hour, 20 min.
Directed by Gordon Hunt. Musical direction, Joseph Thalken. Set, Michael Devine; lighting, John De Santis. Producer, Tammy Taylor.
It has been a few years since singer/actress B.J. Ward began her comical sojourn through the great operatic arias in a series of Sunday brunch performances at Hollywood's

Gardenia cabaret. Under the direction of longtime ally Gordon Hunt, Ward has refined her often hilarious musings on the works of such European stalwarts as Verdi, Puccini, Bizet and Mozart into a seamless interaction of music and comedy that is greatly enhanced by music director/pianist Joseph Thalken, who serves as both accompanist and foil. But what makes this latest "Stand-Up" routine memorable is Ward's poignant, deeply introspective side trips into the English-language works of Carlisle Floyd, Gian Carlo Menotti and George Gershwin.

Ward possesses a wonderfully malleable vocal instrument but does not present the effortless vocal control and range of a Kathleen Battle or Cecilia Bartoli. Striding about the stage and occasionally into the audience dressed in a black suit and tennis shoes, she exudes an aura of hard work as she tackles Verdi's challenging "Sempre Libera" (*La Traviata*), the recitative-rich "Si. Mi chiamana Mimi" (*La Bohème*) or Bizet's zesty "Seguidilla" (*Carmen*). It is that very effort, however, that sets up her droll between-aria chatter. Collapsing on the floor after the stratospheric "Sempre Libera," Ward complains, "There is no need for a note to be that high." Commenting on the tragic social life of Puccini's Mimi, she informs the audience, "Nineteenth-century Paris was a tough dating town." Later, she sums up Musetta's self-serving "Quando me 'n vo'" (*La Bohème*) by calling it an "Italian 'My Way.'"

The comedic high point of the evening comes when Ward enlists the aid of Thalken to perform Mozart's duet, "La ci darem la mano" (*Don Giovanni*). The two exhibit Marx Brothers-like fluidity, timing and zaniness as they alternate on both the vocal and piano duties without missing a beat. For the first-act closer, Ward demonstrates she is an actress of considerable skill, offering Gian Carlo Menotti's "To This We've Come" (*The Consul*), a deeply moving indictment of the monolithic government bureaucracies that have been set up to thwart immigrants seeking a better life.

In the second act, she continues her beautifully introspective English-language musings with Floyd's tender folk opera aria, "Ain't It a Pretty Night!" (*Susannah*). Ward quickly gets back on the comedy track when explaining that the opera's heroine, Susannah, was plagued by the narrow-mindedness of the local clergy. "It just goes to show that evangelists do more than lay people," she shrugs.

Ward is known for her surprises. Announcing she has added Gershwin's "I Loves You Porgy" (*Porgy and Bess)* to the program, she launches into the passion-filled aria only to have baritone Michael Smith rise unannounced out of the audience to provide an exquisite rendering of Porgy's "Bess You Is My Woman Now."

"Stand-Up Opera" is aided by the simple but mood-enhancing scenery and lighting of Michael Devine and John De Santis, respectively.

Anita O'Day
Reviewed Aug. 17, 1999.
Band: Marty Harris, Jim DiJulio, Jack LeConte.
Between the three 40-minute sets Anita O'Day performed Tuesday, a screen drops behind the Atlas stage, and the singer is seen in her early 20s bouncing, dancing and singing with a rowdy Gene Krupa behind the drums and Roy Eldridge delivering a mighty trumpet solo over Krupa's fierce big band. It's a welcome sign that O'Day is so willing to address the ghosts that surround her return –in the lobby she sells her autobiog-

raphy that ends with her kicking heroin in the late 1960s – that it's easy to accept what age and a destructive lifestyle have done to her voice.

O'Day turns 80 next month and has considerably cleaned up her act in the three years since she was hospitalized, and some say near death, after a fall at her trailer in the desert town of Hemet. Her return, which included a gig at Gotham's Avery Fisher Hall in June with the Manhattan Transfer, has been accompanied by an eye-opening box set from the mail order reissue label Mosaic of Stamford, Conn. The nine-CD set, *The Complete Anita O'Day Verve/Clef Sessions*, showcases her recordings from 1952 to 1962 and delivers a sturdy argument that revolutionary jazz singing wasn't limited to Ella Fitzgerald and Sarah Vaughan as revisionist historians have argued.

Tuesday evening, O'Day was four lines into "Let's Fall in Love" and already showing she had lost none of her phrasing skills. The absence of held notes, the subtle gaps in lines, the scatting and the dropping in, for effect, of "la-la-la" phrases dominated her perf. O'Day turns Louis Jordan's jumpy "Is You or Is You Ain't (My Baby)" into a slow blues, singing against Jim DiJulio's walking bass and emphasizing the heartache of the lyric with a crack and, unlike other jazz singers, virtually no quiver in the higher register.

Tales have long been told of O'Day's demands of sidemen, and she asserts her musical mind onstage, calling out keys and tempos, giving soloists a specific number of bars and then counting them off, and then questioning a move she wasn't quite prepared for after a song ends. Pianist Marty Harris backs her with understatement and fluidity. Through it all, she sings admirably, a touch groggy but always emotional and always in key. Her range was never that wide to start, and as more and more septuagenarians step to the stage – Jimmy Scott, John Lee Hooker, Ruth Brown – there's a sense of forgiveness between audience and performer that has its rightful place.

O'Day keeps her sets short, singing four songs and handing the microphone to Mark Miller, an engaging if dry mellow-voiced tenor.

Lyle Lovett
Presented by Universal Concerts/Discover Today Motorcycling. Reviewed: Aug. 11, 1999.
Band: Lyle Lovett, John Hagen, Buck Reid, Ray Herndon, Tim Ray, Dan Tomlinson, Gene Elders, Viktor Krauss, Steve Marsh, Harvey Thompson, Vinnie Ciesielski, Charles Rose, Francine Reed, Sir Harry Bowens, Sweet Pea Atkinson, Willie Greene Jr.
The return of the Large Band behind Texas troubadour Lyle Lovett is no nostalgic exercise. After a three-year absence, during which time Lovett converted his backing unit to an all-string band steeped in bluegrass and then turned his attention to other writers' songs, the band shines in its collective polish and in solo turns. And Lovett is the grand captain, quiet in his command of the troops and the stage, telling new and quirky stories, and an absolute delight weaving through well-worn material.

Show emphasized material from the new MCA disc *Live in Texas* (it rhymes with give) and its predecessor, *Step Inside This House*. The *Live* album is culled from a 1995 performance, guaranteeing that Wednesday's show would be a bevy of familiar favorites and songs written for the larger ensemble. While Francine Reed's stellar blues rave-up "Wild Women Don't Get the Blues" and the Reed-Lovett duet on "What Do You Do" were note-for-note recreations of the live versions, the two-hour show was filled with sufficient nuance and shifting settings to all seem fresh again.

Lovett, who started the horn 'n' gospel Large Band in 1989 after establishing himself as a new-breed country singer-songwriter, continues to escape any pigeonholing. Wednesday's show began in a Southern soul instrumental, wandered into vintage country ("Stand By Your Man"), a fusion of folk and funk ("Penguins"), Texas swing ("That's Right [You're Not From Texas]"), gospel ("Church") and soft-spoken Texas balladry ("North Dakota").

The subject matter, as always, is love, the varying degrees of dependence and tributes to the diversity of the Lone Star State. It doesn't get any more American. And as performing in the 1990s goes, it doesn't get any better.

Santana & Mana

Presented by Nederlander. Reviewed: Aug. 13, 1999.
Bands: (Santana) Carlos Santana, Tony Lindsay, Benny Rietveld, Chester D. Thompson, Rodney Holmes, Karl Perazzo, Raul Rekow; (Mana) Fher Gonzalez, Sergio Vallin, Juan Calleros, Alex Gonzalez.
It was old-school versus new-school in a battle of Latin Rock generations at the sold-out Anaheim Pond on Friday. The third of four co-headlining shows paired original Woodstock veteran Carlos Santana and his band with Mana – the current Rock en Espanol kings – and the clear winner was the diverse audience, treated to a long and rewarding evening of uplifting cross-cultural music.

Following a triumphant opening performance by L.A.'s eclectic Ozomatli – which consummated with the band's traditional drum parade into and through the cheering audience – the anticipation in the air was palpable for Guadalajara's Mana, an entirely unremarkable rock outfit that's all the rage in Latin music circles.

Long-haired frontman Fher Gonzalez sang (in Spanish) about love, life and liberty, while his three bandmates produced a string of mostly simplistic songs that, sung in English, surely would have appealed to Bon Jovi and Journey fans back in the '80s. Mana (which alternates set slots each night with Santana during their month-long tour of the U.S. south-west and west) easily won over the crowd with an energetic and infectious approach that had the fans up front screaming for their favorite members, namely guitarist Segio Vallin and drummer Alex Gonzalez, both of whom scored bouquets of flowers from enraptured females.

Nearly everyone in attendance seemed to know the words to all the songs, the best of which were the sweeping ballad and big radio hit "Como Questa" and a tune whose title translates into "I Don't Care," which the fans responded to by throwing panties and hats onto the stage.

Visionary guitarist-composer Carlos Santana didn't play his usual hits-filled set, but instead took advantage of the many talented musicians on hand and the open-minded audience, while offering a dramatic lesson in grace and imagination. The opening trio of songs, notably old favorite "Everybody's Everything," featured the always-festive Ozomatli horn section. The 90-minute production featured a host of Santana's more obscure, jam-oriented material that gave room for all the talented players to shine, though each song ultimately rose and fell on the beautiful tones and breathtaking leads and solos from Mr. Santana's six strings.

Show closed with a pair of classics, the newly arranged "Black Magic Woman" and a party version of "Oye Como Va" that nearly had Santana in tears, as he told the audience that, "This has been the best tour of my whole life."

Brian Setzer Orchestra

Presented by Nederlander. Reviewed: Aug. 14, 1999.
Band: Ray Herrmann, Tim Misica, Steve Marsh, Rick Rossi, Don Roberts, Dan Fornero, John Fumo, Kevin Norton, Dennis Farias, George McMullen, Michael Vlatkovich, Mark Jones, Robbie Hioki, Ernie Nunez, Tony Garner, Bernie Dresel.
Brian Setzer capped the most successful tour of his solo career with a luau-themed party Saturday night at the near-full Greek, the second of two nights at the Griffith Park site, where the former Stray Cats leader and his big band celebrated one of the biggest, if not most unlikely, comebacks of the '90s. Opener "Let's Live It Up" (also the name of the tour), from Setzer's platinum-plus 1998 Interscope album *The Dirty Boogie*, set the no-holds-barred tone for the evening.

The guitarist-vocalist and his snap 17-piece orchestra (reeds on the left, horns on the right) then train-rolled through a satisfying set of rocking originals, such as "This Cat's on a Hot Tin Roof"; classics such as Santa & Johnny's 1959 No. 1 instrumental "Sleep Walk" and encore "Mack the Knife"; and souped-up versions of Stray Cats hits "Stray Cat Strut" and "Rumble in Brighton," which featured a nifty lead-and-follow between Setzer's fiery guitar and the playful horn section.

Show was a bit too similar to last summer's appearance at the same venue (though where was Gwen Stefani to sing "You're the Boss" this time?), and Setzer's bragging about the two Grammy Awards was a bit off-putting. But the musician, whose career appeared permanently in the dumper early this decade, looks to the next one having cashed in, after an inauspicious restart in 1994, on his second chance at success.

Watcha Tour

Presented by Nederlander & WARP magazine. Reviewed: Aug. 15, 1999.
Bands: Molotov, Cafe Tacuba, Fishbone, Control Machete, Illya Kuryaki, Puya, Bersuit, Chris Perez Band, others.
The same folks who gave punk rock fans a safe outdoor place to play in the summer, via the successful Warped Tour, have this year launched the Latin Rock-themed Watcha Tour, which hopes to give an annual national outlet for both established and rising artists of the Rock en Espanol persuasion.

This year's model, featuring such stars as double-bass hard rockers Molotov, L.A. funk-rock merchants Fishbone and the twisted Cafe Tacuba, ended its two-week, 10-city run through the south and south-west U.S. at the three-fourths full Greek Theater on sunny Sunday, where singing, dancing and indulging in food and drink was the order of the long day. The above-mentioned groups provided most of the highlights during the six-hour production, though a revolving stage that kept all of the bands' 30-minute sets on or near schedule allowed for a total of 12 acts to perform, also including the Chris Perez Band, led by the widower of slain star Selena, as well as the aggressive sounds of Puerto Rican metal act Puya and East L.A. punks Union 13.

Fishbone – which earlier had played an entirely different set at an afternoon benefit for ill Circle Jerks singer Keith Morris at the Whisky – was the post-sunset trigger that finally set off the tired audience, which was composed almost entirely of young Latinos. Bald 'Bone singer Angelo Moore stirred the crowd's fire by leaping into the audience and performing 1991's "Sunless Saturday" while riding over the kids' upstretched hands, ignoring the guy who threw an entire drink on his head.

Mexico City's Cafe Tacuba's unique sound, which combines traditional Mexican songwriting with modern alt-rock flourishes, stood out from much of the less-imaginative music around it. They were the most impressive performers of the day, particularly bassist Quique Rangel, whose screeching upright instrument made a lasting impression.

Headliner Molotov brought the show to a close with a heavy, Led Zep-informed style that included such crowd faves as the reggae-flavoured "Chinga tu Madre" and the musical fiesta "Molotov Cocktail Party," where the drummer and the singer switched places.

The Cult
Reviewed: Aug. 16, 1999.
Band: Ian Astbury, Billy Duffy, Matt Sorum, Martyne LeNoble, Mike Dimkich.
What could reasonably be called a new and improved edition of popular '80s and early '90s hard rockers The Cult opened an unprecedented seven-night sold-out run at the Sunset Strip's House of Blues.

The sound at the packed club was fattened by the recent addition of second guitarist Mike Dimkich, who added heft to the familiar riffs and solos of original six-stringer Billy Duffy. Long-haired frontman Ian Astbury easily fell back into the role of rock star, barking at fans with insults that were intended, no doubt, to incite the crowd members to mosh faster and cheer louder.

Ninety-minute show was a virtual greatest-hits run-through, including such enduring radio station fodder as "Fire Woman," "Sweet Soul Sister" (the band's catchiest), "Lil' Devil" and a smoking take on "She Sells Sanctuary." Following a quick break, Astbury and the band (which recently inked a new deal with Atlantic Records) returned to the stage, where the singer – who looks and sings quite like Jim Morrison – quipped, "Perhaps you're witnessing the most misunderstood band since the Doors."

The group then launched into the surprise track of the night, a trippy rendition of their semi-obscure 1985 gem "Phoenix" (which Astbury introduced as "Kitty Litter Disco"), followed by the adrenaline-pumping closer "Love Removal Machine."

Chris Isaak
Presented by Nederlander. Reviewed: Aug. 29, 1999.
Band: Kenny Dale Johnson, Rowland Sallie, Hershel Yatovitz.
Musical swashbuckler Chris Isaak had 'em dancing, rolling and swooning in the aisles at his good-time concert at the Greek on Sunday, a winning 110-minute production that featured plenty of musical skill, casual but undeniable sexiness, and gut-busting humor – the unbeatable combination that generally makes Isaak's shows something special.

Dressed in shocking purple suits, Isaak and his superb long-time band Silvertone (guitarist Hershel Yatovitz is a relatively recent addition) displayed an audacious and unusual sense of timing – not to mention dexterity – as they seamlessly shifted between painful ballads like 1995's "Somebody's Crying" and all-out rockers like "Speak of the Devil," the title track from Isaak's recent seventh album for Reprise/Warner Bros.

Isaak – who looks like James Dean, sings like Roy Orbison and cracks wise like a less-frantic Jim Carrey – offered a smoldering version of "Baby Did a Bad, Bad Thing," his 1995 song that was featured in this summer's *Eyes Wide Shut*, and a festive cover of "Diddley Daddy" (which he intro'd by disclosing his discovery that "all L.A. people are freaks," which he seemed to mean as a compliment).

The encore marked the return of Isaak's show-stopping "human mirrorball" suit, which the audience greeted with uproarious laughter, even though he set about performing such heart-wrenching material as 1993's "Can't Do a Thing to Stop Me." A medley of "Blue Moon" and "Only the Lonely" left many in the orchestra section weak-kneed, while "San Francisco Nights" helped close the show on a celebratory note.

Banned From Utopia
Reviewed: Aug. 27, 1999.
Band: Arthur Barrow, Bruce Fowler, Walt Fowler, Ralph Humphrey, Ed Mann, Kurt McGettrick, Robert Martin, Tommy Mars, Mike Miller.
Musical iconoclast Frank Zappa took as his motto the Edgard Varese quotation, "The present-day composer refuses to die!" Now many of the revolving cast of characters that comprised Zappa's touring and recording bands have seen to it that this late great musician's output – a massive body of uncategorizable work that radio and retail had little idea what to do with – continues to be heard by those who will listen, at least in a live context.

A loose, motley looking bunch onstage (group coalesced for a Zappa tribute in Germany in 1995), all are consummate, in-demand players – having been put through their paces over the years by the legendary discriminating bandleader and wearing it like a badge of honour – and each would have his moment to show off during the first of four capacity weekend shows. But possessed solos in particular from Kurt McGettrick – whose weathered baritone sax nearly outweighed him – and guitarist Mike Miller practically brought down the roof on the tightly configured venue. (Miller couldn't exactly fit onstage with the other musicians, and Arthur Barrow, ably filling in for bassist Tom Fowler who's touring with Ray Charles in Europe, knocked over drummer Ralph Humphrey's music sheet reading light early on adjusting to the cramped quarters.)

But read Zappa's complicated charts they did, what with their bewildering melange of tones, tempos and styles – often within a mere musical passage of one song. Smiles and hoots were in abundance from the predominantly male Zappa-tistas in the aud in instant recognition of such fan faves as "Inca Roads," "Peaches en Regalia," "Montana" and an encore of "Zombie Woof," all among Zappa's more melodically friendly fusion fare. The sound was quite extraordinary, given a nine-piece electric ensemble with brass was squeezed into a stage and seating area the size of an extra-large living room. Venue, opened in January, is run by the son of Don Randi, owner of the original jazz club in Studio City since 1970, and offers some welcome booking competition to Catalina and the Jazz Bakery.

And while Zappa's unique ringmaster stage persona and musicianship were sorely missed – much less his own satirical potshots at politics and religion (some comical references to candidate George W. Bush were offered up in the spirit), Banned From Utopia is vital living proof that his compositional efforts will not soon be forgotten.

Africa Fete

Presented by Grand Performances and the Kennedy Center, Palm Pictures, American Express. Reviewed: Aug. 29, 1999. **Performers: Baaba Maal, Kulanjan (Taj Mahal & Toumani Diabate), Oliver Mtukudzi.**

The exuberance and charisma of Baaba Maal were a much-needed pack of adrenaline at Sunday's three-and-a-half-hour African music festival. Were it not for the Senegalese singer's exemplary show of percussion, dancing and costumes, the evening would have sagged under the weight of foreign language troubadours whose messages were lost on the crowd that packed every nook and cranny of the California Plaza.

Oliver Mtukudzi of Zimbabwe and the cross-cultural collaboration between Taj Mahal and Mali's Toumani Diabate – it's called Kulanjan – had their moments, yet felt less than inspired and even out of sorts. Neither act lived up to the quality of their new discs: Mtukudzi, whose *Tuku Music* appears on Putumayo, settled into a folk groove with his acoustic guitar and seven-member troupe that suffered from too much sameness of spirit until his closing numbers, among them "Ndima Ndapedza," which showed his affinity for spry dance music in the southern African tradition.

Mahal, who began his band's 55-minute set by stating they were headed back to 1235 AD for a musical source, began in duet with his steel guitar and a troupe member's antecedent of the banjo on "Catfish Blues," pleasantly marrying two rural styles from two continents. After that, with the arrival of an eight-member band that showcased Diabate on the kora, a 21-string lute-like instrument, the music turned into a hypnotic collection of clinks, clacks and shimmering metal, much of it slow and moody. The extended vocal lines approached rapture, but felt disembodied from the accompaniment; only when Mahal ventured into the funky style of hunter music, wassoulou, did it recall the cultural give-and-take that makes Kulanjan's disc on the Hannibal label an inviting listen.

To close the evening, Maal's act entered the stage possessed. A trio of drummers fortified Maal's introduction with a whirling demonstration of polyrhythmic bliss. The 12 members of the band progressively took the stage until Maal, with the deportment of a superstar, stepped to the microphone and delivered otherworldy singing. Here there was no language barrier.

Where Mtukudzi's socially charged lyrics required translation and Kulanjan needed a more coherent infrastructure, Maal tapped into a melange of African elements, taking the roots of yela rhythms and applying Western instrumentation to his personal hybrid of Mali, Senegal and the Ivory Coast. Maal is a magnanimous performer – this was his second well-received visit to downtown's California Plaza – and his music makes a viscerally potent statement for music without boundaries.

Billy Bragg and the Blokes

Reviewed: Aug. 30, 1999.
Band: Billy Bragg, Ian McLagan, Ben Mandelson, Lu Edmonds, Simon Edwards, Martyn Barker.
Woody Guthrie, brilliant pop melodies and chats about fascism are still a healthy part of Billy Bragg's stage show one year removed from the release of his acclaimed Guthrie project *Mermaid Avenue* in which he penned music for the folksinger's unfinished works. There's a bright disposition that favours romance over monologues at the front end of this 85-minute show that suggests Bragg has finally succeed-

ed in evenhandedly dealing with one of pop's most curious blends.

Not that Bragg has ever had a problem onstage. Since his arrival in 1985 as a leftist folk troubadour with his heart resting right above a union patch on his sleeve, he has always been a fascinating and pointed monologist capable of spinning delicious melodies and attacking society's ills in a single turn. Monday's show tapped Bragg's catalog of 10 or so albums – for an artist so tied to era-specific lyrics (Reagan and Thatcher were always big faves), nothing comes out dated.

Bragg's most dramatic speech preceded a rambunctious reading of Guthrie's "Eisler on the Go," in which Bragg detailed the House Unamerican Activities Committee gaining its Hollywood access first through Hanns Eisler. Bragg suggested that only illness kept the left-leaning Guthrie away from HUAC's witness stand, depriving America of what was potentially some of "the greatest theater of the 1950s."

The sweet Guthrie/Bragg ballad "Way Over Yonder in the Minor Key" stood out along with longtime favorites "Greetings to the New Brunette" (now dubbed "Shirley"), a group sing-along on "A New England" and the impressive "Sulk," a B-side from 1992 that's part of Rhino's rarities compilation *Reaching to the Converted (Minding the Gaps)* that was released Tuesday.

Back-up band featured exotic instrumentation that included two bouzoukis that, rather than conjure Russian dances, sparked the rock songs with a cross between mandolin and guitar. Ian McLagan of the Faces was, as expected, spectacular on the keyboards, particularly when they dove into his old band's songbook for the eloquent "Glad and Sorry" from the pen of the late Ronnie Lane.

Hans Joachim Roedelius; Roger Eno & Lol Hammond

Presented by Curious Music in association with All Saints Records and Thirsty Ear Records. Reviewed: Sept. 3, 1999.
Hans Joachim Roedelius has been a steady presence in the electronic arts since his duo, Cluster, produced *Cluster and Eno*, the 1977 album that brought producer-performer Brian Eno into the ambient fold before his acclaimed solo projects such as *Music For Airports*. After 30 years of performing and 80 albums to his credit, Roedelius, at the age of 65, is on his first solo tour, performing quaint piano works and dabbling in atmospheric sound portraits.

Roedelius and Roger Eno (Brian's brother) each performed at LunaPark for 40 minutes and the two gave distinctly different impressions of what it means to be a performer-composer in this arty camp at the close of the millennium. Roedelius, on four songs of varying lengths, has a fully linear style that goes against the grain of repetition that many younger electronic artists favor. What he shares with contemporaries such as the Orb is an ability to be open-ended and evoke a collection of emotions by shading a work toward extremes; in his first piece, for example, he slowed to a deliberate cascade of four or five notes at a time before shifting to a rolling and eerie passage that gave way to sounds of sheer terror. All it needed was a silent film to accompany.

Roger Eno, on the other hand, shows more of a virtuoso hand as he executes soft melodies with new age flourishes. His version of a habanera was quite watered down and on his finale he echoed a portion of the Beatles' "Eleanor Rigby," yet beyond that his music feels uncategorizable. It lacks the weight of Roedelius but it has a level of sophistication that can't be dismissed.

Eno was joined by dance remixer Lol Hammond and a third musician, the two of whom provided drones, nature noises and spaceship sounds to his soothing electric piano. It didn't live up to the adventurous stroll through a castle soundscape that Roedelius had created earlier. His knob-twirling tune had enough variations to hold the interest, from a key dropping to an electric guitar to a house beat to very Cluster-like drones; his keyboard voicings reached back to the electronic vibraphone/piano sound Brian Eno used on side two of *Before and After Science*, which left the music hanging in a gently soothing and blissful state.

McCoy Tyner

Reviewed: Sept. 7, 1999.
Band: McCoy Tyner, Avery Sharpe, Aaron Scott.
Charlie Mingus once titled a tune "If Charlie Parker was a Gunslinger, There'd be a Whole Lot of Dead Copycats" (a.k.a. "Gunslinging Bird"). That's the influence McCoy Tyner has today, for it often seems as if almost every young neo-bopper in front of a grand piano sounds either like Tyner, Bill Evans or both. He likes to change the context in which he performs – earlier this year, he toured with a Latin jazz band and put out a cooking CD, *McCoy Tyner and the Latin All-Stars* (Telarc) – but his basic two-fisted, densely chorded, life-affirming style generally doesn't change.

With just his trio on hand this time, Tyner's opening set was plagued with sonic gremlins that still crop up on occasion in the over-resonant Jazz Bakery. During the ensemble passages of the opening number, "Changes," the pickup of Tyner's piano was blaring and blurred, Aaron Scott's drums sounded overbearing and Avery Sharpe's bass was almost inaudible. It seemed as if each musician was playing in his own world, unable to hear each other, eventually competing with a frenzy that generated unintentional chaos rather than excitement.

Under these conditions, the only way to be understood is to tone it down, leave space between the notes, play more subtly and responsively – which the trio did on "My Romance" and in spots elsewhere. Tyner's solos vibrated with rapid right-hand patterns, contrary scales and, of course, those big tremolos and dense, affirmative chords that all the young cats adore. Sharpe handled his bass with an agility and powerful strumming technique that almost resembled flamenco, and Scott could generate some genuinely romping drive.

Yet a good deal of the time, this trio was projecting outward as if this were Carnegie Hall, firing away like Mingus's gunslinger. Such concentrated energy can lead to ecstasy, but in this acoustical space, it felt like a mugging.

Samson et Dalila

The L.A. Opera presented Camille Saint-Saens' three-act opera; text by Ferdinand Lemaire, based on the *Book of Judges*. Reviewed: Sept. 8, 1999. Running time: 2 hours 45 min.
Conductor, Lawrence Foster, with the Los Angeles Opera Chorus and Orchestra; director, Nicolas Joel. Set designer, Douglas Schmidt; costumes, Carrie Robbins; lighting designer, Kurt Landisman; choreographer, Daniel Pelzig. Placido Domingo (Samson), Denyce Graves (Dalila), Richard Bernstein (Abimelech), Gregory Yurisich (High Priest). With: Coke Morgan, Cedric Perry, Bruce Sledge, Louis Lebherz.

Tattered baggage though it be, *Samson et Dalila* maintains its place in the opera repertory on the strength of its glittering surface. Sure, it has only one tune worth remembering, and its ballet is the ancestor of all cornball hootchy-kootch. Given a fair serving of charismatic lung-power in its two name roles, however, and a stage setting evocative of a fondly imagined Loew's Babylon lobby, it can still dupe an undemanding audience into an illusion of some kind of masterpiece.

Credit composer Camille Saint-Saens as the opera's masterful string-puller. Samson is a role fashioned in tenor heaven, from his first lurching onstage with his mighty battle cry to his heartrending laments in Philistine captivity. Does it matter that nothing remains in the memory once the song is sung? No; what remains is the sound, if not the shape, of Placido Domingo's white-hot outbursts: opera at its most elemental.

Dalila is fashioned out of friendlier stuff; she has her one memorable tune in the act two love/hate duet, although it's a long time in coming. Denyce Graves, apparently put on earth to take over and inflame all of opera's bad-girl mezzo-soprano roles (of which there are many) – with flashing eyes that could seduce any tenor within miles to abandon home, hearth and hairdo – was, in a word, sensational. (She even tried a few dance steps during the Bacchanale, a welcome contrast to choreographer Daniel Pelzig's Muscle Beach stuff.)

Douglas Schmidt's production – garishly lit by Kurt Landisman from Thomas E. Munn's original design – is on loan from the San Francisco Opera. It nicely matched the music's tendency toward the ponderous overstatement: a heavy impasto of burnished color (as from watching 10 Gustave Moreau paintings at once) and, for the final temple scene, a terrific jumble of pseudo-Oriental statuary where you might search in vain for the popcorn stand. Nicolas Joel's tidy and unremarkable staging at least nicely accomplished the final catastrophe that everyone sits still for; it brought down the house.

Samson marks the start of the L.A. Opera's 14th season, the last for outgoing founder and general director Peter Hemmings; it served as well to trumpet the imminent arrival of incoming artistic director Domingo (with the rest of the new administrative team as yet unannounced). In a sense, the production also honoured the sweep of history over those 14 years. Conductor Lawrence Foster, who led his usual capable if unremarkable reading of Saint-Saens' score, was on the podium for the company's inaugural *Otello* in October 1986, with Domingo in the title role. Bass-baritones Richard Bernstein and Louis Lebherz, the Abimelech and Old Hebrew in this *Samson*, were L.A. Opera resident artists, nicely honed within the company for the major careers they now enjoy worldwide.

Big Band Alumni All-Stars;
Clayton-Hamilton Jazz Orchestra

Presented by Los Angeles Philharmonic Assn. Reviewed: Sept. 8, 1999.
Performers: Big Band Alumni All-Stars (Frank Wess, Danny House, Frank Foster, Pete Christlieb, Jack Nimitz, Dennis Wilson, Charlie Loper, Benny Powell, Bill Reichenbach, Byron Stripling, Frank Szabo, Bob Summers, Ron Stout, Gerald Wiggins, Randy Napolean, Peter Washington, Ed Shaughnessy); Clayton-Hamilton Jazz Orchestra; Carmen Bradford.
It was obvious it would be a good outing for the Clayton-Hamilton Jazz Orchestra when its marvelous plunger-mute

trumpeter Snooky Young – hitherto silent through most of the summer – took the first swinging solo Wednesday. Indeed Snooky, a venerable alumnus of the Count Basie band, set the tone for the evening – an often electric look back at the Basie-Ellington axis by two big bands, enhanced by modern technology.

With the help of a camera crew and a video screen left over from recent L.A. Philharmonic multimedia concerts, the audience got to see some close-up action via ultra-sharp HDTV images. At last, the personal connection with the audience that John Clayton had been talking about all summer had been achieved, for the images were highly communicative – the sheer joy on Clayton's face as he led the band, the competitive fire that lit up the duelling soloists, the titterings from the crowd whenever baby-faced guitarist Randy Napolean appeared onscreen. If budget allows, video ought to be a permanent feature here for jazz concerts.

The main event was a monster stunt that worked – a recreation of the surprisingly successful merger of the Basie and Ellington orchestras on a 1961 Columbia album, *First Time: The Count Meets The Duke*. (Coincidentally, Columbia Legacy just reissued the disc.) The Big Band Alumni All-Stars was assembled mostly from Basie veterans and local stalwarts and was wheeled out in a duplicate bandstand next to the CHJO. Together, the two bands revved it up on three cleverly arranged selections from the Basie-Ellington album, passing the baton masterfully from one rhythm section to the other, the reed and brass sections playing together with amazing precision.

On their own, the All-Stars revealed a solid, undiminished feeling for the Basie idiom as they played a powerhouse set ("Shiny Stockings," "Lil' Darlin'," "Rollercoaster"), with former Basie band leader Frank Foster as de facto leader from his chair in the sax section. As good as the CHJO sounded in their own set earlier, the All-Stars outdid them in the crucial area of swing – and much of that advantage could be attributed to the subtle, effortlessly percolating beat of the underappreciated drummer of the Carson-era *Tonight Show* band, Ed Shaughnessy.

Almost but not quite overlooked in the shuffle was a video tribute to the late Joe Williams – who had been originally booked for this gig – and another multimedia stunt where the CHJO sympathetically accompanied a tape of Williams singing "You Are So Beautiful." Former Basie vocalist Carmen Bradford revealed a duskier, more matured style in a brief set with the CHJO.

Cesaria Evora

Presented by UCLA Performing Arts. Reviewed: Sept. 18, 1999.
Band: Cesaria Evora, Antonio Gomes Fernandes, Fernando Lopes Andrade, Aderito Goncalves, Pontes, Joao Pina Alves, Virgilio Duarte, Antonio Pina Alves, Carlos Monteiro, Julian Subida, Leonel Bermudez Hernandez, Daniel Rodriguez Rodriguez.
In the years prior to the escalation of his public profile through the movie *Round Midnight*, the late jazz saxophonist Dexter Gordon had the nasty habit of taking any tune – whether bossa nova, Gershwin or blues – and embellishing it with a furious bebop solo that had more to do with his history than the composition's structure. The solo wouldn't match the introductory theme, but isolated, it was always beautiful

music: the audience was in the presence of a master. And so it goes with Cesaria Evora – quite possibly the most lauded female vocalist in "world music" in the 1990s.

Evora's music is a graceful blend of Africa, Portugal, Brazil and Cuba. This native of Africa's Cape Verde Islands has made four exceptional albums, the latest being *Cafe Atlantico*, her first for RCA Victor. Their popularity has reached the point where she can sell out two shows at Royce. And with her spectacular band, featuring the effervescent saxophonist and percussionist Antonio Gomes Fernandes and the fleet and rich pianistics of Fernando Lopes Andrade, Evora coasted.

She delivered her 85-minute perf with so little emotion, however, that it actually seemed cold at times. Her music, particularly the newer works recorded in Paris and Havana, reach across the globe, tapping traditions as varied as the bolero, Cuba's danzon, the Afro-Brazilian dance music of Bahia and the solemn Portuguese morna, for which she is best known. Unfortunately, the morna style informed virtually every number she performed Saturday. As they began, songs were spirited and contained various rhythms; once Evora entered, though, it took only a few bars until the meter had been slowed to fit her sense of timing. Initially, it was a fascinating juxtaposition: Evora, 59, so consumed by the pain and passion of a lyric that her deliberate delivery defies the joyful backing supplied by her acoustic-guitar-heavy backing.

But it wore thin, her lack of movement and facial expression proving detrimental to the enjoyment of her gorgeous, pleasantly pitched voice. (Her album covers and press photos often emphasize her smiling and dancing.) The voice is indeed a jewel and as a solo instrument, Evora displayed it impeccably.

Latin Jazz Festival

Presented by the Latin Jazz Institute and Festival Los Angeles. Reviewed Sept. 18, 1999.
Performers: Lalo Schifrin Big Band with David Sanchez, Jon Faddis, Ignacio Berroa, Alex Acuna; Chucho Valdes Quartet; Manny Oquendo and Libre; Eliades Ochoa y Cuarteto Patria.
For a while, it looked as if opening night at the third annual Latin Jazz Festival would play to large patches of empty seats. Indeed, many were filled only when those with cheap tickets were allowed to come down into the seating area in California Plaza's stunning outdoor Watercourt. Perhaps it was the unfamiliar location deep in downtown L.A. that kept attendance down, or the overcast weather. It couldn't have been the strong and diverse line-up.

Things got off to a fine start with veteran bandleader/ timbales player Manny Oquendo's highly unusual 11-piece Latin jazz band. It stacks four trombones in its five-man brass section, yet the texture wasn't at all overweight: There was plenty of fascinating interplay among the brasses, and the rhythm section was powerful enough to lift the mambos well off the ground (though Marvin Gaye's "I Want You" was an awkward fit).

Chucho Valdes dropped in to show off his bewildering arsenal of piano fireworks, throwing in everything from Lisztian classical flash to some funk as he mixed it up with his high-energy Afro-Cuban quartet. Valdes centered his set around tunes from his latest album, *Briyumba Palo Congo* (Blue Note) – including a splashy, mostly solo excursion on "Embraceable You." Another Cuban rediscovery from the ranks of the Buena Vista Social Club, Eliades Ochoa delivered a short set of soaring high-tenor vocals and melodic acoustic guitar over basic, hypnotically revolving vamps. It wasn't Latin jazz per se, but it swung – with help from the illuminated dancing fountains in the rear.

For Argentinean native Lalo Schifrin, who long ago veered off the Latin path into jazz, Hollywood, classical music and everything else, the U.S. premiere of his hour-long, six-movement *Latin Jazz Suite* – performed brilliantly by Cologne's WDR Big Band on a new Aleph CD – was a split decision. Only in the last three movements, "Fiesta," "Ritual" and "Manaos," did the performance (and the piece) hit its stride, with pungent Schifrin harmonic signatures and some nasty grooves kicking in to drive trumpeter Jon Faddis's breathtaking mastery of Dizzy Gillespie idioms, as well as the substantial bop tenor sax of David Sanchez. Earlier on, "Pampas" sounded like a generic movie theme and "Martinique" seemed like a neighbour of "St. Thomas."

Phish

Presented by Avalon Concerts. Reviewed: Sept. 19, 1999.
Band: Trey Anastasio, Mike Gordon, Jonathan Fishman, Page McConnell.
In the Vermont band's biggest and most impressive L.A.-area show to date, on a cool Sunday evening at Irvine Meadows, improv-jam rockers Phish took nearly the length of their first, 65-minute set to get warmed up, with a series of brand new and otherwise obscure tunes, before catching fire with an inspired second-half program that's sure to have the group's rabid fans talking for some time.

Following the well-received opener "NICU," a six-year-old, unrecorded track, the quartet (Trey Anastasio on guitar, Mike Gordon on bass, Jon Fishman on drums, Page McConnell on keyboards; they all sing) set a mellow and experimental tone during the first set, with such new band compositions as "Heavy Things" as well as at least one Anastasio solo tune, leaving the quietly animated Gordon, as well as some in the crowd, appearing less than thrilled with the song selection.

But the pace and the energy began to pick up an hour into the sold-out show with "Stash," a fan favorite with a long, Grateful Dead-like intro that included one of the evening's many chances for audience participation. Most of the dancing attendees knew just when to clap during the ambitious number, which lit into a long jam built around a fixed chord progression. First set closed with a laugh with the four-part barbershop harmonies (they just can't resist) of "Hello My Baby."

Guitarist Anastasio, who sings lead vocals on many of the genre-hopping songs (he also writes the concert set list), and whose inventive and biting style bears influence from Jimi Hendrix, Carlos Santana, Bob Marley and Jerry Garcia, was the star of the show's second set (which followed a 30-minute break). The pretty strumming of encore "Guyute" (from last year's Elektra album *The Story of the Ghost*), the eclectic strains of 1990's "The Squirming Coil," and the stretched-out, magical six-string work of "Wading in the Velvet Sea" were among the many "Trey-lights," though as usual, all four members delivered impressive performances.

Technically speaking, the evening's involving and dramatically executed light show was nearly as diverse and surprising as the music that it enhanced, while the show's sound was next to spectacular when measured against most outdoor amphitheater shows.

Chris Cornell

Presented by Nederlander/Goldenvoice. Reviewed: Sept. 21, 1999.
Band: Alain Johannes, Natasha Schneider, Ric Markmann, Greg Upchurch.
Soundgarden singer Chris Cornell made his local solo concert debut Tuesday at the sold-out Fonda, the first of two hot-ticket nights, where the Seattle native sang emotional songs of love, pain and regret to a seated audience that heard an engaging, if somewhat abbreviated, sampling of the talented and expressive vocalist's ample skills.

Following a brief instrumental opening from Cornell's backing band (which includes partners Alain Johannes and Natasha Schneider of the L.A. band Eleven), Cornell quickly put his majestic voice to work on such tunes as "Preaching the End of the World," his current psychedelic radio hit "Can't Change Me," and the delicate "Flutter Girl," where Cornell's sensual body movements thoroughly matched his soaring vocals.

The 65-minute show's songs, many taken from Cornell's likable new album *Euphoria Morning* (A&M/Interscope), generally steered clear of the often-bombastic sound of Soundgarden (which has been on extended hiatus since 1997), and featured a pleasing variety of styles and moods – courtesy of the fab backing musicians – influenced by the likes of the Beatles, Otis Redding and Pink Floyd. Cornell drew the loudest cheers for two familiar Soundgarden-era tracks, "Seasons," which he contributed to the 1992 film *Singles*, and band hit "Like Suicide," which was offered in a spooky, stripped-down version similar to his solo version found on the *S.W.F.* soundtrack.

"Pillow of Your Bones," a song of complete emotional devotion, was among the show's other highlights; keyboard played Natasha Schneider effectively matched vocals with Cornell, giving the engrossing song extra impact.

Stefon Harris

Jazz Bakery. Reviewed: Sept. 22, 1999.
Band: Stefon Harris, Billy Childs, Tarus Mateen, Nasheet Waits.
Stefon Harris's second album for Blue Note, *Black Action Figure*, is the most exciting new jazz disc of the year. With a seven-piece unit, the young vibraphonist Harris demonstrates that he has the goods to propel jazz into the 21st century without resting on the accomplishments of his predecessors. He paid tribute to one of those earlier vibe masters, Bobby Hutcherson, in his first set Wednesday and demonstrated how much he can bring to quartet jazz, providing spark after spark in a driving and unrelenting ensemble performance.

Harris tackled the title track from his new album first, weaving solos that wander down linear avenue after linear avenue. His band engaged him in a nice tug of war at times, providing a roaring undercurrent that gave the music a refreshing density. Pianist Billy Childs presented a slicing counterpoint to Harris's melodic strings, prodding rather than duelling as they embarked on a journey of reinforced steps. Best of all, Harris and his band deliver invigorating music at every turn, boldly stating phrase upon phrase, even turning the ballad "Collage" into a call to arms.

When Harris took a break, though, the band's swirling music was sometimes difficult to assimilate as each instrumentalist pushed individual personalities onto the melodies. With a ferocity that recalled early Tony Williams, drummer

Nasheet Waits delivered a lengthy solo that evoked a war zone. It started with the tom-toms replicating a march and the barking of orders as the snare suggested gunfire; as the solo built up speed, the mayhem of a guerrilla attack took shape until Waits returned his slightly orchestrated solo to tenuous calm. Had he been displaying a variety of rhythmic patterns throughout the evening, his solos would have been more impressive, but in this context he was a propeller on overdrive.

Childs, as usual, presented a distinct approach to the piano that pays little heed to the instrument's dominant forefathers. He gave Harris room to let his mallets fly and quickly dove into a maelstrom when the leader completed his solos. Tonally, Childs revealed complexities that haven't shown up on his solo albums yet commanded the small audience's attention from start to finish.

No Doubt
Reviewed: Oct. 6, 1999.
Band: Gwen Stefani, Tony Kanal, Tom Dumont, Adrian Young, Gabe McNair, Steve Bradley.
After a two-year hiatus from the local concert scene, Orange County multi-platinum rockers No Doubt brought a confident and exciting performance to the sold-out House of Blues on Wednesday that served as a compelling preview of the band's upcoming, highly anticipated fourth album.

No Doubt opened the 80-minute show (the fifth in a series of eight West Coast club gigs) to very loud cheers with "New," the group's propulsive contrib to the recent *Go* soundtrack. Set featured many of the group's bright hit songs, including "Excuse Me Mr.," "Just a Girl" and encore "Spiderwebs," plus a version of "Jumping Someone Else's Train" by the Cure. But the most impressive aspect of the fun show (which was opened by San Diego punk band Unwritten Law) was the nice mix of sounds and styles evident in the outstanding new material, due for album release by Interscope in February.

Tunes like "Marry Me" and the charming "Bathtub" showed off creative new songwriting and musical twists, as did "Simple Life," which kicked off with a sweet acoustic guitar intro. The band's punch was further spiked by tasty brass and keyboard fills from Gabe McNair and Steve Bradley, who were clad in matching neon green jumpsuits. Radiant in pink hair and clothes, beaming singer Gwen Stefani sounded and looked great, and she elicited screams and waves wherever she looked around the packed room.

Ibrahim Ferrer; Ruben Gonzalez
Reviewed: Nov. 18, 1999.
Band: Orlando "Cachaito" Lopez, Adolfo Pichardo, Ruben Gonzalez, Angel "Pangle" Terry, Robertico "El Millonario" Garcia, Filiberto Sanchez, Alejandro Pichardo, Guajiro Mirabal, Jesus "Aguaje" Ramos, Demetrio Muniz, Jimmy Jenks, Tony Jimencz, Ventura Garcia, Julian Sanchez, Jose Nurquez, Omara Portuondo, Manolo Galban.
Time stands still when these two stars of the Buena Vista Social Club perform together. Playing nearly forgotten traditional Cuban music, singer Ibrahim Ferrer and pianist Ruben Gonzalez led their respective groups through bliss-inducing tunes that emphasized melody on par with rhythm and showcased the pre-revolution musical give-and-take between America and Cuba.

With four members of the BVSC – in addition to the leaders – on board, this is the closest we in the States are going to get to revisiting the magical moments that defined the *Buena Vista* and *Afro Cuban All-stars* discs as well as the film of their collaboration in Cuba. Quite rightfully, the package is selling out venues everywhere in record time.

In his hour-long set, the 77-year-old Gonzalez shied away from the jazz influences he exhibited on his debut disc *Introducing* (Nonesuch), choosing instead to play free-flowing ballads and lightly swinging boleros and dance numbers. After starting solo with a number that could've been taken from a silent movie, band members came onstage progressively until they numbered seven. Gonzalez was at his rhapsodic best when accompanied by the understated bass of Orlando "Cachaito" Lopez, four percussionists and the muted trumpet of Guajiro Mirabal. Gonzalez loves long-flowing, hand over hand movements that use almost all of the 88s; with a touch of humor in his presentation, coupled with his richly orchestrated style, he conjures a recurring image of the under-appreciated Chico Marx, a big band leader of his own in the 1940s when Gonzalez was doing pioneering work with the legendary Arsenio Rodriguez.

Before Ry Cooder's experiment became the Buena Vista Social Club, and in turn became a million-selling phenomenon that has spawned a Wim Wenders docu and a national tour, Ferrer, 72, was an absolute unknown. Whereas the others have had careers reborn, Ferrer was just getting started. Ferrer's voice is a heavenly blend of 1950s balladeers Johnny Ray and Jimmy Scott with a dash of Nat (King) Cole thrown in. As much as he's a throwback to the middle of the century, so, too, is the music – within his first five-minute rumba there were echoes of doo-wop and Duke Ellington woodwind voicings. Demetrio Muniz's first trombone solo was awash in big band influences, stunningly smooth and in no hurry to keep up with the steady rhythm set by the 12 musicians behind him.

Singer Omara Portuondo, a popular member of the BVSC, lent a considerable feistiness to the proceedings, singing first with Gonzalez and later in several duets with Ferrer. The real discovery here, though, is electric guitarist Manolo Galban (the original BVSC guitarist, Compay Segundo, just released his second solo album and is successfully touring on his own as a leader). In a rock or jazz setting, Galban would be perceived as a Dadaist, a musician who drew on the work of Gary Lucas with Captain Beefheart's Magic Band and the late experimentalist Sonny Sharrock. Galban's playing is all over the map, and he seemingly won't stop at anything in his terse and jagged solos, running up and down the fret board with chordings and single guitar lines that are never less than riveting.

A real woman is never too old.
(Cher, Mermaids)

Video

Variety's coverage of video cannot match that of its sister publication, *Video Business*, but since the technology's inception in the 1970s the paper has devoted numerous articles and news items to its fortunes. In a mere 20 years, the home-entertainment scene has undergone a revolution. The choice has expanded from cumbersome, horrendously expensive cassettes on three competing formats to the current buffet of DVDs and bargain cassettes. Rental remains the engine-room of the industry, but "sell-through" is catching up fast, with a release like *The Lion King* or *Titanic* capable of generating $200 million and more in a single week's sales across the U.S. Now DVD has catapulted the home cinema industry into the 21st century. And for an ill-reviewed, low-budget film, the modern equivalent of the old "supporting movie," the video shelves represent a last bid for survival if not for salvation.

U.K. video rental: 1999

1.	There's Something About Mary	Fox-Pathe
2.	Armageddon	Buena Vista
3.	Saving Private Ryan	CIC
4.	Enemy of the State	Buena Vista
5.	Lock, Stock and Two Smoking Barrels	Universal
6.	Blade	EV
7.	Lethal Weapon 4	Warner
8.	The Truman Show	CIC
9.	Payback	Buena Vista
10.	Dr. Dolittle	Fox Pathe

Source: BVA/Rental Monitor

U.K. video sales: 1999

1.	A Bug's Life	Buena Vista
2.	The Lion King 2: Simba's Pride	Buena Vista
3.	Notting Hill	Universal
4.	The Matrix	Warner
5.	Saving Private Ryan	CIC
6.	Mulan	Buena Vista
7.	Antz	CIC
8.	Lock, Stock and Two Smoking Barrels	Universal
9.	Dr. Dolittle	Fox
10.	George of the Jungle	Buena Vista

Source: BVA/CIN

U.K. DVD sell-through: 1999

1.	The Matrix	Warner
2.	Armageddon	Buena Vista
3.	Blade	EV
4.	Lock, Stock and Two Smoking Barrels	Universal
5.	A Bug's Life	Buena Vista
6.	Enemy of the State	Buena Vista
7.	Notting Hill	Universal
8.	Lethal Weapon 4	Warner
9.	The Exorcist	Warner
10.	Ronin	MGM

Source: BVA/CIN

U.S. DVD sell-through: 1999

1.	The Matrix
2.	Blade
3.	Armageddon
4.	A Bug's Life
5.	Enemy of the State
6.	Lock, Stock and Two Smoking Barrels
7.	Lethal Weapon 4
8.	Notting Hill
9.	Ronin
10.	The Exorcist

Source: Blockbuster

U.S. DVD sales: 1999

1.	The Matrix	Warner
2.	Saving Private Ryan	Universal
3.	The Mummy	Universal
4.	Austin Powers, The Spy...	New Line
5.	Armageddon	Disney
6.	American Pie	Universal
7.	Titanic	Paramount
8.	Enemy of the State	Disney
9.	Big Daddy	Columbia
10.	Blade	New Line

Source: VideoScan

Top 10 U.S. renting VHS titles: 1999

1. *There's Something About Mary*	Fox	6. *The Truman Show*	Paramount
2. *Rush Hour*	New Line	7. *You've Got Mail*	Warner
3. *Saving Private Ryan*	DreamWorks	8. *Stepmom*	Columbia TriStar
4. *The Waterboy*	BV/Touchstone	9. *Lethal Weapon 4*	Warner
5. *Enemy of the State*	BV/Touchstone	10. *The Matrix*	Warner

Source: VSDA VidTrac

Top 10 U.S. renting DVD titles: 1999

1. *The Matrix*	Warner	6. *8MM*	Columbia TriStar
2. *Enemy of the State*	BV/Touchstone	7. *Big Daddy*	Columbia TriStar
3. *The Mummy*	Universal	8. *The Siege*	Fox
4. *Payback*	Paramount	9. *A Civil Action*	BV/Touchstone
5. *Analyze This*	Warner	10. *The Waterboy*	BV/Touchstone

Source: VSDA VidTrac

Video Business Video Hall of Fame honorees: 1999

Jerry Bruckheimer (producer *The Rock, Armageddon, Top Gun, Beverly Hills Cop, Crimson Tide, Enemy of the State*)

David Mount (chairman and CEO Warner/Elektra/Atlantic, manufacturer of almost 40% of DVDs sold worldwide)

Tim Shannahan (president and CEO Video Products Distributors, the West Coast's most formidable video software wholesaler)

The Brave New World of DVD

DVD is now recognized as the fastest growing home technology in recent memory. More DVD machines are being installed, faster, than either VCRs or CD players were in the initial period following their launch.

In the United States, DVD has almost achieved mainstream status, with 4 million players active and some 6,000 film titles available. The new technology has been embraced because it fills a vacuum, replacing fuzzy NTSC images with a crystal-clear picture and digital sound. Laser Discs were magnificent for their time, but their unwieldy format and high price restricted their use to an elite ownership. The wonders of digital TV and widescreen monitors have not been promoted heavily in the U.S., leaving the field free for DVD to prosper.

Not so in Europe or the Far East, where consumers (and, more significantly retailers) have become obsessed with the digital revolution. Many more millions subscribe to the various digital services than will – at least in the medium term – ever purchase DVD players. Indeed the average consumer in Europe is unlikely to convert to DVD until programmes and movies can be recorded on to the shiny platter. The development of broad-band telephony implies a home delivery system so sophisticated that a movie will soon be downloadable to a PC within minutes, not hours, for storage on the user's hard disk.

However, DVD will accomplish its goals in the short term through the home PC, with DVD drives a commonplace among machines now on the market. High-resolution monitors allow films to be viewed in the office or in the work room at home, albeit without the dramatic benefits that a large screen and five-speaker surround configuration can add to the home cinema experience.

Don't take the quality for granted, however. The major studios (led by Warner Bros, Columbia TriStar, and Buena Vista) have taken pains to preserve their older films under good conditions, and to effect an excellent "transfer" from the 35mm inter-negative to DVD. They, along with the Criterion Collection in New York, spend long hours in restoring sound and particularly image to its pristine state, eliminating flecks and tears with the aid of sophisticated computer gadgetry.

Many smaller companies have not followed this path, because it's too costly. Releases from Artisan and Fox-Lorber, for example, often rely on inferior elements, and offer little in the way of bonus materials. Many of the classic works of Truffaut and Rohmer are released by Fox-Lorber, and yet look no better than a good 16mm copy.

The sound quality constitutes one of DVD's most seductive advantages. Dolby Digital 5.1 is standard on most receivers, and when that red light glows on the console you know that even a 30-year-old movie will sound dramatically better than it ever has on VHS.

The growth of DVD outside the U.S. has been inhibited by the studios' insistence on regionalization. Hollywood's stance was prompted by fears of brand-new titles being "pirated" and released abroad ahead of their theatrical bows in certain territories. The world has been divided into six regions, with the U.S. number 1, Europe number 2, etc. Most DVD players from the reputable manufacturers are encoded to accept just one region. So if you buy a DVD while Christmas shopping in New York, you will not able to play it back in Britain or Australia – *unless* you have your machine clandestinely adapted (which costs around $150), so that its innards are fooled into believing they are back in their original factory in Asia before the encoding was set.

The problem with regionalization is that the amount of software (read: movies) available in territories outside the U.S. is restricted to titles the major distributors feel will sell to a mass public. Indie and foreign titles get short shrift. Classics such as Fellini's *Amarcord* and *Nights of Cabiria*, Cocteau's *Beauty and* the *Beast*, and Bergman's *The Seventh Seal* can be found in sparkling transfers in the States, but not in Britain or Germany. Many observers feel that the studios will quietly abandon the regional encoding within the next two years. Besides, most new Hollywood pictures reach other countries within 2-3 months now, and the DVD release in the States is rarely permitted within a six-month window.

For many enthusiasts, the appeal of DVD lies in the bonus "extras" included on most discs. The Criterion edition of *Armageddon* (available in the States) contains a commentary by director Michael Bay that you can hear by pressing the "audio" button on your remote – and it's so calm and cogent that it almost convinces you that *Armageddon* is an interesting movie. The DVD of *Saving Private Ryan* offers "an exclusive message from Steven Spielberg," two theatrical trailers, production notes, and biographies of cast and director. *Apocalypse Now* contains the fabled "compound conflagration" sequence, with Francis Coppola talking over the images and explaining why it had to be omitted from the finished film.

A majority of DVDs provide a full menu of subtitles. In Europe, that might be anything from Arabic to Icelandic and even Serbo-Croat. In the States, it's more likely to be Spanish or French. The subtitles are accessed via the DVD menu that's called up at the start of the film. They can be switched on and off at will and often run below the image, thus not interfering with the visual quality of the film in any way.

A further benefit of DVD is the chapter encoding. This allows a viewer to access a specific scene or "chapter" in the film, rather as specific tracks can be played on a music CD. This naturally delights consumers who have been long frustrated by having to rewind video cassette tapes in the vain hope of locating the right moment or sequence.

Finally, DVD may have resolved the long-running debate over "widescreen" versions on video. The discs usually have sufficient "depth" to offer a widescreen version on one side, and a squeezed "full-screen" version on the other. **Peter Cowie**

A selection of recommended DVD's available in the U.S. and/or Europe:

Apocalypse Now (Paramount Home Video)
Armageddon (Criterion 16720)
Black Orpheus (Criterion BLA070)
Brazil (Criterion BRA100, 3 discs)
Bug's Life, A (Disney 16698)
City of Angels (Warner 16320)

Das Boot (Columbia TriStar)
Exorcist, The (Warner 16176)
Fargo (PolyGram 047 798 2)
Godzilla (Columbia TriStar 23126)
GoldenEye (MGM DO 56035)
Gone With the Wind (MGM 906311)

Heat (Warner 14192)
Jeremiah Johnson (Warner D011061)
Mask of Zorro, The (Columbia TriStar 03008)
Matrix, The (Warner 17737)
Mummy, The (Universal 20636)
My Fair Lady (Warner 16668)
Nanook of the North (Criterion, with new music score)
Nights of Cabiria (Criterion NIG040)
Picnic at Hanging Rock (Criterion PIC100)
Psycho (Universal 20538, 1998 version)

Règle du Jeu, La (Editions Montparnasse, Paris)
Saving Private Ryan (DreamWorks 84433 in UK)
Secret Garden, The (Warner ZI19000)
Seventh Seal, The (Criterion SEV100)
Silence of the Lambs, The (Criterion CC1530D)
Starship Troopers (Columbia TriStar)
Summertime (Criterion SUM060)
Thin Red Line, The (Fox 4111850)
Yellow Submarine (MGM 907508)

Sundry data for U.S. in 1999:

DVD sales: 22.7 million units (VideoScan) compared with 9.3 million in 1998
DVD hardware: 3.9 million units shipped in U.S. (Consumer Electronics Association), and 8.5 million units worldwide
DVD purchase volume: $592.8 million; 1998, $676.3 million

> *Why should people go out and
> pay money to see bad films
> when they can stay at home and
> see bad television for nothing?
> (Samuel Goldwyn)*

Books

Under the rubric "Literati," *Variety* throughout its existence has covered the book scene to a greater or lesser extent. In the late 1990s, book-selling weathered the tides of recession better than almost any other consumer sector. Superstores are opening in practically every main street and shopping mall, alongside the explosion of online bookstores on the internet, and each year literally hundreds of thousands of new titles appear in the Anglo-Saxon world. We include here some of the key literary awards on both sides of the Atlantic, along with the critical bestselling lists for 1999.

The Pulitzer Prize, fiction awards: 1965-1999

1965: *The Keepers of the House*, Shirley Ann Grau
1966: *Collected Stories*, Katherine Anne Porter
1967: *The Fixer*, Bernard Malamud
1968: *The Confessions of Nat Turner*, William Styron
1969: *House Made of Dawn*, N. Scott Momaday
1970: *Collected Stories*, Jean Stafford
1971: No Award
1972: *Angle of Repose*, Wallace Stegner
1973: *The Optimist's Daughter*, Eudora Welty
1974: No Award
1975: *The Killer Angels*, Michael Shaara
1976: *Humboldt's Gift*, Saul Bellow
1977: No Award
1978: *Elbow Room*, James Alan McPherson
1979: *The Stories of John Cheever*, John Cheever
1980: *The Executioner's Song*, Norman Mailer
1981: *A Confederacy of Dunces*, John Kennedy Toole
1982: *Rabbit Is Rich*, John Updike
1983: *The Color Purple*, Alice Walker

1984: *Ironweed*, William Kennedy
1985: *Foreign Affairs*, Alison Lurie
1986: *Lonesome Dove*, Larry McMurtry
1987: *A Summons to Memphis*, Peter Taylor
1988: *Beloved*, Toni Morrison
1989: *Breathing Lessons*, Anne Tyler
1990: *The Mambo Kings Play Songs of Love*, Oscar Hijuelos
1991: *Rabbit at Rest*, John Updike
1992: *A Thousand Acres*, Jane Smiley
1993: *A Good Scent from a Strange Mountain*, Robert Olen Butler
1994: *The Shipping News*, E. Annie Proulx
1995: *The Stone Diaries*, Carol Shields
1996: *Independence Day*, Richard Ford
1997: *Martin Dressler: The Tale of an American Dreamer*, Steven Millhauser
1998: *American Pastoral*, Philip Roth
1999: *The Hours*, Michael Cunningham

U.S. National Book Awards, finalists and winners: 1999

YOUNG PEOPLE'S LITERATURE
Finalists: Laurie Halse Anderson, *Speak* (FSG); Louise Erdrich, *The Birchbark House* (Hyperion); Polly Horvath, *The Trolls* (FSG); Walter Dean Myers, *Monster* (HarperCollins)
Winner: Kimberly Willis Holt, *When Zachary Beaver Came to Town* (Holt)

NON-FICTION
Finalists: Natalie Angier, *Woman: An Intimate Geography* (Houghton Mifflin); Mark Bowden, *Black Hawk Down: A Story of Modern War* (Atlantic Monthly Press); John Phillip Santos, *Places*

Unfinished at the Time of Creation (Viking); Judith Thurman, *Secrets of the Flesh: A Life of Colette* (Knopf)
Winner: John W. Dower, *Embracing Defeat: Japan in the Wake of World War II* (Norton/New Press publication)

POETRY
Finalists: Louise Gluck, *Vita Nova: Poems* (Ecco Press); Clarence Major, *Configurations: New & Selected Poems* (Copper Canyon); Sherod Santos, *The Pilot Star Elegies* (Norton)
Winner: Ai, *Vice: New and Selected Poems* (Norton)

FICTION

Finalists: Andre Dubus III, *House of Sand and Fog* (Norton); Kent Haruf, *Plainsong* (Knopf); Patricia Henley, *Hummingbird House* (MacMurray & Beck); Jean Thompson Short Story Collection, *Who Do You Love?* (Harcourt Brace)

Winner: Ha Jin, *Waiting* (Pantheon)

Booker Prize: 1969–1999

1969: *Something to Answer For*, P.H. Newby
1970: *The Elected Member*, Bernice Rubens
1971: *In a Free State*, V.S. Naipaul
1972: *G*, John Berger
1973: *The Siege of Krishnapur*, J.G. Farrell
1974: *The Conservationist*, Nadine Gordimer
1975: *Heat and Dust*, Ruth Prawer Jhabvala
1976: *Saville*, David Storey
1977: *Staying on*, Paul Scott
1978: *The Sea, The Sea*, Iris Murdoch
1979: *Offshore*, Penelope Fitzgerald
1980: *Rites of Passage*, William Golding
1981: *Midnight's Children*, Salman Rushdie
1982: *Schindler's Ark*, Thomas Keneally
1983: *Life & Times of Michael K*, J.M. Coetzee
1984: *Hotel du Lac*, Anita Brookner

1985: *The Bone People*, Keri Hulme
1986: *The Old Devils*, Kingsley Amis
1987: *Moon Tiger*, Penelope Lively
1988: *Oscar and Lucinda*, Peter Carey
1989: *The Remains of the Day*, Kazuo Ishiguro
1990: *Possession*, A.S. Byatt
1991: *The Famished Road*, Ben Okri
1992: *The English Patient*, Michael Ondaatje; *Sacred Hunger*, Barry Unsworth
1993: *Paddy Clarke, Ha Ha Ha*, Roddy Doyle
1994: *How Late It Was, How Late*, James Kelman
1995: *The Ghost Road*, Pat Barker
1996: *Last Orders*, Graham Swift
1997: *The God of Small Things*, Arundhati Roy
1998: *Amsterdam*, Ian McEwan
1999: *Disgrace*, J.M. Coetzee

Nobel Prize for Literature: 1901–1999

1901: René François Armand (France)
1902: Theodor Mommsen (Germany)
1903: Björnstjerne Björnson (Norway)
1904: Jose Echegaray (Spain) and Frédéric Mistral (France)
1905: Henryk Sienkiewicz (Poland)
1906: Giosue Carducci (Italy)
1907: Rudyard Kipling (United Kingdom)
1908: Rudolf Eucken (Germany)
1909: Selma Lagerlöf (Sweden)
1910: Paul von Heyse (Germany)
1911: Maurice Maeterlinck (Belgium)
1912: Gerhart Hauptmann (Germany)
1913: Rabindranath Tagore (India)
1914: No Award
1915: Romain Rolland (France)
1916: Verner von Heidenstam (Sweden)
1917: Karl Gjellerup (Denmark) and Henrik Pontoppidan (Denmark)
1918: No Award
1919: Carl Spitteler (Switzerland)
1920: Knut Hamsun (Norway)
1921: Anatole France (France)

1922: Jacinto Benavente (Spain)
1923: William Butler Yeats (Ireland)
1924: Wladyslaw Reymont (Poland)
1925: George Bernard Shaw (United Kingdom)
1926: Grazia Deledda (Italy)
1927: Henri Bergson (France)
1928: Sigrid Undset (Norway)
1929: Thomas Mann (Germany)
1930: Sinclair Lewis (U.S.A.)
1931: Erik Axel Karlfeldt (Sweden)
1932: John Galsworthy (United Kingdom)
1933: Ivan Bunin (U.S.S.R.)
1934: Luigi Pirandello (Italy)
1935: No Award
1936: Eugene O'Neill (U.S.A.)
1937: Roger Martin du Gard (France)
1938: Pearl S. Buck (U.S.A.)
1939: F E Sillanpää (Finland)
1940: No Award
1941: No Award
1942: No Award
1943: No Award
1944: Johannes V. Jensen (Denmark)

1945: Gabriela Mistral (Chile)
1946: Hermann Hesse (Switzerland)
1947: André Gide (France)
1948: T. S. Eliot (United Kingdom)
1949: William Faulkner (U.S.A.)
1950: Bertrand Russell (United Kingdom)
1951: Pär Lagerkvist (Sweden)
1952: François Mauriac (France)
1953: Winston Churchill (United Kingdom)
1954: Ernest Hemingway (U.S.A.)
1955: Halldór Laxness (Iceland)
1956: J. R. Jiménez (Spain)
1957: Albert Camus (France)
1958: Boris Pasternak (U.S.S.R.)
1959: Salvatore Quasimodo (Italy)
1960: Saint-John Perse (France)
1961: Ivo Andrić (Yugoslavia)
1962: John Steinbeck (U.S.A.)
1963: Giorgos Seferis (Greece)
1964: Jean-Paul Sartre (France) *(declined)*
1965: Mikhail Sholokhov (U.S.S.R.)
1966: Shmuel Y. Agnon (Israel) and Nelly Sachs
(Germany)
1967: Miguel A. Asturias (Guatemala)
1968: Yasunari Kawabata (Japan)
1969: Samuel Beckett (Ireland)
1970: Aleksandr I. Solzhenitsyn (U.S.S.R.)
1971: Pablo Neruda (Chile)

1972: Heinrich Böll (Germany)
1973: Patrick White (Australia)
1974: Eyvind Johnson (Sweden)
1975: Eugenio Montale (Italy)
1976: Saul Bellow (U.S.A.)
1977: Vicente Aleixandre (Spain)
1978: Isaac Bashevis Singer (U.S.A.)
1979: Odysseus Elytis (Greece)
1980: Czeslaw Milosz (Poland/U.S.A.)
1981: Elias Canetti (United Kingdom)
1982: Gabriel García Márquez (Colombia)
1983: William Golding (United Kingdom)
1984: Jaroslav Seifert (Czechoslovakia)
1985: Claude Simon (France)
1986: Wole Soyinka (Nigeria)
1987: Joseph Brodsky (U.S.A.)
1988: Naguib Mahfouz (Egypt)
1989: Dr. Camilo José Cela (Spain)
1990: Octavio Paz (Mexico)
1991: Nadine Gordimer (South Africa)
1992: Derek Walcott (St. Lucia)
1993: Toni Morrison (U.S.A.)
1994: Kenzaburo Oe (Japan)
1995: Seamus Heaney (Ireland)
1996: Wislawa Szymborska (Poland)
1997: Dario Fo (Italy)
1998: José Saramago (Portugal)
1999: Günter Grass (Germany)

UK fastselling paperbacks: 1999

The 100 titles on this list were published for the first time in paperback in 1999. Below this cut-off point, 39 other titles passed the 100,000 units mark; the largest number since these records were first kept in 1979. The phenomenon of 1999 was the huge surge in the sales of the children's author, J.K. Rowling, whose total for three Harry Potter adventures passed 4m in the U.K. and 16m in America. She is one of 45 women authors, the highest percentage yet. Between them the top 100 sold 28m in British markets. Paperback figures are not yet much affected by unprecedented sales for a score or so of heavily discounted new hardcover titles, including 485,000 for Sir Alex Ferguson's *Managing My Life* and 663,000 for Thomas Harris's bizarre thriller *Hannibal*. Healthy rises appear generally for sporting biography, self-help, urban comedies of the flat-dwelling young and – with improved government subvention in schools – children's books. **Alex Hamilton**

Title, Author, Imprint	Total
1 *Tara Road*, Maeve Binchy, Orion	1,108,933
2 *H. Potter: Chamber of Secrets*, J.K. Rowling, Bloomsbury	1,024,972
3 *The Street Lawyer*, John Grisham, Arrow	993,401
4 *Point of Origin*, Patricia Cornwell, Warner	651,262
5 *About a Boy*, Nick Hornby, Phoenix	548,620
6 *Rainbow Six*, Tom Clancy, Penguin	546,119
7 *The Long Road Home*, Danielle Steel, Corgi	539,179
8 *Mirror Image*, Danielle Steel, Corgi	501,543
9 *Eleventh Commandment*, Jeffrey Archer, HarperCollins	501,170

10 *Who Wants To Be A Millionaire?,* Various, Boxtree	486,280
11 *The Solace of Sin,* Catherine Cookson, Corgi	474,522
12 *Archangel,* Robert Harris, Arrow	470,159
13 *Bag of Bones,* Stephen King, NEL	467,854
14 *The Loop,* Nicholas Evans, Corgi	453,534
15 *The Klone and I,* Danielle Steel, Corgi	450,172
16 *Tell Me Your Dreams,* Sidney Sheldon, HarperCollins	445,740
17 *Charlotte Gray,* Sebastian Faulks, Vintage	433,623
18 *When the Wind Blows,* James Patterson, Feature	427,687
19 *Field of 13,* Dick Francis, Pan	412,679
20 *Carpe Jugulum,* Terry Pratchett, Corgi	395,583
21 *Riley,* Catherine Cookson, Corgi	383,689
22 *Notes From a Big Country,* Bill Bryson, Black Swan	378,175
23 *Southern Cross,* Patricia Cornwell, Warner	361,783
24 *Other People's Children,* Joanna Trollope, Black Swan	361,566
25 *The Last Continent,* Terry Pratchett, Corgi	337,768
26 *The Breaker,* Minette Walters, Pan	328,404
27 *The Gilded Cage,* Josephine Cox, Headline	325,353
28 *Widow For One Year,* John Irving, Black Swan	313,287
29 *Tomorrow the World,* Josephine Cox, Headline	312,028
30 *Sight For Sore Eyes,* Ruth Rendell, Arrow	302,198
31 *A Certain Justice,* P.D. James, Penguin	297,456
32 *Come Together,* Lloyd & Rees, Arrow	296,096
33 *Mr Maybe,* Jane Green, Penguin	293,229
34 *Blast From the Past,* Ben Elton, Black Swan	284,517
35 *Angels Flight,* Michael Connelly, Orion	282,616
36 *Net Force: Hidden Agendas,* Tom Clancy, Feature	280,507
37 *Sudden Change of Heart,* Barbara T. Bradford, HarperCollins	267,214
38 *Snap Happy,* Fiona Walker, Coronet	249,729
39 *Net Force: Night Moves,* Tom Clancy, Feature	248,168
40 *Stalingrad,* Antony Beevor, Penguin	243,870
41 *Amsterdam,* Ian McEwan, Vintage	240,804
42 *Shadow Watch,* Tom Clancy, Penguin	232,922
43 *Dead Souls,* Ian Rankin, Orion	231,522
44 *The Hammer of Eden,* Ken Follett, Pan	227,071
45 *Star Wars: Episode 1,* Patricia C. Wrede, Scholastic	223,644
46 *Suddenly Single,* Sheila O'Flanagan, Headline	223,445
47 *Seize the Night,* Dean Koontz, Headline	223,019
48 *Charlie,* Lesley Pearse, Penguin	218,129
49 *Black Notice,* Patricia Cornwell, Little Brown	217,588
50 *She's the One,* Cathy Kelly, Headline	216,358
51 *The Chimney Sweeper's Boy,* Barbara Vine, Penguin	214,503
52 *Last Chance Saloon,* Marian Keyes, Penguin	213,850
53 *A Patchwork Planet,* Anne Tyler, Vintage	210,659
54 *Driving Over Lemons,* Chris Stewart, Sort of Books	201,532
55 *The Tesseract,* Alex Garland, Penguin	195,437
56 *The Waiting Time,* Gerald Seymour, Corgi	190,156
57 *No Safe Place,* Richard N Patterson, Arrow	189,883
58 *Moon Island,* Rosie Thomas, Arrow	187,884
59 *Ralph's Party,* Lisa Jewell, Penguin	187,772
60 *Every Dead Thing,* John Connolly, Coronet	183,847
61 *OP Centre State of Siege,* Tom Clancy, HarperCollins	182,336
62 *Monsoon,* Wilbur Smith, Macmillan	180,502
63 *The Hanging Garden,* Ian Rankin, Orion	180,218
64 *The Kissing Garden,* Charlotte Bingham, Bantam	179,686
65 *Georgiana,* Amanda Foreman, HarperCollins	175,902
66 *Polly,* Freya North, Arrow	174,565
67 *My Legendary Girlfriend,* Mike Gayle, Flame	174,300
68 *Rosie Meadows Regrets,* Catherine Alliott, Headline	173,195
69 *Filth,* Irvine Welsh, Vintage	172,035
70 *Flight of Eagles,* Jack Higgins, Penguin	171,215
71 *Hanna's Daughters,* Marianne Fredericksson, Phoenix	169,800
72 *Day of Confession,* Alan Folsom, Warner	169,382
73 *The English,* Jeremy Paxman, Penguin	166,669
74 *LA Connections: The Novel,* Jackie Collins, Pan	165,472
75 *Snow Falcon,* Stuart Harrison, HarperCollins	165,193
76 *The Surgeon of Crowthorne,* Simon Winchester, Penguin	164,381
77 *Armadillo,* William Boyd, Penguin	164,224
78 *Head Over Heels,* Jill Mansell, Headline	161,526
79 *Aches & Pains,* Maeve Binchy, Orion	157,400
80 *The New Flower Expert,* D.G. Hessayon, Expert	156,901

81 Pilot's Wife, Anita Shreve, Abacus	152,785
82 Message in a Bottle, Nicholas Sparks, Bantam	151,875
83 When Morning Comes, Audrey Howard, Coronet	150,759
84 A Man in Full, Tom Wolfe, Picador	147,501
85 Losing My Virginity, Richard Branson, Virgin	147,135
86 Sharpe's Triumph Hist., Bernard Cornwell, HarperCollins	146,248
87 Ashes to Ashes, Tami Hoag, Orion	144,500
88 City Woman, Patricia Scanlan, Bantam	143,123
89 The Ties That Bind, Lyn Andrews, Headline	141,175
90 Southern Cross, Patricia Cornwell, Little Brown	140,832
91 The Corner House, Ruth Hamilton, Corgi	140,317
92 Beyond the Shining Water, Audrey Howard, Coronet	139,782
93 The Lazarus Child, Robert Mawson, Bantam	139,022
94 Kremlin Device, Chris Ryan, Arrow	138,412
95 Speaking in Tongues, Jeffery Deaver, Coronet	138,223
96 Making of Minty Malone, Isabel Wolff, HarperCollins	138,016
97 Buried Alive!, Jacqueline Wilson, Yearling	134,764
98 The Keys to the Garden, Susan Sallis, Corgi	131,700
99 Star Wars Storybook, George Lucas, Scholastic	130,851
100 Birthday Letters, Ted Hughes, Faber	129,262

Publishers Weekly's U.S. paperback bestsellers: 1999

Title, Author, Publisher   **Weeks on '99 List**

MASSMARKET
*Dr. Atkins' New Diet Revolution, Robert C. Atkins, Avon (99), 51
Protein Power, Drs. Michael R. Eades & Mary Dan Eades, Bantam (24), 6
* The Street Lawyer, John Grisham, Dell/Island, 23
* Summer Sisters, Judy Blume, Dell, 22
*Message in a Bottle, Nicholas Sparks, Warner, 17
*The Notebook, Nicholas Sparks, Warner, 16

TRADE
*Memoirs of a Geisha, Arthur Golden, Vintage, 47
*Where the Heart Is, Billie Letts, Warner (1), 46
Divine Secrets of the Ya-Ya Brotherhood, Rebecca Wells, Harper Perennial (45), 41
*The Pilot's Wife, Anita Shreve, Little, Brown/Back Bay, 36
*The Seat of the Soul, Cary Zukav, S&S/Fireside (9), 35

*The Reader, Bernard Schlink, Vintage, 33
*Angela's Ashes, Frank McCourt, S&S/Touchstone, 29
Don't Sweat the Small Stuff, Dr. Richard Carlson. Hyperion (88), 27
*Chicken Soup For the Teenage Soul II, J. Canfield, M.V. Hanson & K. Kirberger, Health Communications, 23
Left Behind, Tim LaHaye and Jerry B. Jenkins, Tyndale House, 22
A Walk in the Woods, Bill Bryson, Broadway, 21
I Know This Much Is True, Wally Lamb, HarperCollions/ReganBooks, 19
Midwives, Chris Mohjalian, Vintage (7), 16
Charming Billy, Alice McDermott, Delta, 16
Suzanne Somers' Eat Great, Lose Weight, Suzanne Somers, Three Rivers, 16

* These titles achieved the #1 spot during
their 1999 presence on PW's bestseller list.
Numbers in parentheses show how many
weeks the book was on PW's list prior to 1999.

> *I exercise extreme self-control.*
> *I never drink anything stronger*
> *than gin before breakfast.*
> *(W.C. Fields)*

Announcements

Marriages

Alex Kingston (35), actress, married Florian Haertel (34), journalist in January.

Caroline of Monaco married Ernst of Hanover in January.

Charles Bronson (77) married Kim Weeks (36) in January.

Christopher Lambert (42), actor, married Jaymis Haft (22) in February.

Diane Ladd, actress, wed enterpreneur Robert Charles Hunter on February 14.

Jason Priestley, *Beverly Hills 90210* star, married Ashlee Peterson, makeup artist in February.

Rufus Sewell (32), actor, married Yasmin Abdallah, fashion buyer in March.

Gary Webster (35), actor, married Wendy Turner, actress and sister of TV presenter Anthea Turner, in March.

Blue Peter's Katy Hill (28) wed childhood sweetheart Andrew Frampton (31), songwriter and record producer, in March.

Sarah O'Hare (26), Australian model, married Lachlan Murdoch (27), Rupert Murdoch's son, in late March.

Nigel Planer, ex *Young Ones* star, married Frankie Park, actress and writer, on April 3.

Lysette Anthony (35), actress, married David Price, producer and director, in April.

Joe Millson, actor, married actress Caroline Fitzgerald in May.

James Major (24), son of the former prime minister John Major married model, TV presenter, and actress Emma Noble (27) in May.

Stella Tennant (28), supermodel, married David Lasnet, French photographer in May.

Andrea McLean (29), GMTV weathergirl, married BBC science researcher Nick Green (29), in May.

Esther Rantzen, TV presenter, and her husband of 21 years, Desmond Wilcox, presenter, renewed their vows in May.

Greg Kinnear, American actor, married his British girlfriend, former glamor model Helen Labdon, in May.

Richard Dreyfuss (51), actor, married his girlfriend of six years Janelle Lacey (33), accountant, in June.

Grace Kennedy (41), singer, married Nigel Angel, top celebrity lawyer, in June.

Frankie Lane (86), singer, married Marcia Kline (61) in June.

Esther Cañadas (22), Spanish top model, married Mark Vanderloo (31), Dutch model, in June.

Sean Pertwee (35), actor, married the Hon. Jacqueline Hamilton-Smith (32), makeup artist and daughter of Lord Colwyn, in June.

Tony Robinson, member of the pop group *The Beautiful South*, married Rachael Kelham in June.

Rupert Murdoch (68) married Wendy Deng (31) in June, only three weeks after completing his divorce from Anna Murdoch.

Zac Goldsmith (24), journalist son of late billionaire businessman James Goldsmith, married Sheherazade Ventura Bentley (24) in June.

Courtney Cox (35), *Friends* star, and David Arquette (27), actor, married in June.

Clasically trained singers Charlotte Page (31) and Joe Shovelton (31) married on 27 June.

Phil Collins (48), singer, married Orianne Cevey (27) in July.

Martin Scorsese (56), director, married Helen S. Morris in July. This is his fifth marriage.

Posh Spice married soccer star David Beckham in July.

Helen Hunt (36), Oscar-winner, married her longtime boyfriend Hank Azaria (35) in July.

Raquel Welch (58), Hollywood star, married Richard Palmer (45), restaurant-chain owner, at her home in Beverly Hills in July.

Daniel Stewart (29), son of Patrick Stewart, married Mary Stillwagon in July.

Seraphina Watts (31), daughter of Charlie Watts the famous Rolling Stone, married Nicholas Hoskins, lawyer, in July.

Johnny Vaughan, *Big Breakfast* presenter, married his longtime girlfriend Antonia in the summer.

Peri Gilpin, wisecracking Roz from *Frasier*, married Christian Vincent in August.

Zoe Ball (28), British DJ, married Norman Cook (aka Fatboy Slim) in August.

Nicholas Lyndhurst, actor known for his role in *Only Fools and Horses*, married Lucy Smith in September.

Tam Williams (27), actor, married Serena Burke, trainee surgeon, in September.

Kirsty Young, TV presenter, married Nick Jones, hotel entrepreneur in September.

Richard Widmark (84), veteran film star, married Susan Blanchard (Henry Fonda's third wife) in November.

Evel Knievel (61), former stunt-rider, married Krystal Kennedy (30) in November.

Jacquie Leavy, *Sky News* sports presenter, married Brazilian website designer Eduardo Beltrao in December.

Jerry Seinfeld (45), actor, and Jessica Sklar (28), publicist, married on Christmas Day.

Births

Janet Dibley, actress, and Tyler Butterworth, actor, celebrated the birth of their son, Todd William Tyler, in January.

Mel B (Scary Spice) and Jimmy Gulzar celebrated the birth of their first child, daughter Phoenix Chi, in February.

Mel Gibson and wife Robyn celebrated the birth of their seventh child, a son, early in the year.

Kate Beckinsale and partner Michael Sheen celebrated the birth of a daughter in February.

Victoria Adams (Posh Spice) and David Beckham, soccer star, celebrated the birth of their first child, son Brooklyn Joseph, in March.

Michael Le Vell star of *Coronation Street*, and wife Janette celebrated the birth of their son, Finley, in March.

Boyzone's Ronan Keating and wife Yvonne celebrated the birth of their first child, Jack, in March.

Former *EastEnders* star Gillian Taylforth and long-time partner Geoff Knights celebrated the birth of a son in March.

Emma Forbes, TV presenter, and husband Graham Clempson celebrated the birth of a baby boy in March.

Kevin Pallister, actor, and actress wife Theresa Kartell celebrated the birth of their first child, son George, in April.

Berni Nolan, of the Nolan Sisters and husband Steve Doneathy celebrated the birth of a baby girl, Erin Kate, in April.

Mary McCartney, Paul McCartney's daughter, and husband Alistair Donald celebrated the birth of their first child, a boy, in April.

Julio Iglesias and partner Miranda Rijnsburger celebrated the birth of their second son, Rodrigo, in April.

It was reported in April that Woody Allen and wife Soon-Yi had become parents. The baby girl, Bechet Dumaine Allen, was adopted.

David Duchovny, *X-Files* star, and wife Tea Leoni celebrated the birth of their first child, a daughter, on April 24.

Christian Slater and girlfriend Ryan Haddon celebrated the birth of their child in spring.

Luciana Morad, Brazilian model, gave birth to a boy, Lucas, in May. The father is Mick Jagger.

Johnny Depp and French actress Vanessa Paradis celebrated the birth of their first child, daughter Lily-Rose, in May.

Fiona Phillips, GMTV presenter, and husband, GMTV's chief reporter Martin Frizell, celebrated the birth of son, Nathaniel, on May 28.

Cindy Crawford supermodel, and husband Rande Gerber, wealthy nightclub owner, celebrated the birth of their first child, son Presley Walker, on July 2.

Marie Osmond, singer and American TV host, and husband Brian Blosil celebrated the birth of their seventh child, son Mathew, in July.

Caroline (daughter of the screen legend Grace Kelly and Prince Ranier of Monaco) and Ernst of Hanover celebrated the birth of their daughter, Alexandra, on July 20.

Lucy Lawless, aka Xena, Warrior Princess, and husband Robert Tapert celebrated the birth of their son, Julius Robert Bay Tapert, in September.

Patsy Kensit, model and actress, and Liam Gallagher celebrated the birth of their son, Lennon, in October.

Lisa Maxwell, West End actress, and Paul Jessup, design consultant, celebrated the birth of their daughter, Beau, in November.

Martin Clunes, actor, and his wife Philippa Braithwaite celebrated the birth of their daughter, Emily, in November.

Emma Thompson, actor and Greg Wise, actor, celebrated the birth of their first child, daughter Maya, on December 4.

Notable separations

Rod Stewart rock star, and Rachel Hunter, model, separated in January after eight years of marriage.

Gwyneth Paltrow and Ben Affleck separated in January.

Carol Barnes TV news presenter, separated from husband Nigel Thomson, cameraman, in January.

Rock band **The Verve** split up in April.

Ruthie Henshall, singer and dancer, split with her longtime partner, actor John Gordon Sinclair, in June.

Jonathan Ross TV presenter, and his wife Jane Goldman, best-selling author, separated in June.

Robson Green, star of *Soldier, Soldier* and *Reckless*, and wife Alison separated in July after seven years together.

Andie MacDowell and husband Paul Qualey separated in July after 13 years of marriage.

Claudia Schiffer, supermodel and actress, separated from boyfriend David Copperfield, magician, in September after six years.

Tim Allen, star of *Home Improvement*, separated from his wife of 15 years, Laura Deibel, in November.

Divorces

Heather Previn filed for divorce from conductor **André Previn** in February.

Lynn Redgrave filed for divorce from her husband of 32 years, John Clark, in February.

Brooke Shields, actress, and Andre Agassi, tennis star, divorced in April after a two-year marriage.

Rita Rusic filed for separation from Italy's top film producer-distributor, **Vittorio Cecchi Gori**, in April.

Ex-*Baywatch* star **Carmen Electra** filed for divorce just five months after marrying basketball-star Dennis Rodman.

Donald Trump, New York property tycoon, and Marla Maples, actress, divorced in June.

Mick Jagger and **Jerry Hall's** marriage was finally declared null and void in July.

Divorce proceedings were underway for actress **Samantha Janus** and her husband of two years, Mauro, in November.

Bonnie Raitt, recording star, and her husband of eight years, actor Michael O'Keefe, filed for divorce in November.

Nature, Mr. Allnut, is
what we are put in this
world to rise above.
(Katharine Hepburn,
The African Queen)

Obituaries

From its earliest years *Variety* has been tracking the quick and the dead, the latter often under the somewhat mordant banner of "Necrology." Shorn of sentiment and tightly compiled, these obituaries focus on the facts in the careers of everyone from superstars to the humblest journalist or technician. The important names appear in the weekly edition of *Variety*, while those lesser mortals whose reputation might be familiar only to Los Angelinos figure in *Daily Variety*.

Variety journalists are taught to be rigorous in their pursuit of accurate facts about the newly departed, and ascertaining the cause of death remains a priority. Indeed, our venerable gossip columnist, Army Archerd, has for decades been the first person to be entrusted with bad news – notably Rock Hudson's contracting AIDS, Henry Mancini's battle with cancer, or Jimmy Stewart's death in 1997. For the purposes of this *Almanac* we have selected some of the more noteworthy obituaries, along with a checklist of all those published during 1999. The full-length "Obits." can be accessed through our website, at www.Variety.com.

Obituaries for 1999

Martin Agronsky, broadcast journalist, died July 25 of congestive heart failure at his home in Washington, DC. He was 84.

Jeffrey D. Alderman, a pioneering polling expert for *ABC News* and a former editor with The Associated Press, died November 15 in New York following a battle with cancer. He was 56.

David Allen, an Oscar-nominated visual-effects director for *Young Sherlock Holmes*, died August 16 in Santa Ana, CA. He was 54.

Rex Allen, the last of Hollywood's singing cowboy stars, died at a Tucson hospital on December 17 after a friend accidentally ran over him in his driveway.

William Allyn, television and film producer, died January 3 of complications from heart disease at Cedars Sinai Medical Center in Los Angeles . He was 71.

Fabrizio De Andre, singer-songwriter, whose politicized, poetic ballads made him one of the most important and enduring influences on Italian music of the past 30 years, died January 11 of cancer in a Milan clinic. He was 58.

Meir Ariel, Israeli singer-songwriter, died July 18 of an infection in Tel Aviv. He was 57.

Graham Armitage, actor-director and winner of a Cannes supporting actor award for his role as Louis XIII in Ken Russell's *The Devils*, died March 6 at his home in South Africa. He was 63.

Michael Avallone, a mystery writer who penned the Ed Noon series and whose novels were based on the TV series *The Man From U.N.C.L.E.* and *Hawaii Five-*

0, died February 26 at his home in Los Angeles. He was 74.

Hoyt Axton, the folksy singer, songwriter, and character actor, died October 26 at his ranch in Victor, MT. He was 61.

Adele Balkan, a costume designer whose career encompassed 40 years, died November 20 of cancer in Los Angeles. She was 92.

Ian Bannen, stage and film actor, died November 3 in an auto accident. He was 71.

Lionel Bart, the lyricist and composer who created *Oliver!* and other musicals, died April 3 of cancer. He was 68.

William Benedict, film and TV character actor, died November 25 of complications from heart surgery in Los Angeles. He was 82.

Rick Bennewitz, an Emmy-winning director of the NBC soap *Santa Barbara* and the senior director of *Sunset Beach*, died January 9 of a heart attack in Los Angeles. He was 62.

Hugh Benson, television executive and producer, died October 28 of cancer in Reseda, CA. He was 82.

Mary Kay Bergman, versatile voiceover artist, committed suicide November 11 at her home in Los Angeles. She was 38.

Phil Berle, legendary comedian and Milton Berle's brother, who enjoyed a successful career in the entertainment business in his own right, died January 2 in Tampa, FL. He was 97.

John Berry, the film and theater director whose blacklist-disrupted career spanned working with Orson Welles' Mercury Theater Troupe in the 1930s to his upcoming film adaptation of Athol Fugard's *Boesman and Lena*, died November 29 in Paris after a bout with pleurisy. He was 82.

Dirk Bogarde, British actor who segued from frothy comedies to serious dramas, died May 8 of a heart attack at his London home. He was 78.

Alberto Bolet, the Havana-born conductor who led orchestras on three continents and spread Cuban rhythms throughout the world, died November 10 of natural causes in Teaneck, NJ. He was 94.

Dalla Bower, a pioneer television producer who began his career in early radio and cinema, died October 18 at his home in London. He was 92.

Lester Bowie, trumpeter, a leading contributor to the jazz avant-garde and a founding member of the Art Ensemble of Chicago, died of complications from liver cancer November 8 at his Brooklyn home. He was 58.

Paul Bowles, novelist, composer, poet, and quintessential icon of individualism died November 18 of a heart attack in Tangiers, Morocco, where he had lived since 1947. He was 88.

Betty Evelyn Box, one of the most successful producers of post-World War II British films, died January 15. She was 78.

Richard Boone, American-born trombonist and scat singer, died in February at 68 in Copenhagen. The date and cause of death were not available.

Junior Braithwaite, a member of Bob Marley's Wailers, was shot dead in Jamaica in June. He was 47.

Eleanor Breese, novelist and executive story editor, died October 13 of natural causes in Santa Monica. She was 87.

Robert Bresson, the master director once described by Jean-Luc Godard as the Dostoevsky of French cinema, died December 18 in Paris. He was 98.

Robert Benjamin Bring, Emmy-nominated film editor, died August 4 of brain cancer at his home in Valley Village, CA. He was 60.

Kenn Brodziak, Australian legit legend, died June 3 of unreported causes in Melbourne. He was 86.

Hillary Brooke, the elegant blonde actress who perfected the "other woman" role in dozens of films and played Gales Storm's adversary in the 1950s sitcom *My Little Margie*, died May 25 in Bonsall, CA. She was 84.

Charles Brown, blues pianist, singer, and composer, died January 21 of heart failure at Summit Medical Center in Oakland. He was 76.

Dennis Brown, Jamaican-born singer, known as the Crown Prince of Reggae, died in July at the age of 42.

Vanessa Brown, the actress-writer who escaped Nazi Europe to become a celebrated radio Quiz Kid, Jane

opposite Lex Barker's film Tarzan, and respected as the author of a book on labor policy, died May 21 of cancer in Woodland Hills, CA. She was 71.

Bobbe Brox, the last surviving member of the singing Brox Sisters trio of the 1920s and widow of songwriter Jimmy van Heusen, died May 2 of natural causes in Glens Falls, NY. She was 98.

Charlie Byrd, guitarist, an ambassador of Brazilian jazz, died November 30 of cancer at his home in Annapolis, MD. He was 74.

Rory Calhoun, actor, producer, and writer best remembered for his 1950s Western films and TV series *The Texan*, died in Los Angeles on April 28 after being hospitalized for 10 days, suffering from emphysema and diabetes. He was 76.

As a young man, the L.A. native got in trouble for a string of car robberies that landed him in a federal reformatory. Upon his release he held a number of rough jobs, working as a logger in California's redwood forests, a miner in Nevada, a cowpuncher in Arizona, and a forest firefighter. But his big career break came when he met Alan Ladd on a bridle path in the Hollywood Hills and the Western star persuaded him to take a screen test.

Calhoun enjoyed his heyday as a Western star in the 1950s, establishing himself as one of the country's leading screen cowboys in 1952 with *Way of a Gaucho*. He went on to star in such films as *Four Guns to the Border*, *The Treasure of Pancho Villa*, *The Hired Gun*, and *Powder River*.

On *The Texan*, a CBS Western that ran for two seasons beginning in 1958, Calhoun played Bill Longley, who traveled helping those in need in the years following the Civil War.

He also appeared in anthology series, including *Ford Television Theater*, *Death Valley Days*, and *Zane Theater*, and served as host of the syndicated *Western Star Theater*. He produced, directed, and scripted the 1957 motion picture *Domino Kid*. He co-scripted *Shotgun* and wrote the novels *The Man From Padera* and *Cerrado*. In the 1980s he returned to TV in the CBS soap *Capitol* and to the big screen with *Angel*.

Ernesto Calindri, a doyen of the Italian stage whose distinguished career in theater, films, and television spanned more than 70 years, died June 8 in a Milan clinic after a brief illness. He was 90.

Flora Carabella, Italian actress and the widow of actor Marcello Mastroianni, died April 20 of bone cancer at her home in Rome. She was 73.

John Carmody, who created the *Washington Post*'s television column and wrote it for 21 years, died March 1 of cancer in Washington, DC. He was 74.

Allan Carr, the producer best known for the films

Grease and *Grease 2*, died June 29 at his home in Beverly Hills. He was 62.

Anita Carter, who played standup bass and sang soprano as a member of the country music group The Carter Family, died July 29 in Nashville, TN, of undisclosed causes. She was 66.

Peggy Cass, a comedienne who won an Oscar nomination for reprising her Tony-winning role as Agnes Gooch in *Auntie Mame*, died March 8 of heart failure in New York. She was 74.

Marguerite Chapman, a prolific leading lady in 1940s Columbia features who played Miss Morris in *The Seven Year Itch*, died August 31 at Providence St. Joseph Medical Center in Burbank, CA. The cause of death was not disclosed. She was 82.

Claudie Cheval, director of France's Ateliers du Cinéma Européen (ACE), a training institute for film producers, died July 30 of cancer. She was 48.

Minoru Chiaki, the last surviving actor to play one of the Seven Samurai in the renowned film by Akira Kurosawa, died November 2 in Tokyo at the age of 82.

Roy Chiao, an actor who had a long career in Hong Kong films, died April 16 of a heart attack in the U.S. He was 72.

Ellen Cobry, the Emmy-winning and Oscar-nominated actress, best known as the grandmother on the hit 1970s TV series *The Waltons*, died April 14. She was 87.

Bob Cochran, one of the original on-air personalities for former Pittsburgh TV station WIIC, died May 30 of unreported causes in Atlanta. He was 68.

Iron Eyes Cody the actor known for playing American Indians in many movies, died January 4 of natural causes in Los Angeles. He was in his late eighties or early nineties.

Thomas E. Coffin, an NBC researcher, died May 13 in Stanton, CA. He was 83.

Philip Cohan, longtime radio producer and director from its golden age, died November 27 of natural causes in Pacific Palisades, CA. He was 94.

John Leon Collis, retired Rear Admiral, a former commander of the Pearl Harbor Naval Shipyard who wrote several popular songs, died January 12 of natural causes in Honolulu. He was 92.

Christopher Cordeaux, film editor, died 2 September of unreported causes in Sydney. He was 57.

Stuart Craig, chairman and CEO of Craig Broadcasting Systems, Canada's largest owned broadcasting company, died October 30 of pancreatic cancer at his home in Brandon, Manitoba. He was 66.

Jill Craigie, actress, author, film director, and wife of former Labor leader Michael Foot, died in December at the age of 85.

Harry Crane, the comedy writer whose writing credits span more than half a century, died September 16 of cancer at his Beverly Hills home. He was 85.

Charles Crichton, the British helmer who directed some of the brightest Ealing Studio film comedies during the 1940s and 1950s and after a long hiatus enjoyed a comeback decades later with *A Fish Called Wanda*, died September 14 at his home in London following a short illness. He was 89.

Quentin Crisp, the eccentric writer, performer, and ranconteur best known for his autobiography *The Naked Civil Servant*, died on November 21 in Manchester Royal Infirmary. He was 90.

Mary Jane Croft Lewis, who worked opposite Lucille Ball on the TV series *I Love Lucy*, *The Lucy Show*, and *Here's Lucy*, died August 24 of natural causes at her home in Century City, CA. She was 83.

John Crohan, founder and former president of Talk America Radio Networks, died July 25 in Canton, MA, following a lengthy illness. He was 69.

Stanley Dance, Grammy-winning jazz critic and confidant to jazz greats Duke Ellington and Earl Hines, died February 23 of pneumonia at the Remington Rehabilitation Center in Rancho Bernardo, CA. He was 88.

Jill Dando, BBC host and one of Britain's best-liked TV stars, was shot dead April 26 outside her West London home. She was 37.

Rick Danko, the bassist whose high-pitched and soulful voice shaped the music of The Band, died at his home in upstate New York on December 10, the day after he turned 56.

Charles G. 'Bud' Dant, band leader and composer, died October 31 of natural causes at Kona Community Hospital in Hawaii. He was 92.

Jeanne-Marie Darre, French pianist, died January 26 at her home in Port Marly, France. She was 93.

Martin Davis, former media baron and chairman of Paramount Communications, died October 4 of a heart attack in New York City. He was 72.

Danny Dayton, actor and director perhaps best remembered for his recurring role as Hak Pivnik on *All in the Family*, died February 6 of emphysema in Cedars-Sinai Medical Center in Los Angeles. He was 75.

Eddie Dean the cowboy singer who appeared in numerous B Westerns during the 1930s and 1940s, died March 4 of natural causes in Thousand Oaks, CA. He was 91.

Sarah Delany, who with her sister wrote a memoir that became a play and telefilm, *Having Our Say*, died January 25 in her sleep at her suburban New York City home in Mount Vernon. She was 109.

Frank DeVol, the prolific Oscar-nominated composer who wrote the theme music for the original *Brady Bunch* and *My Three Sons* TV series, died October 27 of natural causes in Lafayette, CA. He was 88.

Gerald Dickler, an entertainment attorney whose efforts helped lead to the creation of AFTRA and who represented radio and TV personalities blacklisted during the McCarthy era, died February 13 of pneumonia in New York. He was 86.

Joe DiMaggio, baseball legend, also famous for his brief marriage to Marilyn Monroe, died March 8 after losing his battle against lung cancer. He was 84.

Joe DiMaggio Jr., son of the baseball legend, died in California, apparently of natural causes. He was 57.

Shirley Dinsdale Layburn, a ventriloquist who won the very first Emmy Award for 1948 and later moved on to a career in health care, died May 9 of cancer at her home in Stony Brook, N.Y. She was 72.

Edward Dmytryk, who directed such pics as *Murder My Sweet*, *The Caine Mutiny*, and *Raintree County*, and served a year in federal prison as one of Hollywood's Unfriendly 10 during the HUAC anti-Communist hearings of the late 1940s, died July 1 of heart and kidney failure at his home in Encino, California. He was 90.

Robert Douglas a prolific British stage and screen actor of the 1930s and 1940s who became a successful TV director, died January 11 of natural causes at his home in Encinitas, CA. He was 89.

Richard S. Dubelman, producer, cinematographer, and director, died July 1 in Englewood Cliffs, NJ. He was 69.

Anthony Duquette, Tony Award-winning costume designer, died September 9 of complications resulting from a heart attack at the UCLA Medical Center. He was 85.

Stanley Durwood, feisty and controversial theater exhibition magnate, died July 14 at the age of 78.

Harry 'Sweets' Edison, trumpeter and master jazz accompanist for singers ranging from Frank Sinatra to Ella Fitzgerald, died July 27 following a 14-year battle with cancer. He was 83.

Hans Ehrmann, a 40-year contributor to *Variety*, died in Santiago, Chile on August 21 of complications from a respiratory illness. He was 74.

Ross Elliott, a prolific character actor whose four-decade career spanned Broadway, TV and feature films, died August 12 at the Motion Picture Home in Los Angeles, following a lengthy battle with cancer. He was 82.

Jimmy Ellis, known nationally for his impersonations of Elvis Presley, was shot to death December 12 inside a pawn and package store he owned in Orrville, Alabama. He was 53.

Ruth Enders Tripp, children's TV actress, died July 28 in New York after a long illness. She was 79.

Francine Everett, an entertainer known for her roles in all-black films of the 1930s and 1940s, died May 27 of unreported causes in New York. She was probably in her early 80s.

Clifton Fadiman, editor, essayist, critic, a founder of the Book-of-the-Month Club and host of 1930s radio show *Information Please*, died of pancreatic cancer June 20 at his son's home on Sanibel Island, FL. He was 95.

Hyman R. Faine, a labor executive with the American Guild of Musical Artists who helped establish the Management in the Arts program at UCLA, died April 8 in Los Angeles from pneumonia. He was 88.

Luis M. Farias, a founder of Mexico's radio announcers' union who later became a senator, died April 3. The cause of death was not reported, but he had suffered from Parkinson's Disease. He was 78.

Art Farmer, a jazz musician who developed a hybrid of the trumpet and flugelhorn that he called a "flumpet," died October 4 of a heart attack in New York. He was 71.

Fred Feast, the British actor best known for his role in *Coronation Street*, died after a long illness in July. He was 69.

Rudi Fehr, the Oscar-nominated film editor for 1985's *Prizzi's Honor* who worked at Warner Bros. for 40 years, died of a heart attack April 16 in Los Angeles. He was 88.

Magdalene Ferguson, a long-time publicist who promoted such films as *The African Queen* and *Lawrence of Arabia*, died January 24 in Toluca Lake, California. She was 91.

Manfredo Fest, a jazz pianist and a pioneer of the Brazilian *bossa nova* movement, died October 8 in Palm Harbor, FL, while awaiting a liver transplant. He was 63.

William Fineshriber, vice-president of the Motion Picture Association. of America from 1960 to 1984 and a longtime broadcast exec, died November 6 of natural causes at his home in Century City, CA. He was 90.

Fred Ford, saxophonist and a versatile jazz and rhythm and blues musician, died November 26 in Memphis, TN, following a battle with cancer. He was 69.

George Forrest, the Oscar nominated composer-lyricist who wrote numerous songs for stage and film, died October 10 in Miami of natural causes. He was 84.

Helen Forrest, one of the top vocalists from the big-band era, died July 11 of heart failure at the Motion Picture Country Home and Hospital in Woodland Hills, CA. She was 82.

John Fowler, Australian radio, TV, and theater stalwart, died May 27 of unreported causes. He was 71.

Van Arsdale France, who created highly successful training programs for Disneyland workers beginning in 1955, died October 13 of pneumonia at Hoag Memorial Hospital Presbyterian in Newport Beach, CA. He was 87.

Harry S. Franklin, writer-director, died March 7 after a brief illness at Cedars-Sinai Medical Center in Los Angeles. He was 88.

Lowell Fulson, blues guitarist and singer, died March 7 of kidney and congestive heart failure at Pacific Hospital in Long Beach, CA. He was 77.

Allen Funt, creator and original host of *Candid Camera,* died September 5 in Pebble Beach, CA, of complications resulting from a serious stoke he suffered in 1993. He was 84.

Felix Galimar, renowned violinist and chamber musician, died November 10 in New York of natural causes. He was 89.

Andrew Gardner, who presented the first *News at Ten* in 1967, died of a heart attack in April. He was 66.

Frances Gershwin Godowsky, sister of George and Ira Gershwin who later won renown as a respected painter in her own right, died January 18 in New York City. She was 92.

Betty Lou Gerson, the actress who provided voice of the villainess Cruella De Vil in Disney's animated feature *101 Dalmatians,* died January 12 in Los Angeles after suffering a massive stroke. She was 84.

Edmund Gilbert, an ubiquitous voiceover artist and actor who enjoyed a 40-year career in TV and films, died May 8 at his home in Beverly Hills following a lengthy battle with lung cancer. He was 67.

Hamilton Gilkison, singer-songwriter who wrote an eclectic range of music spanning folk to calypso to songs for Disney animation, died October 15 in Austin, TX, of natural causes. He was 83.

Kenneth Glancy, former RCA Records president, died May 23 in New York of unreported causes. He was 74.

Ernest Gold, Oscar-winning composer who wrote scores for *Exodus, It's a Mad, Mad, Mad World, On the Beach,* and *The Secret of Santa Vittoria,* died March 17 from stroke complications. He was 77.

Leonard Goldenson, a founding father of network television, died December 27 at his home in Sarasota, FL. He was 94.

David Golding, studio publicist who once served as Samuel Goldwyn's publicity chief and was a managing editor of *Stars and Stripes* during World War II, died February 14 of undisclosed causes in Santa Monica. He was 85.

James Goldstone, the Emmy-winning director who helmed the pilot episode of *Star Trek,* died November 5 of cancer at his home in Shaftsbury, VT. He was 68.

Dias Gomes, a highly successful Brazilian TV scribe who was also an accomplished playwright and novelist, died May 18 in a car crash in Sao Paulo. He was 76.

William Goodhart, screenwriter and creator of the 1960s hit Broadway comedy *Generation,* died of heart disease October 20 at his home on Shelter Island, NY. He was 74.

Sandra Gould, the actress best known as nosy next-door neighbor Gladys Kravitz on the popular TV series *Bewitched,* died July 20 of a stroke. She was 73.

Ronny Graham, who wrote for *M*A*S*H* and *The Mary Tyler Moore Show,* died July 4 in Century City, CA, of unreported causes. He was 79.

Joseph Green, writer and director, died September 1 from liver failure at St. Luke's Roosevelt Hospital in New York. He was 71.

Leo Greenfield, a distribution executive for several top studios including Warner Bros. and MGM, died October 3 of cancer at Cedars-Sinai Medical Center in Los Angeles. He was 84.

Howard Griffiths, pioneering Australian television scriptwriter, died October 24 of leukaemia in Sydney. He was 64.

Sam Grossman, writer and director, died of cancer February 22. He was 53.

Jerzy Grotowski, avant-garde Polish director and one of modern theater's most influential innovators, died January 14 at his home in Pontedera, near Pisa, Italy. He was 65 and had been suffering from leukemia and a heart condition.

Anne Haddy, veteran Australian actress, died June 6 in Melbourne after long battles with cancer, kidney and heart problems. She was 71.

Huntz Hall, the rubber-faced actor, one of the original Dead End Kids in the popular films of the late 1930s, died of heart failure January 30 at his North Hollywood home. He was 78.

James Hammerstein, legit director/producer and son of Oscar Hammerstein, died of a heart attack January 7 in New York. He was 57.

Hilary Harris, Academy Award-winning experimental filmmaker and kinetic sculptor, died 26 October of kidney failure at Mount Sinai Medical Center in New York. He was 69.

Mike Harris, journalist, film and TV critic and former *Variety* staffer and contributor, died August 7 of liver cancer in Sydney. He was 64.

Stefan Hatos, longtime radio and television writer and producer, died March 2 of a heart ailment in Toluca Lake, CA. He was 78.

Joseph Heller, novelist, TV writer, playwright, and screenwriter famous for his darkly comic first novel (later a movie) *Catch-22*, died December 12 of a heart attack at his Long Island home. He was 76.

Shirley Hemphill, actress and comedian died December 10 of natural causes at her home in West Covina, CA. She was 52.

Bob Herbert, who created the Spice Girls, died August 9 in a car accident in the U.K. He was 57.

Ed Herlihy, a radio announcer who was the voice of Kraft Foods for 40 years, died January 30 of natural causes in New York. He was 89.

Al Hicks, a longtime freelance writer who worked for several of the big Hollywood studios as a publicist in Europe, died March 7 of heart failure at Hollywood Presbyterian Hospital. He was 81.

George Higgins, the prosecutor-turned-novelist who put Boston organized-crime figures in both prison and fiction (including his bestseller *The Friends of Eddie Coyle*) was found dead, apparently from natural causes, November 6 in his Milton, MA, home. He was 59.

Bill Hillman, the San Francisco news broadcaster who served as national president of AFTRA from 1979 to 1984, died August 3 of congestive heart failure. He was 76.

Al Hirt, Grammy-winning trumpeter, died April 26 in New Orleans of liver failure. He was 76.

L.C. 'Speedy' Huggins, a legend of Kansas City jazz, died February 20 of pulmonary infection. He was 85.

Gordon Hughes, a director-writer whose career spanned a half-century of work on stage, radio, and TV, died April 19 of heart failure in a Montecito, CA, nursing home. He was 89.

Marilyn Jackson Wells, a longtime studio session singer who enjoyed a four-decade career, died May 24 of cancer at her home in Santa Monica, CA. She was 70.

Milt Jackson, jazz vibraphonist and master improviser and a 40-year veteran of the Modern Jazz Quartet, died October 9 of liver cancer in Teaneck, NJ. He was 76.

Brion James, who played Leon the murderous replicant in *Blade Runner* and appeared in character roles in more than 100 other movies, died August 7 at UCLA Medical Center after suffering a heart attack in his Malibu home. He was 54.

Jim Jensen, popular anchorman for New York's WCBS-TV from 1964-95, died October 15 of an apparent heart attack at Lenox Hill Hospital in New York. He was 73.

Calvin Jones, TV and PR exec, died of natural causes July 8 in Katy, TX. He was 74.

Henry Jones, Tony Award-winning actor, whose career on Broadway, film and television spanned more than half a century, died May 17 in Los Angeles from injuries suffered in a fall at his Santa Monica home. He was 86.

Madeline Kahn, the offbeat comedienne and singer who won a Tony Award and earned back-to-back Oscar nominations for her work in *Paper Moon* and *Blazing Saddles*, died December 3 in New York of ovarian cancer. She was 57.

Sarah Kane, who caused a sensation with her graphic and violent first play, *Blasted*, was found hanged in her apartment February 20, an apparent suicide, according to Scotland Yard. She was 28.

Garson Kanin, the writer and director who successfully commuted between stage and screen and was responsible for such memorable works as *Born Yesterday* and *A Double Life*, died of heart failure at his Manhattan home on March 13 after a long illness. He was 86.

Kanin co-wrote several films with his wife, actress Ruth Gordon, including the Katharine Hepburn and Spencer Tracy starrers *Adam's Rib* and *Pat and Mike*. His brother, Michael, was the Oscar-winning co-writer of *Woman of the Year*, the first Hepburn-Tracy pairing, and producer of Kanin's and Gordon's *A Double Life*.

Before marrying Gordon in 1942, Kanin had prospered as a Hollywood director at RKO, most prominently with the comedies *Bachelor Mother*, *Tom, Dick, and Harry*, *My Favorite Wife*, and the drama *They Knew What They Wanted*.

Born on November 24, 1912, in Rochester, NY, he dropped out of high school following the Wall Street crash of 1929 and worked as a messenger for Western Union and as a salesman. Having studied clarinet and saxophone, he secured work for a jazz band and segued into vaudeville and radio performances.

Kanin studied at the American Academy of Dramatic Arts. His first Broadway role, in *Little Ol' Boy*, came on the heels of his graduation in 1933, and he worked steadily in feature roles in such productions as *Three Men on a Horse, Boy Meets Girl, The Body Beautiful,* and *Star Spangled.* He also worked as an assistant to director George Abbott on several plays, including *Brother Rat* and *Room Service.* Abbott encouraged him to direct the 1936 and 1937 productions *Hitch Your Wagon* and *Too Many Heroes.*

Samuel Goldwyn hired him in 1937 as a director on his production staff. But he and Goldwyn frequently feuded, and the contract was soon terminated; Kanin then moved to RKO. His first assignment, 1938's *A Man To Remember*, received such good notices that the studio bumped him up to higher profile pictures such as *Next Time I Marry*, with Lucille Ball, and the John Barrymore vehicle *The Great Man Votes*.

He was then handed *Bachelor Mother*, written by Norman Krasna, to star the queen of the RKO lot, Ginger Rogers. He passed the test with flying colors but then went on suspension after refusing to direct *Anne of the Windy Poplars*, which brother Michael had been asked to write. He returned in 1940 for *My Favorite Wife* with Irene Dunne and Cary Grant.

Fearing he'd be typecast as a comedy director, he directed an adaptation of Sidney Howard's play *They Knew What They Wanted*, starring Carole Lombard and Charles Laughton, but in 1941 he helmed another Rogers comedy, *Tom, Dick, and Harry*. He was also responsible for the idea behind *Woman of the Year*, which his brother Michael co-wrote with Ring Lardner Jr., although Kanin received no credit on the film. He made similar uncredited contributions to *The More the Merrier* and *A Lady Takes a Chance* (both in 1943). That same year Kanin entered the Army and was stationed in Fort Monmouth, NJ with the Training Film Laboratory, where he directed the short *Night Shift* and *Ring of Steel*. He served for a year during World War II as a sergeant in the Air Force and, in 1943, became a captain in the OSS, where he and British director Carol Reed co-directed the Oscar-winning documentary *The True Glory*. He also directed *Fellow Americans, Battle Stripes* and, with Jean Renoir, *Salute to France*, released in 1946.

In December 1942, Kanin married actress-writer Ruth Gordon and directed her in *Years Ago* (1946). He spent the next few years on Broadway directing *How I Wonder* and *The Leading Lady*. But his biggest success was 1946's *Born Yesterday*, which he wrote. It starred Judy Holliday and ran for more than 1,600 performances. (A film version directed by George Cukor won Holliday a 1950 Best Actress Oscar.)

Other writing-directing credits for the stage during this period include *Smile of the World* and *The Rat Race*. Kanin even tried his hand at opera, crafting an English-language libretto for a production of Strauss' *Die Fledermaus* at the Metropolitan Opera in 1950. Gordon and Kanin's first screenwriting collaboration, *A Double Life*, earned them an Oscar nomination and brought an Oscar to the film's star,

Ronald Colman. The duo were also nominated for Oscars for the Hepburn-Tracy comedies *Adam's Rib* and *Pat and Mike*. The story for Frank Tashlin's *The Girl Can't Help It* in 1957 came from Kanin's play *Do Re Mi*. He also provided the story for the 1960 Bing Crosby vehicle *High Time*. And he wrote and directed *The Rat Race* in 1960 (from his play). His brother and sister-in-law, Michael and Fay Kanin, adapted *The Right Approach* from Kanin's *The Live Wire* in 1961.

Kanin returned to the stage to direct such Broadway productions as *The Diary of Anne Frank* and *Funny Girl*, which catapulted Barbra Streisand to fame.

In 1969 he returned to the screen with two middling writing-directing assignments: *Where It's At*, starring David Janssen, and *Some Kind of Nut*, with Dick Van Dyke. In 1980 he and Gordon collaborated on the TV movie *Hardhat and Legs*. But for most of the later years of his life, Kanin turned to biography and fiction, including *Tracy and Hepburn* and the novel *Moviola*.

Following Gordon's death in 1985, Kanin married actress Marian Seldes.

Ferenc Kardos, Hungarian director of such films as *Red-Letter Days*, *Petofi '73* and *Truants*, died March 6 of a heart attack at his home in Budapest. He was 62.

David Karps, novelist, screenwriter and television writer, died September 11 of bladder cancer in Pittsfield, MA. He was 77.

Richard Katz, a *Variety* reporter, died September 28 in New York of respiratory failure. He was 33.

Ira Kaye, who brought multiplexes to Hong Kong, died June 6 in that city. He was 81.

Rosalind Keene, Australian opera singer and television performer, died July 21 in Sydney, Australia, of unreported causes. She was 67.

Thomas Kellard, a contract player at 20th Century Fox during the 1930s, died March 16 of respiratory complications following a brief illness at his home in Lancaster, CA. He was 85.

Daniel Patrick Kelley, a talent agent for MCA, died October 21 of natural causes in Burbank, CA. He was 80.

DeForest Kelley, known to millions of TV viewers and filmgoers as Dr. Leonard 'Bones' McCoy from the original *Star Trek* TV series, died June 11 at the Motion Picture and Television Fund Hospital in Los Angeles. He was 79.

Paul Edward Kelly, longtime Dickinson Theaters exec, died March 30 of Alzheimer's Disease at the home of his son in Kansas City. He was 83.

Nerine Kidd, wife of *Star Trek* actor William Shatner, was found dead in the swimming pool of their Los Angeles home in August. She was 40.

Lynne Rae Kieser Stoutenborough, Emmy Award-winning sports producer for Cincinnati's WKRC-TV, died June 9 of brain cancer in Cincinnati. She was 39.

Richard Kiley, Tony and Emmy-winning thesp, Broadway's original *Man of LaMancha* and a durable musical and dramatic presence on stage, film and TV for more than 40 years, died March 5 in Warwick, NY. He was 76.

It was in *La Mancha* that Kiley, singing "The Impossible Dream," had his biggest success. He won a Tony Award for his role as Don Quixote in the musical, which opened in 1965 and ran for more than five years. He returned to Broadway in revivals of the show in 1972 and 1977. He also received a Tony in 1959 for his turn in *Redhead*, a Victorian murder-mystery musical that starred Gwen Verdon and was directed by Bob Fosse.

Kiley first gained notice in New York in 1953, appearing in a revival of George Bernard Shaw's *Misalliance* and winning a Theater World Award, given to promising newcomers. Later that year he played the caliph in *Kismet* and sang the show's hit song, "Stranger in Paradise."

Born in Chicago, Kiley studied at Loyola University and Barnum Dramatic School, and after serving in the Navy during World War II, he got his first break touring in the national company of *A Streetcar Named Desire*, replacing Anthony Quinn in the role of Stanley Kowalski. He starred with Diahann Carroll in 1962's controversial *No Strings*, the only Broadway musical for which Richard Rodgers wrote the music and lyrics. In that tale of an interracial romance, Carroll played a high-fashion model and Kiley, a jaded, prize-winning novelist.

Also on Broadway, Kiley appeared in an adaptation of Allen Drury's *Advise and Consent* in 1960, Alan Ayckbourn's comedy *Absurd Person Singular* in 1974 and 1987's praised revival of Arthur Miller's *All My Sons*.

On TV, he appeared in *The Thorn Birds*, one of the most popular miniseries ever, and for which he won an Emmy Award. He also won Emmys for the TV series *A Year in the Life* and *Picket Fences*.

Films of Kiley's four-decade career included *Looking For Mr. Goodbar*, *The Blackboard Jungle*, *The Little Prince*, *Endless Love*, and *Patch Adams*.

Kiley's first marriage, to Mary Bell Wood, ended in divorce. They had six children. In 1968, he married Pat Ferrier, a dancer he had met in *Redhead*.

Brett King, a prolific actor who starred in dozens of film and TV projects, died January 14 of leukemia in Palm Beach, FL. He was 79.

Jim King, a 40-year veteran of print, radio and television news, collapsed and died January 2 of an apparent heart attack in Moline, IL. He was 65.

Stewart Klein, three-time Emmy Award-winner and legit/film reporter, died May 10 of colon cancer at his home in New York. He was 66.

Herbert Kline, Oscar-nominated documentary director who captured the outbreak of World War II on film in *Lights Out in Europe*, died February 5 at Cedars-Sinai Medical Center in Los Angeles after a long illness. He was 89.

Herb Klynn, animation leader, the producer and graphic designer who formed his own successful animation company, died February 3 after a lengthy illness at Tarzana California's Medical Center. He was 83.

Frank Kowalski, an industry veteran who began his career in Hollywood as a child actor and later served as a script supervisor and screenwriter, died June 3 in Panorama City, CA, following a lengthy battle with Parkinson's Disease. He was 73.

Robert Kramer, American movie director who devoted his career to capturing dissident movements, died November 10 in Paris of meningitis. He was 60.

Stanley Kubrick, the brilliant, eccentric, and ground-breaking director of such classic films as *The Killing, Paths of Glory, Dr. Strangelove, 2001: A Space Odyssey* and *A Clockwork Orange*, died of a heart attack on March 7 at his home in Hertfordshire, north of London. He was 70.

The expatriate American, who lived for more than half his life in England, made only 13 films in 40 years. Starting with his feature debut in 1953, *Fear and Desire*, Kubrick made seven films within 11 years. But in the 20 years between 1968 (*2001*) and 1987 (*Full Metal Jacket*), he directed only five pics – thus making the arrival of each new Kubrick work even more of an event.

He enjoyed an unprecedented agreement with Warner Bros., dating back to the early '70s, which allowed him virtual carte blanche, and privileges such as final cut – rare even for the most heralded of directors. He was always a cinematic innovator: even *The Killing* in 1956, ostensibly a pulp-genre quickie, featured a fragmented time structure that enhanced the narrative suspense. In the 1960s *Lolita* brought a deft comic touch to the subject of paedophilia, and *Dr. Strangelove or: How I Learned to Stop Worrying and Love the Bomb* mocked nuclear annihilation at the height of the Cold War.

Some detractors dubbed his films bloodless, misanthropic and cold, but that was frequently his intention: starting with *2001*, which revolutionized film technology, his works explored the slow dehumanization of mankind. Though his film stories spanned decades and genres, they all shared a dark, ironic perspective. His esteem as a filmmaker was enhanced by his reputation as an idiosyncratic and secretive perfectionist." Kubrick did not like to be photographed and had not given an interview in 20 years.

Production designer Ken Adam (*Dr. Strangelove, Barry Lyndon*) told *Daily Variety*, "He was brilliant, and without doubt the best director I ever worked with, and he came with all the problems of near genius. Kubrick was accused of being egocentric, uncompromising and brutal to his actors, sometimes demanding 60–100 takes of scenes. Kirk Douglas, who starred in *Paths of Glory* and *Spartacus*, once called him "a cold bastard." On the other hand, Terry Semel, co-chairman and co-CEO of Warner Bros., said, "He was a unique and thoroughly satisfying individual with a great sense of humor and an amazing range of passions and interests. I just adored the guy." Sony Pictures Entertainment chairman John Calley agreed. "He was one of the few people in my life that I feel was a defining person. His life and his family were thrilling. They lived an artist's life in the best possible sense. He was completely unique and wise and supportive. An amazing man and an amazing friend."

Kubrick fought for and received veto rights over where his films would screen; chose when and whether he would screen for studio execs; often cut his own trailers; and rarely ventured outside a 50-mile radius from his home. One industry titan who was close to him observed, "He really did become a genuine recluse. Dinner with him consisted of sitting in Stanley's kitchen with his wife and his dogs."

Kubrick refused to fly, once commenting, "I love airplanes but I don't like to be in them." Adam theorized that was based on an incident when the director was learning to fly in New York. "On his first solo flight, he forgot to switch on the second magneto, which is a flying term, but it caused his plane to stagger into the air, and he just managed to land without crashing. I think it gave him an enormous shock ... I think it was the last time he ever flew in an aircraft."

Kubrick was born in the Bronx on July 26, 1928. His first love was photography, a childhood hobby that developed into an obsession. In high school he sold his first photo, of a grieving news-stand man surrounded by headlines announcing the death of President Franklin Roosevelt.

After graduating from William Howard Taft High, he briefly attended City College, leaving to join *Look*'s photo staff – at the age of 17. But a few years later he bought a 35mm newsreel camera; with friend Alex Singer, he made a 15-minute documentary about boxer Walter Cartier, *The Day of the Fight*. They sold the $3,800 short to RKO Pathe News for $4,000. RKO Pathe that year financed another docu, *Flying Padre*, about Reverend Fred Stadtmeuller, who traversed New Mexico in a plane to minister to his flock. He also directed a 1953 short, *The Seafarers*.

Written by Howard Sackler, his first fiction film was the war-themed *Fear and Desire*, shot in the San Gabriel Mountains for $50,000. Though visually adept, its fable-like quality left most critics cold and confused. His second film, 1955's *Killer's Kiss*, was a tight melodrama of revenge. United Artists paid him $75,000 for it and agreed to advance him $100,000 for another "quickie."

With James B. Harris he formed Harris-Kubrick Films in 1955 and bought rights to Lionel White's *Clean Break*, about a racetrack robbery. Budgeted at about $300,000 (partly from UA and Harris), *The Killing*, starring Sterling Hayden, was widely praised for its fractured time structure, although it didn't make back its investment. *The Killing* caught the eye of MGM production head Dore Schary, who offered Harris-Kubrick a 40-week contract to find the right project. Kubrick chose Humphrey Cobb's novel *Paths of Glory*, and secured Kirk Douglas to star. Shot on an $850,000 budget, the World War I-era film only broke even, but has since become a model of the anti-war genre.

When Anthony Mann departed *Spartacus* in 1960, Douglas convinced Kubrick to tackle the $12 million spectacle, to which Kubrick brought a great deal of intimate drama. The film garnered an Oscar for Peter Ustinov as well as Oscars for cinematography and costume design.

He worked for a time with Marlon Brando on *One Eyed Jacks* (1961), but ultimately bowed out; Brando himself took the reins of the existential Western. Kubrick's epiphany at the time was that, to survive the Hollywood system, he had to remove himself from Southern California and prying studio chiefs.

Taking up permanent residence in England, Kubrick chose a project with a decidedly American backdrop, an adaptation of Vladimir Nabokov's *Lolita*. The nymphet in her early teens was made a few years older in deference to censorship standards in 1962, but the cast of James Mason, Peter Sellers and Shelley Winters managed to capture the novel's dark humor. Critical response, however, was mixed at best – though credited with the script, Nabokov initially denounced the adaptation.

Kubrick's next film, the 1964 release *Dr. Strangelove*, proved to be one of the great black comedies in screen history. The adaptation of the book *Red Alert* was originally to be a faithful, sober-sided adaptation; Kubrick's novel take resulted in the breakup of his partnership with Harris. Referring to the director's perfectionism, designer Adam cited several examples of scenes that pleased everyone except Kubrick. The original ending was a gigantic pie fight, but Kubrick vetoed it at the last minute. "We all ganged up on him and said it was brilliant, but he insisted. It was the pie fight to end all pie fights, but when I saw that ending later, I knew that Stanley had made the right decision. To work with him, one had to be enormously flexible, and not panic. It was a trying, but great experience." *Strangelove*, Kubrick, Peter Sellers and the adapted script by Kubrick, Peter George and Terry Southern received Oscar nominations.

Kubrick pulled down another Oscar nomination as director in 1968 for *2001* – based on the novel by Arthur C. Clarke – a state-of-the-art film that instantly achieved cult status with the '60s psychedelic culture. Following blah response to a conventional space-travel ad push, the film underwent a promotional about-face, with ads tagging it "the ultimate trip." The pic went on to become a classic. It would also inspire future filmmakers such as George Lucas and Steven Spielberg.

Following *2001*, Kubrick was pursued by several studios and accepted an unprecedented deal from Warner Bros. and John Calley that allowed him enormous artistic and technical latitude. Kubrick planned to make one of his dream projects, *Napoleon*, but was persuaded to postpone the mammoth undertaking to do a more manageable picture.

The prescient *A Clockwork Orange*, based on Anthony Burgess' novel, was another dark comic venture, a study of casual violence that imagined a future where youth gangs terrorize cities. The highly stylized film once again copped Oscar picture, director and screenplay nominations for Kubrick, and the film was voted the year's best by the New York Film Critics, with Kubrick picking up the directing prize. It was a major international box-office hit.

In 1975 Kubrick dropped back into the past, adapting William Makepeace Thackeray's 18th-century-set novel *Barry Lyndon*, shot over the better part of a year with Ryan O'Neal in the lead. Kubrick again picked up picture, director and writing Oscar nominations. The sumptuously shot film won an Academy Award for John Alcott's camerawork, but didn't connect commercially in the U.S. More popular internationally, the expensive period piece took years to recoup its cost.

Partly a result of the director's hermetic existence, his films did not always reflect the zeitgeist, with many achieving a certain timelessness. Perhaps as a result, his work seemed to take on greater weight as the years went by, thanks to the quality of his craftsmanship and the universality of his themes.

The Shining, starring Jack Nicholson, diverged wildly from the conventional thriller elements of the Stephen King novel, with Kubrick creating a unique and innovative horror film edged with dark humor. It was a worldwide box-office success. Though set in the American West, it was filmed in England, and Kubrick directed the opening Oregon helicopter shots via radio hookup and from aerial photographs at his disposal.

It was seven years before Kubrick returned to the screen, this time with the anti-war piece *Full Metal Jacket* (again filmed in England over a long shooting schedule). *Jacket* was different from all other movies on the Vietnam War, and eventually became as definitive and persuasive a statement about the nature of war as his earlier *Paths of Glory*.

For the next decade Kubrick toyed with several projects, including the World War II piece *Aryan Papers*, and a sci-fi project, *A.I.* (an acronym for artificial intelligence.) The former, a tale of refugees, was to star Jodie Foster and Joseph Mazzello, and locations had been chosen in Denmark (the first time Kubrick had ventured outside Britain in two decades) prior to a last-minute change of heart that associates said was due to the release of *Schindler's List*.

Then, in 1995, Kubrick secured Tom Cruise and Nicole Kidman to star in *Eyes Wide Shut*. The film broke *Lawrence of Arabia*'s record as the major-studio film with the longest shooting schedule; its July 1999 release finally came more than a year after its bow was first scheduled.

In 1997 he received the D.W. Griffith award for career achievement from the Directors Guild. In his videotaped acceptance speech, Kubrick said, "Anyone who has ever been privileged to direct a film also knows that, although it can be like trying to write *War and Peace* in a bumper car at an amusement park, when you finally get it right, there are not many joys in life that can equal the feeling."

Kubrick was married first to Toba Metz, a former high-school classmate, and then to dancer Ruth Sobotka. His third wife was actress Suzanne Christiane Harlan – who appeared as the singer at the close of *Paths of Glory*. [*Eyes Wide Shut* opened posthumously.]

Buzz Kulik, highly regarded prolific TV director known for eliciting strong performances from his thesps, died January 13 of heart failure in Los Angeles. He was 76.

Kulik, whose career began shortly after World War II, is perhaps best remembered for helming *Brian's Song*, the celebrated 1971 TV movie that depicted the friendship between Chicago Bears football players Gayle Sayers and terminally ill Brian Piccolo. *Brian's Song* was so popular that it received a theatrical release. Kulik also directed the Emmy-winning "Hallmark Hall of Fame" presentation *A Storm in Summer* (1970).

Born in Kearney, NJ, Seymour "Buzz" Kulik served as a first lieutenant in the Army during World War II. After his discharge in 1945, he worked in the mail room of New York ad agency J. Walter Thompson. His world changed when he responded to a notice asking for volunteers to work as directors in a new medium called television. He first directed cameras at Yankee Stadium and subsequently helmed live episodes of such golden-age TV shows as *Kraft Television Theater*, *Playhouse 90*, *Lux Video Theater*, *Climax* and *You Are There*. He then served as a staff writer for CBS in the 1950s and directed episodes of legendary TV series such as *Gunsmoke*, *The Twilight Zone* and *The Defenders*.

During his career, Kulik received five Emmy nominations and an award from the Directors Guild of America for *Brian's Song*. A sampling of miniseries directed by Kulik includes *From Here to Eternity*, *Kane & Abel*, *Around the World in 80 Days* and *Jackie Collins' Lucky/Chances*.

Kulik also served as TV advisor to Sen. Edmund Muskie, D-Maine, during his 1972 presidential campaign. Kulik's foray into feature directing included the Burt Reynolds-starrer *Shamus* (1973) and Steve McQueen's last film, *The Hunter* (1980).

Frances Lafferty, a radio actress during the 1940s, died September 15 of undisclosed causes at her home in Brentwood. She was 79.

Rene Lecavalier, who hosted French-language NHL games for Radio-Canada for more than 30 years, died September 6 in Montreal of natural causes. He was 81.

Martin Leeds, entertainment lawyer and executive who represented Lassie, died January 28 in Santa Monica following a heart attack. He was 82.

Bethel Leslie, Tony and Emmy-nominated actress, died November 28 in New York after a brief illness. She was 70.

Roger Levin, distribution executive for several top studios including Warner Bros. and Disney, died October 11 of cancer at Cedars-Sinai Medical Center in Los Angeles. He was 61.

Gene Levitt, a writer, producer and director who created the original *Fantasy Island* series, died November 15 of prostate cancer in Los Angeles. He was 79.

Desmond Llewelyn, who played eccentric scientist Q in a string of James Bond films, was killed in a car accident on December 19. He was 85.

Lucy Lichtig, a continuity director who in the course of a career spanning more than 50 years worked with the cream of European and American directors, died August 19 in Brest, France. She was 87.

Bobby Limb, Oz television star died September 14 in Sydney of cancer. He was 74.

Ron Link, who helped pioneer the experimental Off Off Broadway theater movement of the 1970s and '80s and became one of Los Angeles' prominent stage directors, died June 7 of a pulmonary embolism. He was 54.

Robert Linn, classical composer, died October 28 in L.A. from cancer complications. He was 74.

Joan Long, award-winning Australian producer, screen-writer and noted film historian, died January 2 in Sydney. She was 73.

Lucille Lortel, an actress whose stage renown was far eclipsed by her later work as a producer and supporter of Off Broadway theater, died April 4 at New York Presbyterian Hospital following a brief illness. She was 98.

Charles Lowe, the writer-producer of the George Burns/Gracie Allen TV program *The Burns and Allen Show*, died September 2 at Cedars-Sinai Medical Center in Los Angeles following a long illness. He was 87.

Marc A. Lustgarten, Madison Square Garden chairman and Cablevision's vice chairman, died of cancer August 30 in New York. He was 52.

Jo Lustig, American press agent, producer and manager who lived and worked in London, died May 29 in Cambridge, England, of pancreatic cancer. He was 74.

Mungo MacCallum, Australian broadcaster, journalist and author, died July 12 in Sydney from bronchitis. He was 85.

J.H.C. Macgregor Scott, former exec at Warner-Pathe Distributors and Commonwealth United International., died January 13 in Arcadia, CA. He was 94.

Pupella Maggio, renowned Italian stage and film actress, died December 8 in a Rome hospital after a cerebral haemorrhage. She was 89.

Terence Mahony, former vice president for government relations at NBC and most recently of the law firm Holland & Knight, died February 5 of an apparent heart attack. He was 54.

Corrado Mantoni, veteran radio and television presenter, one of Italy's best-loved media personalities, died June 8 in Rome after a brief illness. He was 74.

Larry Markes, longtime film and TV writer, died May 19 in Los Angeles following complications resulting from a fall he suffered at his home in March. He was 77.

Margaret Mason, the actress whose credits ranged from *The Manchurian Candidate* in 1962 to recent daytime soaps, died of a heart attack March 26 at her home in Silverdale, Washington. She was 58.

Ed Margulies, a columnist for the Mr. Showbiz website who also served as a co-editor for *Movieline* magazine, died November 16 in Los Angeles of a heart attack. He was 48.

Victor Mature, the beefy leading man of the '40s and '50s whose films included *Kiss of Death* and *Samson and Delilah*, died August 4 in Rancho Santa Fe following a three-year battle with cancer. He was 86.

Though he admitted to being a better golfer than actor, Mature, who had leading roles in almost 50 films, came along at a time when inscrutable leading men with muscular physiques were in fashion. Never averse to publicity, he played up his sobriquet "the Hunk," which gave him needed visibility to compete with some of his more talented contemporaries like Charlton Heston and Robert Mitchum.

He is best remembered for biblical spectacles including Cecil B. DeMille's *Samson and Delilah* and *The Robe*, but turned in some of his best work in *film noir* like *Kiss of Death* and *Cry of the City* as well as John Ford's classic Western *My Darling Clementine*.

But since the late '50s, except for occasional small roles as in the early '80s TV remake of *Samson and Delilah*, Mature rarely worked in the business. He never took acting too seriously, he confessed. Nor marriage, to some extent: he was wed five times.

Born in Louisville, KY, Mature left school in his teens and became a successful candy wholesaler. With that money he started a restaurant in 1935 only to sell it a short time later to head to California where he intended to become an actor. He studied at Pasadena Playhouse's drama school and in 1936 made his debut there in *Paths of Glory*.

A year later while acting in Ben Hecht's *To Quito and Back*, he was spotted by producer Hal Roach, who gave him a small role in *The Housekeeper's Daughter* with Joan Bennett. The brief appearance resulted in a deluge of fan mail, and he was thrown into a leading role in *One Million B.C.*, a sub-par caveman tale. The poorly reviewed film gave him a profile as a brawny, he-man type, and he capitalized on the attendant publicity. In 1940, Roach sold half of Mature's $250-a-week, seven-year contract to RKO, which put him in the film version of *No, No Nanette*. He continued in a musical vein, moving on to Broadway in Moss Hart's play with music *Lady in the Dark* opposite Gertrude Lawrence. It was here that the description "hunk" was ascribed to him. And it stuck.

Of his early films, the thriller *I Wake Up Screaming*, co-starring Betty Grable, was one of his better efforts, but not *Shanghai Gesture*, also in 1941. At this point, Fox took over his contract and paid him $1,200 a week while casting him in musical vehicles with Grable and Rita Hayworth such as *Song of the Islands* and *My Gal Sal*.

During the war, Mature signed up with the Coast Guard and was assigned to duty patroling the North Atlantic. His only acting work during the period was the musical *Tars and Spars* for recruitment purposes.

After the war he landed a plum role in *My Darling Clementine*. Other strong vehicles included *Moss Rose* in 1947 and the noir *Cry of the City*. His biggest success would be as Samson in DeMille's 1950 version of *Samson and Delilah*, for which he was paid $50,000. Neither he nor co-star Hedy Lamarr was right for the roles, but DeMille worked his usual unintentionally campy magic.

Mature worked in a range of films throughout the '50s, from musical comedies like *Wabash Avenue* and *Million Dollar Mermaid* to Westerns like *Chief Crazy Horse* and action films such as *Dangerous Mission* and *Betrayed*. But he is best remembered for beefcake spectacles like *Androcles and the Lion*, *The Robe*, *Demetrius and the Gladiators* and *The Egyptian*.

After such a spate, it was hard to see him in anything else, which is why by the early '60s he'd joined the exodus of American actors to Italy, where he starred in *Hannibal* and *The Tartars*. But by the end of the decade he was reduced mostly to cameos, some spoofing his persona such as *After the Fox*, a comedy with Peter Sellers, and the Monkees' *Head*. His wife, Lorey, was a former Chicago opera singer.

Eddie Maxwell, longtime comedy writer and lyricist during Hollywood's golden age, died November 21 of natural causes in Studio City. He was 87.

Curtis Mayfield, composer and songwriter, died December 26. He was 57. Immediate cause of death was unknown.

Donal McCann, Irish actor, died July 18 in Harold's Cross, Ireland, after a 20-month battle with cancer. He was 56. Best known in America for his work in films, McCann appeared in *Out of Africa*, *Stealing Beauty* and John Huston's final film, *The Dead*.

He was especially proud of his starring role in *The*

Dead because it was based on a piece from fellow Irishman James Joyce's short-story collection, *Dubliners.*

In his native country, McCann is most celebrated for his work on stage in plays such as Sean O'Casey's *Juno and the Paycock* and Brian Friel's *The Faith Healer* and *Translations.* Although he performed primarily at Dublin's Abbey and Gate theaters, he also worked on the West End and Broadway.

The thesp came from a celebrated Dublin family: his father was Lord Mayor of the city as well as a playwright. After brief and unsuccessful stints studying architecture and working as a newspaper copy boy, McCann turned to acting. He studied at the Queen's Theatre and the Abbey School of Acting.

McCann became an international star in 1968 when he appeared in a production of Dion Boucicault's *The Shaughraun* in London. Soon thereafter he starred in *The Pallisers,* a British TV series based on the novels of Anthony Trollope. He went on to work in dozens of films and a number of TV series, but he always returned to his first love: the stage.

McCann was most recently seen on stage in Sebastian Barry's *The Steward of Christendom,* which ran in Dublin, London and New York.

Joe Dowling, who directed McCann in a number of plays, including the original production of *The Faith Healer,* noted that the actor never sought the limelight. "He had the opportunity to be a star, but he went against that," Dowling told *Daily Variety.* "Donal turned down an enormous amount of things because they weren't for him. There was an enormous integrity there."

He is survived by his partner, Beau, a sister, nieces, aunts and cousins.

Elizabeth McCormick, a pioneer of Off Broadway theater and a writer, director, and producer, died August 15 in New York after a long illness. She was 89.

Louis Melvin McCreary, whose trombone could be heard on numerous recordings by such artists as the Tijuana Brass, the Beach Boys and the Rolling Stones, died January 20 of cancer in Encino, CA. He was 71.

Grace McDonald, 1940s actress and dancer, died October 30 after a battle with double pneumonia at Scottsdale Healthcare Clinic in Arizona. She was 81.

Shepard Menken, actor and voiceover artist, died January 2 of natural causes in Woodland Hills, CA. He was 77.

Yehudi Menuhin, the violinist whose astonishing youthful virtuosity matured to make him into one of the great musical talents of the 20th century, died March 12 of heart failure in Berlin's Martin Luther Hospital while battling pneumonia. He was 82 and

had been sharing his love of music with audiences around the world for 75 years.

"He was a giant in this century, as a violinist, musician, personality within the musical world ... and of course the most phenomenal child prodigy that ever existed, certainly in this century," said violinist Itzhak Perlman.

Menuhin, who lived in London and in Gstaad, Switzerland, was born in New York of Russian Jewish parents who had emigrated from Israel. He was only seven years old when he astonished a San Francisco audience with a brilliant debut violin performance. Four years later he played at New York's Carnegie Hall with the New York Symphony Orchestra. By 13, he had already won accolades in Berlin, Paris and London.

During World War II Menuhin gave 500 concerts for U.S. and Allied troops and for Red Cross funds. Although known as a humanitarian and nurturer of young musicians, he offended many by performing for Germans in Berlin only two years after the war. He said he did so to further tolerance and "the brotherhood of man." He was in Berlin at the time of his death to prepare for a concert on March 16.

He toured India at the invitation of the government and began to bring Indian music and musicians to the West. Open to many kinds of music, he was an admirer of the early Beatles, played jazz with Stephane Grappelli, and performed with Ravi Shankar.

Menuhin married twice. His first wife was Nola Nicholas, daughter of an Australian industrialist, whom he married in 1938. They had a son and daughter. After a 1947 divorce Menuhin married Diana Gould, a British ballerina and actress with whom he had two sons. His second wife and children survive him.

Buster Merryfield, who played Uncle Albert in *Only Fools and Horses,* died of a brain tumor in June in London. He was 78.

Byron F. Meyers, a veteran industryite who served in numerous production capacities during his career, died November 1 of cancer in Los Angeles. He was 59.

Paul J. Micale, actor, died January 16 of complications from Alzheimer's Disease at the Motion Picture and Television Home in Woodland Hills, CA. He was 83.

Mickey S. Michaels, movie and TV set decorator who worked on the 1995 pic *Crimson Tide,* died March 20 in Los Angeles of natural causes. He was 67.

Buzz Miller, Broadway and film dancer, died February 23 from complications of emphysema. He was 75.

Harvey Miller, an Oscar-nominated screenwriter for

the 1980 feature *Private Benjamin*, died January 8 of heart failure at his home in Los Angeles. He was 63.

Donald Mills, last surviving member of the world-famous singing Mills Brothers, died November 13 in Los Angeles of complications from pneumonia. He was 84.

Gilbert Millstein, former news editor of *NBC Nightly News*, died May 7 in New York of kidney failure. He was 83.

Meyer Mishkin, legendary theatrical agent who early in his career helped discover such stalwarts as Tyrone Power, Gregory Peck, and Kirk Douglas, died October 9 of natural causes in Los Angeles. He was 87.

Kazuo Miyagawa, the man behind the lens of *Rashomon* and some of Japan's other most famous films, died August 7 of kidney failure in Tokyo. He was 91. Miyagawa worked with legendary director Akira Kurosawa on the award-winning *Rashomon* and other films. In *Rashomon*, the breathtaking black-and white film that put Japanese cinema on the global map, Miyagawa caught the attention of audiences with his shots of sunlight seeping through trees. He also worked with famed director Kenji Mizoguchi on *Ugetsu Monogatari*, which won the Silver Lion at the Venice Film Festival in 1953.

Miyagawa started in the movie business in 1926 when he joined Nikkatsu Studio. He became a cameraman in 1935 and made a name for himself with the 1943 hit movie *Muhomatsu no Issho*, directed by Hiroshi Inagaki. His final film credit as a cinematographer was for the 1989 film *Maihime* from Masahiro Shinoda.

Jay Moloney, former CAA agent was found dead in his home early on November 16, just two days after turning 35. He hanged himself.

Clayton Moore, TV's Lone Ranger, died of a heart attack December 28 in West Hills, CA. He was 85.

Jim Moran, known for outrageous publicity stunts in the 1940s and 1950s, died 18 October of natural causes in Newark, NJ. He was 91.

Akio Morita, co-founder of Sony Corp. and the man who gave the world the Walkman, died October 3 of pneumonia in a Tokyo hospital, the company said. He was 78.

While responsible for some of Sony's most successful innovations, Morita was also its marketing mastermind and a high-profile envoy for Japan Inc. at the peak of its global presence in the 1980s.

The heir to one of Japan's oldest sake-brewing families, Morita declined to take over the family business and in 1946 founded, with inventor Masaru Ibuka, the firm that was to become a world electronic and entertainment giant.

First called Tokyo Tsushin Denki, the company was rechristened "Sony" – from the Latin "sonus" for sound – in 1958. "We wanted a new name that could be recognized anywhere in the world, one that could be pronounced the same in any language," Morita wrote in his book *Made in Japan*. Sony then went on to invent and market a host of household consumer products, introducing stereo into Japan and inventing the Trinitron system, a method of projecting color images on to a television tube. The firm also built the world's first videocassette recorder for home use, the Betamax, a product now remembered as the loser in a marketing battle with rival Matsushita's VHS brand.

Morita's most famous brainchild, the Walkman, first appeared in 1979 after he overrode opposition from those within his own company who saw no future for the product.

In 1989, Sony made world headlines with its $3.4 billion buyout of Columbia Pictures, an ill-starred investment that failed to deliver on its promise. Morita, an energetic charmer easily recognized by his full tuft of silky white hair, was a key player in efforts to smooth often testy U.S.-Japan economic ties. He helped General Motors in its talks on buying 35% of truckmaker Isuzu in the early 1970s.

A ceaseless explainer of the differences between Japanese and U.S. business styles, he advocated traditional Japanese values such as job security. "Who owns a company anyway? Is it the managers, the shareholders or the workers?" he wrote. "In Japan, we feel that the company must be as much concerned with the workers as the shareholders."

Morita, who became the president of Sony in 1971 and chairman in 1976, suffered a stroke in late 1993 while playing tennis and withdrew from business and public activities.

Gary Morton, the comedian who, as Lucille Ball's husband and executive producer warmed up the audiences of several of her TV series after *I Love Lucy*, died March 30 of lung cancer in Palm Springs. He was 74.

John T. 'Jack' Mullin, a Hollywood audio and video engineer who helped revolutionize the entertainment industry by bringing audio magnetic tape recording to America in the late 1940s, died June 24 of heart failure. He was 85.

Dame Iris Murdoch, one of the greatest British novelists of the 20th century, died at the age of 79 on 8 February from Alzheimer's Disease.

Kathryn Murray, whose ballroom dancing inspired millions of students in dance schools run by her late husband Arthur Murray, died August 6 in Hawaii of natural causes. She was 92.

Tatsuji 'Tats' Nagashima, a Japanese concert promoter perhaps best remembered for bringing the Beatles to Tokyo in 1966, died May 2 of pneumonia in Tokyo. He was 73.

Anthony Newley, the British actor who found success as singer, playwright, composer and lyricist, died April 14 at his home in Jensen Beach, FL. Newley was 67. He had been diagnozed with renal-cell cancer in 1985 and, after the cancer went into remission for many years, found it had returned in 1997.

Newley shot to fame as a 17-year-old playing the Artful Dodger in the film version of *Oliver Twist*, only his fourth film and a mere three years removed from his job as an office-boy for an insurance company. His fruitful film career throughout the 1950s and early '60s – he appeared in 28 pix between 1950 and 1963 – gave way to a musical and Broadway run that found him winning the 1962 Grammy for song of the year and half a dozen Tony nominations for the musicals *Stop the World, I Want to Get Off* and *Roar of the Greasepaint, Smell of the Crowd*.

Born September 24, 1931, in London, Newley trained for the stage with the Dewsbury Repertory Company and Italia Conti. He made his film debut at the age of 14 as the lead in *The Adventures of Dusty Bates*. His breakthrough came in 1948 in *Oliver Twist*, which led to a string of roles for Brit studio pics. He made his U.S. debut in 1956, appearing in six films that year.

His film credits include 1967's *Doctor Doolittle*, *Sweet November*, which he produced in 1968, and *Can Heironymus Merkin Ever Forget Mercy Humpe and Find True Happiness?* in 1969, which he produced and directed. His last film was 1975's *Old Dracula*.

Newley's stage career also began in 1946 with *The Wind of Heaven* at the Colchester Repertory Co. in England. With partner Leslie Bricusse, he wrote the book, music and lyrics for *Stop the World, I Want to Get Off*. He starred as Littlechap in *Stop the World*, first in London in 1961 and then on Broadway. He also starred as Cocky in *Roar of the Greasepaint*, for which he wrote music and lyrics with Bricusse, in England (1964) and on Broadway (1965). In 1983, he penned, directed and starred in *Chaplin* at the Dorothy Chandler Pavilion in L.A.; it is one of his six stage directing credits.

Stop the World, which was turned into a film, spawned the hit songs *What Kind of Fool Am I?* and *Gonna Build a Mountain*. It was for the former that Newley won the Grammy for 1962 Song of the Year. Additionally, Newley and Bricusse composed the lyrics for the James Bond theme *Goldfinger*. Newley also composed the score for 1971's *Willy Wonka and the Chocolate Factory* and the song *The Candy Man*, which was a No. 1 hit for Sammy Davis Jr.

After spending 1971 as host of his own show on ABC, Newley devoted much of the 1970s to his work as a nightclub performer. He made regular appearances in the 1980s on network variety shows and featured in several TV movies.

He was married three times, once to actress Joan Collins (1963–71), and is survived by his mother, Grace, of Surrey, England; and four children, Tara, Alexander, Shelby and Christopher.

David Nicolette, a theater writer and former city editor of the Grand Rapids (Mich.) Press, died June 6 of natural causes in Grand Rapids. He was 80.

Jabu Nkosi, a jazz keyboardist, died in early June of heart failure in Johannesburg, South Africa. He was 46.

Lillias (Scotty) Norel, legit wardrobe mistress died January 23. She was 88.

Red Norvo, musician who introduced the xylophone and vibraphone to jazz, died April 6 at Fireside Convalescent Home in Santa Monica, CA. He was 91.

Mike Ockrent, helmer of smash Broadway musicals *Me and My Girl* and *Crazy for You*, died December 2 of acute leukemia in New York. He was 53.

Sean O'Halloran, lawyer-turned-television executive, died in mid-October of undetermined causes near Melbourne. He was 38.

Bill Orr, Australian theater entrepreneur, died June 14 of heart failure in Sydney. He was 79.

Bill Owen, the actor known as Compo in the *Last of the Summer Wine*, died on 12 July of pancreatic cancer. He was 85.

Richard M. Pack, *Television Quarterly* editor, former NBC and Group W exec, died July 1 from heart complications in Laguna Hills, CA. He was 83.

Peter Pagan, Sydney-born actor, died June 2 in New York of unreported causes. He was 77.

Jonni Paris, an actress who got her start in the *Our Gang* comedies, died January 26 following a lengthy fight with cancer. She was 66.

Edward L. Palmer, one of the minds behind *Sesame Street* and founder of the media consulting firm World Media Partners, died August 1 of prostate cancer in Ithaca, NY. He was 66.

Jennifer Paterson, television chef and half of the hit British cooking duo *Two Fat Ladies*, died August 10 of lung cancer. She was 71.

Kathryn Paterson, Australian chief censor, died of cancer September 20 in Sydney. She was 36.

Dick Patterson, versatile actor-writer with many legit and TV credits, died September 20 after a long illness in Los Angeles. He was 70.

Bob Peck, British actor who played a game warden in

Steven Spielberg's *Jurassic Park*, died April 4 in London after a lengthy struggle with cancer. He was 53.

Gil Perkins, a stuntman and film and TV actor, died March 28 of natural causes at the Motion Picture and TV Hospital in Woodland Hills, CA. He was 91.

Michel Petrucciani, a jazz pianist who waged a lifelong battle against a crippling disease that stunted his growth and made his bones dangerously brittle, died January 6 in New York City. He was 36.

Lee Philips, prolific TV director died at his Brentwood, California, home March 3 of complications from a Parkinson's-like illness. He was 72.

Charles Pierce, renowned female impersonator who gained fame for his characterizations of Hollywood stars, died May 31 of cancer in his home in Toluca Lake, CA. He was 72.

Noam Pitlik, television director, who went from acting to directing such TV shows as *Barney Miller*, for which he won an Emmy, died February 18 after a year-long battle with lung cancer. He was 66.

Dana Plato, actress, who like her fellow *Diff'rent Strokes* child co-stars had seen legal troubles since the show was canceled, died of an apparently accidental drug overdose May 8. She was 34.

Hal Polaire, a film producer whose 40-year career included work as an assistant director in Billy Wilder films *The Apartment* and *Irma La Douce*, died July 11 of heart failure at his home in Honduras. He was 81.

Abraham Polonsky, the acclaimed postwar writer and director whose career was curtailed by the Hollywood blacklist, died October 26 at his home in Beverly Hills, apparently of heart failure. He was 88.

In the wake of such hardhitting, gritty scripts as *Body and Soul* and *Force of Evil* (which he also directed), Polonsky's career was taking off in the late '40s. But in 1951 he was called before the House Un-American Activities Committee and refused to cooperate with its investigation into his past or present political affiliations. As a result, he was placed on Hollywood's blacklist and was, thus, unemployable at the major studios. During this period, he continued to write for television and to doctor scripts, although it was not until the late 1960s that he was again credited for his screen work.

Just this year, the feisty, ever-energetic Polonsky had returned to the limelight in a major way. In January, he received the Career Achievement award from the Los Angeles Film Critics Association., and for the next three months he was the most outspoken opponent of the Academy of Motion Picture Arts & Sciences' decision to give a special Oscar to Elia Kazan, whom Polonsky never forgave for naming names during the blacklist period.

Born to Russian-Jewish immigrants on December 5, 1910, in New York City, where he maintained he had "the usual, restless street life," he graduated from CCNY and then attended Columbia University Law School. He taught at City College from 1932 until serving in the OSS in Europe during World War II. During that period he launched his writing career along several different paths. He worked on some radio scripts for the likes of Orson Welles and for the serial *The Goldbergs*, and turned out political essays with a socialist slant, an orientation he took from his pharmacist father. A novel, *The Discoverers*, was initially accepted, then rejected by a publisher.

In 1945 he moved to Los Angeles to start working as a writer at Paramount, where he had signed a contract just before the war. His first credit (shared) was on Mitchell Leisen's *Golden Earrings*, in which little of his own work survived. It was only after he left Paramount that his career gathered speed. His original screenplay for *Body and Soul*, a tough boxing drama directed by Robert Rossen and starring John Garfield, brought Polonsky an Oscar nomination in 1947. Garfield and producer Bob Robertson then asked him to adapt the novel *Tucker's People*, which became *Force of Evil*, and convinced Polonsky to direct. While *Body and Soul* was successful, *Force of Evil* was considered too dark and unpleasant a gangster drama to be popular in 1948. Recognized by only a handful of critics at the time, the film has subsequently been upgraded by critics and historians to classic status.

After a stay in Europe to prepare a film version of Thomas Mann's *Mario the Magician*, Polonsky had just signed a directing deal at 20th Century Fox when he was summoned by HUAC; upon refusing to cooperate with the committee, he was effectively blacklisted. *I Can Get It For You Wholesale*, released in 1951, was, for 17 years, the last feature to bear his name.

In Martin Ritt's film *The Front*, written by Walter Bernstein, a blacklisted writer continues to work for television and films under pseudonyms or by using other writers as a front. This is essentially what Polonsky did, carving out regular work in TV (primarily the *You Are There* series) as well as some script-doctoring work – all without credit.

The best-known film written pseudonymously by Polonsky was Robert Wise's 1959 crime melodrama *Odds Against Tomorrow*, of which the Writers Guild of America recently officially acknowledged him as the author. Polonsky also wrote fiction and short stories.

Polonsky's name finally appeared on a movie again in 1968, on Don Siegel's New York cop drama *Madigan*.

Newly in demand, Polonsky returned as a writer-director with *Tell Them Willie Boy Is Here*, a revisionist Western starring Robert Redford and Robert Blake that was well received upon its release in 1970.

The next year, his final directorial effort, *Romance of a Horsethief*, did not succeed, and thereafter Polonsky worked only sporadically in Hollywood, contributing the script to the negligible 1979 release *Avalanche Express* and co-scripting the turgid Vatican melodrama *Monsignor* in 1981.

Shortly thereafter, he almost succeeded in launching *Mario the Magician* and was commissioned to adapt Church of Scientology founder L. Ron Hubbard's novel *Battlefield Earth* for the screen, but neither film was ever made.

By the 50th anniversary of the blacklist, Polonsky was feted by the Writer's Guild for his intestinal fortitude, and retrospectives of his few films were common. The Cal State Northridge Press has recently published his scripts for *Force of Evil*, *Odds Against Tomorrow* and the *You Are There* series, and is preparing to bring out *Body and Soul*.

Polonsky's wife, Sylvia, died several years ago. He is survived by his son Hank, daughter Susan and several grandchildren and great-grandchildren.

Albert Popwell, Broadway dancer-turned-actor, died April 9, during open-heart surgery in Los Angeles. He was 72.

Mario Puzo, author of the bestselling novel *The Godfather* that spawned the Mafia film trilogy, died July 2 of apparent heart failure at his Long Island home. He was 78. Puzo's literary agent, Neil Olson, said the author has been in poor health for several years and had a history of diabetes and heart trouble.

Puzo, who won screenplay Oscars for *The Godfather* and *The Godfather, Part II*, had just completed his latest book on organized crime, *Omerta*, which Random House plans to publish next year.

Born in the tough New York neighborhood of Hell's Kitchen on Manhattan's West Side, Puzo wrote several other novels chronicling organized crime families, including *The Sicilian* (1984) and *The Last Don* (1996), which was made into a hit 1997 television miniseries.

"Puzo was candid about the fact that he'd written *The Godfather* for money," recalled Peter Bart, editor-in-chief of Variety Inc. who, as Paramount's vice president for production at the time, acquired the option on the book for $10,000. "He had struggled so long to support his family from his writings that he had become desperate."

"When I first met him he said, 'Look, I know I look fat, but I'm practically starving. I need to write a commercial book.'" Hoping to elicit a sale, Bart said, Puzo had packed all of the best moments of *The Godfather* into a 60-page package. "It was not so much a novel as a sort of literary highlight reel," Bart said. Still, the material faced daunting obstacles at the studio. The Mafia-themed movie *The Brotherhood* had failed at the box office, and "the conventional wisdom was that gangster stories, like Westerns, were passé," Bart said.

A number of directors backed away from the project on those grounds, but some also felt that "the novel glamorized the mob," Bart recalled. Puzo himself was baffled by this argument, since he'd felt he had presented a starkly realistic view of the Mafia family even though he had relied on research rather than personal contact.

The 1969 saga of the Corleone family became one of the bestselling books of all time (more than 21 million copies), and the films *The Godfather* (1972) and *The Godfather, Part II* (1974) both won the Best Picture Oscar. The first film also won a Best Actor Oscar for Brando, whose portrayal of Vito Corleone became one of his trademark roles. It was a casting decision for which Puzo took partial credit. "That was my suggestion," he told Larry King on CNN.

Born in 1920 to illiterate Italian immigrants, Puzo served in Germany during World War II and attended New York's City College on the G.I. bill. He started writing pulp stories for *Male* and other men's magazines and published his first novel, *The Dark Arena*, in 1955 to enthusiastic reviews.

Puzo took nine years to write his second book, *The Fortunate Pilgrim* (1964), an autobiographical family novel about Italian immigrants that brought Puzo some of his strongest reviews. Puzo himself said it was his best book, but when it did not bring in a lot of money, the author said he "looked around and I said ... 'I'd better make some money,' and he set out to do just that, with a $5,000 advance from Putnam. The result was *The Godfather*.

Puzo also wrote the screenplays or stories for films that ranged from hits to flops, including *Earthquake* (1974), *Superman* (1978), *The Cotton Club* (1984) and *Christopher Columbus: The Discovery* (1992).

Puzo enjoyed what he called a "bourgeois life," with homes in Los Angeles and Long Island and frequent gambling trips to Las Vegas, augmented by avid tennis playing and sports enthusiasm.

Puzo is survived by his children, Anthony, Dorothy, Eugene, Virginia and Joseph; a sister, Evely Murphy; a brother, Anthony Cleri; and his companion of 20 years, Carol Gino. His wife, Erika, died in 1978.

John Quinn, longtime correspondent for *Variety* and *Daily Variety*, died July 3 from a short illness in St. Luke's Hospital in Kansas City. He was 88.

Robert J. Quinn, Emmy-nominated director of *The Tonight Show With Johnny Carson* for more than two decades, died October 21 of cancer at his Malibu, CA, home. He was 72.

Jose Quintero, Tony Award-winning theater director, died February 27 of cancer in New York. He was 74.

Anthony Radziwill, an executive at HBO and longtime ABC News producer, died August 10 in New York following a 10-year battle with cancer. He was 40.

Gene Rayburn, the jocular TV gameshow host, died November 29. He was 81.

Oliver Reed, the feisty, hard-drinking British actor who was as well-known for his antics offscreen as he was for his performances onscreen, died May 2 in Malta. He was 61.

Reed, who was on the Mediterranean island filming *The Gladiator*, died on the way to the hospital about 15 minutes after taking ill in a bar in Valetta, Malta, police said.

Reed's screen credits ranged from Ken Russell's 1969 film *Women in Love*, which featured nude wrestling and the first screen scene showing a bare penis, to the family musical *Oliver!* and *Castaway*, the story of a man who spends a year alone with a woman on a desert island.

In later years his acting was overshadowed by the drunken binges and bar brawls that over 40 years had become the stuff of British tabloid legend.

Born on February 13, 1938, in Wimbledon, south London, the nephew of famed Brit director Carol Reed, the thesp made his screen debut in 1960 and landed his first leading role in 1961 in *The Curse of the Werewolf*. He quickly became typecast as a villain, perhaps best remembered for his portrayal of violent hard-drinking rogue Bill Sykes in *Oliver!*

His 1986 role in *Castaway*, based on the true story of adult magazine editor Gerald Kingsland, had him cavorting nude around a desert island with Amanda Donohoe as the young blonde who answered an ad to become his girl Friday.

He lived in Ireland with his wife, Josephine, who he met when he was 42 and she was 16. Reed is survived by his wife and a daughter, Sarah.

Pee Wee Reese, the Hall of Fame shortstop for the Brooklyn Dodgers and sports broadcaster, died August 14 after battling cancer. He was 81.

Bert Remsen, notable character actor, died of natural causes on April 22 at his home in L.A.'s San Fernando Valley. He was 74.

Georgy Rerberg, perhaps the most heralded Russian cinematographer of the last 30 years, died July 28 in Moscow. He was 62.

Norman Reyes, a Filipino-American radio broadcaster, died January 7 in his sleep in San Pablo City in Laguna, south of Manila. He was 76.

Lee Richardson, Tony-nominated stage, film and TV actor, died October 2 in New York of cardiac arrest. He was 73.

Don Roberts, prolific production designer, died January 10 of a brain tumor in Woodland Hills. He was 64.

Judee Roberts, who worked at Universal Studios for 36 years, died October 3 of cancer at Providence St. Joseph's Hospital in Burbank, CA. She was 75.

Stephen Roberts, longtime character actor who started his career with Orson Welles' Mercury Theater, died October 26 of cancer in Woodland Hills, CA. He was 82.

Joaquin Rodrigo, known for his haunting 1939 masterpiece Concierto de Aranjuez, died July 6 in Madrid of natural causes. He was 97.

Buddy Rogers, the affable star of *Wings*, the first winner of the Best Picture Oscar, died April 12. He was 94.

Helen Rollason, BBC sports presenter, died of cancer in August. She was 43.

Ruth Roman, popular leading lady of film and TV during the 1940s and 1950s who parlayed a co-starring role with Kirk Douglas in *Champion* into a studio contract at Warner Bros., died September 9 at her home in Laguna Beach. She was 75.

Although she had appeared in a handful of films during the early 1940s including *Stage Door Canteen*, *Since You Went Away* and the serial *The Jungle Queen*, Roman hit her stride in 1949 with the Stanley Kramer-produced *Champion*. She nonetheless made her mark by portraying intelligent, strong-willed characters.

After signing with Warner Bros. she worked with Bette Davis in *Beyond the Forest* and *Three Secrets* and Farley Granger in the Alfred Hitchcock-helmed *Strangers on a Train*. In 1952 she worked with fading screen legend Errol Flynn in *Maru Maru* and appeared with Gary Cooper in *Dallas* and *Blowing Wild*. During the 1950s she divided her work schedule equally between television and features, appearing in numerous New York-based TV shows including *Playhouse 90*.

Additional TV credits included *Studio One*, numerous Philco productions and a recurring role with Edmund O'Brien on the TV series *Long Hot Summer* during the 1965–66 season. Roman also appeared with regularity on such TV shows as *Route 66, Naked City, The Defenders, Dr. Kildare, Marcus Welby, M.D., Murder, She Wrote* and *Knots Landing*.

A native of Boston, she began acting in community plays at age nine and garnered a scholarship to the Bishop Lee Dramatic School. She tried Broadway without success and wound up working as a model. She then headed to Hollywood and Universal Studios, where a bit part in *Stage Door Canteen* led to bigger roles and eventual success.

She is survived by her son, Richard Roman Hall.

Norman E. Rothstein, theatrical-entertainment producer, general manager and consultant for more than 40 years, died December 23 of cancer. He was 63.

Martha Rountree, co-creator and first moderator of the NBC News program *Meet the Press*, died August 23 in Washington of natural causes. She was 87.

Mary Allen Rowlands, artist-actress, mother of actress Gena Rowlands, died of heart failure May 28 in Woodland Hills, CA. She was 94.

Milton 'Mickey' Rudin, a showbiz attorney who repped Frank Sinatra, Lucille Ball and Marilyn Monroe in 52 years of bare-knuckled practice, died December 13 of pneumonia in Beverly Hills. He was 79.

Andrew Russell, Emmy-winning scribe died November 18 in Los Angeles of natural causes. He was 84.

João Saad, Brazilian broadcasting magnate, died October 9 in Sao Paulo following a two-year fight with cancer. He was 80.

Doug Sahm, legendary Texas musician who formed Texas Tornados, was found dead November 18 in a Taos, NM, hotel room. He was 58.

Elsie F. Samuelson, director and co-founder of New York's Stagedoor Manor Performing Arts Training Center, died November 26 of cancer in New Rochelle, NY. She was 72.

Masaru Sato, the music director for filmmaker Akira Kurosawa, died December 5 after falling ill at a party in his honor. He was 71.

Stefan Schnabel, who starred as Dr. Steven Jackson in *Guiding Light* for 16 years and performed with the Old Vic, died March 11 at his home on Lake Como, Italy. He was 87.

Judy Schoen, theatrical agent, died October 29 of lung cancer in L.A. She was 57.

Amanda Schofield, publicity manager of Eon Productions, maker of the James Bond 007 films, died October 24 in London of natural causes. She was 39.

George C. Scott, the gravel-voiced and granite-faced actor who was best at portraying the vulnerability beneath the gruff exterior of his characters, died September 22 at his home in Westlake Village. He was 71. Scott, who had been in ill health in recent years,

died from a rupture of a major blood vessel in his abdomen, according to Craig Stevens, senior deputy coroner for Ventura County.

At his best, George Campbell Scott was considered peerless in his film and TV work, though he professed to prefer the stage. From the late 1950s through the 1970s, he expertly played intelligent characters who seemed beaten by life and often seemed on the verge of exploding. In pics such as *The Hustler, Dr. Strangelove, Petulia, The Hospital* and *Islands in the Stream*, his surly image made his expressions of self-doubt and tenderness all the more effective.

But while Scott was a respected figure in show business, he was never a beloved one. He was often obstinate and contrary. His relationship with the industry often seemed contentious, as when he publicly refused the Best Actor Oscar for 1970's *Patton* (he had rejected earlier Academy Award nominations as well). He later turned down an Emmy for Arthur Miller's *The Price*.

Problems with alcohol dependency marred his career and, in later years, rendered his work erratic and infrequent, though he did some fine TV work in the '80s, in such telefilms as Charles Dickens' *Oliver Twist* and *A Christmas Carol*.

Born in Wise, VA, on October 18, 1927, Scott was raised in Detroit and showed early signs of talent in writing and on the baseball diamond. After graduating from Redford High School, he enlisted in the Marines and spent four years after World War II burying bodies at Arlington National Cemetery.

In the late 1940s, he enrolled in the University of Missouri's school of journalism. But in college his fancy turned to performing. "The minute I got onstage, I knew ... that this was what I wanted to do," he told *Life* magazine. He dropped out of college in 1953 and spent several years touring in stock around the country. In between he worked in construction. His problems with drinking erupted in public fights and the deterioration of his first marriage to aspiring actress Carolyn Hughes. Settling in New York and continuing his struggle in the mid-1950s, he married singer Patricia Reed; through a friend, he was introduced to New York Shakespeare Festival producer Joseph Papp. He made his debut for Papp in *Richard III*, garnering raves and an agent, Jane Deacy.

In 1957 he won the Clarence Derwent award for his role as Jaques in *As You Like It*. Further awards piled up for *Children of Darkness*, a production in which he met actress Colleen Dewhurst, who was to become his third wife. That tempestuous union led to divorce, remarriage and divorce again in 1972; their son is actor-director Campbell Scott.

Scott's Broadway debut came in 1958's *Comes a Day*, opposite Judith Anderson, and was followed by *The Andersonville Trial* (in which he later appeared on TV) and *The Wall*. His film debut came in 1959 in *The Hanging Tree*, starring Gary Cooper.

That year he also played a razor-sharp prosecuting attorney in Otto Preminger's *Anatomy of a Murder*, which brought him his first Oscar nomination. He asked that his nomination be withdrawn but was ignored. The same thing happened in 1961 when he was cited again by the Academy, this time for his role as a riveting antagonist opposite Paul Newman in *The Hustler*.

In 1961, Scott and Theodore Mann founded the Theater of Michigan to promote regional plays. After a few flops, Scott folded the company and personally paid off its debts in 1962. He continually worked on television in the 1950s and 1960s on such programs as *Playhouse 90*, *Hallmark Hall of Fame* and series such as *Ben Casey*, for which he won an Emmy nomination in 1962. He starred in the short-lived but widely praised urban drama *East Side, West Side* in 1963 on CBS, copping another Emmy nom. He said script arguments with censors made it impossible for him to continue the show.

On film, his work included John Huston's 1963 *List of Adrian Messenger* and *The Bible* (1966), but his best early '60s perf was as Gen. Buck Turgidson in Stanley Kubrick's masterpiece *Dr. Strangelove or: How I Learned to Stop Worrying and Love the Bomb*.

His theatrical reputation grew with the 1967 revival of *The Little Foxes* and his pairing with Maureen Stapleton in Neil Simon's *Plaza Suite* in 1968. He was splendid in Richard Lester's 1968 drama *Petulia*, and his next film was *Patton* (which won Best Pic for 1970.) Though he refused the Oscar, Scott accepted the New York Film Critics award.

They Might be Giants (1971), with Joanne Woodward, was an overlooked gem. *The Hospital*, with a memorable script by Paddy Chayevsky, earned Scott another Oscar nomination. He fought with Huston, who walked off 1971's *The Last Run* (most of the film was helmed by Richard Fleischer). Many of his other films of that decade were of mixed quality, including *The New Centurions* (1972), *Day of the Dolphins* (in which he starred with new wife Trish Van Devere), *Oklahoma Crude* and *The Hindenberg* (1975.) Better were the Franklin J. Schaffner-directed 1977 Hemingway adaptation *Islands in the Stream*, Stanley Donen's 1978 two-part spoof *Movie, Movie* and Paul Schrader's *Hardcore*.

In 1970, Scott did his first Hollywood directing gig, the TV version of *The Andersonville Trial*. (He directed only two films, 1972's *Rage* and *The Savage Is Loose* in 1974.) His theater credits in the 1970s included an all-star version of *Uncle Vanya* in 1973, *Death of a Salesman* with Teresa Wright in 1975 and *Sly Fox*, a popular 1976 adaptation of *Volpone*. He worked less frequently in films during the 1980s, appearing to some good effect in *The Formula* and *Taps* and less so in *Firestarter* and *The Exorcist III* (1990.) He had a small role in 1993's *Malice*, the 1995 *Angus* and this year's remake of *Gloria*, his last bigscreen appearance.

He often had better luck on TV. He did well by Arthur Miller's *The Crucible* in 1967, 1970's *Jane Eyre* (originally made for theatrical release) and 1975's *Fear on Trial*. He was a memorable Fagin in *Oliver Twist* in 1982 and an effective Scrooge in *A Christmas Carol* in 1984. He also starred in *Mussolini: The Untold Story* and *The Last Days of Patton* on the small screen. But his 1987 TV series, *Mr. President*, on the fledgling Fox network, lasted less than a season.

His theater appearances were less frequent during the 1980s and 1990s. Among his credits during that period were Noel Coward's *Present Laughter* in 1982, which he starred in and directed, and *Design For Living*, which he helmed two years later.

In 1996 he starred in the National Actors Theater's Broadway revival of *Inherit the Wind*. Despite his recent ill health, Scott had still been working frequently. Among his recent TV projects were the remakes of *Inherit the Wind*, which bowed in May, and *12 Angry Men*, for which he won an Emmy Award last year.

Scott is survived by six children.

Marian Searchiner, theatrical agent and former VP of NBC, died March 15 of natural causes in Santa Barbara, CA. She was 81.

Al Shapiro, New Line's prexy of domestic theatrical distribution who was largely responsible for transforming the niche-oriented film company into a Hollywood studio, died of cancer September 12. He was 57.

Robert Shaw, multi Grammy-winning chorale director, died of a stroke January 25 at a hospital in New Haven, CT. He was 82.

Jean Shepherd, writer, PBS host and radio performer, died October 16 of natural causes in Sanibel Island, FL. He was 78.

Mercedes Shirley, longtime legit and TV actress, died January 29 of natural causes at her home in Sherman Oaks, CA. She was 71.

Richard Shull, character actor, died of a heart attack October 13 only a few hours after performing the role of D.W. Dewitt in the Broadway production of *Epic Proportions*. He was 70.

Robert F. Shugrue, an Emmy-winning film editor who worked on TV movies, miniseries and feature films, died November 27 of heart failure in Los Angeles. He was 62.

Sylvia Sidney, whose career on stage and screen spanned seven decades, died July 1 of complications from throat cancer. She was 88.

The actress, with her saucer-shaped eyes and low voice, could play tough or vulnerable, and her work was always intelligent and never sentimental. She was rarely recognized with awards, perhaps because she made it look easy. Being a star never attracted her, she often said, "being an actress did."

Already an established stage name, she made her film debut playing herself in the 1927 *Broadway Nights*. She went on to star in such pics as *Street Scene, An American Tragedy* (both 1931), Alfred Hitchcock's *Sabotage*, and two 1937 hits, Fritz Lang's *You Only Live Once* and William Wyler's *Dead End*.

In later years she shone in character roles in such films as the 1973 *Summer Wishes, Winter Dreams*, where her performance as Joanne Woodward's cantankerous mother earned Sidney her single Oscar nomination (and the National Board of Review Award) as supporting actress. More recently she co-starred with Shirley MacLaine and Jessica Tandy in *Used People* and did hilarious turns in two Tim Burton films *Beetlejuice* (1988) and *Mars Attacks!* (1996).

On TV, she made numerous guest appearances and was nominated for Emmys for *The Defenders* (1962–63) and the AIDS telepic *An Early Frost* (1985). She had a recurring role in the 1998 revival of *Fantasy Island*.

Sidney was born Sophia Kosow in the Bronx on August 8, 1910. She adopted the surname Sidney from her stepfather and changed her first name to Sylvia for her stage debut in *Prunella* at the age of 15. She reached Broadway a year later in *The Squall* and after a brief film detour returned to the stage. Paramount's B.P. Schulberg was so impressed by her performance in *Bad Girl* that he offered her the female lead in Sergei Eisenstein's proposed film version of *An American Tragedy*. When the pic was postponed, Sidney took a role originally meant for Clara Bow in Rouben Mamoulian's crime drama *City Streets* opposite Gary Cooper.

Josef von Sternberg eventually directed an otherwise disappointing adaptation of Theodore Dreiser's *American Tragedy*, and Sidney was considered the best thing about the pic. As a contract player at Paramount, she became one of the studio's top leading ladies in the 1930s, along with Miriam Hopkins, Claudette Colbert and Marlene Dietrich.

She starred in the occasional comedy such as the 1932 *Merrily We Go to Hell* directed by Dorothy Arzner, but mostly she was cast in social dramas such as King Vidor's *Street Scene* (adapted from Elmer Rice's play).

Sidney went to England to star in Alfred Hitchcock's '36 *Sabotage* and returned to the U.S. for two of Lang's best American films, *Fury* (1936) and *You Only Live Once* the next year. Also in 1937, she got top billing in William Wyler's *Dead End*, though she was outshone by Humphrey Bogart and the Dead End kids.

In 1938 she returned to Broadway in Ben Hecht's short-lived *To Quito and Back* and in the Group Theater's presentation of *The Gentle People*, by Irwin Shaw. She toured in *Pygmalion* and Noël Coward's *Tonight at 8:30*. Her appearance in the thriller *Angel Street* was the sensation of the 1941–42 Broadway season.

In the 1950s she frequently appeared on live dramatic shows, including *Playhouse 90* and *Broadway TV Theater*. Her screen roles were intermittent. Of note were the 1952 *Les Miserables* and 1955's *Violent Saturday* with Lee Marvin. Her sandpaper voice and strychnine personality were put to good use in a variety of later film roles, such as *I Never Promised You a Rose Garden* (1977), *Damien: Omen II* (1978) and *Hammett* (1983), TV series *Route 66, The Nurses, My Three Sons* and *Starsky and Hutch* and the soap *Ryan's Hope*.

Her first marriage to publisher Bennet Cerf was brief. A second marriage to actor Luther Adler produced a son Jacob (Jody), whose later battle with Lou Gehrig's Disease turned Sidney into a volunteer for the National ALS Foundation. A third marriage to publicist Carlton Alsop also ended in divorce.

Maurice 'Red' Silverstein, longtime international film distribution exec, died September 6 of complications from a fall he suffered three years ago. He was 89.

Shel Silverstein, lyricist, Oscar-nominated songwriter and author, was found dead May 10 at his home in Key West, FL. An autopsy showed he died of a massive heart attack. He was 66.

Stanley Simmons, Broadway costume and set designer, died September 4 in Los Angeles of heart failure. He was 71.

Gene Siskel, *Chicago Tribune* film columnist and critic, died February 20 after a year-long battle with complications from a brain tumor. He was 53.

Michael Smith, an award-winning former advertising executive at Warner Bros. and a photographer, died July 21 in Santa Fe, NM, of AIDS complications. He was 45.

Hank Snow, whose gaudy rhinestone suits and million-selling hit song "I'm Movin' On" made him a country music legend for more than 40 years, died December 20 at his home. He was 85.

Stanley Soble, legit casting director, died July 6 due to surgery complications. He was 59.

Mario Soldati, film director and prolific writer of books, poems and screenplays, died June 19 of natural causes in Rome. He was 92.

Born in Turin, Italy, Soldati, a graduate of the University of Turin, came to the United States in his late twenties to study and subsequently teach at Columbia U. while he moonlighted as a correspondent for a Genoa newspaper.

Although Soldati directed some 30 films from 1931 to 1960 and served as second-unit director on *Ben Hur* (1959), his strongest talent was considered his narrative style of writing. He often delved into the whimsical strangeness of life in some three dozen works. His novels won occasional Italian literary prizes, but had little commercial success. His first widely recognized book was *Lettere da Capri*, written in 1953.

He adapted easily to television, working with the medium in the early 1950s in its very first years in Italy. He was also considered the father of Italian TV criticism.

Among the more acclaimed of his films was *Piccolo Mondo Antico*, and *La Provinciale*, based on a novel by Alberto Moravia.

Dusty Springfield, the British pop singer known for her soulful style and hit singles in the 1960s, died March 2 of cancer, only days before she was to be honored for her career. She was 59.

Donald E. Stewart, Academy Award-winning screenwriter died April 28 in Los Angeles of lung cancer. He was 69.

Michael Stewart, international music publisher and former UA Music chief, died at his Beverly Hills home on March 22 after a long battle with cancer. He was 70.

Shirley Stoler, actress who enjoyed a five-decade career on stage, television and in films, died February 17 of heart failure. She was 70.

Jesse Stone, who wrote "Shake, Rattle and Roll" and helped develop many of Atlantic Records' biggest rock 'n' roll hits, died in New York on April 1 after a long illness. He was 97.

Walter Stone, comedy writer, one of the original *Honeymooners* writers and one of comedian Jackie Gleason's chief writers, died October 20 of natural causes in Miami. He was 79.

Susan Strasberg, actress daughter of fabled acting coach Lee Strasberg and a close friend of Marilyn Monroe, died January 21 of cancer at her apartment in New York City. She was 60.

David Strickland, who featured in the NBC sitcom *Suddenly Susan* and appears in *Forces of Nature*, was found hanged in a motel room near the Las Vegas Strip on March 22. He was 29.

Darrell Sweet, drummer and founding member of the Scottish group Nazareth, died April 30 of a heart attack as the band was embarking on the second leg of its American tour. He was 51.

William Targ, the editor who agreed to publish Mario Puzo's *The Godfather* sight unseen with a $5,000 advance, died July 22 of natural causes at his home in New York City. He was 92.

Frank Tarloff, who not only survived the Hollywood blacklist of the 1950s but went on to win an Academy Award a decade later, died June 25 of lung cancer at his home in Beverly Hills. He was 83.

Michael Thompson, theatrical producer of OffBroadway's *Life on the Third Rail*, died September 24 in Fort Lauderdale, FL. He was 54.

Italo Tinari, veteran film-stock and colour specialist, who formerly was managing director of Technicolor Italy, died August 26 of complications arising from leukemia in Rome. He was 75.

Mel Torme, jazz and pop singer, whose crooning vocals led to the unwanted nickname "the Velvet Fog," died June 5 in Los Angeles. He was 73.

Torme, who had suffered a mild stroke three years ago, died of complications from that stroke. He began singing professionally at the age of four and went on to have a performing career of almost 70 years. Although he never achieved the career heights of his peers and suffered a professional setback during the advent of rock, he eventually acquired a substantial following and appeared continually in clubs and jazz concerts over the latter part of his life.

His voice actually improved with age. So did his technique and his command of the jazz/pop idiom. Except for Ella Fitzgerald, Torme was probably the most daring and successful practitioner of 'scat' improvisational singing. He received a Lifetime Achievement award from the National Academy of Recording Arts and Sciences at the Grammy Awards in February 1999.

Torme also wrote more than 300 songs, the most famous of which, "The Christmas Song" (aka "Chestnuts Roasting on an Open Fire") became a holiday standard immortalized by Nat King Cole. A proficient drummer, he often sat in on the instrument with bands and orchestras.

In addition, he appeared in several movies, on

television (working behind the camera, as well, on some occasions), recorded dozens of albums (he approved of only a few later ones), and even published books. The most famous was a brutally honest but appreciative recollection of Judy Garland, *The Other Side of the Rainbow* (1970).

He was born Melvin Howard Torme in Chicago on September 13, 1925, and reportedly sang his first complete song before he was a year old. When he was four his parents took him to the Blackhawk restaurant to watch the Coon-Sanders band perform. Torme sang along at his table; during the intermission, he was invited by band drummer Carlton Coon to sing a number with the band. His rendition of "You're Driving Me Crazy" earned him a steady Monday night gig at $15 a week.

In 1933 he won a children's division radio audition at the Chicago World's Fair and from there won roles on radio soap operas like *Song of the City, Romance of Helen Trent* and *Little Orphan Annie*. He also developed a great ear for mimicry and would impersonate major stars of the day, including Gary Cooper.

Through drummer Ben Pollack, Torme landed in Los Angeles, where he toured with Chico Marx's band for one year, until it broke up. But an RKO executive saw him perform and championed him for a role in the Frank Sinatra musical *Higher and Higher* (1943). Over the next five years he appeared in *Pardon My Rhythm, Let's Go Steady, Good News,* and *Words and Music.*

Torme was asked to take over a Los Angeles vocal group, the School Kids; redubbed the Mel-Tones in 1943, they became his backup singers and were eventually signed by the Decca label. During these years Torme also recorded separately on Musicraft Records and sat in on drums with the likes of Artie Shaw, Stan Kenton and Tommy Dorsey. Appearing as a soloist at the Copacabana at 21, Torme was convinced he would conquer New York. But the reviews ranged from generous to scathing, and Torme retreated to England, where appreciation of his technique was already strong.

When he returned to the U.S. in the early '50s, he emphasized the jazz aspect of his singing and began to appear regularly on TV as a singer and actor. His 1957 drama *The Comedian,* starring Mickey Rooney, earned him a Best Supporting Actor Emmy nomination. He also took on some gangster-style roles in films like *Girls Town* and *The Big Operator.*

Las Vegas emerged as an important entertainment venue in the early '60s, and Torme fitted right into the large clubs. By then he was recording for Capitol, Coral, and Bethlehem; he would eventually add Columbia and Atlantic to the list. With lyricist Robert Wells he wrote *The Christmas Song.* A major Nat King Cole hit, it has been recorded by at least 500 other performers. His only self-sung hit was the minor "Comin' Home, Baby" in 1962.

With rock 'n' roll dominating the '60s, Torme's style went out of fashion. He worked as a writer and adviser for *The Judy Garland Show* on CBS. He also wrote scripts for television, including the series *Run For Your Life* and *The Virginian.*

Easing into the '70s, Torme exec-produced the CBS special *The Singers* and hosted an ABC documentary series, *It Was a Very Good Year.* Then his career took an upswing. His 1970 single "Games People Play" became a moderate hit, and his vocal technique evolved, giving him a greater range and clarity. He attributed this to singing from the diaphragm, rather than from his head, as he had done for most of his career (the "velvet" in his voice may have been the result of partially re-grown tonsils after a childhood tonsillectomy.)

By the mid '70s there was a major jazz revival in the U.S., and Torme was one of the beneficiaries, playing at clubs with big bands, singing at the Newport and other prominent jazz festivals, and even performing with symphonic orchestras in major cities.

Over his career he recorded about 50 albums.

Torme had a large gun collection, and was a licensed pilot, writing for aviation magazines from time to time. His temper and temperament improved over the years, he claimed, thanks in part to therapy, though he was unable to succeed at three of his four marriages, the first to actress Candy Toxton (1949–55), the second to model Arlene Miles, which lasted for a decade starting in 1956, and the third to British thesp Janette Scott (1966–77). Torme is survived by his wife, Ali, and five children – Steve, Melissa, Tracy, Daisy and James.

Coles Trapnell, writer-producer of the hit TV series *Maverick,* died January 29 of a heart attack at a retirement home in Los Angeles. He was 88.

Bobby Troup, musician-actor, died February 7 of congestive heart failure, in Sherman Oaks, California Hospital and Health Center. He was 80.

Alison Trumpy, VP for sales at Goldcrest Films Intl., died in early May of cancer in London. She was 39.

Nicola Trussardi, Italian fashion designer, died April 14 after falling into a coma after brain and abdominal surgery. He was 56.

David Tyrell, a comedic stage actor who worked with Burgess Meredith and Gloria Swanson, died July 5 in Los Angeles of natural causes. He was 86.

Jean Vander Pyl, veteran actress and voiceover artist best known as the voice of Wilma Flintstone, died April 10 in her Dana Point, CA, home following an eight-month battle with lung cancer. She was 79.

Frankie Vaughan, the 1950s matinee idol who starred opposite Marilyn Monroe in *Let's Make Love*, died September 17 of a heart condition at his home in Buckinghamshire, England. He was 71.

Virginia Verrill, musical voice of Jean Harlow, later a popular radio star, died January 18 of complications following a lengthy battle with Alzheimer's Disease in Raleigh, NC. She was 82.

Frantisek Vlacil, Czech film director, died January 8 in Prague, following a long illness. He was 74.

Lucille Vore, who starred as Baby Lucille in the original silent *Our Gang* comedy films, died April 8 of congestive heart failure in San Diego. She was 82.

Frank Wagner, choreographer, director and teacher, died September 12 of complications from multiple myeloma in Fr. Myers, FL. He was 77.

Billy Ree Wallace, actress who appeared in numerous TV series, died March 3 of respiratory failure and emphysema in Los Angeles. She was 73.

Peter Warg, a correspondent for *Variety* in the Middle East, died March 18 of liver failure in Cairo. He was 61.

Grover Washington Jr., renowned American jazz saxophonist, died December 17 from an apparent heart attack, minutes after taping a performance for CBS' *Early Show* in New York. He was 56.

Vincent Wasilewski, head of the National Assn. of Broadcasters for 17 years, died September 9 of heart failure at Washington Hospital Center. He was 76.

Bobs Watson, actor best-known as Peewee in *Boys' Town*, died June 26 of cancer at home in Laguna Beach. He was 68.

Jack Watson, British actor, died at 84 on 4 July.

Julius Wechter, leader of the Baja Marimba Band died February 1 of lung cancer at his home in Calabasas, CA. He was 63.

Herman Wedemeyer, an all-American running back who became a series regular on *Hawaii Five-O*, died January 25 at the Queen's Medical Center in Honolulu. He was 74.

Gene Weed, prolific TV producer-director died of cancer at home in Chatsworth, CA on August 5.

Senor Wences, the master ventriloquist who delighted *Ed Sullivan Show* audiences, died April 20 at his home in New York City. He was 103.

Bill Wendell, veteran radio and TV announcer, died April 14 of complications from cancer. He was 75.

Stuart Werbin, a film and TV writer and a journalist for *Rolling Stone*, died of complications from cancer October 7 at his Los Angeles home. He was 52.

Morris West, Australian thriller writer whose best-selling novels were turned into movies, died October 9 of natural causes in Sydney. He was 83.

Norman Wexler, the Oscar-nominated scribe who wrote *Saturday Night Fever*, *Staying Alive*, and *Serpico*, died August 23 of a heart attack in Washington, DC. He was 73.

Andrew White, a prolific creator, writer and producer for radio, television, and film died March 29, of natural causes in Studio City, CA. He was 82.

Joan White, actress, director and producer, died June 8 of natural causes in Middlesex, England. She was 89.

Albert Whitlock, an Oscar-winning visual-effects artist, died October 26 in Santa Barbara, CA, after a lengthy illness. He was 84.

Ernie Wilkins, composer and saxophonist, died June 5 of a stroke in Copenhagen. He was 79.

Joe Williams, one of the great male jazz vocalists, collapsed on a Las Vegas street March 29. He was 80.

Larry Williams, photographer who also directed music videos, commercials and episodic TV, died May 31 of a heart attack in Los Angeles. He was 84.

BoxCar Willie, country singer, died April 12 of leukemia. He was 67.

Orlandus Wilson, one of the founders of the Golden Gate Quartet of the 1930s and 1940s, died December 30 of unreported causes in Paris. He was 81.

William Winter, the first *Voice of America* radio commentator whose World War II broadcasts were heard throughout Asia, died November 3 of natural causes in Woodland Hills, CA. He was 92.

Ernie Wise, whose partnership with Eric Morecambe was one of the most popular in U.K. showbusiness, died from heart failure on March 21. He was 73.

John Woolf, British film producer died of unreported causes June 28 in his London home. He was 86.

Jerry Wunderlich, a two-time Oscar-nominated set director for *The Exorcist* (1973) and *The Last Tycoon* (1976), died May 14 of a heart attack at his home in North Hollywood. He was 74.

Marv Ystrom, veteran optical-effects specialist, died June 4 at Sherman Oaks Community Hospital of a ruptured aneurism. He was 70.

Joseph D. Zaleski, a 32-year syndication-sales veteran who shattered industry records with his campaign on behalf of *The Cosby Show*, died August 6 of cancer in Los Angeles. He was 66.

Patricia Zipprodt, Tony Award-winning costume designer died July 17 of cancer in New York. She was 74.

Stella Zucco, former actress and widow of the 1940s villain George Zucco, died April 5 of natural causes. She had just celebrated her 99th birthday.